PHILIP'S NAVIG
TRUCKER'S Britain

NEW EDITION

NAVIGATOR

NAV I

www.philips-maps.co.uk
First published in 2009 by Philip's
a division of Octopus Publishing Group Ltd
www.octopusbooks.co.uk
Carmelite House
50 Victoria Embankment
London EC4Y 0DZ
An Hachette UK Company
www.hachette.co.uk
Fifth edition 2016
Second impression 2016
ISBN 978-1-84907-404-9
Cartography by Philip's
Copyright © 2016 Philip's

Map data

This product includes mapping data licensed from
Ordnance Survey®, with the permission of the
Controller of Her Majesty's Stationery Office.
© Crown copyright 2016. All rights reserved.
Licence number 100011710

Data for the speed cameras provided by PocketGPSWorld.com Ltd.

Data for the caravan sites provided by The Camping and Caravanning Club.

Information for the selection of Wildlife Trust nature reserves provided by
The Wildlife Trusts.

Information for National Parks, Areas of Outstanding Natural Beauty, National Trails
and Country Parks in Wales supplied by the Countryside Council for Wales.

Information for National Parks, Areas of Outstanding Natural Beauty, National Trails
and Country Parks in England supplied by Natural England. Data for Regional Parks,
Long Distance Footpaths and Country Parks in Scotland provided by
Scottish Natural Heritage.

Information for Forest Parks supplied by the Forestry Commission

Information for the RSPB reserves provided by the RSPB

Gaelic name forms used in the Western Isles provided by Comhairle nan Eilean.

Data for the National Nature Reserves in England provided by Natural England.
Data for the National Nature Reserves in Wales provided by Countryside Council for
Wales. Darparwyd data'n ymwneud â Gwarchodfeydd Natur Cenedlaethol Cymru gan
Gyngor Cefn Gwlad Cymru.

Information on the location of National Nature Reserves in Scotland was provided
by Scottish Natural Heritage.

Data for National Scenic Areas in Scotland provided by the Scottish Executive Office.
Crown copyright material is reproduced with the permission of the Controller of HMSO
and the Queen's Printer for Scotland. Licence number C02W0003960.

Printed in China

Contents

II Key to map symbols

III Mobile Layby Cafés – gourmet or gruesome?

VI Restricted motorway junctions

VIII Route planning maps

XIV Distances and journey times

1 Road maps of Britain

315 Urban approach maps

315 Bristol *approaches*
316 Birmingham *approaches*
318 Cardiff *approaches*
319 Edinburgh *approaches*
320 Glasgow *approaches*
321 Leeds *approaches*
322 London *approaches*
326 Liverpool *approaches*
327 Manchester *approaches*
328 Newcastle *approaches*
329 Nottingham *approaches*
330 Sheffield *approaches*

331 Town plans

331 Aberdeen, Aberystwyth, Ashford, Ayr, Bangor, Barrow-in-Furness, Bath, Berwick-upon-Tweed

332 Birmingham, Blackpool, Bournemouth, Bradford, Brighton, Bristol, Bury St Edmunds

333 Cambridge, Canterbury, Cardiff, Carlisle, Chelmsford, Cheltenham, Chester, Chichester, Colchester

334 Coventry, Derby, Dorchester, Dumfries, Dundee, Durham, Edinburgh, Exeter

335 Fort William, Glasgow, Gloucester, Grimsby, Hanley, Harrogate, Holyhead, Hull

336 Inverness, Ipswich, Kendal, King's Lynn, Leeds, Lancaster, Leicester, Lewes

337 Lincoln, Liverpool, Llandudno, Llanelli, Luton, Macclesfield, Manchester

338 London

340 Maidstone, Merthyr Tydfil, Middlesbrough, Milton Keynes, Newcastle, Newport, Newquay, Newtown, Northampton

341 Norwich, Nottingham, Oban, Oxford, Perth, Peterborough, Plymouth, Poole, Portsmouth

342 Preston, Reading, St Andrews, Salisbury, Scarborough, Shrewsbury, Sheffield, Southampton

343 Southend-on-Sea, Stirling, Stoke, Stratford-upon-Avon, Sunderland, Swansea, Swindon, Taunton, Telford

344 Torquay, Truro, Wick, Winchester, Windsor, Wolverhampton, Worcester, Wrexham, York

345 Index to town plans

361 Index to road maps of Britain

402 County and unitary authority boundaries

Road map symbols

Motorway

Motorway junctions – full access, restricted access

Toll motorway

Motorway service area

Motorway under construction

Primary route – dual, single carriageway, services
– under construction, narrow

Primary destination

Numbered junctions – full, restricted access

A road – dual, single carriageway
– under construction, narrow

B road – dual, single carriageway
– under construction, narrow

Minor road – dual, single carriageway

Drive or track

Urban side roads (height, weight and width restrictions not shown)

Height restriction, width restriction – feet and inches

Tunnel, weight restriction – tonnes

Distance in miles

Roundabout, multi-level junction,

Toll, steep gradient – points downhill

Speed camera – single, multiple

National trail – England and Wales

Long distance footpath – Scotland

Railway with station, level crossing, tunnel

Preserved railway with level crossing, station, tunnel

Tramway

National boundary

County or unitary authority boundary

Car ferry, catamaran

Passenger ferry, catamaran

Hovercraft

Internal ferry – car, passenger

Principal airport, other airport or airfield

Area of outstanding natural beauty, National Forest – England and Wales, Forest park, National park, National scenic area – Scotland, Regional park

Woodland

Beach – sand, shingle

Navigable river or canal

Lock, flight of locks, canal bridge number

Caravan or camping sites
– CCC* Club Site, Ready Camp Site, Camping in the Forest Site
– CCC Certificated Site, Listed Site
*Categories defined by The Camping and Caravanning Club of Great Britain

Viewpoint, park and ride, spot height – in metres

Linear antiquity

Adjoining page number, OS National Grid reference – see page 402

Road map scale 1: 100 000 or 1.58 miles to 1 inch

Road map scale (Isle of Man and parts of Scotland)
1: 200 000 or 3.15 miles to 1 inch

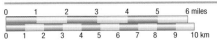

Tourist information

BYLAND ABBEY ✠ Abbey or priory

WOODHENGE 🏛 Ancient monument

SEALIFE CENTRE 🐬 Aquarium or dolphinarium

CITY MUSEUM AND ART GALLERY ⊠ Art collection or museum

TATE ST IVES 🖼 Art gallery

1644 ⚔ Battle site and date

ABBOTSBURY SWANNERY 🦅 Bird sanctuary or aviary

BAMBURGH CASTLE 🏰 Castle

YORK MINSTER ✝ Cathedral

SANDHAM MEMORIAL CHAPEL ⛪ Church of interest

SEVEN SISTERS 🌲 Country park
– England and Wales

LOCHORE MEADOWS 🌲 – Scotland

ROYAL BATH & WEST SHOWGROUND 🐄 County show ground

MONK PARK FARM 🐕 Farm park

HILLIER GARDENS AND ARBORETUM ❀ Garden, arboretum

ST ANDREWS ⛳ Golf course – 18-hole

TYNTESFIELD 🏠 Historic house

SS GREAT BRITAIN 🚢 Historic ship

HATFIELD HOUSE 🏡 House and garden

CUMBERLAND PENCIL MUSEUM 🏛 Museum

MUSEUM OF DARTMOOR LIFE – Local

NAT MARITIME MUSEUM ◇ – Maritime or military

⚓ Marina

SILVERSTONE 🏁 Motor racing circuit

Nature reserves

HOLTON HEATH 🍁 – National nature reserve

BOYTON MARSHES RSPB – RSPB reserve

DRAYCOTT SLEIGHTS – Wildlife Trust reserve

Ⓟ Picnic area

WEST SOMERSET RAILWAY 🚂 Preserved railway

THIRSK 🏇 Racecourse

LEAHILL TURRET 🏛 Roman antiquity

THRIGBY HALL ⓨ Safari park

FREEPORT BRAINTREE 🛍 Shopping village

MILLENNIUM STADIUM 🏟 Sports venue

ALTON TOWERS 🎡 Theme park

Tourist information centres
🅸 – open all year
🅘 – open seasonally

NATIONAL RAILWAY MUSEUM 🚃 Transport collection

LEVANT MINE ◉ World heritage site

HELMSLEY △ Youth hostel

MARWELL 🐘 Zoo

SUTTON BANK VISITOR CENTRE •∗• Other place
GLENFIDDICH DISTILLERY ✦ of interest

Approach map symbols

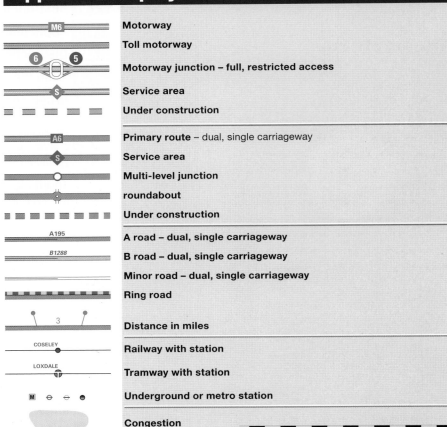

Motorway

Toll motorway

Motorway junction – full, restricted access

Service area

Under construction

Primary route – dual, single carriageway

Service area

Multi-level junction

roundabout

Under construction

A road – dual, single carriageway

B road – dual, single carriageway

Minor road – dual, single carriageway

Ring road

Distance in miles

Railway with station

Tramway with station

Underground or metro station

Congestion charge area

Speed Cameras

Fixed camera locations are shown using the 🄴🄾 symbol. In congested areas the 🄴🄾 symbol is used to show that there are two or more cameras on the road indicated.

Due to the restrictions of scale the camera locations are only approximate and cannot indicate the operating direction of the camera. Mobile camera sites, and cameras located on roads not included on the mapping are not shown. Where two or more cameras are shown on the same road, drivers are warned that this may indicate that a SPEC system is in operation. These cameras use the time taken to drive between the two camera positions to calculate the speed of the vehicle. At the time of going to press, some local authorities were considering decommissioning their speed cameras.

Load and vehicle restrictions – please read

Any information on height, width and weight restrictions in the UK as noted on pages 1–314 of this atlas has been derived from the relevant OS material used to compile this atlas. Any information on height, width and weight restrictions on the Isle of Man has been derived from the relevant information as supplied by the Isle of Man Highways Department. Where a warning sign is displayed, any height obstructions, including but not limited to low bridges and overhead cables, are shown in the atlas where such obstructions cross navigable roads selected for inclusion. Height restrictions lower than 16'6" and width restrictions narrower than 13 feet, are all shown in 3 inch multiples and have been rounded down where necessary. Weight restrictions indicate weak bridges and the maximum gross weight which could be supported is shown in tonnes. While every effort has been made to include all relevant and accurate information, due to limitations of scale a single symbol may be used to indicate more than one feature and it is not possible to show restrictions on urban side roads.

Mobile Layby Cafés – gourmet or gruesome?

Do you drive on by?

Stephen Mesquita,
Philip's On the Road Correspondent

Roadside snack van sign in Herefordshire *Jeff Morgan / Alamy*

Have you ever done this? You're driving along on one of Britain's A-Roads. It's sometime between 6am and 2pm. You're feeling a bit peckish. You see a layby coming up. There's a notice by the road. Something about hot food. There's a van flying a Union Jack. There are a couple of truck drivers there, queueing up. You might even catch a tempting whiff of something frying.

And you drive straight past. Not really for you? You've never eaten in a layby so you'll wait for a place you know and recognise. Or buy a sandwich at the next petrol station.

Well, that's what I've always done. Up until yesterday. That's when I set out, with my trusty accomplice (and Philip's Sales Supremo) Stuart, to see if my lifelong prejudices were justified.

Butty Vans

A quick word about terminology first. We're going to drop the 'Mobile Layby Cafés' and go with 'Butty Vans'. Stuart and I were out to beat The Breakfast Buns from Butty Vans in One Morning Record.

And so it was with some trepidation that we set off from Northampton and headed for our first Butty Van. Here's confession number one: as soon as we'd photographed the bacon roll that we'd ordered, we polished it off.

This was a good start – and in stark contrast to our Motorway Service Area research, where the fare was so unappetising that we tried only a tiny portion of each item and left the rest.

And as the day started, so it went on. Of the eight buns, only one really disappointed. The other seven were tasty, hot, great value and came with friendly chat. Stuart and I polished almost all of them off – and two especially good ones were down the gullets of Philip's intrepid breakfast critics before you could say 'another bacon roll please'.

▲ The first bacon butty of the day in a layby alongside the A43

Eight in a Day

Would I recommend eight in a day? As a gastronomic experience, no. It's too much salt intake (my car was littered with empty bottles of water by the end of the day). And I did long for a freshly made flat white by the end of the day.

But a Butty Van breakfast or snack every now and again? Absolutely. Now I've done it once, I'll be very happy to do it again. In fact, I'm rather ashamed I hadn't managed to overcome my prejudices before now.

So to answer my question. Gourmet: no. Gruesome: certainly not. A tasty roadside snack, piping hot, cooked to order and served with a smile – definitely. I'll have one of those.

Butty Vans vs. Motorway Service Areas– how they compare

If you're expecting Butty Vans to serve up the fare you get at your local deli, you probably don't need to read on. The buns are not made of artisanal sourdough ciabatta. The butter isn't Danish unsalted. The bacon didn't cost £15 a kilo. The eggs probably aren't fresh from the farm that morning. Butty Vans aren't posh.

But the point is this – all the Butty Vans we ate at were owned by people who took great pride in what they did. We met one real foody proprietor who told us he'd been to a burger fair the weekend before and always offered specials ('Codfinger'; 'Blue Burger Special'). All of them were aware that, to compete against the big brands, they had to offer good food at good prices.

The ingredients were perfectly decent. The bacon was almost universally of a better quality than we tasted last year in our Full English Breakfast campaign in Motorway Service Areas. And it was all cooked to order in front of you, which gave it one spectacular advantage over the Motorway Service Areas. It was hot.

And it was a fraction of the price.

The only disappointment was the tea and coffee. But at £0.70–£0.80 a cup, you should know what you're getting and you get what you pay for – although at one Butty Van, the teabags were Yorkshire Tea.

You can compare further in our
Butty Van vs. Motorway Service Area checklist:

	Butty Vans	Motorway Service Areas
Good Value for Money	✔	✗
Proud of what they do	✔	✗
Cooked to Order	✔	rarely
Meal Hot	✔	✗
Quality of ingredients	See above	See above
Quality of hot drinks	✗	✗
Friendly Service	✔	✗
Parking	✔	✔
Easy to find	✗	✔

Meal in a Bun One:

Location	A43 West of Northampton
Meal:	Bacon roll plus tea
Price:	£2.50 plus £0.60

Verdict: Generous helping of tasty bacon, cooked in front of us and piping hot. The tea was wet and warm.

Meal in a Bun Two:

Location:	A43 Brackley
Meal:	Sausage and Bacon roll plus tea
Price:	£3.20 plus £0.50

Verdict: A breakfast on its own served with a smile and lots of chat. The ingredients were nothing special but all tasty.

Meal in a Bun Three:

Location:	A422 between Buckingham and Milton Keynes
Meal:	Bacon and Egg roll plus coffee
Price:	£3.00 plus £0.80

Verdict: Another very decent breakfast in a bun, with the egg cooked to order. Yorkshire Tea teabags spurned for instant coffee. Should have had the tea.

Meal in a Bun Five:

Location:	Yardley Road Industrial Estate, Olney
Meal:	Double egg roll
Price:	£2.50

Verdict: I was stupid. I had a double egg sandwich (which was tasty) but I was rightly berated by Mr Sizzler for not being more adventurous and having one of his speciality burgers or chicken dishes. The things I sacrifice to make these surveys fair.

Meal in a Bun Six:

Location:	A505 West of Royston
Meal:	Bacon Roll
Price:	£2.00

Verdict: The best bread (slightly toasted) and loads of decent bacon for £2.00. I rest my case. I should have added: cooked by Italians. They know how to cook, the Italians. Even good old English Bacon butties. Buonissimo!

Meal in a Bun Seven:

Location:	A505 West of Royston
Meal:	Bacon Roll
Price:	£2.50

Verdict: A bit disappointing. Bread tough, bacon tough. Our only below par experience of the day.

Roadside snack van, Perthshire *Mar Photographics / Alamy*

Butty Vans – what you need to know

- **Layby cafes are licensed by the local authority**, normally annually, to do business in a particular layby.
- **Food Hygiene is an important part of their credibility** – most of them display their certificates prominently.
- **You can't go there for dinner.** Most open early (often around 6am) and shut up around 2pm (sometimes 3pm).
- **They aren't just found in laybys on A Roads.** Some are on industrial estates and business parks.
- **The good ones are there come rain or shine** (bad weather can be good for business) most days of the year.

- **Most of them have a name:** we sampled the fare at Dom's Doorsteps, Taste Buds Snacks, Sizzlers, Delicias and Smell the Bacon.
- **It's a competitive business** – and their regulars (mostly truck drivers and white van men on A Roads) are discerning customers who expect tasty food at reasonable prices. We heard one van driver say he draws the line at paying £1 for a cup of tea.
- **We were made very welcome**, even though it was obvious we weren't their usual clientele.

Our thanks to all the proprietors who answered our questions about their businesses so openly.

Meal in a Bun Four:

Location:	Harding Road, Milton Keynes
Meal:	Sausage and Egg roll plus tea
Price:	£2.25 plus £0.50

Verdict: Sausage and egg: not expensive ingredients but properly cooked, nice and hot and at a nugatory price.

Meal in a Bun Eight:

Location:	A505 East of Royston
Meal:	Sausage roll
Price:	£3.00

Verdict: This café was called Smell the Bacon but the sausages were from Musks of Newmarket. They were delicious! They seemed to disappear remarkably quickly, Stuart.

DOM'S DOORSTEPS
Est 1997
Phone Orders Taken

Hotdog	£1.75
Hotdog With Cheese	£1.95
Bacon	£1.75
Egg (2 Eggs)	£1.75
Sausage	£1.75
Sausage & Onion	£1.75
Sausage & Mushroom	£1.75
Sausage With Cheese	£2.25
Sausage & Tomato	£1.95
Sausage & Bacon	£2.25
Sausage & Egg	£2.25
Sausage & Egg With Cheese	£2.25
Sausage & Bacon With Cheese	£2.45
Sausage & Egg With Mushroom	£2.45
Sausage & Bacon With Mushroom	£2.75
Egg & Bacon	£2.75
Bacon & Mushroom	£2.25
Egg & Mushroom	£2.25
Egg & Bacon With Mushroom	£2.25
Egg & Cheese	£2.25
Sausage & Egg With Bacon	£1.95
Sausage & Egg With Bacon + Cheese	£2.75
Sausage & Egg With Bacon + Mushroom	£2.95
Sausage & Egg With Bacon + Tomato	£3.25
	£3.25

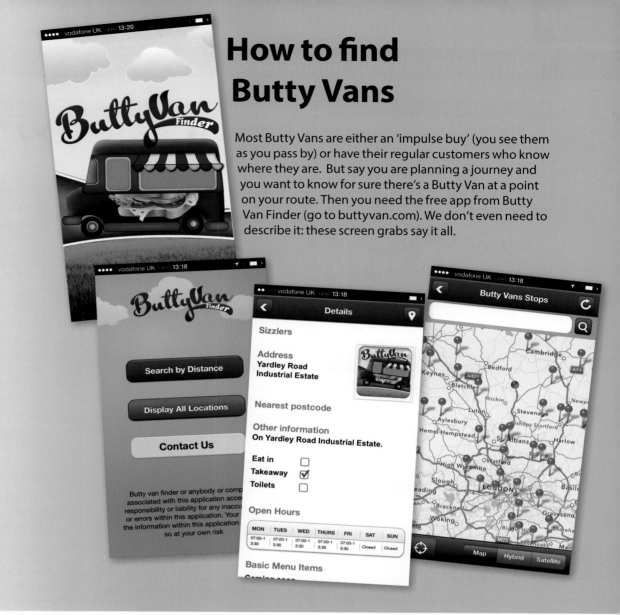

How to find Butty Vans

Most Butty Vans are either an 'impulse buy' (you see them as you pass by) or have their regular customers who know where they are. But say you are planning a journey and you want to know for sure there's a Butty Van at a point on your route. Then you need the free app from Butty Van Finder (go to buttyvan.com). We don't even need to describe it: these screen grabs say it all.

Enter the Butty Van Competition

Send us your personal recommendations for _Breakfast On the Move_ (Butty Vans or anywhere else) by email, with pictures if possible, and tell us why you recommend them – or any amusing stories you have.

Send them by 31st December 2017.

The 25 best entries in our opinion will each receive a free copy of the _Philip's Royal Geographical Society Essential World Atlas_ (worth £25).

Email your entries to buttyvan@octopusbooks.co.uk

Restricted motorway junctions

M1 Junction 34

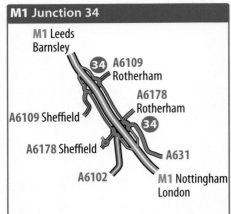

M1 Junctions 6, 6A
M25 Junctions 21, 21A

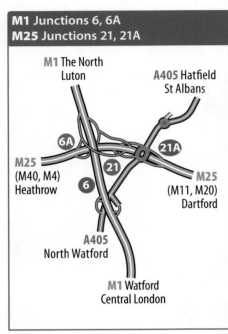

M4 Junctions 25, 25A, 26

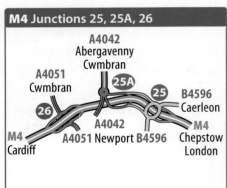

M8 Junctions 8, 9 · M73 Junctions 1, 2 · M74 Junctions 2A, 3, 3A, 4

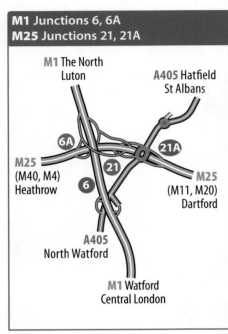

M1	Northbound	Southbound
2	No exit	No access
4	No exit	No access
6A	No exit. Access from M25 only	No access. Exit to M25 only
7	No exit. Access from A414 only	No access. Exit to A414 only
17	No access. Exit to M45 only	No exit. Access from M45 only
19	No exit to A14	No access from A14
21A	No access	No exit
23A		Exit to A42 only
24A	No exit	No access
35A	No access	No exit
43	No access. Exit to M621 only	No exit. Access from M621 only
48	No exit to A1(M) southbound	

M3	Eastbound	Westbound
8	No exit	No access
10	No access	No exit
13	No access to M27 eastbound	
14	No exit	No access

M4	Eastbound	Westbound
1	Exit to A4 eastbound only	Access from A4 westbound only
2	Access from A4 eastbound only	Access to A4 westbound only
21	No exit	No access
23	No access	No exit
25	No exit	No access
25A	No exit	No access
29	No exit	No access
38		No access
39	No exit or access	No exit
41	No access	No exit
41A	No exit	No access
42	Access from A483 only	Exit to A483 only

M5	Northbound	Southbound
10	No exit	No access
11A	No access from A417 eastbound	No exit to A417 westbound

M6	Northbound	Southbound
3A	No access. Exit to M42 northbound only	No exit. Access from M6 eastbound only
4A	No exit. Access from M42 southbound only	No access. Exit to M42 only
5	No access	No exit
10A	No access. Exit to M54 only	No exit. Access from M54 only
11A	No exit. Access from M6 Toll only	No access. Exit to M6 Toll only
20	No exit to M56 eastbound	No access from M56 westbound
24	No exit	No access
25	No access	No exit
30	No exit. Access from M61 northbound only	No access. Exit to M61 southbound only
31A	No access	No exit
45	No access	No exit

M6 Toll	Northbound	Southbound
T1		No exit
T2	No exit, no access	No access
T5	No exit	No access
T7	No access	No exit
T8	No access	No exit

M8	Eastbound	Westbound
8	No exit to M73 northbound	No access from M73 southbound
9	No access	No exit
13	No exit southbound	Access from M73 southbound only
14	No access	No exit
16	No access	No exit
17	No exit	No access
18		No access
19	No exit to A814 eastbound	No access from A814 westbound
20	No exit	No access
21	No access from M74	No access
22	No exit. Access from M77 only	No access. Exit to M77 only
23	No exit	No access
25	Exit to A739 northbound only. Access from A739 southbound only	Access from A739 southbound only
25A	No exit	No access
28	No exit	No access
28A	No exit	No access

M9	Eastbound	Westbound
1A	No exit	No access
2	No access	No exit
3	No exit	No access
6	No access	No exit
8	No exit	No access

M5 Junction 11A

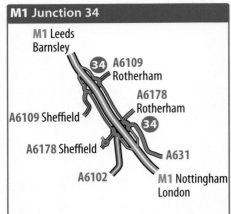

M11	Northbound	Southbound
4	No exit	No access
5	No access	No exit
9	No access	No exit
13	No access	No exit
14	No exit to A428 westbound	No exit. Access from A14 westbound only

M20	Eastbound	Westbound
2	No access	No exit
3	No exit Access from M26 eastbound only	No access Exit to M26 westbound only
11A	No access	No exit

M23	Northbound	Southbound
7	No exit to A23 southbound	No access from A23 northbound
10A	No exit	No access

M25	Clockwise	Anticlockwise
5	No exit to M26 eastbound	No access from M26 westbound
19	No access	No exit
21	No exit to M1 southbound. Access from M1 southbound only	No exit to M1 southbound. Access from M1. southbound only
31	No exit	No access

M27	Eastbound	Westbound
10	No exit	No access
12	No access	No exit

M40	Eastbound	Westbound
3	No exit	No access
7	No exit	No access
8	No exit	No access
13	No exit	No access
14	No access	No exit
16	No access	No exit

M42	Northbound	Southbound
1	No exit	No access
7	No access Exit to M6 northbound only	No exit Access from M6 northbound only
7A	No access. Exit to M6 southbound only	No exit
8	No exit. Access from M6 southbound only	Exit to M6 northbound only. Access from M6 southbound only

M45	Eastbound	Westbound
M1 J17	Access to M1 southbound only	No access from M1 southbound
With A45	No access	No exit

M48	Eastbound	Westbound
M4 J21	No exit to M4 westbound	No access from M4 eastbound
M4 J23	No access from M4 westbound	No exit to M4 eastbound

M49	Southbound	Northbound
18A	No exit to M5 northbound	No access from M5 southbound

M53	Northbound	Southbound
11	Exit to M56 eastbound only. Access from M56 westbound only	Exit to M56 eastbnd only. Access from M56 westbound only

M56	Eastbound	Westbound
2	No exit	No access
3	No access	No exit
4	No exit	No access
7		No access
8	No exit or access	No exit
9	No access from M6 northbound	No access to M6 southbound
15	No exit to M53	No access from M53 northbound

M57	Northbound	Southbound
3	No exit	No access
5	No exit	No access

M58	Eastbound	Westbound
1	No exit	No access

M60	Clockwise	Anticlockwise
2	No exit	No access
3	No exit to A34 northbound	No exit to A34 northbound
4	No access from M56	No exit to M56
5	No exit to A5103 southbound	No exit to A5103 northbound
14	No exit	No access
16	No exit	No access
20	No access	No exit
22		No access
25	No access	
26		No exit or access
27	No exit	No access

M61	Northbound	Southbound
2	No access from A580 eastbound	No exit to A580 westbound
3	No access from A580 eastbound. No access from A666 southbound	No exit to A580 westbound
M6 J30	No exit to M6 southbound	No access from M6 northbound

M62	Eastbound	Westbound
23	No access	No exit

M65	Eastbound	Westbound
9	No access	No exit
11	No exit	No access

M66	Northbound	Southbound
1	No access	No exit

M67	Eastbound	Westbound
1A	No access	No exit
2	No exit	No access

M69	Northbound	Southbound
2	No exit	No access

M73	Northbound	Southbound
2	No access from M8 or A89 eastbound. No exit to A89	No exit to M8 or A89 westbound. No access from A89

M74	Northbound	Southbound
3	No access	No exit
3A	No exit	No access
7	No exit	No access
9	No exit or access	No access
10		No exit
11	No exit	No access
12	No access	No exit

M77	Northbound	Southbound
4	No exit	No access
6	No exit	No access
7	No exit or access	
8	No access	No access

M80	Northbound	Southbound
4A	No access	No exit
6A	No exit	
8	Exit to M876 northbound only. No access	Access from M876 southbound only. No exit

M90	Northbound	Southbound
2A	No access	No exit
7	No exit	No access
8	No access	No exit
10	No access from A912	No exit to A912

M180	Eastbound	Westbound
1	No access	No exit

M621	Eastbound	Westbound
2A	No exit	No access
4	No exit	
5	No exit	No access
6	No access	No exit

M876	Northbound	Southbound
2	No access	No exit

A1(M)	Northbound	Southbound
2	No access	No exit
3		No access
5	No exit	No access
14	No exit	No access
40	No access	No exit
43	No exit. Access from M1 only	No access. Exit to M1 only
57	No access	No exit
65	No access	No exit

A3(M)	Northbound	Southbound
1	No exit	No access
4	No access	No exit

A38(M) with Victoria Rd, (Park Circus) Birmingham	
Northbound	No exit
Southbound	No access

A48(M)	Northbound	Southbound
M4 Junc 29	Exit to M4 eastbound only	Access from M4 westbound only
29A	Access from A48 eastbound only	Exit to A48 westbound only

A57(M)	Eastbound	Westbound
With A5103	No access	No exit
With A34	No access	No exit

A58(M)		Southbound
With Park Lane and Westgate, Leeds		No access

A64(M)	Eastbound	Westbound
With A58 Clay Pit Lane, Leeds	No access	No exit
With Regent Street, Leeds	No access	No access

A74(M)	Northbound	Southbound
18	No access	No exit
22		No exit

A194(M)	Northbound	Southbound
A1(M) J65 Gateshead Western Bypass	Access from A1(M) northbound only	Exit to A1(M) southbound only

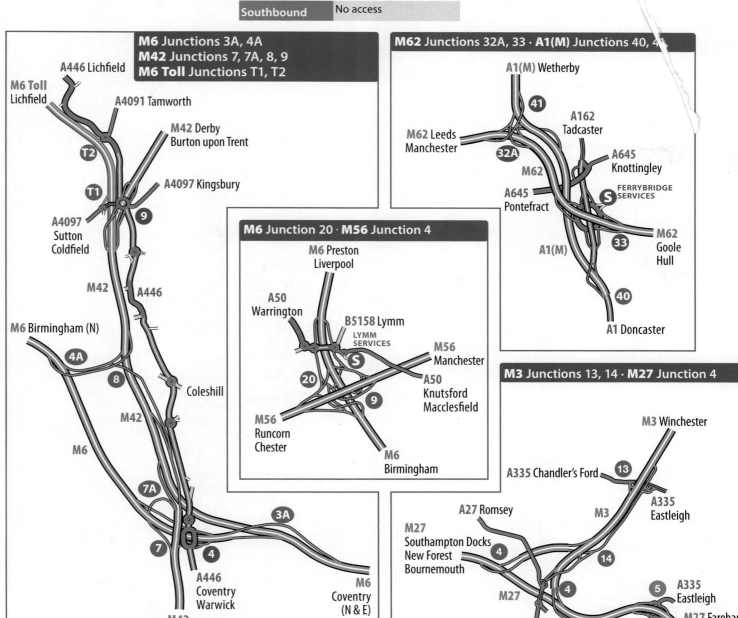

M6 Junctions 3A, 4A
M42 Junctions 7, 7A, 8, 9
M6 Toll Junctions T1, T2

A446 Lichfield
M6 Toll Lichfield
A4091 Tamworth
M42 Derby Burton upon Trent
T2
A4097 Kingsbury
T1
A4097 Sutton Coldfield
9
M42
A446
M6 Birmingham (N)
4A
8
Coleshill
M42
M6
7A
3A
7
4
A446 Coventry Warwick
M42 Birmingham (S)
M6 Coventry (N & E)

M62 Junctions 32A, 33 · A1(M) Junctions 40, 41
A1(M) Wetherby
41
A162 Tadcaster
M62 Leeds Manchester
32A
A645 Knottingley
M62
A645 Pontefract
FERRYBRIDGE SERVICES
S
A1(M)
33
M62 Goole Hull
40
A1 Doncaster

M6 Junction 20 · M56 Junction 4
M6 Preston Liverpool
A50 Warrington
B5158 Lymm
LYMM SERVICES
S
M56 Manchester
20
A50 Knutsford Macclesfield
9
M56 Runcorn Chester
M6 Birmingham

M3 Junctions 13, 14 · M27 Junction 4
M3 Winchester
A335 Chandler's Ford
13
A335 Eastleigh
A27 Romsey
M3
M27 Southampton Docks New Forest Bournemouth
4
14
4
A335 Eastleigh
5
M27
A33 Southampton
M27 Fareham Portsmouth

NORTH SEA

Distances and journey times

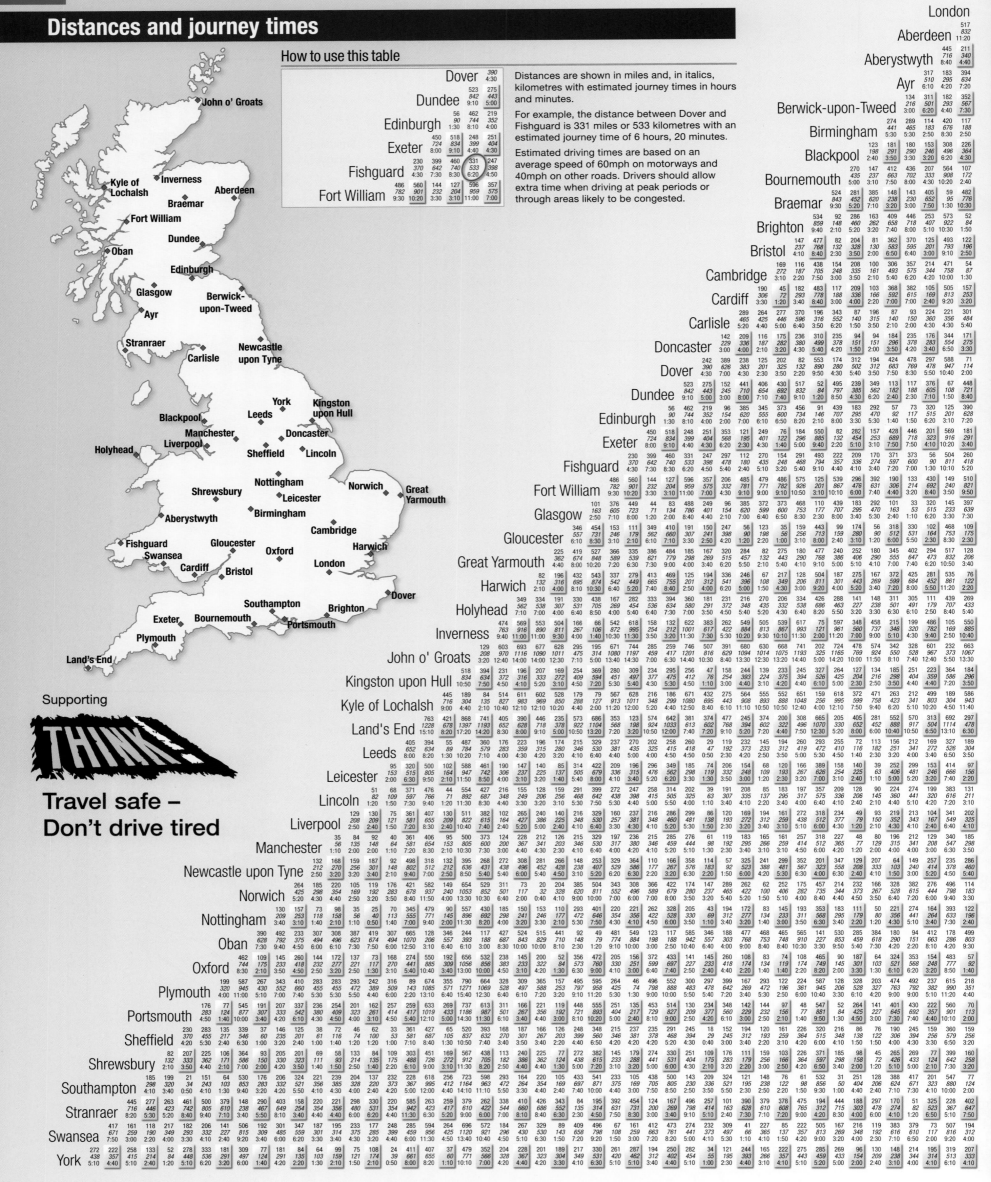

How to use this table

Distances are shown in miles and, in italics, kilometres with estimated journey times in hours and minutes.

For example, the distance between Dover and Fishguard is 331 miles or 533 kilometres with an estimated journey time of 6 hours, 20 minutes.

Estimated driving times are based on an average speed of 60mph on motorways and 40mph on other roads. Drivers should allow extra time when driving at peak periods or through areas likely to be congested.

Supporting

THINK!

Travel safe –
Don't drive tired

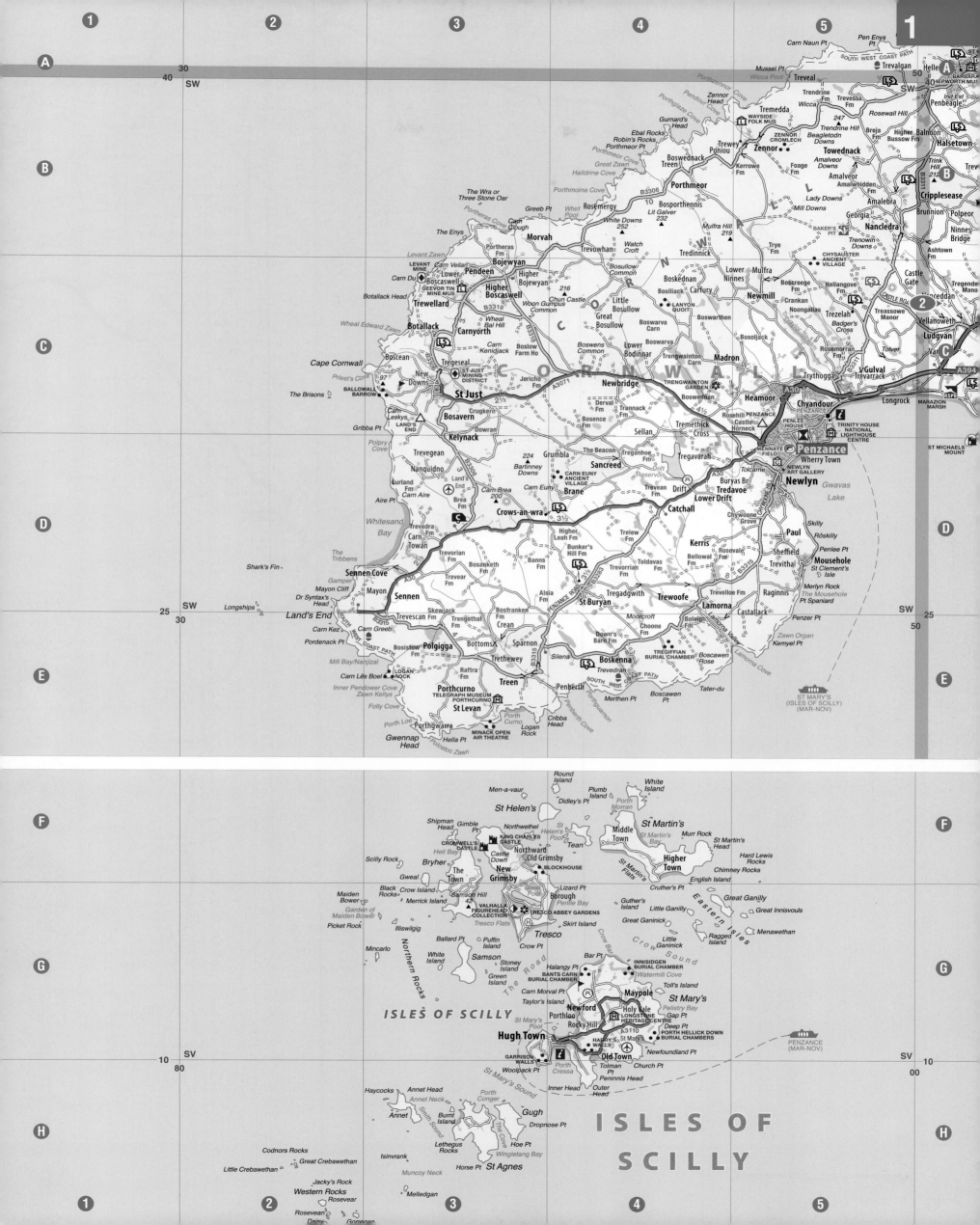

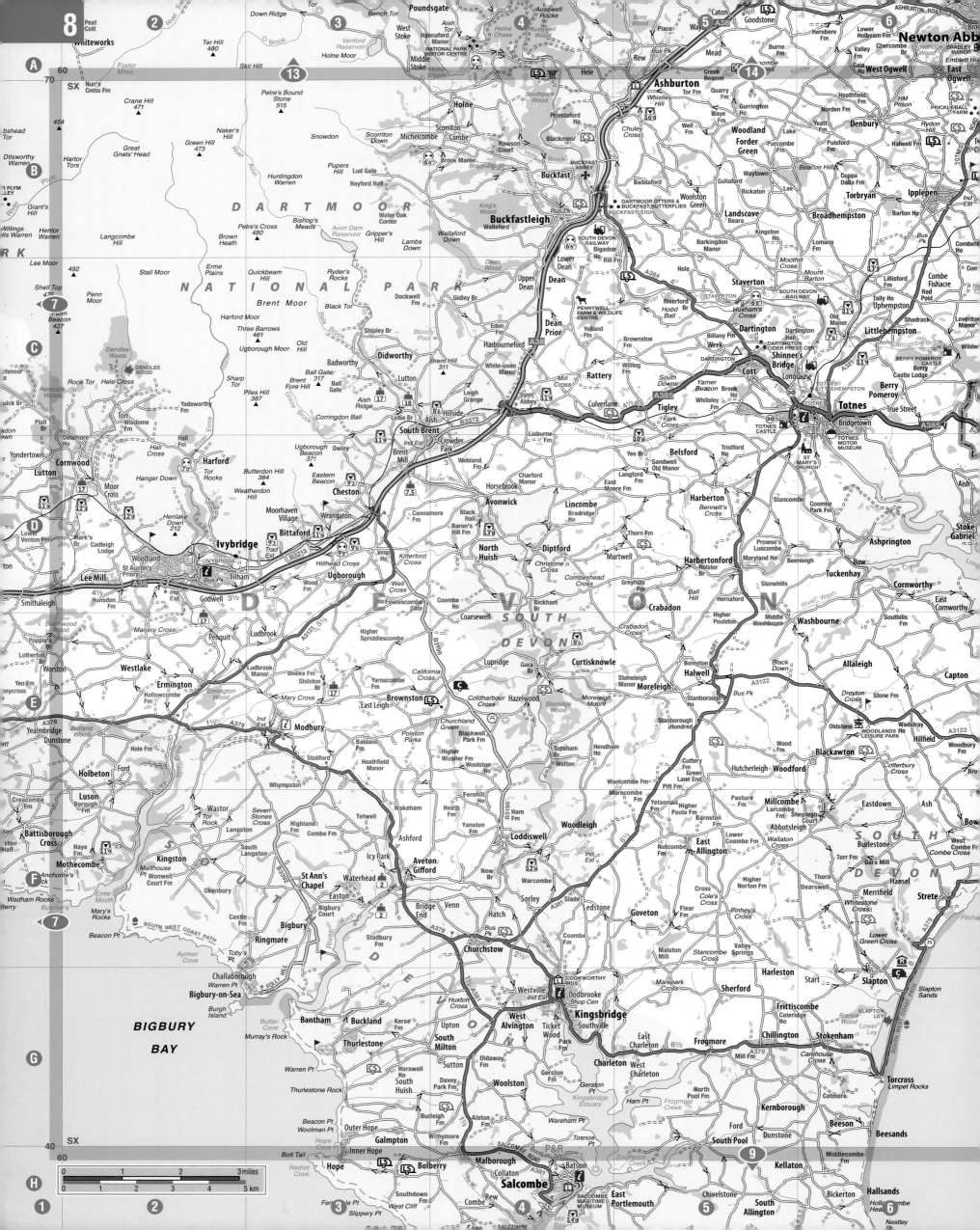

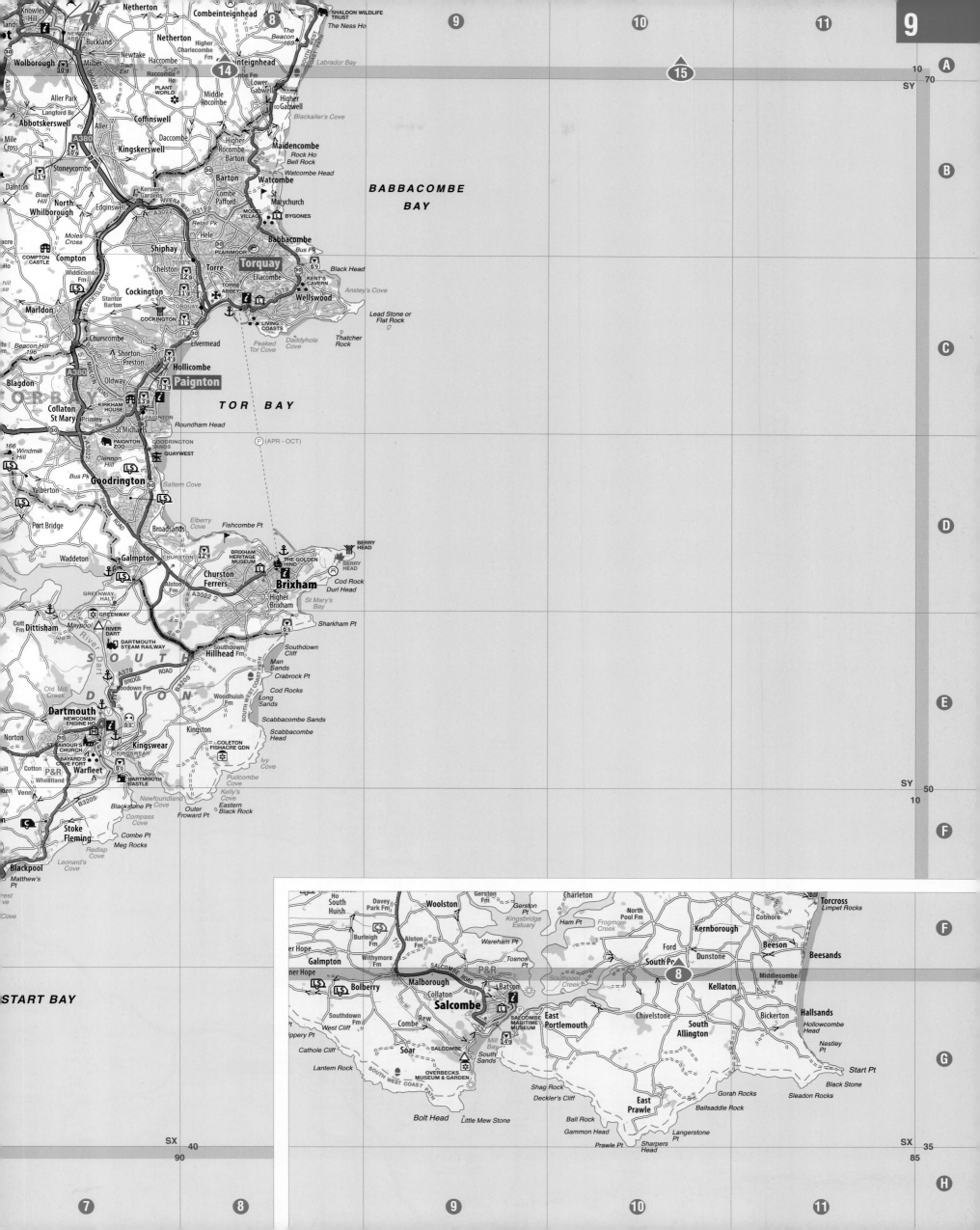

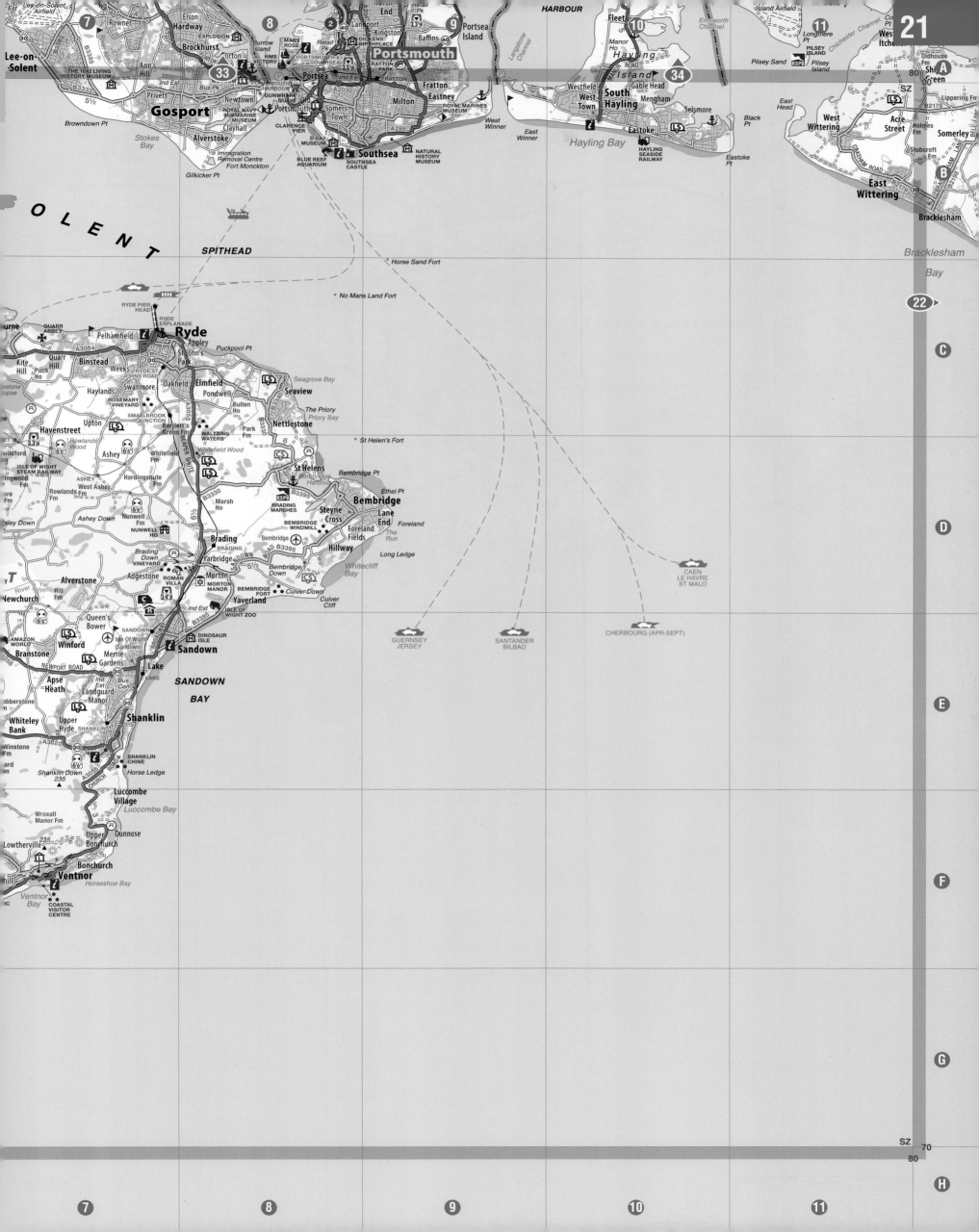

SOLENT

SPITHEAD

Lee-on-Solent

Gosport

Brockhurst

Portsmouth

Southsea

Hayling Island

South Hayling

Hayling Bay

West Wittering

East Wittering

Bracklesham

Bracklesham Bay

Ryde

Ryde Pier Head

Seaview

Nettlestone

St Helens

Bembridge

Brading

Sandown

SANDOWN BAY

Shanklin

Luccombe Village

Ventnor

GUERNSEY JERSEY

SANTANDER BILBAO

CHERBOURG (APR-SEPT)

CAEN LE HAVRE ST MALO

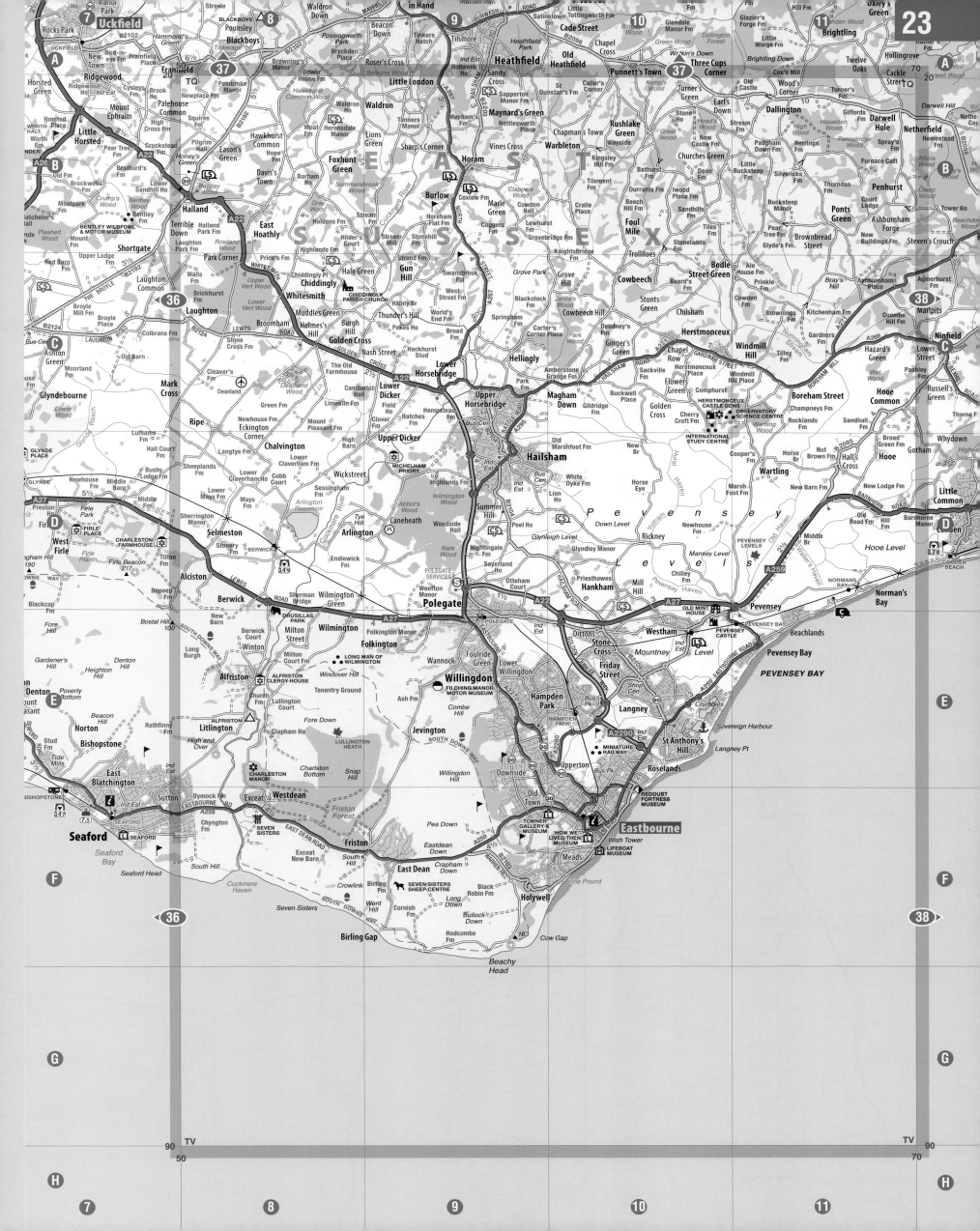

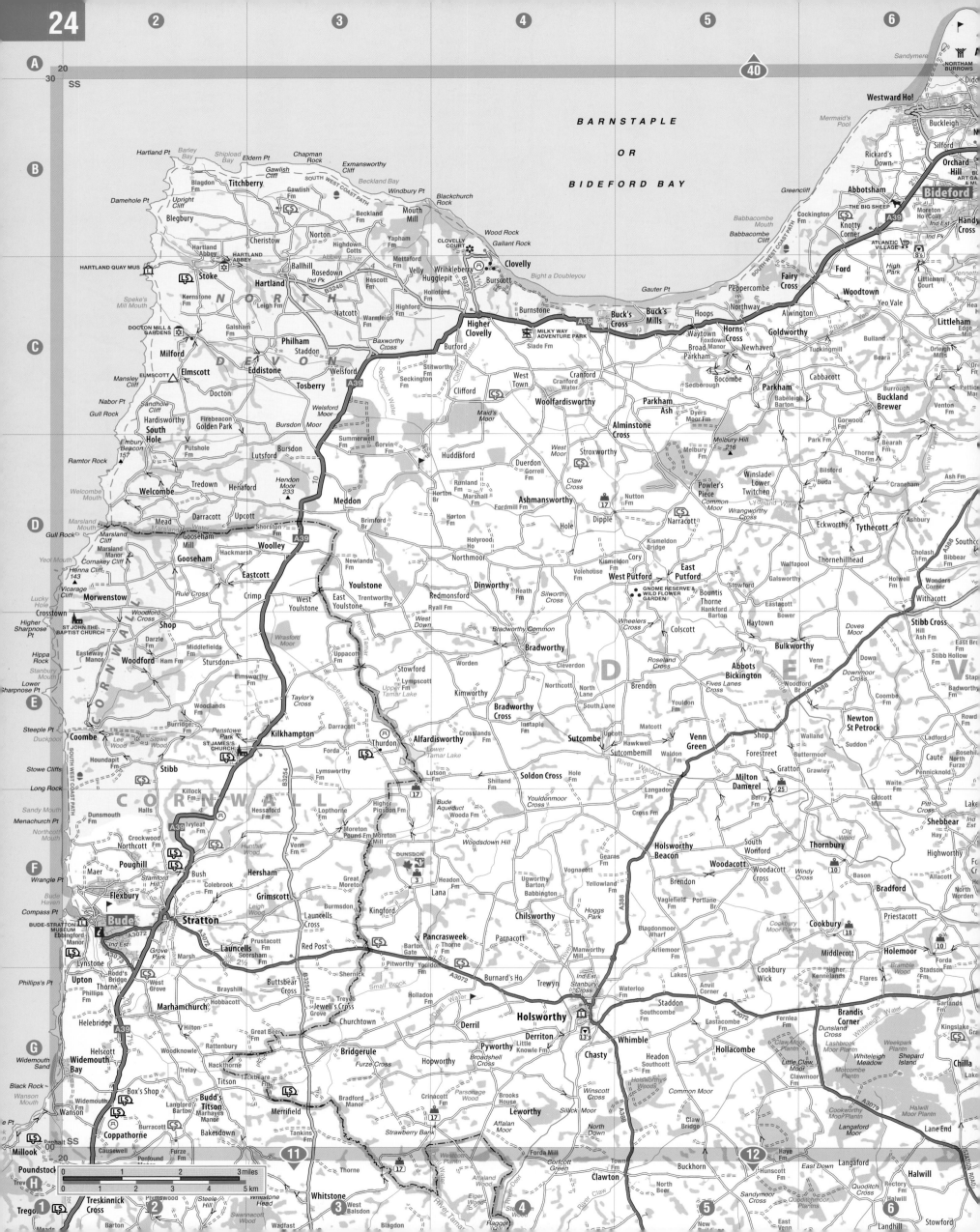

Lundy

Hen & Chickens
North West Pt
Seals' Rock
North East Pt
Gannets' Rock
Gannets' Bay
St James's Stone
Tibbetts Hill 138
Tibbett's Pt
LUNDY MARINE NATURE RESERVE
Jenny's Cove
Dead Cow Pt
Ackland's Moor 142
Lundy Roads
BIDEFORD (MAR-OCT)
ILFRACOMBE (MAR-OCT)
Halftide Rock
Beacon Hill
Castle Hill
Rat Island
South West Pt
Surf Pt

LUNDY (MAR-OCT)
Capstone Pt
Samson's Bay
Hele Bay
Water Mouth
WATERMOUTH CASTLE
Rawn's Rocks
Blackstone Pt
Elwill Bay
Trentishoe

Ilfracombe
Hele
OLD CORN MILL
Hole Fm
Hangman Pt
Little Hangman 218
Gt Hangman 318
SOUTH WEST COAST PATH
Holdstone Down 349
South Dean Fm
MUSEUM
Chambercombe
CHAMBERCOMBE MANOR
Gooseswell
Hole Fm
Lester Cliff
Girt Fm
Girt Down
Trentishoe Down
Holdstone
Trentishoe

Bull Pt
Pensport Rock
Shag Pt
Flat Pt
Lee Bay
Lincombe
Higher Slade
NORTH DEVON
Berrynarbor
Lee
Combe Martin
Warmscombe Fm
Sterridge
Knap Down
Verwill Fm
Walner Fm
Tattiscombe

Morte Pt
Rockham Bay
North Morte Fm
Lee
Higher Warcombe
Whitestone
Lower Slade
Slade Resr
Oakridge Fm
Two Pots
Ruggaton Fm
Bowden Fm
Henstridge
Stoneditch Hill
WILDLIFE & DINOSAUR PARK
Stony Corner
Truckham Fm
Dean
Westleigh
Cowley Wood

Mortehoe
Borough Cross
Little Shelfin Fm
Ind Est
Hore Down Fm
Outer Narracott Fm
Stapleton Fm
Berry Down
South Ley
LONG LANE
Kentisbury
Higher Week Fm
Kentisbury Down
Preston Ho

Grunta Pool
Trimstone
Cheglinch
Hore Down Fm
Hillcrest Fm
Cleave Fm
Highlands Fm
Bugford
Stonecombe

Woolacombe
Mill Rock
Ossaborough
Willingcott
Dean
Higher Aylescott
Century
Bittadon
Collacott Fm
Wigmore Fm
Dingles Fm
Clifton
East Down
Patchole
Kentisbury Ford
Bridwick
Fm

Morte Bay
Ivycott
Bradwell
Dean Cross
Fullabrook
Burland Fm
Little Silver
Hewish Down
Bowden Corner
Northcote Fm
Churchill
Arlington Beccott
Halls Cross
Hallsdown Fm

Black Rock
Putsborough Sand
Pickwell Down
North Downs
West Down
Fullabrook Down
Metcombe Fm
Whitefield Down
Churchill Down
ARLINGTON COURT
Arlington
Arlington Court
Wistlandpound Reservoir
Halls Cross

Baggy Pt
SOUTH WEST COAST PATH
Pickwell
Castle Street Fm
Buckland Down
Stoneyard Wood
Okewill Cross
Garman's Down
White Cawsey
Deerpark Wood
Huckham Fm
Besshill Fm
Rye Park

Vention
Putsborough
Georgeham
North Buckland
Winsham Down Ho
Halsinger Down
Beara Down
Patsford
Swindon Down
Gipsy Corner
Milltown
Viveham Fm
Woolley Wood
Loxhore
Tidicombe Fm

Croyde Bay
Ora Hill
Croyde
Forda
Darracott
Nethercott
Upcott
Halsinger
Winsham
Whiddon
South Woolley Fm
Loxhore Cott
Lower Loxhore

Croyde Bay
Cross
South Hole Fm
Incledon Fm
Knowle
Beara
Middle Marwood
Crockers
Higher Muddiford
Muddiford
The Warren
Chilbridge

Saunton
Sandy Lane
Lobb
Buckland Manor
Boode
Pippacott
Whitehall
Marwood
MARWOOD HILL
Guineaford
Plaistow Mill
Plaistow Barton
Shirwell Cross
Shirwell
Lower Loxhore

CROYDE ROAD
SAUNTON ROAD 4½
Braunton
Luscott Barton
Mainstone
Whitehall
Kingsheanton
Prixford
BROOMHILL SCULPTURE GARDENS
Varley Cross
South Hill
Youlston Wood

Braunton
Shop Cent
Braunton Down
Knowl Water
Heanton Punchardon
West Ashford
Springfield Cross
Waytown Fm
Sepscott Fm
Bratton Cross
Birch

Braunton Burrows
Velator
Wrafton
Ashford
Upcott Ho
Burridge
Pitt Fm
Brightlycott
Chelfham
Horridge
Stoke Rivers
Bratton Fleming

Saunton Sands
SOUTH WEST COAST PATH
Braunton Marsh
CHIVENOR
Penhill Pt
Allen's Rock
Bradiford
Raleigh
Kingdon's Gardens
Snapper
Northleigh
Hutcherton Down

Danger area
Horsey Island
Saltpill Duck Pond
Penhill
Pilton
Pottington
Derby
Waytown
Youlden Ho
Coombe Willesleigh
Dean Head
Gunn
Stone Cross

Airy Pt
Chivenor
River Taw
BARNSTAPLE
ST ANNE'S CHAPEL & MUSEUM
MUSEUM OF BARNSTAPLE & NORTH DEVON
Westacott
East Acland
Sandick

LUNDY (MAR-OCT)
Lower Yelland
Broad Sands
Crow Pt
Muddlebridge
BICKINGTON ROAD
Sticklepath
Ind Est
Lake
P&R
Newport
Portmor
Landkey
Harford
Hurscott
Sandick Cross

Crow Rock
Instow Sands
Yelland
Fremington
Combrew
Bickington
Brynsworthy
Bradiford
Derby
Rumsam
Swimbridge Newland
Yeoland Newland
Riverton

Sandymere
Instow
Worlington
The Quay
Brake Plantns
Bickleton
Collacott Fm
Roundswell
Upcott Fm
Hollamoor Clump
Bishops Tawton
Swimbridge Newland

Appledore
N DEVON MARITIME MUSEUM
NORTHAM BURROWS
Diddywell
Instow Fm
Huish
St John's Chapel
Eastacombe
Tawstock
Hannaford
Swimbridge
Kerscott

Westleigh
Northam
Silford
TAPELEY PARK GARDENS
Coombe
Trayhill
Huish Moor
Stonyland
Uppacott
Downrew Ho
Hangman's Hill
Bydown Ho
Lane End Fm

Rickard's
A39
Holmacott
Eastleigh Manor
Holmacott
Horwood
Rushcott Fm
Prospect Corner
Halmpstone Manor
Summer

0 1 2 3 miles
0 1 2 3 4 5 km

BRISTOL CHANNEL

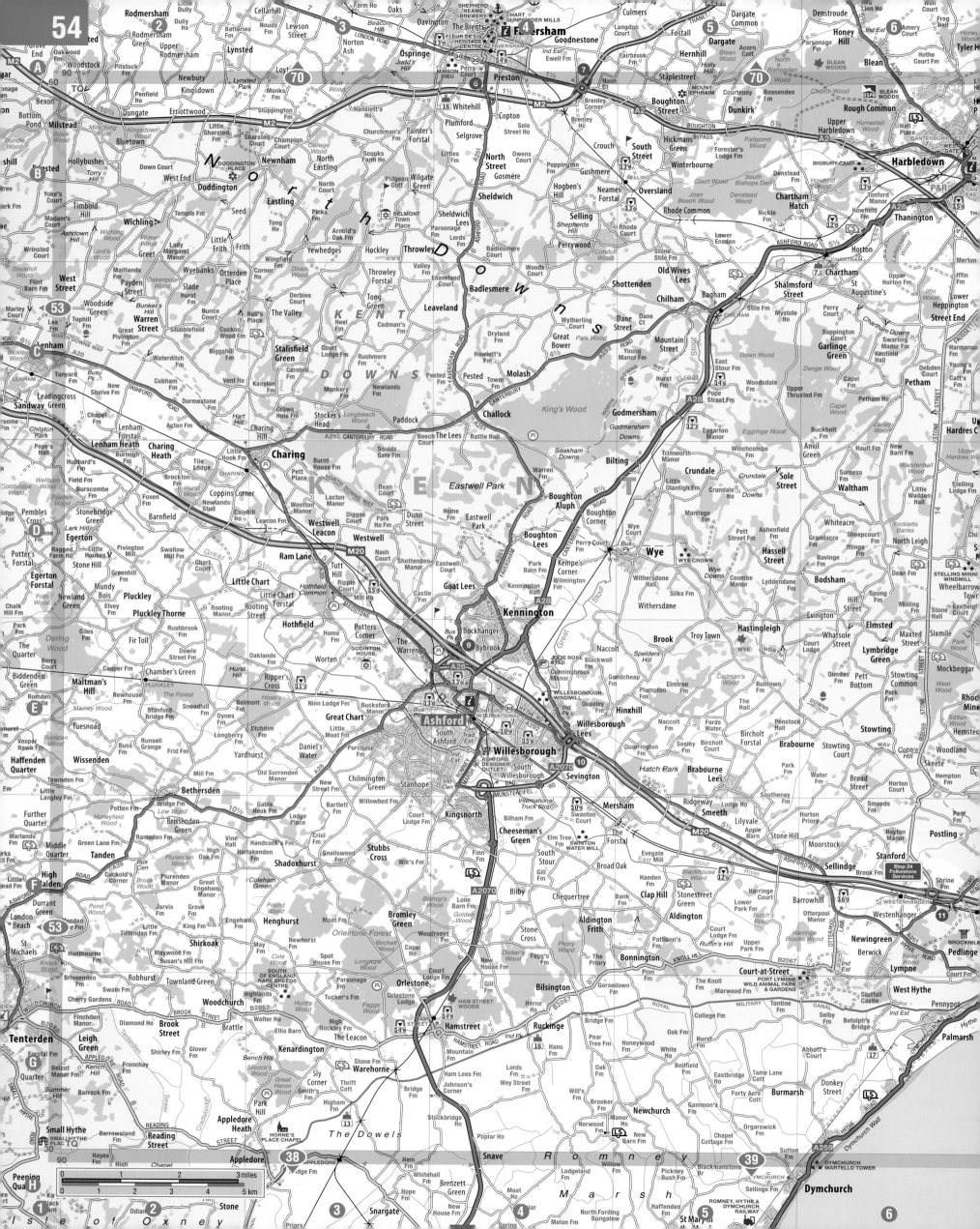

RHOSSILI
BAY

THE GOWER

Gower Peninsula

GWYR

OXWICH BAY
BAE OXWICH

PORT EYNON
BAY

BRISTOL CHANNE

MÔR HAFREN

0   1   2   3miles
0   1   2   3   4   5 km

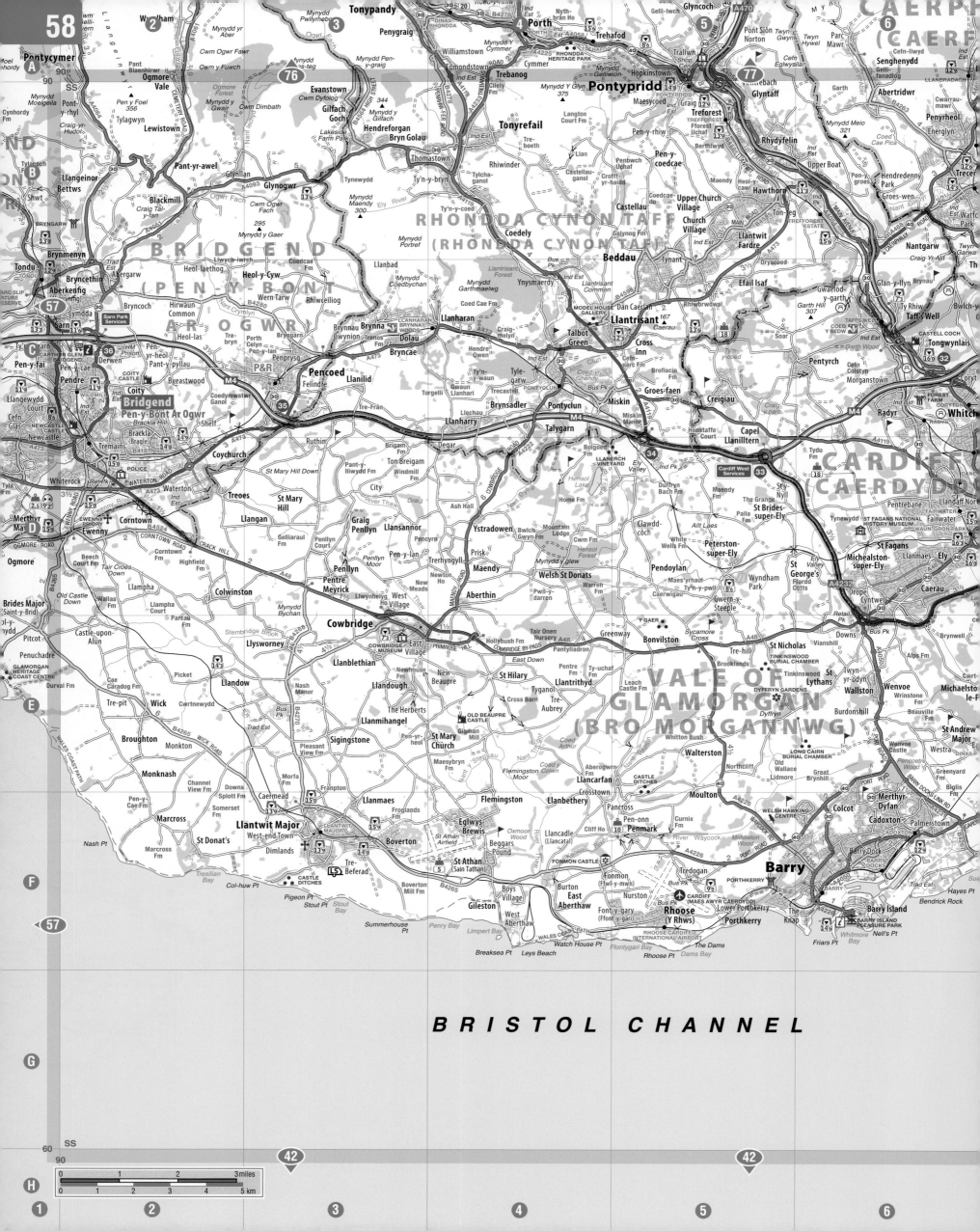

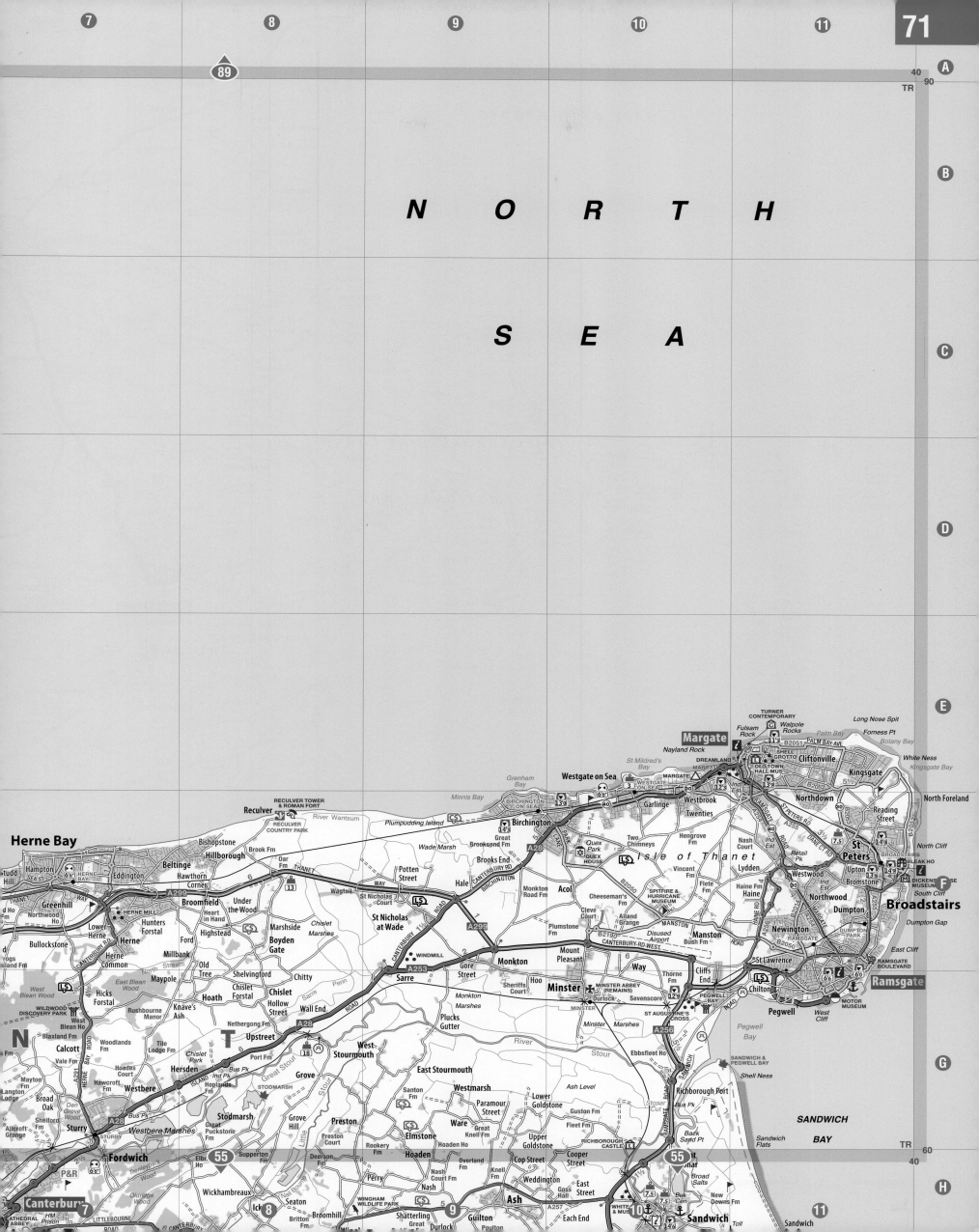

NORTH

SEA

Margate
Cliftonville
Kingsgate
North Foreland
Westgate on Sea
Westbrook
Northdown
Reading Street
North Cliff
Reculver
Birchington
Garlinge
Twenties
St Peters
Herne Bay
Bishopstone
Hillborough
Brook Fm
Isle of Thanet
Broadstairs
Hampton
Beltinge
Hawthorn Corner
Under the Wood
Quex House
Two Chimneys
Hengrove Fm
Lydden
Westwood
Bromstone
Dumpton Gap
Greenhill
Broomfield
Heart in Hand
St Nicholas Court
Hale
Acol
Spitfire & Hurricane Museum
Newington
Northwood
Dumpton
Eddington
Hunters Forstal
Highstead
Marshside
Boyden Gate
Chitty
Chislet Marshes
Monkton Road Fm
Cheeseman's Fm
Cleve Court
Alland Grange
Haine
East Cliff
Herne
Herne Common
Millbank
Old Tree
Shelvingford
Chislet
Windmill
Sarre
Gore Street
Monkton
Mount Pleasant
Way
Manston
Thorne Fm
Cliffs End
St Lawrence
Ramsgate
Hicks Forstal
Maypole
Hoath
Chislet Forstal
Hollow Street
Wall End
Sheriffs Court
Minster
Durlock
St Augustine's Cross
Sevenscore
Pegwell
West Cliff
Motor Museum
Wildwood Discovery Park
West Blean Wood
Rushbourne Manor
Knave's Ash
Plucks Gutter
Monkton Marshes
Minster Marshes
Pegwell Bay
Calcott
Upstreet
West Stourmouth
Port Fm
East Stourmouth
River Stour
Ebbsfleet Ho
Sandwich & Pegwell Bay
Shell Ness
Westbere
Hersden
Grove
Westmarsh
Lower Goldstone
Richborough Port
Fordwich
Stodmarsh
Grove Hill
Preston
Ware
Upper Goldstone
Guston Fm
Fleet Fm
Richborough Castle
Sandwich Flats
Sturry
Westbere Marshes
Great Puckstone
Elmstone
Hoaden
Cooper Street
Sandwich Bay
Canterbury
Wickhambreaux
Wingham Wildlife Park
Ash
Ash
Sandwich

ST BRIDES BAY

BAIE SAIN FFRAID

PEMBROKESHIRE COAST

NATIONAL PARK

Milford Haven
Aberdaugleddau

Milford Haven
Aberdaugleddyf

PEMBROKESHIRE

COAST NATIONAL PARK

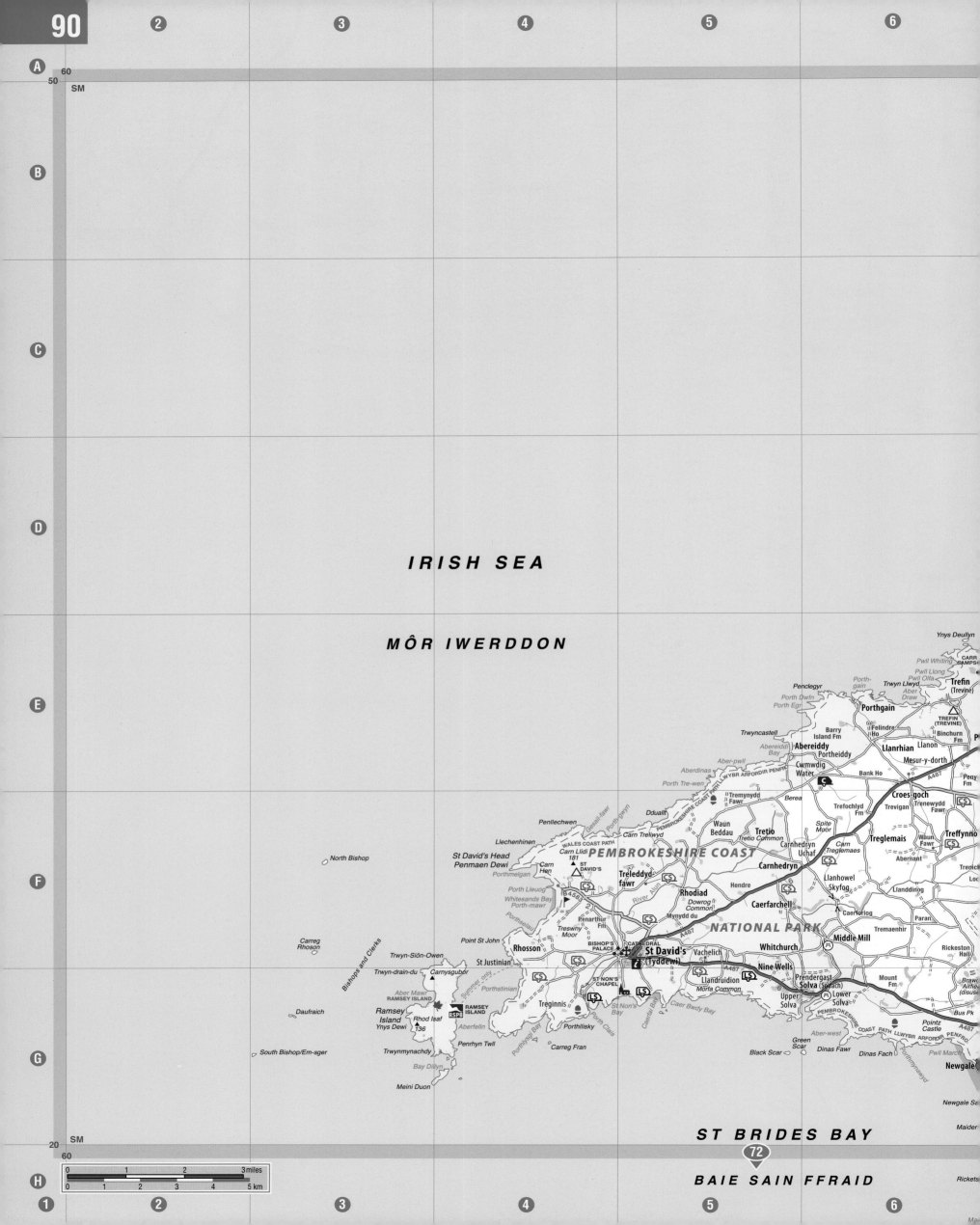

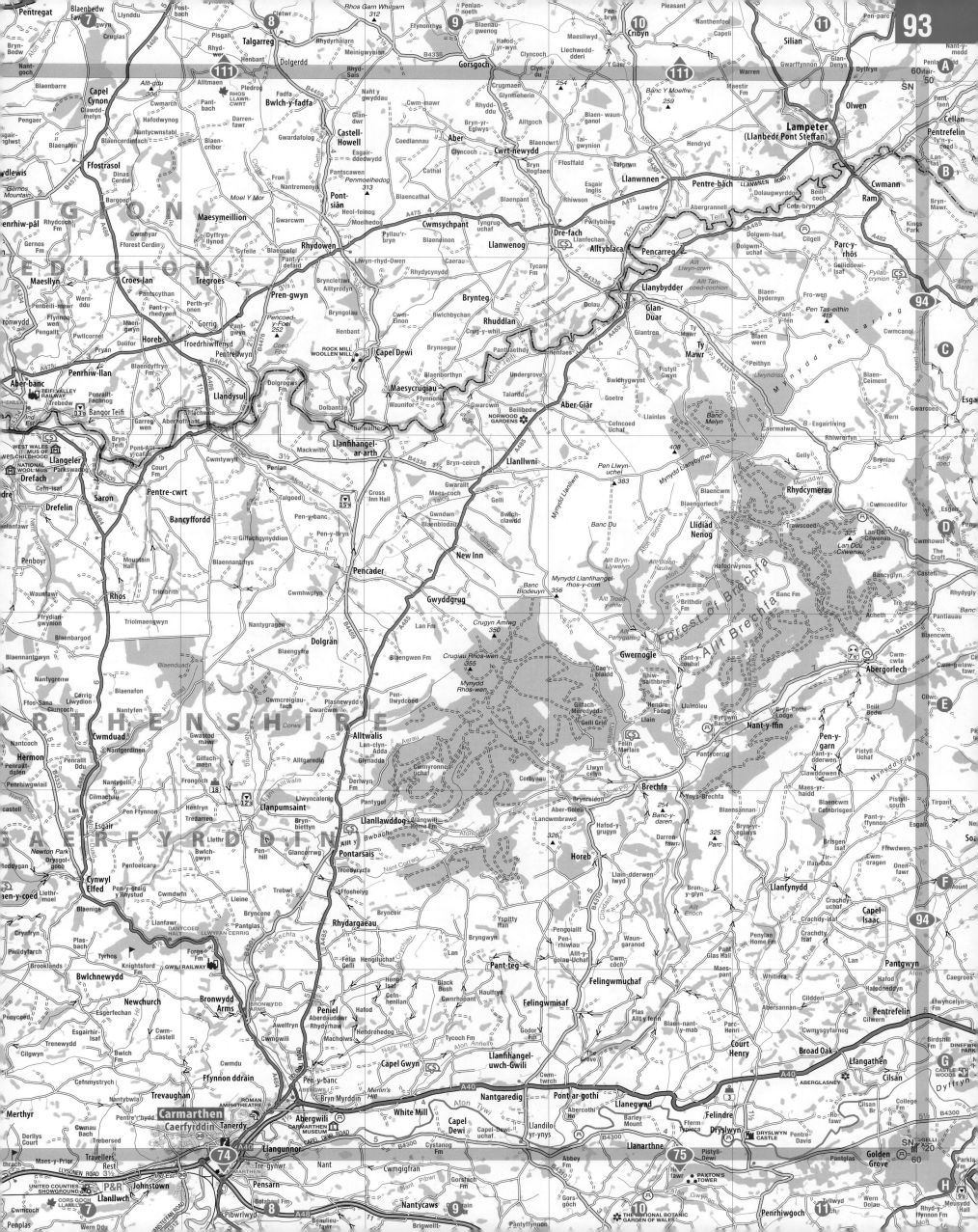

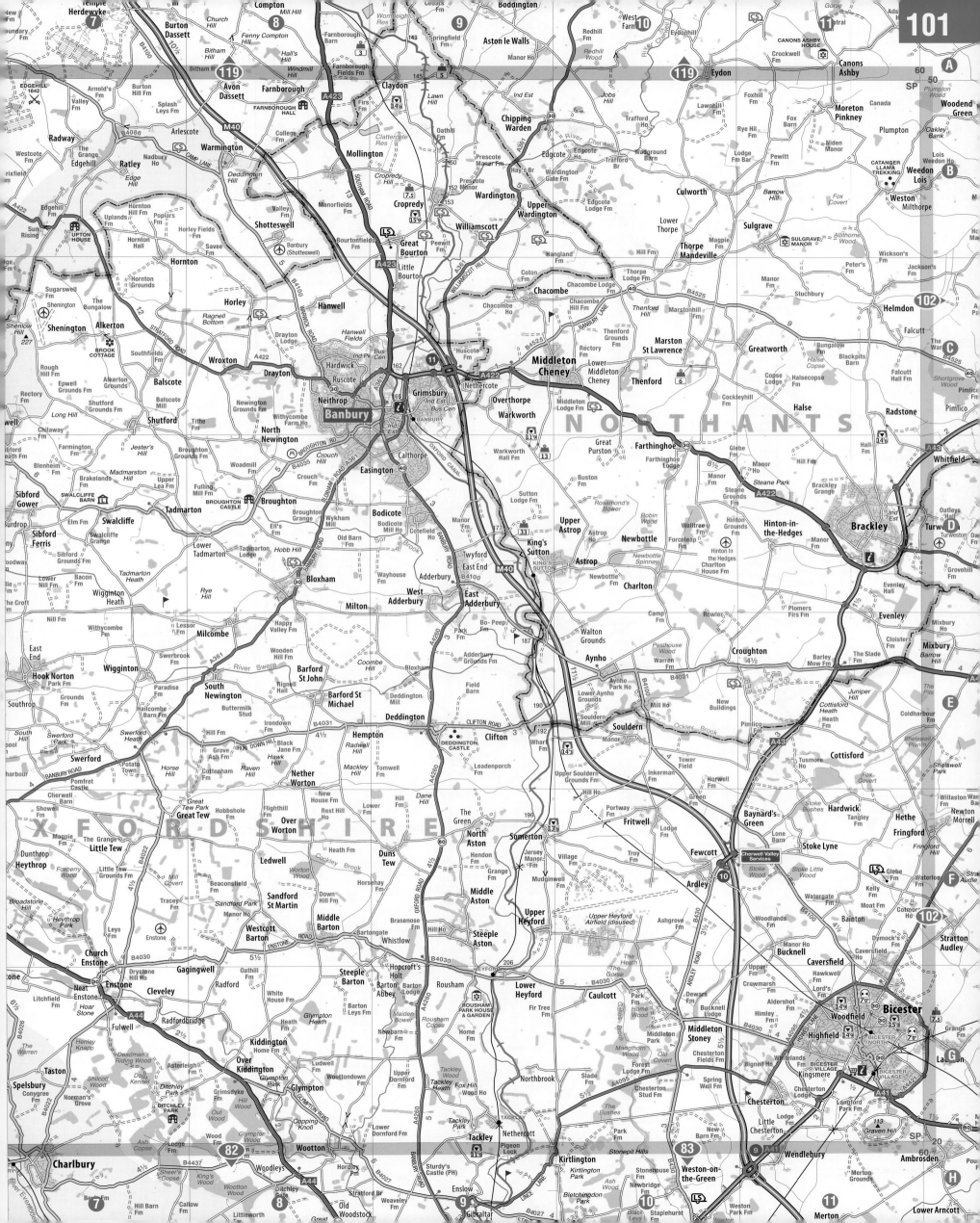

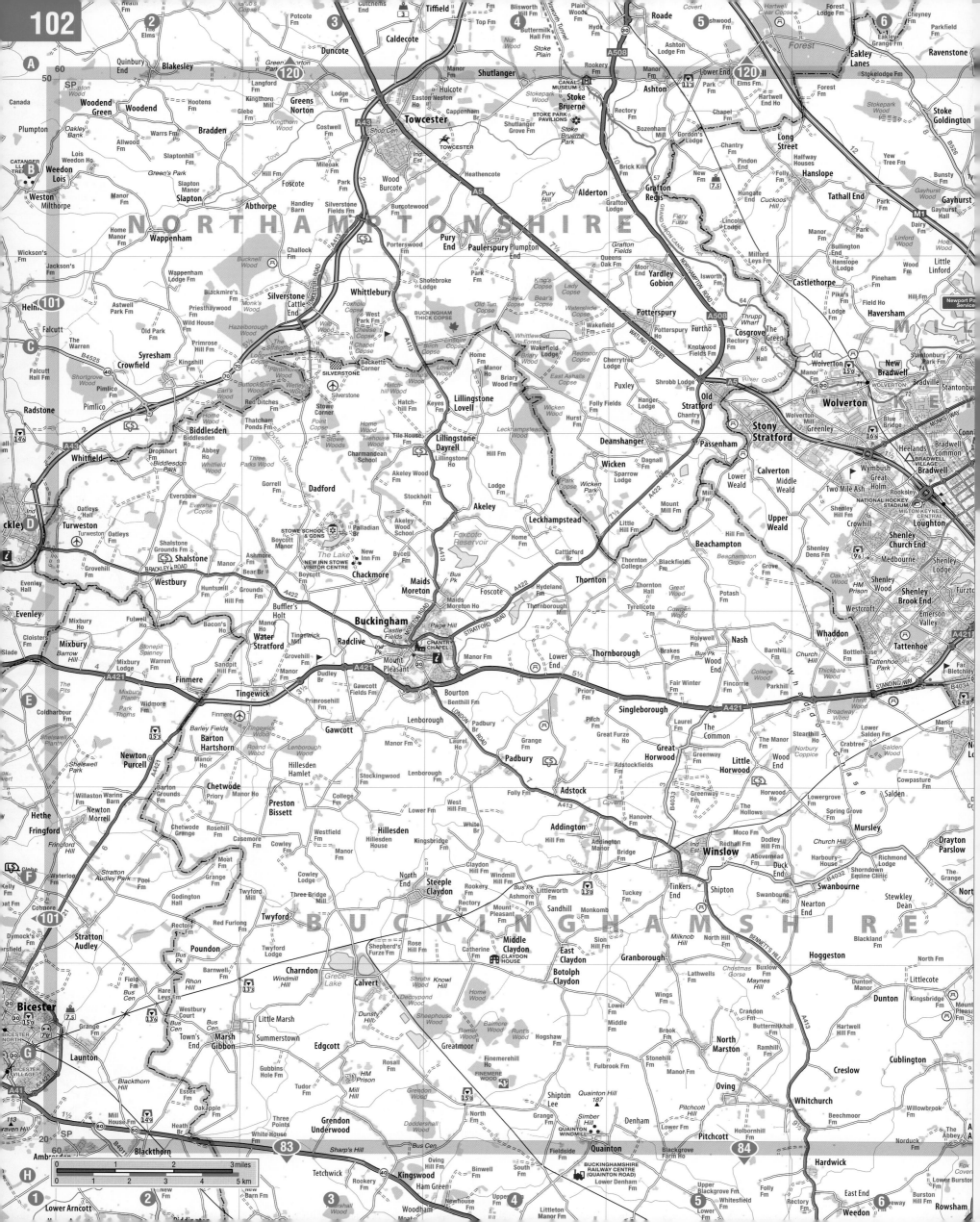

NORTH

SEA

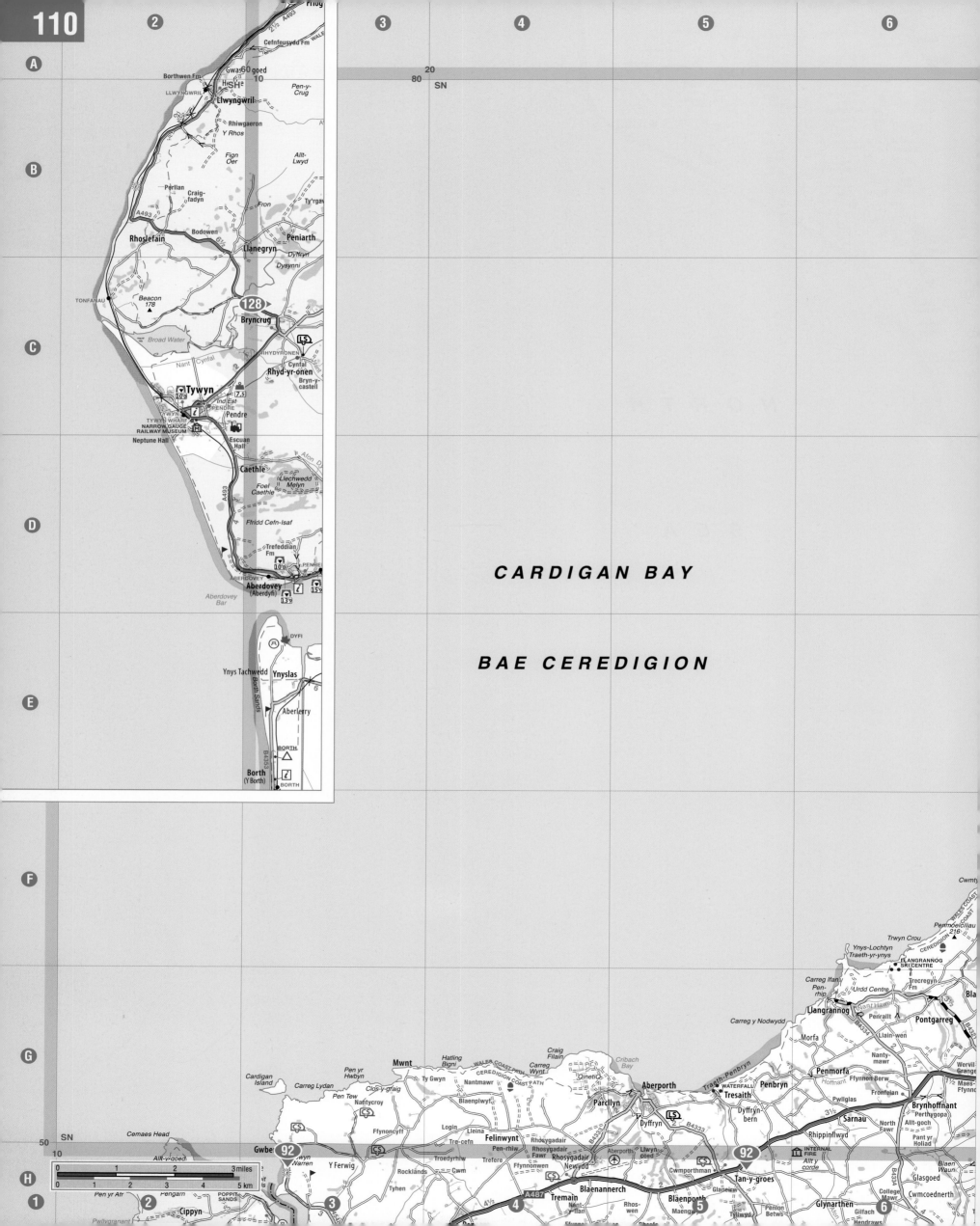

CARDIGAN BAY

BAE CEREDIGION

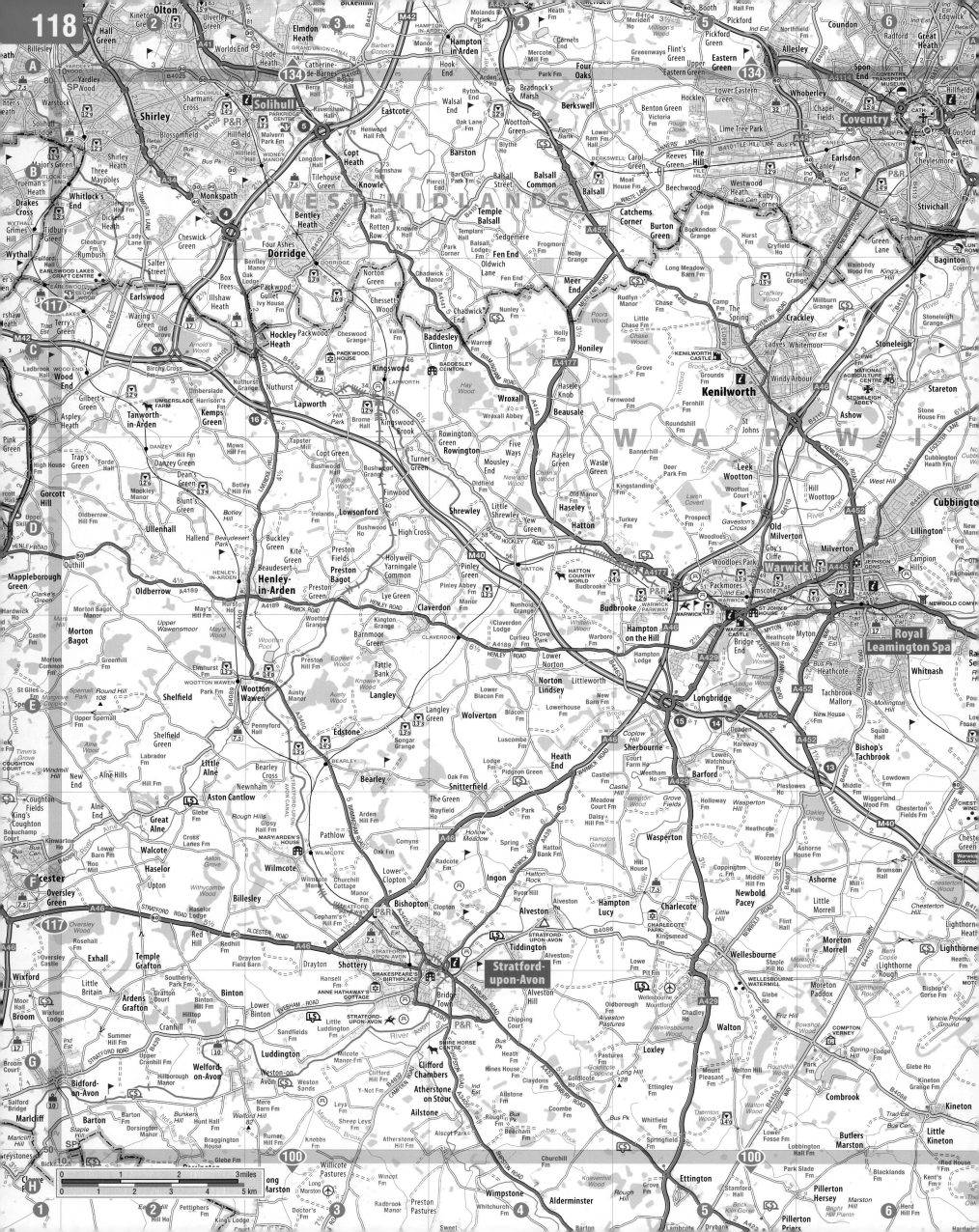

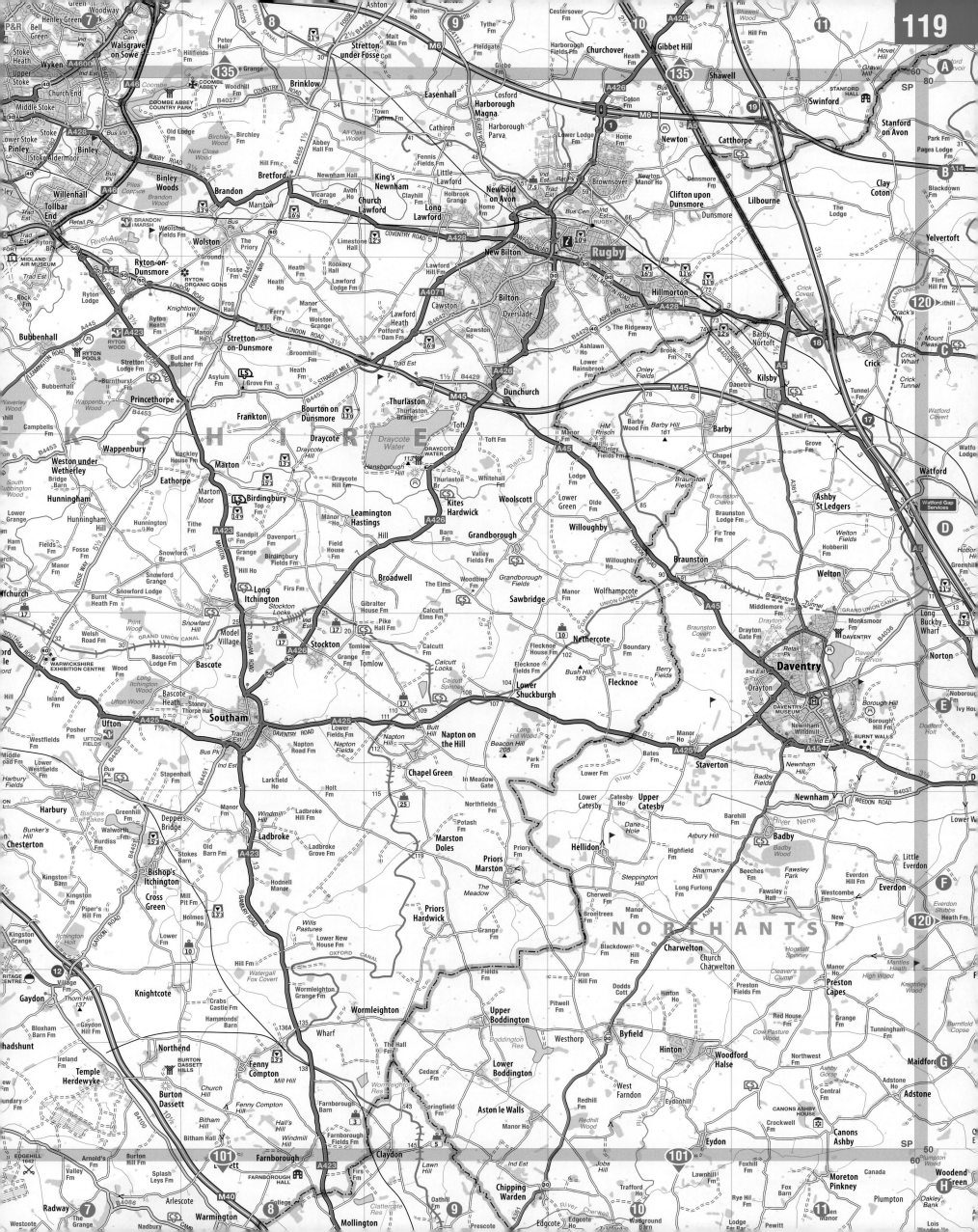

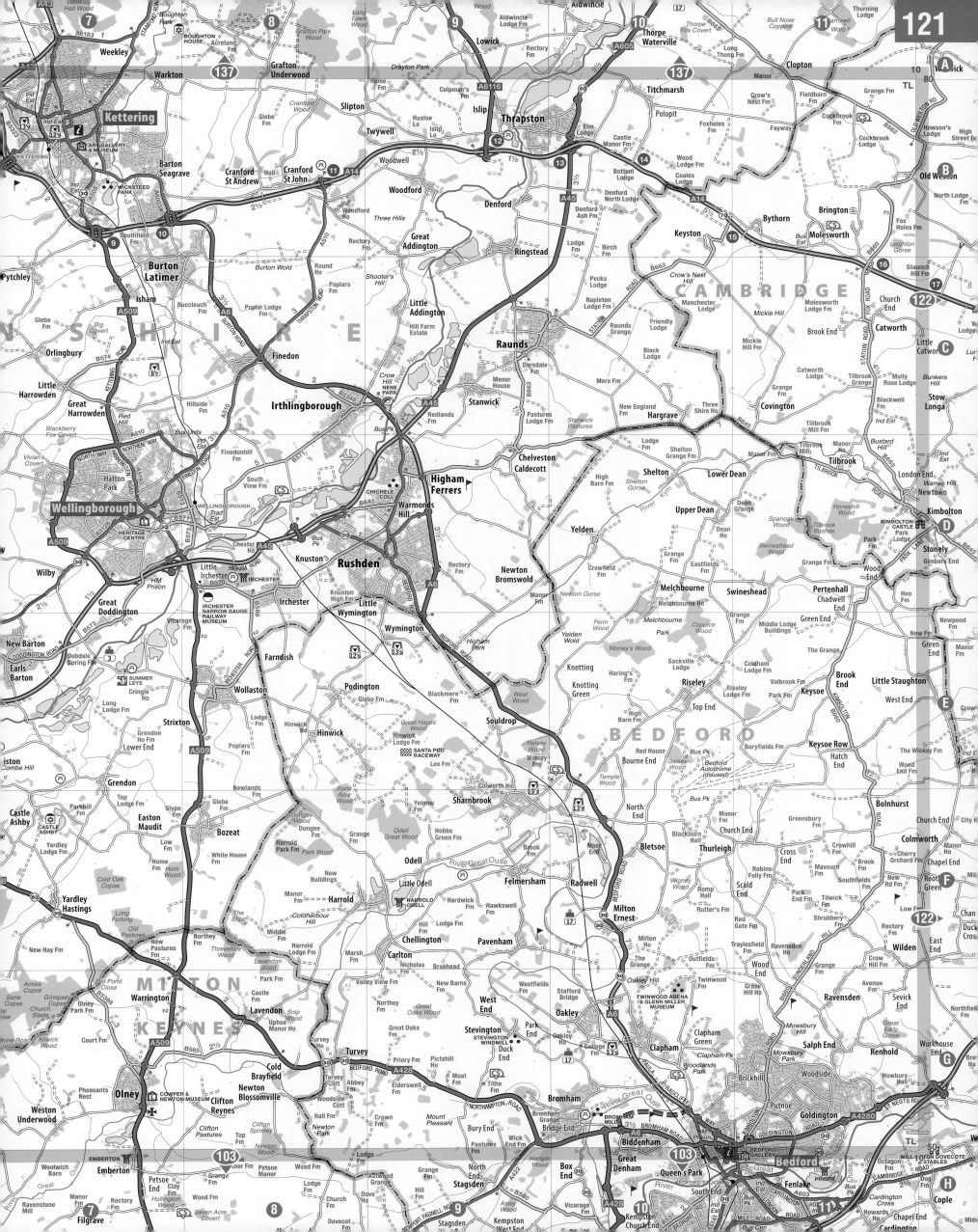

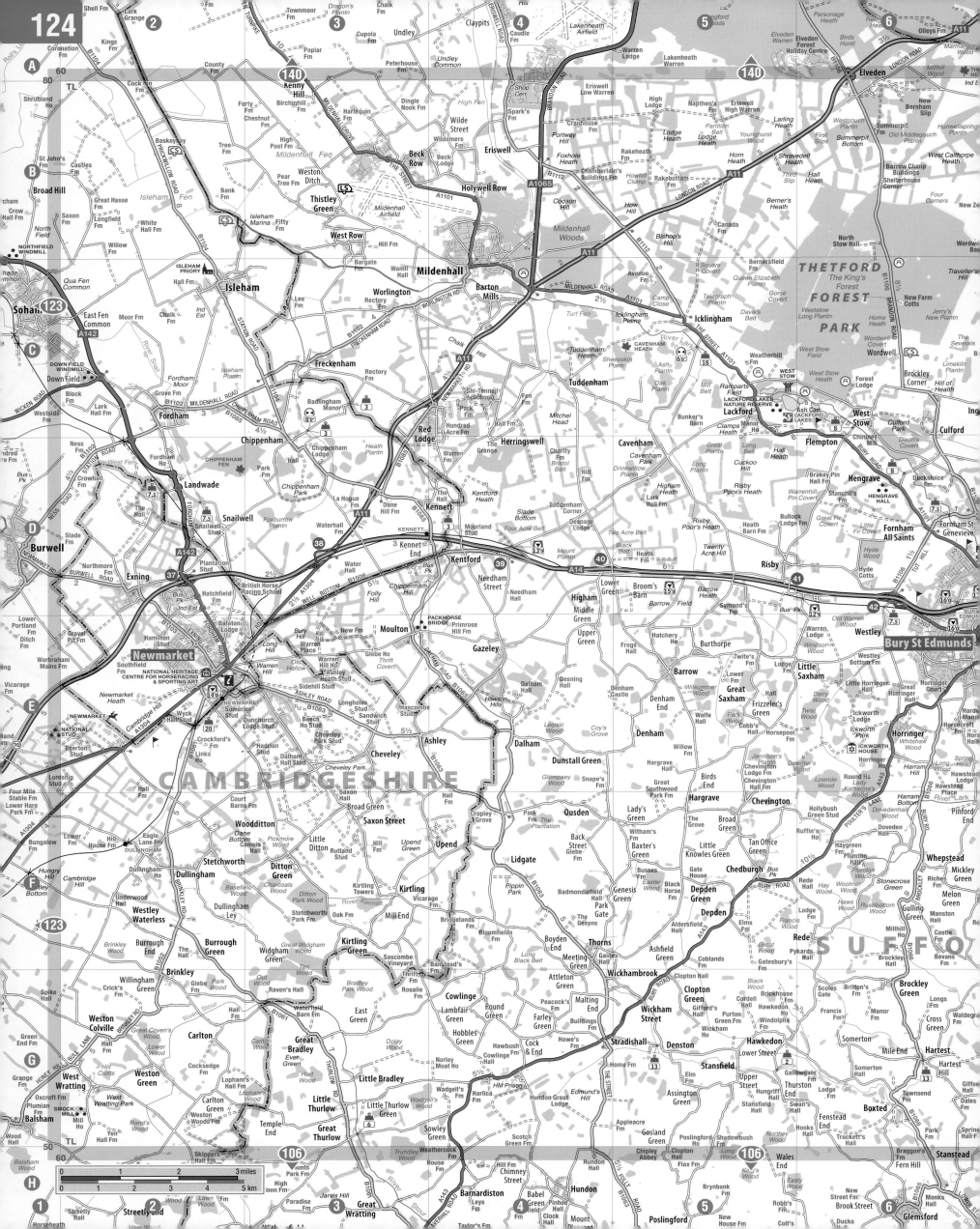

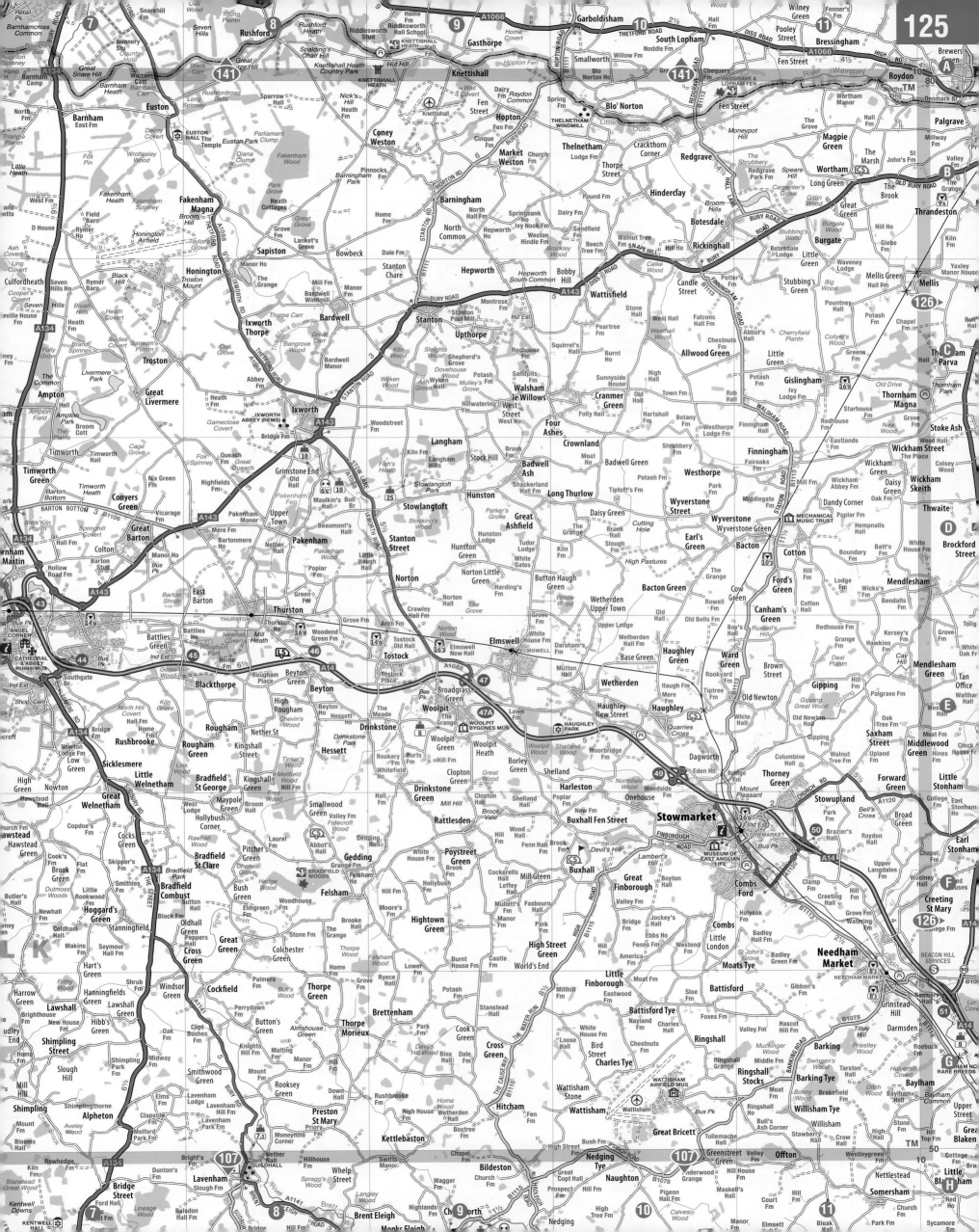

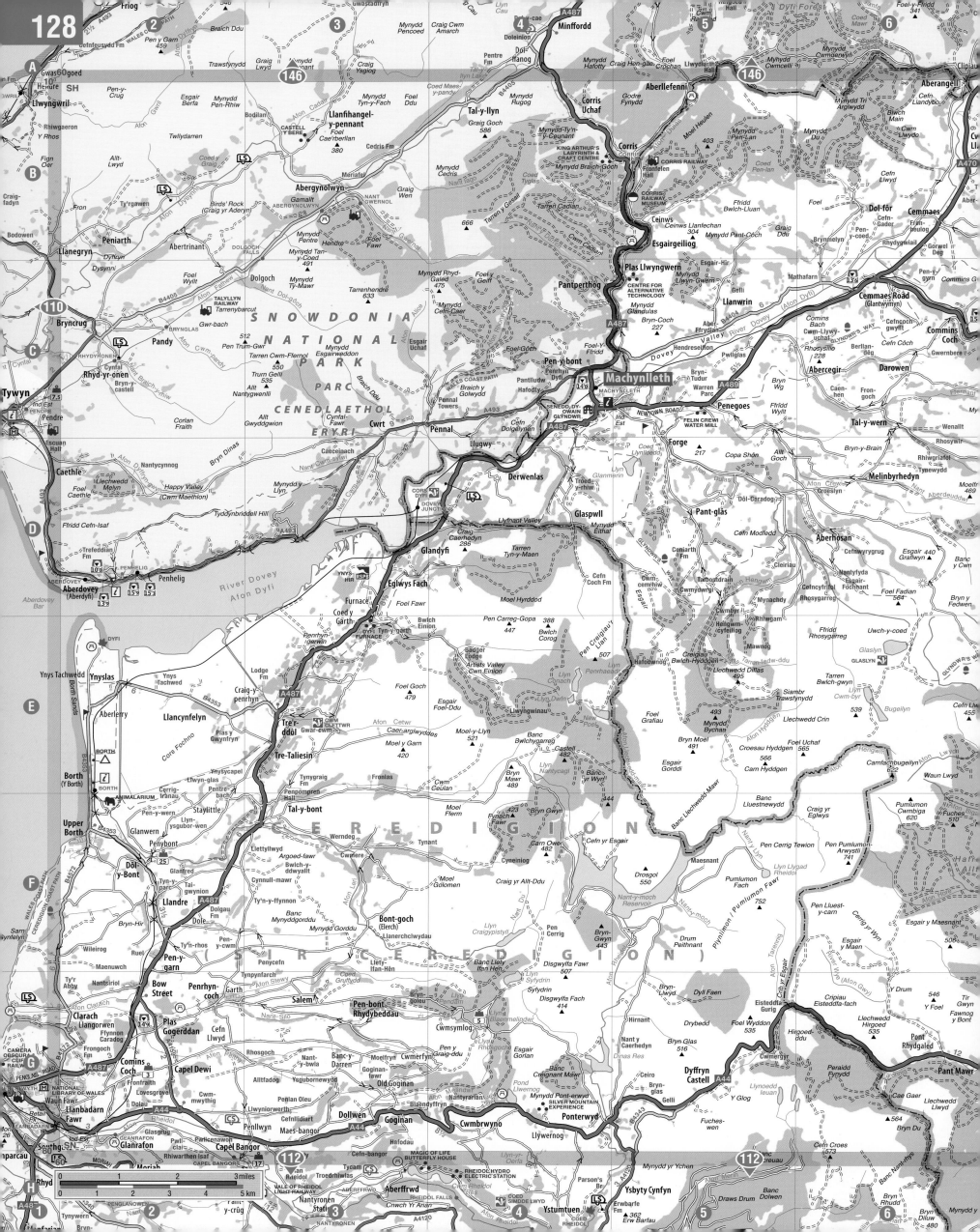

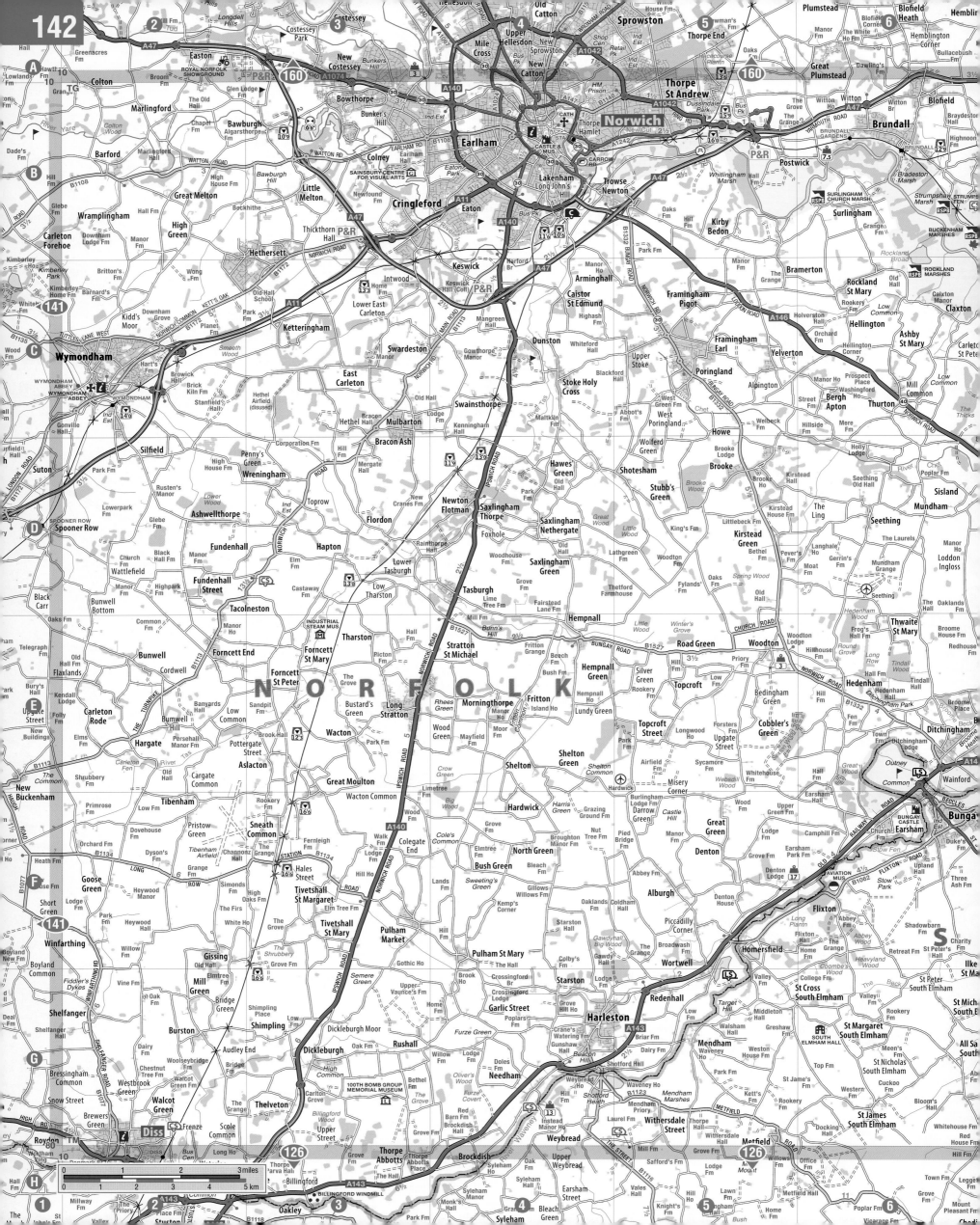

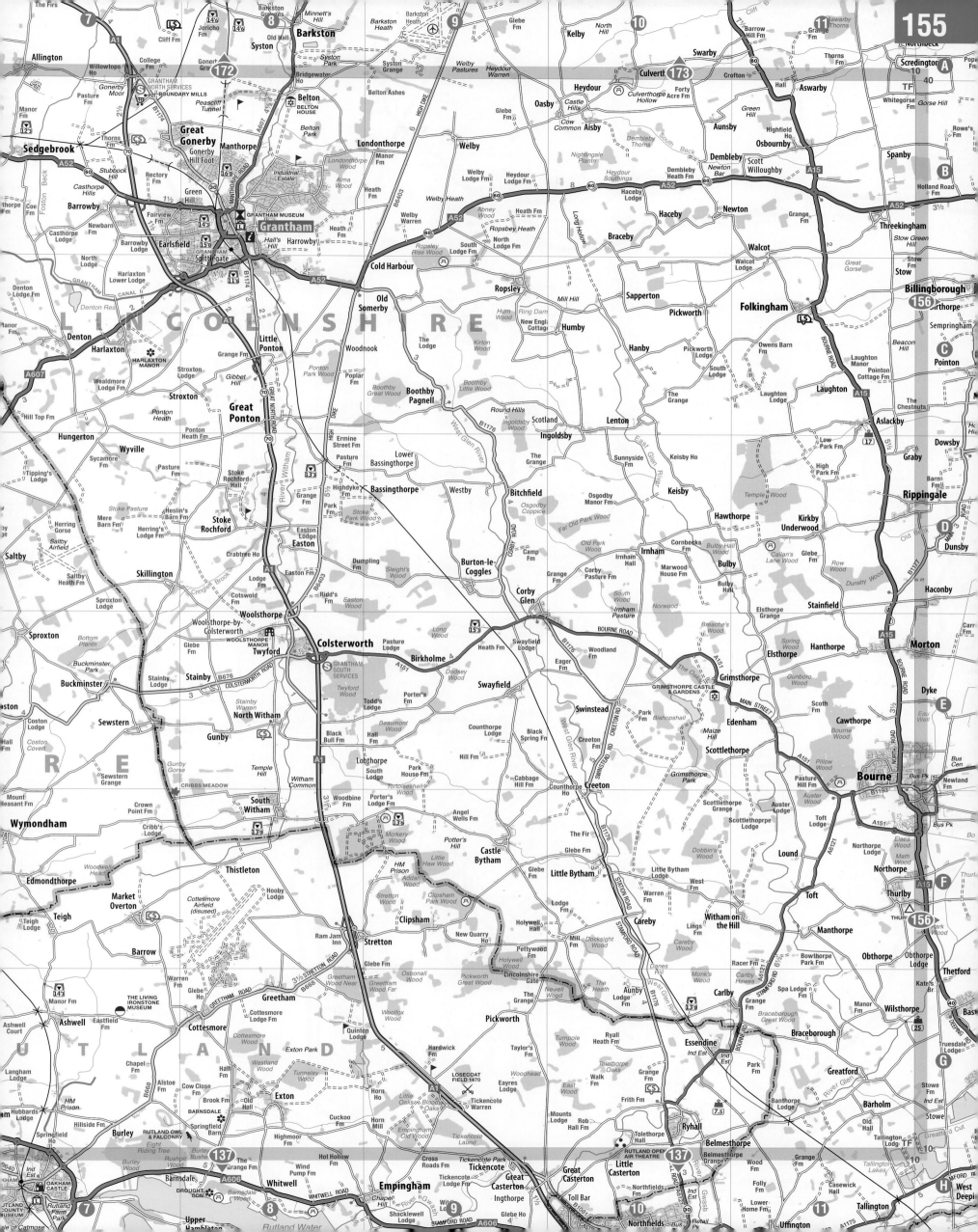

NORTH SEA

NORFOLK COAST

Keswick
Walcott
Rookery Fm
Ostend
lington
Walcott
Walcott Ho
Walcott Hall
Happisburgh
Whimpwell Green
Eccles on Sea
Fox Hill
East Ruston Hall
Mill Fm
Bush Estate
Grove Ho
Happisburgh Common
EAST RUSTON OLD VICARAGE GDN
Manor Ho
Castle Fm
ilcock's Fm
Lessingham
Manor Hill Hall
Hempstead
Hampstead Marshes
Sea Palling
Ingham Corner
New Hall
Heath Fm
Great Moss Fen
WAXHAM GREAT BARN
Brunstead Grange
Brunstead Hall
The Grove
Manor Ho
Randall's Mill
Waxham
Brumstead Common
Ingham
Old Hall
Lound Fm
Brograve Fm
Manor Ho
Stalham
Walnut Fm
Warren Fm
Chapel Field
MUSEUM OF THE BROADS
Stalham Green
Whinmere Fm
Hickling
Eastfield Fm
Horsey Corner
Berry Hall
Sutton Hall
Sutton
Bray Fm
Hickling Green
Stubb
Brayden Marshes
The Hall HORSEY WINDMILL
Horsey
Middle Marsh
Longmoor Fm
Hickling Heath
Hill Common
HICKLING BROAD NR
Stubb Mill
WINTERTON DUNES
nnygate
Wood Fm
Wood Street
Catfield
Heath Fm
HICKLING BROAD
Rush Hill
Horsey Mere
Blackfleet Broad
Winterton Holmes
Barton Turf
Hall Fm
Barton Broad
Catfield Hall
Catfield Common
Swim Coots
White Slea
Hundred Stream
Somerton Holmes
ANT BROADS & MARSHES
Sound Plantn
Heigham Sound
MARTHAM BROAD
Meadow Dyke
THE BROADS
Workhouse common
Irstead
Hall Fen
Rookery Fm
Fritton
Sharp Street
Walton Fm
Potter Heigham
Damgate
West Somerton
Burnley Hall
East Somerton
hammer on
Crome's Broad
How Hill
Ludham
River Thurne
Mustard Hyrn
High Barn Fm
Winterton-on-Sea
Neatishead Hall
Turf Fen
Ludham Hall
Ludham Marshes
White Gate Fm
Thunder Hill
Blood Hills
Mill Fm
eet
AIR DEFENCE DAR MUSEUM
Johnson Street
Bastwick
Cess
Grange Fm
Martham
7½
Cold Harbour Fm
Hundred Dike
Repps
Ashby Hall
Hemsby
Newport
Upper Street
Thurne
Rollesby
Main Road
Decoy Fm
Dowe Hill
Scratby Hall
Sand Cliffs
Ranworth Marshes
Ward Marsh
Boundary Ho
Ormesby Broad
Ormesby St Michael
Ormesby St Margaret
Scratby
Ranworth
Clippesby
Narrowgate Corner
7½
California
FAIRHAVEN WOODLAND & WATER GARDEN
Pilson Green
Manor Fm
Clippesby Ho
Burgh St Margaret (Fleggburgh)
Lily Broad
Rollesby Broad
A149
Nova Scotia Fm
South Walsham
Low Fm
Newgate Corner
A1064
6
Filby Broad
Filby Heath
ROMAN TOWN
Tyegate Green
Town Green
Highfield
Upton
Upton Green
Billockby
Charity Fm
Filby
A1064
Mautby
Caister Hall
Caister-on-Sea
Watt's Hall Fm
Thrigby
THRIGBY HALL WILDLIFE GARDENS
Mautby Lodge
Lower Caister Castle & Wood Fm Motor Museum
Long Plantn
Burlingham Green
Fishley
Whitegate
Winsford Hall
Woodlands
Barn Fm
West End
West Caister
Caister Pt
North Burlingham
Acle
CANDLEMAKER WORKSHOP
Stokesby
Runham
Manor Fm
Decoy Fm
Gt Yarmouth North Denes
North Denes
Lingwood
Lingwood Lodge
Damga
143
A47
NEW ROAD
8
Mautby Marsh Fm
Ashtree Fm
New Road
Newtown
North Beach
North Burlingham
Beighton
Moulton St Mary
Tunstall
Britannia
Runham Vauxhall
Runham
10
143
Great Yarmouth

CAERNARFON

BAY

BAE CAERNARFON

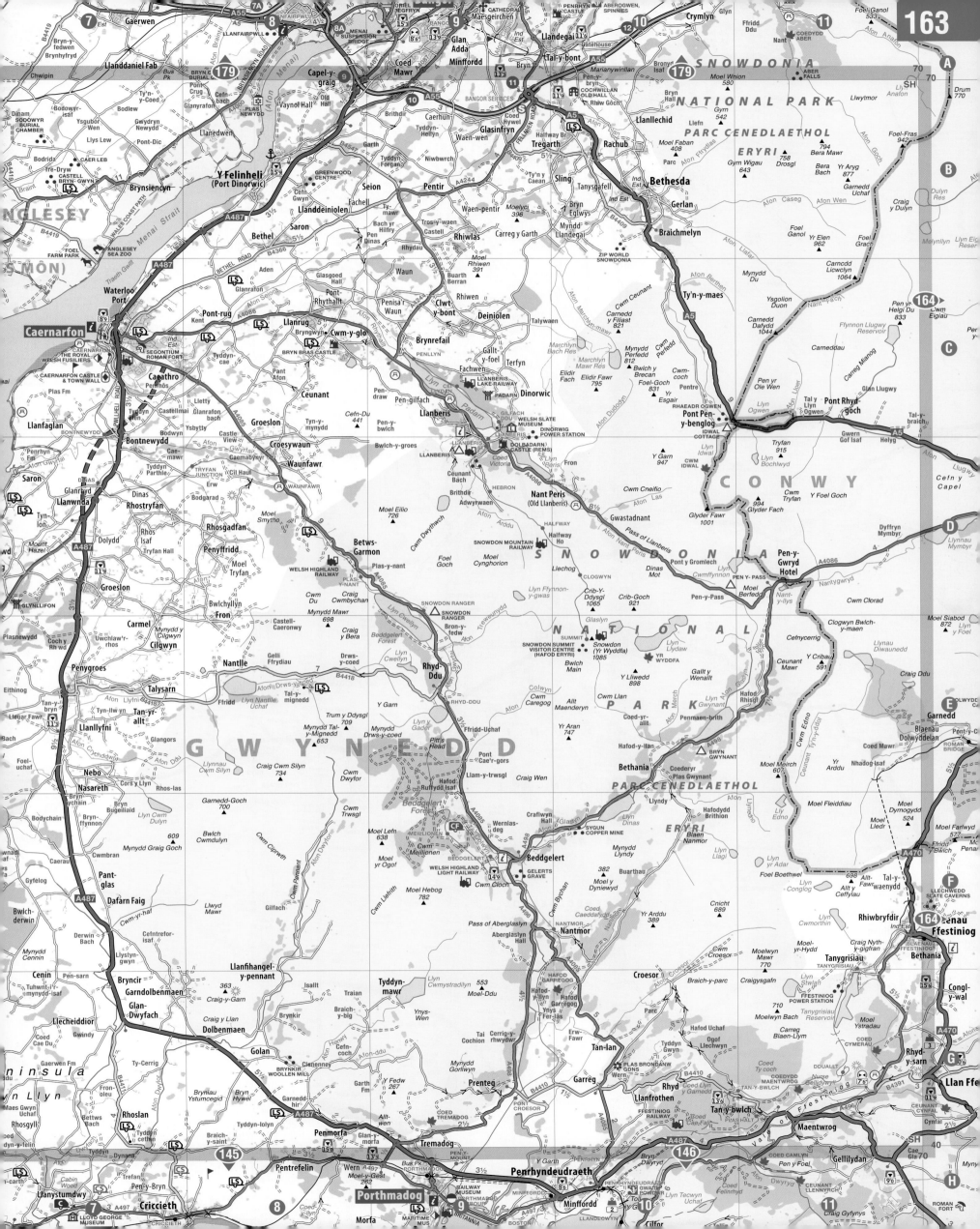

THE WASH

182

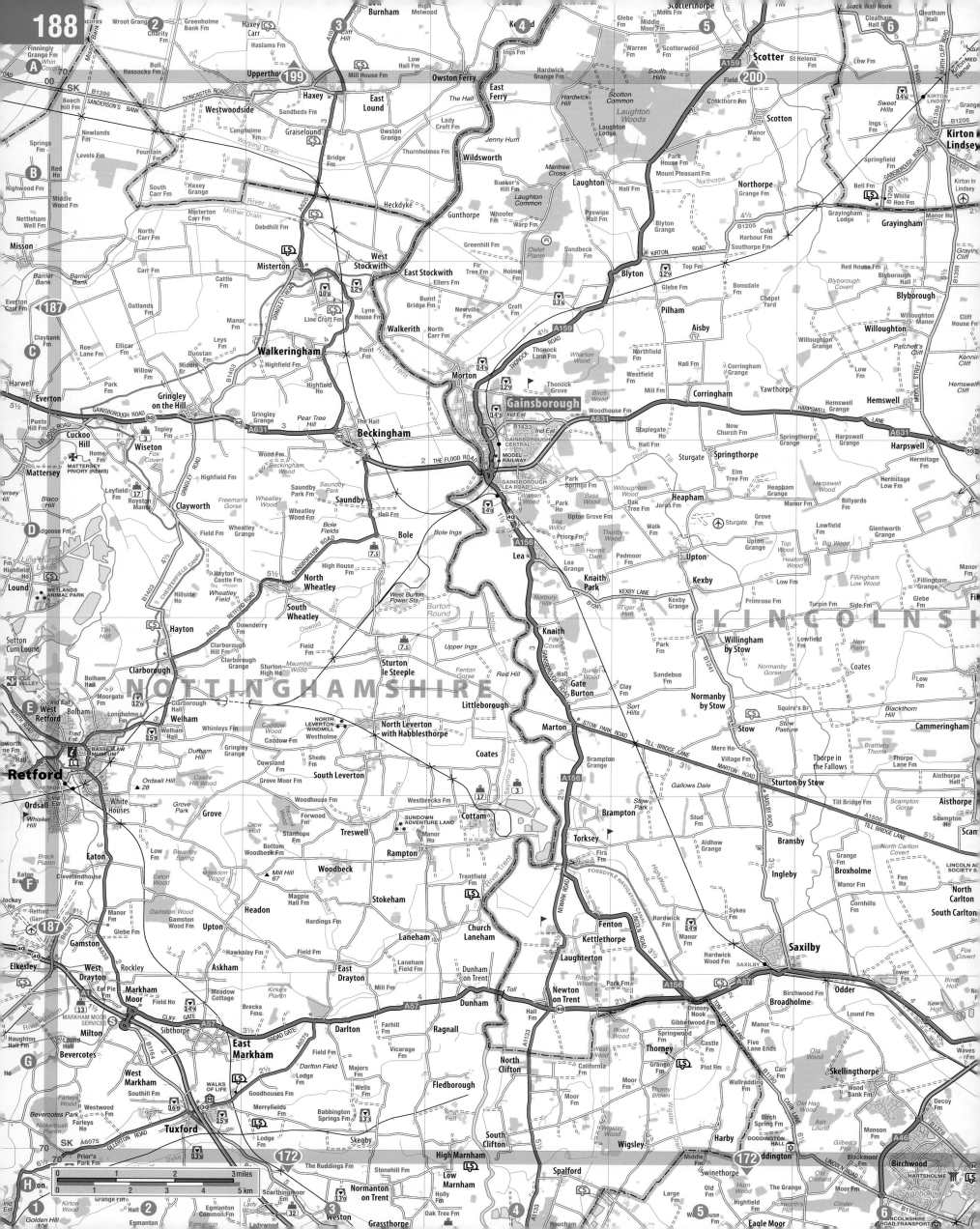

N O R T H

S E A

Saltfleet

Saltfleetby
All Saints

Theddlethorpe
St Helen

Theddlethorpe
All Saints

North End

THE SEAL SANCTUARY
& NATURE CENTRE

Meers
Bridge

FUN FAIR

Mablethorpe

Trusthorpe

Strubby

Maltby le Marsh

Thorpe

Sutton on Sea

Sandilands

Beesby

Hagnaby

Saleby

Hannah

Sea Bank
Fm

Markby

Asserby

Black
House Fm

Bilsby

Wold
Sea Fm

Huttoft

Anderby Creek

Alford

Anderby

Thurlby

Wolla Bank

Mumby

Chapel Six Marshes

Farlesthorpe

Chapel Pt

Authorpe
Row

Cumberworth

Helsey

Hogsthorpe

Chapel St Leonards

Willoughby

Sloothby

Hasthorpe

Slackholme
End

HARDY'S
ANIMAL FARM

Ingoldmells

Habertoft

Addlethorpe

FANTASY ISLAND

Welton
Marsh

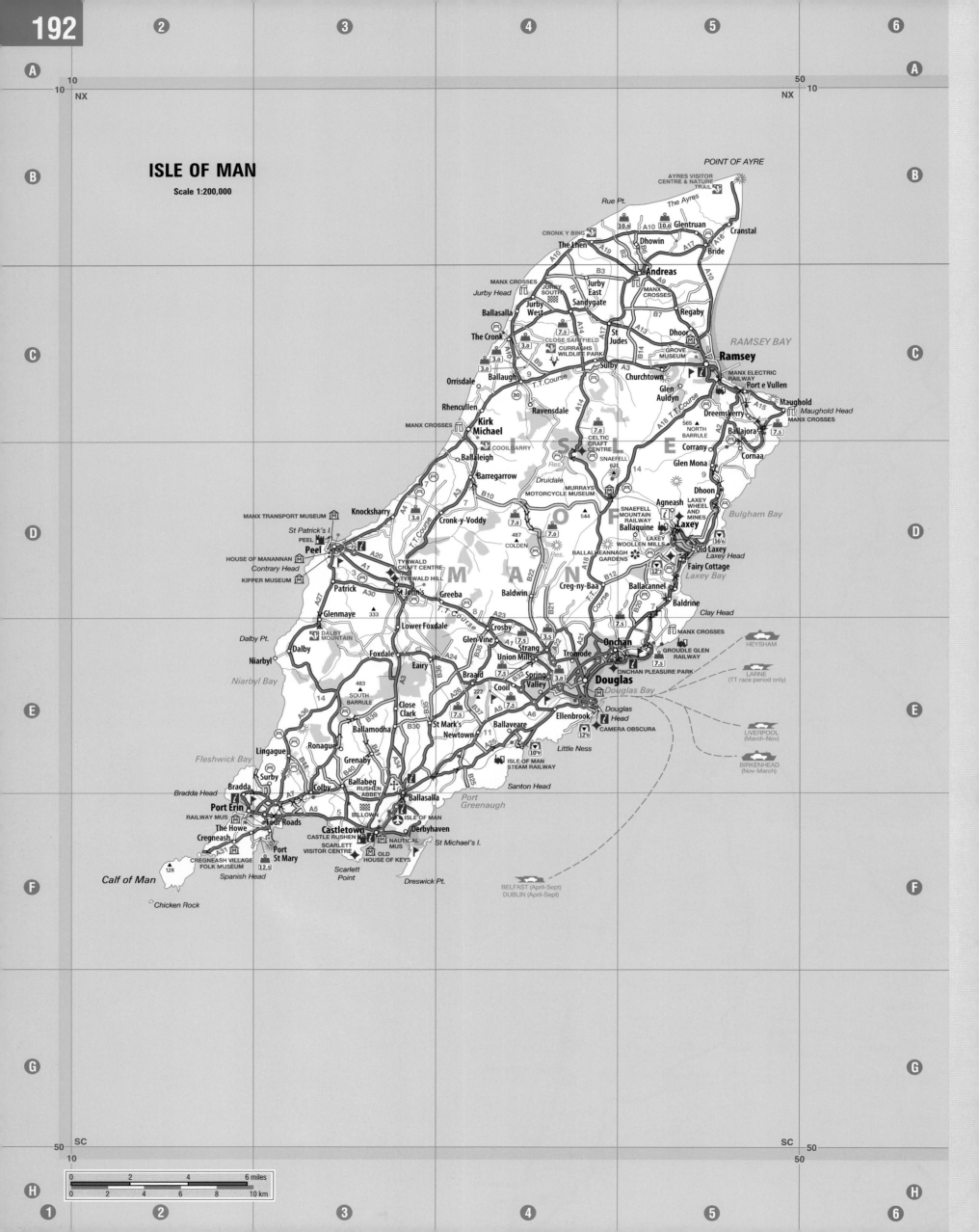

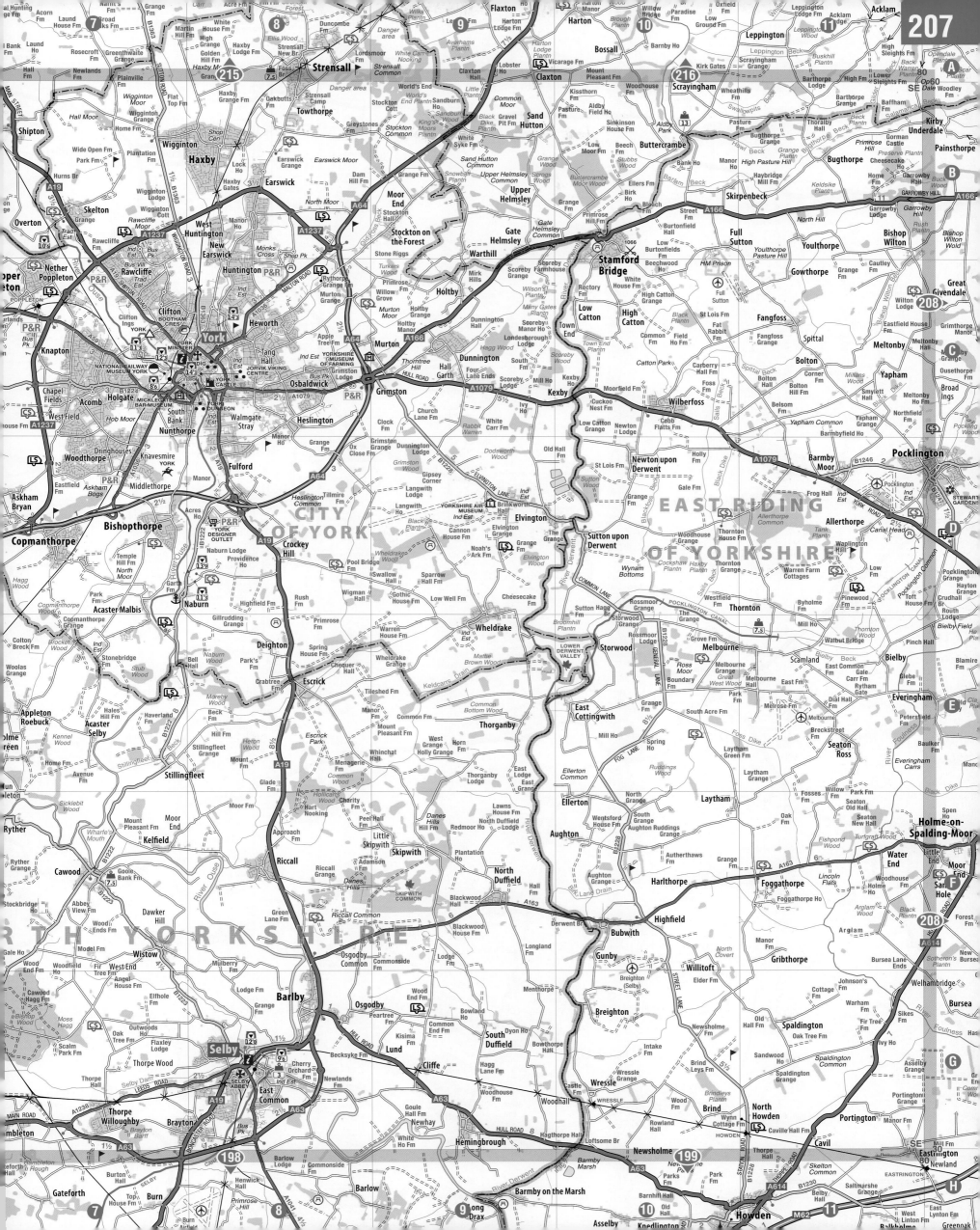

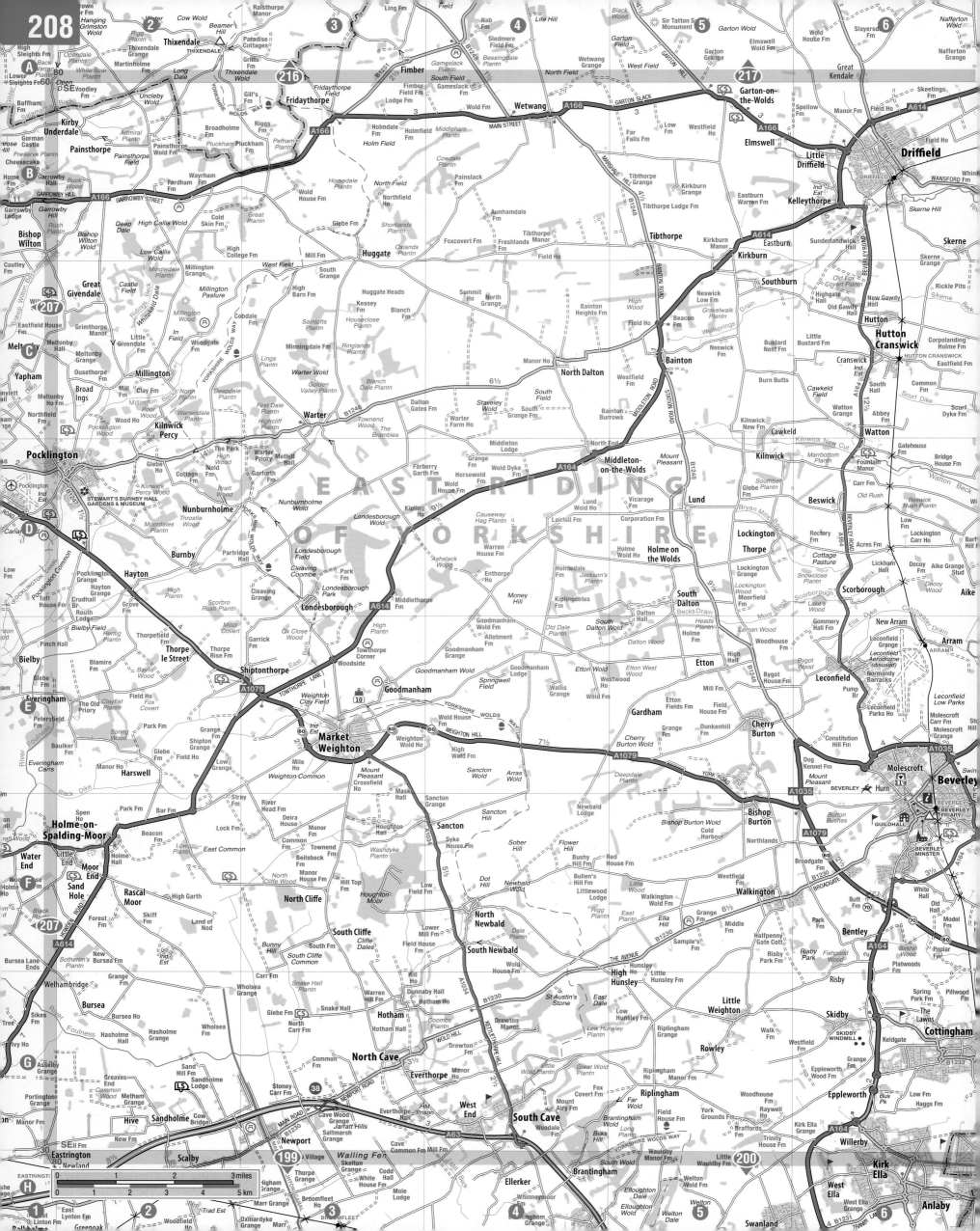

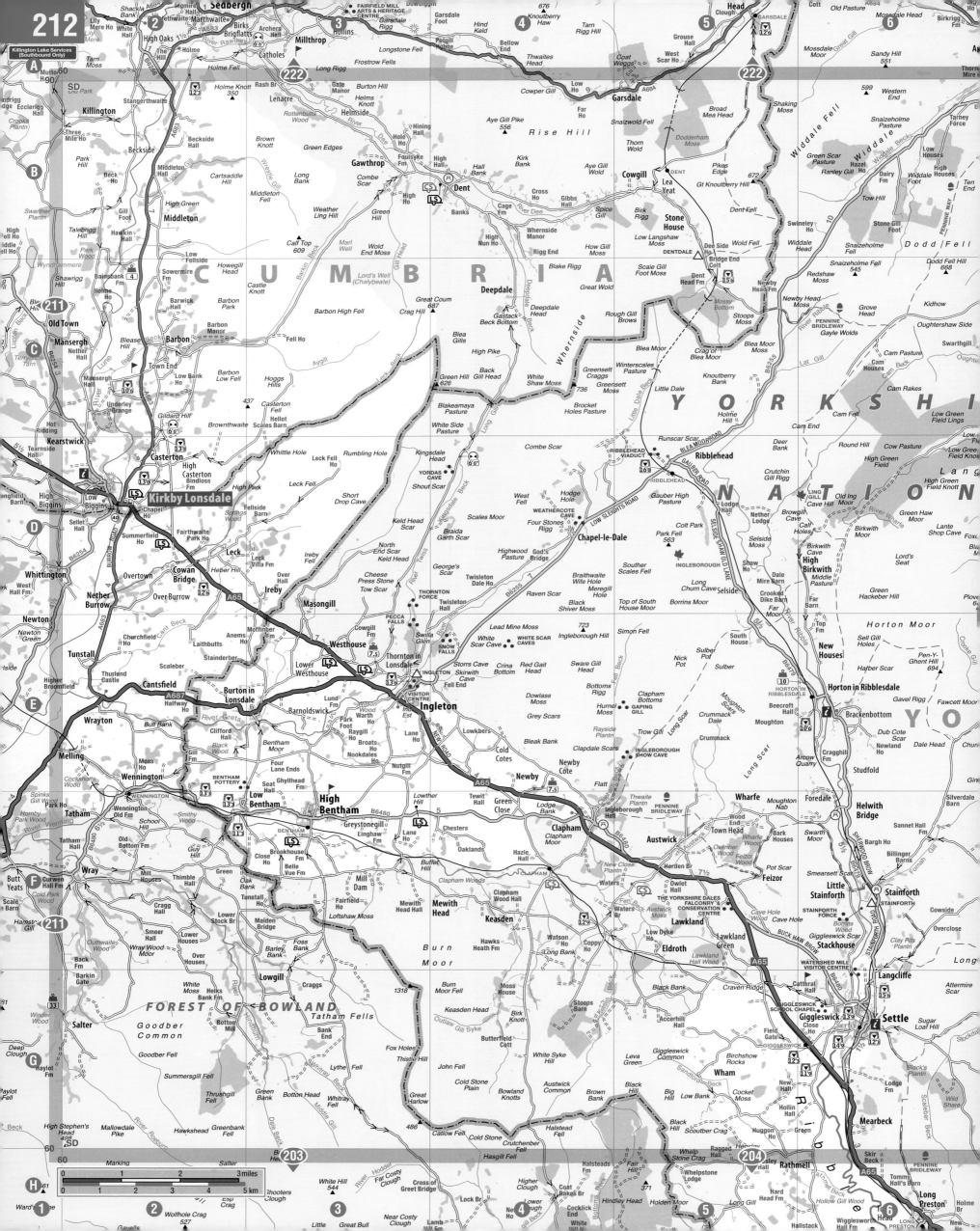

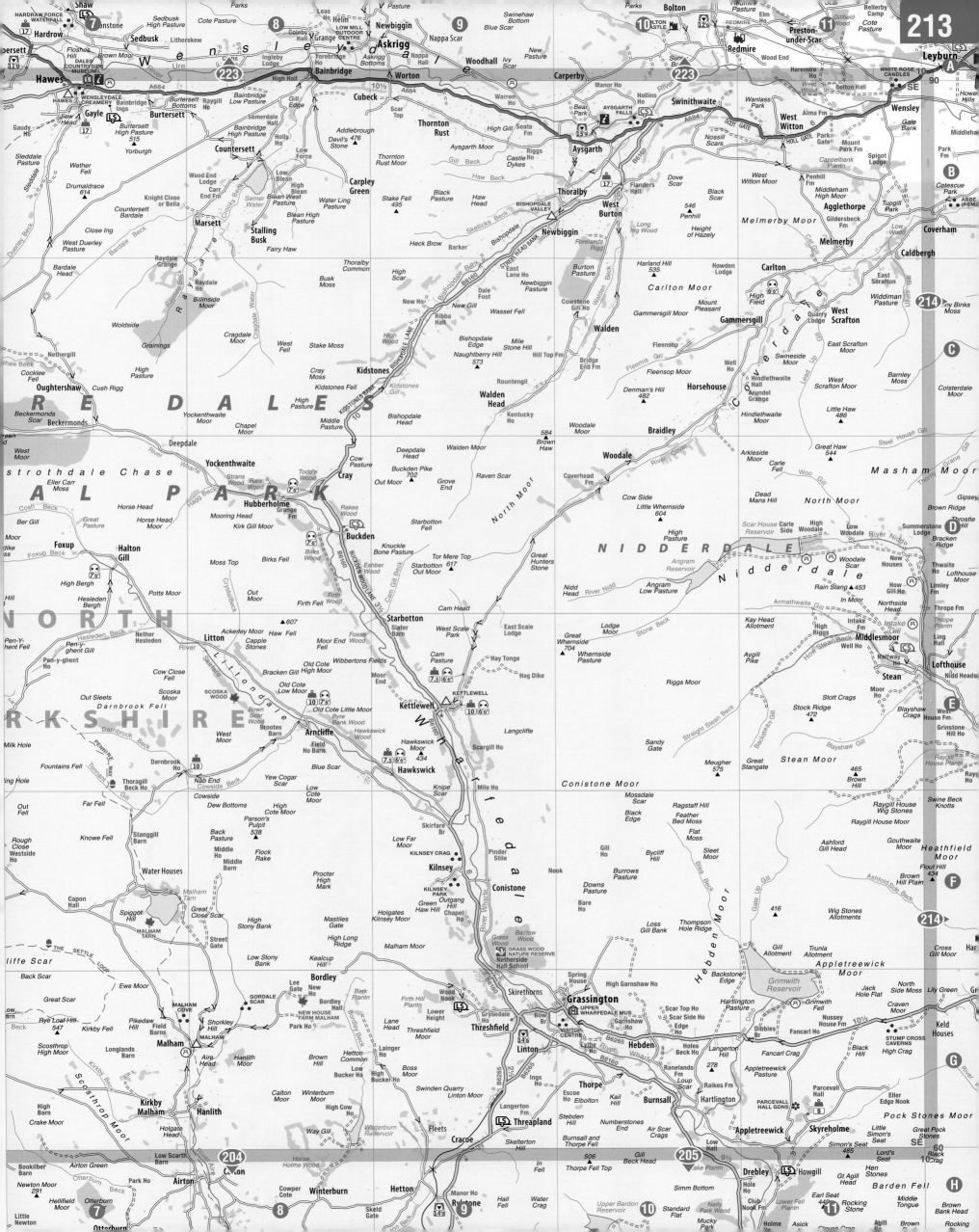

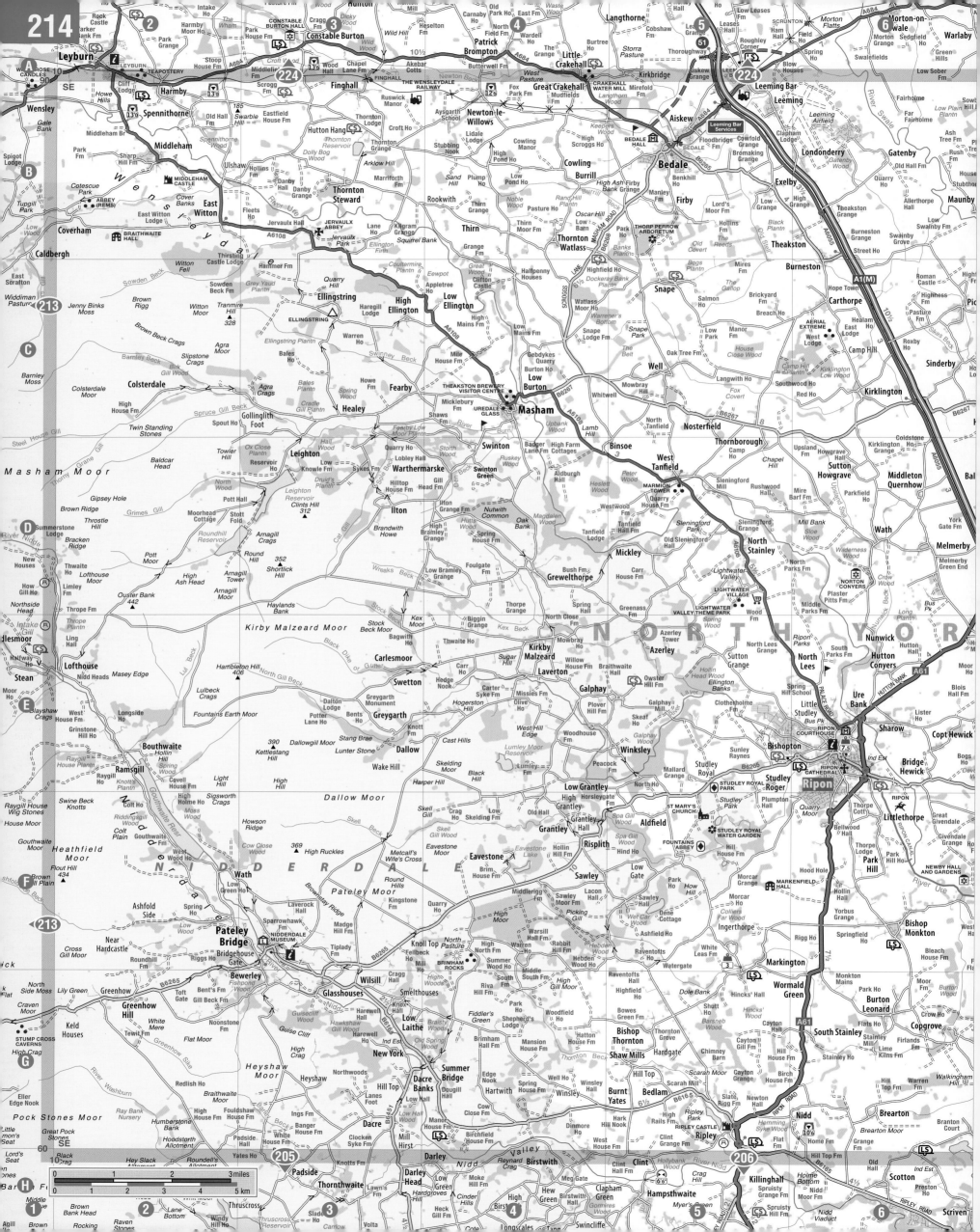

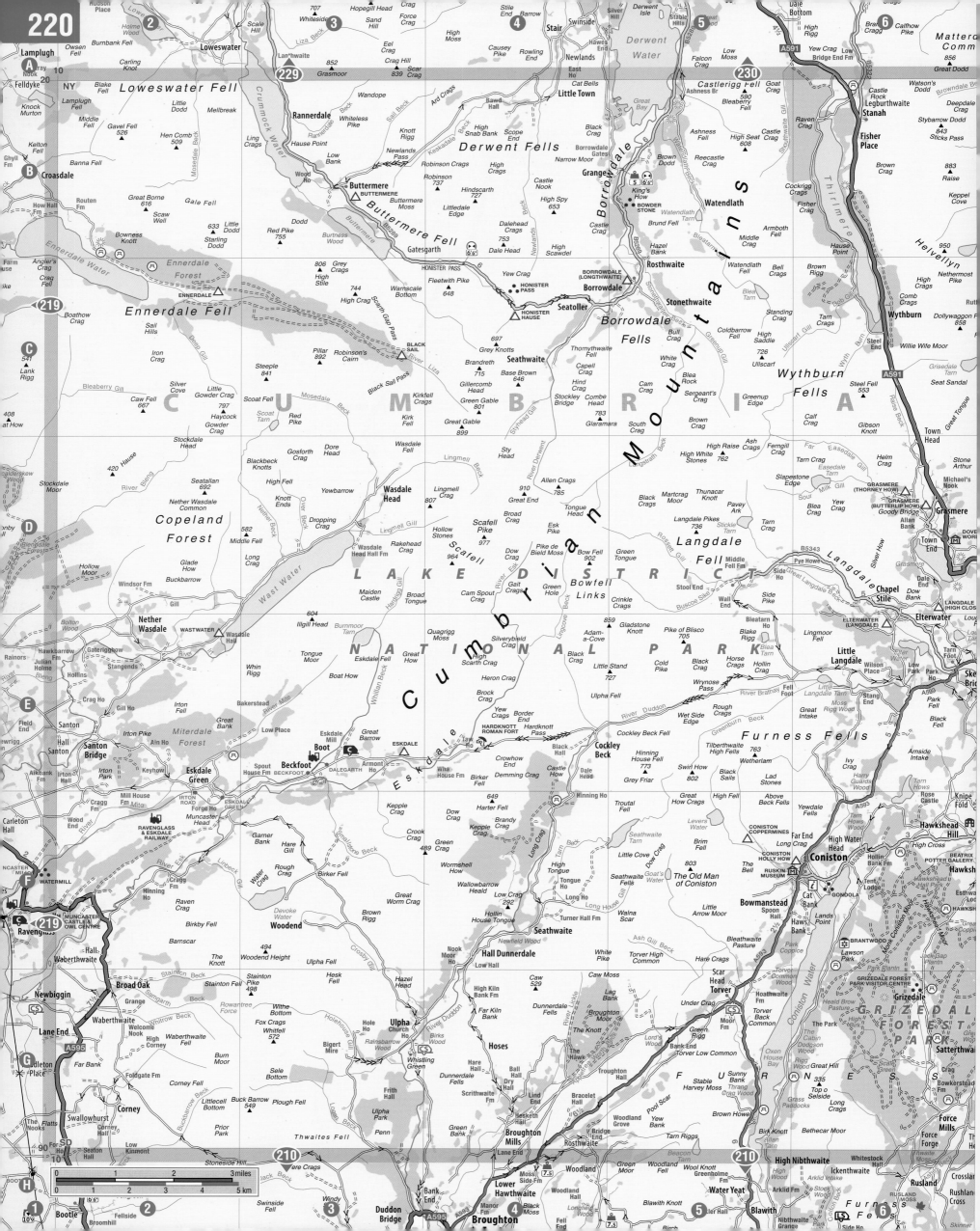

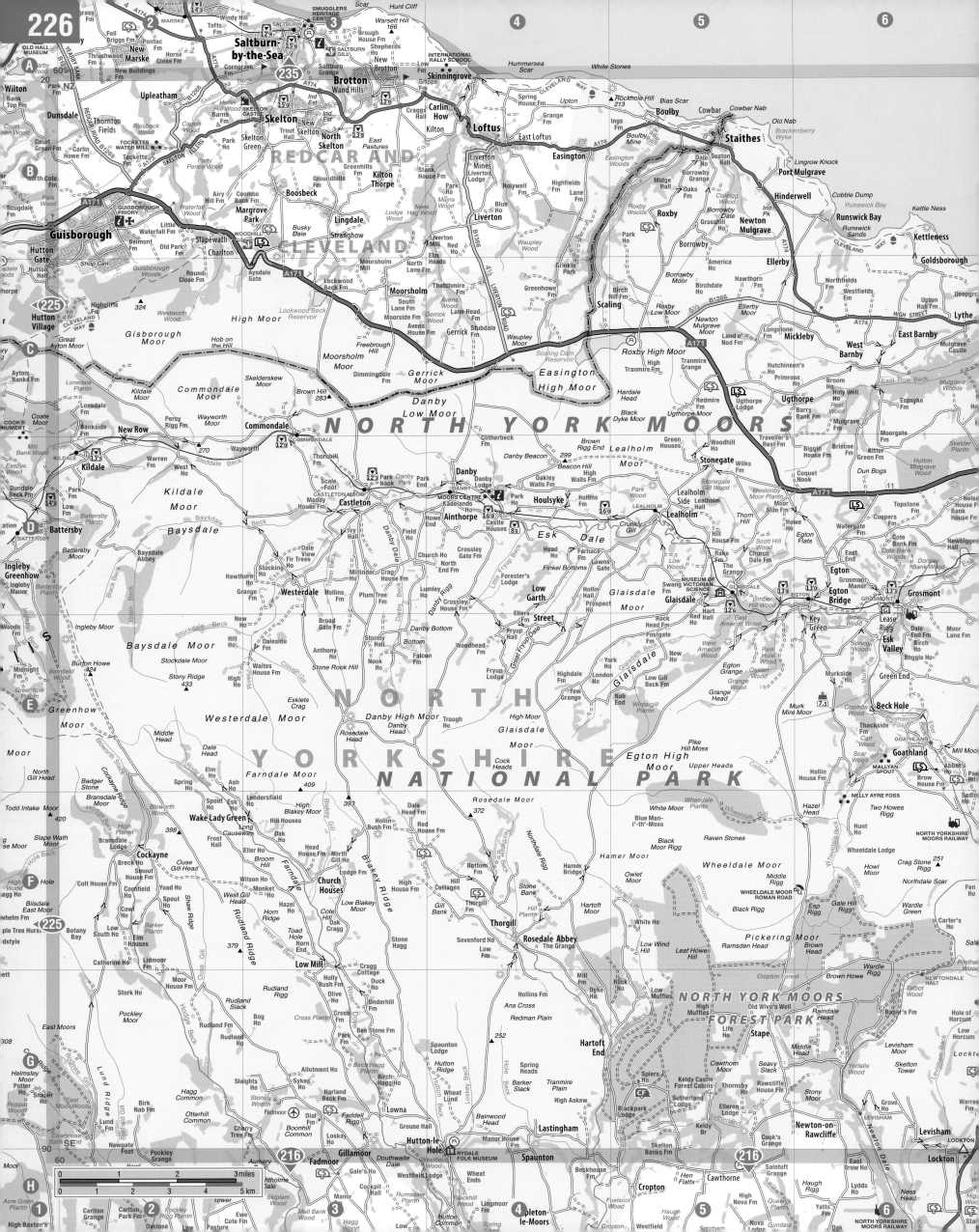

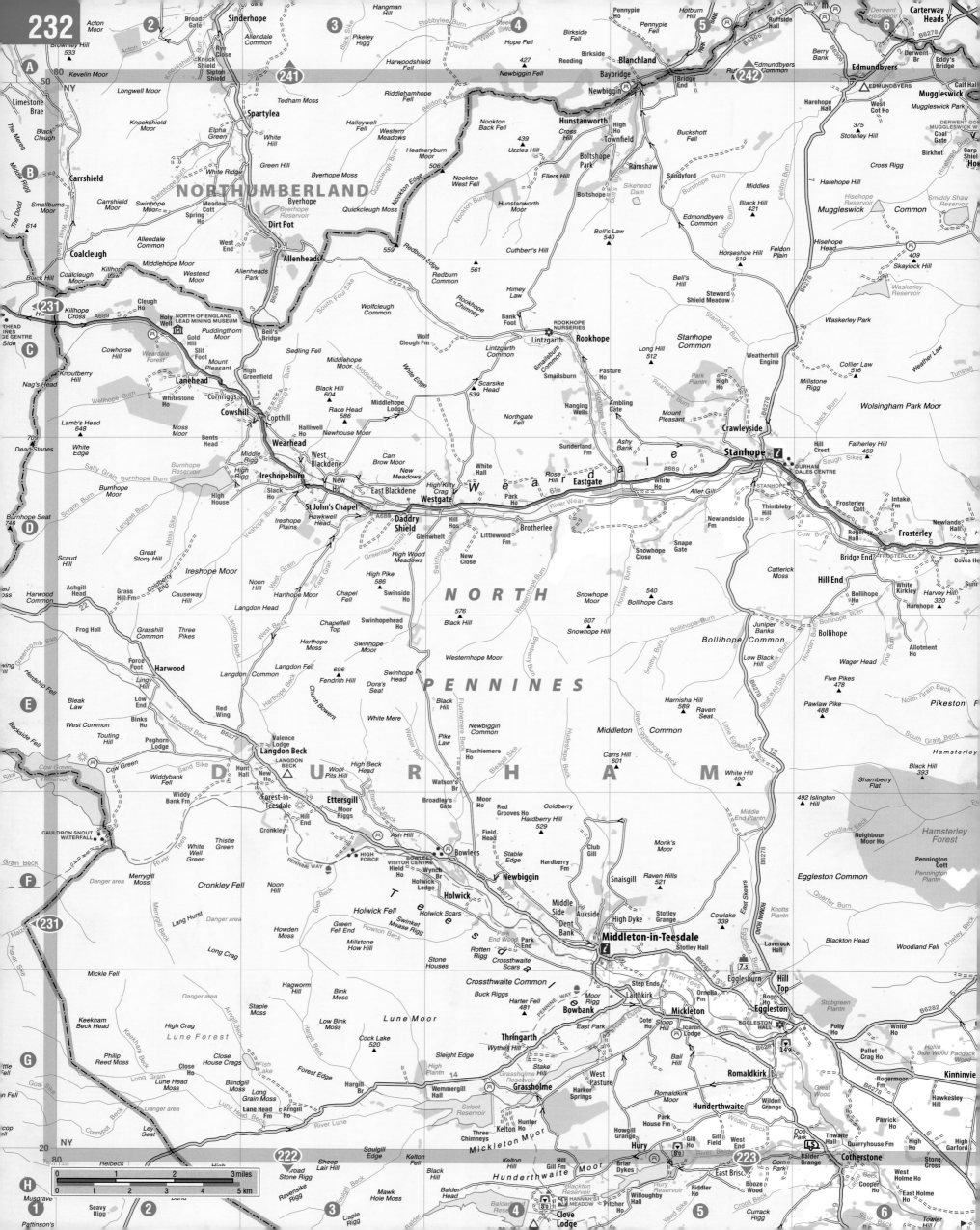

NORTH SEA

TEES BAY

Bran Sands

Coatham Sands

West Scar   Salt Scar

Redcar Rocks   The Flashes

Grangetown Works

COATHAM MARSH

Coatham

Warrenby

BRITISH STEEL REDCAR

TRUNK ROAD

Westfield

Redcar

Mill Howle

REDCAR EAST

Redcar Racecourse

REDCAR CENTRAL

REDCAR LANE

COAST ROAD

Scanbeck Howle

Dormanstown

B1269

Marske-by-the-Sea

Stone Gap

Kirkleatham

Grewgrass Fm

LONGBECK

A174

MARSKE

Windy Hill

Tofts Fm

SALTBURN

Saltburn Gill

SMUGGLERS HERITAGE CENTRE

Saltburn Scar   Hunt Cliff

Brough House Fm

Warsett Hill 166

Wilton Chemical Works

OLD HALL MUSEUM

Yearby

Fell Briggs Fm

Pontac Fm

New Marske

Horse Close Fm

Corngrave Fm

Saltburn-by-the-Sea

Saltburn Grange

Shepherds Ho

New Brotton

INTERNATIONAL RALLY SCHOOL

Low Fm

Hummersea Scar   White Stones

Yearby Wood

New Buildings Fm

Brotton

Wand Hills

Skinningrove

Gripps

SPring House Fm

Upton

226

Rockhole Hill 213

Bias Scar

Lazenby

Wilton

Wilton Bank

Park Fm

B1269

225

Upleatham

Skelton

Craggs Hall

Carlin How

Kilton

Grange Fm

Boulby Mine

Boulby

Cowbar   Cowbar Nab

A1053

Lackenby

Lazenby Bank

Wilton Bank Top Fm

Dunsdale

Thornton Fields

Reisbeck Wood

Capon Wood

SKELTON CASTLE

Hollin Hill Wood

Ind Est

Ind Est

Skelton

Skelton Green

Trout Hall

New Skelton

Park Ho

Skelton

East Pastures

Loftus

Liverton

East Loftus

A174

Easington

Ings Fm

Boulby Cliffs

Old Nab

Brackenberry Wyke

Park Seaton

Staithes

242

GREYSTONE ROAD

REDCAR ROAD B1269

Court Green Wood

Carlin Howe Fm

TOCKETTS WATER MILL

SKELTON ELLERS

REDCAR AND

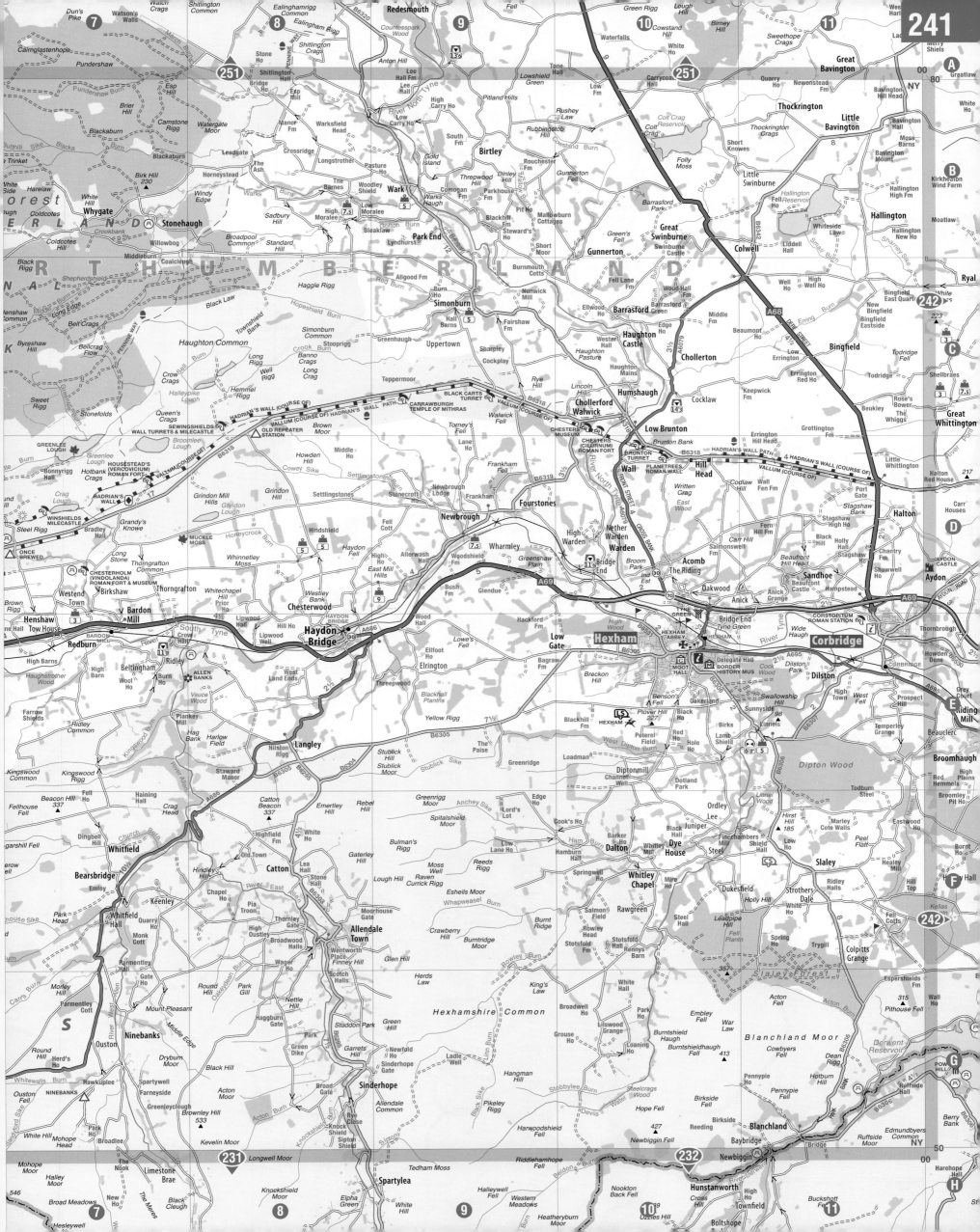

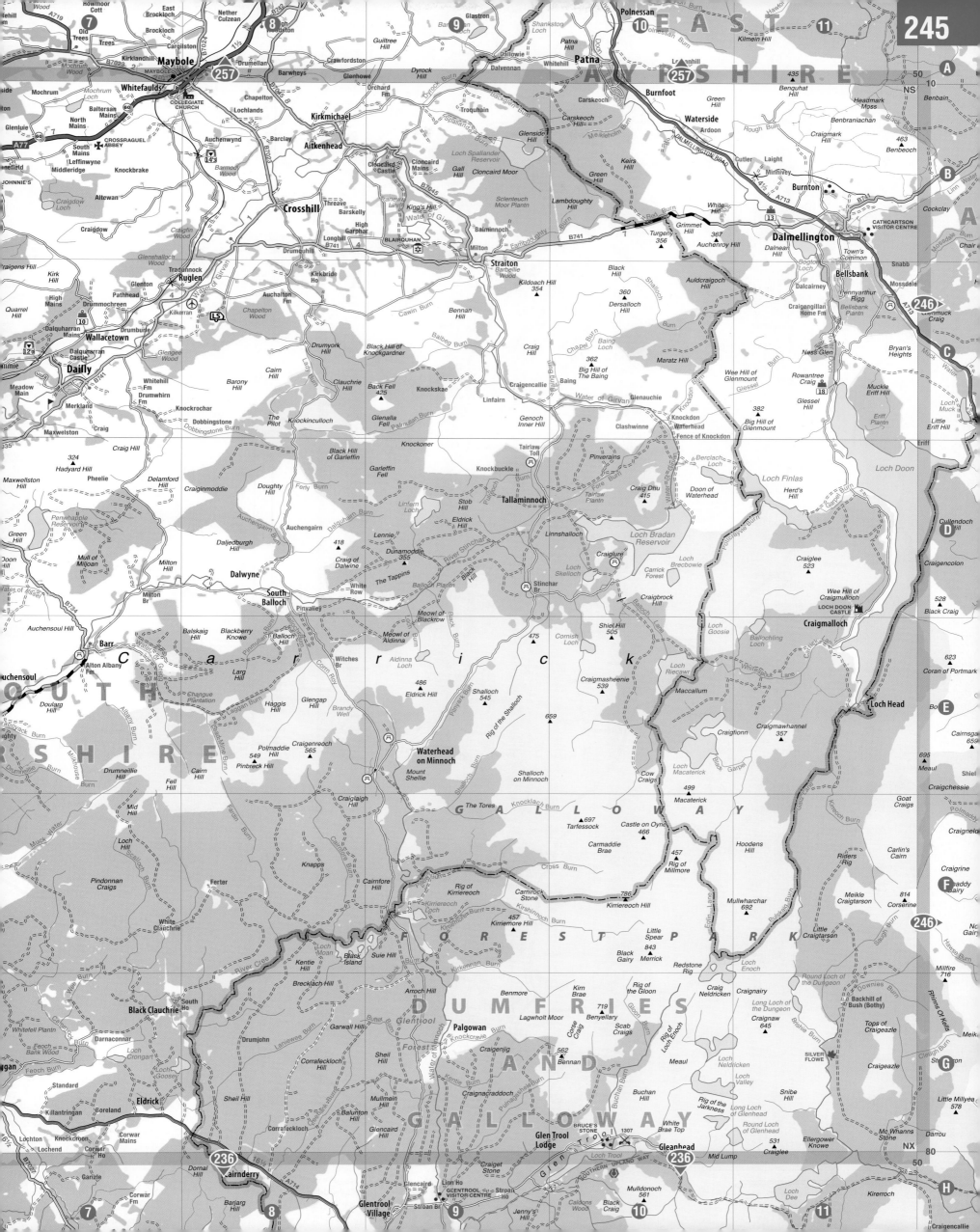

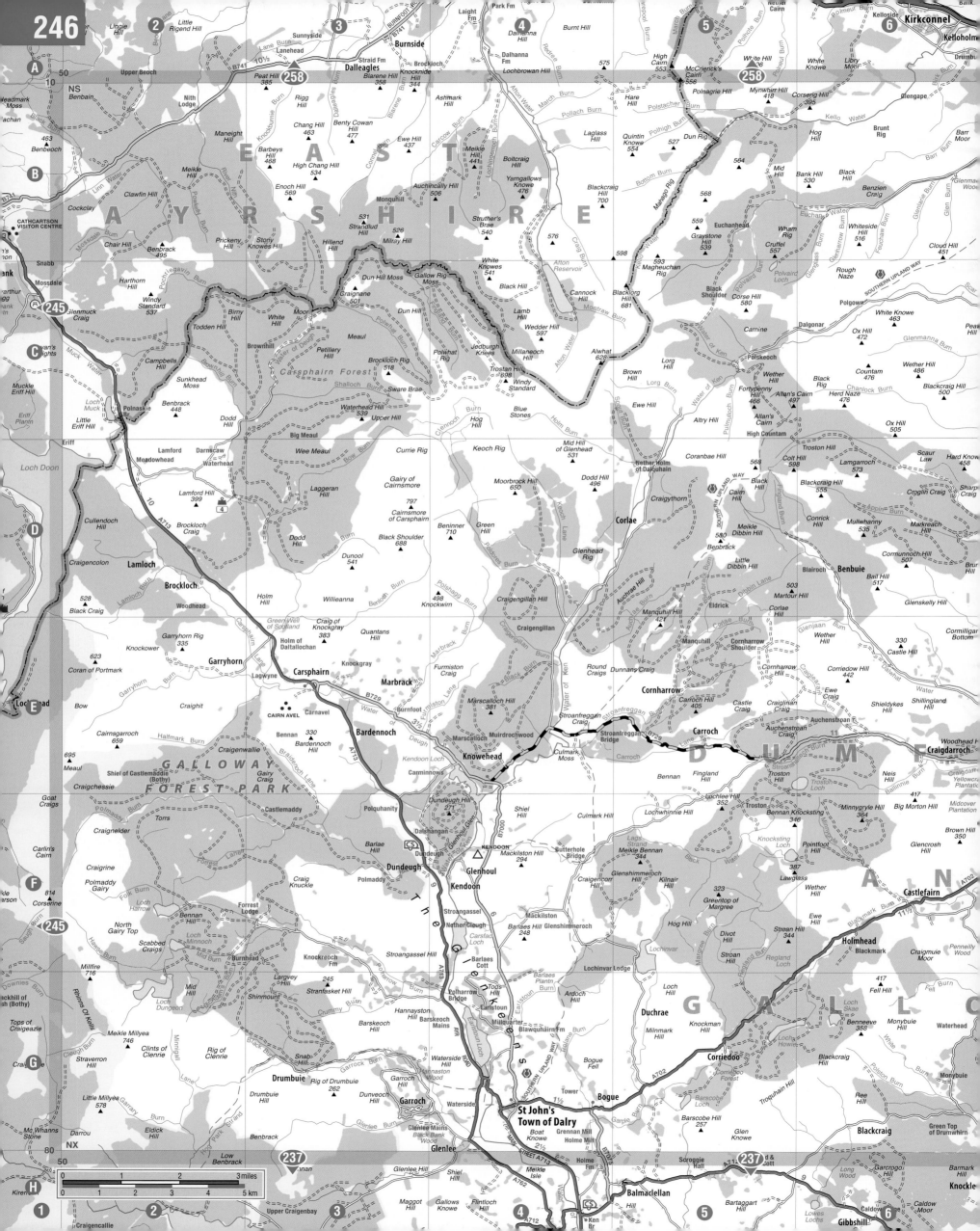

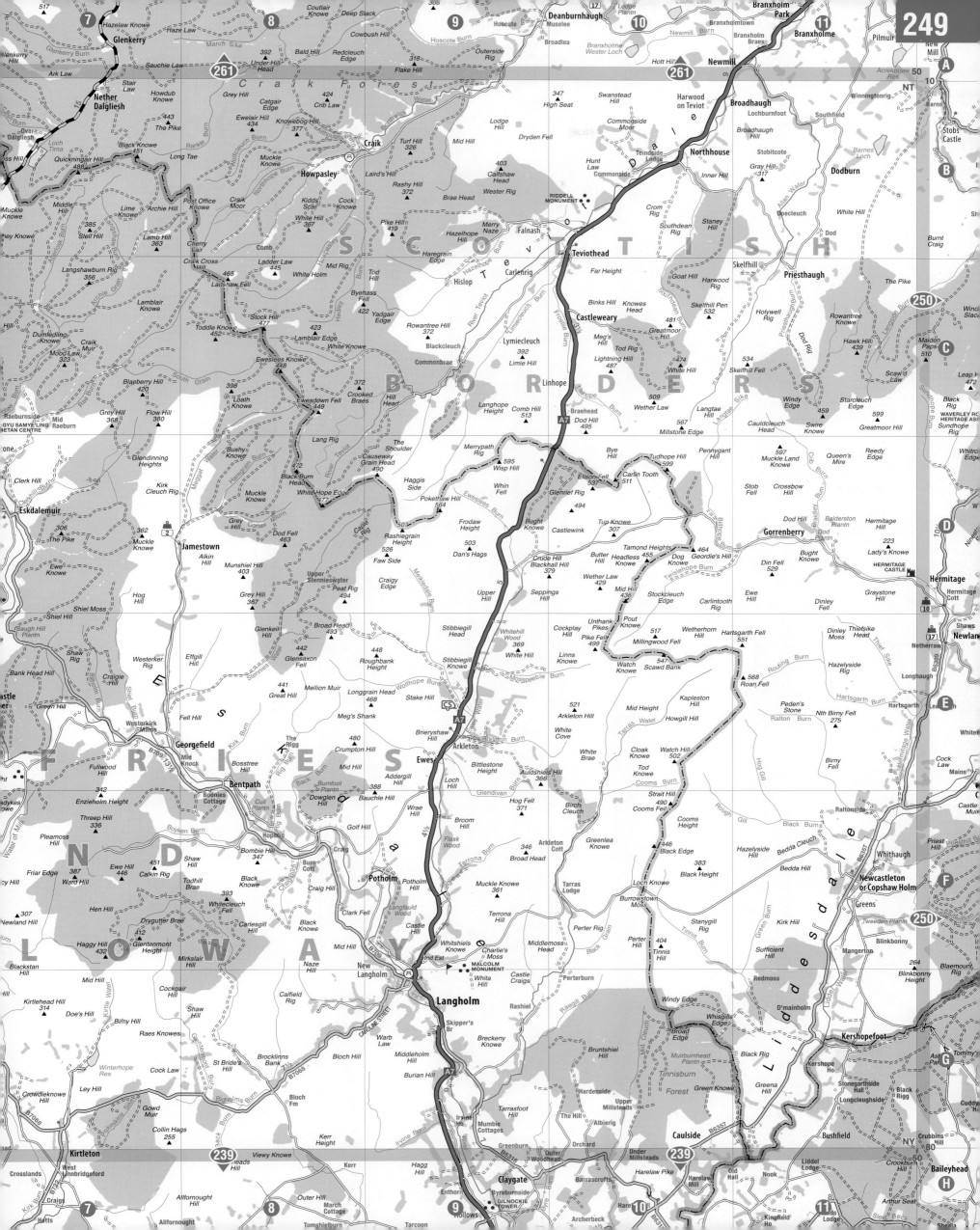

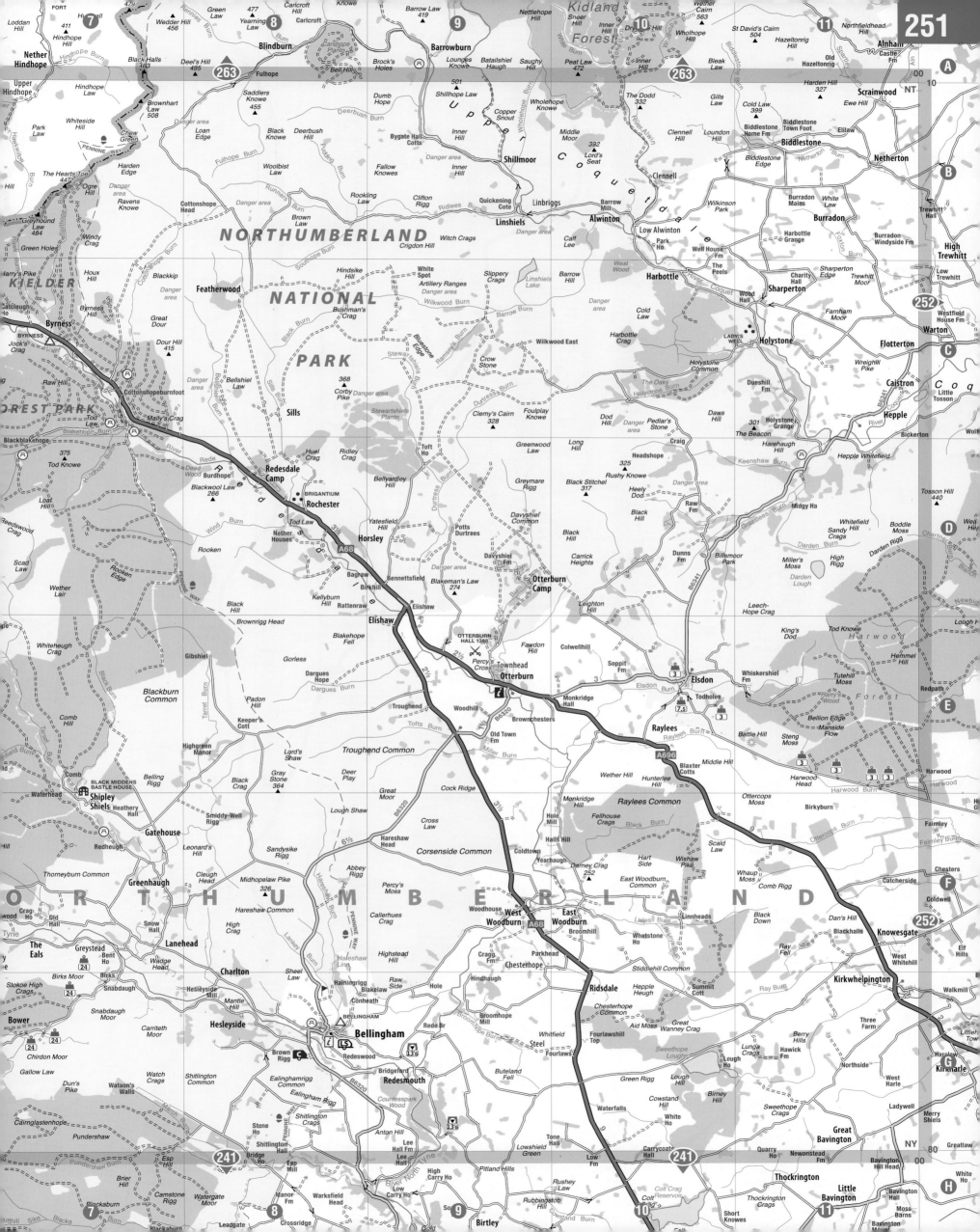

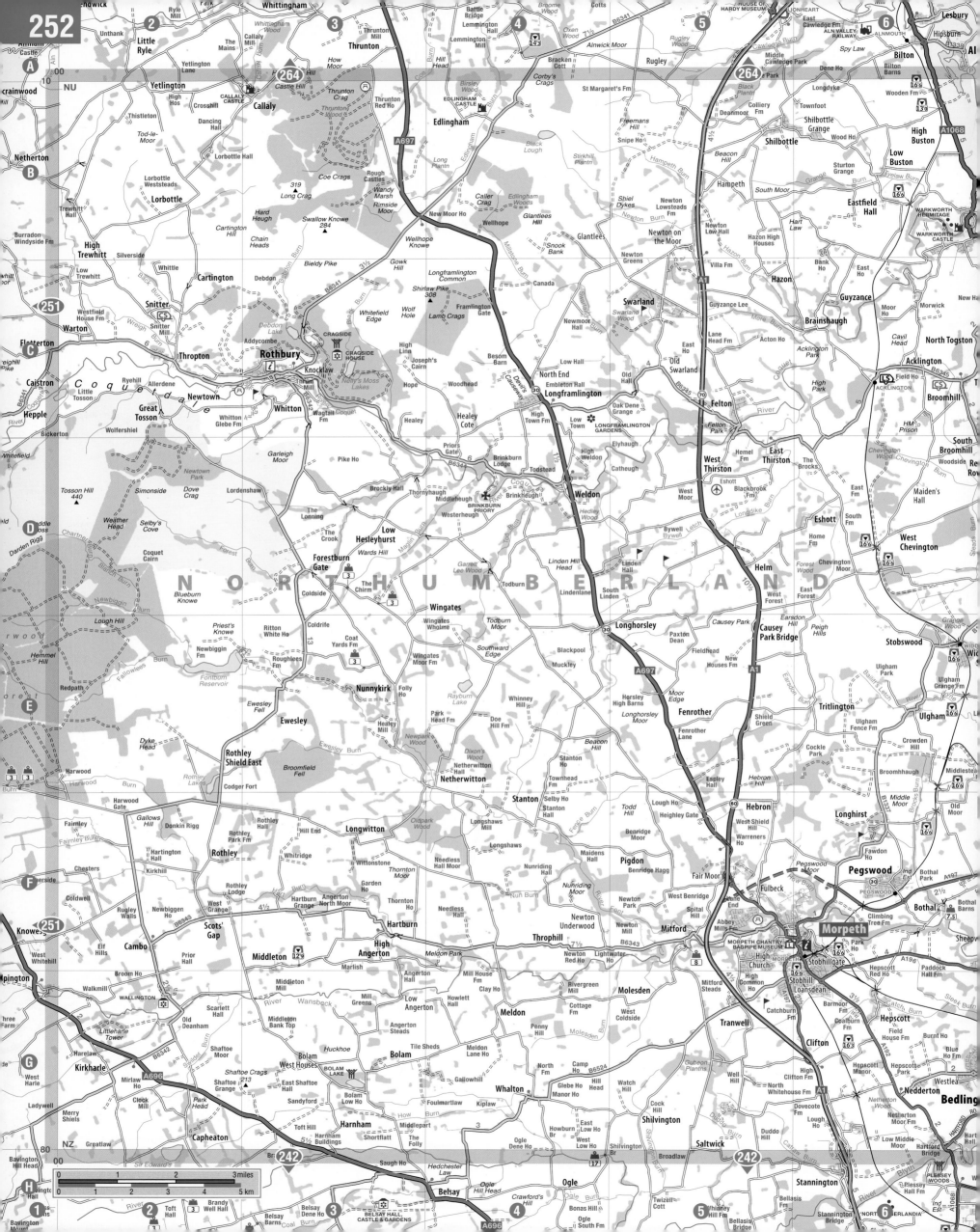

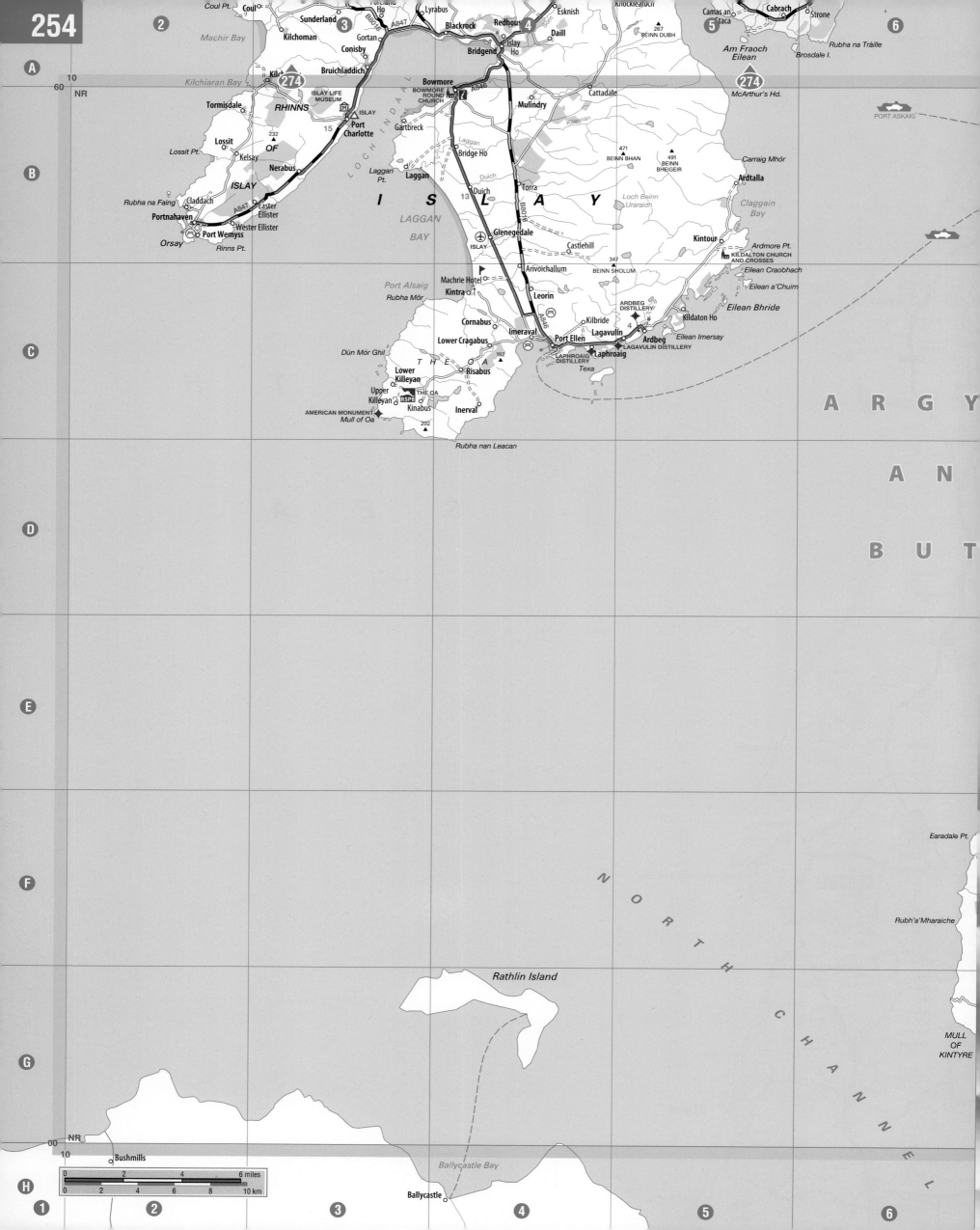

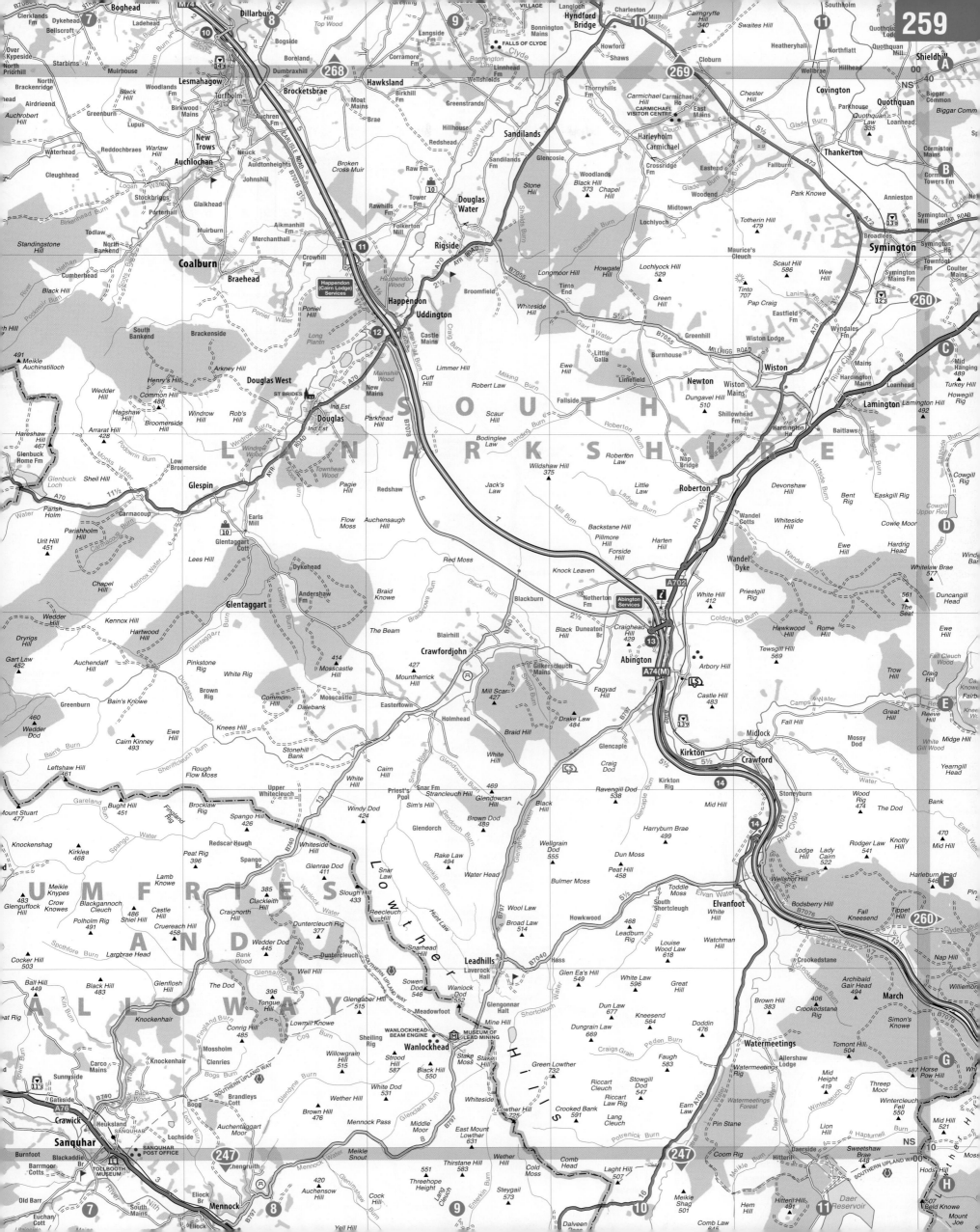

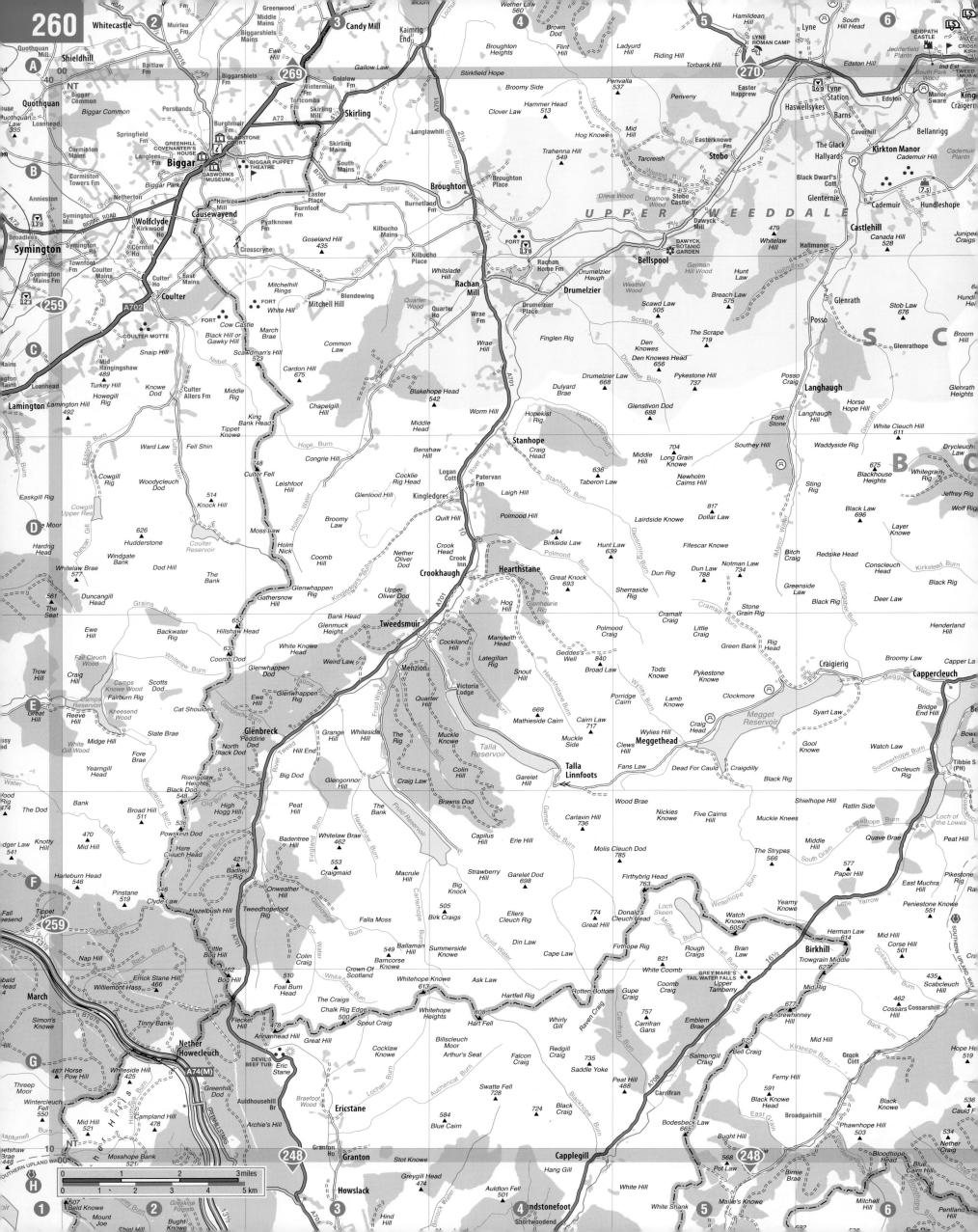

A
50
40
NU

B

C

ngstone

Car

D

N O R T H

S E A

Embleton
Bay

E

Castle Pt
DUNSTANBURGH
CASTLE
Queen
Margaret's Cove

wton Pt

Craster

Cullernose Pt

Howick

F

Rumbling Kern

Red
Stead

Howick
Haven

Sugar Sands

Low
Stead

Howdiemont Sands

ghoughton

Red Ends

G

Boulmer

Boulmer
Haven

Field
Ho

Seaton Pt

Marden Rocks

nmouth

Alnmouth
Bay

NU
10
50

253

253

H

EAST LOTHIAN

SCOTTISH BORDERS

Grid/places (top): Dod · Rammer Wood · Blaik Law · Lothian Edge · High Wood · Needle Hill · Berry Hill · Blackcastle · Oldhamstocks Mains · DUNGLASS COLLEGIATE CHURCH · Belvidere Wood · Cockburnspath · Cove · Cove Harbour · Pease Bay · Red Rock · Greenheugh Pt · Siccar Pt

NUNRAW ABBEY · Garvald Mains · Robin Tup's Plantn · Common Plantn · Moorcock Hall · Deuchrie Edge · Elmsleugh Wood · Oldhamstocks · Dovecot Hall · PEASE DEAN · Meikle Poo Craig · Hirst Rocks

Dunbar Common · Mid Hill · Clints Dod 399 · Eachil Rig · Friardykes Dod · Bransly Hill · Birny Knowe · Wightman Hill · Dod Hill · Ecclaw · Ewieside Hill · Old Cambus Townhead · Old Townhead · Old Cambus · Greenside Hill · Meikle Black Law · Old Cambus Wood

WHITE CASTLE (FORT) · Snawdon Wood · 400 Rangely Kip · Wool Hill · Ling Rig · Saddle Hill · Dogbush Knowe · Sting Hill · Heart Law 392 · Ewelairs Hill · Corse Law · Paits Hill · Ecclaw Hill · Bowshiel Wood · Penmanshiel Wood · Penmanshiel · Gowel Hill · Bell Hill · Drone Hill

Darent Ho · Bleak Law · Nine Stones · Spartleton · Birk Cleugh Hill · Bothwell Hill · Crichness Law · Crichness · Duddy Hill · Black Law · Nether Monynut · Dunglass Common · Blackburn · Blackburn Ho · Blackburn Mill · Blackburning Wood · Roadside Woods · Grantshouse · Brockholes Wood · Renton Barns · Renton Ho · Atton Cott · Dalks Law · Houn

Green Castle · 423 · Newlands Hill · Moss Law · Lammermuir Hills · Kingside Hill · Summer Hill · Peat Law · Inner Hill · Laughing Law · Quixwood Moor · Landsend Wood · Berryhill Cott · Fawcett Wood · Horseley Hill · Green Wood

271 Side · Wanside Rig · Faseny Cott · Dod Hill · Penshiel Hill · Whiteadder Reservoir · The Bell · Harehead · Dunter Law · Blakerstone Moor · SOUTHERN UPLAND WAY · Abbey St Bathans · Hill Wood · Drakemyre · Greenburn Plantn

Collar Law · Little Says Law · Herd's Hill · Priestlaw Hill · Cranshaws · Dog Law · Barnside Hill · Whiteadder Water · Blackerstone · Drakemire Strips

Hareshaw Knowe · Killpallet Heights · Duddy Bank · Cranshaws Hill · Hill Wood · Long Wood · High Strip · Catch Hill · Moorlaw Strips · Ellemford Covert · Roughside Wood · Abbey Hill (Inner) · EDINSHALL BROCH · Slighhouses · Lintlaw

Little Law 456 · Wether Law · Comfortlee · Ellemford · Ellemford Bridge · Ellem Lodge · Fellcleugh Old Wood · Humbles Knowe · Preston Plantn · Billiem · Byden

Meikle Law · Byrecleugh Ridge · Mutiny Stones · Horseupcleugh Rig · Black Hill · Lamb Hill · Wester Burn · Wrunk Law · Moor Plantn · Lodge Wood · Cockburn Law · Cockburn · Baird's Covert · Bishop's Well Plantn · Bunkle Wood

Meikle Namels Ridge · Whinrig Hill · Scar Law · Longformacus · Dye Water · Owl Wood · Millburn · Br · Preston Haugh · Preston · Cruxfield · Blanerne

Wedder Lairs · Upper Knowe · Philips Knowe · Dunside Hill · SOUTHERN UPLAND WAY · Moor Plantn · Black Hill · Mill Burn · Kidshielhaugh · Plendernethy Hill · Castle Mains · Oxendean Tower · Cumledge Mill · B6355 · Broomhouse Mains · NORMAN ARCH · EDROM CHURCH · Edrom Mains · Edrom

Blythe Edge · 450 Pulpit Law · Watch Water · Watch Water Reservoir · Edfast Plantn · Cowhill Plantn · Feuar's Moor · Dirrington Hill · Dunterlee Plantn · Knock Hill · Young Jeanie's Wood · Harelawcraigs Plantn · Duns Wood · Duns Law 218 · Rulesmains Fm · Buxley · MANDERSTON · Whitemire

Twin Law 447 · Sting Law · Rawburn Cott · Old Plantn · Southside Plantn · Dirrington 398 · Dirrington Gt Law · Henlaw Wood · Hardens Hill · Langton Edge · Wellrig Burn · Langton Wood · St Mary's Cott · Castle Wood · Whin Covert · Brieryhill · Kelloe Mains · Blackadder Mains

Harecleugh Forest · Eve Law 311 · Dronshiel Hill · Inch Moor · Blackrig Plantn · Duns Castle · JIM CLARK ROOM · Duns · Clockmill · Cheeklaw · Wedderburn Castle · Kelloe Mains · Blackadder West

Bondreigh Burn · Cralaw · Flass Hill · Loch Wood · Dirrington Lit Law 363 · White Knowe · Sale Moss · Shiningpool Moss · Lees Hill · Raecleugh Head · Langton Mill · Duns Mill · Putton Mill · Kimmerghame Ho · Joshua Plantn

Raidshawrig · Flass Wood · Wedderlie · Hurd Law · Bedshiel · B6456 · Camp Moor · Choicelee · Woodend · Gavinton · Nisbet Hill · Sinclair's Hill · Kimmerghame Mains · Laws Moor Plantn

Peat Law · Raecleugh · Millknowe Burn · Polwarth Moss · Backlea Plantn · Kyles Hill · Polwarth · Kirk Burn · Caldra House · Cairn's Mill · Mount Pleasant · Greenriggs · Swinton Quarter

Bruntaburn Mill · Jordanlaw Moss · Westruther · Westruther Mains · Dogden Moss · Hule Moss · Greenlaw Moor · Howe Burn · Marchmont Ho · Sisterpath · Fogo · Fogo Mains · Bogend · Harcarse Hill · Swinton · SWINTON KIRK · Swinton Hill

Cambridge · Whiteburn · Thornydykes · Hare Law · Harelaw Moor · Meikle Harelaw · Moss Road Plantn · Piersknowe Plantn · Fogorig · Fogo · Hunthall · Ryslaw · Longbank · Swinton Mill · Merse

271 · Corsbie Moor · Houndslow · Lill Rig · A697 · Crawlee Plantn · Blackadder Water · Charterhall Wood · Cleughead · Angelrow Fm · Charterhall · Mount Pleasant · Swintonmill · Little Swinton

Eden Burn · Bassendeanhill · Bassendean · Rumbleton · Halliburton · Greenlaw · Rumbletonlaw · Castle Mill · B6460 · Angelrow Fm · Kames East Mains · Earnslaw · Kames West Mains · B6461 · Marlfield · Butterlaw · Simprim Burn

Knock Hill 272 · Macks Mill · A6105 · Catmoss · Foulshot Law · Crumrig · Purves Hall · Mersington Ho · Leitholm · Crosshall

Kirkhill · Corsbie · Green Knowe Tower · West Mains · Gordon · Byrewalls · Middlethird · Todrig · Gordonbank · Ploughlands · A697 · Lambden Ho · Pittlesheugh · Stainrigg Mains · Anton's Hill · Hawkslaw · Skaithmuir

Legerwood · Huntlywood · East Morriston · Gordon East Mains · Easter Howlaws · Wester Howlaws · Lambden · Viewfield · Stonefold · Hardacres · Orange Lane · Darnchester West Mains · Kincham Wood

West Morriston · Fans · Fans Hill · Littlehill Plantn · Whitehill Ho · Hume Crags · Hume Platn · Hassington East Mains · Eccles · Eccles Ho · Brae Dunstan · Fernyrig Cott · Crown Gorse · Dunglass Wood · THE HIRSEL · Wester Park

EAST END · Darlingfield · Falsidehill · Hardiesmill Place · Hume · Hume Mill · Harehaugh Craigs · Blue Houses · Hassington West Mains · Wormerlaw · Eccles Newton · Bartleyhill · Birgham · Birgham Wood · Coldstream

262 · Blinkbonny · Lurgie Craigs · Stichill Home Fm · Sweethope Hill · Stichill Eastfield · Harpertoun · Saint Foin · Lochton · Springhill · Gallows Law · West

263 · Cowdenknowes · Rachelfield · Girrick · Stichill · Kaimflat · Caldronbrae · Sheep Covert · Parkend · Eden Hall · Carham Hall · Carham · Jark

Scale: 0–3 miles · 0–5 km

A **10** 20 NM

B

C OBAN

D COLONSAY
Oronsay

E (Summer Only)

F JURA

G ISLAY

H RHINS OF ISLAY

60 NR 10

0   2   4   6 miles
0   2   4   6   8   10 km

Fast Castle Head
Wheat Stack
Telegraph Hill
FAST CASTLE
Oatlee Hill
Dowlaw Burn
Lumsdaine
ingham mmon
Lumsdaine Moor
Coldingham Loch
Cross Law
Moorside

273
St Abb's Head
ST ABB'S HEAD
Horsecastle Bay
Mire Loch
Bell Hill
Starney Bay

273

Lumsdaine
Coldingham Loch
Moorside
Common
Oatlee Hill
Dowlaw Burn
Telegraph Hill
Wheat Stack
Fast Castle Head
FAST CASTLE
Lumsdaine Moor

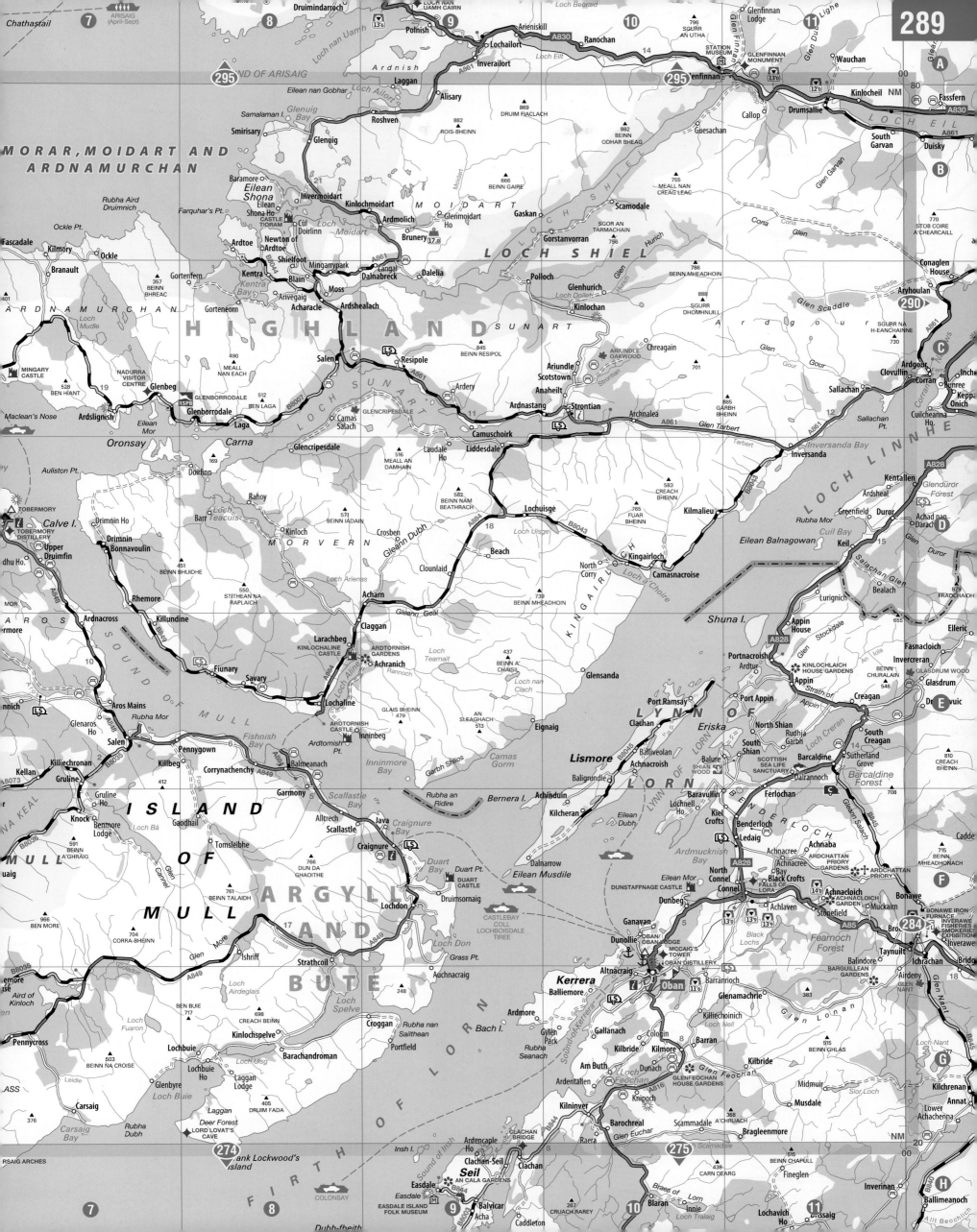

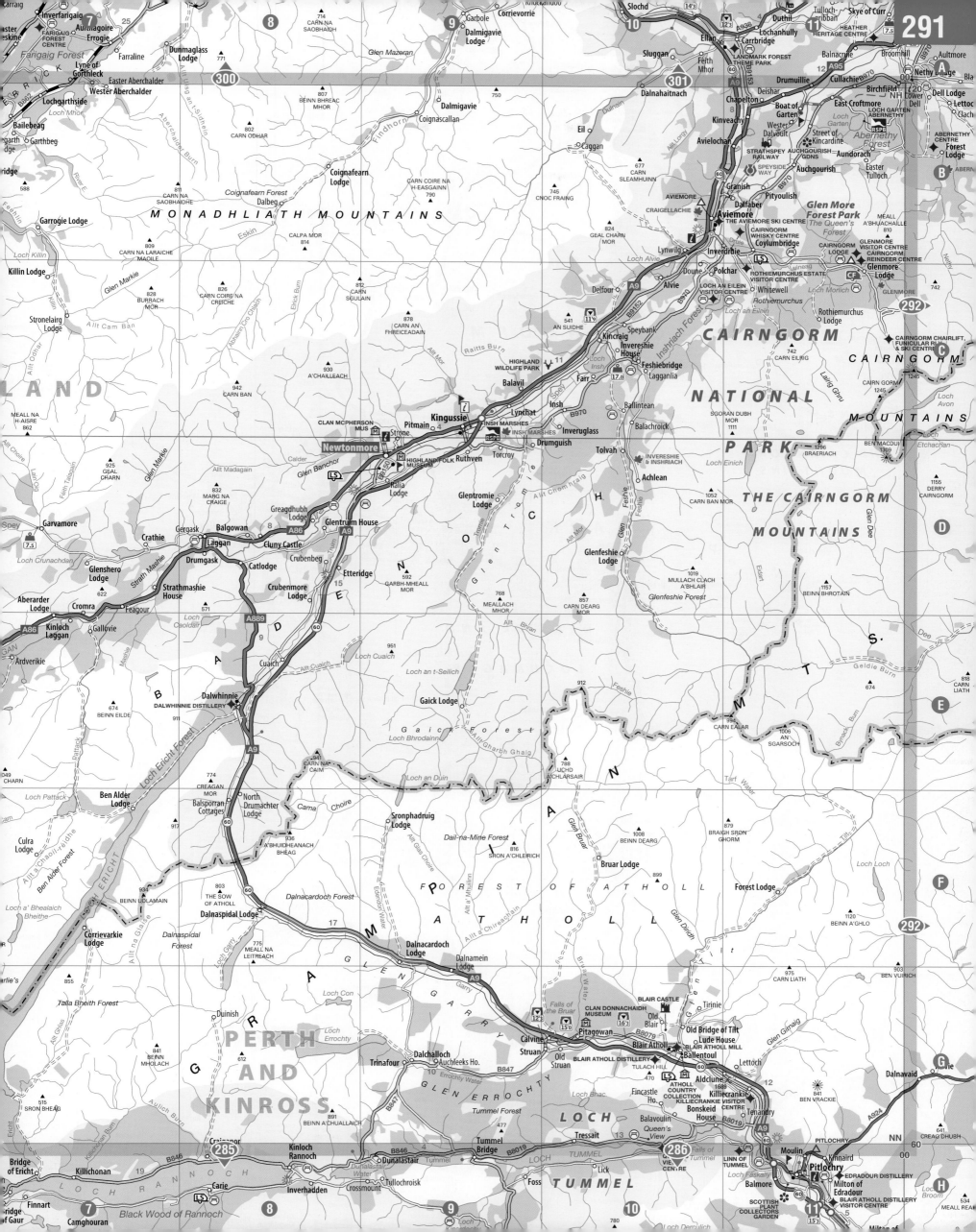

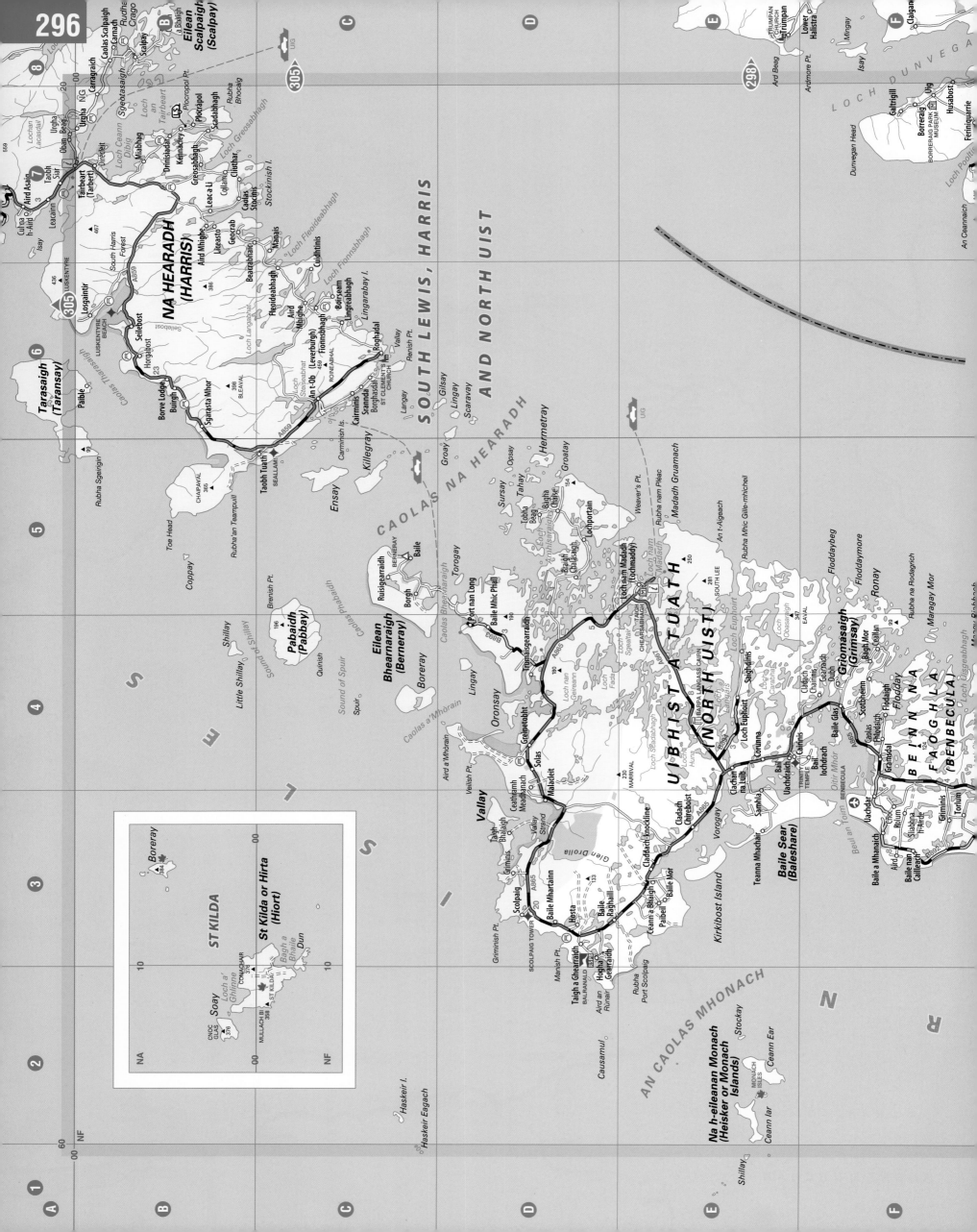

SOUTH LEWIS, HARRIS

AND NORTH UIST

NA HEARADH (HARRIS)

UIBHIST A TUATH

NORTH UIST

CAOLAS NA HEARADH

St KILDA

St Kilda or Hirta (Hiort)

Na h-eileanan Monach
(Heisker or Monach Islands)

Tarasaigh (Taransay)

Pabaidh (Pabbay)

Eilean Bhearnaraigh (Berneray)

BEINN NA FAOGHLA (BENBECULA)

Baile Sear (Baleshare)

Griomasaigh (Grimsay)

Eilean Scalpaigh (Scalpay)

LOCH DUNVEGAN

AN CAOLAS MHONACH

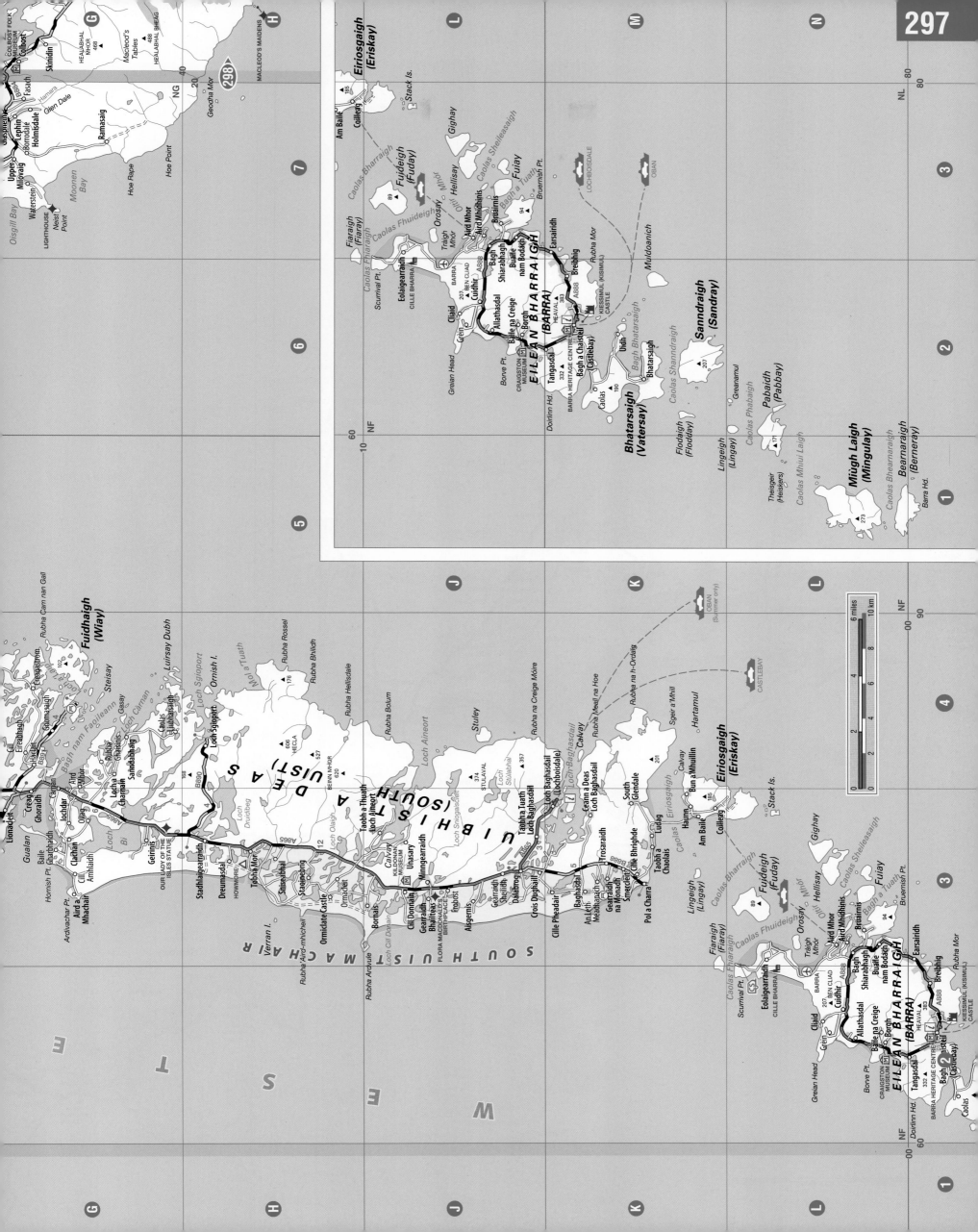

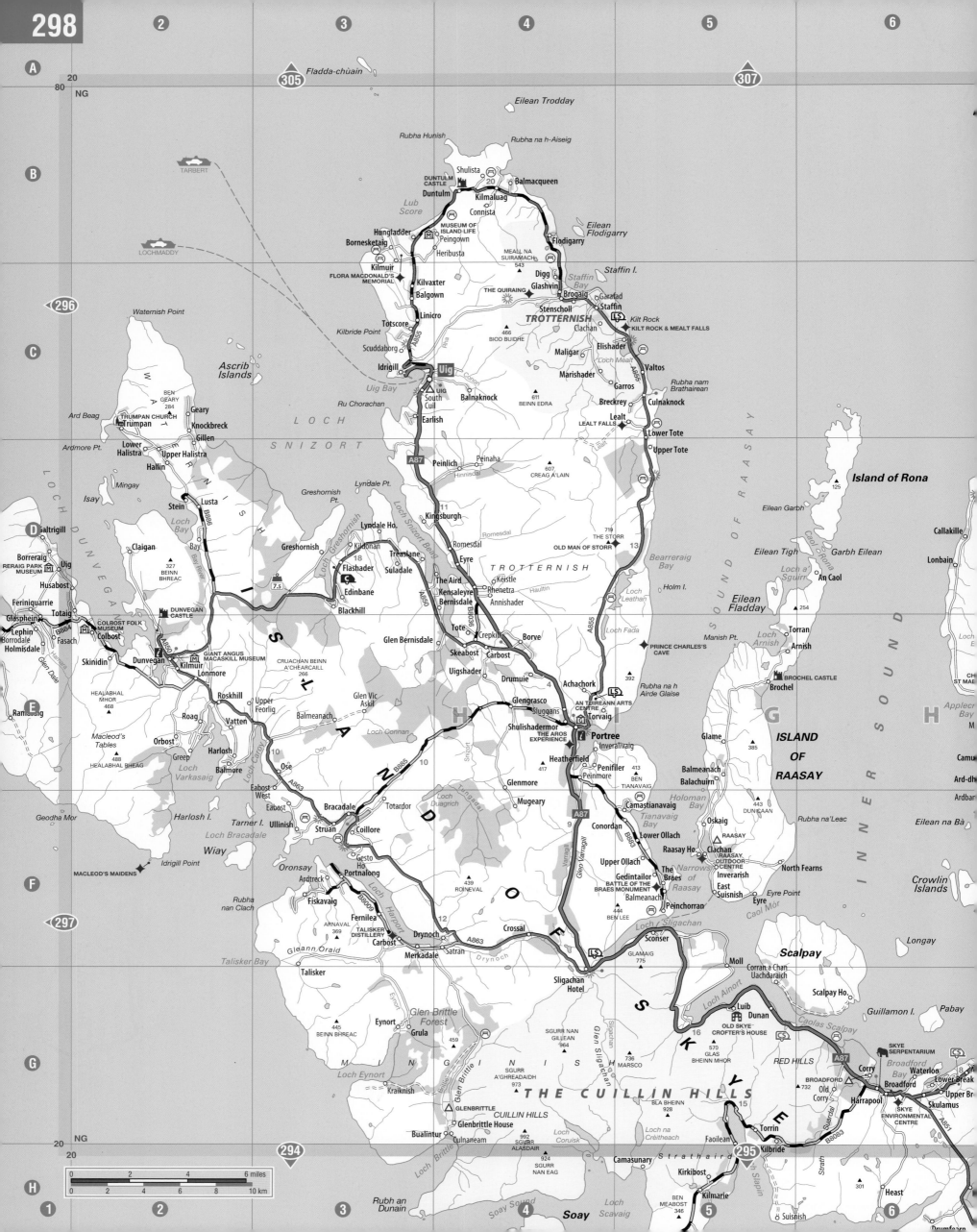

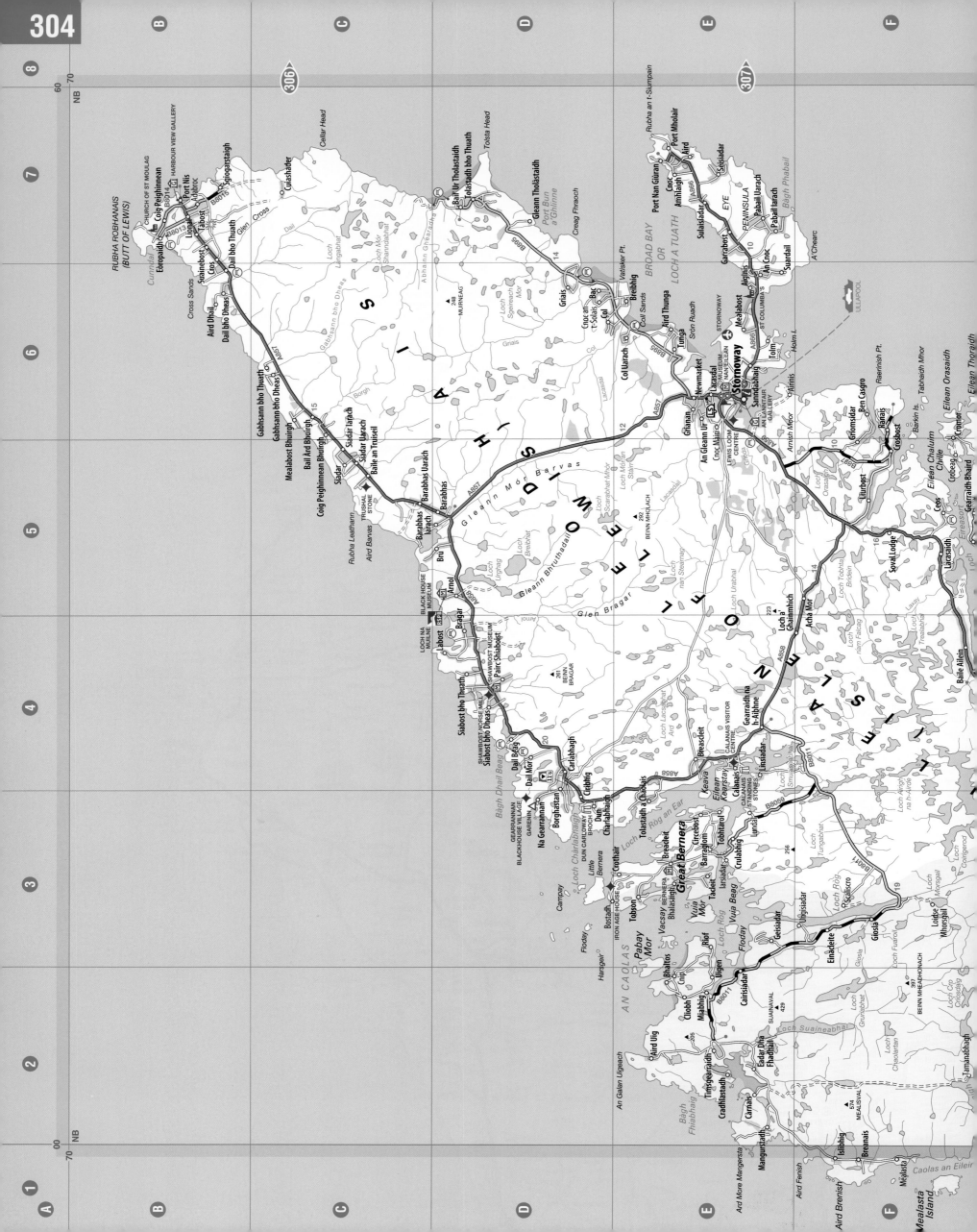

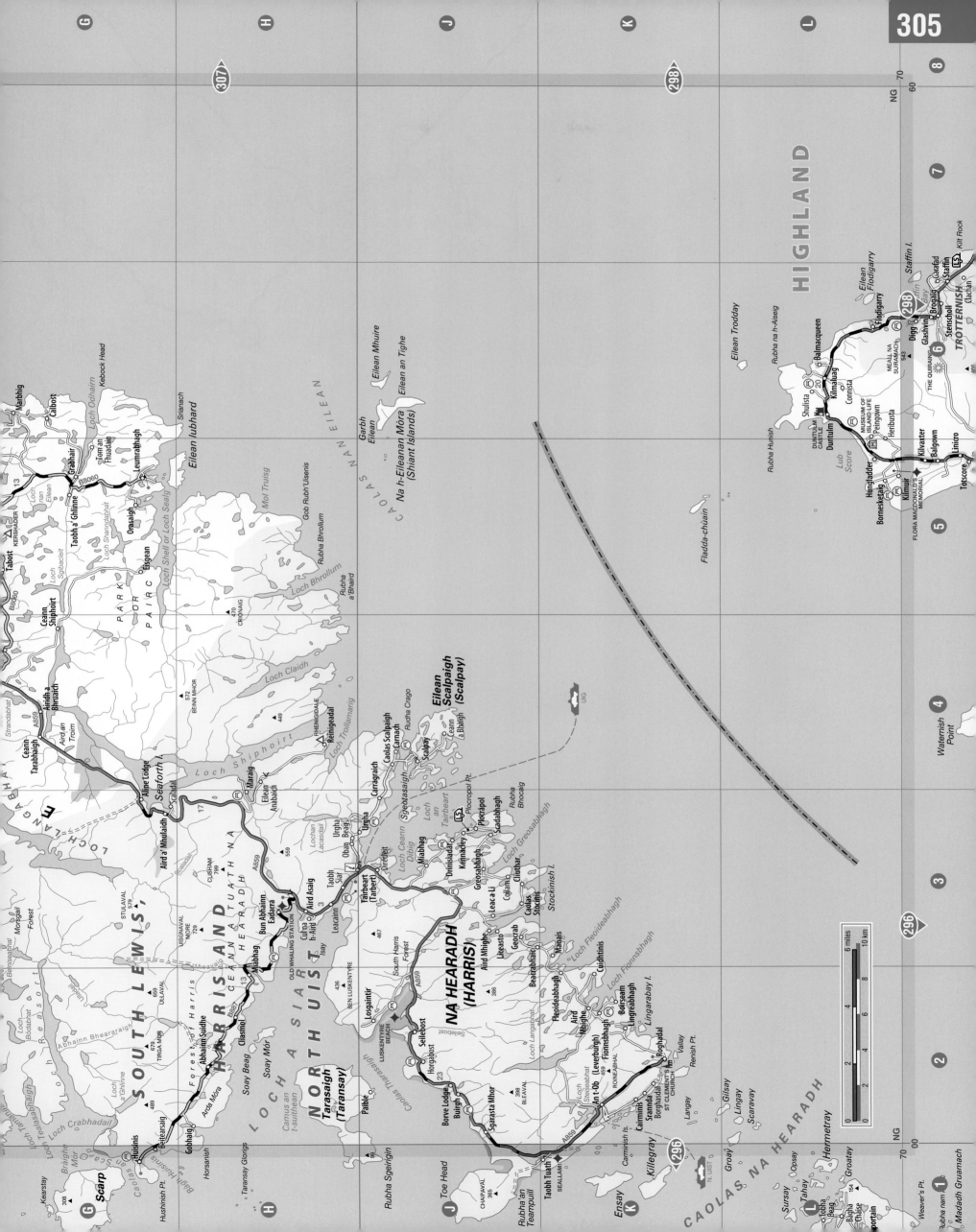

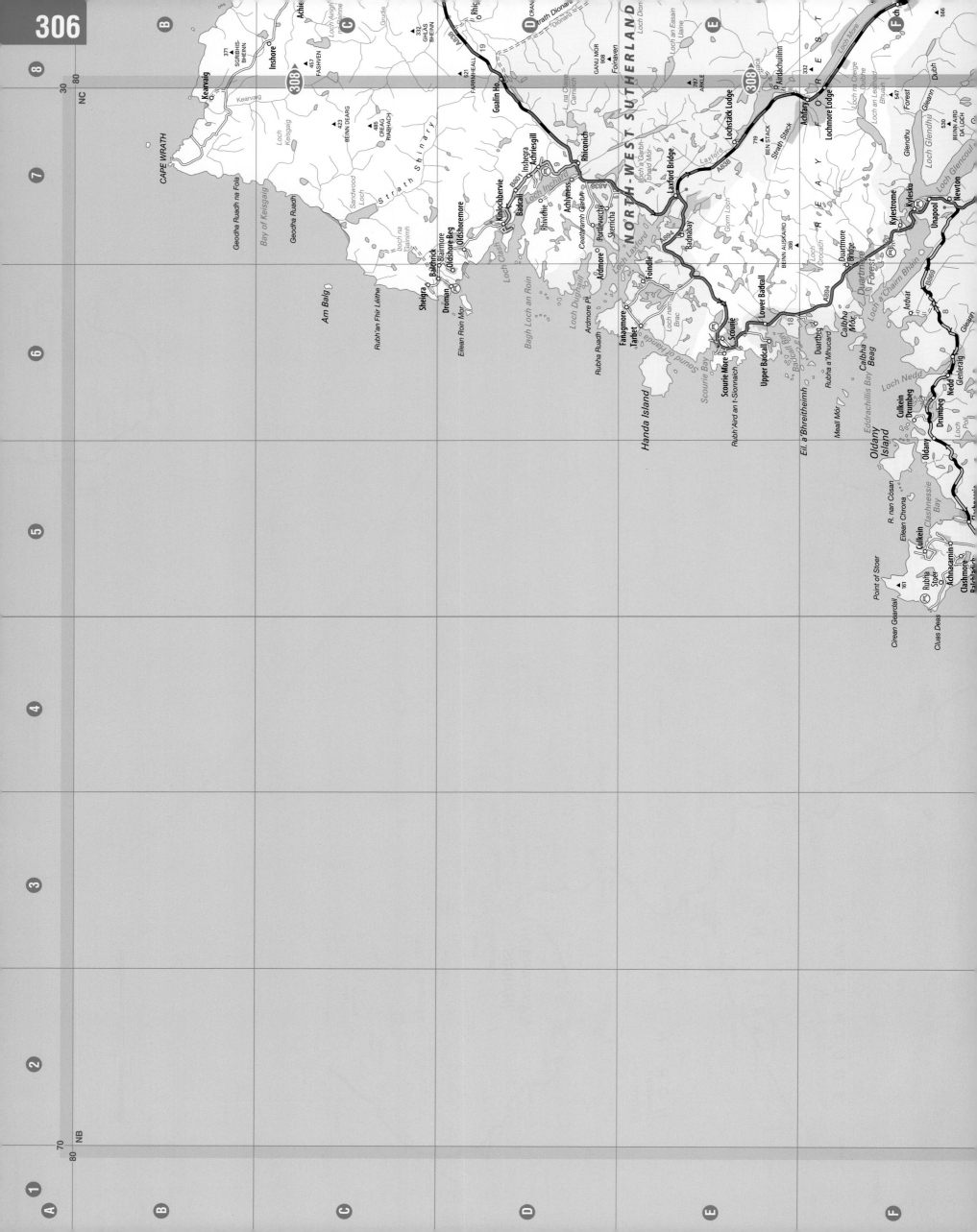

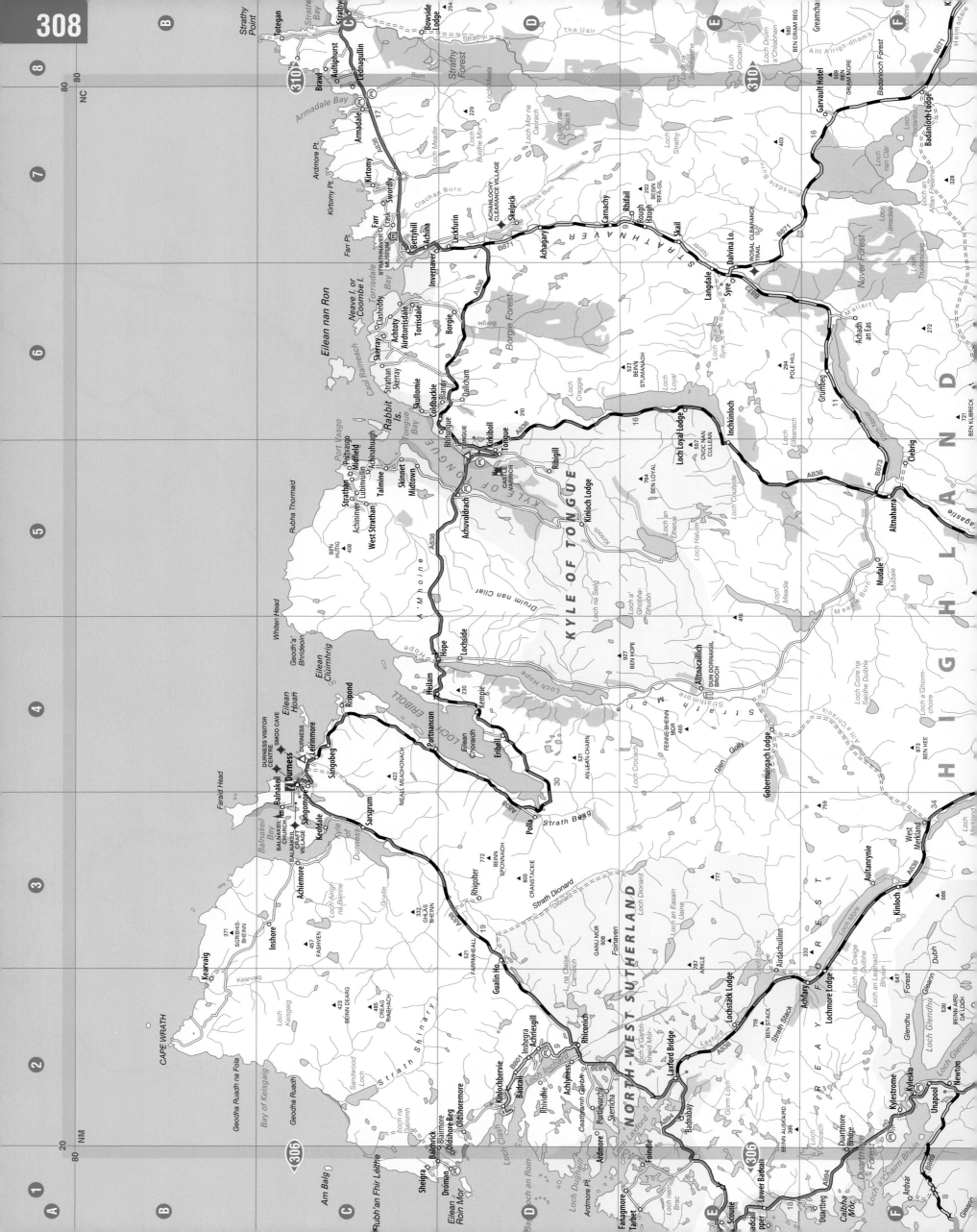

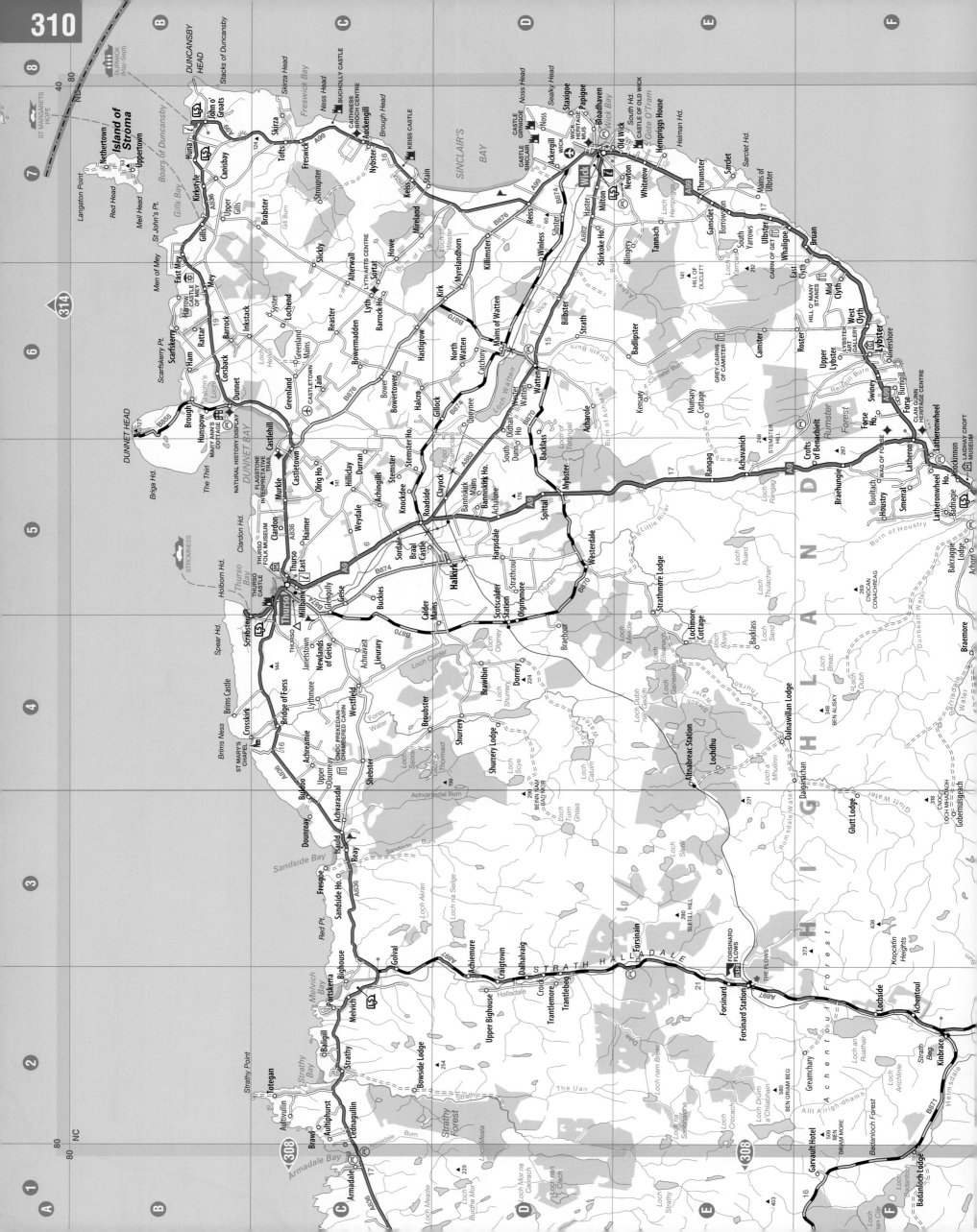

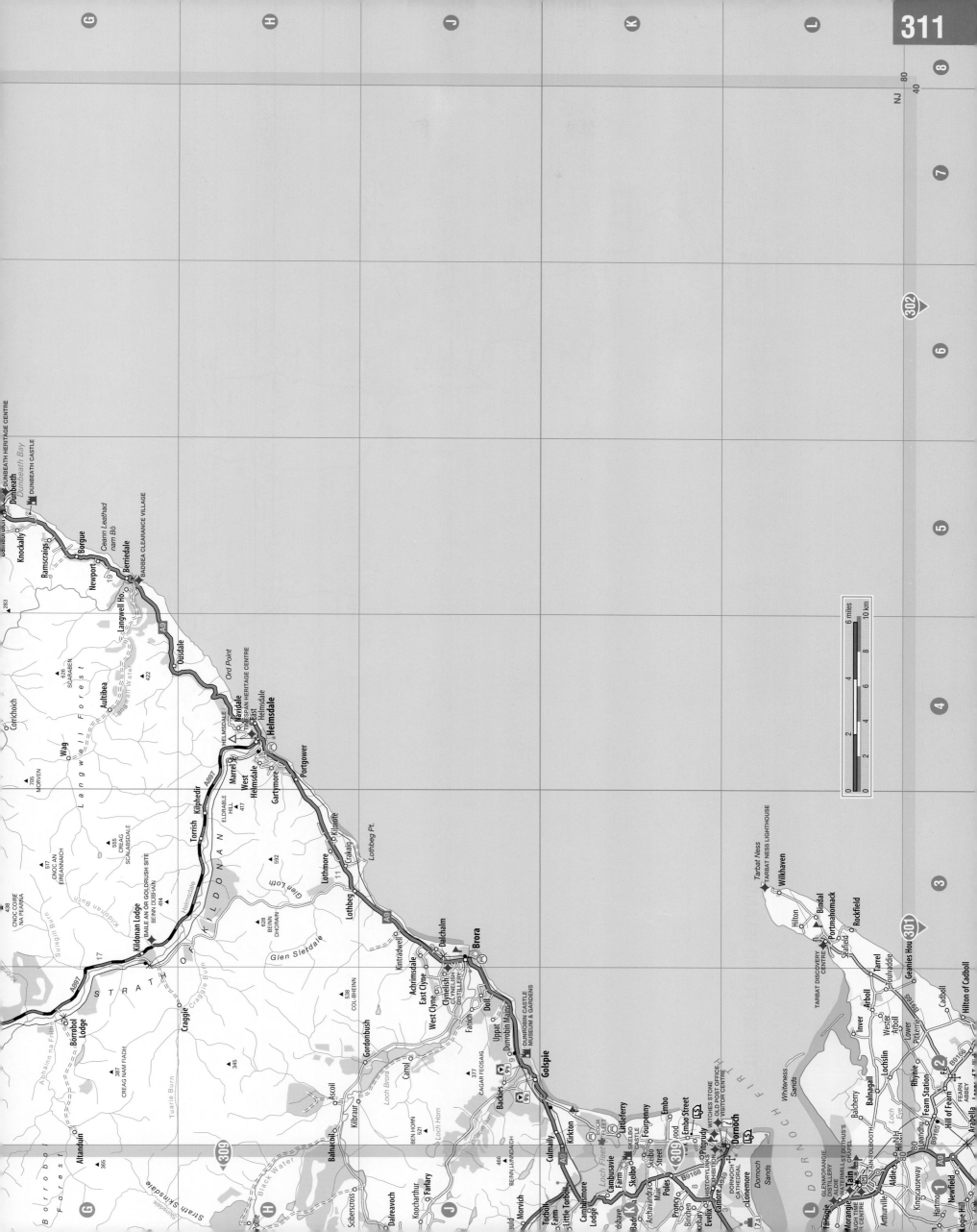

Dunbeath
Dunbeath Bay
DUNBEATH HERITAGE CENTRE
DUNBEATH CASTLE
Knockally
Ramscraig
Borgue
Newport
Ceann Leathad
nam Bb
Berriedale
Langwell Ho.
BADBEA CLEARANCE VILLAGE
19
283
A9
Ousdale
Corrichoich
Ord Point
626
SCARABEN
422
Aultibea
Langwell Water
HELMSDALE
Marrel
TIMESPAN HERITAGE CENTRE
Helmsdale East
Helmsdale
Helmsdale
Wag
West
Helmsdale
Portgower
705
MORVEN
46
Gartymore
A897
Torrish
Kilphedir
ELDRABLE HILL
417
Kilmote
517
CNOC AN
ÉREANNAICH
555
CREAG
SCALABSDALE
Lothmore
11
Crakaig
Lothbeg Pt.
438
CNOC COIRE
NA PEARNA
BAILE AN OR GOLDRUSH SITE
BEINN DUBHAIN
414
Kildonan Lodge
592
Glen Loth
Lothbeg
Tarbat Ness
TARBAT NESS LIGHTHOUSE
Wilkhaven
Himsdale
KILDONAN
628
BEINN
DHORAIN
Glen Sletdale
STRATH OF
Kintradwell
Dalchalm
Brora
TARBAT DISCOVERY CENTRE
Hilton
Bindal
Portmahomack
Clynelish
CLYNELISH
DISTILLERY
Achrimsdale
East Clyne
Scafield
Rockfield
Borrobol
Lodge
538
COL-BHEINN
West Clyne
Fanich
DUNROBIN CASTLE
MUSEUM & GARDENS
Uppat
Doll
Inver
Wester
Arboll
Arboll
Tarrel
Foulyvaddie
Geanies Hou
301
Altanduin
387
CREAG NAM FIADH
345
Craggie
Ascoil
Carrol
377
CAGAR FEOSAIG
Backies
Golspie
99
Lower
Pitkerrie
FEARN
ABBEY
Lochslin
Cadboll
Hilton of Cadboll
365
Balnacoil
Kilbraur
BEN HORN
521
Loch Horn
Loch Brora
Backies
Golspie
99
Inver
Rhynie
B9165
Balchary
Loch Fleet
Littleferry
Fourpenny
Embo
Embo Street
WITCHES STONE
OLD POST OFFICE
VISITOR CENTRE
Balnagall
Fearn Station
Dalreavoch
Sciberscross
Knocharthur
466
BENN LUNNDAIDH
Gordonbush
Culmally
Kirkton
Pitgrudy
Skelbo
Castle
Skelbo
Street
HISTORYLINKS
EXHIBITION
Dornoch
Whiteness
Sands
Loch
Eye
Lochslin
Balchery
Fearn Abbey
Farlary
Cambusavie
Cambusmore
Lodge
Little Torboll
Poles
B9168
DORNOCH
CATHEDRAL
GLENMORANGIE
DISTILLERY
WATERMILL DUTHUS'S
HIGH TIDE
CENTRE
Dornoch
Sands
Tain
Morangie
Newfield
Cambusavie
Muir
Skelbo
Balnacoil
Cuthill
Proncy
Evelix
Clonemore
Tain
Aldie
Arboll
Hill of Fearn
Torboll
Farm
Morvich
Kirkton
Torroble
Hilton
A9
Altass
Clashmore
Loch
Skibo
Ledmore

STRATH SKINSDALE

Craggie Burn

Kildonan Burn

Susgill Burn

Tuatie Burn

Black Water

Abhainn na Frithe

Borrobol
Forest

Loch Fleet

DORNOCH FIRTH

NJ 80 40
80

311

A897

309

309

302

301

Scale:
6 miles
10 km
0 2 4
0 2 4 6 8

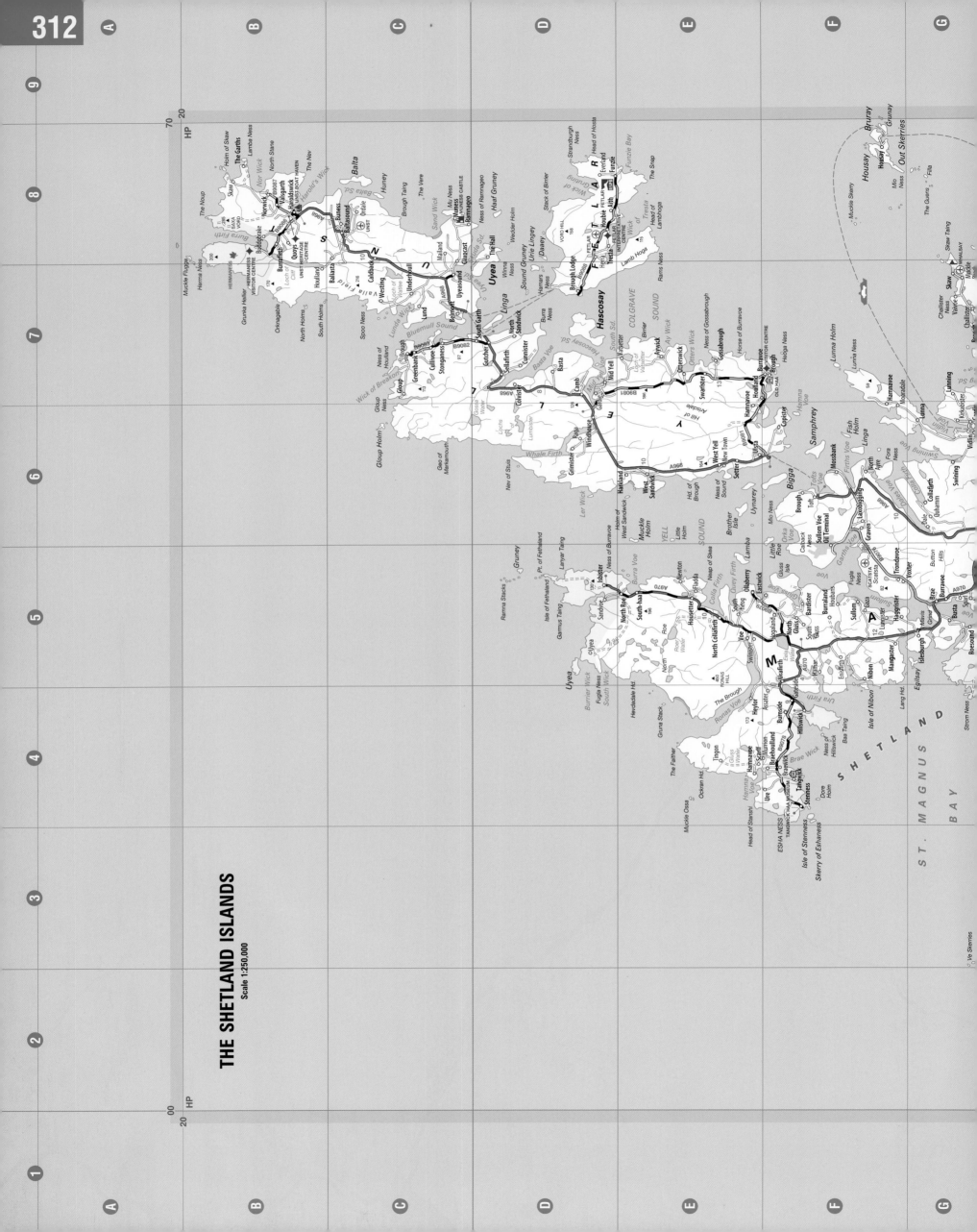

THE SHETLAND ISLANDS

Scale 1:250,000

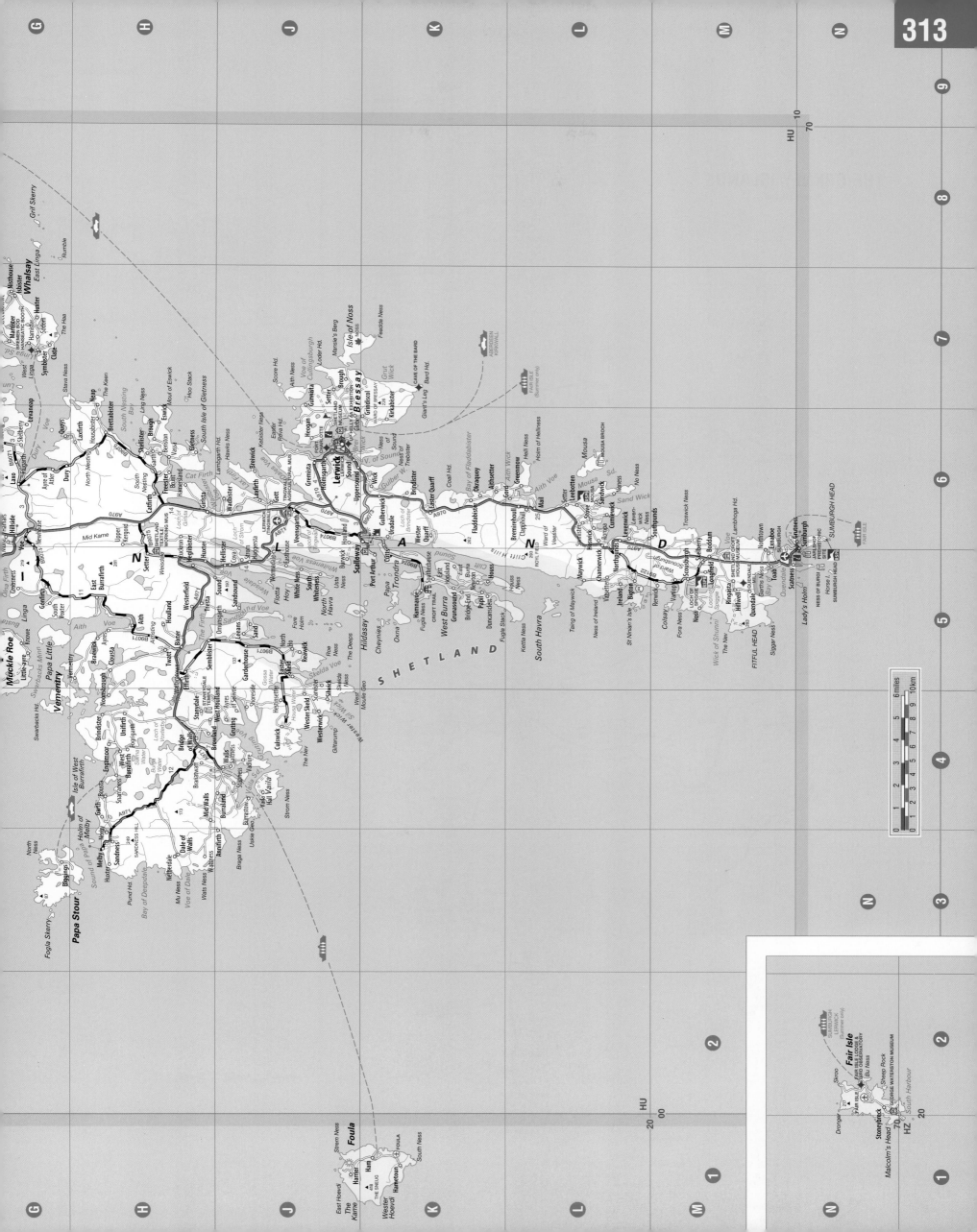

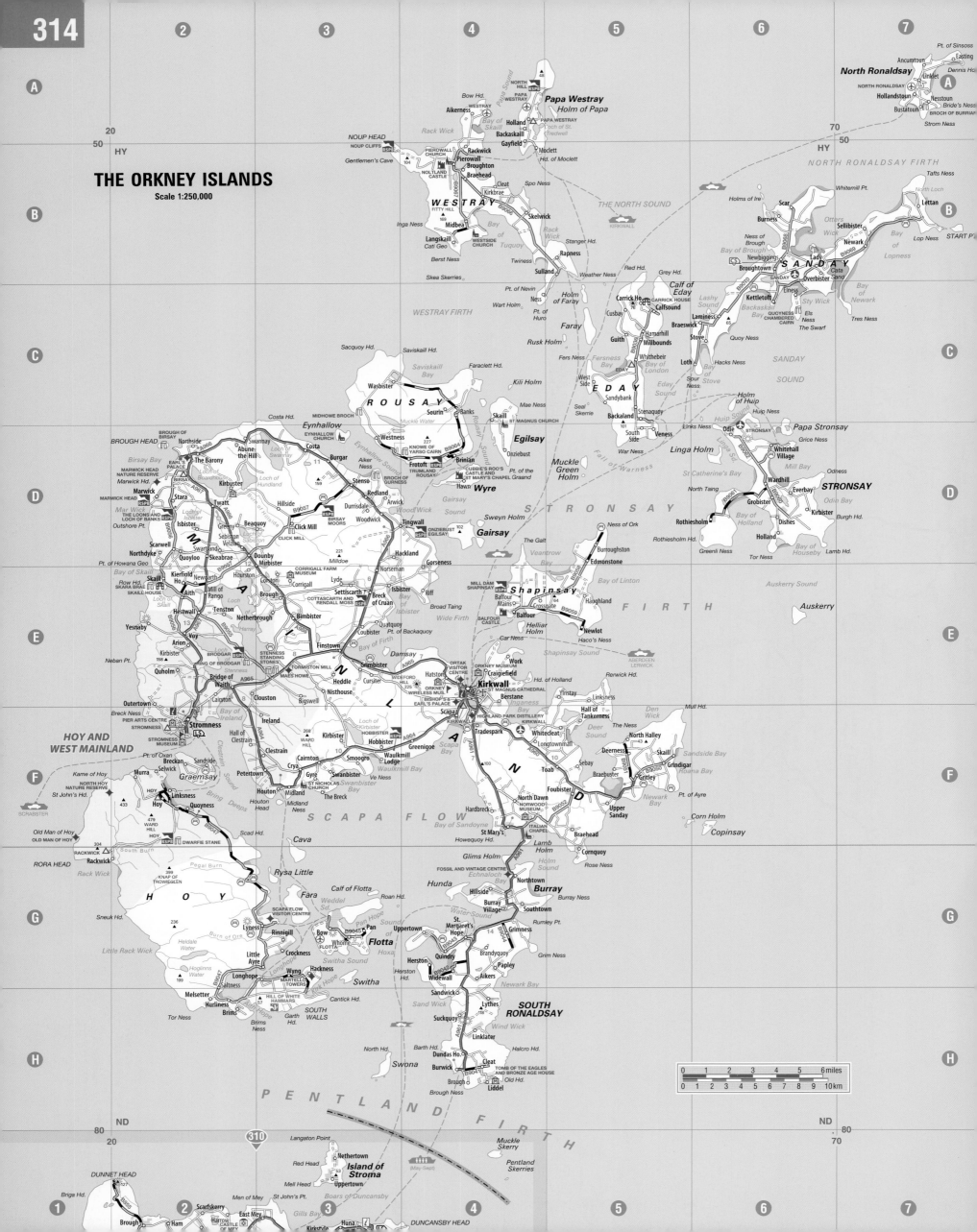

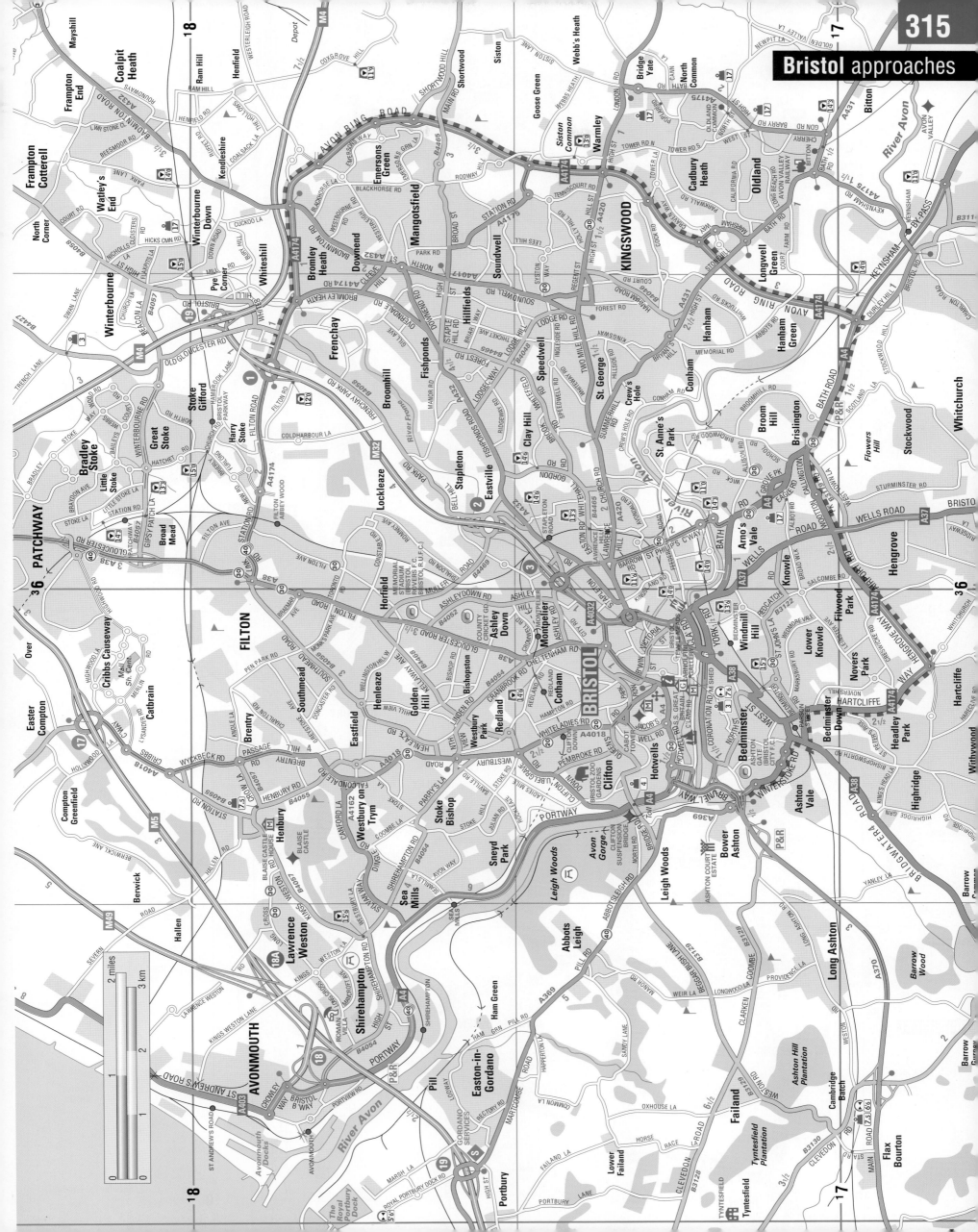

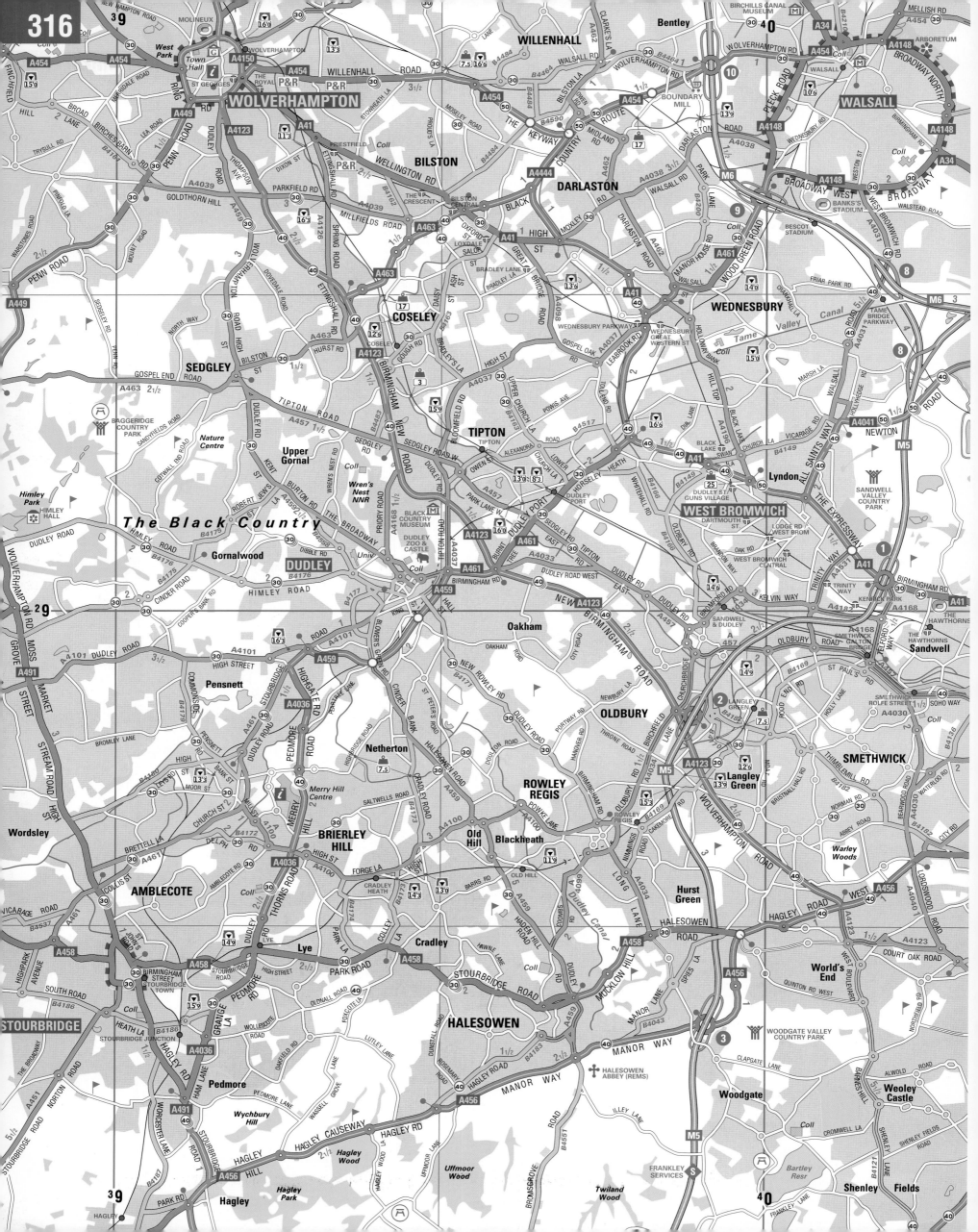

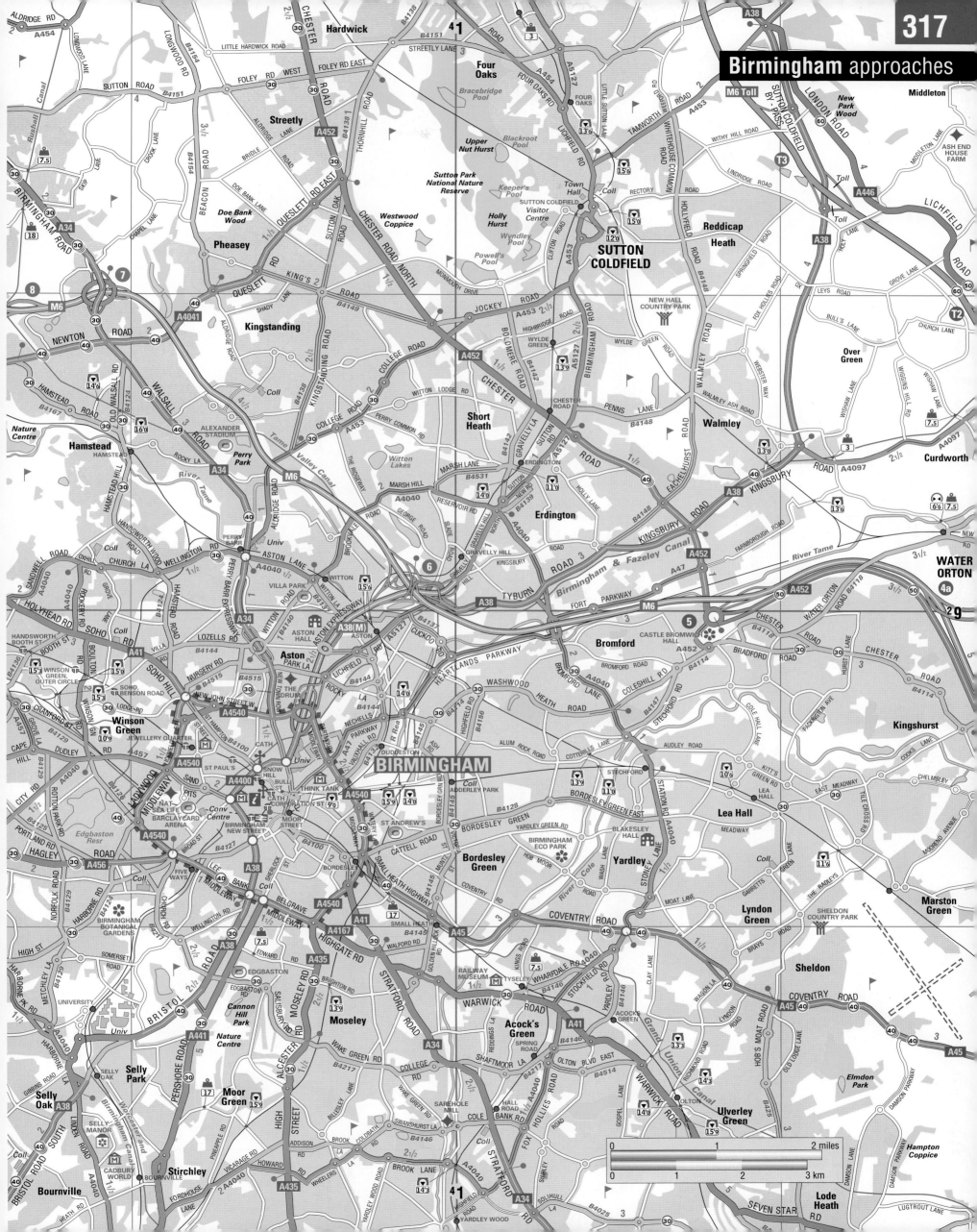

Birmingham approaches

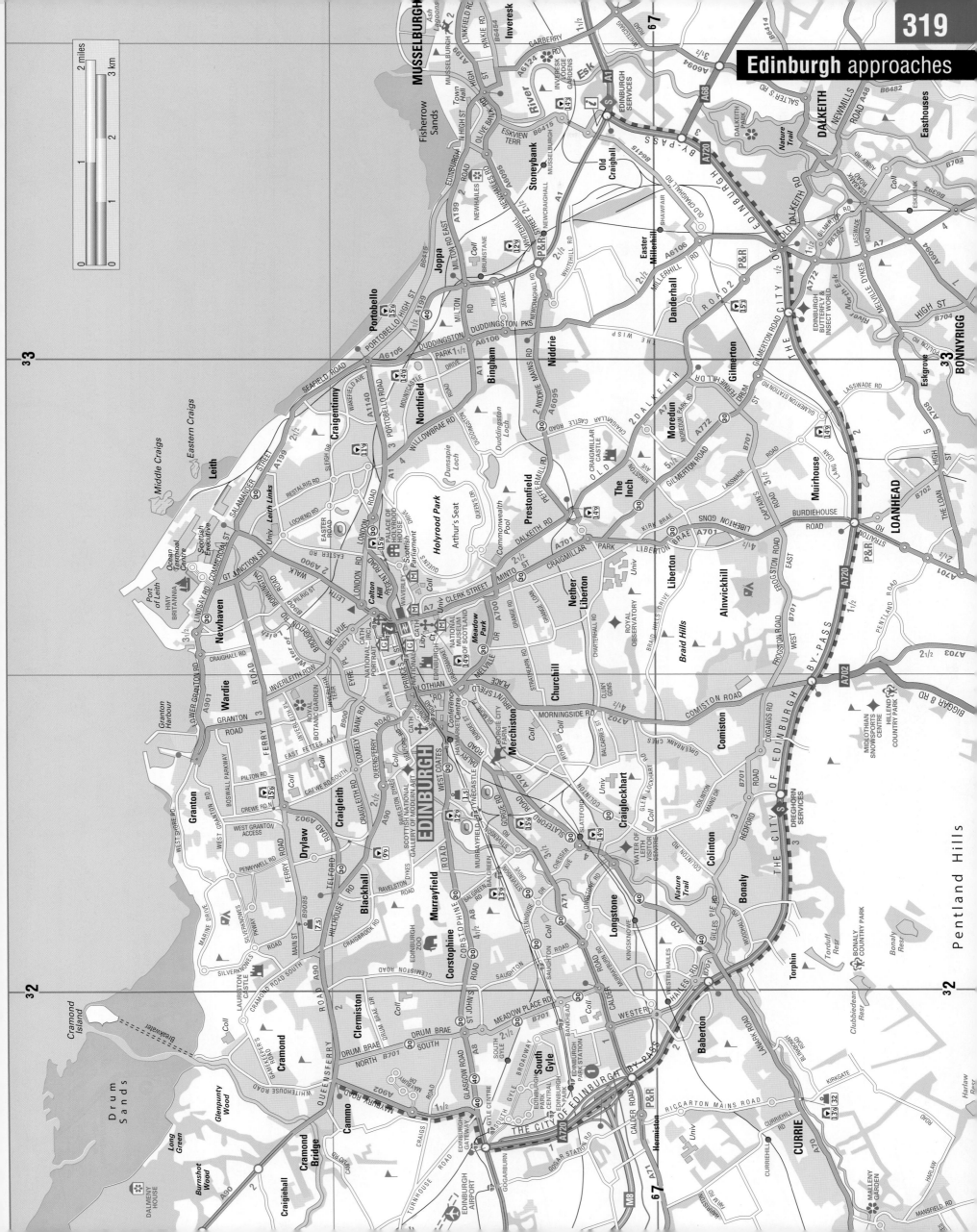

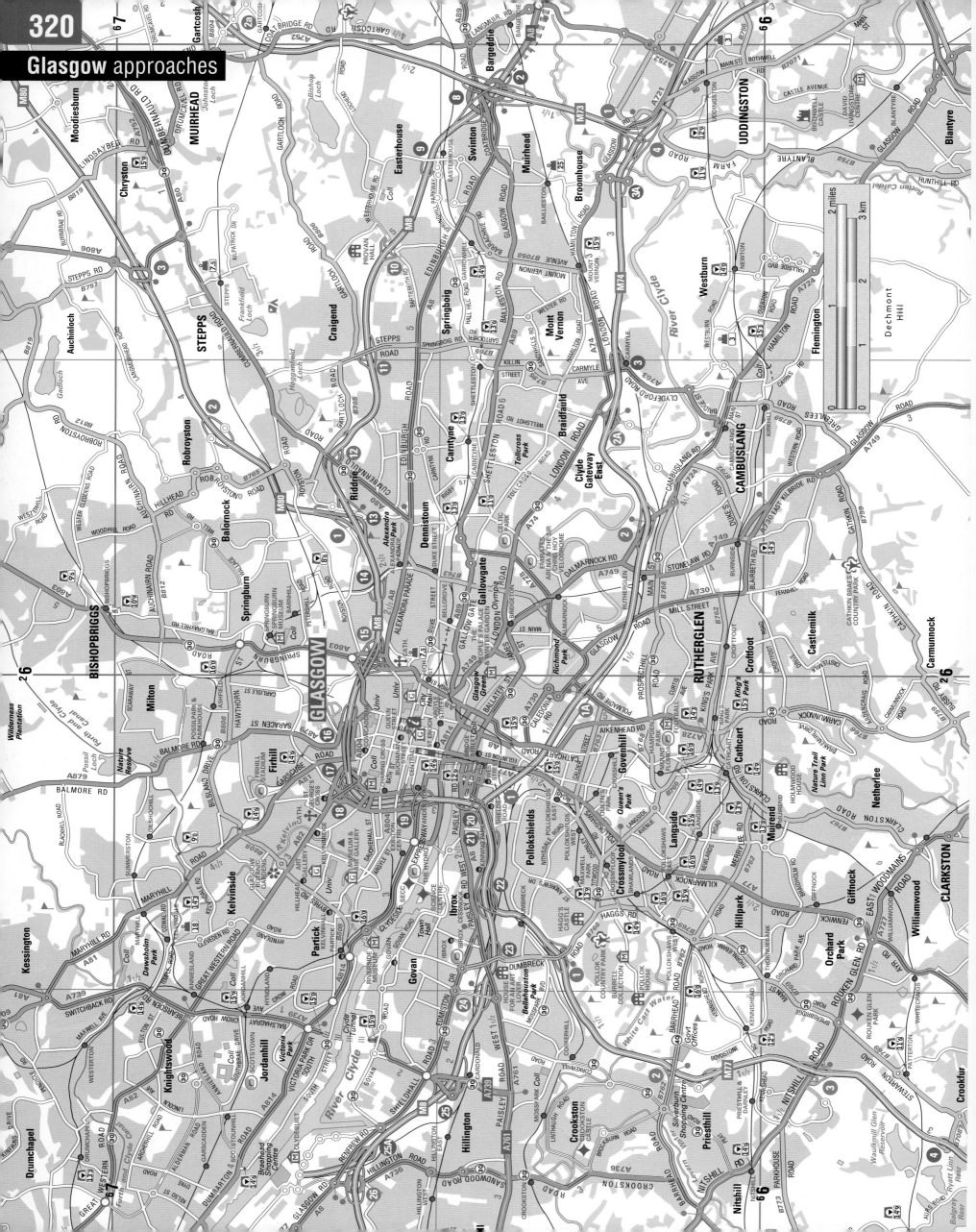

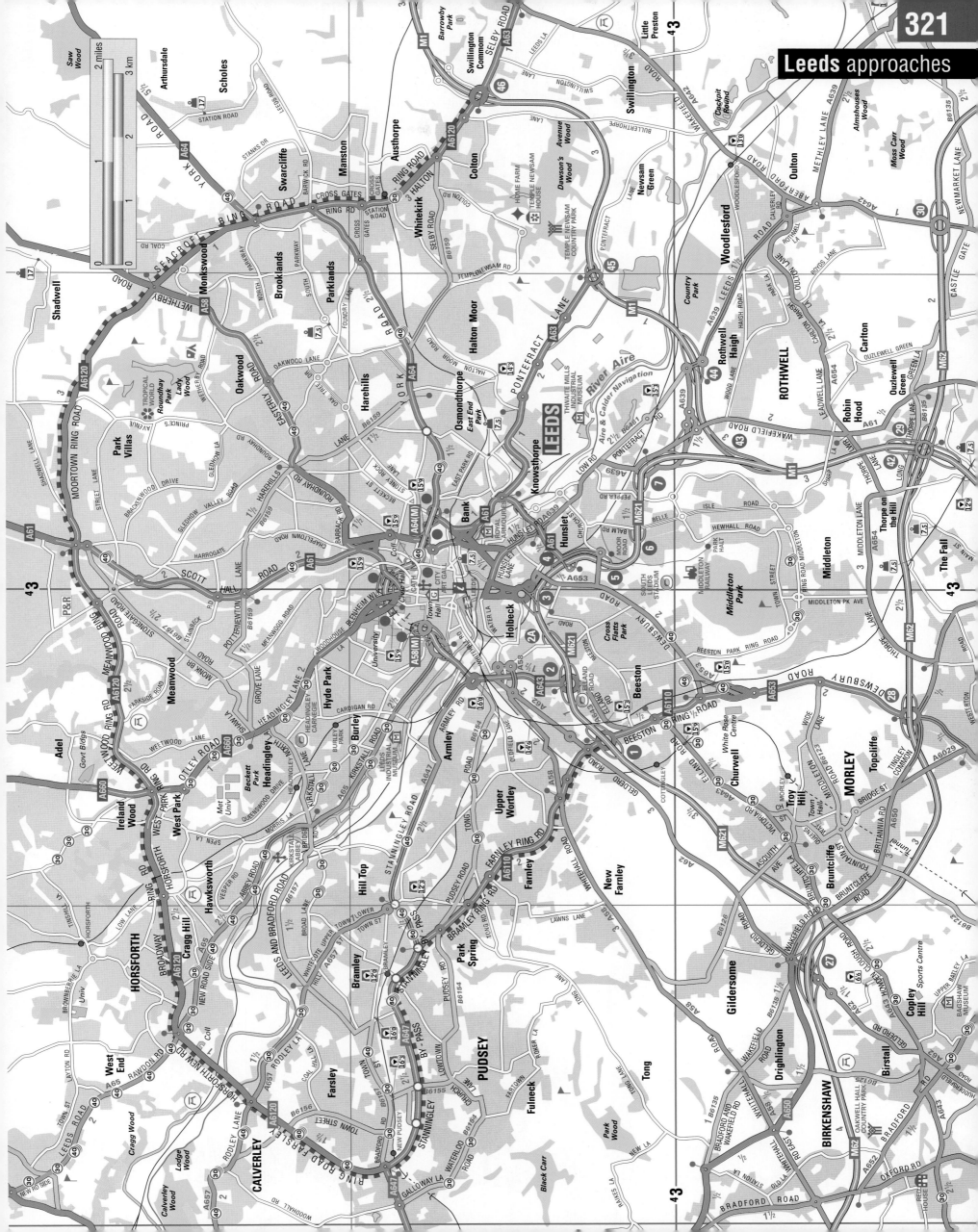

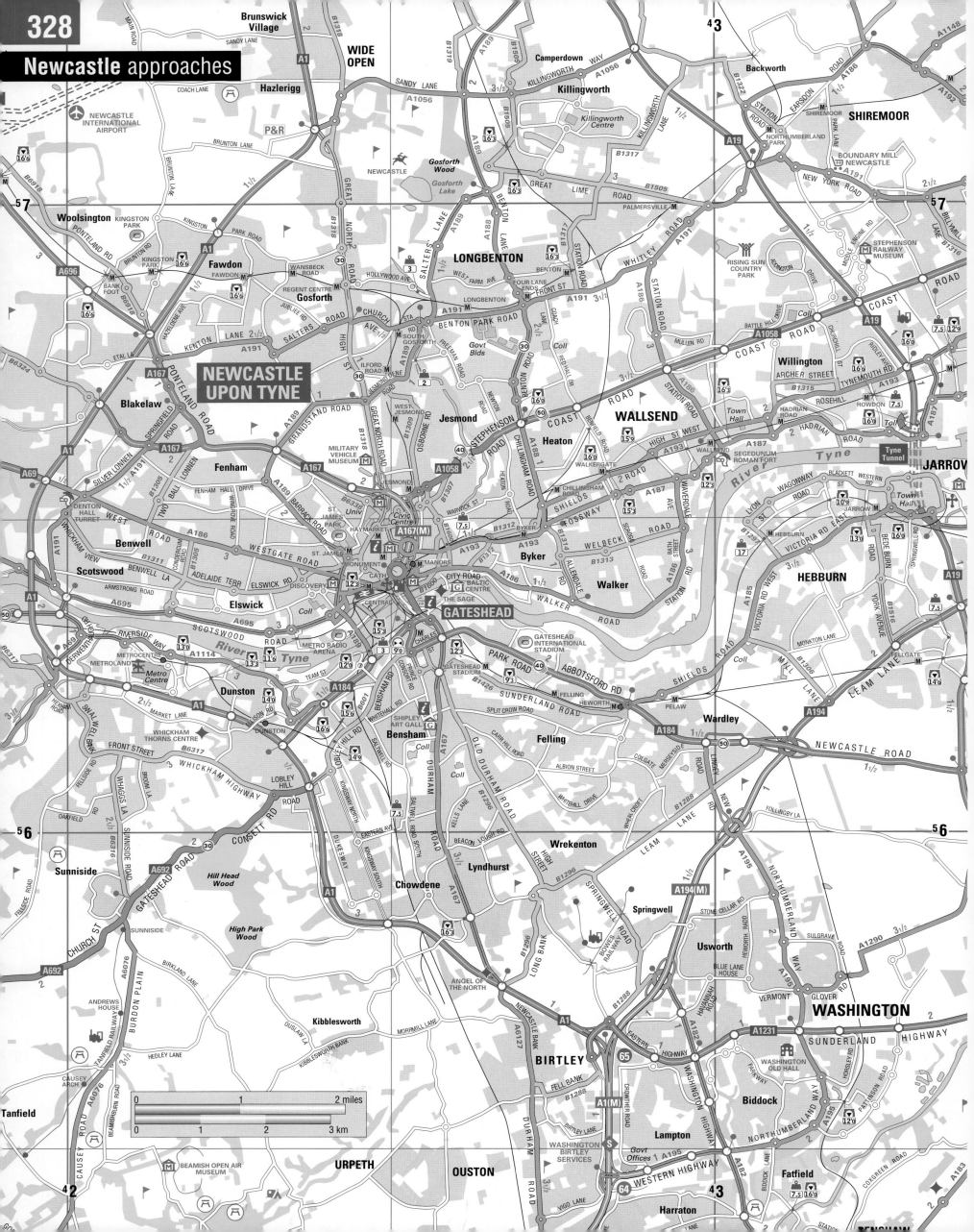

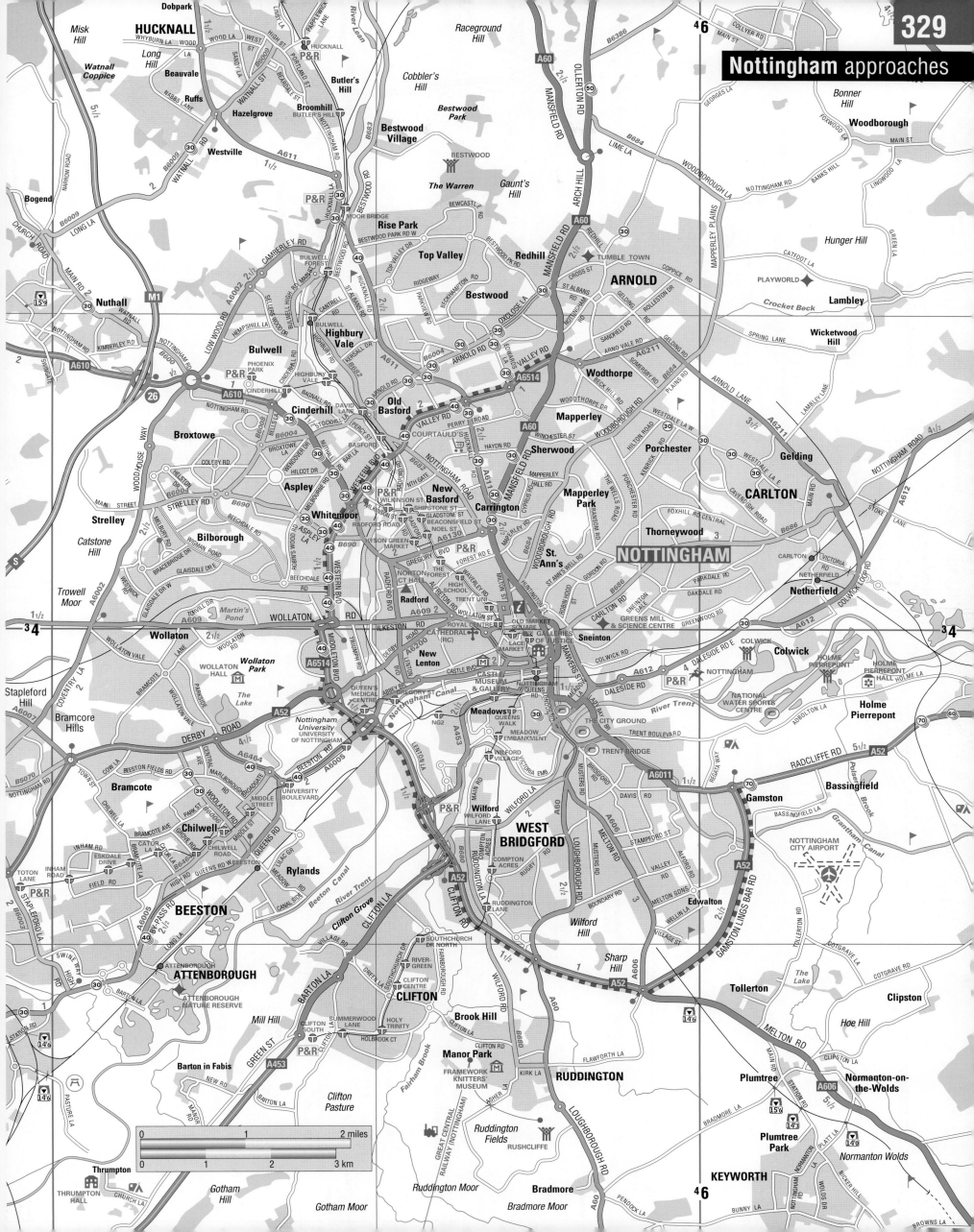

Aberdeen page 293 • Aberystwyth page 128 • Ashford page 54 • Ayr page 257 • Bangor page 179 • Barrow-in-Furness page 210 • Bath page 61 • Berwick-upon-Tweed page 273

331

Town plan symbols

Motorway
Primary route – dual, single carriageway
A road – dual, single carriageway
B road – dual, single carriageway

Minor through road
One-way street
Pedestrian roads
Shopping streets

Railway with station
Tramway with station
Underground or Metro station

H Hospital
P Parking
Police, Post Office
Shopmobility
Youth hostel

Bus or railway station building
Shopping precinct or retail park
Park
Congestion charge zone

✝ Abbey or cathedral
Ancient monument
Aquarium
Art gallery
Bird collection or aviary
Building of interest
Castle
Church of interest
Cinema
Garden
Historic ship
House
House and garden
Museum
Preserved railway
Roman antiquity
Safari park
Theatre
Tourist information centre
Zoo
✦ Other place of interest

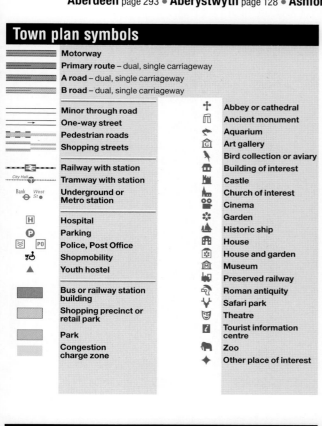

Aberdeen

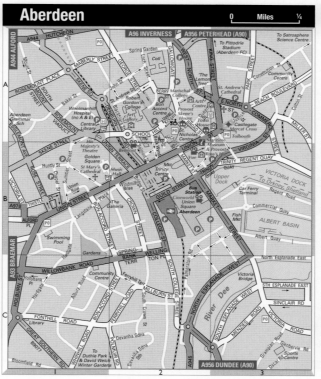

Aberystwyth

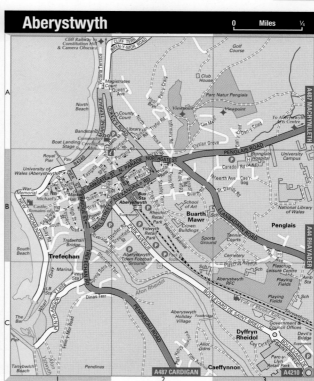

Ashford

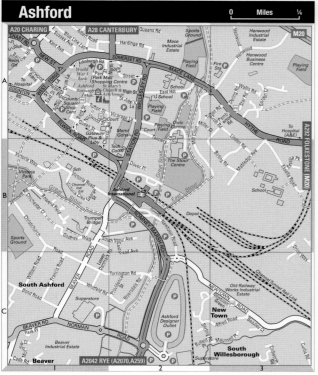

Ayr

Bangor

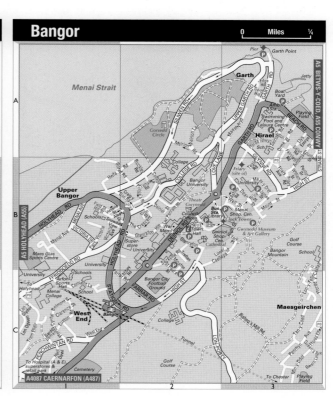

Barrow-in-Furness

Bath

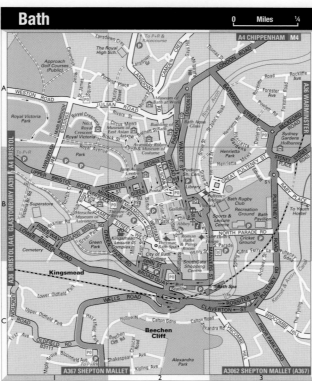

Berwick-upon-Tweed

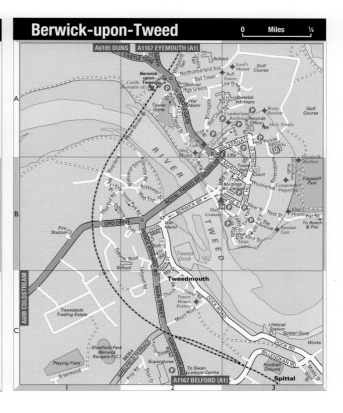

Birmingham

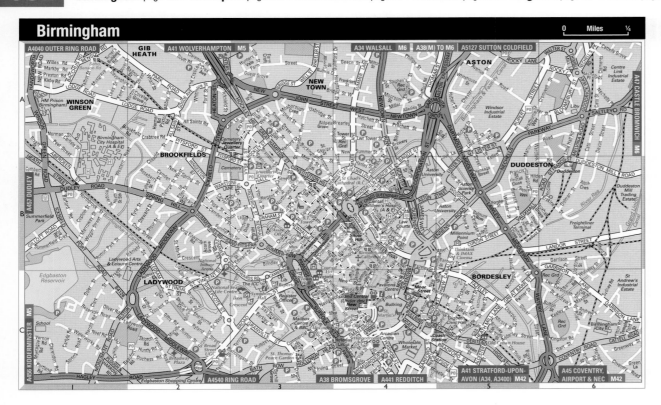

Blackpool

Bournemouth

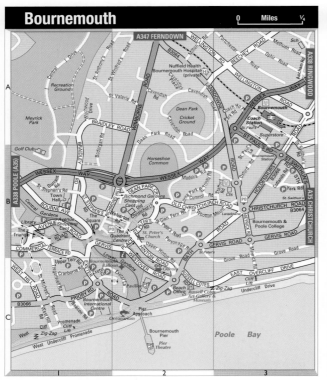

Bradford

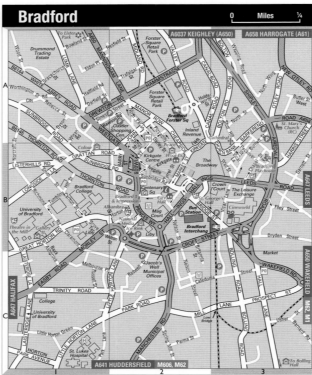

Brighton

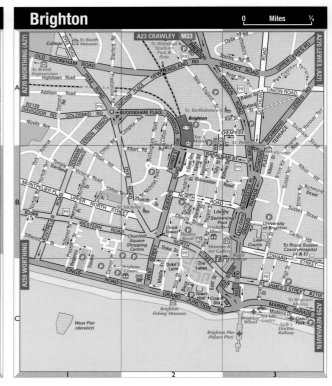

Bristol

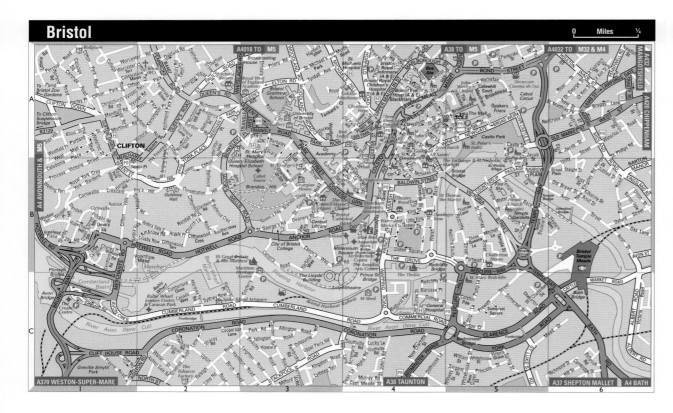

Bury St Edmunds

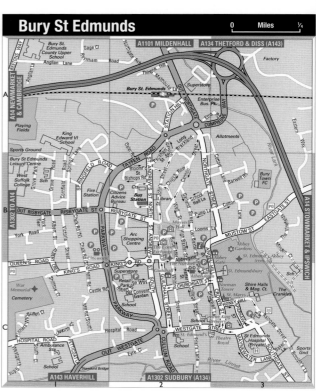

Cambridge page 123 ● Canterbury page 54 ● Cardiff page 59 ● Carlisle page 239 ● Chelmsford page 88 ● Cheltenham page 99 ● Chester page 166 ● Chichester page 22 ● Colchester page 107

333

Cambridge

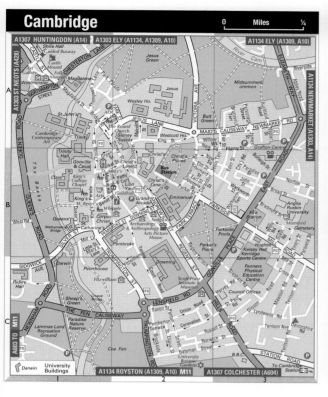

Canterbury

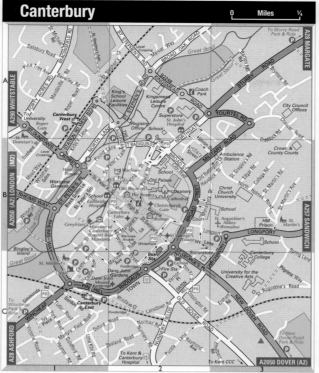

Cardiff / Caerdydd

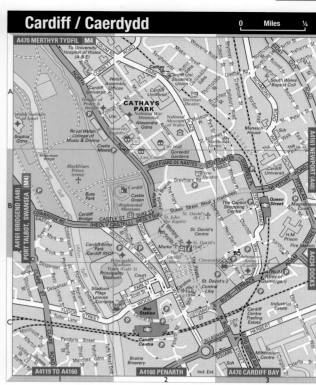

Carlisle

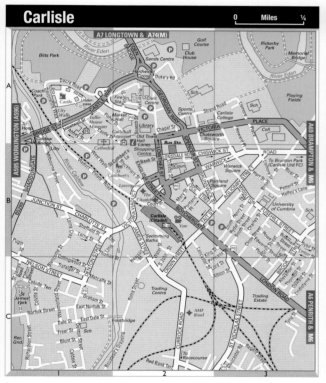

Chelmsford

Cheltenham

Chester

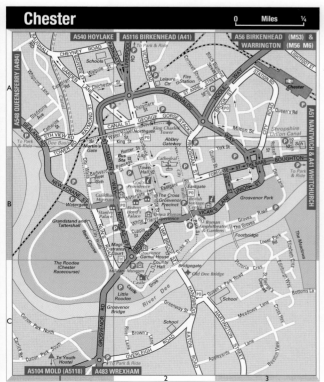

Chichester

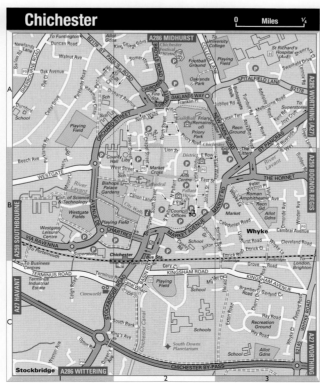

Colchester

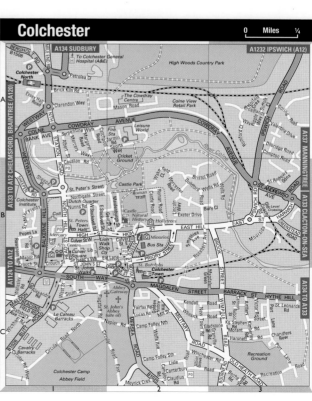

Coventry

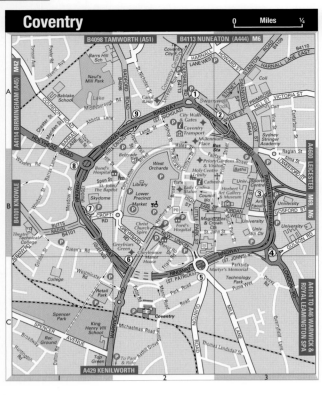

Derby

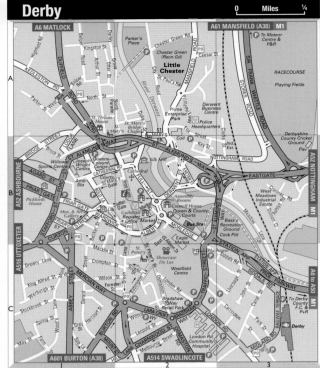

Dorchester

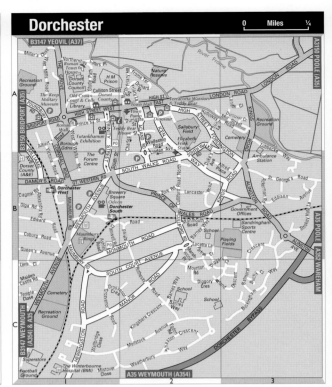

Dumfries

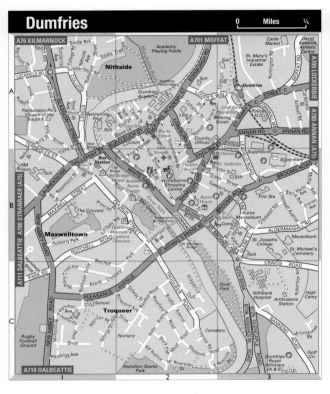

Dundee

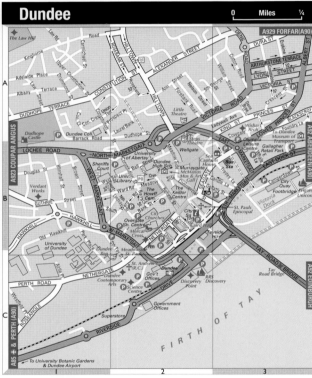

Durham

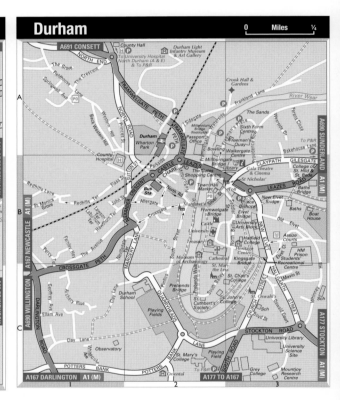

Edinburgh

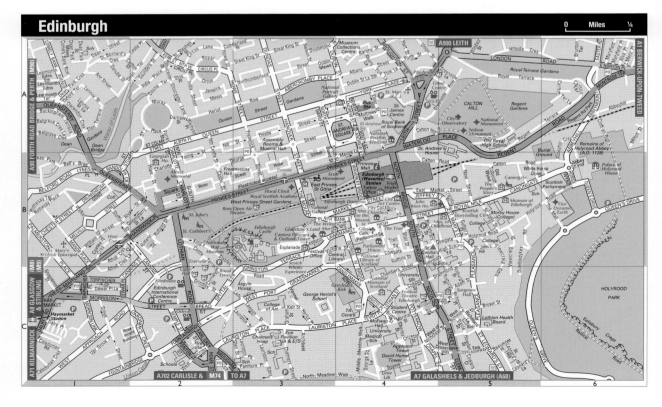

Exeter

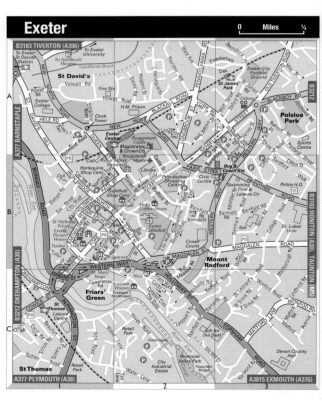

Fort William page 290 • **Glasgow** page 267 • **Gloucester** page 80 • **Grimsby** page 201 • **Hanley (Stoke-on-Tent)** page 168 • **Harrogate** page 206 • **Holyhead** page 178 • **Hull** page 200

335

Fort William

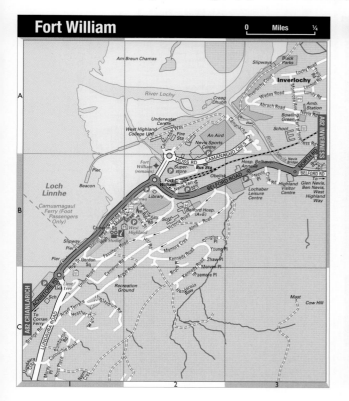

Glasgow

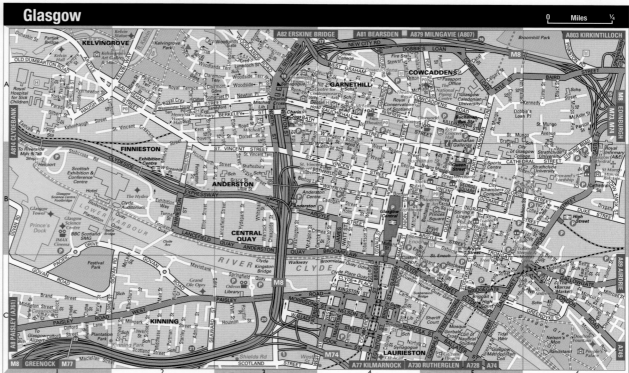

Gloucester

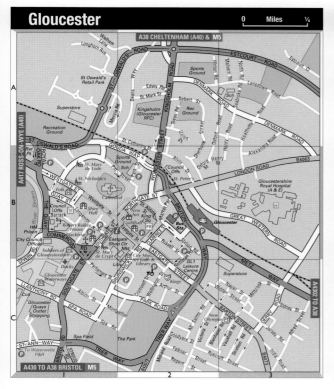

Grimsby

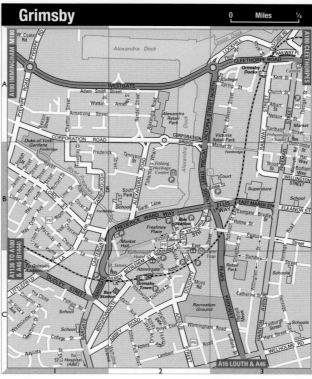

Hanley (Stoke-on-Trent)

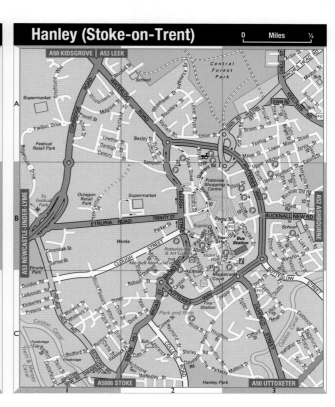

Harrogate

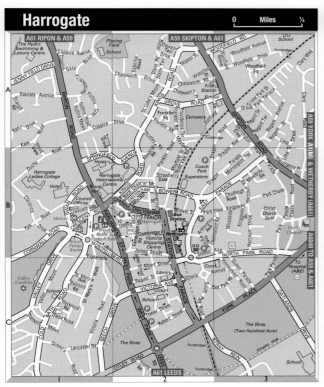

Holyhead / Caergybi

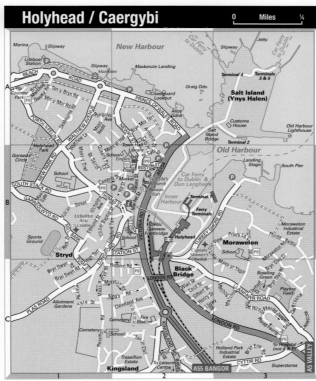

Hull

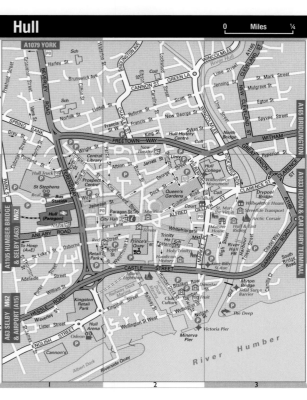

Inverness
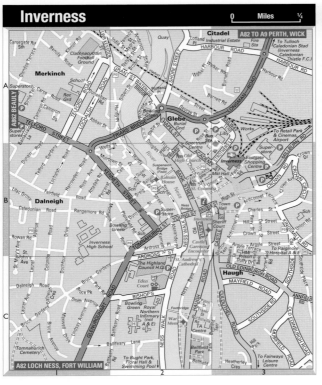

Ipswich
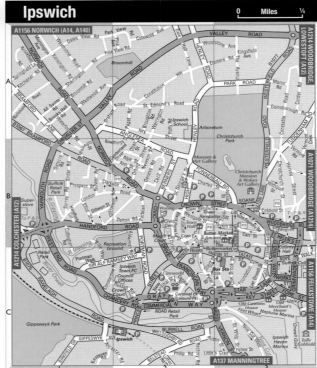

Kendal
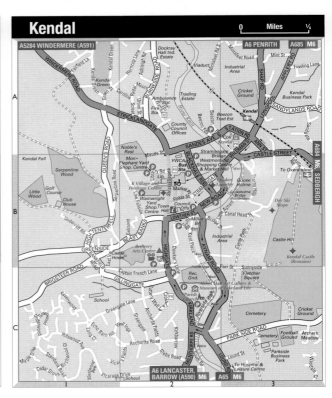

King's Lynn
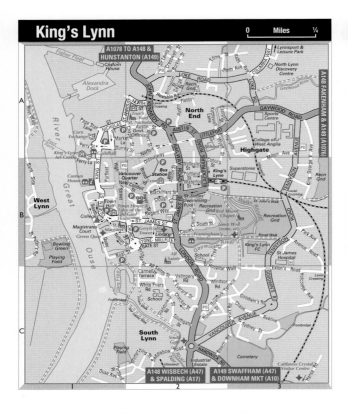

Leeds
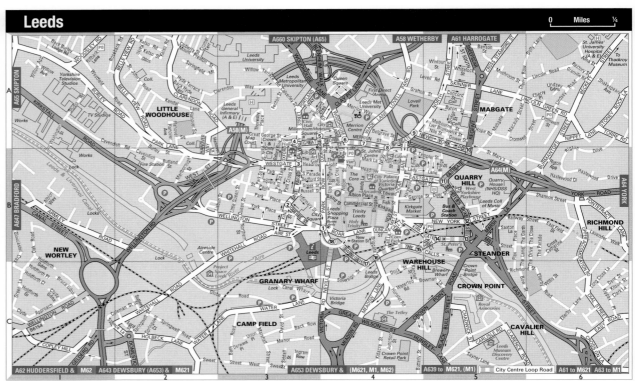

Lancaster
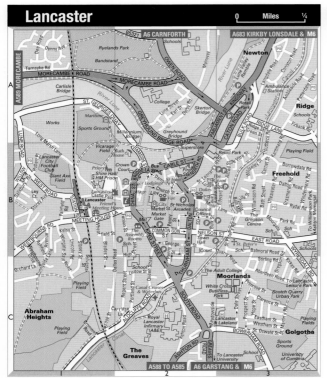

Leicester
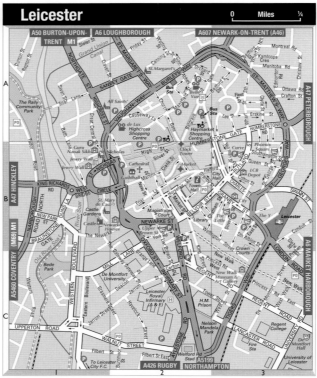

Lewes
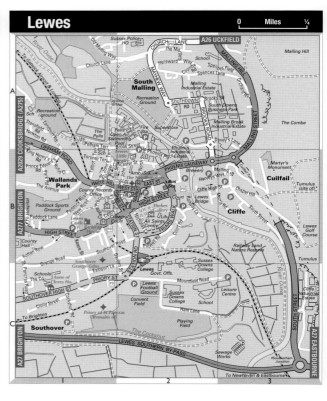

Lincoln

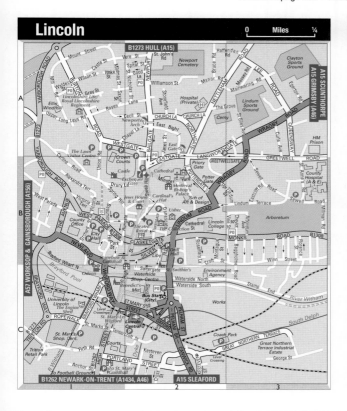

Liverpool

Llandudno

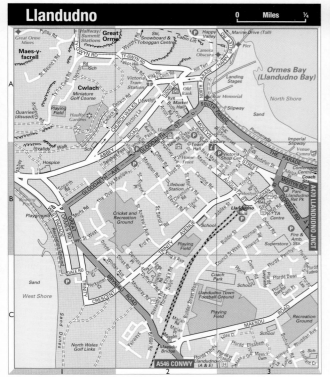

Llanelli

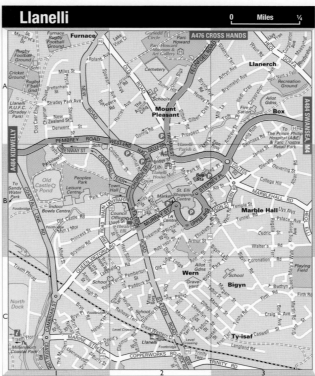

Luton

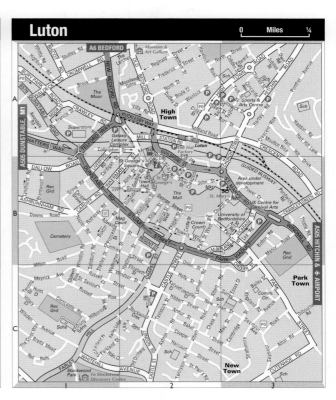

Macclesfield

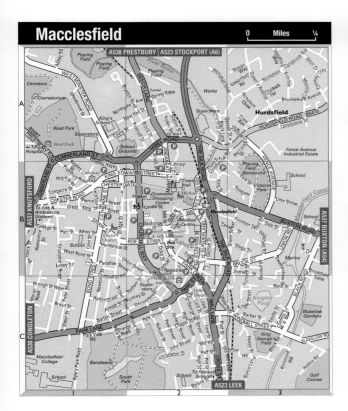

Manchester

Maidstone

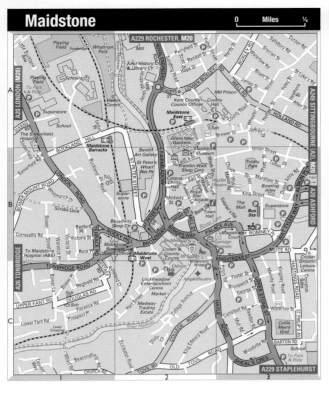

Merthyr Tydfil / Merthyr Tudful

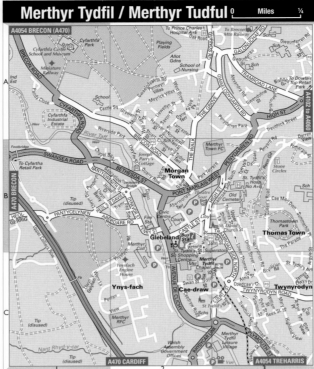

Middlesbrough

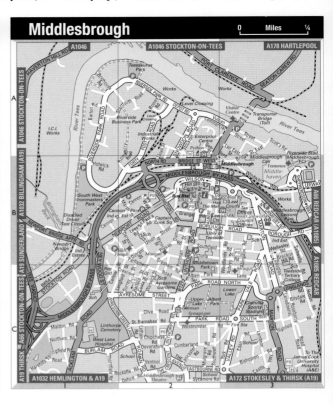

Milton Keynes

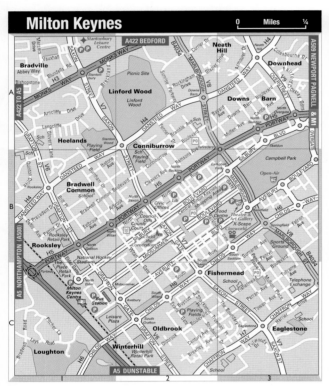

Newcastle upon Tyne

Newport / Casnewydd

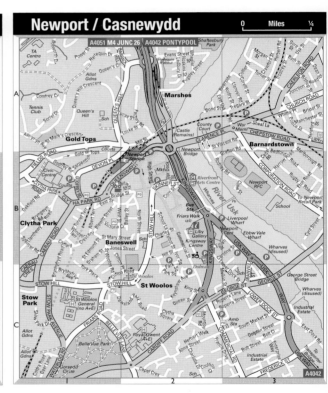

Newquay

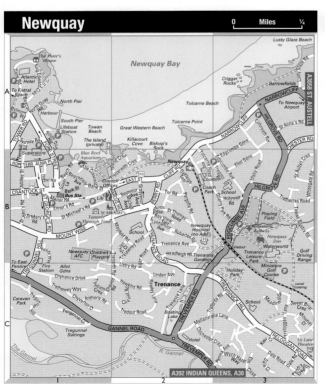

Newtown / Y Drenewydd

Northampton

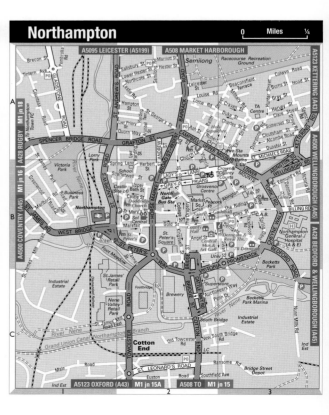

Norwich page 142 • **Nottingham** page 153 • **Oban** page 289 • **Oxford** page 83 • **Perth** page 286 • **Peterborough** page 138 • **Plymouth** page 7 • **Poole** page 18 • **Portsmouth** page 21

341

Norwich
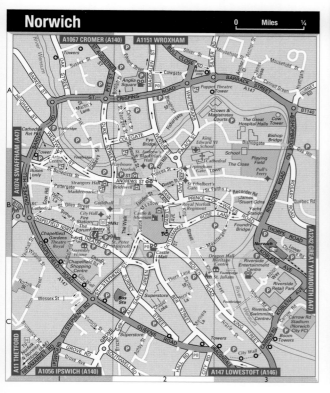

Nottingham
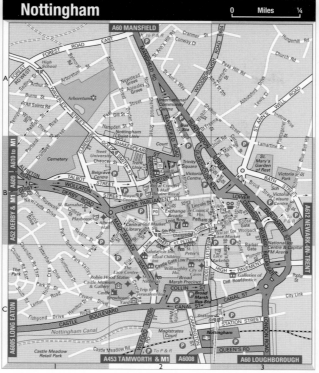

Oban
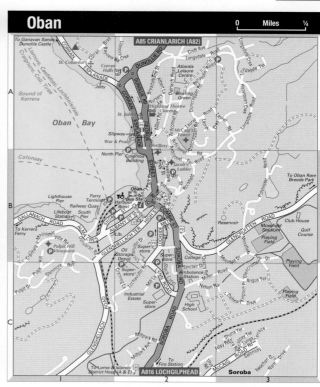

Oxford
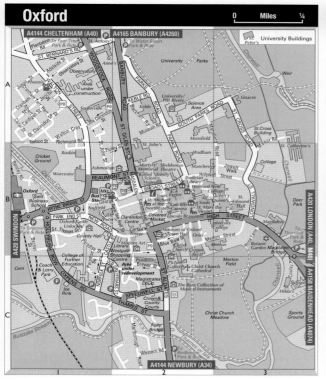

Perth
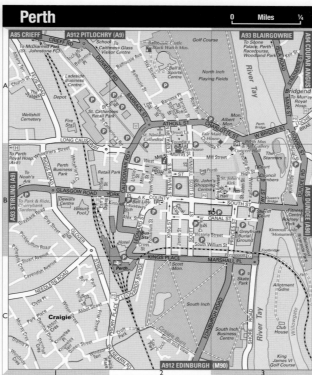

Peterborough
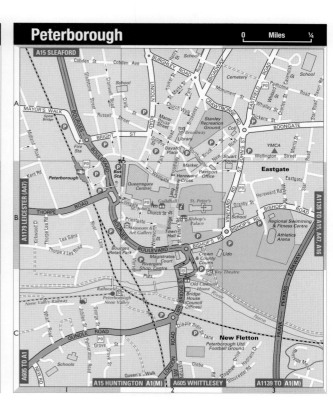

Plymouth

Poole
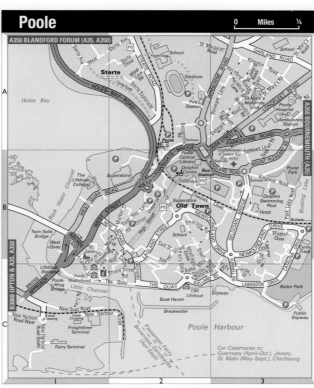

Portsmouth
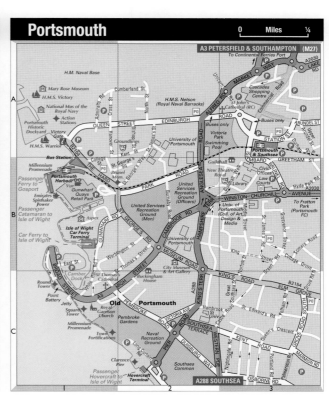

Preston
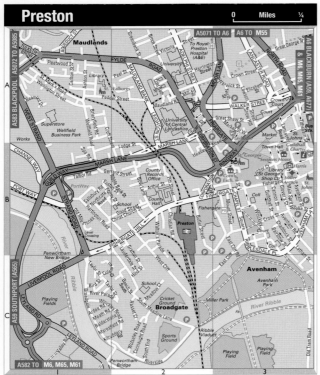

Reading
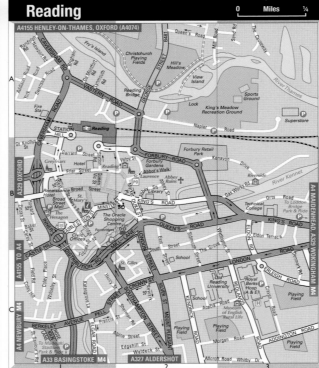

St Andrews
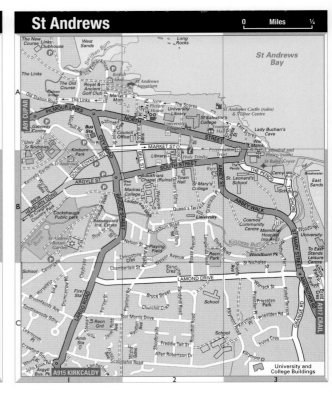

Salisbury
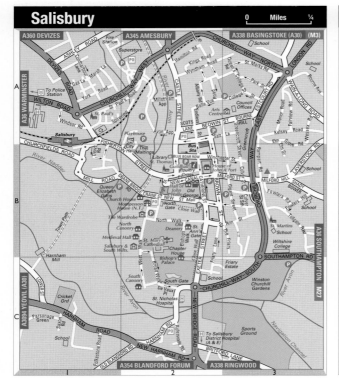

Scarborough
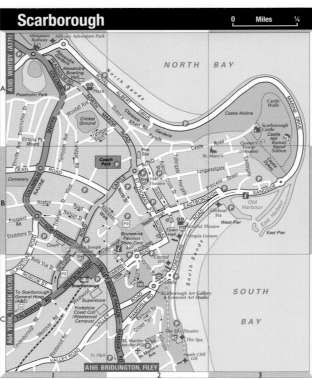

Shrewsbury
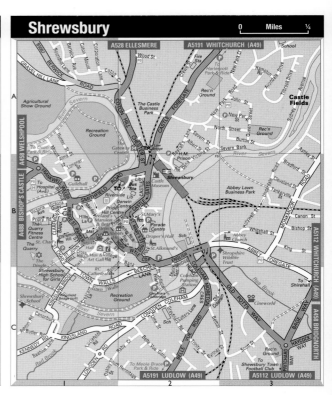

Sheffield
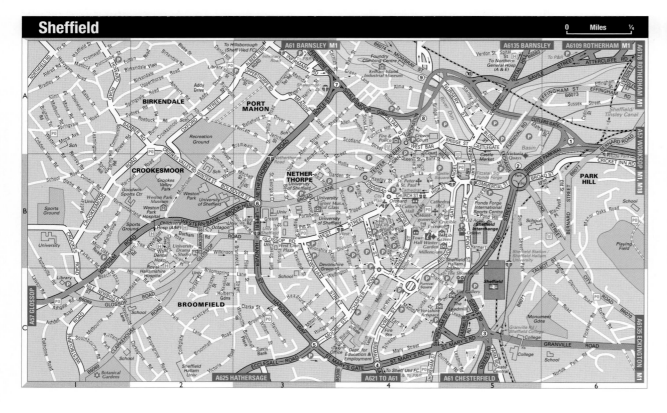

Southampton
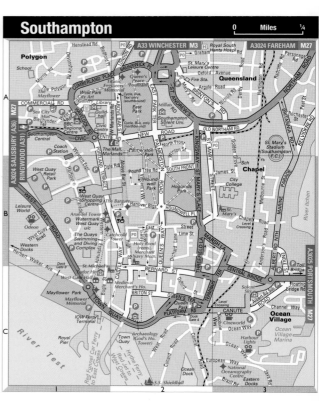

Southend page 69 • Stirling page 278 • Stoke page 168 • Stratford-upon-Avon page 118 • Sunderland page 243 • Swansea page 56 • Swindon page 63 • Taunton page 28 • Telford page 132

343

Southend-on-Sea

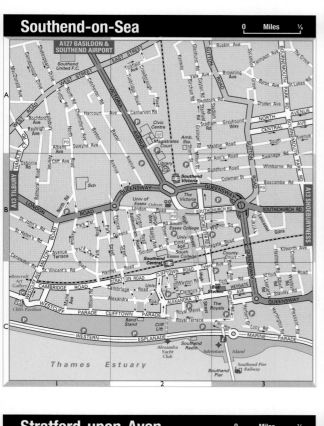

Stirling

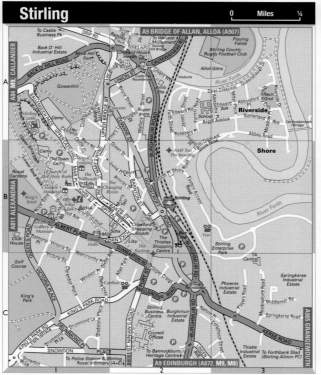

Stoke

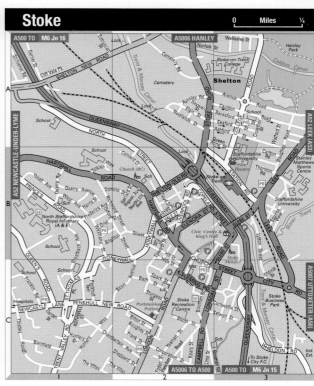

Stratford-upon-Avon

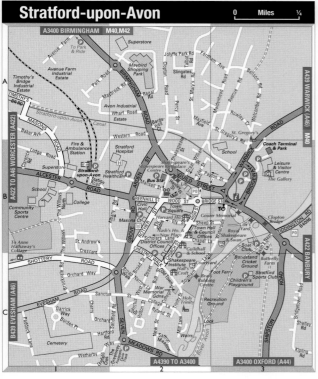

Sunderland

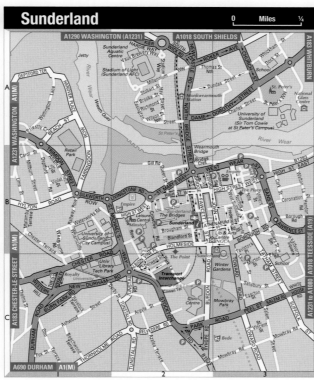

Swansea / Abertawe

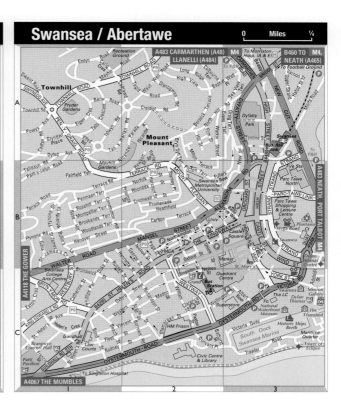

Swindon

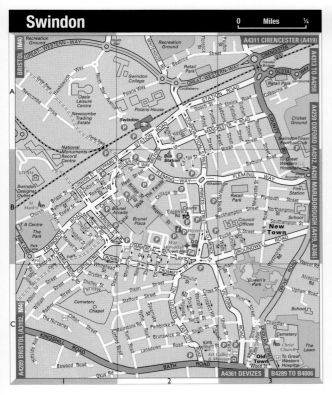

Taunton

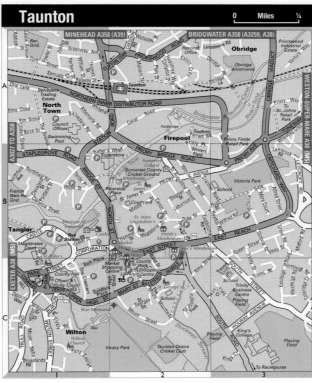

Telford

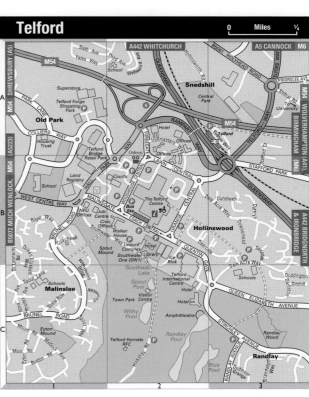

Torquay

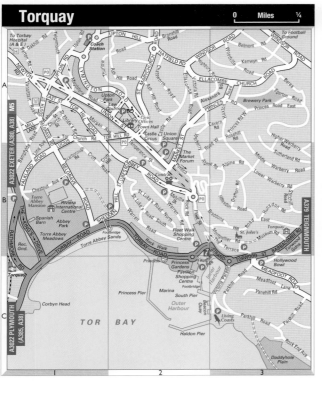

Truro

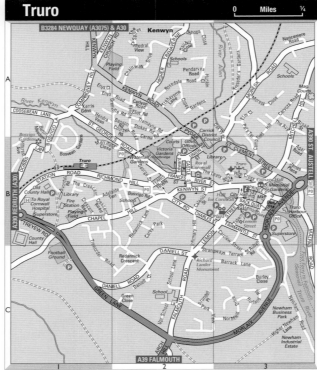

Wick

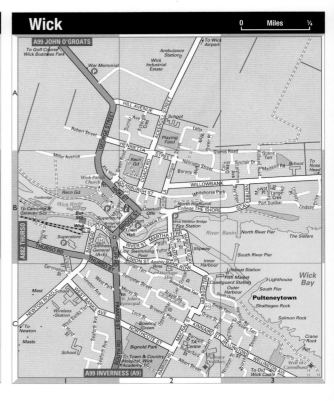

Winchester

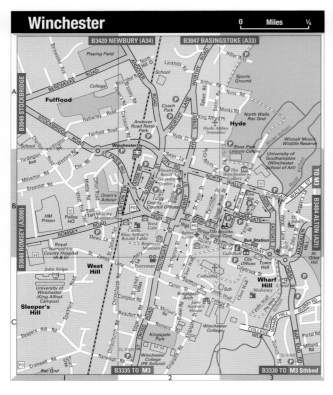

Windsor

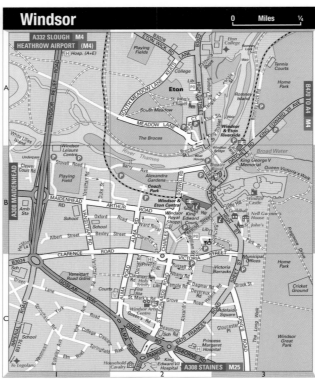

Wolverhampton

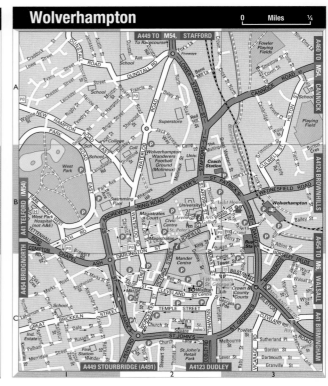

Worcester

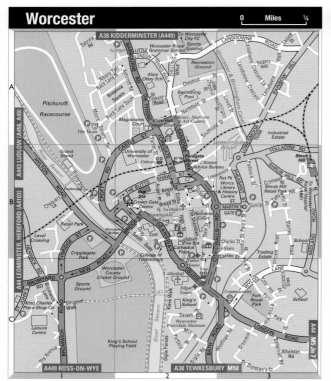

Wrexham / Wrecsam

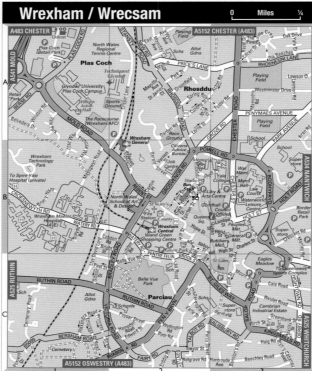

York

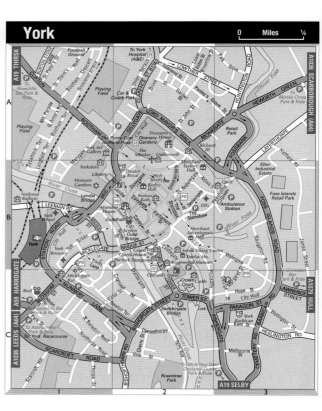

Town plan indexes

Aberdeen 331

Aberdeen ⇌ B2
Aberdeen Grammar
School A1
Academy, The A1
Albert Basin B3
Albert Quay C1
Albury Rd C1
Alford Pl B2
Art Gallery 龠 A2
Arts Centre 龠 A2
Back Wynd A2
Baker St A2
Beach Blvd A3
Belmont ⌂ B2
Belmont St B2
Berry St A2
Blackfriars St A2
Bloomfield Rd C1
Bon Accord Centre A2
Bon-Accord St B1/C1
Bridge St B2
Broad St A2
Bus Station B2
Car Ferry Terminal B3
Castlegate A2
Central Library A1
Chapel St A1
Cineworld ⌂ B2
College B2
College St B2
Commerce St A3
Commercial Quay C3
Community Centre A3/C1
Constitution St A3
Cotton St A3
Crown St B2
Denburn Rd A1
Devanha Gdns C2
Devanha Gdns South . .C2
East North St A3
Esslemont Ave A1
Ferryhill Rd C2
Ferryhill Terr C2
Fish Market B3
Fonthill Rd C1
Galleria, The A3
Gallowgate A2
George St A2
Glenbervie Rd C3
Golden Sq A2
Grampian Rd C3
Great Southern Rd C1
Guild St B2
Hardgate B1/C1
His Majesty's
Theatre ⌂ A1
Holburn St C1
Hollybank Pl C1
Huntly St B1
Hutcheon St A1
Information Ctr ⓘ A2
John St A2
Justice St A3
King St A3
Langstane Pl B1
Lemon Tree, The A2
Library C1
Loch St A2
Maberly St A1
Marischal College 龠 . . .A2
Maritime Mus &
Provost Ross's Ho 龠 . .B2
Market B2/B3
Menzies Rd C3
Mercat Cross ✦ A3
Millburn St C2
Miller St A3
Market B2
Mount St A1
Music Hall ⌂ B1
North Esp East C3
North Esp West C3
Oscar Rd C3
Palmerston Rd C2
Park St A3
Police Station ▣ A2
Polmuir Rd C2
Post Office
ⓟ A1/A2/A3/B1/C3
Provost Skene's Ho 龠 . .A2
Queen St A2
Regent Quay A3
Regent Road A3
Robert Gordon's Coll. . . .A2
Rose St B1
Rosemount Pl A1
Rosemount Viaduct A1
St Andrew St A2
St Andrew's Cath † A3
St Mary's Cathedral † . . .B1
St Nicholas Centre A2
St Nicholas St A2
School Hill A2
Sinclair Rd C3
Skene Sq A1
Skene St A1
South College St C2
South Crown St C2
South Esp East C3
South Esp West C3
South Mount St A1
Sports Centre A3
Spring Garden A2
Springbank Terr B2
Summer St B1
Swimming Pool B1
Thistle St B1
Tolbooth 龠 A2
Town House 龠 A2
Trinity Centre B2
Trinity Quay B3
Union Row B1
Union Square B2
Union St B1/B2
Upper Dock B3
Upper Kirkgate A2
Victoria Bridge C3
Victoria Rd C3

Victoria Rd. C3
Victoria St B2
Virginia St A3
Vue ⌂ B2
Wellington Pl B2
West North St A2
Whinhill Rd C1
Willowbank Rd C1
Windmill Brae B2
Woolmanhill Hospl Ⓗ . . .A1

Aberystwyth 331

Aberystwyth Holiday
Village C2
Aberystwyth RFC C3
Aberystwyth Sta ⇌ B2
Aberystwyth Town
Football Ground C2
Alexandra Rd. B2
Ambulance Station C3
Baker St B1
Banadl Rd C1
Bandstand A1
Bath St B1
Boat Landing Stage A1
Bvd de Saint-Brieuc C3
Bridge St B1
Bronglais Hospital Ⓗ . . .B3
Bryn-y-Mor Rd A2
Buarth Rd. B2
Bus Station B2
Cae Ceredig. C3
Cae Melyn B3
Cae'r-Gog A3
Cambrian St B2
Caradoc Rd A3
Caravan Site C2
Castle (Remains of) 龠 . .A1
Castle St A1
Cemetery. B3
Ceredigion Mus 龠 B2
Chalybeate St B1
Cliff Terr. A2
Club House A2
Commodore ⌂ A1
County Court. B2
Crown Buildings B2
Dan-y-Coed A3
Dinas Terr C1
Eastgate. B1
Edge-hill Rd B3
Elm Tree Ave B2
Elysian St B2
Felin-y-Mor Rd. C1
Fifth Ave. C2
Fire Station B1
Glanrafon Terr B1
Glyndŵr Rd B3
Golf Course A3
Government &
Council Offices. C3
Gray's Inn Rd. B1
Great Darkgate St B1
Greenfield St C2
Heol-y-Bryn A3
High St B1
Infirmary Rd B3
Information Ctr ⓘ B2
Iorwerth Ave C3
King St B1
Lauraplace B1
Lifeboat Station C1
Llanbadarn Rd B3
Loveden Rd B3
Magistrates Court A1
Marina C1
Marine Terr A1
Market Hall B1
Mill St B1
Moor La A2
National Liby of Wales. . .B3
New Promenade. B1
New St B1
North Beach A1
North Parade B2
North Rd A2
Northgate St A2
Parc Natur Penglais. . . .A3
Parc-y-Llyn Retail Pk . . .C3
Park & Ride B2
Park Ave. B1
Pavillion B1
Pendinas C1
Penglais Rd. B3
Penrheidol C2
Pen-y-Craig A3
Pen-yr-angor C1
Pier St A1
Plas Ave B1
Plas Helyg C2
Plascrug Ave B2/C3
Plascrug Leisure Ctr C2
Police Station ▣ C2
Poplar Row B1
Portland Rd. B2
Portland St A2
Post Office ⓟ B1/B3
Powell St B1
Prospect St B1
Quay Rd B1
Queen St B1
Queen's Ave. A2
Queen's Rd B2
Rheidol Retail Park B2
Riverside Terr. B2
St Davids St B3
St Michael's ⌂ A1
School of Art B2
Seaview Pl A1
South Beach B1
South Rd B1
Sports Ground C1
Spring Gdns. C1
Stanley Terr. B2
Swimming Pool & L CtrC3
Superstore B3
Tanybwlch Beach C1
Tennis Courts B3

Terrace Rd B1
The Bar. C1
Library A2
Trefechan Bridge B1
Trefechan Rd. C2
Trefor Rd A2
Trinity Rd B2
University Campus B3
University of Wales
(Aberystwyth) B1
Vale of Rheidol
Railway ⌂ C2
Vaynor St. C1
Victoria Terr A1
Viewpoint ❋ A1
Viewpoint ❋ A3
War Memorial. B1
Wharf Quay C1
Y Lanfa C1
Ystwyth Retail Park B2

Ashford 331

Albert Rd A1
Alfred Rd A3
Apsley St A2
Ashford Borough
Museum 龠 A1
Ashford Int Sta ⇌ B2
Bank St A1
Barrowhill Gdns A1
Beaver Industrial Est . . .C1
Beaver Rd C1
Beazley Ct C3
Birling Rd. B3
Blue Line La B1
Bond Rd C1
Bowens Field B1
Bulleid Pl C2
Cade Rd C1
Chart Rd. A1
Chichester Cl B1
Christchurch Rd B1
Chunnel Industrial Est. . .B1
Church Rd A2
Civic Centre. A2
County Square Sh Ctr . .A1
Court A2
Court A1
Croft Rd A3
Cudworth Rd C3
Curtis Rd C3
Dering Rd A3
Dover Pl B2
Drum La A3
East Hill A2
East St A1
Eastmead Ave B2
Edinburgh Rd A1
Elwick Rd A2
Essella Pk B3
Essella Rd B3
Fire Sta. A1
Forge La. A1
Francis Rd A2
George St A1
Godfrey Walk A2
Gordon Cl. A1
Hardinge Rd A2
Henwood A3
Henwood Bsns Ctr A3
Henwood Ind Est A3
High St A2
Hythe Rd C1
Information Ctr ⓘ A2
Jemmett Rd. B1
Kent Ave A1
Library A1
Linden Rd. B3
Lower Denmark Rd C1
Mabledon Ave B1
Mace Industrial Est B1
Mace La A2
Maunsell Pl B3
McArthur Glen
Designer Outlet C2
Memorial Gdns A2
Mill Ct A2
Miller Cl C3
Mortimer Cl. C1
New St A2
Newtown Green C3
Newtown Rd B2/C3
Norman Rd A2
North St A2
Norwood Gdns C2
Norwood St C2
Old Railway Works
Industrial Estate. C3
Orion Way B3
Pk Mall Shopping Ctr. . .A1
Park Pl C1
Park St A1/A2
Pemberton Rd. A2
Police Station ▣ B2
Post Office ⓟ A1/A3
Providence St A1
Queen St B1
Queens Rd A1
Regents Pl A1
Riversdale Rd B1
Romney Marsh Rd B2
St John's La A2
St Mary's Church & Arts
Venue ⌂ A2
Somerset Rd C3
South Stour Ave B2
Star Rd B3
Station Rd A1
Stirling Rd C2
Stour Centre, The. A2
Sussex Ave A1
Tannery La. A2
Technical College A1
Torrington Rd C2
Trumper Bridge B3
Tufton Rd. A2
Tufton St A2
Vicarage La A1
Victoria Cres B1

Victoria Park B1
Victoria Rd. B1
Victoria Way B1
Wallis Rd A3
West St. A1
Wellesley Rd A2
Whitfeld Rd A1
William Rd C1
World War I Tank ✦ A1

Ayr 331

Ailsa Pl B1
Alexandra Terr A3
Allison St C1
Alloway Pk C1
Alloway Pl C1
Alloway St C2
Arran Mall C2
Arran Terr B1
Arthur St B2
Ashgrove St. C2
Auld Brig B2
Auld Kirk ▲ B2
Ayr ⇌ C2
Ayr Academy B1
Ayr Central Sh Ctr. B2
Ayr Harbour. A1
Back Hawkhill Ave A3
Back Main St B2
Back Peebles St A2
Bath Pl C1
Bellevue Cres C1
Bellevue La C1
Beresford La C2
Beresford Terr C2
Boswell Pk. B2
Britannia Pl A3
Bruce Cres. B1
Burns Statue ✦ C2
Bus Sta. B1
Carrick St C2
Cassillis St B1
Cathcart St C1
Charlotte St. B1
Citadel Leisure Ctr. B1
Citadel Pl. B1
Compass Pier A1
Content Ave. C3
Content St B2
Craigie Ave B3
Craigie Rd. B3
Craigie Way. B3
Cromwell Rd B1
Crown St A2
Dalblair Rd. C2
Dam Park Sports
Stadium C3
Damside A2
Dongola Rd C3
Eglinton Pl. B1
Eglinton Terr. B1
Elba St B2
Elmbank St. B1
Esplanade B1
Euchar Rock A1
Farifield Rd C1
Fort St B1
Fothringham Rd C3
Fullarton St B2
Gaiety ⌂ C2
Garden St B2
George St B2
George's Ave A3
Glebe Cres A2
Glebe Rd A2
Gorden Terr. B2
Green St A2
Green Street La A3
Hawkhill Ave A3
Hawkhill Avenue La A3
High St B2
Holmston Rd C3
Information Ctr ⓘ B1
James St B3
John St B2
King St B2
Kings Ct B2
Kyle Centre B2
Kyle St B2
Library B2
Limekiln Rd B2
Limonds Wynd B2
Lymburn Pl B3
Macadam Pl B2
Main St B2
Mcadam's Monument ✦ .C3
Mccall's Ave A3
Mews La. B1
Mill Brae C3
Mill St A2
Mill Wynd C2
Miller Rd C2
Montgomerie Terr B1
New Bridge B2
New Bridge St B2
New Rd A2
Newmarket St B2
Newton-on-Ayr Sta ⇌ . .A2
North Harbour St B1
North Pier A1
Odeon ⌂ C2
Oswald La C1
Park Circus C1
Park Circus La. C1
Park Terr C1
Pavilion Rd A1
Peebles St A2
Philip Sq. B2
Police Station ▣ B2
Post Office ⓟ A2/B2
Prestwick Rd A2
Princes Ct A2
Queen St B2

Queen's Terr B1
Racecourse Rd C1
River St B2
Riverside Pl B2
Russell Dr A3
St Andrews Church ⌂ . . .B2
St George's Rd A3
Sandgate. B2
Savoy Park. C1
Seabank Rd B1
Smith St C2
Somerset Rd A3
South Beach Rd C1
South Harbour St B1
South Pier A1
Station Rd B2
Strathaye Pl C1
Taylor St. B1
Town Hall B2
Tryfield Pl B2
Turner's Bridge B2
Union Ave. C1
Victoria Bridge C3
Victoria St. B3
Viewfield Rd C2
Virginia Gdns A2
Waggon Rd. A2
Walker Rd A3
Wallace Tower ✦ B2
Weaver St B2
Weir Rd. C2
Wellington La C1
Wellington Sq C1
West Sanquhar Rd A3
Whitletts Rd A3
Wilson St A3
York St B1
York Street La B1

Bangor 331

Abbey Rd C2
Albert St B1
Ambrose St A3
Ambulance Station A3
Arfon Sports Hall B3
Ashley Rd. B3
Bangor City Football
Ground. A2
Bangor Mountain B3
Bangor Station ⇌ B2
Bangor University B2
Beach Rd A2
Belmont St. B2
Bishop's Mill Rd C3
Boat Yard A1
Brick St B3
Buckley St B2
Bus Station B2
Caellepa B2
Caernarfon Rd C1
Cathedral † B2
Cemetery. C1
Clarence St C1
Clock Tower ✦ B2
College B2/C2
College La B2
College Rd B2
Convent La. B2
Council Offices. B2
Craig y Don Rd. B3
Dean St B3
Deiniol Rd B2
Deiniol Shopping Ctr. . . .B2
Deiniol St B2
Edge Hill A3
Euston Rd A2
Fairview Rd C2
Farrar Rd C2
Ffordd Cynfal C1
Ffordd Elfed C2
Ffordd Islwyn A2
Ffordd y Castell C3
Ffriddoedd Rd. B1
Field St B3
Fountain St A3
Friars Ave. B3
Friars Rd B3
Friary (Site of) ✦ B3
Gardd Deman C2
Garth Hill A3
Garth Point A3
Garth Rd. A3
Glanrafon B2
Glanrafon Hill B2
Glynne Rd B3
Golf Course C2
Golf Course C2
Gorad Rd A1
Gorsedd Circle 龠 A2
Gwern Las C2
Gwynedd Museum &
Art Gallery 龠 B2
Heol Dewi C1
High St B3/C2
Hill St A3
Holyhead Rd B1
Hwfa Rd B1
Information Ctr ⓘ B2
James St B2
Library B2
Llys Emrys C1
Lon Ogwen C1
Lon-Pobty C2
Lon-y-Felin C1
Lon-y-Glyder C1
Love La A2
Lower Penrallt Rd B2
Lower St B2
Maes Glas Sports Ctr. . .B2
Maes-y-Dref. C1
Maesyffryd C1
Meirion Rd A2
Meirion Rd B2
Menai Ave B1
Menai College C1
Menai Shopping Ctr. . . .B2
Min-y-Ddol C2
Minafon C2
Mount St B3

Orme Rd B1
Parc Victoria. B1
Penchwintan Rd C1
Penlon St A2
Penrhyn Ave A3
Pier ✦ A3
Police Station ▣ B2
Post Office
ⓟ B2/B3/C1/C3
Prince's Rd. B2
Queen's Ave. B2
St Paul's St B2
Seion Rd A3
Seiriol Rd B2
Siliwen Rd A2
Snowdon View B1
Station Rd C1
Strand St B3
Swimming Pool and
Leisure Centre B3
Tan-y-Coed. C3
Tegid Rd B2
Temple Rd B2
The Crescent. B2
Theatr Gwynedd ⌂ B2
Totton Rd A3
Town Hall B2
Treflan C1
Trem Elidir. C1
Upper Garth Rd. A3
Victoria Ave. B1
Victoria Dr. B1
Victoria St B2
Vron St B2
Well St B3
West End C1
William St B2
York Pl B3

Barrow-in-Furness 331

Abbey Rd A3/B2
Adelaide St B3
Ainslie St A3
Albert St B3
Allison St A3
Anson St A2
Argyle St C1
Arthur St B3
Ashburner Way. A1
Barrow Raiders RLFC . . .C1
Barrow Station ⇌ A2
Bath St A1/B2
Bedford St B3
Bessamer Way A1
Blake St A1/A2
Bridge Rd. C2
Buccleuch Dock C2
Buccleuch Dock
Rd C2/C3
Buccleuch St. B2/B3
Byron St A3
Calcutta St A1
Cameron St. A3
Carlton Ave A3
Cavendish Dock Rd C2
Cavendish St B2/B3
Channelside Walk C1
Channelside Haven. C1
Chatsworth St A3
Cheltenham St A3
Church St A2
Clifford St B2
Clive St A2
Collingwood St B3
Cook St. A2
Cornerhouse Retail Pk . .A2
Cornwallis St A2
Courts A2
Crellin St B3
Cross St C3
Custom House ✦ B2
Dalkeith St B3
Dalton Rd B2/C2
Derby St A3
Devonshire Dock C2
Devonshire Dock Hall . . .B1
Dock Museum, The 龠 . .B1
Drake St A2
Dryden St. A3
Duke St A1/B2/C2
Duncan St B2
Dundee St C2
Dundonald St B2
Earle St. C1
Emlyn St B2
Exmouth St A2
Farm St A2
Fell St A3
Fenton St B2
Ferry Rd C1
Forum, The ⌂ B2
Furness College B1
Glasgow St A3
Goldsmith St A3
Greengate St B3
Hardwick St. A3
Harrison St B3
Hartington St B3
Hawke St A2
Hibbert Rd A2
High Level Bridge. C2
High St A2
Hindpool Retail Park A2
Hindpool Rd A2
Holker St A2
Hollywood Ret & L Pk . .A2
Hood St A1
Howard St. A3
Howe St A2
Information Ctr ⓘ A1/B1
Ironworks Rd. A1
James St B2
Jubliee Bridge C1
Keith St A3
Keyes St A3
Lancaster St A3
Lawson St B2

Bath 331

Alexandra Park. C2
Alexandra Rd. C2
Approach Golf Courses
(Public) A1
Bath Aqua Glass 龠 A2
Archway St C3
Assembly Rooms & Mus
of Costume 龠 A2
Avon St B2
Barton St A2
Bath Abbey † B2
Bath City College A2
Bath Pavilion B3
Bath Rugby Club. B3
Bath Spa Station ⇌ C3
Bathwick St A3
Beckford Road A3
Beechen Cliff Rd. C2
Bennett St A2
Bloomfield Ave. C1
Broad Quay C2
Broad St A2
Brock St A1
Building of Bath
Museum 龠 A2
Bus Station B2
Calton Gdns C2
Calton Rd C2
Camden Cr A2
Cavendish Rd A1
Cemetery. C1
Charlotte St A2
Chaucer Rd C2
Cheap St. B2
Circus Mews A2
Claverton St C2
Corn St B2
Cricket Ground A3
Daniel St A3
Edward St A3
Ferry La B2
First Ave. C1
Forester Ave A3
Forester Rd A3
Gays Hill A2
George St A2
Great Pulteney St. B3
Green Park B1
Green Park Rd B2
Grove St B2
Guildhall 龠 B2
Harley St A2
Hayesfield Park C1
Henrietta Gdns A3
Henrietta Mews A3
Henrietta Park A3
Henrietta Rd A3

Berwick-upon-Tweed 331

Bank Hill B2
Barracks ⊟ A3
Bell Tower ✦ A3
Bell Tower Pl A3
Berwick Br. B2
Berwick Infirmary Ⓗ A1
Berwick-upon-
Tweed ⇌ B2
Billendean Rd C3
Blakewell Gdns C3
Blakewell Rd C3
Brass Bastion ✦ A3
Bridge St B3
Brucegate St A3
Castle (Remains of) 龠 . .A2
Castle Terr A2
Castlegate A2
Chapel St A3
Church Rd A3
Church St B3
Coxon's La. A3
Cumberland
Bastion ✦ A2

Henry St

Henry St. B2
Herschel Museum of
Astronomy 龠 B1
Holburne Museum 龠 . . .B3
Holloway C2
Information Ctr ⓘ B2
James St West B1/B2
Jane Austen Centre 龠 . .B2
Julian Rd A1
Junction Rd C1
Kingsmead L Complex .B2
Kipling Ave C1
Lansdown Cr A1
Lansdown Gr. A2
Lansdown Rd. A2
Library B2
London Rd A3
London St A2
Lower Bristol Rd. B1
Lower Oldfield Park. C1
Lyncombe Hill C3
Manvers St B3
Maple Gr C1
Margaret's Hill A2
Marlborough Bldgs A1
Marlborough La B1
Midland Bridge Rd B1
Milk St B2
Milsom St B2
Monmouth St B2
Morford St A2
Museum of Bath
at Work 龠 A2
Museum of
East Asian Art 龠 A2
New King St B1
No 1 Royal Cres 龠 A1
Norfolk Bldgs B1
Norfolk Cr B1
North Parade Rd B3
Oldfield Rd C1
Paragon A2
Pines Way B1
Podium Shopping Ctr .B2
Police Station ▣ B2
Portland Pl A2
Post Office
ⓟ A1/A3/B2/C1/C2
Postal Museum 龠 A2
Powlett Rd A3
Prior Park Rd C3
Pulteney Bridge ✦ B2
Pulteney Gdns. B3
Pulteney Rd B3/C3
Queen Sq B2
Raby Pl B3
Recreation Ground B3
Rivers St A2
Rockliffe Ave A3
Rockliffe Rd A3
Roman Baths &
Pump Room 龠 B2
Rossiter Rd C3
Royal Ave A1
Royal Cr A1
Royal High School,
The A1
Royal Victoria Park A1
St James Sq. A1
St John's Rd. A3
Shakespeare Ave C2
Southgate C2
South Pde B3
Sports & Leisure Ctr . . .B3
Spring Gdns B3
Stall St B2
Stanier Rd B1
Superstore A2
Sydney Gdns A3
Sydney Pl. B3
Sydney Rd B3
Theatre Royal ⌂ B2
Thermae Bath Spa ✦ . . .B2
The Tyning C3
Thomas St A3
Union St. B2
Upper Bristol Rd. B1
Upper Oldfield Park. C1
Victoria Art Gallery 龠 . . .B2
Victoria Bridge Rd B1
Walcot St A2
Wells Rd C1
Westgate Buildings B2
Westgate St B2
Weston Rd A1
Widcombe Hill C3

Birmingham 332

Abbey St. A2
Aberdeen St A1
Acorn Gr. B1
Adams St A5
Adderley St C5
Albert St B4/B5
Albion St B2
Alcester St. C5
Aldgate Gr A3
Alexandra Theatre ⌂ . . .C3
All Saint's St A1
All Saints Rd A1
Allcock St C5
Allesley St. A4
Allison St C4
Alma Cr B6
Alston Rd C6
Arcadian Centre C4
Arthur St. C6
Assay Office B3
Aston Expressway A5
Aston Science Park A5
Aston St A5
Aston University B4/A5
Avenue Rd A5
BT Tower ✦ B3
Bacchus Rd. A1
Bagot St A4
Banbury St B5

Barford Rd B1
Barford St C4
Barn St C5
Barnwell Rd C6
Barr St A3
Barrack St B5
Bartholomew St C4
Barwick St B4
Bath Row C3
Beaufort Rd C1
Belmont Row B5
Benson Rd A1
Berkley St C3
Bexhill Gr C3
Birchall St C5
Birmingham City FC C6
Birmingham City Hospital (A&E) A1
Bishopsgate St C3
Blews St A4
Bloomsbury St A6
Blucher St C3
Bordesley St C4
Bowyer St C5
Bradburne Way A5
Bradford St C5
Branston St A3
Brearley St A4
Brewery St A4
Bridge St A3
Bridge St C3
Bridge St West A4
Brindley Dr B3
Broad St C3
Broad St UGC C2
Broadway Plaza ✦ C2
Bromley St C5
Bromsgrove St C4
Brookfield Rd A2
Browning St C2
Bryant St A1
Buckingham St A3
Bullring C4
Bull St B4
Cambridge St C3
Camden Dr B3
Camden St B2
Cannon St C4
Cardigan St B5
Carlisle St A1
Carlyle Rd C1
Caroline St B3
Carver St B2
Cato St A6
Cattell Rd C6
Cattells Gr A6
Cawdor Cr C1
Cecil St B4
Cemetery A2/B2
Cemetery La A2
Ctr Link Industrial Est A6
Charlotte St B3
Cheapside C4
Chester St A5
Children's Hospital (A&E) B4
Church St B4
Claremont Rd A2
Clarendon Rd C1
Clark St C1
Clement St B3
Clissold St B2
Cliveland St B4
Coach Station C5
College St B2
Colmore Circus B4
Colmore Row B4
Commercial St C3
Constitution Hill B3
Convention Ctr, The C3
Cope St B2
Coplow St B1
Corporation St B4
Council House B3
County Court B4
Coveley Gr A2
Coventry Rd C6
Coventry St C5
Cox St B3
Crabtree Rd A2
Cregoe St C3
Crescent Ave A2
Crescent Theatre C3
Cromwell St A6
Cromwell St B3
Curzon St B5
Cuthbert Rd B1
Dale End B4
Dart St C6
Dartmouth Circus A4
Dartmouth Middleway A5
Dental Hospital B4
Deritend C5
Devon St A6
Devonshire St A1
Digbeth Civic Hall C5
Digbeth High St C4
Dolman St B6
Dover St A1
Duchess Rd C2
Duddeston B6
Duddeston Manor Rd B5
Duddeston Mill Rd B6
Duddeston Mill Trading Estate B6
Dudley Rd B1
Edgbaston Sh Ctr C2
Edmund St B3
Edward St B3
Elkington St A4
Ellen St B2
Ellis St C3
Erskine St B6
Essex St C4
Eyre St B2
Farm Croft A3
Farm St A3
Fazeley St B4/C5
Felstead Way B5
Finstall Cl B5
Five Ways C2
Fleet St B3
Floodgate St C5
Ford St A2
Fore St C4
Forster St B5
Francis Rd C2
Francis St B5
Frankfort St A4
Frederick St B3
Freeth St C1
Freightliner Terminal B6
Garrison La C6
Garrison St B6
Gas St C3
Geach St A4
George St B3
George St West B2
Gibb St C5
Gillott Rd B1
Gilby Rd C2
Glover St C5
Goode Ave A2
Goodrick Way A6
Gordon St B6
Graham St B3
Granville St C3
Gray St C6
Great Barr St C5
Great Charles St B3
Great Francis St B6
Great Hampton Row A3
Great Hampton St A3
Great King St A3
Great Lister St A5
Great Tindal St C2
Green La C6
Green St C5
Greenway St C6
Grosvenor St West C2
Guest Gr A3
Guild Cl C2
Guildford Dr A4
Guthrie Cl A3
Hagley Rd C1
Hall St B3
Hampton St A3
Handsworth New Rd A1
Hanley St B4
Harford St A3
Harmer Rd A2
Harold Rd C1
Hatchett St A4
Heath Mill La C5
Heath St B1
Heath St South B1
Heaton St A2
Heneage St B5
Henrietta St B4
Herbert Rd C6
High St C4
High St C5
Hilden Rd B5
Hill St C3/C4
Hindlow Cl B6
Hingeston St B2
Hippodrome Theatre C4
HM Prison A1
Hockley Circus A2
Hockley Hill A3
Hockley St A3
Holliday St C3
Holloway Circus C4
Holloway Head C3
Holt St B5
Hooper St B1
Horse Fair C4
Hospital St A4
Howard St B3
Howe St B5
Hubert St A5
Hunters Rd A2
Hunters Vale A3
Huntly Rd C2
Hurst St C4
Icknield Port Rd B1
Icknield Sq B2
Icknield St A2/B2
Ikon Gallery C3
Information Ctr C4
Inge St C4
Irving St C3
Ivy La C5
James Watt Queensway B4
Jennens Rd B5
Jewellery Quarter A3
Jewellery Quarter Museum B3
John Bright St C4
Keeley St C6
Kellett Rd B5
Kent St C4
Kenyon St B3
Key Hill A3
Kilby Ave C2
King Edwards Rd B2
King Edwards Rd C3
Kingston Rd C6
Kirby Rd A1
Ladywood Arts & L Ctr B1
Ladywood Middleway C2/C3
Ladywood Rd C1
Lancaster St B4
Landor St B6
Law Courts B4
Lawford Cl B5
Lawley Middleway B5
Ledbury Cl C2
Ledsam St B2
Lees St A1
Legge La B3
Lennox St A3
Library A6/C3
Library Walk B2
Lighthorne Ave B2
Link Rd B1
Lionel St B3
Lister St B5
Little Ann St C5
Little Hall Rd A6
Liverpool St C5
Livery St B3/B4
Lodge Rd A1
Lord St A5
Love La A5
Loveday St B4
Lower Dartmouth St C6
Lower Loveday St B4
Lower Tower St A4
Lower Trinity St C5
Ludgate Hill B3
Mailbox Centre & BBC C3
Margaret St B3
Markby Rd A1
Marroway St B1
Maxstoke St C6
Melvina Rd A6
Meriden St C4
Metropolitan (RC) † B4
Midland St B6
Milk St C5
Mill St A5
Millennium Point B5
Miller St A4
Milton St A4
Moat La C4
Montague Rd C1
Montague St C5
Monument Rd C1
Moor Street C4
Moor St Queensway C4
Moorsom St A4
Morville St C2
Mosborough Cr A3
Moseley St C4
Mott St B3
Mus & Art Gallery B3
Musgrave Rd A1
National Indoor Arena ✦ C2
National Sea Life Centre C3
Navigation St C3
Nechell's Park Rd A6
Nechells Parkway B5
Nechells Pl A6
New Bartholomew St C4
New Canal St C5
New John St West A3
New Spring St B2
New St C4
New Street C4
New Summer St A4
New Town Row A4
Newhall Hill B3
Newhall St B3
Newton St B4
Newtown A4
Noel Rd C1
Norman St A1
Northbrook St B1
Northwood St B3
Norton St A2
Old Crown House C5
Old Rep Theatre, The C4
Old Snow Hill B4
Oliver Rd C1
Oliver St A5
Osler St C1
Oxford St C5
Pallasades Centre C4
Palmer St C5
Paradise Circus C3
Paradise St C3
Park Rd A2
Park St C4
Pavilions Centre C4
Paxton Rd A2
Peel St A1
Penn St B5
Pershore St C4
Phillips St A4
Pickford St C5
Pinfold St C4
Pitsford St A2
Plough & Harrow Rd C1
Police Station A4/B1/B4/C2/C4
Pope St B2
Portland Rd C1
Post Office A3/A5/B1/B3/B4/B5/C2/C3/C5
Preston Rd A1
Price St B4
Princip St B4
Printing House St B4
Priory Queensway B4
Pritchett St A4
Proctor St A5
Queensway B3
Radnor St A2
Rea St C4
Regent Pl B3
Register Office C3
Repertory Theatre C3
Reservoir Rd C1
Richard St A5
River St C5
Rocky La A5/A6
Rodney Cl C2
Roseberry St B2
Rotton Park St B1
Rupert St A5
Ruston St C2
Ryland St C2
St Andrew's Ind Est C6
St Andrew's Rd C6
St Andrew's St C6
St Bolton St C6
St Chads Queensway B4
St Clements Rd A6
St George's St A3
St James Pl B5
St Marks Cr B2
St Martin's C4
St Paul's B3
St Paul's B3
St Paul's Sq B3
St Philip's † B4
St Stephen's St A4
St Thomas' Peace Garden C3
St Vincent St C2
Saltley Rd A6
Sand Pits Pde B3
Severn St C3
Shadwell St B4
Sheepcote St C2
Shefford Rd A4
Sherborne St C2
Shylton's Croft C2
Skipton Rd C2
Smallbrook Queensway C4
Smith St A3
Snow Hill B4
Snow Hill Queensway B4
Soho, Benson Rd A1
South Rd A2
Spencer St B3
Spring Hill B2
Staniforth St B4
Station St C4
Steelhouse La B4
Stephenson St C4
Steward St B2
Stirling Rd C1
Stour St B2
Suffolk St C3
Summer Hill Rd B2
Summer Hill St B2
Summer Hill Terr B2
Summer La A4
Summer Row B3
Summerfield Cr B1
Summerfield Park B1
Sutton St C3
Swallow St C3
Sydney Rd C6
Symphony Hall C3
Talbot St A1
Temple Row C4
Temple St C4
Templefield St C6
Tenby St B3
Tenby St North B2
Tennant St C2/C3
The Crescent A2
Thimble Mill La A6
Thinktank (Science & Discovery) B5
Thomas St A4
Thorpe St C4
Tilton Rd C6
Tower St A4
Town Hall C3
Trent St C5
Turner's Buildings A1
Unett St A3
Union Terr B5
Upper Trinity St C5
Uxbridge St A3
Vauxhall Gr B5
Vauxhall Rd B5
Vernon Rd C1
Vesey St B4
Viaduct St B5
Victoria Sq C3
Villa St A3
Vittoria St B3
Vyse St B3
Walter St A6
Wardlow Rd A5
Warstone La B2
Washington St C3
Water St B3
Waterworks Rd C1
Watery La C5
Well St A3
Western Rd B1
Wharf St A2
Wheeler St A3
Whitehouse St A5
Whitmore St A2
Whittall St B4
Wholesale Market C4
Wiggin St B1
Willes Rd A1
Windsor Industrial Est A5
Windsor St A5
Windsor St B5
Winson Green Rd A1
Witton St C6
Wolseley St C6
Woodcock St B5

Blackpool 332

Abingdon St A1
Addison Cr A3
Adelaide St B1
Albert Rd B2
Alfred St B2
Ascot Rd A3
Ashton Rd C2
Auburn Gr C3
Bank Hey St B1
Banks St A1
Beech Ave A3
Bela Gr C2
Belmont Ave B2
Birley St A1
Blackpool & Fleetwood Tram B1
Blackpool & The Fylde College B2
Blackpool FC C2
Blackpool North A2
Blackpool Tower ✦ B1
Blundell St C1
Bonny St B1
Breck Rd B3
Bryan Rd A3
Buchanan St A2
Bus Station A2
Cambridge Rd A3
Caunce St A2/A3
Central Dr B1/C2
Central Pier ✦ C1
Central Pier C1
Central Pier Theatre C1
Chapel St C1
Charles St A2
Charnley Rd B2
Church St A1/A2
Clinton Ave B2
Coach Station A2/C1
Cocker St A1
Cocker St A1
Coleridge Rd A3
Collingwood Ave A3
Comedy Carpet ✦ B1
Condor Gr C3
Cookson St A2
Coronation St B1
Corporation St A1
Courts B1
Cumberland Ave B3
Cunliffe Rd C3
Dale St C1
Devonshire Rd A3
Devonshire Sq A3
Dickson Rd A1
Elizabeth St A2
Ferguson Rd C3
Forest Gate B3
Foxhall Rd C1
Foxhall Sq C1
Freckleton St C2
George St A2
Gloucester Ave B3
Golden Mile, The C1
Gorse Rd B3
Gorton St A2
Grand Theatre, The B1
Granville Rd A2
Grasmere Rd C2
Grosvenor St A2
Grundy Art Gallery A1
Harvey Rd B3
Hornby Rd B2
Houndshill Sh Ctr B1
Hull Rd B1
Ibbison Ct C2
Information Ctr A1
Kent Rd C2
Keswick Rd C2
King St A2
Knox Gr C3
Laycock Gate A3
Layton Rd A3
Leamington Rd B2
Leeds Rd B3
Leicester Rd B2
Levens Gr C2
Library A1
Lifeboat Station B1
Lincoln Rd B2
Liverpool Rd B3
Livingstone Rd B2
London Rd A3
Lune Gr C2
Lytham Rd C1
Madame Tussaud's Blackpool B1
Manchester Sq C1
Manor Rd B3
Maple Ave B3
Market St A1
Marlboro Rd B3
Mere Rd B3
Milbourne St A2
Newcastle Ave B3
Newton Dr A3
North Pier ✦ A1
North Pier A1
North Pier Theatre A1
Odeon C2
Olive Gr B3
Palatine Rd B2
Park Rd B2/C3
Peter St A2
Police Station B1
Post Office A1/A3/B1/B2/B3
Princess Pde A1
Princess St C1/C2
Promenade A1/C1
Queen St A1
Queen Victoria Rd C2
Raikes Pde B2
Reads Ave B2
Regent Rd B2
Register Office B2
Ribble Rd B2
Rigby Rd C1/C2
Ripon Rd B3
St Albans Rd B3
St John's Square A1
St Ives Ave C3
St Vincent Ave C3
Salisbury Rd B3
Salthouse Ave C2
Salvation Army Ctr A2
Sands Way C2
Sealife Centre B1
Seasiders Way C1
Selbourne Rd A2
Sharrow Gr C3
Somerset Ave C3
Springfield Rd A1
South King St B2
Sutton Pl B2
Talbot Rd A1/A2
Thornber Gr C2
Topping St A1
Tower B1
Town Hall A1
Tram Depot C1
Tyldesley Rd C1
Vance Rd B1
Victoria St B1
Victory Rd A2
Wayman Rd A3
Westmorland Ave C2/C3
Whitegate Dr B3
Winter Gardens Theatre B1
Woodland Gr B3
Woolman Rd B2

Bournemouth 332

Ascham Rd A3
Avenue Rd B1
Ave Shopping Centre B1
Bath Rd C2
Beacon Rd C1
Beach Office C2
Beechey Rd A3
Bodorgan Rd B1
Bourne Ave B1
Bournemouth A3
Bournemouth & Poole College B3
Bournemouth Balloon ✦ C2
Bournemouth Int Ctr C1
Bournemouth Pier C2
Bournemouth Sta A3
Braidley Rd A1
Cavendish Place A2
Cavendish Rd A2
Central Drive A1
Central Gdns B1
Christchurch Rd B3
Cliff Lift C1/C3
Coach House Pl A3
Coach Station A3
Commercial Rd B1
Cotlands Rd B3
Courts B3
Cranborne Rd C1
Cricket Ground A2
Cumnor Rd B2
Dean Park A2
Dean Park Cr B2
Dean Park Rd A2
Durrant Rd B1
East Overcliff Dr C3
Exeter Cr C1
Exeter La C2
Exeter Rd C1
Gervis Place B1
Gervis Rd B3
Glen Fern Rd B2
Golf Club B1
Grove Rd B3
Hinton Rd C2
Holdenhurst Rd B3
Horseshoe Common B2
Nuffield Health Bournemouth Hospital (private) A2
Information Ctr B2
Lansdowne B3
Lansdowne Rd A2
Lorne Park Rd B2
Lower Gdns B1/C2
Madeira Rd B2
Methuen Rd A3
Meyrick Park A1
Meyrick Rd B3
Milton Rd A2
Oceanarium C2
Odeon Cinema C2
Old Christchurch Rd B2
Ophir Rd A3
Oxford Rd B3
Park Rd A3
Parsonage Rd B2
Pavilion C2
Pier Approach C2
Pier Theatre C2
Police Station A3/B3
Portchester Rd A3
Post Office B1/B3
Priory Rd C1
Quadrant, The B2
Recreation Ground A1
Richmond Gardens Shopping Centre B2
Richmond Hill Rd B1
Russell Cotes Art Gallery & Museum C2
Russell Cotes Rd C2
St Anthony's Rd A1
St Michael's Rd C1
St Paul's A3
St Paul's La B3
St Paul's Rd A3
St Peter's B2
St Peter's B2
St Peter's Rd B2
St Stephen's Rd B1/B2
St Swithun's B3
St Swithun's Rd B3
St Swithun's Rd South B3
St Valerie Rd A2
St Winifred's Rd A2
Stafford Rd B3
Terrace Rd B1
The Square B1
The Triangle B1
Town Hall B1
Tregonwell Rd C1
Trinity Rd B2
Undercliff Drive C3
Upper Hinton Rd B2
Upper Terr Rd C1
Wellington Rd A2/A3
Wessex Way A3/B1/B2
West Cliff Promenade C1
West Hill Rd C1
West Undercliff Prom C1
Westover Rd B2
Wimborne Rd A2
Wootton Mount B2
Wychwood Dr A1
Yelverton Rd B2
York Rd B3
Zig-Zag Walks C1/C3

Bradford 332

Alhambra B2
Back Ashgrove B1
Barkerend Rd A3
Barnard Rd C3
Barry St B2
Bolling Rd C3
Bolton Rd A3
Bowland St A1
Bradford 1 B2
Bradford College B1
Bradford Forster Sq A2
Bradford Interchange B3
Bradford Playhouse B3
Bridge St B2
Britannia St B2
Burnett St B3
Bus Station B2
Butler St West A3
Caledonia St C2
Canal Rd A2
Carlton St B1
Cathedral † A3
Centenary Sq B2
Chapel St B3
Cheapside A2
Church Bank B3
Cineworld B3
City Hall B2
City Rd A1
Claremont B1
Colour Museum B1
Croft St B2
Crown Court B3
Darfield St A1
Darley St A2
Drewton Rd A1
Drummond Trading Estate A1
Dryden St B3
Dyson St A1
Easby Rd C1
East Parade B3
Eldon Pl A1
Filey St B3
Forster Square Ret Pk A2
Gallery II B1
Garnett St B3
Godwin St B2
Gracechurch St A1
Grattan Rd B1
Great Horton Rd B1/B2
Grove Terr B1
Hall Ings B2
Hall La C3
Hallfield Rd A1
Hammstrasse A2
Harris St B3
Holdsworth St A2
Ice Rink ✦ B2
Impressions B2
Information Ctr B2
Ivegate B2
Inland Revenue A2
Jacob's Well Municipal Offices B2
James St A2
John St A2
Kirkgate B2
Kirkgate Centre B2
Laisteridge La C1
Leeds Rd B3
Library B1/B2
Listerhills Rd B1
Little Horton La C1
Little Horton Gn C1
Longside La B1
Lower Kirkgate B2
Lumb La A1
Magistrates Court B2
Manchester Rd C2
Manningham La A1
Manor Row A2
Market C3
Market St B2
Melbourne Place C1
Midland Rd A2
Mill La C2
Morley St B1
National Media B2
Nelson St B2/C2
Nesfield St A2
New Otley Rd A3
Norcroft St B1
North Parade A2
North St A3
North Wing A3
Oastler Shopping Ctr A2
Otley Rd A3
Park Ave C1
Park La C1
Park Rd C2
Parma St C2
Peace Museum B2
Peckover St B3
Piccadilly A2
Police Station B2/C2
Post Office A2/B1/B2/C3
Princes Way B2
Prospect St C3
Radwell Drive C2
Rawson Rd A1
Rebecca St A1
Richmond Rd B1
Russell St C1
St George's Hall B2
St Lukes Hospital C1
St Mary's A3
Shipley Airedale Rd A3/B3
Simes St A1
Smith St B1
Spring Mill St C2
Stott Hill A3
Sunbridge Rd A1/B1/B2
The Leisure Exchange B3
Theatre in the Mill B1
Thornton Rd A1/B1
Trafalgar St A2
Trinity Rd C1
Tumbling Hill St B1
Tyrrel St B2
Univ of Bradford B1/C1
Usher St C3
Valley Rd A2
Vicar La B3
Wakefield Rd C3
Wapping Rd A3
Westgate A1
White Abbey Rd A1
Wigan Rd A1
Wilton St B1
Wood St A1
Wool Exchange B2
Worthington St A1

Brighton 332

Addison Rd A1
Albert Rd B2
Albion Hill B3
Albion St B3
Ann St A3
Baker St A3
Black Lion St C2
Brighton A2
Brighton Centre C2
Brighton Fishing Museum C2
Brighton Pier (Palace Pier) ✦ C3
Brighton Wheel ✦ C3
Broad St C3
Buckingham Pl A2
Buckingham Rd B2
Cannon Pl C1
Carlton Hill B3
Chatham Pl A1
Cheapside A3
Church St B2
Churchill Sq Sh Ctr B2
Clifton Hill B1
Clifton Pl B1
Clifton Rd B1
Clifton St A2
Clifton Terr B1
Clock Tower B2
Coach Station C3
Clyde Rd A3
Coach Park C3
Compton Ave A2
Davigdor Rd A1
Denmark Terr B1
Ditchling Rd A3
Dome B2
Duke St B2
Duke's La C2
Dyke Rd A1/B2
East St C2
Edward St B3
Elmore Rd B3
Frederick St B2
Gardner St B2
Gloucester Pl B3
Gloucester Rd B2
Goldsmid Rd A1
Grand Junction Rd C2
Grand Pde B3
Grove Hill B3
Guildford St A2
Hampton Pl B1
Hanover Terr A3
High St C3
Highdown Rd A1
Information Ctr C2
John St B3
Kemp St B2
Kensington Pl B2
Kings Rd C1
Law Courts B3
Lewes Rd A3
Library B2
London Rd A3
Madeira Dr C3
Marine Pde C3
Middle St C2
Montpelier Pl B1
Montpelier Rd B1
Montpelier St B1
Mus & Art Gallery B3
New England Rd A2
New England St A2
New Rd B2
Nizells Ave A1
Norfolk Rd B1
Norfolk Terr B1
North Rd B2
North St B2
Odeon C2
Old Shoreham Rd A1
Old Steine C3
Osmond Rd A1
Over St B2
Oxford St A3
Park Crescent Terr A3
Phoenix Art Gallery B3
Phoenix Rise A3
Police Station B3
Post Office A1/A2/A3/B1/B2/B3/C3
Preston Rd A2
Preston St B1
Prestonville Rd A1
Queen's Rd B2
Regency Sq C1
Regent St B2
Richmond Pl B3
Richmond St B3
Richmond Terr A3
Rose Hill Terr A3
Royal Alexandra Hospital B1
Royal Pavilion B2
St Bartholomew's A3
St James's St C3
St Nicholas Rd B2
St Nicholas' B2
St Peter's A3
Sea Life Centre C3
Shaftesbury Rd A3
Ship St C2
Sillwood Rd B1
Sillwood St B1
Southover St A3
Spring Gdns B2
Stanford Rd A1
Stanley Rd A3
Surrey St B2
Sussex St B3
Sussex Terr B3
Swimming Pool B3
Sydney St B3
Temple Gdns B1
Terminus Rd A2
The Lanes C2
Theatre Royal B2
Tidy St B2
Town Hall C2
Toy & Model Mus A2
Trafalgar St B2
Union Rd A3
University of Brighton B3
Upper Lewes Rd A3
Upper North St B1
Viaduct Rd A3
Victoria Gdns B3
Victoria Rd B1
Volk's Electric Railway ✦ C3
West Pier (derelict) C1
West St C2
Western Rd B1
Whitecross St B2
York Ave B1
York Pl B3

Bristol 332

Acramans Rd C4
Albert Rd C6
Alfred Hill A4
All Saint's St A4
All Saints' B4
Allington Rd C3
Alpha Rd C4
Ambra Vale B1
Ambra Vale East B2
Ambrose Rd B2
Amphitheatre C3
Anchor Rd B3
Anvil St B6
Architecture Ctr ✦ B4
Argyle Pl B2
Arlington Villas A2
Arnolfini Arts Centre, The ✦ B4
Art Gallery A3
Ashton Gate Rd C2
Ashton Rd C1
at-Bristol ✦ B3
Avon Bridge C1
Avon Cr C1
Avon St B6
Baldwin St B4
Baltic Wharf C2
Baltic Wharf L Ctr & Caravan Pk ✦ C2
Baltic Wharf Marina C2
Barossa Pl C4
Barton Manor B6
Barton Rd B6
Barton Vale B6
Bath Rd C6
Bathurst Basin C4
Bathurst Parade C4
Beauley Rd C3
Bedminster Bridge C5
Bedminster Parade C4
Bellevue B2
Bellevue Cr B2
Bellevue Rd C6
Berkeley Pl A2
Berkeley Sq A3
Birch Rd C2
Blackfriars A4
Bond St A5
Braggs La A6
Brandon Hill B3
Brandon Steep B3
Bristol Bridge B5
Bristol Cath (CE) † B3
Bristol Eye Hospital (A&E) A4
Bristol Grammar School A3
Bristol Harbour Railway C3
Bristol Royal Children's Hospital A4
Bristol Royal Infirmary (A&E) A4
Bristol Temple Meads Station B6
Broad Plain B6
Broad Quay B4
Broad St A4
Broad Weir A5
Broadcasting House A3
Broadmead A5
Brunel Way C1
Brunswick Sq A5
Burton Cl C5
Bus Station A4
Butts Rd B3
Cabot Circus A5
Cabot Tower ✦ B3
Caledonia Pl B1
Callowhill Ct A5
Cambridge St C6
Camden Rd C3
Camp Rd A1
Canada Way C2
Cannon St A4
Canon's Rd B3/B4
Canon's Way B3
Cantock's Cl A3

Canynge Rd . . . A1
Canynge Sq . . . A1
Castle Park . . . A5
Castle St . . . A5
Catherine Meade St . . . A4
Cattle Market Rd . . . C6
Central Library . . . B3
Charles Pl . . . B1
Charlotte St . . . B1
Charlotte St South . . . B1
Chatterton House . . . B5
Chatterton Sq . . . C5
Chatterton St . . . C5
Cheese La . . . B5
Christchurch . . . A4
Christchurch Rd . . . A1
Christmas Steps ♦ . . . A4
Church La . . . B2/B5
Church St . . . B5
City Museum . . . A3
City of Bristol College . . . B3
Clare St . . . B4
Clarence Rd . . . C4
Cliff Rd . . . C1
Clift House Rd . . . C1
Clifton Cath (RC) † . . . A1
Clifton Down . . . A1
Clifton Down Rd . . . A1
Clifton Hill . . . B1
Clifton Park . . . A1/A2
Clifton Park Rd . . . A1
Clifton Pl . . . B2
Cliftonwood Cr . . . B2
Cliftonwood Rd . . . B2
Cliftonwood Terr . . . B2
Clifton Vale . . . B1
Cobblestone Mews . . . A1
College Green . . . B3
College Rd . . . A1
College St . . . B3
Colston Almshouses . . . A4
Colston Ave . . . B4
Colston Hall . . . B4
Colston Parade . . . C5
Colston St . . . B4
Commercial Rd . . . C4
Constitution Hill . . . B2
Cooperage La . . . C4
Corn St . . . B4
Cornwallis Ave . . . B1
Cornwallis Cr . . . B1
Coronation Rd . . . C2/C4
Council House . . . B3
Counterslip . . . B5
Courts . . . B4
Create Centre, The ♦ . . . C1
Crosby Row . . . B2
Culver St . . . B3
Cumberland Basin . . . C1
Cumberland Cl . . . C1
Cumberland Rd . . . C2/C3
David St . . . A6
Dean La . . . A6
Deanery Rd . . . B3
Denmark St . . . B3
Dowry Sq . . . B1
Eaton Cr . . . A2
Elmdale Rd . . . A3
Elton Rd . . . A3
Eugene St . . . A4/A6
Exchange, The and St Nicholas' Mkts . . . B4
Fairfax St . . . A4
Fire Station . . . B5
Floating Harbour . . . C5
Foster Almshouses . . . A4
Frayne Rd . . . C1
Frederick Pl . . . B1
Freeland Pl . . . B1
Frogmore St . . . B3
Fry's Hill . . . B1
Gas La . . . B6
Gasferry Rd . . . C3
General Hospital . . . C4
Georgian House . . . B3
Glendale . . . B1
Glentworth Rd . . . B2
Gloucester St . . . A1
Goldney Hall . . . B1
Goldney Rd . . . B1
Gordon Rd . . . A1
Granby Hill . . . B1
Grange Rd . . . A1
Great Ann St . . . A6
Great George St . . . A6/B3
Great George St . . . B3
Great Western Way . . . B6
Green St North . . . B1
Green St South . . . B1
Greenay Bush La . . . C2
Greenbank Rd . . . C2
Greville Smyth Park . . . C1
Guildhall . . . A4
Guinea St . . . C4
Hamilton Rd . . . C2
Hanbury Rd . . . A2
Hanover Pl . . . C3
Harbour Way . . . B3
Harley Pl . . . A1
Haymarket . . . A5
Hensman's Hill . . . B1
High St . . . B4
Highbury Villas . . . A3
Hill St . . . B3
Hill St . . . C6
Hippodrome . . . B4
Hopechapel Hill . . . B1
Horfield Rd . . . A3
Horton St . . . B6
Host St . . . B3
Hotwell Rd . . . B1/B2
Houlton St . . . A6
Howard Rd . . . C3
IMAX Cinema . . . B4
Information Ctr ℹ . . . B4
Islington Rd . . . C3
Jacob St . . . A5/A6
Jacob's Wells Rd . . . B2
John Carr's Terr . . . B2

John Wesley's Chapel . . . A5
Joy Hill . . . B1
Jubilee St . . . B6
Kensington Pl . . . A2
Kilkenny St . . . A6
King St . . . B4
Kingsland Rd . . . B6
Kingston Rd . . . C3
Lamb St . . . A6
Lansdown Rd . . . A1
Lawford St . . . A6
Lawfords Gate . . . A6
Leighton Rd . . . C3
Lewins Mead . . . B4
Lime Rd . . . C2
Little Ann St . . . A6
Little Caroline Pl . . . B1
Little George St . . . A6
Little King St . . . B4
Litfield Rd . . . A1
Llandoger Trow . . . B4
Lloyds' Building, The . . . C3
Lodge St . . . A4
Lord Mayor's Chapel, The . . . B4
Lower Castle St . . . A5
Lower Church La . . . B3
Lower Clifton Hill . . . B2
Lower Guinea St . . . C4
Lower Lamb St . . . B2
Lower Maudlin St . . . A4
Lower Park Rd . . . A4
Lower Sidney St . . . C2
Lucky La . . . C4
Lydstep Terr . . . C3
Mall (Galleries Shopping Centre), The . . . A5
Manilla Rd . . . A1
Mardyke Ferry Rd . . . C2
Maritime Heritage Centre ♦ . . . B3
Marlborough Hill . . . A4
Marlborough St . . . A4
Marsh St . . . B4
Mead St . . . C5
Merchant Dock . . . C3
Merchant Seamen's Almshouses ♦ . . . A5
Merchants Rd . . . A1
Merchants Rd . . . C1
Meridian Pl . . . A2
Meridian Vale . . . A2
Merrywood Rd . . . C3
Midland Rd . . . A6
Milford St . . . C2
Millennium Sq . . . B3
Mitchell La . . . B5
Mortimer Rd . . . A1
M Shed . . . C4
Murray Rd . . . A2
Myrtle Rd . . . A3
Narrow Plain . . . B5
Narrow Quay . . . B4
Nelson St . . . B4
New Charlotte St . . . C4
New Kingsley Rd . . . B6
New Queen St . . . C5
New St . . . A6
Newgate . . . A5
Newton St . . . A6
Norland Rd . . . A1
North St . . . C3
O2 Academy . . . B3
Oakfield Gr . . . A2
Oakfield Pl . . . A2
Oakfield Rd . . . A2
Old Bread St . . . B6
Old Market St . . . A6
Old Park Hill . . . A4
Oldfield Rd . . . B1
Orchard Ave . . . B4
Orchard La . . . B4
Orchard St . . . B4
Osbourne Rd . . . C1
Oxford St . . . B6
Park Pl . . . B2
Park Rd . . . C4
Park Row . . . A3
Park St . . . A3
Passage St . . . B5
Pembroke Gr . . . A1
Pembroke Rd . . . A1
Pembroke Rd . . . C1
Pembroke St . . . A5
Penn St . . . A5
Pennywell Rd . . . A6
Percival Rd . . . A1
Pero's Bridge . . . B4
Perry Rd . . . B3
Pip & Jay ♣ . . . A5
Plimsoll Bridge . . . B1
Police Sta ▣ . . . A4/A6
Polygon Rd . . . B1
Portland St . . . A1
Portwall La . . . B5
Post Office ⊠ . . . A1/A3/A4/A5/A6/B1/B4/C4/C5
Prewett St . . . C5
Prince St . . . B4
Prince St Bridge . . . C4
Princess St . . . C5
Princess Victoria St . . . B1
Priory Rd . . . A3
Pump La . . . C5
QEH Theatre . . . A2
Queen Charlotte St . . . B4
Quakers Friars . . . A5
Quay St . . . B4
Queen Elizabeth Hospital School . . . B2
Queen Sq . . . A5
Queen's Ave . . . A3
Queen's Parade . . . A3
Queen's Rd . . . A2/A3
Raleigh Rd . . . C1
Randall Rd . . . B2
Redcliffe Backs . . . B5

Redcliffe Bridge . . . B4
Redcliffe Hill . . . C5
Redcliffe Parade . . . C4
Redcliffe St . . . B5
Redcliffe Way . . . B5
Redcross St . . . A6
Redgrave Theatre 🎭 . . . A1
Red Lodge 🏛 . . . A4
Regent St . . . B1
Richmond Hill . . . A2
Richmond Hill Ave . . . A2
Richmond La . . . A2
Richmond Park Rd . . . A2
Richmond St . . . C6
Richmond Terr . . . A2
River St . . . A6
Rownham Mead . . . B2
Royal Fort Rd . . . A3
Royal Park . . . A2
Royal West of England Academy 🏛 . . . A3
Royal York Cr . . . B1
Royal York Villas . . . B1
Rupert St . . . A4
Russ St . . . B6
St Andrew's Walk . . . B2
St George's 🎭 . . . B3
St George's Rd . . . B3
St James 🏛 . . . A4
St John's 🏛 . . . B4
St John's Rd . . . C1
St Luke's Rd . . . C5
St Mary Redcliffe 🏛 . . . C5
St Matthias Park . . . A6
St Michael's Hill . . . A3
St Michael's Hospl 🏥 . . . A3
St Michael's Park . . . A3
St Nicholas St . . . B4
St Paul St . . . A5
St Paul's Rd . . . A2
St Peter's (ruin) 🏛 . . . B5
St Philip's Bridge . . . B5
St Philips Rd . . . A6
St Stephen's 🏛 . . . B4
St Stephen's St . . . B4
St Thomas St . . . B5
St Thomas the Martyr 🏛 . . . B5
Sandford Rd . . . B1
Sargent St . . . C5
Saville Pl . . . B1
Ship La . . . C5
Showcase Cinema de Lux 🎬 . . . A5
Silver St . . . A4
Sion Hill . . . A1
Small St . . . A4
Smeaton Rd . . . C1
Somerset Sq . . . C5
Somerset St . . . C5
Southernhay Ave . . . B2
Southville Rd . . . C4
Spike Island Artspace ♦ . . . C2
Spring St . . . C5
SS Great Britain and The Matthew ♣ . . . C2
Stackpool Rd . . . C3
Staight St . . . B6
Stillhouse La . . . C5
Stracey Rd . . . C2
Sydney Row . . . C2
Tankard's Cl . . . A3
Temple Back . . . B5
Temple Boulevard . . . B5
Temple Bridge . . . B5
Temple Church 🏛 . . . B5
Temple Circus . . . B5
Temple Gate . . . C5
Temple St . . . B5
Temple Way . . . B5
Terrell St . . . A4
The Arcade . . . B4
The Fosseway . . . A2
The Grove . . . B4
The Horsefair . . . A5
The Mall . . . A1
Theatre Royal 🎭 . . . B4
Thekla La . . . B4
Thomas La . . . B5
Three Kings of Cologne 🏛 . . . A4
Three Queens La . . . B5
Tobacco Factory, The 🎭 . . . C4
Tower Hill . . . B5
Tower La . . . A4
Trenchard St . . . A4
Triangle South . . . A3
Triangle West . . . A3
Trinity Rd . . . A6
Trinity St . . . A6
Tyndall Ave . . . A3
Union St . . . A4
Union St . . . B6
Unity St . . . A6
Unity St . . . B3
University of Bristol . . . A3
University Rd . . . A3
Upper Maudlin St . . . A4
Upper Perry Hill . . . C3
Upper Byron Pl . . . A3
Upton Rd . . . C1
Valentine Bridge . . . B6
Victoria Gr . . . C2
Victoria Rd . . . C6
Victoria Rooms 🏛 . . . A2
Victoria Sq . . . A2
Victoria St . . . B5
Vyvyan Rd . . . A1
Vyvyan Terr . . . A1
Wade St . . . A6
Walter St . . . C2
Wapping Rd . . . C4
Water La . . . B5
Waterloo Rd . . . A6
Waterloo St . . . A1
Waterloo St . . . B6

Watershed Media Centre ♦ . . . B4
Welling Terr . . . A6
Welsh Back . . . B4
West Mall . . . A1
West St . . . A6
Westfield Pl . . . A1
Wetherell Pl . . . A2
Whitehouse Pl . . . C5
Whitehouse St . . . C5
Whiteladies Rd . . . A2
Whitson St . . . A4
William St . . . C5
Willway St . . . C5
Windsor Pl . . . B1
Windsor Terr . . . B1
Wine St . . . A4
Woodland Rise . . . A3
Woodland Rd . . . A3
Worcester Rd . . . A1
Worcester Terr . . . A1
YHA ▲ . . . B4
York Gdns . . . C1
York Pl . . . A2
York Rd . . . B6

Bury St Edmunds 332
Abbey Gardens ♦ . . . B3
Abbey Gate 🏛 . . . B3
Abbeygate St . . . B2
Albert Cr . . . B3
Albert St . . . B3
Ambulance Sta . . . C1
Angel Hill . . . B2
Angel La . . . B2
Anglian Lane . . . A2
Arc Shopping Centre . . . B2
Athenaeum 🎭 . . . C2
Baker's La . . . C3
Barwell Rd . . . B3
Beetons Way . . . A1
Bishops Rd . . . B2
Bloomfield St . . . B3
Bridewell La . . . C2
Bullen Cl . . . C1
Bury St Edmunds 🚉 . . . A2
Bury St Edmunds County Upper School . . . C2
Bury St Edmunds L Ctr 🏊 . . . C1
Bury Town FC . . . A3
Bus Station . . . B2
Butter Mkt . . . B2
Cannon St . . . B2
Castle Rd . . . C1
Cemetery . . . C1
Chalk Rd (N) . . . B1
Chalk Rd (S) . . . B1
Church Row . . . B2
Churchgate St . . . C2
Cineworld 🎬 . . . C1
Citizens Advice Bureau . . . C2
College St . . . C2
Compiegne Way . . . A3
Corn Exchange, The 🏛 . . . B2
Cornfield Rd . . . B3
Cotton Lane . . . B3
Courts . . . C2
Covent Garden . . . C2
Crown St . . . C2
Cullum Rd . . . C2
Eastern Way . . . A3
Eastgate St . . . B3
Enterprise Bsns Park . . . A2
Etna Rd . . . B3
Eyre Cl . . . C2
Fire Station . . . C1
Friar's Lane . . . C2
Gage Cl . . . C1
Garland St . . . B2
Greene King Brewery ♦ . . . C3
Grove Park . . . B1
Grove Rd . . . B1
Guildhall 🏛 . . . C2
Guildhall St . . . C2
Hatter St . . . C2
High Baxter St . . . B2
Honey Hill . . . C2
Hospital Rd . . . C1/C2
Ickworth Dr . . . C1
Information Ctr ℹ . . . B2
Ipswich St . . . A2
King Edward VI Sch . . . C1
King's Rd . . . B1/B2
Library . . . A2
Long Brackland . . . A2
Looms La . . . B2
Lower Baxter St . . . B2
Malthouse La . . . B2
Maynewater La . . . C3
Mill Rd . . . C1
Mill Rd (South) . . . C1
Minden Close . . . B2
Moyses Hall 🏛 . . . B2
Mustow St . . . B3
Norman Tower 🏛 . . . C2
Northgate Ave . . . A2
Northgate St . . . B2
Nutshell, The 🏛 . . . B2
Osier Rd . . . A2
Out Northgate . . . A2
Out Risbygate . . . B1
Out Westgate . . . C2
Parkway . . . B1/C2
Peckham St . . . B2
Petticoat La . . . B3
Phoenix Day Hospl 🏥 . . . C1
Pinners Way . . . C3
Police Station 📮 . . . B2
Post Office ⊠ . . . B2/B3
Pump La . . . B2
Raingate St . . . C2
Raynham Rd . . . A1
Retail Park . . . A2
Risbygate St . . . B1/B2
Robert Boby Way . . . B2
St Andrew's St North . . . B2

St Andrew's St South . . . C2
St Botolph's La . . . C3
St Edmunds Hospital (private) 🏥 . . . C1
St Edmund's 🏛 . . . C2
St Edmund's Abbey (Remains) ♦ . . . B3
St Edmundsbury † . . . C3
St John's St . . . B2
St Marys 🏛 . . . C2
School Hall La . . . B2
Shillitoe Cl . . . C1
Shire Halls & Magistrates Ct . . . C3
South Cl . . . C3
Southgate St . . . C3
Sparhawk St . . . C3
Spring Lane . . . B1
Springfield Rd . . . B1
Station Hill . . . A2
Swan La . . . B2
Tayfen Rd . . . B2
The Vinefields . . . B3
Theatre Royal 🎭 . . . C2
Thingoe Hill . . . A2
Victoria St . . . B1
War Memorial ♦ . . . C2
Well St . . . B2
West Suffolk College . . . B1
Westgarth Gdns . . . C1
Westgate St . . . C2
Whiting St . . . C2
York Rd . . . B1
York Terr . . . B1

Cambridge 333
Abbey Rd . . . A3
ADC 🎭 . . . A2
Anglia Ruskin Univ . . . B3
Archaeology & Anthropology 🏛 . . . B2
Art Gallery 🏛 . . . A1
Arts Picture House 🎬 . . . B2
Arts Theatre 🎭 . . . B1
Auckland Rd . . . A2
Bateman St . . . C2
BBC . . . B3
Benet St . . . B1
Bradmore St . . . B3
Bridge St . . . A1
Broad St . . . B3
Brookside . . . C2
Brunswick Terr . . . A3
Burleigh St . . . B3
Bus Station . . . B2
Butt Green . . . A2
Cambridge Contemporary Art Gallery 🏛 . . . B1
Castle Mound 🏛 . . . A1
Castle St . . . A1
Cemetery . . . B3
Chesterton La . . . A1
Christ's (Coll) . . . B2
Christ's Lane . . . B2
Christ's Pieces . . . B2
City Rd . . . B3
Clare (Coll) . . . B1
Clarendon St . . . B2
Coe Fen . . . C2
Coronation St . . . C2
Corpus Christi (Coll) . . . B1
Council Offices . . . C3
Cross St . . . C3
Crusoe Bridge . . . C1
Darwin (Coll) . . . B1
Devonshire Rd . . . C3
Downing (Coll) . . . B2
Downing St . . . B2
Earl St . . . B2
East Rd . . . B3
Eden St . . . B2
Elizabeth Way . . . A3
Elm St . . . B2
Emery St . . . B3
Emmanuel (Coll) . . . B2
Emmanuel Rd . . . B2
Emmanuel St . . . B2
Fair St . . . A3
Fenners Physical Education Centre . . . C3
Fire Station . . . B3
Fitzroy St . . . B3
Fitzwilliam Mus 🏛 . . . C2
Fitzwilliam St . . . C2
Folk Museum 🏛 . . . A1
Glisson Rd . . . C3
Gonville & Caius (Coll) . . . B1
Gonville Place . . . C3
Grafton Centre . . . B3
Grand Arcade . . . B2
Gresham Rd . . . C3
Green St . . . B1
Guest Rd . . . B3
Guildhall 🏛 . . . B2
Harvey Rd . . . C3
Hills Rd . . . C3
Hobson St . . . B2
Hughes Hall (Coll) . . . B3
Information Ctr ℹ . . . B2
James St . . . A3
Jesus (Coll) . . . A2
Jesus Green . . . A2
Jesus La . . . A2
Jesus Terr . . . A3
John St . . . B3
Kelsey Kerridge Sports Centre . . . B3
King St . . . B2
King's (Coll) . . . B1
King's Coll Chapel 🏛 . . . B1
King's Parade . . . B1
Lammas Land Rec Gd . . . C1
Lensfield Rd . . . C2
Library . . . C2
Lion Yard . . . B2
Little St Mary's La . . . B1
Lyndewod Rd . . . C3
Magdalene (Coll) . . . A1

Magdalene St . . . A1
Maid's Causeway . . . A3
Malcolm St . . . A2
Market Hill . . . B1
Market St . . . B1
Mathematical Bridge . . . B1
Mawson Rd . . . C3
Midsummer Common . . . A3
Mill La . . . B1
Mill Rd . . . B3
Mill St . . . C3
Gordon St . . . A1
Napier St . . . A3
New Square . . . B3
Newmarket Rd . . . A3
Newnham Rd . . . C1
Norfolk St . . . B3
Northampton St . . . A1
Norwich St . . . C2
Orchard St . . . B2
Panton St . . . C2
Paradise Nature Reserve . . . C1
Paradise St . . . B3
Park Parade . . . A1
Park St . . . A2
Park Terr . . . B2
Parker St . . . B2
Parker's Piece . . . B2
Parkside . . . B3
Parkside Pools . . . B3
Parsonage St . . . B3
Pemberton Terr . . . C2
Pembroke (Coll) . . . B1
Pembroke St . . . B1
Perowne St . . . B3
Peterhouse (Coll) . . . C1
Petty Cury . . . B2
Police Station 📮 . . . B2
Post Office ⊠ . . . B1/B3/C1/C2/C3
Queens' (Coll) . . . B1
Queen's La . . . B1
Queen's Rd . . . B1
Regent St . . . B2
Regent Terr . . . B2
Ridley Hall (Coll) . . . C1
Riverside . . . A3
Round Church, The 🏛 . . . A1
Russell St . . . C2
St Andrew's St . . . B2
St Benet's 🏛 . . . B1
St Catharine's (Coll) . . . B1
St Eligius St . . . C2
St John's (Coll) . . . A1
St Mary's 🏛 . . . B1
St Paul's Rd . . . C3
Saxon St . . . C2
Scott Polar Institute & Museum 🏛 . . . C2
Sedgwick Museum 🏛 . . . B2
Sheep's Green . . . C1
Shire Hall . . . A1
Sidgwick Ave . . . C1
Sidney St . . . A2
Sidney Sussex (Coll) . . . A2
Silver St . . . B1
Station Rd . . . C3
Tenison Ave . . . C3
Tenison Rd . . . C3
Tennis Court Rd . . . B2
The Backs . . . B1
The Fen Causeway . . . C1
Thompson's La . . . A1
Trinity (Coll) . . . A1
Trinity Hall (Coll) . . . B1
Trinity St . . . B1
Trumpington Rd . . . C2
Trumpington St . . . B1
Union Rd . . . C2
University Botanic Gardens 🌳 . . . C2
Victoria Ave . . . A2
Victoria St . . . B2
Warkworth St . . . B3
Warkworth Terr . . . B3
Wesley House (Coll) . . . A2
West Rd . . . B1
Westcott House (Coll) . . . A2
Westminster (Coll) . . . A1
Whipple 🏛 . . . B2
Willis Rd . . . B3
Willow Walk . . . A2

Canterbury 333
Artillery St . . . A3
Barton Mill Rd . . . A3
Beaconsfield Rd . . . A1
Beaney The 🏛 . . . B2
Beverley Rd . . . A1
Bingley's Island . . . B1
Black Griffin La . . . B1
Broad Oak Rd . . . A2
Broad St . . . B2
Brymore Rd . . . A3
Burgate . . . B2
Bus Station . . . C2
Canterbury College . . . C3
Canterbury Tales, The ♦ . . . B2
Canterbury West 🚉 . . . A1
Castle 🏛 . . . C1
Castle Row . . . C2
Castle St . . . C1
Cathedral † . . . B2
Chaucer Rd . . . A3
Christ Church Univ . . . C3
Christchurch Gate 🏛 . . . B2
City Council Offices . . . B2
City Wall . . . C2
Coach Park . . . B2
College Rd . . . C3
Cossington Rd . . . C2
Court . . . C2
Craddock Rd . . . A3
Crown & County Courts . . . C2
Dane John Gdns . . . C2

Dane John Mound ♦ . . . C1
Deanery . . . B2
Dover St . . . C2
Duck La . . . B2
Eastbridge Hospl 🏛 . . . B1
Edgar Rd . . . B3
Ersham Rd . . . C2
Ethelbert Rd . . . C2
Fire Station . . . C2
Forty Acres Rd . . . A1
Gordon Rd . . . C1
Greyfriars ♦ . . . B1
Guildford Rd . . . C1
Havelock St . . . B2
Heaton Rd . . . C1
High St . . . B2
HM Prison . . . B3
Information Ctr ℹ . . . A2/B2
Ivy La . . . B2
Ivy Pl . . . C1
King St . . . B2
King's School . . . B2/B3
King's School Leisure Facilities . . . A2
Kingsmead Leisure Centre . . . A2
Kingsmead Rd . . . A2
Kirby's La . . . B1
Lansdown Rd . . . C2
Lime Kiln Rd . . . C1
Longport . . . B3
Lower Chantry La . . . C3
Mandeville Rd . . . A1
Market Way . . . A2
Marlowe Arcade . . . B2
Marlowe Ave . . . C2
Marlowe Theatre 🎭 . . . B2
Martyrs Field Rd . . . C1
Mead Way . . . B1
Military St . . . B2
Monastery St . . . B2
Mus of Canterbury (Rupert Bear Mus) 🏛 . . . B1
New Dover Rd . . . C3
Norman Rd . . . C1
North Holmes Rd . . . B3
North La . . . B1
Nunnery Fields . . . C2
Nunnery Rd . . . C2
Oaten Hill . . . C2
Odeon Cinema 🎬 . . . C1
Old Dover Rd . . . C2
Old Palace . . . B2
Old Ruttington La . . . B2
Old Weavers 🏛 . . . B2
Orchard St . . . B1
Oxford Rd . . . C1
Palace St . . . B2
Pilgrims Way . . . C3
Pin Hill . . . C1
Pine Tree Ave . . . A1
Police Station 📮 . . . C1
Post Office ⊠ . . . B2/C1/C2
Pound La . . . B1
Puckle La . . . C2
Raymond Ave . . . C2
Registry Office . . . A2
Rheims Way . . . B1
Rhodaus Cl . . . C2
Rhodaus Town . . . C2
Roman Museum 🏛 . . . B2
Roper Gateway . . . A1
Roper Rd . . . A1
Rose La . . . B2
St Augustine's Abbey (remains) † . . . B3
St Augustine's Rd . . . A3
St Dunstan's St . . . A1
St Dunstan's St . . . A1
St George's Pl . . . C2
St George's St . . . B2
St George's Tower ♦ . . . B2
St Gregory's Rd . . . B3
St John's Hospital 🏛 . . . A2
St Margaret's St . . . B2
St Martin's 🏛 . . . B3
St Martin's Ave . . . B3
St Martin's Rd . . . B3
St Michael's Rd . . . A1
St Mildred's 🏛 . . . C1
St Peter's Gr . . . B1
St Peter's La . . . B1
St Peter's Pl . . . B1
St Radigunds St . . . B2
St Stephen's Ct . . . A1
St Stephen's Path . . . A1
St Stephen's Rd . . . A1
Salisbury Rd . . . A1
Simmonds Rd . . . C1
Spring La . . . C3
Station Rd West . . . B1
Stour St . . . B1
Sturry Rd . . . A3
The Causeway . . . A2
The Friars . . . B2
Tourtel Rd . . . A2
Tudor Rd . . . C1
Union St . . . B2
University for the Creative Arts . . . C3
Vernon Pl . . . C2
Victoria Rd . . . C1
Watling St . . . C2
Westgate Gdns . . . B1
Westgate Towers 🏛 . . . B1
Whitefriars . . . B2
Whitehall Gdns . . . B1
Whitehall Rd . . . B1
Wincheap . . . C1
York Rd . . . C2
Zealand Rd . . . C2

Cardiff Caerdydd 333
Adam St . . . B3
Alexandra Gdns . . . A2
Allerton St . . . C1
Arran St . . . A3

ATRiuM (Univ of Glamorgan) . . . C3
Beauchamp St . . . C1
Bedford St . . . A3
Blackfriars Priory (rems) † . . . B2
Boulevard De Nantes . . . B2
Brains Brewery ♦ . . . C2
Brook St . . . B1
Bus Station . . . B2
Bute Park . . . B1
Bute St . . . C2
Bute Terr . . . C3
Callaghan Sq . . . C2
Capitol Sh Ctr, The . . . B3
Cardiff Arms Park (Cardiff RFC) . . . B2
Cardiff Bridge . . . B1
Cardiff Castle 🏛 . . . B2
Cardiff Central Sta 🚉 . . . C2
Cardiff Ctr Trading Est . . . C3
Cardiff Univ . . . A1/A2/B2
Cardiff University Student's Union . . . A2
Caroline St . . . C2
Castle Green . . . B2
Castle Mews . . . A1
Castle St (Heol y Castell) . . . B2
Cathays Station 🚉 . . . A2
Celerity Drive . . . C3
Central Library . . . C2
Central Sq . . . C2
Charles St (Heol Siarl) . . . B3
Churchill Way . . . B3
City Hall . . . A2
City Rd . . . A3
Clare Rd . . . C1
Clare St . . . C1
Coburn St . . . A3
Coldstream Terr . . . B1
College Rd . . . A1
Colum Rd . . . A1
Court . . . C2
Court Rd . . . C1
Craiglee Drive . . . C3
Cranbrook St . . . A3
Customhouse St . . . C2
Cyfartha St . . . A3
Despenser Place . . . C1
Despenser St . . . C1
Dinas St . . . C1
Duke St (Heol y Dug) . . . B2
Dumfries Place . . . B3
East Grove . . . A3
Ellen St . . . C3
Fire Station . . . B3
Fitzalan Place . . . B3
Fitzhamon Emb . . . C1
Fitzhamon La . . . C1
Gloucester St . . . C1
Glynrhondda St . . . A2
Gordon Rd . . . A3
Gorsedd Gdns . . . A2
Green St . . . B1
Greyfriars Rd . . . B2
HM Prison . . . B3
Hafod St . . . C1
Herbert St . . . C3
High St . . . B2
Industrial Estate . . . C3
John St . . . C3
Jubilee St . . . C1
King Edward VII Ave . . . A1
Kingsway (Ffordd y Brenin) . . . B2
Knox Rd . . . B3
Law Courts . . . B2
Llanbleddian Gdns . . . A2
Llantwit St . . . A2
Lloyd George Ave . . . C3
Lower Cathedral Rd . . . B1
Lowther Rd . . . A3
Magistrates Court . . . B3
Mansion House . . . A3
Mardy St . . . C1
Mark St . . . B1
Market . . . B2
Mary Ann St . . . C3
Merches Gdns . . . C1
Mill La . . . C2
Millennium Bridge . . . B1
Miskin St . . . A2
Monmouth St . . . C1
Motorpoint Arena Cardiff ♦ . . . C3
Museum Ave . . . A2
Museum Place . . . A2
National Museum of Wales 🏛 . . . A2
National War Meml ♦ . . . A2
Neville Place . . . B1
New Theatre 🎭 . . . B2
Newport Rd . . . B3
Northcote La . . . A3
Northcote St . . . A3
Park Grove . . . A2
Park Place . . . A2
Park St . . . C2
Penarth Rd . . . C2
Pendyris St . . . C1
Plantagenet St . . . C1
Principality Stadium . . . B1
Principality Stadium Tours (Gate 3) ♦ . . . B2
Quay St . . . B2
Queen Anne Sq . . . A1
Queen St (Heol y Frenhines) . . . B3
Queen St Station 🚉 . . . B3
Regimental Museums 🏛 . . . A1
Rhymney St . . . A3
Richmond Rd . . . A3
Royal Welsh College of Music and Drama ♦ . . . A1
Russell St . . . A3
Ruthin Gdns . . . A2
St Andrews Place . . . A2

St David's † . . . B2
St David's 2 . . . C2
St David's Centre . . . B2
St David's Hall ♦ . . . B2
St John The Baptist 🏛 . . . B2
St Mary St (Heol Eglwys Fair) . . . B2
St Peter's St . . . A3
Salisbury Rd . . . A3
Sandon St . . . C3
Schooner Way . . . C3
Scott Rd . . . C3
Scott St . . . C2
Senghennydd Rd . . . A2
Sherman Theatre 🎭 . . . A2
Sophia Gardens . . . A1
South Wales Baptist College . . . A3
Stadium Plaza Leisure Complex ♦ . . . C1
Stafford Rd . . . C1
Station Terr . . . C3
Stuttgarter Strasse . . . B2
Sussex St . . . C1
Taffs Mead Emb . . . C1
Talworth St . . . A3
Temple of Peace & Health ♦ . . . A1
The Cardiff Story 🏛 . . . B2
The Friary . . . B2
The Hayes . . . C2
The Parade . . . A3
The Walk . . . A3
Treharris St . . . A3
Trinity St . . . B2
Tudor La . . . C1
Tudor St . . . C1
Welsh Assembly Offices . . . A1
West Grove . . . A3
Westgate St (Heol y Porth) . . . B2
Windsor Place . . . B3
Womanby St . . . B2
Wood St . . . C2
Working St . . . B2
Wyeverne Rd . . . A2

Carlisle 333
Abbey St . . . A1
Aglionby St . . . C3
Albion St . . . C3
AMF Bowl ♦ . . . C2
Annetwell St . . . A1
Bank St . . . B2
Bitts Park . . . A1
Blackfriars St . . . B2
Blencome St . . . C1
Blunt St . . . C1
Botchergate . . . C2
Boustead's Grassing . . . C3
Bowman St . . . B3
Broad St . . . B3
Bridge St . . . A1
Brook St . . . C3
Brunswick St . . . B2
Bus Station . . . B2
Caldew Bridge . . . A1
Caldew St . . . C1
Carlisle (Citadel) Station 🚉 . . . B2
Carlisle College . . . A2
Castle 🏛 . . . A1
Castle St . . . A1
Castle Way . . . A1
Cathedral † . . . B2
Cecil St . . . B3
Chapel St . . . B2
Charles St . . . C3
Charlotte St . . . C1
Chatsworth Square . . . B2
Chiswick St . . . B3
Citadel, The ♦ . . . B2
City Walls . . . B1
Civic Centre . . . B2
Clifton St . . . C1
Close St . . . C3
Collingwood St . . . C2
Colville St . . . C1
Colville Terr . . . C1
Court . . . B2
Court St . . . B2
Crosby St . . . B2
Crown St . . . C2
Currock Rd . . . C2
Dacre Rd . . . B1
Dale St . . . C1
Denton St . . . C1
Devonshire Walk . . . A1
Duke's Rd . . . A3
East Dale St . . . C1
East Norfolk St . . . C1
Eden Bridge . . . A2
Edward St . . . C3
Elm St . . . C2
English St . . . B2
Fire Station . . . C2
Fisher St . . . B2
Flower St . . . C3
Freer St . . . C3
Fusehill St . . . C3
Georgian Way . . . B2
Gloucester Rd . . . C2
Golf Course . . . A3
Graham St . . . C1
Grey St . . . C3
Guildhall Museum 🏛 . . . B2
Halfey's La . . . A3
Hardwicke Circus . . . A2
Hart St . . . C3
Hewson St . . . C1
Howard Pl . . . B3
Howe St . . . C3
Information Ctr ℹ . . . A2
James St . . . B2
Junction St . . . C1
King St . . . B2

Lancaster St B2
Lanes Shopping Ctr B2
Laserquest A2/B1
Library A2/B1
Lime St B2
Lindisfarne St C3
Linton St B2
Lismore Pl A3
Lismore St A2
London Rd C3
Lonsdale Rd B2
Lord St B2
Lorne Cres B1
Lorne St B1
Lowther Rd B3
Market Hall A2
Mary St B2
Memorial Bridge A3
Metcalfe St C1
Milbourne St C1
Myddleton St B3
Nelson St C1
Norfolk St C1
Old Town Hall A2
Oswald St C3
Peter St B2
Petteril St B3
Police Station B2
Portland Pl B2
Portland Sq B2
Post Office
. . . . A2/B2/B3/C1/C3
Princess St C2
Pugin St B1
Red Bank Terr C3
Regent St C3
Richardson St C1
Rickerby Park A3
Rickergate B2
River St B2
Rome St B3
Rydal St B3
St Cuthbert's B2
St Cuthbert's La B2
St James' Park B3
St James' Rd C1
St Nicholas St C2
Sands Centre A2
Scotch St B2
Shaddongate B1
Sheffield St B3
South Henry St B3
South John St C2
South St B2
Spencer St A2
Sports Centre A2
Strand Rd C2
Swimming Baths C2
Sybil St B3
Tait St B3
Thomas St B3
Thomson St C3
Trafalgar St C1
Tullie Ho Museum B2
Tyne St A1
University of Cumbria . . . B3
Viaduct Estate Rd B2
Victoria Pl B2
Victoria Viaduct B2
Vue B2
Warwick Rd C3
Warwick Sq B3
Water St B2
West Walls B2
Westmorland St C1

Chelmsford   333

Ambulance Station . . . B1
Anchor St C1
Anglia Ruskin Univ . . . C3
Arbour La C1
Baddow Rd B2/C3
Baker St C2
Barrack Sq B2
Bellmead B2
Bishop Hall La A2
Bishop Rd A2
Bond St B2
Boswells Dr B3
Boudicca Mews C2
Bouverie Rd A1
Bradford St B2
Braemar Ave C1
Brook St B2
Broomfield Rd A1
Burns Cres C2
Bus Station B2
Can Bridge Way B2
Cedar Ave A3
Cedar Ave West A3
Cemetery A2
Cemetery B3
Cemetery C1
Central Park B2
Chelmsford B3
Chelmsford A3
Chichester Dr A3
Chinery Cl C3
Cinema B2
Civic Centre B1
Civic Theatre B1
College C1
Cottage Pl B2
County Cricket
  Ground B2
County Hall B2
Coval Ave C1
Coval La C1
Coval Wells C1
Crown Court B2
Duke St B2
Elm Rd C1
Elms Dr A1
Essex Record Office,
  The B3
Fairfield Rd B2
Falcons Mead A3
George St A2
Glebe Rd C1

Godfrey's Mews C2
Goldlay Ave C3
Goldlay Rd C3
Grove Rd C2
HM Prison A3
Hall St C1
Hamlet Rd C2
Hart St C1
Henry Rd A2
High Bridge Rd B2
High Chelmer Sh Ctr . . B2
High St B2
Hill Cres B3
Hill Rd Sth B3
Hill Rd B3
Hillview Rd A3
Hoffmans Way A2
Hospital B2
Lady La C2
Langdale Gdns C3
Legg St B2
Library B2
Library B2
Lionfield Terr A3
Lower Anchor St C1
Lynmouth Ave C2
Lynmouth Gdns C2
Magistrates Court B2
Maltese Rd A2
Manor Rd C2
Marconi Rd A2
Market B2
Market Rd B2
Marlborough Rd C1
Meadows Sh Ctr, The . . B2
Meadowside A3
Mews Ct C1
Mildmay Rd C2
Moulsham Dr C2
Moulsham Mill C3
Moulsham St C1/C2
Navigation Rd A2
New London Rd B2/C1
New St A2/B2
New Writtle St B1
Nursery Rd A2
Orchard St C2
Park Rd B1
Parker Rd C2
Parklands Dr A3
Parkway A1/B1/B2
Police Station B2
Post Office A3/B2/C2
Primrose Hill A2
Prykes Dr B1
Queen's Rd C1
Queen's Rd B3
Railway St A1
Rainsford Rd A1
Ransomes Way A2
Rectory La A2
Regina Rd A2
Riverside Ice & L Ctr . B2
Riverside Retail Park . A3
Rosebery Rd C1
Rothesay Ave C1
St John's Rd C2
Sandringham Pl B3
Seymour St B3
Shrublands Cl B3
Southborough Rd C1
Springfield Basin . . . B3
Springfield Rd . . A3/B2/B3
Stapleford Cl C1
Swiss Ave A1
Telford Pl A3
The Meades B1
Tindal St B2
Townfield St A1
Trinity Rd B1
University B1
Upper Bridge Rd C1
Upper Roman Rd C2
Van Dieman's Rd C1
Viaduct Rd B1
Vicarage Rd B2
Victoria Rd A2
Victoria Rd South . . . C2
Vincents Rd C2
Waterloo La B1
Weight Rd B2
Westfield Ave A1
Wharf Rd B1
Writtle Rd C1
YMCA C1
York Rd C1

Cheltenham   333

Albert Rd B3
Albion St B3
All Saints Rd B3
Ambrose St B2
Andover Rd C1
Art Gallery & Mus . . . B2
Axiom Centre B3
Back Montpellier Terr . C2
Bandstand C2
Bath Pde B2
Bath Rd C2
Bays Hill Rd C1
Beechwood Sh Ctr . . . B3
Bennington St B2
Berkeley St B2
Brewery The A2
Brunswick St South . . A2
Bus Station B2
CAB A2
Carlton St B3
Central Cross Road . . A3
Cheltenham College . . C2
Cheltenham FC A3
Cheltenham General
  (A&E) C3
Cineworld B2
Christchurch Rd C1
Clarence Rd B2
Clarence Sq A2
Clarence St B2
Cleeveland St A1

Coach Park A2
College Baths Road . . A3
College Rd C2
Colletts Dr A1
Corpus St C3
Devonshire St A2
Douro Rd B1
Duke St B3
Dunalley Pde A2
Dunalley St A2
Everyman B2
Evesham Rd B2
Fairview Rd B3
Fairview St B3
Fire Station C3
Folly La A1
Gloucester Rd A1
Grosvenor St B3
Grove St A1
Gustav Holst A3
Hanover St A2
Hatherley St C1
Henrietta St A2
Hewlett Rd B3
High St B2/B3
Hudson St B2
Imperial Gdns C2
Imperial La C2
Imperial Sq C2
Information Ctr B2
Keynsham Rd C3
King St A2
Knapp Rd A2
Ladies College B2
Lansdown Cr C1
Lansdown Rd C1
Leighton Rd B3
Library B2
London Rd C3
Lypiatt Rd C2
Malvern Rd B1
Manser St A2
Market St A1
Marle Hill Pde A2
Marle Hill Rd A2
Millbrook St A1
Milsom St A1
Montpellier Gdns . . . C2
Montpellier Gr C2
Montpellier Pde C2
Montpellier Spa Rd . . C2
Montpellier St C1
Montpellier Terr C2
Montpellier Walk . . . C2
New St A1
North Pl B2
Old Bath Rd C3
Oriel Rd B2
Overton Park Rd B1
Overton Rd B1
Oxford St C3
Parabola Rd C1
Park Pl C1
Park St A1
Pittville Circus A3
Pittville Cr A3
Pittville Lawn A3
Pittville Park A2
Playhouse B2
Police Station B1/C1
Portland St B3
Post Office B2/C2
Prestbury Rd A3
Prince's Rd C1
Priory St B3
Promenade B2
Queen St A1
Recreation Ground . . A2
Regent Arcade B2
Regent St B2
Rodney Rd B2
Royal Cr B2
Royal Wells Rd B2
St George's Pl B1
St Georges Rd B1
St Gregory's B2
St James St B1
St John's Ave B3
St Luke's Rd C2
St Margarets Rd A2
St Matthew's B2
St Paul's La A2
St Paul's Rd A1
St Paul's St A1
St Stephen's Rd C1
Sandford Lido C3
Sandford Mill Road . . C3
Sandford Park C2
Sandford Rd C2
Selkirk St B3
Sherborne Pl B3
Sherborne St B3
Suffolk Pde C2
Suffolk Rd C2
Suffolk Sq C1
Sun St A1
Swindon Rd B2
Sydenham Villas Rd . . C3
Tewkesbury Rd A1
The Courtyard B1
Thirlstaine Rd C2
Tivoli Rd C1
Tivoli St C1
Town Hall & Theatre . . B2
Townsend St A1
Trafalgar St C2
Union St B3
Univ of Gloucestershire
  (Francis Cl Hall) . . C3
Univ of Gloucestershire
  (Hardwick) A1
Victoria Pl A1
Victoria St A2
Vittoria Walk C2
Wel Pl B2
Wellesley Rd A2
Wellington La A3
Wellington Rd A3
Wellington Sq A3
West Drive A3
Western Rd A1
Winchcombe St B3
Winston Churchill
  Memorial Gardens . . A1

Chester   333

Abbey Gateway B2
Appleyards La C3
Bedward Row B1
Beeston View C1
Bishop Lloyd's Pal . . B2
Black Diamond St A2
Bottoms La C2
Boughton B3
Bouverie St A1
Bridge St B2
Bridgegate C2
British Heritage Ctr . . B2
Brook St A3
Brown's La A3
Bus Station A1
Cambrian Rd A1
Canal St B1
Carrick Rd C1
Castle C2
Castle Dr C2
Cathedral B2
Catherine St C1
Chester A3
Cheyney Rd A1
Chichester St A1
City Rd A3
City Walls B1/B2
City Walls Rd B1
Cornwall St A2
County Hall B2
Cross Hey C3
Cuppin St B2
Curzon Park North . . . C1
Curzon Park South . . . C1
Dee Basin B1
Dee La B3
Delamere St A2
Dewa Roman
  Experience B2
Duke St B2
Eastgate B2
Eastgate St B2
Eaton Rd C2
Edinburgh Way C3
Elizabeth Cr A3
Fire Station A2
Foregate St B2
Frodsham St A2
Gamul House B2
Garden La A1
George St A2
Gladstone Ave A1
God's Providence
  House B2
Gorse Stacks A2
Greenway St C2
Grosvenor Bridge . . . C1
Grosvenor Mus B2
Grosvenor Park B3
Grosvenor Precinct . . B2
Grosvenor Rd C2
Grosvenor St B2
Groves Rd B3
Guildhall Museum . . . B1
Handbridge C2
Hartington St C3
Hoole Way A2
Hunter St B2
Information Ctr B2
King Charles' Tower . . A2
King St A2
Leisure Centre B2
Library B2
Lightfoot St A3
Little Roodee C2
Liverpool Rd A1
Love St B3
Lower Bridge St B2
Lower Park Rd B3
Lyon St A2
Magistrates Court . . . B2
Meadows La C3
Military Museum A3
Milton St A3
New Crane St B1
Nicholas St B2
Northgate A2
Northgate St B2
Nun's Rd B2
Old Dee Bridge C2
Overleigh Rd C2
Park St B2
Police Station B2
Post Office
  . . . . A2/A3/B2/C2
Princess St B2
Queen St B2
Queen's Park Rd C3
Queen's Rd A3
Race Course B1
Raymond St A1
River La C2
Roman Amphitheatre
  & Gardens B2
Roodee, The (Chester
  Racecourse) B1
Russell St A3
St Anne St A2
St George's Cr C3
St Martin's Gate B1
St Martin's Way B1
St Oswalds Way A2
Saughall Rd A1
Sealand Rd A1
South View Rd A1
Stanley Palace B1
Station Rd A3
Steven St A3
The Bars B3
The Cross B2
The Groves B3
The Meadows C3

Tower Rd B1
Town Hall B2
Union St B3
Vicar's La B2
Victoria Cr A2
Victoria Rd A1
Walpole St A1
Water Tower St A1
Watergate B2
Watergate St B2
Whipcord La A1
White Friars B2
York St B3

Chichester   333

Adelaide Rd A3
Alexandra Rd A3
Arts Centre B2
Ave de Chartres . . . B1/B2
Barlow Rd A1
Basin Rd C2
Beech Ave B1
Bishops Pal Gardens . . B2
Bishopsgate Walk . . . A3
Bramber Rd C3
Broyle Rd A2
Bus Station B2
Caledonian Rd B3
Cambrai Ave B3
Canal Wharf C2
Canon La C2
Cathedral B2
Cavendish St A1
Cawley Rd C2
Cedar Dr A1
Chapel St A2
Cherry Orchard St . . . A3
Chichester By-
  Pass C2/C3
Chichester Cinema . . B3
Chichester Festival
  Theatre A2
Chichester B2
Churchside A2
Cineworld C1
City Walls B2
Cleveland Rd B3
College La B1
Coll of Science &
  Technology B1
Cory Cl C2
Council Offices B2
County Hall B2
Courts B2
District B2
Duncan Rd A1
Durnford Cl A1
East Pallant B2
East Row B2
East St B2
East Walls B3
Eastland Rd C3
Ettrick Cl C3
Ettrick Rd C3
Exton Rd A3
Fire Station A2
Football Ground A3
Franklin Pl A2
Friary (Rems of) . . . A2
Garland Cl C3
Green La A3
Grove Rd C3
Guilden Rd C3
Hawthorn Cl A1
Hay Rd C3
Henty Gdns C1
Herald St C3
Information Ctr B2
John's St A2
Joys Croft A3
Jubilee Pk A3
Jubilee Rd A3
Juxon Cl B2
Kent Rd A1
King George Gdns . . . A2
King's Ave C2
Kingsham Ave C3
Kingsham Rd C3
Laburnum Gr C2
Leigh Rd C1
Lennox Rd A3
Lewis Rd A3
Library B2
Lion St B2
Litten Terr B3
Little London B2
Lyndhurst Rd B3
Market B2
Market Ave C1
Market Cross B2
Melbourne Rd A3
Mount La B1
New Park Rd A3
Newlands La A1
North Pallant B2
North St B2
North Walls B2
Northgate A2
Oak Ave A1
Oak Cl A1
Oaklands Park A2
Oaklands Way A1
Orchard Ave A2
Orchard St A1
Ormonde Ave B3
Pallant House B2
Parchment St A1
Parklands Rd A1/B1
Peter Weston Pl C3
Police Station A1
Post Office . . . A1/B2/B3
Priory La B2
Priory Park B2
Priory Rd B2
Queen's Ave C1
Riverside A3

Roman Amphitheatre . B3
St Cyriacs A2
St Pancras A3
St Paul's Rd A2
St Richard's Hospital
  (A&E) A1
Shamrock Cl A1
Sherborne Rd A1
Somerstown A1
South Bank C2
South Downs
  Planetarium C2
South Pallant B2
South St B2
Southgate B2
Spitalfield La B3
Stirling Rd B3
Stockbridge Rd . . . C1/C2
Swanfield Dr A3
Terminus Ind Est C1
Terminus Rd C1
The Hornet B3
The Litten B3
Tower St A2
Tozer Way A3
Turnbull Rd A3
Upton Rd C3
Velyn Ave B3
Via Ravenna B1
Walnut Ave A1
West St B2
Westgate B1
Westgate Fields B1
Westgate Leisure Ctr . B1
Weston Ave C2
Whyke Cl C3
Whyke La B3
Winden Ave B3

Colchester   333

Abbey Gateway C2
Albert St A1
Albion Grove C2
Alexandra Rd C1
Artillery St C3
Arts Centre B1
Balkerne Hill B1
Barrack St C3
Beaconsfield Rd C1
Beche Rd C3
Bergholt Rd A1
Bourne Rd C3
Brick Kiln Rd A1
Bristol Rd B2
Broadlands Way A3
Brook St B3
Bury Cl C3
Bus Sta B2
Butt Rd C2
Camp Folley North . . C3
Camp Folley South . . C3
Campion Rd C2
Cannon St C2
Canterbury Rd C2
Castle B2
Castle Park B2
Castle Rd B2
Catchpool Rd A1
Causton Rd B1
Cavalry Barracks . . . C2
Chandlers Row C3
Circular Rd East . . . C2
Circular Rd North . . C1
Circular Rd West . . . C1
Clarendon Way C1
Claudius Rd C2
Colchester Camp Abbey
  Field C2
Colchester Institute . B1
Colchester C2
Colchester Town C2
Colne Bank Ave A1
Colne View Retail Pk . A2
Compton Rd A3
Cowdray Ave A1/A2
Cowdray Centre, The . . A1
Crouch St B1
Crowhurst Rd B1
Culver Square Sh Ctr . B2
Culver St East B2
Culver St West B2
Dilbridge Rd A3
East Hill B2
East St B2
East Stockwell St . . . B2
Eld La B2
Essex Hall Rd A1
Exeter Dr B2
Fairfax Rd C2
Fire Station A2
Flagstaff Rd C2
George St B2
Gladstone Rd C2
Golden Noble Hill . . C2
Goring Rd A3
Granville Rd C2
Greenstead Rd B3
Guildford Rd C2
Harsnett Rd C3
Harwich Rd B3
Head St B1
High St B2
High Woods Ctry Park . A3
Hollytrees B2
Hythe Hill C3
Information Ctr B2
Ipswich Rd A3
Jarmin Rd A1
Kendall Rd C2
Kimberley Rd C3
King Stephen Rd C3
Le Cateau Barracks . . C1
Leisure World A2
Library B1
Lincoln Way A2
Lion Walk Sh Ctr . . . B2
Lisle Rd C3
Lucas Rd C2

Magdalen Green C3
Magdalen St C2
Maidenburgh St B2
Maldon Rd C1
Manor Rd B1
Margaret Rd A1
Mason Rd A2
Mercers Way A1
Mersea Rd C2
Meyrick Cr C2
Mile End Rd A1
Military Rd C2
Minories B2
Moorside B3
Morant Rd C2
Napier Rd C2
Natural History B2
New Town Rd C2
Norfolk Cr C3
North Hill B1
North Station Rd . . . A1
Northgate St B1
Nunns Rd B1
Odeon B1
Old Coach Rd A2
Old Heath Rd C3
Osborne St B2
Petrolea Cl A1
Popes La B2
Port La C3
Post Office B2
Priory St B2
Queen St B2
Rawstorn Rd B1
Rebon St C3
Recreation Rd C3
Ripple Way A3
Roman Rd B2
Roman Wall B2
Romford Cl A3
Rosebery Ave B2
St Andrews Ave B3
St Andrews Gdns B3
St Botolph St B2
St Botolphs B2
St John's Abbey
  (site of) C2
St John's St B1
St Johns Walk Sh Ctr . B2
St Leonards Rd C3
St Marys Fields B1
St Peters B1
St Peter's St B1
Salisbury Ave C1
Serpentine Walk A1
Sheepen Pl B1
Sheepen Rd B1
Sir Isaac's Walk B2
Smythies Ave B2
South St C1
South Way C1
Sports Way A2
Suffolk Cl A3
Town Hall B2
Valentine Dr A3
Victor Rd C2
Wakefield Cl B2
Wellesley Rd C1
Wells Rd B2/B3
West St C1
West Stockwell St . . . B2
Weston Rd C3
Westway C1
Wickham Rd C2
Wimpole Rd C3
Winchester Rd C2
Winnock Rd C2
Wolfe Ave C2
Worcester Rd C2

Coventry   334

Abbots La A1
Albany Rd B1
Alma St B3
Art Faculty B3
Asthill Grove C2
Bablake School A1
Barras La A1/B1
Barrs Hill School . . . A1
Belgrade B2
Bishop Burges St . . . A2
Bishopgate Green . . . A2
Bond's Hospital B1
Broad Gate B2
Broadway C1
Burges A2
Butts Radial B1
Canal Basin A2
Canterbury St A3
Cathedral B2
Chester St A1
Cheylesmore Manor
  House B2
Christ Church Spire . . B2
City Walls & Gates . . A2
Corporation St B1
Council House B2
Coundon Rd A1
Coventry Station . . . C1
Coventry Transport
  Museum A2
Cox St A3
Croft Rd B1
Dalton Rd C1
Deasy Rd C2
Earl St B2
Eaton Rd C1
Fairfax St B2
Foleshill Rd A2
Ford's Hospital B2
Fowler Rd A1
Friars Rd C2
Gordon St C1
Gosford St B3
Greyfriars Green . . . B2
Greyfriars Rd B2
Gulson Rd B3

Hales St A2
Harnall Lane East . . . A3
Harnall Lane West . . . A2
Herbert Art Gallery &
  Museum B2
Hertford St B2
Hewitt Ave A1
High St B2
Hill St B1
Holy Trinity B2
Holyhead Rd A1
Howard St A3
Huntingdon Rd C1
Information Ctr B2
Jordan Well B2
King Henry VIII Sch . . C1
Lady Godiva Statue . . B2
Lamb St A2
Leicester Row A2
Library B2
Little Park St B2
London Rd C3
Lower Ford St A3
Magistrates & Crown
  Courts A2
Manor House Drive . . . B2
Manor Rd C2
Market B2
Martyr's Memorial . . C2
Meadow St B1
Meriden St A2
Michaelmas Rd C2
Middleborough Rd . . . A1
Mile La C3
Millennium Place . . . A2
Much Park St B2
Naul's Mill Park . . . A1
New Union B2
Park Rd C2
Parkside C2
Post Office B2
Primrose Hill St . . . A3
Priory Gardens &
  Visitor Centre . . . B2
Priory St B2
Puma Way C3
Quarryfield La C3
Queen's Rd B1
Quinton Rd C2
Radford Rd A2
Raglan St B3
Retail Park B3
Ringway (Hill Cross) . A1
Ringway (Queens) . . . B1
Ringway (Rudge) B1
Ringway (St Johns) . . B3
Ringway (St Nicholas) . A2
Ringway (St Patricks) . C2
Ringway (Swanswell) . A2
Ringway (Whitefriars) . B3
St John St B2
St John The Baptist . . B2
St Nicholas St A2
Skydome B1
Spencer Ave C1
Spencer Park C1
Spon St B1
Sports Centre B3
Stoney Rd C2
Stoney Stanton Rd . . . A3
Swanswell Pool A2
Sydney Stringer Acad . A3
Technical College . . . B1
Technology Park C3
The Precinct B2
Theatre B2
Thomas Landsail St . . B3
Tomson Ave A1
Top Green A1
Trinity St B2
University B3
University Sports Ctr . B3
Upper Hill St A1
Upper Well St A2
Victoria St A3
Vine St A3
Warwick Rd C2
Waveley Rd B1
Westminster Rd C1
White St A3
Windsor St B1

Derby   334

Abbey St C1
Agard St B1
Albert St B2
Albion St B2
Ambulance Station . . A2
Arthur St A1
Ashlyn Rd B3
Assembly Rooms B2
Babington La C2
Becket St B1
Belper Rd A1
Bold La B2
Bradshaw Way C2
Bradshaw Way Ret Pk . C2
Bridge St B1
Brook St B1
Burton Rd C1
Bus Station B3
Caesar St A2
Canal St C3
Carrington St C3
Cathedral B2
Charnwood St C2
Chester Green Rd . . . A2
City Rd A2
Clarke St A3
Cock Pitt B3
Council House B2
Courts B2
Cranmer Rd B3
Crompton St C1
Curzon St B1
Darley Grove A1

Derby C3
Derbyshire County
  Cricket Ground . . . A3
Derwent Bsns Centre . A2
Derwent St B2
Drewry La C1
Duffield Rd A1
Duke St A2
Dunton Cl B3
Eagle Market C2
Eastgate B3
East St B2
Exeter St B3
Farm St C1
Ford St B1
Forester St C1
Fox St A2
Friar Gate B1
Friary St B1
Full St B2
Gerard St C1
Gower St C2
Green La C2
Grey St C1
Guildhall B2
Harcourt St C3
Highfield Rd A1
Hill La A2
Information Ctr B2
Iron Gate B2
John St C3
Joseph Wright Ctr . . . B2
Kedleston Rd A1
Key St B2
King Alfred St C1
King St B1
Kingston St A1
Lara Croft Way C3
Leopold St C2
Library B1
Liversage St C3
Lodge La A1
London Rd C3
London Rd Community
  Hospital C3
Macklin St C1
Mansfield Rd A3
Market B2
Market Pl B2
May St C1
Meadow La B3
Melbourne St C2
Mercian Way C1
Midland Rd C3
Monk St C1
Morledge B2
Mount St C1
Mus & Art Gallery . . . B1
Noble St C1
North Parade A1
North St A1
Nottingham Rd B3
Osmaston Rd C2
Otter St A1
Park St C2
Parker St A1
Pickfords House B1
Playhouse A2
Police HQ A2
Police Station B2
Post Office
  . . A1/A2/B1/B2/C2/C3
Prime Enterprise Park A2
Pride Parkway C1
Prime Parkway A2
Queens Leisure Ctr . . B1
Racecourse A3
Railway Terr C3
Register Office B2
Sadler Gate B2
St Alkmund's Way . . B1/B2
St Helens House A1
St Mary's A2
St Mary's Bridge . . . A2
St Mary's Bridge
  Chapel A2
St Mary's Gate B2
St Paul's Rd A1
St Peter's St C2
Showcase De Lux . . . C3
Siddals Rd C3
Silk Mill B2
Sir Frank Whittle Rd . A3
Spa La C1
Spring St B1
Stafford St B1
Station Approach . . . C3
Stockbrook St C1
Stores Rd A3
Traffic St C2
Wardwick B1
Werburgh St C1
West Ave A1
Westfield Centre . . . C2
West Meadows Ind Est B3
Wharf Rd A2
Wilmot St C2
Wilson St C1
Wood's La C1

Dorchester   334

Ackerman Rd B3
Acland Rd B2
Albert Rd A1
Alexandra Rd B2
Alfred Place B3
Alfred Rd B2
Alington Ave B3
Alington Rd A3
Ambulance Station . . B1
Ashley Rd C1
Balmoral Cres C1
Barnes Way B2/C2
Borough Gdns B1
Brewery Sq B1
Bridport Rd A1
Buckingham Way C3
Caters Place A1

Cemetery A3/C1
Charles St A2
Coburg Rd B1
Colliton St B2
Cornwall Rd A1
Cromwell Rd B2
Culliford Rd B2
Culliford Rd North B1
Dagmar Rd B1
Damer's St A2
Diggory Cres C2
Dinosaur Museum A2
Dorchester Bypass B1
Dorchester South
   Station B1
Dorchester West
   Station A1
Dorset County
   Council Offices A1
Dorset County
   (A&E) H B1
Dorset County Mus . . . A1
Duchy Close C3
Duke's Ave B2
Durngate St A2
Durnover Court A3
Eddison Ave B3
Edward Rd B1
Egdon Rd C2
Elizabeth Frink
   Statue ◆ B2
Farfrae Cres B3
Forum Centre, The B1
Friary Hill B1
Friary Lane A2
Frome Terr A2
Garland Cres C3
Glyde Path Rd A1
Government Offices . . . B3
Grosvenor Cres C1
Grosvenor Rd C1
H M Prison A1
Herrington Rd C1
High St East A2
High St Fordington . . . A2
High Street West A1
Holloway Rd A2
Icen Way A2
Keep Military Museum,
   The A3/B3
Kings Rd B1
Kingsbere Cres B2
Lancaster Rd B2
Library C1
Lime Cl C1
Linden Ave B1
London Cl A3
London Rd A2/A3
Lubbecke Way A3
Lucetta La C1
Maiden Castle Rd C1
Manor Rd C2
Marshwood Pl B1
Maumbury Rd B1
Maumbury Rings B1
Mellstock Ave C2
Mill St A3
Miller's Cl A1
Mistover Cl B1
Monmouth Rd B1/B2
Moynton Rd B2
Nature Reserve A2
North Sq. A2
Northernhay A1
Odeon ♥ B1
Old Crown Court &
   Cells ☆ A1
Olga Rd B1
Orchard St A2
Police Station ◙ B1
Post Office ⬤ A1/B1
Pound Lane A2
Poundbury Rd A1
Prince of Wales Rd . . . B1
Prince's Rd B1
Queen's Ave B1
Roman Town House ☆ . A1
Roman Wall ☆ A1
Rothesay Rd B1
St George's Rd B3
Salisbury Field A2
Sandringham Sports
   Centre B3
Shaston Cres C2
Smokey Hole La A3
South Court Ave C1
South St A2
South Walks Rd B2
Superstore B3
Teddy Bear House ♦ . . A1
Temple Cl C2
Terracotta Warriors &
   Teddy Bear Mus ♦ . . . A2
The Grove A1
Town Hall ♦ A2
Town Pump ◆ A2
Trinity St A1
Tutankhamun Ex ♦ . . . A2
Victoria Rd B1
Weatherbury Way C3
Wellbridge Cl C1
West Mills Rd A2
West Walks Rd A1
Weymouth Ave C1
Williams Ave B1
Winterbourne (BMI)
   H C1
Wollaston Rd B2
York Rd B2

Dumfries   334

Academy St A2
Aldermanhill Rd B3
Ambulance Station A3
Annan Rd A3
Ardwall Rd A3
Ashfield Dr A1
Atkinson Rd C1

Averill Cres C1
Balliol Ave C1
Bank St B2
Bankend Rd C3
Barn Slaps B3
Barrie Ave C1
Beech Ave A1
Bowling Green A3
Brewery St B2
Brodie Ave C2
Brooke St B2
Broomlands Dr C1
Brooms Rd B3
Buccleuch St A2
Burns House ♦ B2
Burns Mausoleum B3
Burns St B2
Burns Statue ◆ A2
Bus Station B1
Cardoness St A3
Castle St A2
Catherine St A2
Cattle Market A3
Cemetery B3
Cemetery C2
Church Cres A2
Church St B2
College Rd A1
College St A1
Corbelly Hill B1
Convent, The B1
Corberry Park B1
Cornwall Mt A3
County Offices A2
Court A2
Craigs Rd C3
Cresswell Rd B3
Cresswell Hill B3
Cumberland St B2
David Keswick
   Athletic Centre A3
David St B1
Dock Park C3
Dockhead B2
Dumfries ♦ A3
Dumfries Academy A2
Dumfries Museum &
   Camera Obscura ♦ . . . B2
Dumfries Royal
   Infirmary (A&E) H . . . A1
East Riverside Dr C3
Edinburgh Rd A3
English St B2
Fire Station B3
Friar's Vennel A2
Galloway St B1
George Douglas Dr . . . C1
George St A2
Gladstone Rd C2
Glasgow St A1
Glebe St A2
Glencaple Rd C3
Goldie Ave A1
Goldie Cres A1
Golf Course C2
Greyfriars ♦ A2
Grierson Ave B3
HM Prison B1
Hamilton Ave C1
Hamilton Starke Park . C2
Hazelrigg Ave C1
Henry St B3
Hermitage Dr C1
High Cemetery B1
High St A2
Hill Ave C2
Hill St B1
Holm Ave C2
Hoods Loaning A3
Howgate St B1
Huntingdon Rd A3
Information Ctr ℹ B2
Irish St B2
Irving St A1
King St A1
Kingholm Rd C2
Kirkpatrick Ct C2
Laurieknowe B1
Leafield Rd B3
Library A2
Lochfield Rd A1
Loreburn Pk A3
Loreburn St A2
Loreburne Sh Ctr A2
Lover's Walk A2
Martin Ave C1
Maryholm Dr A1
Maxwell St B1
McKie Ave C1
Mews La A2
Mid Steeple ◆ B2
Mill Green A2
Mill Rd A2
Moat Rd C2
Moffat Rd A3
Mountainhall Pk C3
Nelson St B1
New Abbey Rd B1/C1
New Bridge B1
Newall Terr A2
Nith Ave A3
Nith Bank C2
Nithbank Hospital H . . C3
Nithside Ave A3
Odeon ♥ B2
Old Bridge B1
Old Bridge House ♦ . . . B1
Palmerston Park (Queen
   of the South FC) A1
Park Rd A2
Pleasance Ave A1
Police HQ ◙ B2
Portland Dr C1
Post Office
   ⬤ A2/B1/B2/B3/B3
Priestlands Dr C1
Primrose St B2
Queen St B3

Queensberry St A2
Rae St A2
Richmond Ave C1
Robert Burns Ctr ♦ . . . B2
Roberts Cres C1
Robertson Ave C1
Robinson Dr C1
Rosefield Rd C2
Rosemount St B1
Rotchell Park B1
Rotchell Rd B1
Rugby Football Gd C1
Ryedale Rd A2
St Andrews
   St John the
   Evangelist ♦ A2
St Josephs College B3
St Mary's Ind Est A3
St Mary's St A3
St Michael's ♦ B2
St Michael's Bridge B2
St Michael's Bridge Rd B2
St Michael's Cemetery B3
Shakespeare St B2
Solway Dr C2
Stakeford St A1
Stark Cres C2
Station Rd A3
Steel Ave A1
Sunderries Ave A1
Sunderries Rd A1
Suspension Brae B2
Swimming Pool A1
Terregles St A1
Theatre Royal ♥ B2
Troqueer Rd C2
Union St A1
Wallace St B3
Welldale A3
West Riverside Dr C2
White Sands B2

Dundee   334

Adelaide Pl A1
Airlie Pl C1
Albany Terr A1
Albert St A3
Alexander Cr A2
Alexander St A2
Ann St A2
Arthurstone Terr A3
Bank St B2
Barrack Rd B2
Barrack St B2
Bell St B2
Blackscroft A3
Blinshall St B1
Brown St B1
Bus Station B3
Caird Hall B2
Camperdown St B3
Candle La B3
Carmichael St A1
City Churches ♦ B2
City Quay C3
City Sq B2
Commercial St B2
Constable St A3
Constitution Ct A1
Constitution Cres A1
Constitution St A1/B2
Cotton Rd A3
Courthouse Sq B1
Cowgate B3
Crescent St A3
Crichton St B2
Dens Brae A3
Dens Rd A3
Discovery Point ◆ C2
Douglas St B1
Drummond St A1
Dudhope Castle ♦ A1
Dudhope St B2
Dudhope Terr A1
Dundee ♦ B2
Dundee College A1
Dundee Contemporary
   Arts ♦ C2
Dundee High School . . B2
Dundee Repertory ♥ . . C2
Dura St A3
East Dock St C3
East Whale La B3
East Marketgait B3
Erskine St A3
Euclid Cr B2
Forebank Rd A2
Foundry La A3
Frigate Unicorn ◆ C3
Gallagher Retail Park . B3
Gellatly St B3
Government Offices . . . B1
Guthrie St B1
Hawkhill B1
Hilltown A2
Howff Cemetery, The . . B2
Information Ctr ℹ C2
King St A3
Kinghorne Rd A1
Ladywell Ave A3
Laurel Bank A2
Law Rd A1
Law St A1
Law, The ◆ A1
Library A2
Little Theatre ♥ A2
Lochee Rd B1
Lower Princes St A3
Lyon St A3
McManus Museum &
   Art Gallery ♦ B2
Meadow Side B2
Meadowside St
   Pauls ♦ B2
Mercat Cross ◆ B2
Murraygate B2
Nelson St A2
Nethergate B2/C1
North Marketgait B2

North Lindsay St B2
Old Hawkhill B1
Olympia Leisure Ctr . . . C3
Overgate Shopping Ctr B2
Park Pl C1
Perth Rd C1
Police Station ◙ A2/B2
Post Office ⬤ B3
Princes St A3
Prospect Pl A2
Reform St B2
Riverside Dr C1
Roseangle C1
Rosebank St A2
RRS Discovery ♦ C2
St Andrew's ♦ B3
St Pauls Episcopal † . . B3
Science Centre ♦ C2
Seagate B3
Sheriffs Court B1
South George St A2
South Marketgait B3
South Tay St B2
South Ward Rd B2
Steps ◆ B2
Tay Road Bridge ◆ . . . C3
Tayside House B3
Trades La B3
Union St B2
Union Terr A1
University Library C1
University of Abertay . . B2
University of Dundee . . B1
Upper Constitution St . A1
Verdant Works ♦ B1
Victoria Dock C3
Victoria Rd A2
Victoria St A3
West Marketgait . . . B1/B2
Ward Rd B2
Wellgate B2
West Bell St B1
Westfield Pl C1
William St A3
Wishart Arch ◆ A3

Durham   334

Alexander Cr A1
Allergate B1
Archery Rise C1
Assize Courts A2
Back Western Hill A1
Bakehouse La B3
Baths B3
Baths Bridge B3
Boat House B3
Bowling A2
Boyd St C3
Bus Station B2
Castle ♦ B2
Castle Chare B2
Cathedral † C2
Church St C3
Clay La C3
Claypath B3
College of St Hild &
   St Bede A3
County Hall B1
County Hospital H B1
Crook Hall &
   Gardens ◆ A3
Crossgate B2
Crossgate Peth C1
Darlington Rd C1
Durham ♦ B2
Durham Light Infantry
   Mus & Arts Gallery ♦ A2
Durham School C2
Ellam Ave C1
Elvet Bridge B2
Elvet Court B3
Farnley Hey A1
Ferens Cl A3
Fieldhouse La A1
Flass St B1
Framwelgate B2
Framwelgate Bridge . . . B2
Framwelgate Peth A2
Framwelgate
   Waterside A2
Frankland La A3
Freeman's Pl A3
Freeman's Quay L Ctr . A3
Gala Theatre &
   Cinema ♥ B3
Gates Sh Ctr, The B2
Geoffrey Ave C1
Gilesgate B3
Grey College C3
Hallgarth St C3
Hatfield College B2
Hawthorn Terr B1
Heritage Centre ♦ B3
HM Prison B3
Information Ctr ℹ B3
John St B1
Kingsgate Bridge B3
Laburnum Terr B1
Lawson Terr A1
Leazes Rd B2/B3
Library C1
Margery La B2
Market B2
Mavin St C3
Millburngate B2
Millburngate Bridge . . B2
Millennium Bridge
   (foot/cycle) A2
Mountjoy Research
   Centre C3
Museum of
   Archaeology ♦ B2
Nevilledale Terr B1
New Elvet B3
New Elvet Bridge B3
North Bailey C2
North End A2
North Rd A1/B2
Observatory C1

Old Elvet B3
Oriental Museum ♦ . . . C2
Oswald Court C3
Parkside C3
Passport Office A2
Percy Terr B1
Pimlico C2
Police Station ◙ B1
Post Office ⬤ A1/B2
Potters Bank C1/C2
Prebends Bridge C2
Prebends Walk C2
Prince Bishops Sh Ctr . B3
Princes St A1
Providence Row A3
Quarryheads La C2
Redhills B1
Redhills Terr B1
Saddler St B2
St Chad's College C3
St Cuthbert's Society . . C2
St John's College C2
St Margaret's ♦ B2
St Mary The Less ♦ . . . C2
St Mary's College C2
St Monica Grove B1
St Nicholas' ♦ B2
St Oswald's ♦ C3
Sidegate A2
Silver St B2
Add Sixth Form Centre
   (Durham Gilesgate) . . A3
South Bailey C2
South Rd C3
South St B2
Springwell Ave A1
Stockton Rd C3
Students' Rec Centre . . C3
Sutton St A2
The Avenue B1
The Crescent A1
The Grove A3
The Sands A3
Town Hall B2
Treasury Museum ♦ . . . C2
University ♦ B2
University Arts Block . . B3
University Library C3
Univ Science Site C3
Walkergate Centre B3
Wearside Dr A1
Western Hill A1
Wharton Park A1
Whinney Hill C3
Whitehouse Ave C1

Edinburgh   334

Abbey Strand B6
Abbeyhill A6
Abbeyhill Cr. B6
Abbeymount A6
Abercromby Pl A3
Adam St C5
Albany La A4
Albany St A4
Albert Memorial ◆ . . . B2
Albyn Pl A3
Alva Pl A6
Alva St B2
Ann St A1
Appleton Tower C4
Archibald Pl C3
Argyle House B3
Assembly Rooms &
   Musical Hall A3
Atholl Cr. B2
Atholl Crescent La C1
Bank St B4
Barony St A4
Beaumont Pl C5
Belford Rd B1
Belgrave Cr A1
Belgrave Crescent La . . A1
Bell's Brae A1
Blackfriars St B4
Blair St B4
Bread St C2
Bristo Pl C4
Bristo St C4
Brougham St C3
Broughton St A4
Brown St C5
Brunton Terr A6
Buckingham Terr A1
Burial Ground B5
Bus Station A4
Caledonian Cr. C1
Caledonian Rd C1
Calton Hill A5
Calton Hill A4
Calton Rd B4
Camera Obscura &
   Outlook Tower ◆ . . . B4
Candlemaker Row C4
Canning St C1
Canongate B5
Canongate ♦ B5
Carlton St A1
Carlton Terr A6
Carlton Terrace La A6
Castle St B2
Castle Terr B2
Castlehill B3
Central Library B4
Chalmers Hospital H . . C3
Chalmers St C3
Chambers St C4
Chapel St C4
Charles St C4
Charlotte Sq B2
Chester St B1
Circus La A2
Circus Pl. A2
City Art Centre ♦ B4
City Chambers ♦ B4
City Observatory ♦ . . . A5
Clarendon Cr A1
Clerk St C5
Coates Cr B1

Cockburn St B4
College of Art C3
Comely Bank Ave A1
Comely Bank Row A1
Cornwall St C2
Cowans Cl C5
Cowgate B4
Cranston St B5
Crichton St C4
Croft-An-Righ A6
Cumberland St A3
Dalry Pl C1
Dalry Rd C1
Danube St A1
Darnaway St A2
David Hume Tower . . . C4
Davie St C5
Dean Bridge A1
Dean Gdns A1
Dean Park Cr. A1
Dean Park Mews A1
Dean Park St A1
Dean Path B1
Dean St A1
Dean Terr A1
Dewar Pl C1
Dewar Place La C1
Doune Terr A2
Drummond Pl A3
Drummond St C5
Drumsheugh Gdns B1
Dublin Mews A3
Dublin St A4
Dublin Street La S A4
Dumbiedykes Rd B5
Dundas St A3
Earl Grey St C2
East Crosscauseway . . . C5
East Market St. B4
East Norton Pl A6
East Princes St Gdns . . B3
Easter Rd A6
Edinburgh
   (Waverley) ≉ B4
Edinburgh Castle ♦ . . . B3
Edinburgh Dungeon ◆ B4
Edinburgh International
   Conference Ctr. C1
Elder St A4
Esplanade B3
Eton Terr A1
Eye Pavilion H C3
Festival Office B3
Festival Theatre
   Edinburgh ♥ C4
Filmhouse ♥ C2
Fire Station C2
Floral Clock ◆ B3
Forres St A2
Forth St A4
Fountainbridge C2
Frederick St A3
Freemasons' Hall A3
Fruit Market ♦ B4
Gardner's Crescent . . . C1
George Heriot's
   School C3
George IV Bridge B4
George Sq C4
George Sq La C4
George St A2
Georgian House ♦ B2
Gladstone's Land ♦ . . . B4
Glen St C3
Gloucester La A2
Gloucester Pl A2
Gloucester St A2
Graham St C1
Grassmarket B3
Great King St A3
Great Stuart A2
Greenside La A5
Greenside Row A5
Greyfriars Kirk ♦ C4
Grindlay St C2
Grosvenor St C1
Grove St C1
Gullan's Cl B5
Guthrie St B4
Hanover St A3
Hart St A4
Haymarket C1
Haymarket Station ≉ . . C1
Heriot Pl. C3
Heriot Row A2
High School Yard B5
High St B4
Hill Pl C5
Hill St A2
Hillside Cr A5
Holyrood Park C6
Holyrood Rd B5
Home St C2
Hope St B2
Horse Wynd B6
Howden St C5
Howe St A3
India Pl A2
India St A2
Infirmary St C4
Information Ctr ℹ B3
Jamaica Mews A2
Jeffrey St B4
John Knox House ♦ . . . B5
Johnston Terr C3
Keir St C3
Kerr St A2
King's Stables Rd B2
Lady Lawson St C3
Lauriston Gdns C3
Lauriston Park C3
Lauriston Pl. C3
Lauriston St C3
Lawnmarket B4
Learmonth Gdns A1
Learmonth Terr A1
Leith St A4
Lennox St A1
Lennox St La A1
Leslie Pl A2

London Rd A5
Lothian Health Board . C5
Lothian Rd B2
Lothian St C4
Lower Menz Pl A6
Lynedoch Pl. B1
Manor Pl B1
Market St. B4
Marshall St C4
Maryfield A6
Maryfield Pl A6
McEwan Hall C4
Medical School C4
Melville St B1
Meuse La B4
Middle Meadow Walk . C4
Milton St A6
Montrose Terr A6
Moray House (college) B5
Moray Place A2
Morrison Link C1
Morrison St C1
Mound Pl B3
Multrees Walk A4
Mus Collections Ctr . . . A4
Mus of Childhood ♦ . . B5
Mus of Edinburgh ♦ . . B5
Mus on the Mound ♦ . B4
National Gallery ♦ B3
National Library of
   Scotland ♦ B4
National Monument ◆ A5
National Museum of
   Scotland ♦ C4
National Portrait
   Gallery ♦ B4
National Records
   Scotland ♦ A4
Nelson Monument ◆ . . A5
Nelson St A3
New St B5
Nicolson Sq C4
Nicolson St C4
Niddry St B4
North Bridge B4
North Meadow Walk . . C3
North Bank St B4
North Castle St A2
North Charlotte St A2
North St Andrew St . . . A4
North St David St A3
North West Circus Pl . . A2
Northumberland St . . . A3
Odeon ♥ C2
Old Royal High School . A6
Old Tolbooth Wynd . . . B5
Omni Centre ◆ A4
Our Dynamic Earth ◆ . B6
Oxford Terr A1
Pal of Holyrood Ho ♦ . B6
Palmerston Pl B1
Panmure Pl C3
Parliament House ♦ . . . B4
Parliament Sq. B4
People's Story, The ♦ . B5
Playhouse Theatre ♥ . . A4
Pleasance C5
Police Station ◙ A4
Ponton St C2
Post Office ⬤ . . . A3/A4/B5/
   . . . . C1/C2/C4/C5
Potterrow C4
Princes Mall B4
Princes St B3
Princes ≉ B3
Queen St A2
Queen Street Gdns . . . A3
Queen's Dr B6/C6
Queensferry Rd A1
Queensferry St B2
Queensferry Street La . B2
Radical Rd C6
Randolph Cr B1
Regent Gdns A5
Regent Rd A5
Regent Rd Park A6
Regent Terr A5
Remains of Holyrood
   Abbey (AD 1128) B6
Richmond La C5
Richmond Pl C5
Rose St B2
Rosemount Bldgs C1
Ross Open Air
   Theatre ♥ B3
Rothesay Pl B1
Rothesay Terr B1
Roxburgh Pl. C5
Roxburgh St C5
Royal Bank of
   Scotland ♦ A3
Royal Circus A2
Royal Lyceum ♥ C2
Royal Scottish Acad ♦ B3
Royal Terr A5
Royal Terrace Gdns . . . A5
Rutland Sq. B2
Rutland St B2
St Andrew Sq A4
St Andrew Sq ≉ A4
St Andrew's House A4
St Bernard's Cr A1
St Cecilia's Hall B4
St Colme St A2
St Cuthbert's ♦ B2
St Giles' † B4
St James Centre A4
St John St B5
St John's ♦ B2
St John's Hill B5
St Leonard's Hill C5
St Leonard's La C5
St Leonard's St C5
St Mary's ♦
   St Mary's Scottish
   Episcopal † B1
St Mary's St B5
St Stephen St A2
Salisbury Crags C6
Saunders St A2

Scotch Whisky
   Experience ◆ B3
Scott Monument ◆ . . . B4
Scottish Parliament . . . B6
Scottish Storytelling
   Centre ◆ B5
Semple St C2
Shandwick Pl B2
South Bridge B4
South Charlotte St B2
South College St C4
South Learmonth
   Gdns A1
South St Andrew St . . . A4
South St David St B3
Spittal St C2
Stafford St B1
Student Centre C4
Surgeons' Hall ♦ C5
TA Centre A2
Tattoo Office B3
Teviot Pl C4
The Mall B6
The Mound B3
The Royal Mile B4
The Writer's Mus ♦ . . . B4
Thistle St A3
Torphichen Pl C1
Torphichen St C1
Traverse Theatre ♥ . . . B2
Tron Sq. B4
Tron, The ◆ B4
Union St A4
University C4
University Library C4
Upper Grove Pl C1
Usher Hall ♥ C2
Vennel C3
Victoria St B3
Viewcraig Gdns B5
Viewcraig St B5
VUE ♥ A4
Walker St B1
Waterloo Pl A4
Waverley Bridge B4
Wemyss Pl A2
West Approach Rd C1
West Crosscauseway . . C5
West End ≉ B2
West Maitland St C1
West of Nicholson St . . C4
West Port C3
West Princes St Gdns . . B3
West Richmond St C5
West Tollcross C2
White Horse Cl B5
William St B1
Windsor St A5
York La A4
York Pl A4
York Pl ≉ A4
Young St B2

Exeter   334

Alphington St C1
Athelstan Rd B3
Bampfylde St B2
Barnardo Rd C3
Barnfield Hill B3
Barnfield Rd B2/B3
Barnfield Theatre ♥ . . . B3
Bartholomew St East . . B1
Bartholomew St West . B1
Bear St B2
Beaufort Rd C1
Bedford St B2
Belgrave Rd A3
Belmont Rd A3
Blackall Rd A2
Blackboy Rd A3
Bonhay Rd B1
Bull Meadow Rd C2
Bus & Coach Sta B3
Castle St B2
Cecil Rd C1
Cheeke St A3
Church Rd C1
Chute St A3
City Industrial Estate . . C2
City Wall ◆ B2
Civic Centre B2
Clifton Rd B3
Clifton St B3
Clock Tower B1
College Rd C3
Colleton Cr C2
Commercial Rd C1
Coombe St B2
Cowick St C1
Crown Courts B2
Custom House ♦ C2
Danes' Rd A2
Denmark Rd B3
Devon County Hall C3
Devonshire Pl A3
Dinham Rd B1
East Grove Rd C3
Edmund St C1
Elmgrove Rd A3
Exe St B1
Exeter Cathedral † B2
Exeter Central Sta ≉ . . A2
Exeter City Football
   Ground A3
Exeter College A2
Exeter Picture Ho ♥ . . B2
Fire Station A2
Fore St C1
Friars Walk C2
Guildhall ♦ B2
Guildhall Shopping Ctr B2
Harlequins Sh Ctr B1
Haven Rd C2
Heavitree Rd B3
Hele Rd A1
High St B2
HM Prison A2
Holloway St C2
Hoopern St A2

Horseguards A2
Howell Rd A1
Information Ctr ℹ B3
Iron Bridge B1
Isca Rd C1
Jesmond Rd A3
King William St A2
King St B1
Larkbeare Rd C2
Leisure Centre C1
Library B2
Longbrook St A2
Longbrook Terr A2
Lower North St B1
Lucky La C2
Lyndhurst Rd C3
Magdalen Rd B3
Magdalen St C2
Magistrates &
   Crown Courts B2
Market B2
Market St B2
Marlborough Rd C3
Mary Arches St B1
Matford Ave C2
Matford La C3
Matford Rd C3
May St A3
Mol's Coffee House ♦ . B2
New Bridge St B1
New North Rd A1/A2
North St B1
Northernhay St B1
Norwood Ave C3
Odeon ♥ A3
Okehampton St C1
Old Mill Cl C2
Old Tiverton Rd A3
Oxford Rd A3
Paris St B2
Parr St A3
Paul St B2
Pennsylvania Rd A2
Police HQ ◙ B3
Portland Street A3
Post Office
   ⬤ A3/B1/B3/C1
Powderham Cr A3
Preston St B1
Princesshay Sh Ctr . . . B2
Queen St A1
Queens Rd C1
Queen's Terr A1
Radford Rd C2
Richmond Rd A1
Roberts Rd C2
Rougemont Castle ♦ . . A2
Rougemont House ♦ . . B2
Royal Albert Memorial
   Museum ♦ B2
St David's Hill A1
St James' Pk Sta ≉ A2
St James' Rd A2
St Leonard's Rd C3
St Lukes University . . . B3
St Mary Steps ♦ C1
St Nicholas Priory ♦ . . B1
St Thomas Station ≉ . . C1
Sandford Walk B3
School for the Deaf . . . C2
School Rd C1
Sidwell St A3
Smythen St B1
South St B2
Southernhay East B2
Southernhay West B2
Spacex Gallery ♦ B1
Spicer Rd B3
Sports Centre A1
Summerland St A3
Swimming Pool &
   Leisure Ctr C1
Sydney Rd C1
Tan La C2
The Quay C2
Thornton Hill A1
Topsham Rd C2
Tucker's Hall ♦ B1
Tudor St C1
Velwell Rd A1
Verney St A3
Water La C1/C2
Weirfield Rd C2
Well St A3
West Ave A2
West Grove Rd C2
Western Way . . . A3/B1/B2
Wonford Rd B3/C3
York Rd A3

Fort William   335

Abrach Rd A3
Achintore Rd C1
Alma Rd B2
Am Breun Chamas A2
Ambulance Station A3
An Aird A2
Argyll Rd C1
Argyll Terr C1
Bank St B2
Belford Hospital H B2
Belford Rd B2/B3
Black Parks C2
Braemore Pl A2
Bruce Pl B2
Bus Station B2
Camanachd Cr A3/B2
Cameron Rd B2
Cameron Sq B1
Carmichael Way A2
Claggan Rd A3
Connochie Rd A2
Cow Hill C3
Creag Dhubh A3
Croft Rd B3
Douglas Pl B2
Dudley Rd C1
Dumbarton Rd C1

Earl of Inverness Rd . . A3
Fassifern Rd B1
Fire Station A2
Fort William B2
Fort William
(Remains) ✦ B2
Glasdrum Rd C1
Glen Nevis Pl B3
Gordon Sq B1
Grange Rd A4
Heather Croft Rd C2
Henderson Row C2
High St B1
Highland Visitor Ctr. . . .
Hill Rd B2
Hospital Belhaven
Annexe B3
Information Ctr ℤ A3
Inverlochy Ct. . . . .
Kennedy Rd B2/C2
Library A2
Lime Tree Gallery ✦ . . .C1
Linnhe Rd A3
Lochaber Leisure Ctr. . .B3
Lochiel Rd A3
Lochy Rd A3
Lundavra Cres. B3
Lundavra Rd B2
Lundy Rd B2
Mamore Cr. B2
Mary St. B2
Middle St B1
Montrose Ave A3
Moray Pl. C1
Morven Pl C2
Moss Rd B2
Nairn Cres C1
Nevis Bridge B3
Nevis Rd A3
Nevis Sports Centre . . .B2
Nevis Terr B2
North Rd B2
Obelisk B2
Parade Rd C2
Police Station ⌂ . . .A3/C1
Post Office ✉ A3/B2
Ross Pl C2
St Andrews . . . .
Shaw Pl C1
Station Brae B1
Studio 🎦 B2
Treig Rd A3
Underwater Centre ✦ . .A1
Union Rd B2
Victoria Rd. B2
Wades Rd B2
West Highland 🏛 B2
West Highland Collge
UHI A2
Young Pl B2

Glasgow 335

Admiral St C2
Albert Bridge C5
Albion St B5
Anderston ≷ B3
Anderston Centre B3
Anderston Quay B3
Arches ✦ B4
Argyle
St. A1/A2/B3/B4/B5
Argyle Street ≷ B5
Argyll Arcade B5
Arlington St A3
Arts Centre 🏛 B3
Ashley St A3
Bain St C6
Baird St A5
Baliol St A3
Ballater St C5
Barras, The (Market) .C6
Bath St A3
BBC Scotland/SMG . . .C2
Bell St B5
Bell's Bridge C2
Bentinck St A3
Berkeley St A3
Bishop La. B2
Black St A6
Blackburn St C2
Blackfriars St B6
Blantyre St A1
Blythswood Sq B4
Blythswood St. B4
Bothwell St B4
Brand St C1
Breadalbane St. A2
Bridge St C4
Bridge St Ⓜ C4
Bridgegate C5
Briggait C5
Broomhill Park A6
Broomielaw B4
Broomielaw Quay
Gdns B4
Brown St B4
Brunswick St B5
Buccleuch St A3
Buchanan Bus Station.A5
Buchanan Galleries 🏛 .A5
Buchanan St B5
Buchanan St Ⓜ B5
Cadogan St B4
Caledonian University.A5
Calgary St A5
Cambridge St A4
Canal St. A5
Candleriggs B5
Carlton Pl. C4
Carnarvon St A3
Carrick St. B4
Castle St B6
Cathedral Sq. B6
Cathedral St B5
Central College of
Commerce B5
Ctr for Contemporary
Arts 🏛 A4
Centre St C4

Cessnock Ⓜ C1
Charing Cross ≷ A3
Charlotte St. C6
Cheapside St B3
Cineworld 🎦 . . . .
Citizens' Theatre 🎭 . . .C5
City Chambers
Complex. B5
City Halls 🎭 B5
Clairmont Gdns A2
Claremont St. A2
Claremont Terr. A2
Claythorne St A2
Cleveland St A2
Clifford La. C1
Clifford St C1
Clifton Pl A2
Clifton St A2
Clutha St C1
Clyde Arc B2
Clyde Auditorium B2
Clyde Pl C4
Clyde Place Quay C4
Clyde St C5
Clyde Walkway C3
Clydeside Expressway.B2
Coburg St C4
Cochrane St. B5
College of Nautical
Studies C5
College St B6
Collins St B6
Commerce St C4
Cook St C4
Cornwall St C2
Couper St A5
Cowcaddens Ⓜ A4
Cowcaddens Rd A4
Crimea St B3
Custom House C4
Custom Ho Quay Gdns .C4
Dalhousie St A4
Dental Hospital 🏥 A4
Derby St A2
Dobbie's Loan A4/A5
Dobbie's Loan Pl A5
Dorset St A2
Douglas St B4
Doulton Fountain ✦ . . .C6
Dover St A2
Drury St B4
Drygate B6
Duke St B6
Dunaskin St A1
Dunblane St A4
Dundas St B5
Dunlop St C5
East Campbell St C6
Eastvale St A1
Eglinton St C4
Elderslie St A3
Elliot St B2
Elmbank St A3
Esmond St A1
Exhibition Centre ≷ . . .B2
Exhibition Way B2
Eye Infirmary 🏥 A2
Festival Park C1
Film Theatre 🎦 A4
Finnieston Quay B2
Finnieston Sq B2
Finnieston St B2
Fitzroy Pl A2
Florence St C5
Fox St C5
Gallowgate C6
Garnet St A3
Garnethill St A4
Garscube Rd A4
George Sq B5
George St. B5
George V Bridge C4
Gilbert St A1
Glasgow Bridge C4
Glasgow Cathedral † . . .B6
Glasgow Central ≷ B4
Glasgow Green C6
Glasgow Metropolitan
College. B5/C5
Glasgow Tower ✦ B1
Glasgow Science
Centre ✦ B1
Glasgow Science Centre
Footbridge B1
Glassford St B5
Glebe St A6
Gorbals Cross C5
Gorbals St C5
Gordon St B4
Govan Rd B1/C1/C2
Grace St B3
Grand Ole Opry ✦ C1
Grafton Pl A5
Grant St A3
Granville St A3
Gray St A2
Greendyke St C6
Grey Eagle St B7
Harley St C1
Harvie St C1
Haugh Rd A1
Heliport B1
Henry Wood Hall 🎭 . . .A2
High Court. C5
High St B6
High Street ≷ B6
Hill St A3
Holland St A3
Holm St B4
Hope St A5
Houldsworth St B2
Houston Pl C3
Houston St C3
Howard St C5
Hunter St C6
Hutcheson St B5
Hutchesons Hall 🏛 B5
Hydepark St B3
Hydro The ✦ B2

Imax Cinema 🎦 B1
India St A3
Information Ctr ℤ B5
Ingram St B5
Jamaica St B4
James Watt St B4
John Knox St B6
John St B5
Kelvin Hall ✦ A1
Kelvin Statue ✦ A2
Kelvingrove Art Gallery
& Museum 🏛 A1
Kelvingrove Park A2
Kelvingrove St A2
Kelvinhaugh St A1
Kennedy St A6
Kent Rd A2
Killermont St A5
King St B5
King's 🎭 A3
Kingston Bridge C3
Kingston St C4
Kinning Park Ⓜ C2
Kyle St A5
Lancefield Quay B2
Lancefield St B3
Langshot St C1
Lendel Pl C1
Lighthouse ✦ B4
Lister St A6
Little St B3
London Rd C6
Lorne St C1
Lower Harbour B1
Lumsden St A1
Lymburn St A1
Lyndoch Cr A3
Lyndoch Pl A3
Lyndoch St. A3
Maclellan St C1
Mair St C2
Maitland St A4
Mansell St C7
Mavisbank Gdns C2
Mcalpine St B3
Mcaslin St A6
McLean Sq C1
McLellan Gallery 🏛 A4
McPhater St A4
Merchants' House 🏛 . . .B5
Middlesex St C2
Middleton St C1
Midland St B4
Miller St B5
Millroad St C6
Milnpark St C2
Milton St A4
Minerva St B2
Mitchell Library 🏛 A3
Mitchell St West A3
Mitchell Theatre 🎭 A3
Modern Art Gallery 🏛.B5
Moir St. C6
Molendinar St. C6
Moncur St C6
Montieth Row C6
Montrose St B5
Morrison St C3
Mosque 🕌 C5
Nairn St A1
Nelson Mandela Sq ✦ . .B5
Nelson St C4
Nelson's Monument ✦ . .C6
New City Rd A4
Newton St A3
Newton Pl A3
Nicholson St C5
Nile St B5
Norfolk Court C4
Norfolk St C4
North Frederick St. B5
North Hanover St B5
North Portland St B6
North St A3
North Wallace St A5
O2 Academy ✦ C4
Odeon 🎦 C3
Old Dumbarton Rd A1
Osborne St. B5/C5
Oswald St B4
Overnewton St A1
Oxford St C4
Pacific Dr. B1
Paisley Rd C2
Paisley Rd West C1
Park Circus A2
Park Gdns A2
Park St South A2
Park Terr A2
Parkgrove Terr A2
Parnie St C5
Parson St A6
Partick Bridge A1
Passport Office A5
Pavilion Theatre 🎭 A4
Pembroke St A3
People's Palace 🏛 C6
Pinkston Rd A6
Piping Centre, The
National ✦ A5
Pitt St A4/B4
Plantation Park C1
Plantation Quay B1
Police Sta ⌂ . .A4/A6/B5
Port Dundas Rd. A5
Port St B2
Portman St C2
Prince's Dock B1
Princes St C5
Provand's Lordship 🏛 . . .B6
Queen St ≷ B5
Queen Street Ⓜ B5
Renfrew St A3/A4
Renton St A5
Richmond St B5
Robertson St B4
Rose St A4
Rottenrow B6
Royal Concert Hall 🎭 . . .A5

Royal Cr A2
Royal Exchange Sq B5
Royal Highland Fusiliers
Museum 🏛 A3
Royal Hospital For Sick
Children 🏥 A1
Royal Infirmary 🏥 . . . . .
Royal Scottish Academy
of Music & Drama . .A4
Royal Terr A2
Rutland Cr C2
St Kent St A2
St Andrew's (RC) † C6
St Andrew's ⚓ C6
St Andrew's St C6
St Enoch Ⓜ B5
St Enoch Shopping Ctr B5
St Enoch Sq B5
St George's Rd A3
St James Rd B6
St Mungo Ave A5/A6
St Mungo Museum of
Religious Life 🏛 B6
St Mungo St B6
St Vincent Cr. A2
St Vincent Pl B5
St Vincent St B3/B4
St Vincent Street
Church ⛪ B4
St Vincent Terr A2
Saltmarket C5
Sandyford Pl A3
Sauchiehall St. A2/A4
School of Art A4
Sclater St B7
Scotland St C2
Scott St A4
Scottish Exhibition &
Conference Centre . .B2
Seaward St C2
Shaftesbury St B3
Sheriff Court. C5
Shields Rd Ⓜ C3
Shuttle St. B6
Somerset Pl. A2
South Portland St. C4
Springburn Rd A6
Springfield Quay C3
Stanley St C1
Stevenson St C6
Stewart St A4
Stirling Rd B6
Stirling's Library ✦ B5
Stobcross Quay B1
Stobcross Rd B1
Stock Exchange 🏛 B5
Stockwell Pl C5
Stockwell St C5
Stow College A4
Strathclyde Univ.. . . . . .B6
Sussex St C1
Synagogues ⚹ A3/C4
Taylor St A6
Tenement House 🏛 A3
Teviot St A1
Theatre Royal 🎭 A4
Tolbooth Steeple ✦ . . . .
Mercat Cross ✦ C6
Tower St. C2
Trades House 🏛 B5
Tradeston St C4
Transport Museum 🏛 . . .A1
Tron 🎭 B5
Trongate B5
Tunnel St B2
Turnbull St C5
Union St B4
Victoria Bridge C5
Virginia St B5
West Greenhill Pl A2
West Regent St A4
Wallace St C3
Walls St B6
Walmer Cr C1
Warrock St B3
Washington St B3
Waterloo St B4
Watson St B6
Watt St C2
Wellington St B4
West Campbell St B4
West George St B4
West Graham St A4
West Regent St. A4
West St ≷ C4
West St Ⓜ C4
Westminster Terr A2
Whitehall St B3
Wilkes St C7
Wilson St B5
Woodlands Gate A3
Woodlands Rd. A3
Woodside Cr A3
Woodside Pl A3
Woodside Terr A3
York St B4
Yorkhill Pde. A1
Yorkhill St A1

Gloucester 335

Albion St C3
Alexandra Rd C3
Alfred St. C3
All Saints Rd C2
Alvin St B2
Arthur St C2
Barton St C2
Barrack Square B1
Blackfriars † B1
Blenheim Rd C2
Bristol Rd C1
Bruton Way B2
Bus Station B2
City Council Offices . . .B1
City Mus, Art Gall &
Library 🏛 B2

Commercial Rd. B1
Cromwell St. C2
Deans Way A1
Denmark Rd A3
Derby Rd C3
Docks ⚓ C1
Eastgate Shopping Ctr B1
Eastgate St B2
Edwy Pde. A3
Estcourt Cl. A3
Estcourt Rd A3
Falkner St C2
Folk Museum 🏛 B1
GL1 Leisure Centre . . .C2
Gloucester Cath † B1
Gloucester Quays
Outlet Shopping C1
Gloucester Station ≷ . .B2
Gloucestershire Royal
Hospital (A&E) 🏥 . . .A3
Gloucester Waterways
Mus 🏛 C1
Goodyere St C2
Gouda Way A1
Great Western Rd B3
Guildhall 🏛 B2
Heathville Rd. A3
Henry Rd C3
Henry St B3
Hinton Rd A3
HM Prison B1
India Rd C2
Information Ctr ℤ B2
Jersey Rd C3
King's 🏛 C2
King's Sq B2
Kingsholm
(Gloucester RFC) . . .A2
Kingsholm Rd A2
Lansdown Rd. A3
Library B2
Llanthony Rd C1
London Rd B3
Longhorn Ave A1
Longsmith St. B1
Malvern Rd A2
Market Pde B2
Mercia Rd A2
Metz Way C3
Midland Rd C2
Millbrook St C3
Market B2
Montpellier C1
Napier St C3
Nettleton Rd C2
New Inn ✦ B2
New Olympus 🎭 A3
North Rd A2
Northgate St B2
Oxford Rd A2
Oxford St C3
Park Rd C2
Park St B2
Parliament St C1
Pitt St B1
Police Station ⌂ B2
Post Office ✉ B2
Quay St. B1
Recreation Gd. A1/A2
Regent St C2
Robert Raikes Ho 🏛 . . .B1
Royal Oak Rd A2
Russell St B2
Ryecroft St C2
St Aldate St B2
St Ann Way. C1
St Catherine St A2
St Mark St A2
St Mary de Crypt ⛪ . . .B1
St Mary de Lode ⛪ B1
St Nicholas's ⛪ B1
St Oswald's Rd A1
St Oswald's Retail Pk.A1
St Peter's ⛪ B2
Seabroke Rd A3
Sebert St A3
Severn Rd C1
Sherborne St B2
Shire Hall 🏛 B1
Sidney St C3
Soldiers of
Gloucestershire 🏛 . . .B1
Southgate St B1/C1
Spa Field C1
Spa Rd C1
Sports Ground A2/B2
Station Rd B2
Stratton Rd C3
Stroud Rd C1
Superstore A1
Swan Rd A2
The Park. C2
The Quay B1
Trier Way C1/C2
Union St C2
Vauxhall Rd. C3
Victoria St. C2
Walham Lane A1
Wellington St C2
Westgate Retail Park. .B1
Westgate St. B1
Widden St C2
Worcester St B2

Grimsby 335

Abbey Drive East C2
Abbey Drive West. . . .C2
Abbey Park Rd C2
Abbey Rd C2
Abbey Walk B1
Abbeygate Sh Ctr B1
Abbotsway C3
Adam Smith St . .A1/A2
Ainslie St C1
Albert St B3
Alexandra Dock . . .A2/B2
Alexandra Retail Park . .A2
Alexandra Rd. A2/B2

Annesley St A2
Armstrong St A1
Arthur St B1
Augusta St C1
Bargate C1
Beeson St A1
Bethlehem St B1
Bodiam Way B3
Bradley St B3
Brighowgate C1/C2
Bus Station B2/C2
Canterbury Dr A3
Cartergate. B1/C1
Catherine St C3
Caxton 🎭 A3
Chantry La C1
Charlton St A1
Cheapside B3
Church La C2
Church St C2
Cleethorpe Rd A3
College C1
College St C1
Compton Dr C1
Corporation Bridge A1
Corporation Rd B3
Court B3
Crescent St B3
Deansgate C1
Doughty Rd C2
Dover St. B1
Duchess St A2
Dudley St C1
Duke of York Gardens . .B1
Duncombe St B2
Earl La C1
East Marsh St B2
East St B2
Eastgate. B2
Eastside Rd. A3
Eaton Ct B1
Eleanor St C1
Ellis Way. A3
Fisherman's Chapel ⛪.A3
Fisherman's Wharf . . .C1
Fishing Heritage
Centre ✦ B2
Flour Sq. A3
Frederick St B3
Frederick Ward Way . . .B2
Freeman St A3/B3
Freshney Dr B1
Freshney Pl B1
Garden St C2
Garibaldi St A2
Garth La. B2
Grime St B3
Dundas St C1
Dyke St B3
Eastwood Rd C3
Eaton St B1
Etruria Park. B1
Etruria Rd B1
Etruria Vale Rd C1
Festing St A3
Garibaldi St A2
Hainton Ave C3
Har Way B3
Hare St C2
Harrison St B1
Haven Ave B3
Hay Croft Ave B1
Hay Croft St B1
Heneage Rd B3/C3
Henry St. B3
Holme St B3
Hume St C1
James St B1
Joseph St B1
Kent St A3
King Edward St B2
Lambert Rd C2
Library B2
Lime St B2
Lister St B2
Littlefield La C1
Lockhill A3
Lord St B1
Ludford St C3
Macaulay St A2
Mallard Mews C3
Manor Ave. C3
Market A3
Market Hall B2
Market St B2
Moss Rd. C1
Nelson St B1
New St B2
Osborne St B2
Pasture St B3
Peaks Parkway C2
Pelham St A1
Police Station ⌂ B1
Post Office ✉ . .B1/B2/C2
PS Lincoln Castle ⚓ . . .B2
Pyewipe Rd A1
Railway Pl A3
Railway St A3
Recreation Ground C2
Rendel St A2
Retail Park B1
Richard St B1
Ripon St C1
Robinson St East B3
Royal St A3
St Hilda's Ave C1
St James ⛪ B1
Sheepfold St B3/C3
Sixhills St C2
South Park C1
Spring St B1
Superstore A2
Tasburgh St C3
Tennyson St C2
The Close C2
Thesiger St C1
Time Trap ✦ B2
Town Hall 🏛 B2
Veal St B1
Victoria Retail Park . . .A2
Victoria St North A2
Victoria St South B1
Victoria St West. B2
Watkin St A1
Welholme Ave C1
Welholme Rd C1
Wellington St A2
Wellowgate C2

Werneth Rd B3
West Coates Rd. A2
Westgate A2
Westminster Dr C1
Willingham St. C3
Wintringham Rd C3
Wood St B3
Yarborough Dr C1
Yarborough Hotel 🏨 . . .C2

Hanley 335

Acton St B3
Albion St. B2
Argyle St C1
Ashbourne Gr A2
Avoca St. A3
Baskerville Rd. B3
Bedford Rd C1
Bedford St. C1
Bethesda St B2
Bexley St A2
Birches Head Rd. A3
Botteslow St C3
Boundary St A1
Broad St C2
Broom St A2
Bryan St A2
Bucknall New Rd. B3
Bucknall Old Rd B3
Bus Station B2
Cannon St C2
Castlefield St C1
Cavendish St B1
Central Forest Pk.. . . . .A3
Charles St B3
Chell St A3
Clarke St C1
Cleveland Rd C1
Clifford St C3
Clough St B1
Clyde St C2
College Rd C2
Cooper St C2
Corbridge Rd A1
Cutts St C2
Davis St C1
Denbigh St A1
Derby St B3
Dilke St. A3
Dundas St C1
Dundee Rd C1
Dyke St B3
Eastwood Rd C3
Eaton St B1
Etruria Park. B1
Etruria Rd B1
Etruria Vale Rd C1
Festing St A3
Garden St C2
Garth La B2
Grime St B3
Harding Rd C2
Hassall St C3
Havelock Pl C1
Hazlehurst St C3
Hinde St C2
Hope St B2
Houghton St C1
Hulton St A3
Information Ctr ℤ B3
Jasper St C2
Jervis St A3
John Bright St B2
John St B2
Keelings Rd. A3
Kimberley Rd C1
Ladysmith Rd C1
Lawrence St C2
Leek Rd C3
Library B2
Lichfield St B3
Linfield Rd B3
Loftus St C3
Lower Bedford St C1
Lower Bryan St A2
Lower Mayer St A3
Lowther St. A1
Magistrates Court C2
Malham St A2
Marsh St B2
Matlock St C3
Mayer St. A3
Milton St C1
Mitchell Memorial
Theatre 🎭 B2
Morley St C2
Moston St A3
Mount Pleasant C1
Mulgrave St A1
Mynors St B3
Nelson Pl B3
New Century St B1
Octagon Retail Park . . .B1
Ogden Rd C3
Old Hall St. B3
Old Town Rd B3
Pall Mall B2
Palmerston St C1
Park and Ride B2
Parker St B2
Pavilion Dr A1
Pelham St C1
Percy St B2
Piccadilly B2
Picton St A3
Plough St C1

Police Station ⌂ C2
Portland St B1
Post Office ✉ . .A3/B3/C3
Potteries Museum & Art
Gallery 🏛 B1
Potteries Sh Ctr B2
Potteries Way B2
Powell St A1
Pretoria Rd C1
Quadrant Rd B2
Ranelagh St A1
Raymond St A2
Rectory Rd C1
Regent Rd C1
Regent Theatre 🎭 B2
Richmond Terr A2
Ridgehouse Dr A1
Robson St C2
St Ann St B3
St Luke St B3
Sampson St B2
Shaw St A1
Sheaf St C2
Shearer St C1
Shelton New Rd C1
Shirley Rd C1
Slippery La B2
Snow Hill. C2
Spur St A1
Stafford St B3
Statham St A2
Stubbs La C1
Sun St C1
Supermarket A1/B2
Talbot St C2
The Parkway C1
Town Hall 🏛 B2
Town Rd A3
Trinity St B2
Union St C3
Upper Hillchurch St. . . .A3
Upper Huntbach St B3
Victoria Hall
Theatre 🎭 B3
Warner St A1
Warwick St C1
Waterloo Rd A1
Waterloo St. B3
Well St. A3
Wellesley St B1
Wellington Rd B3
Wellington St B3
Whitehaven Dr A2
Whitmore St A2
Windermere St A1
Woodall St A1
Yates St C2
York St. A2

Harrogate 335

Albert St C2
Alexandra Rd A2
Arthington Ave B2
Ashfield Rd A2
Back Cheltenham
Mount A2
Beech Grove C1
Belmont Rd C1
Bilton Dr A2
Bower Rd B2
Bower St B2
Bus Station B2
Cambridge Rd B2
Cambridge St B2
Cemetery A1
Chatsworth Pl A2
Chatsworth Grove A2
Chatsworth Rd A2
Chelmsford Rd B3
Cheltenham Cr B2
Cheltenham Mt. B2
Cheltenham Pde. B2
Christ Church ⛪ B3
Christ Church Oval B3
Chudleigh Rd B3
Clarence Dr B1
Claro Rd A3
Claro Way A3
Coach Park B2
Coach Rd B3
Cold Bath Rd C1
Commercial St B2
Coppice Ave A1
Coppice Dr. A1
Coppice Gate A1
Cornwall Rd B1
Council Offices B2
Court C2
Crescent Gdns B1
Crescent Rd B1
Dawson Terr A1
Devonshire Pl A3
Diamond Mews C1
Dixon Rd. A2
Dixon Terr. A2
Dragon Ave A3
Dragon Parade A2
Dragon Rd A2
Duchy Rd B1
East Parade B2
East Park Rd C3
Esplanade B1
Fire Station A2
Franklin Mount A2
Franklin Rd B2
Franklin Square A2
Glebe Rd C1
Grove Park Ct A3
Grove Park Terr. A3
Hampsthwaite Rd A1
Harcourt Dr B3
Harcourt Rd B3
Harrogate 🏛 B3
Harrogate Int Ctr B1
Harrogate Ladies Coll . .B1
Harrogate Theatre 🎭 . .B2
Heywood Rd C1
Hollins Cres. A1

Hollins Mews A1
Hollins Rd A1
Homestead Rd C3
Hydro Leisure Ctr, The .B1
Information Ctr ℤ B1
James St B2
Jenny Field Dr. A1
John St. B2
Kent Dr A1
Kent Rd A1
Kings Rd A1
Kingsway. B3
Kingsway Dr A3
Lancaster Rd C1
Leeds Rd B3
Lime Grove B3
Lime St. A3
Mayfield Grove B2
Mayfield Pl B2
Mercer 🏛 B1
Montpellier Hill B1
Mornington Cr A3
Mornington Terr. A2
Mowbray Sq A3
North Park Rd B3
Nydd Vale Rd A2
Oakdale Ave A1
Oatlands Dr C3
Odeon 🎦 B2
Osborne Rd C1
Otley Rd C1
Oxford St B2
Park Chase B3
Park Parade B3
Park View. B2
Parliament St B1
Police Station ⌂ B1
Post Office ✉ B2/C1
Providence Terr A1
Queen Parade B3
Queen's Rd C1
Raglan St C2
Regent Ave A3
Regent Grove. A3
Regent Parade A3
Regent St A3
Regent Terr A3
Rippon Rd A1
Robert St C1
Royal Baths &
Turkish Baths ✦ B1
Royal Pump Room 🏛 . .B1
St Luke's Mount A2
St Mary's Ave C1
St Mary's Walk C1
Scargill Rd A1
Skipton Rd A3
Skipton St. A3
Slingsby Walk C3
South Park Rd C2
Spring Grove A1
Springfield Ave. B1
Station Ave B2
Station Parade B2
Strawberry Dale A2
Stray Rein C3
Studley Rd A2
Superstore B2
Swan Rd B1
The Parade B2
The Stray C2/C3
Tower St C2
Trinity Rd C2
Union St B2
Valley Dr. C1
Valley Gardens C1
Valley Mount C1
Victoria Ave. C2
Victoria Rd. C1
Victoria Shopping Ctr .B2
Waterloo Rd A3
West Park C2
West Park St C2
Wood View A1
Woodfield Ave A3
Woodfield Dr. A3
Woodfield Grove A3
Woodfield Rd A3
Woodfield Square A3
Woodside. B3
York Pl B1
York Rd B1

Holyhead Caergybi 335

Armenia St A2
Arthur St C2
Beach Rd B3
Boston St B2
Bowling Green C1
Bryn Erw Rd C2
Bryn Glas Cl. C3
Bryn Glas Rd C3
Bryn Gwyn Rd C1
Bryn Marchog A1
Bryn Mor Terr A2
Bryngoleu Ave A1
Cae Braenar C2
Cambria St B1
Captain Skinner's
Obelisk ✦ B2
Cecil St. C2
Celtic Gateway
Footbridge B2
Cemetery C1/C2
Cleveland Ave C2
Coastguard Lookout ✦ . .A3
Court B2
Customs House. B3
Cybi Pl B2
Cyttir Rd C3
Edmund St B2
Empire 🎦 B2
Ferry Terminals B2
Fford Beibio B3
Fford Feurig C1
Fford Hirnos C1
Fford Jasper C3
Fford Tudur. B3
Fire Station B3

Garreglwyd Rd B1
Gilbert St C2
Gorsedd Circle B1
Gwelfor Ave. A1
Harbour View B1
Henry St C1
High Terr C1
Hill St B2
Holborn Rd C3
Holland Park Ind Est C3
Holyhead Park B1
Holyhead Station ≥ B2
Information Ctr ℤ B2
King's Rd C2
Kingsland Rd. C3
Lewascote C3
Library A1
Lifeboat Station A1
Llanfwr Cl C3
Llanfwr Rd. C3
Lligwy St C2
Lon Deg C2
London Rd B1
Longford Rd B1
Longford Terr. B1
Maes Cybi B2
Maes Hedd. A1
Maes-Hyfryd Rd. C2
Maes-y-Dref B1
Maes-yr-Haf A2/B2
Maes-yr-Ysgol C3
Marchog A3
Marina B2
Maritime Museum 🏛 B1
Market B2
Market St B2
Mill Bank B1
Min-y-Mor Rd. B2
Morawelon Ind Est B3
Morawelon Rd. B1
Moreton Rd C1
New Park Rd B1
Newry St B1
Old Harbour
   Lighthouse A3
Plas Rd C1
Police Station 🏛 C2
Porth-y-Felin Rd A1
Post Office
   🏤 A1/B1/B2/B3/C2/C3
Prince of Wales Rd B1
Priory La B3
Pump St C1
Queens Park C1
Reseifion Rd C1
Rock St B2
Roman Fort 🏛 B2
St Cybi St B2
St Cybi's Church B2
St Seiriol's Cl. B2
Salt Island Bridge A2
Seabourne Rd C3
South Stack Rd B1
Sports Ground B1
Stanley St. B2
Station St B2
Tan-y-Bryn Rd A1
Tan-yr-Efail C3
Tara St C1
Thomas St B1
Town Hall A2
Treseifion Estate C2
Turkey Shore Rd B2
Ucheldre Arts Ctr ✦ B1
Ucheldre Ave. B1
Upper Baptist St. B1
Victoria Rd B2
Victoria Terr B2
Vulcan St B2
Walthew Ave A1
Walthew La A1
Wian St C2

Hull 335

Adelaide St C1
Albert Dock. C1
Albion St B2
Alfred Gelder St B2
Anlaby Rd. C1
Arctic Corsair ✦ B3
Beverley Rd A2
Blanket Row C2
Bond St. B2
Bridlington Ave. A2
Brook St B1
Brunswick Ave A1
Bus Station B1
Camilla Cl A2
Cannon St A2
Cannon's C1
Caroline St. A2
Carr La B2
Castle St C2
Central Library B1
Charles St A2
Citadel Way B3
City Hall B2
City Hall Theatre B2
Clarence St A3
Cleveland St. A2
Clifton St A1
Club Culture 🏛 C2
Colonial St B1
Court B2
Deep, The 🐟. C3
Dock Office Row. B2
Dock St. B2
Dinostar 🏛. C2
Drypool Bridge B3
Egton St A3
English St. C1
Ferens Gallery 🏛 B1
Fernsway A2
Francis St A2
Francis St West. A2
Freehold St A2
Freetown Way. A2
Fruit Theatre 🏛 C1
Garrison Rd B3

George St B2
Gibson St A2
Great Thornton St B1
Great Union St A3
Green La A1
Grey St A1
Grimston St B2
Grosvenor St A1
Guildhall 🏛 B2
Guildhall Rd. B2
Hands-on History 🏛 B2
Harley St A1
Hessle Rd C1
High St B3
Holy Trinity ♦. B2
Hull & East Riding
   Museum 🏛 B3
Hull Arena C1
Hull College B3
Hull History Centre A2
Hull (Paragon) Sta ≥ B1
Hull Truck Theatre 🎭. B1
Humber Dock Marina C2
Humber Dock St C2
Humber St. C2
Hyperion St A3
Information Ctr ℤ. B2
Jameson St B1
Jarratt St B2
Jenning St A3
King Billy Statue ✦ C2
King Edward St B2
King St B2
Kingston Retail Park C1
Kingston St. C2
Liddell St A1
Lime St. A3
Lister St C1
Lockwood St A3
Maister House 🏛 B2
Maritime Museum 🏛. B2
Market B2
Market Place B2
Minerva Pier C2
Mulgrave St A3
Myton Bridge C2
Myton St B1
NAPA (Northern Acad of
   Performing Arts) 🏛 B1
Nelson St C2
New Cleveland St A3
New George St B2
New Theatre 🎭 A2
Norfolk St. A1
North Bridge A3
North St B1
Odeon 🎬 C1
Old Harbour. C2
Osborne St B1
Paragon St B1
Park St B1
Percy St B1
Pier St. C2
Police Station 🏛 C2
Post Office 🏤 . . .A1/B1/B2
Porter St C1
Portland St B1
Posterngate B2
Prince's Quay B2
Prospect Centre. B1
Prospect St A2
Queen's Gdns B2
Railway Dock Marina C2
Railway St C2
Real 🏛 B3
Red Gallery 🏛 A2
Reform St A2
Retail Park. C1
River Hull Footbridge B3
Riverside Quay C2
Roper St B1
St James St A1
St Luke's St B1
St Mark St A3
St Mary the Virgin ♦. A2
St Stephens Sh Ctr. B1
Scott St A2
South Bridge Rd B3
Spring Bank. A1
Spring St B1
Spurn Lightship ⚓. C2
Spyvee St A3
Streetlife Transport
   Museum 🏛 B3
Sykes St A2
Tidal Surge Barrier ✦ C2
Tower St. B3
Trinity House B2
University A2
Vane St A1
Victoria Pier ⚓ C2
Waterhouse La B1
Waterloo St A1
Waverley St C1
Wellington St C2
Wellington St West C1
West St B1
Whitefriargate. B2
Wilberforce Dr A2
Wilberforce House 🏛. B3
Wilberforce
   Monument ✦ B3
William St A1
Wincolmlee A3
Witham A3
Wright St A1

Inverness 336

Abban St A1
Academy St B2
Alexander Pl B2
Anderson St A2
Annfield Rd C3
Ardconnel St C2
Ardconnel Terr. C3
Ardross Pl B2
Ardross St C2
Argyle St C2
Argyle Terr C3

Attadale Rd B1
Ballifeary La C1
Ballifeary Rd C1/C2
Balnacraig La A1
Balnain House 🏛 B2
Balnain St B2
Bank St B2
Bellfield Park C3
Bellfield Terr. C3
Benula Rd A1
Birnie Terr A1
Bishop's Rd C1
Bowling Green A2
Bowling Green B2
Bridge St B2
Brown St A2
Bruce Ave. C1
Bruce Gdns C1
Bruce Pk C1
Burial Ground A2
Burnett Rd A3
Bus Station. B3
Caledonian Rd B1
Cameron Rd A1
Cameron Sq A1
Carse Rd. A1
Carsegate Rd Sth A1
Castle Garrison
   Encounter ✦ B2
Castle Rd B2
Castle St B3
Celt St B2
Chapel St A2
Charles St B3
Church St. B2
Clachnacuddin
   Football Ground A1
Columba Rd B1/C1
Crown Ave B3
Crown Circus B3
Crown Dr B3
Crown Rd B3
Crown St B3
Culduthel Rd C3
Dalneigh Cres B1
Dalneigh Rd B1
Denny St. C3
Dochfour Dr B1/C1
Douglas Row A2
Duffy Dr C1
Dunabban Rd A1
Dunain Rd B1
Duncraig St B2
Eastgate Shopping Ctr . . .B3
Eden Court 🎭 C2
Fairfield Rd B1
Falcon Sq. B3
Fire Station B2
Fraser St B2
Fraser St C2
Friars' Bridge A2
Friars' La. B2
Friars' St A2
George St. A2
Gilbert St A1
Glebe St A2
Glendoe Terr. A1
Glenurquhart Rd C1
Gordon Terr. B3
Gordonville Rd C2
Grant St A2
Greig St B2
HM Prison A3
Harbour Rd. A3
Harrowden Rd B1
Haugh Rd. C2
Heatherley Cres C3
High St B3
Highland Council HQ,
   The B2
Hill Park C3
Hill St. B3
Huntly Pl A1
Huntly St B2
India St A1
Industrial Estate. A3
Information Ctr ℤ. B2
Innes St B3
Inverness ≥ B3
Inverness College
   (Midmills Campus). B3
Inverness College UHI. . . .A2
Inverness High School . . .B1
Inverness Museum 🏛 B2
Jamaica St A2
Kenneth St B1
Kilmuir Rd. A1
King St B2
Kingsmills Rd B3
Laurel Ave B1/C1
Library B2
Lilac Gr. C3
Lindsay Ave C1
Lochalsh Rd. A1/B1
Longman Rd A3
Lotland Pl A2
Lower Kessock St A1
Madras St A2
Market Hall B2
Maxwell Dr C1
Mayfield Rd C3
Millburn Rd B3
Mitchell's La B3
Montague Row B2
Muirfield Rd C3
Muirtown St B1
Nelson St A2
Ness Bank. C2
Ness Bridge B2
Ness Walk B2
Old Edinburgh Rd. C3
Old High Church ♦ B2
Park Rd C1
Paton St C3
Perceval Rd B2
Planefield Rd B1
Police Station 🏛 A3
Porterfield Bank C3
Porterfield Rd C3

Portland Pl A2
Post Office
   🏤. A2/B1/B2/B3
Queen St B2
Queensgate B2
Railway Station ≥. B3
Rangemore Rd B1
Reay St. B3
Riverside St A2
Rose St B2
Ross Ave B1
Rowan Rd. B1
Royal Northern
   Infirmary 🏥 C2
St Andrew's Cath ♦ C2
St Columba ♦ B2
St John's Ave C1
St Mary's Ave C1
Sheriff Court. B2
Shore St A2
Smith Ave C1
Southside Pl C3
Southside Rd C3
Spectrum Centre B2
Strothers La. B3
Superstore B2
TA Centre C2
Telford Gdns B1
Telford Rd A1
Telford St. A1
Tomnahurich
   Cemetery. C1
Tomnahurich St B2
Town Hall B2
Union Rd B3
Union St B2
Walker Pl A2
Walker Rd A2
War Memorial ✦ C2
Waterloo Bridge. A2
Wells St B1
Young St B2

Ipswich 336

Alderman Rd B2
All Saints' Rd. A1
Alpe St B2
Ancaster Rd. C1
Anglesea Rd B2
Ann St B2
Arboretum. A2
Austin St C2
Belstead Rd C1
Berners St B2
Bibb Way B1
Birkfield Dr C1
Black Horse La B1
Bolton La A3
Bond St. C3
Bowthorpe Cl B2
Bramford La A1
Bramford Rd A1
Bridge St C2
Brookfield Rd. A1
Brooks Hall Rd A1
Broomhill A2
Broomhill Rd. A1
Broughton Rd A2
Bulwer Rd B1
Burrell Rd C2
Butter Market. B2
Buttermarket Shopping
   Centre, The. B2
Cardinal Park L Park C2
Carr St. B3
Cecil Rd C1
Cecilia St B2
Chancery Rd C2
Charles St. B2
Chevallier St A1
Christchurch Mansion &
   Wolsey Art Gallery 🏛. . . .A3
Christchurch Park A3
Christchurch St B3
Cineworld 🎬 C2
Civic Centre B2
Civic Dr. B2
Clarkson St B1
Cobbold St. A3
Commercial Rd. C2
Constable Rd A3
Constantine Rd. C1
Constitution Hill A2
Corder Rd A3
Corn Exchange B2
Cotswold Ave A1
Council Offices B2
County Hall B2
Crown Court B2
Crown St B2
Cullingham Rd. B1
Cumberland St A3
Curriers La. B2
Dale Hall La A1
Dales View Rd A1
Dalton Rd B2
Dillwyn St B2
Elliot St. C2
Elm St B2
Elsmere Rd A3
Falcon St B2
Felaw St C3
Flint Wharf C3
Fonnereau Rd. A2
Fore St C3
Foundation St B3
Franciscan Way B2
Friars St B2
Gainsborough Rd. A3
Gatacre Rd B1
Geneva Rd A2
Gippeswyk Ave C1
Gippeswyk Park C1
Grafton Way C2
Graham Rd A1
Grimwade St B3
Great Whip St C3
Handford Cut B1

Handford Rd B1
Henley Rd. A2
Hervey St A3
High St B2
Holly Rd A2
Information Ctr ℤ B2
Ipswich Haven
   Marina ⚓ C3
Ipswich School A2
Ipswich Station ≥ C2
Ipswich Town FC
   (Portman Road). C2
Ivry St A2
Kensington Rd A1
Kesteven Rd C1
Key St C3
Kingsfield Ave. A2
Kitchener Rd. A1
Little's Cr. C2
London Rd B1
Low Brook St B3
Lower Orwell St C3
Luther Rd C1
Manor Rd A3
Mornington Ave A1
Museum St B2
Mus & Art Gallery 🏛 B2
Neale St A2
New Cardinal St C2
New Cut East C3
New Cut West C3
New Wolsey 🎭 B2
Newson St. B2
Norwich Rd A1/B1
Oban St A1
Old Customs House 🏛 . . .C3
Old Foundry Rd B3
Old Merchant's Ho 🏛 C3
Orford St A2
Paget Rd A2
Park Rd. A3
Park View Rd A3
Peter's St C2
Philip Rd C1
Pine Ave A1
Pine View Rd A1
Police Station 🏛 B2
Portman Rd B1
Portman Walk. C2
Post Office 🏤 B2/B3
Princes St B2
Prospect St B1
Queen St B2
Ranelagh Rd C1
Recreation Ground B1
Rectory Rd A1
Regent Theatre 🎭 B3
Retail Park B3
Retail Park C2
Richmond Rd A1
Rope Walk B3
Rose La. C2
Russell Rd C2
St Edmund's Rd. A2
St George's Rd B2
St Helen's St B3
Sherrington Rd. A1
Silent St B2
Sir Alf Ramsey Way C1
Sirdar Rd A1
Soane St B3
Springfield La A1
Star La C3
Stevenson Rd B1
Suffolk College B3
Suffolk Retail Park. B1
Superstore B3
Surrey Rd B1
Tacket St B3
Tavern St B2
The Avenue A3
Tolly Cobbold Mus 🏛 C3
Tower Ramparts B2
Tower Ramparts
   Shopping Centre B2
Tower St B2
Town Hall 🏛 B2
Tuddenham Rd A3
Upper Brook St B2
Upper Orwell St B3
University C3
Valley Rd A2
Vermont Cr A3
Vermont Rd A3
Vernon St. C3
Warrington Rd A1
Waterloo Rd A1
Waterworks St B3
Wellington St A2
West End Rd B1
Westerfield Rd A2
Westgate St B2
Westholme Rd A1
Westwood Ave A1
Willoughby Rd C1
Withipoll St A3
Woodbridge Rd B3
Woodstone Ave A3
Yarmouth Rd. A1

Kendal 336

Abbot Hall Art Gallery &
   Museum of Lakeland
   Life 🏛 C2
Ambulance Station A2
Anchorite Fields C2
Anchorite Rd. C2
Ann St A3
Appleby Rd A3
Archers Meadow B2
Ashleigh Rd A2
Aynam Rd. B2
Bankfield Rd B1
Beast Banks B1
Beezon Fields A2
Beezon Rd A2
Beezon Trad Est A2
Belmont B2

Birchwood Cl C1
Blackhall Rd B2
Brewery Arts Ctr 🏛🎭 B1
Bridge St. B2
Brigsteer Rd C1
Burneside Rd A2
Bus Station. B2
Buttery Well La C2
Canal Head North B3
Captain French La C2
Caroline St A1
Castle Hill B3
Castle Howe B1
Castle Rd B3
Cedar Gr C1
Council Offices B2
County Council
   Offices A2
Cricket Ground A2
Cricket Ground C3
Cross La C2
Dockray Hall Ind Est A2
Dowker's La B2
Dry Ski Slope ✦. A3
East View A3
Echo Barn Hill C1
Elephant Yard Sh Ctr B2
Fairfield La. A1
Finkle St B2
Fire Station B3
Fletcher Square. C3
Football Ground. A3
Fowling La A3
Gillinggate C2
Glebe Rd C1
Golf Course B1
Goose Holme. B3
Gooseholme Bridge B2
Green St. A1
Greengate C1
Greengate La C1/C2
Greenside C1
Greenwood C1
Gulfs Rd B2
High Tenterfell B1
Highgate B2
Hillswood Ave C1
Horncop La A2
Information Ctr ℤ B2
K Village and Heritage
   Centre 🏛 C2
Kendal Business Park A3
Kendal Castle
   (Remains) ✦ B3
Kendal Fell B1
Kendal Green A1
Kendal Station ≥. B2
Kent Pl A2
Kirkbarrow C2
Kirkland. C2
Library B2
Library Rd B2
Little Aynam B3
Little Wood. C1
Long Cl C1
Longpool A2
Lound Rd B3
Lound St C2
Low Fellside. B1
Lowther St B2
Maple Dr A3
Market Pl B2
Maude St B2
Miller Bridge B2
Milnthorpe Rd. C1
Mint St A2
Mintsfeet Rd A2
Mintsfeet Rd South A2
New Rd. B2
Noble's Rest B1
Parish Church ♦ C2
Park Side Rd C2
Parkside Bsns Park C2
Parr St C2
Queen St B2
Police Station 🏛 A2
Post Office 🏤 . .A3/B2/C2
Quaker Tapestry ✦ B2
Red Mount Chapel ♦ A2
Regent Way B2
Riverside Walk C3
Rydal Mount C1
Sandes Ave. A2
Sandgate. B3
Sandylands Rd A3
Serpentine Rd B1
Serpentine Wood A1
Shap Rd A3
South Rd C2
Stainbank Rd. C1
Station Rd A2
Stramongate B2
Stramongate Bridge B2
Stricklandgate A2/B2
St Lewis St B2
Sunnyside C2
Thorny Hills B3
Town Hall B2
Undercliff Rd B3
Underwood C1
Union St A2
Vicar's Fields C2
Vicarage Dr. C1
Wainwright Yd Sh Ctr B2
Wasdale Cl. C1
Well Ings B2
Westmorland Shopping
   Centre & Market Hall. . . .B2
Westwood Ave C1
Wildman St A3
Windermere Rd A1
YHA 🏛 B2
YWCA B2

King's Lynn 336

Albert St. A2
Albion St C2
All Saints 🏛 C2
All Saints St C2
Austin Fields A2

Austin St A2
Avenue Rd B3
Bank Side. B1
Beech Rd C2
Birch Tree Cl B3
Birchwood St A2
Blackfriars Rd. B2
Blackfriars St B2
Boal St B1
Bridge St B2
Broad St A2
Broad Walk B3
Burkitt St A2
Bus Station. B2
Carmelite Terr C2
Chapel St A2
Chase Ave C3
Checker St C2
Church St. B2
Clough La B2
Coburg St C2
College of
   West Anglia A3
Columbia Way A3
Corn Exchange 🏛 B2
County Court Rd B2
Cresswell St A2
Custom House 🏛 B1
Eastgate St A2
Edma St A2
Exton's Rd C3
Ferry La. B1
Ferry St A1
Framingham's
   Almshouses ♦ B2
Friars St C2
Friars Walk. C2
Gaywood Rd A3
George St. A2
Gladstone Rd C2
Goodwin's Rd. C3
Green Quay ✦ B1
Greyfriars' Tower ✦ B2
Guanock Terr C2
Guildhall 🏛 B1
Hansa Rd C3
Hardwick Rd C2
Hextable Rd A2
High St B2
Holcombe Ave. C3
Hospital Walk C2
Information Ctr ℤ B1
John Kennedy Rd A2
Kettlewell Lane A2
King George V Ave B3
King's Lynn Art Ctr 🏛 A1
King's Lynn FC A3
King's Lynn Station ≥. B2
King St B1
Library B2
Littleport St A2
Loke Rd A2
London Rd C2
Lynn Museum 🏛 B2
Magistrates Court B1
Market La B1
Millfleet C2
Milton Ave A3
Nar Valley Walk. C1
Nelson St. B1
New Conduit St. B2
Norfolk St B2
North Lynn Discovery
   Centre ✦. A1
North St A2
Oldsunway A2
Ouse Ave C3
Page Stair Lane A1
Park Ave B3
Police Station 🏛 B2
Portland Pl B2
Portland St. B2
Purfleet B1
Queen St B1
Raby Ave A3
Railway Rd A2
River Walk C2
Robert St. A2
Saddlebow Rd. C1
St Ann's St B1
St James' Rd B2
St James Æ Swimming
   Pool B2
St James St B2
St John's Walk B2
St Margaret's ♦. B1
St Nicholas 🏛 A1
St Nicholas St A1
St Peter's Rd B1
Sir Lewis St B2
Smith Ave A3
South Everard St C2
South Gate ♦ C2
South Quay B1
South St C2
Southgate St C2
Stonegate St B2
Surrey St A2
Sydney St C3
Tennyson Ave B2
Tennyson Rd B3
Town Hall 🏛 B1
Town Ho & Tales of
   The Old Gaol Ho 🏛. B1
Town Wall (Remains) C2
True's Yard Mus 🏛 A2
Valingers Rd C2
Vancouver Ave C2
Vancouver Quarter B2
Waterloo St C2
Wellesley St C2
White Friars Rd. C2
Windsor Rd C2
Winfarthing St C2

Wyatt St A2
York Rd A3

Lancaster 336

Aberdeen St A2
Adult College, The C3
Aldcliffe Rd C2
Alfred St B2
Ambleside Rd. A3
Ambulance Sta A1
Ashfield Ave B1
Ashton Rd C2
Assembly Rooms,
   The ♦ B2
Balmoral Rd C3
Bath House ♦ B2
Bath Mill La B3
Bath St. B2
Blades St B1
Borrowdale Rd C3
Bowerham Rd. C3
Brewery La B2
Bridge La B2
Brook St C2
Bulk Rd A3
Bulk St B2
Bus Station. B2
Cable St A2
Canal Cruises &
   Waterbus ✦ C2
Carlisle Bridge A1
Carr House La C2
Castle 🏰 B1
Castle Park B1
Caton Rd A3
China St B2
Church St B2
City Museum 🏛. B2
Clarence St C3
Common Gdn St B2
Coniston Rd C3
Cottage Museum 🏛. B1
Council Offices. B2
Court B1
Cromwell Rd C1
Crown Court B1
Dale St. C3
Dallas Rd B1/C1
Dalton Rd A3
Dalton Sq B2
De Vitre St A3
Dee Rd. A1
Denny Ave A3
Derby Rd A2
Dukes 🎭 B1
Earl St. A2
East Rd B3
Eastham St C3
Edward St C3
Fairfield Rd B1
Fenton St B2
Firbank Rd A3
Fire Station C3
Friend's Meeting Ho 🏛 . . .B1
Garnet St C3
George St B2
Giant Axe Field B1
Grand, The 🎭 B2
Grasmere Rd C3
Greaves Rd C2
Green St A3
Gregson Centre, The C3
Gregson Rd. C3
Greyhound Bridge A2
Greyhound Bridge Rd A2
High St C1
Hill Side C3
Hope St. C3
Hubert Pl A3
Information Ctr ℤ B2
Judges Lodgings 🏛 B1
Kelsy St C3
Kentmere Rd. C3
King St. B2
Kingsway A3
Kirkes Rd C3
Lancaster &
   Lakeland 🏥 C3
Lancaster City
   Football Club B1
Lancaster Station ≥ B1
Langdale Rd A3
Ley Ct A3
Library B2
Lincoln Rd C1
Lindow St C2
Lodge St. A2
Long Marsh La. B1
Lune Rd A1
Lune St A3
Lune Valley Ramble A3
Mainway. A2
Maritime Museum 🏛 A1
Market St B2
Market La. B2
Meadowside C3
Meeting House La B1
Millennium Bridge A2
Moor La B2
Moorgate. B3
Morecambe Rd A1/A2
Nelson St B2
North Rd. B2
Orchard La B1
Owen Rd A2
Park Rd B3
Parliament St A3
Patterdale Rd A3
Penny St B2
Police Station 🏛 C2
Portland St. C2
Post Office
   🏤. A3/B1/B2/B3/C3
Primrose St C3
Priory ♦. B1
Prospect St. C3
Quarry Rd B3
Queen St C2

Regent St C2
Ridge La A3
Ridge St A3
Royal Lancaster
   Infirmary (A&E) 🏥 C2
Rydal Rd B3
Ryelands Park A1
St Georges Quay A1
St John's 🏛 B2
St Leonard's Gate. B2
St Martin's Rd C2
St Nicholas Arcades
   Shopping Centre B2
St Oswald St C3
St Peter's ♦ B3
St Peter's Rd B3
Salisbury Rd B1
Scotch Quarry Urban
   Park C3
Shire Hall/HM Prison B1
Sibsey St B1
Skerton Bridge A2
South Rd C2
Station Rd B1
Stirling Rd C3
Storey Ave B1
Sunnyside La C3
Sylvester St C3
Tarnsyke Rd A1
Thurnham St C2
Town Hall B2
Troutbeck Rd. C3
Ulleswater Rd B3
University of Cumbria C3
Vicarage Field B1
Vue 🎬 B2
West Rd B1
Westbourne Dr C1
Westbourne Rd C1
Westham St. C2
White Cross Bsns Park . . .C2
Wheatfield St B1
Williamson Rd C3
Willow La C1
Windermere Rd C3
Wingate-Saul Rd. B1
Wolseley St C3
Woodville St C3
Wyresdale Rd C1

Leeds 336

Aire St B3
Aireside Centre B3
Albion Pl B4
Albion St B4
Albion Way B1
Alma St A6
Arcades 🏛 B4
Armley Rd B1
Back Burley Lodge Rd . . .A1
Back Hyde Terr A2
Back Row. C3
Bath Rd C3
Beckett St A6
Bedford St. B4
Belgrave St A4
Belle View Rd. A1
Benson St A5
Black Bull St. C5
Blenheim Walk A3
Boar La. B4
Bond St B4
Bow St C5
Bowman La B5
Brewery ✦. C4
Bridge St A5/B5
Briggate B4
Bruce Gdns C1
Burley Rd A1
Burley St A2
Burmantofts St B6
Bus & Coach Station B5
Butterly St C4
Butts Cr B4
Brewery Wharf C5
Byron St A5
Call La. B4
Calverley St A3/B3
Canal St B1
Canal Wharf C3
Carlisle Rd A1
Cavendish Rd A1
Cavendish St. A2
Chadwick St C5
Cherry Pl A6
Cherry Row A5
City Museum 🏛 B4
City Palace of
   Varieties 🏛 B4
City Sq B3
Civic Hall 🏛 A4
Clarence Road C5
Clarendon Rd A2
Clarendon Way. A3
Clark La C6
Clay Pit La A4
Cloberry St A2
Clyde Approach C1
Clyde Gdns. C1
Coleman St C2
Commercial St B4
Concord St A5
Cookridge St A4
Copley Hill C1
Corn Exchange 🏛 B4
Cromer Terr A2
Cromwell St A6
Cross Catherine St B6
Cross Green La. C6
Cross Stamford St A5
Crown & County
   Courts B5
Crown Point Bridge C5
Crown Point Retail Pk C4
Crown Point Rd. C4
David St C3
Dent St C6
Derwent Pl C3
Dial St C6

Dock St. C4
Dolly La A6
Domestic St. C2
Duke St. B5
Duncan St B4
Dyer St B6
East Field St B6
East Pde B3
East St C5
Eastgate. B5
Easy Rd. C6
Edward St B4
Ellerby La. C6
Ellerby Rd C6
Fenton St A3
Fire Station B2
First Direct Arena B4
Fish St. B4
Flax Pl. B5
Gelderd Rd C1
George St. B4
Globe Rd C1
Gloucester Cr B1
Gower St A5
Grafton St A4
Grand Theatre B4
Granville Rd. A6
Great George St C4
Great Wilson St. C4
Greek St. B3
Green La C4
Hanover Ave A2
Hanover La A2
Hanover Sq A2
Hanover Way A2
Harewood St B4
Harrison St B4
Haslewood Cl B6
Haslewood Drive B6
High Court. B5
Holbeck St. C2
Holdforth Cl C1
Holdforth Gdns B1
Holdforth Gr C1
Holdforth Pl C1
Holy Trinity B4
Hope Rd A5
Hunslet La C4
Hunslet Rd. C4
Hyde Terr. A2
Infirmary St B3
Information Ctr B3
Ingram Row C3
Junction St C4
Kelso Gdns A2
Kelso Rd A2
Kelso St A2
Kendal La A2
Kendell St C4
Kidacre St C4
King Edward St B4
King St B3
Kippax Pl C6
Kirkgate B4
Kirkgate Market B4
Kirkstall Rd A1
Kitson St C6
Lady La B4
Lands La B3
Lavender Walk B6
Leeds Art Gallery B3
Leeds Bridge C4
Leeds Coll of Music . . .B5
Leeds General Infirmary
(A&E) A3
Leeds Metropolitan
University A3/A4
Leeds Museum
Discovery Centre C5
Leeds Shopping Plaza .B3
Leeds Station B3
Leeds University. A3
Library B3
Lincoln Green Rd A6
Lincoln Rd A6
Lindsey Gdns A6
Lindsey Rd A6
Lisbon St B3
Little Queen St B3
Long Close La C6
Lord St C1
Lovell Park A4
Lovell Park Rd A4
Lovell Rd A5
Lower Brunswick St. . . .A5
Mabgate. A6
Macauly St A5
Magistrates Court A3
Manor Rd C3
Mark La B4
Marlborough St B2
Marsh La B5
Marshall St C3
Meadow La C4
Meadow Rd C4
Melbourne St A5
Merrion Centre A4
Merrion St A4
Merrion Way A4
Mill St B5
Millennium Sq A3
Mount Preston St A3
Mushroom St A5
Neville St C4
New Briggate A4/B4
New Market St B4
New Station St B4
New York Rd A5
New York St B5
Nile St A4
Nippet La A6
North St A4
Northern St B3
Oak Rd B1
Oxford Pl B3
Oxford Row A3
Park Cross St B3
Park La A2
Park Pl B3
Park Row B4

Park Sq. B3
Park Sq East B3
Park Sq West B3
Park St B3
Police Station B5
Pontefract La B6
Portland Cr A3
Portland Way A4
Post Office B4/B5
Project Space
Leeds C2
Quarry House (NHS/DSS
Headquarters) B6
Quebec St B3
Queen St B3
Railway St B5
Rectory St A6
Regent St. A5
Richmond St C5
Rigton Approach B6
Rigton Dr B6
Rillbank Rd A1
Rosebank Rd A1
Royal Armouries C5
Russell St B3
Rutland St B2
St Anne's Cath (RC) † .A4
St Anne's St A4
St James' Hospital A6
St Johns Centre A3
St John's Rd A2
St Mary's St B5
St Pauls St B3
St Peter's B5
Saxton La B5
Sayner La. C5
Shakespeare Ave A6
Shannon St B6
Sheepscar St South . . .A5
Siddall St C3
Skinner La A5
South Pde B3
Sovereign St C4
Spence La C2
Springfield Mount A2
Springwell Ct C2
Springwell Rd C2
Springwell St C2
Stoney Rock La A6
Studio Rd A1
Sutton St C2
Sweet St C3
Sweet St West C3
Swinegate B4
Templar St B5
The Calls B5
The Close B6
The Core B4
The Drive B6
The Garth. B5
The Headrow. B3/B4
The Lane B5
The Light B4
The Parade B6
The Tetley C4
Thoresby Pl A3
Torre Rd A6
Town Hall A3
Union Pl C3
Union St B4
Upper Accomodation
Rd A6
Upper Basinghall St. . .B4
Vicar La B4
Victoria Bridge. C4
Victoria Quarter B4
Victoria Rd. C3
Vue B4
Wade La A4
Washington St A1
Water La C3
Waterloo Rd C5
Wellington Rd B2/C1
Wellington St B3
West St. B2
West Yorkshire
Playhouse B5
Westfield Rd A1
Westgate. B3
Whitehall Rd B3/C2
Whitelock St A5
Willis St. C6
Willow Approach A1
Willow Ave. A1
Willow Terrace Rd A3
Wintoun St A5
Woodhouse La A3/A4
Woodsley Rd A1
York Pl B3
York Rd. B6
Yorkshire Television
Studios A1

Leicester   336
Abbey St. A2
All Saints' A1
Aylestone Rd C2
Bath La A1
Bede Park C1
Bedford St A3
Bedford St South A3
Belgrave Gate A2
Belle Vue B2
Belvoir St. B2
Braunstone Gate B1
Burleys Way A2
Burnmoor St C2
Bus Station A2
Canning St A2
Carlton St C2
Castle B1
Castle Gardens B1
Cathedral † B2
Causeway La A2
Charles St B3
Chatham St B2
Christow St A3
Church Gate A2
City Gallery B3

Civic Centre. B2
Clank St B2
Clock Tower B2
Clyde St A3
Colton St B3
Conduit St B3
Crafton St A3
Craven St A1
Crown Courts B2
De Lux A2
De Montfort Hall C3
De Montfort St C3
De Montfort Univ C1
Deacon St C2
Dover St B3
Duns La B1
Dunton St A1
East St B3
Eastern Boulevard C1
Edmonton Rd A3
Erskine St A3
Filbert St C1
Filbert St East C2
Fire Station A3
Fleet St A3
Friar La B2
Friday St A2
Gateway St C1
Glebe St B3
Granby St B3
Grange La C2
Grasmere St C1
Great Central St A1
Guildhall B2
Guru Nanak Sikh
Museum B1
Halford St B3
Havelock St. C2
Haymarket Sh Ctr A2
High St B2
Highcross St A1
Highcross Sh Ctr A2
HM Prison B1
Horsefair St B2
Humberstone Gate A2
Humberstone Rd A3
Infirmary St C2
Information Ctr C2
Jarrom St C2
Jewry Wall B1
Kamloops Cr A3
King Richards Rd B1
King St B2
Lancaster Rd C3
LCB Depot B3
Lee St A3
Leicester Royal
Infirmary (A&E) C2
Leicester Station B3
Library B1
Little Theatre, The B3
London Rd C3
Lower Brown St B2
Magistrates Court B2
Manitoba Rd A3
Mansfield St A2
Market B2
Market St B2
Mill La C1
Montreal Rd A3
Narborough Rd North .B1
Nelson Mandela Park . .C2
New Park St B1
New St B2
New Walk C3
New Walk Museum &
Art Gallery C3
Newarke Houses B1
Newarke St B2
Northgate St A1
Orchard St A3
Ottawa Rd A3
Oxford St C2
Upper Brown St B2
Phoenix Square B3
Police Station B5
Post Office
. . . . .A1/B2/C2/C3
Prebend St. C3
Princess Rd East C3
Princess Rd West C3
Queen St B3
Regent College C3
Regent Rd C2/C3
Repton St A1
Rutland St B3
St George St B3
St Georges Way B3
St John St A2
St Margaret's A2
St Margaret's Way A2
St Martins B2
St Mary de Castro B1
St Matthew's Way A3
St Nicholas B1
St Nicholas Circle. B1
Sanvey Gate A2
Silver St B2
Slater St A1
Soar La A1
South Albion St. B3
Southampton St B3
Swain St B3
Swan St A1
The Gateway C2
The Newarke B1
The Rally Com Park . . .A1
Tigers Way C3
Tower St C3
Town Hall B2
Tudor Rd B1
University of Leicester .C3
University Rd C3
Upperton Rd C1
Vaughan Way A1
Walnut St C1
Watling St A1
Welford Rd C2
Welford Rd Stadium . .C2

Lewes   336
Abinger Pl A2
All Saints Centre B2
Ambulance Station A3
Anne of Cleves Ho A1
Barbican Ho Mus B1
Brewery A3
Brook St. A2
Brooks Rd A2
Bus Station B2
Castle Ditch La B1
Castle Precincts B1
Chapel Hill. B1
Church La A1/A2
Cliffe High St B2
Cliffe Industrial Est . . .C3
Cluny St C1
Cockshut Rd C1
Convent Field C2
Coombe Rd A2
County Hall B1
County Records Office .B1
Court B2
Court Rd. B1
Crown Court B2
Cuilfail Tunnel B3
Davey's La A3
East St B2
Eastport La C1
Fire Station B2
Fisher St. B2
Friars Walk B2
Garden St. B2
Government Offices . . .B1
Grange Rd B1
Ham La C3
Harveys Way B2
Hereward Way A2
High St B1/B2
Hop Gallery B2
Information Ctr B2
Keere St. B1
King Henry's Rd C1
Lancaster St B2
Landport Rd A1
Leisure Centre C3
Lewes Bridge B2
Lewes Castle B1
Lewes Football Gd C2
Lewes Golf Course B3
Lewes Southern
By-Pass C2
Lewes Station B2
Library B2
Malling Ind Est A3
Malling Brook Ind Est . .A3
Malling Hill A3
Malling St A3/B3
Market St B2
Martyr's Monument. . . .B2
Mayhew Way A2
Morris Rd A2
Mountfield Rd. C2
New Rd B1
Newton Rd A1
North St A2/B2
Offham Rd B1
Old Malling Way A1
Orchard Rd A3
Paddock La B1
Paddock Rd A1
Paddock Sports Gd B1
Park Rd. B1
Pelham Terr A3
Pells Open Air
Swimming Pool A1
Phoenix Causeway. . . .B2
Phoenix Ind Est. B2
Phoenix Pl B2
Pinwell Rd B2
Police Station B1
Post Office
. . . . A2/B1/B2/C1
Prince Edward's Rd . . .C1
Priory St. C1
Priory of St Pancras
(remains of) C1
Railway La B2
Railway Land Nature
Reserve B3
Rotten Row B1
Rufus Cl B1
St Pancras Rd C1
St John St B2
St John's Terr B1
St Nicholas La B2
Sewage Works C2
South Downs College .C2
South St B3/C3
Southdowns Rd A2
Southerham Junction . .C3
Southover Grange
Gdns B1
Southover High St B1
Southover Rd B1
Spences Field A2
Spences La A2
Stansfield Rd. A2
Station Rd B2
Station St B2
Sun St B1
Sussex Downs College .C2
Sussex Police HQ C1
Talbot Terr. B1
The Avenue B1
The Course C1
The Martlets A2

Lincoln   337
Alexandra Terr B1
Anchor St. C1
Arboretum B3
Arboretum Ave B3
Baggholme Rd B3
Bailgate A2
Beaumont Fee B1
Brayford Way C1
Brayford Wharf East . . .C1
Brayford Wharf North . .B1
Bruce Rd A2
Burton Rd A1
Bus Station (City). B2
Canwick Rd C2
Cardinal's Hat B2
Carline Rd B1
Castle B1
Castle St. A1
Cathedral † B2
Cathedral St B2
Cecil St. A2
Chapel La A2
Cheviot St B3
Church La A2
City Hall B1
Clasketgate B2
Clayton Sports Gd A3
Coach Park C2
Collection, The B2
County Hospl (A&E) . . .B3
County Office C1
Courts B1
Croft St B2
Cross St A2
Crown Courts B1
Curle Ave A3
Danesgate B2
Drill Hall B2
Drury La B1
East Bight A2
East Gate B2
Eastcliff Rd B3
Eastgate. B2
Egerton Rd A3
Ellis Windmill A1
Engine Shed, The C1
Environment Agency . .C2
Exchequer Gate B2
Firth Rd C1
Flaxengate B2
Florence St B3
George St. C2
Good La A2
Gray St A1
Great Northern Terr. . . .C3
Great Northern Terrace
Industrial Estate. C3
Greetwell Rd. B3
Greetwellgate. B3
Haffenden Rd A3
High St B2/C1
HM Prison A2
Hospital (Private) A1
Hungate B2
James St A2
Jews House & Ct B2
Kesteven St C2
Langworthgate A2
Lawn Visitor Centre,
The A1
Lee Rd A2
Library B2
Lincoln College B2
Lincoln Central Sta . . .C2
Lincolnshire Life/Royal
Lincolnshire Regiment
Museum A1
Lindum Rd B2
Lindum Sports Ground .A3
Lindum Terr. B3
Mainwaring Rd A3
Manor Rd A2
Market B2
Massey Rd A3
Medieval Bishop's
Palace B2
Mildmay St A1
Mill Rd A1
Millman Rd B3
Minster Yard B2
Monks Rd B3
Montague St B2
Mount St A1
Nettleham Rd A2
Newland B1
Newport A2
Newport Arch A2
Newport Cemetery A2
Northgate A2
Odeon C1
Orchard St B1
Oxford St C2
Park St C1
Pelham Bridge C2
Pelham St C2
Police Station B2
Portland St C2
Post Office
. . . . . . .A1/A2/B1/B3/C2
Potter Gate A2
Priory Gate B2
Queensway A3
Rasen La A1
Ropewalk. C1
Rosemary La B2
St Anne's Rd B3
St Benedict's B1
St Giles Ave A3
St John's Rd A2

St Marks St C1
St Mark's St C1
St Mary-Le-
Wigford C1
St Mary's St C2
St Nicholas St A2
St Swithin's B2
Saltergate B2
Saxon St A1
Sch of Art & Design . . .B2
Sewell Rd B3
Silver St B2
Sincil St C2
Spital St A2
Spring Hill B1
Stamp End C3
Steep Hill B2
Stonebow &
Guildhall C2
Stonefield Ave A2
Tentercroft St. C1
The Avenue B1
The Grove A3
Theatre Royal B2
Tritton Retail Park C1
Tritton Rd C1
Union Rd B1
University of Lincoln . . .C1
Upper Lindum St B3
Upper Long Leys Rd . .A1
Usher B2
Vere St A2
Victoria St B1
Victoria Terr B1
Vine St B3
Wake St A1
Waldeck St A1
Waterside Sh Ctr C2
Waterside North C2
Waterside South C2
West Pde B1
Westgate. A2
Wigford Way C1
Williamson St A2
Wilson St A1
Winn St B3
Wragby Rd A3
Yarborough Rd A1

Liverpool   337
Abercromby Sq. C5
Acc Liverpool C2
Addison St A3
Adelaide Rd B6
Ainsworth St B4
Albany Rd B6
Albert Dock C2
Albert Edward Rd C6
Angela St C6
Anson St B4
Archbishop Blanche
High School. B6
Argyle St C3
Arrad St C5
Ashton St B5
Audley St A4
Back Leeds St A2
Basnett St B3
Bath St A1
Beatles Story C2
Beckwith St C3
Bedford Close. C5
Bedford St North C5
Bedford St South C5
Benson St C4
Berry St C4
Birkett St A4
Bixteth St. B2
Blackburne Place. C4
Bluecoat B3
Bold Place C4
Bold St C4
Bolton St B3
Bridport St B4
Bronte St B4
Brook St. A1
Brownlow Hill. B4/B5
Brownlow St. B5
Brunswick Rd A5
Brunswick St B2
Bus Station C2
Butler Cr A6
Byrom St A3
Caledonia St C5
Cambridge St C5
Camden St A4
Canada Blvd B1
Canning Dock C2
Canterbury St A4
Cardwell St C6
Carver St A4
Cases St B3
Castle St. B2
Catherine St C5
Cavern Club B3
Central Library A3
Central Station B3
Chapel St B2
Charlotte St. B3
Chatham Place C6
Chatham St C5
Cheapside B2
Chestnut St C5
Christian St A4
Church St. B3
Churchill Way North . . .A3
Churchill Way South . . .B4
Clarence St B4
Coach Station A4
Cobden St A5
Cockspur St A2
College La B3
College St North A5
College St South A5
Colquitt St C4
Comus St A3
Concert St C4
Connaught Rd B6
Cook St B2

Copperas Hill B4
Cornwallis St C3
Covent Garden B2
Craven St A4
Cropper St B3
Crown St B5/C6
Cumberland St B2
Dale St B2
Dansie St B4
Daulby St B5
Dawson St B3
Derby Sq B2
Drury La B2
Duckinfield St C4
Duke St C3
Earle St. A2
East St A2
Eaton St A2
Echo Arena C2
Edgar St A3
Edge La B6
Edinburgh Rd A6
Edmund St B2
Elizabeth St B5
Elliot St B3
Empire Theatre B4
Empress Rd B6
Epworth St A5
Erskine St A5
Everyman Theatre C5
Exchange St East B2
Fact Centre, The C4
Falkland St A5
Falkner St C5/C6
Farnworth St A6
Fenwick St B2
Fielding St A6
Fleet St C3
Fraser St A4
Freemasons Row A2
Gardner Row A3
Gascoyne St. A2
George Pier Head. C1
George St. B2
Gibralter Road A1
Gilbert St C3
Gildart St B4
Gill St B4
Goree B2
Gower St C2
Gradwell St C3
Great Crosshall St A3
Great George St C4
Great Howard St A1
Great Newton St B4
Greek St B4
Green La B3
Greenside A5
Greetham St C4
Gregson St. A5
Grenville St C3
Grinfield St C6
Grove St C5
Guelph St A6
Hackins Hey B2
Haigh St A4
Hall La B6
Hanover St B3
Harbord St C6
Hardman St C4
Harker St B4
Hart St B4
Hatton Garden B2
Hawke St B4
Helsby St B5
Henry St C3
Highfield St A2
Highgate St B6
Hilbre St B4
Hope Place C4
Hope St C4
Houghton St B3
Hunter St A3
Hutchinson St A6
Information Ctr C2
Institute For The
Performing Arts C4
Irvine St B6
Irwell St B2
Islington A4
James St B2
James St Station B2
Jenkinson St A4
Johnson St A3
Jubilee Drive. B6
Kempston St A4
Kensington A6
Kensington Gdns A6
Kensington St A6
Kent St C3
King Edward St B1
Kinglake St B6
Knight St C4
Lace St A3
Langsdale St A4
Law Courts C2
Leece St C4
Leeds St A2
Leopold Rd C6
Lime St B3
Lime St Station B4
Little Woolton St B5
Liver St C2
Liverpool John Moores
University A3/B4/C4
Liverpool Landing
Stage B1
Liverpool One C2
London Rd A4/B4
Lord Nelson St B4
Lord St B2
Lovat St A6
Low Hill A5
Low Wood St A6
Lydia Ann St C3
Mansfield St A4
Marmaduke St B6

Marsden St A6
Martensen St B6
Marybone A3
Maryland St C4
Mason St B6
Mathew St B3
May St. B4
Melville Place C6
Merseyside Maritime
Museum C2
Metquarter B3
Metropolitan Cathedral
(RC) † B5
Midghall St A2
Molyneux Rd A6
Moor Place B4
Moorfields. B2
Moorfields Station B2
Moss St A5
Mount Pleasant B4/B5
Mount St C4
Mount Vernon B6
Mulberry St C5
Municipal Buildings. . . .B2
Mus of Liverpool B1
Myrtle Gdns C6
Myrtle St C5
Naylor St A2
Nelson St C3
Neptune Theatre B3
New Islington A4
New Quay B1
Newington St C3
New John St A4
North St A3
North View B6
Norton St A4
Oakes St B5
Odeon B4
Old Hall St A1
Old Leeds St A2
Oldham Place C4
Oldham St C4
Olive St C6
Open Eye Gallery C3
Oriel St A2
Ormond St B2
Orphan St C6
Overbury St C6
Overton St C6
Oxford St C5
Paisley St A1
Pall Mall A2
Paradise St C3
Park La C3
Parker St B3
Parr St C3
Peach St B5
Pembroke Place B4
Pembroke St B5
Philharmonic Hall C5
Pickop St A2
Pilgrim St C4
Pitt St C3
Playhouse Theatre B3
Pleasant St B4
Police HQ C3
Police Station A4/B4
Pomona St B4
Port of Liverpool
Building B1
Post Office . . A2/A4/A5/A6/
B2/B3/B4/C4
Pownall St C2
Prescot St A5
Preston St B3
Princes Dock A1
Princes Gdns A2
Princes Jetty. A1
Princes Pde B1
Princes St B2
Pythian St A6
Queen Sq Bus Station .B3
Queensland St C6
Queensway Tunnel
(Docks exit). B1
Queensway Tunnel
(Entrance). B3
Radio City B3
Ranelagh St B3
Redcross St B2
Renfrew St B6
Renshaw St C4
Richmond Row A4
Richmond St B3
Rigby St A2
Roberts St A1
Rock St A5
Rodney St C4
Rokeby St A4
Romily St. A6
Roscoe La C4
Roscoe St C4
Rose Hill A4
Royal Court Theatre . . .B3
Royal Liver
Building B1
Royal Liverpool Hospital
(A&E) B5
Royal Mail St B4
Rumford Place B2
Rumford St B2
Russell St B4
St Andrew St B4
St Anne St A4
St Georges Hall B3
St John's Centre B3
St John's Gdns B3
St John's La B3
St Joseph's Cr A4
St Minishull St B5
St Nicholas Place B1
St Paul's Sq A2
St Vincent Way B4
Salisbury St A4
Salthouse Dock C2
Salthouse Quay C2
Sandon St C5

Saxony Rd B6
Schomberg St A6
School La B3
Seel St C3
Seymour St B4
Shaw St A5
Sidney Place C6
Sir Thomas St B3
Skelhorne St B4
Slater St C3
Slavery Museum C2
Smithdown La B6
Soho Sq A4
Soho St A4
South John St B2
Springfield A4
Stafford St A4
Standish St A3
Stanley St B2
Strand St C2
Suffolk St C3
Tabley St C3
Tarleton St B3
Tate Gallery C2
Teck St B6
Temple St B2
The Beacon B3
The Strand B2
Titheharn St A2
Town Hall B2
Traffic Police HQ B4
Trowbridge St B4
Trueman St A3
Union St B2
Unity Theatre C4
University C5
Univ of Liverpool B5
Upper Duke St C4
Upper Frederick St C3
Upper Baker St A6
Vauxhall Rd A2
Vernon St B2
Victoria Gallery &
Museum B5
Victoria St B2
Vine St C5
Wakefield St A4
Walker Art Gallery A3
Walker St A4
Wapping C2
Water St B1/B2
Waterloo Rd A1
Wavertree Rd B6
West Derby Rd A6
West Derby St B5
Whitechapel B3
Western Approaches
War Museum B2
Whitley Gdns A5
William Brown St B3
William Henry St A4
Williamson Sq B3
Williamson St B3
Williamson's Tunnels
Heritage Centre C6
Women's Hospital C6
Wood St C3
World Museum,
Liverpool A3
York St C3

Llandudno   337
Abbey Pl B1
Abbey Rd B1
Adelphi St B2
Alexandra Rd C2
Anglesey Rd A1
Argyll Rd B3
Arvon Ave A2
Atlee Cl. C3
Augusta St B2
Back Madoc St B2
Bodafon St. A3
Bodhyfryd Rd A2
Bodnant Cr C3
Bodnant Rd C2
Bridge Rd C2
Bryniau Rd C1
Builder St C2
Builder St West C2
Cabin Lift A2
Camera Obscura A3
Caroline Rd B2
Chapel St A2
Charlton St B2
Church Cr C1
Church Walks A2
Claremont Rd B2
Clement Ave A3
Clifton Rd B2
Clonmel St B2
Coach Station B2
Conway Rd C2
Council St West C2
Cricket and Rec Gd. . . .C2
Cwlach Rd A1
Cwlach St A1
Cwm Howard La C3
Cwm Pl C3
Cwm Rd C3
Dale Rd C2
Deganwy Ave B2
Denness Pl C2
Dinas Rd B1
Dolydd C3
Erol Pl C2
Ewloe Dr. C3
Fairways C3
Fforter Dewi B3
Fforter Dulyn C2
Fforter Dwyfor C2
Fforter Elisabeth. C3
Fforter Gwynedd. C3
Fforter Las C3
Fforter Morfa C3
Fforter Penrhyn C3
Fforter Tudno C3
Fforter yr Orsedd C3
Fforter Ysbyty C2

Llanelli

Fire & Ambulance Sta .B3
Garage St. B3
George St. A2
Gloddaeth St. C1
Gloddaeth St. B2
Gogarth Rd A2
Great Orme Mines ✦ .A1
Great Ormes Rd A2
Happy Valley A2
Happy Valley Rd A2
Haulfre Gardens ❀ ...A1
Herkomer Cr C1
Hill Terr A2
Home Front Mus 🏛 ...B1
Hospice B1
Howard Rd B3
Information Ctr 🛈 ...B1
Invalids' Walk B1
James St B3
Jubilee St. B3
King's Ave C2
King's Rd C2
Knowles Rd C2
Lees Rd C2
Library B2
Lifeboat Station B2
Llandudno A2
Llandudno (A&E) 🏥 ..C1
Llandudno Station ≷ .B3
Llandudno Town
   Football Ground....C2
Llewelyn Ave A2
Lloyd St West B1
Lloyd St B2
Llwynon Rd A1
Llys Maelgwn B2
Madoc St B2
Maelgwn Rd B2
Maesdu Bridge C2
Maesdu Rd C2/C3
Maes-y-Cwm C3
Maes-y-Orsedd C2
Marian Pl C2
Marian Rd C2
Marine Drive (Toll) ..A3
Market Hall A2
Market St. A2
Miniature Golf Course.A1
Morfa Rd B3
Mostyn 🚏 B3
Mostyn Broadway B3
Mostyn St. B2
Mowbray Rd A2
New St A2
Norman Rd B3
North Parade A2
North Wales Golf
   Links.............C1
Old Bank Gallery 🏛 .A2
Old Rd A2
Oxford Rd B3
Parc Llandudno Ret Pk B3
Pier ✦ A3
Plas Rd A2
Police Station B3
Post Office 📮 B3/C2
Promenade A3
Pyllau Rd A1
Rectory La A2
Rhuddan Ave C2
St Andrew's Ave B2
St Andrew's Pl. B2
St Beuno's Rd A1
St David's B2
St David's Rd B2
St George's Pl B2
St Mary's Rd B2
St Seriol's Rd B2
Salisbury Pass B1
Salisbury Rd B2
Somerset St B3
South Parade A3
Stephen St. B3
TA Centre B2
Tabor Hill A2
The Oval B1
The Parade A3
Town Hall B2
Trinity Ave C1
Trinity Cres C1
Trinity Sq A2
Tudno St. A2
Ty-Coch Rd B2
Ty-Gwyn Rd A1/A2
Ty'n-y-Coed Rd A2
Vaughan St B3
Victoria Shopping Ctr.B3
Victoria Tram Sta 🚋 .A2
War Memorial ✦ A2
Werny Wylan C3
West Parade B1
Whiston Pass A2
Winllan Ave C2
Wyddfyd Rd A1
York Rd A2

Llanelli 337

Alban Rd. B3
Albert St. B3
Als St. B3
Amos St C3
Andrew St A1
Ann St. B3
Annesley St B2
Arfryn Ave A3
Arthur St B2
Belvedere Rd. A1
Bigyn La. B3
Bigyn Park Terr. B3
Bigyn Rd. B3
Bond Ave C3
Brettenham St A2
Bridge St B2
Bryn Pl. B2
Bryn Rd C1
Bryn Terr C1
Brynhyfryd Rd. A2
Brynmelyn Ave A3
Brynmor Rd B1

Bryn-More Rd. C1
Burry St C1
Bus Station C2
Caersalem Terr. C2
Cambrian St C2
Caswell St C3
Cedric St B3
Cemetery A1
Chapman St. A1
Charles Terr A1
Church St. B2
Clos Caer Elms A1
Clos Sant Paul. B2
Coastal Link Rd. B1/C1
Coldstream St B2
Coleshill Terr. B1
College Hill B3
College Sq. B2
Copperworks Rd. C2
Coronation Ave C2
Corporation Ave A3
Council Offices.......B2
Court B2
Cowell St B2
Cradock St C3
Craig Ave C3
Cricket Ground A1
Derwent St A1
Dillwyn St C1
Druce St. C1
Elizabeth St B2
Emma St B2
Erw Rd B1
Felinfoel Rd. A1
Fire Station A3
Firth Rd C3
Fron Terr C3
Furnace Rugby
   Football Ground...A1
Gelli-On B2
George St. C2
Gilbert Cres A3
Gilbert Rd A2
Glanmor Rd C2
Glanmor Terr. C2
Glasfryn Terr A3
Glenalla Rd C1
Glevering St B2
Goring Rd. A2
Gorsedd Circle 🌐 ...A2
Grant St C3
Graveyard B2
Great Western Cl C2
Greenway St B1
Hall St. B2
Harries Ave B2
Hedley Terr B3
Heol Elli B3
Heol Goffa A3
Heol Nant-y-Felin A3
Heol Siloh B2
Hick St C2
High St C2
Indoor Bowls Centre .B1
Inkerman St. B2
Island Pl B2
James St B3
King George Ave B3
Lake View Cl A2
Lakefield Pl. C1
Lakefield Rd C1
Langland Rd C1
Leisure Centre B1
Library B2
Llanelli House 🏛 ...B2
Llanelli Parish
   Church...........B2
Llanelli RUFC
   (Stradey Park)....A1
Llanelli Station ≷ ..C2
Llewellyn St. C2
Lliedi Cres B3
Lloyd St B3
Llys Alys B3
Llys Fran. A3
Llysnewedd C1
Long Row B2
Maes Gors C2
Maesyrhaf A3
Mansel St. B3
Marblehall Rd B3
Marborough Rd A2
Margam St C2
Marged St C2
Marine St. C1
Market B2
Market St. B2
Marsh St. C2
Martin Rd C3
Miles St. A1
Mill La. A3/B2
Mincing La. B2
Murray St. B2
Myn y Mor B1
Nathan St. C1
Nelson Terr C1
Nevill St C2
New Dock Rd B3
New Rd A1
New Zealand St. A1
Old Lodge A2
Old Rd. A2
Paddock St B2
Palace Ave. B3
Parc Howard A2
Parc Howard Museum &
   Art Gallery 🏛....A2
Park Cres B1
Park St. B1
Parkview Terr B1
Pemberton St C2
Pembrey Rd A1
Peoples Park B2
Police Station 🚨 ...B2
Post Office 📮
   ...A1/A2/B2/C1/C2
Pottery Pl. B3
Pottery St B3
Princess St B1

Prospect Pl A2
Pryce St A1
Queen Mary's Walk ...C3
Queen Victoria Rd ...C1
Raby St C1
Railway Terr C2
Ralph St C2
Ralph Terr C1
Regalia Terr. B3
Rhydyrafon A3
Richard St C2
Robinson St. A1
Roland Ave A1
Russell St. C3
St David's Cl C1
St Elli Shopping Ctr .B2
St Margaret's Dr. A1
Spowart Ave A1
Station Rd B2/C2
Stepney Pl. B2
Stepney St. B2
Stewart St. A1
Strady Park Ave A1
Sunny Hill A2
Swansea Rd A2
TA Centre B2
Talbot St. C3
Temple St. B3
The Avenue Cilfig A2
The Mariners C1
Theatr Elli 🎭 B2
Thomas St A2
Toft Pl. A3
Town Hall B2
Traeth Ffordd C1
Trinity Rd C3
Trinity Terr C1
Tunnel Rd B3
Tyisha Rd C2
Union Blgs B2
Upper Robinson St. ...A1
Vauxhall St B2
Walter's Rd B3
Waun Lanyrafon B2
Waun Rd A3
Wern Rd A3
West End A2
Y Bwthyn C3
Zion Row B3

London 338

Abbey Orchard St. E4
Abbey St. E8
Abchurch La D7
Abingdon St E5
Achilles Way D3
Acton St. B5
Addington St E5
Air St. D4
Albany St. A3
Albemarle St. D4
Albert Embankment ...F5
Alberta St. F6
Aldenham St A4
Alderney St F3
Aldersgate St. C7
Aldford St D3
Aldgate ⊖ C8
Aldgate High St. C8
Aldwych C5
Allsop Pl. B2
Alscot Rd E8
Amwell St. B6
Andrew Borde St. C4
Angel ⊖ A6
Appold St C8
Argyle Sq B5
Argyle St B5
Argyll St C4
Arnold Circus B8
Artillery La C8
Artillery Row E4
Ashbridge St. B2
Association of
   Photographers
   Gallery 🏛.........B7
Baker St ⊖ B2
Baker St. B2
Balaclava Rd F8
Balcombe St B2
Baldwin's Gdns C6
Balfour St. F7
Baltic St. B7
Bank ⊖ C7
Bank Museum 🏛 C7
Bank of England C7
Bankside D7
Bankside Gallery 🏛 .D6
Banner St. B7
Barbican ≷⊖ C7
Barbican Gallery 🏛 .C7
Basil St. E2
Bastwick St B7
Bateman's Row B8
Bath St. B7
Bath Terr E7
Bayley St C4
Baylis Rd E6
Bayswater Rd D2
Beak St. D4
Beauchamp Pl. E2
Bedford Row C5
Bedford Sq C4
Bedford St D5
Bedford Way B4
Beech St C7
Belgrave Pl. E3
Belgrave Rd F3
Belgrave Sq. E3
Bell La C8
Belvedere Rd. E5
Berkeley Sq. D3
Berkeley St D3
Bermondsey St. E8
Bernard St B5
Berners Pl. C4
Berners St. C4
Berwick St. C4
Bessborough St F4

Bethnal Green Rd. B8
Bevenden St B7
Bevis Marks. C8
BFI (British Film
   Institute)........D5
BFI London IMAX
   Cinema D6
Bidborough St. B5
Binney St C3
Birdcage Walk E4
Bishopsgate C8
Black Prince Rd F5
Blackfriars ≷⊖ D6
Blackfriars Bridge ..D6
Blackfriars Rd E6
Blandford St. C2
Blomfield St. C7
Bloomsbury St. C4
Bloomsbury Way C5
Bolton St. D3
Bond St ⊖ C3
Borough ⊖ E7
Borough High St. E7
Borough Rd E6
Boswell St. C5
Bourne St. F3
Bow St. C5
Bowling Green La. B6
Brad St. E6
Brandon St. F7
Bressenden Pl. E4
Brewer St. D4
Brick St. D3
Bridge St. E5
Britannia Walk B7
British Film Institute
   (BFI).............D5
British Library 🏛 ..B4
British Museum 🏛 ...C5
Britton St. B6
Broad Sanctuary E4
Broadley St. C2
Broadway. E4
Brompton Rd. E2
Brompton Sq. E2
Brook Dr. F6
Brook St. D3
Brown St C2
Brunswick Pl. B7
Brunswick Sq. B5
Brushfield St. C8
Bruton St. D3
Bryanston St. C2
Bryanston St C2
BT Centre. C7
Buckingham Gate. E4
Buckingham
   Palace 🏛.........E4
Buckingham
   Palace Rd. F3
Bunhill Row B7
Byward St. D8
Cabinet War Rooms &
   Churchill Museum 🏛 E4
Cadogan La E3
Cadogan Pl E3
Cadogan Sq. E2
Cadogan St. F2
Cale St F2
Caledonian Rd A5
Calshot St A5
Calthorpe St B5
Calvert Ave B8
Cambridge Circus C4
Cambridge Sq. C2
Cambridge St. F3
Camomile St. C8
Cannon St. D7
Cannon St ≷⊖ D7
Capland St. B1
Carey St. C5
Carlisle La E5
Carlisle Pl. E4
Carlton House Terr ..D4
Carmelite St. D6
Carnaby St. C4
Carter La. C6
Carthusian St C7
Cartwright Gdns. B5
Castle Baynard St. ...D6
Cavendish Pl. C3
Cavendish Sq. C3
Caxton Hall E4
Caxton St. E4
Central St B7
Chalton St. B4
Chancery Lane ⊖ C6
Chapel St. C2
Chapel St. E3
Charing Cross ≷⊖ ...D5
Charing Cross Rd C4
Charles II St. D4
Charles St. D3
Charlotte Rd B8
Charlotte St. C4
Chart St B7
Charterhouse Sq. C6
Charterhouse St. C6
Chatham St F7
Cheapside C7
Chenies St. C4
Chesham St. E3
Chester Sq. F3
Chester Way F6
Chesterfield Hill. ...D3
Cheval Pl. E2
Chiltern St. C3
Chiswell St. C7
Church St. B2
City Garden Row A6
City Rd B7
City Thameslink ≷ ...C6
City University, The.A6
Claremont Sq. A6
Clarendon St. F3
Clarges St D3
Clerkenwell Cl B6
Clerkenwell Green ...B6
Clerkenwell Rd. B6
Cleveland St. C4

Clifford St D4
Clink Prison Mus 🏛 .D7
Cliveden Pl F3
Clock Museum 🏛 C7
Club Row B8
Cockspur St. D4
Coleman St. C7
Columbia Rd. B8
Commercial Rd. C9
Commercial St B8
Compton St. B6
Conduit St. D3
Congreve St. F8
Connaught Sq. C2
Connaught St. C2
Constitution Hill. ...E3
Copperfield St E6
Coptic St. C5
Cornhill C7
Cornwall Rd. D6
Coronet St B8
County St. E7
Courtenay St. F6
Cowcross St. C6
Cowper St. B7
Crampton St. F6
Cranbourn St. D4
Craven St. D5
Crawford Pl. C2
Crawford St. C2
Creechurch La C8
Cromer St. B5
Cromwell Rd. F1
Crosby Row E7
Crucifix La E8
Cumberland Gate. D2
Cumberland St. F3
Cumberland Terr A3
Cuming Mus 🏛 F7
Curtain Rd. B8
Curzon St. D3
Dante Rd F6
D'arblay St. C4
Davies St. D3
Dean St. C4
Deluxe Gallery 🏛 ...B8
Denbigh Pl. F3
Denman St. D4
Dering St. C3
Devonshire St. C3
Diana, Princess of Wales
   Memorial Garden ✦ .D1
Diana, Princess of Wales
   Memorial Walk E3
Dingley Pl. B7
Dorset St. C2
Doughty St. B5
Douglas St. F4
Dover St. D4
Downing St. E5
Draycott Avenue. F2
Draycott Pl. F2
Druid St E8
Drummond St. B4
Drury La. C5
Drysdale St. B8
Duchess St. C3
Dufferin St. B7
Duke of Wellington Pl .E3
Duke St. C3/D3
Duke St Hill. D7
Duke's Pl. C8
Duncannon St. D5
Dunton Rd. F8
East Rd. B7
East St F7
Eastcastle St. C4
Eastcheap D8
Eastman Dental
   Hospital 🏥.......B5
Eaton Gate. F3
Eaton Pl. E3
Eaton Sq. E3
Eaton Terr. F3
Ebury Bridge. F3
Ebury Bridge Rd. F3
Eccleston Bridge F3
Eccleston St. F3
Edgware Rd. C2
Edgware Rd ⊖ C2
Egerton Gdns. E2
Eldon St. C7
Elephant & Castle ≷ .F7
Elephant and
   Castle ⊖.........E6
Elephant Rd. F7
Elizabeth Bridge. F3
Elizabeth St. F3
Elm Tree Rd. A1
Elystan Pl. F2
Elystan St. F2
Embankment ⊖ D5
Endell St. C5
Endsleigh Pl. B4
Enid St E8
Ennismore Gdns. E2
Erasmus St. F4
Euston ≷⊖ B4
Euston Rd. B4
Euston Square ⊖ B4
Evelina Children's
   Hospital E5
Eversholt St. A4
Exhibition Rd. E1
Exmouth Market. B6
Fair St. E8
Falmouth Rd. E7
Fann St. C7
Farringdon ≷⊖ C6
Farringdon Rd. C6
Farringdon St. C6
Featherstone St. B7
Fenchurch St. D8
Fenchurch St ≷ D8
Fetter La. C6

Finsbury Circus C7
Finsbury Pavement ...C7
Finsbury Sq. C7
Fitzalan St. F6
Fitzmaurice Pl. D4
Fleet St. C6
Fleming Lab. Mus 🏛 .B1
Floral St. D5
Florence Nightingale
   Museum 🏛.........E5
Folgate St. C8
Fore St. C7
Foster La. C7
Francis St. F4
Frazier St. E6
Freemason's Hall C5
Friday St. C7
Fulham Rd. F1
Gainsford St. E8
Garden Row E6
Gee St. B7
Geological Mus 🏛 ...E1
George Row. E9
George St. C2
Gerrard St. D4
Gibson Rd F5
Giltspur St. C6
Glasshouse St. D4
Glasshouse Walk. F5
Gloucester Pl. C2
Gloucester Sq. C1
Gloucester St. F3
Golden Hinde ⚓ D7
Golden La. B7
Golden Sq. D4
Goodge St ⊖ C4
Goodge St. C4
Gordon Hospital 🏥 ..F4
Gordon Sq. B4
Goswell Rd. B6
Gough St. B6
Goulston St. C8
Gower St. B4
Gracechurch St. D7
Grafton Way. B4
Graham Terr. F3
Grange Rd. E8
Grange Walk. E8
Gray's Inn Rd. B5
Great College St. E5
Great Cumberland Pl .C2
Great Dover St. E7
Great Eastern St. B8
Great Guildford St ..D7
Great Marlborough St.C4
Great Ormond Street
   Children's Hosp 🏥.B5
Great Percy St. B5
Great Peter St. E4
Great Portland St ⊖ .B3
Great Portland St. ...C3
Great Queen St. C5
Great Russell St. C4
Great Scotland Yd ...D5
Great Smith St. E4
Great Suffolk St. D6/E6
Great Titchfield St .C4
Great Tower St. D8
Great Windmill St. ...D4
Greek St. C4
Green Park ⊖ D3
Green St. D3
Greencoat Pl. F4
Gresham St. C7
Greville St. B5/C6
Greycoat Hosp Sch. ...E4
Greycoat St. E4
Grosvenor Cres. E3
Grosvenor Gdns. E3
Grosvenor Rd. F3
Grosvenor Sq. D3
Grosvenor St. D3
Grove End Rd. B1
Guards Museum and
   Chapel 🏛.........E4
Guildhall Art
   Gallery 🏛.........C7
Guilford St. B5
Guy's Hospital 🏥 ...D7
Haberdasher St. B7
Hackney Rd. B8
Half Moon St. D3
Halkin St. E3
Hall Pl. B1
Hall St. B6
Hallam St. C3
Hamilton CL B1
Hampstead Rd. B4
Hanover Sq. C3
Hans Cres. E2
Hans Rd. E2
Hanway St. C4
Hardwick St. B6
Harewood Ave. B2
Harley St. C3
Harper Rd. E7
Harrington Rd. F1
Harrison St. B5
Harrowby St. C2
Hasker St. F2
Hastings St. B5
Hatfields D6
Hayles St. F6
Haymarket. D4
Hayne St. C6
Hay's Galleria D8
Hay's Mews. D3
Hayward Gallery 🏛 ..D5
Helmet Row. B7
Herbrand St. B5
Hercules Rd. E5
Hertford St. D3
Heygate St. F7
High Holborn. C5
Hill St. D3
HMS Belfast ⚓ D8
Hobart Pl. E3
Holborn ⊖ C5
Holborn. C6

Holborn Viaduct. C6
Holland St. D6
Holmes Mus 🏛 B2
Holywell La. B8
Horse Guards' Rd. ...E4
Horseferry Rd. F4
Houndsditch. C8
Houses of
   Parliament 🏛.....E5
Howland St. C4
Hoxton Sq. B8
Hoxton St. B8
Hugh St. F3
Hunter St. B5
Hunterian Mus 🏛 C5
Hyde Park D2
Hyde Park Cnr ⊖ E3
Hyde Park Cres. C2
Hyde Park St. C2
Imperial Coll London.E1
Imperial College Rd..E1
Imperial War Mus 🏛 .E6
Inner Circle. B3
Institute of Archaeology
   (London Univ).....B3
Ironmonger Row B7
Jacob St. E9
Jamaica Rd. E9
James St. C3
James St. D5
Jermyn St. D4
Jockey's Fields. C5
John Carpenter St. ..D6
John Fisher St. D9
John Islip St. F5
John St. B5
Johnathan St. F5
Judd St. B5
Kennings Way F6
Kennington ⊖ F6
Kennington La. F6
Kennington Park Rd..F6
Kennington Rd. E6/F6
Kensington Gardens .D1
Kensington Gore E1
Kensington Rd. E1
Keyworth St. E6
King Charles St. E5
King's College
   London. D5
King St D5
King William St. C7
Kingley St. C4
King's Cross ≷ A5
King's Cross Rd. B5
King's Cross
   St Pancras ⊖.....A5
King's Rd. F2
Kingsland Rd. B8
Kingsway. C5
Kinnerton St. E3
Kipling St. E7
Knightsbridge ⊖ E2
Lamb St. C8
Lambeth Bridge. F5
Lambeth High St. F5
Lambeth North ⊖ ...E6
Lambeth Palace. E5
Lambeth Palace Rd. ..E5
Lambeth Rd. F5
Lambeth Walk. F5
Lamb's Conduit St. ..C5
Lancaster Gate ⊖ ..D1
Lancaster Pl. D5
Lancaster St. E6
Lancaster Terr. D1
Langham Pl. C3
Lant St. E7
Leadenhall St. C8
Leake St. E5
Leather La. C6
Leathermarket St. ...E8
Leicester Sq ⊖ D4
Leicester St. D4
Leonard St. B7
Leroy St. E8
Lever St. B7
Lexington St. D4
Lidlington Pl. A4
Lime St. D8
Lincoln's Inn Fields.C5
Lindsey St. C6
Lisle St. D4
Lisson Gr. B1
Lisson St. B2
Liverpool St. C8
Liverpool St ≷⊖ C8
Lloyd Baker St. B6
Lloyd Sq. B6
Lodge Rd. B2
Lollard St. F6
Lombard St. C7
London Aquarium ✦ ..E5
London Bridge ⊖ ...D7
London Bridge
   Hospital 🏥.......D7
London City Hall 🏛 .D8
London Dungeon ✦ ...D8
London Film Mus ✦ ..E5
London Guildhall Univ.C7
London Rd. E6
London Transport
   Museum 🏛.........D5
London Wall. C7
London-Eye ✦ E5
London-Eye ⊖ E5
Long Acre. D5
Long La. C6
Long La. E7
Longford St. B3
Lord's Cricket Gd (MCC
   & Middlesex CCC)..B1
Lower Belgrave St. ...E3
Lower Grosvenor Pl. .E3
Lower Marsh E5
Lower Sloane St. F2
Lower Thames St. D7
Lowndes St. E2
Ludgate Circus C6
Ludgate Hill. C6

Luxborough St. C3
Lyall St. E3
Macclesfield Rd. B7
Madame Tussaud's ✦ .B3
Maddox St. D3
Malet St. C4
Maltby St. E8
Manchester Sq. C3
Manchester St. C3
Manciple St. E7
Mandela Way. F8
Mandeville Pl. C3
Mansell St. D8
Mansion House ⊖ ...C7
Mansion House. C7
Maple St. C4
Marble Arch ⊖ D2
Marble Arch. D2
Marchmont St. B5
Margaret St. C4
Margery St. B6
Mark La. D8
Marlborough Rd. D4
Marshall St. C4
Marshalsea Rd. E7
Marsham St. E4
Marylebone ≷⊖ B2
Marylebone High St. .C3
Marylebone La. C3
Marylebone Rd. B3/C2
Marylebone St. C3
Mecklenburgh Sq. B5
Middle Temple La. ...C6
Middlesex St
   (Petticoat La).....C8
Midland Rd. A4
Millbank. F5
Milner St. F2
Minories. C8
Monck St. E4
Monkton St. F6
Monmouth St. C5
Montagu Pl. C2
Montagu Sq. C2
Montagu St. C5
Montague Pl. C4
Montpelier St. E2
Montpelier Walk. E2
Monument ⊖ D7
Monument St. D7
Monument, The ✦ D7
Moor La. C7
Moorfields Eye
   Hospital 🏥.......B7
Moorgate ⊖ C7
Moorgate. C7
Moreland St. B6
Morley St. E6
Mortimer St. C4
Mossop St. F2
Mount Pleasant B6
Mount St. D3
Murray Gr A7
Mus of Gdn History 🏛.E5
Museum of London 🏛 .C7
Museum St. C5
Myddelton Sq. B6
Myddelton St. B6
National Gallery 🏛 .D4
National Hospital 🏥 .B5
National Portrait
   Gallery D4
Natural History
   Museum 🏛.........E1
Neal St. C5
Nelson's Column ✦ ..D5
Neville St. F1
New Bond St. C3/D3
New Bridge St. C6
New Cavendish St. ...C3
New Change C7
New Fetter La. C6
New Inn Yard. B8
New Kent Rd. F7
New North Rd. A7
New Oxford St. C4
New Scotland Yard ...E4
Newburn St. F5
Newcomen St. E7
Newgate St. C6
Newington Butts. F6
Newington Cswy. E6
Newton St. C5
Nile St. B7
Noble St. C7
Noel St. C4
Norfolk Cres. C2
Norfolk Sq. C1
North Audley St. D3
North Carriage Dr ...D2
North Cres. C4
North Ride. D2
North Row. D3
North Wharf Rd. C1
Northampton Sq. B6
Northington St. B5
Northumberland Ave. .D5
Norton Folgate. C8
Nottingham Pl. C3
Old Bailey C6
Old Broad St. C7
Old Brompton Rd. F1
Old Compton St. C4
Old County Hall. E5
Old Gloucester St. ...C5
Old Jamaica Rd. E9
Old Kent Rd. F8
Old King Edward St. ..C7
Old Marylebone Rd ...C2
Old Montague St. C8
Old Nichol St. B8
Old Paradise St. F5
Old St B7
Old St ≷⊖ B7
Old Vic ✦ E6
Onslow Gdns. F1
Onslow Sq. F1
Ontario St. E6

Open Air Theatre 🎭 .B3
Operating Theatre
   Museum 🏛.........D7
Orange St. D4
Orchard St. C3
Ossulston St. A4
Outer Circle. B2
Ovington Sq. E2
Oxford Circus ⊖ ...C4
Oxford St. C3/C4
Paddington ≷⊖ C1
Paddington Green
   Hospital 🏥.......C2
Page's Walk. F8
Palace St. E4
Pall Mall. D4
Pall Mall East D4
Pancras Rd. A5
Panton St. D4
Paris Gdn. D6
Park Cres. B3
Park La. D3
Park Rd. B2
Park St. D3
Park St. D7
Parker St. C5
Parliament Sq. E5
Parliament St. E5
Paternoster Sq. C7
Paul St. B7
Pear Tree St. B6
Pelham Cres. F2
Pelham St. F2
Penfold St. C2
Penton Pl. F6
Penton Rise. B5
Penton St. A6
Pentonville Rd. A5/A6
Percival St. B6
Petticoat La
   (Middlesex St)....C8
Petty France E4
Phoenix Pl. B5
Phoenix Rd. A4
Photo Gallery 🏛 D4
Piccadilly. D3
Piccadilly Circus ⊖ .D4
Pilgrimage St. E7
Pimlico ⊖ F4
Pimlico Rd. F3
Pitfield St. B8
Pollock's Toy Mus 🏛 .A4
Polygon Rd. A4
Pont St E2
Porchester Pl. C2
Portland Pl. C3
Portman Mews. C3
Portman Sq. C3
Portman St. C3
Portugal St. C5
Poultry. C7
Praed St. C1
Primrose St. C8
Prince Consort Rd. ..E1
Prince's Gdns. E1
Prince's St. C7
Princes St. C3
Procter St. C5
Provost St. B7
Quaker St. B8
Queen Anne St. C3
Queen Elizabeth
   Hall 🏛...........D5
Queen Elizabeth St. .E8
Queen St. D7
Queen St. D7
Queen Street Pl. D7
Queen Victoria St. ..D6
Queens Gallery 🏛 ...E4
Queensberry Pl. F1
Quilter St. B8
Radnor St. B7
Rathbone Pl. C4
Rawlings St. F2
Rawstorne St. B6
Red Lion Sq. C5
Red Lion St. C5
Redchurch St. B8
Redcross Way. E7
Reedworth St. F6
Regency St. F4
Regent St. C4
Regent St. D4
Regent's Park B3
Richmond Terr. E5
Ridgmount St. C4
Riley Rd. E8
Rivington St. B8
Robert St. A3
Rochester Row. F4
Rockingham St. E7
Rodney Rd. F7
Rolls Rd. F8
Ropemaker St. C7
Rosebery Ave. B6
Rossmore Rd. B2
Rothsay St. E8
Rotten Row E1
Roupell St. D6
Royal Academy of Arts 🏛.D4
Royal Academy of
   Dramatic Art......B4
Royal Acad of Music 🏛.E1
Royal Albert Hall 🏛 .E1
Royal Artillery
   Memorial ✦.......E2
Royal Brompton
   Hosp 🏥...........F1
Royal Brompton
   Hospital 🏥.......F2
Royal Coll of Nursing.C3
Royal Coll of Surgeons C5
Royal Festival Hall 🏛.D5
Royal London Hospital
   for Integrated
   Medicine 🏥.......C5
Royal Marsden
   Hospital 🏥.......F1
Royal National
   Theatre D6

Royal National Throat, Nose and Ear Hospital H....B5
Royal Opera House 🎭....D5
Rushworth St....E6
Russell St....B4
Russell Square ⊖....B5
Rutland Gate....E2
Sackville St....D4
Sadlers Wells 🎭....B6
Saffron Hill....C6
Sale Pl....C2
Sancroft St....F5
Savile Row....D4
Savoy Pl....D5
Savoy St....D5
School of Hygiene & Tropical Medicine....C4
Science Mus 🏛....E1
Scrutton St....B8
Sekforde St....C6
Serpentine Gallery 🏛....E1
Serpentine Rd....D2
Seven Dials....C5
Seward St....B6
Seymour Pl....C2
Seymour St....C2
Shad Thames....D8/E8
Shaftesbury Ave....D4
Shakespeare's Globe Theatre 🎭....D7
Shepherd Market....D3
Sherwood St....D4
Shoe La....C6
Shoreditch High St....B8
Shoreditch High St ⊖....B8
Shorts Gdns....C5
Shouldham St....C2
Sidmouth St....B5
Silk St....C7
Sir John Soane's Museum 🏛....C5
Skinner St....B6
Sloane Ave....F2
Sloane Sq....F2
Sloane Square ⊖....F3
Sloane St....E2
Snow Hill....C6
Soho Sq....D4
Somerset House 🏛....D5
South Audley St....D3
South Carriage Dr....E2
South Eaton Pl....F3
South Kensington ⊖....F1
South Molton St....D3
South Parade....F1
South Pl....C7
South St....D3
South Terr....F2
South Wharf Rd....C1
Southampton Row....C5
Southampton St....D5
Southwark ⊖....D6
Southwark Bridge....D7
Southwark Bridge Rd....D7
Southwark Cath †....D7
Southwark Park Rd....F8
Southwark St....D7
Spa Rd....E8
Speakers' Corner....D2
Spencer St....B6
Spital Sq....C8
Spring St....C1
St Alban's St....D4
St Andrew St....C6
St Barnabas St....F3
St Bartholomew's Hospital H....C6
St Botolph St....C8
St Bride St....C6
St George's Circus....F6
St George's Dr....F4
St George's Rd....E6
St George's Sq....F4
St Giles High St....C4
St James's Palace 🏛....D4
St James's Park ⊖....E4
St James's St....D4
St John St....B6
St John's Wood Rd....B1
St Margaret St....E5
St Mark's Hosp H....B6
St Martin's La....D5
St Martin's Le Grand....C7
St Mary Axe....C8
St Mary's Hosp H....C1
St Pancras Int ≷....A5
St Paul's ⊖....C7
St Paul's Cath †....C7
St Paul's Churchyard....C6
St Thomas' Hosp H....E5
St Thomas St....D7
Stamford St....D6
Stanhope St....B4
Stanhope Terr....D1
Stephenson Way....A4
Stock Exchange....C6
Stoney St....D7
Strand....C6
Strathearn Pl....D2
Stratton St....D3
Sumner St....D6
Sussex Gdns....C1
Sussex Pl....C1
Sussex Sq....D1
Sussex St....F3
Sutton's Way....B7
Swan St....E7
Swanfield St....B8
Swinton St....B5
Sydney Pl....F2
Sydney St....F2
Tabard St....E7
Tabernacle St....B7
Tachbrook St....F4
Tanner St....E8
Tate Britain 🏛....F5
Tate Modern 🏛....D7
Tavistock Pl....B5
Tavistock Sq....B4

Tea & Coffee Mus 🏛....D7
Temple ⊖....D6
Temple Ave....D6
Temple Pl....D5
Terminus Pl....E3
Thayer St....C3
The Barbican Centre for Arts....C7
The Brunswick Sh Ctr....B5
The Cut....E6
The Mall....D4
Theobald's Rd....C5
Thorney St....F5
Threadneedle St....C7
Throgmorton St....C7
Thurloe Pl....F1
Thurloe Sq....F2
Tonbridge St....B5
Tooley St....D7
Torrington Pl....B4
Tothill St....E4
Tottenham Court Rd ⊖....C4
Tottenham Ct Rd ⊖....C4
Tottenham St....C4
Tower Bridge....D8
Tower Bridge App....D8
Tower Bridge Rd....E8
Tower Hill....D8
Tower Hill ⊖....D8
Tower of London, The 🏛....D8
Toynbee St....C8
Trafalgar Square....D4
Trinity Sq....D8
Trinity St....E7
Trocadero Centre....D4
Tudor St....D6
Turin St....B8
Turnmill St....C6
Tyers St....F5
Ufford St....E6
Union St....D6
Univ Coll Hospl H....B4
University of London....C4
Univ of Westminster....B4
University St....B4
Upper Belgrave St....E3
Upper Berkeley St....C2
Upper Brook St....D3
Upper Grosvenor St....D3
Upper Ground....D6
Upper Montague St....C2
Upper St Martin's La....D5
Upper Thames St....D7
Upper Wimpole St....C3
Upper Woburn Pl....B4
Vauxhall Bridge Rd....F4
Vauxhall St....F5
Vere St....C3
Vernon Pl....C5
Vestry St....B7
Victoria ≷⊖....E3
Victoria and Albert Museum 🏛....E1
Victoria Coach Sta....F3
Victoria Embankment....D5
Victoria Pl Sh Ctr....F3
Victoria St....E4
Villiers St....D5
Vincent Sq....F4
Vinopolis City of Wine....D7
Virginia Rd....B8
Wakley St....B6
Walbrook....C7
Walcot Sq....E6
Wallace Collection 🏛....C3
Walnut Tree Walk....F6
Walton St....F2
Walworth Rd....F7
Wardour St....C4/D4
Warner St....B6
Warren St ⊖....B4
Warren St....B4
Warwick Sq....F4
Warwick Way....F3
Waterloo ≷⊖....E6
Waterloo Bridge....D5
Waterloo East ≷....D6
Waterloo Rd....E6
Watling St....C7
Webber St....E6
Welbeck St....C3
Wellington Arch ✦....E3
Wellington Mus 🏛....E3
Wellington Rd....B2
Wellington Row....B9
Wells St....C4
Wenlock St....A7
Wentworth St....C8
West Carriage Dr....D2
West Smithfield....C6
West Sq....E6
Westbourne St....D1
Westbourne Terr....C1
Westminster ⊖....E5
Westminster Abbey †....E5
Westminster Bridge....E5
Westminster Bridge Rd....E6
Westminster Cathedral (RC) †....E4
Westminster City Hall....E4
Westminster Hall 🏛....E5
Weston St....E7
Weymouth St....C3
Wharf Rd....A7
Wharton St....B5
Whitcomb St....D4
White Cube 🏛....B8
White Lion Hill....D6
White Lion St....A6
Whitechapel Rd....C9
Whitecross St....B7
Whitehall....D5
Whitehall Pl....D5
Wigmore Hall....C3
Wigmore St....C3
William IV St....D5

Willow Walk....F8
Wilmington Sq....B6
Wilson St....C7
Wilton Cres....E3
Wilton Rd....F4
Wimpole St....C3
Winchester St....F3
Wincott St....F6
Windmill Walk....D6
Woburn Pl....B5
Woburn Sq....B4
Wood St....C7
Woodbridge St....B6
Wootton St....D6
Wormwood St....C8
Worship St....B7
Wren St....B5
Wynyatt St....B6
York Rd....E5
York St....C2
York Terrace East....B3
York Terrace West....B3
York Way....A5

Luton   337
Adelaide St....B1
Albert Rd....B2
Alma St....B2
Alton Rd....A2
Anthony Gdns....C1
Arthur St....C2
Ashburnham Rd....B1
Ashton Rd....C2
Avondale Rd....A1
Back St....A2
Bailey St....A2
Baker St....C2
Biscot Rd....A1
Bolton Rd....B3
Boyle Cl....B1
Brantwood Rd....C1
Bretts Mead....C1
Bridge St....B2
Brook St....A2
Brunswick St....A3
Burr St....A3
Bury Park Rd....A1
Bute St....B2
Buxton Rd....B2
Cambridge St....C2
Cardiff Grove....B1
Cardiff Rd....B1
Cardigan St....A2
Castle St....B2/C2
Chapel St....A3
Charles St....A3
Chase St....A3
Cheapside....B2
Chequer St....B2
Chiltern Rise....C1
Church St....B2/B3
Cinema 🎬....A2
Cobden St....A1
Collingdon St....A1
Community Centre....C3
Concorde Ave....A3
Corncastle Rd....C1
Cowper St....C2
Crawley Green Rd....B3
Crawley Rd....A1
Crescent Rise....A3
Crescent Rd....A3
Cromwell Rd....A1
Cross St....A2
Crown Court....B2
Cumberland St....B1
Cutenhoe Rd....C3
Dallow Rd....B1
Downs Rd....B1
Dudley St....A2
Duke St....A2
Dumfries St....B1
Dunstable Place....B2
Dunstable Rd....A1/B1
Edward St....C2
Elizabeth St....C3
Essex Cl....C3
Farley Hill....C1
Farley Lodge....C1
Flowers Way....B2
Francis St....A1
Frederick St....A1
Galaxy L Complex....B2
George St....B2
George St West....B2
Gillam St....A3
Gordon St....B2
Grove Rd....B1
Guildford St....B2
Haddon Rd....A3
Harcourt St....C2
Hart Hill Drive....B3
Hart Hill Lane....A3
Hartley Rd....A3
Hastings St....B2
Hat Factory, The 🎭....B2
Hatters Way....A1
Havelock Rd....A2
Hibbert St....C2
High Town Rd....A3
Highbury Rd....A1
Hightown Community Sports & Arts Centre....A3
Hillary Cres....C1
Hillborough Rd....C1
Hitchin Rd....C2
Holly St....C2
Holm....C2
Hucklesby Way....A2
Hunts Cl....C1
Information Ctr 🛈....B2
Inkerman St....A2
John St....B2
Jubilee St....A3
Kelvin Cl....C2
King St....B2
Kingsland Rd....C2
Latimer Rd....C1
Lawn Gdns....C2

Lea Rd....B3
Library....B2
Library Rd....B2
Liverpool Rd....B1
London Rd....B3
Luton Station ≷....A2
Lyndhurst Rd....A3
Magistrates Court....B2
Mall, The....B2
Manchester St....B2
Manor Rd....B3
May St....C3
Meyrick Ave....C1
Midland Rd....A2
Mill St....A2
Milton Rd....C1
Moor St....A1
Moor, The....A1
Moorland Gdns....A2
Moulton Rise....A3
Museum & Art Gallery....B3
Napier Rd....B1
New Bedford Rd....A1
New Town St....C2
North St....A2
Old Bedford Rd....A2
Old Orchard....C2
Osbourne Rd....C3
Oxen Rd....A3
Park Sq....B2
Park St....B3/C3
Park St West....B2
Park Viaduct....B2
Parkland Drive....C1
Police Station 🛈....B1
Pomfret Ave....A3
Pondwicks Rd....B3
Post Office ⊠....A1/A2/B2/C3
Power Court....B2
Princess St....B1
Red Rails....C1
Regent St....B2
Reginald St....A2
Rothesay Rd....B1
Russell Rise....C1
Russell St....C1
St Ann's Rd....B3
St George's 🎭....B2
St George's Square....B2
St Mary's 🏛....B2
St Marys Rd....B2
St Paul's Rd....C2
St Saviour's Cres....C1
Salisbury Rd....B1
Seymour Ave....C3
Seymour Rd....C3
Silver St....B2
South Rd....C2
Stanley St....B1
Station Rd....A2
Stockwood Cres....C2
Stockwood Park....C1
Strathmore Ave....B3
Stuart St....B2
Studley Rd....A3
Surrey St....C3
Sutherland Place....C1
Tavistock St....C2
Taylor St....A3
Telford Way....A1
Tennyson Rd....B1
Tenzing Grove....C1
The Cross Way....C1
The Larches....A2
Thistle Rd....C2
Town Hall....B2
Townsley Cl....C2
UK Centre for Carnival Arts ✦....B3
Union St....A2
Univ of Bedfordshire....B3
Upper George St....B2
Vicarage St....B3
Villa Rd....A3
Waldeck Rd....A1
Wellington St....B1/B2
Wenlock St....A2
Whitby Rd....C1
Whitehill Ave....C1
William St....C2
Wilsden Ave....C1
Windmill Rd....B3
Windsor St....C2
Winsdon Rd....B1
York St....A3

Macclesfield   337
108 Steps....B2
Abbey Rd....A1
Alton Dr....A3
Armett St....C1
Athey St....B1
Bank St....C3
Barber St....C1
Barton St....C1
Beech La....C1
Beswick St....B1
Black La....A3
Black Rd....C2
Blakelow Gardens....C3
Blakelow Rd....C3
Bond St....B1/C1
Bread St....B1
Bridge St....B1
Brock St....C2
Brocklehurst Ave....B3
Brook St....B3
Brookfield La....C3
Brough St West....B1
Brown St....C1
Brynton Rd....A2
Buckley St....C2
Bus Station....B2
Buxton Rd....B3
Byrons St....C2
Canal St....B3
Carlsbrook Ave....A3

Castle St....B2
Catherine St....B1
Cemetery....A1
Chadwick Terr....A3
Chapel St....C2
Charlotte St....B2
Chester Rd....A3
Chestergate....B1
Christ Church 🏛....B1
Churchill Way....B2
Coare St....A1
Commercial Rd....B2
Conway Cres....A3
Copper St....C3
Cottage St....B2
Court....A2
Court....A2
Crematorium....A1
Crew Ave....A3
Crompton Rd....B1/C1
Cross St....C2
Crossall St....C1
Cumberland St....A1/B1
Dale St....B3
Duke St....B2
Eastgate....B3
Exchange St....B3
Fence Ave....B3
Fence Ave Ind Est....A3
Flint St....A3
Foden St....A2
Fountain St....B2
Garden St....A3
Gas Rd....B2
George St....B2
Glegg St....B3
Golf Course....C3
Goodall St....C1
Grange Rd....C1
Great King St....B1
Green St....B3
Grosvenor Sh Ctr....B2
Gunco La....C2
Half St....C2
Hallefield Rd....B3
Hatton St....C2
Hawthorn Way....A3
Heapy St....C2
Henderson St....B1
Heritage Centre & Silk Museum 🏛....B2
Hibel Rd....A2
High St....C2
Hobson St....C2
Hollins Rd....C3
Hope St West....B1
Horseshoe Dr....B1
Hurdsfield Rd....A3
Information Ctr 🛈....B2
James St....C2
Jodrell St....B3
John St....C2
Jordangate....A2
King Edward St....B2
King George's Field....C3
King St....C2
King's School....C1
Knight Pool....C1
Knight St....C2
Lansdowne St....A3
Library....A2
Lime Gr....B3
Little Theatre 🎭....C2
Loney St....B1
Longacre St....A3
Lord St....C2
Lowe St....C2
Lowerfield Rd....A3
Lyon St....B1
Macclesfield College....B2
Macclesfield Sta ≷....B2
Marina....B3
Market....B3
Market Pl....A2
Masons La....A3
Mill La....C1
Mill Rd....C2
Mill St....B2
Moran Rd....C1
New Hall St....C2
Newton St....C1
Nicholson Ave....A3
Nicholson Cl....A3
Northgate Ave....A2
Old Mill La....C2
Paradise Mill 🏛....B1
Paradise St....B1
Park Green....B2
Park La....C1
Park Rd....C1
Park Vale Rd....C1
Parr St....C2
Peel St....C2
Percyvale St....A2
Peter St....C1
Pickford St....B2
Pierce St....B1
Pinfold St....C2
Pitt St....C2
Pool St....B2
Poplar Rd....C3
Post Office ⊠....B1/B2/B3
Pownall St....A2
Prestbury Rd....A1/B1
Queen Victoria St....B2
Queen's Ave....C3
Registrar....A2
Richmond Hill....C3
Riseley St....A1
Roan Ct....A3
Roe St....B2
Rowan Way....A3
Ryle St....C2
Ryle's Park Rd....C1
St George's St....C2
St Michael's 🏛....B2
Samuel St....B2

Saville St....C3
Shaw St....B1
Slater St....C1
Snow Hill....C1
South Park....C1
Spring Gdns....A2
Statham St....C2
Station St....A2
Steeple St....A3
Sunderland St....B2
Superstore....A1/A2/C2
Swettenham St....A3
The Silk St 🏛....A2/B2
Thistleton Cl....C2
Thorp St....B2
Town Hall....B2
Townley St....C3
Turnock St....C3
Union Rd....B2
Union St....B3
Victoria Park....C1
Vincent St....C2
Waters Green....B2
Waterside....C2
West Bond St....B1
West Park....A1
West Park Museum 🏛....A1
Westbrook Dr....A1
Westminster Rd....A1
Whalley Hayes....B1
Windmill St....C3
Withyfold Dr....A2
York St....B3

Maidstone   340
Albion Pl....B2
All Saints 🏛....B2
Allen St....A3
Amphitheatre ✦....B2
Archbishop's Pal 🏛....B2
Bank St....B2
Barker Rd....C2
Barton Rd....C2
Beaconsfield Rd....C1
Bedford Pl....B1
Bentlif Art Gallery 🏛....B2
Bishops Way....B2
Bluett St....A3
Bower La....C1
Bower Mount Rd....B1
Bower Pl....C1
Bower St....A3
Bowling Alley....B3
Boxley Rd....A3
Brenchley Gardens....A2
Brewer St....A3
Broadway....B2
Broadway Sh Ctr....B2
Brunswick St....C3
Buckland Hill....A1
Buckland Rd....B1
Bus Station....B3
Campbell Rd....C3
Carriage Museum 🏛....B2
Church Rd....C2
Church St....B3
Cinema 🎬....B2
College Ave....C2
College Rd....C2
Collis Memorial Gdn....C3
Cornwallis Rd....A2
Corpus Christi Hall....B2
County Hall....A2
County Rd....A3
Crompton Gdns....C3
Crown & County Courts....B2
Curzon Rd....A3
Dixon Cl....C2
Douglas Rd....C1
Earl St....B2
Eccleston Rd....C2
Fairmeadow....B2
Fisher St....A2
Florence Rd....C1
Foley St....A3
Foster St....C2
Fremlin Walk Sh Ctr....B2
Gabriel's Hill....B3
George St....C3
Grecian St....A3
Hardy St....A3
Hart St....C2
Hastings Rd....C3
Hayle Rd....C3
Hazlitt Theatre 🎭....B2
Heathorn St....A3
Hedley St....A3
High St....B2
HM Prison....A3
Holland Rd....A3
Hope St....A2
Information Ctr 🛈....B2
James St....A3
James Whatman Way....A2
Jeffrey St....A3
Kent County Council Offices....B2
Kent History & Library Centre....A2
King Edward Rd....C2
King St....B3
Kingsley Rd....C3
Knightrider St....B2
Launder Way....C1
Lesley Pl....A1
Little Buckland Ave....A1
Lockmeadow Leisure Complex....B1
London Rd....B1
Lower Boxley Rd....A2
Lower Fant Rd....C1
Magistrates Court....B3
Maidstone Barracks Station ≷....A1
Maidstone Borough Council Offices....B2
Maidstone East Sta ≷....A2
Maidstone Museum 🏛....B2

Maidstone West Sta ≷....B2
Market....C2
Market Buildings....B2
Marsham St....B3
Medway St....B2
Medway Trading Est....C2
Melville Rd....C2
Mill St....B2
Millennium Bridge....C2
Mote Rd....B3
Muir Rd....A3
Old Tovil Rd....C3
Palace Ave....B2
Perryfield St....A2
Police Station 🛈....C3/C2
Post Office ⊠....A2/B2/B3/C3
Priory Rd....C1
Prospect Pl....C1
Pudding La....B2
Queen Anne Rd....B3
Queens Rd....A1
Randall St....A2
Rawdon Rd....C3
Reginald St....C1
Rock Pl....B1
Rocky Hill....B1
Romney Pl....B2
Rose Yard....B2
Rowland Cl....A3
Royal Engineers' Rd....A2
Royal Star Arcade....B2
St Annes St....A3
St Faith's St....A2
St Luke's Rd....A3
St Peter's Br....C2
St Peter's Wharf Retail Park....B2
St Peter St....B2
St Philip's Ave....C3
Salisbury Rd....A3
Sandling Rd....A2
Scott St....A2
Scrubs La....A3
Sheal's Cres....C3
Somerfield La....B1
Somerfield Rd....B1
Staceys St....A2
Station Rd....A2
Superstore....A1/B2/B3
Terrace Rd....B1
The Mall....B2
Tonbridge Rd....C1
Tovil Rd....C3
Town Hall....B2
Trinity Park....B3
Tufton St....B3
Union St....B2
Upper Fant Rd....C1
Upper Stone St....C3
Victoria St....B1
Visitor Centre....A1
Warwick Pl....B1
Wat Tyler Way....B3
Waterloo St....C3
Waterlow Rd....A3
Week St....B2
Well Rd....A3
Westree Rd....C1
Wharf Rd....C2
Whatman Park....A1
Wheeler St....A3
Whitchurch Cl....B1
Woodville Rd....C3
Wyatt St....B2
Wyke Manor Rd....B3

Manchester   337
Adair St....B6
Addington St....A5
Adelphi St....A3
Air & Space Gallery 🏛....B2
Albert St....B4
Albion St....C4
AMC Great Northern 🎬....C3
Ancoats Gr....B6
Ancoats Gr North....B6
Angela St....C2
Aquatic Centre....C4
Ardwick Green Park....C5
Ardwick Green North....C5
Ardwick Green South....C5
Arlington St....A3
Artillery St....B3
Arundel St....C3
Atherton St....B3
Atkinson St....B3
Aytoun St....B4
Back Piccadilly....A4
Baird St....B5
Balloon St....A4
Bank Pl....A3
Baring St....B5
Barrack St....C1
Barrow St....A3
BBC TV Studios....A5
Bendix St....A5
Bengal St....A5
Berry St....C5
Blackfriars Rd....A3
Blackfriars St....B3
Blantyre St....C2
Bloom St....B4
Blossom St....A5
Boad St....B5
Bombay St....C4
Booth St....A3
Booth St....B4
Bootle St....B3
Brazennose St....B3
Brewer St....A5
Bridge St....A3
Bridgewater Hall....B3
Bridgewater Pl....A4
Brook St....C4

Holland St....A6
Hood St....A5
Hope St....B1
Hope St....B4
Houldsworth St....A5
Hoyle St....C6
Hulme Hall Rd....A1
Hulme St....A1
Hulme St....C3
Hyde Rd....C6
Information Ctr 🛈....B3
Irwell St....A2
Islington St....A2
Jackson Cr....C1
Jackson's Row....B3
James St....A1
Jenner Cl....C2
Jersey St....A5
John Dalton St....A1
John Dalton St....B3
John Ryland's Liby 🏛....B3
John St....A2
Kennedy St....B3
Kincardine Rd....C5
King St....A3
King St West....A3
Law Courts....B3
Laystall St....B5
Lever St....A4
Library....A5
Linby St....C2
Little Lever St....A4
Liverpool Rd....B2
Liverpool St....B1
Lloyd St....C3
Lockton Cl....C5
London Rd....B5
Long Millgate....A3
Longacre St....B6
Loom St....A5
Lower Byrom St....B2
Lower Mosley St....B3
Lower Moss La....C2
Lower Ormond St....C4
Loxford St....C4
Luna St....A5
Major St....B4
Manchester Arndale....A4
Manchester Art Gallery 🏛....B4
Manchester Central Convention Complex....B3
Manchester Metropolitan University....B4/C4
Manchester Piccadilly Station ≷....B5
Manchester Technology Centre....C4
Mancunian Way....C3
Manor St....C5
Marble St....A4
Market St....A4
Market St ⊖....A4
Market St ⊖....A4
Marsden St....A3
Marshall St....A5
Mayan Ave....C2
Medlock St....C3
Middlewood St....B1
Miller St....A4
Minshull St....B4
Mosley St....A4
Mount St....B3
Mulberry St....B3
Murray St....A5
Museum of Science & Industry (MOSI) 🏛....B2
Nathan Dr....A4
National Football Mus 🏛....A4
Naval St....A5
New Bailey St....A2
New Elm St....B2
New Islington ⊖....A6
New Islington Sta ⊖....B6
New Quay St....B2
New Union St....A6
Newgate St....A4
Newton St....A5
Nicholas St....B4
North Western St....C6
Oak St....A4
Odeon 🎬....A4
Old Mill St....A6
Oldfield Rd....A1/C1
Oldham Rd....A4
Oldham St....A4
Opera House 🎭....B3
Ordsall La....C1
Oxford Rd....C4
Oxford Rd ≷....C4
Oxford St....B4
Paddock St....C6
Palace Theatre 🎭....B4
Pall Mall....A3
Palmerston St....B6
Park St....A1
Parker St....B4
Peak St....B5
Penfield Cl....C4
Peoples' History Museum 🏛....A2
Peru St....A1
Peter St....B3
Piccadilly....A4
Piccadilly ≷....B4
Piccadilly Gdns ⊖....B4
Piercy St....A6
Poland St....A5
Police Museum 🏛....A5
Police Station 🛈....B3/B5
Pollard St....B6
Port St....A5
Portland St....B4
Portugal St East....B5
Post Office ⊠....A1/A4/A5/B3
Potato Wharf....B2
Princess St....B3/C4

Pritchard St. ... C4
Quay St. ... A2
Quay St. ... B2
Queen St. ... B3
Radium St. ... A5
Redhill St. ... A5
Regent Rd ... A2
Renold Theatre ... A2
Retail Park. ... A2
Rice St. ... B2
Richmond St. ... B4
River St. ... C3
Roby St. ... B5
Rodney St. ... A6
Roman Fort ... B2
Rosamond St. ... A4
Royal Exchange ... A3
Sackville St. ... B4
St Andrew's St ... B6
St Ann St ... A3
St Ann's ... A3
St George's Ave ... C1
St James St ... A4
St John St. ... B3
St John's Cath (RC) ... A2
St Mary's ... B3
St Mary's Gate. ... A3
St Mary's Parsonage ... A3
St Peter's Sq ... C5
St Stephen St ... A2
Salford Approach. ... A4
Salford Central ... A2
Sheffield St. ... B5
Shepley St. ... B5
Sherratt St. ... A4
Shudehill ... A4
Shudehill ... A4
Sidney St. ... C4
Silk St. ... B3
Silver St. ... B4
Skerry Cl ... C5
Snell St. ... B6
South King St ... A3
Sparkle St. ... B5
Spear St. ... A4
Spring Gdns. ... A4
Stanley St. ... A2/B2
Station Approach. ... A5
Store St. ... B5
Swan St. ... A4
Tariff St. ... B5
Tatton St. ... B6/C6
Temperance St. ... B6/C6
The Triangle ... B3
Thirsk St. ... C6
Thomas St. ... A4
Thompson St. ... A5
Tib La ... B3
Tib St ... A4
Town Hall (Manchester) ... B3
Town Hall (Salford) ... A2
Trafford St. ... C3
Travis St. ... B5
Trinity Way ... A2
Turner St. ... A4
Union St. ... C6
University of Manchester (Sackville Street Campus) ... C5
Upper Brook St. ... C5
Upper Cleminson St. ... A1
Upper Wharf St. ... A1
Vesta St. ... B6
Victoria ... A4
Victoria Station ... A4
Victoria St. ... A3
Wadesdon Rd ... C5
Water St. ... B2
Watson St. ... B3
West Fleet St. ... B1
West King St. ... A2
West Mosley St. ... B4
West Union St. ... B1
Weybridge Rd ... A6
Whitworth St. ... B4
Whitworth St West. ... C3
Wilburn St. ... B1
William St. ... A2
William St. ... C6
Wilmott St. ... C3
Windmill St. ... B3
Windsor Cr ... A1
Withy Gr. ... A4
Woden St. ... C1
Wood St. ... B3
Woodward St. ... A6
Worrall St. ... C1
Worsley St. ... C2
York St. ... B4
York St ... A3
York St ... C4

Merthyr Tydfil
Merthyr Tudful 340

Aberdare Rd ... B2
Abermorlais Terr ... B2
Alexandra Rd. ... A3
Alma St. ... C3
Arfryn Pl ... C3
Argyle St. ... C3
Avenue De Clichy ... C2
Bethesda St. ... B2
Bishops Gr. ... A3
Brecon Rd ... A1/B2
Briarmead ... A3
Bryn St ... C3
Bryntirion Rd ... B3/C3
Bus Station ... B2
Caedraw Rd. ... C2
Cae Mari Dwn ... B3
Castle Sq. ... A1
Castle St. ... B2
Chapel ... C2
Chapel Bank ... B1
Church St. ... B2
Civic Centre. ... B2
Coedcae'r Ct ... B2
Court ... B3

Courts ... B2
Court St ... C3
Cromwell St. ... B2
Cyfarthfa Castle School and Museum ... A1
Cyfarthfa Ind Est ... A1
Cyfarthfa Park ... A1
Cyfarthfa Rd ... A2
Dane St. ... A2
Dane Terr. ... A2
Danyparc ... B3
Darren View ... A2
Dixon St ... B2
Dyke St. ... C3
Dynevor St ... C3
Elwyn Dr. ... C3
Fire Station ... B2
Fothergill St. ... B3
Galonuchaf Rd ... A3
Garth St. ... B2
Georgetown ... A2
Grawen Terr ... A2
Grove Pk ... A2
Gurnos St ... A2
Gwaelodygarth Rd ... A2/A3
Gwaunfarren Gr ... A3
Gwaunfarren Rd ... A3
Gwendoline St ... A3
Hampton St. ... C3
Hanover St. ... C3
Heol S O Davies ... B1
Heol-Gerrig ... A3
Highland View ... A3
High St ... A3/B2/B3/C2
Howell Cl ... B1
Information Ctr ... B2
Jackson's Bridge ... B2
James St ... B2
John St. ... B2
Joseph Parry's Cottage ... B2
Lancaster St ... B2
Library ... B2
Llewellyn St ... B2
Llwyfen St ... B2
Llwyn Berry ... B1
Llwyn Dic Penderyn. ... C1
Llwyn-y-Gelynen. ... C1
Lower Thomas St ... B3
Market ... C2
Mary St. ... C3
Masonic St. ... C2
Merthyr College ... B2
Merthyr RFC ... B2
Merthyr Town FC ... B2
Merthyr Tydfil Leisure Village ... C3
Merthyr Tydfil Sta ... B2
Meyrick Villas ... B3
Miniature Railway ... A1
Mount St. ... B2
Nantygwenith St. ... B1
Norman Terr. ... B2
Oak Rd ... B3
Old Cemetery ... B3
Pandy Cl. ... A2
Pantycelynen ... B1
Park Terr ... C3
Penlan View ... C1
Penry St ... C3
Pentwyn Villas ... A2
Penyard Rd ... A3
Penydarren Park ... A3
Penydarren Rd ... A3
Plymouth St. ... C3
Police Station ... B2
Pont Marlais West ... B2
Post Office ... A3/B2/C2
Quarry Row ... B2
Queen's Rd ... B3
Rees St. ... C3
Rhydycar Link ... C2
Riverside Park ... A1
St David's ... B2
St Tydfil's ... B2
St Tydfil's Hospital (No A+E) ... B2
St Tydfil's Sq Sh Ctr ... B2
Saxon St. ... A2
School of Nursing ... A2
Seward St ... A3
Shiloh La ... A3
Stone Circles ... B3
Stuart St. ... A3
Summerhill Pl. ... B3
Superstore ... B2
Swan St ... B2
Swansea Rd. ... B3
Taff Glen View. ... C3
Taff Vale Ct ... B3
Theatre Soar ... B2
The Grove ... B3
The Parade ... B3
The Walk ... B3
Thomastown Park ... B3
Tramroad La ... A3
Tramroad Side ... B2
Tramroad Side North ... B3
Tramroad Side South ... C3
Trevithick Gdns ... C3
Trevithick St ... B2
Tudor Terr ... B2
Twynyrodyn Rd ... C3
Union St ... B2
Upper Colliers Row ... B1
Upper Thomas St ... B3
Victoria St ... C3
Vue ... C3
Vulcan Rd. ... B2
Warlow St ... C3
Well St ... A3
Welsh Assembly Government Offices ... C2
Wern La ... C3
West Gr ... C3
William St ... C2
Yew St. ... C3
Ynysfach Engine Ho ... C2
Ynysfach Rd. ... C2

Middlesbrough 340

Abingdon Rd ... C3
Acklam Rd ... C3
Albert Park ... C3
Albert Rd ... B2
Albert Terr. ... C2
Aubrey St. ... C2
Ayresome Gdns. ... C2
Ayresome Green La ... C2
Ayresome St. ... C2
Barton Rd ... A1
Bilsdale Rd ... C3
Bishopton Rd ... C2
Borough Rd ... B2/B3
Bowes Rd. ... A1
Breckon Hill Rd. ... C3
Bridge St East ... B3
Bridge St West ... B2
Brighouse Rd ... A1
Burlam Rd ... C1
Bus Station ... B2
Cannon Park ... B1
Cannon Park Way ... B2
Cannon St ... B2
Captain Cook Sq. ... B2
Carlow St. ... C1
Castle Way. ... C3
Chipchase Rd ... C2
Cineworld ... B3
Clairville Sports Stadium ... C3
Cleveland Centre ... B2
Clive Rd ... C2
Commercial St. ... A2
Corporation Rd. ... B2
Costa St ... C2
Council Offices ... B2
Crescent Rd. ... C2
Cumberland Rd. ... C2
Depot Rd ... A2
Derwent St ... B2
Devonshire Rd ... C2
Diamond Rd. ... A2
Disabled Driver Test Circuit ... B1
Dorman Museum ... C2
Douglas St. ... B3
Eastbourne Rd ... C2
Eden Rd ... C2
Enterprise Centre ... A2
Forty Foot Rd ... A2
Gilkes St. ... B2
Gosford St. ... B3
Grange Rd ... B2
Gresham Rd. ... C2
Harehills Rd. ... C1
Harford St ... C2
Hartington Rd ... B2
Haverton Hill Rd. ... A1
Hey Wood St ... B1
Highfield Rd ... C3
Hill St Centre. ... B2
Holwick Rd. ... A1
Hutton Rd ... C3
ICI Works ... A1
Information Ctr ... B2
Lambton Rd. ... C2
Lancaster Rd. ... C2
Lansdowne Rd ... C3
Latham Rd ... C2
Law Courts ... B2/B3
Lees Rd. ... C2
Leeway ... C3
Linthorpe Cemetery ... C1
Linthorpe Rd. ... B2
Lloyd St. ... B2
Longford St. ... C2
Longlands Rd ... C3
Lower East St ... A3
Lower Lake ... C3
Maldon Rd ... C1
Manor St. ... B2
Marsh St. ... B2
Marton Rd. ... B3
Middlehaven. ... A2
Middlesbrough By-Pass ... B2/C1
Middlesbrough Coll. ... A3
Middlesbrough L Park. ... B3
Middlesbrough Sta ... B2
Middlesbrough Theatre ... C2
Middleton Park ... C3
MIMA ... B2
Mosque ... B2
Mosque ... C3
Mulgrave Rd ... C2
North Ormesby Rd ... B3
Newport Bridge ... A1
Newport Bridge Approach Rd ... A1
Newport Rd ... B2
North Rd ... B2
Northern Rd ... C1
Outram St ... B2
Oxford Rd. ... C2
Park La ... B2
Park Rd North ... C2
Park Rd South ... C2
Park Vale Rd ... C3
Parliament Rd. ... B1
Police Station ... B2
Port Clarence Rd ... A3
Portman St ... B2
Princes Rd. ... B2
Python ... B2
Riverside Bsns Park. ... A2
Riverside Park Rd. ... A1
Riverside Stadium (Middlesbrough FC) ... B3
Rockliffe Rd ... C2
Romaldkirk Rd ... B1
Roman Rd ... C2
Roseberry Rd ... C3
St Barnabas' Rd ... C2
St Paul's Rd ... B2
Saltwells Rd ... B3

Scott's Rd ... A3
Seaton Carew Rd ... A3
Shepherdson Way ... B3
Sikh Temple ... B2
Snowdon Rd. ... B2
South West Ironmasters Park. ... B1
Southfield Rd ... C2
Southwell Rd. ... C2
Springfield Rd. ... C1
Startforth Rd. ... A2
Stockton Rd. ... C1
Stockton St ... A2
Surrey St. ... C2
Sycamore Rd. ... C2
Synagogue ... B2
Tax Offices. ... B2
Tees Viaduct ... C1
Teessaurus Park. ... A2
Teesside Tertiary Coll ... B3
Temenos ... B3
The Avenue ... C2
The Crescent. ... C2
Thornfield Rd ... C1
Town Hall. ... B2
Transporter Bridge (Toll). ... A3
Union St. ... B2
University of Teesside ... B2
Upper Lake ... C3
Valley Rd ... C2
Ventnor Rd. ... C2
Victoria Rd. ... B2
Visitor Centre ... A3
Vulcan St ... A2
Warwick St ... C2
Wellesley Rd ... B3
West Lane Hospital ... C1
Westminster Rd ... C2
Wilson St ... B2
Windward Way ... B3
Woodlands Rd ... B2
York Rd. ... C3

Milton Keynes 340

Abbey Way ... B1
Arbrook Ave ... A1
Armourer Dr ... A3
Arncliffe Dr ... A1
Avebury ... C2
Avebury Blvd. ... C2
Bankfield ... B3
Bayard Ave. ... A2
Belvedere ... A2
Bishopstone ... A1
Blundells Rd. ... A1
Boycott Ave. ... C2
Bradville Comm Blvd. ... B1
Bradwell Rd. ... C1
Bramble Ave ... A1
Brearley Ave ... C3
Breckland ... A2
Brill Place ... A3
Burnham Dr. ... A1
Bus Station ... B2
Campbell Park ... B3
Cantle Ave. ... A3
Central Milton Keynes Shopping Area ... C2
Century Ave. ... C2
Chaffron Way ... C3
Childs Way ... C1
Christ the Cornerstone ... B2
Cineworld ... B2
Civic Offices ... B2
Cleavers Ave ... A2
Colesbourne Dr ... A3
Conniburrow Blvd ... A2
County Court. ... B2
Currier Dr ... A2
Dansteed Way. ... A2/A3/B1
Deltic Ave ... B1
Downs Barn ... A2
Downs Barn Blvd ... A2
Eaglestone ... C3
Eelbrook Ave. ... C1
Elder Gate ... B1
Evans Gate ... C2
Fairford Cr. ... A1
Falcon Ave ... A2
Fennel Dr. ... A2
Fishermead Blvd ... C3
Food Centre ... B2
Fulwoods Dr ... C3
Glazier Dr. ... A1
Glovers La ... A1
Grafton Gate ... C1
Grafton St ... A1/C2
Gurnards Ave ... A3
Harrier Dr ... A3
Ibstone Ave ... A1
Langcliffe Dr. ... A1
Leys Rd ... A1
Library ... B2
Linford Wood ... A2
Marlborough Gate ... B2
Marlborough St ... A2/B3
Mercers Dr ... A2
Midsummer ... B2
Midsummer Blvd ... C2
Milton Keynes Central ... C1
Monks Way ... A1
Mullen Ave. ... A3
Mullion Pl ... C3
National Hockey Stadium ... A2
Neath Hill ... A3
North Elder ... C3
North Grafton ... C1
North Overgate ... C3
North Row ... A3
North Saxon ... B2
North Secklow ... B2
North Skeldon ... C3
North Witan ... B2
Oakley Gdns ... A3

Oldbrook Blvd. ... C2
Open-Air Theatre ... B3
Overgate ... A3
Overstreet. ... A3
Patriot Dr. ... B1
Pencarrow Pl ... B3
Penryn Ave ... B3
Perran Ave ... C1
Pitcher La ... C1
Place Retail Park, The ... C1
Point Centre, The. ... B2
Police Station ... B2
Portway ... A1
Post Office ... A2/B2/C2
Precedent Dr ... B1
Quinton Dr. ... C1
Ramsons Ave. ... A2
Rockingham Dr. ... A2
Rooksley ... C1
Rooksley Retail Park . C1
Saxon Gate ... B2
Saxon St. ... A1/C3
Secklow Gate ... B2
Shackleton Pl ... C3
Silbury Blvd. ... B2
Skeldon ... C3
South Grafton ... C2
South Row ... C2
South Saxon ... C2
South Secklow ... B3
South Witan ... C2
Springfield ... C3
Stanton Wood ... A1
Stantonbury ... A1
Stantonbury L Ctr ... A1
Strudwick Dr. ... C3
Sunrise Parkway ... A2
Telephone Exchange. ... B2
The Boundary ... C3
Theatre & Art Gallery ... B2
Tolcarne Ave ... C3
Towan Ave ... C3
Trueman Pl ... C2
Vauxhall ... B2
Winterhill Retail Park .C2
Witan Gate. ... B2
X-Scape ... B3

Newcastle upon Tyne 340

Albert St. ... A3
Argyle St. ... B3
Back New Bridge St ... B3
BALTIC Centre for Contemporary Art ... C3
Barker St. ... A3
Barrack Rd. ... B1
Bath La ... B1
Bell's Court ... B2
Bessie Surtees Ho ... C2
Bigg Market. ... C2
Biscuit Factory ... A3
Black Gate ... C2
Blackett St. ... B2
Blandford Sq. ... C1
Boating Lake. ... A1
Boyd St. ... B3
Brandling Park ... A2
Bus Station ... B2
Buxton St. ... B3
Byron St. ... A3
Camden St. ... A3
Castle Keep ... C2
Central ... C1
Central Library ... B2
Central Motorway ... B2
Chester St. ... A3
City Hall. ... B2
City Road ... B3/C3
City Walls ... C1
Civic Centre. ... A2
Claremont Rd. ... A1
Clarence St ... B3
Clarence Walk ... B3
Clayton St. ... C1/B1
Clayton St West ... C1
Coach Station ... B2
College St ... B2
Collingwood St ... C2
Copland Terr. ... B3
Coppice Way. ... B3
Corporation St ... B1
Courts ... B3
Crawhall Rd. ... B3
Dean St. ... C2
Discovery ... C1
Dinsdale Pl ... A3
Dinsdale Rd. ... A3
Doncaster Rd ... A3
Durant Rd. ... B2
Eldon Sq. ... B1
Eldon Sq Shopping Ctr. ... B2
Ellison Pl ... B2
Empire ... B1
Eskdale Terr ... A2
Eslington Terr. ... A2
Exhibition Park. ... A1
Falconar St. ... B3
Fenkle St. ... C1
Forth Banks. ... C1
Forth St. ... C1
Gallowgate ... B1
Gateshead Heritage @ St Mary's ... C2
Gateshead Millennium Bridge ... C3
Gibson St. ... B3
Goldspink La ... A3
Grainger Market. ... B2
Grainger St ... C2
Grantham Rd. ... A3
Granville Rd. ... A2
Great North Mus: Hancock ... A2
Grey St. ... C2
Groat Market. ... C2

Guildhall ... C2
Hancock St. ... A2
Hanover St. ... C2
Hatton Gallery ... A1
Hawks Rd. ... C3
Heber St. ... B1
Helmsley Rd ... A3
High Bridge ... C2
High Level Bridge. ... C2
Hillgate ... C3
Howard St. ... B3
Hutton Terr ... A3
Information Ctr ... A2
Jesmond ... A2
Jesmond Rd. ... A2/A3
John Dobson St ... B2
John George Joicey Museum ... C2
Jubilee Rd ... B3
Kelvin Gr ... A3
Kensington Terr. ... A2
Laing Gallery ... B2
Lambton Rd. ... A2
Leazes Cres ... B1
Leazes La ... B1
Leazes Park ... B1
Leazes Park Rd ... B1
Leazes Terr. ... B1
Live ... C2
Low Friar St. ... C1
Manor Chare. ... C2
Manors ... B2
Manors Station ... B3
Market St. ... B2
Melbourne St ... B3
Mill Rd ... C3
Mill Volvo Tyne ... C1
Monument ... B2
Monument Mall Sh Ctr B2
Morpeth St. ... A1
Mosley St. ... C2
Napier St. ... A3
Nazareth House ... A1
New Bridge St. ... B2/B3
Newcastle Central Station ... C1
Newcastle University ... A1
Newgate Shopping Ctr. ... B1
Newgate St. ... B1
Newington Rd ... A3
Northern Stage Theatre ... A1
Northumberland Rd ... B2
Northumberland St ... B2
Northumbria Univ ... A2
Northwest Radial Rd ... A1
O2 Academy ... C1
Oakwellgate ... C2
Orchard St. ... C2
Osborne Rd ... A2
Osborne Terr. ... A3
Pandon. ... B3
Pandon Bank. ... B3
Park Terr ... A1
Percy St. ... B1
Pilgrim St. ... B2
Pipewellgate. ... C2
Pitt St ... B1
Plummer Tower ... B2
Police Station ... B1
Portland Rd. ... A3/B3
Portland Terr. ... A3
Post Office ... A3/B1/B2/B3
Pottery La ... C1
Prudhoe Pl. ... B1
Prudhoe St. ... B1
Quayside ... C2
Queen Elizabeth II Bridge ... C3
Queen Victoria Rd ... A1
Richardson Rd ... A1
Ridley Pl. ... B2
Rock Terr ... B3
Rosedale Terr. ... A3
Royal Victoria Infirmary ... A1
Sage Gateshead, The ... C3
St Andrew's St ... B1
St James ... B1
St James' Blvd ... C1
St James' Park (Newcastle Utd FC) .. B1
St Mary's Place. ... B2
St Nicholas ... C2
St Nicholas St ... C2
St Thomas' St. ... B1
Sandyford Rd ... A2/A3
Science Park. ... B3
Shield St. ... B3
Shieldfield. ... B3
Simpson Terr. ... B3
South Shore Rd. ... C3
South St. ... C1
Starbeck Ave. ... A3
Stepney Rd. ... B3
Stoddart St. ... B3
Stowell St. ... B1
Strawberry Pl ... B1
Swing Bridge. ... C2
Temple St. ... C1
Terrace Pl ... B1
The Close. ... C2
The Gate ... B1
The Side. ... C2
Times Sq ... C1
Tower St. ... B3
Trinity House. ... C2
Tyne Bridge. ... C2
Tyneside ... B2
Victoria Sq. ... A2
Warwick St. ... A3
Waterloo St. ... C1
Wellington St. ... B1

Westgate Rd ... C1/C2
Windsor Terr. ... A2
Worswick St. ... B2
Wretham Pl. ... B3

Newport Casnewydd 340

Albert Terr. ... B1
Allt-yr-Yn Ave. ... A1
Alma St. ... C2
Ambulance Station ... A2
Bailey St. ... B2
Barrack Hill ... A2
Bath St ... A3
Bedford Rd ... C3
Belle Vue La ... C1
Belle Vue Park ... C1
Bishop St. ... A3
Blewitt St. ... B1
Bolt Cl. ... C3
Bolt St. ... C3
Bond St. ... A2
Bosworth Dr ... A1
Bridge St ... B1
Bristol St. ... A3
Bryngwyn Rd. ... B1
Brynhyfryd Ave. ... C1
Brynhyfryd Rd. ... C1
Bus Station ... B2
Caerau Cres. ... C1
Caerau Rd. ... B1
Caerleon Rd ... A3
Capel Cres. ... C2
Cardiff Rd ... C2
Caroline St. ... B3
Castle (Remains) ... A2
Cedar Rd ... A3
Charles St. ... B2
Charlotte Dr ... C2
Chepstow Rd ... A3
Church Rd ... A3
City Cinema ... B1
Civic Centre. ... B1
Clarence Pl ... A2
Clifton Pl ... B1
Clifton Rd. ... C1
Clyffard Cres. ... B1
Clytha Park Rd ... B1
Clytha Sq ... C2
Coldra Rd. ... C1
Collier St ... A3
Colne St. ... B3
Commercial Rd. ... C3
Commercial St. ... B2
Corelli St ... A3
Corn St. ... B2
Corporation Rd. ... B3
Coulson Cl ... C2
County Court. ... A1
Courts ... A1
Courts ... B2
Crawford St. ... A3
Cyril St. ... B3
Dean St. ... A3
Devon Pl. ... A1
Dewsland Park Rd ... C1
Dolphin St. ... C3
East Dock Rd. ... C3
East St. ... A1
East Usk Rd ... A3
Ebbw Vale Wharf ... A3
Emlyn St. ... B2
Enterprise Way ... B3
Eton Rd. ... A3
Evans St ... A2
Factory Rd ... A2
Fields Rd ... B1
Francis Dr ... C2
Frederick St ... C3
Friars Rd ... C1
Gaer La ... B1
George St. ... C2
George Street Bridge ... C2
Godfrey Rd ... B1
Gold Tops. ... B1
Gore St ... A3
Gorsedd Circle ... C1
Grafton Rd. ... A3
Graham St ... B1
Granville St. ... C3
Harlequin Dr ... C3
Harrow Rd ... A3
Herbert Rd. ... A3
Herbert Walk ... C2
Hereford St. ... A3
High St. ... B2
Hill St. ... B2
Hoskins St. ... A2
Ivor Sq ... A3
Jones St. ... B1
Junction Rd. ... A3
Keynsham Ave. ... C2
King St. ... C2
Kingsway ... B2
Kingsway Centre ... B2
Ledbury Dr. ... A2
Library ... B2
Liverpool Wharf ... B3
Llanthewy Rd. ... B1
Llanvair Rd ... A3
Locke St. ... A2
Lower Dock St. ... C2
Lucas St. ... A2
Manchester St. ... A3
Market ... B2
Marlborough Rd ... A3
Mellon St. ... C3
Mill St. ... A2
Morgan St. ... A3
Mountjoy Rd ... C1
Newport Bridge ... A2
Newport Ctr ... B2
Newport RFC. ... B3
Newport Station ... B2

Oakfield Rd ... C1
Park Sq. ... C2
Police Station ... A3/C2
Post Office ... B1/B2/C1/C3
Power St. ... A1
Prince St. ... A3
Pugsley St. ... A2
Queen St. ... B2
Queen's Cl ... A1
Queen's Hill ... A1
Queen's Hill Cres ... A1
Queensway ... B2
Railway St ... B2
Riverfront Arts Centre ... B2
Riverside ... A3
Rodney Rd ... C2
Royal Gwent (A&E) ... C2
Rudry St ... A3
Rugby Rd ... B3
Ruperra La ... C3
Ruperra St ... C3
St Edmund St. ... B1
St Mark's Cres. ... A1
St Mary St ... A1
St Vincent Rd ... A3
St Woolos ... C2
St Woolos General (no A+E) ... C1
St Woolos Rd. ... B1
School La. ... C1
Serpentine Rd. ... B1
Sheaf La. ... A2
Skinner St ... B2
Sorrel Dr ... A3
South Market St ... C3
Spencer Rd. ... A1
Stow Hill. ... B2/C1/C2
Stow Park Ave. ... C1
Stow Park Dr. ... C1
TA Centre. ... A3
Talbot St. ... B2
Tennis Club ... A1
Tregare St. ... A3
Trostrey St. ... A3
Tunnel Terr. ... B1
Turner St. ... A3
Upper Dock St. ... B2
Usk St. ... A3
Usk Way. ... B3/C3
Victoria Cr. ... C1
War Memorial ... B1
Waterloo Rd. ... C1
West St. ... B1
Wharves. ... A3
Wheeler St. ... A2
Whitby Pl ... B3
Windsor Terr. ... B1
York Pl ... C1

Newquay 340

Agar Rd ... B2
Alma Pl. ... B2
Ambulance Station ... A2
Anthony Rd ... C3
Atlantic Hotel ... A1
Bank St. ... B1
Barrowfields. ... C3
Bay View Terr ... B2
Beach Rd ... B2
Beacon Rd ... B1
Belmont Pl. ... B1
Berry Rd. ... B2
Blue Reef Aquarium ... B1
Boating Lake. ... C2
Bus Station ... B2
Chapel Hill. ... C2
Chester Rd. ... A3
Cheviot Rd ... C1/C2
Chichester Cres ... C2
Chynance Dr ... C1
Chyverton Cl ... C1
Cliff Rd. ... B1
Coach Park ... B2
Colvreath Rd ... B3
Council Ofices ... A2
Crantock St ... B1
Criggar Rocks ... A3
Dale Cl ... C3
Dale Rd. ... C3
Dane Rd ... B1
East St. ... B2
Edgcumbe Ave ... B2
Edgcumbe Gdns ... B2
Eliot Gdns ... B2
Elm Cl ... A3
Ennor's Rd. ... B2
Fernhill Rd. ... B1
Fire Station ... A2
Fore St. ... B1
Gannel Rd. ... C1
Golf Driving Range. ... A1
Gover La. ... B1
Great Western Beach .A2
Grosvenor Ave. ... B2
Harbour. ... A1
Hawkins Rd. ... C2
Headleigh Rd. ... B2
Hilgrove Rd ... A3/B3
Holywell Rd. ... B1
Hope Terr. ... B1
Huer's House, The ... A1
Information Ctr ... B1
Island Cres. ... B1
Jubilee St. ... B1
Kew Cl. ... C2
Killacourt Cove. ... A2
King Edward Cres. ... A2
Lanhenvor Ave. ... B2
Library ... B2
Lifeboat Station ... A1
Linden Ave. ... C2
Listry Rd. ... C1
Lusty Glaze Beach ... A3
Lusty Glaze Rd. ... A3

Manor Rd. ... B1
Marcus Hill ... B2
Mayfield Rd. ... B2
Meadowside ... C2
Mellanvrane La. ... C2
Michell Ave ... B2
Miniature Golf Course .C3
Miniature Railway ... B1
Mount Wise. ... B1
Mowhay Cl. ... C3
Narrowcliff ... A3
Newquay ... B2
Newquay Hospital (no A&E) ... B2
Newquay Town Football Ground ... B3
Newquay Zoo ... C3
North Pier ... A1
North Quay Hill ... A1
Oakleigh Terr ... B2
Pargolla Rd ... B2
Pendragon Cres ... C3
Pengannel Cl. ... C1
Penina Ave. ... C3
Police Sta & Courts ... B2
Post Office ... B1/B2
Quarry Park Rd ... C2
Rawley La. ... C2
Reeds Way ... B1
Robartes Rd ... B2
St Anne's Rd ... A3
St Aubyn Cres ... B2
St George's Rd ... B1
St John's Rd. ... B1
St Mary's Rd ... B1
St Michael's ... B1
St Michael's Rd. ... B1
St Thomas' Rd. ... B2
Seymour Ave. ... B2
South Pier ... A1
South Quay Hill ... A1
Sweet Briar Cres ... C2
Sydney Rd ... A1
The Crescent. ... A2
Tolcarne Beach. ... A2
Tolcarne Point ... A2
Tolcarne Rd. ... B2
Tor Rd. ... B2
Towan Beach ... A1
Towan Blystra Rd ... B2
Tower Rd. ... A1
Trebarwith Cres ... B2
Tredour Rd. ... C3
Treforda Rd. ... C3
Tregoss Rd. ... C3
Tregunnel Hill. ... B1/C1
Tregunnel Saltings ... C1
Trelawney Rd ... B2
Treloggan La. ... C3
Treloggan Rd. ... C3
Trembath Cres ... C3
Trenance Ave ... B2
Trenance Gardens. ... B2
Trenance La. ... C2
Trenance Leisure Park B3
Trenance Rd ... B2
Trenarth Rd. ... C2
Treninnick Hill ... C3
Tretherras Rd ... A3
Trethewey Way ... C1
Trevemper Rd. ... C2
Tunnels Through Time ... B1
Ulalia Rd. ... B2
Vivian Cl. ... B2
Waterworld. ... C3
Whitegate Rd ... B3
Wych Hazel Way ... C3

Newtown Y Drenewydd 340

Ash Cl. ... A3
Back La. ... B2
Baptist Chapel ... B2
Barn La. ... A2
Bear Lanes Sh Ctr. ... B2
Beech Cl. ... A3
Beechwood Dr ... A2
Brimmon Cl. ... C2
Brimmon Rd ... C2
Broad St. ... B2
Bryn Bank ... A1
Bryn Cl ... A2
Bryn Gdns ... A1
Bryn House ... A1
Bryn La. ... A1/A2
Bryn Meadows ... A1
Bryn St ... A2
Brynglais Ave ... B1
Brynglais Cl. ... B1
Bus Station ... B2
Byrnwood Dr. ... A1
Cambrian Bridge ... B3
Cambrian Gdns. ... B3
Cambrian Way. ... B2
Canal Rd. ... A3
Castle Mound ... C2
Cedewain. ... C3
Cefnaire ... C2
Cefnaire Coppice ... C2
Ceiriog ... C3
Cemetery. ... A3
Church (Remains of). ... B2
Churchill Dr. ... A1
Cledan ... B3
Colwyn ... B3
Commercial St ... B2
Council Offices. ... B1
Crescent St ... A2
Cwm Llanfair. ... A2
Davies Memorial Gallery ... B2
Dinas ... B3
Dolafon Rd ... B3
Dolerw Park ... B1
Dolfor Rd ... C1
Eirianell ... C2
Fairfield Dr ... A2
Fferdd Croesawdy ... A2

Fire Station C1
Frankwell St A2
Frolic St B2
Fron La A1
Garden La A2
Gas St B2
Glyndŵr C1
Golwgydre La B2
Gorsedd Circle B1
Great Brimmon Farm C3
Hafren B2
Halfpenny Bridge B2
High St B2
Hillside Ave A3
Hoel Treowen C2
Information Ctr B2
Kerry Rd B3
Ladywell Shopping
  Centre B2
Library B1
Llanfair St A2
Llanidloes Rd C1
Llys Ifor A2
Lon Cerddyn B1
Lonesome La. . . . A3
Long Bridge A2
Lon Helyg C2
Lower Canal Rd B3
Maldwyn Leisure Ctr C1
Market B2
Market St B2
Milford Rd B1
Mill Cl B1
Miniature Railway ◆ B1
Mwyn Fynydd A3
New Church St B2
New Rd B2
Newtown Football Gd B1
Newtown Infirmary A2
Newtown Station A2
Oak Tree Ave A3
Old Kerry Rd B3
Oldbarn La. . . . A2
Park Cl A2
Parklands B1
Park La. . . . B2
Park St B2
Pavillion Ct C1
Plantation La. . . . C2
Police Station B1
Pont Brynfedw A2
Pool Rd B3
Poplar St B2
Post Office B2/C1
Powys B2
Powys Theatre ◆ A2
Pryce Jones Stores &
  Museum ◆ B2
Quaker Meeting Ho B1
Regent B2
Robert Owen House B2
Robert Owen Mus B2
Rugby Club A3
St David's B2
School La. . . . A2
Sheaf St B3
Short Bridge St. . . . B2
Stone St B2
Sycamore Dr A2
Textile Museum B2
The Bryn A1
The Park. . . . B2
Town Hall B2
Union St A2
Upper Brimmon C3
Vastre Industrial Est B3
War Memorial B2
WHSmith Museum C1
Wynfields C1
Y Ffrydd A3

Northampton 340

78 Derngate B3
Abington Sq B3
Abington St B3
Alcombe St A3
All Saints' B2
Ambush St B1
Angel St B2
Arundel St A2
Ash St A2
Auctioneers Way A2
Bailiff St A2
Barrack Rd A2
Beaconsfield Terr A3
Becketts Park C3
Becketts Park Marina C3
Bedford Rd B3
Billing Rd B3
Brecon St A1
Brewery C2
Bridge St B2
Broad St B2
Burns St A3
Bus Station B2
Campbell St. . . . A2
Castle (Site of) B2
Castle St. . . . B2
Cattle Market Rd C2
Central Museum &
  Art Gallery B2
Charles St A3
Cheyne Walk B3
Church La. . . . A2
Clare St A3
Cloutsham St. . . . A3
College St B2
Colwyn Rd B2
Cotton End. . . . C2
Countess Rd A1
County Hall B2
Court A3
Craven St A3
Crown & County
  Courts B3
Denmark Rd B3
Derngate B3
Derngate & Royal
  Theatres ◆ B3

Doddridge Church ◆ B2
Duke St. . . . A3
Dunster St A3
Earl St A3
Euston Rd C2
Fire Station A3
Foot Meadow B2
Gladstone Rd. . . . A1
Gold St B2
Grafton St A2
Gray St A3
Green St B1
Greenwood Rd B1
Greyfriars B2
Grosvenor Centre B2
Grove Rd A3
Guildhall ◆ B2
Hampton St A2
Harding Terr A1
Hazelwood Rd B3
Herbert St B1
Hervey St A3
Hester St A2
Holy Sepulchre ◆ A2
Hood St A3
Horse Market B2
Hunter St A3
Information Ctr B1
Kettering Rd A3
Kingswell St B2
Lady's La B2
Leicester St A2
Leslie Rd A2
Library B3
Lorne Rd A2
Lorry Park A1
Louise Rd A1
Lower Harding St A2
Lower Hester St A2
Lower Mounts. . . . B3
Lower Priory St A2
Main Rd C1
Marefair B2
Market Sq B2
Marlboro Rd B1
Marriott St A2
Military Rd A3
Mounts Baths L Ctr. . . . A2
Nene Valley Retail Pk. . . . C1
New South Bridge Rd. . . . C2
Northampton General
  Hospital (A&E) C3
Northampton Sta A2
Northcote St A2
Nunn Mills Rd C3
Old Towcester Rd C2
Overstone Rd A3
Peacock Pl. . . . B2
Pembroke Rd A1
Penn Court C2
Police Station B2
Post Office
  . . . . A1/A2/B3/C2
Quorn Way. . . . A2
Ransome Rd C3
Regent Sq A2
Robert St A2
St Andrew's Rd A1
St Andrew's St A1
St Edmund's Rd B3
St George's St A2
St Giles B2
St Giles St B3
St Giles' Terr B3
St James' Mill Rd B1
St James' Mill Rd East C1
St James Park Rd B1
St James Retail Park B1
St James Rd B1
St Leonard's Rd C2
St Mary's St B2
St Michael's Rd A3
St Peter's B2
St Peter's Square
  Shopping Precinct. . . . B2
St Peter's Way. . . . B2
Salisbury Rd B1
Scarletwell St B2
Semilong Rd A2
Sheep St. . . . B2
Sol Central (L Ctr) B2
Somerset St A3
South Bridge. . . . C2
Southfield Ave C2
Spencer Bridge Rd. . . . A1
Spencer Rd A2
Spring Gdns. . . . B2
Spring La B2
Swan St C2
TA Centre A3
Tanner St B2
The Drapery B2
The Ridings B3
Tintern Ave A1
Towcester Rd C2
Upper Bath St B2
Upper Mounts. . . . B2
Victoria Park A1
Victoria Promenade B2
Victoria Rd B3
Victoria St. . . . B2
Wellingborough Rd B3
West Bridge. . . . B1
York Rd B3

Norwich 341

Albion Way C3
All Saints Green C2
Anchor Cl. . . . A3
Anchor St. . . . A3
Anglia Sq B2
Argyle St C3
Arts Centre B1
Ashby St C2
Assembly House B1
Bank Plain B2
Barker St A2
Barn Rd A2
Barrack St A3

Ber St C2
Bethel St B1
Bishop Bridge A3
Bishopbridge Rd. . . . A3
Bishopgate B3
Blackfriars St A2
Botolph St A2
Braconde C2
Brazen Gate. . . . C2
Bridewell ◆ B2
Brunswick Rd C1
Bull Close Rd A2
Bus Station C2
Calvert St B2
Cannell Green. . . . A3
Carrow Rd C3
Castle Mall. . . . B2
Castle Meadow. . . . B2
Castle & Museum ◆ B2
Cathedral † B2
Cathedral Retail Park A1
Cattlemarket St B2
Chantry Rd. . . . C1
Chapel Loke C2
Chapelfield East. . . . B1
Chapelfield Gdns B1
Chapelfield North B1
Chapelfield Rd B1
Chapelfield Sh Ctr C1
City Hall B1
City Rd C2
City Wall C1/C3
Colegate A2
Coslany St B1
Cow Hill B1
Cow Tower ◆ A3
Cowgate A2
Crown & Magistrates
  Courts B2
Dragon Hall Heritage
  Centre ◆ C3
Duke St. . . . A1
Edward St A2
Elm Hill. . . . B2
Erpingham Gate ◆. . . . B2
Fire Station B1
Fishergate. . . . A2
Foundry Bridge B3
Fye Bridge A2
Garden St. . . . C2
Gas Hill. . . . B3
Grapes Hill. . . . B1
Great Hospital
  Halls, The. . . . A3
Grove Ave. . . . C1
Grove Rd C1
Guildhall ◆ B1
Gurney Rd A3
Hall Rd C2
Heathgate. . . . A3
Heigham St A1
Horn's La C2
Information Ctr B1
Ipswich Rd C1
James Stuart Gdns B3
King Edward VI
  School ◆ B2
King St B2
King St C3
Koblenz Ave. . . . C3
Library B1
London St B2
Lower Clarence Rd. . . . B3
Lower Cl. . . . B3
Maddermarket ◆ B1
Magdalen St A2
Mariners La C2
Market B2
Market Ave B2
Mountergate. . . . B3
Mousehold St A3
Newmarket Rd C1
Norfolk Gallery ◆ B2
Norfolk St C1
Norwich City FC C3
Norwich Station B3
Oak St A1
Palace St B2
Pitt St A2
Playhouse ◆ B2
Post Office A2/B2/C2
Pottergate. . . . B1
Prince of Wales Rd. . . . B2
Princes St B2
Pull's Ferry ◆ B3
Puppet Theatre ◆ B2
Quebec Rd B3
Queen St B2
Queens Rd C2
RC Cathedral † B1
Recorder Rd B3
Riverside Entertainment
  Centre B3
Riverside Swimming
  Centre B3
Riverside Retail Park. . . . C3
Riverside Rd B3
Rosary Rd B3
Rose La. . . . B2
Rouen Rd B2
Royal Norfolk Regiment
  Museum ◆ B2
St Andrew's &
  Blackfriars Hall ◆ B2
St Andrews St B2
St Augustines St. . . . A1
St Benedicts St B1
St Ethelbert's Gate ◆ B2
St Faiths La B3
St Georges St A2
St Giles St B1
St James Cl A3
St Julians C2
St Martin's La A1
St Peter Mancroft † B1
St Peters St B2
St Stephens Rd C1
St Stephens St C1
Silver Rd A2
Silver St A2

Southwell Rd. . . . C2
Strangers Hall ◆ B1
Superstore C2
Surrey St A1
Sussex St A1
The Close. . . . B3
The Forum ◆ B1
The Walk B2
Theatre Royal ◆ B1
Theatre St B1
Thorn La. . . . B2
Thorpe Rd B3
Tombland B2
Union St C1
Vauxhall St B1
Victoria St. . . . C1
Walpole St. . . . B1
Wensum St A2
Wessex St C1
Westwick St A1
Wherry Rd C3
Whitefriars A2
Willow La. . . . B1
Yacht Station B3

Nottingham 341

Abbotsford Dr. . . . A3
Addison St A1
Albert Hall ◆ B1
Alfred St South A3
Alfreton Rd A1
All Saints St A1
Annesley Gr. . . . A1
Arboretum ❀ A1
Arboretum St A1
Arthur St A1
Arts Theatre ◆ B3
Ashforth St A2
Balmoral Rd A1
Barker Gate. . . . B3
Bath St B3
Belgrave Centre B1
Bellar Gate B3
Belward St B3
Blue Bell Hill Rd. . . . A3
Brewhouse Yard ◆ C2
Broad Marsh Bus Sta. . . . C2
Broad Marsh Precinct C2
Broad St. . . . B3
Brook St. . . . B3
Burns St. . . . A1
Burton St B2
Bus Station C2
Canal St. . . . C2
Carlton St. . . . B3
Carrington St C2
Castle Blvd. . . . C1
Castle ☐ C1
Castle Gate. . . . C2
Castle Mdw Retail Pk. . . . C1
Castle Meadow Rd ☐. . . . C1
Castle Museum &
  Gallery ◆ C1
Castle Rd C2
Castle Wharf C2
Cavendish Rd East C1
Cemetery. . . . B1
Chaucer St. . . . B1
Cheapside B2
Church Rd. . . . A2
City Link. . . . C3
City of Caves ◆ C2
Clarendon St B1
Cliff Rd C2
Clumber Rd East. . . . C1
Clumber St B2
College St B1
Collin St C2
Conway Cl B3
Council House ◆ B2
Court B3
Cranbrook St. . . . B3
Cranmer St A2
Cromwell St. . . . B1
Curzon St B2
Derby Rd B1
Dryden St A1
Exchange Arcade ◆ B2
Fishpond Dr. . . . C1
Fletcher Gate B3
Forest Rd East. . . . A1
Forest Rd West A1
Friar La. . . . C2
Galleries of Justice ☐ B3
Gedling Gr A1
Gedling St B3
George St B3
Gill St A2
Glasshouse St B2
Goldsmith St B1
Goose Gate B3
Great Freeman St. . . . A2
Guildhall ☐ B2
Hamilton Dr. . . . C1
Hampden St A1
Heathcote St B3
High Pavement C3
High School ☐ A1
Holles Cr C1
Hope Dr C1
Hungerhill Rd A3
Huntingdon Dr B1
Huntingdon St A2
Information Ctr B2
Instow Rise A2
International Com Ctr A2
Kent St B3
King St B2
Lace Centre, The C2
Lace Market ☐ B3
Lace Mkt Theatre ◆ B3
Lamartine St B3
Lenton Rd C1
Lewis Cl A3
Lincoln St B2
London Rd C3
Long Row B2
Low Pavement C2
Lower Parliament St B3

Magistrates Court C2
Maid Marian Way B2
Mansfield Rd A2/B2
Middle Hill. . . . C2
Milton St B2
Mount St C1
National Ice Centre C3
Newcastle Dr. . . . B1
Newstead Gr A2
North Sherwood St A2
Nottingham Arena C3
Nottingham Sta ◆ C2
Nottingham Trent
  University A2/B2
Old Market Square ◆ B2
Oliver St A1
Park Dr C1
Park Row B1
Park Terr B1
Park Valley C1
Peas Hill Rd A3
Peel St A1
Pelham St B3
Peveril Dr. . . . C1
Plantagenet St A3
Playhouse Theatre ◆ B1
Plumptre St C3
Police Station B2
Poplar St C3
Portland Rd B1
Post Office C3
Queen's Rd C3
Raleigh St A1
Regent St B1
Rick St B3
Robin Hood Statue ◆ C2
Robin Hood St. . . . B3
Royal Centre ◆ B2
Royal Children Inn ☐ C2
Royal Concert Hall ◆ B2
St Ann's Hill Rd A2
St Ann's Way A2
St Ann's Well Rd A3
St Barnabas † B1
St James' St B2
St Mark's St B2
St Mary's Gdn of Rest. . . . B3
St Mary's Gate. . . . B3
St Nicholas † C2
St Peter's † B2
St Peter's Gate B2
Salutation Inn ☐ C2
Shakespeare St B2
Shelton St A2
South Pde B2
South Rd C1
South Sherwood St B2
Station St C3
Station Street ◆ C2
Stoney St B3
Talbot St. . . . B1
Tattershall Dr C1
Tennis Dr B1
Tennyson St A1
The Park. . . . C1
The Ropewalk B1
Theatre Royal ◆ B2
Trent St C2
Trent University ◆ B2
Trinity Square Sh Ctr B2
Trip to Jerusalem
  Inn ☐ C2
Union Rd B3
Upper Parliament St B2
Victoria Centre B2
Victoria Leisure Ctr B3
Victoria Park B3
Victoria St B2
Walter St A1
Warser Gate B3
Watkin St A2
Waverley St A1
Wheeler Gate B2
Wilford Rd C2
Wilford St C2
Willoughby House ◆ C2
Wollaton St B1
Woodborough Rd. . . . A2
Woolpack La B3
York St A2

Oban 341

Aird's Cres. . . . C2
Albany St B2
Albert La A2
Albert Rd A2
Alma Cres B1
Ambulance Station C3
Angus Terr. . . . C3
Ardconnel Rd B2
Ardconnel Terr. . . . B2
Argyll Sq B2
Argyll St B2
Atlantis Leisure Ctr A2
Bayview Rd A1
Benvoulin Rd B1
Bowling Green A2
Breadalbane St B2
Bus Station B2
Campbell St B2
College. . . . B2
Colonsay Terr. . . . A1
Columba Building B2
Combie St B2
Corran Brae. . . . A1
Corran Esplanade A1/A2
Corran Halls ◆ A2
Court B2
Crannaig-a-
  Mhinisteir C2
Crannog La C1
Croft Ave B2
Dalintart Dr C2
Dalriach Rd B2
Distillery ◆ B2
Drummore Rd C1
Duncraggan Rd B2
Dunollie Rd A2
Dunuaran Rd B2

Feochan Gr C3
Ferry Terminal B1
Gallanach Rd. . . . C1
George St. . . . A2
Glencruitten Dr C3
Glencruitten Rd B3
Glenmore Rd C1
Glenshellach Rd C1
Glenshellach Terr C1
Harbour Bowl A2
Hazeldean Cres A3
High St A2
Highland Theatre
  Cinema ☐ A2
Hill St B2
Industrial Estate. . . . C3
Information Ctr B2
Islay St B2
Jacob's Ladder ◆ C3
Jura Rd C3
Knipoch Pl. . . . C3
Laurel Cres A2
Laurel Rd A2/A3
Library B1
Lifeboat Station B1
Lighthouse Pier B1
Lismore Cres A1
Lochavullin Dr C1
Lochavullin Rd C1
Lochside St C2
Longsdale Cres. . . . A2
Longsdale Rd A2/A3
Longsdale Terr A1
Lunga Rd C3
Lynn Rd C2
Market St B2
McCaig Rd C3
McCaig's Tower ◆ B2
Mill La. . . . C2
Miller Rd. . . . B2
Millpark Ave C1
Millpark Rd C1
Mossfield Ave B3
Mossfield Dr B3
Mossfield Stadium B3
Nant Dr C2
Nelson Rd A3
North Pier A1
Nursery La A2
Oban ◆ B2
Police Station B2
Polvinister Rd B3
Post Office A2/B2
Pulpit Dr C1
Pulpit Hill. . . . C1
Pulpit Hill
  Viewpoint ◆ C1
Quarry Rd. . . . C2
Queen's Park Pl B2
Railway Quay. . . . B1
Rockfield Rd B2
St Columba's † A1
St John's † B1
Scalpay Terr C3
Shore St B1
Shuna Terr. . . . C3
Sinclair Dr C2
Soroba Rd B2/C2
South Pier B1
Stevenson St B2
Tweedale St B2
Ulva Rd B1
Villa Rd B1
War & Peace ◆ B1

Oxford 341

Adelaide St A1
Albert St. . . . A1
All Souls (Coll) B2
Ashmolean Mus ☐ B1
Balliol (Coll) B2
Banbury Rd A2
Bate Collection of
  Musical
  Instruments ☐ C2
Beaumont St B1
Becket St B1
Blackhall Rd A2
Blue Boar St B2
Bodleian Library ☐ B2
Botanic Garden ❀ B3
Brasenose (Coll) B2
Brewer St C2
Broad St B2
Burton-Taylor
  Theatre ◆ B2
Bus Station B1
Canal St A1
Cardigan St A1
Carfax Tower ◆ B2
Castle ☐ B1
Castle St. . . . B2
Catte St B2
Cemetery. . . . C1
Christ Church (Coll). . . . B2
Christ Church Cath † C2
Christ Church Mdw C2
Clarendon Centre B2
Coach & Lorry Park C1
College. . . . B2
Coll of Further Ed C1
Cornmarket St B2
Corpus Christi (Coll) B2
County Hall B1
Covered Market B2
Cowley Pl. . . . B3
Cranham St A1
Cranham Terr. . . . A1
Cricket Ground B1
Crown & County
  Courts C2
Deer Park. . . . B3
Exeter (Coll) B2
Folly Bridge C2
George St B1
Great Clarendon St A1
Hart St A1
Hertford (Coll) B2
High St B2

Hollybush Row B1
Holywell St B2
Hythe Bridge St B1
Ice Rink C1
Information Ctr B2
Jericho St A1
Jesus (Coll) B2
Jowett Walk B3
Juxon St A1
Keble (Coll) A2
Keble Rd A2
Library B3
Linacre (Coll) A3
Lincoln (Coll) B2
Little Clarendon St. . . . A1
Longwall St B3
Magdalen (Coll) B3
Magdalen Bridge B3
Magdalen St B2
Magistrate's Court. . . . B1
Manchester (Coll) B2
Manor Rd B3
Mansfield (Coll) A3
Mansfield Rd A2
Market B2
Marlborough Rd C1
Merton Field C2
Merton (Coll) B3
Merton St. . . . B2
Mus of Modern Art ☐ B2
Museum of Oxford ☐ B2
Museum Rd A2
New College (Coll) B3
New Inn Hall St B2
New Rd B1
New Theatre ◆ B2
Norfolk St C1
Nuffield (Coll) B1
Observatory A1
Observatory St A1
Odeon ☐ B1/B2
Old Fire Station ◆ B1
Old Greyfriars St C2
Oriel (Coll) B2
Oxford Station ◆ B1
Oxford Story, The ◆ B2
Oxford University
  Research Centres A2
Oxpens Rd C1
Paradise Sq. . . . C1
Paradise St B1
Park End St B1
Parks Rd A2/B2
Pembroke (Coll) C2
Phoenix ☐ A1
Picture Gallery ◆ C2
Plantation Rd A1
Playhouse ◆ B2
Police Station B2
Post Office A1/B2
Pusey St B2
Queen's La B3
Queen's (Coll) B2
Radcliffe Camera ☐ B2
Rewley Rd B1
Richmond Rd A1
Rose La. . . . B3
Ruskin (Coll) B1
Saïd Business School B1
St Aldates C2
St Anne's (Coll) A1
St Antony's (Coll) A1
St Bernard's Rd A1
St Catherine's (Coll) B3
St Cross Building A3
St Cross Rd A3
St Edmund Hall (Coll) B3
St Giles St B2
St Hilda's (Coll) C3
St John St B2
St John's (Coll) B2
St Mary the Virgin † B2
St Michael at the
  Northgate † B2
St Peter's (Coll) B1
St Thomas St B1
Science Area. . . . A2
Science Museum ☐ B2
Sheldonian
  Theatre ◆ B2
Somerville (Coll) A1
South Parks Rd A2
Speedwell St C2
Sports Ground C3
Thames St C1
Town Hall B2
Trinity (Coll) B2
Turl St. . . . B2
University Coll (Coll). . . . B3
Univ Mus & Pitt
  Rivers Mus ☐ A2
University Parks A2
Wadham (Coll) B2
Walton Cr. . . . A1
Walton St A1
Western Rd C2
Westgate Sh Ctr B2
Woodstock Rd A1
Worcester (Coll) B1

Perth 341

A K Bell Library B2
Abbot Cres. . . . C1
Abbot St. . . . C1
Albany Terr A1
Albert Monument. . . . A2
Alexandra St B2
Atholl St A2
Balhousie Ave A2
Balhousie Castle Black
  Watch Museum ◆ A2
Balhousie Rd A2
Ballantine Pl A1
Barossa Pl A2
Barossa St A2
Barrack St A2
Bell's Sports Centre. . . . A1
Bellwood B3

Blair St B1
Burn Park. . . . C1
Bus Station B2
Caledonian Rd B2
Canal Cres. . . . B2
Canal St B2
Cavendish Ave. . . . C1
Charles St B2
Charlotte Pl. . . . A2
Charlotte St. . . . A3
Church St B2
City Hall B3
Club House C1
Commercial St B2
Concert Hall ◆ B3
Council Chambers B2
County Pl B2
Court B2
Craigie Pl A1
Crieff Rd. . . . A1
Croft Park C2
Cross St B2
Darnhall Cres C1
Darnhall Dr C1
Dewars Centre B1
Dundee Rd B3
Dunkeld Rd A1
Earl's Dykes. . . . B1
Edinburgh Rd C3
Elibank St C1
Fair Maid's House ◆ A3
Fergusson ☐ B2
Feus Rd A1
Fire Station B1
Fitness Centre B1
Foundary La C1
Friar St C1
George St. . . . B2
Glamis Pl. . . . C1
Glasgow Rd B1
Glenearn Rd C2
Glover St B1/C1
Golf Course A2
Gowrie St A3
Gray St C1
Graybank Rd B1
Greyfriars Burial
  Ground A3
Hay St A2
High St B2/B3
Hotel. . . . B3
Inchaffray St A1
Industrial/Retail Park. . . . B1
Information Ctr B2
Isla Rd A3
James St B2
Keir St A1
King Edward St B2
King James VI
  Golf Course C3
King St B2
Kings Pl C2
Kinnoull Causeway B1
Kinnoull Aisle
  'Monument' ◆ B3
Kinnoull St B2
Knowelea Pl C1
Knowelea Terr. . . . C1
Ladeside Bsns Centre A1
Leisure Pool A3
Leonard St B2
Lickley St A3
Lochie Brae A3
Long Causeway A1
Low St. . . . A3
Main St. . . . B3
Marshall Pl C2
Melville St A2
Mill St B2
Milne St B2
Murray Cres. . . . C1
Murray St. . . . B2
Needless Rd C1
New Rd B1
North Inch A2
North Methven St B1
Park Pl C1
Perth ☐ B2
Perth Bridge A3
Perth Business Park C1
Perth Museum & Art
  Gallery ☐ B3
Perth Station ◆ B1
Pickletullum Rd. . . . C1
Pitheavlis Cres C1
Playhouse ◆ B2
Police Station A2
Pomarium St B1
Post Office A3/B2/C2
Princes St B3
Priory Pl C1
Queen St C2
Queen's Bridge B3
Riggs Rd B1
Riverside B3
Riverside Park A3
Rodney Park C3
Rose Terr A2
St Catherines Ret Pk A1
St Catherine's Rd A1/A2
St John's Kirk † B2
St John's Shopping Ctr B2
St Leonards Bridge C2
St Ninians Cathedral † A2
Scott Monument C2
Scott St B2
Sheriff Court. . . . B2
Shore Rd C3
Skate Park A3
South Inch C2
South Inch Bsns Ctr C2
South Inch Park C2
South Inch View. . . . C2
South Methven St B2
South William St B2
Stormont St A2
Strathmore St A3

Stuart Ave C1
Tay St B3
The Stables A1
The Stanners B3
Union La B2
Victoria St B2
Watergate B2
Wellshill Cemetery A1
West Bridge St A3
West Mill St B2
Whitefriars Cres. . . . B1
Whitefriars St B1
Wilson St C1
Windsor Terr. . . . C1
Woodside Cres C1
York Pl B2
Young St C1

Peterborough 341

Athletics Arena. . . . A3
Bishop's Palace ☐ B2
Bishop's Rd B2/B3
Boongate A3
Bourges Boulevard A2
Bourges Retail Pk B1/B2
Bridge House
  (Council Offices) C2
Bridge St B2
Bright St. . . . A1
Broadway ◆ A2
Brook St A2
Burghley Rd. . . . A2
Bus Station A2
Cavendish St A3
Charles St A2
Church St. . . . B2
Church Walk A2
Cobden Ave A3
Cobden St A1
Cowgate. . . . B2
Craig St A2
Crawthorne Rd A2
Cripple Sidings La C2
Cromwell Rd A1
Dickens St A3
Eastfield Rd. . . . A3
Eastgate. . . . B3
Fire Station A3
Fletton Ave C2
Frank Perkins
  Parkway C3
Geneva St A2
George St C1
Gladstone St A1
Glebe Rd A2
Gloucester Rd C3
Granby St B3
Grove St C1
Guildhall ☐ B2
Hadrians Ct C1
Henry St A2
Hereward Cross (Sh). . . . B2
Hereward Rd B3
Information Ctr B2
Jubilee St C1
Key Theatre ◆ C2
Kent Rd. . . . A1
Kirkwood Cl B1
Lea Gdns B1
Library A2
Lincoln Rd A2
London Rd C2
Long Causeway B2
Lower Bridge St C2
Magistrates Court B2
Manor House St A2
Mayor's Walk A1
Midland Rd A2
Monument St A3
Morris St A3
Mus & Art Gallery ☐ B2
Nene Valley
  Railway ◆ C1
New Rd A2
New Rd A2
Northminster A2
Old Customs House ☐ C2
Oundle Rd C1
Padholme Rd. . . . A3
Palmerston Rd C1
Park Rd A2
Passport Office A2
Peterborough Sta ◆ B1
Peterborough Nene
  Valley ◆ C1
Peterborough United
  FC C2
Police Station B2
Post Office
  . . . . A3/B1/B2/B3/C1
Priestgate B2
Queen's Walk C1
Queensgate Centre B2
Railworld ◆ C1
Regional Swimming &
  Fitness Centre B3
River La B1
Rivergate Sh Ctr B2
Riverside Mead. . . . C3
Russell St A1
St John's ◆ B2
St John's St A2
St Marks St A2
St Peter's † B2
St Peter's Rd B2
Saxon Rd A3
Spital Bridge A1
Stagshaw Dr C3
Star Rd A3
Thorpe Lea Rd. . . . B1
Thorpe Rd B1
Thorpe's Lea Rd B1
Tower St. . . . A2
Town Hall B2
Viersen Platz. . . . B2
Vineyard Rd B2
Wake Rd A3
Wellington St A2

Plymouth • Poole • Portsmouth • Preston • Reading • St Andrews • Salisbury • Scarborough • Sheffield 357

Wentworth St B2
Westgate B2
Whalley St A3
Wharf Rd C1
Whitsed St A3
YMCA A3

Plymouth 341

Alma Rd A1
Anstis St B1
Armada Centre B2
Armada St A3
Armada Way B2
Arts Centre B2
Athenaeum B1
Athenaeum St C1
Barbican C3
Barbican C3
Baring St A3
Bath St B1
Beaumont Park B3
Beaumont Rd B3
Black Friars Gin Distillery C2
Breton Side B3
Bus Station B2
Castle St C3
Cathedral (RC) B1
Cecil St B1
Central Park A1
Central Park Ave A2
Charles Church B3
Charles Cross B3
Charles St B2
City Museum & Art Gallery B2
Citadel Rd C2
Citadel Rd East C2
Civic Centre B2
Cliff Rd C1
Clifton Pl A3
Cobourg St A2
College of Art B2
Continental Ferry Port B1
Cornwall St B2
Dale Rd A2
Deptford Pl A3
Derry Ave A2
Derry's Cross B1
Drake Circus B2
Drake Cir Sh Ctr B2
Drake's Memorial C2
Drum B2
Eastlake St B2
Ebrington St B3
Elizabethan House C3
Elliot St C1
Endsleigh Pl A2
Exeter St B3
Fire Station A3
Fish Quay C3
Gibbons St A3
Glen Park Ave A2
Grand Pde C1
Great Western Rd C1
Greenbank Rd A3
Greenbank Terr A3
Guildhall B2
Hampton St B3
Harwell St B1
Hill Park Cr A3
Hoe Approach B2
Hoe Rd C2
Hoegate St C2
Houndiscombe Rd A2
Information Ctr C3
James St A2
Kensington Rd A3
King St B1
Lambhay Hill C3
Leigham St C1
Library B2
Lipson Rd A3/B3
Lockyer St C2
Lockyers Quay C3
Madeira Rd C2
Marina B3
Market Ave B1
Martin St B1
Mayflower Stone and Steps C3
Mayflower St B2
Mayflower Visitor Centre C3
Merchants House B2
Millbay Rd B1
National Marine Aquarium C3
Neswick St B1
New George St B2
New St C3
North Cross A2
North Hill A3
North Quay B2
North Rd East A2
North Rd West A1
North St B3
Notte St B2
Octagon St B1
Pannier Market B1
Pennycomequick A1
Pier St C1
Plymouth Pavilions B1
Plymouth Station A2
Police Station B3
Portland Sq A2
Post Office A1/B1/B2
Princess St B2
Prysten House B2
Queen Anne's Battery Seasports Centre C3
Radford Rd C1
Regent St B3
Rope Walk C3
Royal Citadel C2
Royal Pde B2
St Andrew's B2
St Andrew's Cross B2
St Andrew's St B2
St Lawrence Rd A2
Saltash Rd A2
Smeaton's Tower C2
Southern Terr A3
Southside St C2
Stuart Rd A1
Sutherland Rd A2
Sutton Rd B3
Sydney St A1
Teats Hill Rd C3
The Crescent B1
The Hoe C2
The Octagon B1
The Promenade C2
Tothill Ave B3
Union St B1
Univ of Plymouth A2
Vauxhall St B2/3
Victoria Park A1
West Hoe Rd C1
Western Approach B1
Whittington St A1
Wyndham St B1
YMCA B2
YWCA C2

Poole 341

Ambulance Station A3
Baiater Gdns C2
Baiter Park C3
Ballard Cl C2
Ballard Rd C2
Bay Hog La B1
Bridge Approach C1
Bus Station B2
Castle St B2
Catalina Dr B3
Chapel La B2
Church St B1
Cinnamon La B1
Colborne Cl B3
Dear Hay La B2
Denmark La A3
Denmark Rd A3
East St B2
Elizabeth Rd A3
Emerson Rd B2
Ferry Rd C1
Ferry Terminal C1
Fire Station A2
Freightliner Terminal C1
Furnell Rd B3
Garland Rd A3
Green Rd B2
Heckford La A3
Heckford Rd A3
High St B2
High St North A3
Hill St B2
Holes Bay Rd A1
Hospital (A&E) A3
Information Ctr C2
Kingland Rd B3
Kingston Rd A3
Labrador Dr C3
Lagland St B2
Lander Cl C3
Old Lifeboat C2
Lighthouse – Poole Centre for the Arts B3
Longfleet Rd A3
Maple Rd A3
Market Cl B2
Market St B2
Mount Pleasant Rd B3
New Harbour Rd C1
New Harbour Rd S C1
New Harbour Rd W C1
New Orchard B1
New Quay Rd C1
New St B2
Newfoundland Dr B2
North St B2
Old Orchard B2
Parish Rd A3
Park Lake Rd B3
Parkstone Rd A3
Perry Gdns B2
Pitwines Cl B2
Police Station A2
Poole Central Library B2
Poole Lifting Bridge C1
Poole Park B2
Poole Station A2
Poole Waterfront Museum C1
Post Office A2/B2
St John's Rd A3
St Margaret's Rd A2
St Mary's Maternity Unit A3
St Mary's Rd A3
Seldown Bridge B3
Seldown La B3
Seldown Rd B3
Serpentine Rd A2
Shaftesbury Rd A3
Skinner St B2
Slipway B1
Stanley Rd C2
Sterte Ave A2
Sterte Ave West A1
Sterte Cl A2
Sterte Esplanade A2
Sterte Rd A2
Strand St C2
Swimming Pool B3
Taverner Cl B3
Thames St B1
The Lifeboat College B2
The Quay C2
Towngate Bridge B2
Vallis Cl C3
Waldren Cl B3
West Quay B1
West Quay Rd B1
West St B1
West View Rd A2
Whatleigh Cl B2
Wimborne Rd A3

Portsmouth 341

Action Stations C1
Admiralty Rd A1
Alfred Rd A2
Anglesea Rd B2
Arundel St B3
Aspex B1
Bishop St A2
Broad St C1
Buckingham House C2
Burnaby Rd B2
Bus Station B1
Camber Dock C1
Cambridge Rd B2
Car Ferry to Isle of Wight B1
Cascades Sh Ctr A3
Castle Rd C3
City Museum & Art Gallery B2
Civic Offices B3
Clarence Pier C2
College St B1
Commercial Rd A3
Cottage Gr B3
Cross St A1
Cumberland St A2
Duisburg Way C2
Durham St A3
East St B1
Edinburgh Rd A2
Elm Gr C3
Great Southsea St C3
Green Rd B3
Greetham St B3
Grosvenor St B3
Groundlings A2
Grove Rd North C3
Grove Rd South C3
Guildhall B3
Guildhall Walk B3
Gunwharf Quays Retail Park B1
Gunwharf Rd B1
Hambrook St C2
Hampshire Terr B2
Hanover St A1
High St C2
HM Naval Base A1
HMS Nelson (Royal Naval Barracks) A2
HMS Victory A1
HMS Warrior A1
Hovercraft Terminal C2
Hyde Park Rd B3
Information Ctr A1/B3
Isambard Brunel Rd B3
Isle of Wight Car Ferry Terminal B1
Kent Rd C3
Kent St A2
King St B3
King's Rd C3
King's Terr C2
Lake Rd A3
Law Courts B3
Library B3
Long Curtain Rd C2
Market Way A3
Marmion Rd C3
Mary Rose Museum A1
Middle St B3
Millennium Prom B1/C1
Museum Rd B2
National Museum of the Royal Navy A1
Naval Recreation Gd C2
Nightingale Rd C3
Norfolk St B3
North St A2
Osborne Rd C3
Park Rd B2
Passenger catamaran to Isle of Wight B1
Passenger ferry to Gosport B1
Pelham Rd C3
Pembroke Gdns C2
Pier Rd C2
Point Battery C1
Police Station B3
Portsmouth & Southsea A3
Portsmouth Harbour B1
Portsmouth Historic Dockyard A1
Post Office A2/A3/B1/B3/C3
Queen St A1
Queen's Cr C3
Round Tower C1
Royal Garrison Church C1
St Edward's Rd C3
St George's Rd B2
St George's Sq B1
St George's Way B2
St James's Rd B3
St James's St A2
St John's Cath (RC) A3
St Thomas's Cath C1
St Thomas's St B2
Somers Rd B3
Southsea Common C2
Southsea Terr C2
Spinnaker Tower B1
Square Tower C1
Station St A3
Swimming Pool A2
The Hard B1
Town Fortifications C1
Unicorn Rd A2
United Services Recreation Ground B2
University of Portsmouth A2/B2
University of Portsmouth – College of Art, Design and Media B3
Upper Arundel St A3
Victoria Ave C2
Victoria Park A2
Victory Gate A1
Vue B1
Warblington St B1
Western Pde C2
White Hart Rd C1
Winston Churchill Ave B3

Preston 342

Adelphi St A2
Anchor Ct B3
Aqueduct St A1
Ardee Rd C1
Arthur St B2
Ashton St A1
Avenham La B3
Avenham Park C3
Avenham Rd B3
Avenham St B3
Bairstow St B3
Balderstone Rd C1
Beamont Dr A1
Beech St South C2
Bird St C1
Bow La B2
Brieryfield Rd A1
Broadgate C1
Brook St A2
Bus Station A3
Butler St B2
Cannon St B3
Carlton St A1
Chaddock St B3
Channel Way B1
Chapel St B3
Christ Church St B2
Christian Rd B2
Cold Bath St A2
Coleman Ct C1
Connaught Rd C2
Corn Exchange B3
Corporation St A2/B2
County Hall B2
County Records Office B2
Court A3
Court B3
Cricket Ground C2
Croft St A1
Cross St B3
Crown Court A3
Crown St A3
East Cliff C3
East Cliff Rd B3
Edward St A2
Elizabeth St A3
Euston St B1
Fishergate B2/B3
Fishergate Hill B2
Fishergate Sh Ctr B2
Fitzroy St B1
Fleetwood St A1
Friargate A3
Fylde Rd A1/A2
Gerrard St B2
Glover's Ct B3
Good St B2
Grafton St B2
Great George St A3
Great Shaw St A3
Greenbank St A2
Guild Way B1
Guildhall & Charter B3
Guildhall St B3
Harrington St A2
Harris Museum B3
Hartington Rd B1
Hasset Cl C2
Heatley St B2
Hind St C2
Information Ctr B3
Kilruddery Rd C1
Lancaster Rd A3/B3
Latham St B3
Lauderdale St C2
Lawson St A3
Leighton St A2
Leyland Rd C1
Library A1
Library B3
Liverpool Rd C1
Lodge St B2
Lune St B3
Main Sprit West B3
Maresfield Rd C1
Market St West A3
Marsh La B1/B2
Maudland Bank A2
Maudland Rd A2
Meadow Ct C2
Meath Rd C1
Mill Hill A2
Miller Arcade B3
Miller Park C3
Moor La A3
Mount St B3
North Rd A3
North St A3
Northcote Rd B1
Old Milestones B1
Old Tram Rd C3
Pedder St A1/A2
Peel St A2
Penwortham Bridge C2
Penwortham New Bridge C1
Pitt St B2
Playhouse A3
Police Station A3
Port Way B1
Post Office B3
Preston Station B2
Ribble Bank St B2
Ribble Viaduct C2
Ribblesdale Pl B3
Ringway B3
River Parade C1
Riverside C2
St Georges B3
St George's Sh Ctr B3
St Johns B3
St Johns Shopping Ctr A3
St Mark's Rd A1
St Walburges A1
Salisbury Rd B1
Sessions House B3
Snow Hill A3
South End C2
South Meadow La C2
Spa Rd B1
Sports Ground C2
Strand Rd B1
Syke St B3
Talbot Rd B1
Taylor St C1
Tithebarn St A3
Town Hall B3
Tulketh Brow A1
University of Central Lancashire A2
Valley Rd C1
Victoria St A2
Walker St A3
Walton's Parade B2
Warwick St A3
Wellfield Bsns Park A1
Wellfield Rd A1
Wellington St A1
West Cliff C2
West Strand A1
Winckley Rd C1
Winckley Square B3
Wolseley Rd C2

Reading 342

Abbey Ruins B2
Abbey Sq B2
Abbey St B2
Abbot's Walk B2
Acacia Rd C2
Addington Rd C3
Addison Rd A1
Allcroft Rd C3
Alpine St C2
Baker St B1
Berkeley Ave C1
Bridge St B1
Brigham Rd A1
Broad St B1
Broad Street Mall B1
Carey St B1
Castle Hill C1
Castle St B1
Caversham Rd A1
Christchurch Playing Fields A2
Magistrate's Court B1
Civic Offices B1
Coley Hill C1
Coley Pl C1
Craven Rd C3
Crown St C2
De Montfort Rd A1
Denmark Rd C3
Duke St B2
East St B2
Edgehill St C2
Eldon Rd B3
Eldon Terr B3
Elgar Rd C1
Erleigh Rd C3
Field Rd C1
Fire Station A1
Fobney St B1
Forbury Gdns B2
Forbury Retail Park B2
Forbury Rd B2
Francis St C1
Friar St B1
Garrard St B1
Gas Works Rd B3
George St A2
Great Knollys St B1
Greyfriars B1
Gun St B1
Henry St C1
Hexagon Theatre, The B1
Hill's Meadow A2
Howard St B1
Information Ctr B1
Inner Distribution Rd B1
Katesgrove La C1
Kenavon Dr B2
Kendrick Rd C2
King's Meadow Recreation Ground A2
King's Rd B2
Library B2
London Rd C3
London St B2
Lynmouth Rd A1
Market Pl B2
Mill La B2
Mill Rd A2
Minster St B1
Morgan Rd C3
Mount Pleasant C2
Museum of English Rural Life C3
Napier Rd A2
Newark St C2
Newport Rd A1
Old Reading Univ C3
Oracle Sh Ctr, The B1
Orts Rd B3
Pell St C1
Queen Victoria St B1
Queen's Rd A2
Queen's Rd B2
Police Station B1
Post Office B2
Randolph Rd A1
Reading Bridge A2
Reading Station A1
Redlands Rd C3
Renaissance Hotel B1
Riverside Museum B3
Rose Kiln La C1
Royal Berks Hospital (A&E) C3
St Giles C2
St Laurence B2
St Mary's B1
St Mary's Butts B1
St Saviour's Rd C1
Send Rd A3
Sherman Rd C2
Sidmouth St B2
Silver St C2
South St B2
Southampton St C2
Station Hill A1
Station Rd B1
Superstore A3
Swansea Rd A1
Technical College B3
The Causeway A3
The Grove B2
Valpy St B2
Vastern Rd A1
Vue B2
Waldeck St C2
Watlington St B3
West St B1
Whitby Dr C3
Wolseley St C1
York Rd A1
Zinzan St B1

St Andrews 342

Abbey St B2
Abbey Walk B3
Abbotsford Cres A1
Albany Pk C3
Allan Robertson Dr C2
Ambulance Station C1
Anstruther Rd C3
Argyle St B1
Argyll Business Park C1
Auld Burn Rd B2
Bassaguard Ind Est B1
Bell St B2
Blackfriars Chapel (Ruins) B2
Boase Ave B2
Braid Cres C3
Brewster Pl C3
Bridge St B1
British Golf Mus A1
Broomfaulds Ave C1
Bruce Embankment A1
Bruce St C2
Bus Station A1
Byre B2
Canongate C1
Cathedral and Priory (Ruins) B3
Cemetery B3
Chamberlain St C1
Church St B2
Churchill Cres C2
City Rd A1
Claybraes C1
Cockshaugh Public Pk B1
Cosmos Com Centre B3
Council Office A2
Crawford Gdns C1
Doubledykes Rd B1
Drumcarrow Rd C1
East Sands B3
East Scores A3
Fire Station C1
Forrest St C1
Fraser Ave C1
Freddie Tait St C2
Gateway Centre A1
Glebe Rd B2
Golf Pl A1
Grange Rd C3
Greenside Pl B2
Greyfriars Gdns A2
Hamilton Ave C2
Hepburn Gdns B1
Holy Trinity B2
Horseleys Park C1
Information Ctr B2
Irvine Cres C3
James Robb Ave C1
James St B1
John Knox Rd C1
Kennedy Gdns B1
Kilrymont Cl C3
Kilrymont Pl C3
Kilrymont Rd C3
Kinburn Park B1
Kinkell Terr C3
Kinnesburn Rd B2
Ladebraes Walk B2
Lady Buchan's Cave A3
Lamberton Pl C1
Lamond Dr C2
Langlands Rd B2
Largo Rd C1
Learmonth Pl C1
Library B2
Links Clubhouse A1
Links, The A1
Livingstone Cres B2
Long Rocks A2
Madras College B2
Market St A2
Martyr's Monument A1
Memorial Hospital (No A+E) B3
Murray Pk A2
Murray Pl A2
Nelson St B2
New Course, The A1
New Picture House A2
North Castle St A3
North St A2
Old Course, The A1
Old Station Rd A1
Pends, The B3
Pilmour Links A1
Pipeland Rd B2/C2
Police Station A2
Post Office B2
Preservation Trust B3
Priestden Pk C3
Priestden Pl C3
Priestden Rd C3
Queen's Gdns B2
Queen's Terr B2
Roundhill Rd C2
Royal & Ancient Golf Club A1
St Andrews B1
St Andrews Aquarium A2
St Andrews Botanic Garden B1
St Andrews Castle (Ruins) & Visitor Centre A2
St Leonard's School B3
St Mary St B3
St Mary's College B2
St Nicholas St C3
St Rules Tower B3
St Salvator's College A2
Sandyhill Cres C2
Sandyhill Rd C2
Scooniehill Rd C2
Shields Ave C3
Shoolbraids C2
Sloan St B1
South St B2
Spottiswoode Gdns C1
Station Rd A1
Swilcen Bridge A1
The Scores A2
The Shore B3
Tom Morris Dr C2
Tom Stewart La C1
Town Hall B2
Union St A2
University Chapel A2
University Library A2
Univ of St Andrews A1
Viaduct Walk B1
War Memorial A3
Wardlaw Gdns B1
Warrack St C3
Watson Ave B2
West Port B2
West Sands A1
Westview B2
Windmill Rd A1
Winram Pl C1
Wishart Gdns C2
Woodburn Pk B3
Woodburn Pl B3
Woodburn Terr B3
Younger Hall A2

Salisbury 342

Albany Rd A2
Arts Centre A3
Ashley Rd A1
Avon Approach A2
Ayleswade Rd C2
Bedwin St A2
Belle Vue A2
Bishop's Palace C2
Bishops Walk B2
Blue Boar Row B2
Bourne Ave A3
Bourne Hill A3
Britford La C2
Broad Walk C2
Brown St B2
Bus Station B2
Castle St A2
Catherine St B2
Chapter House B2
Church House B2
Churchfields Rd B1
Churchill Way East B3
Churchill Way North A3
Churchill Way South C2
Churchill Way West A1
City Hall B2
Close Wall B2
Coldharbour La A1
College St A3
Council Offices A3
Court A1
Crane Bridge Rd B2
Crane St B2
Cricket Ground C1
Culver St South B3
De Vaux Pl C2
Devizes Rd A1
Dews Rd B1
Elm Grove B3
Elm Grove Rd A3
Endless St A2
Estcourt Rd A3
Exeter St C2
Fairview Rd A3
Fire Station A1
Fisherton St A1
Folkestone Rd C1
Fowlers Hill B3
Fowlers Rd B3
Friary Estate C3
Friary La B2
Gas La A1
Gigant St B3
Greencroft B3
Greencroft St A3
Guildhall B2
Hall of John Halle B2
Hamilton Rd A2
Harnham Mill B1
Harnham Rd C1/C2
High St B2
Hospital A1
Ho of John A'Port B2
Information Ctr B2
Kelsey Rd A3
King's Rd A2
Laverstock Rd B3
Library B2
London Rd A3
Lower St C1
Maltings, The B2
Manor Rd A3
Marsh La A1
Medieval Hall B2
Milford Hill B3
Milford St B3
Mill Rd B1
Millstream Approach A2
Mompesson House (NT) B2
New Bridge Rd C2
New Canal B2
New Harnham Rd C2
New St B2
North Canonry B2
North Gate B2
North Walk B2
Old George Hall B2
Old Blandford Rd C1
Old Deanery B2
Park St A3
Parsonage Green C1
Playhouse Theatre A2
Post Office A2/B2/C2
Poultry Cross B2
Queen Elizabeth Gdns B1
Queen's Rd A3
Rampart Rd B3
St Ann's Gate B2
St Ann St B2
St Marks Rd A3
St Martins B3
St Mary's Cathedral B2
St Nicholas Hosp C2
St Paul's A1
St Paul's Rd A1
St Thomas B2
Salisbury & South Wiltshire Museum B2
Salisbury General Hospital (A&E) C2
Salisbury Station A1
Salt La A3
Saxon Rd C1
Scots La A2
Shady Bower B3
South Canonry C2
South Gate C2
Southampton Rd B2
Spire View A1
Sports Ground C3
The Friary B3
Tollgate Rd B3
Town Path B1
Wain-a-Long Rd A3
Wardrobe, The B2
Wessex Rd A3
West Walk C2
Wilton Rd A1
Wiltshire College B3
Winchester St B3
Windsor Rd A1
Winston Churchill Gdns C3
Wyndham Rd A2
YHA B3
York Rd A1

Scarborough 342

Aberdeen Walk B2
Albert Rd A2
Albion Rd C2
Alexandra Bowling Hall A1
Alexandra Gardens A1
Auborough St B2
Belle Vue St C1
Belmont Rd C2
Brunswick Pavilion Shopping Centre B2
Castle Dykes B3
Castlegate B3
Castle Holms A3
Castle Hill A3
Castle Rd B2
Castle Walls A3
Cemetery B1
Central Lift C2
Clarence Gardens A2
Coach Park B1
Columbus Ravine A1
Court B1
Cricket Ground A1
Cross St B2
Crown Terr C2
Dean Rd B1
Devonshire Dr A1
East Harbour B3
East Pier B3
Eastborough B2
Elmville Ave B1
Esplanade C2
Falconers Rd B2
Falsgrave Rd C1
Fire Station B2
Foreshore Rd B2
Friargate B2
Futurist Theatre B2
Gladstone Rd B1
Gladstone St B1
Hoxton Rd B1
Information Ctr B2/B3
King St B2
Library B2
Lifeboat Station B3
Londesborough Rd C1
Longwestgate B3
Marine Dr A3
Military Adventure Pk A1
Miniature Railway A1
Nelson St B1
Newborough B2
Nicolas St B2
North Marine Rd A1
North St B2
Northway B1
Old Harbour B3
Olympia Leisure B2
Peasholm Park A1
Peasholm Rd A1
Plaza A1
Police Station B1
Post Office B2/C1
Princess St B3
Prospect Rd B1
Queen St B2
Queen's Parade A2
Queen's Tower (Remains) A3
Ramshill Rd C2
Roman Signal Sta A3
Roscoe St C1
Rotunda Museum C2
Royal Albert Dr A2
St Martin-on-the-Hill C2
St Martin's Ave C2
St Mary's B3
St Thomas St B2
Sandside B3
Scarborough Art Gallery and Crescent Art Studio C2
Scarborough Castle A3
Scarborough C1
Somerset Terr C2
South Cliff Lift C2
Spa, The C2
Spa Theatre, The C2
Stephen Joseph Theatre B1
Tennyson Ave B1
The Crescent C2
Tollergate B2
Town Hall B2
Trafalgar Rd B1
Trafalgar Square A1
Trafalgar St West B1
Valley Bridge Parade C2
Valley Rd C1
Vernon Rd C2
Victoria Park Mount A1
Victoria Rd B1
West Pier B3
Westborough C1
Westover Rd C1
Westwood C1
Woodall Ave A1
YMCA Theatre B2
York Pl B2
Yorkshire Coast College (Westwood Campus) C1

Sheffield 342

Addy Dr A2
Addy St A2
Adelphi St A3
Albert Terrace Rd A3
Albion St A2
Aldred Rd A1
Allen St A4
Alma St A4
Angel St B5
Arundel Gate B5
Arundel St C4
Ashberry Rd A2
Ashdell Rd C1
Ashgate Rd C1
Athletics Centre B2
Attercliffe Rd A6
Bailey St B4
Ball St A4
Balm Green B4
Bank St B4
Barber Rd A2
Bard St B5
Barker's Pool B4
Bates St A1
Beech Hill Rd C1
Beet St B3
Bellefield St A3
Bernard Rd A6
Bernard St B6
Birkendale A2
Birkendale Rd A2
Birkendale View A1
Bishop St C4
Blackwell Pl B6
Blake St A2
Blonk St A5
Bolsover St B2
Botanical Gdns C1
Bower Rd A1
Bradley St A1
Bramall La C4
Bramwell St A3
Bridge St A4/A5
Brighton Terrace Rd A1
Broad La B3
Broad St B6
Brocco St A3
Brook Hill B3
Broomfield Rd C1
Broomgrove Rd C2
Broomhall Pl C3
Broomhall Rd C2
Broomhall St C3
Broomspring La C2
Brown St C5
Brunswick St B3
Burgess St B4
Burlington St A2
Burns Rd A2
Cadman St A6
Cambridge St B4
Campo La B4
Carver St B4
Castle Market B5
Castle Square B5

Castlegate A5
Cathedral (RC) ✝ B4
Cathedral 🚊 B4
Cavendish St B3
Charles St C4
Charter Row C4
Children's Hospital (A&E) 🏥 B2
Church St B4
City Hall 🎭 B4
City Hall 🚊 B4
City Rd C6
Claremont Cr B2
Claremont Pl B2
Clarke St C3
Clarkegrove Rd C2
Clarkehouse Rd C1
Clarkson St B2
Cobden View Rd A1
Collegiate Cr C2
Commercial St B5
Commonside A1
Conduit Rd B1
Cornish St A3
Corporation St A4
Court B4
Cricket Inn Rd B6
Cromwell St A1
Crookes Rd B1
Crookes Valley Park B2
Crookes Valley Rd B2
Crookesmoor Rd A2
Crown Court A4
Crucible Theatre 🎭 B5
Cutlers Gate A6
Cutler's Hall 🏛 B4
Daniel Hill A2
Dental Hospital 🏥 B2
Dept for Education & Employment C4
Devonshire Green B3
Devonshire St B3
Division St B4
Dorset St C2
Dover St A3
Duchess Rd C5
Duke St B5
Duncombe St A1
Durham Rd B2
Earl St C4
Earl Way C4
Ecclesall Rd C3
Edward St B3
Effingham Rd A6
Effingham St A6
Egerton St C3
Eldon St B3
Elmore Rd B1
Exchange St B5
Eyre St C4
Fargate B4
Farm Rd C5
Fawcett St A3
Filey St B3
Fire & Police Mus 🏛 A4
Fire Station C4
Fir St A1
Fitzalan Sq/ Ponds Forge 🚊 B5
Fitzwater Rd C6
Fitzwilliam Gate C4
Fitzwilliam St B3
Flat St B5
Foley St A6
Foundry Climbing Ctr A4
Fulton Rd A1
Furnace Hill A4
Furnival Rd A5
Furnival Sq C4
Furnival St C4
Garden St B3
Gell St B3
Gibraltar St A4
Glebe Rd B1
Glencoe Rd C6
Glossop Rd B2/B3/C1
Gloucester St C2
Granville Rd C6
Granville Rd/ Sheffield College 🚊 C5
Graves Gallery 🏛 B5
Greave Rd B3
Green La A4
Hadfield St A1
Hanover St C3
Hanover Way C3
Harcourt Rd B1
Harmer La B5
Havelock St C2
Hawley St B4
Haymarket B5
Headford St C3
Heavygate Rd A1
Henry St A3
High St B4
Hodgson St C3
Holberry Gdns C2
Hollis Croft B4
Holly St B4
Hounsfield Rd B3
Howard Rd A1
Hoyle St A3
Hyde Park 🚊 A6
Infirmary Rd A3
Infirmary Rd 🚊 A3
Information Ctr ℹ B4
Jericho St A3
Johnson St A5
Kelham Island Industrial Museum 🏛 A4
Lawson Rd C1
Leadmill Rd C5
Leadmill St C5
Leadmill, The C5
Leamington St A1
Leavy Rd B3
Lee Croft B4
Leopold St B4
Leveson St A6
Library A2
Library B5
Library C1
Lyceum Theatre 🎭 B5
Malinda St A3
Maltravers St A5
Manor Oaks Rd B6
Mappin St B3
Marlborough Rd B1
Mary St C4
Matilda St C4
Matlock Rd A1
Meadow St A3
Melbourn Rd A1
Melbourne Ave C1
Millennium Galleries 🏛 B5
Milton St C3
Mitchell St B3
Mona Ave A1
Mona Rd A1
Montgomery Terr Rd A3
Montgomery Theatre 🎭 B4
Monument Gdns C6
Moor Oaks Rd B1
Moore St C3
Mowbray St A4
Mushroom La B2
Netherthorpe Rd B3
Netherthorpe Rd 🚊 B3
Newbould La C1
Nile St C1
Norfolk Park Rd C6
Norfolk Rd C6
Norfolk St B4
North Church St B4
Northfield Rd A1
Northumberland Rd B1
Nursery St A5
O2 Academy 🎭 B5
Oakholme Rd C1
Octagon B2
Odeon 🎦 B5
Old St B6
Orchard Square B4
Oxford St A2
Paradise St B4
Park La C2
Park Sq B5
Parker's Rd B1
Pearson Building (Univ) C2
Penistone Rd A3
Pinstone St B4
Pitt St B3
Police Station 👮 A4/B5
Pond Hill B5
Pond St B5
Ponds Forge Int Sports Ctr B5
Portobello St B3
Post Office 📮 A1/A2/B3/B4/B5/B6/C1/C3/C4/C6
Powell St A2
Queen St B4
Queen's Rd C5
Ramsey Rd B1
Red Hill B3
Redcar Rd B1
Regent St B3
Rockingham St B4
Roebuck Rd A2
Royal Hallamshire Hospital 🏥 C2
Russell St A4
Rutland Park C1
St George's Cl B3
St Mary's Gate C3
St Mary's Rd C4/C5
St Peter & St Paul Cathedral ✝ B4
St Philip's Rd A3
Savile St A5
School Rd B1
Scotland St A4
Severn Rd B1
Shalesmoor A4
Shalesmoor 🚊 A3
Sheaf St B5
Sheffield Hallam Univ B5
Sheffield Ice Sports Ctr – Skate Central C5
Sheffield Interchange B5
Sheffield Parkway A6
Sheffield Station ⇌ C5
Sheffield Sta/ Sheffield Hallam Univ 🚊 B5
Sheffield University B2
Shepherd St A3
Shipton St A2
Shoreham St C4
Showroom, The 🎦 C5
Shrewsbury Rd C5
Sidney St C4
Site Gallery 🏛 C5
Slinn St A1
Smithfield A4
Snig Hill A5
Snow La A4
Solly St B3
Southbourne Rd C1
South La C4
South Street Park B5
Spital Hill A5
Spital St A5
Spring Hill B1
Spring Hill Rd B1
Springvale Rd A1
Stafford Rd C6
Stafford St B6
Stanley St A5
Suffolk Rd C5
Summer St B2
Sunny Bank C3
Surrey St B4
Sussex St A6
Sutton St B3
Sydney Rd A2
Sylvester St C4
Talbot St B5
Taptonville Rd B1
Tax Office C4
Tenter St B4
The Moor C4
Town Hall 🏛 B4
Townend St A1
Townhead St B4
Trafalgar St B4
Tree Root Walk B2
Trinity St A4
Trippet La B4
Turner Mus of Glass 🏛 B3
Union St B4
Univ Drama Studio 🎭 B2
Univ of Sheffield 🚊 B3
Upper Allen St A3
Upper Hanover St B3
Upperthorpe Rd A2/A3
Verdon St A5
Victoria Quays ✦ B5
Victoria Rd C2
Victoria St B3
Waingate B5
Watery St A3
Watson Rd C1
Wellesley Rd B2
Wellington St C3
West Bar A4
West Bar Green A4
West One Plaza B3
West St B3
West St 🚊 B4
Westbourne Rd C1
Western Bank B2
Western Rd A1
Weston Park B2
Weston Park Hospl 🏥 B2
Weston Park Mus 🏛 B2
Weston St B2
Wharncliffe Rd C3
Whitham Rd B1
Wicker A5
Wilkinson St B2
William St C3
Winter Garden ✦ B4
Winter St B2
York St B4
Yorkshire Artspace C5
Young St C4

Shrewsbury 342

Abbey Church ⛪ B3
Abbey Foregate B3
Abbey Lawn Bsns Park B3
Abbots House 🏛 B2
Agricultural Show Gd A1
Albert St A2
Alma St B1
Ashley St A3
Ashton Rd C1
Avondale Dr A3
Bage Way C3
Barker St B1
Beacall's La A2
Beeches La C2
Beehive La C1
Belle Vue Gdns C2
Belle Vue Rd C2
Belmont Bank C1
Berwick Ave A1
Berwick Rd A1
Betton St C2
Bishop St B3
Bradford St B3
Bridge St B1
Bus Station B2
Butcher Row B2
Burton St A3
Butler Rd C1
Bynner St C2
Canon St B3
Canonbury C1
Castle Bsns Park, The A2
Castle Foregate A2
Castle Gates B2
Castle Museum 🏰 B2
Castle St B2
Cathedral (RC) ✝ C1
Chester St A2
Cineworld 🎦 C3
Claremont Bank B1
Claremont Hill B1
Cleveland St B3
Coleham Head B2
Coleham Pumping Station 🏛 C2
College Hill B1
Corporation La A1
Coton Cres A1
Coton Hill A2
Coton Mount A1
Crescent La C1
Crewe St A2
Cross Hill B1
Darwin Centre B2
Dingle, The ❀ B1
Dogpole B2
Draper's Hall 🏛 B2
English Bridge B2
Fish St B2
Frankwell B1
Gateway Ctr, The 🏛 A2
Gravel Hill La A1
Greyfriars Rd C2
Guildhall 🏛 B1
Hampton Rd A3
Haycock Way C3
HM Prison B2
High St B1
Hills La B1
Holywell St B3
Hunter St A1
Information Ctr ℹ B1
Ireland's Mansion & Bear Steps 🏛 B1
John St A3
Kennedy Rd C1
King St B3
Kingsland Bridge C1
Kingsland Bridge (toll) C1
Kingsland Rd C1
Library B2
Lime St C2
Longden Coleham C2
Longden Rd C1
Longner St B1
Luciefelde Rd C1
Mardol B1
Market B1
Marine Terr C2
Monkmoor Rd B3
Moreton Cr C2
Mount St A1
New Park Cl A3
New Park Rd A2
New Park St A3
North St A2
Oakley St C1
Old Coleham C2
Old Market Hall 🎦 B1
Old Potts Way C3
Parade Centre B2
Police Station 👮 B1
Post Office 📮 A2/B1/B2/B3
Pride Hill B1
Pride Hill Centre B1
Priory Rd B1
Pritchard Way C3
Queen St A3
Raby Cr C2
Rad Brook C1
Rea Brook C3
Riverside B1
Roundhill La A1
St Alkmund's ⛪ B2
St Chad's ⛪ B1
St Chad's Terr B1
St John's Hill B1
St Julians Friars C2
St Mary's ⛪ B2
St Mary's St B2
Salters La C2
Scott St C3
Severn Bank A3
Severn St A2
Shrewsbury ⇌ B2
Shrewsbury High School for Girls C1
Shrewsbury Museum & Art Gallery 🏛 B1
Shrewsbury School ✦ C1
Shropshire Wildlife Trust ✦ B3
Smithfield Rd B1
South Hermitage C1
Swan Hill B1
Sydney Ave A3
Tankerville St B3
The Dana B2
The Quarry B1
The Square B1
Tilbrook Dr A3
Town Walls C1
Trinity St C2
Underdale Rd B3
Victoria Ave B1
Victoria Quay B1
Victoria St B2
Welsh Bridge B1
Whitehall St B3
Wood St A2
Wyle Cop B2

Southampton 342

Above Bar St A2
Albert Rd North B3
Albert Rd South C3
Anderson's Rd B3
Archaeology Mus (God's Ho Tower) 🏛 C2
Argyle Rd A2
Arundel Tower ✦ B1
Bargate, The ✦ B2
BBC Regional Centre A1
Bedford Pl A1
Belvidere Rd A3
Bernard St C2
Blechynden Terr A1
Brazil Rd C3
Brinton's Rd A2
Britannia Rd A3
Briton St C2
Brunswick Pl A1
Bugle St C1
Canute Rd C3
Castle Way C2
Catchcold Tower ✦ B1
Central Bridge C3
Central Rd C2
Channel Way C3
Chapel Rd B3
Cineworld 🎦 C3
City Art Gallery 🏛 A1
City College B3
Civic Centre A1
Civic Centre Rd A1
Coach Station B1
Commercial Rd A1
Cumberland Pl A1
Cunard Rd C2
Derby Rd A3
Devonshire Rd A1
Dock Gate 4 C2
Dock Gate 8 B1
East Park A2
East Park Terr A2
East St B2
Endle St B3
European Way C2
Fire Station A2
Floating Bridge Rd C3
Golden Gr A3
Graham Rd A2
Guildhall A1
Hanover Bldgs B2
Harbour Lights 🎦 C3
Harbour Pde B1
Hartington Rd A3
Havelock Rd A1
Henstead Rd A1
Herbert Walker Ave B1
High St B2
Hoglands Park B2
Holy Rood (Rems), Merchant Navy Memorial ⛪ B2
Houndwell Park B2
Houndwell Pl B2
Hythe Ferry C2
Information Ctr ℹ A1
Isle of Wight Ferry Terminal C1
James St B3
Java Rd C3
Kingsway A2
Leisure World B1
Library A1
Lime St B2
London Rd A2
Marine Pde B3
Marsh La B2
Mayflower Meml ✦ C1
Mayflower Park C1
Mayflower Theatre, The 🎭 A1
Medieval Merchant's House 🏛 C1
Melbourne St B3
Millais 🏛 A2
Morris Rd A1
National Oceanography Centre ✦ C3
Neptune Way C3
New Rd A2
Nichols Rd A3
North Front A2
Northam Rd A3
Ocean Dock C2
Ocean Village Marina C3
Ocean Way C3
Odeon 🎦 B1
Ogle Rd B1
Old Northam Rd A2
Orchard La B2
Oxford Ave A2
Oxford St C2
Palmerston Park A2
Palmerston Rd A2
Parsonage Rd A3
Peel St A3
Platform Rd C2
Police Station 👮 A1
Portland Terr B1
Post Office 📮 A2/A3/B2
Pound Tree Rd B2
Quays Swimming & Diving Complex, The B1
Queen's Park C2
Queen's Peace Fountain ✦ A2
Queen's Terr C2
Queen's Way B2
Radcliffe Rd A3
Rochester St A3
Royal Pier C1
Royal South Hants Hospital 🏥 A2
Sea City Mus 🏛 A1
St Andrew's Rd A2
St Mary St A2
St Mary's ⛪ B3
St Mary's Leisure Ctr A2
St Mary's Pl B2
St Mary's Rd A2
St Mary's Stadium (Southampton FC) A3
St Michael's ⛪ C1
Solent Sky 🏛 C3
South Front B2
Southampton Central Station ⇌ A1
Southampton Solent University A2
SS Shieldhall ⛴ C2
Terminus Terr C2
The Mall, Marlands A1
The Polygon A1
Threefield La B2
Titanic Engineers' Memorial ✦ A2
Town Quay C1
Town Walls B2
Tudor House 🏛 C1
Vincent's Walk B2
West Gate Hall 🏛 C1
West Marlands Rd A1
West Park A1
West Park Rd A1
West Quay Rd B1
West Quay Retail Park B1
West Quay Sh Ctr B1
West Rd C2
Western Esplanade B1
Winton St A2

Southend-on-Sea 343

Adventure Island ✦ C3
Albany Ave A1
Albert Rd C3
Alexandra Rd C2
Alexandra St C2
Alexandra Yacht Club ✦ C2
Ashburnham Rd B2
Ave Rd B1
Avenue Terr B1
Balmoral Rd B1
Baltic Ave B3
Baxter Ave A2/B2
Beecroft Art Gallery 🏛 C1
Bircham Rd A2
Boscombe Rd B3
Boston Ave A1/B2
Bournemouth Park Rd A3
Browning Ave A3
Bus Station C3
Byron Ave A3
Cambridge Rd C1/C2
Canewdon Rd B1
Carnarvon Rd A2
Central Ave A3
Chelmsford Ave A1
Chichester Rd B2
Church Rd C3
Civic Centre A2
Clarence Rd C2
Clarence St C2
Cliff Ave B1
Cliffs Pavilion 🎭 C1
Clifftown Parade C2
Clifftown Rd C2
Colchester Rd A1
College Way B2
Coleman St B3
County Court B3
Cromer Rd B3
Crowborough Rd A2
Dryden Ave A3
East St A2
Elmer App B2
Elmer Ave B2
Gainsborough Dr A1
Gayton Rd A2
Glenhurst Rd A2
Gordon Pl B2
Gordon Rd B2
Grainger Rd A2
Greyhound Way A3
Guildford Rd B3
Hamlet Ct Rd B1
Hamlet Rd C1
Harcourt Ave A1
Hartington Rd C3
Hastings Rd B3
Herbert Gr C3
Heygate Ave C3
High St B2/C2
Information Ctr ℹ C3
Kenway A2
Kilworth Ave B3
Lancaster Gdns B3
Library B2
London Rd B1
Lucy Rd C3
MacDonald Ave A1
Magistrates Court A2
Maldon Rd A2
Maine Ave C1
Marine Rd C1
Marine Parade C3
Milton Rd B1
Milton St B2
Napier Ave B2
North Ave A3
North Rd A1/B1
Odeon 🎦 B2
Osborne Rd B1
Park Cres B1
Park Rd B1
Park St B1
Park Terr B1
Pier Hill C3
Pleasant Rd C3
Police Station 👮 A2
Post Office 📮 B2/B3
Princes St B2
Queens Rd B2
Queensway B2/B3/C3
Rayleigh Ave A1
Redstock Rd A2
Rochford Ave A1
Royal Mews C2
Royal Terr C2
Royals Sh Ctr, The C3
Ruskin Ave A3
St Ann's Rd B3
St Helen's Rd B1
St John's Rd B1
St Leonard's Rd C3
St Lukes Rd A3
St Vincent's Rd C1
Salisbury Ave A1/B1
Scratton Rd C2
Shakespeare Dr A1
Short St A2
South Ave A3
Southchurch Rd B3
South Essex College B2
Southend Central ⇌ B2
Southend Pier Railway 🚂 C3
Southend Radio C2
Southend United FC A1
Southend Victoria ⇌ B2
Stadium Rd A2
Stanfield Rd A2
Stanley Rd C3
Sutton Rd A3/B3
Swanage Rd B3
Sweyne Ave A1
Sycamore Gr A3
Tennyson Ave A3
The Grove A3
Tickfield Ave A2
Tudor Rd A1
Tunbridge Rd A2
Tylers Ave B3
Tyrrel Dr B3
Univ of Essex B2/C2
Vale Ave A2
Victoria Ave A2
Victoria Sh Ctr, The B2
Warrior Sq B3
Wesley Rd C3
West Rd A1
West St A1
Westcliff Ave C1
Westcliff Parade C1
Western Esplanade C1
Weston Rd C2
Whitegate Rd B3
Wilson Rd C1
Wimborne Rd B3
York Rd C3

Stirling 343

Abbey Rd A3
Abbotsford Pl A3
Abercromby Pl C1
Albert Halls 🎭 B1
Albert Pl B1
Alexandra Pl A3
Allan Park C2
Ambulance Station A2
AMF Ten Pin Bowling ✦ B2
Argyll Ave A3
Argyll's Lodging ✦ B1
Back O' Hill Ind Est A1
Back O' Hill Rd A1
Baker St B2
Ballengeich Pass A1
Balmoral Pl B1
Barn Rd B1
Barnton St B2
Bow St B1
Bruce St A2
Burghmuir Ind Est C2
Burghmuir Rd A2/B2/C2
Bus Station B2
Cambuskenneth Bridge A3
Carlton 🎦 C2
Castle Ct B1
Causewayhead Rd A2
Cemetery A1
Church of the Holy Rude ⛪ B1
Clarendon Pl C1
Club House B1
Colquhoun St C3
Corn Exchange B2
Council Offices C2
Court B2
Cowane 🎭 A2
Cowane St A2
Cowane's Hospital 🏛 B1
Crawford Sh Arc B2
Crofthead Rd A1
Dean Cres A3
Douglas St A2
Drip Rd A1
Drummond La C1
Drummond Pl C1
Drummond Pl La C1
Dumbarton Rd C2
Eastern Access Rd B2
Edward Ave A3
Edward Rd A2
Forrest Rd A2
Fort A1
Forth Cres B2
Forth St A2
Gladstone Pl C1
Glebe Ave C1
Glebe Cres C1
Golf Course C1
Goosecroft Rd B2
Gowanhill A1
Greenwood Ave B1
Harvey Wynd A1
Information Ctr ℹ B1
Irvine Pl B2
James St A2
John St B1
Kerse Rd C3
King's Knot ✦ B1
King's Park C1
King's Park Rd C1
Laurencecroft Rd A2
Leisure Pool B2
Library B2
Linden Ave C2
Lovers Wk A2
Lower Back Walk B1
Lower Bridge St A2
Lower Castlehill A1
Mar Pl B1
Meadow Pl A3
Meadowforth Rd C3
Middlemuir Rd C3
Millar Pl A3
Morris Terr B2
Mote Hill A1
Murray Pl B2
Nelson Pl C2
Old Town Cemetery B1
Old Town Jail ✦ B1
Orchard House Hospital (No A+E) 🏥 A2
Park Terr C1
Phoenix Industrial Est C3
Players Rd C3
Port St C2
Princes St B2
Queen St B2
Queen's Rd B1
Queenshaugh Dr A3
Rainbow Slides B2
Ramsay Pl A2
Riverside Dr A3
Ronald Pl A2
Rosebery Pl A2
Royal Gardens B1
Royal Gdns B1
St Mary's Wynd B1
St Ninian's Rd C2
Scott St A2
Seaforth Pl B2
Shore Rd B2
Smith Art Gallery & Museum 🏛🏛 B1
Snowdon Pl C1
Snowdon Pl La C1
Spittal St B2
Springkerse Ind Est C3
Springkerse Rd C3
Stirling Bsns Centre C2
Stirling Castle 🏰 A1
Stirling County Rugby Football Club A3
Stirling Enterprise Pk B3
Stirling Old Bridge A2
Stirling Station ⇌ B2
Superstore A2
Sutherland Ave A3
TA Centre C3
Tannery La A2
The Bastion ✦ C2
The Changing Room 🏛 B1
Thistle Industrial Est C3
Thistles Sh Ctr, The B2
Tollbooth, The ✦ B1
Town Wall B1
Union St A2
Upper Back Walk B1
Upper Bridge St A1
Upper Castlehill B1
Upper Craigs C2
Victoria Pl C1
Victoria Rd B1
Victoria Sq B1/C1
Vue 🎦 B2
Wallace St A2
Waverley Cres A3
Wellgreen Rd C2
Windsor Pl C1
YHA ▲ B1

Stoke 343

Ashford St A3
Avenue Rd A3
Aynsley Rd A2
Barnfield C1
Bath St C2
Beresford St A3
Bilton St C2
Boon Ave C2
Booth St C2
Boothen Rd C2/C3
Boughey St C2
Boughley Rd B3
Brighton St B1
Campbell Rd C2
Carlton Rd B3
Cauldon Rd A3
Cemetery A2
Cemetery Rd A2
Chamberlain Ave C1
Church (RC) ⛪ B2
Church St C2
City Rd C3
Civic Centre & King's Hall 🏛 B3
Cliff Vale Pk A1
College Rd A2
Convent Cl B2
Copeland St B2
Cornwallis St C3
Corporation St C2
Crowther St A3
Dominic St B1
Elenora St B2
Elgin St B2
Epworth St A3
Etruscan St A1
Film Theatre 🎦 B3
Fleming Rd C2
Fletcher Rd C2
Floyd St B2
Foden St C2
Frank St C2
Franklin Rd C1
Frederick Ave B1
Garden St C1
Garner St A1
Gerrard St B2
Glebe St B3
Greatbach Ave B1
Hanley Park A3
Harris St B1
Hartshill Rd B1
Hayward St A2
Hide St B2
Higson Ave B2
Hill St B2
Honeywall B2
Hunters Dr C1
Hunters Way C1
Keary St C2
Kingsway B2
Leek Rd B3
Library C2
Lime St C2
Liverpool Rd B2
London Rd C2
Lonsdale St C2
Lovatt St B2
Lytton St B3
Market C2
Newcastle La C1
Newlands St A2
Norfolk St A2
North St A1/B2
North Staffordshire Royal Infirmary (A&E) 🏥 B1
Northcote Ave B2
Oldmill St C3
Oriel St B1
Oxford St B1
Penkhull New Rd C1
Penkhull St C1
Police Station 👮 C2
Portmeirion Pottery ✦ C2
Post Office 📮 A3/B1/B3/C1/C2
Prince's Rd B1
Pump St B2
Quarry Ave B1
Quarry Rd B1
Queen Anne St A3
Queen's Rd C1
Queensway A1/B2/C3
Richmond St B1
Rothwell St C1
St Peter's ⛪ B3
St Thomas Pl C1
Scrivenor Rd A1
Seaford St A3
Selwyn St C3
Shelton New Rd A1
Shelton Old Rd B2
Sheppard St C2
Spark St C2
Spencer Rd B3
Spode St C2
Squires View B3
Staffordshire Univ B3
Stanley Matthews Sports Centre B3
Station Rd B3
Stoke Business Park C3
Stoke Recreation Ctr C2
Stoke Rd A2
Stoke-on-Trent Coll A3
Stoke-on-Trent Sta ⇌ B3
Sturgess St C2
The Villas C1
Thistley Hough C1
Thornton Rd B3
Tolkien Way B1
Trent Valley Rd C1
Vale St B2
Watford St A3
Wellesley St A3
West Ave B1
Westland St B1
Yeaman St C2
Yoxall Ave B1

Stratford-upon-Avon 343

Albany Rd B1
Alcester Rd B1
Ambulance Station B1
Arden St B2
Avenue Farm A1
Ave Farm Ind Est A1
Avenue Rd A3
Avon Industrial Estate A2
Baker Ave A1
Bandstand C3
Benson Rd A3
Birmingham Rd A2
Boat Club B3
Borden Pl C1
Brass Rubbing Ctr ✦ C2
Bridge St B2
Bridgetown Rd C3
Bridgeway B3
Broad St C2
Broad Walk C2
Brookvale Rd C1
Bull St C2
Bus Station B2
Butterfly Farm ✦ C3
Cemetery C1
Chapel La B2
Cherry Orchard C1
Chestnut Walk B2
Children's Playground C3
Church St C2
Civic Hall B2
Clarence Rd B1
Clopton Bridge ✦ B3
Clopton Rd A2
Coach Terminal & Park B3
College B1
College La C2
College St C2
Com Sports Centre B1
Council Offices (District) B2
Courtyard 🎭 C2
Cox's Yard ✦ B3
Cricket Ground C3
Ely Gdns B2
Ely St B2
Evesham Rd C1
Fire Station B1
Foot Ferry C3
Fordham Ave A2
Gallery, The 🏛 B3
Garrick Way C1
Gower Memorial ✦ B3
Great William St B2
Greenhill St B2
Grove Rd B2
Guild St B2
Guildhall & School 🏛 B2
Hall's Croft 🏛 C2
Hartford Rd C1
Harvard House 🏛 B2
Henley St B2
High St B2
Holton St C2
Holy Trinity ⛪ C2
Information Ctr ℹ B3
Jolyffe Park Rd A2
Kipling Rd C3
Leisure & Visitor Ctr B3
Library B2
Lodge Rd B1
Maidenhead Rd A3
Mansell St B2
Masons Court B2
Masons Rd A1
Maybird Shopping Pk A2
Maybrook Rd A1
Mayfield Ave A2
Meer St B2
Mill La C2
Moat House Hotel B3
Narrow La C2
Nash's Ho & New Pl 🏛 B2
New St C2
Old Town C2
Orchard Way C1
Paddock La C1
Park Rd A1
Payton St B2
Percy St A2
Police Station 👮 B2
Post Office 📮 B2/B3
Recreation Ground C2
Regal Road A2
Rother St B2
Rowley Cr A3

Royal Shakespeare Theatre....B3
Ryland St....C2
Saffron Meadow....C2
St Andrew's Cr....B2
St Gregory's....A3
St Gregory's Rd....B2
St Mary's Rd....A2
Sanctus Dr....C1
Sanctus St....C1
Sandfield Rd....B2
Scholars La....B2
Seven Meadows Rd....C2
Shakespeare Ctr ✦....B2
Shakespeare Institute..C2
Shakespeare St....B2
Shakespeare's Birthplace ✦....B2
Sheep St....B2
Shelley Rd....C3
Shipston Rd....B1
Shottery Rd....C1
Slingates Rd....A2
Southern La....C1
Station Rd....B1
Stratford Healthcare [H]....
Stratford Hospital [H]....A1
Stratford Sports Club....B1
Stratford-upon-Avon Station ≷....B1
Swan's Nest La....B2
Swan Theatre 🏛....B2
Talbot Rd....A2
The Greenway....C2
The Willows....B1
The Willows North....B1
Tiddington Rd....B3
Timothy's Bridge Industrial Estate....A1
Timothy's Bridge Rd..A1
Town Hall & Council Offices....B2
Town Sq....B2
Trinity St....B2
Tyler St....B2
War Memorial Gdns....B3
Warwick Rd....B3
Waterside....A3
Welcombe Rd....A3
West St....A2
Western Rd....A2
Wharf Rd....B2
Wood St....B2

Sunderland 343
Albion Pl....C2
Alliance Pl....B1
Argyle St....C1
Ashwood St....C1
Athenaeum St....B2
Azalea Terr....C1
Beach St....A1
Bede Theatre 🏛....C3
Bedford St....C1
Beechwood Terr....C1
Belvedere Rd....C1
Blandford St....B2
Borough Rd....B3
Bridge Cr....B2
Bridge St....B2
Brooke St....A2
Brougham St....B2
Burdon Rd....C1
Burn Park....C1
Burn Park Rd....C1
Burn Park Tech Park..C1
Carol St....A3
Charles St....A3
Chester Rd....C1
Chester Terr....B1
Church St....A3
Civic Centre....C2
Cork St....B3
Coronation St....B3
Cowan Terr....C2
Crowtree Rd....B2
Dame Dorothy St....B1
Deptford Rd....B1
Deptford Terr....A1
Derby St....B2
Derwent St....B2
Dock St....A3
Dundas St....A2
Durham Rd....C2
Easington St....A2
Egerton St....C3
Empire 🏛....B2
Empire Theatre 🏛....B2
Farringdon Row....B1
Fawcett St....B2
Fox St....C1
Foyle St....B2
Frederick St....B3
Gill Rd....C3
Hanover Pl....A1
Havelock Terr....C1
Hay St....A3
Headworth Sq....B3
Hendon Rd....C3
High St East....B3
High St West....B2/3
Holmeside....B2
Hylton Rd....B1
Information Ctr [i]....B2
John St....B2
Kier Hardie Way....A2
Lambton St....B2
Laura St....C3
Lawrence St....B3
Leisure Centre....B3
Library & Arts Centre.B3
Lily St....B1
Lime St....B1
Livingstone Rd....B2
Low Row....B2
Matamba Terr....B1
Millburn St....B1
Millennium Way....A2

Minster 🏛....B2
Monkwearmouth Station Museum 🏛..A2
Mowbray Park....C3
Mowbray Rd....C3
Murton St....C3
National Glass Ctr ✦..A2
New Durham Rd....C1
Newcastle Rd....A2
Nile St....B3
Norfolk St....C3
North Bridge St....B1
Northern Gallery for Contemporary Art 🏛.B2
Otto Terr....C1
Park La....C1
Park Lane Ⓜ....C2
Park Rd....C2
Paul's Rd....B1
Peel St....C1
Police Station 🔖....B2
Post Office 🏤....A1
Priestly Cr....A1
Queen St....B2
Railway Row....B1
Retail Park....C3
Richmond St....A2
Roker Ave....A2
Royalty Theatre 🏛....C1
Ryhope Rd....C2
St Mary's Way....B2
St Michael's Way....B2
St Peter's 🚉....A3
St Peter's Ⓜ....A3
St Peter's Way....B3
Salem Rd....C3
Salem St....C3
Salisbury St....C3
Sans St....B3
Silkworth Row....B1
Southwick Rd....A1
Stadium of Light (Sunderland AFC)...A1
Stadium Way....A1
Stobart St....A1
Stockton Rd....C2
Suffolk St....C3
Sunderland Aquatic Centre....A2
Sunderland Ⓜ....B2
Sunderland Mus 🏛....B2
Sunderland Station ≷.B2
Sunderland St....B3
Tatham St....C3
Tavistock Pl....B3
The Bridges....B2
The Place....B1
The Royalty....C1
Thelma St....C1
Thomas St North....A2
Thornholme Rd....C1
Toward Rd....C3
Transport Interchange....C2
Trimdon St Way....B1
Tunstall Rd....C1
University Ⓜ....C1
University Library....C1
University of Sunderland (City Campus)....B1
University of Sunderland (Sir Tom Cowie at St Peter's Campus)...B1
Vaux Brewery Way....A2
Villiers St....B3
Villiers St South....B3
Vine Pl....B2
Violet St....A3
Walton La....B3
Waterworks Rd....B2
Wearmouth Bridge....A2
Wellington La....A1
West Sunniside....B3
West Wear St....B3
Westbourne Rd....C1
Western Hill....C1
Wharncliffe....B1
Whickham St....A3
White House Rd....C3
Wilson St North....B1
Winter Gdns....C3
Wreath Quay....A1

Swansea Abertawe 343
Adelaide St....C3
Albert Row....C3
Alexandra Rd....B2
Argyle St....C1
Baptist Well Pl....A2
Beach St....C1
Belle Vue Way....B3
Berw Rd....A1
Berwick Terr....A1
Bond St....C1
Brangwyn Concert Hall 🏛...C1
Bridge St....A3
Brookands Terr....B1
Brunswick St....C1
Bryn-Syfi Terr....A2
Bryn-y-Mor Rd....C1
Bullins La....A2
Burrows Rd....C1
Bus/Rail link....B2
Bus Station....C2
Cadfan Rd....A1
Cadrawd Rd....A1
Caer St....B3
Carig Cr....A1
Carlton Terr....B2
Carmarthen Rd....A2
Castle Square....B3
Castle St....B3
Catherine St....C1
Cinema 🎦....C2
Civic Centre & Library.C2
Clarence St....C2
Colbourne Terr....A2

Constitution Hill....B1
Court....B3
Creidiol Rd....A2
Cromwell St....B2
Duke St....B1
Dunvant Pl....C2
Dyfatty Park....A3
Dyfatty St....A3
Dyfed Ave....A1
Dylan Thomas Ctr ✦..B3
Dylan Thomas Theatre 🏛....B3
Eaton Cr....C1
Eigen Cr....A1
Elfed Rd....A2
Emlyn Rd....A1
Evans Terr....A3
Fairfield Terr....B1
Ffynone Dr....B1
Ffynone Rd....B1
Fire Station....A2
Firm St....A2
Fleet St....C1
Francis St....C1
Fullers Row....B2
George St....B2
Glamorgan St....C2
Glyndŵr Pl....A1
Graig Terr....A3
Grand Theatre 🏛....C2
Granogwen Rd....A2
Guildhall....C1
Guildhall Rd South....C1
Gwent Rd....A1
Gwynedd Ave....A1
Hafod St....A3
Hanover St....B1
Harcourt St....B2
Harries St....A2
Heathfield....B2
Henrietta St....B1
Hewson St....A2
High St....A3/B3
High View....A2
Hill St....A2
Historic Ships Berth 🚢....C3
HM Prison....B3
Information Ctr [i]....C2
Islwyn Rd....A1
King Edward's Rd....C1
Law Courts....B2
Long Ridge....A2
Madoc St....C2
Mansel St....B2
Maritime Quarter....C3
Market....B3
Mayhill Gdns....B1
Mayhill Rd....B1
Mega Bowl 🎳....B3
Milton Terr....A2
Mission Gallery 🏛....C3
Montpellier Terr....A3
Morfa Rd....A3
Mount Pleasant....B2
National Waterfront Museum 🏛....C3
Nelson St....C2
New Cut Rd....A3
New St....A3
Nicander Pde....A2
Nicander Pl....A2
Nicholl St....B2
Norfolk St....B1
North Hill Rd....A2
Northampton La....B2
Orchard St....B3
Oxford St....C1
Oystermouth Rd....C1
Page St....C2
Pant-y-Celyn Rd....B1
Parc Tawe Link....B3
Parc Tawe North....B3
Parc Tawe Sh & L Ctr.B3
Patti Pavilion 🏛....C1
Paxton St....C1
Penmaen Terr....B1
Pen-y-Graig Rd....A1
Phillips Pde....C1
Picton Terr....B2
Plantasia ❁....B3
Police Station 🔖....B2
Post Office 🏤....A1/A2/B2/C1
Powys Ave....A1
Primrose St....B2
Princess Way....B2
Promenade....B2
Pryder Gdns....A1
Quadrant Centre....C2
Quay Park....B3
Rhianfa La....B1
Rhondda St....B2
Richardson St....C2
Rodney St....C1
Rose Hill....B1
Rosehill Terr....B1
Russell St....B1
St Helen's Ave....C1
St Helen's Cr....C1
St Helen's Rd....C1
St James Gdns....B1
St James's Cr....B1
St Mary's 🚉....B3
Sea View Terr....A3
Singleton St....C2
South Dock....C3
Stanley Pl....A3
Strand....B3
Swansea Castle 🏰....B3
Swansea Coll Arts Ctr.B3
Swansea Metropolitan University....C1
Swansea Museum 🏛....C3
Swansea Station ≷....B1
Taliesin Rd....A1
Tan y Marian Rd....A1
Tegid Rd....A1
Teilo Cr....A1
Terrace Rd....B1/B2

The Kingsway....B2
The LC....C3
Tontine St....A3
Tower of Eclipse ✦....B2
Townhill Rd....A1
Tramshed The 🏛....C3
Trawler Rd....C3
Union St....B2
Upper Strand....A3
Vernon St....B2
Victoria Quay....C3
Victoria Rd....B3
Vincent St....C1
Walter Rd....B1
Watkin St....A2
Waun-Wen Rd....A2
Wellington St....C2
Westbury St....C1
Western St....C1
Westway....C2
William St....B2
Wind St....B3
Woodlands Terr....B1
YMCA....B2
York St....B2

Swindon 343
Albert St....C3
Albion St....C2
Alfred St....A2
Alvescot Rd....C3
Art Gallery & Mus 🏛..C3
Ashford Rd....C1
Aylesbury St....A2
Bath Rd....C2
Bathampton St....B1
Bathurst Rd....B3
Beatrice St....A2
Beckhampton St....B3
Bowood Rd....C1
Bristol St....B1
Broad St....A3
Brunel Arcade....B2
Brunel Plaza....B2
Brunswick St....C2
Bus Station....B2
Cambria Bridge Rd....C1
Cambria Place....C1
Canal Walk....B2
Carfax St....B2
Carr St....B1
Cemetery....C1/C3
Chandler Cl....C3
Chapel....A3
Chester St....B1
Christ Church 🏛....B3
Church Place....B2
Cirencester Way....A3
Clarence St....B2
Clifton St....C1
Cockleberry ❁....A2
Colbourne ❁....A3
Colbourne St....A3
College St....B2
Commercial Rd....B2
Corporation St....A2
Council Offices....B3
County Rd....A3
Courts....B2
Cricket Ground....C3
Cricklade Street....A3
Crombey St....B1/C2
Cross St....C2
Curtis St....B1
Deacon St....C2
Designer Outlet (Great Western)....B1
Dixon St....C2
Dover St....C2
Dowling St....A2
Drove Rd....C3
Dryden St....C1
Durham St....C2
East St....A2
Eastcott Hill....C2
Eastcott Rd....C2
Edgeware Rd....B2
Edmund St....C2
Elmina Rd....A3
Emlyn Square....B1
Euclid St....B2
Exeter St....B1
Fairview....C1
Faringdon Rd....B1
Farnsby St....B1
Fire Station....B2
Fleet St....B2
Fleming Way....B2/B3
Florence St....A2
Gladstone St....A3
Gooch St....A3
Graham St....A3
Great Western Way....A1/A2
Groundwell Rd....B3
Hawksworth Way....A1
Haydon St....A2
Henry St....C2
Hillside Ave....C1
Holbrook Way....B2
Hunt St....C1
Hydro....B1
Hythe Rd....C2
Information Ctr [i]....B2
Joseph St....C2
Kent Rd....C2
King William St....C1
Kingshill Rd....C1
Lansdown Rd....C2
Leicester St....B3
Library....B2
Lincoln St....B3
Little London....C3
London St....B2
Magic ❁....B3
Maidstone Rd....C1
Manchester Rd....A3
Maxwell St....B1
Milford St....B2

Milton Rd....B1
Morse St....C3
National Monuments Record Centre....B1
Newcastle St....B3
Newcombe Drive....A1
Newcombe Trading Estate....A1
Newhall St....C2
North St....C2
North Star Ave....A1
North Star ❁....A1
Northampton St....B3
Oasis Leisure Centre..A1
Ocotal Way....A3
Okus Rd....C2
Old Town....C3
Oxford St....B1
Park Lane....B1
Park Lane ❁....B1
Pembroke St....C2
Plymouth St....B3
Polaris House....A2
Polaris Way....A2
Police Station 🔖....B2
Ponting St....A2
Post Office 🏤....B1/B2/C1/C3
Poulton St....A3
Princes St....B2
Prospect Hill....C2
Prospect Place....C2
Queen St....B2
Queen's Park....C3
Radnor St....C2
Read St....C2
Reading St....B1
Regent St....B2
Retail Park....A2/A3/B3
Rosebery St....A3
St Mark's 🏛....B1
Salisbury St....A2
Savernake St....C2
Shelley St....C1
Sheppard St....B1
South St....C2
Southampton St....B3
Spring Gardens....B3
Stafford Street....C2
Stanier St....C2
Station Road....A2
STEAM 🏛....B1
Swindon College....A2
Swindon Rd....C2
Swindon Station ≷....A2
Swindon Town Football Club....A3
T A Centre....A3
Tennyson St....B1
The Lawn....C3
The Nurseries....C1
The Parade....B2
The Park....B3
Theobald St....C1
Town Hall....B2
Transfer Bridges ❁....A3
Union St....C2
Upham Rd....C3
Victoria Rd....B3
Walcot Rd....B3
War Memorial ✦....B2
Wells St....B3
Western St....B3
Westmorland Rd....B3
Whalebridge ❁....B2
Whitehead St....C1
Whitehouse Rd....A2
William St....C1
Wood St....C3
Wyvern Theatre & Arts Centre 🏛....B2
York Rd....B3

Taunton 343
Addison Gr....A1
Albemarle Rd....A1
Alfred St....B3
Alma St....B3
Bath Pl....B2
Belvedere Rd....A2
Billet St....B2
Billetfield....C2
Birch Gr....A1
Brewhouse Theatre 🏛.B2
Bridge St....B1
Bridgwater & Taunton Canal....A3
Broadlands Rd....C1
Burton Pl....C1
Bus Station....B1
Canal Rd....A2
Cann St....C1
Canon St....B2
Castle 🏰....B1
Castle St....B1
Cheddon Rd....A2
Chip Lane....A1
Clarence St....B3
Cleveland St....B1
Clifton Terr....A2
Coleridge Cres....A3
Compass Hill....C1
Compton Cl....A2
Corporation St....B1
Council Offices....B1
County Walk Sh Ctr....C2
Courtyard....B2
Cranmer Rd....B2
Critchard Way....B3
Cyril St....A3
Deller's Wharf....B1
Duke St....B2
East Reach....B3
East St....B3
Eastbourne Rd....B3
Eastleigh Rd....B3
Eaton Cres....A1
Elm Gr....A1
Elms Cl....A1

Fons George....C1
Fore St....B2
Fowler St....A1
French Weir Rec Grd..B1
Geoffrey Farrant Wk..B2
Grays Rd....C1
Greenway Ave....A1
Guildford Pl....A1
Hammet St....B2
Haydon Rd....B3
Heavitree Way....A2
Herbert St....A1
High St....C2
Holway Ave....C3
Hugo St....B3
Huish's Almshouses 🏛..B2
Hurdle Way....C2
Information Ctr [i]....C2
Jubilee St....A1
King's College....A1
Kings Cl....C3
Laburnum St....C3
Lambrook Rd....B3
Lansdowne Rd....A3
Leslie Ave....A1
Leycroft Rd....C3
Library....C2
Linden Gr....C2
Magdalene St....B2
Magistrates Court....B1
Malvern Terr....C2
Market House 🏛....B2
Mary St....C2
Middle St....B2
Midford Rd....C1
Mitre Court....B3
Mount Nebo....C1
Mount St....C2
Mountway....C2
Mus of Somerset 🏛....B1
North St....B2
Northfield Ave....B1
Northfield Rd....B1
Northleigh Rd....A2
Obridge Allotments....A3
Obridge Lane....A3
Obridge Rd....A2
Obridge Viaduct....A3
Old Mkt Shopping Ctr.B2
Osborne Way....C1
Park St....C1
Paul St....C2
Plais St....C3
Playing Field....C3
Police Station 🔖....A1
Portland St....C1
Post Office 🏤....B1/B2/C1
Priorswood Ind Est....A3
Priorswood Rd....A2
Priory Ave....B3
Priory Bridge Rd....A2
Priory Fields Retail Pk.A3
Priory Park....A3
Priory Way....A3
Queen St....B3
Railway St....A2
Records Office....A2
Recreation Grd....A1
Riverside Place....B1
St Augustine St....B2
St George's....C2
St Georges Sq....C2
St James St....B2
St John's....C1
St John's Rd....B2
St Josephs Field....C1
St Mary Magdalene's 🏛....B2
Samuels Ct....A1
Shire Hall & Law Courts....C1
Somerset County Cricket Ground....A2
Somerset County Hall.C1
Somerset Cricket 🏛....A2
South Rd....C3
South St....C2
Staplegrove Rd....A1
Station Rd....A1
Stephen St....B2
Swimming Pool....A1
Tancred St....B2
Tauntfield Cl....C3
Taunton Dean Cricket Club....C3
Taunton Station ≷....A2
The Avenue....C1
The Crescent....C1
The Mount....C2
Thomas St....A1
Toneway....A2
Tower St....B2
Trevor Smith Pl....A3
Trinity Bsns Centre....C2
Trinity Rd....C3
Trinity St....C2
Trull Rd....C1
Tudor House 🏛....B2
Upper High St....B2
Venture Way....A3
Victoria Gate....B3
Victoria Park....B3
Victoria St....B3
Viney St....B3
Vivary Park....C1
Vivary Rd....C1
War Memorial ✦....C1
Wellesley St....A1
Wheatley Cres....A1
Whitehall....C1
Wilfred Rd....B3
William St....A1
Wilton Church 🏛....C1
Wilton Cl....C1
Wilton Gr....C1
Wilton St....C1
Winchester St....B2

Winters Field....B2
Wood St....B3
Yarde Pl....B1

Telford 343
Alma Ave....C3
Amphitheatre....B2
Bowling Alley....B2
Brandsfarm Way....C3
Brunel Rd....B1
Bus Station....B2
Buxton Rd....C1
Central Park....A2
Civic Offices....B2
Coach Central....B1
Coachwell Cl....B1
Colliers Way....A1
Courts....B2
Dale Acre Way....B3
Darliston....C3
Deepdale....B3
Deercote....B2
Dinthill....C3
Doddington....B3
Dodmoor Grange....C3
Downemead....B3
Duffryn....B3
Dunsheath....B3
Euston Way....A3
Eyton Mound....C1
Eyton Rd....C1
Forgegate....A2
Grange Central....B2
Hall Park Way....B2
Hinkshay Rd....C2
Hollinsworth Rd....A2
Holyhead Rd....A3
Housing Trust....A1
Ice Rink....B2
Information Ctr [i]....B2
Ironmasters Way....A2
Job Centre....B1
Land Registry....B1
Lawn Central....B2
Lawnswood....C1
Library....B2
Malinslee....C2
Matlock Ave....C1
Moor Rd....C1
Mount Rd....C1
NFU Offices....B1
Odeon 🎦....B2
Park Lane....A1
Police Station 🔖....B2
Priorslee Ave....A3
Queen Elizabeth Ave..C3
Queen Elizabeth Way..B1
Queensway....A2/B3
Rampart Way....B1
Randlay Ave....C3
Randlay Wood....C3
Rhodes Ave....C3
Royal Way....B1
St Leonards Rd....B2
St Quentin Gate....B2
Shifnal Rd....C1
Sixth Ave....A1
Southwater One (SW1)....A2
Southwater Way....B1
Spout Lane....C1
Spout Mound....C1
Spout Way....C1
Stafford Court....B3
Stafford Park....C3
Stirchley Ave....C3
Stone Row....C1
Telford Bridge Ret Pk.A1
Telford Central Sta ≷.A3
Telford Centre, The...B2
Telford Forge Sh Pk...A1
Telford Hornets RFC..C2
Telford Int Ctr....B2
Telford Rd....A3
Third Ave....A1
Town Park....B2
Town Park Visitor Ctr.B2
Walker House....B2
Wellswood Ave....A2
West Centre Way....B1
Withywood Drive....C1
Woodhouse Central....B3
Yates Way....A1

Torquay 344
Abbey Rd....B2
Alexandra Rd....A2
Alpine Rd....B3
Ash Hill Rd....A2
Babbacombe Rd....B3
Bampfylde Rd....B1
Barton Rd....A1
Beacon Quay....C2
Belgrave Rd....A1/B1
Belmont Rd....A3
Berea Rd....A3
Braddons Hill Rd East.B3
Brewery Park....A3
Bronshill Rd....A3
Castle Circus....A2
Castle Rd....A2
Cavern Rd....A2
Central 🛍....B2
Chatsworth Rd....A2
Chestnut Ave....B1
Church St....A2
Civic Offices....A2
Coach Station....B1
Corbyn Head....C1
Croft Hill....B2
Croft Rd....B2
Daddyhole Plain....C3
East St....A1
Egerton Rd....A3
Ellacombe Church Rd.A3
Ellacombe Rd....A3
Falkland Rd....B1
Fleet St....B2

Fleet Walk Sh Ctr....B2
Grafton Rd....B3
Haldon Pier....C2
Hatfield Rd....A2
Highbury Rd....A2
Hillesdon Rd....B2
Hollywood Bowl 🎳....A3
Hoxton Rd....A3
Hunsdon Rd....B3
Information Ctr [i]....B2
Inner Harbour....A3
Kenwyn Rd....A3
Laburnum St....A1
Law Courts....B2
Library....A1
Lime Ave....B1
Living Coasts ❁....C3
Lower Warberry Rd....B3
Lucius St....B1
Lymington Rd....A1
Magdalene Rd....A1
Marina....C2
Market Forum The....B2
Market St....B2
Meadfoot Lane....C3
Meadfoot Rd....C3
Melville St....B2
Middle Warberry Rd...B3
Mill Lane....A1
Montpellier Rd....B3
Morgan Ave....A1
Museum Rd....B3
Newton Rd....A1
Oakhill Rd....A1
Outer Harbour....C2
Parkhill Rd....C3
Pavilion Shopping Ctr.C2
Pimlico....B2
Police Station 🔖....B2
Post Office 🏤....A1/B2
Princes Rd....A3
Princes Rd East....A3
Princes Rd West....A3
Princess Gdns....C2
Princess Pier....C2
Princess Theatre 🏛....C2
Rathmore Rd....B1
Recreation Grd....B1
Riviera Int Ctr....B1
Rock End Ave....C3
Rock Rd....B2
Rock Walk....B2
Rosehill Rd....A3
St Efride's Rd....A1
St John's....B3
St Luke's Rd....B2
St Luke's Rd North....B2
St Luke's Rd South....B2
St Marychurch Rd....A2
Scarborough Rd....B1
Shedden Hill....B1
South Pier....C2
South St....A1
Spanish Barn 🏛....B1
Stitchill Rd....B3
Strand....B2
Sutherland Rd....A3
Teignmouth Rd....A1
Temperance St....B2
The King's Drive....B1
The Terrace....B3
Thurlow Rd....A1
Tor Bay....C2
Tor Church Rd....A1
Tor Hill Rd....A1
Torbay Rd....B2
Torquay Museum 🏛....B3
Torquay Station ≷....C1
Torre Abbey Mansion 🏛....B1
Torre Abbey Meadows.B1
Torre Abbey Sands....B1
Torwood Gdns....B3
Torwood St....C3
Town Hall....A2
Union Square....A2
Union St....A1
Upton Hill....A2
Upton Park....A2
Upton Rd....A1
Vanehill Rd....C3
Vansittart Rd....A1
Vaughan Parade....C2
Victoria Parade....C2
Victoria Rd....A2
Warberry Rd West....B2
Warren Rd....B2
Windsor Rd....A2/A3
Woodville Rd....A3

Truro 344
Adelaide Ter....A1
Agar Rd....B3
Arch Hill....C2
Arundell Pl....C2
Avondale Rd....B1
Back Quay....B2
Barrack La....C2
Barton Meadow....A1
Benson Rd....C3
Bishops Cl....A3
Bosvean Gdns....C1
Bosvigo Gardens ❁....B1
Bosvigo La....B1
Bosvigo Rd....B1
Broad St....C3
Burley Cl....C3
Bus Station....B2
Calenick St....C2
Campfield Hill....C2
Carclew St....C2
Carew Rd....A2

Chapel Hill....B1
Charles St....C2
City Hall....B3
City Rd....B2
Coinage Hall 🏛....B3
Comprigney Hill....A1
Coosebean La....A1
Copes Gdns....A2
County Hall....B1
Courtney Rd....A2
Crescent Rd....B1
Crescent Rise....B1
Daniell Court....C1
Daniell Rd....C2
Daniell St....C2
Daubuz Cl....A2
Dobbs La....B1
Edward St....B2
Eliot Rd....A3
Elm Court....A3
Enys Cl....A1
Enys Rd....A1
Fairmantle St....B3
Falmouth Rd....C1
Ferris Town....B2
Fire Station....B1
Frances St....B2
George St....B2
Green Cl....C1
Green La....C1
Grenville Rd....A2
Hall For Cornwall 🏛...B3
Hendra Rd....A2
Hendra Vean....A1
High Cross....B3
Higher Newham La....C3
Higher Trehaverne....A2
Hillcrest Ave....B1
Hospital [H]....B1
Hunkin Cl....C2
Hurland Rd....C3
Infirmary Hill....B2
James Pl....B3
Kenwyn Church Rd....A1
Kenwyn Rd....A2
Kenwyn St....B2
Kerris Gdns....A1
King St....B2
Lemon Quay....B2
Lemon St Gallery 🏛....B2
Library....B1/B3
Malpas Rd....A3
Market....B2
Memorial Gdns....C2
Merrifield Close....A3
Mitchell Hill....B1
Moresk Cl....A3
Moresk Rd....A3
Morlaix Ave....C2
Nancemere Rd....A3
Newham Bsns Park...C3
Newham Industrial Est.C3
Newham Rd....C2
Northfield Dr....A3
Oak Way....A3
Old County Hall 🏛....B1
Pal's Terr....A3
Park View....C2
Pendarves Rd....B2
Plaza Cinema 🎦....B3
Police Station 🔖....B2
Post Office 🏤....B2/B3
Prince's St....B3
Pydar St....B2
Quay St....B3
Redannick Cres....C2
Redannick La....B2
Richard Lander Monument ✦....C2
Richmond Hill....B1
River St....B2
Rosedale Rd....A3
Royal Cornwall Mus 🏛.B2
St Aubyn St....B3
St Clement St....B3
St George's Rd....B1
School La....C2
Station Rd....B1
Stokes Rd....A2
Strangways Terr....C2
Tabernacle St....B3
The Avenue....A3
The Crescent....B2
The Leats....B2
The Spires....A1
Trehaverne La....A2
Tremayne Rd....A2
Treseder's Gdns....A3
Treworder Rd....B1
Treyew Rd....C1
Truro Cathedral ✝....B3
Truro Harbour Office..B3
Truro Station ≷....B2
Union St....B2
Upper School La....B3
Victoria Gdns....B2
Waterfall Gdns....B2

Wick 344
Ackergill Cres....A2
Ackergill St....A2
Albert St....B2
Ambulance Station....A2
Argyle Sq....B2
Assembly Rooms....B2
Bank Row....B3
Bankhead....B1
Barons Well....A2
Barrogill St....B2
Bay View....B3
Bexley Terr....A1
Bignold Park....A1
Bowling Green....B1
Breadalbane Terr....B1
Bridge of Wick....B1
Bridge St....B2
Brown Pl....B2
Burn St....B2

Bus Station B1
Caithness General
  Hospital (A&E) H B1
Cliff Rd B1
Coach Rd A2
Coastguard Station . . . C3
Corner Cres B3
Coronation St C1
Council Offices C2
  Court B2
Crane Rock C3
Dempster St C2
Dunnet Ave A2
Fire Station B2
Fish Market C3
Francis St C2
George St A1
Girnigoe St B2
Glamis Rd B2
Gowrie Pl B2
Grant St C2
Green Rd B2
Gunns St B3
Harbour Quay C3
Harbour Rd C3
Harbour Terr C2
Harrow Hill C2
Henrietta St A2/B2
Heritage Museum 🏛 . . B2
High St B2
Hill Ave A2
Hillhead Rd B2
Hood St C1
Huddart St B3
Information Ctr 🅭 C1
Kenneth St C1
Kinnaird St B1
Kirk Hill B1
Langwell Cres A2
Leishman Ave A1
Leith Walk A2
Library C2
Lifeboat Station C3
Lighthouse C2
Lindsay Dr B2
Lindsay Pl B2
Loch St B2
Louisburgh St B2
Lower Dunbar St C2
Macleay La B2
Macleod St B3
MacRae St C2
Martha Terr B2
Miller Ave C2
Miller St B1
Moray St C1
Mowat Pl A2
Murchison St C3
Newton Ave C1
Newton Rd C1
Nicolson St C2
North Highland Coll. . . C1
North River Pier C3
Northcote St C2
Owen Pl A2
Police Station 🅟 B1
Port Dunbar B3
Post Office 🄿 B2/C2
Pulteney Distillery ♦ . C2
River St B2
Robert St A1
Rutherford St C2
St John's Episcopal ⛪ . B3
Sandigoe Rd B3
Scalesburn C1
Seaforth Ave C1
Shore La A1
Sinclair Dr B3
Sinclair Terr B3
Smith Terr C3
South Pier C3
South Quay C3
South Rd C2
South River Pier B3
Station Rd B1
Swimming Pool C2
TA Centre C2
Telford St B2
The Shore B2
Thurso Rd B1
Thurso St B1
Town Hall B2
Union St B2
Upper Dunbar St. C2
Vansittart St C3
Victoria Pl C2
War Memorial C2
Well of Cairndhuna ♦ . C3
Wellington Ave C3
Wellington St C3
West Banks Ave C1
West Banks Terr C1
West Park C1
Whitehorse Park B2
Wick Harbour Bridge . . B2
Wick Industrial Estate . A2
Wick Parish Church ⛪ . B1
Wick Stations ⛭ B1
Williamson St C1
Willowbank B2

Winchester 344

Andover Rd A1
Andover Rd Retail Pk. . A1
Archery La C2
Arthur Rd A2
Bar End Rd C3
Beaufort Rd C2
Beggar's La B2
Bereweke Ave A1
Bereweke Rd A1

Boscobel Rd A2
Brassey Rd A2
Broadway B3
Brooks Sh Ctr, The . . . B3
Bus Station B3
Butter Cross ♦ B2
Canon St C2
Castle Wall C2
Castle, King Arthur's
  Round Table 🏛 B2
Cathedral ✝ C2
Cheriton Rd A1
Chesil St C3
Chesil Theatre ⛭ C3
Christchurch Rd C1
City Mill 🏛 B3
City Museum 🏛 B2
City Offices C3
City Rd B2
Clifton Rd B1
Clifton Terr B2
Close Wall C2/C3
Coach Park A2
Colebrook St C3
College St C2
College Walk C3
Compton Rd C2
County Council
  Offices B2
Cranworth Rd A2
Cromwell Rd C1
Culver Rd C3
Domum Rd C3
Durngate Pl B3
Eastgate St B3
Edgar Rd C2
Egbert Rd A2
Elm Rd B1
Everyman 🎭 C2
Fairfield Rd A1
Fire Station B3
Fordington Ave. B1
Fordington Rd. A1
Friarsgate B3
Gordon Rd B3
Greenhill Rd A1
Guildhall 🏛 B3
HM Prison B1
Hatherley Rd A1
High St B2
Hillier Way A3
Hyde Abbey
  (Remains) ✝ A2
Hyde Abbey Rd B2
Hyde Cl A2
Hyde St A2
Information Ctr 🅭 B2
Jane Austen's Ho 🏛 . . C2
Jewry St B2
John Stripe Theatre ⛭ . C1
King Alfred Pl A2
Kingsgate Arch C2
Kingsgate Park C2
Kingsgate Rd C2
Kingsgate St C2
Lankhills Rd A1
Library B2
Lower Brook St B3
Magdalen Hill B3
Market La B2
Mews La B1
Middle Brook St B3
Middle Rd B1
Military Museums 🏛 . . B2
Milland Rd C3
Milverton Rd A1
Monks Rd A3
North Hill Cl. A3
North Walls B2
North Walls Rec Gnd . . A3
Nuns Rd C3
Oram's Arbour B1
Owen's Rd A2
Parchment St B2
Park & Ride C3
Park Ave. B3
Playing Field A1
Police HQ 🅟 B1
Police Station 🅟 B3
Portal Rd C3
Post Office 🄿 B2/C1
Quarry Rd C3
Ranelagh Rd C2
Regiment Museum 🏛 . B2
River Park Leisure Ctr . B3
Romans' Rd C2
Romsey Rd B2
Royal Hampshire County
  Hospital (A&E) H . . . B1
St Cross Rd C1
St George's St B2
St Giles Hill B2
St James' La B1
St James' Terr. B1
St James Villas C2
St John's 🏛 B3
St John's St B3
St Michael's Rd C2
St Paul's Hill B1
St Peter St B2
St Swithun St C2
St Thomas St C2
Saxon Rd A2
School of Art. B3
Sleepers Hill Rd C1
Southgate St C2
Sparkford Rd C1
Staple Gdns B2
St Leonards Rd C2
Step Terr B1
Stockbridge Rd. A1
Stuart Cres C1

Sussex St B2
Swan Lane B2
Tanner St B3
The Square B2
The Weirs C3
The Winchester
  Gallery 🏛 A2
Theatre Royal ⛭ B2
Tower St B2
Town Hall C2
Union St B3
Univ of Southampton
  (Winchester School
  of Art) B3
Univ of Winchester (King
  Alfred Campus) C1
Upper Brook St. B2
Wales St B2
Water Lane B3
West End Terr B1
West Gate 🏛 B2
Western Rd A1
Wharf Hill C3
Winchester College. . . C2
Winchester Sta ⛭ A2
Winnall Moors
  Wildlife Reserve A3
Wolvesey Castle 🏛 . . . C3
Worthy Lane A2
Worthy Rd A2

Windsor 344

Adelaide Sq. C3
Albany Rd C2
Albert St. B1
Alexandra Gdns C2
Alexandra Rd. C2
Alma Rd C2
Ambulance Station . . . B1
Arthur Rd B2
Bachelors Acre B2
Barry Ave C1
Beaumont Rd C2
Bexley St B1
Boat House B2
Brocas St B2
Brook St. C3
Bulkeley Ave C1
Castle Hill B2
Charles St. B2
Claremont Rd C2
Clarence Cr B2
Clarence Rd. B1
Clewer Court Rd. C1
Coach Park B1
College Cr C2
Courts C2
Cricket Ground C2
Dagmar Rd C2
Datchet Rd. B3
Devereux Rd C2
Dorset Rd C2
Duke St B1
Elm Rd C2
Eton College ♦ A3
Eton Ct A2
Eton Sq A2
Eton Wick Rd A2
Fire Station B1
Farm Yard B3
Frances Rd C2
Frogmore Dr B3
Gloucester Pl C3
Goslar Way C1
Goswell Hill B2
Goswell Rd B2
Green La C1
Grove Rd C2
Guildhall 🏛 B2
Helena Rd C2
Helston La B1
High St A2/B3
Holy Trinity ⛪ C2
Hospital (Private) H . . C2
Household Cavalry C2
Imperial Rd C1
Information Ctr 🅭 . . B2/B3
Keats La C2
King Edward Ct. B2
King Edward VII Ave. . . A3
King Edward VII
  Hospital H C3
King George V Meml . . B3
King's Rd C2
King Stable St A2
Library C2
Maidenhead Rd B1
Meadow La A2
Municipal Offices C3
Nell Gwynne's Ho 🏛 . . B3
Osborne Rd C2
Oxford Rd B1
Park St B2
Peascod St B2
Police Station 🅟 B2
Post Office 🄿 A2
Princess Margaret
  Hospital H C2
Queen Victoria's Walk. B3
Queen's Rd C2
River St. B2
Romney Island A3
Romney Lock. A3
Romney Lock Rd. A3
Russell St C2
St John's ⛪ B3
St John's Chapel ⛪ . . . A2
St Leonards Rd C2
St Mark's Rd C2
Sheet St C2
South Meadow A2

South Meadow La A2
Springfield Rd. C1
Stovell Rd B1
Sunbury Rd A2
Tangier La A2
Tangier St A3
Temple Rd B3
Thames St B3
The Brocas A2
The Home Park A3/C3
The Long Walk C3
Theatre Royal ⛭ B3
Trinity Pl C2
Vansittart Rd. B1/C1
Vansittart Rd Gdns. . . . C1
Victoria Barracks C1
Victoria St C2
Ward Royal B2
Westmead C1
White Lilies Island A1
William St B2
Windsor Arts Ctr 🎭 . . . B2
Windsor Castle 🏛 B2
Windsor & Eton
  Central ⛭ B2
Windsor & Eton
  Riverside ⛭ A3
Windsor Bridge B2
Windsor Great Park. . . C2
Windsor Leisure Ctr. . . B1
Windsor Relief Rd A1
Windsor Royal Sh C1
York Ave C1
York Rd C1

Wolverhampton 344

Albion St B3
Alexandra St A1
Arena 🏟 B2
Arts Gallery 🏛 B2
Ashland St C1
Austin St A1
Badger Dr A3
Bailey St. B2
Bath Ave. A1
Bath Rd. C2
Bell St B2
Berry St B3
Bilston Rd C3
Bilston St. C2
Birmingham Canal . . . A3
Bone Mill La. A2
Brewery Rd A2
Bright St. A1
Burton Cres. B3
Bus Station B3
Cambridge St A3
Camp St B2
Cannock Rd A3
Castle St. C2
Chapel Ash C1
Cherry St C1
Chester St A1
Church La C2
Church St C2
Civic Centre. B2
Clarence Rd. B2
Cleveland St C2
Clifton St C1
Coach Station B2
Compton Rd B1
Corn Hill B3
Coven St A2
Craddock St. A1
Cross St North A2
Crown & County
  Courts C3
Crown St B2
Culwell St B3
Dale St C1
Darlington St. C1
Dartmouth St C2
Devon Rd A1
Drummond St B2
Dudley Rd C2
Dudley St C2
Duke St C3
Dunkley St A1
Dunstall Ave A2
Dunstall Hill A2
Dunstall Rd A1/A2
Evans St A1
Fawdry St A1
Field St. B3
Fire Station B1
Fiveways ⌛ C1
Fowler Playing Fields . . A3
Fox's La. A2
Francis St A2
Fryer St B3
Gloucester St C1
Gordon St C3
Graiseley St C1
Grand 🎭 B3
Granville St C2
Great Brickkiln St. C1
Great Hampton St A1
Great Western St A1
Grimstone St. B3
Harrow St A1
Hilton St A3
Horseley Fields. C3
Humber Rd C1
Jack Hayward Way. . . . A2
Jameson St A1
Jenner St. C3
Kennedy Rd B3
Kimberley St C1
King St B2
Laburnum St C1
Lansdowne Rd B1

Leicester St A1
Lever St C3
Library B2
Lichfield St B2
Light House 🎬 B2
Little's La B3
Lock St B3
Lord St C1
Lowe St A2
Lower Stafford St. A2
Magistrates Court. C2
Mander Centre B2
Mander St C1
Market St. B2
Market B2
Melbourne St C3
Merridale St C1
Middlecross A3
Molineux St. A2
Mostyn St A1
New Hampton Rd East . A1
Nine Elms La A3
North Rd A2
Oaks Cres. C1
Oxley St A2
Paget St A1
Park Ave. B1
Park Road East B1
Park Road West B1
Paul St C2
Pelham St. C1
Penn Rd C1
Piper's Row B3
Pitt St C1
Police Station 🅟 B3
Pool St C2
Poole St A3
Post Office 🄿
  . . . . . . A1/A2/B2/B2
Powlett St C3
Queen St B3
Raby St. C1
Railway Dr B3
Red Hill St B2
Red Lion St B2
Retreat St. C1
Ring Rd B2
Rugby St A1
Russell St C1
St Andrew's B1
St David's C2
St George's C3
St George's Parade . . . C2
St James St C3
St John's C2
St John's Retail Park . . C2
St John's Square. C2
St Mark's C1
St Marks Rd C1
St Marks St C1
St Patrick's B2
St Peter's B2
St Peter's ⛪ B2
Salisbury St C1
Salop St C2
School St C2
Sherwood St. A2
Smestow St A3
Snowhill C2
Springfield Rd. A3
Stafford St. B3
Staveley Rd A1
Steelhouse La C3
Stephenson St C1
Stewart St C2
Sun St B3
Sutherland Pl C3
Tempest St C2
Temple St C2
Tettenhall Rd B1
The Maltings A2
The Royal 🚊 C3
Thomas St C2
Thornley St B2
Tower St B3
University B2
Upper Zoar St C1
Vicarage Rd C3
Victoria St C2
Walpole St A1
Walsall St C3
Ward St C3
Warwick St C3
Water St A3
Waterloo Rd B2
Wednesfield Rd B3
West Pk (not A&E) H . . B1
West Park Swimming
  Pool B1
Wharf St C3
Whitmore Hill B2
Wolverhampton 🚊 B2
Wolverhampton St
  George's 🚊 C2
Wolverhampton
  Wanderers Football
  Gnd (Molineux) A2
Worcester St. C2
Wulfrun Centre C2
Yarwell Cl A3
York St C1
Zoar St C1

Worcester 344

Albany Terr A1
Alice Otley School A2
Angel Pl B2
Angel St B2
Ashcroft Rd A2

Athelstan Rd C3
Back Lane North A1
Back Lane South A1
Barbourne Rd A2
Bath Rd C2
Battenhall Rd C3
Bridge St B2
Britannia Sq A1
Broad St B2
Bromwich La C1
Bromwich Rd C1
Bromyard Rd. C1
Bus Station B2
Carden St. B3
Castle St A2
Cathedral ✝ C2
Cathedral Plaza B2
Charles St B3
Chequers La B3
Chestnut St A2
Chestnut Walk A2
Citizens' Advice
  Bureau B2
City Walls Rd B2
Cole Hill C3
College of Technology . B2
College St C2
Commandery 🏛 C3
Cripplegate Park B1
Croft Rd B1
Cromwell St B3
CrownGate Centre B2
Deansway B2
Diglis Pde C2
Diglis Rd C2
Edgar Tower ♦ C2
Farrier St A2
Fire Station B3
Foregate St A2
Foregate Street ⛭ A2
Fort Royal Hill C3
Fort Royal Park C3
Foundry St B3
Friar St C2
George St B3
Grand Stand Rd. B1
Greenhill C3
Greyfriars 🏛 B2
Guildhall 🏛 B2
Henwick Rd B1
High St B2
Hill St B3
Huntingdon Hall 🎭 . . . B2
Hylton Rd B1
Information Ctr 🅭 B2
King Charles Pl
  Shopping Centre C1
King's School C2
King's School
  Playing Field C2
Kleve Walk C2
Lansdowne Cr A3
Lansdowne Rd A3
Lansdowne Walk A3
Laslett St A3
Leisure Centre A3
Library, Museum &
  Art Gallery 🏛 A2
Little Chestnut St A2
Little London C3
London Rd C3
Lowell St A2
Lowesmoor B2
Lowesmoor Terr. A3
Lowesmoor Wharf A3
Magistrates Court B3
Midland Rd B3
Mill St C2
Moors Severn Terr A1
New Rd B1
New St B2
Northfield St A3
Odeon 🎬 B2
Padmore St B3
Park St C3
Pheasant St B3
Pitchcroft
  Racecourse A1
Police Station 🅟 A2
Portland St C2
Post Office 🄿 B2
Quay St B2
Queen St B2
Rainbow Hill A3
Recreation Ground . . . A1
Reindeer Court. B2
Rogers Hill A3
Sabrina Rd A1
St Dunstan's Cr C3
St John's C1
St Martin's Gate B3
St Oswald's Rd A2
St Paul's St B3
St Swithin's Church . . . B2
St Wulstans Cr C3
Sansome Walk A2
Severn St C2
Shaw St B2
Shire Hall Crown Ct . . . A2
Shrub Hill 🚊 B3
Shrub Hill Retail Park . . B3
Shrub Hill Rd B3
Slingpool Walk C1
South Quay C2
Southfield St A2
Sports Ground A2/C1
Stanley Rd A3
Swan, The 🎭 A1
Swimming Pool A2
Tallow Hill B3
Tennis Walk A2
The Avenue C1

The Butts B2
The Cross B2
The Shambles B2
The Tything A2
Tolladine Rd B3
Tybridge St B1
Univ of Worcester B3
Vincent Rd B3
Vue 🎬 A3
Washington St A3
Woolhope Rd C3
Worcester Bridge. B2
Worcester County
  Cricket Ground C1
Worcester Library &
  History Centre C3
Worcester Porcelain
  Museum 🏛 C2
Worcester Royal
  Grammar School A2
Wylds La C3

Wrexham Wrecsam 344

Abbot St B2
Acton Rd A3
Albert St C2
Alexandra Rd. C1
Aran Rd A3
Barnfield C3
Bath Rd C2
Beechley Rd C3
Belgrave Rd C2
Belle Vue Park C2
Belle Vue Rd C2
Belvedere Dr A1
Bennion's Rd C3
Berse Rd A1
Bersham Rd C1
Birch St B3
Bodhyfryd B3
Border Retail Park B2
Bradley Rd C2
Bright St B1
Bron-y-Nant A3
Brook St C2
Bryn-y-Cabanau Rd. . . C3
Bury St A2
Bus Station B2
Butchers Market B2
Caia Rd C3
Cambrian Ind Est C3
Caxton Pl B2
Cemetery A3
Centenary Rd C1
Chapel St C2
Charles St B3
Chester Rd A3
Chester St B3
Cilcen Gr A3
Citizens Advice
  Bureau B2
Cobden Rd B1
Council Offices B3
County 🏛 B2
Crescent Rd. C3
Crispin La A2
Croesnewyth Rd. B1
Cross St A2
Cunliffe St C2
Derby Rd B3
Dolydd Rd B1
Duke St. B2
Eagles Meadow. C3
Earle St C2
East Ave A3
Edward St C2
Egerton St B2
Empress Rd C1
Erddig Rd C2
Fairy Rd C2
Fire Station B3
Foster Rd A3
Foxwood Dr A1
Garden Rd A2
General Market B2
Gerald St B2
Greenbank St C3
Greenfield A2
Grosvenor Rd B2
Grove Park 🎭 B3
Grove Park Rd B3
Grove Rd A3
Guildhall B2
Haig Rd C3
Hampden Rd C1
Hazel Gr A3
Henblas St B2
High St B2
Hightown Rd C3
Hill St B2
Holt Rd B3
Holt St B3
Hope St B2
Huntroyde Ave C3
Information Ctr 🅭 B2
Island Gn Sh Ctr B2
Job Centre. B2
Jubilee Rd B2
King St B2
Kingsmills Rd C3
Lambpit St B2
Lawson Cl A3
Lawson Rd A3
Lea Rd C2
Library & Arts Centre . . B2
Lilac Way B1

Llys David Lord B1
Lorne St B2
Maesgwyn Rd B1
Maesydre Rd A3
Manley Rd B3
Market St. B3
Mawddy Ave A3
Mayville Ave A3
Memorial Gallery 🏛 . . . B2
Memorial Hall B3
Mold Rd A1
Mount St C2
Neville Cres A3
New Rd A2
North Wales Regional
  Tennis Centre A1
North Wales School of
  Art & Design B3
Oak Dr A3
Park Ave. A3
Park St C2
Peel St C1
Pentre Felin C2
Pen y Bryn. B2
Penymaes Ave A3
Peoples Market. B3
Percy St C2
Plas Coch Retail Park . . A1
Plas Coch Rd A1
Police Station 🅟 C2
Poplar Rd C3
Post Office 🄿
  . . . . . . A2/B2/C2/C3
Powell Rd B3
Poyser St C3
Price's La B1
Primose Way B1
Princess St C1
Queen St B3
Queens Sq B2
Regent St B2
Rhosddu Rd A2/B2
Rhosnesni La. A3
Rivulet Rd C3
Ruabon Rd C1
Ruthin Rd C1/C2
St Giles ⛪ B3
St Giles Way C3
St James Ct A2
St Mary's ✝ B2
Salisbury Rd C3
Salop Rd C3
Sontley Rd C2
Spring Rd A3
Stanley St C2
Stansty Rd A2
Station Approach. B2
Studio 🎭 B2
Talbot Rd C2
Techniquest
  Glyndŵr 🏛 B1
The Beeches A3
The Pines A3
Town Hill B2
Trevor St C2
Trinity St B2
Tuttle St C3
Vale Park A1
Vernon St. B2
Vicarage Hill C2
Victoria Rd C2
Walnut St B3
War Memorial B3
Waterworld L Ctr ♦ . B1/B2
Watery Rd B1/B2
Wellington Rd C2
Westminster Dr A3
William Aston Hall 🎭 . . A1
Windsor Rd C1
Wrexham AFC A1
Wrexham Central ⛭ . . . B2
Wrexham General ⛭ . . . B2
Wrexham Maelor
  Hospital (A&E) H B1
Wrexham Technology
  Park B1
Wynn Ave A2
Yale College A2
Yale Gr A3
Yorke St C3

York 344

Aldwark B2
Ambulance Station . . . B3
Barbican Rd C3
Barley Hall 🏛 B2
Bishopgate St C2
Bishopthorpe Rd C2
Blossom St C1
Bootham A1
Bootham Cr A1
Bootham Terr A1
Bridge St B2
Brook St A2
Brownlow St A2
Burton Stone La A1
Castle Museum 🏛 C2
Castlegate B2
Cemetery Rd C2
Cherry St C2
City Screen 🎬 B2
City Wall A2/B1/C3
Clarence St A2
Clementhorpe C2
Clifford St B2
Clifford's Tower 🏛 C2
Clifton A1
Coach park B1
Coney St B2
Cromwell Rd C2
Crown Court C2

Davygate B2
Deanery Gdns A2
DIG 🏛 B2
Ebor Industrial Estate . . B3
Fairfax House 🏛 B2
Fishergate C2
Foss Islands Retail Pk . B3
Foss Islands Rd B3
Fossbank A3
Garden St A2
George St C2
Gillygate A2
Goodramgate B2
Grand Opera House 🎭 . B2
Grosvenor Terr A1
Guildhall B2
Hallfield Rd B3
Heslington Rd C3
Heworth Green A3
Holy Trinity ⛪ B2
Hope St C2
Huntington Rd A3
Information Ctr 🅭 B2
James St B3
Jorvik Viking Ctr 🏛 . . . B2
Kent St C3
Lawrence St C3
Layerthorpe A3
Leeman Rd B1
Lendal B2
Lendal Bridge B1
Library B1
Longfield Terr. A1
Lord Mayor's Walk A2
Lower Eldon St A3
Lowther St A2
Mansion House 🏛 B2
Margaret St C3
Marygate A1
Melbourne St C2
Merchant Adventurer's
  Hall 🏛 B2
Merchant Taylors'
  Hall 🏛 B2
Micklegate B1
Micklegate Bar 🏛 C1
Minster, The ✝ A2
Monkgate A2
Moss St C1
Museum Gdns ✤ B1
Museum St B2
National Railway
  Museum 🏛 B1
Navigation Rd B3
Newton Terr C2
North Parade A1
North St B2
Nunnery La C1
Nunthorpe Rd C1
Ouse Bridge B2
Paragon St C3
Park Gr A3
Park St C1
Parliament St B2
Peasholme Green B3
Penley's Grove St A2
Piccadilly B2
Police Station 🅟 A2
Post Office 🄿 . . . B1/B2/C3
Priory St C1
Purey Cust Nuffield
  Hospital, The H A2
Queen Anne's Rd A1
Quilt Museum 🏛 B3
Reel 🎬 C1
Regimental
  Museum 🏛 B2
Richard III Museum 🏛 . A2
Roman Bath 🏛 B2
Rowntree Park C2
St Andrewgate B2
St Benedict Rd C1
St John St A2
St Olave's Rd A1
St Peter's Gr A1
St Saviourgate B2
Scarcroft Hill C1
Scarcroft Rd C1
Skeldergate C2
Skeldergate Bridge . . . C2
Station Rd B1
Stonegate B2
Sycamore Terr A1
Terry Ave C2
The Shambles B2
The Stonebow B2
Theatre Royal ⛭ B2
Thorpe St C1
Toft Green B1
Tower St C2
Townend St A2
Treasurer's House 🏛 . . A2
Trinity La B1
Undercroft Mus 🏛 A2
Union Terr A2
Victor St C2
Vine St C2
Walmgate B3
Wellington St C3
York Art Gallery 🏛 . . . A1
York Barbican C3
York Brewery ♦ C1
York Dungeon, The 🏛 . B2
York Station ⛭ B1

Abbreviations used in the index

Aberdeen	Aberdeen City	Dorset	Dorset	Luton	Luton	Plym	Plymouth
Aberds	Aberdeenshire	Dumfries	Dumfries and Galloway	M Keynes	Milton Keynes	Poole	Poole
Ald	Alderney	Dundee	Dundee City	M Tydf	Merthyr Tydfil	Powys	Powys
Anglesey	Isle of Anglesey	Durham	Durham	Mbro	Middlesbrough	Ptsmth	Portsmouth
Angus	Angus	E Ayrs	East Ayrshire	Medway	Medway	Reading	Reading
Argyll	Argyll and Bute	E Dunb	East Dunbartonshire	Mers	Merseyside	Redcar	Redcar and Cleveland
Bath	Bath and North East Somerset	E Loth	East Lothian	Midloth	Midlothian	Renfs	Renfrewshire
Bedford	Bedford	E Renf	East Renfrewshire	Mon	Monmouthshire	Rhondda	Rhondda Cynon Taff
Bl Gwent	Blaenau Gwent	E Sus	East Sussex	Moray	Moray	Rutland	Rutland
Blackburn	Blackburn with Darwen	E Yorks	East Riding of Yorkshire	N Ayrs	North Ayrshire	S Ayrs	South Ayrshire
Blackpool	Blackpool	Edin	City of Edinburgh	N Lincs	North Lincolnshire	S Glos	South Gloucestershire
Bmouth	Bournemouth	Essex	Essex	N Lanark	North Lanarkshire	S Lanark	South Lanarkshire
Borders	Scottish Borders	Falk	Falkirk	N Som	North Somerset	S Yorks	South Yorkshire
Brack	Bracknell	Fife	Fife	N Yorks	North Yorkshire	Scilly	Scilly
Bridgend	Bridgend	Flint	Flintshire	NE Lincs	North East Lincolnshire	Shetland	Shetland
Brighton	City of Brighton and Hove	Glasgow	City of Glasgow	Neath	Neath Port Talbot	Shrops	Shropshire
Bristol	City and County of Bristol	Glos	Gloucestershire	Newport	City and County of Newport	Slough	Slough
Bucks	Buckinghamshire	Gtr Man	Greater Manchester	Norf	Norfolk	Som	Somerset
C Beds	Central Bedfordshire	Guern	Guernsey	Northants	Northamptonshire	Soton	Southampton
Caerph	Caerphilly	Gwyn	Gwynedd	Northumb	Northumberland	Staffs	Staffordshire
Cambs	Cambridgeshire	Halton	Halton	Nottingham	City of Nottingham	Southend	Southend-on-Sea
Cardiff	Cardiff	Hants	Hampshire	Notts	Nottinghamshire	Stirling	Stirling
Carms	Carmarthenshire	Hereford	Herefordshire	Orkney	Orkney	Stockton	Stockton-on-Tees
Ceredig	Ceredigion	Herts	Hertfordshire	Oxon	Oxfordshire	Stoke	Stoke-on-Trent
Ches E	Cheshire East	Highld	Highland	Pboro	Peterborough	Suff	Suffolk
Ches W	Cheshire West and Chester	Hrtlpl	Hartlepool	Pembs	Pembrokeshire	Sur	Surrey
Clack	Clackmannanshire	Hull	Hull	Perth	Perth and Kinross		
Conwy	Conwy	IoM	Isle of Man			Swansea	Swansea
Corn	Cornwall	IoW	Isle of Wight			Swindon	Swindon
Cumb	Cumbria	Invclyd	Inverclyde			T&W	Tyne and Wear
Darl	Darlington	Jersey	Jersey			Telford	Telford & Wrekin
Denb	Denbighshire	Kent	Kent			Thurrock	Thurrock
Derby	City of Derby	Lancs	Lancashire			Torbay	Torbay
Derbys	Derbyshire	Leicester	City of Leicester			Torf	Torfaen
Devon	Devon	Leics	Leicestershire			V Glam	The Vale of Glamorgan
		Lincs	Lincolnshire			W Berks	West Berkshire
		London	Greater London			W Dunb	West Dunbartonshire
						W Isles	Western Isles
						W Loth	West Lothian
						W Mid	West Midlands
						W Sus	West Sussex
						W Yorks	West Yorkshire
						Warks	Warwickshire
						Warr	Warrington
						Wilts	Wiltshire
						Windsor	Windsor and Maidenhead
						Wokingham	Wokingham
						Worcs	Worcestershire
						Wrex	Wrexham
						York	City of York

Index to road maps of Britain

How to use the index

Example **Blatherwycke** Northants **137 D9**

- grid square
- page number
- county or unitary authority

A

Aaron's Hill Sur 50 E3
Aaron's Town Cumb 240 E2
Abbas Combe Som 30 C2
Abberley Worcs 116 D5
Abberton Essex 89 B8
— Worcs 117 G9
Abberwick Northumb 264 G4
Abbess End Essex 87 C9
Abbess Roding Essex 87 C9
Abbey Devon 27 E10
Abbeycwmhir Powys 113 C11
Abbey-cwm-hir Powys 113 C11
Abbeydale Glos 80 B5
— S Yorks 186 E4
Abbeydale Park S Yorks 186 E4
Abbey Dore Hereford 97 E7
Abbey Field Essex 107 G9
Abbey Gate Kent 53 B9
Abbey Green Shrops 149 C10
— Staffs 169 D7
Abbey Hey Gtr Man 184 B5
Abbey Hulton Stoke 168 F6
Abbey Mead Sur 66 F4
Abbey St Bathans
— Borders 272 C5
Abbeystead Lancs 203 C7
Abbey Town Cumb 238 G5
Abbey Village Lancs 194 C6
Abbey Wood London 68 D3
Abbots Bickington Devon 24 E5
Abbots Bromley Staffs 151 E11
Abbotsbury Dorset 17 D7
Abbotsford S Wus 46 B4
Abbotsham Devon 24 B6
Abbotskerswell Devon 9 B7
Abbots Langley Herts 85 E9
Abbotsleigh Devon 8 F6
Abbots Leigh N Som 60 E4
Abbotsley Cambs 122 F4
Abbot's Meads Ches W 166 B5
Abbots Morton Worcs 117 F10
Abbots Ripton Cambs 122 B4
Abbots Salford Warks 117 G11
Abbotstone Hants 48 G5
Abbotswood Hants 32 C5
— Sur 50 C4
Abbots Worthy Hants 48 G3
Abbotts Ann Hants 47 E10
Abcott Shrops 115 B7
Abdon Shrops 131 F11
Abdy S Yorks 186 B6
Aber Ceredig 93 B9
Aberaeron Ceredig 111 E9
Aberaman Rhondda 77 E8
Aberangell Gwyn 146 G6
Aber-Arad Carms 92 D6
Aberarder Highld 290 E6
Aberarder House Highld 300 G6
Aberarder Lodge Highld 291 E7
Aberargie Perth 286 F5
Aberarth Ceredig 111 E9
Aberavon Neath 57 C8
Aber-banc Ceredig 93 C7
Aberbargoed Caerph 77 E11
Aberbechan Powys 130 E2
Aberbeeg Bl Gwent 78 E2
Aberbran Powys 95 F9
Abercanaid M Tydf 77 F9
Abercarn Caerph 78 G2
Abercastle Pembs 91 E7
Abercegir Powys 128 C6
Aberchalder Highld 290 C5
Aberchirder Aberds 302 D6
Aber Cowarch Gwyn 147 F7
Abercraf Powys 76 C4
Abercregan Neath 57 B11
Abercrombie Fife 287 G8
Abercwmboi Rhondda 77 F8
Abercych Pembs 92 C4
Abercynafon Powys 77 B9
Abercynffig / Aberkenfig
— Bridgend 57 E11
Abercynon Rhondda 77 F9
Aberdalgie Perth 286 E4
Aberdâr / Aberdare
— Rhondda 77 E7
Aberdare / Aberdâr
— Rhondda 77 E7

Aberdaron Gwyn 144 D3
Aberdeen Aberdeen 293 C11
Aberdesach Gwyn 162 E6
Aberdour Fife 280 D3
Aberdovey / Aberdyfi
— Gwyn 128 D2
Aberdulais Neath 76 E3
Aberdyfi / Aberdovey
— Gwyn 128 D2
Aberedw Powys 95 B11
Abereiddy Pembs 90 E5
Abererch Gwyn 145 B7
Aberfan M Tydf 77 E9
Aberfeldy Perth 286 C2
Aberffraw Anglesey 162 B5
Aberffrwd Ceredig 112 B3
Aberford W Yorks 206 F4
Aberfoyle Stirl 285 G9
Abergarw Bridgend 58 C2
Abergarwed Neath 76 E4
Abergavenny Mon 78 C5
Abergele Conwy 180 F6
Aber-Giâr Carms 93 C10
Abergorlech Carms 93 E11
Abergwaun / Fishguard
— Pembs 91 D9
Abergwesyn Powys 113 G7
Abergwili Carms 93 G8
Abergwynant Gwyn 146 F3
Aber-gwynfi Neath 57 B11
Abergwyngregyn Gwyn 179 G11
Abergynolwyn Gwyn 128 B3
Aber-Hirnant Gwyn 147 C9
Aberhosan Powys 128 D6
Aberkenfig / Abercynffig
— Bridgend 57 E11
Aberlady E Loth 281 E9
Aberlemno Angus 287 B9
Aberllefenni Gwyn 128 E2
Aberllydan / Broad Haven
— Pembs 72 C5
Aberllynfi / Three Cocks
— Powys 96 D3
Abermagwr Ceredig 112 C3
Abermaw / Barmouth
— Gwyn 146 F2
Abermeurig Ceredig 111 F11
Aber miwl / Abermule
— Powys 130 E3
Abermorddu Flint 166 D4
Abermule / Aber-miwl
— Powys 130 E3
Abernant Powys 148 E2
Abernant Carms 92 G6
— Powys 130 D3
Aber-nant Rhondda 77 E8
Abernethy Perth 286 F5
Abernyte Perth 286 D6
Aber-oer Wrex 166 F3
Aberogwr / Ogmore by Sea
— V Glam 57 F11
Aberpennar / Mountain Ash
— Rhondda 77 F8
Aberporth Ceredig 110 G5
Aber-Rhiwlech Gwyn 147 E8
Aberriw / Berriew
— Powys 130 C3
Abersoch Gwyn 144 D6
Abersychan Torf 78 E3
Abertawe / Swansea
— Swansea 56 C6
Aberteifi / Cardigan
— Ceredig 92 B3
Aberthin V Glam 58 D4
Abertillery Bl Gwent 78 E2
Abertridwr Caerph 58 B6
— Powys 147 F10
Abertrinant Gwyn 128 B2
Abertysswg Caerph 77 D10
Aberuchill Castle
— Perth 285 E11
Aberuthven Perth 286 F3
Aber-Village Powys 96 G2
Aberyscir Powys 95 F9
Aberystwyth Ceredig 111 A11
Abhainn Suidhe
— W Isles 305 H2
Abingdon-on-Thames
— Oxon 83 F7
Abinger Common Sur 50 D6

Abinger Hammer Sur 50 D5
Abington Northants 120 E5
— S Lanark 259 E10
Abington Pigotts Cambs 104 C6
Abington Vale Northants 120 E5
Abingworth W Sus 35 D10
Ab Kettleby Leics 154 E4
Ab Lench Worcs 117 G10
Ablington Glos 81 D10
— Wilts 47 E11
Abney Derbys 185 F11
Aboyne Aberds 293 D7
Abraham Heights Lancs 211 G9
Abram Gtr Man 194 G6
Abriachan Highld 300 F5
Abridge Essex 87 F7
Abronhill N Lnrk 278 G5
Abshot Hants 33 F8
Abson S Glos 61 E7
Abthorpe Northants 102 B2
Abune-the-Hill Orkney 314 D2
Aby Lincs 190 F6
Acaster Malbis York 207 D7
Acaster Selby N Yorks 207 E7
Accrington Lancs 195 B9
Acha Argyll 274 F6
Achabraid Argyll 275 E8
Achachork Highld 298 E4
Achadh an Eas Highld 308 F2
Achadunan Argyll 284 F5
Achafolla Argyll 275 B8
Achagary Highld 308 D7
Achaglass Argyll 255 C8
Achahoish Argyll 275 E8
Achalader Perth 286 C5
Achallader Argyll 285 C7
Achalone Highld 310 D5
Acha Mor W Isles 304 F5
Achanalt Highld 300 C2
Achanamara Argyll 275 E8
Achandunie Highld 300 B6
Achaneich Argyll 275 E11
Ach'an Todhair Highld 290 F2
Achany Highld 309 J5
Achaphubuil Highld 290 F2
Acharacle Highld 289 C8
Acharn Highld 289 D9
— Perth 285 C11
Acharole Highld 310 D6
Acharossan Argyll 275 F10
Acharry Muir Highld 309 K6
Achath Aberds 293 B9
Achavanich Highld 310 E5
Achavelgin Highld 301 D9
Achavraat Highld 301 E9
Achddu Carms 74 E6
Achdregnie Moray 302 G2
Achduart Highld 307 J5
Achentoul Highld 310 F2
Achfary Highld 306 F7
Achfrish Highld 309 H5
Achgarve Highld 307 K3
Achiemore Highld 308 C3
— Highld 310 D2
A'Chill Highld 294 E4
Achiltibuie Highld 307 J5
Achina Highld 308 C7
Achinahuagh Highld 308 C5
Achindaul Highld 290 E3
Achindown Highld 301 E8
Achinduich Highld 309 J5
Achinduin Argyll 289 F10
Achingills Highld 310 C5
Achininver Highld 308 C5
Achintee Highld 299 E8
— Highld 290 F3
Achintraid Highld 295 B10
Achlaven Argyll 289 F11
Achleck Argyll 288 E6
Achlorachan Highld 300 D3
Achluachrach Highld 290 E4
Achlyness Highld 306 D7
Achmelvich Highld 307 G5
Achmore Highld 295 B10
— Stirl 285 D9
Achnaba Argyll 275 E10
Achnabat Highld 300 F5
Achnabreck Argyll 275 D9

Achnacarnin Highld 306 F5
Achnacarry Highld 290 E3
Achnacloich Argyll 289 F11
— Highld 295 E7
Achnaconeran Highld 290 B6
Achnacraig Argyll 288 E6
Achnacree Argyll 289 F11
Achnacree Bay Argyll 289 F11
Achnacroish Argyll 289 E10
Achnadrish Argyll 288 D6
Achnafalnich Argyll 284 E6
Achnagarron Highld 300 C6
Achnaha Highld 288 C6
Achnahanat Highld 309 K5
Achnahannet Highld 301 G9
Achnairn Highld 309 H5
Achnaluachrach Highld 309 J6
Achnandarach Highld 295 B10
Achnanellan Highld 290 E2
Achnasaul Highld 290 E3
Achnasheen Highld 299 D11
Achnashellach Highld 299 E9
Achnavast Highld 310 C4
Achneigie Highld 299 B10
Achormlarie Highld 309 K6
Achorn Highld 310 F5
Achosnich Highld 288 C6
Achranich Highld 289 E9
Achreamie Highld 310 C4
Achriabhach Highld 290 G3
Achriesgill Highld 306 D7
Achrimsdale Highld 311 J3
Achtoty Highld 308 C6
Achurch Northants 137 G10
Achuvoldrach Highld 308 D5
Achvaich Highld 309 K7
Achvarasdal Highld 310 C3
Ackenthwaite Cumb 211 C10
Ackergill Highld 310 D7
Acklam Mbro 225 B9
— N Yorks 216 G5
Ackleton Shrops 132 D5
Acklington Northumb 252 C6
Ackton W Yorks 198 C2
Ackworth Moor Top
— W Yorks 198 D2
Acle Norf 161 G8
Acock's Green W Mid 134 G2
Acol Kent 71 F10
Acomb Northumb 241 D10
— York 207 C7
Aconbury Hereford 97 E10
Acre Gtr Man 195 F9
— Lancs 195 C9
Acrefair Wrex 166 G3
Acres Nook Staffs 168 E4
Acre Street W Sus 21 B11
Acton Ches E 167 E10
— Dorset 18 F5
— London 67 C8
— Shrops 130 G6
— Staffs 168 G4
— Suff 107 C7
— Worcs 116 E6
— Wrex 166 E4
Acton Beauchamp
— Hereford 116 G3
Acton Bridge Ches W 183 F9
Acton Burnell Shrops 131 C10
Acton Green Hereford 116 G3
— London 67 D8
Acton Pigott Shrops 131 C10
Acton Place Suff 107 B7
Acton Reynald Shrops 149 E10
Acton Round Shrops 132 D2
Acton Scott Shrops 131 F9
Acton Trussell Staffs 151 F8
Acton Turville S Glos 61 C10
Adabroc W Isles 304 B7
Adambrae W Loth 269 A10
Adam's Green Dorset 29 E8
Adber Dorset 29 C9
Adderbury Oxon 101 D9
Adderley Shrops 150 B3
Adderley Green Stoke 168 G6
Adderstone Northumb 264 C4
Addiewell W Loth 269 C9
Addingham W Yorks 205 D7
Addingham Moorside
— W Yorks 205 D7
Addington Bucks 102 F4

Addington Borders 271 E10
Addiscombe London 67 F10
Addlestone Sur 66 G5
Addlestonemoor Sur 66 F4
Addlethorpe Lincs 175 B8
Adel W Yorks 205 F11
Adeney Telford 150 F4
Adeyfield Herts 85 D9
Adfa Powys 129 C11
Adforton Hereford 115 C8
Adgestone IoW 21 D7
Adisham Kent 55 C8
Adlestrop Glos 100 F4
Adlingfleet E Yorks 199 C10
Adlington Ches E 184 E6
— Lancs 194 E6
Adlington Park Lancs 194 E5
Admaston Staffs 151 E10
— Telford 150 G2
Admington Warks 100 B4
Adpar Ceredig 92 C6
Adsborough Som 28 B3
Adscombe Som 43 F7
Adstock Bucks 102 E4
Adstone Northants 119 G11
Adswood Gtr Man 184 D5
Adversane W Sus 35 C9
Advie Highld 301 F11
Adwalton W Yorks 197 B8
Adwell Oxon 83 F11
Adwick le Street
— S Yorks 198 F4
Adwick upon Dearne
— S Yorks 198 G3
Ae Dumfries 247 F11
Ae Village Dumfries 247 F11
Affetside Gtr Man 195 E9
Affleck Aberds 303 G8
Affpuddle Dorset 18 C2
Affric Lodge Highld 299 G11
Afon Eitha Wrex 166 F3
Afon-wen Flint 181 G10
Afon Wen Gwyn 145 B8
Afton IoW 20 D2
Agar Nook Leics 153 G9
Agbrigg W Yorks 197 D10
Aggborough Worcs 116 B6
Agglethorpe N Yorks 213 B11
Aglionby Cumb 239 F10
Agneash IoM 192 D5
Aifft Denb 165 B10
Aigburth Mers 182 D5
Aiginis W Isles 304 E6
Aike E Yorks 209 D7
Aikenway Moray 302 E2
Aikerness Orkney 314 A4
Aikers Orkney 314 G4
Aiketgate Cumb 230 B5
Aikton Cumb 239 G7
Ailby Lincs 190 F6
Ailey Hereford 96 B6
Ailstone Warks 118 G4
Ailsworth Pboro 138 D2
Aimes Green Essex 86 E5
Ainderby Quernhow
— N Yorks 214 B6
Ainderby Steeple
— N Yorks 224 G6
Aingers Green Essex 108 G2
Ainley Top W Yorks 196 D6
Ainsdale Mers 193 E10
Ainsdale-on-Sea Mers 193 E10
Ainstable Cumb 230 B6
Ainsworth Gtr Man 195 E9
Ainthorpe N Yorks 226 D4
Aintree Mers 182 B5
Aird Argyll 275 C8
— Dumfries 236 C2
— Highld 295 B7
— W Isles 305 F11
Aird a' Mhachair
— W Isles 297 G3
Aird a' Mhulaidh
— W Isles 305 G3
Aird Asaig W Isles 305 H3
Aird Dhail W Isles 304 B6
Airdens Highld 309 K6

Airdeny Argyll 289 G11
Aird Mhidhinis W Isles 297 L3
Aird Mhighe W Isles 296 C6
— W Isles 305 J3
Aird Mhòr W Isles 297 G4
Aird Mhòr W Isles 297 L3
Aird of Sleat Highld 295 E7
Airdrie N Lanark 268 B5
Airds of Kells Dumfries 237 B8
Aird Thunga W Isles 304 E6
Airdtorrisdale Highld 308 C6
Aird Uig W Isles 304 E2
Airedale W Yorks 198 B3
Airidh a Bhruaich
— W Isles 305 G4
Airieland Dumfries 237 D9
Airinis W Isles 304 E6
Airlie Angus 287 B7
Airlies Dumfries 236 D5
Airmyn E Yorks 199 B8
Airntully Perth 286 D4
Airor Highld 295 E9
Airth Falk 279 D7
Airthrey Castle Stirl 278 B6
Airton N Yorks 204 B4
Airyhassen Dumfries 236 E5
Airy Hill N Yorks 227 D7
Airyligg Dumfries 236 C4
Aisby Lincs 188 C5
— Lincs 155 B10
Aisgernis W Isles 297 J3
Aish Devon 8 D6
— Devon 8 D6
Aisholt Som 43 F7
Aiskew N Yorks 214 B5
Aislaby N Yorks 216 B5
— N Yorks 227 D7
— Stockton 225 C8
Aisthorpe Lincs 188 E6
Aith Orkney 314 E2
— Shetland 312 D8
— Shetland 313 H5
Aithnen Powys 148 E4
Aithsetter Shetland 313 K6
Akeld Northumb 263 D11
Akeley Bucks 102 D4
Akenham Suff 108 B2
Albany T&W 243 F7
Albaston Corn 12 G4
Alberbury Shrops 149 G7
Albert Town Pembs 72 B6
Albert Village Leics 152 F6
Albourne W Sus 36 D3
Albourne Green W Sus 36 D3
Albrighton Shrops 132 C6
— Shrops 149 F9
Albro Castle Ceredig 92 B3
Alburgh Norf 142 F5
Albury Herts 105 G8
— Sur 50 D5
Albury End Herts 105 G8
Albury Heath Sur 50 D5
Alby Hill Norf 160 C3
Alcaig Highld 300 D5
Alcaston Shrops 131 F9
Alcester Warks 117 F11
Alcester Lane's End
— W Mid 133 G11
Alciston E Sus 23 D8
Alcombe Som 42 D3
— Wilts 61 F10
Alconbury Cambs 122 B3
Alconbury Weston
— Cambs 122 B3
Aldborough Norf 160 C3
— N Yorks 215 F8
Aldborough Hatch
— London 68 B3
Aldbourne Wilts 63 D9
Aldbrough E Yorks 209 F10
Aldbrough St John
— N Yorks 224 C4
Aldbury Herts 85 C7
Aldcliffe Lancs 211 G9
Aldclune Perth 291 G10
Aldeburgh Suff 127 F9
Aldeby Norf 143 E8

Aar–Alm

Alkrington Garden Village
— Gtr Man 195 G11
Alladale Lodge Highld 309 L4
Allaleigh Devon 8 E6
Allanaquoich Aberds 292 D3
Allanbank Borders 271 F10
— N Lnrk 268 D6
Allangrange Mains
— Highld 300 D6
Allanshaugh Borders 271 F8
Allanshaws Borders 271 G9
Allanton Borders 273 E7
— N Lnrk 269 D7
— S Lnrk 268 E4
Allaston Glos 79 E10
Allathasdal W Isles 297 L2
Allbrook Hants 33 C7
All Cannings Wilts 62 G5
Allendale Town
— Northumb 241 F8
Allen End Warks 134 D3
Allenheads Northumb 232 B3
Allensford Durham 242 G3
Allensmore Hereford 97 D9
Allenton Derby 153 C7
Allenwood Cumb 239 F11
Aller Devon 9 B7
— Dorset 30 G3
— Som 28 B6
Allerby Cumb 229 D7
Allerford Devon 27 F11
— Som 42 D2
Aller Park Devon 9 B7
Allerston N Yorks 217 C7
Allerthorpe E Yorks 207 D11
Allerton Mers 182 D6
— W Yorks 205 G8
Allerton Bywater
— W Yorks 198 B2
Allerton Mauleverer
— N Yorks 206 B4
Allesley W Mid 134 G6
Allestree Derby 152 B6
Allet Corn 4 F5
Allexton Leics 136 C6
Allgreave Ches E 169 B7
Allhallows Medway 69 D10
Allhallows-on-Sea
— Medway 69 D10
Alligin Shuas Highld 299 D9
Allimore Green Staffs 151 F7
Allington Lincs 172 G5
— Wilts 47 F8
— Wilts 61 D11
— Wilts 62 G3
Allington Bar Wilts 61 E11
Allithwaite Cumb 211 D7
Alloa Clack 279 C7
Allonby Cumb 229 C7
Allostock Ches W 184 G2
Alloway S Ayrs 257 F8
Allowenshay Som 28 E4
All Saints South Elmham
— Suff 142 G6
Allscot Shrops 132 D4
Allscott Telford 150 G2
All Stretton Shrops 131 D9
Allt Carms 75 E9
Alltami Flint 166 B3
Alltbeithe Highld 290 C2
Alltchaorunn Highld 284 B4
Alltforgan Powys 147 E9
Alltmawr Powys 95 B11
Alltnacaillich Highld 308 E4
Allt na h-Airbhe
— Aberds 292 E4
Allt-nan-sùgh Highld 295 C11
Alltsigh Highld 290 B6
Alltwalis Carms 93 E8
Alltwen Neath 76 E2
Alltyblaca Ceredig 93 B10
Allt-yr-yn Newport 59 B9
Allwood Green Suff 125 C10
Alma Notts 171 E7

Almagill Dumfries 238 B3
Almeley Hereford 114 G6
Almeley Wooton
Hereford 114 G6
Almer Dorset 18 B4
Almholme S Yorks 198 F5
Almington Staffs 150 C4
Alminstone Cross Devon . 24 C4
Almondbank Perth 286 E4
Almondbury W Yorks 197 D2
Almondsbury S Glos 60 C6
Almondvale W Loth 269 B11
Almshouse Green
Essex 106 E5
Alne N Yorks 215 F9
Alne End Warks 118 F2
Alne Hills Warks 118 E2
Alness Highld 300 C6
Alnessferry Highld 300 C6
Alne Station N Yorks 215 F10
Alnham Northumb 263 G11
Alnmouth Northumb 264 G6
Alnwick Northumb 264 G5
Alperton London 67 C7
Alphamstone Essex 107 D7
Alpheton Suff 125 G7
Alphington Devon 14 C4
Alpington Norf 142 C5
Alport Derbys 170 C2
Alpraham Ches E 167 D9
Alresford Essex 107 G11
Alrewas Staffs 152 F3
Alsager Ches E 168 D3
Alsagers Bank Staffs 168 F4
Alscot Bucks 84 E4
Alsop en le Dale
Derbys 169 D11
Alston Cumb 231 B10
Devon 28 G4
Alstone Glos 99 G8
Glos 99 G8
Som 43 D10
Alstonefield Staffs 169 D10
Alston Sutton Som 44 C2
Alswear Devon 26 C2
Alt Gtr Man 196 G2
Altandhu Highld 307 H4
Altanduin Highld 311 G2
Altarnun Corn 11 E10
Altass Highld 309 J4
Altbough Hereford 97 E10
Altdargue Aberds 293 C7
Alterwall Highld 310 C6
Altham Lancs 203 G11
Althorne Essex 88 F6
Althorpe N Lincs 199 F10
Alticane S Ayrs 244 F6
Alticry Dumfries 236 D4
Altmore Windsor 65 D11
Altnabreac Station
Highld 310 E4
Altnacealgach Hotel
Highld 307 H7
Altnacraig Argyll 289 G10
Altnafeadh Highld 284 B6
Altnaharra Highld 308 F5
Altofts W Yorks 197 C11
Alton Derbys 170 C5
Hants 49 F8
Staffs 169 G9
Wilts 47 D7
Alton Barnes Wilts 62 G6
Altonhill E Ayrs 257 B10
Alton Pancras Dorset 30 G2
Alton Priors Wilts 62 G6
Altonside Moray 302 D2
Altour Highld 290 E4
Altrincham Gtr Man 184 D3
Altrua Highld 290 E4
Altskeith Stirl 285 G8
Altyre Ho Moray 301 D10
Alva Clack 279 B7
Alvanley Ches W 183 G7
Alvaston Derby 153 C7
Alvechurch Worcs 117 C10
Alvecote Warks 134 C4
Alvediston Wilts 31 C7
Alveley Shrops 132 G5
Alverdiscott Devon 25 B8
Alverstoke Hants 21 B7
Alverstone IoW 21 D7
Alverthorpe W Yorks 197 C10
Alverton Notts 172 G3
Alves Moray 301 C11
Alvescot Oxon 82 E3
Alveston S Glos 60 B6
Warks 118 F4
Alveston Down S Glos 60 B6
Alveston Hill Warks 118 G4
Alvie Highld 291 C10
Alvingham Lincs 190 C5
Alvington Glos 79 E10
Som 29 D8
Alwalton Cambs 138 D2
Alway Newport 59 B10
Alweston Dorset 29 E11
Alwington Devon 24 C6
Alwinton Northumb 251 B10
Alwoodley W Yorks 205 E11
Alwoodley Gates
W Yorks 206 E2
Alwoodley Park
W Yorks 205 E11
Alyth Perth 286 C6
Amalebra Corn 1 B5
Amalveor Corn 1 B5
Amatnatua Highld 309 K4
Am Baile W Isles 297 K3
Ambaston Derbys 153 C8
Ambergate Derbys 170 E4
Amber Hill Lincs 174 F2
Amberley Glos 80 E5
Hereford 97 B10
W Sus 35 E8
Amble Northumb 253 C7
Amblecote W Mid 133 F7
Ambler Thorn W Yorks . . . 196 B5
Ambleside Cumb 221 E7
Ambleston Pembs 91 F10
Ambrosden Oxon 83 B10
Am Buth Argyll 289 G10
Amcotts N Lincs 199 E11
Amen Corner Brack 65 F10
Amersham Bucks 85 F7
Amersham Common
Bucks 85 F7
Amersham Old Town
Bucks 85 F7
Amersham on the Hill
Bucks 85 F7
Amerton Staffs 151 D9
Amesbury Bath 45 B7
Wilts 47 E7
Ameysford Dorset 31 G9
Amington Staffs 134 C4
Amisfield Dumfries 247 G11

Amlwch Anglesey 178 C6
Amlwch Port Anglesey 179 C7
Ammanford / Rhydaman
Carms 75 C10
Ammerham Som 28 F5
Amod Argyll 255 D8
Amotherby N Yorks 216 E4
Ampfield Hants 32 C6
Ampleforth N Yorks 215 D11
Ampney Crucis Glos 81 E9
Ampney St Mary Glos 81 E9
Ampney St Peter Glos 81 E9
Amport Hants 47 E9
Ampthill C Beds 103 D10
Ampton Suff 125 C7
Amroth Pembs 73 D11
Amulree Perth 286 D2
Anagach Highld 301 G10
Anaheilt Highld 289 C10
Ancaster Lincs 173 G7
Anchor Shrops 130 G3
Anchorage Park Ptsmth . . . 33 G11
Anchor Corner Norf 141 D10
Anchorsholme Blkpool 202 E2
Anchor Street Norf 160 E6
An Caol Highld 298 D6
Ancroft Northumb 273 F9
Ancrum Borders 262 E4
Ancton W Sus 35 G7
Ancumtoun Orkney 314 A12
Anderby Lincs 191 F8
Anderby Creek Lincs 191 F8
Andersea Som 43 G8
Anderson Dorset 18 B3
Anderton Ches W 183 F10
Corn 7 E8
Lancs 194 E6
Andertons Mill Lancs 194 E4
Andover Hants 47 D11
Andover Down Hants 47 D11
Andoversford Glos 81 B8
Andreas IoM 192 C5
Andwell Hants 49 C7
Anelog Gwyn 144 D3
Anerley London 67 F10
Anfield Mers 182 C5
Angarrack Corn 2 B3
Angarrick Corn 3 B7
Angelbank Shrops 115 B11
Angersleigh Som 27 D11
Angerton Cumb 238 F6
An Gleann Ur W Isles 304 E6
Angmering W Sus 35 G9
Angram N Yorks 206 D6
N Yorks 223 F7
Anick Northumb 241 D11
Anie Stirl 285 F9
Ankerdine Hill Worcs 116 F4
Ankerville Highld 301 B8
Anlaby E Yorks 200 B4
Anlaby Park Hull 200 B5
An Leth Meadhanach
W Isles 297 K3
Anmer Norf 158 D4
Anmore Hants 33 E11
Annan Dumfries 238 D5
Annaside Cumb 210 B1
Annat Argyll 284 E4
Highld 290 D5
Highld 299 D8
Anna Valley Hants 47 E10
Annbank S Ayrs 257 E10
Annesley Notts 171 E8
Annesley Woodhouse
Notts 171 E7
Annfield Plain Durham . . . 242 G5
Anniesland Glasgow 267 B10
Annifirth Shetland 313 J3
Annishader Highld 298 D4
Annis Hill Suff 143 F7
Annitsford T&W 243 C7
Annscroft Shrops 131 B9
Annwell Place Derbys 152 F6
Ansdell Lancs 193 B10
Ansells End Herts 85 B11
Ansford Som 44 G6
Ansley Warks 134 E5
Ansley Common Warks . . . 134 E6
Anslow Staffs 152 D4
Anslow Gate Staffs 152 D3
Ansteadbrook Sur 50 G2
Anstey Herts 105 E8
Leics 135 B10
Anstruther Easter Fife . . . 287 G9
Anstruther Wester Fife . . . 287 G9
Ansty Hants 49 E8
Warks 135 G7
Wilts 31 B7
W Sus 36 C3
Ansty Coombe Wilts 31 B7
Ansty Cross Dorset 30 G3
Anthill Common Hants . . . 33 E10
Anthony Corn 7 E7
Anthony Passage Corn 7 E8
Anthorn Cumb 238 F5
Antingham Norf 160 C5
An t-Ob W Isles 296 C6
Anton's Gowt Lincs 174 F3
Antonshill Falk 279 E7
Antony Corn 7 E7
Antrobus Ches W 183 F10
Anvil Green Kent 54 D6
Anvilles W Berks 63 F10
Anwick Lincs 173 E10
Anwoth Dumfries 237 D7
Aonachan Highld 290 E4
Aoradh Argyll 274 G3
Apedale Staffs 168 F4
Aperfield London 52 B2
Apes Dale Worcs 117 C9
Apes Hall Cambs 139 E11
Apethorpe Northants 137 D10
Apeton Staffs 151 F7
Apley Lincs 189 F10
Apley Forge Shrops 132 D4
Apperknowle Derbys 186 F5
Apperley Glos 99 F7
Apperley Bridge
W Yorks 205 F9
Apperley Dene
Northumb 242 F3
Appersett N Yorks 223 G7
Appin Argyll 289 E11
Appin House Argyll 289 E11
Appleby N Lincs 200 E3
Appleby-in-Westmorland
Cumb 231 G9
Appleby Magna Leics 134 B6
Appleby Parva Leics 134 B6
Applecross Highld 299 E7

Applecross Ho Highld . . . 299 E7
Appledore Devon 27 E9
Devon 40 G3
Kent 39 B7
Appledore Heath Kent . . . 54 G3
Appleford Oxon 83 G8
Applegarthtown
Dumfries 248 G4
Applehouse Hill Windsor . 65 C10
Applemore Hants 32 F5
Appleshaw Hants 47 D10
Applethwaite Cumb 229 F11
Appleton Halton 183 D8
Oxon 82 E6
Appleton-le-Moors
N Yorks 216 B4
Appleton-le-Street
N Yorks 216 E4
Appleton Park Warr 183 E10
Appleton Roebuck
N Yorks 207 E7
Appleton Thorn Warr 183 E10
Appleton Wiske N Yorks . 225 E7
Appletreehall Borders 262 F2
Appletreewick
N Yorks 213 G11
Appley IoW 21 C8
Som 27 C9
Appley Bridge Lancs 194 F4
Apse Heath IoW 21 E7
Apsey Green Suff 126 E5
Apsley Herts 85 D9
Apsley End Herts 104 E2
Apuldram W Sus 22 C4
Aqueduct Telford 132 B3
Aquhythie Aberds 293 B9
Arabella Highld 301 B8
Arbeadie Aberds 293 D8
Arberth / Narberth
Pembs 73 C10
Arbirlot Angus 287 C10
Arboll Highld 311 L2
Arborfield Wokingham 65 F9
Arborfield Cross
Wokingham 65 F9
Arborfield Garrison
Wokingham 65 F9
Arbourthorne S Yorks 186 D5
Arbroath Angus 287 C10
Arbury Cambs 123 E8
Arbuthnott Aberds 293 F9
Archdeacon Newton
Darl 224 B5
Archenfield Hereford 96 C5
Archiestown Moray 302 E2
Archnalea Highld 289 C10
Arclid Ches E 168 C3
Arclid Green Ches E 168 C3
Ardachu Highld 309 J6
Ardailly Argyll 255 B7
Ardalanish Argyll 274 B4
Ardallie Aberds 303 F10
Ardalum Ho Argyll 288 F6
Ardamaleish Argyll 275 G11
Ardaneaskan Highld 295 B10
Ardanstur Argyll 275 B9
Ardargie House Hotel
Perth 286 F4
Ardarroch Highld 295 B10
Ardban Highld 295 B9
Ardbeg Argyll 254 C5
Argyll 276 E3
Ardcharnich Highld 307 L6
Ardchiavaig Argyll 274 B4
Ardchonnell Argyll 275 B10
Ardchronie Highld 309 L6
Ardchuilk Highld 300 F2
Ardchullarie More Stirl . . 285 F9
Ardchyle Stirl 285 E9
Ardclach Highld 301 E9
Ardconnel Argyll 289 G7
Arddleen Powys 148 F5
Ardechive Highld 290 D3
Ardelve Highld 295 C10
Arden Argyll 277 E7
E Renf 267 D10
Ardencaple Ho Argyll 275 B8
Ardendrain Highld 300 F5
Arden Park Gtr Man 184 C6
Ardens Grafton Warks 118 G2
Ardentallen Argyll 289 G10
Ardentraive Argyll 275 F11
Ardeonaig Stirl 285 D10
Ardersier Highld 301 D7
Ardery Highld 289 C9
Ardessie Highld 307 L5
Ardfern Argyll 275 C9
Ardfernal Argyll 274 F6
Ardgartan Argyll 284 G6
Ardglassie Aberds 303 C10
Ardgour Highld 290 C2
Ardgye Moray 301 C11
Ardheslaig Highld 299 D7
Ardiecow Moray 302 C5
Ardinamir Argyll 275 B8
Ardindrean Highld 307 L6
Ardingly W Sus 36 B4
Ardington Oxon 64 B3
Ardington Wick Oxon 64 B3
Ardintoul Highld 295 C10
Ardlair Aberds 302 G5
Highld 299 B9
Ardlamont Ho Argyll 275 G10
Ardleigh Essex 107 F11
Ardleigh Green London . . . 68 B4
Ardleigh Heath Essex 107 E10
Ardler Perth 286 C6
Ardley Oxon 101 F10
Ardley End Essex 87 C8
Ardlui Argyll 285 E7
Ardlussa Argyll 275 E7
Ardmair Highld 307 K6
Ardmay Argyll 284 G6
Ardmenish Argyll 274 F6
Ardminish Argyll 255 C7
Ardmolich Highld 289 B9
Ardmore Argyll 289 G9
Highld 306 D7
Highld 309 L7
Highld 311 L2
Ardnacross Argyll 289 E7
Ardnadam Argyll 276 E3
Ardnagowan Argyll 284 G4
Ardnagrask Highld 300 E5
Ardnahein Argyll 276 D3
Ardnarff Highld 295 B10
Ardnastang Highld 289 C10
Ardnave Argyll 274 F3
Ardno Argyll 284 G5
Ardo Aberds 303 F8
Ardoch Argyll 277 F7
Perth 286 D4
Stirl 285 F9
Ardochy House Highld . . . 290 C4

Ardo Ho Aberds 303 G9
Ardoyne Aberds 302 G6
Ardpatrick Argyll 275 G8
Ardpatrick Ho Argyll 255 B8
Ardpeaton Argyll 276 D4
Ardradnaig Perth 285 C11
Ardrishaig Argyll 275 E9
Ardross Fife 287 G9
Highld 300 B6
Ardrossan N Ayrs 266 G4
Ardross Castle Highld 300 B6
Ardshave Highld 309 K7
Ardsheal Highld 289 C10
Ardshealach Highld 289 C8
Ardslignish Argyll 289 C7
Ardtalla Argyll 254 B5
Ardtalnaig Perth 285 D11
Ardtaraig Argyll 275 E11
Ardtoe Highld 289 B8
Ardtreck Highld 294 B5
Ardtrostan Perth 285 E10
Arduaine Argyll 275 B8
Ardullie Highld 300 C5
Ardvannie Highld 309 L6
Ardvar Highld 306 F6
Ardvasar Highld 295 E8
Ardverikie Highld 291 E7
Ardvorlich Perth 285 E10
Ardwell Dumfries 236 E3
Moray 302 F3
S Ayrs 244 E5
Ardwell Mains Dumfries . . 236 E3
Ardwick Gtr Man 184 B5
Areley Kings Worcs 116 C6
Arford Hants 49 F10
Argoed Caerph 77 F11
Powys 113 E9
Powys 130 E5
Shrops 130 G6
Argos Hill E Sus 37 B9
Arichamish Argyll 275 C10
Arichastlich Argyll 284 D6
Arielod Highld 288 D3
Arinacrinachd Highld 299 D7
Arinagour Argyll 288 D4
Arinthluic Argyll 299 E9
Arion Orkney 314 E2
Arisaig Highld 295 G8
Ariundle Highld 289 C10
Arivegaig Highld 289 C8
Arivoichallum Argyll 254 C4
Arkendale N Yorks 215 G7
Arkesden Essex 105 E9
Arkholme Lancs 211 E11
Arkleby Cumb 229 D8
Arkleton Dumfries 249 E9
Arkle Town N Yorks 223 E10
Arkley London 86 F2
Arksey S Yorks 198 F5
Arkwright Town Derbys . . 186 G6
Arle Glos 99 G8
Arlebrook Glos 80 D4
Arlecdon Cumb 219 B10
Arlescote Warks 101 B7
Arlesey C Beds 104 D3
Arleston Telford 150 G3
Arley Green Ches E 183 E11
Arlingham Glos 80 C2
Arlington Devon 40 E6
E Sus 23 D8
Glos 81 D10
Arlington Beccott Devon . . 40 E6
Armadale Highld 308 C7
W Loth 269 B8
Armadale Castle Highld . . 295 E8
Armathwaite Cumb 230 B6
Armigers Essex 105 F11
Arminghall Norf 142 C5
Armitage Staffs 151 F11
Armitage Bridge
W Yorks 196 E6
Armley W Yorks 205 G11
Armscote Warks 100 C4
Armsdale Staffs 150 C5
Armshead Staffs 168 F6
Armston Northants 137 F11
Armthorpe S Yorks 198 F6
Arnabost Argyll 288 D4
Arnaby Cumb 210 C3
Arncliffe N Yorks 213 E8
Arncroach Fife 287 G9
Arndilly Ho Moray 302 E2
Arne Dorset 18 D5
Arnesby Leics 136 E2
Arngask Perth 286 F5
Arnisdale Highld 295 D10
Arnish Highld 298 E5
Arniston Midloth 270 C6
Arnol W Isles 304 D5
Arnold E Yorks 209 E8
Notts 171 F9
Arno's Vale Bristol 60 E6
Arnprior Stirl 278 C2
Arnside Cumb 211 D9
Aros Mains Argyll 289 E7
Arowry Wrex 149 B9
Arpafeelie Highld 300 D6
Arpinge Kent 55 F7
Arrad Foot Cumb 210 C6
Arram E Yorks 208 E6
Arrathorne N Yorks 224 G4
Arreton IoW 20 D6
Arrington Cambs 122 G6
Arrivain Argyll 284 D6
Arrochar Argyll 284 G6
Arrow Warks 117 F11
Arrowe Hill Mers 182 D3
Arrowfield Top Worcs 117 C10
Arrow Green Hereford 115 F8
Arscaig Highld 309 H5
Arscott Shrops 131 B9
Arthill Ches E 184 D2
Arthington W Yorks 205 E11
Arthingworth
Northants 136 G5
Arthog Gwyn 146 G2
Arthrath Aberds 303 F9
Arthursdale W Yorks 206 F3
Arthurstone Perth 286 C6
Arthurville Highld 309 L7
Artington Sur 50 D3
Artrochie Aberds 303 F10
Arundel W Sus 35 F8
Arwick Orkney 314 D3
Aryhoulan Highld 290 G2
Asby Cumb 229 G2
Ascog Argyll 266 C2
Ascoil Highld 311 H2
Ascot Windsor 66 F2
Ascott Warks 100 E6
Ascott d'Oyley Oxon 82 B4
Ascott Earl Oxon 82 B3

Ascott-under-Wychwood
Oxon 82 B4
Ascreavie Angus 25 E10
Asenby N Yorks 215 D7
Asfordby Leics 154 E4
Asfordby Hill Leics 154 F4
Asgarby Lincs 173 F11
Lincs 174 B4
Ash Devon 8 F6
Dorset 30 E5
Hereford 115 C10
Kent 276 F4
Kent 102 B5
Northants 137 F11
Som 29 D7
Sur 49 C11
Som 44 D2
Ash Common Wilts 45 B11
Ashampstead W Berks 64 D5
Ashampstead Green
W Berks 64 D5
Ashansworth Hants 48 B2
Ashbank Lincs 53 C10
Ash Bank Staffs 168 F6
Ashbeer Som 42 F5
Ashbocking Suff 126 G3
Ashbourne Derbys 169 F11
Ashbrittle Som 27 C9
Ashbrook Shrops 131 E9
Ashburnham Place
E Sus 23 B11
Ashburnham Forge
E Sus 23 B11
Ashburton Devon 8 B5
Ashbury Devon 12 B6
Oxon 63 C9
Ashby N Lincs 200 F2
Ashby by Partney Lincs . . 174 B6
Ashby cum Fenby
NE Lincs 201 G9
Ashby de la Launde
Lincs 173 D9
Ashby Folville Leics 154 G4
Ashby Hill NE Lincs 201 G8
Ashby Magna Leics 135 F10
Ashby Parva Leics 135 F10
Ashby Puerorum Lincs . . . 190 G4
Ashby St Ledgers
Northants 119 D11
Ashby St Mary Norf 142 C6
Ashchurch Glos 99 E8
Ashcombe Devon 14 G4
Ashcombe Park N Som . . . 59 G10
Ashcott Som 44 F2
Ashcott Corner Som 44 F2
Ashculme Devon 27 D10
Ashdon Essex 105 C11
Ashe Hants 48 D4
Asheldham Essex 89 E7
Ashen Essex 106 C4
Ashendon Bucks 84 C2
Asheridge Bucks 84 E6
Ashey IoW 21 D7
Ashfield Argyll 275 E8
Carms 94 F3
Hants 32 D5
Hereford 97 G11
Shrops 148 D6
Stirl 285 G11
Suff 126 E4
Ashfield Cum Thorpe
Suff 126 E4
Ashfield Green Suff 124 G4
Suff 126 C5
Ashfields Shrops 150 D4
Ashfold Crossways
W Sus 36 B2
Ashfold Side N Yorks 214 F2
Ashford Devon 8 F3
Devon 40 F4
Hants 31 E10
Kent 54 E4
Sur 66 E5
Ashford Bowdler
Shrops 115 C10
Ashford Carbonell
Shrops 115 C10
Ashford Common
Sur 66 E5
Ashford Hill Hants 64 G5
Ashford in the Water
Derbys 185 G11
Ashgate Derbys 186 G5
Ashgill S Lnrk 268 F5
Ash Green Sur 50 D2
Warks 134 F6
Ashgrove Bath 45 B9
Ash Grove Wrex 166 G5
Ash Hill Devon 14 G4
Ashiestiel Borders 261 B10
Ashill Devon 27 E9
Norf 141 C7
Som 28 D4
Ashingdon Essex 88 G5
Ashington Northumb 253 F7
Poole 18 B6
Som 29 C9
W Sus 35 D11
Ashintully Castle Perth . . 292 G3
Ashkirk Borders 261 E11
Ashlett Hants 33 G7
Ashleworth Glos 98 F6
Ashley Cambs 124 E3
Ches E 184 E3
Devon 25 E10
Glos 80 G6
Hants 19 B11
Hants 32 D5
Kent 55 E8
Northants 136 E6
Staffs 150 B4
Wilts 61 G11
Ashley Dale Staffs 150 B5
Ashley Down Bristol 60 D5
Ashley Green Bucks 85 E7
Ashley Heath Dorset 31 G10
Ashley Heath Ches E 184 D3
Dorset 31 G10
Staffs 150 B4
Ashley Moor Hereford 115 D9
Ashley Park Sur 66 F6
Ash Magna Shrops 149 B11
Ashmanhaugh Norf 160 E6
Ashmansworth Hants 48 B3
Ashmansworthy Devon . . . 24 D4
Ashmead Green Glos 80 F3
Ashmill Devon 12 B3
Ash Mill Devon 26 C3
Ash Moor Devon 26 D3
Ashmore Dorset 30 D6
Ashmore Green W Berks . . 64 F4
Ashmore Green W Mid . . . 133 D9
Ashmore Lake W Mid 133 D9
Ashnashellach Lodge
Highld 299 D10
Ashopton Derbys 185 D11
Ashore Wood Argyll 118 F6
Ashorne Warks 118 F6
Ashott Som 170 C4
Ashover Derbys 170 C4
Ashow Warks 118 C6
Ash Parva Shrops 149 B11
Ashperton Hereford 98 C2

Ash Priors Som 27 B11
Ashreigney Devon 25 E10
Ashridge Court Glos 25 G11
Ash Street Suff 107 B10
Ashtead Sur 51 B7
Ash Thomas Devon 27 E8
Ashton Corn 2 D4
Hereford 115 E10
Involyd 276 F4
Northants 102 B5
Northants 137 F11
Pboro 138 B2
Som 44 D2
Ashton Common Wilts 45 B11
Ashton Gate Bristol 60 E5
Ashton Green E Sus 23 C7
Ashton Hayes Ches W 167 B8
Ashton Heath Halton 183 F9
Ashton-in-Makerfield
Gtr Man 183 B9
Ashton Keynes Wilts 81 G8
Ashton under Hill Worcs . 99 D9
Ashton-under-Lyne
Gtr Man 184 B6
Ashton upon Mersey
Gtr Man 184 C3
Ashton Vale Bristol 60 E5
Ashurst Hants 32 E4
Kent 52 F4
Lancs 194 F3
Som 35 11
W Sus 35 G8
Ashurst Bridge Hants 32 E4
Ashurstwood W Sus 52 F2
Ashvale Bl Gwent 77 C10
Ash Vale Sur 49 C11
Ashwater Devon 12 B3
Ashwell Devon 14 E2
Herts 104 D5
Rutland 155 G7
Som 28 D5
Ashwell End Herts 104 C5
Ashwellthorpe Norf 142 D2
Ashwick Som 44 D6
Ashwicken Norf 158 F4
Ashwood Staffs 133 F7
Ashybank Borders 262 F2
Askam in Furness Cumb . . 210 D4
Askern S Yorks 198 E5
Askerswell Dorset 16 C6
Askerton Hill Lincs 172 F4
Askett Bucks 84 E4
Askham Notts 188 G3
Askham Bryan York 207 D7
Askham Richard York 206 D6
Asknish Argyll 275 D10
Askrigg N Yorks 223 G8
Askwith N Yorks 205 E9
Aslackby Lincs 155 C11
Aslacton Norf 142 E3
Aslockton Notts 154 B4
Asloun Aberds 293 B7
Aspall Suff 126 D3
Aspatria Cumb 229 C8
Aspenden Herts 105 F7
Asperton Lincs 156 B5
Aspley Nottingham 171 G8
Staffs 150 C6
Aspley Guise C Beds 103 D8
Aspley Heath C Beds 103 D8
Warks 117 C11
Aspull Gtr Man 194 F6
Aspull Common
Gtr Man 183 B10
Assater Shetland 312 F4
Asselby E Yorks 199 B8
Asserby Lincs 191 F7
Asserby Turn Lincs 191 F7
Assington Suff 107 D8
Assington Green Suff 124 G5
Assynt Ho Highld 300 C5
Astbury Ches E 168 C4
Astcote Northants 120 G3
Asterby Lincs 190 F4
Asterley Shrops 131 B7
Asterton Shrops 131 E7
Asthall Oxon 82 C3
Asthall Leigh Oxon 82 C4
Astle Ches E 184 G4
Highld 309 K7
Astley Gtr Man 195 G8
Shrops 149 F10
Warks 134 F6
Worcs 116 D5
Astley Abbotts Shrops . . . 132 D4
Astley Bridge Gtr Man . . . 195 E8
Astley Cross Worcs 116 D6
Astley Green Gtr Man 184 B2
Aston Ches E 167 F10
Ches W 183 F9
Derbys 152 C3
Derbys 185 E11
Flint 166 B4
Hereford 115 C9
Hereford 115 E8
Oxon 82 E4
Shrops 132 B3
Shrops 149 F11
S Yorks 187 D7
Staffs 150 B4
Telford 132 B2
W Mid 133 F11
Wokingham 65 D9
Aston Abbotts Bucks 102 G6
Aston Bank Worcs 116 C2
Aston Botterell Shrops . . . 132 G2
Aston-by-Stone Staffs . . . 151 C8
Aston Cantlow Warks 118 F2
Aston Clinton Bucks 84 C5
Aston Crews Hereford 98 G3
Aston Cross Glos 99 E8
Aston End Herts 104 G5
Aston Eyre Shrops 132 E3
Aston Fields Worcs 117 D9
Aston Flamville Leics 135 E9
Aston Ingham Hereford . . 98 G3
Aston juxta Mondrum
Ches E 167 D11
Aston le Walls Northants 119 G9
Aston Magna Glos 100 D3
Aston Munslow Shrops . . . 131 F10
Aston on Carrant Glos . . . 99 E8
Aston on Clun Shrops 131 G7
Aston-on-Trent Derbys . . 153 D8
Aston Pigott Shrops 130 B6
Aston Rogers Shrops 130 B6
Aston Rowant Oxon 84 F2
Aston Sandford Bucks . . . 84 D3
Aston Somerville Worcs . . 99 D10
Aston Square Shrops 148 D6
Aston Subedge Glos 100 C2
Aston Tirrold Oxon 64 B5
Aston Upthorpe Oxon 64 B5

Astrope Herts 84 C5
Astwick C Beds 104 D4
Astwith Derbys 170 C6
Astwood M Keynes 103 B8
Worcs 117 D8
Worcs 117 F7
Astwood Bank Worcs 117 E10
Aswarby Lincs 173 G9
Aswardby Lincs 190 G5
Atch Lench Worcs 117 G10
Atcham Shrops 131 B10
Athelhampton Dorset 17 C11
Athelington Suff 126 C4
Athelney Som 28 B4
Athelstaneford E Loth . . . 281 F10
Atherfield Green IoW 20 F5
Atherington Devon 25 C9
W Sus 35 G8
Athersley North
S Yorks 197 F11
Athersley South
S Yorks 197 F11
Atherstone Som 28 D5
Warks 134 D6
Atherstone on Stour
Warks 118 G4
Atherton Gtr Man 195 G7
Athnamulloch Highld 299 G11
Athron Hall Perth 286 G4
Atley Hill N Yorks 224 E5
Atlow Derbys 170 F2
Attadale Highld 295 B11
Attadale Ho Highld 295 C11
Attenborough Notts 153 B10
Atterby Lincs 189 C7
Attercliffe S Yorks 186 D5
Atterley Shrops 132 D2
Atterton Leics 135 E7
Attleborough Norf 141 D10
Warks 135 E7
Attlebridge Norf 160 F2
Attleton Green Suff 124 G4
Atwick E Yorks 209 D9
Atworth Wilts 61 F11
Auberrow Hereford 97 B9
Aubourn Lincs 172 C6
Auchagallon N Ayrs 255 D9
Auchallater Aberds 292 E3
Auchareoch N Ayrs 255 E10
Aucharnie Aberds 302 E6
Auchattie Aberds 293 D8
Auchavan Angus 292 G3
Auchbreck Moray 302 G2
Auchenback E Renf 267 D10
Auchenbainzie Dumfries . 247 D8
Auchenblae Aberds 293 F9
Auchenbrack Dumfries . . . 247 D7
Auchenbreck Argyll 255 C7
Argyll 275 E11
Auchencairn Dumfries . . . 237 D9
Dumfries 247 G11
N Ayrs 256 D2
Auchencairn Ho
Dumfries 237 D10
Auchencar N Ayrs 255 D9
Auchencarroch W Dunb . . 277 E8
Auchencrow Borders 273 C7
Auchendinny Midloth 270 C5
Auchengray S Lnrk 269 E9
Auchenhalrig Moray 302 C3
Auchenharvie N Ayrs 266 G5
Auchenheath S Lnrk 268 G6
Auchenhew N Ayrs 256 E2
Auchenlaich Stirl 285 G10
Auchenlochan Argyll 275 F10
Auchenmalg Dumfries . . . 236 D4
Auchenreoch E Dunb 278 F3
Auchensoul S Ayrs 245 E7
Auchentiber S Ayrs 266 F6
Auchenvennel Argyll 276 D5
Auchertyre Highld 295 C10
Auchgourish Highld 291 B11
Auchinairn E Dunb 268 B2
Auchindrean Highld 307 L6
Auchininna Aberds 302 E6
Auchinleck Dumfries 236 B6
E Ayrs 258 E3
Auchinloch N Lnrk 278 G3
Auchinner Perth 285 F10
Auchinraith S Lnrk 268 D3
Auchinstarry N Lnrk 278 F4
Auchintoul Aberds 293 B7
Highld 309 K5
Auchiries Aberds 303 F10
Auchlee Aberds 293 D10
Auchleeks Ho Perth 291 G10
Auchlevan Aberds 302 G6
Auchlochan S Lnrk 259 B8
Auchlossan Aberds 293 C7
Auchlunachan Highld 307 L6
Auchlunies Aberds 293 D10
Auchlyne Stirl 285 E9
Auchmacoy Aberds 303 F9
Auchmair Moray 302 G3
Auchmantle Dumfries 236 C3
Auchmillan E Ayrs 258 D2
Auchmithie Angus 287 C10
Auchmore Highld 300 D4
Auchmuirbridge Fife 286 G6
Auchmull Angus 293 F7
Auchnacraig Argyll 289 G9
Auchnafree Perth 286 D2
Auchnagallin Highld 301 F10
Auchnagarron Argyll 275 E11
Auchnagatt Aberds 303 E9
Auchnaha Argyll 275 E10
Auchnahillin Highld 301 F7
Auchnarrow Moray 302 G2
Auchnashelloch Perth . . . 285 F11
Auchtascailt Highld 299 B9
Aucholzie Aberds 292 D5
Auchrannie Angus 286 B6
Auchroisk Highld 301 G10
Auchronie Angus 292 E6
Auchterarder Perth 286 F3
Auchtercairn Highld 299 B7
Auchterderran Fife 280 B4
Auchterhouse Angus 287 D7
Auchtermuchty Fife 286 F6
Auchterneed Highld 300 D4
Auchtertool Fife 280 C4
Auchtertyre Moray 301 D11
Stirl 285 D7
Auchtubh Stirl 285 E9
Auckengill Highld 310 C7
Auckley S Yorks 198 G6
Audenshaw Gtr Man 184 B6
Audlem Ches E 167 G11
Audley Staffs 168 E4
Audley End Essex 105 D10
Essex 106 D6

Norf 142 G5
Suff 125 G7
Auds Aberds 302 C6
Aughertree Cumb 229 D11
Aughton E Yorks 207 F10
Lancs 193 F11
Lancs 211 F10
S Yorks 187 D7
Wilts 47 B8
Aughton Park Lancs 194 F2
Aukside Durham 232 F4
Auldearn Highld 301 D9
Aulden Hereford 115 G9
Auldgirth Dumfries 247 F10
Auldhame E Loth 281 E11
Auldhouse S Lnrk 268 E2
Auldtown of Carnoustie
Aberds 302 E6
Ault a'chruinn Highld . . . 295 C11
Aultanrynie Highld 308 F3
Aultbea Highld 307 L3
Aultdearg Highld 300 C2
Aultgrishan Highld 307 L2
Aultguish Inn Highld 300 B3
Ault Hucknall Derbys 171 B7
Aultibea Highld 311 G4
Aultiphurst Highld 310 C2
Aultivullin Highld 310 C2
Aultmore Highld 301 G10
Moray 302 D4
Aultnagoire Highld 300 G5
Aultnamain Inn Highld . . 309 L6
Aultnaslat Highld 290 C3
Aulton Aberds 302 G6
Aulton of Atherb Aberds 303 E9
Aultvaich Highld 300 E5
Aunby Lincs 155 G10
Aundorach Highld 291 B11
Aunk Devon 27 G8
Aunsby Lincs 155 B10
Auquhorthies Aberds 303 G8
Aust S Glos 60 B5
Austendike Lincs 156 E5
Austen Fen Lincs 190 C5
Austerfield S Yorks 187 C11
Austerlands Gtr Man 196 F3
Austhorpe W Yorks 206 G3
Austrey Warks 134 B5
Austwick N Yorks 212 F5
Authorpe Lincs 190 E6
Authorpe Row Lincs 191 G8
Avebury Wilts 62 F6
Avebury Trusloe Wilts . . . 62 F5
Aveley Thurrock 68 C5
Avening Glos 80 F5
Avening Green S Glos 80 G2
Averham Notts 172 E3
Avernish Highld 295 C10
Avery Hill London 68 E2
Aveton Gifford Devon 8 F3
Avielochan Highld 291 B11
Aviemore Highld 291 B10
Avington Hants 48 G4
W Berks 63 F11
Avoch Highld 301 D7
Avon Hants 19 B8
Wilts 62 D3
Avonbridge Falk 279 G8
Avoncliff Wilts 45 B10
Avon Dassett Warks 101 B8
Avonmouth Bristol 60 D4
Avonwick Devon 8 D4
Awbridge Hants 32 C4
Awhirk Dumfries 236 D2
Awkley S Glos 60 B5
Awliscombe Devon 27 G10
Awre Glos 80 D2
Awsworth Notts 171 G7
Axbridge Som 44 C2
Axford Hants 48 E6
Wilts 63 F8
Axmansford Hants 64 G5
Axminster Devon 15 B11
Axmouth Devon 15 C11
Aycliff Kent 55 E10
Aycliffe Durham 233 G11
Aydon Northumb 242 D2
Aykley Heads Durham . . . 233 C11
Aylburton Glos 79 E10
Aylburton Common
Glos 79 E10
Ayle Northumb 231 B10
Aylesbeare Devon 14 C6
Aylesbury Bucks 84 C4
Aylesby NE Lincs 201 F8
Aylescott Kent 53 B8
Aylesham Kent 55 C9
Aylestone Leicester 135 C11
Aylestone Hill Hereford . . 97 C10
Aylestone Park
Leicester 135 C11
Aylmerton Norf 160 B3
Aylsham Norf 160 D3
Aylton Hereford 98 D3
Aylworth Glos 100 G3
Aymestrey Hereford 115 D8
Aynho Northants 101 E10
Ayot Green Herts 86 C2
Ayot St Lawrence Herts . . 85 B11
Ayot St Peter Herts 86 B2
Ayr S Ayrs 257 E8
Ayre of Atler Shetland . . . 313 G6
Ayres End Herts 85 C11
Ayres of Selivoe
Shetland 313 J4
Ayres Quay T&W 243 F9
Aysgarth N Yorks 213 B10
Ayshford Devon 27 D8
Ayside Cumb 211 C7
Ayston Rutland 137 C7
Aythorpe Roding Essex . . 87 B9
Ayton Borders 273 C8
T&W 243 F7
Ayton Castle Borders 273 C8
Aywick Shetland 312 E7
Azerley N Yorks 214 E5

B

Babbacombe Torbay 9 B8
Babbington Notts 171 G7
Babbinswood Shrops 148 C6
Babbs Green Herts 86 B5
Babcary Som 29 B9
Babel Carms 94 D6
Babel Green Suff 106 B4
Babell Flint 181 G11
Babeny Devon 13 F9
Bableigh Norf 158 D3
Babraham Cambs 123 G10
Babworth Notts 187 E11
Bac W Isles 304 D6
Bachau Anglesey 178 E6
Bache Shrops 131 G9
Bacheldre Powys 130 E4

Bachelor's Bump E Sus 38 E4
Bache Mill Shrops 131 F10
Bach-y-gwreiddyn
Swansea 75 E10
Backaland Orkney 314 C5
Backaskaill Orkney 314 A4
Backbarrow Cumb 211 C7
Backbower Gtr Man 185 C7
Backburn Aberds 293 D10
Backe Carms 74 B3
Backfolds Aberds 303 D10
Backford Ches W 182 G6
Backford Cross Ches W . 182 G5
Backhill Aberds 303 F7
Aberds 303 F10
Backhill of Clackriach
Aberds 303 E9
Backhill of Fortree
Aberds 303 E9
Backhill of Trustach
Aberds 293 D8
Backies Highld 311 J2
Backlass Highld. 310 D6
Highld 310 E4
Back Muir Perth 279 D11
Back of Keppoch Highld. 295 G8
Back o' th' Brook Staffs. 169 E7
Back Rogerton E Ayrs . . 258 E3
Back Street Suff 124 F4
Backwell N Som. 60 F3
Backwell Common
N Som 60 F3
Backwell Green N Som . . .60 F3
Backworth T&W 243 C8
Bacon End Essex 87 B10
Bacon's End W Mid . . . 134 F3
Baconsthorpe Norf . . . 160 B2
Bacton Hereford 97 E7
Norf 160 C6
Suff 125 D11
Bacton Green Norf 160 C6
Suff 125 D11
Bacup Lancs 195 C11
Badachonacher Highld. 300 B6
Badachro Highld 299 B7
Badanloch Lodge Highld 308 F7
Badarach Highld 309 K5
Badavanich Highld. . . . 299 D11
Badbea Highld 307 K5
Badbury Swindon 63 C7
Badbury Wick Swindon . . .63 C7
Badby Northants 119 F11
Badcall Highld 306 D7
Badcaul Highld 307 K5
Baddeley Edge Stoke . . 168 E6
Baddeley Green Stoke . . 168 E6
Baddesley Clinton
Warks 118 C3
Baddesley Ensor Warks. 134 D5
Baddidarach Highld. . . 307 G5
Baddock Aberds 292 E3
Baddock Highld 301 D7
Baddow Park Essex 88 E2
Badeach Moray 302 F2
Badenscallie Highld. . . 307 J5
Badenscoth Aberds . . . 303 F7
Badentoy Park Aberds . 293 D11
Badgenyon Aberds 292 E5
Badgall Corn 11 D10
Badgeney Cambs 139 D8
Badger Shrops 132 D5
Badgergate Stirl. 278 B5
Badger's Hill Worcs. 99 B10
Badger's Mount Kent . . 68 G3
Badger Street Som 28 D3
Badgeworth Glos 80 B6
Badgworth Som 43 C11
Badharlick Corn 11 D11
Badicaul Highld 295 C9
Badingair Highld 309 H4
Badlesmere Kent 54 C4
Badlipster Highld 310 E6
Badluarch Highld 307 K4
Badminton S Glos 61 C10
Badnaban Highld 307 G5
Badnabay Highld 306 E7
Badnagie Highld 310 F5
Badninish Highld 309 K7
Badrallach Highld. 307 K5
Badsey Worcs 99 C11
Badshalloch W Dunb . . 277 D9
Badshot Lea Sur 49 D11
Badsworth W Yorks . . . 198 E3
Badwell Ash Suff 125 D9
Badwell Green Suff . . . 125 D10
Bae Cinmel / Kinmel Bay
Conwy 181 E7
Bae Colwyn / Colwyn Bay
Conwy 180 F4
Bae Penrhyn / Penrhyn Bay
Conwy 180 G4
Baffins Ptsmth. 33 G11
Bagber Dorset 30 E3
Bagby N Yorks 215 C9
Bagby Grange N Yorks . 215 C9
Bag Enderby Lincs 190 G5
Bagendon Glos 81 D8
Bagginswood Shrops . . 132 G3
Baggrow Cumb 229 C9
Bàgha Chàise W Isles . . 296 D5
Bagh a Chaisteil
W Isles 297 M2
Bagham Kent 54 C5
Baghasdal W Isles 297 K3
Bagh Mor W Isles 296 F4
Bagh Shiarabhagh
W Isles 297 L3
Bagillt Flint 182 F2
Baginton Warks 118 C6
Baglan Neath 57 C8
Bagley Shrops 149 D8
Som 44 D3
W Yorks 205 F9
Bagley Green Som 27 D10
Bagley Marsh Shrops . . 149 D7
Bagmore Hants 49 E7
Bagnall Staffs 168 E6
Bagnor W Berks 64 F3
Bagpath Glos 80 F4
Glos 80 G4
Bagshaw Derbys 185 E9
Bagshot Sur 66 G2
Wilts 63 F10
Bagshot Heath Sur 66 G2
Bagslate Moor
Gtr Man 195 E11
Bagstone S Glos 61 B7
Bagthorpe Norf 158 C5
Notts 171 E7
Baguley Gtr Man. 184 D4
Bagworth Leics 135 B8
Bagwyllydiart Hereford . .97 F8
Bagwy Llydiart Hereford .97 F8
Bail Ard Bhuirgh
W Isles 304 C6
Bailbrook Bath 61 F9
Baildon W Yorks 205 F9
Baildon Green W Yorks . 205 F8

Baile W Isles 296 C5
Baile Ailein W Isles . . . 304 F4
Baile a Mhanaich
W Isles 296 F3
Baile an Truiseil
W Isles 304 C5
Bailebeag Highld 291 B7
Baile Boidheach Argyll. 275 F8
Baile Gharbhaidh
W Isles 297 G3
Baile Glas Argyll 296 F4
Baile Mhartainn
W Isles 296 D3
Baile Mhic Phail
W Isles 296 D4
Baile Mor Argyll 288 G4
W Isles 296 E3
Baile na Creige W Isles . 297 L2
Baile Raghaill W Isles . 296 D3
Bailey Green Hants 33 B11
Baileyhead Cumb 240 B2
Bailiesward Aberds . . . 302 F4
Bailieston Glasgow 268 C3
Bail' Iochdrach W Isles . 296 F4
Bailrigg Lancs 202 B5
Bail Uachdraich
W Isles 296 E4
Bail' Ur Tholastaidh
W Isles 304 D7
Bainbridge N Yorks . . . 223 G8
Bainsford Falk. 279 E7
Bainshole Aberds 302 F6
Bainton E Yorks 208 C5
Oxon 101 F11
Pboro. 137 B11
Bucks 84 E6
Bairnkine Borders 262 F5
Baker's Cross Kent. 53 F9
Bakers End Herts 86 B5
Baker's Hill Glos 79 C9
Baker Street Thurrock . . .68 C6
Baker's Wood Bucks 66 B4
Bakesdown Corn 24 G2
Bakestone Moor Derbys . 187 F6
Bakewell Derbys 170 B2
Balachreick Highld . . . 291 C10
Balachuirn Highld. 298 E5
Balallan W Isles 304 F4
Balaswitch Highld 291 C9
Balavil Highld 291 C9
Balavoulin Perth. 291 G10
Balbeg / Y Bala Gwyn. . 147 B8
Balbeg Highld 300 G4
Highld 300 G5
Balbeggie Perth 286 E5
Balblair Highld 300 E5
Highld 301 C7
Highld 309 K5
Balby S Yorks 198 G5
Balcherry Highld 311 L2
Balchladich Highld. . . . 306 F5
Balchraggan Highld . . . 300 E5
Highld 300 G5
Balchrystie Fife 287 G8
Balcladaich Highld . . . 300 G2
Balcombe Lane W Sus . . 51 G10
Balcomie Fife 287 F10
Balcraggie Lodge Highld 310 F5
Balcurvie Fife 287 G7
Baldersby N Yorks 215 D7
Baldersby St James
N Yorks 215 D7
Balderstone Gtr Man . . 196 E2
Balderton Ches W 166 C5
Notts 172 E4
Baldhu Corn 4 G5
Baldingstone Gtr Man . 195 E10
Baldinnie Fife 287 F8
Baldock Herts 104 E4
Baldoon Row Oxon 83 E9
Baldoon Highld 300 B6
Baldovie Dundee 287 D8
Baldrine IoM 192 D5
Baldslow E Sus. 38 E3
Baldwin IoM 192 D4
Baldwinholme Cumb . . 239 G8
Baldwin's Gate Staffs. . 168 G3
Baldwins Hill W Sus 51 F11
Balearn Aberds 303 D10
Balemartine Argyll. . . . 288 E1
Balephuil Argyll 288 E1
Balerno Edin 270 B3
Balerominor Argyll. . . . 274 D7
Balevullin Argyll 288 E1
Balfield Angus 293 G7
Balfour Orkney 314 E4
Balfour Mains Orkney . 314 E4
Balfron Stirl 277 D10
Balfron Station Stirl. . . 277 D10
Balgaveny Aberds 302 E6
Balgavies Angus 287 B9
Balgonar Fife 279 C10
Balgove Aberds 303 F8
Balgowan Highld 291 D8
Highld 300 E5
Highld 298 E3
Perth 286 D4
Balgown Highld. 298 C3
Balgrennie Aberds 292 C6
Balgrochan E Dunb . . . 278 F2
Balgy Highld 299 D8
Balhaldie Stirl 286 G3
Balhalgardy Aberds . . . 303 G7
Balham London 67 E9
Balhary Perth. 286 C6
Baliasta Shetland 312 C8
Baligill Highld. 310 C2
Baligortan Argyll 288 E5
Baligrundle Argyll 289 G10
Balindore Argyll 289 F11
Balinoe Argyll 288 E1
Balintore Angus 286 B6
Highld 301 B8
Balintraid Highld. 301 B7
Balintuim Aberds 292 C3
Balk N Yorks 215 C9
Balkeerie Angus 287 C7
Balkemback Angus . . . 287 D7
Balk Field Notts 188 E2
Balkholme E Yorks 199 B9
Ball Corn 10 G6
Shrops 148 D6
Ballacannel IoM. 192 E3
Ballachrochin Highld. . 301 F8
Ballachulish Highld . . . 284 B4
Balladen Lancs 195 C10
Ballajora IoM 192 C5
Ballaleigh IoM 192 D4
Ballamodha IoM 192 E3
Ballantrae S Ayrs 244 G3

Ballaquine IoM 192 D5
Ballard's Ash Wilts 62 C5
Ballards Gore Essex. . . . 88 G6
Ballard's Green Warks . 134 E5
Ballasalla IoM 192 C4
IoM 192 E3
Ballater Aberds 292 D5
Ballathie Perth 286 D5
Ballaugh IoM 192 C4
Ballaveare IoM 192 E4
Ballcorach Moray 301 G11
Ballechin Perth. 286 B3
Balleigh Highld 309 L7
Ballencrieff E Loth . . . 281 F9
Ballencrieff Toll
W Loth 279 G9
Ballentoul Perth. 291 G10
Ball Green Stoke 168 E5
Ball Haye Green Staffs . 169 D7
Ballhill Devon 24 C3
Ball Hill Hants 64 G2
Ballidon Derbys 170 E2
Ballimore N Ayrs 255 D9
Ballimore Argyll 275 E11
Argyll 289 G10
Ballinaby Argyll 274 G3
Ballindean Perth 286 E6
Ballingdon Suff 107 C7
Ballinger Common Bucks 84 E6
Ballingham Hereford . . .97 E11
Ballingham Hill Hereford 97 E11
Ballingry Fife 280 B3
Ballinlick Perth 286 C3
Ballinluig Perth 286 B4
Ballintean Highld 291 C10
Ballintuim Perth 286 B5
Balliveolan Argyll 289 E10
Balloch Angus 287 B7
Highld 301 E7
N Lnrk 278 G4
W Dunb 277 E7
Ballochan Aberds 293 D7
Ballochearn Stirl 277 D11
Ballochford Moray. . . . 302 F2
Ballochmorrie S Ayrs . . 244 G6
Ballo' Ditton Halton. . . 183 D7
Ballogie Aberds 293 D7
Balls Cross W Sus 35 B7
Balls Green Essex 107 G11
E Sus 52 F3
Sur 35 C10
Ball's Green Glos 80 F5
Balls Hill W Mid 133 E9
Ballygown Argyll 288 E6
Ballygrant Argyll 274 G4
Ballygroggan S Ayrs . . . 255 F7
Ballyhaugh Argyll 288 D3
Balmacara Highld 295 C10
Balmacara Square
Highld 295 C10
Balmaclellan Dumfries . 237 B8
Balmacneil Perth. 286 B3
Balmacqueen Highld . . 298 B4
Balmae Dumfries 237 E8
Balmaha Stirl 277 C8
Balmalcolm Fife 287 G7
Balmeanach Argyll . . . 289 E8
Argyll 289 E8
Highld 295 B7
Highld 298 E3
Highld 298 E5
Balmedie Aberds 293 B11
Balmer Heath Shrops . . 149 C8
Balmerino Fife 287 E7
Balmerlawn Hants 32 G4
Balmesh Dumfries. 236 D3
Balmichael N Ayrs 255 D10
Balminnoch Dumfries . . 236 C4
Balmirmer Angus 287 D9
Balmoral Borders 261 B11
Balmore Highld 298 E2
Highld 300 F2
Highld 301 G8
Perth 286 B3
Balmule Fife 280 D4
Balmullo Fife 287 E8
Balmungie Highld 301 D7
Balmurrie Dumfries . . . 236 C4
Balnaboth Angus 292 G5
Balnabreich Moray . . . 302 D3
Balnabruaich Highld. . . 301 C7
Balnabruich Highld . . . 311 G5
Balnacoil Highld 311 H2
Balnacra Highld 299 E9
Balnacruie Highld 301 G9
Balnafoich Highld 300 F6
Balnagall Highld 311 L2
Balnaglaic Highld. 300 F4
Balnagowan Aberds . . . 293 C7
Balnaguard Perth. 286 B3
Balnaguisich Highld. . . 300 C6
Balnahanaid Perth. . . . 285 C10
Balnahard Argyll 274 D5
Argyll 288 F6
Balnain Highld 300 F4
Balnakeil Highld 308 C3
Balnaknock Highld . . . 298 C4
Balnamoon Aberds . . . 303 D9
Angus 293 G7
Balnapaling Highld . . . 301 C7
Balne N Yorks 198 D5
Balnoon Corn 2 B2
Balochroy Argyll 255 B8
Balole Argyll 274 G4
Balone Fife 287 F8
Balornock Glasgow . . . 268 B2
Balquharn Perth 286 D4
Balquhidder Stirl 285 E9
Balquhidder Station
Highld 285 E9
Balsall W Mid 118 B4
Balsall Common W Mid . 118 B4
Balsall Heath W Mid . . 133 G11
Balsall Street W Mid . . 118 B4
Balsam Cambs 123 G11
Balscote Oxon 101 C7
Balscott Oxon 101 C7
Balsham Cambs 123 G11
Balsporran Cottages
Highld 291 F8
Balstonia Thurrock 69 C7
Balterley Staffs 168 E3
Balterley Green Staffs . 168 E3
Balterley Heath Staffs . 168 E2

Baltersan Dumfries . . . 236 C6
Balthangie Aberds . . . 303 D8
Balthayock Perth 286 E5
Baltonsborough Som . . 44 G4
Balure Argyll 289 E11
Balvaird Highld 300 D5
Balvenie Moray 302 E3
Balvicar Argyll 275 B8
Balvraid Highld 295 D10
Highld 301 F8
Balwest Corn 2 C3
Bamber Bridge Lancs . . 194 B5
Bamber's Green Essex . 105 G11
Bamburgh Northumb . . 264 C5
Bamff Perth 286 B6
Bamford Derbys 186 E2
Gtr Man 195 E11
Bampton Cumb 221 B10
Devon 27 C7
Oxon 82 E4
Bampton Grange Cumb 221 B10
Banavie Highld 290 F3
Banbury Oxon 101 C9
Bancffosfelen Carms . . .75 C7
Banchor Highld 301 E9
Banchory Aberds 293 D8
Banchory-Devenick
Aberds 293 C11
Bancycapel Carms. 74 B6
Banc-y-Darren Ceredig . 128 G3
Bancyfelin Carms. 74 B4
Bancyffordd Carms 93 D8
Bandirran Perth 286 D6
Bandonhill London 67 G9
Bandrake Head Cumb . . 210 B6
Banff Aberds 302 C6
Bangor Gwyn 179 G9
Bangor is y coed / Bangor
on Dee Wrex 166 F5
Bangor on Dee / Bangor-is-
y-coed Wrex 166 F5
Bangors Corn 11 B10
Bangor Teifi Ceredig . . .93 C7
Banham Norf 141 F11
Bank Hants 32 F3
Bankend Dumfries 238 D2
Bank End Cumb 210 B3
Cumb 228 D6
Bank Fold Blkburn 195 C8
Bankfoot Perth 286 D4
Bankglen E Ayrs 258 G4
Bankhead Aberdeen . . 293 B10
Aberds 293 C8
Dumfries 236 C2
Falk 278 E6
S Lnrk 269 G7
Bank Houses Lancs . . . 202 C4
Bankland Som 28 B4
Bank Lane Gtr Man . . . 195 D9
Bank Newton N Yorks . 204 C4
Banknock Falk. 278 F5
Banks Cumb 240 E3
Lancs 193 C11
Orkney 314 C4
Bank's Green Worcs . . . 117 D9
Bankshill Dumfries . . . 248 G4
Bankside Falk 279 E7
Bank Street Worcs. 116 E2
Bank Top Gtr Man. 195 E8
Lancs 194 F4
Stoke 168 E5
T&W 242 D4
W Yorks 196 C6
W Yorks 205 F9
Banners Gate W Mid . . 133 D11
Banningham Norf 160 D4
Banniskirk Ho Highld . 310 D5
Bannister Green Essex . 106 G3
Bannockburn Stirl. . . . 278 C5
Barns Corn 4 F4
Banstead Sur 51 B8
Bantam Grove W Yorks . 197 B9
Bantaskin Falk 279 F7
Bantham Devon 8 G3
Banton N Lnrk. 278 F5
Banwell N Som 43 B11
Banyard's Green Suff . . 126 C5
Bapchild Kent 70 G2
Baptist End W Mid . . . 133 F8
Bapton Wilts 46 F3
Barabhas W Isles 304 C5
Barabhas Iarach
W Isles 304 D5
Barabhas Uarach
W Isles 304 C5
Barachander Argyll 289 G10
Baramore Highld 289 B8
Barassie S Ayrs 257 C8
Baravullin Argyll 289 F10
Barbadoes Stirl 277 B11
Barbaraville Highld . . . 301 B7
Barber Booth Derbys . . 185 E10
Barber Green Cumb. . . 211 C7
Barber's Moor Lancs . . 194 D3
Barbican Plym 7 E9
Barbieston S Ayrs 257 F10
Barbon Cumb 212 C2
Barbreck Ho Argyll . . . 275 C9
Barbridge Ches E 167 D10
Barbrook Devon 41 D8
Barby Northants 119 C10
Barby Nortoft
Northants 119 C10
Barcaldine Argyll 289 E11
Barcelona Corn 6 E4
Barcheston Warks 100 D5
Barclose Cumb 239 E10
Barcombe E Sus 36 E6
Barcombe Cross E Sus . 36 D6
Barcroft W Yorks 204 F6
Barden N Yorks. 224 G2
Barden Park Kent 52 D5
Barden Scale N Yorks . 205 B7
Bardfield End Green
Essex 106 E2
Bardfield Saling Essex . 106 F3
Bardister Shetland . . . 312 F5
Bardnabeinne Highld . . 309 K7
Bardney Lincs 173 B10
Bardon Leics 153 G8
Bardon Mill Northumb . 241 E7
Bardowie E Dunb 277 G11
Bardown E Sus. 37 B11
Bardrainney Invclyd . . 276 G6
Bardsea Cumb 210 D6
Bardsey W Yorks 206 E3
Bardsey Suff. 125 G8
Bardwell Suff 125 C8
Bare Lancs 211 C9
Bare Ash Northumb . . . 263 D6
Bareppa Corn 3 D7
Barford Norf 142 B2
Sur 49 F11
Warks 118 E5
Barford St John Oxon . 101 E8
Barford St Martin Wilts . 46 G5
Barford St Michael
Oxon 101 E8
Barfrestone Kent 55 C9
Bargaly Dumfries 236 C6
Bargarran Renfs 277 G9
Bargate Derbys 170 F5
Bargeddie N Lnrk 268 C4
Bargoed Caerph 77 F10
Bargrennan Dumfries . 236 B5
Barham Cambs 122 B2
Kent 55 C8
Suff 126 G2
Barharrow Dumfries . . 237 D8
Barhill Dumfries. 237 D10
Bar Hill Cambs 123 E7
Lancs 155 G11
Barholm Lincs 155 G11
Dumfries 237 D7
Barkby Leics 136 B2
Barkby Thorpe Leics . . 136 B2
Barkers Green Shrops . 149 D10
Barkers Hill Wilts 30 B6
Barkestone-le-Vale
Leics 154 C5
Barkham Wokingham . . .65 F9
Barking London 68 C2
Suff 125 G11
Barkingside London 68 B2
Barking Tye Suff 125 G11
Barkisland W Yorks . . . 196 D5
Barkla Shop Corn 4 E4
Barkston Lincs 172 G6
N Yorks 206 F5
Barkston Ash N Yorks . 206 F5
Barkway Herts 105 D7
Barlake Som 45 D7
Barlanark Glasgow . . . 268 C3
Barland Powys 114 E5
Barland Common
Swansea 56 C5
Barlavington W Sus 35 D7
Barlborough Derbys . . 187 F7
Barlby N Yorks 207 G8
Barley Herts 105 D7
Lancs 204 E2
Barleycroft End Herts . 105 F8
Barley End Bucks 85 C7
Barley Green Lancs . . . 204 E2
Barley Mow T&W 243 G7
Barleythorpe Rutland . 136 B6
Barling Essex 70 B2
Barlings Lincs 189 G9
Barlow Derbys 186 G4
N Yorks 198 B6
T&W 242 E5
Barmby Moor E Yorks . 207 D11
Barmby on the Marsh
E Yorks 199 B7
Barmer Norf 158 C6
Barming Heath Kent . . . 53 B8
Barmollack Argyll 255 D8
Barmoor Castle
Northumb 263 B11
Barmoor Lane End
Northumb 264 B2
Barmouth / Abermaw
Gwyn. 146 F2
Barmpton Darl 224 B6
Barmston E Yorks 209 B9
T&W 243 F8
Barmulloch Glasgow . . 268 B2
Barnaby Green Suff. . . 127 B9
Barnacabber Argyll . . . 276 D3
Barnacle Warks 135 G7
Barnaline Argyll 275 B10
Barnard Castle Durham 223 B11
Barnardiston Suff 106 B4
Barnard Gate Oxon . . . 82 C6
Barnbarroch Dumfries . 237 D10
Barnburgh S Yorks . . . 198 G3
Barnby Suff 143 F9
Barnby Dun S Yorks . . 198 G6
Barnby in the Willows
Notts 172 E5
Barnby Moor Notts . . . 187 E11
Barnes London 67 D8
IoW 20 D6
Barnes Cray London 68 D4
Barnes Hall S Yorks . . . 186 B4
Barnes Street Kent 52 D6
Barnetby le Wold
N Lincs 200 F5
Barnet Gate London 86 F2
Barnetby-le-Wold
N Lincs 200 F5
Barnet London 86 F3
Barnetby le Wold
N Lincs 200 F5
Barnet Gate London 86 F2
Barnetbrook Worcs. . . 117 B10
Barrhead E Renf 267 D9
Barrhill S Ayrs 244 G6
Barrington Cambs 105 B7
Som 28 D5
Barripper Corn 2 B4
Barrmill N Ayrs 267 E7
Barrock Highld 310 B6
Barrock Ho Highld . . . 310 C6
Barrow Glos 99 G7
Lancs 203 F10
Rutland 155 F7
Som 44 E5
Som 46 B2
Suff 124 E5
S Yorks 186 B5
Barroway Drove Norf . 139 C11
Barrow Bridge Gtr Man . 195 E7
Barrowburn Northumb . 263 G9
Barrowby Lincs 155 B7
Barrowburn Northumb . 251 C11
Barrow Common
N Som 60 F4
Barrowden Rutland . . . 137 C8
Barrowford Lancs 204 F3
Barrow Green Kent 70 G3
Barrow Gurney N Som . .60 F4
Barrow Haven N Lincs . 200 C5
Barrow Hill Derbys . . . 186 F6
Dorset 18 B5
Barrow-in-Furness
Cumb 210 F4
Barrow Island Cumb . . 210 F3
Barrow Nook Lancs . . . 194 G2
Barrows Green Ches E . 167 B10
Cumb 211 B10
Barrow's Green Mers . . 183 D8
Barrow Street Wilts 45 G11
Barrow upon Humber
N Lincs 200 C5
Barrow upon Soar
Leics 153 F11
Barrow upon Trent
Derbys 153 D7
Barrow Vale Bath 60 G6
Barrow Wake Glos 80 B6
Barry Angus 287 D9
V Glam 58 F6
Barry Dock V Glam 58 F6
Barry Island V Glam 58 F6
Barsby Leics 154 G3
Barsham Suff. 143 F7
Barston W Mid 118 B4
Bartestree Hereford. . . .97 C11
Barthol Chapel Aberds . 303 F8
Bartholomew Green
Essex 106 G4
Barthomley Ches E . . . 168 E3
Bartington Ches W . . . 183 F10
Bartley Hants 32 E4
Bartley Green W Mid . . 133 G10
Bartlow Cambs 105 B11
Barton Cambs 123 F8
Ches W 166 D6
Glos 99 F11
IoW 20 D6
Lancs 193 D9
N Som 43 B10
Oxon 83 D9
Torbay 9 B8
Warks 118 G2
Barton Abbey Oxon . . . 101 G9
Barton Bendish Norf. . 140 B4
Barton Court Hereford . .98 C4
Barton End Glos 80 F4
Barton Green Staffs . . 152 F3
Barton Hartshorn Bucks 102 E2
Barton Hill Bristol 60 E6
Staffs. 152 F2
N Yorks 216 F4
Barton in Fabis Notts . 153 C10
Barton in the Beans
Leics 135 B7
Barton-le-Clay C Beds . 103 E11
Barton-le-Street
N Yorks 216 E4
Barton-le-Willows
N Yorks 216 F4
Barton Mills Suff 124 C4
Barton on Sea Hants . . . 19 C10
Barton on the Heath
Warks 100 E5
Barton St David Som. . . 44 G4
Barton Seagrave
Northants 121 B7
Bartonsham Hereford . . .97 D10
Barton Stacey Hants . . .48 E2
Barton Town Devon . . . 41 E7
Barton Turf Norf 161 E7
Barton Turn Staffs . . . 152 F4
Barton-under-Needwood
Staffs 152 F3
Barton-upon-Humber
N Lincs 200 C4
Barton Upon Irwell
Gtr Man 184 B3
Bardsley Gtr Man. 196 G2
Bardwell Suff. 125 C8
Bare Lancs 211 C9
Bare Ash Northumb . . . 263 D6
Barton Waterside
N Lincs 200 C4
Barugh S Yorks 197 F10
Barugh Green S Yorks . 197 F10
Barway Cambs 123 B11
Barwell Leics 135 D8

Barwick Devon 25 F7
Herts 86 B5
Som 29 E9
Barwick in Elmet
W Yorks 206 F3
Baschurch Shrops . . . 149 E8
Bascote Warks 119 E8
Bascote Heath Warks . 119 E7
Base Green Suff 125 E10
Basford Shrops 131 F7
Staffs 168 F5
Basford Green Staffs . . 169 E7
Bashall Eaves Lancs . . 203 E9
Bashley Hants 19 B10
Bashley Park Hants 19 B10
Basildon Essex 69 B8
Basingstoke Hants 48 C6
Baslow Derbys 186 G3
Bason Bridge Som 43 D10
Bassaleg Newport. 59 B9
Bassenthwaite Cumb . 229 G10
Bassett Soton. 32 D6
S Yorks 186 B3
Bassett Green Soton . . 32 D6
Bassingbourn Cambs . 104 C6
Bassingbourne Herts . . 104 C6
Bassingfield Notts . . . 154 B2
Bassingham Lincs . . . 172 C6
Bassingthorpe Lincs . . 155 D9
Bassus Green Herts . . . 104 F6
Basta Shetland 312 D7
Basted Kent 52 B6
Baston Lincs 156 G2
Bastonford Worcs 116 G6
Bastwick Norf 161 F8
Baswich Staffs 151 E8
Baswick Steer E Yorks . 209 D7
Batavaime Stirl 285 D8
Batch Som 43 B10
Batchcott Shrops 115 C9
Batchfields Hereford . . .98 B3
Batchley Worcs 117 D10
Batchworth Herts 85 G9
Batchworth Heath Herts . 85 G9
Batcombe Dorset 29 F10
Som 45 E7
Bate Heath Ches E . . . 183 F11
Bateman's Green
Worcs 117 B11
Bateman's Hill Pembs . .73 E8
Batemoor S Yorks 186 E5
Batford Herts 85 B10
Bath Bath. 61 F9
Bathampton Bath. 61 F9
Bathealton Som 27 C9
Batheaston Bath. 61 F9
Bathford Bath 61 F9
Bathgate W Loth 269 B9
Bathley Notts 172 D3
Bathpool Corn 11 G11
Som 28 B2
Bath Side Essex 108 E5
Bath Vale Ches E 168 C5
Bathville W Loth 269 B8
Bathway Som 44 C5
Bathwick Bath. 61 F9
Batley W Yorks 197 C8
Batley Carr W Yorks . . 197 C8
Batsford Glos. 100 E3
Batson Devon 9 G9
Batsworthy Devon 26 D3
Batten's Green Som . . . 28 D3
Battenton Green Worcs . 116 D5
Battersby N Yorks 225 D11
Battersea London 67 D9
Battisborough Cross
Devon 7 F11
Battisford Suff 125 G11
Battisford Tye Suff . . . 125 G10
Battle E Sus. 38 D2
Powys 95 G11
Battledown Glos. 99 G9
Battlefield Shrops . . . 149 F10
Battle Hill T&W 243 D8
Battlescombe Glos 80 D6
Battlesbridge Essex . . . 88 G3
Battlesden C Beds . . . 103 F9
Battlesea Green Suff . . 126 B4
Battleton Som 26 B6
Battles Green Essex . . 125 E7
Battram Leics 135 B8
Battramsley Hants 20 B2
Battramsley Cross Hants . 20 B2
Batt's Corner Hants 49 E10
Batworthy Devon 13 D10
Baugh Argyll 288 E2
Baughton Worcs 99 C7
Baughurst Hants 48 B5
Baulking Oxon 82 G4
Baumber Lincs 190 G2
Baunton Glos. 81 E8
Baverstock Wilts 46 G4
Bawburgh Norf 142 B3
Bawdeswell Norf 159 E10
Bawdrip Som 43 F10
Bawdsey Suff 108 C6
Bawsey Norf. 158 F3
Bawtry S Yorks 187 C11
Baxenden Lancs 195 B9
Baxterley Warks 134 D5
Baxter's Green Suff . . . 124 F5
Bay Dorset 30 B4
Highld 298 D2
Baybridge Hants 33 C8
Northumb 241 G10
Baycliff Cumb 210 E5
Baydon Wilts 63 D9
Bayford Herts 86 D4
Som 30 B2
Bayles Cumb 231 C10
Bayley's Hill Kent 52 C4
Baylham Suff 126 G2
Baynard's Green Oxon . 101 F10
Baynham's Green
Essex 106 F2
Baysham Hereford 97 G11
Bayston Hill Shrops . . 131 B9
Bayswater London 67 C9
Baythorne End Essex . . 106 C4
Baythorpe Lincs 174 G3
Bayton Worcs 116 C3
Bayton Common Worcs . 116 C4
Bayworth Oxon 83 E8
Beach Highld 289 D9
S Glos 61 E8
Beachampton Bucks . . 102 D5
Beachamwell Norf. . . . 140 B4
Beachborough Kent . . . 55 F7
Beach Hay Worcs 116 C4
Beachlands E Sus 23 E11
Beachley Glos 79 G9
Beacon Corn 2 B5

London 67 G7
Devon 27 F11
Devon 28 F2
Beacon Down E Sus 37 C9
Beacon End Essex . . . 107 G9
Beaconhill Northumb . . 243 B7
Beacon Hill Bath. 61 F9
Bucks. 84 G6
Cumb 210 E4
Dorset 18 C5
Kent. 53 C9
Notts 172 E4
Suff 108 B4
Sur 49 F11
Beacon Lough T&W . . 243 F7
Beacon's Bottom Bucks . 84 F3
Beaconsfield Bucks 66 B2
Beaconside Staffs 151 E8
Beacrabhaic W Isles . . 305 J3
Beadlam N Yorks 216 C3
Beadlow C Beds 104 D2
Beadnell Northumb . . . 264 D6
Beaford Devon 25 E7
Beal Northumb 273 G11
N Yorks 198 B4
Bealach Highld 289 D11
Bealach Maim Argyll . . 275 D10
Bealbury Corn 7 B7
Beal's Green Kent 53 G9
Bealsmill Corn 12 F3
Beambridge Shrops . . 131 F10
Beam Bridge Som 27 D10
Beam Hill Staffs 152 D4
Beamhurst Staffs 151 B11
Beamhurst Lane
Staffs 151 B11
Beaminster Dorset. . . . 29 G7
Beamish Durham. 242 G6
Beamond End Bucks . . .84 F6
Beamsley N Yorks 205 C7
Bean Kent 68 E5
Beanacre Wilts 62 F2
Beancross Falk 279 F8
Beanhill M Keynes . . . 103 D7
Beanley Northumb . . . 264 F3
Beansburn E Ayrs 257 B10
Beanthwaite Cumb . . . 210 C4
Beaquoy Orkney 314 D3
Bear Cross Bmouth 19 B7
Beard Hill Som 44 E6
Beardly Batch Som 44 E6
Beardwood Blkburn . . 195 B7
Beare Devon 27 G7
Beare Green Sur. 51 E7
Bearley Warks 118 E3
Bearley Cross Warks . . 118 E3
Bearnus Argyll 288 E5
Bearpark Durham 233 C10
Bearsbridge Northumb . 241 F7
Bearsden E Dunb 277 G10
Bearsted Kent 53 B9
Bearstone Shrops 150 B4
Bearwood Hereford . . . 115 F7
Poole 18 B6
W Mid 133 G10
Beasley Staffs 168 F4
Beattock Dumfries . . . 248 C3
Beauchamp Roding
Essex 87 C9
Beauchief S Yorks. 186 E4
Beaudesert Warks 118 D3
Beaufort BI Gwent 77 C11
Beaufort Castle Highld. 300 E5
Beaulieu Hants 32 G5
Beaulieu Park Essex . . .88 C2
Beaulieu Wood Dorset . .30 F2
Beauly Highld 300 E5
Beaumaris Anglesey . . 179 F10
Beaumont Cumb 239 F8
Essex 108 G3
Windsor 66 E3
Beaumont Hill Darl . . . 224 B5
Beaumont Leys
Leicester. 135 B11
Beausale Warks 118 C4
Beauvale Notts 171 F8
Beauworth Hants 33 B9
Beavan's Hill Hereford . 98 G3
Beaworthy Devon 12 B5
Beazley End Essex . . . 106 F4
Bebington Mers 182 E4
Bebside Northumb . . . 253 G7
Beccles Suff 143 E8
Becconsall Lancs 194 C2
Beck Bottom W Yorks . 197 C10
Beckbury Shrops 132 C5
Beckces Cumb 230 F4
Beckenham London 67 F11
Beckermet Cumb 219 D10
Beckermonds N Yorks . 213 C7
Beckery Som 44 F3
Beckett End Norf 140 D5
Beckfoot Cumb 220 E3
Cumb 229 B7
W Yorks 205 F8
Beckford Worcs 99 D9
Beckhampton Wilts 62 F5
Beck Head Cumb 211 C8
Beck Houses N Yorks . . 221 F11
Beck Houses Lincs . . . 174 F2
Beckingham Lincs . . . 172 E5
Notts 188 D3
Beckington Som 45 D10
Beckjay Shrops 115 B7
Beckley E Sus 38 C5
Hants 19 B10
Oxon 83 C9
Beckley Furnace E Sus . 38 C4
Beck Row Suff 124 B3
Beckside Cumb 212 B2
Beck Side Cumb 210 C4
Cumb 211 C7
Beckton London 68 C2
Beckwith N Yorks 205 C11
Beckwithshaw
N Yorks 205 C11
Becontree London 68 B3
Bedale N Yorks 214 B5
Bedburn Durham 233 E8
Beddau Rhondda 58 B5
Beddgelert Gwyn 163 F10
Beddingham E Sus 36 F6
Beddington London . . . 67 G10
Beddington Corner
London 67 G9
Bedfield Suff. 126 D4
Bedford Beds. 121 G10
Gtr Man 183 B11
Bedford Park London. . .67 C8
Bedgebury Cross Kent . 53 G8
Bedgrove Bucks 84 C4
Bedham W Sus 35 C8
Bedhampton Hants 22 B2
Bedingfield Suff. 126 D3
Bedingham Green Norf . 142 E5

Bedlam N Yorks 214 G5
Som 45 D9
Bedlam Street W Sus 36 D3
Bedlar's Green Essex 105 G10
Bedlington Northumb 253 G7
Bedlington Station
Northumb 253 G7
Bedlinog M Tydf 77 E9
Bedminster Bristol 60 E5
Bedminster Down Bristol 60 F5
Bedmond Herts 85 E9
Bednall Staffs 151 F9
Bednall Head Staffs 151 F9
Bedrule Borders 262 F4
Bedstone Shrops 115 B7
Bedwas Caerph 59 B7
Bedwell Herts 104 G4
Wrex 166 F5
Bedwellty Caerph 77 E11
Bedwellty Pits Bl Gwent 77 D11
Bedwlwyn Wrex 148 B4
Bedworth Warks 135 F7
Bedworth Heath Warks 134 F6
Bedworth Woodlands
Warks 134 F6
Bed-y-coedwr Gwyn 146 D4
Beeby Leics 136 B3
Beech Hants 49 F7
Staffs 151 B7
Beechcliff Staffs 151 B7
Beechcliffe W Yorks 205 E7
Beechen Cliff Bath 61 G9
Beech Hill Gtr Man 194 F5
W Berks 65 G7
Beechingstoke Wilts 46 B5
Beech Lanes W Mid 133 F10
Beechwood Halton 183 E8
Newport 59 B10
W Mid 118 B5
W Yorks 206 F2
Beecroft C Beds 103 G10
Beedon W Berks 64 D3
Beedon Hill W Berks 64 D3
Beeford E Yorks 209 C8
Beeley Derbys 170 B3
Beelsby NE Lincs 201 G8
Beenham W Berks 64 F5
Beenham's Heath
Windsor 65 D10
Beenham Stocks
W Berks 64 F5
Beeny Corn 11 C8
Beer Devon 15 D10
Som 44 G2
Beercrocombe Som 28 C4
Beer Hackett Dorset 29 E9
Beesands Devon 8 G6
Beesby Lincs 191 E7
Beeslack Midloth 270 C4
Beeson Devon 8 G6
Beeston C Beds 104 B3
Ches W 167 D8
Norf 159 F8
Notts 153 B10
W Yorks 205 G11
Beeston Hill W Yorks 205 G11
Beeston Park Side
W Yorks 197 B9
Beeston Regis Norf 177 E11
Beeston Royds
W Yorks 205 G11
Beeston St Lawrence
Norf 160 E6
Beeswing Dumfries 237 C10
Beetham Cumb 211 D9
Som 28 E3
Beetley Norf 159 F9
Beffcote Staffs 150 F6
Began Cardiff 59 C8
Begbroke Oxon 83 C7
Begdale Cambs 139 B9
Begelly Pembs 73 D10
Beggar Hill Essex 87 E10
Beggarington Hill
W Yorks 197 C9
Beggars Ash Hereford 98 D4
Beggars Bush W Sus 35 F11
Beggar's Bush Powys 114 E5
Beggars Pound V Glam 58 F4
Beggearn Huish Som 42 F4
Beguildy Powys 114 B3
Beighton Norf 143 B7
S Yorks 186 E6
Beighton Hill Derbys 170 E3
Beili-glas Mon 78 C4
Beitearsaig W Isles 305 G1
Beith N Ayrs 266 E6
Bekesbourne Kent 55 B7
Bekesbourne Hill Kent 55 B7
Belah Cumb 239 F9
Belan Powys 130 C4
Belaugh Norf 160 F5
Belbins Hants 32 C5
Belbroughton Worcs 117 B8
Belchalwell Dorset 30 F3
Belchalwell Street Dorset 30 F3
Belchamp Otten Essex 106 C6
Belchamp St Paul Essex 106 C5
Belchamp Walter Essex 106 C6
Belcher's Bar Leics 135 B8
Belchford Lincs 190 F3
Beleybridge Fife 287 F9
Belfield Gtr Man 196 E2
Belford Northumb 264 C4
Belgrano Conwy 181 F7
Belgrave Ches W 166 C5
Leicester 135 B11
Staffs 134 C4
Belgravia London 67 D9
Belhaven E Loth 282 F3
Belhelvie Aberds 293 B11
Belhinnie Aberds 302 G4
Bellabeg Aberds 292 B5
Bellamore S Ayrs 244 F6
Bellanoch Argyll 275 D8
Bellanrigg Borders 260 B6
Bellasize E Yorks 199 B10
Bellaty Angus 286 B6
Bell Bar Herts 86 D3
Bell Busk N Yorks 204 B4
Bell Common Essex 86 E6
Belleau Lincs 190 F6
Belle Eau Park Notts 171 D11
Belle Green S Yorks 197 F11
Bellehiglash Moray 301 F11
Belle Isle W Yorks 197 B10
Bell End Worcs 117 B8
Bellerby N Yorks 224 G2
Belle Vale Mers 182 D6
W Mid 133 G9
Bellever Devon 13 F9
Bellevue Worcs 117 C9
Belle Vue Cumb 229 E8
Cumb 239 F9
Gtr Man 184 B5
Shrops 149 G9
S Yorks 198 G5
W Yorks 197 D10
Bellfield E Ayrs 257 B10
Bellfields Sur 50 C3
Bell Green London 67 E11
W Mid 135 G7
Bell Heath Worcs 117 B9
Bell Hill Hants 34 C2
Belliehill Angus 293 G7
Bellingdon Bucks 84 D6
Bellingham London 67 E11
Northumb 251 G8
Bellmount Norf 157 E10
Belloch Argyll 255 D7
Bellochantuy Argyll 255 D7
Bell o' th' Hill Ches W 167 F8
Bellsbank E Ayrs 245 C11
Bell's Close T&W 242 E5
Bell's Corner Suff 107 D9
Bellshill N Lnrk 268 C4
Northumb 264 C4
Bellside N Lnrk 268 D6
Bellsmyre W Dunb 277 F8
Bellspool Borders 260 B5
Bellsquarry W Loth 269 C10
Bells Yew Green E Sus 52 F6
Belluton Bath 60 G6
Bellyeoman Fife 280 D2
Belmaduthy Highld 300 D6
Belmesthorpe Rutland 155 G10
Belmont Blkburn 195 D7
Durham 234 C2
E Sus 38 E4
Harrow 67 G9
Oxon 63 B11
S Ayrs 257 E8
Shetland 312 C7
Sutton 85 G11
Belnacraig Aberds 292 B5
Belnagarrow Moray 302 E3
Belnie Lincs 156 C5
Belowda Corn 5 C9
Belper Derbys 170 F4
Belper Lane End Derbys 170 F4
Belph Derbys 187 F8
Belsay Northumb 242 B4
Belses Borders 262 D3
Belsford Devon 8 D5
Belsize Herts 85 E8
Belstead Suff 108 C2
Belston S Ayrs 257 E9
Belstone Devon 13 C8
Belstone Corner Devon 13 B8
Belthorn Blkburn 195 C8
Beltinge Kent 71 F7
Beltingham Northumb 241 E7
Beltoft N Lincs 199 F10
Belton Leics 153 E8
Lincs 155 B8
N Lincs 199 F9
Norf 143 C9
Belton in Rutland
Rutland 136 C6
Beltring Kent 53 D7
Belts of Collonach
Aberds 293 D8
Belvedere London 68 D3
W Loth 269 B9
Belvoir Leics 154 C6
Bembridge IoW 21 D8
Bemersyde Borders 262 C3
Bemerton Wilts 46 G6
Bemerton Heath Wilts 46 G6
Bempton E Yorks 218 E3
Benacre Suff 143 G10
Ben Alder Lodge Highld 291 F7
Ben Armine Lodge
Highld 309 H7
Benbuie Dumfries 246 D6
Ben Casgro W Isles 304 F6
Benchill Gtr Man 184 D4
Bencombe Glos 80 F3
Benderloch Argyll 289 F11
Bendish Herts 104 G3
Bendronaig Lodge
Highld 299 F10
Benenden Kent 53 G10
Benfield Dumfries 236 C5
Benfieldside Durham 242 G3
Bengal Pembs 91 E9
Bengate Norf 160 D6
Bengeo Herts 86 C4
Bengeworth Worcs 99 C10
Bengrove Glos 99 E9
Benhall Glos 99 G8
Benhall Green Suff 127 E7
Benhall Street Suff 127 E7
Benhilton London 67 F9
Benholm Aberds 293 G10
Beningbrough N Yorks 206 B6
Benington Herts 104 G5
Lincs 174 F5
Benington Sea End
Lincs 174 F6
Benllech Anglesey 179 E8
Benmore Argyll 276 E2
Stirl 285 E8
Benmore Lodge Argyll 289 F7
Highld 309 H3
Bennacott Corn 11 C11
Bennah Devon 14 E2
Bennan N Ayrs 255 E10
Bennane Lea S Ayrs 244 F3
Bennetland E Yorks 199 B10
Bennetsfield Highld 300 D6
Bennett End Bucks 84 F3
Bennetts End Herts 85 D9
Benniworth Lincs 190 E2
Benover Kent 53 D8
Ben Rhydding W Yorks 205 D8
Bensham T&W 242 E6
Benslie N Ayrs 266 G6
Benson Oxon 83 G10
Benston Shetland 313 H6
Bent Aberds 293 F8
Benter Som 44 D6
Bentfield Bury Essex 105 F9
Bentfield Green Essex 105 F10
Bentgate Gtr Man 196 E2
Bent Gate Lancs 195 C9
Benthall Northumb 264 D6
Shrops 132 C3
Bentham Glos 80 B6
Benthoul Aberdeen 293 C10
Bentilee Stoke 168 F6
Bentlass Pembs 73 E7
Bentlawnt Shrops 130 C6
Bentley Essex 87 F9
E Yorks 208 F6
Hants 49 E9
Suff 108 D2
S Yorks 198 F5
Warks 134 D5
W Mid 133 D9
Worcs 117 D9
Bentley Common Warks 134 D5
Bentley Heath Herts 86 F2
W Mid 118 B3
Bentley Rise S Yorks 198 G5
Benton Devon 41 F7
Benton Green W Mid 118 B5
Bentpath Dumfries 249 E8
Bents W Loth 269 C9
Bents Head W Yorks 205 F7
Bentwichen Devon 41 G8
Bentworth Hants 49 E7
Benvie Dundee 287 D7
Benville Dorset 29 G8
Benwell T&W 242 E6
Benwick Cambs 138 E6
Beobridge Shrops 132 E5
Beoley Worcs 117 D11
Beoraidbeg Highld 295 F8
Bepton W Sus 34 D5
Berden Essex 105 F9
Bere Alston Devon 7 B8
Berechurch Essex 107 G9
Bere Ferrers Devon 7 C9
Berefold Aberds 303 F9
Berepper Corn 2 E5
Bere Regis Dorset 18 C2
Bergh Apton Norf 142 C6
Berghers Hill Bucks 66 B2
Berhill Som 44 F2
Berinsfield Oxon 83 F9
Berkeley Glos 79 F11
Berkeley Heath Glos 79 F11
Berkeley Road Glos 80 E2
Berkeley Towers
Ches E 167 E11
Berkhamsted Herts 85 D7
Berkley Som 45 D10
Berkley Down Som 45 D9
Berkley Marsh Som 45 D10
Berkswell W Mid 118 B4
Bermondsey London 67 D10
Bermuda Warks 135 F7
Bernards Heath Herts 85 D11
Bernera Highld 295 C10
Berner's Cross Devon 25 F10
Berner's Hill E Sus 53 G8
Berners Roding Essex 87 D10
Bernice Argyll 276 C2
Bernisdale Highld 298 D4
Berrick Salome Oxon 83 G10
Berriedale Highld 311 G5
Berrier Cumb 230 F3
Berriew / Aberriw
Powys 130 C3
Berrington Northumb 273 G10
Shrops 131 B10
Worcs 115 D11
Berrington Green
Worcs 115 D11
Berriowbridge Corn 11 F11
Berrow Som 43 C10
Worcs 98 E5
Berrow Green Worcs 116 F4
Berry Swansea 56 D3
Berry Brow W Yorks 196 E6
Berry Cross Devon 25 E7
Berry Down Cross Devon 40 E5
Berryfield Wilts 61 G11
Berrygate Hill E Yorks 201 C8
Berry Hill Glos 79 C9
Pembs 91 C11
Stoke 168 F6
Worcs 117 E7
Berryhillock Moray 302 C5
Berrylands London 67 F7
Berry Moor S Yorks 197 G9
Berrynarbor Devon 40 D5
Berry Pomeroy Devon 8 C6
Berrysbridge Devon 26 G6
Berry's Green London 52 B2
Bersham Wrex 166 F4
Berstane Orkney 314 E4
Berth-ddu Flint 166 B2
Berthengam Flint 181 F10
Berwick E Sus 23 D8
Kent 54 F6
S Glos 60 C5
Berwick Bassett Wilts 62 E5
Berwick Hill Northumb 242 B5
Berwick Hills Mbro 225 B10
Berwick St James Wilts 46 F5
Berwick St John Wilts 30 C6
Berwick St Leonard
Wilts 46 G2
Berwick-upon-Tweed
Northumb 273 E9
Berwick Wharf Shrops 149 G10
Berwyn Denb 165 G11
Bescaby Leics 154 D6
Bescar Lancs 193 E11
Bescot W Mid 133 D10
Besford Shrops 149 E11
Worcs 99 C8
Bessacarr S Yorks 198 G6
Bessels Green Kent 52 B4
Bessels Leigh Oxon 83 E7
Besses o' th' Barn
Gtr Man 195 F10
Bessingby E Yorks 218 F3
Bessingham Norf 160 B3
Best Beech Hill E Sus 52 G6
Besthorpe Norf 141 D11
Notts 172 C4
Bestwood Nottingham 171 G9
Bestwood Village Notts 171 F9
Beswick E Yorks 208 D6
Gtr Man 184 B5
Betchcott Shrops 131 D8
Betchton Heath Ches E 168 C3
Betchworth Sur 51 D8
Bethania Ceredig 111 E11
Gwyn 163 E10
Gwyn 164 F2
Bethany Corn 6 D6
Bethel Anglesey 178 G5
Corn 5 E10
Gwyn 147 B9
Gwyn 163 B8
Bethelnie Aberds 303 F7
Bethersden Kent 54 E2
Bethesda Gwyn 163 B10
Pembs 73 B9
Bethlehem Carms 94 F3
Bethnal Green London 67 C10
Betley Staffs 168 F3
Betley Common Staffs 168 F2
Betsham Kent 68 E6
Betteshanger Kent 55 C10
Bettiscombe Dorset 16 B3
Bettisfield Wrex 149 B9
Betton Shrops 130 C6
Shrops 150 B3
Betton Strange Shrops 131 B10
Bettws Bridgend 58 B2
Mon 78 B3
Newport 78 G3
Bettws Cedewain Powys 130 D2
Bettws Gwerfil Goch
Denb 165 F8
Bettws Ifan Ceredig 92 B6
Bettws Newydd Mon 78 D5
Bettws-y-crwyn Shrops 130 G4
Bettyhill Highld 308 C7
Betws Bridgend 57 D11
Carms 75 C10
Betws Bledrws Ceredig 111 G11
Betws-Garmon Gwyn 163 D8
Betws Ifan Ceredig 92 B6
Betws-y-Coed Conwy 164 D4
Betws-yn-Rhos Conwy 180 G6
Beulah Ceredig 92 B5
Powys 113 G8
Bevendean Brighton 36 F4
Bevercotes Notts 187 G11
Bevere Worcs 116 F6
Beverley E Yorks 208 F6
Beverston Glos 80 G5
Bevington Glos 79 F11
Bewaldeth Cumb 229 E10
Bewbush W Sus 51 F8
Bewcastle Cumb 240 C3
Bewdley Worcs 116 B5
Bewerley N Yorks 214 G3
Bewholme E Yorks 209 C9
Bewley Common Wilts 62 F2
Bewlie Borders 262 D3
Bewlie Mains Borders 262 D3
Bewsey Warr 183 D9
Bexfield Norf 159 D10
Bexhill E Sus 38 F2
Bexley London 68 E3
Bexleyheath London 68 D3
Bexleyhill W Sus 34 B6
Bexon Kent 53 B11
Bexwell Norf 140 C2
Beyton Suff 125 E8
Beyton Green Suff 125 E8
Bhalasaigh W Isles 304 E3
Bhaltos W Isles 304 E2
Bhatarsaigh W Isles 297 M2
Bhlàraidh Highld 290 B5
Bibstone S Glos 79 G11
Bibury Glos 81 D10
Bicester Oxon 101 G11
Bickenhall Som 28 D3
Bickenhill W Mid 134 G3
Bicker Lincs 156 B4
Bicker Bar Lincs 156 B4
Bicker Gauntlet Lincs 156 B4
Bickershaw Gtr Man 194 G6
Bickerstaffe Lancs 194 G2
Bickerton Ches E 167 E8
Devon 9 G11
N Yorks 206 C5
Bickford Staffs 151 G7
Bickham Som 42 E3
Bickingcott Devon 26 B3
Bickington Devon 13 G11
Devon 40 G4
Bickleigh Devon 7 C10
Devon 26 F6
Bickleton Devon 40 G4
Bickley Ches W 167 F8
London 68 F2
Worcs 116 C2
Bickley Moss Ches W 167 F8
Bickley Town Ches W 167 F8
Bickleywood Ches W 167 F8
Bickmarsh Warks 100 B2
Bicknacre Essex 88 E3
Bicknoller Som 42 F6
Bicknor Kent 53 B11
Bickton Hants 31 E11
Bicton Hereford 115 E9
Pembs 72 D4
Shrops 130 G5
Shrops 149 F8
Bicton Heath Shrops 149 G9
Bidborough Kent 52 E5
Bidden Hants 49 D8
Biddenden Kent 53 F11
Biddenden Green Kent 53 E11
Biddenham Beds 103 B10
Biddestone Wilts 61 E11
Biddick T&W 243 F8
Biddick Hall T&W 243 E9
Biddisham Som 43 C11
Biddlesden Bucks 102 C2
Biddlestone Northumb 251 B11
Biddulph Staffs 168 D5
Biddulph Moor Staffs 168 D6
Bideford Devon 25 B7
Bidford-on-Avon Warks 118 G2
Bidlake Devon 12 D5
Bidston Mers 182 C3
Bidston Hill Mers 182 D3
Bidwell C Beds 103 G10
Bielby E Yorks 207 E11
Bieldside Aberdeen 293 C10
Bierley IoW 20 F6
W Yorks 205 G9
Bierton Bucks 84 B4
Bigbury Devon 8 F3
Bigbury-on-Sea Devon 8 G3
Bigby Lincs 200 F5
Bigfrith Windsor 65 C11
Biggar Cumb 210 F3
S Lnrk 260 B2
Biggar Road N Lnrk 268 C5
Biggin Derbys 169 D11
Derbys 170 F3
N Yorks 206 F6
Thurrock 69 D7
Biggings Shetland 313 G3
Biggin Hill London 52 B2
Biggleswade C Beds 104 C3
Bighouse Highld 310 C2
Bighton Hants 48 G6
Biglands Cumb 239 G7
Big Mancot Flint 166 B4
Bignall End Staffs 168 E4
Bignor W Sus 35 E7
Bigods Essex 106 G2
Bigram Stirl 285 G10
Bigrigg Cumb 219 C10
Big Sand Highld 299 B7
Bigswell Orkney 314 E3
Bigton Shetland 313 L5
Bilberry Corn 5 C10
Bilborough Nottingham 171 G8
Bilbrook Som 42 E4
Staffs 133 C7
Bilbrough N Yorks 206 D6
Bilbster Highld 310 D6
Bilby Notts 187 E10
Bildershaw Durham 233 G10
Bildeston Suff 107 B9
Billacombe Plym 7 E10
Billacott Corn 11 C11
Billericay Essex 87 G11
Billesdon Leics 136 C4
Billesley Warks 118 F2
W Mid 133 G11
Billesley Common
W Mid 133 G11
Billingborough Lincs 156 C2
Billinge Mers 194 G4
Billingford Norf 126 B3
Norf 159 E10
Billingham Stockton 234 G5
Billinghay Lincs 173 E11
Billingley S Yorks 198 G2
Billingshurst W Sus 35 B9
Billingsley Shrops 132 F4
Billington C Beds 103 G8
Lancs 203 F10
Staffs 151 E7
Billockby Norf 161 G8
Bill Quay T&W 243 E7
Billy Mill T&W 243 D8
Billy Row Durham 233 D9
Bilmarsh Shrops 149 D9
Bilsborrow Lancs 202 F6
Bilsby Lincs 191 F7
Bilsby Field Lincs 191 F7
Bilsdon Devon 14 C2
Bilsham W Sus 35 G7
Bilsington Kent 54 G4
Bilson Green Glos 79 C11
Bilsthorpe Notts 171 C10
Bilsthorpe Moor Notts 171 D11
Bilston Midloth 270 C5
W Mid 133 D9
Bilstone Leics 135 B7
Bilting Kent 54 D5
Bilton E Yorks 209 G9
Northumb 264 G6
N Yorks 206 B2
Warks 119 C9
Bilton Haggs N Yorks 206 D5
Bilton in Ainsty N Yorks 206 D5
Bimbister Orkney 314 E3
Binbrook Lincs 190 C2
Binchester Blocks
Durham 233 E10
Bincombe Dorset 17 E9
Som 43 F7
Bindal Highld 311 L3
Bindon Som 27 C10
Binegar Som 44 D6
Bines Green W Sus 35 D11
Binfield Brack 65 E10
Binfield Heath Oxon 65 D8
Bingfield Northumb 241 C11
Bingham Edin 280 G6
Notts 154 B4
Bingley W Yorks 205 F8
Bings Heath Shrops 149 F10
Binham Norf 159 B9
Binley Hants 48 C2
W Mid 119 B7
Binley Woods Warks 119 B7
Binnegar Dorset 18 D3
Binniehill Falk 279 G7
Binscombe Sur 50 D3
Binsey Oxon 83 D7
Binsoe N Yorks 214 D4
Binstead Hants 49 E9
IoW 21 C7
Binsted Hants 49 E9
W Sus 35 F7
Binton Warks 118 G2
Bintree Norf 159 E10
Binweston Shrops 130 C6
Birch Essex 88 B6
Gtr Man 195 F11
Birch Acre Worcs 117 C11
Birchall Hereford 98 D3
Staffs 169 E7
Bircham Newton Norf 158 C5
Bircham Tofts Norf 158 C5
Birchan Coppice Worcs 116 C6
Birchanger Essex 105 G10
Birch Berrow Worcs 116 E4
Birchburn N Ayrs 255 E10
Birch Cross Staffs 152 C2
Birchden E Sus 52 F4
Birchencliffe W Yorks 196 D6
Birchend Hereford 98 C3
Birchendale Staffs 151 B11
Bircher Hereford 115 D9
Birches Green W Mid 134 E2
Birches Head Stoke 168 F5
Birchett's Green E Sus 53 G7
Birchfield Highld 301 G9
W Mid 133 E11
Birch Green Essex 88 B6
Herts 86 C3
Lancs 194 F3
Worcs 99 B7
Birchgrove Cardiff 59 D7
E Sus 36 B6
Swansea 57 B8
Birchhall Corner Essex 107 E10
Birch Heath Ches W 167 C8
Birch Hill Brack 65 F11
Ches W 183 G8
Birchill Devon 28 G4
Birchills W Mid 133 D10
Birchington Kent 71 F9
Birchley Heath Warks 134 E5
Birchmoor Warks 134 C5
Birchmoor Green
C Beds 103 E8
Bircholt Forstal Kent 54 E5
Birchover Derbys 170 C2
Birch Vale Derbys 185 D8
Birchwood Herts 86 D2
Lincs 172 B6
Som 28 E2
Warr 183 C10
Birchy Hill Hants 19 B11
Bircotes Notts 187 C10
Birdbrook Essex 106 C4
Birdbush Wilts 30 C6
Birdfield Argyll 275 D10
Birdforth N Yorks 215 D9
Birdham W Sus 22 D4
Birdholme Derbys 170 B5
Birdingbury Warks 119 D8
Birdlip Glos 80 C6
Birdsall N Yorks 216 F6
Birds Edge W Yorks 197 F8
Birds End Suff 124 E5
Birdsgreen Shrops 132 F5
Birds Green Essex 87 D9
Birdsmoorgate Dorset 28 G5
Birdston E Dunb 278 F3
Bird Street Suff 125 G10
Birdwell S Yorks 197 G10
Birdwood Glos 80 B2
Birgham Borders 263 B7
Birichen Highld 309 K7
Birkacre Lancs 194 D5
Birkby Cumb 229 D7
N Yorks 224 E6
W Yorks 196 D6
Birkdale Mers 193 D10
Birkenbog Aberds 302 C5
Birkenhead Mers 182 D4
Birkenhills Aberds 303 E7
Birkenshaw N Lnrk 268 C3
S Lnrk 268 F5
W Yorks 197 B8
Birkenshaw Bottoms
W Yorks 197 B8
Birkenside Borders 271 G11
Birkett Mire Cumb 230 G2
Birkhall Aberds 292 D5
Birkhill Angus 287 D7
Borders 260 F6
Borders 271 G11
Birkholme Lincs 155 E9
Birkhouse W Yorks 197 C7
Birkin N Yorks 198 B4
Birks Cumb 222 G3
W Yorks 197 B9
Birkshaw Northumb 241 D7
Birley Hereford 115 G9
Birley Carr S Yorks 186 C4
Birley Edge S Yorks 186 C4
Birleyhay Derbys 186 E5
Birling Kent 69 G7
Northumb 252 B6
Birling Gap E Sus 23 F9
Birlingham Worcs 99 C8
Birmingham W Mid 133 F11
Birnam Perth 286 C4
Birniehill S Lnrk 268 E2
Birse Aberds 293 D7
Birsemore Aberds 293 D7
Birstall Leics 135 B11
W Yorks 197 B8
Birstall Smithies
W Yorks 197 B8
Birstwith N Yorks 205 B10
Birthorpe Lincs 156 C2
Birtle Gtr Man 195 E10
Birtley Hereford 115 D7
Northumb 241 B9
Shrops 131 E9
T&W 243 F7
Birtley Green Sur 50 E4
Birtsmorton Worcs 98 D6
Birts Street Worcs 98 D5
Bisbrooke Rutland 137 D7
Biscathorpe Lincs 190 D2
Biscombe Som 27 E11
Biscot Luton 103 G11
Biscovey Corn 5 E11
Bisham Windsor 65 C10
Bishampton Worcs 117 G9
Bish Mill Devon 26 B2
Bishon Common Hereford 97 C8
Bishop Auckland
Durham 233 F10
Bishopbridge Lincs 189 C8
Bishopbriggs E Dunb 278 G2
Bishop Burton E Yorks 208 F5
Bishopdown Wilts 47 G7
Bishop Kinkell Highld 300 D5
Bishop Middleham
Durham 234 E2
Bishopmill Moray 302 C2
Bishop Monkton
N Yorks 214 F6
Bishop Norton Lincs 189 C7
Bishopsbourne Kent 55 C7
Bishops Cannings Wilts 62 G4
Bishop's Castle Shrops 130 F6
Bishop's Caundle Dorset 29 E11
Bishop's Cleeve Glos 99 F9
Bishop's Down Dorset 29 E11
Bishops Frome Hereford 98 B3
Bishopsgarth Stockton 234 G4
Bishopsgate Sur 66 E3
Bishops Green Essex 87 B5
Bishop's Green W Berks 64 G4
Bishop's Hull Som 28 C2
Bishop's Itchington
Warks 119 F7
Bishops Lydeard Som 27 B11
Bishop's Norton Glos 98 G6
Bishops Nympton Devon 26 C3
Bishop's Offley Staffs 150 D5
Bishop's Quay Corn 2 D6
Bishop's Stortford
Herts 105 G9
Bishop's Sutton Hants 48 G6
Bishop's Tachbrook
Warks 118 E6
Bishops Tawton Devon 40 G5
Bishopsteignton Devon 14 G4
Bishopstoke Hants 33 D7
Bishopston Bristol 60 D5
Swansea 56 D5
Bishopstone Bucks 84 C4
E Sus 23 E7
Hereford 97 C8
Kent 71 F8
Swindon 63 C8
Wilts 31 B9
Bishopstrow Wilts 45 E11
Bishop Sutton Bath 44 B5
Bishop's Waltham Hants 33 D9
Bishopswood Som 28 E3
Bishop's Wood Staffs 132 B6
Bishopsworth Bristol 60 F5
Bishop Thornton
N Yorks 214 G5
Bishopthorpe York 207 D7
Bishopton Darl 234 G3
Dumfries 236 E6
N Yorks 214 E6
Renfs 277 G8
Warks 118 F3
Bishopwearmouth T&W 243 F9
Bishop Wilton E Yorks 207 B11
Bishpool Newport 59 B10
Bishton Newport 59 B11
Staffs 151 E10
Bisley Glos 80 D6
Sur 50 B3
Bisley Camp Sur 50 B2
Bispham Blkpool 202 E2
Bispham Green Lancs 194 E3
Bissoe Corn 4 G5
Bissom Corn 3 C7
Bisterne Hants 31 G10
Bisterne Close Hants 32 G2
Bitchet Green Kent 52 C5
Bitchfield Lincs 155 D9
Bittadon Devon 40 E4
Bittaford Devon 8 D3
Bittering Norf 159 F8
Bitterley Shrops 115 B11
Bitterne Soton 33 E7
Bitterne Park Soton 32 E6
Bitterscote Staffs 134 C4
Bitteswell Leics 135 F10
Bittles Green Dorset 30 C5
Bitton S Glos 61 F7
Bix Oxon 65 B8
Bixter Shetland 313 H5
Blaby Leics 135 D11
Blackacre Dumfries 248 E2
Blackadder West
Borders 272 E6
Blackawton Devon 8 E6
Black Bank Cambs 139 F10
Warks 135 F7
Black Banks Darl 224 C5
Black Barn Lincs 157 D8
Blackbeck Cumb 219 D10
Blackbird Leys Oxon 83 E9
Blackborough Devon 27 F9
Norf 158 G3
Blackborough End Norf 158 G3
Black Bourton Oxon 82 E3
Blackboys E Sus 37 C8
Blackbraes Aberds 293 B10
Blackbrook Derbys 170 F4
Derbys 185 E9
Mers 183 B8
Staffs 150 B5
Sur 51 D7
Blackburn Aberds 293 B10
Aberds 302 F5
Blkburn 195 B7
S Yorks 186 C5
W Loth 269 B9
Black Callerton T&W 242 D5
Black Carr Norf 141 D11
Blackcastle Midloth 271 D8
Blackchambers Aberds 293 B9
Black Clauchrie S Ayrs 245 G7
Black Corner W Sus 51 F9
Black Corries Lodge
Highld 284 B6
Blackcraig Dumfries 246 G6
Blackcraigs Angus 293 E7
Black Crofts Argyll 289 F11
Black Cross Corn 5 C8
Black Dam Hants 48 C6
Blackden Heath Ches E 184 G3
Blackditch Oxon 82 D6
Blackdog Aberds 293 B11
Black Dog Devon 26 F4
Blackdown Dorset 28 G5
Hants 33 C8
Warks 118 D6
Blackdyke Cumb 238 G4
Blackdykes E Loth 281 E11
Blacker Hill S Yorks 197 G11
Blacketts Kent 70 F2
Blackfell T&W 243 F7
Blackfen London 68 E3
Blackfield Hants 32 G6
Blackford Cumb 239 E9
Dumfries 248 G4
Perth 286 G2
Shrops 131 G11
Som 29 B11
Som 42 D2
Som 44 D2
Blackford Bridge
Gtr Man 195 F10
Blackfordby Leics 152 F6
Blackfords Staffs 151 G9
Blackgang IoW 20 F5
Blackgate Angus 287 B8
Blackhall Aberds 293 D8
Edin 280 G4
Renfs 267 C9
Blackhall Colliery
Durham 234 D5
Blackhall Mill T&W 242 F4
Blackhall Rocks Durham 234 D5
Blackham E Sus 52 F3
Blackhaugh Borders 261 B10
Blackheath Essex 107 G10
London 67 D11
Suff 127 C8
Sur 50 D4
W Mid 133 F9
Blackheath Park London 68 D2
Black Heddon Northumb 242 B3
Blackhill Aberds 303 D10
Aberds 303 E10
Aberds 303 F10
Durham 242 G3
Hants 32 D4
Highld 298 D3
Black Hill W Yorks 204 E6
Blackhillock Moray 302 E4
Blackhills Highld 301 D9
Moray 302 D2
Swansea 56 C5
Blackhorse Devon 14 C5
S Glos 61 D7
Black Horse Drove
Cambs 139 E11
Blackjack Lincs 156 B5
Black Lake W Mid 133 E9
Blackland Wilts 62 F4
Blacklands E Sus 38 E4
Hereford 98 C2
Black Lane Gtr Man 195 F9
Blacklaw Aberds 302 D6
Blackleach Lancs 202 G5
Blackley Gtr Man 195 G11
W Yorks 196 D6
Blacklunans Perth 292 G3
Black Marsh Shrops 130 D6
Blackmarstone Hereford 97 D10
Blackmill Bridgend 58 B2
Blackminster Worcs 99 C11
Blackmoor Bath 60 G5
Gtr Man 195 G7
Hants 49 G9
N Som 60 G3
Som 27 D11
Black Moor Lancs 196 E4
W Yorks 205 F11
Blackmoorfoot W Yorks 196 E5
Blackmoor Gate Devon 41 E7
Blackmore Essex 87 E10
Shrops 130 B6
Blackmore End Essex 106 E4
Herts 85 B11
Worcs 98 C6
Black Mount Argyll 284 C6
Blackness Aberds 293 D8
E Sus 52 G4
Falk 279 F11
Blacknest Hants 49 E9
Windsor 66 F3
Blacknoll Dorset 18 D2
Black Notley Essex 106 G5
Blacko Lancs 204 E3
Blackoe Shrops 149 B10
Blackpark Dumfries 236 C5
Black Park Wrex 166 G4
Black Pill Swansea 56 C6
Blackpole Worcs 117 F7
Black Pole Lancs 202 F5
Blackpool Blkpool 202 F2
Devon 7 E11
Devon 9 F7
Devon 14 G2
Pembs 73 C9
Blackpool Gate Cumb 240 B2
Blackridge W Loth 269 B7
Blackrock Argyll 274 G4
Bath 60 F6
Mon 78 C2
Black Rock Brighton 36 G4
Corn 2 C5
Blackrod Gtr Man 194 E6
Blackshaw Dumfries 238 D2
Blackshaw Head
W Yorks 196 B3
Blackshaw Moor Staffs 169 D8
Blacksmith's Corner
Suff 108 C2
Blacksmith's Green Suff 126 D2
Blacksnape Blkburn 195 C8
Blackstone Worcs 116 C5
W Sus 36 D2
Black Street Suff 143 F10
Black Tar Pembs 73 D7
Blackthorn Oxon 83 B10
Blackthorpe Suff 125 E8
Blacktoft E Yorks 199 C10
Blacktop Aberdeen 293 C10
Black Torrington Devon 25 F7
Blacktown Newport 59 C9
Black Vein Caerph 78 G2
Blackwall Derbys 170 F3
London 67 C11
Blackwall Tunnel
London 67 C11
Blackwater Corn 4 F4
Dorset 19 B8
Hants 49 B11
IoW 20 D6
Norf 159 E11
Som 28 D3
Blackwaterfoot N Ayrs 255 E9
Blackwater Lodge
Moray 302 G3
Blackweir Cardiff 59 D7
Blackwell Cumb 239 G10
Darl 224 C5
Derbys 170 D6
Derbys 185 G10
Devon 27 B8
Warks 100 C4
Worcs 117 C9
W Sus 51 F11
Blackwood Caerph 77 F11
S Lnrk 268 G5
Warr 183 C10
Blackwood Hill Staffs 168 D6
Blacon Ches W 166 B5
Bladbean Kent 55 D7
Blades N Yorks 223 F9
Bladnoch Dumfries 236 D6
Bladon Oxon 82 C6
Blaenannerch Ceredig 92 B4
Blaenau Carms 75 C10
Flint 166 D2
Blaenau Dolwyddelan
Conwy 164 E2
Blaenau Ffestiniog
Gwyn 164 F2
Blaenau-Gwent Bl Gwent 78 E2
Blaenavon Torf 78 D3
Blaenbedw Fawr
Ceredig 111 G7
Blaencaerau Bridgend 57 C11
Blaencelyn Ceredig 111 G7
Blaen-Cil-Llech Ceredig 92 B6
Blaen Clydach Rhondda 77 G7
Blaencwm Rhondda 76 F6
Blaendulais / Seven Sisters
Neath 76 D4
Blaendyryn Powys 95 D8
Blaenffos Pembs 92 D3
Blaengarw Bridgend 76 G6
Blaengwrach Neath 76 D5
Blaengwynfi Neath 57 B11
Blaenllechau Rhondda 77 F8
Blaen-pant Ceredig 92 C5
Blaenpennal Ceredig 112 E2
Blaenplwyf Ceredig 111 B11
Blaenporth Ceredig 92 B5
Blaenrhondda Rhondda 76 E6
Blaenwaun Carms 92 F4
Blaen-waun Carms 92 F4
Blaen-y-coed Carms 92 F6
Blaenycwm Ceredig 112 B6
Blaen-y-cwm Bl Gwent 77 C10
Denb 147 C10
Gwyn 146 E4
Powys 147 E11
Blagdon N Som 44 B4
Torbay 9 C7
Blagdon Hill Som 28 D2
Blagill Cumb 231 B10
Blaguegate Lancs 194 F3
Blaich Highld 290 F2
Blain Highld 289 C8
Blaina Bl Gwent 78 D2
Blainacraig Ho Aberds 293 D7
Blair Fife 280 C6
Blair Atholl Perth 291 G10
Blairbeg N Ayrs 256 C2
Blairburn Fife 279 D9
Blairdaff Aberds 293 B8
Blair Drummond Stirl 278 B4
Blairdryne Aberds 293 D9
Blairglas Argyll 276 D6
Blairgorm Highld 301 G10
Blairgowrie Perth 286 C5
Blairhall Fife 279 D10
Blairhill N Lnrk 268 B4
Blairingone Perth 279 B9
Blairland N Ayrs 266 F6
Blairlinn N Lnrk 278 G5
Blairlogie Stirl 278 B6
Blairlomond Argyll 276 B3
Blairmore Argyll 276 E3
Highld 306 D6
Blairnamarrow Moray 292 B4
Blairquhosh Stirl 277 E10
Blair's Ferry Argyll 275 G10
Blairskaith E Dunb 277 F11
Blaisdon Glos 80 B2
Blaise Hamlet Bristol 60 D5
Blakebrook Worcs 116 B6
Blakedown Worcs 117 B7
Blake End Essex 106 G4
Blakelands M Keynes 103 C7
Blakelaw Borders 263 C7
T&W 242 D6
Blakeley Staffs 133 E7
Blakeley Lane Staffs 169 F7
Blakelow Ches E 167 E11
Blakemere Hereford 97 C7
Blakenall Heath
W Mid 133 C10
Blakeney Glos 79 D11
Norf 177 E8
Blakenhall Ches E 168 F2
W Mid 133 D8
Blakeshall Worcs 132 G6
Blakesley Northants 120 G2
Blanchland Northumb 241 G11
Blandford Camp Dorset 30 F6
Blandford Forum Dorset 30 F5
Blandford St Mary Dorset 30 F5
Bland Hill N Yorks 205 C10
Blandy Highld 308 D6
Blanefield Stirl 277 F11
Blanerne Borders 272 D6
Blank Bank Staffs 168 F4
Blankney Lincs 173 C9
Blantyre S Lnrk 268 D3
Blar a'Chaorainn Highld 290 G3
Blaran Argyll 275 B9
Blarghour Argyll 275 B10
Blarmachfoldach Highld 290 G2
Blarnalearoch Highld 307 K6
Blasford Hill Essex 88 C2
Blashford Hants 31 F11
Blaston Leics 136 D6
Blatchbridge Som 45 D9
Blatherwycke Northants 137 D9
Blawith Cumb 210 B5
Blaxhall Suff 127 F7
Blaxton S Yorks 199 G7
Blaydon T&W 242 E5
Blaydon Burn T&W 242 E5
Blaydon Haughs T&W 242 E5
Bleach Green Cumb 219 B9
Suff 126 B4
Bleadney Som 44 D3
Bleadon N Som 43 B10
Bleak Acre Hereford 98 B2
Bleak Hall M Keynes 103 D7
Bleak Hey Nook
Gtr Man 196 F4

Bleak Hill Hants 31 E10
Blean Kent 70 G6
Bleasby Lincs 189 E10
Notts 172 F2
Bleasby Moor Lincs 189 E10
Bleasdale Lancs 203 D7
Bleatarn Cumb 222 C4
Blebocraigs Fife 287 F8
Bleddfa Powys 114 D4
Bledington Glos 100 G4
Bledlow Bucks 84 E3
Bledlow Ridge Bucks 84 F3
Bleet Wilts 45 B11
Blegbie E Loth 271 C9
Blegbury Devon 24 B2
Blencarn Cumb 231 E8
Blencogo Cumb 229 B9
Blendworth Hants 34 E2
Blenheim Oxon 83 D9
Oxon 83 E9
Blenheim Park Norf 158 C6
Blenkinsopp Hall
Northumb 240 E5
Blennerhasset Cumb 229 C9
Blervie Castle Moray 301 D10
Bletchingdon Oxon 83 B8
Bletchingley Sur 51 C10
Bletchley M Keynes 103 E7
Shrops 150 C2
Bletherston Pembs 91 G11
Bletsoe Beds 121 F10
Blewbury Oxon 64 B4
Bliby Kent 54 F4
Blickling Norf 160 D3
Blidworth Notts 171 D9
Blidworth Bottoms
Notts 171 E9
Blidworth Dale Notts 171 E9
Blindburn Northumb 263 G8
Blindcrake Cumb 229 E8
Blindley Heath Sur 51 D11
Blindmoor Som 28 E3
Blingery Highld 310 E7
Blisland Corn 11 G8
Blissford Hants 31 E11
Bliss Gate Worcs 116 C4
Blisworth Northants 120 G4
Blithbury Staffs 151 E11
Blitterlees Cumb 238 G4
Blockley Glos 100 D3
Blofield Norf 142 B6
Blofield Heath Norf 160 G6
Blo' Norton Norf 125 B10
Bloodman's Corner
Suff 143 D10
Bloomfield Bath 45 B7
Bath 61 G8
Borders 262 E3
W Mid 133 E9
Bloomsbury London 67 C10
Blore Staffs 150 C4
Staffs 169 F10
Bloreheath Staffs 150 B4
Blossomfield W Mid 118 B2
Blount's Green Staffs 151 C11
Blowick Mers 193 D11
Blowinghouse Corn 4 E4
Bloxham Oxon 101 D8
Bloxholm Lincs 173 E9
Bloxwich W Mid 133 C9
Bloxworth Dorset 18 C3
Blubberhouses N Yorks 205 B9
Blue Anchor Corn 5 D8
Som 42 E4
Swansea 56 B4
Bluebell Telford 149 G11
Blue Bell Hill Kent 69 G8
Bluecairn Borders 271 G10
Blue Hill Herts 104 G5
Blue Row Essex 89 C8
Bluetown Kent 54 B2
Blue Town Kent 70 D2
Blue Vein Wilts 61 F10
Bluewater Kent 68 E5
Blughasary Highld 307 J6
Blundellsands Mers 182 B4
Blundeston Suff 143 D10
Blundies Staffs 132 F6
Blunham C Beds 122 G3
Blunsdon St Andrew
Swindon 62 B6
Bluntington Worcs 117 C7
Bluntisham Cambs 123 C7
Blunts Corn 6 C6
Blunt's Green Warks 118 D2
Blurton Stoke 168 G5
Blyborough Lincs 188 C6
Blyford Suff 127 B8
Blymhill Staffs 150 G6
Blymhill Lawns Staffs 150 G6
Blyth Borders 270 F2
Northumb 253 G8
Notts 187 D10
Blyth Bridge Borders 270 F2
Blythburgh Suff 127 B9
Blythe Borders 271 F11
Blythe Bridge Staffs 169 G7
Blythe Marsh Staffs 169 G7
Blyth End Warks 134 E4
Blythswood Renfs 267 B10
Blyton Lincs 188 C5
Boarhills Fife 287 F9
Boarhunt Hants 33 F10
Boarsgreave Lancs 195 C10
Boarshead E Sus 52 G4
Boars Hill Oxon 83 E7
Boarstall Bucks 83 C10
Boasley Cross Devon 12 C5
Boath Highld 300 B5
Boat of Garten Highld 291 B11
Bobbing Kent 69 F11
Bobbington Staffs 132 E6
Bobbingworth Essex 87 D8
Bobby Hill Suff 125 C10
Boblainy Highld 300 F4
Bocaddon Corn 6 D3
Bochastle Stirl 285 G10
Bockhanger Kent 54 E4
Bocking Essex 106 G5
Bocking Churchstreet
Essex 106 F5
Bocking's Elm Essex 89 B11
Bockleton Worcs 115 E11
Bockmer End Bucks 65 B10
Bocombe Devon 24 C5
Bodantionail Highld 299 B7
Boddam Aberds 303 E11
Shetland 313 M5
Bodden Som 44 E6
Boddington Glos 99 F7
Bodedern Anglesey 178 E4
Bodellick Corn 10 G5
Bodelva Corn 5 E11
Bodelwyddan Denb 181 F8
Bodenham Hereford 115 G10
Wilts 31 B11
Bodenham Bank Hereford 98 E2
Bodenham Moor
Hereford 115 G10
Bodermid Gwyn 144 D3
Bodewryd Anglesey 178 C5
Bodfari Denb 181 G9
Bodffordd Anglesey 178 F6
Bodham Norf 177 E10
Bodiam E Sus 38 B3
Bodicote Oxon 101 D9
Bodiechell Aberds 303 E7
Bodieve Corn 10 G5
Bodiggo Corn 5 D10
Bodilly Corn 2 C5
Bodinnick Corn 6 E2
Bodle Street Green
E Sus 23 C11
Bodley Devon 41 D7
Bodmin Corn 5 B11
Bodmiscombe Devon 27 F10
Bodney Norf 140 D6
Bodorgan Anglesey 162 B5
Bodsham Kent 54 D6
Boduan Gwyn 144 B6
Boduel Corn 6 C4
Bodwen Corn 5 C10
Bodymoor Heath Warks 134 D4
Bofarnel Corn 6 C2
Bogallan Highld 300 D6
Bogbrae Aberds 303 F10
Bogend Borders 272 F5
Notts 171 F7
S Ayrs 257 C9
Bogentory Aberds 293 C9
Boghall Midloth 270 B4
W Loth 269 B9
Boghead Aberds 293 D8
S Lnrk 268 G5
Bogmoor Moray 302 C3
Bogniebrae Aberds 302 E5
Aberds 302 E6
Bognor Regis W Sus 22 D6
Bograxie Aberds 293 B9
Bogs Aberds 302 G5
Bogs Bank Borders 270 E3
Bogside N Lnrk 268 E6
Bogthorn W Yorks 204 F6
Bogton Aberds 302 D6
Bogtown Aberds 302 C5
Bogue Dumfries 246 G4
Bohemia E Sus 38 E4
Wilts 32 D2
Bohenie Highld 290 E4
Bohetherick Corn 7 B8
Bohortha Corn 3 C9
Bohuntine Highld 290 E4
Bohuntinville Highld 290 E4
Boirseam W Isles 296 C6
Bojewyan Corn 1 C3
Bokiddick Corn 5 C11
Bolahaul Fm Carms 74 B6
Bolam Durham 233 G9
Northumb 252 G3
Bolam West Houses
Northumb 252 G3
Bolas Heath Telford 150 E3
Bolberry Devon 9 G8
Bold Heath Mers 183 D8
Boldmere W Mid 134 E2
Boldon T&W 243 E9
Boldon Colliery T&W 243 E8
Boldre Hants 20 B2
Boldron Durham 223 C10
Bole Notts 188 D3
Bolehall Staffs 134 C4
Bolehill Derbys 170 E3
Derbys 186 G6
S Yorks 186 E5
Bole Hill Derbys 186 G4
Bolenowe Corn 2 B5
Boleside Borders 261 C11
Boley Park Staffs 134 B2
Bolham Devon 27 E7
Notts 188 E2
Bolham Water Devon 27 E11
Bolholt Gtr Man 195 E9
Bolingey Corn 4 E5
Bolitho Corn 2 C5
Bollihope Durham 232 E6
Bollington Ches E 184 F6
Bollington Cross Ches E 184 F6
Bolney W Sus 36 C3
Bolnhurst Beds 121 F11
Bolnore W Sus 36 C4
Bolshan Angus 287 B10
Bolsover Derbys 187 G7
Bolsterstone S Yorks 186 B3
Bolstone Hereford 97 E11
Boltby N Yorks 215 B9
Bolter End Bucks 84 G3
Bolton Cumb 231 G8
E Loth 281 G10
E Yorks 207 C11
Gtr Man 195 F8
Northumb 264 G4
W Yorks 205 F9
Bolton Abbey N Yorks 205 C7
Bolton Bridge N Yorks 205 C7
Bolton-by-Bowland
Lancs 203 D11
Boltonfellend Cumb 239 D11
Boltongate Cumb 229 C10
Bolton Green Lancs 194 D5
Bolton Houses Lancs 202 G4
Bolton-le-Sands Lancs 211 F9
Bolton Low Houses
Cumb 229 C10
Bolton New Houses
Cumb 229 C10
Bolton-on-Swale
N Yorks 224 F5
Bolton Percy N Yorks 206 E6
Bolton Town End Lancs 211 F9
Bolton upon Dearne
S Yorks 198 G3
Bolton Wood Lane
Cumb 229 C11
Bolton Woods W Yorks 205 F9
Boltshope Park Durham 232 B4
Bolventor Corn 11 F9
Bomarsund Northumb 253 G7
Bombie Dumfries 237 D9
Bomby Cumb 221 B10
Bomere Heath Shrops 149 F9
Bonaly Edin 270 B4
Bonar Bridge Highld 309 K6
Bonawe Argyll 284 D4
Bonby N Lincs 200 D4
Boncath Pembs 92 D4
Bonchester Bridge
Borders 262 G3
Bonchurch IoW 21 F7
Bondend Glos 80 B5
Bond End Staffs 152 F2
Bondleigh Devon 25 G11
Bondman Hays Leics 135 B9
Bonds Lancs 202 E5
Bondstones Devon 25 F9
Bonehill Devon 13 F10
Staffs 134 C3
Bo'ness Falk 279 E9
Bonhill W Dunb 277 F7
Boningale Shrops 132 C6
Bonjedward Borders 262 E5
Bonkle N Lnrk 268 D6
Bonnavoulin Highld 289 D7
Bonning Gate Cumb 221 F9
Bonnington Borders 261 B7
Edin 270 B2
Kent 54 F5
Bonnybank Fife 287 G7
Bonnybridge Falk 278 E6
Bonnykelly Aberds 303 D8
Bonnyrigg and Lasswade
Midloth 270 B6
Bonnyton Aberds 302 F6
Angus 287 B10
Angus 287 D7
E Ayrs 257 B10
Bonsall Derbys 170 D3
Bonskeid House Perth 291 G10
Bonson Som 43 E8
Bont Mon 78 B5
Bontddu Gwyn 146 F3
Bont-Dolgadfan Powys 129 C7
Bont Fawr Carms 94 F4
Bont goch / Elerch
Ceredig 128 F3
Bonthorpe Lincs 191 G7
Bontnewydd Ceredig 112 D2
Gwyn 163 D7
Bont-newydd Conwy 181 G8
Bont Newydd Gwyn 146 E5
Gwyn 164 G2
Bontuchel Denb 165 D9
Bonvilston / Tresimwn
V Glam 58 E5
Bon-y-maen Swansea 57 B7
Boode Devon 40 F4
Booker Bucks 84 G4
Bookham Dorset 30 G2
Booleybank Shrops 149 D11
Boon Borders 271 F11
Boon Hill Staffs 168 E4
Boorley Green Hants 33 E8
Boosbeck Redcar 226 B3
Boose's Green Essex 106 E6
Boot Cumb 220 E3
Booth Staffs 151 D10
W Yorks 196 B4
Booth Bank Ches E 184 D2
Booth Bridge Lancs 204 D4
Boothby Graffoe Lincs 173 D7
Boothby Pagnell Lincs 155 C9
Boothen Stoke 168 G5
Boothferry E Yorks 199 B8
Boothgate Derbys 170 F5
Booth Green Ches E 184 E6
Boothroyd W Yorks 197 C8
Boothsdale Ches W 167 B8
Boothstown Gtr Man 195 G8
Boothtown W Yorks 196 B5
Boothville Northants 120 E5
Booth Wood W Yorks 196 D4
Bootle Cumb 210 B2
Mers 182 B4
Booton Norf 160 E2
Boots Green Ches W 184 G3
Boot Street Suff 108 B4
Booze N Yorks 223 E10
Boquhan Stirl 277 D10
Boquio Corn 2 C5
Boraston Shrops 116 D2
Boraston Dale Shrops 116 C2
Borden Kent 69 G11
W Sus 34 C4
Border Cumb 238 G5
Bordesley W Mid 133 F11
Bordesley Green W Mid 134 F2
Bordlands Borders 270 F3
Bordley N Yorks 213 G8
Bordon Hants 49 F10
Bordon Camp Hants 49 F9
Boreham Essex 88 D3
Wilts 45 E11
Boreham Street E Sus 23 C11
Borehamwood Herts 85 F11
Boreland Dumfries 236 C5
Dumfries 248 E5
Fife 280 C6
Stirl 285 D9
Boreland of Southwick
Dumfries 237 C11
Boreley Worcs 116 D6
Borestone Stirl 278 C5
Borgh W Isles 296 C5
W Isles 297 L2
Borghasdal W Isles 296 C6
Borghastan W Isles 304 D4
Borgie Highld 308 D6
Borgue Dumfries 237 E8
Highld 311 G5
Borley Essex 106 C6
Borley Green Essex 106 C6
Suff 125 E9
Bornais W Isles 297 J3
Bornesketaig Highld 298 B3
Borness Dumfries 237 E8
Borough Scilly 1 G3
Boroughbridge N Yorks 215 F7
Borough Green Kent 52 B6
Borough Marsh
Wokingham 65 D9
Borough Park Staffs 134 B4
Borough Post Som 28 C4
Borras Wrex 166 E4
Borras Head Wrex 166 E5
Borreraig Highld 296 F7
Borrobol Lodge Highld 311 G2
Borrodale Highld 297 G7
Borrohill Aberds 303 D9
Borrowash Derbys 153 C8
Borrowby N Yorks 215 B8
N Yorks 226 B5
Borrowdale Cumb 220 C5
Borrowfield Aberds 293 D10
Borrowston Highld 310 E7
Borrowstoun Mains
Falk 279 E9
Borstal Medway 69 F8
Borthwick Midloth 271 D7
Borthwickbrae Borders 261 G10
Borthwickshiels
Borders 261 F10
Borth / Y Borth Ceredig 128 E2
Borth-y-Gest Gwyn 145 B11
Borve Highld 298 E4
Borve Lodge W Isles 305 J2
Borwick Lancs 211 E10
Borwick Rails Cumb 210 D3
Bosavern Corn 1 C3
Bosbury Hereford 98 C3
Boscadjack Corn 2 C5
Boscastle Corn 11 C8
Boscean Corn 1 C3
Boscombe Bmouth 19 C8
Wilts 47 F8
Boscomoor Staffs 151 G8
Boscoppa Corn 5 E10
Boscreege Corn 2 C3
Bosham W Sus 22 C4
Bosham Hoe W Sus 22 C4
Bosherston Pembs 73 G7
Boskednan Corn 1 C4
Boskenna Corn 1 E4
Bosleake Corn 4 G3
Bosley Ches E 168 B6
Boslowick Corn 3 C7
Boslymon Corn 5 C11
Bosoughan Corn 5 C7
Bosporthennis Corn 1 B4
Bossall N Yorks 216 G4
Bossiney Corn 11 D7
Bossingham Kent 54 D6
Bossington Hants 47 G10
Kent 55 B8
Som 41 D11
Bostadh W Isles 304 D3
Bostock Green Ches W 167 B11
Boston Lincs 174 G4
Boston Long Hedges
Lincs 174 F5
Boston Spa W Yorks 206 D4
Boston West Lincs 174 F3
Boswednack Corn 1 B4
Boswin Corn 2 C5
Boswinger Corn 5 G9
Boswyn Corn 2 B5
Botallack Corn 1 C3
Botany Bay London 86 F3
Mon 79 E8
Botcherby Cumb 239 F10
Botcheston Leics 135 B9
Botesdale Suff 125 B10
Bothal Northumb 252 F6
Bothampstead W Berks 64 D4
Bothamsall Notts 187 G11
Bothel Cumb 229 D9
Bothenhampton Dorset 16 C5
Bothwell S Lnrk 268 D4
Bothy Highld 290 F4
Botley Bucks 85 E7
Hants 33 E8
Oxon 83 D7
Botloe's Green Glos 98 F4
Botolph Claydon Bucks 102 G4
Botolphs W Sus 35 F11
Bottacks Highld 300 C4
Botternell Corn 11 G11
Bottesford Leics 154 B6
N Lincs 199 F11
Bottisham Cambs 123 E10
Bottlesford Wilts 46 B6
Bottom Boat W Yorks 197 C11
Bottomcraig Fife 287 E7
Bottom House Staffs 169 E8
Bottomley W Yorks 196 D5
Bottom of Hutton Lancs 194 B3
Bottom o' th' Moor
Gtr Man 195 E7
Bottom Pond Kent 53 B11
Bottreaux Mill Devon 26 B4
Bottrells Close Bucks 85 G7
Botts Green Warks 134 E4
Botusfleming Corn 7 C8
Botwnnog Gwyn 144 C5
Bough Beech Kent 52 D3
Boughrood Powys 96 D2
Boughrood Brest Powys 96 D2
Boughspring Glos 79 F9
Boughton Ches W 166 B6
Lincs 173 F10
Norf 140 C3
Northants 120 D5
Notts 171 B11
Boughton Aluph Kent 54 D4
Boughton Corner Kent 54 D4
Boughton Green Kent 53 C9
Boughton Heath
Ches W 166 B6
Boughton Lees Kent 54 D4
Boughton Malherbe
Kent 53 D11
Boughton Monchelsea
Kent 53 C9
Boughton Street Kent 54 B5
Bougton End C Beds 103 D9
Boulby Redcar 226 B5
Bould Oxon 100 G4
Boulden Shrops 131 F10
Boulder Clough
W Yorks 196 C4
Bouldnor IoW 20 D3
Bouldon Shrops 131 F10
Boulmer Northumb 265 G7
Boulsdon Glos 98 G4
Boulston Pembs 73 C7
Boultenstone Aberds 292 B6
Boultham Lincs 173 B7
Boultham Moor Lincs 173 B7
Boulton Derbys 153 C7
Boulton Moor Derbys 153 C7
Boundary Leics 152 F6
Staffs 169 G7
Boundstone Sur 49 E10
Bountis Thorne Devon 24 D5
Bourn Cambs 122 F6
Bournbrook W Mid 133 G10
Bourne Lincs 155 E11
N Som 44 B3
Bourne End Beds 121 E10
Bucks 65 B11
C Beds 103 C9
Herts 85 D8
Bournemouth Bmouth 19 C7
Bournes Green Glos 80 E6
Sthend 70 B2
Worcs 117 C8
Bourne Vale W Mid 133 D11
Bourne Valley Poole 19 C7
Bournheath Worcs 117 C9
Bournmoor Durham 243 G8
Bournside Glos 99 G8
Bournstream Glos 80 G2
Bournville W Mid 133 G10
Bourton Bucks 102 E4
Dorset 45 G9
N Som 59 G11
Oxon 63 B8
Shrops 131 D11
Wilts 62 G4
Bourton on Dunsmore
Warks 119 C8
Bourton-on-the-Hill
Glos 100 E3
Bourton-on-the-Water
Glos 100 G3
Bourtreehill N Ayrs 257 B8
Bousd Argyll 288 C4
Bousta Shetland 313 H4
Boustead Hill Cumb 239 F7
Bouth Cumb 210 B6
Bouthwaite N Yorks 214 E2
Bouts Worcs 117 F10
Bovain Stirl 285 D9
Boveney Bucks 66 D2
Boveridge Dorset 31 E9
Boverton V Glam 58 F3
Bovey Tracey Devon 14 F2
Bovingdon Herts 85 E8
Bovingdon Green Bucks 65 B10
Herts 85 E8
Bovinger Essex 87 D8
Bovington Camp Dorset 18 D2
Bow Borders 271 G9
Devon 8 D6
Devon 26 G2
Orkney 314 G3
Oxon 82 G4
Bowbank Durham 232 G4
Bowbeck Suff 125 B8
Bow Brickhill M Keynes 103 E8
Bowbridge Glos 80 E5
Bowbrook Shrops 149 G9
Bow Broom S Yorks 187 B7
Bowburn Durham 234 D2
Bowcombe IoW 20 D5
Bow Common London 67 C11
Bowd Devon 15 C8
Bowden Borders 262 C3
Devon 8 F6
Dorset 30 C3
Bowden Hill Wilts 62 F2
Bowdens Som 28 B6
Bowderdale Cumb 222 E3
Bowdon Gtr Man 184 D3
Bower Highld 310 C6
Northumb 251 G7
Bower Ashton Bristol 60 E5
Bowerchalke Wilts 31 C8
Bower Heath Herts 85 B10
Bowerhill Wilts 62 G2
Bower Hinton Som 29 D7
Bowerhope Borders 261 E7
Bower House Tye Suff 107 C9
Bowermadden Highld 310 C6
Bowers Staffs 150 B6
Bowers Gifford Essex 69 B9
Bowershall Fife 279 C11
Bowertower Highld 310 C6
Bowes Durham 223 C9
Bowes Park London 86 G4
Bowgreave Lancs 202 E5
Bowgreen Gtr Man 184 D3
Bowhill Borders 261 D10
Fife 280 B4
Bowhouse Dumfries 238 D2
Bowhousebog or Liquo N
Lnrk 269 D7
Bowing Park Mers 182 D6
Bowismiln Borders 262 E2
Bowithick Corn 11 E9
Bowker's Green Lancs 194 G2
Bowland Bridge Cumb 211 B8
Bowldown Wilts 62 D2
Bowlee Gtr Man 195 F10
Bowlees Durham 232 F4
Bowler's Town E Sus 38 C6
Bowley Hereford 115 G10
Bowley Lane Hereford 98 C3
Bowley Town Hereford 115 G10
Bowlhead Green Sur 50 F2
Bowling W Dunb 277 G9
W Yorks 205 G9
Bowling Alley Hants 49 D9
Bowling Bank Wrex 166 F5
Bowling Green Corn 5 D10
Corn 12 G3
Glos 81 E8
Hants 19 B11
Shrops 150 D2
W Mid 133 F8
Worcs 116 G6
Bowlish Som 44 E6
Bowmans Kent 68 E4
Bowmanstead Cumb 220 F6
Bowmore Argyll 254 B4
Bowness-on-Solway
Cumb 238 E6
Bowness-on-Windermere
Cumb 221 F8
Bow of Fife Fife 287 F7
Bowridge Hill Dorset 30 B4
Bowrie-fauld Angus 287 C9
Bowsden Northumb 273 G9
Bowsey Hill Windsor 65 C10
Bowshank Borders 271 G9
Bowside Lodge Highld 310 C2
Bowston Cumb 221 F9
Bow Street Ceredig 128 G2
Norf 141 D10
Bowthorpe Norf 142 B3
Bowyer's Common Hants 34 B3
Box Glos 80 E5
Wilts 61 F10
Boxbush Glos 80 C2
Glos 98 G3
Box End Beds 103 B10
Boxford Suff 107 C9
W Berks 64 E2
Boxgrove W Sus 22 B6
Box Hill Sur 51 C7
Wilts 61 F10
Boxley Kent 53 B9
Boxmoor Herts 85 D9
Box's Shop Corn 24 G2
Boxted Essex 107 E9
Suff 124 G6
Boxted Cross Essex 107 E10
Boxted Heath Essex 107 E10
Box Trees W Mid 118 C2
Boxwell Glos 80 G4
Boxworth Cambs 122 E6
Boxworth End Cambs 123 D7
Boyatt Wood Hants 32 C6
Boyden End Suff 124 F4
Boyden Gate Kent 71 F8
Boyland Common Norf 141 G11
Boylestone Derbys 152 B3
Boylestonfield Derbys 152 B3
Boyndie Aberds 302 C6
Boyn Hill Windsor 65 C11
Boynton E Yorks 218 F2
Boysack Angus 287 C9
Angus 287 C10
Boys Hill Dorset 29 E11
Boys Village V Glam 58 F4
Boythorpe Derbys 186 G5
Boyton Corn 12 C2
Suff 109 B7
Wilts 46 F3
Boyton Cross Essex 87 D10
Boyton End Essex 106 E2
Suff 106 C4
Bozeat Northants 121 F8
Bozen Green Herts 105 F8
Braaid IoM 192 E4
Braal Castle Highld 310 C5
Brabling Green Suff 126 E5
Brabourne Kent 54 E5
Brabourne Lees Kent 54 E5
Brabster Highld 310 C7
Bracadale Highld 294 B5
Bracara Highld 295 F9
Braceborough Lincs 155 G11
Bracebridge Lincs 173 B7
Bracebridge Heath
Lincs 173 B7
Bracebridge Low Fields
Lincs 173 B7
Braceby Lincs 155 B10
Bracewell Lancs 204 D3
Bracken Bank W Yorks 204 F6
Brackenber Cumb 222 B4
Brackenbottom N Yorks 212 E6
Brackenfield Derbys 170 D5
Brackenhall W Yorks 197 D7
Bracken Hill W Yorks 197 C7
Brackenlands Cumb 229 B11
Bracken Park W Yorks 206 E3
Brackenthwaite Cumb 229 B11
Cumb 229 G9
N Yorks 205 C11
Brackla / Bragle
Bridgend 58 D2
Bracklamore Aberds 303 D8
Bracklesham W Sus 22 D4
Brackletter Highld 290 E3
Brackley Argyll 255 C8
Northants 101 D11
Brackloch Highld 307 G6
Bracknell Brack 65 F11
Braco Perth 286 G2
Bracobrae Moray 302 D5
Braco Castle Perth 286 F2
Bracon N Lincs 199 F9
Bracon Ash Norf 142 D3
Braco Park Aberds 303 C9
Bracorina Highld 295 F9
Bradaford Devon 12 C3
Bradbourne Derbys 170 E2
Bradbury Durham 234 F2
Bradda IoM 192 F2
Bradden Northants 102 B2
Braddock Corn 6 C3
Braddocks Hay Staffs 168 D5
Bradeley Stoke 168 E5
Bradeley Green Ches E 167 G8
Bradenham Bucks 84 F4
Norf 141 B8
Bradenstoke Wilts 62 D4
Brades Village W Mid 133 E9
Bradfield Devon 27 F9
Essex 108 E2
Norf 160 C5
W Berks 64 E6
Bradfield Combust Suff 125 F7
Bradfield Green
Ches E 167 D11
Bradfield Heath Essex 108 F2
Bradfield St Clare Suff 125 F8
Bradfield St George
Suff 125 E8
Bradford Corn 11 F8
Derbys 170 C2
Devon 24 F6
Gtr Man 184 B5
Northumb 264 C5
W Yorks 205 G9
Bradford Abbas Dorset 29 E9
Bradford Leigh Wilts 61 G10
Bradford-on-Avon
Wilts 61 G10
Bradford-on-Tone Som 27 C11
Bradford Peverell Dorset 17 C9
Bradgate S Yorks 186 C6
Bradiford Devon 40 G5
Brading IoW 21 D8
Bradley Derbys 170 F2
Glos 80 G3
Hants 48 E6
NE Lincs 201 F8
Staffs 151 F7
W Mid 133 D8
Wrex 166 E4
W Yorks 197 C7
Bradley Cross Som 44 C3
Bradley Fold Gtr Man 195 F9
Bradley Green Ches W 167 F8
Glos 80 G2
Som 43 F9
Warks 134 C5
Worcs 117 E9
Bradley in the Moors
Staffs 169 G9
Bradley Mills W Yorks 197 D7
Bradley Mount Ches E 184 F6
Bradley Stoke S Glos 60 C6
Bradlow Hereford 98 D4
Bradmore Notts 153 C11
W Mid 133 D7
Bradney Shrops 132 D5
Som 43 F10
Bradninch Devon 27 G8
Bradnock's Marsh
W Mid 118 B4
Bradnop Staffs 169 D8
Bradnor Green Hereford 114 F5
Bradpole Dorset 16 C5
Bradshaw Gtr Man 195 E8
Staffs 168 D6
W Yorks 196 E5
W Yorks 205 G7
Bradstone Devon 12 E3
Bradville M Keynes 102 C6
Bradwall Green Ches E 168 C3
Bradway S Yorks 186 E4
Bradwell Derbys 185 E11
Devon 40 E3
Essex 106 G6
M Keynes 102 D6
Norf 143 C10
Staffs 168 F4
Bradwell Common
M Keynes 102 D6
Bradwell Grove Oxon 82 D2
Bradwell Hills Derbys 185 E11
Bradwell on Sea Essex 89 D8
Bradwell Waterside
Essex 89 D7
Bradworthy Devon 24 E4
Bradworthy Cross Devon 24 E4
Brae Dumfries 237 B10
Highld 307 L3
Highld 309 J4
Shetland 312 G5
Braeantra Highld 300 B5
Braebuster Orkney 314 F5
Braedownie Angus 292 F4
Braeface Falk 278 E5
Braefield Highld 300 F4
Braefindon Highld 300 D6
Braegrum Perth 286 E4
Braehead Dumfries 236 D6
Orkney 314 B4
Orkney 314 F5
S Ayrs 257 E8
S Lnrk 259 C8
S Lnrk 267 D11
S Lnrk 269 E9
Stirl 278 C6
Braehead of Lunan
Angus 287 B10
Braehoulland Shetland 312 F4
Braehour Highld 310 D4
Braehungie Highld 310 F5
Braeintra Highld 295 B10
Braelangwell Lodge
Highld 309 K5
Braemar Aberds 292 D3
Braemore Highld 299 B11
Highld 310 F4
Brae of Achnahaird
Highld 307 H5
Brae of Boquhapple
Stirl 285 G10
Braepark Edin 280 F3
Brae Roy Lodge Highld 290 D5
Braeside Invclyd 276 F4
Braes of Enzie Moray 302 D3
Braes of Ullapool Highld 307 K6
Braeswick Orkney 314 C6
Braevallich Argyll 275 C10
Braewick Shetland 312 F4
Shetland 313 H5
Brafferton Darl 233 G11
N Yorks 215 E8
Brafield-on-the-Green
Northants 120 F6
Bragar W Isles 304 D4
Bragbury End Herts 104 G5
Bragenham Bucks 103 F8
Bragle / Brackla
Bridgend 58 D2
Bragleenmore Argyll 289 G11
Braichmelyn Gwyn 163 B10
Braichyfedw Powys 129 E7
Braid Edin 280 G4
Braides Lancs 202 C4
Braidfauld Glasgow 268 C2
Braidley N Yorks 213 C10
Braids Argyll 255 C8
Braidwood S Lnrk 268 F6
Braigh Chalasaigh
W Isles 296 D5
Braigo Argyll 274 G3
Brailsford Derbys 170 G3
Brailsford Green Derbys 170 G3
Braingortan Argyll 275 F11
Brain's Green Glos 79 D11
Brainshaugh Northumb 252 C6
Braintree Essex 106 G5
Braiseworth Suff 126 C2
Braishfield Hants 32 B5
Braiswick Essex 107 F9
Braithwaite Cumb 229 G10
S Yorks 198 E6
W Yorks 204 E6
Braithwell S Yorks 187 C8
Brakefield Green Norf 141 B10
Brakenhill W Yorks 198 D2
Bramber W Sus 35 E11
Bramblecombe Dorset 30 G3
Brambridge Hants 33 C7
Bramcote Notts 153 B10
Warks 135 F8
Bramcote Hills Notts 153 B10
Bramcote Mains Warks 135 F8
Bramdean Hants 33 B10
Bramerton Norf 142 C5
Bramfield Herts 86 B3
Suff 127 C7
Bramford Suff 108 B2
W Mid 133 E8
Bramhall Gtr Man 184 D5
Bramhall Moor Gtr Man 184 D6
Bramhall Park Gtr Man 184 D5
Bramham W Yorks 206 E4
Bramhope W Yorks 205 E11
Bramley Derbys 186 F6
Hants 48 B6
Sur 50 D4
S Yorks 187 C7
W Yorks 205 F10
Bramley Corner Hants 48 B6
Bramley Green Hants 49 B7
Bramley Head N Yorks 205 B8
Bramley Vale Derbys 171 B7
Bramling Kent 55 B8
Brampford Speke Devon 14 B4
Brampton Cambs 122 C4
Cumb 231 G9
Cumb 240 E2
Derbys 186 G5
Hereford 97 D8
Lincs 188 F4
Norf 160 E4
Suff 143 G8
S Yorks 198 G2
Brampton Abbotts
Hereford 98 F2
Brampton Ash Northants 136 F5
Brampton Bryan
Hereford 115 C7
Brampton en le Morthen
S Yorks 187 D7
Brampton Park Cambs 122 C4
Brampton Street Suff 143 G8
Bramshall Staffs 151 C11
Bramshaw Hants 32 D3
Bramshill Hants 65 G8
Bramshott Hants 49 G10
Bramwell Som 28 B6
Branatwatt Shetland 313 H4
Branault Highld 289 C7
Branbridges Kent 53 D7
Brancaster Norf 176 E3
Brancaster Staithe Norf 176 E3
Brancepeth Durham 233 D10
Branch End Northumb 242 E3
Branchill Moray 301 D10
Branchton Invclyd 276 F4
Brand End Lincs 174 F5
Branderburgh Moray 302 B2
Brandesburton E Yorks 209 D8
Brandeston Suff 126 E4
Brand Green Glos 98 F4
Hereford 98 C5
Brandhill Shrops 115 B8
Brandis Corner Devon 24 G6
Brandish Street Som 42 D2
Brandiston Norf 160 E2
Brandlingill Cumb 229 F8
Brandon Durham 233 D10
Lincs 172 F6
Northumb 264 F2
Suff 140 F5
Warks 119 B8
Brandon Bank Cambs 140 F2
Brandon Creek Norf 140 E2
Brandon Parva Norf 141 B11
Brandsby N Yorks 215 E11
Brands Hill Windsor 66 D4
Brandwood Shrops 149 D9
Brandwood End
W Mid 117 B11
Brandy Carr W Yorks 197 C10
Brandy Hole Essex 88 F4
Brandyquoy Orkney 314 G4
Brandy Wharf Lincs 189 B8
Brane Corn 1 D4
Bran End Essex 106 F3
Branksome Darl 224 B5
Poole 18 C6
Branksome Park Poole 19 C7
Bransbury Hants 48 E2
Bransby Lincs 188 F5
Branscombe Devon 15 D9
Bransford Worcs 116 G5
Bransgore Hants 19 B9
Branshill Clack 279 C7
Bransholme Hull 209 G8
Branson's Cross Worcs 117 C11
Branston Leics 154 D6
Lincs 173 B8
Staffs 152 E4
Branston Booths Lincs 173 B9
Branstone IoW 21 E7
Bransty Cumb 219 B9
Brant Broughton Lincs 172 E6
Brantham Suff 108 E2
Branthwaite Cumb 229 D11
Cumb 229 G7
Branthwaite Edge
Cumb 229 G7
Brantingham E Yorks 200 B2
Branton Northumb 264 F2
S Yorks 198 G6
Branton Green N Yorks 215 G8
Branxholme Borders 261 G11
Branxholm Park
Borders 261 G11
Branxton Northumb 263 B9
Brascote Leics 135 C8
Brassey Green Ches W 167 C8
Brassington Derbys 170 E2
Brasted Kent 52 C3
Brasted Chart Kent 52 C3
Brathens Aberds 293 D8
Bratoft Lincs 175 B7
Brattle Kent 54 G2
Brattleby Lincs 188 E6
Bratton Som 42 D2
Telford 150 G2
Wilts 46 C2
Bratton Clovelly Devon 12 C5
Bratton Fleming Devon 40 F6
Bratton Seymour Som 29 B11
Braughing Herts 105 F7
Braughing Friars Herts 105 G8
Braulen Lodge Highld 300 F2
Braunston Northants 119 D10
Braunstone Leics 135 C11
Braunstone Town
Leicester 135 C11
Braunston-in-Rutland
Rutland 136 B6
Braunton Devon 40 F3
Brawby N Yorks 216 D4
Brawith N Yorks 225 D10
Brawl Highld 310 C2
Brawlbin Highld 310 D4
Bray Windsor 66 D2
Braybrooke Northants 136 G5
Braydon Side Wilts 62 B4
Brayford Devon 41 G7
Brayfordhill Devon 41 G7
Brays Grove Essex 87 D7
Bray Shop Corn 12 G2
Braystones Cumb 219 D10
Brayswick Worcs 98 B6
Braythorn N Yorks 205 D10
Brayton N Yorks 207 G8
Braytown Dorset 18 D2
Bray Wick Windsor 65 D11
Braywoodside Windsor 65 D11
Brazacott Corn 11 C11
Brazenhill Staffs 151 E7
Brea Corn 4 G3
Breach Bath 60 G6
Kent 69 F10
W Sus 22 B3
Breachacha Castle
Argyll 288 D3
Breachwood Green
Herts 104 G2
Breacleit W Isles 304 E3
Breaden Heath Shrops 149 B8
Breadsall Derbys 153 B7
Breadsall Hilltop Derby 153 B7
Breadstone Glos 80 E2
Bread Street Glos 80 D4
Breage Corn 2 D4
Breakachy Highld 300 E4
Brealeys Devon 25 D8
Bream Glos 79 D10
Breamore Hants 31 D11
Bream's Meend Glos 79 D9
Brean Som 43 B9
Breanais W Isles 304 F1
Brearley W Yorks 196 B4
Brearton N Yorks 214 G6
Breascleit W Isles 304 E4
Breaston Derbys 153 C9
Brechfa Carms 93 E10
Brechin Angus 293 G7
Breckan Orkney 314 F2
Breckles Norf 141 E9
Breck of Cruan Orkney 314 E3
Breckrey Highld 298 C5
Brecks S Yorks 187 C7
Brecon Powys 95 F10
Bredbury Gtr Man 184 C6
Bredbury Green
Gtr Man 184 C6
Brede E Sus 38 D4
Bredenbury Hereford 116 F2
Bredfield Suff 126 G5
Bredgar Kent 69 G11
Bredhurst Kent 69 G9
Bredicot Worcs 117 G8
Bredon Worcs 99 D8
Bredon's Hardwick
Worcs 99 D8
Bredon's Norton Worcs 99 D8
Bredwardine Hereford 96 C6
Breedon on the Hill
Leics 153 E8
Breeds Essex 87 C11
Breedy Butts Lancs 202 E2
Breibhig W Isles 297 M2
W Isles 304 E6
Breich W Loth 269 C9
Breightmet Gtr Man 195 F8
Breighton E Yorks 207 G10
Breinton Hereford 97 D9
Breinton Common
Hereford 97 C9
Breiwick Shetland 313 J6
Brelston Green
Hereford 97 G11
Bremhill Wilts 62 E3
Bremhill Wick Wilts 62 E3
Bremirehoull Shetland 313 L6
Brenachoile Lodge Stirl 285 G8
Brenchley Kent 53 E7
Brenchoillie Argyll 284 G4
Brendon Devon 24 E5
Devon 24 F5
Devon 41 D9
Brenkley T&W 242 B6
Brent Corn 6 E4
Brent Eleigh Suff 107 B8
Brentford London 67 D7
Brentford End London 67 D7
Brentingby Leics 154 F5
Brent Knoll Som 43 C10
Brent Mill Devon 8 D3
Brent Pelham Herts 105 E8
Brentry Bristol 60 D5
Brentwood Essex 87 G9
Brenzett Kent 39 B8
Brenzett Green Kent 39 B8
Brereton Staffs 151 F11
Brereton Cross Staffs 151 F11
Brereton Green Ches E 168 C3
Brereton Heath Ches E 168 C4
Breretonhill Staffs 151 F11
Bressingham Norf 141 G11

Bressingham Common Norf. . . 141 G11
Bretby Derbys . . . 152 E5
Bretford Warks . . . 119 B8
Bretforton Worcs . . . 99 C11
Bretherdale Head Cumb. . . 221 E11
Bretherton Lancs . . . 194 C3
Brettabister Shetland . . . 313 H6
Brettenham Norf . . . 141 G8
 Suff . . . 125 G9
Bretton Derbys . . . 186 F2
 Flint . . . 166 C5
 Pboro. . . 138 C3
Brewer's End Essex . . . 105 G11
Brewers Green Norf . . . 142 G2
Brewer Street Sur . . . 51 C10
Brewlands Bridge Angus . . . 292 G3
Brewood Staffs . . . 133 B7
Briach Moray . . . 301 D10
Briants Puddle Dorset . . . 18 C2
Briar Hill Northants . . . 120 F4
Brick End Essex. . . 105 F11
Bricket Wood Herts. . . 85 E10
Brickfields Worcs. . . 117 F7
Brickhill Beds . . . 121 G11
Brick Hill Sur . . . 66 G3
Brick House End Essex. . . 105 F9
Brickhouses Ches E . . . 168 C3
Brick Houses S Yorks . . . 186 E4
Brick-kiln End Notts . . . 171 D9
Bricklehampton Worcs . . . 99 C9
Bride IoM . . . 192 B5
Bridekirk Cumb . . . 229 E8
Bridell Pembs . . . 92 C3
Bridestowe Devon . . . 12 D6
Brideswell Aberds . . . 302 F5
Bridford Devon . . . 14 D2
Bridfordmills Devon . . . 14 D2
Bridge Corn . . . 4 G3
 Corn . . . 55 C7
 Som . . . 28 F5
Bridge Ball Devon . . . 41 D8
Bridge End Beds . . . 121 G10
 Cumb . . . 230 B3
 Devon . . . 8 F3
 Durham . . . 232 D6
 Essex . . . 106 E3
 Flint . . . 166 D4
 Hereford . . . 98 B2
 Lincs . . . 156 B2
 Northumb . . . 241 D10
 Northumb . . . 241 E10
 Oxon . . . 83 G9
Bridge-End Shetland . . . 313 K5
Bridge End Sur . . . 50 E5
 Warks . . . 118 E5
 Worcs . . . 98 E6
Bridgefoot Aberds . . . 292 C6
 Angus . . . 287 D7
 Cumb . . . 229 F7
Bridge Green Essex . . . 105 D9
 Norf . . . 142 G2
Bridgehampton Som . . . 29 C9
Bridge Hewick N Yorks . . . 214 E6
Bridgehill Durham . . . 242 G3
Bridge Ho Argyll . . . 254 B4
Bridgeholm Green Derbys . . . 185 E8
Bridgehouse Gate N Yorks . . . 214 F3
Bridgelands Borders . . . 261 C11
Bridgemary Hants . . . 33 G9
Bridgemere Ches E . . . 168 F2
Bridgemont Derbys . . . 185 E8
Bridgend Aberds . . . 293 B7
 Aberds . . . 302 F5
 Angus . . . 293 G7
 Argyll . . . 255 D8
 Argyll . . . 274 G4
 Argyll . . . 275 D9
 Corn . . . 6 D2
 Cumb . . . 221 C7
 Devon . . . 7 F11
 Fife . . . 287 F7
 Glos . . . 80 E4
 Highld . . . 300 D3
 Invclyd . . . 276 F5
 Moray . . . 302 F3
 N Lnrk . . . 278 G3
 Pembs . . . 92 B3
 W Loth . . . 279 F10
Bridgend of Lintrathen Angus . . . 286 B6
Bridgend / Pen-y-Bont ar-ogwr Bridgend . . . 58 C2
Bridgeness Falk . . . 279 E10
Bridge of Alford Aberds . . . 293 B7
Bridge of Allan Stirl . . . 278 B5
Bridge of Avon Moray . . . 301 F11
 Moray . . . 301 G11
Bridge of Awe Argyll . . . 284 E4
Bridge of Balgie Perth . . . 285 C9
Bridge of Cally Perth . . . 286 B5
Bridge of Canny Aberds . . . 293 D8
Bridge of Craigisla Angus . . . 286 B6
Bridge of Dee Dumfries . . . 237 D9
Bridge of Don Aberdeen . . . 293 B11
Bridge of Dun Angus . . . 287 B10
Bridge of Dye Aberds . . . 293 E8
Bridge of Earn Perth . . . 286 F5
Bridge of Ericht Perth . . . 285 B9
Bridge of Feugh Aberds . . . 293 D9
Bridge of Forss Highld . . . 310 C4
Bridge of Gairn Aberds . . . 292 D5
Bridge of Gaur Perth . . . 285 B9
Bridge of Lyon Perth . . . 285 C11
Bridge of Muchalls Aberds . . . 293 D10
Bridge of Muick Aberds . . . 292 D5
Bridge of Oich Highld . . . 290 C5
Bridge of Orchy Argyll . . . 284 D6
Bridge of Waith Orkney . . . 314 E2
Bridge of Walls Shetland . . . 313 H4
Bridge of Weir Renfs . . . 267 B7
Bridge Reeve Devon . . . 25 E11
Bridgerule Devon . . . 24 G3
Bridges Corn . . . 5 D9
 Shrops . . . 131 D7
Bridge Sollers Hereford . . . 97 C8
Bridge Street Suff . . . 107 B7
Bridgeton Glasgow . . . 268 C2
Bridgetown Corn . . . 8 C6
 Devon . . . 8 C6
 Som . . . 42 G2
 Staffs . . . 133 B9
Bridge Town Warks . . . 118 G4
Bridge Trafford Ches W . . . 183 G7
Bridgham Norf . . . 141 F9
Bridgnorth Shrops . . . 132 E4

Bridgtown Staffs . . . 133 B9
Bridgwater Som . . . 43 F10
Bridlington E Yorks . . . 218 F3
Bridport Dorset . . . 16 C5
Bridstow Hereford . . . 97 G11
Brierfield Lancs . . . 204 F2
Brierholme Carr S Yorks . . . 199 E7
Brierley Glos . . . 79 B10
 Hereford . . . 115 F9
 S Yorks . . . 198 E2
Brierley Hill W Mid . . . 133 F8
Brierton Hrtlpl . . . 234 E5
Briery Cumb . . . 229 G11
Briery Hill Bl Gwent . . . 77 D11
Briestfield W Yorks . . . 197 D8
Brigflatts Cumb . . . 222 G2
Brigg N Lincs . . . 200 F4
Briggate Norf . . . 160 D6
Briggswath N Yorks . . . 227 D7
Brigham Cumb . . . 229 E7
 Cumb . . . 229 G11
 E Yorks . . . 209 C7
Brighouse W Yorks . . . 196 C6
Brighstone IoW . . . 20 E4
Brightgate Derbys . . . 170 D3
Brighthampton Oxon . . . 82 E5
Brightholmlee S Yorks . . . 186 B3
Brightley Devon . . . 13 B7
Brightling E Sus . . . 37 C11
Brightlingsea Essex . . . 89 B9
Brighton Brighton . . . 36 G4
 Corn . . . 5 E8
Brighton le Sands Mers . . . 182 B4
Brightons Falk . . . 279 F8
Brightside S Yorks . . . 186 D5
Brightwalton W Berks . . . 64 D2
Brightwalton Green W Berks . . . 64 D2
Brightwalton Holt W Berks . . . 64 D2
Brightwell Suff . . . 108 C4
Brightwell Baldwin Oxon . . . 83 F11
Brightwell cum Sotwell Oxon . . . 83 G9
Brigmerston Wilts . . . 47 D7
Brignall Durham . . . 223 C11
Brig o'Turk Stirl . . . 285 G9
Brigsley NE Lincs . . . 201 G9
Brigsteer Cumb . . . 211 B9
Brigstock Northants . . . 137 F8
Brill Bucks . . . 83 C11
 Corn . . . 2 D6
Brilley Hereford . . . 96 B5
Brilley Mountain Powys . . . 114 G5
Brimaston Pembs . . . 91 G8
Brimfield Hereford . . . 115 D10
Brimington Derbys . . . 186 G6
Brimington Common Derbys . . . 186 G6
Brimley Devon . . . 13 F11
 Devon . . . 28 G4
Brimpsfield Glos . . . 80 C6
Brimps Hill Glos . . . 79 B11
Brimpton W Berks . . . 64 G5
Brimpton Common W Berks . . . 64 G5
Brims Orkney . . . 314 H2
Brims Castle Highld . . . 310 B4
Brimscombe Glos . . . 80 E5
Brimsdown London . . . 86 F5
Brimstage Mers . . . 182 E4
Brinacory Highld . . . 295 F9
Brincliffe S Yorks . . . 186 D4
Brind E Yorks . . . 207 G10
Brindham Som . . . 44 E4
Brindister Shetland . . . 313 H4
 Shetland . . . 313 K6
Brindle Lancs . . . 194 C6
Brindle Heath Gtr Man . . . 195 G10
Brindley Ches E . . . 167 E9
Brindley Ford Stoke . . . 168 E5
Brindwoodgate Derbys . . . 186 F4
Brineton Staffs . . . 150 G6
Bringewood Forge Hereford . . . 115 C9
Bringhurst Leics . . . 136 E6
Bringsty Common Hereford . . . 116 F4
Brington Cambs . . . 121 B11
Brinian Orkney . . . 314 D4
Briningham Norf . . . 159 C10
Brinkhill Lincs . . . 190 G5
Brinkley Cambs . . . 124 G2
 Notts . . . 172 E2
Brinklow M Keynes . . . 103 D8
 Warks . . . 119 B8
Brinkworth Wilts . . . 62 C4
Brinmore Highld . . . 300 G6
Brinnington Gtr Man . . . 184 C6
Brinscall Lancs . . . 194 C6
Brinsea N Som . . . 60 G2
Brinsford Staffs . . . 133 B8
Brinsley Notts . . . 171 F7
Brinsop Hereford . . . 97 C8
Brinsworth S Yorks . . . 186 D6
Brinsworthy Devon . . . 41 G9
Brinton Norf . . . 159 B10
Brisco Cumb . . . 239 G10
Briscoe Cumb . . . 219 C10
Briscoerigg N Yorks . . . 205 C11
Brisley Norf . . . 159 E8
Brislington Bristol . . . 60 E6
Brissenden Green Kent . . . 54 F2
Bristnall Fields W Mid . . . 133 F9
Bristol Bristol . . . 60 E5
Briston Norf . . . 159 C11
Britain Bottom S Glos . . . 61 B9
Britannia Lancs . . . 195 C11
Britford Wilts . . . 31 B11
Brithdir Caerph . . . 77 E11
 Ceredig . . . 92 B6
 Gwyn . . . 146 F5
Brithem Bottom Devon . . . 27 E8
Briton Ferry / Llansawel Neath . . . 57 C8
Britten's Bath . . . 45 B7
Britwell Slough . . . 66 C3
Britwell Salome Oxon . . . 83 G11
Brixham Torbay . . . 9 D8
Brixton Devon . . . 7 E11
 London . . . 67 D10
Brixton Deverill Wilts . . . 45 F11
Brixworth Northants . . . 120 C4
Brize Norton Oxon . . . 82 D4
Broad Alley Worcs . . . 117 D7
Broad Blunsdon Swindon . . . 81 G11
Broadbottom Gtr Man . . . 185 C7
Broadbridge W Sus . . . 22 B4
Broadbridge Heath W Sus . . . 50 G6

Broad Campden Glos . . . 100 D3
Broad Carr W Yorks . . . 196 D5
Broad Chalke Wilts . . . 31 B8
Broad Clough Lancs . . . 195 C11
Broadclyst Devon . . . 14 B5
Broad Colney Herts . . . 85 E11
Broad Common Worcs . . . 117 D7
Broadfield Gtr Man . . . 195 E10
 Invclyd . . . 276 G6
 Lancs . . . 194 C4
 Lancs . . . 195 B8
 Pembs . . . 73 E10
 W Sus . . . 51 G9
Broadford Highld . . . 295 C8
Broad Ford Kent . . . 53 E8
Broadford Bridge W Sus . . . 35 C9
Broadgate Hants . . . 32 C6
Broadgrass Green Suff . . . 125 E9
Broad Green Cambs . . . 124 F3
 C Beds . . . 103 C9
 Essex . . . 105 D8
 Essex . . . 107 G2
 London . . . 67 F10
 Mers . . . 182 C6
 Suff . . . 124 F5
 Suff . . . 125 F11
 Worcs . . . 116 F5
 Worcs . . . 117 C9
Broadgreen Wood Herts . . . 86 D4
Broadhalgh Gtr Man . . . 195 E11
Broadham Green Sur . . . 51 C11
Broadhaugh Borders . . . 249 B10
Broadhaven Highld . . . 310 D7
Broad Haven / Aberllydan Pembs . . . 72 C5
Broadheath Gtr Man . . . 184 D3
Broad Heath Powys . . . 114 E6
 Staffs . . . 151 D7
 Worcs . . . 116 D3
Broadhembury Devon . . . 27 G10
Broadhempston Devon . . . 8 B6
Broad Hill Cambs . . . 123 B11
Broad Hinton Wilts . . . 62 D6
Broadholme Derbys . . . 170 F6
 Lincs . . . 188 G5
Broad Ings S Yorks . . . 208 C2
Broadland Row E Sus . . . 38 D4
Broadlands Devon . . . 14 G3
Broadlane Corn . . . 2 C4
Broad Lane Corn . . . 4 G3
Broad Lanes Shrops . . . 132 F5
Broadley Lancs . . . 195 D11
 Moray . . . 302 C3
Broadley Common Essex . . . 86 D6
Broadleys Aberds . . . 303 C8
Broad Marston Worcs . . . 100 B2
Broadmayne Dorset . . . 17 D10
Broad Meadow Staffs . . . 168 F4
Broadmeadows Borders . . . 261 C10
Broadmere Hants . . . 48 D6
Broadmoor Pembs . . . 73 D9
 Sur . . . 50 D6
Broadmoor Common Hereford . . . 98 D2
Broadmore Green Worcs . . . 116 G6
Broadoak Dorset . . . 16 B4
 Glos . . . 80 C2
 Hants . . . 33 G8
 Hants . . . 149 F9
 Wrex . . . 166 D5
Broad Oak Carms . . . 93 G11
 Cumb . . . 220 G2
 Dorset . . . 16 B3
 E Sus . . . 37 C10
 E Sus . . . 38 D4
 Hants . . . 49 C9
 Hereford . . . 97 G9
 Kent . . . 54 F4
 Kent . . . 71 G7
 Mers . . . 183 B8
 Shrops . . . 132 F5
Broadoak End Herts . . . 86 C4
Broad Oak Park Gtr Man . . . 195 G9
Broad Parkham Devon . . . 24 C5
Broadplat Oxon . . . 65 C8
Broadrashes Moray . . . 302 D4
Broadrock Glos . . . 79 F8
Broadsea Aberds . . . 303 C9
Broad's Green Essex . . . 87 C11
 Essex . . . 62 F3
Broadshard Som . . . 28 E6
Broadstairs Kent . . . 71 F11
Broadstone Kent . . . 53 D11
 Mon . . . 79 E8
 Poole . . . 18 B6
 Shrops . . . 131 F10
Broad Street E Sus . . . 23 C8
 Kent . . . 53 B10
 Kent . . . 54 E6
 Kent . . . 55 E7
 Medway . . . 69 E9
 Suff . . . 107 C9
 Wilts . . . 46 B6
Broad Street Green Essex . . . 88 D5
Broad Tenterden Kent . . . 53 G11
Broad Town Wilts . . . 62 D5
Broadwas Worcs . . . 116 F5
Broadwater Herts . . . 104 G4
Broadwater Down Kent . . . 52 F5
Broadwaters Worcs . . . 116 B6
Broadwath Cumb . . . 239 F11
Broadway Carms . . . 74 D3
 Carms . . . 74 D5
 Pembs . . . 72 C5
 Som . . . 28 D4
 Som . . . 127 B7
 Suff . . . 126 B5
 Worcs . . . 99 D11
Broadway Lands Hereford . . . 97 E11
Broadwell Glos . . . 79 C9
 Glos . . . 100 F4
 Oxon . . . 82 E3
 Warks . . . 119 D9
Broadwey Dorset . . . 17 E9
Broadwindsor Dorset . . . 28 G6
Broadwood Kelly Devon . . . 25 F10
Broadwoodwidger Devon . . . 12 D4
Brobury Hereford . . . 96 C6
Brochel Highld . . . 298 E5
Brochroy Argyll . . . 284 D4
Brock Lancs . . . 202 E6
Brockamin Worcs . . . 116 G5
Brockbridge Hants . . . 33 D10
Brockdish Norf . . . 126 B4
Brockencote Worcs . . . 117 C7
Brockenhurst Hants . . . 32 G4
Brocketsbrae S Lnrk . . . 259 B8
Brockfield Devon . . . 28 F4
Brockford Green Suff . . . 126 D2

Brockford Street Suff . . . 126 D2
Brockhall Northants . . . 120 E2
Brockhall Village Lancs . . . 203 F10
Brockham Sur . . . 51 D7
Brockham End Bath . . . 61 F8
Brockham Park Sur . . . 51 D8
Brockhampton Glos . . . 99 B8
 Glos . . . 99 G10
 Hants . . . 22 B2
 Hereford . . . 97 E11
Brockhampton Green Dorset . . . 30 F2
Brockhill Borders . . . 261 E9
Brock Hill Essex . . . 88 F2
Brockholes W Yorks . . . 197 E7
Brockhollands Glos . . . 79 D10
Brockhurst Derbys . . . 170 C4
 Hants . . . 33 G10
 Warks . . . 135 G9
Brocklebank Cumb . . . 230 C2
Brocklehirst Dumfries . . . 238 C3
Brocklesby Lincs . . . 200 E6
Brockley London . . . 67 E11
 N Som . . . 60 F3
Brockley Corner Suff . . . 124 C6
Brockley Green Suff . . . 106 B4
 Suff . . . 124 G6
Brockleymoor Cumb . . . 230 D5
Brockloch Dumfries . . . 246 D2
Brockmanton Hereford . . . 115 F10
Brockmoor W Mid . . . 133 F8
Brockscombe Devon . . . 12 C5
Brock's Green Hants . . . 64 G4
Brock's Watering Norf . . . 142 E2
Brockton Shrops . . . 130 C6
 Shrops . . . 130 F6
 Shrops . . . 131 E11
 Shrops . . . 132 C4
 Shrops . . . 132 E5
 Staffs . . . 150 B5
 Telford . . . 150 F4
Brockweir Glos . . . 79 E8
Brockwell Som . . . 42 E2
Brockwood Hants . . . 33 B11
Brockworth Glos . . . 80 B5
Brocton Corn . . . 5 B10
 Staffs . . . 151 F9
Brodick N Ayrs . . . 256 B2
Brodie Moray . . . 301 D10
Brodsworth S Yorks . . . 198 F4
Brogaig Highld . . . 298 C4
Brogborough C Beds . . . 103 D9
Broke Hall Suff . . . 108 C3
Brokenborough Wilts . . . 62 B2
Broken Cross Ches E . . . 184 G5
 Ches W . . . 183 G11
Broken Green Herts . . . 105 G8
Bromborough Mers . . . 182 E4
Bromborough Pool Mers . . . 182 D4
Bromdon Shrops . . . 132 G2
Brome Suff . . . 126 B2
Brome Street Suff . . . 126 B3
Bromeswell Suff . . . 126 G6
Bromfield Cumb . . . 229 B9
 Shrops . . . 115 B9
Bromford W Mid . . . 134 E2
Bromham Beds . . . 121 G10
 Wilts . . . 62 G3
Bromley Herts . . . 105 G8
 London . . . 67 C11
 London . . . 68 F2
 Shrops . . . 132 D4
 S Yorks . . . 149 D8
 W Mid . . . 133 F8
Bromley Common London . . . 68 F2
Bromley Cross Essex . . . 107 F11
 Gtr Man . . . 195 E8
Bromley Green Kent . . . 54 F3
Bromley Hall Staffs . . . 150 C5
Bromley Heath S Glos . . . 61 D7
Bromley Park London . . . 67 F11
Bromley Wood Staffs . . . 152 E2
Bromlow Shrops . . . 130 C6
Brompton London . . . 67 D9
 Medway . . . 69 F9
 N Yorks . . . 217 C8
 N Yorks . . . 225 F7
 Notts . . . 171 B9
Brompton-by-Sawdon N Yorks . . . 217 C9
Brompton-on-Swale N Yorks . . . 224 F4
Brompton Ralph Som . . . 42 G5
Brompton Regis Som . . . 42 G3
Bromsash Hereford . . . 98 G2
Bromsberrow Glos . . . 98 E4
Bromsberrow Heath Glos . . . 98 E4
Bromsgrove Worcs . . . 117 C9
Bromstead Common Staffs . . . 150 F5
Bromstead Heath Staffs . . . 150 F6
Bromstone Kent . . . 71 F11
Bromyard Hereford . . . 116 G3
Bromyard Downs Hereford . . . 116 F3
Bronaber Gwyn . . . 146 C4
Broncroft Shrops . . . 131 F10
Brondesbury London . . . 67 C8
Brondesbury Park London . . . 67 C8
Brongest Ceredig . . . 92 B6
Brongwyn Ceredig . . . 92 B5
Bronington Wrex . . . 149 B9
Bronllys Powys . . . 96 D2
Bronnant Ceredig . . . 112 D2
Bronwydd Ceredig . . . 93 C7
Bronwydd Arms Carms . . . 93 G8
Bronydd Powys . . . 96 B4
Bronygarth Shrops . . . 148 B5
Brook Carms . . . 74 D3
 Devon . . . 12 G5
 Devon . . . 14 C2
 Hants . . . 32 B4
 Hants . . . 32 E3
 IoW . . . 20 E3
 Kent . . . 54 E5
 Sur . . . 50 E3
 Sur . . . 50 F2
Brook Bottom Gtr Man . . . 185 D7
 Gtr Man . . . 196 G3
 Lancs . . . 202 E6
Brook End Beds . . . 121 E11
 Beds . . . 121 C10
 C Beds . . . 103 B9
 Herts . . . 104 F5
 M Keynes . . . 103 C8
 Cambs . . . 122 B5
 Wilts . . . 61 C10
Brookend Glos . . . 79 E11

Flint . . . 166 C4
 Hants . . . 47 G10
 Lancs . . . 203 G7
 Lancs . . . 202 F6
 M Keynes . . . 103 C7
 N Lincs . . . 200 F3
 Northants . . . 120 B6
 N Yorks . . . 204 C4
 N Yorks . . . 216 E5
 Orkney . . . 314 B4
 Oxon . . . 101 D8
 Shrops . . . 131 E11
 Shrops . . . 132 E6
 Staffs . . . 150 C5
 Staffs . . . 58 G2
Brookfield Derbys . . . 185 B8
 Lancs . . . 203 G7
 Lancs . . . 202 E6
 Mbro . . . 225 B9
 Renfs . . . 267 C8
Brookfoot W Yorks . . . 196 C6
Brookgreen IoW . . . 20 E3
Brook Green London . . . 67 D8
 Suff . . . 125 C7
Brookhampton Oxon . . . 83 F10
 Som . . . 29 B10
 Som . . . 131 E11
Brook Hill Hants . . . 153 C11
Brookhouse Blkburn . . . 203 F11
 Ches E . . . 184 F6
 Denb . . . 165 B9
 Lancs . . . 211 G10
 S Yorks . . . 187 D8
 W Yorks . . . 196 B5
Brookhouse Green Ches E . . . 168 C4
Brookhouses Derbys . . . 185 E8
 Staffs . . . 169 G7
Brookhurst Mers . . . 182 E4
Brookland Kent . . . 39 B7
Brooklands Dumfries . . . 237 B10
 Gtr Man . . . 184 C3
 Shrops . . . 167 G8
 Sur . . . 66 G5
Brookleigh Devon . . . 14 B5
Brookmans Park Herts . . . 86 E2
Brookpits W Sus . . . 35 G8
Brook Place Sur . . . 66 G3
Brook's End Kent . . . 71 F9
Brooks Green W Sus . . . 35 C10
Brookside Brack . . . 66 E2
 Derbys . . . 186 G5
Brook Street Essex . . . 87 G9
 Kent . . . 52 D5
 Kent . . . 54 G2
 Suff . . . 106 B6
 W Sus . . . 36 B4
Brookthorpe Glos . . . 80 C4
Brookville Norf . . . 140 D4
Brookwood Sur . . . 50 B2
Broom Beds . . . 104 C3
 Cumb . . . 231 G9
 Devon . . . 28 G4
 E Renf . . . 267 D10
 Fife . . . 287 G7
 S Yorks . . . 186 C5
 Warks . . . 117 G11
Broome Norf . . . 143 E7
 Shrops . . . 131 D10
 Shrops . . . 131 G8
 Worcs . . . 117 B8
Broomedge Warr . . . 184 D2
Broome Park Northumb . . . 264 G4
Broomer's Corner W Sus . . . 35 C10
Broomershill W Sus . . . 35 D9
Broomfield Aberds . . . 303 F9
 Cumb . . . 230 B2
 Essex . . . 88 C2
 Kent . . . 54 C3
 Kent . . . 71 F7
 Som . . . 43 G8
Broomfields Shrops . . . 149 F8
Broomfleet E Yorks . . . 199 B11
Broom Green Norf . . . 159 E9
Broomhall Ches E . . . 167 F10
 Windsor . . . 66 F3
Broomhall Green Ches E . . . 167 F10
Broomham E Sus . . . 23 C8
Broomhaugh Northumb . . . 242 E3
Broomhill Borders . . . 261 D11
 Bristol . . . 60 D6
 Highld . . . 301 G9
 Kent . . . 39 C8
 Norf . . . 140 C2
 N Yorks . . . 217 C8
 S Yorks . . . 186 B4
Broom Hill Bristol . . . 60 E6
 Dorset . . . 31 G8
 Durham . . . 242 G4
 Kent . . . 68 F3
 Som . . . 43 G10
 Som . . . 117 B8
Broomhill Bank E Sus . . . 52 E5
Broomholm Norf . . . 160 C6
Broomhouse Glasgow . . . 268 C3
Broomlands N Ayrs . . . 257 B8
Broomley Northumb . . . 242 E2
Broompark Durham . . . 233 C10
Broom's Barn Suff . . . 124 E5
Broom's Green Glos . . . 98 E4
Broomsgrove E Sus . . . 38 E4
Broomston Norf . . . 158 D6
Broom Street Kent . . . 70 G4
Brora Highld . . . 311 J3
Broseley Shrops . . . 132 C3
Brotherhouse Bar Lincs . . . 156 G5
Brotheridge Green Worcs . . . 98 C6
Brotherlee Durham . . . 232 D4
Brotherstone Borders . . . 262 B4
Brothertoft Lincs . . . 174 F3
Brotherton N Yorks . . . 198 B3
Brothybeck Cumb . . . 230 C2
Brotton Redcar . . . 226 B3
Broubster Highld . . . 310 C4
Brough Cumb . . . 222 C5
 Derbys . . . 185 E11
 E Yorks . . . 200 B2
 Highld . . . 310 B6
 Notts . . . 172 D4
 Orkney . . . 314 B4
 Orkney . . . 314 F3
 Shetland . . . 312 F7
 Shetland . . . 312 G7
 Shetland . . . 313 H6
 Shetland . . . 313 J7
Broughall Shrops . . . 167 G9
Brough Lodge Shetland . . . 312 D7
Brough Sowerby Cumb . . . 222 C5
Broughton Borders . . . 260 B4
 Bucks . . . 84 C5
 Cambs . . . 122 B5
 Flint . . . 166 C4

Neath . . . 57 C10
 Powys . . . 130 C3
 Rhondda . . . 76 D6
 Shrops . . . 130 D5
 W Berks . . . 64 E4
Bucklandwharf Bucks . . . 84 C5
Bucklebury W Berks . . . 64 E5
Bucklebury Alley W Berks . . . 64 E4
Bucklegate Lincs . . . 156 B6
Buckleigh Devon . . . 24 B6
Bucklerheads Angus . . . 287 D8
Bucklers Hard Hants . . . 20 B4
Bucklesham Suff . . . 108 C4
Buckley / Bwcle Flint . . . 166 C3
Buckley Green Warks . . . 118 D3
Buckley Hill Mers . . . 182 B4
Buckminster Leics . . . 155 E7
Buckmoorend Bucks . . . 84 E4
Bucknall Lincs . . . 173 B11
 Stoke . . . 168 F6
Bucknell Oxon . . . 101 F11
 Shrops . . . 115 C7
Buckoak Ches W . . . 183 G8
Buckover S Glos . . . 79 G11
Buckpool Moray . . . 302 C4
 W Mid . . . 133 F7
Buckridge Worcs . . . 116 C4
Bucksburn Aberdeen . . . 293 C10
Buck's Cross Devon . . . 24 C4
Bucks Green W Sus . . . 50 G5
Buckshaw Village Lancs . . . 194 C5
Bucks Hill Herts . . . 85 E9
Bucks Horn Oak Hants . . . 49 E10
Buckskin Hants . . . 48 C6
Buck's Mills Devon . . . 24 C5
Buckton E Yorks . . . 218 E3
 Hereford . . . 115 C7
 Northumb . . . 264 B3
Buckton Vale Gtr Man . . . 196 G3
Buckworth Cambs . . . 122 B2
Budbrooke Warks . . . 118 D5
Budby Notts . . . 171 B10
Buddbrake Shetland . . . 312 B6
Buddileigh Staffs . . . 168 F3
Budd's Titson Corn . . . 24 F2
Bude Corn . . . 24 F2
Budge's Shop Corn . . . 5 D9
Budlake Devon . . . 14 B5
Budle Northumb . . . 264 B5
Budleigh Salterton Devon . . . 15 E7
Budlett's Common E Sus . . . 37 C7
Budock Water Corn . . . 3 C7
Buersil Head Gtr Man . . . 196 E2
Buerton Ches E . . . 167 G11
Buffler's Holt Bucks . . . 102 C3
Bufton Leics . . . 135 B8
Bugbrooke Northants . . . 120 F3
Bugford Devon . . . 9 E7
Buglawton Ches E . . . 168 C5
Bugle Corn . . . 5 D10
Bugle Gate Worcs . . . 116 D6
Bugley Dorset . . . 30 C3
 Wilts . . . 45 E11
Bugthorpe E Yorks . . . 207 B11
Building End Essex . . . 105 D7
Buildwas Shrops . . . 132 C2
Builth Road Powys . . . 113 G10
Builth Wells Powys . . . 113 G10
Buirgh W Isles . . . 305 J2
Bulbourne Herts . . . 84 C6
Bulby Lincs . . . 155 D11
Bulcote Notts . . . 171 G11
Buldoo Highld . . . 310 C3
Bulford Wilts . . . 47 E7
Bulford Camp Wilts . . . 47 E7
Bulkeley Ches E . . . 167 E8
Bulkeley Hall Shrops . . . 168 G2
Bulkington Warks . . . 135 F7
 Wilts . . . 46 B2
Bulkworthy Devon . . . 24 E5
Bullamoor N Yorks . . . 225 G7
Bull Bay / Porthllechog Anglesey . . . 178 C6
Bullbridge Derbys . . . 170 E5
Bullbrook Brack . . . 65 F11
Bulleign Kent . . . 53 G11
Bullenhill Wilts . . . 45 B11
Bulley Glos . . . 80 B3
Bullgill Cumb . . . 229 D7
Bull Hill Hants . . . 20 B2
Bullinghope Hereford . . . 97 D10
Bullington Hants . . . 48 E3
 Lincs . . . 189 F9
Bull's Hill Hereford . . . 97 G11
Bullockstone Kent . . . 71 F7
Bulls Cross London . . . 86 F4
Bulls Green Norf . . . 143 D8
Bull's Green Herts . . . 86 B3
Bullwood Argyll . . . 276 G3
Bullyhole Bottom Mon . . . 79 F7
Bulmer Essex . . . 106 C6
 N Yorks . . . 216 F3
Bulmer Tye Essex . . . 106 D6
Bulphan Thurrock . . . 68 B6
Bulstrode Herts . . . 85 E8
Bulthy Shrops . . . 148 G6
Bulverhythe E Sus . . . 38 F3
Bulwark Aberds . . . 303 E9
 Mon . . . 79 G8
Bulwell Nottingham . . . 171 G8
Bulwell Forest Nottingham . . . 171 F8
Bulwick Northants . . . 137 E7
Bumble's Green Essex . . . 86 D6
Bun Abhainn Eadarra W Isles . . . 305 H3
Bunacaimb Highld . . . 295 G8
Buna'Mhuilinn W Isles . . . 297 K3
Bunarkaig Highld . . . 290 E3
Bunbury Ches E . . . 167 D9
Bunbury Heath Ches E . . . 167 D9
Bunce Common Sur . . . 51 D8
Bunchrew Highld . . . 300 E6
Bundalloch Highld . . . 295 C10
Buness Shetland . . . 312 C8
Bunessan Argyll . . . 288 G5
Bungay Suff . . . 142 G6
Bunkers Hill Gtr Man . . . 184 D6
 Oxon . . . 83 B7
Bunker's Hill Cambs . . . 139 B8
 Lincs . . . 174 E3
 Lincs . . . 188 G6
 Norf . . . 142 B7
 Suff . . . 143 C10
Bunloit Highld . . . 300 G5
Bun Loyne Highld . . . 290 C4
Bunnahabhain Argyll . . . 274 F5
Bunny Notts . . . 153 D11
Bunny Hill Notts . . . 153 D11
Bunree Highld . . . 290 G2
Bunroy Highld . . . 290 E4
Bunsley Bank Ches E . . . 167 G11

Bunstead Hants . . . 32 C6
Buntait Highld . . . 300 F3
Buntingford Herts . . . 105 F7
Bunting's Green Essex . 106 E6
Bunwell Norf . . . 142 E2
Bunwell Bottom Norf . . 142 D2
Buoltach Highld . . . 310 F5
Burbage Derbys . . . 185 G8
　Leics . . . 135 E8
　Wilts . . . 63 G8
Burcher Hereford . . . 114 E6
Burchett's Green
　Windsor . . . 65 C10
Burcombe Wilts . . . 46 G5
Burcot Oxon . . . 83 F9
　Worcs . . . 117 C9
　Som . . . 44 D4
Burdiehouse Edin . . . 270 B5
Burdon T&W . . . 243 G9
Burdonshill V Glam . . . 58 E6
Burcote Shrops . . . 132 D4
　Bucks . . . 103 G7
　Som . . . 44 D4
Bures Suff . . . 107 E8
Bures Green Suff . . . 107 D8
Burford . . . 167 G10
　Devon . . . 24 C4
　Oxon . . . 82 C3
　Shrops . . . 115 D11
　Som . . . 44 E5
Burg Argyll . . . 288 E5
　Argyll . . . 288 G6
Burgar Orkney . . . 314 D3
Burgate Hants . . . 31 D11
　Suff . . . 125 B11
Burgates Hants . . . 34 B3
Burgedin Powys . . . 148 G4
Burge End Herts . . . 104 E2
Burgess Hill W Sus . . . 36 D4
Burgh Suff . . . 126 G4
Burgh by Sands Cumb . 239 F8
Burgh Castle Norf . . . 143 B9
Burghclere Hants . . . 64 G3
Burghclere Common
　Hants . . . 64 G3
Burghead Moray . . . 301 C10
Burghfield W Berks . . . 65 F7
Burghfield Common
　W Berks . . . 64 F6
Burghfield Hill W Berks . .65 F7
Burgh Heath Sur . . . 51 B8
Burgh Hill E Sus . . . 23 C8
　E Sus . . . 38 B2
Burghill Hereford . . . 97 C9
Burgh le Marsh Lincs . . 175 B8
Burgh Muir Aberds . . . 293 B9
　Aberds . . . 303 G7
Burgh next Aylsham
　Norf . . . 160 D4
Burgh on Bain Lincs . . . 190 D2
Burgh St Margaret /
　Fleggburgh Norf . . . 161 G8
Burgh St Peter Norf . . 143 E9
Burgh Stubbs Norf . . . 159 C10
Burghwallis S Yorks . . 198 E4
Burgois Corn . . . 10 G4
Burham Kent . . . 69 G8
Buriton Hants . . . 34 C2
Burland Ches E . . . 167 E10
Burlawn Corn . . . 10 G5
Burleigh Brack . . . 65 E11
　Glos . . . 80 E5
Burlescombe Devon . . . 27 D9
Burleston Dorset . . . 17 C11
Burlestone Devon . . . 8 F6
Burley Hants . . . 32 G2
　Rutland . . . 155 G7
　Shrops . . . 131 G9
　W Yorks . . . 205 G11
Burley Beacon Hants . . 32 G2
Burley Gate Hereford . . 97 B11
Burley in Wharfedale
　W Yorks . . . 205 D9
Burley Lawn Hants . . . 32 G2
Burley Lodge Hants . . .32 F2
Burley Street Hants . . . 32 G2
Burley Woodhead
　W Yorks . . . 205 E9
Burlinch Som . . . 28 B3
Burlingham Green Norf. 161 G7
Burlingjobb Powys . . . 114 F5
Burlish Park Worcs . . . 116 C6
Burlorne Tregoose Corn . .5 B10
Burlow E Sus . . . 23 D8
Burlton Shrops . . . 149 D9
Burmantofts W Yorks . . 206 G2
Burmarsh Hereford . . . 97 B10
　Kent . . . 54 G5
Burmington Warks . . . 100 D5
Burn N Yorks . . . 198 B5
Burnage Gtr Man . . . 184 C5
Burnard's Ho Devon . . . 24 G4
Burnaston Derbys . . . 152 C5
Burnbank S Lnrk . . . 268 D4
Burn Bridge N Yorks . . 206 C2
Burnby E Yorks . . . 208 D2
Burncross S Yorks . . . 186 B4
Burndell W Sus . . . 35 G7
Burnden Gtr Man . . . 195 F8
Burnedge Gtr Man . . . 196 E2
Burnend Aberds . . . 303 E8
Burneside Cumb . . . 221 F10
Burness Orkney . . . 314 B6
Burneston N Yorks . . . 214 B6
Burnett Bath . . . 61 F7
Burnfoot Borders . . . 261 G10
　Borders . . . 262 F2
　Dumfries . . . 239 C7
　Dumfries . . . 247 E11
　E Ayrs . . . 245 B10
　N Lnrk . . . 268 B5
　Perth . . . 286 G3
Burngreave S Yorks . . . 186 D5
Burnham Bucks . . . 66 C2
　N Lincs . . . 200 D5
Burnham Deepdale
　Norf . . . 176 A4
Burnham Green Herts . .86 B3
Burnham Market Norf. . 176 E4
Burnham Norton Norf . 176 E4
Burnham-on-Crouch
　Essex . . . 89 F7
Burnham-on-Sea Som . 43 D10
Burnham Overy Staithe
　Norf . . . 176 E4
Burnham Overy Town
　Norf . . . 176 E4
Burnham Thorpe Norf . 176 E5
Burnhead Aberds . . . 293 D10
　Borders . . . 262 F2
　Dumfries . . . 247 D9
　Dumfries . . . 247 G10
　S Ayrs . . . 244 C6
Burnhervie Aberds . . . 293 B9
Burnhill Green Staffs . . 132 C5
Burnhope Durham . . . 233 B9
Burnhouse N Ayrs . . . 267 E7

Burnhouse Mains
　Borders . . . 271 F8
Burniere Corn . . . 10 G5
Burniestrype Moray . . . 302 C3
Burniston N Yorks . . . 227 G10
Burnley Lancs . . . 204 G2
Burnley Lane Lancs . . . 204 G2
Burnley Wood Lancs . . 204 G2
Burnmouth Borders . . . 273 C9
Burn Naze Lancs . . . 202 E2
Burnmouth Durham . . . 242 F5
Burnopfield Durham . . 242 F5
Burnrigg Cumb . . . 239 F11
Burnsall N Yorks . . . 213 G10
Burnside Aberds . . . 303 E8
　Angus . . . 287 B9
　E Ayrs . . . 258 G3
　Fife . . . 286 G5
　Perth . . . 286 G5
　Shetland . . . 312 F4
　S Lnrk . . . 268 C2
　W Loth . . . 279 G11
Burnside of Duntrune
　Angus . . . 287 D8
Burnstone Devon . . . 24 C4
Burnswark Dumfries . . 238 B5
Burnt Ash Glos . . . 80 E5
Burntcommon Sur . . . 50 C4
Burntheath Derbys . . . 152 C4
Burnt Heath Derbys . . 186 F2
　Essex . . . 107 F11
Burnt Hill W Berks . . . 64 E5
Burnthouse Corn . . . 3 B7
Burnt Houses Durham . 233 G8
Burntisland Fife . . . 280 D4
Burnt Mills Essex . . . 88 G2
Burnt Oak E Sus . . . 37 B8
　London . . . 86 G2
Burnt Tree W Mid . . . 133 E9
Burnturk Fife . . . 287 G7
Burntwood Staffs . . . 133 B11
Burntwood Green
　Staffs . . . 133 B11
Burntwood Pentre Flint. 166 C3
Burnt Yates N Yorks . . 214 G5
Burnworthy Som . . . 27 D11
Burpham Sur . . . 50 C4
　W Sus . . . 35 F8
Burradon Northumb . . 251 B11
　T&W . . . 243 C7
Burrafirth Shetland . . . 312 B8
Burraland Shetland . . . 312 F5
　Shetland . . . 313 J5
Burras Corn . . . 2 C5
Burrastow Shetland . . 313 J4
Burraton Corn . . . 7 D8
Burraton Coombe Corn . 7 D8
Burravoe Shetland . . . 312 F7
　Shetland . . . 313 J4
Burray Village Orkney . 314 G4
Burreldales Aberds . . . 303 F7
Burrells Cumb . . . 222 B3
Burrelton Perth . . . 286 D6
Burridge Devon . . . 28 F4
　Devon . . . 40 F5
　Hants . . . 33 E8
Burrigill Highld . . . 310 F6
Burrill N Yorks . . . 214 B4
Burringham N Lincs . . 199 F10
Burrington Devon . . . 25 D10
　Hereford . . . 115 C9
　N Som . . . 44 B3
Burrough End Cambs . . 124 F2
Burrough Green Cambs . 124 F2
Burrough on the Hill
　Leics . . . 154 G5
Burroughs Grove Bucks . 65 B10
Burroughston Orkney . . 314 D5
Burrow Devon . . . 28 G5
　Som . . . 28 B6
　Som . . . 42 E2
Burrowbridge Som . . . 43 G11
Burrow-bridge Som . . .28 B5
Burrowhill Sur . . . 66 G3
Burrows Cross Sur . . . 50 D5
Burrowsmoor Holt
　Notts . . . 172 G2
Burrswood Kent . . . 52 F4
Burry Swansea . . . 56 C3
Burry Green Swansea . . 56 C3
Burry Port / Porth Tywyn
　Carms . . . 74 E6
Burscott Devon . . . 24 C4
Burscough Lancs . . . 194 E2
Burscough Bridge Lancs 194 E2
Bursdon Devon . . . 24 D3
Bursea E Yorks . . . 208 G2
Burshill E Yorks . . . 209 D7
Bursledon Hants . . . 33 F7
Burslem Stoke . . . 168 F5
Burstall Suff . . . 107 C11
Burstallhill Suff . . . 107 B11
Burstock Dorset . . . 28 G6
Burston Devon . . . 26 G2
　Norf . . . 142 G2
　Staffs . . . 151 C8
Burstow Sur . . . 51 E10
Burstwick E Yorks . . . 201 B8
Burtersett N Yorks . . . 213 B7
Burtholme Cumb . . . 240 E2
Burthorpe Suff . . . 124 E5
Burthwaite Cumb . . . 230 B4
Burtle Som . . . 43 E11
Burtle Hill Som . . . 43 E11
Burtoft Lincs . . . 156 B5
Burton Ches W . . . 167 C8
　Ches W . . . 182 G4
　Dorset . . . 17 C9
　Dorset . . . 19 C9
　Lincs . . . 189 G7
　Northumb . . . 264 C5
　Pembs . . . 73 D7
　Som . . . 29 E8
　Som . . . 43 E7
　V Glam . . . 58 F4
　Wilts . . . 45 G10
　Wilts . . . 61 D10
　Wrex . . . 166 D5
Burton Agnes E Yorks . 218 G2
Burton Bradstock Dorset 16 D5
Burton Corner Lincs . . 174 F4
Burton Dassett Warks . 119 F7
Burton End Cambs . . . 106 B2
　Essex . . . 105 G10
Burton Ferry Pembs . . . 73 D7
Burton Fleming
　E Yorks . . . 217 E11
Burton Green Essex . . 106 C1
　W Mid . . . 118 B5
　Wrex . . . 166 D4
Burton Hastings Warks. 135 E8
Burton-in-Kendal
　Cumb . . . 211 D10
Burton in Lonsdale
　N Yorks . . . 212 E3

Burton Joyce Notts . . . 171 G10
Burton Latimer
　Northants . . . 121 C8
Burton Lazars Leics . . . 154 F5
Burton-le-Coggles
　Lincs . . . 155 D9
Burton Leonard
　N Yorks . . . 214 G6
Burton Manor Staffs . . 151 E8
Burton on the Wolds
　Leics . . . 153 E11
Burton Overy Leics . . . 136 D3
Burton Pedwardine
　Lincs . . . 173 G10
Burton Pidsea E Yorks . 209 G10
Burton Salmon N Yorks. 198 B3
Burton Stather N Lincs . 199 D11
Burton upon Stather
　N Lincs . . . 199 D11
Burton upon Trent
　Staffs . . . 152 E5
Burton Westwood
　Shrops . . . 132 D2
Burntwood Warr . . . 183 C9
Burwardsley Ches W . . 167 D8
Burwarton Shrops . . . 132 F2
Burwash E Sus . . . 37 C11
Burwash Common
　E Sus . . . 37 C10
Burwash Weald E Sus . 37 C10
Burwell Cambs . . . 123 D11
　Lincs . . . 190 F5
Burwen Anglesey . . . 178 C6
Burwick Orkney . . . 314 H4
　Shetland . . . 313 J5
Burwood Shrops . . . 131 F9
Burwood Park Sur . . . 66 G5
Bury Cambs . . . 138 G5
　Gtr Man . . . 195 E10
　Som . . . 26 B6
　W Sus . . . 35 E8
Buryas Br Corn . . . 1 D4
Burybank Staffs . . . 151 B7
Bury End Beds . . . 121 G9
　Beds . . . 104 E2
　Worcs . . . 99 D11
Bury Green Herts 86 E4
　Herts . . . 105 G8
Bury Hollow W Sus 35 E8
Bury Park Luton . . . 103 G11
Bury St Edmunds Suff. . 125 E7
Bury's Bank W Berks . . 64 F3
Burythorpe N Yorks . . 216 G5
Busbiehill N Ayrs . . . 257 B9
Busbridge Sur . . . 50 E3
Busby E Renf . . . 267 D11
　E Renf . . . 267 D11
Buscot Oxon . . . 82 F2
Buscott Oxon . . . 44 F2
Bush Aberds . . . 293 G9
　Corn . . . 24 F2
Bush Bank Hereford . . 115 G9
Bushbury W Mid . . . 133 C8
Bushby Leics . . . 136 C3
Bush Crathie Aberds . . 292 D4
Bush End Essex 87 B9
Bush Estate Norf . . . 161 D8
Bushey Dorset . . . 18 E5
　Herts . . . 85 G10
Bushey Ground Oxon . . 82 D4
Bushey Heath Herts . . 85 G11
Bushey Mead London . . 67 F8
Bushfield Cumb . . . 249 G11
Bush Green Norf . . . 141 D10
　Norf . . . 142 F4
　Suff . . . 125 F8
Bush Hill Park London . .86 F4
Bushley Worcs . . . 99 E7
Bushley Green Worcs . . 99 E7
Bushmead Beds . . . 122 E2
Bushmoor Shrops . . . 131 F8
Bushton Wilts . . . 62 D5
Bushy Common Norf . . 159 G9
Bushy Hill Sur . . . 50 C4
Busk Cumb . . . 231 C8
　Gtr Man . . . 196 F2
Buslingthorpe Lincs . . 189 D9
Bussage Glos . . . 80 E5
Bussex Som . . . 43 F11
Busta Shetland . . . 312 G5
Bustard Green Norf . . 142 E3
Bustard's Green Norf . 142 E3
Bustatoun Orkney . . . 314 A7
Busveal Corn . . . 4 G4
Butcher's Common Norf 160 E6
Butcher's Cross E Sus . . 37 B9
Butcombe N Som . . . 60 G4
Bute Town Caerph . . . 77 D10
Butetown Cardiff . . . 59 D7
Butleigh Head Shrops . 149 G8
Butleigh Som . . . 44 G4
Butleigh Wootton Som . 44 G4
Butlersbank Shrops . . 149 E11
Butlers Cross Bucks . . 84 D5
Butler's End Warks . . . 134 F4
Butler's Hill Notts . . . 171 F8
Butlers Marston Warks . 118 G6
Butley Suff . . . 127 G7
Butley High Corner Suff 109 B7
Butley Low Corner Suff. 109 B7
Butley Town Ches E . . 184 F6
Butlocks Heath Hants . .33 F7
Butterbank Staffs . . . 151 E7
Butterburn Cumb . . . 240 D4
Buttercrambe N Yorks . 207 B10
Butterknowle Durham . 233 F8
Butterleigh Devon . . . 27 F7
Butterley Derbys . . . 170 E5
　Derbys . . . 170 E6
Buttermere Cumb . . . 220 B3
　Wilts . . . 63 G10
Butterow Glos . . . 80 E5
Butters Green Staffs . . 168 E4
Buttershaw W Yorks . . 196 B6
Butterstone Perth . . . 286 C4
Butterton Staffs . . . 168 G4
　Staffs . . . 169 D9
Butterwick Cumb . . . 221 B10
　Durham . . . 234 F3
　Lincs . . . 174 G5
　N Yorks . . . 216 D6
　N Yorks . . . 217 D9
Butt Green Ches E . . . 167 E11
Buttington Powys . . . 130 B5
Buttonbridge Shrops . . 116 B4
Button Haugh Green
　Suff . . . 125 D9
Buttonoak Worcs . . . 116 B5
Button's Green Suff . . 125 G8
Butts Devon . . . 14 D2
Buttsash Hants . . . 32 F6
Buttsbear Cross Corn . . 24 E2
Buttsbury Essex . . . 87 F11
Butt's Green Essex . . 105 E9
Butt's Green Hants . . . 32 B4
Buttsole Kent . . . 55 C10

Butt Yeats Lancs . . . 211 F11
Buxhall Suff . . . 125 F10
Buxhall Fen Street
　Suff . . . 125 F10
Buxley Borders . . . 272 E6
Buxted E Sus . . . 37 C7
Buxton Derbys . . . 185 G9
　Norf . . . 160 E4
Buxworth Derbys . . . 185 E8
Bwcle / Buckley Flint . 166 C3
Bwlch Flint . . . 181 G11
　Powys . . . 96 G2
Bwlch-derwin Gwyn . . 163 F7
Bwlchgwyn Wrex . . . 166 E3
Bwlch-Llan Ceredig . . 111 F11
Bwlchnewydd Carms . . 93 G7
Bwlchtocyn Gwyn . . . 144 D6
Bwlch-y-cibau Powys . 148 F3
Bwlch-y-cwm Cardiff . . 58 C6
Bwlch-y-fadfa Ceredig . .93 B8
Bwlch-y-ffridd Powys . 129 D10
Bwlchygroes Pembs . . 92 D4
Bwlchllyn Gwyn . . . 163 D8
Bwlch-y-Plain Powys . 114 B4
Bwlch-y-sarnau Powys 113 C10
Bybrook Kent . . . 54 E4
Bycross Hereford . . . 97 C7
Byeastwood Bridgend . 58 C2
Byebush Aberds . . . 303 F7
Bye Green Bucks . . . 84 C5
Byerhope Northumb . . 232 B3
Byermoor T&W . . . 242 F5
Byers Green Durham . . 233 E10
Byfield Northants . . . 119 G10
Byfleet Sur . . . 66 G5
Byford Hereford . . . 97 C7
Bygrave Herts . . . 104 D5
Byker T&W . . . 243 E7
Byland Abbey N Yorks . 215 D10
Bylchau Conwy . . . 165 C7
Byley Ches W . . . 168 B2
Bynea Carms . . . 56 B4
Byram N Yorks . . . 198 B3
Byrness Northumb . . . 251 C7
Bythorn Cambs . . . 121 B11
Byton Hereford . . . 115 E7
Byton Hand Hereford . 115 E7
Bywell Northumb . . . 242 E2
Byworth W Sus . . . 35 C7

C

Cabbacott Devon . . . 24 C6
Cabbage Hill Brack . . 65 E11
Cabharstadh W Isles . . 304 F5
Cabin Shrops . . . 130 F6
Cablea Perth . . . 286 D3
Cabourne Lincs . . . 200 G6
Cabrach Argyll . . . 274 G5
　Moray . . . 302 G3
Cabrich Highld . . . 300 E5
Cabus Lancs . . . 202 D5
Cackle Hill Lincs . . . 157 D7
Cackleshaw W Yorks . . 204 F6
Cackle Street E Sus . . 23 B11
　E Sus . . . 37 B7
　E Sus . . . 38 D4
Cadboll Highld . . . 301 B8
Cadbury Devon . . . 26 G6
Cadbury Barton Devon . 25 D11
Cadbury Heath S Glos . .61 E7
Cadder E Dunb . . . 278 G2
Cadderlie Argyll . . . 284 D4
Caddington C Beds . . . 85 B9
Caddleton Argyll . . . 275 B8
Caddonfoot Borders . . 261 C10
Caddonlee Borders . . 261 B10
Cadeby Leics . . . 135 C8
　S Yorks . . . 198 G4
Cadeleigh Devon . . . 26 F6
Cademuir Borders . . . 260 B6
Cade Street E Sus . . . 37 C10
Cader Denb . . . 165 C8
Cadger Path Angus . . 287 B8
Cadgwith Corn . . . 2 G6
Cadham Fife . . . 286 G6
Cadishead Gtr Man . . 184 C2
Cadle Swansea . . . 56 B6
Cadley Lancs . . . 202 G6
　Wilts . . . 47 C8
　Wilts . . . 63 F8
Cadmore End Bucks . . 84 G3
Cadnam Hants . . . 32 E3
Cadney N Lincs . . . 200 G4
Cadney Bank Wrex . . 149 C9
Cadole Flint . . . 166 C2
Cadoxton V Glam . . . 58 F6
Cadoxton-Juxta-Neath
　Neath . . . 57 B9
Cadshaw Blkburn . . . 195 D8
Cadwell Herts . . . 104 E3
Cadzow S Lnrk . . . 268 E4
Caeathro Gwyn . . . 163 C7
Cae Clyd Gwyn . . . 164 G2
Cae-gors Carms . . . 75 E9
Caehopkin Powys . . . 76 C4
Caemorgan Ceredig . . 92 B3
Caenby Lincs . . . 189 D9
Caenby Corner Lincs . 189 D7
Caerau Bridgend . . . 57 C11
　Cardiff . . . 58 D6
Caerau Park Newport . 59 B9
Cae'r-bont Powys . . . 76 C4
Cae'r-bryn Carms . . . 75 C9
Caerdeon Gwyn . . . 146 F2
Caer Farchell Pembs . . .90 F5
Caergeiliog Anglesey . 178 F4
Caergwrle Flint . . . 166 D4
Caergybi / Holyhead
　Anglesey . . . 178 E2
Caerhendy Neath . . . 57 C9
Caerhun Conwy . . . 180 G2
Cae'r-Lan Powys . . . 76 C4
Caerleon Newport . . . 78 G4
Caer Llan Mon . . . 79 D7
Caermead V Glam . . . 58 F3
Caermeini Pembs . . . 92 E2
Caernarfon Gwyn . . . 163 C7
Caerphilly / Caerffili
　Caerph . . . 59 B7
Caersws Powys . . . 129 E10
Caerwedros Ceredig . . 111 F7
Caerwent Mon . . . 79 G7
Caerwent Brook Mon . 60 B3
Caerwych Gwyn . . . 146 B2
Caerwys Flint . . . 181 G10
Caethle Gwyn . . . 128 G2
Cage Green Kent . . . 52 D5
Caggan Highld . . . 291 B10
Caggle Street Mon . . . 78 B5

Cailness Stirl . . . 285 G7
Caim Anglesey . . . 179 E10
Caio Carms . . . 94 D3
Cairinis W Isles . . . 296 E4
Cairisiadar W Isles . . 304 E2
Cairminis W Isles . . . 296 C6
Cairnargat Moray . . . 302 F4
Cairnbaan Argyll . . . 275 D9
Cairnbanno Ho Aberds . 303 E8
Cairnborrow Aberds . . 302 E4
Cairnbrogie Aberds . . 303 G8
Cairnbulg Castle
　Aberds . . . 303 C10
Cairncross Angus . . . 292 F6
　Borders . . . 273 C7
Cairndow Argyll . . . 284 F5
Cairness Aberds . . . 303 C10
Cairneyhill Fife . . . 279 D10
Cairnfield Ho Moray . . 302 C4
Cairngaan Dumfries . . 236 F3
Cairngarroch Dumfries. 236 E2
Cairnhill Aberds . . . 303 D7
　Aberds . . . 303 F7
　N Lnrk . . . 268 C5
Cairnie Aberds . . . 293 C10
　Aberds . . . 302 E4
Cairnlea S Ayrs . . . 244 G6
Cairnleith Crofts Aberds 303 E9
Cairnmuir Aberds . . . 303 E8
Cairnorrie Aberds . . . 303 E8
Cairnpark Aberds . . . 293 B10
Cairnryan Dumfries . . 236 C2
Cairnton Orkney . . . 314 F2
Cairston Orkney . . . 314 E2
Caister-on-Sea Norf . . 161 G10
Caistron Northumb . . 251 C11
Caitha Bowland Borders 271 G9
Cakebole Worcs . . . 117 C7
Calais Street Suff . . . 107 D9
Calanais W Isles . . . 304 E4
Calbost W Isles . . . 305 G6
Calbourne IoW . . . 20 D4
Calceby Lincs . . . 190 F5
Calcoed Flint . . . 181 G11
Calcot Glos . . . 81 D9
　W Berks . . . 65 E7
Calcot Row W Berks . . 65 E7
Calcott Kent . . . 71 G7
　Shrops . . . 149 G8
Calcott's Green Glos . . 80 B3
Calcutt N Yorks . . . 206 B2
　Wilts . . . 81 G10
Caldback Shetland . . . 312 C8
Caldbeck Cumb . . . 230 D2
Caldbergh N Yorks . . 213 B11
Caldecote Cambs . . . 122 F6
　Cambs . . . 138 F2
　Herts . . . 104 D4
　Northants . . . 120 G3
　Warks . . . 135 E7
Caldecote Hill Herts . . 85 G11
Caldecott Northants . . 121 D9
　Oxon . . . 83 F7
　Rutland . . . 137 E7
Caldecotte M Keynes . 103 D7
Calderbank N Lnrk . . 268 C5
Calder Bridge Cumb . . 219 D10
Calderbrook Gtr Man . 196 D2
Caldercruix N Lnrk . . 268 B6
Calder Grove W Yorks . 197 D10
Calder Hall Cumb . . . 219 D10
Calder Mains Highld . . 310 D4
Caldermill S Lnrk . . . 268 G3
Caldermoor Gtr Man . . 196 D2
Calderstones Mers . . 182 D6
Calder Vale Lancs . . . 202 D6
Calderwood S Lnrk . . 268 D2
Caldhame Angus . . . 287 C8
Caldicot / Cil-y-coed
　Mon . . . 60 B3
Caldmore W Mid . . . 133 D10
Caldwell Derbys . . . 152 F5
　N Yorks . . . 224 C3
Caldy Mers . . . 182 D2
Caldy Island Pembs . . 73 E10
Caledrhydiau Ceredig . 111 F9
Cale Green Gtr Man . . 184 D5
Calenick Corn . . . 4 G6
Caleys Fields Worcs . . 100 C4
Calf Heath Staffs . . . 133 B8
Calford Green Suff . . 106 B3
Calfsound Orkney . . . 314 C5
Calgary Argyll . . . 288 D5
Caliach Argyll . . . 288 D5
Calianach Highld . . . 289 D8
California Cambs . . . 139 G10
　Falk . . . 279 F8
　Norf . . . 161 G10
California / Crai Powys . 95 G9

Calver Derbys . . . 186 G2
Calverhall Shrops . . . 150 B2
Calver Hill Hereford . . 97 B7
Calverleigh Devon . . . 26 E6
Calverley W Yorks . . . 205 F10
Calvert Bucks . . . 102 G3
Calverton M Keynes . . 102 D5
　Notts . . . 171 F10
Calvine Perth . . . 291 G10
Calvo Cumb . . . 238 G4
Cam Glos . . . 80 F3
Camaghael Highld . . . 290 F3
Camas an Staca Argyll . 274 G5
Camas-luinie Highld . . 295 C11
Camasnacroise Highld . 289 D10
Camastianavaig Highld. 295 B7
Camas Salach Highld . . 289 C8
Camasunary Highld . . 295 D7
Camault Muir Highld . . 300 E5
Camb Shetland . . . 312 D7
Camber E Sus . . . 39 D7
Camberley Sur . . . 65 G11
Camberwell London . . 67 D10
Camblesforth N Yorks . 199 B7
Cambo Northumb . . . 252 F2
Cambois Northumb . . 253 G8
Camborne Corn . . . 4 G3
Cambourne Cambs . . 122 F6
Cambridge Borders . . 271 F11
　Glos . . . 80 E3
Cambridge Batch N Som . 60 F4
Cambridge Town Sthend. 70 C2
Cambrose Corn . . . 4 G3
Cambus Clack . . . 279 C7
Cambusavie Farm
　Highld . . . 309 K7
Cambusbarron Stirl . . 278 C5
Cambusdrenny Stirl . . 278 C5
Cambuskenneth Stirl . . 278 C6
Cambuslang S Lnrk . . 268 D2
Cambusmore Lodge
　Highld . . . 309 K7
Cambusnethan N Lnrk . 268 D6
Camden London . . . 67 C9
Camden Park Kent . . 52 F5
Cameley Bath . . . 44 B6
Camelford Corn . . . 11 E8
Camel Green Dorset . . 31 E10
Camelon Falk . . . 279 E7
Camelsdale Sur . . . 49 G11
Camer Kent . . . 69 F7
Cameron Bridge Fife . . 280 B6
Camer's Green Worcs . . 98 D5
Camerton Bath . . . 45 B7
　Cumb . . . 228 E6
　E Yorks . . . 201 B8
Cammachmore Aberds . 293 D11
Cammeringham Lincs . 188 E6
Camnant Powys . . . 113 F11
Camore Highld . . . 309 K7
Camp Corner Oxon . . 83 E7
Campdown T&W . . . 243 C7
Camphill Derbys . . . 185 F11
Campion Hills Warks . . 118 D6
Campions Essex . . . 87 C7
Cample Dumfries . . . 247 E9
Campmuir Perth . . . 286 D6
Campsall S Yorks . . . 198 E4
Campsea Ashe Suff . . 126 F6
Camps End Cambs . . 106 C2
Campsey Ash Suff . . 126 F6
Campsfield Oxon . . . 83 B7
Camps Heath Suff . . 143 E10
Campton C Beds . . . 104 D2
Camptoun E Loth . . . 281 F10
Camptown Borders . . 262 F5
Camp Town W Yorks . . 206 F2
Camquhart Argyll . . . 275 E10
Camrose Pembs . . . 91 G8
Camserney Perth . . . 286 C2
Camster Highld . . . 310 E6
Camuscross Highld . . 295 D8
Camusnagaul Highld . . 290 F2
　Highld . . . 307 L5
Camusrory Highld . . . 295 F10
Camusteel Highld . . . 299 E7
Camusterrach Highld . . 299 E7
Camusvrachan Perth . . 285 C10
Canada Hants . . . 32 D3
Canadia E Sus . . . 38 D2
Canal Foot Cumb . . . 210 D6
Canal Side S Yorks . . 199 E7
Canbus Clack . . . 279 C7
Candacraig Ho Aberds . 292 B5
Candlesby Lincs . . . 175 C7
Candle Street Suff . . 125 C10
Candy Mill S Lnrk . . . 269 G11
Cane End Oxon . . . 65 D7
Caneheath E Sus . . . 23 D9
Canewdon Essex . . . 88 G5
Canford Bottom Dorset. 31 G8
Canford Cliffs Poole . . 19 D7
Canford Heath Poole . 18 B6
Canford Magna Poole . 18 B6
Cangate Norf . . . 160 F6
Canham's Green Suff . 125 D10
Canholes Derbys . . . 185 G8
Canisbay Highld . . . 310 B7
Canklow S Yorks . . . 186 C6
Canley W Mid . . . 118 B6
Cann Dorset . . . 30 C5
Cann Common Dorset . 30 C5
Cannalidgey Corn . . . 5 B8
Cannard's Grave Som . . 44 E6
Cann Common Dorset . 30 C5
Cannich Highld . . . 300 F3
Cannington Som . . . 43 F9
Canning Town London . 68 C2
Cannock Staffs . . . 133 B9
Cannock Wood Staffs . 151 F10
Cannon's Green Essex . 87 D9
Canon Bridge Hereford. 97 C8
Canon Frome Hereford . 98 C3
Canon Pyon Hereford . .97 B9
Canons Ashby
　Northants . . . 119 G11
Canonsgrove Som . . . 28 C2
Canons Park London . . 85 G11
Canon's Town Corn . . .2 B2
Canterbury Kent . . . 54 B6
Cantley Norf . . . 143 B7
　S Yorks . . . 198 G6
Cantlop Shrops . . . 131 B10

Canton Cardiff . . . 59 D7
Cantraybruich Highld . . 301 E7
Cantraydoune Highld . . 301 E7
Cantraywood Highld . . 301 E7
Cantsfield Lancs . . . 212 E2
Canvey Island Essex . . 69 C9
Canwick Lincs . . . 173 B7
Canworthy Water Corn . 11 D10
Caol Highld . . . 290 F3
Caolas Argyll . . . 288 E2
　W Isles . . . 297 M2
Caolas Fhlodaigh
　W Isles . . . 296 F4
Caolas Liubharsaigh
　W Isles . . . 297 G4
Caolas Scalpaigh
　W Isles . . . 305 J4
Caol Ila Argyll . . . 274 F5
Caolas Stocinis W Isles . 305 J3
Caol Lanna con Highld. 290 G3
Capel Carms . . . 75 E8
　Kent . . . 52 E6
　Sur . . . 51 E7
Capel Bangor Ceredig . 128 G3
Capel Betws Lleucu
　Ceredig . . . 112 F2
Capel Carmel Gwyn . . 144 D3
Capel Coch Anglesey . 179 E7
Capel Cross Kent . . . 53 E8
Capel Curig Conwy . . 164 D2
Capel Cynon Ceredig . . 93 B7
Capel Dewi Carms . . . 93 G9
　Ceredig . . . 93 C9
　Ceredig . . . 128 G3
Capel Garmon Conwy . 164 D4
Capel Green Suff . . . 109 B7
Capel-gwyn Carms . . 93 G9
Capel Gwyn Anglesey . 178 F4
Capel Gwynfe Carms . . 94 G4
Capel Hendre Carms . . 75 C9
Capel Hermon Gwyn . . 146 D4
Capel Isaac Carms . . . 93 F11
Capel Iwan Carms . . . 92 D5
Capel-le-Ferne Kent . . 55 F8
Capel Llanilltern Cardiff 58 C5
Capel Mawr Anglesey . 178 F6
Capel Newydd / Newchapel
　Pembs . . . 92 D4
Capel Parc Anglesey . 178 D6
Capel St Andrew Suff . 109 B7
Capel St Mary Suff . . 107 D11
Capel Seion Carms . . 75 C8
　Ceredig . . . 112 B2
Capel Siloam Conwy . . 164 E6
Capel Tygwydd Ceredig . 92 C5
Capel Uchaf Gwyn . . 162 E6
Capel-uchaf Conwy . . 180 F2
Capel-y-ffin Powys . . 96 E5
Capel-y-graig Gwyn . . 163 B8
Capenhurst Ches W . . 182 G5
Capernwray Lancs . . 211 E10
Capheaton Northumb . 252 G2
Capland Som . . . 28 D4
Cappercleuch Borders . 260 E6
Capplegill Dumfries . . 248 B4
Capstone Medway . . . 69 F9
Captain Fold Gtr Man . 195 E11
Capton Devon . . . 8 E6
　Som . . . 42 F5
Caputh Perth . . . 286 D4
Caradon Town Corn . . 11 G11
Carbis Corn . . . 5 D10
Carbis Bay Corn . . . 2 B2
Carbost Highld . . . 294 B5
　Highld . . . 298 E4
Carbrain N Lnrk . . . 278 G5
Carbrook S Yorks . . . 186 D5
Carbrooke Norf . . . 141 C9
Carburton Notts . . . 187 G10
Carcant Borders . . . 271 E7
Carcary Angus . . . 287 B10
Carclaze Corn . . . 5 D10
Carclew Corn . . . 3 B7
Car Colston Notts . . . 172 G2
Carcroft S Yorks . . . 198 E4
Cardenden Fife . . . 280 C4
Cardeston Shrops . . . 149 G7
Cardew Cumb . . . 230 B2
Cardewlees Cumb . . . 239 G8
Cardiff Cardiff . . . 59 D7
Cardigan / Aberteifi
　Ceredig . . . 92 B3
Cardinal's Green Cambs 106 B2
Cardington Beds . . . 103 B11
　Shrops . . . 131 D10
Cardinham Corn . . . 6 B2
Cardonald Glasgow . . 267 C10
Cardow Moray . . . 301 E11
Cardrona Borders . . . 261 C7
Cardross Argyll . . . 276 E6
Cardurnock Cumb . . . 238 F5
Careby Lincs . . . 155 F10
Careston Castle Angus . 287 B9
Care Village Leics . . . 136 D4
Carew Pembs . . . 73 E8
Carew Cheriton Pembs . 73 E8
Carew Newton Pembs . 73 E8
Carey Hereford . . . 97 E11
Carey Park Corn . . . 6 E4
Carfin N Lnrk . . . 268 D5
Carfrae E Loth . . . 271 B11
Carfury Corn . . . 1 C4
Cargate Common Norf . 142 E2
Cargenbridge Dumfries 237 B11
Cargill Perth . . . 286 D5
Cargo Cumb . . . 239 F9
Cargo Fleet Mbro . . . 234 G6
Cargreen Corn . . . 7 C8
Carham Northumb . . 263 B8
Carharrack Corn . . . 4 G4
Carie Perth . . . 285 B10
　Perth . . . 285 D10
Carines Corn . . . 4 D5
Carisbrooke IoW . . . 20 D5
Cark Cumb . . . 211 D7
Carkeel Corn . . . 7 C8
Carlabhagh W Isles . . 304 D4
Carland Cross Corn . . .5 E7
Carlbury N Yorks . . . 224 B5
Carlby Lincs . . . 155 G11
Carlecotes S Yorks . . 197 G7
Carleen Corn . . . 2 C4
Carlenrig Borders . . . 249 C9
Carlesmoor N Yorks . . 214 E3
Carleton Cumb . . . 219 D10
　Cumb . . . 230 G6
　Cumb . . . 239 F10
　Lancs . . . 202 E3
　N Yorks . . . 204 D5
Carleton Forehoe Norf . 141 B11
Carleton Hall Cumb . . 219 F11
Carleton-in-Craven
　N Yorks . . . 204 D5
Carleton Rode Norf . . 142 E2
Carleton St Peter Norf. 142 C6
Carley Hill T&W . . . 243 F9
Carlidnack Corn . . . 3 D7
Carlin How Redcar . . 226 B4
Carlingcott Bath . . . 45 B7
Carlinghow W Yorks . . 197 C8
Carlingwark Devon . . 27 E11
Carlisle Cumb . . . 239 F10
Carloggas Corn . . . 5 B7
　Corn . . . 5 C9
Carloonan Argyll . . . 284 F4
Carlops Borders . . . 270 D3
Carlton Beds . . . 121 F9
　Cambs . . . 124 G2
　Leics . . . 135 C7
　Notts . . . 171 G10
　N Yorks . . . 198 C6
　N Yorks . . . 213 C11
　N Yorks . . . 216 B2
　N Yorks . . . 224 C3
　Stockton . . . 234 G3
　Suff . . . 127 E7
　S Yorks . . . 197 E11
　W Yorks . . . 197 B10
Carlton Colville Suff . . 143 F10
Carlton Curlieu Leics . 136 D3
Carlton Green Cambs . 124 G2
Carlton Husthwaite
　N Yorks . . . 215 D9
Carlton in Cleveland
　N Yorks . . . 225 E10
Carlton in Lindrick
　Notts . . . 187 E9
Carlton le Moorland
　Lincs . . . 172 D6
Carlton Miniott N Yorks 215 C7
Carlton on Trent Notts . 172 C3
Carlton Purlieus
　Northants . . . 136 F6
Carlton Scroop Lincs . 172 G6
Carluddon Corn . . . 5 D10
Carluke S Lnrk . . . 268 E6
Carlyon Bay Corn . . . 5 E11
Carmarthen /
　Caerfyrddin Carms . . 93 G8
Carmel Anglesey . . . 178 E5
　Carms . . . 75 B9
　Flint . . . 181 G10
　Gwyn . . . 163 E7
　Powys . . . 113 E11
Carmichael S Lnrk . . 259 B10
Carminow Cross Corn . .5 B11
Carmont Aberds . . . 293 E10
Carmunnock Glasgow . 268 D2
Carmyle Glasgow . . . 268 C2
Carmyllie Angus . . . 218 F2
Carnach Highld . . . 299 G11
　Highld . . . 307 K5
　W Isles . . . 305 J4
Carnachy Highld . . . 308 D7
Càrnais W Isles . . . 304 E2
Càrnan W Isles . . . 297 G3
Carn Arthen Corn . . . 2 B5
Carnbahn Perth . . . 285 C10
Carnbee Fife . . . 287 G9
Carnbo Perth . . . 286 G4
Carnbrea Corn . . . 4 G3
Carn Brea Village Corn . 4 G3
Carnbroe N Lnrk . . . 268 C4
Carndu Highld . . . 295 C10
Carnduff S Lnrk . . . 268 E3
Carnduncan Argyll . . 274 G3
Carne Corn . . . 3 B10
　Corn . . . 3 E7
　Corn . . . 5 D9
Carnebone Corn . . . 2 C6
Carnedd Powys . . . 129 E10
Carnetown Rhondda . . 77 G9
Carnforth Lancs . . . 211 E10
　Lancs . . . 211 E10
Carnglas Swansea . . 56 C6
Carn-gorm Highld . . . 295 C11
Carnhedryn Pembs . . .90 F6
Carnhedryn Uchaf
　Pembs . . . 90 F5
Carnhell Green Corn . . 2 B4
Carnhot Corn . . . 4 G4
Carnkie Corn . . . 2 B5
　Corn . . . 2 C6
Carnkief Corn . . . 4 E5
Carno Powys . . . 129 D9
Carnoch Highld . . . 300 D3
　Highld . . . 300 F3
Carnock Fife . . . 279 D10
Carnon Downs Corn . . 4 G5
Carnousie Aberds . . . 302 D6
Carnoustie Angus . . . 287 D9
Carnsmerry Corn . . . 5 D10
Carn Towan Corn . . . 1 D3
Carntyne Glasgow . . . 268 B2
Carnwadric E Renf . . 267 D10
Carnwath S Lnrk . . . 269 F9
Carnyorth Corn . . . 1 C3
Caroe Corn . . . 11 C9
Carol Green W Mid . . 118 B5
Carpalla Corn . . . 5 E9
Carpenders Park Herts . 85 G10
Carpenter's Hill
　Worcs . . . 117 C11
Carperby N Yorks . . . 213 B10
Carpley Green N Yorks . 213 B8
Carr Gtr Man . . . 195 D9
　S Yorks . . . 187 D7
Carradale Argyll . . . 255 D9
Carragraich W Isles . . 305 J3
Carr Bank Cumb . . . 211 D9
Carrbridge Highld . . . 301 G9
Carrbrook Gtr Man . . 196 G3
Carr Cross Lancs . . . 193 E11
Carreglefn Anglesey . . 178 D5
Carreg-wen Pembs . . 92 C4
Carr Gate W Yorks . . 197 C10
Carr Green Gtr Man . . 184 D2
Carr Hill T&W . . . 243 E7
Carrhouse Devon . . . 26 F4
Carr Houses Mers . . . 193 G10
Carrick Argyll . . . 275 E10
　Dumfries . . . 237 D7
　Fife . . . 287 E8
Carrick Castle Argyll . 276 C3
Carrick Ho Orkney . . 314 C5
Carriden Falk . . . 279 E9
Carrington Gtr Man . . 184 C2
　Lincs . . . 174 E4
　Midloth . . . 270 C6
　Nottingham . . . 171 G9
Carroch Dumfries . . . 246 E5
Carrog Conwy . . . 164 F3
　Denb . . . 165 G10
Carroglen Perth . . . 285 E11
Carrol Highld . . . 311 J2
Carron Falk . . . 279 E7
　Moray . . . 302 E2
Carronbridge Dumfries. 247 D9
Carron Bridge Stirl . . 278 E4
Carronshore Falk . . . 279 E7
Carrow Hill Mon . . . 78 G6
Carr Shield Northumb . 232 B2

Carrutherstown Dumfries 238 C4
Carr Vale Derbys 171 B7
Carrville Durham 234 C2
Carry Argyll 275 G10
Argyll 289 G7
Carscreugh Dumfries 236 D4
Carsegowan Dumfries 236 D6
Carse Gray Angus 287 B8
Carse Ho Argyll 275 G8
Carseriggan Dumfries 236 C5
Carsethorn Dumfries 237 D11
Carshalton London 67 G9
Carshalton Beeches London 67 G9
Carshalton on the Hill London 67 G9
Carsington Derbys 170 E3
Carskiey Argyll 255 G7
Carsluith Dumfries 236 D6
Carsphairn Dumfries 246 E3
Carstairs S Lnrk 269 F8
Carstairs Junction S Lnrk 269 F8
Carswell Marsh Oxon 82 F4
Cartbridge Sur 50 B4
Carterhaugh Borders 261 D10
Carter Knowle S Yorks 186 E4
Carter's Clay Hants 32 C4
Carter's Green Essex 87 C8
Carter's Hill Wokingham 65 F9
Carterspiece Glos 79 C9
Carterton Oxon 82 D3
Carterway Heads Northumb 242 G2
Carthamartha Corn 12 F3
Carthew Corn 2 B5
Corn 5 D10
Carthorpe N Yorks 214 C6
Cartington Northumb 252 C2
Cartland S Lnrk 269 F7
Cartledge Derbys 186 F4
Cartmel Cumb 211 D7
Cartmel Fell Cumb 211 B8
Cartsdyke Inclyd 276 F5
Cartworth W Yorks 196 F6
Carty Port Dumfries 236 C6
Carway Carms 75 D7
Carwinley Cumb 239 C10
Cary Fitzpaine Som 29 B9
Carzantic Corn 12 E3
Carzield Dumfries 247 G11
Carzise Corn 2 C3
Cascob Powys 114 D4
Cascob Green Glos 80 D4
Cashlie Perth 285 C8
Cashmoor Dorset 31 E7
Cas Mael / Puncheston Pembs 91 F10
Cassey Compton Glos 81 C9
Cassington Oxon 83 C7
Cassop Durham 234 D2
Castallack Corn 1 D5
Castell Conwy 164 B3
Denb 165 B10
Castellau Rhondda 58 B5
Castell-Howell Ceredig 93 B8
Castell nedd / Neath Neath 57 B8
Castell Newydd Emlyn / Newcastle Emlyn Carms 92 C6
Castell-y-bwch Torf 78 G3
Castell-y-rhingyll Carms 75 C9
Casterton Cumb 212 D2
Castle Devon 28 G4
Som 27 B9
Castle Acre Norf 158 F6
Castle Ashby Northants 121 F7
Castle Bolton N Yorks 223 G10
Castle Bromwich W Mid 134 F2
Castle Bytham Lincs 155 F9
Castlebythe Pembs 91 F10
Castle Caereinion Powys 130 B3
Castle Camps Cambs 106 C2
Castle Carlton Lincs 190 E5
Castle Carrock Cumb 240 F2
Castlecary N Lnrk 278 F5
Castle Cary Som 44 G6
Castle Combe Wilts 61 D10
Castlecraig Highld 301 C8
Castle Craig Borders 270 G2
Castlecroft Staffs 133 D7
Castle Donington Leics 153 D8
Castle Douglas Dumfries 237 C9
Castle Eaton Swindon 81 F10
Castle Eden Durham 234 D4
Castle End Pboro 138 B2
Castlefairn Dumfries 246 F6
Castlefields Halton 183 E8
Castle Fields Shrops 149 G10
Castle Forbes Aberds 293 B8
Castleford W Yorks 198 B2
Castle Frome Hereford 98 B3
Castle Gate Corn 1 C5
Castlegreen Shrops 130 F6
Castle Green London 68 C3
Sur 66 G3
S Yorks 197 G9
Castle Gresley Derbys 152 F5
Castlehead Renfs 267 C9
Castle Heaton Northumb 273 G8
Castle Hedingham Essex 106 D5
Castlehill Argyll 254 B4
Borders 260 B6
Highld 310 C5
S Ayrs 257 E9
W Dunb 277 F7
Castle Hill E Sus 37 B9
Gtr Man 184 C6
Kent 53 E7
Suff 108 B3
Worcs 116 F5
Castle Huntly Perth 287 E7
Castle Kennedy Dumfries 236 D3
Castlemaddy Dumfries 246 F3
Castlemartin Pembs 72 E6
Castlemilk Dumfries 238 B5
Glasgow 268 C2
Castlemorris Pembs 91 E8
Castlemorton Worcs 98 D5
Castle O'er Dumfries 248 E6
Castlerigg Cumb 229 G11
Castle Rising Norf 158 E3
Castleside Durham 233 B7
Castle Street W Yorks 196 C3
Castle Stuart Highld 301 E7
Castlethorpe M Keynes 102 C6
N Lincs 200 F3
Castleton Angus 287 C7
Argyll 275 G9
Derbys 185 E11
Gtr Man 195 E11
Moray 301 G11

Newport 59 C9
N Yorks 226 D3
Castleton Village Highld 300 E6
Castle Toward Argyll 266 B2
Castletown Ches W 167 B7
Cumb 230 E6
Dorset 17 G9
Highld 301 E7
Highld 310 C5
IoM 192 F3
Staffs 151 E8
T&W 243 F9
Castle Town W Sus 35 E2
Castleump Glos 98 F4
Castle-upon-Alun V Glam 58 E2
Castle Vale W Mid 134 E2
Castleweary Borders 249 C10
Castlewigg Dumfries 236 E6
Castley N Yorks 205 D11
Castling's Heath Suff 107 C9
Caston Norf 141 D9
Castor Pboro 138 D2
Caswell Swansea 56 D5
Catacol N Ayrs 255 C10
Cat Bank Cumb 220 F6
Catbrain S Glos 60 C5
Catbrook Mon 79 E8
Catch Flint 182 G2
Catchall Corn 1 D4
Catchems Corner W Mid 118 B4
Catchems End Worcs 116 B5
Catchgate Durham 242 G5
Catchory Highld 310 D6
Catcleugh Northumb 250 C6
Catcliffe S Yorks 186 D6
Catcomb Wilts 62 D4
Catcott Som 43 F11
Caterham Sur 51 B10
Catfield Norf 161 E7
Catfirth Shetland 313 H6
Catford London 67 E11
Catforth Lancs 202 F5
Cathays Cardiff 59 D7
Cathays Park Cardiff 59 D7
Cathcart Glasgow 267 C11
Cathedine Powys 96 F2
Catherine-de-Barnes W Mid 134 G3
Catherine Slack W Yorks 196 B5
Catherington Hants 33 E11
Catherton Shrops 116 C2
Cat Hill S Yorks 197 F8
Cathiron Warks 119 B9
Catholes Cumb 222 G3
Cathpair Borders 271 F9
Catisfield Hants 33 F8
Catley Lane Head Gtr Man 195 D11
Catley Southfield Hereford 98 C3
Catlodge Highld 291 D8
Catlowdy Cumb 239 B11
Catmere End Essex 105 D9
Catmore W Berks 64 C3
Caton Devon 13 G11
Lancs 211 G10
Caton Green Lancs 211 F10
Catrine E Ayrs 258 D2
Cat's Ash Newport 78 G5
Cat's Common Norf 160 E6
Cats Edge Staffs 169 E7
Catsfield E Sus 38 E2
Catsfield Stream E Sus 38 E2
Catsgore Som 29 B8
Catsham Som 44 G5
Catshaw S Yorks 197 G8
Catshill W Mid 133 B11
Worcs 117 C9
Cat's Hill Cross Staffs 150 C6
Catslackburn Borders 261 D8
Catslip Oxon 65 B8
Catstree Shrops 132 D4
Cattadale Argyll 274 G4
Cattal N Yorks 206 C4
Cattawade Suff 108 E2
Cattedown Plym 7 E9
Catteralls Lancs 202 E5
Catterick N Yorks 224 F4
Catterick Bridge N Yorks 224 F4
Catterick Garrison N Yorks 224 F3
Catterlen Cumb 230 E5
Catterline Aberds 293 F10
Catterton N Yorks 206 D6
Catteshall Sur 50 E3
Catthorpe Leics 119 B11
Cattistock Dorset 17 B7
Cattle End Northants 102 C3
Catton Northumb 241 F8
N Yorks 215 D7
Catwick E Yorks 209 D8
Catworth Cambs 121 C11
Caudle Green Glos 80 C6
Caudlesprings Norf 141 C8
Caulcott C Beds 103 C9
Oxon 101 G10
Cauld Borders 261 G11
Cauldcoats Holdings Falk 279 F10
Cauldcots Aberds 287 C10
Cauldhame Stirl 278 C2
Cauldmill Borders 262 G2
Cauldon Staffs 169 F9
Cauldon Lowe Staffs 169 F9
Cauldwells Aberds 303 D7
Caulkerbush Dumfries 237 D11
Caulside Dumfries 239 B9
Caundle Marsh Dorset 29 E11
Caunsall Worcs 132 G6
Caunton Notts 172 D2
Causeway Hants 33 E11
Hants 34 C2
Mon 60 B2
Causewayend S Lnrk 260 B2
Causeway End Cumb 210 C6
Cumb 211 B9
Dumfries 236 C6
Essex 87 B11
Wilts 62 C4
Causeway Foot W Yorks 197 E7
W Yorks 205 G7
Causeway Green W Mid 133 F9
Causewayhead Cumb 238 G4
Stirl 278 B6
Causewaywood Shrops 131 D10
Causey Durham 243 G7
Causey Park Bridge Northumb 252 E5
Causeyton Aberds 293 B8
Caute Devon 24 E6
Cautley Cumb 222 G3
Cavendish Suff 106 B5
Cavendish Bridge Leics 153 D8
Cavenham Suff 124 D5
Cavers Carre Borders 262 E2
Caversfield Oxon 101 F11

Caversham Reading 65 E8
Caversham Heights Reading 65 D8
Caverswall Staffs 169 G7
Cavil E Yorks 207 G11
Cawdor Highld 301 D10
Cawkeld E Yorks 208 C5
Cawkwell Lincs 190 F3
Cawood N Yorks 207 F7
Cawsand Corn 7 E8
Cawston Norf 160 E2
Warks 119 C9
Cawthorne Lincs 155 E11
S Yorks 197 F9
Cawthorpe Lincs 155 E11
Cawton N Yorks 216 D2
Caxton Cambs 122 F6
Caynham Shrops 115 C11
Caythorpe Lincs 172 F6
Notts 171 F11
Cayton N Yorks 217 C11
Ceallan W Isles 296 F4
Ceann a Bhaigh W Isles 296 F3
Ceann a Bhàigh W Isles 305 J4
Ceannacroc Lodge Highld 290 B4
Ceann a Deas Loch Baghasdail W Isles 297 K3
Ceann Shiphoirt W Isles 305 G4
Ceann Tarabhaigh W Isles 305 G4
Cearsiadair W Isles 304 F5
Ceathramh Meadhanach W Isles 296 D4
Cefn Newport 59 B9
Powys 148 G5
Cefn Berain Conwy 165 B7
Cefn-brith Conwy 164 E6
Cefn-bryn-brain Carms 76 C2
Cefn-bychan Swansea 56 B4
Cefncaeau Carms 56 B4
Cefn Canol Powys 148 C4
Cefn-coch Conwy 164 B5
Cefn Coch Powys 129 C10
Powys 148 D2
Cefn-coed-y-cymmer M Tydf 77 D9f
Cefn Cribbwr Bridgend 57 E11
Cefn Cross Bridgend 57 E11
Cefn-ddwysarn Gwyn 147 B9
Cefn Einion Shrops 130 F5
Cefneithin Carms 75 C9
Cefn-eurgain Flint 166 B2
Cefn Fforest Caerph 77 F11
Cefn Glas Bridgend 57 E11
Cefn Golau Bl Gwent 77 D10
Cefn-gorwydd Powys 95 B8
Cefn Hengoed Caerph 77 F10
Cefn-hengoed Swansea 57 B7
Cefn Llwyd Ceredig 128 G2
Cefn-mawr Wrex 166 F3
Cefnpennar Rhondda 77 E8
Cefn Rhigos Rhondda 76 D5
Cefn-y-bedd Flint 166 D4
Cefn-y-Crib Torf 78 F2
Cefn-y-Garth Swansea 76 E2
Cefn-y-pant Carms 92 F3
Cegidfa / Guilsfield Powys 148 G4
Cei-bach Ceredig 111 F8
Ceinewydd / New Quay Ceredig 111 F7
Ceint Anglesey 179 F7
Ceinws Powys 128 B5
Cellan Ceredig 94 B2
Cellarhead Staffs 169 F7
Cellarhill Kent 70 G3
Celyn-Mali Flint 165 B11
Cemaes Anglesey 178 C5
Cemmaes Powys 128 B6
Cemmaes Road / Glantwymyn Powys 128 C6
Cenarth Carms 92 C5
Cenin Gwyn 163 F7
Central Inclyd 276 F5
Central Milton Keynes M Keynes 102 D6
Ceos W Isles 304 F5
Ceres Fife 287 F8
Ceri / Kerry Powys 130 F2
Cerne Abbas Dorset 29 G11
Cerney Wick Glos 81 F9
Cerrigceinwen Anglesey 178 G6
Cerrig Llwydion Neath 57 C9
Cerrig-mân Anglesey 179 C7
Cerrigydrudion Conwy 165 F7
Cess Norf 161 F8
Cessford Borders 262 E6
Ceunant Gwyn 163 C8
Chaceley Hole Glos 98 E6
Chaceley Stock Glos 99 F7
Chacewater Corn 4 G4
Chackmore Bucks 102 D3
Chacombe Northants 101 C9
Chadbury Worcs 99 B10
Chadderton Gtr Man 196 F2
Chadderton Fold Gtr Man 195 F11
Chaddesden Derby 153 B7
Chaddesley Corbett Worcs 117 C7
Chaddlehanger Devon 12 F5
Chaddlewood Plym 7 D11
Chadkirk Gtr Man 184 D6
Chadlington Oxon 100 G6
Chadshunt Warks 118 G6
Chadsmoor Staffs 151 G9
Chadstone Northants 121 F7
Chad Valley W Mid 133 F10
Chadwell Leics 154 E5
Shrops 150 G5
Chadwell End Beds 121 D11
Chadwell Heath London 68 B3
Chadwell St Mary Thurrock 68 D6
Chadwick S Glos 116 D6
Chadwick End W Mid 118 C4
Chadwick Green Mers 183 B8
Chaffcombe Som 28 E5
Chafford Hundred Thurrock 68 D5
Chagford Devon 13 D10
Chailey E Sus 36 D5
Chainbridge Cambs 139 C8
Chain Bridge Lincs 174 G4
Chainhurst Kent 53 D8
Chalbury Dorset 31 F8
Chalbury Common Dorset 31 F8
Chaldon Sur 51 B10
Chaldon Herring or East Chaldon Dorset 17 E11
Chale IoW 20 F5
Chale Green IoW 20 F5
Chalfont Common Bucks 85 G8
Chalfont Grove Bucks 85 G7
Chalfont St Giles Bucks 85 G7

Chalfont St Peter Bucks 85 G8
Chalford Glos 80 E5
Oxon 84 E2
Wilts 45 C11
Chalford Hill Glos 80 E5
Chalgrave C Beds 103 F10
Chalgrove Oxon 83 F10
Chalk Kent 69 E7
Chalk End Essex 87 C10
Chalkhouse Green Oxon 65 D8
Chalkhill Norf 141 C7
Chalksole Kent 55 E9
Chalkway Som 28 F5
Chalkwell Kent 69 G11
S'thend 69 B11
Challaborough Devon 8 G3
Challacombe Devon 41 E7
Challister Shetland 312 G7
Challoch Dumfries 236 C5
Challock Kent 54 C4
Chalmington Dorset 29 G9
Chalton C Beds 103 F10
Devon 8 G5
Hants 34 D2
Chalvedon Essex 69 B8
Chalvey Slough 66 D3
Chalvington E Sus 23 D8
Chambercombe Devon 40 D4
Chamber's Green Kent 54 E2
Champson Devon 26 B4
Chance Inn Fife 287 F7
Chancery / Rhydgaled Ceredig 111 B11
Chance's Pitch Hereford 98 C4
Chandler's Cross Herts 85 F9
Worcs 98 D5
Chandler's Ford Hants 32 C6
Channel's End Beds 122 F2
Channel Tunnel Kent 55 F7
Channerwick Shetland 313 L6
Chantry Devon 25 C9
Som 45 D8
Suff 108 C2
Chapel Corn 4 C6
Cumb 229 E10
Chapel Allerton Som 44 C2
W Yorks 206 F2
Chapel Amble Corn 10 F5
Chapel Brampton Northants 120 D4
Chapel Chorlton Staffs 150 B6
Chapel Cleeve Som 42 E4
Chapel Cross E Sus 37 C10
Chapel End Beds 122 F2
Beds 103 B11
Cambs 138 G2
C Beds 103 C11
Ches E 167 G11
Essex 105 G11
Northants 138 F2
Warks 134 E6
Chapel-en-le-Frith Derbys 185 E9
Chapel Field Gtr Man 195 F9
Norf 161 E7
Chapel Fields W Mid 118 B6
York 207 C7
Chapelgate Lincs 157 E8
Chapel Green Herts 104 D6
Warks 119 E9
Warks 134 F5
Chapel Haddlesey N Yorks 198 B5
Chapelhall N Lnrk 268 C5
Chapel Head Cambs 138 G6
Chapelhill Dumfries 248 E3
Highld 301 B8
N Ayrs 266 G4
Perth 286 D4
Perth 286 E3
Perth 286 E6
Chapel Hill Aberds 303 F10
Glos 79 E10
Lincs 174 D2
Mon 79 E8
N Yorks 206 D2
Chapel House Lancs 194 F3
Chapel Knapp Wilts 61 F11
Chapelknowe Dumfries 239 C8
Chapel Lawn Shrops 114 B6
Chapel-le-Dale N Yorks 212 D4
Chapel Leigh Som 27 B10
Chapel Mains Borders 271 G11
Chapel Milton Derbys 185 E9
Chapel of Garioch Aberds 303 G7
Chapel of Stoneywood Aberdeen 293 B10
Chapel on Leader Borders 271 G11
Chapel Outon Dumfries 236 E6
Chapel Plaister Wilts 61 F10
Chapel Row Essex 88 E3
E Sus 23 C10
W Berks 64 F5
Chapels Blkburn 195 C7
Cumb 210 C4
Chapel St Leonards Lincs 191 G9
Chapel Stile Cumb 220 D6
Chapelthorpe W Yorks 197 D10
Chapelton Angus 287 C10
Devon 25 B9
Devon 13 D8
Highld 291 B11
S Lanark 268 F4
Chapeltown Blkburn 195 D8
Moray 302 G2
S Yorks 186 B5
W Yorks 206 F2
Chapmanslade Wilts 45 D10
Chapman's Town E Sus 23 B10
Chapman's Well Devon 12 C3
Chapmore End Herts 86 B4
Chappel Essex 107 F7
Charaton Cross Corn 6 B6
Charcott Kent 52 D4
Chard Som 28 F4
Chard Junction Dorset 28 G4
Chardleigh Green Som 28 E4
Chardstock Devon 28 G4
Charfield S Glos 80 G2
Charfield Green S Glos 80 G2
Charfield Hill S Glos 80 G2
Charford Worcs 117 D9
Chargrove Glos 80 B6
Charing Kent 54 D3
Charing Cross Dorset 31 E10
Charing Heath Kent 54 D3
Charing Hill Kent 54 C3
Charingworth Glos 100 D4
Charlbury Oxon 82 B5
Charlcombe Bath 61 F8
Charlcutt Wilts 62 D3
Charlecote Warks 118 F5

Charlemont W Mid 133 E10
Charles Devon 41 G7
Charles Bottom Devon 41 G7
Charlesfield Borders 262 D3
Dumfries 238 D5
Charleshill Sur 49 E11
Charleston Angus 287 C7
Renfs 267 C9
Charlestown Aberdeen 293 C11
Corn 5 E10
Derbys 185 C8
Dorset 17 F9
Fife 279 E11
Gtr Man 195 G10
Gtr Man 195 G11
Highld 299 B8
Highld 300 E6
W Yorks 196 B3
W Yorks 205 F9
Charlestown of Aberlour Moray 302 E2
Charles Tye Suff 125 G10
Charlesworth Derbys 185 C8
Charlton Devon 8 G5
Devon 41 F8
Hants 47 D11
Herts 104 F3
London 68 D2
Northants 101 D10
Northumb 251 E8
Oxon 64 B2
Redcar 226 B2
Som 28 B3
Som 44 E6
Som 45 C7
Som 45 D7
Telford 149 G11
Wilts 30 C6
Wilts 46 B6
Wilts 62 G3
Worcs 99 B10
Worcs 116 C6
W Sus 35 E4
Charlton Abbots Glos 99 G10
Charlton Adam Som 29 B8
Charlton-All-Saints Wilts 31 C11
Charltonbrook S Yorks 186 B4
Charlton Down Dorset 17 C9
Charlton Horethorne Som 29 C11
Charlton Kings Glos 99 G9
Charlton Mackrell Som 29 B8
Charlton Marshall Dorset 30 G5
Charlton Musgrove Som 30 B2
Charlton on Otmoor Oxon 83 B9
Charlton on the Hill Dorset 30 G5
Charlton Park Glos 99 G9
Charlton St Peter Wilts 46 B6
Charlwood E Sus 51 G11
Sur 51 E9
Sur 51 F8
Charman Dean W Sus 35 F11
Charminster B'mouth 19 C8
Dorset 17 C9
Charmouth Dorset 16 C5
Charnage Wilts 45 G10
Charndon Bucks 102 G3
Charnes Staffs 150 C5
Charney Bassett Oxon 82 G5
Charnock Green Lancs 194 D5
Charnock Hall S Yorks 186 E5
Charnock Richard Lancs 194 D5
Charsfield Suff 126 F5
Chart Corner Kent 53 C9
Charter Alley Hants 48 B5
Charterhouse Som 44 B3
Charterville Allotments Oxon 82 C4
Chartham Kent 54 C6
Chartham Hatch Kent 54 C6
Chart Hill Kent 53 D9
Chartridge Bucks 84 E6
Chart Sutton Kent 53 D10
Charvil Wokingham 65 D9
Charwelton Northants 119 F10
Chase Cross London 87 G8
Chase End Street Worcs 98 D5
Chase Hill S Glos 61 B8
Chase Terrace Staffs 133 B10
Chasetown Staffs 133 B10
Chasty Devon 24 G4
Chatburn Lancs 203 E11
Chatcull Staffs 150 C5
Chatford Shrops 131 B9
Chatham Caerph 59 B8
Medway 69 F9
Chatham Green Essex 88 C2
Chathill Northumb 264 D5
Chat Hill W Yorks 205 G8
Chatley Worcs 117 E7
Chattenden Medway 69 E9
Chatter End Essex 105 F9
Chatteris Cambs 139 F7
Chatterley Staffs 168 E4
Chatterton Lancs 195 D9
Chattisham Suff 107 C11
Chattle Hill Warks 134 E3
Chatto Borders 263 F7
Chatton Northumb 264 D3
Chaul End C Beds 103 G11
Chavel Shrops 149 G8
Chavenage Green Glos 80 F5
Chavey Down Brack 65 F11
Chawleigh Devon 26 E2
Chawley Oxon 83 E7
Chawson Worcs 117 E7
Chawston Beds 122 F3
Chawton Hants 49 F8
Chaxhill Glos 80 C2
Chazey Heath Oxon 65 D7
Cheadle Gtr Man 184 D5
Cheadle Staffs 169 G8
Cheadle Heath Gtr Man 184 D5
Cheadle Hulme Gtr Man 184 D5
Cheadle Park Staffs 169 G8
Cheam London 67 G8
Cheapside Herts 85 C10
Sur 50 B4
Chearsley Bucks 84 C2
Chebsey Staffs 151 D7
Checkendon Oxon 65 C7
Checkley Ches E 168 F2
Hereford 97 D11
Staffs 169 G8
Checkley Green Ches E 168 F2
Chedburgh Suff 124 F5
Cheddar Som 44 C3
Cheddington Bucks 84 B6
Cheddleton Staffs 169 E7
Cheddleton Heath Staffs 169 E7

Cheddon Fitzpaine Som 28 B2
Chedglow Wilts 80 G6
Chedgrave Norf 143 D7
Chedington Dorset 29 F7
Chediston Suff 127 B7
Chediston Green Suff 127 B7
Chedworth Glos 81 C9
Chedworth Laines Glos 81 C8
Chedzoy Som 43 F10
Cheeklaw Borders 272 E5
Cheeseman's Green Kent 54 F4
Cheetam Hill Gtr Man 195 G10
Cheglinch Devon 40 E4
Chegworth Kent 53 C10
Cheldon Devon 26 E2
Chelfham Devon 40 F6
Chelford Ches E 184 G4
Chellaston Derby 153 C7
Chell Heath Stoke 168 E5
Chellington Beds 121 F9
Chells Herts 104 F5
Chelmarsh Shrops 132 F4
Chelmer Village Essex 88 D2
Chelmick Shrops 131 E9
Chelmondiston Suff 108 D4
Chelmorton Derbys 169 B10
Chelmsford Essex 88 D2
Chelmsine Som 27 D11
Chelmsley Wood W Mid 134 F3
Chelsea London 67 D9
Chelsfield London 68 G2
Chelsham Sur 51 B11
Chelston Som 27 C11
Torbay 9 C7
Chelston Heathfield Som 27 C11
Chelsworth Suff 107 B9
Chelsworth Common Suff 107 B9
Cheltenham Glos 99 G8
Chelveston Northants 121 D9
Chelvey N Som 60 F3
Chelvey Batch N Som 60 F3
Chelwood Bath 60 G6
Chelwood Common E Sus 36 B6
Chelwood Gate E Sus 36 B6
Chelworth Wilts 81 G7
Chelworth Lower Green Wilts 81 G9
Chelworth Upper Green Wilts 81 G9
Chelynch Som 45 E7
Chemistry Shrops 167 G8
Cheney Longville Shrops 131 G8
Chenhalls Corn 2 B3
Chenies Bucks 85 F8
Cheny Longville Shrops 131 G8
Chepstow Mon 79 G8
Chequerbent Gtr Man 195 F7
Chequerfield W Yorks 198 C3
Chequers Corner Norf 139 B9
Chequertree Kent 54 F4
Cherhill Wilts 62 E4
Cherington Glos 80 F6
Warks 100 D5
Cheriton Devon 41 D8
Hants 33 B9
Kent 55 F7
Pembs 73 F7
Som 24 B3
Swansea 56 C3
Cheriton Bishop Devon 13 C11
Cheriton Cross Devon 13 C11
Cheriton Fitzpaine Devon 26 F5
Cheriton or Stackpole Elidor Pembs 73 F7
Cherrington Telford 150 E3
Cherrybank Perth 286 E5
Cherry Burton E Yorks 208 E5
Cherry Green Essex 105 F11
Herts 105 F7
Cherry Hinton Cambs 123 F9
Cherry Orchard Shrops 149 G9
Worcs 117 G7
Cherry Tree Blkburn 195 B7
Gtr Man 185 C7
Cherrytree Hill Derby 153 B7
Cherry Willingham Lincs 189 G8
Chertsey Sur 66 F4
Chertsey Meads Sur 66 F5
Cheselbourne Dorset 17 B11
Chesham Bucks 85 E7
Gtr Man 195 E10
Chesham Bois Bucks 85 F7
Cheshunt Herts 86 E5
Chesley Kent 69 G11
Cheslyn Hay Staffs 133 B9
Chessetts Wood Warks 118 C3
Chessington London 67 G7
Chessmount Bucks 85 E7
Chestall Staffs 151 G11
Chester Ches W 166 B6
Chesterblade Som 45 E7
Chesterfield Derbys 186 G5
Staffs 134 B2
Chesterhill Midloth 271 B7
Chesterhope Northumb 251 F9
Chesterknowes Borders 262 D2
Chester-le-Street Durham 243 G7
Chester Moor Durham 233 B11
Chesters Borders 262 E4
Borders 262 G4
Chesterton Cambs 123 E9
Cambs 138 D2
Glos 81 E8
Oxon 101 G11
Shrops 132 D5
Staffs 168 F4
Warks 118 F6
Chesterton Green Warks 118 F6
Chesterwood Northumb 241 D8
Chestfield Kent 70 F6
Chestnut Hill Cumb 229 G11
Chestnut Street Kent 69 G11
Cheston Devon 8 D3
Cheswardine Shrops 150 D4
Cheswell Telford 150 F4
Cheswick Northumb 273 F10
Cheswick Buildings Northumb 273 F10
Cheswick Green W Mid 118 C2
Chetnole Dorset 29 E10
Chettiscombe Devon 27 E7
Chettisham Cambs 139 G10
Chettle Dorset 31 E7
Chetton Shrops 132 E3
Chetwode Bucks 102 F2
Chetwynd Aston Telford 150 F5
Chetwynd Park Shrops 150 E4
Cheveley Cambs 124 E3
Chevening Kent 52 B3
Cheverell's Green Herts 85 B9
Chevin End W Yorks 205 E9
Chevington Suff 124 F5
Chevithorne Devon 27 D7
Chew Magna Bath 60 G5
Chew Moor Gtr Man 195 F7
Chew Stoke Bath 60 G5

Chitcombe E Sus 38 C4
Chithurst W Sus 34 C4
Chittering Cambs 123 C9
Chitterley Devon 26 G6
Chitterne Wilts 46 E3
Chittlehamholt Devon 25 C10
Chittlehampton Devon 25 B10
Chitts Hills Essex 107 F9
Chitty Kent 71 G8
Chivelstone Devon 9 G11
Chivenor Devon 40 G4
Chivery Bucks 84 D6
Chobham Sur 66 G3
Choicelee Borders 272 E4
Cholderton Wilts 47 E8
Cholesbury Bucks 84 D6
Chollerford Northumb 241 C10
Chollerton Northumb 241 C10
Cholmondeston Ches E 167 C10
Cholsey Oxon 64 B5
Cholstrey Hereford 115 F8
Cholwell Bath 44 B6
Chop Gate N Yorks 225 F11
Choppington Northumb 253 G7
Chopwell T&W 242 F4
Chorley Ches E 167 E9
Lancs 194 D5
Shrops 132 G3
Staffs 151 G11
Chorley Common W Sus 34 B4
Chorleywood Herts 85 F8
Chorleywood Bottom Herts 85 F8
Chorleywood West Herts 85 F8
Chorlton Ches E 168 E2
Chorlton-cum-Hardy Gtr Man 184 C4
Chorlton Lane Ches W 167 F7
Choulton Shrops 131 F7
Chowdene T&W 243 F7
Chowley Ches W 167 D7
Chownes Mead W Sus 36 C4
Chreagain Highld 289 C10
Chrishall Essex 105 D8
Christchurch Cambs 139 D9
Dorset 19 C9
Glos 79 C9
Newport 59 B10
Christian Malford Wilts 62 D3
Christleton Ches W 166 B6
Christmas Common Oxon 84 G2
Christon N Som 43 B11
Christon Bank Northumb 264 D6
Christow Devon 14 D2
Christ's Hospital W Sus 35 C11
Chryston N Lanark 278 G3
Chub Tor Devon 7 B11
Chuck Hatch E Sus 52 G3
Chudleigh Devon 14 F3
Chudleigh Knighton Devon 14 F2
Chulmleigh Devon 25 E11
Chunal Derbys 185 C8
Church Lancs 195 B8
Churcham Glos 80 B3
Church Aston Telford 150 F4
Churchbank Shrops 114 B6
Church Brampton Northants 120 D4
Churchbridge Corn 6 D4
Staffs 133 B9
Church Brough Cumb 222 C5
Church Broughton Derbys 152 C3
Church Charwelton Northants 119 F10
Church Clough Lancs 204 F3
Church Common Hants 34 B2
Church Coombe Corn 4 G3
Church Cove Corn 2 F6
Church Crookham Hants 49 C10
Churchdown Glos 80 B5
Church Eaton Staffs 150 F6
Churchend Essex 89 G8
Essex 88 C6
Essex 100 G2
Glos 80 F3
Newport 59 B10
S Glos 80 G2
Church End Barnet 86 G2
Beds 121 C10
Beds 122 F2
Brent 67 C8
Bucks 84 B6
Bucks 84 D2
Cambs 121 C11
Cambs 123 F7
Cambs 138 E5
C Beds 103 E9
C Beds 103 E10
C Beds 103 F7
C Beds 103 F8
C Beds 103 G9
E Yorks 209 C7
Essex 87 B11
Essex 88 B2
Essex 105 E10
Essex 106 D4
Essex 106 F4
Glos 80 D2
Glos 99 D7
Hants 48 F5
Herts 85 B10
Herts 85 F9
Herts 104 D4
Herts 105 D8
Lincs 156 C6
Lincs 190 F2
Lincs 201 G7
Oxon 82 B5
Oxon 100 G6
Suff 108 B4
Sur 50 B5
Warks 134 F5
Warks 134 E4
Wilts 62 E2
W Mid 119 B7
Worcs 117 D10
Church Enstone Oxon 101 G7
Churches Green E Sus 23 B10
Church Fenton N Yorks 206 F6
Churchfield Hereford 98 B4
Hereford 133 E10
Churchfields Wilts 31 B10
Churchgate Herts 86 E5
Churchgate Street Essex 87 C7
Church Green Devon 15 B9
Corn 141 G11
Church Gresley Derbys 152 F5
Church Hanborough Oxon 82 C6
Church Hill Ches W 167 C10
Pembs 73 C7
W Mid 133 D9
Worcs 117 D10
Church Hougham Kent 55 E9
Church Houses N Yorks 226 F2
Churchill Devon 28 G4

Devon 40 E5
N Som 44 B2
Oxon 100 C3
Worcs 117 B7
Worcs 117 G8
Churchill Green N Som 60 G2
Churchinford Som 28 E2
Church Knowle Dorset 18 E4
Church Laneham Notts 188 F4
Church Langton Leics 136 E4
Highld 290 F3
Perth 285 D11
Church Lawford Warks 119 B8
Church Lawton Ches E 168 D4
Church Leigh Staffs 151 B10
Church Lench Worcs 117 G10
Church Mayfield Staffs 169 G11
Ches E
Church Minshull 167 C11
Ches E
Churchmoor Rough 131 E8
Shrops
Church Norton W Sus 22 D5
Church Oakley Hants 48 C5
Churchover Warks 135 G10
Church Preen Shrops 131 D10
Church Pulverbatch 131 C8
Shrops
Churchstanton Som 27 E11
Churchstoke Powys 130 E5
Churchstow Devon 8 F4
Church Stowe Northants 120 F2
Churchtown Pembs 73 D10
Churchtown Corn 11 F7
Cumb 230 C3
Derbys 170 C3
Devon 24 G3
Devon 41 E7
IoM 192 C5
Lancs 202 E5
Mers 193 D11
Shrops 130 F5
Som 42 F3
Church Town Corn 4 G3
Leics 153 F7
N Lincs 199 F9
Som 51 C11
Church Village Rhondda 58 B5
Church Warsop Notts 171 C11
Church Westcote Glos 100 G4
Church Whitfield Kent 55 D10
Church Wilne Derbys 153 C8
Churchwood W Sus 35 D8
Churnet Grange Staffs 169 E7
Churnsike Lodge
Northumb 240 B5
Churscombe Torbay 9 C7
Churston Ferrers Torbay 9 D8
Churt Sur 49 F11
Churton Ches W 166 D6
Churwell W Yorks 197 B9
Chute Cadley Wilts 47 C10
Chute Standen Wilts 47 C10
Chwefforf Conwy 180 G4
Chwilog Gwyn 145 B8
Chwitffordd / Whitford
Flint 181 F10
Chyandour Corn 1 C5
Chyanvounder Corn 2 E5
Chycoose Corn 3 C4
Chynhale Corn 2 C4
Chynoweth Corn 2 E5
Chyvarloe Corn 2 E5
Cicelyford Mon 79 E8
Cilan Uchaf Gwyn 144 E5
Cilau Pembs 91 D8
Cilcain Flint 165 B11
Cilcennin Ceredig 111 E10
Cilcewydd Powys 130 C4
Cilfor Gwyn 146 B2
Cilfrew Neath 76 E3
Cilfynydd Rhondda 77 G9
Cilgerran Pembs 92 C3
Cilgwyn Carms 94 F4
Ceredig 92 C6
Gwyn 163 E7
Pembs 91 D11
Ciliau Aeron Ceredig 111 F9
Cill Amhlaidh W Isles 297 G3
Cill Donnain W Isles 297 J3
Cille Bhrighde W Isles 297 K3
Cille Eireabhagh W Isles 297 K3
Cille Pheadair W Isles 297 K3
Cilmaengwyn Neath 76 D2
Cilmery Powys 113 G10
Cilsan Carms 93 G11
Ciltalgarth Gwyn 164 G5
Ciltwrch Powys 96 C3
Cilybebyll Neath 76 E2
Cil y coed / Caldicot
Mon 60 B3
Cilycwm Carms 94 D5
Cimla Neath 57 B9
Cinderford Glos 79 C11
Cinderhill Derbys 170 F5
Nottingham 171 G8
Cinder Hill Gtr Man 195 F9
Kent 52 D4
W Mid 133 E8
W Sus 36 B5
Cinnamon Brow Warr 183 C10
Cippenham Slough 66 C2
Cippyn Pembs 92 B2
Circebost W Isles 304 E3
Cirencester Glos 81 E8
City London 67 C10
Powys 130 F4
V Glam 58 D3
City Dulas Anglesey 179 D7
Clabhach Argyll 288 D3
Clachaig Argyll 276 E2
Highld 292 B2
N Ayrs 255 E10
Clachan Argyll 255 B8
Argyll 275 B8
Argyll 284 C5
Highld 289 C10
Highld 295 B7
Highld 298 C4
Highld 307 L6
W Isles 297 G3
Clachaneasy Dumfries 236 B5
Clachanmore Dumfries 236 E2
Clachan na Luib
W Isles 296 E4
Clachan of Campsie
E Dunb 278 F2
Clachan of Glendaruel
Argyll 275 E10
Clachan-Seil Argyll 275 B8
Clachan Strachur Argyll 284 G4
Clachbreck Argyll 275 F8
Clachnabrain Angus 292 G5
Clachtoll Highld 307 G5
Clackmannan Clack 279 C8
Clackmarras Moray 302 D2
Clacton-on-Sea Essex 89 B11
Cladach Chairinis
W Isles 296 F4

Cladach Chireboist
W Isles 296 E3
Claddach Argyll 254 B2
Claddach Knockline
W Isles 296 E3
Cladich Argyll 284 E4
Cladich Steading Argyll 284 E4
Cladswell Worcs 117 F10
Claggan Highld 289 E8
Highld 290 F3
Claigan Highld 298 D2
Claines Worcs 117 F7
Clandown Bath 45 B7
Clanfield Hants 33 D11
Oxon 82 E3
Clanking Bucks 84 D4
Clanville Hants 47 D10
Som 44 G6
Wilts 62 D2
Claonaig Argyll 255 B9
Claonel Highld 309 J5
Clapgate Dorset 31 G8
Herts 105 G8
Clapham Beds 121 G10
Devon 14 D3
London 67 D9
N Yorks 212 F4
W Sus 35 F9
Clapham Green Beds 121 G10
N Yorks 205 B10
Clapham Hill Kent 70 G6
Clapham Park London 67 E9
Clap Hill Kent 54 F5
Clappers Borders 273 D8
Clappersgate Cumb 221 E7
Clapphoull Shetland 313 L6
Clapton Som 28 F6
Som 44 C6
Clapton in Gordano
N Som 60 E3
Clapton-on-the-Hill
Glos 81 B11
Clapton Park London 67 C10
Clapworthy Devon 25 C11
Clarach Ceredig 128 G2
Clarack Aberds 292 D6
Clara Vale T&W 242 E4
Clarborough Notts 188 E2
Clardon Highld 310 C5
Clare Oxon 83 F11
Suff 106 B5
Clarebrand Dumfries 237 C9
Claregate W Mid 133 C7
Claremont Park Sur 66 G6
Claremount W Yorks 196 B5
Clarencefield Dumfries 238 D3
Clarence Park N Som 59 G10
Clarendon Park
Leicester 135 C11
Clareston Pembs 73 C7
Clarilaw Borders 262 D3
Borders 262 F2
Clarken Green Hants 48 C5
Clark Green Ches E 184 F6
Clarksfield Gtr Man 196 G2
Clark's Green Sur 51 F7
Clark's Hill Lincs 157 E7
Clarkston E Renf 267 D11
N Lnrk 268 B5
Clase Swansea 57 B7
Clashandorran Highld 300 E5
Clashcoig Highld 309 K6
Clashgour Argyll 284 C6
Clashindarroch Aberds 302 F4
Clashmore Highld 306 F5
Highld 309 L7
Clashnessie Highld 306 F5
Clashnoir Moray 302 G2
Clate Shetland 313 G7
Clatford Wilts 63 F7
Clatford Oakcuts Hants 47 F10
Clathy Perth 286 F3
Clatt Aberds 302 G5
Clatter Powys 129 E9
Clatterford IoW 20 D5
Clatterford End Essex 87 C10
Essex 87 D9
Essex 87 E8
Clatterin Bridge Aberds 293 F8
Clatto Fife 287 F8
Clatworthy Som 42 G5
Clauchlands N Ayrs 256 C2
Claughton Lancs 202 E6
Lancs 211 F11
Mers 182 D4
Clavelshay Som 43 G9
Claverdon Warks 118 E3
Claverham N Som 60 F2
Claverhambury Essex 86 E6
Clavering Essex 105 E9
Claverley Shrops 132 E5
Claverton Bath 61 G9
Claverton Down Bath 61 G9
Clawdd-côch V Glam 58 D5
Clawdd-newydd Denb 165 E9
Clawdd Poncen Denb 165 G9
Clawthorpe Cumb 211 D10
Clawton Devon 12 B3
Claxby Lincs 189 C10
Lincs 191 G7
Claxby St Andrew 191 G7
Claxton Norf 142 C6
N Yorks 216 A3
Claybokie Aberds 292 D2
Claybrooke Magna Leics 135 F9
Claybrooke Parva Leics 135 F9
Clay Common Suff 143 G9
Clay Coton Northants 119 B11
Clay Cross Derbys 170 C5
Claydon Oxon 119 G8
Suff 126 G2
Clay End Herts 104 F6
Claygate Dumfries 239 B9
Kent 52 E6
Kent 53 E8
Sur 66 G6
Claygate Cross Kent 52 B6
Clayhall Hants 21 B8
London 86 G6
Clayhanger Devon 27 D8
Som 43 G7
W Mid 133 C10
York 207 C7
Clayhidon Devon 27 D11
Clayhill E Sus 38 C4
Hants 32 F4
Clay Hill Bristol 60 D6
W Berks 64 E5
Clayhithe Cambs 123 E10
Clayholes Angus 287 D9
Clay Lake Lincs 156 E5
Clayland Stirl 277 D11
Clay Mills Derbys 152 D5

Clayock Highld 310 D5
Claypit Hill Cambs 123 G7
Claypits Devon 27 B7
Glos 80 D3
Kent 54 G4
Suff 140 G4
Claypole Lincs 172 F5
Clays End Bath 61 G8
Claythorpe Lincs 190 F6
Clayton Gtr Man 184 B5
Staffs 168 G5
S Yorks 198 F3
W Sus 36 E3
W Yorks 205 G8
Clayton Brook Lancs 194 C5
Clayton Green Lancs 194 C5
Clayton Heights
W Yorks 205 G8
Clayton-le-Dale Lancs 203 G9
Clayton-le-Moors
Lancs 203 G10
Clayton-le-Woods
Lancs 194 C5
Clayton West W Yorks 197 E9
Clayworth Notts 188 D2
Cleadale Highld 294 G6
Cleadon T&W 243 E9
Cleadon Park T&W 243 E9
Clearbrook Devon 7 B10
Clearwell Glos 79 D9
Newport 59 B9
Clearwood Wilts 45 D10
Cleasby N Yorks 224 C5
Cleat Orkney 314 H4
Orkney 314 H4
Cleatlam Durham 224 B2
Cleator Cumb 219 C10
Cleator Moor Cumb 219 B10
Cleave Devon 28 G2
Clebrig Highld 308 F5
Cleckheaton W Yorks 197 B8
Cleddon Mon 79 E8
Cleedownton Shrops 131 G11
Cleehill Shrops 115 B11
Cleekhimin N Lnrk 268 D5
Cleemarsh Shrops 131 G11
Clee St Margaret
Shrops 131 G11
Suff 126 C4
Cleestanton Shrops 115 B11
Cleethorpes NE Lincs 201 F10
Cleeton St Mary Shrops 116 B2
Cleeve N Som 60 F3
Oxon 64 C6
Cleeve Hill Glos 99 G9
Cleeve Prior Worcs 99 B11
Cleghorn S Lnrk 269 F8
Clegyrnant Powys 129 B8
Clehonger Hereford 97 D9
Cleirwy / Clyro Powys 96 C4
Cleish Perth 279 B11
Cleland N Lnrk 268 D5
Clement's End C Beds 85 B8
Clement Street Kent 68 E4
Clench Wilts 63 G7
Clench Common Wilts 63 F7
Clenchwarton Norf 157 E11
Clennell Northumb 251 B10
Clent Worcs 117 B8
Cleobury Mortimer
Shrops 116 B3
Cleobury North Shrops 132 F2
Cleongart Argyll 255 D7
Clephanton Highld 301 D8
Clerkenwater Corn 5 B11
Clerkenwell London 67 C10
Clerk Green W Yorks 197 C8
Clerklands Borders 262 E2
Clermiston Edin 280 G3
Clestrain Orkney 314 F3
Cleuch Head Borders 262 G3
Cleughbrae Dumfries 238 C3
Clevancy Wilts 62 D5
Clevans Renfs 267 B7
Clevedon N Som 60 E2
Cleveley Oxon 101 G7
Cleveleys Lancs 202 E2
Cleverton Wilts 62 B3
Clevis Bridgend 57 F10
Clewer Bath 44 C2
Clewer New Town
Windsor 66 D2
Clewer Village Windsor 66 D3
Cley next the Sea Norf 177 E8
Cliaid W Isles 297 L2
Cliasmol W Isles 305 H2
Cliburn Cumb 231 G7
Click Mill Orkney 314 D3
Cliddesden Hants 48 D6
Cliff Derbys 185 D8
Warks 134 D4
Cliffburn Angus 287 C10
Cliffe Lancs 203 G10
Medway 69 D8
N Yorks 207 G9
N Yorks 224 B4
Cliff End E Sus 38 E5
W Yorks 196 D6
Cliffe Woods Medway 69 E8
Clifford Devon 24 C4
Hereford 96 B4
W Yorks 206 E4
Clifford Chambers
Warks 118 G3
Clifford's Mesne Glos 98 G4
Cliffs End Kent 71 G10
Clifftown Shend 69 B11
Clifton Bristol 60 E5
C Beds 104 D3
Ches W 183 F8
Cumb 230 F6
Derbys 169 G11
Devon 40 E5
Gtr Man 195 G9
Lancs 202 G5
Northum 252 A6
Nottingham 153 C11
N Yorks 205 D9
Oxon 101 E9
Stirl 285 D7
S Yorks 186 C6
S Yorks 187 B8
Worcs 98 B6
W Yorks 197 C10
York 207 C7
Clifton Campville Staffs 152 G5
Cliftoncote Borders 263 E8
Clifton Green Gtr Man 195 G9
Clifton Hampden Oxon 83 F8
Clifton Junction
Gtr Man 195 G9
Clifton Manor C Beds 104 D3
Clifton Maybank Dorset 29 E9
Clifton Reynes
M Keynes 121 G8
Clifton upon Dunsmore
Warks 119 B10

Clifton upon Teme
Worcs 116 E4
Cliftonville Kent 71 E11
N Lnrk 268 B4
Climping W Sus 35 G8
Climpy S Lnrk 269 D8
Clink Som 45 D9
Clinkham Wood Mers 183 B8
Clint N Yorks 205 B11
Clint Green Norf 159 G10
Clintmains Borders 262 C4
Cliobh W Isles 304 E2
Clipiau Gwyn 146 G6
Clippesby Norf 161 G8
Clippings Green Norf 159 G10
Clipsham Rutland 155 F9
Clipston Northants 136 G4
Notts 154 C2
Clipstone Swindon 63 C7
Notts 171 C9
Clitheroe Lancs 203 E10
Cliuthar W Isles 305 J3
Clive Ches W 167 B11
Shrops 149 E10
Clive Green Ches W 167 C11
Clive Vale E Sus 38 E4
Clivocast Shetland 312 C8
Clixby Lincs 200 G6
Cloatley Wilts 81 G7
Cloatley End Wilts 81 G7
Clocaenog Denb 165 E9
Clochan Aberds 303 E9
Moray 302 C4
Clock Face Mers 183 C8
Clock House London 67 G9
Clockmill Borders 272 E5
Clock Mills Hereford 96 B5
Cloddiau Powys 130 B4
Cloddymoss Moray 301 D9
Clodock Hereford 96 F6
Cloford Som 45 E8
Cloford Common Som 45 E8
Cloigyn Carms 74 C6
Clola Aberds 303 E11
Clophill C Beds 103 D11
Clopton Northants 137 G11
Suff 126 G4
Clopton Corner Suff 126 G4
Clopton Green Suff 124 G4
Closeburn Dumfries 247 E9
Close Clark IoM 192 E3
Close House Durham 233 F10
Closworth Som 29 E9
Clothall Herts 104 E5
Clothall Common Herts 104 E5
Clotton Ches W 167 C8
Clotton Common
Ches W 167 C8
Cloudesley Bush Warks 135 F9
Clouds Hereford 97 D11
Clough Gtr Man 196 D2
Gtr Man 196 E5
Clough Dene Durham 242 F5
Cloughfold Lancs 195 C10
Clough Foot W Yorks 196 C2
Clough Hall Staffs 168 E4
Clough Head W Yorks 196 C5
Cloughton N Yorks 227 G10
Cloughton Newlands
N Yorks 227 F10
Clounlaid Highld 289 D9
Clousta Shetland 313 H5
Clouston Orkney 314 E2
Clova Aberds 302 G4
Angus 292 F5
Clovelly Devon 24 C4
Clove Lodge Durham 223 B8
Clovenfords Borders 261 B10
Clovenstone Aberds 293 B9
Cloves Moray 301 C11
Clovullin Highld 290 G2
Clowance Wood Corn 2 C4
Clow Bridge Lancs 195 B10
Clowne Derbys 187 F7
Clows Top Worcs 116 C4
Cloy Wrex 166 G5
Cluanie Inn Highld 290 B2
Cluanie Lodge Highld 290 B2
Clubmoor Mers 182 C5
Clubworthy Corn 11 C11
Cluddley Telford 150 G2
Clun Shrops 130 G6
Clunbury Shrops 131 G7
Clunderwen Carms 73 B10
Clune Highld 301 G9
Clunes Highld 290 E4
Clungunford Shrops 115 B7
Clunie Aberds 302 D6
Perth 286 C5
Clunton Shrops 130 G6
Cluny Fife 280 B4
Cluny Castle Aberds 293 B8
Highld 291 D8
Clutton Bath 44 B6
Ches W 167 E7
Clwt-grugoer Conwy 165 C7
Clwt-y-bont Gwyn 163 C9
Clwydfagwyr M Tydf 77 D8
Clydach Mon 78 C2
Swansea 75 E11
Clydach Terrace Powys 77 C11
Clydach Vale Rhondda 77 G7
Clydebank W Dunb 277 G9
Clyffe Pypard Wilts 62 D5
Clynder Argyll 276 E4
Clyne Neath 76 E4
Clynelish Highld 311 J2
Clynnog-fawr Gwyn 162 F6
Clyro / Cleirwy Powys 96 C4
Clyst Honiton Devon 14 C5
Clyst Hydon Devon 27 G8
Clyst St George Devon 14 D5
Clyst St Lawrence Devon 27 G8
Clyst St Mary Devon 14 C5
Cnip W Isles 304 E2
Cnoc Amhlaigh W Isles 304 E7
Cnoc an t-Solais
W Isles 304 D6
Cnocbreac Argyll 274 F5
Cnoc Fhionn Highld 295 D10
Cnoc Màiri W Isles 304 E6
Cnoc Rolum W Isles 296 F3
Cnwch-coch Ceredig 112 B3
Coachford Aberds 302 E4
Coad's Green Corn 11 F11
Coal Aston Derbys 186 F5
Coalbank Telford 150 C2
Coalbrookdale Telford 132 B3
Coalbrookvale Bl Gwent 77 D11
Coalburn S Lnrk 259 C8
Coalburns T&W 242 E4
Coalcleugh Northum 232 B2
Coaley Glos 80 E3
Coaley Peak Glos 80 E3
Coalford Aberds 293 D10

Coalhall E Ayrs 257 F10
Coalhill Essex 88 F3
Coalmoor Telford 132 B3
Coalpit Field Warks 135 F7
Coalpit Heath S Glos 61 C7
Coalport Telford 132 C3
Coalsnaughton Clack 279 B8
Coaltown of Balgonie
Fife 280 B5
Coaltown of Wemyss
Fife 280 B5
Coalville Leics 153 G8
Coalway Glos 79 C9
Coanwood Northumb 240 F5
Coarsewell Devon 8 E4
Coat Som 29 C7
Coatbridge N Lnrk 268 C4
Coatdyke N Lnrk 268 C5
Coate Swindon 63 C7
Wilts 62 G4
Coates Cambs 138 D6
Glos 81 E7
Lancs 204 D3
Lincs 188 E6
Midloth 270 C4
Notts 188 E4
W Sus 34 D6
Coatham Redcar 235 F7
Coatham Mundeville
Darl 233 G11
Cobairdy Aberds 302 E5
Cobbaton Devon 25 B10
Cobbler's Corner Worcs 116 F5
Cobbler's Green Norf 142 E5
Cobbler's Plain Mon 79 E7
Cobbs Warr 183 D10
Cobb's Cross Glos 98 E5
Cobbs Fenn Essex 106 E4
Cobby Syke N Yorks 205 B9
Coberley Glos 81 B7
Cobhall Common
Hereford 97 D9
Cobham Kent 69 F7
Sur 66 G6
Cobleland Stirl 277 B10
Cobler's Green Essex 87 B11
Cobley Dorset 31 C8
Cobley Hill Worcs 117 C10
Cobnash Hereford 115 F9
Cock Alley Derbys 186 G6
Cock and End Suff 124 G4
Cockayne N Yorks 226 F2
Cock Bank Wrex 166 F5
Cock Bevington Warks 117 G11
Cock Bridge Aberds 292 C4
Cockburnspath Borders 282 G5
Cock Clarks Essex 88 E4
Cocken Durham 234 C2
Cockenzie and Port Seton
E Loth 281 F8
Cocker Bar Lancs 194 C4
Cockerham Lancs 202 C5
Cockermouth Cumb 229 E8
Cockernhoe Herts 104 G2
Cockernhoe Green
Herts 104 G2
Cockersdale W Yorks 197 B8
Cockett Swansea 56 C6
Cocketty Aberds 293 F9
Cockfield Durham 233 G8
Suff 125 G8
Cockfosters London 86 F3
Cock Gate Hereford 115 D9
Cock Green Essex 87 B11
Cockhill Som 44 G6
Cock Hill N Yorks 206 B2
Cocking W Sus 34 D5
Cocking Causeway
W Sus 34 D5
Cocklake Som 44 C2
Cocklaw Northum 241 C10
Cockleford Glos 81 C7
Cockley Beck Cumb 220 E4
Cockley Cley Norf 140 C5
Cockley Hill W Yorks 197 D7
Cock Marling E Sus 38 D5
Cocknowle Dorset 18 E4
Cockpole Green
Wokingham 65 C9
Cocks Corn 4 E5
Cocks Green Suff 125 F7
Cockshead Ceredig 112 F2
Cockshutford Shrops 131 F11
Cockshutt Shrops 149 D8
Shrops 149 E8
Cock Street Kent 53 C9
Suff 107 D7
Cockthorpe Norf 177 E7
Cockwells Corn 2 C2
Cockwood Devon 14 E5
Devon 43 E8
Cockyard Derbys 185 E8
Hereford 97 E8
Codda Corn 11 F9
Coddenham Suff 126 G3
Coddenham Green Suff 126 F3
Coddington Ches W 167 D7
Hereford 98 C4
Notts 172 D5
Codford St Mary Wilts 46 F3
Codford St Peter Wilts 46 F3
Codicote Herts 86 B2
Codicote Bottom Herts 86 B2
Codmore Hill W Sus 35 C9
Codnor Derbys 170 F6
Codnor Breach Derbys 170 F6
Codnor Gate Derbys 170 F6
Codnor Park Derbys 170 F6
Codrington S Glos 61 D8
Codsall Staffs 133 C7
Codsall Wood Staffs 132 B6
Codsend Som 41 F11
Coed Cae Bl Gwent 77 D11
Coedcae Bl Gwent 77 D11
Coed Cwnwr Mon 78 E6
Coedely Rhondda 58 B4
Coed Eva Torf 78 G3
Coedkernew Newport 59 C9
Coed Llai / Leeswood
Flint 166 D3
Coel Mawr Gwyn 179 G9
Coalpoeth Neath 76 E4
Coed-Talon Flint 166 D3
Coed-y-bryn Ceredig 93 C7
Coed-y-caerau Newport 78 G5
Coed-y-fedw Mon 78 D6

Coed-y-paen Mon 78 F4
Coed-y-parc Gwyn 163 B10
Coed-yr-ynys Powys 96 G3
Coed Ystumgwern
Gwyn 145 E11
Coed-y-wlad Gwyn 130 B4
Coffee Hall M Keynes 103 D7
Coffinswell Devon 14 C5
Cofton Devon 14 C5
Cofton Common
Glos 80 C4
Cofton Hackett Worcs 117 B10
Cog V Glam 59 F7
Cogan V Glam 59 E7
Cogenhoe Northants 120 E6
Cogges Oxon 82 D5
Coggeshall Essex 106 G6
Coggeshall Hamlet
Essex 107 G7
Coggins Mill E Sus 37 B9
Coignafearn Lodge
Highld 291 B8
Coignascallan Highld 291 B9
Coig Peighinnean
W Isles 304 B7
Coig Peighinnean Bhuirgh
W Isles 304 C6
Coilacriech Aberds 292 D5
Coilantogle Stirl 285 G8
Coilessan Argyll 284 G6
Coileag W Isles 297 K3
Coillaig Argyll 284 E5
Coille Mhorgil Highld 290 B5
Coillore Highld 294 B5
Coirea-chrombe Stirl 285 G9
Coisley Hill S Yorks 186 E6
Coity Bridgend 58 C2
Cokenach Herts 105 E8
Cokhay Green Derbys 152 D5
Col W Isles 304 D6
Colaboll Highld 309 H5
Colan Corn 5 C7
Colaton Raleigh Devon 15 D7
Colbost Highld 298 E2
Colburn N Yorks 224 F3
Colby Cumb 231 G9
IoM 192 E3
Norf 160 C4
Colchester Essex 107 G10
Colchester Green Suff 125 F8
Cold Ash W Berks 64 F4
Cold Ashby Northants 120 B3
Cold Ash Hill Hants 49 G10
Cold Ashton S Glos 61 E9
Cold Aston Glos 81 B10
Coldbackie Highld 308 D6
Coldbeck Cumb 222 E4
Cold Bevington Warks 117 G11
Cold Blow Pembs 73 C10
Cold Brayfield
M Keynes 121 G8
Coldbrook Powys 96 D3
Cold Christmas Herts 86 B5
Cold Cotes N Yorks 212 E4
Coldean Brighton 36 F4
Coldeast Devon 14 G2
Coldeaton Derbys 169 D10
Cold Elm Glos 98 E6
Colden Common Hants 33 C7
Coldfair Green Suff 127 E8
Coldham Cambs 139 C8
Staffs 133 B7
Coldham's Common
Cambs 123 F9
Cold Hanworth Lincs 189 E8
Coldharbour Corn 4 F5
Devon 27 G9
Dorset 31 G8
Glos 79 E9
London 68 C4
Sur 50 E6
Cold Harbour Dorset 18 B5
Herts 85 B10
Kent 69 G11
Lincs 155 C9
Oxon 64 D6
Wilts 45 B11
Windsor 65 D10
Cold Hatton Telford 150 E2
Cold Hatton Heath
Telford 150 E2
Cold Hesledon Durham 234 B4
Cold Hiendley W Yorks 197 E11
Cold Higham Northants 120 G3
Coldingham Borders 273 B8
Cold Inn Pembs 73 D10
Cold Kirby N Yorks 215 C10
Coldmeece Staffs 151 C7
Cold Moss Heath
Ches E 168 C3
Cold Newton Leics 136 B4
Cold Northcott Corn 11 D10
Cold Norton Essex 88 E4
Coldoch Stirl 278 B3
Cold Overton Leics 154 G6
Coldra Newport 59 B11
Coldrain Perth 286 G4
Coldred Kent 55 D9
Coldridge Devon 25 F11
Coldrife Northumb 252 E4
Cold Row Lancs 202 E4
Coldstream Angus 287 D7
Borders 263 B8
Coldwaltham W Sus 35 D8
Cold Well Staffs 151 G11
Coldwells Aberds 303 E11
Coldwells Croft Aberds 302 G5
Colebatch Shrops 130 F6
Colebrook Devon 27 F8
Colebrooke Devon 13 B11
Coleburn Moray 302 D2
Coleby Lincs 173 C7
N Lincs 199 E11
Cole End Essex 105 F11
Warks 134 F4
Colegate End Norf 142 F3
Coleford Devon 26 G3
Glos 79 C9
Som 45 D7
Cole Green Herts 86 C3
Herts 105 E8
Colehall W Mid 134 F2
Coleman Green Herts 85 C11
Coleman's Hatch E Sus 52 G3
Colemere Shrops 149 C8
Colemore Hants 49 G8
Colemore Green Shrops 132 D4
Colenden Perth 286 E5
Cole Park London 67 E7
Colerne Wilts 61 E10
Cole Row Lancs 202 E4
Colesbourne Glos 81 C8
Colesbrook Dorset 30 B3
Cole's Cross Dorset 28 C5
Colesden Beds 122 F2
Coles Green Suff 107 C11
Worcs 116 G5
Coleshill Bucks 85 F7
Oxon 82 G2
Warks 134 F4
Coles Meads Sur 51 C9
Colestocks Devon 27 G9
Colethrop Glos 80 C4
Coley Bath 44 B5
Reading 65 E8
W Yorks 196 B6
Colfin Dumfries 236 D2
Colgate W Sus 51 G8
Colgrain Argyll 276 E6
Colham Green London 66 C5
Colinsburgh Fife 287 G8
Colinton Edin 270 B4
Colintraive Argyll 275 F11
Colkirk Norf 159 D8
Suff 197 D8
Collace Perth 286 D6
Collafield Glos 79 C11
Collafirth Shetland 312 G6
Collam W Isles 305 J3
Collamoor Head Corn 11 C5
Collaton Corn 9 G9
Collaton St Mary Torbay 9 D7
College Milton S Lnrk 268 D2
College of Roseisle
Moray 301 C11
College Park London 67 C8
College Town Brack 65 G11
Collennan S Ayrs 257 C8
Collessie Fife 286 F6
Colleton Mills Devon 25 D11
Collett's Br Norf 139 B9
Collett's Green Worcs 116 G6
Collier Row London 87 G8
Collier's End Herts 105 G7
Collier's Green E Sus 38 C3
Kent 53 F9
Colliers Hatch Essex 87 E8
Collier Street Kent 53 D8
Collier's Wood London 67 E9
Colliery Row T&W 234 B2
Collieston Aberds 303 G10
Collin Dumfries 238 C3
Collingbourne Ducis
Wilts 47 C8
Collingbourne Kingston
Wilts 47 C8
Collingham Notts 172 C4
W Yorks 206 D3
Collington Hereford 116 E2
Collingtree Northants 120 F5
Collingwood Northumb 243 B7
Collins End Oxon 65 D7
Collins Green Warr 183 C9
Worcs 116 F4
Collipriest Devon 27 E8
Colliston Angus 287 C10
Collycroft Warks 135 F7
Collynie Aberds 303 F8
Collyweston Northants 137 C9
Colmonell S Ayrs 244 F4
Colmslie Borders 262 B2
Colmsliehill Borders 271 G10
Colmworth Beds 122 F2
Colnabaichin Aberds 292 C4
Colnbrook Slough 66 D4
Colne Cambs 123 B8
Lancs 204 E3
Colne Bridge W Yorks 197 C7
Colne Edge Lancs 204 E3
Colne Engaine Essex 107 E7
Colnefields Cambs 123 B8
Coln Rogers Glos 81 D9
Coln St Aldwyns Glos 81 D10
Coln St Dennis Glos 81 C9
Cologin Argyll 289 G10
Colpitts Grange
Northumb 241 F10
Colpy Aberds 302 F6
Colquhar Borders 270 G6
Colscott Devon 24 E5
Colshaw Staffs 169 B8
Colsterdale N Yorks 214 C2
Colsterworth Lincs 155 E8
Colston E Dunb 268 B2
Pembs 73 C7
Colston Bassett Notts 154 C3
Colstrope Bucks 65 B9
Coltfield Moray 301 C11
Colt Hill Hants 49 C8
Colthouse Cumb 221 F7
Colthrop W Berks 64 F4
Coltishall Norf 160 F5
Coltness N Lnrk 268 D6
Colton Cumb 210 B6
Norf 142 B3
N Yorks 206 E6
Staffs 151 E11
Suff 125 D7
W Yorks 206 G3
Colt Park Cumb 210 D6
Col's Green S Glos 61 C8
Colt's Green S Glos 61 C8
Col Uarach W Isles 304 E6
Columbia T&W 243 F8
Columbjohn Devon 14 B5
Colva Powys 96 B4
Colvend Dumfries 237 D10
Colvister Shetland 312 D7
Colwall Hereford 98 C4
Colwall Green Hereford 98 C4
Colwall Stone Hereford 98 C4
Colwell IoW 20 D2
Northumb 241 B11
Colwich Staffs 151 E10
Colwick Notts 171 G10
Colwinston / Tregolwyn
V Glam 58 D2
Colworth W Sus 22 C6
Colwyn Bay / Bae Colwyn
Conwy 180 F4
Colychurch Bridgend 58 C2
Colyford Devon 15 C10
Colyton Devon 15 C10
Colzie Fife 286 F6
Combe Devon 7 D11
Devon 8 B4
Hereford 115 E7
Oxon 82 B6
Som 28 B6
Combe Almer Dorset 18 B5
Combe Common Sur 50 F2
Combe Down Bath 61 G9
Combe Fishacre Devon 8 C6
Combe Florey Som 43 G7
Combe Hay Bath 45 B8
Combeinteignhead
Devon 14 G4
Combe Martin Devon 40 D5
Combe Moor Hereford 115 E7
Combe Pafford Torbay 9 B8
Combe Raleigh Devon 27 G11
Comberbach Ches W 183 F10
Comberford Staffs 134 B3
Comberton Cambs 123 F7
Hereford 115 D9
Combe St Nicholas Som 28 E4
Combe Throop Som 30 C2
Combpyne Devon 15 C11
Combrew Devon 40 G4
Combridge Staffs 151 B11
Combrook Warks 118 G6
Combs Derbys 185 F8
Suff 125 F11
W Yorks 197 D8
Combs Ford Suff 125 F11
Combwich Som 43 E9
Comers Aberds 293 C8
Come-to-Good Corn 4 G5
Comeytrowe Som 28 C2
Comford Corn 2 B6
Comfort Corn 2 D6
Comhampton Worcs 116 D6
Comins Coch Ceredig 128 G2
Comiston Edin 270 B4
Comley Shrops 131 D9
Commercial End
Cambs 123 E11
Commins Denb 165 C10
Commins Capel Betws
Ceredig 112 F2
Commins Coch Powys 128 C5
Common Cefn-llwyn
Mon 78 G4
Commondale N Yorks 226 C3
Common Edge Blkpool 202 G2
Common End Cumb 228 G6
Derbys 170 C6
Common Hill Hereford 97 E11
Common Moor Corn 6 B4
Common Platt Wilts 62 B6
Commonside Ches W 183 G8
Derbys 170 G2
Notts 171 G7
Common Side Ches W 167 B9
Derbys 170 C6
Derbys 186 F4
Common-y-coed Mon 60 B3
Comp Kent 52 B6
Compass Som 43 G9
Compstall Gtr Man 185 C7
Compton Derbys 169 F11
Devon 9 C7
Farnham, Sur 49 D11
Hants 32 B4
Hants 33 G8
Plym 7 D9
Staffs 132 G6
Sur 50 D3
W Berks 64 D4
Wilts 46 C6
W Mid 133 D7
W Sus 34 E3
W Yorks 206 E3
Compton Abbas Dorset 30 D5
Compton Abdale Glos 81 B9
Compton Bassett Wilts 62 E5
Compton Beauchamp
Oxon 63 B9
Compton Bishop Som 43 B11
Compton Chamberlayne
Wilts 31 B8
Compton Common Bath 60 G6
Compton Dando Bath 60 G6
Compton Dundon Som 44 G3
Compton Durville Som 28 D6
Compton End Hants 33 B7
Compton Green Glos 98 F4
Compton Greenfield
S Glos 60 C5
Compton Martin Bath 44 B4
Compton Pauncefoot
Som 29 B10
Compton Valence
Dorset 17 C7
Comrie Fife 279 D10
Highld 300 D4
Perth 285 E11
Comrue Dumfries 248 F3
Conaglen House Highld 290 G2
Conanby S Yorks 187 B7
Conchra Argyll 275 E11
Highld 295 C10
Concord T&W 243 F8
Concraig Perth 286 F2
Concraigie Perth 286 C5
Conder Green Lancs 202 B5
Conderton Worcs 99 D8
Condicote Glos 100 F3
Condorrat N Lnrk 278 G5
Condover Shrops 131 B9
Coney Hall London 67 G11
Coney Hill Glos 80 B5
Coneyhurst W Sus 35 C10
Coneysthorpe N Yorks 216 E4
Coneythorpe N Yorks 206 B3
Coney Weston Suff 125 B9
Conford Hants 49 G10
Congash Highld 301 G10
Congdon's Shop Corn 11 F11
Congeith Dumfries 237 C10
Congelow Kent 53 D7
Congerstone Leics 135 B7
Congham Norf 158 E4
Congleton Ches E 168 C5
Congleton Edge Ches E 168 C5
Congl-y-wal Gwyn 164 G2
Congresbury N Som 60 G2
Congreve Staffs 151 G8
Conham Bristol 60 E6
Conicavel Moray 301 D9
Coningsby Lincs 174 D2
Conington Cambs 122 D6
Cambs 138 F3
Conisbrough S Yorks 187 B8
Conisby Argyll 274 G3
Conisholme Lincs 190 B6
Coniston Cumb 220 F6
E Yorks 209 F9
Coniston Cold N Yorks 204 B4
Conistone N Yorks 213 E8
Conkwell Wilts 61 G10
Connah's Quay Flint 166 B4
Connel Argyll 289 F11
Connel Park E Ayrs 258 G4
Conniburrow M Keynes 103 D7

Connista Highld. 298 B4
Connon Corn 6 C3
Connor Downs Corn 2 B3
Conock Wilts 46 B5
Conon Bridge Highld. . . . 300 D5
Conon House Highld 300 D5
Cononish Stirl 285 E7
Cononley N Yorks 204 D5
Cononley Woodside
N Yorks 204 D5
Cononsyth Angus 287 C9
Conordan Highld. 295 B7
Conquermoor Heath
Telford 150 F3
Consall Staffs. 169 F7
Consett Durham 242 G4
Constable Burton
N Yorks 224 G3
Constable Lee Lancs. . . 195 C10
Constantine Corn. 2 D6
Constantine Bay Corn. . . . 10 G3
Contin Highld 300 D4
Contlaw Aberdeen. 293 C10
Conwy Conwy. 180 F3
Conyer Kent 70 G3
Conyers Green Suff. 125 D7
Cooden E Sus 38 F2
Cooil IoM 192 E4
Cookbury Devon 24 F6
Cookbury Wick Devon 24 F5
Cookham Windsor 65 B11
Cookham Dean Windsor. 65 C11
Cookham Rise Windsor . 65 C11
Cookhill Worcs 117 F11
Cookley Suff 126 B6
Worcs 132 G6
Cookley Green Oxon 83 G11
Cookney Aberds 293 D10
Cookridge W Yorks. 205 E11
Cooksbridge E Sus. 36 E6
Cooksey Corner Worcs. . 117 D8
Cooksey Green Worcs . . 117 D8
Cook's Green Essex. 89 B11
Suff 125 G9
Cookshill Staffs. 168 G6
Cooksland Corn 5 B11
Cooksmill Green Essex . 87 D10
Cooksongreen Ches W . . 183 G9
Coolham W Sus 35 C10
Cooling Medway 69 D9
Coolinge Kent 55 F8
Cooling Street Medway . . . 69 E8
Coombe Bucks. 84 D4
Corn. 4 G2
Corn. 4 G5
Corn. 4 G6
Corn. 5 E9
Corn. 6 C4
Corn. 24 E2
Devon 14 G4
Devon 27 D8
Glos 80 G3
Hants. 33 C11
Kent. 55 B9
London. 67 E8
Som 28 B3
Som 28 F6
Wilts 30 C5
Wilts 47 C7
Coombe Bissett Wilts. . . . 31 B10
Coombe Dingle Bristol . . . 60 D5
Coombe Hill Glos 99 F7
Coombe Keynes Dorset . . . 18 E2
Coombes W Sus. 35 F11
Coombesdale Staffs 150 B6
Coombeswood W Mid . . . 133 F9
Coomb Hill Kent 69 G7
Coombs End S Glos. 61 C9
Coombses Som 28 F4
Coopersale Common
Essex 87 E7
Coopersale Street Essex. . 87 E7
Cooper's Corner Kent. . . . 52 D3
Cooper's Green E Sus 37 C7
Herts 85 D11
Cooper's Hill C Beds . . . 103 D10
Sur. 66 E3
Cooper Street Kent 55 B10
Cooper Turning
Gtr Man. 194 F6
Cootham W Sus 35 E9
Copcut Worcs 117 E7
Copdock Suff. 108 C2
Coped Hall Wilts. 62 C5
Copenhagen Denb 165 B8
Copford Essex. 107 G8
Copford Green Essex . . . 107 G8
Copgrove N Yorks 214 G6
Copister Shetland 312 F6
Cople Beds 104 B2
Copley Durham 233 F7
Gtr Man 185 B7
W Yorks 196 C5
Copley Hill W Yorks 197 B8
Coplow Dale Derbys . . . 185 F11
Copmanthorpe York 207 D7
Copmere End Staffs 150 D6
Copnor Ptsmth. 33 G11
Copp Lancs 202 F4
Coppathorne Corn. 24 G2
Coppenhall Ches E. 168 D2
Staffs. 151 F8
Coppenhall Moss
Ches E. 168 D2
Copperhouse Corn 2 B3
Coppice Gtr Man 196 G2
Coppicegate Shrops 132 G4
Coppingford Cambs 138 G3
Coppins Corner Kent 54 D2
Coppleham Som. 42 G2
Copplestone Devon 26 G3
Coppull Lancs 194 E5
Coppull Moor Lancs 194 E5
Copsale W Sus 35 C11
Copse Hill London. 67 E8
Copster Green Lancs. . . . 203 G9
Copster Hill Gtr Man. 196 G2
Copston Magna Warks . . 135 F9
Cop Street Kent. 55 B9
Copt Green Warks 118 D3
Copthall Green Essex. 86 E6
Copt Heath W Mid. 118 B3
Copt Hewick N Yorks 214 E6
Copthill Durham 232 C3
Copthorne Ches E. 167 G11
Corn. 11 C11
Shrops 149 G9
Sur. 51 F10
Coptiviney Shrops 149 B8
Copt Oak Leics. 153 G9
Copton Kent 54 B4
Copy's Green Norf 159 B8
Copythorne Hants 32 E4
Corbets Tey London 68 B5
Corbridge Northumb . . . 241 E11
Corbriggs Derbys 170 B6
Corby Northants. 137 F7
Corby Glen Lincs. 155 E9
Corby Hill Cumb 239 F11
Cordon N Ayrs 256 C2
Cordwell Norf 142 E2
Coreley Shrops 116 C2
Cores End Bucks 66 B2
Corfe Som. 28 D2
Corfe Castle Dorset 18 E5
Corfe Mullen Dorset 18 B5
Corfton Shrops 131 F9
Corfton Bache Shrops . . . 131 F9
Corgarff Aberds 292 C4
Corgee Corn. 5 C10
Corhampton Hants 33 C10
Corlae Dumfries. 246 D5
Corlannau Neath 57 C9
Corley Warks 134 F6
Corley Ash Warks. 134 F5
Corley Moor Warks 134 F5
Cornaa IoM 192 D5
Cornabus Argyll 254 C4
Cornaigbeg Argyll 288 E1
Cornaigmore Argyll. 288 C4
Argyll 288 E1
Cornard Tye Suff 107 C8
Cornbank Midloth 270 C4
Cornbrook Shrops 116 B2
Corncatterach Aberds . . . 302 F5
Cornel Conwy. 164 C2
Corner Row Lancs 202 F4
Cornett Hereford. 97 B11
Corney Cumb 220 G2
Cornforth Durham 234 E2
Cornharrow Dumfries 246 E5
Cornhill Aberds 302 D5
Powys 96 C2
Stoke. 168 E5
Cornhill-on-Tweed
Northumb 263 B9
Cornholme W Yorks 196 B2
Cornish Hall End Essex . 106 D3
Cornquoy Orkney 314 G5
Cornriggs Durham 232 C2
Cornsay Durham 233 C8
Cornsay Colliery
Durham. 233 C9
Cornton Stirl 278 B5
Corntown Highld. 300 D5
V Glam 58 D2
Cornwell Oxon. 100 F5
Cornwood Devon 8 D2
Cornworthy Devon. 8 D6
Corpach Highld 290 F2
Corpusty Norf 160 C2
Corran Highld. 290 G2
Highld 295 E10
Corran a Chan Uachdaraich
Highld 295 C7
Corranbuie Argyll. 275 G9
Corrany IoM. 192 D5
Corrichoich Highld. 311 G4
Corrie N Ayrs 255 C11
Corrie Common
Dumfries. 248 F6
Corriecravie N Ayrs 255 E10
Corriecravie Moor
N Ayrs 255 E10
Corriedoo Dumfries 246 G5
Corriegarth Lodge
Highld 291 B7
Corriemoillie Highld 300 C3
Corriemulzie Lodge
Highld 309 K3
Corrievarkie Lodge
Perth. 291 F7
Corrievorrie Highld 301 G7
Corrigall Orkney 314 E3
Corrimony Highld. 300 F3
Corringham Lincs 188 C5
Thurrock 69 C8
Corris Gwyn 128 B5
Corris Uchaf Gwyn. 128 B4
Corrour Highld. 290 G5
Corrour Shooting Lodge
Highld 290 G6
Corrow Argyll. 284 G5
Corry Highld 295 C8
Corrybrough Highld. 301 G8
Corrydon Perth 292 G3
Corryghoil Argyll 284 E5
Corrykinloch Highld 309 G3
Corrylach Argyll 255 D8
Corrymuckloch Perth. . . . 286 D2
Corrynachenchy Argyll . 289 E8
Corry of Ardnagrask
Highld 300 E5
Corsback Highld 310 B6
Corscombe Dorset. 29 F8
Corse Aberds 302 E6
Glos 98 F5
Corse Lawn Worcs 98 E6
Corse of Kinnoir Aberds. 302 E5
Corsewall Dumfries 236 C2
Corsham Wilts. 61 E11
Corsindae Aberds. 293 C8
Corsley Wilts 45 D10
Corsley Heath Wilts 45 D10
Corsock Dumfries 237 B9
Corston Bath 61 F7
Orkney. 314 E3
Wilts 62 C2
Corstorphine Edin 280 G3
Cors-y-Gedol Gwyn 145 E11
Cortachy Angus. 287 B7
Corton Suff. 143 D10
Wilts 46 E2
Corton Denham Som 29 C10
Cortworth S Yorks 186 B6
Coruanan Lodge Highld . 290 G2
Corunna W Isles 296 E4
Corvast Highld 309 K5
Corwen Denb. 165 G9
Cory Devon 24 D5
Coryates Dorset 17 D8
Coryton Cardiff. 58 C6
Devon 12 E5
Thurrock 69 C8
Còsag Highld. 295 D10
Cosby Leics. 135 E10
Coscote Oxon. 64 B4
Coseley W Mid 133 E8
Cosford Warks. 119 B9
Cosgrove Northants 102 C5
Cosham Ptsmth 33 F11
Cosheston Pembs. 73 E8
Cosmeston V Glam 59 F7
Cosmore Dorset 29 F11
Cossall Notts 171 G7
Cossall Marsh Notts 171 G7
Cosses S Ayrs 244 G4
Cossington Leics 154 G2
Som 43 E11
Costa Orkney 314 D3
Costessey Norf 160 G3
Costessey Park Norf 160 G3
Costhorpe Notts. 187 D9
Costislost Corn 10 G6
Costock Notts 153 D11
Coston Leics. 154 E6
Norf 141 B11
Coswinsawsin Corn. 2 B4
Cote Oxon 82 E4
Som 43 E10
W Sus. 35 F10
Cotebrook Ches W 167 B9
Cotehill Cumb 239 G11
Cotes Cumb. 211 B9
Leics 153 E11
Staffs. 150 C6
Cotesbach Leics 135 G10
Cotes Heath Staffs. 150 C6
Cotes Park Derbys 170 E6
Cotford St Lukes Som. . . 27 B11
Cotgrave Notts 154 B2
Cothall Aberds. 293 B10
Cotham Bristol 60 E5
Notts 172 F3
Cothelstone Som 43 G7
Cotheridge Worcs 116 G5
Cotherstone Durham. . . . 223 B10
Cothill Oxon 83 F7
Cotland Mon. 79 E8
Cotleigh Devon 28 G2
Cotmanhay Derbys. 171 G7
Cotmarsh Wilts. 62 D5
Cotmaton Devon. 15 D8
Coton Cambs 123 F8
Northants 120 C3
Shrops. 149 C10
Staffs. 134 B3
Staffs. 150 E6
Staffs. 151 C9
Coton Clanford Staffs. . . 151 E7
Coton Hayes Staffs 151 C9
Coton Hill Shrops 149 G9
Staffs. 151 C9
Coton in the Clay Staffs . 152 D3
Coton in the Elms
Derbys 152 F4
Coton Park Derbys. 152 F5
Cotonwood Shrops 149 B10
Staffs. 150 E6
Cotswold Community
Wilts 81 F8
Cott Devon. 8 C5
Cottam E Yorks. 217 F9
Lancs 202 G6
Notts 188 F4
Cottartown Highld 301 F10
Cottenham Cambs 123 D8
Cottenham Park London . . 67 F8
Cotterdale N Yorks 222 G6
Cottered Herts 104 F6
Cotterhill Woods
S Yorks 187 E9
Cotteridge W Mid 117 B10
Cotterstock Northants . 137 E10
Cottesbrooke Northants. 120 C4
Cottesmore Rutland. 155 G8
Cotteylands Devon. 26 E6
Cottingham E Yorks 208 G6
Northants 136 E6
Cottingley W Yorks. 205 F8
Cottisford Oxon 101 E11
Cotton Staffs 169 F9
Suff 125 D11
Cotton End Beds. 103 B11
Northants 120 F5
Cotton Stones W Yorks . . 196 C4
Cotton Tree Lancs 204 F4
Cottonworth Hants 47 F11
Cottown Aberds 293 B9
Aberds. 302 G5
Aberds. 303 E8
Cotts Devon 7 B8
Cottwood Devon. 25 E10
Cotwall Telford 150 F2
Cotwalton Staffs. 151 B8
Coubister Orkney 314 E3
Couch Green Hants 48 G4
Couch's Mill Corn. 6 D2
Coughton Hereford 97 G11
Warks 117 E11
Coughton Fields Warks 117 F11
Cougie Highld. 300 G2
Coulaghailtro Argyll 275 G8
Coulags Highld. 299 E9
Coulby Newham Mbro . 225 B10
Coulderton Cumb. 219 D9
Couldoran Highld 299 E8
Couligartan Stirl 285 G8
Coulin Highld 299 D10
Coulin Lodge Highld . . . 299 D10
Coull Aberds. 293 C7
Argyll 274 G3
Coulmony Ho Highld 301 E9
Coulport Argyll 276 D4
Coulsdon London 51 B9
Coulshill Perth 286 G3
Coulston Wilts. 46 C3
Coulter S Lnrk 260 C2
Coultings Som. 43 E8
Coulton N Yorks 216 E2
Coultra Fife 287 E7
Cound Shrops. 131 C11
Coundlane Shrops 131 B11
Coundmoor Shrops 131 C11
Coundon Durham 233 F10
W Mid 134 G6
Coundongate Durham. . 233 F10
Coundon Grange
Durham. 233 F10
Counters End Herts. 85 D8
Countersett N Yorks. 213 B8
Countess Wilts 47 E7
Countess Cross Essex. . . 107 E7
Countess Wear Devon. . . . 14 D4
Countesthorpe Leics . . 135 D11
Countisbury Devon 41 D8
County Oak W Sus 51 F9
Coupar Angus Perth 286 C6
Coup Green Lancs 194 B5
Coupland Cumb. 222 B4
Northumb 263 C10
Cour Argyll 255 C9
Courance Dumfries. 248 E3
Coursley Som. 42 G6
Court-at-Street Kent 54 F5
Court Barton Devon. 14 D2
Court Colman Bridgend . 57 E11
Court Corner Hants. 48 B6
Courteenhall Northants . 120 G5
Court Henry Carms 93 G11
Courthill Perth 286 C5
Court House Green
W Mid 135 G7
Courtsend Essex 89 G8
Courtway Som. 43 G8
Cousland Midloth 271 B7
Cousley Wood E Sus 53 G7
Couston Argyll. 275 F11
Cova Shetland. 313 J5
Cove Argyll 276 E4
Borders 282 G5
Devon 27 D7
Hants. 49 B11
Highld 307 K3
Cove Bay Aberdeen. 293 C11
Cove Bottom Suff. 127 B9
Covehithe Suff 143 G10
Coven Staffs. 133 B8
Covender Hereford. 98 C2
Coveney Cambs. 139 G9
Covenham St Bartholomew
Lincs 190 C4
Covenham St Mary
Lincs 190 C4
Coven Heath Staffs 133 C8
Coven Lawn Staffs 133 B8
Coventry W Mid. 118 B6
Coverack Corn. 3 F7
Coverack Bridges Corn 2 C5
Coverham N Yorks. 214 B2
Covesea Moray 301 B11
Covingham Swindon. 63 B7
Covington Cambs 121 C11
S Lnrk 259 B11
Cowan Bridge Lancs 212 D2
Cow Ark Lancs 203 D9
Cowbar Redcar 226 B5
Cowbeech E Sus 23 C10
Cowbeech Hill E Sus 23 C10
Cowbit Lincs. 156 F5
Cowbog Aberds. 303 D8
Cowbridge Lincs. 174 F4
Som 42 E3
Cowbridge / Y Bont-Faen
V Glam. 58 E3
Cowcliffe W Yorks. 196 D6
Cowdale Derbys 185 G9
Cowden Kent 52 E3
Cowdenbeath Fife 280 C3
Cowdenburn Borders . . . 270 E4
Cowen Head Cumb. 221 F9
Cowers Lane Derbys 170 F4
Cowes IoW 20 B5
Cowesby N Yorks 215 B9
Cowesfield Green Wilts. . 32 C3
Cowfold W Sus. 36 C2
Cowgill Cumb 212 B5
Cow Green Suff. 125 D11
Cowgrove Dorset 18 B5
Cowhill Derbys 170 F5
S Glos. 79 G10
Cow Hill Lancs 203 G7
Cowhorn Hill S Glos. 61 E7
Cowie Aberds. 293 E10
Stirl 278 D6
Cowlands Corn 4 G6
Cowleaze Corner Oxon. . . . 82 E4
Cowley Derbys. 186 F4
Devon 14 B4
Glos 81 C7
London. 66 C5
Oxon 83 E8
Cowleymoor Devon 27 E7
Cowley Peachy London . . . 66 C5
Cowling Lancs 194 D5
N Yorks. 204 E5
N Yorks. 214 B4
Cowlinge Suff 124 G4
Cowlow Derbys 185 G9
Cowmes W Yorks. 197 D7
Cowpe Lancs 195 C10
Cowpen Northumb 253 G7
Cowpen Bewley
Stockton 234 G5
Cowplain Hants. 33 E11
Cow Roast Herts. 85 C7
Cowshill Durham. 232 C3
Cowslip Green N Som 60 G3
Cowstrandburn Fife . . . 279 C10
Cowthorpe N Yorks. 206 C4
Coxall Hereford 115 C7
Coxbank Ches E 167 G11
Coxbench Derbys 170 G5
Coxbridge Som 44 F4
Cox Common Suff 143 G8
Coxford Corn. 11 B9
Norf 158 D6
Soton 32 D5
Coxgreen Staffs 132 F6
Cox Green Gtr Man 195 E8
Sur. 50 G5
Windsor. 65 D11
Coxheath Kent. 53 C8
Coxhill Kent 55 D8
Cox Hill Corn 4 G4
Coxhoe Durham. 234 D2
Coxley Som. 44 E4
W Yorks 197 D9
Coxley Wick Som 44 E4
Coxlodge T&W 242 D6
Cox Moor Notts. 171 D8
Coxpark Corn. 12 G4
Coxtie Green Essex 87 F9
Coxwold N Yorks 215 D10
Coychurch Bridgend. 58 D2
Coylton S Ayrs 257 E10
Coylumbridge Highld . . 291 B11
Coynach Aberds 292 C6
Coynachie Aberds 302 F4
Coytrahen Bridgend. 57 D11
CoytrahÛn Bridgend. 57 D11
Crabadon Devon 8 E5
Crabbet Park W Sus. 51 F10
Crabble Kent 55 E9
Crabbs Cross Worcs . . . 117 E10
Crabbs Green Herts 105 F9
Crabgate Norf 159 D11
Crab Orchard Dorset. 31 F9
Crabtree Plym 7 D10
W Sus. 36 B2
Crabtree Green Wrex . . . 166 G4
Crackaig Argyll 274 G6
Crackenedge W Yorks . . . 197 C8
Crackenthorpe Cumb . . . 231 G9
Crackington Haven Corn. . 11 B8
Crackley Staffs 168 E4
Warks 118 C5
Crackleybank Shrops . . . 150 G5
Crackpot N Yorks. 223 F9
Crackthorn Corner
Suff. 125 B10
Cracoe N Yorks. 213 G9
Cracow Moss Ches E 168 F2
Staffs. 168 F3
Craddock Devon 27 E9
Cradhlastadh W Isles . . . 304 E2
Cradle Edge W Yorks 205 F7
Cradle End Herts 105 G9
Cradley Hereford. 98 B4
W Mid 133 G8
Cradley Heath W Mid. . . . 133 F8
Cradoc Powys 95 E10
Crafthole Corn 7 E7
Crafton Bucks 84 B5
Crag Bank Lancs 211 E9
Crag Foot Lancs 211 E9
Craggan Highld 301 G10
Moray 301 F11
Stirl 285 E9
Cragganvallie Highld. . . . 300 F5
Craggenmore Moray. . . . 301 F11
Cragg Hill W Yorks 205 F10
Craggie Highld. 301 F7
Highld 311 H2
Craggiemore Highld 309 J7
Cragg Vale W Yorks 196 C4
Craghead Durham. 242 G6
Crahan Corn. 2 C5
Crai Powys 95 G7
Craibstone Moray. 302 D4
Craichie Angus 287 C9
Craig Dumfries. 237 B8
Dumfries 237 C8
Highld 299 E10
Craiganor Lodge Perth 285 B10
Craig Berthlwyd M Tydf . . . 77 F9
Craig Castle Aberds 302 G4
Craig-cefn-parc
Swansea. 75 E11
Craigdallie Perth 286 E6
Craigdam Aberds 303 F8
Craigdarroch Dumfries. . 246 E6
Highld 300 D4
Craigdhu Highld 300 E4
Craig Douglas Borders . . 261 E7
Craigearn Aberds 293 B9
Craigellachie Moray 302 E2
Craigencallie Ho
Dumfries. 237 B7
Craigencross Dumfries . . 236 C2
Craigend Borders 271 F9
Glasgow. 268 B3
Perth 286 E3
Perth 286 E5
Stirl 278 D5
Craigendive Argyll 275 E11
Craigendoran Argyll 276 E6
Craigendowie Angus. . . . 293 G7
Craigends Renfs 267 B8
Craigens Argyll 274 G3
E Ayrs. 258 F3
Craigentinny Edin 280 G5
Craigerne Borders 261 B7
Craighall Perth 286 C5
Craighat Stirl. 277 E9
Craighead Fife 287 G10
Highld 301 C7
Craighill Aberds 303 E7
Craighlaw Mains
Dumfries. 236 C5
Craighouse Argyll. 274 G6
Craigie Aberds. 293 B11
Dundee 287 D8
Perth 286 C5
Perth 286 E5
S Ayrs. 257 C10
S Ayrs. 257 E8
Craigiefield Orkney 314 E4
Craigiehall Edin 280 F3
Craigielaw E Loth 281 F9
Craigierig Borders 260 E6
Craigleith Edin 280 G4
Craig Llangiwg Neath. . . . 76 D2
Craig-llwyn Shrops 148 D4
Craiglockhart Edin 280 G4
Craig Lodge Argyll 275 G10
Craigmalloch E Ayrs . . . 245 E11
Craigmaud Aberds 303 D8
Craigmill Stirl 278 B6
Craigmillar Edin 280 G5
Craigmore Argyll 266 B2
Craig-moston Aberds. . . . 293 F8
Craignant Shrops 148 B5
Craignell Dumfries 237 B7
Craigneuk N Lnrk 268 C5
N Lnrk 268 D5
Craignish Castle Argyll. . 275 C8
Craignure Argyll 289 F9
Craigo Angus 293 G8
Craigow Perth 286 G4
Craig Penllyn V Glam 58 D3
Craigrory Highld 300 E6
Craigrothie Fife 287 F7
Craigroy Moray 301 D11
Craigruie Stirl 285 E8
Craig's End Essex. 106 D4
Craigsford Mains
Borders. 262 B3
Craigshall Dumfries 237 D10
Craigshill W Loth. 269 B11
Craigside Durham. 233 D8
Craigston Castle Aberds 303 D7
Craigton Aberdeen 293 C10
Angus 287 B7
Angus 287 D9
Glasgow. 267 C10
Highld 300 E6
Highld 309 H6
Highld 309 K6
Craigtown Highld 310 D2
Craig-y-don Conwy 180 E3
Craig-y-Duke Swansea. . . . 76 E2
Craig-y-nos Powys 76 B4
Craig-y-penrhyn
Ceredig. 128 E3
Craig-y-Rhacca Caerph. . . 59 B7
Craik Borders 249 B8
Crail Fife 287 G10
Crailing Borders 262 E5
Crailinghall Borders 262 E5
Crakaig Highld. 311 H3
Crakehill N Yorks. 215 E8
Crakemarsh Staffs. 151 B11
Crambe N Yorks 216 G4
Crambeck N Yorks 216 F4
Cramhurst Sur 50 E2
Cramlington Northumb. . 243 B7
Cramond Edin 280 F3
Cramond Bridge Edin. . . . 280 F3
Crampmoor Hants. 32 C5
Cranage Ches E 168 B3
Cranberry Staffs. 150 B6
Cranborne Dorset 31 E9
Cranbourne Brack 66 E2
Hants. 48 C6
Cranbrook Devon 14 B6
Kent. 53 F9
London. 68 B2
Cranbrook Common Kent. 53 F9
Crane Moor S Yorks 197 G10
Crane's Corner Norf 159 G8
Cranfield C Beds 103 C9
Cranford Devon. 24 C4
London. 66 D6
Cranford St Andrew
Northants. 121 B8
Cranford St John
Northants. 121 B8
Cranham Glos 80 C5
London. 68 B5
Cranhill Glasgow. 268 B2
Warks 118 G2
Crank Mers. 183 B8
Crankwood Gtr Man 194 G6
Crank Wood Gtr Man 194 G6
Cranleigh Sur 50 F5
Cranley Suff. 126 C3
Cranley Gardens London . . 67 B9
Cranmer Green Suff . . . 125 C10
Cranmore IoW 20 D3
Som 45 E7
Cranna Aberds. 302 D6
Crannich Argyll 289 E7
Crannoch Moray. 302 D4
Cranoe Leics 136 D5
Cransford Suff 126 E6
Cranshaws Borders 272 C3
Cranstal IoM 192 B5
Cranswick E Yorks 208 C6
Crantock Corn. 4 C5
Cranwell Lincs. 173 F8
Cranwich Norf. 140 E5
Cranworth Norf 141 C9
Craobh Haven Argyll 275 C8
Crapstone Devon 7 B10
Crarae Argyll 275 D10
Crask Highld 308 C7
Crask Inn Highld 309 G5
Craskins Aberds 293 C7
Crask of Aigas Highld . . . 300 E4
Craster Northumb 265 F7
Craswall Hereford. 96 D5
Crateford Shrops 132 F4
Staffs. 133 B8
Cratfield Suff. 126 B6
Crathes Aberds 293 D9
Crathie Aberds. 292 D4
Highld 291 D7
Crathorne N Yorks 225 D8
Craven Arms Shrops 131 G8
Crawcrook T&W 242 E4
Crawford Lancs. 194 G3
S Lnrk 259 E11
Crawforddyke S Lnrk. . . . 269 F7
Crawfordjohn S Lnrk 259 E9
Crawick Dumfries 259 G7
Crawley Devon. 28 F3
Hants. 48 G2
Oxon 82 C4
W Sus. 51 F9
Crawley Down W Sus. 51 F10
Crawley End Essex. 105 C8
Crawley Hill Sur 65 G11
Crawleyside Durham 232 C5
Crawshaw W Yorks 197 E8
Crawshawbooth Lancs. 195 B10
Crawton Aberds 293 F10
Cray N Yorks 213 D8
Perth 292 G3
Crayford London 68 E4
Crayke N Yorks 215 E11
Craymere Beck Norf . . . 159 C11
Crays Hill Essex. 88 G2
Cray's Pond Oxon. 64 C6
Crazies Hill Wokingham. . . 65 C9
Creacombe Devon 26 D4
Creagan Argyll. 289 E11
Creagan Sithe Argyll 284 G6
Creag Aoil Highld 290 F3
Creagastrom W Isles . . . 297 G4
Creag Ghoraidh
W Isles 297 G3
Creaguaineach Lodge
Highld 290 G5
Creaksea Essex. 88 F6
Creamore Bank Shrops 149 C10
Crean Corn 1 E3
Creaton Northants 120 C4
Creca Dumfries 238 C6
Credenhill Hereford. 97 C9
Crediton Devon 26 G4
Creebridge Dumfries. . . . 236 C6
Creech Dorset 18 E4
Creech Bottom Dorset 18 E4
Creech Heathfield Som . . . 28 B3
Creech St Michael Som . . . 28 B3
Creed Corn 5 F8
Creediknowe Shetland . . 312 G7
Creegbrawse Corn. 4 G4
Creekmoor Poole. 18 C6
Creekmouth London 68 C3
Creeksea Essex. 88 F6
Creeting Bottoms Suff. . 126 F2
Creeting St Mary Suff. . 125 F11
Creeton Lincs. 155 E10
Creetown Dumfries 236 D6
Creggans Argyll 284 G4
Cregneash IoM. 192 F2
Creg-ny-Baa IoM. 192 D4
Cregrina Powys. 114 G2
Creich Fife 287 E7
Creigau Mon 79 F7
Creighton Staffs. 151 B11
Creigiau Cardiff. 58 C5
Crelly Corn 2 C5
Cremyll Corn 7 E9
Crendell Dorset. 31 E9
Crepkill Highld. 298 E4
Creslow Bucks. 102 G6
Cressage Shrops. 131 C11
Cressbrook Derbys 185 G11
Cresselly Pembs 73 D9
Cressex Bucks 84 G4
Cress Green Glos 80 E3
Cressing Essex 106 G5
Cresswell Northumb. 253 E7
Staffs. 151 B9
Cresswell Quay Pembs . . . 73 D9
Creswell Derbys 187 G8
Staffs. 151 D7
Staffs. 151 D8
Creswell Green Staffs . 151 G11
Cretingham Suff. 126 E4
Cretshengan Argyll 275 G8
Creunant / Crynant
Neath 76 E3
Crewe Ches E 168 D2
Ches W. 166 E6
Crewe-by-Farndon
Ches W 166 E6
Crewgarth Cumb. 231 E8
Crewgreen Powys 148 F6
Crewkerne Som 28 F6
Crews Hill London. 86 F4
Crew's Hole Bristol 60 E6
Crewton Derby 153 C7
Crianlarich Stirl 285 E7
Cribbs Causeway S Glos. . 60 C5
Cribden Side Lancs 195 C9
Cribyn Ceredig 111 G10
Criccieth Gwyn 145 B9
Crich Derbys. 170 E5
Crich Carr Derbys. 170 E4
Crichie Aberds. 303 E9
Crichton Midloth 271 C7
Crick Mon 79 G7
Northants 119 C11
Crickadarn Powys 95 C11
Cricket Hill Hants. 65 G10
Cricket Malherbie Som . . . 28 E5
Cricket St Thomas Som . . . 28 F5
Crickham Som. 44 D2
Crickheath Shrops 148 E5
Crickheath Wharf
Shrops 148 E5
Crickhowell Powys 78 B2
Cricklade Wilts 81 G10
Cricklewood London 67 B8
Crickmery Shrops. 150 D3
Crick's Green Hereford. . 116 G2
Criddlestyle Hants. 31 E11
Cridling Stubbs N Yorks . 198 C4
Cridmore IoW 20 E5
Crieff Perth. 286 E2
Criggan Corn 5 C10
Criggion Powys. 148 F5
Crigglestone W Yorks . . 197 D10
Crimble Gtr Man 195 E11
Crimchard Som. 28 F4
Crimdon Park Durham . . 234 D5
Crimond Aberds 303 D10
Crimonmogate Aberds. 303 D10
Crimp Corn 24 D3
Crimplesham Norf. 140 C3
Crimscote Warks 100 B4
Crinan Argyll 275 D8
Crinan Ferry Argyll. 275 D8
Crindau Newport. 59 B10
Crindledyke N Lnrk. 268 D6
Cringleford Norf. 142 B3
Cringles W Yorks 204 D6
Cringletie Borders 270 G4
Crinow Pembs 73 C10
Cripple Corner Essex . . . 107 E7
Cripplesease Corn. 2 B2
Cripplestyle Dorset 31 E9
Cripp's Corner E Sus 38 C3
Crispie Argyll 275 F10
Crist Derbys 185 E8
Critchell's Green Hants . . . 32 B3
Critchill Som 45 D9
Critchmere Sur. 49 G11
Crit Hall Kent 53 G9
Crizeley Hereford 97 E8
Croanford Corn. 10 G6
Croasdale Cumb 219 B11
Crobeag W Isles 304 F5
Crockenhill Kent 68 F4
Crocker End Oxon 65 B8
Crockerhill Hants. 33 F9
W Sus. 22 B6
Crockernwell Devon 13 C11
Crockers Devon. 40 F5
Crocker's Ash Hereford . . . 79 B8
Crockerton Wilts 45 E11
Crockerton Green Wilts 45 E11
Crocketford or Ninemile Bar
Dumfries. 237 B10
Crockey Hill York 207 D8
Crockham Heath
W Berks 64 G2
Crockham Hill Kent. 52 C2
Crockhurst Street Kent . . . 52 E6
Crockleford Heath
Essex 107 F10
Crockleford Hill Essex. 107 F10
Crockness Orkney 314 G3
Crock Street Som. 28 E4
Croesau Bach Shrops . . . 148 D4
Croeserw Neath 57 B11
Croes-goch Pembs 87 E11
Croes-Hywel Mon 78 C4
Croes-lan Ceredig 93 C7
Croes Llanfair Mon 78 D4
Croesor Gwyn 163 G10
Croespenmaen Caerph. . 77 F11
Croes-wian Flint. 181 G10
Croesyceiliog Carms. 74 B6
Torf 78 F4
Croes-y-mwyalch Torf . . 78 G4
Croes y pant Mon 78 E4
Croesywaun Gwyn. 163 D8
Croft Hereford 115 D9
Leics 135 D10
Lincs 175 C8
Pembs 92 C3
Warr 183 C10
Croftamie Stirl 277 D9
Croftfoot S Lnrk 268 C2
Crofthandy Corn. 4 G4
Croftlands Cumb. 210 D5
Croftmalloch W Loth 269 C8
Croft Mitchell Corn 2 B5
Croftmoraig Perth. 285 C11
Croft of Tillymaud
Aberds 303 F11
Crofton Cumb 239 G8
London. 68 F2
Wilts 63 G9
W Yorks 197 D11
Croft-on-Tees N Yorks . . 224 D5
Crofts Dumfries 237 B9
Crofts Bank Gtr Man. 184 B3
Crofts of Benachielt
Highld 310 F5
Crofts of Haddo Aberds . 303 F8
Crofts of Inverthernie
Aberds 303 E7
Crofts of Meikle Ardo
Aberds 303 E8
Crofty Swansea 56 B4
Croggan Argyll 289 G9
Croglin Cumb 231 B7
Croich Highld 309 K4
Croick Highld 310 D2
Croig Argyll. 288 D5
Crois Dughaill W Isles . . 297 J3
Cromarty Highld 301 C7
Cromasaig Highld. 299 C10
Crombie Fife 279 D10
Crombie Castle Aberds. . 302 D5
Cromblet Aberds. 303 F7
Cromdale Highld. 301 G10
Cromer Herts. 104 F5
Norf 160 A4
Cromer-Hyde Herts 86 C2
Cromford Derbys 170 D3
Cromhall S Glos. 79 G11
Cromhall Common
S Glos 61 B7
Cromor W Isles 304 F6
Crompton Fold Gtr Man . 196 F2
Cromra Highld 291 D7
Cromwell Notts. 172 C3
Cromwell Bottom
W Yorks. 196 C6
Cronberry E Ayrs. 258 E4
Crondall Hants 49 D9
Cronk-y-Voddy IoM 192 D4
Cronton Mers 183 D7
Crook Cumb 221 G9
Devon 27 G11
Durham 233 D9
Crookdake Cumb 229 C9
Crooke Gtr Man 194 F5
Crooked Billet London 67 E8
Crookedholm E Ayrs . . . 257 B11
Crooked Soley Wilts 63 E10
Crooked Withies Dorset . . 31 F9
Crookes S Yorks. 186 D4
Crookesmoor S Yorks . . . 186 D4
Crookfur E Renf. 267 D10
Crookgate Bank Durham 242 F5
Crookhall Durham 242 G4
Crookham Northumb . . . 263 B10
W Berks. 64 G4
Crookham Village Hants . 49 C9
Crookhaugh Borders. . . . 260 D4
Crookhill T&W. 242 E5
Crookhouse Borders 263 D7
Crooklands Cumb. 211 C10
Crook of Devon Perth . . . 286 G4
Crookston Glasgow 267 C10
Cropredy Oxon 101 B9
Cropston Leics 153 G11
Cropthorne Worcs 99 C9
Cropton N Yorks. 216 B5
Cropwell Bishop Notts. . 154 B3
Cropwell Butler Notts . . 154 B3
Cros W Isles 304 B7
Crosben Highld 289 D9
Crosbost W Isles. 304 F5
Crosby Cumb 229 D7
IoM 192 E4
Mers 182 B4
N Lincs. 199 E11
Crosby Court N Yorks. . . . 225 G7
Crosby Garrett Cumb . . . 222 D4
Crosby-on-Eden Cumb 239 F11
Crosby Ravensworth
Cumb. 222 C2
Crosby Villa Cumb 229 D7
Croscombe Som. 44 E5
Crosemere Shrops. 149 D8
Crosland Edge W Yorks. . 196 E6
Crosland Hill W Yorks . . . 196 E6
Crosland Moor W Yorks . 196 D6
Croslands Park Cumb . . . 210 E4
Cross Devon 40 F3
Devon 40 G6
Shrops. 149 B7
Som 44 C2
Crossaig Argyll 255 B9
Crossal Highld 294 B6
Crossapol Argyll. 288 E1
Cross Ash Mon. 78 B6
Cross-at-Hand Kent 53 D9
Cross Bank Worcs 116 C4
Crossbrae Aberds. 302 D6
Crossburn Falk 279 G7
Crossbush W Sus 35 F8
Crosscanonby Cumb 229 D7
Cross Coombe Corn 4 E4
Crosscrake Cumb 211 B10
Crossdale Street Norf . . 160 B4
Cross End Beds. 121 F11
Essex. 107 E7
M Keynes 103 D8
Crossens Mers 193 D11
Crossflatts W Yorks 205 E8
Crossford Fife. 279 D11
S Lnrk 268 F6
Crossgate Lincs 156 D4
Orkney. 314 E4
Staffs. 151 B8
Cross Gate W Sus 35 E8
Crossgatehall E Loth 271 B7
Crossgates Cumb 229 G7
Fife 280 D2
N Yorks. 217 C10
Powys 113 E11
Cross Gates W Yorks 205 F7
W Yorks 206 G3
Crossgill Cumb 231 C10
Lancs 211 G11
Crossgreen Shrops 149 F9
Cross Green Devon 12 D3
Staffs. 133 B8
Suff 124 G6
Suff 125 F7
Suff 125 G9
Telford. 150 G2
Warks 119 F7
W Yorks 206 G2
Crosshands Carms. 92 G3
Cross Hands Carms 75 C9
Cross-hands Carms. 92 G3
Cross Hands Pembs. 73 C9
Cross Heath Staffs. 168 F4
Crosshill E Ayrs 257 E11
Fife 280 B3
S Ayrs. 245 B8
Cross Hill Corn 10 G6
Derbys 170 F6
Glos 79 F9
Cross Hills N Yorks 204 E6
Cross Holme N Yorks 225 F11
Crosshouse E Ayrs 257 B9
Cross Houses Shrops . . . 131 B10
Shrops. 132 E3
Crossings Cumb 240 B2
Cross in Hand E Sus. 37 C9
Leics 135 G10
Cross Inn Carms 74 C3
Ceredig 111 E10
Ceredig 111 F7
Rhondda 58 C5
Crosskeys Caerph. 78 G2
Cross Keys Kent 52 C4
Wilts 61 E11
Crosskirk Highld 310 B4
Crosslands Cumb 210 B6
Cross Lane Ches E. 167 C11
Cross Lane Head Shrops 132 D4
Crosslanes Shrops 148 F6
Cross Lanes Corn. 2 E5
Dorset 30 G3
N Yorks. 215 F10
Oxon 65 D7
Wrex 166 F5
Crosslee Borders 261 F8
Renfs 267 B8
Crossley Hall W Yorks . . 205 G8
Cross Llyde Hereford. 97 F8
Crossmichael Dumfries . 237 C9
Crossmill E Renf 267 D10
Crossmoor Lancs 202 F4
Crossmount Perth 285 B11
Cross Oak Powys. 96 G2
Cross of Jackston
Aberds 303 F7
Cross o' th' hands
Derbys 170 F3
Cross o' th' Hill Ches W. . 167 F7
Crosspost W Sus. 36 C3
Crossroads Aberds 293 D9
E Ayrs. 257 C11
Fife 281 B7
Cross Roads Devon 12 D5
W Yorks 204 F6
Cross Stone Aberds 303 G9
Cross Street Suff 126 B3
Crosston Angus. 287 B9
Crosstown Corn 24 D2
V Glam 58 F4
Cross Town Ches E 184 F3
Crosswater Sur. 49 F11
Crossway Hereford. 98 E2
Mon 78 B6
Powys 113 F11
Crossway Green Mon 79 G8
Worcs 116 D6
Crossways Dorset. 17 D11
Kent. 68 D5
Mon 96 G6
S Glos. 79 G11
Sur. 49 F11
Crosswell / Ffynnongroes
Pembs. 92 D2
Crosswood Ceredig 112 C3
Crosthwaite Cumb 221 G8
Croston Lancs 194 D3
Crostwick Norf 160 F5
Crostwight Norf 160 D6
Crothair W Isles 304 E3
Crouch Kent. 52 B6
Kent. 54 B5
Crouch End London 67 B9
Crouchers W Sus 22 C4
Croucheston Wilts. 31 B9
Crouch Hill Dorset 30 E2
Crouch House Green
Kent. 52 D2
Croughly Moray. 301 G11
Croughton Northants. . . 101 E10

Crovie Aberds....303 C8
Crow Hants....31 G11
Crowan Corn....2 C4
Crowborough E Sus....52 G4
Staffs....168 D6
Crowborough Warren E Sus....52 G4
Crowcombe Som....42 F6
Crowcroft Worcs....116 G5
Crowden Derbys....185 B9
Devon....12 B5
Crowder Park Devon....8 D4
Crowdhill Hants....33 C7
Crowdicote Derbys....169 B10
Crowdleham Kent....52 B5
Crowdon N Yorks....227 F9
Crowell Oxon....84 F2
Crowell Hill Oxon....84 F2
Crowfield Northants....102 C2
Suff....126 F2
Crowgate Street Norf....160 E6
Crowgreaves Shrops....132 D4
Crow Green Essex....87 F9
Crowhill Gtr Man....184 B6
M Keynes....102 D6
Crow Hill Hereford....98 F2
Crowhole Derbys....186 F4
Crowhurst E Sus....38 E3
Sur....51 D11
Crowhurst Lane End Sur....51 D11
Crowland Lincs....156 G4
Crowlas Corn....2 C2
Crowle N Lincs....199 E9
Worcs....117 F8
Crowle Green Worcs....117 F8
Crowle Hill N Lincs....199 E9
Crowle Park N Lincs....199 E9
Crowmarsh Gifford Oxon....64 B6
Crown Corner Suff....126 C5
Crown East Worcs....116 G6
Crow Nest W Yorks....205 F8
Crownfield Bucks....84 F4
Crownhill Plym....7 D9
Crown Hills Leicester....136 C2
Crownland Suff....125 D10
Crownpits Sur....50 E3
Crownthorpe Norf....141 C11
Crowntown Corn....2 C4
Crown Wood Brack....65 F11
Crows-an-wra Corn....1 D3
Crow's Green Essex....106 F3
Crowshill Norf....141 B8
Crowsley Oxon....65 D8
Crowsnest Shrops....131 C7
Crow's Nest Corn....6 C1
Crowther's Pool Powys....96 B4
Crowthorne Brack....65 G10
Crowton Ches W....183 G8
Crow Wood Halton....183 D8
Croxall Staffs....152 G3
Croxby Lincs....189 B11
Croxby Top Lincs....189 B11
Croxdale Durham....233 D11
Croxden Staffs....151 B11
Croxley Green Herts....85 F9
Croxteth Mers....182 B6
Croxton Cambs....122 E4
N Lincs....200 E5
Norf....141 F7
Norf....159 C9
Staffs....150 C5
Croxtonbank Staffs....150 C5
Croxton Green Ches W....167 E8
Croxton Kerrial Leics....154 D6
Croy Highld....301 E7
N Lnrk....278 F4
Croyde Devon....40 F2
Croyde Bay Devon....40 F2
Croydon Cambs....104 B6
London....67 F10
Crozen Hereford....97 B11
Crubenbeg Highld....291 D8
Crubenmore Lodge Highld....291 D8
Cruckmeole Shrops....131 B8
Cruckton Shrops....149 G8
Cruden Bay Aberds....303 F10
Crudgington Telford....150 F2
Crudie Aberds....303 D7
Crudwell Wilts....81 G7
Crug Powys....114 C3
Crugmeer Corn....10 F4
Crugybar Carms....94 D3
Cruise Hill Worcs....117 E10
Crulabhig W Isles....304 E3
Crumlin Caerph....78 F2
Crumplehorn Corn....6 E4
Crumpsall Gtr Man....195 G10
Crumpsbrook Shrops....116 B2
Crumpton Hill Worcs....98 B5
Crundale Kent....54 D5
Pembs....73 B7
Cruwys Morchard Devon....26 E5
Crux Easton Hants....48 B2
Cruxton Dorset....17 B8
Crwbin Carms....75 C7
Crya Orkney....314 F3
Cryers Hill Bucks....84 F5
Crymlyn Gwyn....179 G10
Crymych Pembs....92 E3
Cryant / Creunant Neath....76 E3
Crynfryn Ceredig....111 E11
Cuaich Highld....291 E8
Cuaig Highld....299 D7
Cuan Argyll....275 B8
Cubbington Warks....118 D6
Cubeck N Yorks....213 B9
Cubert Corn....4 D5
Cubitt Town London....67 D11
Cubley S Yorks....197 G8
Cubley Common Derbys....152 B3
Hereford....97 D8
Cuckfield W Sus....36 B4
Cucklington Som....30 B3
Cuckney Notts....187 G9
Cuckold's Green Suff....143 G9
Wilts....46 B3
Cuckoo Green Suff....143 C10
Cuckoo Hill Notts....188 C2
Cuckoo's Corner Hants....49 E8
Wilts....46 B4
Cuckoo's Knob Wilts....63 G7
Cuckoo Tye Suff....107 C7
Cuckron Shetland....313 H6
Cucumber Corner Norf....143 B7
Cuddesdon Oxon....83 E10
Ches W....183 G10
Cuddington Heath Ches W....167 F7
Cuddy Hill Lancs....202 F5
Cudham London....52 B2
Cudliptown Devon....12 F6
Cudworth Som....28 E5
Sur....51 E8
S Yorks....197 F11

Cudworth Common S Yorks....197 F11
Cuerden Green Lancs....194 C5
Cuerdley Cross Warr....183 D8
Cufaude Hants....48 B6
Cuffern Pembs....91 G7
Cuffley Herts....86 E4
Cuiashader W Isles....304 C7
Cuidhir W Isles....297 L2
Cuidhtinis W Isles....296 C6
Cuiken Midloth....270 C4
Cuilcheanna Ho Highld....290 G2
Cuin Argyll....288 D6
Culbo Highld....300 C6
Culbokie Highld....300 D6
Culburnie Highld....300 E4
Culcabock Highld....300 E6
Culcairn Highld....300 C6
Culcharry Highld....301 D8
Culcheth Warr....183 B11
Culdoich Highld....301 E7
Culduie Highld....299 E7
Culeave Highld....309 K5
Culford Suff....124 D6
Culfordheath Suff....125 C7
Culfosie Aberds....293 C9
Culgaith Cumb....231 F8
Culham Oxon....83 F8
Culkein Highld....306 F5
Culkein Drumbeg Highld....306 F6
Culkerton Glos....80 F6
Cullachie Highld....301 G9
Cullen Moray....302 C5
Cullercoats T&W....243 C9
Cullicudden Highld....300 C6
Cullingworth W Yorks....205 F7
Cullipool Argyll....275 B8
Cullivoe Shetland....312 C7
Culloch Perth....285 F11
Culloden Highld....301 E7
Cullompton Devon....27 F8
Culmaily Highld....311 K2
Culmazie Dumfries....236 D5
Culm Davy Devon....27 D10
Culmer Sur....50 F2
Culmers Kent....70 G5
Culmington Shrops....131 G9
Culmore Stirl....278 B3
Culmstock Devon....27 E10
Culnacraig Highld....307 J5
Cul na h-Aird W Isles....305 H3
Culnaightrie Dumfries....237 D9
Culnaknock Highld....298 C5
Culnaneam Highld....294 C6
Culpho Suff....108 B4
Culrain Highld....309 K5
Culross Fife....279 D9
Culroy S Ayrs....257 G8
Culscadden Dumfries....236 E6
Culsh Aberds....292 D5
Aberds....303 E8
Culshabbin Dumfries....236 D5
Culswick Shetland....313 J4
Cultercullen Aberds....303 G9
Cults Aberdeen....293 C10
Aberds....302 E5
Dumfries....236 E6
Fife....287 G7
Culverlane Devon....8 C4
Culverstone Green Kent....68 G6
Culverthorpe Lincs....173 G8
Culworth Northants....101 B10
Culzie Lodge Highld....300 B5
Cumberlow Green Herts....104 E6
Cumbernauld N Lnrk....278 F5
Cumbernauld Village N Lnrk....278 F5
Cumber's Bank Wrex....149 B8
Cumberton Herts....104 E5
Cumberworth Lincs....191 G8
Cumdivock Cumb....230 B2
Cumeragh Village Lancs....203 F7
Cuminestown Aberds....303 D8
Cumledge Borders....272 D5
Cumlewick Shetland....313 L6
Cumlodden Argyll....275 D11
Cumloden Dumfries....236 C6
Cummersdale Cumb....239 G9
Cummerton Aberds....303 C8
Cummertrees Dumfries....238 D4
Cummingston Moray....301 C11
Cumnock E Ayrs....258 E3
Cumnor Oxon....83 E7
Cumnor Hill Oxon....83 D7
Cumrew Cumb....240 G2
Cumwhinton Cumb....239 G10
Cumwhitton Cumb....240 G2
Cundall N Yorks....215 E8
Cundy Cross S Yorks....197 F11
Cundy Hos S Yorks....186 B4
Cunninghamhead N Ayrs....267 G7
Cunnister Shetland....312 D7
Cupar Fife....287 F7
Cupar Muir Fife....287 F7
Cupernham Hants....32 C5
Cupid Green Herts....85 D9
Cupid's Hill Mon....97 F8
Curbar Derbys....186 G3
Curborough Staffs....152 G2
Curbridge Hants....33 E8
Oxon....82 D4
Curdridge Hants....33 E8
Curdworth Warks....134 E3
Curgurrell Corn....3 B9
Curin Highld....300 D3
Curland Som....28 D3
Curland Common Som....28 D3
Curlew Green Suff....127 D7
Curling Tye Green Essex....88 D4
Curload Som....28 B4
Currarie S Ayrs....244 E5
Curran Vale Corn....5 D9
Curridge W Berks....64 E3
Currie Edin....270 B3
Currock Cumb....239 G10
Curry Lane Corn....11 C11
Curry Mallet Som....28 C4
Curry Rivel Som....28 C4
Cursiter Orkney....314 E3
Curteis' Corner Kent....53 F11
Curtisden Green Kent....53 E8
Curtisknowle Devon....8 E4
Cusbay Orkney....314 C5
Cusgarne Corn....4 G5
Cushuish Som....43 G7
Cusop Hereford....96 C4
Custards Hants....32 F3
Custom House London....68 C2
Cusworth S Yorks....198 G4
Cutcloy Dumfries....236 F6
Cutcombe Som....42 F2
Cutgate Gtr Man....195 E11
Cuthill W Isles....281 G7
Cutiau Gwyn....146 F2

Cutlers Green Essex....105 E11
Cutler's Green Som....44 C5
Cutmadoc Corn....5 C11
Cutmere Corn....6 C6
Cutnall Green Worcs....117 D7
Cutsdean Glos....99 E11
Cutsyke W Yorks....198 C2
Cutteslowe Oxon....83 C8
Cutthorpe Derbys....186 G4
Cuttiford's Door Som....28 E4
Cutts Shetland....313 K6
Cuttybridge Pembs....72 B6
Cuttyhill Aberds....303 D10
Cuxham Oxon....83 F11
Cuxton Medway....69 F8
Cuxwold Lincs....201 G7
Cwm Bl Gwent....77 D11
Denb....181 F9
Neath....57 C10
Powys....129 D11
Cwmafan Neath....57 C9
Cwmaman Rhondda....77 F8
Cwmann Carms....93 B11
Cwmavon Torf....78 D3
Cwmbach Carms....75 D7
Carms....92 F5
Powys....96 D3
Rhondda....77 F8
Cwmbâch Rhondda....77 F8
Cwmbach Llechrhyd Powys....113 G10
Cwmbelan Powys....129 G8
Cwmbran Torf....78 G3
Cwmbrwyno Ceredig....128 G4
Cwm-byr Carms....94 E3
Cwm Capel Carms....75 E7
Cwmcarn Caerph....78 G2
Cwmcarvan Mon....79 D7
Cwm-celyn Bl Gwent....78 D2
Cwm-cou Ceredig....92 C5
Cwmcoednerth Ceredig....92 B6
Cwmcrawnon Powys....77 B10
Cwmcych Carms....92 D5
Cwmdare Rhondda....77 E7
Cwm Dows Caerph....78 F2
Cwmdu Carms....94 E2
Powys....96 G3
Cwmduad Carms....93 E7
Cwm-Dulais Swansea....75 E10
Cwmdwr Carms....94 E4
Cwmerfyn Ceredig....128 G3
Cwmfelin Bridgend....57 D11
M Tydfil....77 F9
Cwmfelin Boeth Carms....73 B11
Cwmfelinfach Caerph....77 G11
Cwm felin fach Caerph....77 G11
Cwmfelin Mynach Carms....92 G4
Cwmffrwd Carms....74 B6
Cwm Ffrwd-oer Torf....78 E3
Cwm-Fields Torf....78 E3
Cwmgiedd Powys....76 C3
Cwmgors Neath....76 C2
Cwmgwili Carms....75 C9
Cwmgwrach Neath....76 E4
Cwm Gwyn Swansea....56 C6
Cwm Head Shrops....131 F8
Cwm-hesgen Gwyn....146 D5
Cwmhiraeth Carms....92 D5
Cwm-hwnt Rhondda....76 D6
Cwmifor Carms....94 F3
Cwm Irfon Powys....95 B7
Cwmisfael Carms....75 B7
Cwmllynfell Neath....76 C2
Cwm-mawr Carms....75 C8
Cwm-miles Carms....92 G3
Cwm Nant-gam Bl Gwent....78 C2
Cwmorgan Pembs....92 D5
Cwmpar Rhondda....77 F7
Cwm-parc Rhondda....76 F6
Cwmpengraig Carms....92 D6
Cwm Penmachno Conwy....164 F3
Cwmpennar Rhondda....77 E8
Cwm Plysgog Ceredig....92 C3
Cwmrhos Powys....96 G3
Cwmrhydyceirw Swansea....57 B7
Cwmsychpant Ceredig....93 B8
Cwmsyfiog Caerph....77 E11
Cwmsymlog Ceredig....128 G4
Cwmtillery Bl Gwent....78 D2
Cwm-twrch Isaf Powys....76 C3
Cwm-twrch Uchaf Powys....76 C3
Cwmwdig Water Pembs....90 E6
Cwmwysg Powys....95 F7
Cwm-y-glo Carms....75 B9
Gwyn....163 C8
Cwmyoy Mon....96 G5
Cwmystwyth Ceredig....112 C5
Cwrt Gwyn....128 C3
Cwrt-newydd Ceredig....93 B9
Cwrt-y-cadno Carms....94 C3
Cwrt-y-gollen Powys....78 B2
Cydweli / Kidwelly Carms....74 D6
Cyffordd Llandudno / Llandudno Junction Conwy....180 F3
Cyffylliog Denb....165 D9
Cyfronydd Powys....130 B2
Cymau Flint....166 D3
Cymdda Bridgend....58 C2
Cymer Neath....57 B10
Cymmer Rhondda....77 G8
Cyncoed Cardiff....59 C7
Cynghordy Carms....94 C6
Cynheidre Carms....75 D8
Cynonville Neath....57 B10
Cyntwell Cardiff....58 D6
Cynwyd Denb....165 G9
Cynwyl Elfed Carms....93 F7
Cywarch Gwyn....147 F7

D

Daccombe Devon....9 B8
Dacre Cumb....230 F5
N Yorks....214 G3
Dacre Banks N Yorks....214 G3
Daddry Shield Durham....232 D3
Dadford Bucks....102 D3
Dadlington Leics....135 D8
Dafarn Faig Gwyn....163 F7
Dafen Carms....75 E8
Daffy Green Norf....141 B9
Dagdale Staffs....151 C11
Dagenham London....68 C3
Daggons Dorset....31 E10
Daglingworth Glos....81 D7
Dagnall Bucks....85 B7
Dagtail End Worcs....117 E10
Dagworth Suff....125 E10
Dail Beag W Isles....304 D4
Dail bho Dheas W Isles....304 B6

Dail bho Thuath W Isles....304 B6
Daill Argyll....274 G4
Dailly S Ayrs....245 C7
Dail Mor W Isles....304 D4
Dainton Devon....9 B7
Dairsie or Osnaburgh Fife....287 F8
Daisy Green Suff....125 D10
Suff....125 D7
Daisy Hill Gtr Man....195 G2
W Yorks....197 B9
W Yorks....205 G8
Daisy Nook Gtr Man....196 G2
Dalabrog W Isles....297 J3
Dalavich Argyll....275 B10
Dalbeattie Dumfries....237 C10
Dalbeg Highld....291 B8
Dalblair E Ayrs....258 F4
Dalbog Angus....293 F7
Dalbury Derbys....152 C5
Dalby IoM....192 E3
Lincs....190 G6
N Yorks....216 E2
Dalchalloch Perth....291 G9
Dalchalm Highld....311 J3
Dalchenna Argyll....284 G4
Dalchirach Moray....301 F11
Dalchonzie Perth....285 E11
Dalchork Highld....309 H5
Dalchreichart Highld....290 B4
Dalchruin Perth....285 F11
Dalderby Lincs....174 B2
Dale Cumb....230 C6
Gtr Man....196 F3
Pembs....72 D4
Shetland....312 G6
Dale Abbey Derbys....153 B8
Dalebank Derbys....170 C6
Dale Bottom Cumb....229 G11
Dale Brow Ches E....184 F6
Dale End Derbys....170 C2
N Yorks....204 D5
Dale Head Cumb....221 B8
Dale Hill E Sus....53 G7
E Sus....53 G8
Dalelia Highld....289 C9
Dale Moor Derbys....153 B8
Dale of Walls Shetland....313 H3
Dales Brow Gtr Man....195 G9
Dales Green Staffs....168 D5
Daless Highld....301 F8
Dalestie Moray....292 B3
Dalestorth Notts....171 C8
Dalfaber Highld....291 B11
Dalfoil Stirl....277 D11
Dalganachan Highld....310 E4
Dalgarven N Ayrs....266 F5
Dalgety Bay Fife....280 E3
Dalginross Perth....285 E11
Dalguise Perth....286 C3
Dalhalvaig Highld....310 D2
Dalham Suff....124 E4
Dalhastnie Angus....293 F7
Dalhenzean Perth....292 G3
Dalinlongart Argyll....276 E2
Dalkeith Midloth....270 B6
Dallam Warr....183 C9
Dallas Moray....301 D11
Dallas Lodge Moray....301 D11
Dallcharn Highld....308 D6
Dalleagles E Ayrs....258 G3
Dallicott Shrops....132 E5
Dallimores IoW....20 C6
Dallinghoo Suff....126 G5
Dallington E Sus....23 B11
Northants....120 E4
Dallow N Yorks....214 E3
Dalmadilly Aberds....293 B9
Dalmally Argyll....284 E5
Dalmarnock Glasgow....268 C2
Perth....286 C3
Dalmary Stirl....277 B10
Dalmellington E Ayrs....245 B11
Dalmeny Edin....280 F2
Dalmigavie Highld....291 B9
Dalmigavie Lodge Highld....301 G10
Dalmilling S Ayrs....257 E9
Dalmore Highld....300 C6
Highld....309 H3
Dalmuir W Dunb....277 G10
Dalnabreck Highld....289 C8
Dalnacardoch Lodge Perth....291 F9
Dalnacroich Highld....300 D3
Dalnaglar Castle Perth....292 G3
Dalnahaitnach Highld....301 G8
Dalnamein Lodge Perth....291 G9
Dalnarrow Argyll....289 F7
Dalnaspidal Lodge Perth....291 F8
Dalnavaid Perth....292 G2
Dalnavie Highld....300 B6
Dalnaw Dumfries....236 B5
Dalnawillan Lodge Highld....310 E4
Dalness Highld....284 B5
Dalnessie Highld....309 H6
Dalphaid Highld....309 H3
Dalqueich Perth....286 G4
Dalreavoch Highld....309 J7
Dalriach Highld....301 F10
Dalrigh Stirl....285 E7
Dalrymple E Ayrs....257 G9
Dalscote Northants....120 G3
Dalserf S Lnrk....268 E5
Dalshannon N Lnrk....278 G4
Dalston Cumb....239 G9
London....67 C10
Dalswinton Dumfries....247 F10
Dalton Cumb....211 D10
Dumfries....238 C4
Lancs....194 F3
Northumb....241 F10
Northumb....242 C4
N Yorks....215 D8
N Yorks....224 D2
S Lnrk....268 D3
S Yorks....187 C7
W Yorks....197 D7
Dalton-in-Furness Cumb....210 E4
Dalton-le-Dale Durham....234 B4
Dalton Magna S Yorks....187 C7
Dalton-on-Tees N Yorks....224 D5
Dalton Parva S Yorks....187 C7
Dalton Piercy Hrtlpl....234 E5
Dalveen Dumfries....247 C9
Dalveich Stirl....285 E10
Dalvina Lo Highld....308 E6
Dalvraid Highld....308 D5
Dalwey Telford....132 B3
Dalwhinnie Highld....291 E8
Dalwood Devon....28 G3
Dalwyne S Ayrs....245 D8
Damask Green Herts....104 F5
Damems W Yorks....204 F6

Damerham Hants....31 D10
Damery Glos....80 G2
Damgate Norf....143 B8
Norf....161 F9
Dam Green Norf....141 F11
Damhead Moray....301 D10
Dam Head W Mid....196 B6
Damhead Holdings Midloth....270 B5
Dam Mill Staffs....133 C7
Dammaglaur Dumfries....236 F3
Dam of Quoigs Perth....286 G2
Damside Borders....270 F3
Danaway Kent....69 G11
Danbury Essex....88 E3
Danbury Common Essex....88 E3
Danby N Yorks....226 D4
Danby Wiske N Yorks....224 F6
Dancers Hill Herts....86 F2
Dancing Green Hereford....98 G2
Dandaleith Moray....302 E2
Danderhall Midloth....270 B6
Dandy Corner Suff....125 D11
Danebank Ches E....185 E7
Dane Bank Gtr Man....184 B6
Danebridge Ches E....169 B7
Dane End Herts....104 G6
Danegate E Sus....52 G5
Danehill E Sus....36 B6
Danemoor Green Norf....141 B11
Danesbury Herts....86 B2
Danesfield Bucks....65 C10
Danesford Shrops....132 E4
Danesmoor Derbys....170 C6
Danes Moss Ches E....184 G6
Dane Street Kent....54 C5
Daneway Glos....80 E6
Dangerous Corner Gtr Man....195 G7
Lancs....194 D4
N Yorks....204 D5
Daniel's Water Kent....54 E3
Danna na Cloiche Argyll....275 F7
Dannonchapel Corn....10 E6
Danskine E Loth....271 B11
Danthorpe E Yorks....209 G10
Danygraig Caerph....78 G2
Danzey Green Warks....118 D2
Dapple Heath Staffs....151 D10
Darby End W Mid....133 F9
Darby Green Hants....65 G10
Darbys Green Worcs....116 F4
Darby's Hill W Mid....133 F9
Darcy Lever Gtr Man....195 F8
Dardy Powys....78 B2
Darenth Kent....68 E5
Daresbury Halton....183 E9
Daresbury Delph Halton....183 E9
Darfield S Yorks....198 G2
Darfoulds Notts....187 F9
Dargate Kent....70 G5
Dargate Common Kent....70 G5
Darite Corn....6 B5
Darland Wrex....166 D5
Darlaston W Mid....133 D9
Darlaston Green W Mid....133 D9
Darley N Yorks....205 B9
Darley Abbey Derby....153 B7
Darley Bridge Derbys....170 C3
Darley Dale Derbys....170 C3
Darleyford Corn....11 G11
Darley Green Warks....118 C3
Darleyhall Herts....104 G2
Darley Head N Yorks....205 B9
Darley Hillside Derbys....170 C3
Darlingscott Warks....100 C4
Darlington Darl....224 C5
Darliston Shrops....149 C11
Darlton Notts....188 G3
Darmsden Suff....125 G11
Darn Hill Gtr Man....195 E10
Darnall S Yorks....186 D5
Darnford Staffs....134 B2
Darnhall Ches W....167 C10
Darnhall Mains Borders....270 F4
Darnick Borders....262 C2
Darowen Powys....128 C6
Darra Aberds....303 E7
Darracott Devon....24 D2
Devon....40 F3
Darras Hall Northumb....242 C5
Darrington W Yorks....198 D3
Darrow Green Norf....142 F5
Darsham Suff....127 D8
Darshill Som....44 E6
Dartford Kent....68 E4
Dartford Crossing Kent....68 D5
Dartington Devon....8 C5
Dartmeet Devon....13 G9
Dartmoor Devon....13 G7
Dartmouth Devon....8 E6
Dartmouth Park London....67 B9
Darvel E Ayrs....258 B3
Darvillshill Bucks....84 F4
Darwell Hole E Sus....23 B11
Darwen Blkburn....195 C7
Dassels Herts....105 F7
Datchet Windsor....66 D3
Datchworth Herts....86 B3
Datchworth Green Herts....86 B3
Daubhill Gtr Man....195 F8
Daugh of Kinermony Moray....302 E2
Dauntsey Wilts....62 C3
Dauntsey Lock Wilts....62 C3
Dava Moray....301 F10
Davenham Ches W....183 G11
Davenport Ches E....184 G5
Gtr Man....184 D6
Davenport Green Ches E....184 F4
Gtr Man....184 C4
Daventry Northants....119 D10
Davidson's Mains Edin....280 F4
Davidstow Corn....11 D9
David Street Kent....68 F6
David's Well Powys....113 B11
Davington Dumfries....248 C6
Kent....70 G4
Daviot Aberds....303 G7
Highld....301 E7
Davis's Town E Sus....23 B8
Davoch of Grange Moray....302 D4
Davyhulme Gtr Man....184 B3
Daw Cross N Yorks....205 C11
Dawdon Durham....234 B4
Dawes Green Sur....51 D8
Dawesgreen Sur....51 D8

Dawley Bank Telford....132 B3
Dawlish Devon....14 F5
Dawlish Warren Devon....14 F5
Dawn Conwy....180 G5
Daw's Cross Essex....107 E7
Daws Green Som....27 C11
Daws Heath Essex....69 B10
Dawshill Worcs....116 G6
Daw's House Corn....12 E2
Dawsmere Lincs....157 C8
Day Green Ches E....168 D3
Dayhills Staffs....151 C9
Dayhouse Bank Worcs....117 B9
Daylesford Glos....100 F4
Ddol Flint....181 G10
Ddôl Cownwy Powys....147 F10
Ddrydwy Anglesey....178 G3
Deacons Hill Herts....85 F11
Deadman's Cross C Beds....104 C2
Deadman's Green Staffs....151 B10
Deadwater Hants....49 F10
Northumb....250 D4
Deaf Hill Durham....234 D3
Deal Kent....55 C11
Deal Hall Essex....89 F8
Dean Cumb....229 F7
Devon....8 D6
Devon....40 D6
Devon....41 D8
Dorset....31 D7
Edin....280 G4
Hants....33 D9
Hants....48 G2
Lancs....195 B11
Oxon....100 G6
Som....45 E7
Dean Bank Durham....233 E11
Deanburnhaugh Borders....261 G9
Dean Court Oxon....83 D7
Dean Cross Devon....40 E4
Dean Gtr Man....195 F7
Hants....48 C4
Deanend Dorset....31 D7
Deane Gtr Man....195 F8
Hants....48 C5
Deanich Lodge Highld....309 L3
Deanland Dorset....31 D7
Deanlane End W Sus....34 E2
Dean Lane Head W Yorks....205 G7
Dean Park Renfs....267 B10
Dean Prior Devon....8 C4
Dean Row Ches E....184 E5
Deans W Loth....269 B10
Deans Bottom Kent....69 G11
Deanscales Cumb....229 F7
Deansgreen Ches E....183 D11
Dean's Green Warks....118 D2
Deanshanger Northants....102 D5
Deanshaugh Moray....302 E3
Deanston Stirl....285 G11
Dearham Cumb....229 D7
Dearnley Gtr Man....196 D2
Debach Suff....126 G4
Debden Essex....105 E10
Debden Cross Essex....105 E11
Debden Green Essex....86 F6
Essex....105 E11
Debenham Suff....126 E3
Deblin's Green Worcs....98 B6
Dechmont W Loth....279 G10
Deckham T&W....243 E7
Deddington Oxon....101 E9
Dedham Essex....107 E11
Dedham Heath Essex....107 E11
Dedridge W Loth....269 B11
Dedworth Windsor....66 D2
Deebank Aberds....293 D8
Deecastle Aberds....292 D6
Deene Northants....137 E7
Deenethorpe Northants....137 E7
Deepcar S Yorks....186 B3
Deepclough Derbys....185 B8
Deepcut Sur....50 B2
Deepdale Cumb....212 C4
N Yorks....213 D7
Deepdene Sur....51 D7
Deepfields W Mid....133 E8
Deeping Gate Lincs....138 B3
Deeping St James Lincs....138 B3
Deeping St Nicholas Lincs....156 F4
Deepthwaite Cumb....211 C10
Deepweir Mon....60 B3
Deerhill Moray....302 D4
Deerhurst Glos....99 F7
Deerhurst Walton Glos....99 F7
Deerland Pembs....73 C7
Deerness Orkney....314 F5
Deer's Green Essex....105 E9
Deerstones N Yorks....205 C7
Deerton Street Kent....70 G3
Defford Worcs....99 C8
Defynnog Powys....95 F8
Deganwy Conwy....180 F3
Degar V Glam....58 D4
Degibna Corn....2 D5
Deighton N Yorks....225 D7
W Yorks....197 D7
York....207 D8
Deiniolen Gwyn....163 C9
Deishar Highld....291 B11
Delabole Corn....11 E7
Delamere Ches W....167 B9
Delfrigs Aberds....303 G9
Delliefure Highld....301 F10
Dell Lodge Highld....292 B2
Dell Quay W Sus....22 C4
Delly End Oxon....82 C5
Delnabo Moray....292 C4
Delnadamph Aberds....292 C4
Delnamer Angus....292 G3
Delph Gtr Man....196 F3
Delves Durham....233 B8
Delvine Perth....286 C5
Dembleby Lincs....155 B10
Demelza Corn....5 C9
Denaby Main S Yorks....187 B8
Denbeath Fife....281 B7
Denbury Devon....8 B6
Denby Derbys....170 F6
Denby Bottles Derbys....170 F6
Denby Common Derbys....170 F6
Denby Dale W Yorks....197 F8
Denchworth Oxon....82 G6
Dendron Cumb....210 E4
Denel End C Beds....103 D10

Denend Aberds....302 F6
Deneside Durham....234 B4
Denford Northants....121 B9
Staffs....169 E7
Dengie Essex....89 E7
Denham Bucks....66 B4
Suff....124 E5
Suff....126 C3
Denham Corner Suff....126 C3
Denham End Suff....124 E5
Denham Green Bucks....66 B4
Denham Street Suff....126 C3
Denhead Aberds....303 D9
Fife....287 F8
Denhead of Arbilot Angus....287 C9
Denhead of Gray Dundee....287 D7
Denholm Borders....262 F3
Denholme W Yorks....205 G7
Denholme Clough W Yorks....205 G7
Denholme Edge W Yorks....205 G7
Denholme Gate W Yorks....205 G7
Denio Gwyn....145 B7
Denmead Hants....33 E11
Denmore Aberdeen....293 B11
Denmoss Aberds....302 E6
Dennington Suff....126 D5
Dennington Corner Suff....126 D5
Dennington Hall Suff....126 D5
Denny Falk....278 E6
Denny Bottom Kent....52 F5
Denny End Cambs....123 D9
Dennyloanhead Falk....278 E6
Denny Lodge Hants....32 F4
Dennystown W Dunb....277 F7
Denside Aberds....293 D10
Densole Kent....55 E8
Denston Suff....124 G5
Denstone Staffs....169 G9
Denstroude Kent....70 G6
Dent Cumb....212 B4
Dent Bank Durham....232 F4
Denton Cambs....138 F2
Darl....224 B4
E Sus....23 E7
Gtr Man....184 B6
Kent....55 D8
Kent....69 E7
Lincs....155 C7
Norf....142 F5
Northants....120 F6
N Yorks....205 D8
Oxon....83 E9
S Yorks....187 D8
Denton Burn T&W....242 D5
Denton Holme Cumb....239 G10
Denton's Green Mers....183 B7
Denver Norf....140 C2
Denvilles Hants....22 B2
Denwick Northumb....264 G6
Deopham Norf....141 C11
Deopham Green Norf....141 D10
Deopham Stalland Norf....141 C11
Depden Suff....124 F5
Depden Green Suff....124 F5
Deppers Bridge Warks....119 F7
Deptford London....67 D11
T&W....243 F9
Wilts....46 F4
Derby Derbys....153 B7
Devon....40 G5
Derbyhaven IoM....192 F3
Derbyshire Hill Mers....183 C8
Dereham Norf....159 G9
Dergoals Dumfries....236 D4
Deri Caerph....77 E10
Derril Devon....24 G4
Derringstone Kent....55 D8
Derrington Shrops....132 F3
Staffs....151 E7
Derriton Devon....24 G4
Derry Stirl....285 E10
Derrydarroch Stirl....285 E7
Derry Downs London....68 F3
Derry Fields Wilts....81 G8
Derry Hill Wilts....62 E3
Derry Lodge Aberds....292 D4
Derrythorpe N Lincs....199 F10
Dersingham Norf....158 C3
Derwen Bridgend....58 C2
Denb....165 E9
Derwen-fawr Carms....92 G5
Derwenlas Powys....128 D4
Derwydd Carms....75 B10
Desborough Northants....136 G6
Desford Leics....135 C9
Deskryshiel Aberds....292 B6
Detchant Northumb....264 B3
Detling Kent....53 B9
Deuchar Angus....292 G6
Deuddwr Powys....148 F4
Deuxhill Shrops....132 F3
Devauden Mon....79 F7
Devil's Bridge / Pontarfynach Ceredig....112 B4
Devitts Green Warks....134 E5
Devol Invclyd....276 G6
Devonport Plym....7 E9
Devonside Clack....279 B8
Devon Village Clack....279 B8
Devoran Corn....3 B7
Dewar Borders....270 F6
Dewartown Midloth....271 C7
Dewes Green Essex....105 E9
Dewlands Common Dorset....31 F9
Dewlish Dorset....17 B11
Dewsbury W Yorks....197 C8
Dewsbury Moor W Yorks....197 C8
Dewshall Court Hereford....97 E9
Dhoon IoM....192 D5
Dhoor IoM....192 C5
Dhowin IoM....192 B5
Dial Post W Sus....35 D11
Dibberford Dorset....29 G7
Dibden Hants....32 F6
Dibden Purlieu Hants....32 F6
Dickens Heath W Mid....118 B2
Dickleburgh Norf....142 G3
Dickleburgh Moor Norf....142 G3
Dickon Hills Lincs....175 D7
Didbrook Glos....99 E11
Didcot Oxon....64 B4
Diddington Cambs....122 D3
Diddlebury Shrops....131 F10
Diddywell Devon....25 B7

Didley Hereford....97 E9
Didling W Sus....34 D4
Didlington Norf....140 D5
Didmarton Glos....61 B10
Didsbury Gtr Man....184 C4
Didworthy Devon....8 C3
Diebidale Highld....309 L4
Digbeth W Mid....133 F11
Digby Lincs....173 E9
Digg Highld....298 C4
Diggle Gtr Man....196 F4
Diglis Worcs....116 G6
Digmoor Lancs....194 F3
Digswell Herts....86 C2
Digswell Park Herts....86 C3
Dihewyd Ceredig....111 F9
Dilham Norf....160 D6
Dilhorne Staffs....169 G7
Dillarburn S Lnrk....268 G6
Dill Hall Lancs....195 B8
Dillington Cambs....122 D2
Som....28 D5
Dilston Northumb....241 E11
Dilton Marsh Wilts....45 D11
Dilwyn Hereford....115 G8
Dimlands V Glam....58 F3
Dimmer Som....44 G6
Dimple Derbys....170 C3
Gtr Man....195 D8
Dimsdale Staffs....168 F4
Dimson Corn....12 G4
Dinas Carms....92 E5
Corn....10 G4
Gwyn....144 B5
Gwyn....163 D7
Dinas Cross Pembs....91 D10
Dinas Dinlle Gwyn....162 D6
Dinas-Mawddwy Gwyn....147 G2
Dinas Mawr Conwy....164 E4
Dinas Powys V Glam....59 E7
Dinbych / Denbigh Denb....165 C9
Dinbych-y-Pysgod / Tenby Pembs....73 E10
Dinckley Lancs....203 F10
Dinder Som....44 E5
Dinedor Hereford....97 E10
Dinedor Cross Hereford....97 E10
Dines Green Worcs....116 F6
Dingestow Mon....79 C7
Dinghurst N Som....44 B2
Dingle Mers....182 D5
Dingleden Kent....53 G10
Dingleton Borders....262 C2
Dingley Northants....136 F5
Dingwall Highld....300 D5
Dinlabyre Borders....250 E2
Dinmael Conwy....165 G8
Dinmore Hereford....115 G10
Dinnet Aberds....292 D6
Dinnington Som....28 D6
S Yorks....187 D8
T&W....242 C6
Dinorwic Gwyn....163 C9
Dinton Bucks....84 C3
Wilts....46 G4
Dinworthy Devon....24 D4
Dipford Som....28 C2
Dipley Hants....49 B8
Dippenhall Sur....49 D10
Dippertown Devon....12 E4
Dippin N Ayrs....256 E2
Dipple Devon....24 C4
Moray....302 D3
S Ayrs....245 C7
Diptford Devon....8 D4
Dipton Durham....242 G5
Diptonmill Northumb....241 E10
Dirdhu Highld....301 G10
Direcleit W Isles....305 J3
Dirleton E Loth....281 E10
Dirt Pot Northumb....232 B3
Discoed Powys....114 E5
Discove Som....45 G7
Diseworth Leics....153 E9
Dishes Orkney....314 D6
Dishforth N Yorks....215 E7
Disley Ches E....185 E7
Diss Norf....126 B2
Disserth Powys....113 F10
Distington Cumb....228 G5
Ditchampton Wilts....46 G5
Ditcheat Som....44 F6
Ditchfield Bucks....84 G4
Ditchford Hill Worcs....100 D4
Ditchingham Norf....142 E6
Ditchling E Sus....36 D4
Ditherington Shrops....149 G10
Ditteridge Wilts....61 F10
Dittisham Devon....8 E6
Ditton Halton....183 D7
Kent....53 B8
Ditton Green Cambs....124 F3
Ditton Priors Shrops....132 F2
Dittons E Sus....23 E10
Divach Highld....300 G4
Divlyn Carms....94 D5
Dixton Glos....99 F9
Mon....79 C8
Dizzard Corn....11 B9
Dobcross Gtr Man....196 F3
Dobs Hill Flint....166 C4
Dobson's Bridge Shrops....149 C9
Dobwalls Corn....6 C4
Doccombe Devon....13 D11
Dochamroch Highld....300 F6
Dochfour Ho Highld....300 F6
Dochgarroch Highld....300 F6
Dockenfield Sur....49 E10
Docker Lancs....211 E11
Docking Norf....158 B5
Docklow Hereford....115 F11
Dockray Cumb....230 G3
Dockroyd W Yorks....204 F6
Doc Penfro / Pembroke Dock Pembs....73 E7
Docton Devon....24 C2
Dodbrooke Devon....8 G4
Dodburn Borders....249 B11
Doddenham Worcs....116 F5
Doddinghurst Essex....87 F9
Doddington Cambs....139 E7
Kent....54 B2
Lincs....188 G6
Northumb....263 C11
Shrops....115 B11
Doddiscombsleigh Devon....14 D3
Dodford Northants....120 E2
Worcs....117 C8
Dodington S Glos....61 C9
Som....43 E7
Dodleston Ches W....166 C5
Dodmarsh Hereford....97 C11
Dodscott Devon....25 D8
Dods Leigh Staffs....151 C10

Dodworth S Yorks . . . 197 F10
Dodworth Bottom
  S Yorks . . . 197 G10
Dodworth Green
  S Yorks . . . 197 G10
Doe Bank W Mid . . . 134 D2
Doe Green Warr . . . 183 D9
Doehole Derbys . . . 170 D5
Doe Lea Derbys . . . 171 B7
Doffcocker Gtr Man . . . 195 F7
Dogdyke Lincs . . . 174 D2
Dog Hill Gtr Man . . . 196 F3
Dogingtree Estate
  Staffs . . . 151 G9
Dogley Lane W Yorks . . . 197 E7
Dogmersfield Hants . . . 49 C9
Dogridge Wilts . . . 62 B5
Dogsthorpe Pboro . . . 138 C3
Dog Village Devon . . . 14 B5
Doirlinn Highld . . . 289 D8
Dolanog Powys . . . 147 G11
Dolau Powys . . . 114 D2
  Rhondda . . . 58 C3
Dolbenmaen Gwyn . . . 163 G8
Dole Ceredig . . . 128 F2
Dolemeads Bath . . . 45 C6
Doley Staffs . . . 150 D4
Dolfach Powys . . . 129 C8
Dol-ffanog Gwyn . . . 146 G4
Dolfor Powys . . . 130 F2
Dol-för Powys . . . 128 B6
Dolgarrog Conwy . . . 164 B3
Dolgellau Gwyn . . . 146 F4
Dolgerdd Ceredig . . . 111 G8
Dolgoch Gwyn . . . 128 C3
Dolgran Carms . . . 93 E8
Dolhelfa Powys . . . 113 C8
Dolhendre Gwyn . . . 147 C7
Doll Highld . . . 311 J2
Dollar Clack . . . 279 B9
Dolley Green Powys . . . 114 D6
Dollis Hill London . . . 67 B8
Dollwen Ceredig . . . 128 G3
Dolphin Flint . . . 181 G11
Dolphingstone E Loth . . . 281 G7
Dolphinholme Lancs . . . 202 C6
Dolphinston Borders . . . 262 F5
Dolphinton S Lnrk . . . 270 F2
Dolton Devon . . . 25 E9
Dolwen Conwy . . . 180 G5
  Powys . . . 180 F4
Dolwyd Conwy . . . 180 F4
Dolwyddelan Gwyn . . . 164 E2
Dôl-y-Bont Ceredig . . . 128 F2
Dol-y-cannau Powys . . . 96 B3
Dolydd Gwyn . . . 163 D7
Dolymelynllyn
  Gwyn . . . 146 E4
Dolyhir Powys . . . 114 F4
Dolwern Wrex . . . 148 B4
Domewood Sur . . . 51 E10
Domgay Powys . . . 148 F5
Dommett Som . . . 28 E3
Doncaster S Yorks . . . 198 G5
Doncaster Common
  S Yorks . . . 198 G6
Dones Green Ches W . . . 183 F10
Donhead St Andrew
  Wilts . . . 30 C6
Donhead St Mary Wilts . . . 30 C6
Donibristle Fife . . . 280 D3
Doniford Som . . . 42 E5
Donington Lincs . . . 156 B4
  Shrops . . . 132 C6
Donington Eaudike
  Lincs . . . 156 B4
Donington le Heath
  Leics . . . 153 G8
Donington on Bain
  Lincs . . . 190 E2
Donington South Ing
  Lincs . . . 156 C4
Donisthorpe Leics . . . 152 G6
Don Johns Essex . . . 106 F6
Donkey Street Kent . . . 54 G6
Donkey Town Sur . . . 66 G2
Donna Nook Lincs . . . 190 B6
Donnington Glos . . . 100 F3
  Hereford . . . 98 E4
  Shrops . . . 131 B11
  Telford . . . 150 G4
  W Berks . . . 64 F3
  W Sus . . . 22 C5
Donnington Wood
  Telford . . . 150 G4
Donwell T&W . . . 243 F7
Donyatt Som . . . 28 E4
Doomsday Green
  W Sus . . . 35 B11
Doonfoot S Ayrs . . . 257 F8
Dora's Green Hants . . . 49 D10
Dorback Lodge Highld . . . 292 B2
Dorcan Swindon . . . 63 C7
Dorchester Dorset . . . 17 C9
  Oxon . . . 83 G9
Dordale Worcs . . . 117 C8
Dordon Warks . . . 134 C5
Dore S Yorks . . . 186 E4
Dores Highld . . . 300 F5
Dorking Sur . . . 51 D7
Dorking Tye Suff . . . 107 D8
Dorley's Corner Suff . . . 127 D7
Dormansland Sur . . . 52 E2
Dormans Park Sur . . . 51 E11
Dormanstown Redcar . . . 235 G7
Dormer's Wells London . . . 66 C6
Dormington Hereford . . . 97 D11
Dormston Worcs . . . 117 F9
Dorn Glos . . . 100 E4
Dornal S Ayrs . . . 236 B4
Dorney Bucks . . . 66 D2
Dorney Reach Bucks . . . 66 D2
Dorn Hill Worcs . . . 100 E3
Dornie Highld . . . 295 C10
Dornoch Highld . . . 309 L7
Dornock Dumfries . . . 238 D6
Dorrery Highld . . . 310 D4
Dorridge W Mid . . . 118 B3
Dorrington Lincs . . . 173 E9
  Shrops . . . 131 C9
Dorsington Warks . . . 100 B2
Dorstone Hereford . . . 96 C6
Dorton Bucks . . . 83 C11
Dorusduain Highld . . . 295 C11
Doseley Telford . . . 132 B3
Dosmuckeran Highld . . . 300 C4
Dosthill Staffs . . . 134 C4
  Staffs . . . 134 C4
Dothan Anglesey . . . 178 G5
Dothill Telford . . . 150 G2
Dottery Dorset . . . 16 B5
Doublebois Corn . . . 6 C3
Double Hill Bath . . . 45 B8
Dougarie N Ayrs . . . 255 D9
Doughton Glos . . . 80 G5
  Norf . . . 159 D7
Douglas IoM . . . 192 E4
  S Lnrk . . . 259 C8

Douglas & Angus
  Dundee . . . 287 D8
Douglastown Angus . . . 287 C8
Douglas Water S Lnrk . . . 259 B9
Douglas West S Lnrk . . . 259 C8
Doulting Som . . . 44 E6
Dounby Orkney . . . 314 D2
Doune Highld . . . 291 C10
  Highld . . . 309 J4
  Stirl . . . 285 G11
Doune Park Aberds . . . 303 C7
Douneside Aberds . . . 292 C6
Dounie Argyll . . . 275 D8
  Highld . . . 309 K5
  Highld . . . 309 L6
Dounreay Highld . . . 310 C3
Dousland Devon . . . 7 B10
Dovaston Shrops . . . 149 E7
Dovecot Mers . . . 182 C6
Dovecothall Glasgow . . . 267 D10
Dove Green Notts . . . 171 E7
Dove Holes Derbys . . . 185 F9
Dovenby Cumb . . . 229 E7
Dovendale Lincs . . . 190 E4
Dove Point Mers . . . 182 C2
Dover Gtr Man . . . 194 G6
  Kent . . . 55 E10
Dovercourt Essex . . . 108 E5
Doverdale Worcs . . . 117 D7
Doverhay Som . . . 41 D11
Doveridge Derbys . . . 152 C2
Doversgreen Sur . . . 51 D9
Dowally Perth . . . 286 C4
Dowanhill Glasgow . . . 267 B11
Dowbridge Lancs . . . 202 G4
Dowdeswell Glos . . . 81 B7
Dowe Hill Norf . . . 161 F10
Dowlais M Tydf . . . 77 D10
Dowlais Top M Tydf . . . 77 D9
Dowland Devon . . . 25 E9
Dowles Worcs . . . 116 B5
Dowlesgreen Wokingham . . . 65 F10
Dowlish Ford Som . . . 28 E5
Dowlish Wake Som . . . 28 E5
Downall Green Gtr Man . . . 194 G5
Down Ampney Glos . . . 81 F10
Downan Moray . . . 301 F11
  S Ayrs . . . 244 G3
Downcraig Ferry
  N Ayrs . . . 266 D3
Downderry Corn . . . 6 E6
Downe London . . . 68 G2
Downend Glos . . . 80 F4
  IoW . . . 20 D6
  S Glos . . . 60 D6
  W Berks . . . 64 D3
Down End Som . . . 43 E10
Downfield Dundee . . . 287 D7
Down Field Cambs . . . 124 C2
Downgate Corn . . . 11 G11
  Corn . . . 12 G3
Down Hall Corn . . . 239 G7
Downham Essex . . . 88 F2
  Lancs . . . 203 E11
  London . . . 67 E11
  Northumb . . . 263 C9
Downham Market Norf . . . 140 C2
Down Hatherley Glos . . . 99 G7
Downhead Som . . . 29 B9
  Som . . . 45 D7
Downhead Park
  M Keynes . . . 103 C7
Downhill Corn . . . 5 B7
  Perth . . . 286 D4
  T&W . . . 243 F9
Downholland Cross
  Lancs . . . 193 F11
Downholme N Yorks . . . 224 F2
Downicary Devon . . . 12 C3
Downies Aberds . . . 293 D11
Downinney Corn . . . 11 C10
Downley Bucks . . . 84 G4
Down Park W Sus . . . 51 F10
Downs V Glam . . . 58 E6
Down St Mary Devon . . . 26 G2
Downside C Beds . . . 103 G10
  E Sus . . . 23 E9
  N Som . . . 44 D6
  Som . . . 44 D6
  Sur . . . 50 B6
  Sur . . . 51 B7
Down Street E Sus . . . 36 C6
Down Thomas Devon . . . 7 E10
Downton Hants . . . 19 C11
  Powys . . . 114 E4
  Shrops . . . 149 G10
  Wilts . . . 31 C11
Downton on the Rock
  Hereford . . . 115 C8
Dowsby Lincs . . . 156 D2
Dowsdale Lincs . . . 156 G5
Dowslands Som . . . 28 C2
Dowthwaitehead Cumb . . . 230 G3
Doxey Staffs . . . 151 E8
Doxford Park T&W . . . 243 G9
Doynton S Glos . . . 61 E8
Drabblegate Norf . . . 160 D4
Draethen Newport . . . 59 B8
Draffan S Lnrk . . . 268 F5
Dragley Beck Cumb . . . 210 D5
Dragonby N Lincs . . . 200 D2
Dragons Green W Sus . . . 35 C10
Drakehouse S Yorks . . . 186 E6
Drakeland Corner Devon . . . 7 D11
Drakelow Worcs . . . 132 G6
Drakemyre Aberds . . . 303 F9
  N Ayrs . . . 266 E5
Drake's Broughton Worcs . . . 99 B8
Drakes Cross Worcs . . . 117 B11
Drakestone Green Suff . . . 107 B9
Drakewalls Corn . . . 12 G4
Draughton Northants . . . 120 B5
  N Yorks . . . 204 C6
Drawbridge Corn . . . 6 B3
Drax N Yorks . . . 199 B7
Draycot Oxon . . . 83 D10
Draycot Cerne Wilts . . . 62 D2
Draycote Warks . . . 119 C8
Draycot Fitz Payne Wilts . . . 62 G6
Draycot Foliat Swindon . . . 63 D7
Draycott Derbys . . . 153 C8
  Glos . . . 80 E2
  Glos . . . 100 D3
  Som . . . 29 C8
  Som . . . 44 C3
  Worcs . . . 99 B7
Draycott in the Clay
  Staffs . . . 152 D3
Draycott in the Moors
  Staffs . . . 169 G6
Drayford Devon . . . 26 E3
Drayton Leics . . . 136 E6
  Lincs . . . 156 B4
  Norf . . . 160 G3
  Northants . . . 119 E11
  Oxon . . . 83 G7
  Oxon . . . 101 C8
  Ptsmth . . . 33 F11
  Som . . . 28 C6

Som . . . 29 D7
  Warks . . . 118 F3
  Worcs . . . 117 B8
Drayton Bassett Staffs . . . 134 C3
Drayton Beauchamp
  Bucks . . . 84 C6
Drayton Parslow Bucks . . . 102 F6
Drayton St Leonard
  Oxon . . . 83 F10
Drebley N Yorks . . . 205 B7
Dreemskerry IoM . . . 192 C5
Dreenhill Pembs . . . 72 C6
Drefach Carms . . . 75 C8
  Carms . . . 92 G5
  Carms . . . 93 D7
Dre-fach Carms . . . 75 B11
Drefelin Carms . . . 93 D7
Dreggie Highld . . . 301 G10
Dreghorn Edin . . . 270 B4
  N Ayrs . . . 257 B9
Dre-gôch Denb . . . 165 B10
Drellingore Kent . . . 55 E8
Drem E Loth . . . 281 F10
Dresden Stoke . . . 168 G6
Dreumasdal W Isles . . . 297 H3
Drewsteignton Devon . . . 13 C10
Driby Lincs . . . 190 G5
Driffield E Yorks . . . 208 B6
  Glos . . . 81 F9
Drift Corn . . . 1 D4
Drigg Cumb . . . 219 F11
Drighlington W Yorks . . . 197 B8
Drimnin Highld . . . 289 D7
Drimnin Ho Highld . . . 289 D7
Drimpton Dorset . . . 28 F6
Drimsynie Argyll . . . 284 G5
Dringhoe E Yorks . . . 209 C9
Dringhouses York . . . 207 D7
Drinisiadar W Isles . . . 305 J3
Drinkstone Suff . . . 125 E9
Drinkstone Green Suff . . . 125 E9
Drishaig Argyll . . . 284 F5
Drissaig Argyll . . . 275 B10
Drive End Dorset . . . 29 F9
Driver's End Herts . . . 86 B2
Drochedlie Aberds . . . 302 C5
Drochil Borders . . . 270 G3
Droitwich Spa Worcs . . . 117 E7
Droman Highld . . . 306 D6
Dromore Dumfries . . . 237 C7
Dron Perth . . . 286 F5
Dronfield Derbys . . . 186 F5
Dronfield Woodhouse
  Derbys . . . 186 F4
Drongan E Ayrs . . . 257 F10
Dronley Angus . . . 287 D7
Droop Dorset . . . 30 F3
Drope Cardiff . . . 58 D6
Dropping Well S Yorks . . . 186 C5
Droughdool Dumfries . . . 236 D3
Droxford Hants . . . 33 D10
Droylsden Gtr Man . . . 184 B6
Drub W Yorks . . . 197 B8
Druggers End Worcs . . . 98 D5
Druid Denb . . . 165 G8
Druids Green V Glam . . . 58 E4
Druidston Pembs . . . 72 B5
Druim Highld . . . 301 D9
Druimarbin Highld . . . 290 F2
Druimavuic Argyll . . . 284 C4
Druimdrishaig Argyll . . . 275 F8
Druimindarroch Highld . . . 295 G8
Druimkinnerras Highld . . . 300 F4
Druimnacroish Argyll . . . 288 E6
Druimsornaig Argyll . . . 289 F9
Druimyeon More Argyll . . . 255 B7
Drum Argyll . . . 275 F10
  Edin . . . 270 B6
  Perth . . . 286 G4
Drumardoch Stirl . . . 285 F10
Drumbeg Highld . . . 306 F6
Drumblade Aberds . . . 302 E5
Drumblair Aberds . . . 302 E6
Drumbuie Dumfries . . . 246 G3
  Highld . . . 295 B9
Drumburgh Cumb . . . 239 F7
Drumburn Dumfries . . . 237 C11
Drumchapel Glasgow . . . 277 G10
Drumchardine Highld . . . 300 D5
Drumchork Highld . . . 307 L3
Drumclog S Lnrk . . . 258 B4
Drumdelgie Aberds . . . 302 E4
Drumderfit Highld . . . 300 D6
Drumdollo Aberds . . . 302 F6
Drumeldrie Fife . . . 287 G8
Drumelzier Borders . . . 260 C4
Drumfearn Highld . . . 295 D8
Drumgask Highld . . . 291 D8
Drumgelloch N Lnrk . . . 268 B5
Drumgley Angus . . . 287 B8
Drumgreen Aberds . . . 292 F6
Drumguish Highld . . . 291 D9
Drumhead Aberds . . . 293 D8
Drumin Moray . . . 301 F11
Drumlasie Aberds . . . 293 C8
Drumlean Stirl . . . 285 G8
Drumlemble Argyll . . . 255 F7
Drumliah Highld . . . 309 K6
Drumligair Aberds . . . 293 B11
Drumlithie Aberds . . . 293 E9
Drumloist Stirl . . . 285 G10
Drummersdale Lancs . . . 193 E11
Drummick Perth . . . 286 E3
Drummond Highld . . . 300 C6
Drummoddie Dumfries . . . 236 E5
Drummuir Moray . . . 302 E3
Drummuir Castle Moray . . . 302 E3
Drumnadrochit Highld . . . 300 G5
Drumnagorrach Moray . . . 302 D5
Drumness Perth . . . 286 F2
Drumoak Aberds . . . 293 D9
Drumore Argyll . . . 255 E8
Drumpark Dumfries . . . 247 G9
Drumpellier N Lnrk . . . 268 B4
Drumphail Dumfries . . . 236 C4
Drumrash Dumfries . . . 237 B8
Drumrunie Highld . . . 307 J6
Drumry W Dunb . . . 277 G10
Drums Aberds . . . 303 G9
Drumsallie Highld . . . 289 B11
Drumstinchall Dumfries . . . 237 D10
Drumsturdy Angus . . . 287 D8
Drumtochty Castle
  Aberds . . . 293 F8
Drumtroddan Dumfries . . . 236 E5
Drumuie Highld . . . 298 E4
Drumuillie Highld . . . 301 G9
Drumvaich Stirl . . . 285 G11
Drumwalt Dumfries . . . 236 D5
Drumwhindle Aberds . . . 303 F9
Drunkendub Angus . . . 287 C10
Drury Flint . . . 166 C3
Drurylane Norf . . . 141 C8
Drury Square Norf . . . 159 F8
Drybeck Cumb . . . 222 B3

Drybridge Moray . . . 302 C4
  N Ayrs . . . 257 B9
Drybrook Glos . . . 79 B10
Dryburgh Borders . . . 262 C3
Dryden Borders . . . 261 E11
Dry Doddington Lincs . . . 172 F4
Dry Drayton Cambs . . . 123 E7
Dryhill Kent . . . 52 B3
Dry Hill Hants . . . 49 F7
Dryhope Borders . . . 261 E7
Drylaw Edin . . . 280 F4
Drym Corn . . . 2 C4
Drymen Stirl . . . 277 D9
Drymere Norf . . . 140 B5
Drymuir Aberds . . . 303 E9
Drynain Argyll . . . 276 D3
Drynham Wilts . . . 45 B11
Drynie Park Highld . . . 300 D5
Drynoch Highld . . . 294 B6
Dry Sandford Oxon . . . 83 E7
Dryslwyn Carms . . . 93 G11
Dry Street Essex . . . 69 B7
Dryton Shrops . . . 131 B11
Drywells Aberds . . . 302 D6
Duag Bridge Highld . . . 309 K3
Duartbeg Highld . . . 306 F6
Duartmore Bridge
  Highld . . . 306 F6
Dubbs Cross Devon . . . 12 C3
Dubford Aberds . . . 303 C8
Dubhchladach Argyll . . . 275 G9
Dublin Suff . . . 126 D3
Dubton Angus . . . 287 B9
Dubwath Cumb . . . 229 E9
Duchally Highld . . . 309 H3
Duchlage Argyll . . . 276 D6
Duchrae Dumfries . . . 237 B7
Duck Corner Suff . . . 109 C7
Duck End Beds . . . 103 C11
  Beds . . . 121 G9
  Bucks . . . 102 F5
  Cambs . . . 122 E4
  Essex . . . 105 G10
  Essex . . . 106 E3
  Essex . . . 106 F3
Duckend Green Essex . . . 106 G4
Duckhole S Glos . . . 79 G10
Duckington Ches W . . . 167 E7
Ducklington Oxon . . . 82 D5
Duckmanton Derbys . . . 186 G6
Duck's Cross Beds . . . 122 F2
Ducks Island London . . . 86 F2
Duckswich Worcs . . . 98 D6
Duddenhoe End Essex . . . 105 D9
Duddingston Edin . . . 280 G5
Duddington Northants . . . 137 C9
Duddlestone Som . . . 28 C2
Duddleswell E Sus . . . 37 B7
Duddlewick Shrops . . . 132 G3
Duddo Northumb . . . 273 G8
Duddon Ches W . . . 167 C8
Duddon Bridge Cumb . . . 210 B3
Duddon Common
  Ches W . . . 167 B8
Dudleston Shrops . . . 148 B6
Dudleston Grove Shrops . . . 149 B7
Dudleston Heath (Criftins)
  Shrops . . . 149 B7
Dudley T&W . . . 243 C7
  W Mid . . . 133 E8
Dudley Hill W Yorks . . . 205 G9
Dudley Port W Mid . . . 133 E9
Dudley's Fields W Mid . . . 133 C9
Dudley Wood W Mid . . . 133 F8
Dudlows Green Warr . . . 183 E10
Dudsbury Dorset . . . 19 B7
Dudswell Herts . . . 85 D7
Dudwells Pembs . . . 91 G8
Duerdon Devon . . . 24 D4
Duffield Derbys . . . 170 G4
Duffieldbank Derbys . . . 170 F5
Duffryn Neath . . . 57 B10
  Newport . . . 59 B9
Dufftown Moray . . . 302 F3
Duffus Moray . . . 301 C11
Dufton Cumb . . . 231 F9
Duggleby N Yorks . . . 217 F7
Duich Argyll . . . 254 B4
Duileter Argyll . . . 284 D5
Duinish Perth . . . 291 G8
Duirinish Highld . . . 295 B9
Duisdalebeg Highld . . . 295 D9
Duisdalemore Highld . . . 295 D9
Duisky Highld . . . 290 F2
Duke End Warks . . . 134 F4
Dukesfield Northumb . . . 241 F10
Dukestown Bl Gwent . . . 77 C10
Dukinfield Gtr Man . . . 184 B6
Dulas Anglesey . . . 179 D7
Dulcote Som . . . 44 E5
Dulford Devon . . . 27 F9
Dull Perth . . . 286 C2
Dullatur N Lnrk . . . 278 F4
Dullingham Cambs . . . 124 F2
Dullingham Ley Cambs . . . 124 F2
Dulnain Bridge Highld . . . 301 G9
Duloch Fife . . . 280 D2
Duloe Beds . . . 122 E3
  Corn . . . 6 D4
Dulsie Highld . . . 301 E9
Dulverton Som . . . 27 B7
Dulwich London . . . 67 E10
Dulwich Village London . . . 67 E10
Dumbarton W Dunb . . . 277 F7
Dumbleton Glos . . . 99 D10
Dumcrieff Dumfries . . . 248 C4
Dumfries Dumfries . . . 237 B11
Dumgoyne Stirl . . . 277 E10
Dummer Hants . . . 48 D5
Dumpford W Sus . . . 34 C4
Dumpinghill Devon . . . 24 F6
Dumpling Green Norf . . . 159 G10
Dumpton Kent . . . 71 F11
Dun Angus . . . 287 B10
Dunach Argyll . . . 289 G10
Dunadd Argyll . . . 275 D9
Dunain Ho Highld . . . 300 E6
Dunalastair Perth . . . 285 B11
Dunan Highld . . . 295 C7
Dunans Argyll . . . 275 D11
Dunball Som . . . 43 E10
Dunbar E Loth . . . 282 F3
Dunbeath Highld . . . 311 G5
Dunbeg Argyll . . . 289 G10
Dunblane Stirl . . . 285 G11

Duncote Northants . . . 120 G3
Duncow Dumfries . . . 247 G11
Duncraggan Stirl . . . 285 G9
Duncrievie Perth . . . 286 G5
Duncroisk Stirl . . . 285 D9
Duncton W Sus . . . 34 H4
Dundee Dundee . . . 287 D8
Dundeugh Dumfries . . . 246 F3
Dundon Som . . . 44 G3
Dundonald Fife . . . 280 C4
  S Ayrs . . . 257 C9
Dundon Hayes Som . . . 44 G3
Dundraw Cumb . . . 229 B10
Dundreggan Highld . . . 290 B5
Dundreggan Lodge
  Highld . . . 290 B5
Dundrennan Dumfries . . . 237 E9
Dundridge Hants . . . 33 D9
Dundry N Som . . . 60 F5
Dunecht Aberds . . . 293 C9
Dunfermline Fife . . . 279 D11
Dunfield Glos . . . 81 F10
Dunford Bridge S Yorks . . . 197 G8
Dungate Kent . . . 54 B2
Dunge Wilts . . . 45 C11
Dungeness Kent . . . 39 D9
Dungworth S Yorks . . . 186 D3
Dunham-on-the-Hill
  Ches W . . . 183 G7
Dunham on Trent Notts . . . 188 G4
Dunhampstead Worcs . . . 117 E8
Dunhampton Worcs . . . 116 D6
Dunham Town Gtr Man . . . 184 D2
Dunham Woodhouses
  Gtr Man . . . 184 D2
Dunholme Lincs . . . 189 F8
Dunino Fife . . . 287 F9
Dunipace Falk . . . 278 E6
Dunira Perth . . . 285 E11
Dunkeld Perth . . . 286 C4
Dunkerton Bath . . . 45 B8
Dunkeswell Devon . . . 27 F10
Dunkeswick N Yorks . . . 206 D2
Dunkirk Cambs . . . 139 F10
  Ches W . . . 182 G5
  Kent . . . 54 B5
  Norf . . . 160 D4
  Nottingham . . . 153 B11
  S Glos . . . 61 B9
  Staffs . . . 168 E4
  Wilts . . . 62 G3
Dunk's Green Kent . . . 52 C6
Dunlappie Angus . . . 293 G7
Dunley Hants . . . 48 C3
  Worcs . . . 116 D5
Dunlichity Lodge Highld . . . 300 F6
Dunlop E Ayrs . . . 267 F8
Dunmaglass Lodge
  Highld . . . 300 G5
Dunmere Corn . . . 5 B10
Dunmore Argyll . . . 275 G8
  Falk . . . 279 D7
  Highld . . . 300 E5
Dunnerholme Cumb . . . 210 D4
Dunnet Highld . . . 310 B6
Dunnichen Angus . . . 287 C9
Dunnikier Fife . . . 280 C5
Dunninald Angus . . . 287 B11
Dunning Perth . . . 286 F4
Dunnington E Yorks . . . 209 C9
  Warks . . . 117 G11
  York . . . 207 C9
Dunnockshaw Lancs . . . 195 B10
Dunnose IoW . . . 21 F7
Dunns Heath Shrops . . . 149 F9
Dunn Street Kent . . . 54 D3
  Kent . . . 69 G9
  Shrops . . . 130 G4
Dunollie Argyll . . . 289 F10
Dunoon Argyll . . . 276 F3
Dunragit Dumfries . . . 236 D3
Dunrobin Mains Highld . . . 311 J2
Dunrostan Argyll . . . 275 E8
Duns Borders . . . 272 E5
Dunsa Derbys . . . 186 G2
Dunsby Lincs . . . 156 D2
Dunscar Gtr Man . . . 195 E8
Dunscore Dumfries . . . 247 G9
Dunscroft S Yorks . . . 199 F7
Dunsdale Redcar . . . 226 B2
Dunsden Green Oxon . . . 65 D8
Dunsfold Sur . . . 50 F4
Dunsfold Common Sur . . . 50 F4
Dunsfold Green Sur . . . 50 F4
Dunsford Devon . . . 14 D2
  Sur . . . 50 F4
Dunshalt Fife . . . 286 F6
Dunshillock Aberds . . . 303 E9
Dunsinnan Perth . . . 286 D5
Dunskey Ho Dumfries . . . 236 D2
Dunslea Corn . . . 11 G11
Dunsley N Yorks . . . 227 C7
  Staffs . . . 133 G7
Dunsmore Bucks . . . 84 D5
  Warks . . . 119 D10
Dunsop Bridge Lancs . . . 203 C9
Dunstable C Beds . . . 103 G10
Dunstall Staffs . . . 152 E3
Dunstall Common Worcs . . . 99 C7
Dunstall Green Suff . . . 124 E4
Dunstall Hill W Mid . . . 133 C8
Dunstan Northumb . . . 265 F7
Dunstan Steads
  Northumb . . . 264 E6
Dunster Som . . . 42 E4
Duns Tew Oxon . . . 101 F9
Dunston Derbys . . . 186 G5
  Lincs . . . 173 C9
  Norf . . . 142 C4
  Staffs . . . 151 F8
  T&W . . . 242 E6
Dunston Heath Staffs . . . 151 F8
Dunston Hill T&W . . . 242 E6
Dunsville S Yorks . . . 198 F6
Dunswell E Yorks . . . 209 F7
Dunsyre S Lnrk . . . 269 F11
Dunterton Devon . . . 12 F3
Dunthrop Oxon . . . 101 F7
Duntisbourne Abbots
  Glos . . . 81 D7
Duntisbourne Leer Glos . . . 81 D7
Duntisbourne Rouse
  Glos . . . 81 D7
Duntish Dorset . . . 29 F11
Duntocher W Dunb . . . 277 G9
Dunton Bucks . . . 102 G5
  C Beds . . . 104 C4
  Norf . . . 159 C7
Dunton Bassett Leics . . . 135 E10

Dunton Green Kent . . . 52 B4
Dunton Patch Norf . . . 159 C7
Dunton Wayletts Essex . . . 87 G11
Duntrune Castle Argyll . . . 275 D8
Duntulm Highld . . . 298 B4
Dunure S Ayrs . . . 257 F7
Dunvant / Dynfant
  Swansea . . . 56 C5
Dunvegan Highld . . . 298 E2
Dunveth Corn . . . 10 G5
Dunwear Som . . . 43 F10
Dunwich Suff . . . 127 C9
Dunwood Staffs . . . 168 D6
Dupplin Castle Perth . . . 286 F4
Durdar Cumb . . . 239 G10
Durgan Corn . . . 3 D7
Durgates E Sus . . . 52 G6
Durham Durham . . . 233 C11
Durisdeer Dumfries . . . 247 C9
Durisdeermill Dumfries . . . 247 C9
Durkar W Yorks . . . 197 D10
Durleigh Som . . . 43 F9
Durleighmarsh W Sus . . . 34 C3
Durley Hants . . . 33 D8
  Wilts . . . 63 G8
Durley Street Hants . . . 33 D8
Durlock Kent . . . 55 B9
Durlow Common
  Hereford . . . 98 D2
Durn Gtr Man . . . 196 D2
Durnamuck Highld . . . 307 K5
Durness Highld . . . 308 C4
Durno Aberds . . . 303 G7
Durns Town Hants . . . 19 B11
Duror Highld . . . 289 D11
Durran Argyll . . . 275 C10
  Highld . . . 310 C5
Durrant Green Kent . . . 53 F11
Durrants Hants . . . 22 B2
Durrington Wilts . . . 47 E7
  W Sus . . . 35 G10
Durrisdale Orkney . . . 314 D3
Dursley Glos . . . 80 F3
Dursley Cross Glos . . . 98 G3
Durston Som . . . 28 B3
Durweston Dorset . . . 30 F5
Dury Shetland . . . 313 G6
Duryard Devon . . . 14 C4
Duston Northants . . . 120 E4
Dutch Village Essex . . . 69 C9
Duthil Highld . . . 301 G9
Dutlas Powys . . . 114 B4
Duton Hill Essex . . . 106 F2
Dutson Corn . . . 12 D2
Dutton Ches W . . . 183 F9
Duxford Cambs . . . 105 B9
  Oxon . . . 82 F5
Dwygyfylchi Conwy . . . 180 F2
Dwyran Anglesey . . . 162 B6
Dwyrhiw Powys . . . 129 C11
Dyce Aberdeen . . . 293 B10
Dyche Som . . . 43 E7
Dye House Northumb . . . 241 F10
Dyer's Common S Glos . . . 60 C5
Dyer's Green Cambs . . . 105 B7
Dyffryn Bridgend . . . 57 C11
  Carms . . . 92 G6
  Ceredig . . . 110 G5
  Pembs . . . 91 E8
  V Glam . . . 58 D5
Dyffryn Ardudwy Gwyn . . . 145 E11
Dyffryn-bern Ceredig . . . 110 G5
Dyffryn Castell Ceredig . . . 128 G5
Dyffryn Ceidrych Carms . . . 94 F4
Dyffryn Cellwen Neath . . . 76 D5
Dyke Argyll . . . 275 E8
  Lincs . . . 156 E2
  Moray . . . 301 D9
Dykehead Angus . . . 292 G5
  N Lnrk . . . 268 D6
  Stirl . . . 277 B11
Dykelands Aberds . . . 293 G9
Dykends Angus . . . 286 B6
Dykeside Aberds . . . 303 E7
Dykesmains N Ayrs . . . 266 G5
Dylife Powys . . . 129 E7
Dymchurch Kent . . . 39 B9
Dymock Glos . . . 98 E4
Dynfant / Dunvant
  Swansea . . . 56 C5
Dyrham S Glos . . . 61 D8
Dysart Fife . . . 280 C6
Dyserth Denb . . . 181 F9

E

Eabost Highld . . . 294 B5
Eabost West Highld . . . 294 B5
Each End Kent . . . 55 B10
Eachway Worcs . . . 117 B9
Eachwick Northumb . . . 242 C4
Eadar Dha Fhadhail
  W Isles . . . 304 E2
Eagland Hill Lancs . . . 202 D4
Eagle Lincs . . . 172 B5
Eagle Barnsdale Lincs . . . 172 B5
Eagle Moor Lincs . . . 172 B5
Eaglescliffe Stockton . . . 225 C8
Eaglesfield Cumb . . . 229 F7
  Dumfries . . . 238 C6
Eaglesham E Renf . . . 267 E11
Eaglethorpe Northants . . . 137 E11
Eagle Tor Derbys . . . 170 C2
Eagley Gtr Man . . . 195 E8
Eairy IoM . . . 192 E3
Eakley Lanes M Keynes . . . 120 G6
Eakring Notts . . . 171 C11
Ealand N Lincs . . . 199 E9
Ealing London . . . 67 C7
Eals Northumb . . . 240 F5
Eamont Bridge Cumb . . . 230 F6
Earby Lancs . . . 204 D3
Earcroft Blkburn . . . 195 C7
Eardington Shrops . . . 132 E4
Eardisland Hereford . . . 115 F8
Eardisley Hereford . . . 96 B6
Eardiston Shrops . . . 149 D7
  Worcs . . . 116 D4
Earith Cambs . . . 123 C7
Earl Soham Suff . . . 126 E4
Earl Sterndale Derbys . . . 169 B9
Earl Stonham Suff . . . 126 F2
Earlish Highld . . . 298 C3
Earlsdon W Mid . . . 118 B6
Earl's Down E Sus . . . 23 B10
Earlsferry Fife . . . 281 B9
Earlsfield Lincs . . . 155 B8
  London . . . 67 E9
Earlsford Aberds . . . 303 F8
Earl's Green Suff . . . 125 D10
Earl Shilton Leics . . . 135 D9
Earlsmill Moray . . . 301 D9
Earl's Common Worcs . . . 117 F9
Earl's Court London . . . 67 D9
Earl's Croome Worcs . . . 99 C7
Earlsdon...
Earlsheaton W Yorks . . . 197 C9
Earlston Borders . . . 262 B2
  E Ayrs . . . 257 C9
Earl Stonham...
Earlswood Mon . . . 79 F7
  Sur . . . 51 D9
  Warks . . . 118 C2
Earnley W Sus . . . 22 D4
Earnock S Lnrk . . . 268 E3
Earnshaw Bridge Lancs . . . 194 C4
Earsairidh W Isles . . . 297 M3
Earsdon T&W . . . 243 C8
Earsham Norf . . . 142 F6
Earsham Street Suff . . . 126 B4
Earswick York . . . 207 B8
Eartham W Sus . . . 22 B6
Earthcott Green S Glos . . . 61 B7
Easby N Yorks . . . 225 D11
  N Yorks . . . 224 D3
Easdale Argyll . . . 275 B8
Easebourne W Sus . . . 34 C5
Easenhall Warks . . . 119 B9
Eashing Sur . . . 50 E2
Easington Bucks . . . 83 C11
  Durham . . . 234 C4
  E Yorks . . . 201 C11
  Lancs . . . 203 C10
  Northumb . . . 264 C4
  Oxon . . . 83 F11
  Oxon . . . 101 C9
  Redcar . . . 226 B4
Easington Colliery
  Durham . . . 234 C4
Easington Lane T&W . . . 234 B3
Easingwold N Yorks . . . 215 F10
Easole Street Kent . . . 55 C9
Eason's Green E Sus . . . 23 B8
Eassie Angus . . . 287 C7
East Aberthaw V Glam . . . 58 F4
Eastacombe Devon . . . 25 B8
  Devon . . . 25 C10
Eastacott Devon . . . 25 C10
East Acton London . . . 67 C8
East Adderbury Oxon . . . 8 F5
East Allington Devon . . . 8 F5
East Amat Highld . . . 309 K4
East Anstey Devon . . . 26 B5
East Anton Hants . . . 47 D11
East Appleton N Yorks . . . 224 F4
East Ardsley W Yorks . . . 197 B10
East Ashling W Sus . . . 22 B4
East Aston Hants . . . 48 D3
East Auchronie Aberds . . . 293 C10
East Ayton N Yorks . . . 217 B9
East Bank Bl Gwent . . . 78 D2
East Barkwith Lincs . . . 189 E11
East Barming Kent . . . 53 C8
East Barnby N Yorks . . . 226 C6
East Barnet London . . . 86 F3
East Barns E Loth . . . 282 F4
East Barsham Norf . . . 159 C9
East Barton Suff . . . 125 D8
East Beach W Sus . . . 22 E5
East Beckham Norf . . . 177 E11
East Bedfont London . . . 66 E5
East Bergholt Suff . . . 107 D11
East Bierley W Yorks . . . 197 B7
East Bilney Norf . . . 159 F9
East Blackdene Durham . . . 232 D3
East Blatchington E Sus . . . 23 E7
East Bloxworth Dorset . . . 18 C3
East Boldon T&W . . . 243 E9
East Boldre Hants . . . 32 G5
East Bonhard Perth . . . 286 E5
Eastbourne Darl . . . 224 C6
  E Sus . . . 23 F10
East Bower Som . . . 43 F10
East Brent Som . . . 43 C10
Eastbridge Suff . . . 127 D9
East Bridgford Notts . . . 171 G11
East Briscoe Durham . . . 223 B9
Eastbrook Som . . . 28 C2
  V Glam . . . 59 F7
East Buckland Devon . . . 41 G7
East Budleigh Devon . . . 15 D7
Eastburn E Yorks . . . 208 B5
  W Yorks . . . 204 E6
East Burnham Bucks . . . 66 C3
East Burrafirth Shetland . . . 313 H5
East Burton Dorset . . . 18 D3
Eastbury Herts . . . 85 G9
  W Berks . . . 63 D11
East Butsfield Durham . . . 233 B8
East Butterwick N Lincs . . . 199 F10
Eastby N Yorks . . . 204 C6
East Cairnbeg Aberds . . . 293 F9
East Calder W Loth . . . 269 B11
East Carleton Norf . . . 142 C3
East Carlton Northants . . . 136 F6
  W Yorks . . . 205 E10
East Chaldon or Chaldon
  Herring Dorset . . . 17 E11
East Challow Oxon . . . 64 B1
East Charleton Devon . . . 8 G5
East Chelborough Dorset . . . 29 F9
East Chiltington E Sus . . . 36 D5
East Chinnock Som . . . 29 E7
East Chisenbury Wilts . . . 46 C6
Eastchurch Kent . . . 70 E3
East Clandon Sur . . . 50 C5
East Claydon Bucks . . . 102 F4
East Clevedon N Som . . . 60 E2
East Clyne Highld . . . 311 J3
East Clyth Highld . . . 310 F7
East Coker Som . . . 29 E8
East Combe Som . . . 43 G7
Eastcombe Glos . . . 80 E5
  Som . . . 43 G7
East Common N Yorks . . . 207 G8
East Compton Dorset . . . 30 D5
  Som . . . 44 E6
East Cornworthy Devon . . . 8 E6
Eastcote London . . . 66 B6
  Northants . . . 120 G2
  W Mid . . . 118 B3
Eastcote Village London . . . 66 B6
Eastcott Corn . . . 24 D3
  Wilts . . . 46 C4
East Cottingwith E Yorks . . . 207 E11
Eastcotts Beds . . . 103 B11
East Cowes IoW . . . 20 B6
East Cowick E Yorks . . . 199 C7
East Cowton N Yorks . . . 224 E6
East Cramlington
  Northumb . . . 243 B7
East Cranmore Som . . . 45 E7
East Creech Dorset . . . 18 E4
East Croachy Highld . . . 300 G6
East Croftmore Highld . . . 291 B11
East Curthwaite Cumb . . . 230 B2

East Dean E Sus . . . 23 F9
  Glos . . . 98 G3
  Hants . . . 32 B3
  W Sus . . . 34 G6
East Dene S Yorks . . . 186 C6
East Denton T&W . . . 242 D6
East Didsbury Gtr Man . . . 184 D4
Eastdon Devon . . . 14 E5
East Down Devon . . . 40 E6
Eastdown Devon . . . 8 F6
East Drayton Notts . . . 188 F3
East Dulwich London . . . 67 E10
East Dundry N Som . . . 60 F5
East Ella Hull . . . 200 B5
Eastend Essex . . . 86 C6
  Oxon . . . 100 G6
East End Beds . . . 122 F2
  Bucks . . . 84 B3
  Bucks . . . 103 G7
  E Yorks . . . 201 B9
  E Yorks . . . 209 B9
  Glos . . . 81 E11
  Hants . . . 20 B3
  Hants . . . 33 C11
  Hants . . . 64 G2
  Herts . . . 105 F9
  Kent . . . 53 E11
  Kent . . . 53 F10
  M Keynes . . . 103 C8
  N Som . . . 60 E3
  Oxon . . . 82 C5
  Oxon . . . 101 D9
  Oxon . . . 101 C9
  S Glos . . . 61 E9
  Som . . . 29 B10
  Suff . . . 108 E2
  Suff . . . 126 C2
East End Green Herts . . . 86 C3
Easter Aberchalder
  Highld . . . 291 B8
Easter Ardross Highld . . . 300 B6
Easter Balgedie Perth . . . 286 G5
Easter Balmoral Aberds . . . 292 D4
Easter Boleskine Highld . . . 300 G5
Easter Brackland Stirl . . . 285 G10
Easter Brae Highld . . . 300 C6
Easter Cardno Aberds . . . 303 C9
Easter Compton S Glos . . . 60 C5
Easter Cringate Stirl . . . 278 D4
Easter Culfosie Aberds . . . 293 C9
Easter Davoch Aberds . . . 292 C6
Easter Earshaig
  Dumfries . . . 248 C2
Easter Ellister Argyll . . . 254 B3
Easter Fearn Highld . . . 309 L6
Easter Galcantray
  Highld . . . 301 E8
Eastergate W Sus . . . 22 B6
Easter Howgate Midloth . . . 270 C4
Easter Howlaws Borders . . . 272 G4
Easter Kinkell Highld . . . 300 D5
Easter Knox Angus . . . 287 C9
Easter Langlee Borders . . . 262 B2
Easter Lednathie Angus . . . 292 G5
Easter Milton Highld . . . 301 D9
Easter Moniack Highld . . . 300 E5
Eastern Green W Mid . . . 134 G5
Easter Ord Aberdeen . . . 293 C10
Easter Quarff Shetland . . . 313 K6
Easter Rhynd Perth . . . 286 F5
Easter Row Stirl . . . 285 G11
Easter Silverford Aberds . . . 303 C7
Easter Skeld Shetland . . . 313 J5
Easter Softlaw Borders . . . 263 C7
Easterton Wilts . . . 46 C4
Easterton of Lenabo
  Aberds . . . 303 E10
Easter Tulloch Highld . . . 291 B10
Easter Whyntie Aberds . . . 302 C6
East Everleigh Wilts . . . 47 C8
East Ewell Sur . . . 67 G8
East Farleigh Kent . . . 53 C8
East Farndon Northants . . . 136 F4
East Fen Common
  Cambs . . . 124 C2
East Ferry Lincs . . . 188 B4
Eastfield Borders . . . 262 D2
  Bristol . . . 60 D5
  N Lnrk . . . 269 C7
  N Lnrk . . . 278 G4
  Northumb . . . 243 B7
  N Yorks . . . 217 C10
  Pboro . . . 138 D4
  S Yorks . . . 197 G8
Eastfield Hall Northumb . . . 252 B6
East Fields W Berks . . . 64 F4
East Finchley London . . . 67 B9
East Finglassie Fife . . . 280 B5
East Firsby Lincs . . . 189 D7
East Fleet Dorset . . . 17 E8
East Fortune E Loth . . . 281 F11
East Garforth W Yorks . . . 206 G4
East Garston W Berks . . . 63 D11
Eastgate Durham . . . 232 D5
  Norf . . . 160 D2
  Pboro . . . 138 D4
East Gateshead T&W . . . 243 E7
East Ginge Oxon . . . 64 B2
East Gores Essex . . . 107 G7
East Goscote Leics . . . 154 G2
East Grafton Wilts . . . 63 G9
East Green Moray . . . 301 C10
  Suff . . . 127 C9
  Suff . . . 124 G5
East Grimstead Wilts . . . 32 B2
East Grinstead W Sus . . . 51 F11
East Guldeford E Sus . . . 38 C6
East Haddon Northants . . . 120 D3
East Hagbourne Oxon . . . 64 B4
East Halton N Lincs . . . 200 D6
Eastham Mers . . . 182 E5
  Worcs . . . 116 E3
East Ham London . . . 68 C2
Easthampstead Brack . . . 65 F11
Easthampton Hereford . . . 115 E8
East Hanney Oxon . . . 82 G6
East Hanningfield Essex . . . 88 E2
East Hardwick W Yorks . . . 198 D3
East Harling Norf . . . 141 F9
East Harlsey N Yorks . . . 225 F8
East Harnham Wilts . . . 31 B10
East Harptree Bath . . . 44 B5

East Hartford Northumb . . 243 B7
East Harting W Sus 34 D3
East Hatch Wilts 30 B6
East Hatley Cambs 122 G5
Easthaugh Norf 159 F11
East Hauxwell N Yorks . . 224 G3
Eastheath Wokingham . . . 65 F10
East Heckington Lincs . . 173 G11
East Hedleyhope
 Durham 233 C9
East Helmsdale Highld . . 311 H4
East Hendred Oxon 64 B3
East Herringthorpe
 S Yorks 187 C7
East Herrington T&W . . . 243 G9
East Heslerton N Yorks . . 217 D8
East Hewish N Som 59 G11
East Hill Kent 68 G5
East Hoathly E Sus 23 B8
East Hogaland Shetland . . 313 K5
East Holme Dorset 18 D3
East Holton Dorset 18 C5
Easthope Shrops 131 D11
Easthopewood Shrops . . 131 D11
East Horndon Essex 68 B6
Easthorpe Essex 107 G8
 Leics 154 B6
 Notts 172 E2
East Horrington Som 44 D5
East Horsley Sur 50 C5
East Horton Northumb . . . 264 C2
Easthouse Shetland 313 J6
Easthouses Midloth 270 B6
East Howdon T&W 243 D8
East Howe Bmouth 19 B7
East Huntspill Som 43 E10
East Hyde C Beds 85 B10
East Ilkerton Devon 41 D8
East Ilsley W Berks 64 C3
Easting Orkney 314 A4
Eastington Devon 26 F2
 Glos 80 D3
 Glos 81 C10
East Keal Lincs 174 C5
East Kennett Wilts 62 F6
East Keswick W Yorks . . . 206 E3
East Kilbride S Lnrk 268 E2
East Kimber Devon 12 B5
East Kingston W Sus 35 G9
East Kirkby Lincs 174 C4
East Knapton N Yorks . . . 217 D7
East Knighton Dorset 18 D2
East Knowstone Devon . . . 26 C4
East Knoyle Wilts 45 G11
East Kyloe Northumb 264 B3
East Kyo Durham 242 G5
East Lambrook Som 28 D6
East Lamington Highld . . 301 B7
East Langdon Kent 55 D10
East Langton Leics 136 E4
East Langwell Highld . . . 309 J7
East Lavant W Sus 22 B5
East Lavington W Sus . . . 34 D6
East Layton N Yorks 224 D3
Eastleach Martin Glos . . . 82 D2
Eastleach Turville Glos . . 81 D11
East Leake Notts 153 D11
East Learmouth
 Northumb 263 B9
Eastleigh Devon 25 B7
 Hants 32 D6
East Leigh Devon 8 E3
 Devon 25 C11
 Devon 26 F4
East Lexham Norf 159 F7
East Lilburn Northumb . . 264 E2
Eastling Kent 54 B3
East Linton E Loth 281 F11
East Liss Hants 34 B3
East Lockinge Oxon 64 B2
East Looe Corn 6 E5
East Lound N Lincs 188 B3
East Lulworth Dorset 18 E3
East Lutton N Yorks 217 F8
East Lydeard Som 27 B11
East Lydford Som 44 G5
East Lyng Som 28 B4
East Mains Aberds 293 D8
 Borders 271 F11
 S Lnrk 268 E2
East Malling Kent 53 B8
East Malling Heath Kent . . 53 B8
East March Angus 287 D8
East Marden W Sus 34 E4
East Markham Notts 188 G2
East Marsh NE Lincs 201 E9
East Martin Hants 31 D9
East Marton N Yorks 204 C4
East Meon Hants 33 C11
East Mere Devon 27 D7
East Mersea Essex 89 C9
East Mey Highld 310 B7
East Molesey Sur 67 F7
Eastmoor Derbys 186 G4
 Norf 140 C4
East Moors Cardiff 59 D7
East Morden Dorset 18 B4
East Morton W Yorks 205 E7
East Moulsecoomb
 Brighton 36 F4
East Ness N Yorks 216 D3
East Newton E Yorks 209 F11
 N Yorks 216 D2
Eastney Ptsmth 21 B9
Eastnor Hereford 98 D4
East Norton Leics 136 C5
East Oakley Hants 48 C5
East Ogwell Devon 14 G2
Eastoke Hants 21 B10
Easton Bristol 60 E6
 Cambs 122 C2
 Cumb 239 C10
 Cumb 239 F7
 Devon 8 F3
 Devon 13 D10
 Dorset 17 G9
 Hants 48 G4
 IoW 20 D2
 Lincs 155 D8
 Norf 160 G2
 Som 44 D5
 W Berks 64 E2
Easton Grey Wilts 61 B11
Easton in Gordano
 N Som 60 D4
Easton Maudit Northants . 121 F7
Easton on the Hill
 Northants 137 C10
Easton Royal Wilts 63 G8
Easton Town Som 44 G5
 Wilts 61 B11

East Orchard Dorset 30 D4
East Ord Northumb 273 E9
Eastover Som 43 F10
East Panson Devon 12 C3
Eastpark Dumfries 238 D2
East Parley Dorset 19 B8
East Peckham Kent 53 D7
East Pennard Som 44 F5
East Perry Cambs 122 D3
East Portholland Corn 5 G9
East Portlemouth Devon . . 9 G6
East Prawle Devon 9 G6
East Preston W Sus 35 G9
East Pulham Dorset 30 F3
East Putford Devon 24 D5
East Quantoxhead Som . . . 42 E6
East Rainton T&W 234 B2
East Ravendale NE Lincs . 201 F9
East Raynham Norf 159 D7
Eastrea Cambs 138 D5
East Rhidorroch Lodge
 Highld 307 K7
Eastriggs Dumfries 238 D6
East Rigton W Yorks 206 E3
Eastrington E Yorks 199 B9
Eastrip Wilts 61 E10
East Rolstone N Som 59 G11
Eastrop Hants 48 C6
East Rounton N Yorks . . . 225 E8
East Row N Yorks 227 C7
East Rudham Norf 158 D6
East Runton Norf 177 E11
East Ruston Norf 160 D6
Eastry Kent 55 C10
East Saltoun E Loth 271 B9
East Sheen London 67 D8
East Skelston Dumfries . . 247 F8
East Sleekburn
 Northumb 253 G7
East Somerton Norf 161 F9
East Stanley Durham 242 G6
East Stockwith Lincs . . . 188 C3
East Stoke Dorset 18 D3
 Notts 172 F3
 Som 29 D7
East Stour Dorset 30 C4
East Stour Common
 Dorset 30 C4
East Stourmouth Kent . . . 71 G9
East Stowford Devon 25 B10
East Stratton Hants 48 F4
East Street Kent 55 B10
 Som 44 F4
East Studdal Kent 55 D10
East Suisnish Highld . . . 295 B7
East Taphouse Corn 6 C3
East-the-Water Devon . . . 25 B7
East Third Borders 262 B4
East Thirston Northumb . . 252 D5
East Tilbury Thurrock 69 D7
East Tisted Hants 49 G8
East Torrington Lincs . . . 189 E10
East Town Som 42 G6
 Som 44 E6
 Wilts 45 B11
East Trewent Pembs 73 F8
East Tuddenham Norf . . 159 G11
East Tuelmenna Corn 6 B2
East Tytherley Hants 32 B3
East Tytherton Wilts 62 E3
East Village Devon 26 F4
 V Glam 58 E3
Eastville Bristol 60 E6
 Lincs 174 D6
East Wall Shrops 131 E10
East Walton Norf 158 F4
East Water Som 44 C4
East Week Devon 13 C9
Eastwell Leics 154 D5
East Wellow Hants 32 C4
Eastwell Park Kent 54 D4
East Wemyss Fife 280 B6
East Whitburn W Loth . . . 269 B9
Eastwick Herts 86 C6
 Shetland 312 F5
East Wickham London . . . 68 D3
East Williamston Pembs . . 73 E9
East Winch Norf 158 F3
East Winterslow Wilts . . . 47 G8
East Wittering W Sus 21 B11
East Witton N Yorks 214 B2
Eastwood Notts 171 F7
 S Yorks 186 C6
 Sthend 69 B10
 W Yorks 196 C4
Eastwood End Cambs . . . 139 E8
Eastwood Hall Notts 171 F7
East Woodburn
 Northumb 251 F10
East Woodhay Hants 64 G2
East Woodlands Som 45 E9
East Worldham Hants 49 F8
East Worlington Devon . . . 26 E2
East Worthing W Sus 35 G11
East Wretham Norf 141 E8
East Youlstone Devon 24 D2
Eathorpe Warks 119 D7
Eaton Ches E 168 B5
 Ches W 167 C9
 Hereford 115 C10
 Leics 154 D5
 Norf 142 B4
 Norf 188 F2
 Oxon 82 E6
 Shrops 131 C11
 Shrops 131 F10
Eaton Bishop Hereford . . . 97 D8
Eaton Bray C Beds 103 G9
Eaton Constantine
 Shrops 131 B11
Eaton Ford Cambs 122 E3
Eaton Green C Beds 103 G9
Eaton Hastings Oxon 82 F3
Eaton Mascott Shrops . . 131 B10
Eaton on Tern Shrops . . . 150 E3
Eaton Socon Cambs 122 F3
Eaton upon Tern Shrops . 150 E3
Eau Brink Norf 157 F11
Eau Withington
 Hereford 97 C10
Eaves Green W Mid 134 G5
Eavestone N Yorks 214 F4
Ebberly Hill Devon 25 D9
Ebberston N Yorks 217 C7
Ebbesbourne Wake Wilts . 31 C7
Ebblake Hants 31 F10
Ebbw Vale BI Gwent 77 D11
Ebchester Durham 242 F4
Ebdon N Som 59 G11
Ebernoe W Sus 35 B7
Ebford Devon 14 D5
Ebley Glos 80 D4
Ebnal Ches W 167 F7
 Hereford 98 D3
Ebnall Hereford 115 E9
Ebreywood Shrops 149 F10
Ebrington Glos 100 C3
Ecchinswell Hants 48 A4
Ecclaw Borders 272 B5
Ecclefechan Dumfries . . . 238 C5
Eccle Riggs Cumb 210 B4

Eccles Borders 272 G5
 Gtr Man 184 B3
 Kent 69 G8
Ecclesall S Yorks 186 E4
Ecclesfield S Yorks 186 C5
Eccles Green Hereford . . . 97 B8
Eccleshall Staffs 150 D6
Eccleshill W Yorks 205 F9
Ecclesmachan W Loth . . . 279 G11
Eccles on Sea Norf 161 D8
Eccles Road Norf 141 G10
Eccleston Ches W 166 C6
 Lancs 194 D4
 Mers 183 B7
Eccleston Park Mers 183 C7
Eccup W Yorks 205 E11
Echt Aberds 293 C9
Eckford Borders 262 D6
Eckfordmoss Borders . . . 262 D6
Eckington Derbys 186 F6
 Worcs 99 C8
Eckington Corner E Sus . . 23 D8
Ecklands S Yorks 197 G8
Eckworthy Devon 24 D6
Ecton Northants 120 E6
 Staffs 169 D9
Ecton Brook Northants . . 120 E6
Edale Derbys 185 D10
Edale End Derbys 185 D11
Edbrook Som 43 E8
Edburton W Sus 36 E3
Edderside Cumb 229 B7
Edderton Highld 309 L7
Eddington Kent 71 F7
 W Berks 63 F10
Eddistone Devon 24 C3
Eddleston Borders 270 F4
Eddlewood S Lnrk 268 E4
Edenbridge Kent 52 D2
Edenfield Lancs 195 D9
Edenhall Cumb 231 E7
Edenham Lincs 155 E11
Eden Mount Cumb 211 C7
Eden Park London 67 F11
Edensor Derbys 170 C2
Edentaggart Argyll 276 C6
Edenthorpe S Yorks 198 F6
Edentown Cumb 239 F9
Eden Vale Durham 234 D4
Ederline Argyll 275 C9
Edern Gwyn 144 B5
Edford Som 45 D7
Edgarley Som 44 F4
Edgbaston W Mid 133 G11
Edgcote Northants 101 B10
Edgcott Bucks 102 G3
 Som 41 F11
Edgcumbe Corn 2 C6
Edge Glos 80 D4
 Shrops 131 B8
Edgebolton Shrops 149 E11
Edge End Glos 79 C9
 Lancs 203 G10
Edgefield Norf 159 C11
Edgefield Street Norf . . . 159 C11
Edge Fold Blkburn 195 D8
Edge Green Ches W 167 E7
 Gtr Man 183 B9
 Norf 141 F10
Edgehill Warks 101 B7
Edge Hill Mers 182 C5
 Warks 134 D4
Edgeley Gtr Man 184 D5
Edge Mount S Yorks 186 C3
Edgeley Shrops 148 F6
Edgerton W Yorks 196 D6
Edgeside Lancs 195 C10
Edgeworth Glos 80 D6
Edginswell Devon 9 B7
Edgiock Worcs 117 E10
Edgmond Telford 150 F4
Edgmond Marsh Telford . 150 E4
Edgton Shrops 131 F7
Edgware London 85 G11
Edgwick W Mid 134 G6
Edgworth Blkburn 195 D8
Edham Borders 262 B6
Edial Staffs 133 B11
Edinample Stirl 285 E9
Edinbane Highld 298 D3
Edinburgh Edin 280 G5
Edinchip Stirl 285 E9
Edingale Staffs 152 G4
Edingight Ho Moray 302 D5
Edinglassie Ho Aberds . . 292 B5
Edingley Notts 171 D11
Edingthorpe Norf 160 C6
Edingthorpe Green Norf . 160 C6
Edington Som 43 F10
 Wilts 46 C2
Edingworth Som 43 C11
Edintore Moray 302 E4
Edistone Devon 24 C2
Edithmead Som 43 D10
Edith Weston Rutland . . . 137 B8
Edlaston Derbys 169 G11
Edlesborough Bucks 85 B7
Edlingham Northumb . . . 252 B5
Edlington Lincs 190 G2
 S Yorks 187 B9
Edmondbyers Durham . . . 242 G2
Edmondsham Dorset 31 E9
Edmondsley Durham . . . 233 B10
Edmondstone Orkney . . . 314 D5
Edmondthorpe Leics . . . 155 F7
Edmonston S Lnrk 269 G11
Edmonstone Orkney 314 D5
Edmonton Corn 10 G5
 London 86 G4
Edmundbyers Durham . . 242 G2
Ednam Borders 262 B6
Ednaston Derbys 170 G2
Edney Common Essex . . . 87 E11
Edradynate Perth 286 B2
Edrom Borders 272 D6
Edstaston Shrops 149 C10
Edstone Warks 118 E3
Edvin Loach Hereford . . . 116 F3
Edwalton Notts 153 B11
Edwardstone Suff 107 C8
Edwardsville M Tydf 77 F9
Edwinsford Carms 94 E2
Edwinstowe Notts 171 B10
Edworth C Beds 104 C4
Edwyn Ralph Hereford . . 116 F2
Edzell Angus 293 G7
Efail-fach Neath 57 B9
Efail Isaf Rhondda 58 C5
Efailnewydd Gwyn 145 B7
Efailwen Carms 92 F2
Efenechtyd Denb 165 D10
Effingham Sur 50 C6
Effirth Shetland 313 H5
Effledge Borders 262 F3
Efflinch Staffs 152 F3
Efford Devon 26 G5
Egbury Hants 48 C2
Egdon Worcs 117 G8

Egerton Gtr Man 195 E8
 Kent 54 D2
Egerton Forstal Kent 53 D11
Egerton Green Kent 167 E8
Egford Som 45 D9
Eggbeare Corn 12 D2
Eggborough N Yorks 198 C5
Eggbuckland Plym 7 D10
Eggesford Station
 Devon 25 E11
Eggington C Beds 103 F9
Egginton Derbys 152 D5
Egginton Common
 Derbys 152 D5
Egglesburn Durham 232 G5
Egglescliffe Stockton . . . 225 C8
Eggleston Durham 232 G5
Egham Sur 66 E4
Egham Hythe Sur 66 E4
Egham Wick Sur 66 E3
Egleton Rutland 137 B7
Eglingham Northumb . . . 264 F4
Egloshayle Corn 10 G5
Egloskerry Corn 11 D11
Eglwys-Brewis V Glam . . 58 F4
Eglwys Cross Wrex 167 G7
Eglwys Fach Ceredig . . . 128 D3
Eglwyswen Pembs 92 D3
Eglwyswrw Pembs 92 D2
Egmanton Notts 172 B2
Egmere Norf 159 B8
Egremont Cumb 219 C10
 Mers 182 C4
Egton N Yorks 226 D6
Egton Bridge N Yorks . . . 226 D6
Egypt Bucks 66 B3
 Hants 48 E3
 W Berks 64 D2
Eiden Highld 309 J7
Eight Ash Green Essex . . 107 F8
Eighton Banks T&W 243 F7
Eignaig Highld 289 E9
Eign Hill Hereford 97 D10
Eilanreach Highld 295 D10
Eilean Anabaich
 W Isles 305 H4
Eilean Darach Highld . . . 307 L6
Eilean Shona Ho Highld . 289 B8
Einacleit W Isles 304 F3
Einsiob / Evenjobb
 Powys 114 E5
Eisgean W Isles 305 G5
Eisingrug Gwyn 146 C2
Eland Green Northumb . . 242 C5
Elan Village Powys 113 D8
Elberton S Glos 60 B6
Elborough N Som 43 B11
Elbridge Shrops 149 E7
 W Sus 22 C6
Elburton Plym 7 E10
Elcho Perth 286 E5
Elcock's Brook Worcs . . . 117 E10
Elcombe Glos 80 F3
 Swindon 62 C6
Elcot W Berks 63 F11
Eldene Swindon 63 C7
Eldernell Cambs 138 D6
Eldersfield Worcs 98 E6
Elderslie Renfs 267 C8
Elder Street Essex 105 E11
Eldmire N Yorks 215 D9
Eldon Durham 233 F10
Eldon Lane Durham 233 F10
Eldrick S Ayrs 245 G7
Eldroth N Yorks 212 F5
Eldwick W Yorks 205 E8
Elemore Vale T&W 234 B3
Elerch / Bont-goch
 Ceredig 128 F3
Elfhowe Cumb 221 F9
Elford Northumb 264 C5
 Staffs 152 G3
Elford Closes Cambs . . . 123 C10
Elgin Moray 302 C2
Elgol Highld 295 D7
Elham Kent 55 E7
Elie Fife 287 G8
Elim Anglesey 178 D5
Eling Hants 32 E5
 W Berks 64 D4
Elishader Highld 298 C5
Elishaw Northumb 251 D10
Elizafield Dumfries 238 C2
Elkesley Notts 187 F11
Elkington Northants 120 B2
Elkins Green Essex 87 E10
Elkstone Glos 81 C7
Ellacombe Torbay 9 C8
Elland W Yorks 196 C6
Elland Lower Edge
 W Yorks 196 C6
Elland Upper Edge
 W Yorks 196 C6
Ellary Argyll 275 F8
Ellastone Staffs 169 G10
Ellel Lancs 202 B5
Ellenbrook Herts 86 D2
Ellenborough Cumb 228 D6
Ellenglaze Corn 4 D5
Ellenhall Staffs 150 D6
Ellen's Green Sur 50 F5
Ellerbeck N Yorks 225 F8
Ellerburn N Yorks 216 C6
Ellerby N Yorks 226 C5
Ellerdine Telford 150 E2
Ellerdine Heath Telford . . 150 E2
Ellerhayes Devon 27 G7
Elleric Argyll 284 C4
Ellerker E Yorks 200 B2
Ellerton E Yorks 207 F10
 N Yorks 224 F3
 Shrops 150 D4
Ellesborough Bucks 84 D4
Ellesmere Shrops 149 C8
Ellesmere Park Gtr Man . 184 B3
Ellesmere Port Ches W . . 182 F6
Ellicombe Som 42 E4
Ellingham Hants 31 F11
 Norf 143 E7
 Northumb 264 D5
Ellingstring N Yorks 214 C3
Ellington Cambs 122 C3
 Northumb 252 E6
Ellington Thorpe Cambs . 122 C3
Elliot Angus 287 D10
Elliots Green Som 45 D9
Elliot's Town Caerph 77 E10
Ellisfield Hants 48 D6
Elliston Borders 262 D2
Ellistown Leics 153 G8
Ellon Aberds 303 F9
Ellonby Cumb 230 D4
Ellough Suff 143 F7

Elloughton E Yorks 200 B2
Ellwood Glos 79 D9
Elm Cambs 139 B9
Elmbridge Glos 80 C5
 Worcs 117 D8
Elm Corner Sur 50 B5
Elm Cross Wilts 62 D6
Elmdon Essex 105 D9
 W Mid 134 G3
Elmdon Heath W Mid . . . 134 G3
Elmer W Sus 35 G7
Elmers End London 67 F11
Elmers Green Lancs 194 F3
Elmer's Marsh W Sus . . . 34 B5
Elmesthorpe Leics 135 E9
Elmfield IoW 21 C8
Elm Hill Dorset 30 B4
Elmhurst Staffs 152 G2
Elmley Castle Worcs 99 C9
Elmley Lovett Worcs 117 D7
Elmore Glos 80 B3
Elmore Back Glos 80 B3
Elm Park London 68 B4
Elmscott Devon 24 C2
Elmsett Suff 107 B11
Elms Green Hereford . . . 116 D4
Elmslack Lancs 211 D9
Elmstead Essex 107 F11
Elmstead Heath Essex . . 107 G11
Elmstead Market
 Essex 107 G11
Elmsted Kent 54 E6
Elmsthorpe Leics 135 D9
Elmstone Kent 71 G9
Elmstone Hardwicke
 Glos 99 F8
Elmswell E Yorks 208 B5
 Suff 125 E9
Elmton Derbys 187 G8
Elness Orkney 314 C6
Elphin Highld 307 H7
Elphinstone E Loth 281 G7
Elrick Aberds 293 C10
 Aberds 302 G5
Elrig Dumfries 236 E5
Elrington Northumb 241 E9
Elscar S Yorks 197 G11
Elsdon Hereford 114 G6
 Northumb 251 E10
Elsecar S Yorks 186 B5
 S Yorks 197 G11
Elsenham Essex 105 F10
Elsenham Sta Essex 105 F10
Elsfield Oxon 83 C8
Elsham N Lincs 200 E4
Elsing Norf 159 F11
Elslack N Yorks 204 D4
Elson Hants 33 G10
 Shrops 149 B7
Elsrickle S Lnrk 269 G11
Elstead Sur 50 E2
Elsted W Sus 34 D4
Elsthorpe Lincs 155 E11
Elstob Durham 234 G2
Elston Devon 26 G3
 Notts 172 F3
 Wilts 46 E5
Elstone Devon 25 D11
Elstow Beds 103 B11
Elstree Herts 85 F11
Elstronwick E Yorks 209 G10
Elswick Lancs 202 F4
 T&W 242 E6
Elswick Leys Lancs 202 F4
Elsworth Cambs 122 E6
Elterwater Cumb 220 E6
Eltham London 68 E2
Eltisley Cambs 122 F5
Elton Cambs 137 E11
 Ches W 183 F7
 Derbys 170 C2
 Glos 80 C2
 Gtr Man 195 E9
 Hereford 115 C9
 Notts 154 B3
 Stockton 225 B8
Elton Green Ches W 183 G7
Elton's Marsh Hereford . . 97 C9
Eltringham Northumb . . . 242 E3
Elvanfoot S Lnrk 259 G11
Elvaston Derbys 153 C8
Elveden Suff 124 B6
Elvet Hill Durham 233 C11
Elvingston E Loth 281 F9
Elvington Kent 55 C9
 York 207 D9
Elwell Devon 41 G7
 Dorset 17 E9
Elworth Ches E 168 C2
Elworthy Som 42 G5
Ely Cambs 139 G10
 Cardiff 58 D6
Emberton M Keynes 103 B7
Embleton Cumb 229 E9
 Durham 234 F4
 Northumb 264 E6
Embo Highld 311 K2
Emborough Som 44 C6
Embo Street Highld 311 K2
Embsay N Yorks 204 C6
Emersons Green S Glos . . 61 D7
Emerson Park London . . . 68 B4
Emerson Valley
 M Keynes 102 E6
Emery Down Hants 32 F3
Emley W Yorks 197 E8
Emmbrook Wokingham . . 65 F9
Emmer Green Reading . . . 65 D8
Emmett Carr Derbys 187 F7
Emmington Oxon 84 E2
Emneth Norf 139 B9
Emneth Hungate Norf . . . 139 B10
Emorsgate Norf 157 E10
Empingham Rutland 137 B8
Empshott Hants 49 F8
Empshott Green Hants . . . 49 G8
Emscote Warks 118 D6
Emsworth Hants 22 B2
Enborne W Berks 64 F2
Enborne Row W Berks . . . 64 G2
Enchmarsh Shrops 131 D10
Enderby Leics 135 D10
Endmoor Cumb 211 C10
Endon Staffs 168 E6
Endon Bank Staffs 168 E6
Energlyn Caerph 58 B6
Enfield London 86 F4
 Worcs 117 D10
Enfield Highway London . . 86 F5
Enfield Lock London 86 F5
Enfield Town London 86 F4
Enfield Wash London 86 F5
Enford Wilts 46 C6
Engamoor Shetland 313 H4
Engedi Anglesey 178 G5

Engine Common S Glos . . 61 C7
Englefield W Berks 64 E6
Englefield Green Sur 66 E3
Englesea-brook Ches E . . 168 E3
English Bicknor Glos 79 B9
Englishcombe Bath 61 G8
English Frankton
 Shrops 149 D9
Engollan Corn 10 G3
Enham Alamein Hants . . . 47 D11
Enis Devon 25 B9
Enmore Som 43 G8
Enmore Field Hereford . . 115 E9
Enmore Green Dorset . . . 30 C5
Ennerdale Bridge
 Cumb 219 B11
Enniscaven Corn 5 D9
Enoch Dumfries 247 C9
Enochdhu Perth 292 G2
Ensay Argyll 288 E5
Ensbury Bmouth 19 B7
Ensbury Park Bmouth . . . 19 C7
Ensdon Shrops 149 F8
Ensis Devon 25 B9
Enslow Oxon 83 B7
Enstone Oxon 101 G7
Enterkinfoot Dumfries . . 247 C9
Enterpen N Yorks 225 D9
Enton Green Sur 50 E3
Enville Staffs 132 F6
Eolaigearraidh W Isles . . 297 L3
Eorabus Argyll 288 G5
Eòropaidh W Isles 304 B7
Epney Glos 80 C3
Epperstone Notts 171 F11
Epping Essex 87 E7
Epping Green Essex 86 D5
 Herts 86 D3
Epping Upland Essex 86 E6
Eppleby N Yorks 224 C3
Eppleworth E Yorks 208 G6
Epsom Sur 67 G8
Epwell Oxon 101 C7
Epworth N Lincs 199 G9
Epworth Turbary
 N Lincs 199 G9
Erbistock Wrex 166 G5
Erbusaig Highld 295 C9
Erchless Castle Highld . . 300 E4
Erddig Wrex 166 E4
Erdington W Mid 134 E2
Eredine Argyll 275 C10
Eriboll Highld 308 D4
Ericstane Dumfries 260 D3
Eridge Green E Sus 52 F4
Erines Argyll 275 F9
Eriswell Suff 124 B4
Erith London 68 D4
Erlestoke Wilts 46 C3
Ermine Lincs 189 G7
Ermington Devon 8 E2
Ernesettle Plym 7 D8
Erpingham Norf 160 C3
Erriottwood Kent 54 B2
Errogie Highld 300 G5
Errol Perth 286 E6
Errol Station Perth 286 E6
Erskine Renfs 277 G9
Erskine Bridge Renfs . . . 277 G9
Ervie Dumfries 236 C2
Erwarton Suff 108 E4
Erwood Powys 95 C11
Eryholme N Yorks 224 D6
Eryrys Denb 166 D2
Escomb Durham 233 E9
Escott Som 42 F5
Escrick N Yorks 207 E8
Esgairdawe Carms 94 C2
Esgairgeiliog Powys 128 B5
Esgyryn Conwy 180 F4
Esh Durham 233 C9
Esher Sur 66 G6
Eshiels Borders 261 B7
Esholt W Yorks 205 E9
Eshott Northumb 252 D6
Eshton N Yorks 204 B4
Esh Winning Durham . . . 233 C9
Eskadale Highld 300 F4
Eskbank Midloth 270 B6
Eskdale Green Cumb 220 E3
Eskdalemuir Dumfries . . 249 E7
Eskham Lincs 190 B5
Esknish Argyll 274 G4
Esk Valley N Yorks 226 D6
Eslington Park
 Northumb 264 G2
Esperley Lane Ends
 Durham 233 G8
Esprick Lancs 202 F4
Essendine Rutland 155 G10
Essendon Herts 86 D3
Essich Highld 300 F6
Essington Staffs 133 B9
Esslemont Aberds 303 G9
Eston Redcar 225 B11
Estover Plym 7 D10
Eswick Shetland 313 H6
Etal Northumb 263 B10
Etchilhampton Wilts 62 G4
Etchingham E Sus 38 B2
Etchinghill Kent 55 F7
 Staffs 151 F10
Etchingwood E Sus 37 C8
Etherley Dene Durham . . 233 F9
Ethie Castle Angus 287 C10
Ethie Mains Angus 287 C10
Etling Green Norf 159 G10
Etloe Glos 79 D11
Eton Windsor 66 D3
Eton Wick Windsor 66 D3
Etruria Stoke 168 F5
Etsell Shrops 131 C7
Etterby Cumb 239 F9
Etteridge Highld 291 D8
Ettersgill Durham 232 F3
Ettingshall W Mid 133 D8
Ettingshall Park W Mid . . 133 E8
Ettington Warks 100 B5
Etton E Yorks 208 D5
 Pboro 138 B2
Ettrick Borders 261 F7
Ettrickbridge Borders . . . 261 E9
Ettrickdale Argyll 275 G11
Ettrickhill Borders 261 F7
Etwall Derbys 152 C5
Etwall Common Derbys . . 152 C5
Eudon Burnell Shrops . . . 132 F3
Eudon George Shrops . . . 132 F3
Euston Suff 125 B7
Euximoor Drove
 Cambs 139 D9
Euxton Lancs 194 D5
Evanstown Bridgend 58 B3
Evanton Highld 300 C6
Evedon Lincs 173 F9
Eve Hill W Mid 133 E8
Evelix Highld 309 K7
Evendine Hereford 98 C5

Evenley Northants 101 E11
Evenlode Glos 100 F4
Even Pits Hereford 97 D11
Even Swindon Swindon . . 62 B6
Evenwood Durham 233 G8
Evenwood Gate Durham . 233 G8
Everbay Orkney 314 D6
Evercreech Som 44 F6
Everdon Northants 119 F11
Everingham E Yorks 208 E2
Everland Shetland 312 D8
Everleigh Wilts 47 C8
Everley N Yorks 217 B9
Eversholt C Beds 103 E9
Evershot Dorset 29 G9
Eversley Hants 65 G9
Eversley Centre Hants . . . 65 G9
Eversley Cross Hants 65 G9
Everthorpe E Yorks 208 G4
Everton C Beds 122 G4
 Hants 19 C11
 Mers 182 C5
 Notts 187 C11
Evertown Dumfries 239 B9
Evesbatch Hereford 98 B3
Evesham Worcs 99 C10
Evington Leicester 136 C2
Ewanrigg Cumb 228 D6
Ewden Village S Yorks . . 186 B3
Ewell Sur 67 G8
Ewell Minnis Kent 55 E9
Ewelme Oxon 83 G10
Ewen Glos 81 F8
Ewenny V Glam 58 D2
Ewerby Lincs 173 F10
Ewerby Thorpe Lincs . . . 173 F10
Ewes Dumfries 249 E10
Ewesley Northumb 252 E3
Ewhurst Sur 50 E5
Ewhurst Green E Sus 38 C3
 Sur 50 F5
Ewloe Flint 166 B4
Ewloe Green Flint 166 B3
Ewood Blkburn 195 B8
Ewood Bridge Lancs 195 C9
Eworthy Devon 12 C5
Ewshot Hants 49 D10
Ewyas Harold Hereford . . 97 F7
Exbourne Devon 25 G10
Exbury Hants 20 B4
Exceat E Sus 23 F8
Exebridge Devon 26 C6
Exelby N Yorks 214 B5
Exeter Devon 14 C4
Exford Som 41 F11
Exfords Green Shrops . . . 131 B9
Exhall Warks 118 F2
 Warks 135 F7
Exlade Street Oxon 65 C7
Exley W Yorks 196 C5
Exley Head W Yorks 204 F6
Exminster Devon 14 D4
Exmouth Devon 14 E6
Exning Suff 124 D2
Exted Kent 55 E7
Exton Devon 14 D5
 Hants 33 C10
 Rutland 155 G8
 Som 42 G2
Exwick Devon 14 C4
Eyam Derbys 186 F2
Eydon Northants 119 G10
Eye Hereford 115 E9
 Pboro 138 C4
 Suff 126 C2
Eye Green Pboro 138 C4
Eyemouth Borders 273 C8
Eyeworth C Beds 104 B4
Eyhorne Street Kent 53 C10
Eyke Suff 126 G6
Eynesbury Cambs 122 F3
Eynort Highld 294 C5
Eynsford Kent 68 F4
Eynsham Oxon 82 D6
Eype Dorset 16 C5
Eyre Highld 298 D4
Eyres Monsell
 Leicester 135 D11
Eythorne Kent 55 D9
Eyton Hereford 115 E9
 Shrops 131 F7
 Shrops 149 B7
 Wrex 166 F5
Eyton on Severn
 Shrops 131 B11
Eyton upon the Weald
 Moors Telford 150 G3

F

Faberstown Wilts 47 C9
Faccombe Hants 47 B11
Faceby N Yorks 225 E9
Fachell Gwyn 163 B8
Fachwen Gwyn 163 C9
Facit Lancs 195 D11
Fackley Notts 171 C7
Faddiley Ches E 167 E9
Faddonch Highld 295 C11
Fadmoor N Yorks 216 B3
Faerdre Swansea 75 E11
Fagley W Yorks 205 F9
Fagwyr Swansea 75 E11
Faichem Highld 290 C4
Faifley W Dunb 277 G10
Failand N Som 60 E4
Failford S Ayrs 257 D11
Failsworth Gtr Man 195 G11
Fain Highld 299 D11
Faindouran Lodge
 Moray 292 C2
Fairbourne Gwyn 146 G2
Fairbourne Heath Kent . . 53 C11
Fairburn N Yorks 198 B3
Fairburn House Highld . . 300 D4
Fair Cross London 68 B3
Fairfield Clack 279 C7
 Derbys 185 G9
 Gtr Man 184 B6
 Kent 39 B7
 Mers 182 C5
 Stockton 225 B9
 Worcs 117 B8
Fairfield Park Bath 61 F9
Fairfields Glos 98 A4
Fairford Glos 81 E11
Fair Green Norf 158 F2
Fairhaven Lancs 193 B10
 N Ayrs 255 C10
Fair Hill Cumb 230 E7
Fairhill S Lnrk 268 E4
Fairlands Sur 50 C3

Fairlie IoW 20 C5
Fairlie N Ayrs 266 D4
Fairlight E Sus 38 E5
Fairlight Cove E Sus 38 E5
Fairlop London 87 G7
Fairmile Devon 15 B7
 Dorset 19 C9
 Sur 66 G6
Fairmilehead Edin 270 B4
Fair Moor Northumb 252 F5
Fairoak Caerph 77 F11
 Staffs 150 C5
Fair Oak Hants 33 D7
 Hants 64 G5
 Lancs 203 D8
Fair Oak Green Hants . . . 65 G7
Fairseat Kent 68 G6
Fairstead Essex 88 B3
 Norf 158 F2
Fairview Glos 99 G9
Fairwarp E Sus 37 B7
Fairwater Cardiff 58 D6
 Torf 78 G3
Fairwood Wilts 45 C10
Fairy Cottage IoM 192 D5
Fairy Cross Devon 24 C6
Fakenham Norf 159 D7
Fakenham Magna Suff . . 125 B8
Fala Midloth 271 C8
Fala Dam Midloth 271 C8
Falahill Borders 271 D7
Falcon Hereford 98 E2
Falcon Lodge W Mid 134 E2
Falconwood London 68 D3
Falcutt Northants 101 C11
Faldingworth Lincs 189 E9
Faldonside Borders 262 C2
Falfield Fife 287 G8
 S Glos 79 G11
Falkenham Suff 108 D5
Falkenham Sink Suff . . . 108 D5
Falkirk Falk 279 F7
Falkland Fife 286 G6
Falla Borders 262 G6
Fallgate Derbys 170 C5
Fallin Stirl 278 C6
Fallinge Derbys 170 C3
Fallings Heath W Mid . . . 133 D9
Fallowfield Gtr Man 184 C5
Fallside N Lnrk 268 C4
Falmer E Sus 36 F5
Falmouth Corn 3 C8
Falnash Borders 249 B9
Falsgrave N Yorks 217 B10
Falside W Loth 269 B9
Falsidehill Borders 272 G3
Falstone Northumb 250 F6
Fanagmore Highld 306 E6
Fancott C Beds 103 F10
Fangdale Beck
 N Yorks 225 G11
Fangfoss E Yorks 207 C11
Fanich Highld 311 J2
Fankerton Falk 278 E5
Fanmore Argyll 288 E6
Fanner's Green Essex . . . 87 C11
Fannich Lodge Highld . . 300 C2
Fans Borders 272 G2
Fanshowe Ches E 184 G5
Fant Kent 53 B8
Faoilean Highld 295 C7
Far Arnside Cumb 211 D8
Far Bank S Yorks 198 E6
Far Banks Lancs 194 C2
Far Bletchley M Keynes . . 103 E7
Farcet Cambs 138 E4
Far Coton Leics 135 C7
Far Cotton Northants . . . 120 F4
Farden Shrops 115 B11
Fareham Hants 33 F9
Far End Cumb 220 F6
Farewell Staffs 151 F11
Far Forest Worcs 116 C4
Farforth Lincs 190 F4
Far Green Glos 80 E3
Farhill Derbys 170 C5
Far Hoarcross Staffs 152 E2
Faringdon Oxon 82 F3
Farington Lancs 194 B4
Farington Moss Lancs . . . 194 B4
Farlam Cumb 240 F3
Farlands Booth Derbys . . 185 D9
Farlary Highld 309 J7
Far Laund Derbys 170 F5
Farleigh N Som 60 F4
 Sur 67 G11
Farleigh Court Sur 67 G11
Farleigh Green Kent 53 C8
Farleigh Hungerford
 Som 45 B10
Farleigh Wallop Hants . . . 48 D6
Farleigh Wick Wilts 61 G10
Farlesthorpe Lincs 191 G7
Farleton Lancs 211 F11
Far Ley Staffs 132 D5
Farley Green Suff 124 G4
 Sur 50 D5
Farley Hill Luton 103 G11
 Wokingham 65 G8
Farleys End Glos 80 B3
Farlington N Yorks 216 F2
 Ptsmth 33 F11
Farlow Shrops 132 G2
Farmborough Bath 61 G7
Farmbridge End Essex . . . 87 C10
Farmcote Glos 99 F11
 Shrops 132 E5
Farmington Glos 81 B10
Farmoor Oxon 82 D6
Far Moor Gtr Man 194 G4
Farms Common Corn 2 C5
Farmtown Moray 302 D5
Farm Town Leics 153 F7
Farnah Green Derbys . . . 170 F4
Farnborough Hants 49 C11
 London 68 G2
 Warks 101 B8
 W Berks 64 C2
Farnborough Green
 Hants 49 B11
Farnborough Park
 Hants 49 B11
Farnborough Street
 Hants 49 B11
Farncombe Sur 50 E3
Farndish Beds 121 D8
Farndon Ches W 166 E6
 Notts 172 E3
Farnell Angus 287 B10
Farnham Dorset 31 E7
 Essex 105 G9

Farnham continued
N Yorks....215 G7
Suff....127 E7
Sur....49 D10
Farnham Common Bucks 66 C3
Farnham Green Essex...105 F9
Farnham Park Bucks....66 C3
Farnham Royal Bucks....66 C3
Farnhill N Yorks....204 D6
Farningham Kent....68 F4
Farnley N Yorks....205 D10
W Yorks....205 G11
Farnley Bank W Yorks...197 E7
Farnley Tyas W Yorks...197 E7
Farnsfield Notts....171 D10
Farnworth Gtr Man....195 F8
Halton....183 D8
Far Oakridge Glos....80 E5
Far Highld....291 C10
Highld....300 F6
Highld....308 C7
Farraline Highld....300 G5
Farr House Highld....300 F6
Farringdon Devon....14 C4
T&W....243 G9
Farrington Dorset....30 D4
Farrington Gurney Bath..44 B6
Far Royds W Yorks....205 G11
Far Sawrey Cumb....221 F7
Farsley W Yorks....205 F10
Farsley Beck Bottom
W Yorks....205 F10
Farther Howegreen
Essex....88 E4
Farthing Corner
Medway....69 G10
Farthing Green Kent....53 D10
Farthinghoe Northants 101 D10
Farthingloe Kent....55 E9
Farthingstone Northants 120 F2
Far Thrupp Glos....80 E5
Fartown W Yorks....196 D6
Farway Devon....15 B9
Farway Marsh Devon....28 G4
Fasach Highld....297 G7
Fasag Highld....299 D8
Fascadale Highld....289 B7
Faslane Port Argyll....284 C4
Fasnacloich Argyll....284 C4
Fasnakyle Ho Highld....300 G3
Fassfern Highld....290 F2
Fatfield T&W....243 G8
Fattahead Aberds....302 D6
Faucheldean W Loth....279 G11
Faugh Cumb....240 G2
Faughill Borders....262 C2
Fauld Staffs....152 D3
Fauldhouse W Loth....269 C8
Fauldiehill Angus....287 D9
Fauldshope Borders....261 D10
Faulkbourne Essex....88 B3
Faulkland Som....45 C8
Fauls Shrops....149 C11
Faverdale Darl....224 B5
Faversham Kent....70 G4
Favillar Moray....302 F2
Fawdington N Yorks....215 E8
Fawdon Northumb....264 F2
T&W....242 D6
Fawfieldhead Staffs....169 C9
Fawkham Green Kent....68 F5
Fawler Oxon....63 B10
Oxon....82 B5
Fawley Bucks....65 B9
Hants....33 G7
W Berks....63 C11
Fawley Bottom Bucks....65 B8
Fawley Chapel Hereford 97 F11
Faxfleet E Yorks....199 C11
Faygate W Sus....51 G8
Fazakerley Mers....182 B5
Fazeley Staffs....134 C4
Feagour Highld....291 D7
Fearby N Yorks....214 C3
Fearn Highld....301 B8
Fearnan Perth....285 C11
Fearnbeg Highld....299 D7
Fearnhead Warr....183 C10
Fearn Lodge Highld....309 L6
Fearnmore Highld....299 C7
Fearn Station Highld....301 B8
Fearnville W Yorks....206 F2
Featherstone Staffs....133 B8
W Yorks....198 C2
Featherwood Northumb 251 C8
Feckenham Worcs....117 E10
Fedw Fawr Anglesey....179 E10
Feering Essex....107 G7
Feetham N Yorks....223 F9
Fegg Hayes Stoke....168 E5
Fèith Mhor Highld....301 G8
Feizor N Yorks....212 F5
Felbridge Sur....51 F11
Felbrigg Norf....160 B4
Felcourt Sur....51 E11
Felden Herts....85 E8
Felderland Kent....55 B10
Feldy Ches E....183 F11
Felhampton Shrops....131 F8
Felin-Crai Powys....95 G7
Felindre Carms....75 C7
Carms....93 D7
Carms....93 G10
Carms....94 E3
Carms....94 F4
Ceredig....111 F10
Powys....96 B3
Powys....96 G3
Powys....130 C3
Powys....130 D4
Rhondda....58 C3
Swansea....75 E10
Felindre Farchog Pembs 92 D2
Felinfach Ceredig....111 F10
Powys....95 E11
Felinfoel Carms....75 E8
Felingwmisaf Carms....93 G10
Felingwmuchaf Carms....93 G10
Felin Newydd Carms....94 D3
Felin-newydd Powys....96 D2
Felin Newydd / New Mills
Powys....129 C11
Felin Puleston Wrex....166 F4
Felin-Wnda Ceredig....92 B6
Felinwynt Ceredig....110 G4
Felixkirk N Yorks....215 C9
Felixstowe Suff....108 E5
Felixstowe Ferry Suff...108 D6
Felkington Northumb....273 G8
Felkirk W Yorks....197 E11
Felldyke Cumb....219 B11
Fell End Cumb....222 F4
Fellgate T&W....243 E8
Felling T&W....243 E7
Felling Shore T&W....243 E7
Fell Lane W Yorks....204 E6
Fellside T&W....242 E5
Fell Side Cumb....230 D2
Felmersham Beds....121 F9

Felmingham Norf....160 D5
Felmore Essex....69 B8
Felpham W Sus....35 H7
Felsham Suff....125 F8
Felsted Essex....106 G3
Feltham London....66 E6
Som....28 D2
Felthamhill London....66 E5
Felthorpe Norf....160 F3
Felton Hereford....97 B11
Northumb....252 D5
N Som....60 F4
Felton Butler Shrops....149 F7
Feltwell Norf....140 E4
Fenay Bridge W Yorks....197 D7
Fence Lancs....204 F2
Fence Houses T&W....243 G8
Fencott Oxon....83 B9
Fen Ditton Cambs....123 E9
Fen Drayton Cambs....122 D6
Fen End Lincs....156 E4
W Mid....118 B4
Fengate Norf....160 E3
Pboro....138 D4
Fenham Northumb....273 G11
T&W....242 D6
Fenhouses Lincs....174 G3
Feniscliffe Blkburn....195 B7
Feniscowles Blkburn....194 B6
Feniton Devon....15 B8
Fenlake Beds....103 B11
Fennington Som....27 B11
Fenn Green Shrops....132 G5
Fenn Street Medway....69 D9
Fenny Bentley Derbys....169 E11
Fenny Bridges Devon....15 B8
Fenny Castle Som....44 E4
Fenny Compton Warks....119 G8
Fenny Drayton Leics....134 D6
Fenny Stratford
M Keynes....103 E7
Fenrother Northumb....252 E5
Fen Side Lincs....174 D4
Fenstanton Cambs....122 D6
Fenstead End Suff....124 G6
Fen Street Norf....141 G11
Suff....125 B9
Fenton Cambs....122 B6
Cumb....240 F2
Lincs....172 E5
Lincs....188 F4
Northumb....263 C11
Stoke....168 F5
Fenton Barns E Loth....281 E10
Fenton Low Stoke....168 F5
Fenton Pits Corn....5 C11
Fenton Town Northumb....263 C11
Fenwick E Ayrs....267 G9
Northumb....242 C3
Northumb....273 G11
S Yorks....198 E5
Feochaig Argyll....255 F8
Feock Corn....3 B8
Feolin Ferry Argyll....274 G5
Ferguslie Park Renfs....267 C9
Ferindonald Highld....295 E8
Feriniquarrie Highld....296 F7
Ferlochan Argyll....289 E11
Fern Angus....292 G6
Bucks....65 B11
Fern Bank Gtr Man....185 B7
Ferndale Kent....52 E5
Rhondda....77 F7
Ferndown Dorset....31 G9
Ferne Wilts....30 C6
Ferness Highld....301 E9
Ferney Green Cumb....221 F8
Fernham Oxon....82 G3
Fernhill Gtr Man....195 E10
Rhondda....77 F8
W Sus....51 E10
Fern Hill Suff....106 B6
Fernhill Gate Gtr Man....195 F7
Fernhill Heath Worcs....117 F7
Fernhurst W Sus....34 B5
Fernie Fife....287 F7
Ferniebrae Aberds....303 D9
Ferniegair S Lanark....268 E4
Ferniehirst Borders....271 G8
Fernilea Highld....294 B5
Fernilee Derbys....185 F8
Fernsplatt Corn....4 G5
Ferrensby N Yorks....215 G7
Ferring W Sus....35 G9
Ferry Hill Cambs....139 G7
Durham....233 E11
Ferryhill Aberdeen....293 C11
Durham....233 E11
Ferryhill Station Durham 234 E2
Ferryside / Glan-y-Ffer
Carms....74 C5
Ferryton Highld....300 C6
Fersfield Norf....141 G11
Fersit Highld....290 F5
Feshiebridge Highld....291 C10
Fetcham Sur....50 B6
Fetterangus Aberds....303 D9
Fettercairn Aberds....293 F8
Fetterdale Fife....287 E8
Fettes Highld....300 D5
Fewcott Oxon....101 F10
Fewston N Yorks....205 C9
Fewston Bents N Yorks....205 C9
Ffairfach Carms....94 G2
Ffaldybrenin Carms....94 C3
Ffarmers Carms....94 C3
Ffawyddog Powys....78 B2
Ffodun / Forden Powys 130 C4
Ffont y gari / Font y gary
V Glam....58 F5
Fforddlas Powys....96 D4
Ffordd-las Denb....165 C10
Ffordd-y-Gyfraith
Bridgend....57 E11
Fforest Carms....75 E9
Fforest-fach Swansea....56 B6
Fforest Gôch Neath....76 E2
Ffostrasol Ceredig....93 B7
Ffos-y-ffin Ceredig....111 E8
Ffos-y-go Wrex....166 E4
Ffridd Powys....130 D3
Ffrith Flint....166 D3
Ffrwd Gwyn....163 D7
Ffwl y mwn / Fonmon
V Glam....58 F4
Ffynnon Carms....74 B5
Ffynnon ddrain Carms....93 G8
Ffynnongroes / Crosswell
Pembs....92 D2
Ffynnon Gron Pembs....91 F8
Ffynnongroyw Flint....181 E10
Ffynnon Gynydd Powys 96 C3
Ffynnon-oer Ceredig....111 G10
Fickleshole Sur....67 G11
Fidden Argyll....288 G5

Fiddes Aberds....293 E10
Fiddington Glos....99 E8
Som....43 E8
Fiddington Sands Wilts 46 C4
Fiddleford Dorset....30 E4
Fiddler's Green Norf....141 D10
Fiddler's Green Glos....99 G8
Hereford....97 D11
Norf....143 B9
Warr....183 D9
Fiddlers Hamlet Essex...87 E7
Field Hereford....114 G6
Som....44 E6
Staffs....151 C10
Field Assarts Oxon....82 C4
Field Broughton Cumb....211 C7
Field Common Sur....66 F6
Field Dalling Norf....159 B10
Field Green Kent....38 B3
Field Head Leics....135 B9
Fields End Herts....85 D8
Field's Place Hereford...115 G8
Fifehead Magdalen
Dorset....30 C3
Fifehead Neville Dorset..30 E3
Fifehead St Quintin
Dorset....30 E3
Fife Keith Moray....302 D4
Fifield Oxon....82 B2
Wilts....46 C6
Windsor....66 D2
Fifield Bavant Wilts....31 B8
Figheldean Wilts....47 D7
Filands Wilts....62 B2
Filby Norf....161 G9
Filby Heath Norf....161 G9
Filchampstead Oxon....83 D7
Filey N Yorks....218 C2
Filgrave M Keynes....103 B7
Filham Devon....8 D2
Filkins Oxon....82 E2
Filleigh Devon....25 B11
Devon....26 E2
Fillingham Lincs....188 D6
Fillongley Warks....134 F5
Filmore Hill Hants....33 B11
Filton S Glos....60 D6
Filwood Park Bristol....60 F5
Fimber E Yorks....217 G7
Finavon Angus....287 B8
Fincastle Ho Perth....291 G10
Finchairn Argyll....275 C10
Fincham Mers....182 C6
Norf....140 B3
Finchampstead
Wokingham....65 G9
Finchdean Hants....34 E2
Finchingfield Essex....106 E3
Finchley London....86 G3
Findern Derbys....152 C6
Findhorn Moray....301 C10
Findhorn Bridge Highld 301 G8
Findochty Moray....302 C4
Findo Gask Perth....286 E3
Findon Aberds....293 D11
W Sus....35 F10
Findon Mains Highld....300 C6
Findon Valley W Sus....35 F10
Findrack Ho Aberds....293 C8
Finedon Northants....121 C8
Fineglen Argyll....275 B10
Fine Street Hereford....96 D6
Fingal Street Suff....126 D4
Fingask Aberds....303 G7
Fingerpost Worcs....116 C4
Fingest Bucks....84 G3
Finghall N Yorks....214 B3
Fingland Cumb....239 F7
Dumfries....259 G11
Fingringhoe Essex....107 G10
Finham W Mid....118 B6
Finkle Street S Yorks....186 B4
Finlarig Stirl....285 D9
Finmere Oxon....102 E2
Finnart Perth....285 B9
Finningham Suff....125 D11
Finningley S Yorks....187 B11
Finnygaud Aberds....302 D5
Finsbury London....67 C10
Finsbury Park London...67 B10
Finstall Worcs....117 D9
Finsthwaite Cumb....211 B7
Finstock Oxon....82 B5
Finstown Orkney....314 E3
Fintry Aberds....303 D7
Dundee....287 D8
Stirl....278 D2
Finwood Warks....118 D3
Finzean Aberds....293 D8
Fionnphort Argyll....288 G5
Fionnsbhagh W Isles....296 C6
Firbank Cumb....222 G2
Firbeck S Yorks....187 D9
Firby N Yorks....214 B5
N Yorks....216 F4
Firemore Highld....307 L3
Firgrove Gtr Man....196 E2
Firkin Argyll....285 G7
Firle E Sus....23 D7
Firsby Lincs....175 C7
Firsdown Wilts....47 G8
First Coast Highld....307 K4
Firs Lane Gtr Man....194 G6
Firswood Gtr Man....184 B4
Firth Borders....271 G8
Firth Moor Darl....224 C6
Firth Park S Yorks....186 C5
Fir Toll Kent....54 E2
Fir Tree Durham....233 E8
Fir Vale S Yorks....186 C5
Firwood Fold Gtr Man....195 E8
Fishbourne IoW....21 C7
W Sus....22 C4
Fishburn Durham....234 E3
Fishcross Clack....279 B7
Fisherford Aberds....302 F6
Fishermead M Keynes....103 D7
Fisher Place Cumb....220 B6
Fisherrow E Loth....280 G6
Fishersgate Brighton....36 F3
Fishers Green Herts....104 F4
Fisher's Pond Hants....33 C7
Fisher's Row Lancs....202 D5
Fisherstreet W Sus....50 G3
Fisherton Highld....301 D7
S Ayrs....257 F7
Fisherton de la Mere
Wilts....46 F4
Fisherwick Staffs....134 B3
Fishery Windsor....65 C11
Fishguard / Abergwaun
Pembs....91 D9
Fishlake S Yorks....199 E7
Fishleigh Devon....25 F8
Fishleigh Barton Devon..25 C9
Fishley Norf....161 G8

Fishmere End Lincs....156 B5
Fishponds Bristol....60 D6
Fishpool Glos....98 F3
Gtr Man....195 F10
Fishpools Powys....114 D3
Fishtoft Lincs....174 G5
Fishtoft Drove Lincs....174 F4
Fishtown of Usan
Angus....287 B11
Fishwick Borders....273 E8
Lancs....194 B5
Fiskavaig Highld....294 B5
Fiskerton Lincs....189 G8
Notts....172 E2
Fitling E Yorks....209 G11
Fittleton Wilts....46 D6
Fittleworth W Sus....35 D8
Fitton End Cambs....157 G8
Fitz Shrops....149 F8
Fitzhead Som....27 B10
Fitzwilliam W Yorks....198 D2
Fiunary Highld....289 E8
Five Acres Glos....79 C9
Five Ash Down E Sus....37 C7
Five Ashes E Sus....37 C9
Five Bells Som....42 E5
Fivecrosses Ches W....183 F8
Fivehead Som....28 C5
Five Houses IoW....20 D4
Five Lane Ends Lancs....202 C6
Fivelanes Corn....11 E10
Five Lanes Mon....78 G6
Five Oak Green Kent....52 D6
Five Oaks W Sus....35 C9
Five Roads Carms....75 D7
Five Ways Warks....118 D4
Five Wents Kent....53 C10
Fixby W Yorks....196 C5
Flackley Ash E Sus....38 C5
Flack's Green Essex....88 B3
Flackwell Heath Bucks...65 B11
Fladbury Worcs....99 B9
Fladbury Cross Worcs....99 B9
Fladda Shetland....312 E5
Fladdabister Shetland....313 K6
Flagg Derbys....169 B10
Flamborough E Yorks....218 E4
Flamstead Herts....85 C9
Flamstead End Herts....86 E4
Flansham W Sus....35 G7
Flanshaw W Yorks....197 C10
Flappit Spring W Yorks...205 F7
Flasby N Yorks....204 B4
Flash Staffs....169 B8
Flashader Highld....298 D3
Flask Inn N Yorks....227 E8
Flathurst W Sus....35 C7
Flaunden Herts....85 E8
Flawborough Notts....172 G3
Flawith N Yorks....215 F9
Flax Bourton N Som....60 F4
Flaxby N Yorks....206 B3
Flaxholme Derbys....170 G4
Flaxlands Norf....142 E2
Flaxley Glos....79 B11
Flaxley Green Staffs....151 F11
Flaxmere Ches W....183 G8
Flax Moss Lancs....195 C9
Flaxpool Som....42 F6
Flaxton N Yorks....216 G3
Fleckney Leics....136 E2
Flecknoe Warks....119 E10
Fledborough Notts....188 G4
Fleet Dorset....17 E8
Hants....22 C2
Hants....49 C11
Lincs....157 E7
Fleetdown Kent....68 E4
Fleet End Hants....33 F8
Fleet Hargate Lincs....157 E7
Fleetlands Hants....33 G9
Fleets N Yorks....213 G9
Fleetville Herts....85 D11
Fleetwood Lancs....202 D2
Fleggburgh / Burgh St
Margaret Norf....161 G8
Fleming Field Durham....234 C3
Flemings Kent....55 B9
Flemingston V Glam....58 F4
Flemington S Lanark....268 D2
S Lanark....268 G4
Flempton Suff....124 D6
Fleoideabhagh W Isles...296 C6
Fletchersbridge Corn....6 B2
Fletcher's Green Kent....52 C4
Fletchertown Cumb....229 C10
Fletching E Sus....36 C6
Fletching Common
E Sus....36 C6
Fleuchary Highld....309 K7
Fleuchlang Dumfries....237 D8
Fleur-de-lis Caerph....77 F11
Flexbury Corn....24 F2
Flexford Sur....50 D2
Flimby Cumb....228 E6
Flimwell E Sus....53 G8
Flint / Fflint....182 G2
Flint Cross Cambs....105 C8
Flintham Notts....172 F2
Flint Hill Durham....242 G5
Flint Mountain / Mynydd
Fflint....182 G2
Flinton E Yorks....209 F10
Flint's Green W Mid....134 G5
Flintsham Hereford....114 F6
Flishinghurst Kent....53 E9
Flitcham Norf....158 D4
Flitholme Cumb....222 B5
Flitton Beds....103 D11
Flitwick Beds....103 D11
Flixborough N Lincs....199 D11
Flixborough Stather
N Lincs....199 D11
Flixton Gtr Man....184 C2
N Yorks....217 D10
Suff....142 G6
Flockton W Yorks....197 E8
Flockton Green
W Yorks....197 D8
Flockton Moor W Yorks..197 E8
Flodaigh W Isles....296 F4
Flodden Northumb....263 B10
Flodigarry Highld....298 B4
Floesfield Moray....301 D11
Flood's Ferry Cambs....139 E7
Flood Street Hants....31 D10
Flookburgh Cumb....211 D7
Flordon Norf....142 D3
Flore Northants....120 E2
Florence Stoke....168 G6
Flotterton Northumb....251 C11
Flowers Bottom Bucks...84 F4
Flowers Green E Sus....23 C10
Flowery Field Gtr Man....184 B6
Flowton Suff....107 B11
Fluchter E Dunb....277 G11
Flugarth Shetland....313 G6

Flushdyke W Yorks....197 C9
Flush House W Yorks....196 F6
Flushing Aberds....303 E10
Corn....3 C8
Corn....3 D7
Flyford Flavell Worcs....117 G9
Foals Green Suff....126 C5
Fobbing Thurrock....69 C8
Fochabers Moray....302 D3
Fochriw Caerph....77 D10
Fockerby N Lincs....199 D10
Fodderletter Moray....301 G11
Fodderstone Gap Norf...140 B3
Foddington Som....29 B9
Foel Powys....147 G9
Foel-gastell Carms....75 C8
Foffarty Angus....287 C8
Foggathorpe E Yorks....207 F11
Foggbrook Gtr Man....184 D6
Fogo Borders....272 F5
Fogorig Borders....272 F5
Fogwatt Moray....302 D2
Foindle Highld....306 E6
Folda Angus....292 G3
Fold Head Lancs....195 D11
Fold Hill Lincs....175 E7
Foldrings S Yorks....186 C3
Fole Staffs....151 B10
Foleshill W Mid....135 G7
Foley Park Worcs....116 B6
Folke Dorset....29 E11
Folkestone Kent....55 F8
Folkingham Lincs....155 C11
Folkington E Sus....23 E9
Folksworth Cambs....138 F2
Folkton N Yorks....217 D11
Folla Rule Aberds....303 F7
Folley Shrops....132 D5
Follifoot N Yorks....206 C2
Folly Dorset....30 G2
Pembs....91 G8
Folly Cross Devon....25 F7
Folly Gate Devon....13 B7
Folly Green Essex....106 F6
Fonmon / Ffwl-y-mwn
V Glam....58 F4
Fonston Corn....11 C10
Fonthill Bishop Wilts....46 G2
Fonthill Gifford Wilts....46 G2
Fontmell Magna Dorset..30 D4
Fontmell Parva Dorset....30 E4
Fontwell W Sus....35 F7
Font-y-gary / Font-y-gari
V Glam....58 F5
Foodieash Fife....287 F7
Foolow Derbys....185 F11
Footbridge Glos....99 F10
Footherley Staffs....134 C2
Footrid Worcs....116 C3
Foots Cray London....68 E3
Forbestown Aberds....292 B5
Force Forge Cumb....220 G6
Force Green Kent....52 B2
Force Mills Cumb....220 G6
Forcett N Yorks....224 C3
Ford Argyll....275 C9
Bucks....84 D3
Derbys....186 E6
Devon....8 G5
Devon....8 F3
Devon....24 C6
Devon....28 G2
Glos....99 F11
Hereford....115 F10
Northumb....263 B10
Plym....7 D9
Shrops....149 G8
Som....27 B9
Som....44 C5
Staffs....169 E8
W Sus....35 G8
Wilts....47 G7
Wilts....61 E10
Forda Devon....12 C6
Devon....40 F3
Fordbridge W Mid....134 F3
Fordcombe Kent....52 E4
Fordell Fife....280 D3
Forden / Ffodun Powys 130 C4
Ford End Essex....87 B11
Forder Corn....7 D8
Forder Green Devon....8 C5
Ford Forge Northumb....263 B10
Fordgate Som....43 G10
Ford Green Lancs....202 D5
Fordham Cambs....124 C2
Essex....107 F8
Norf....140 D2
Fordham Heath Essex....107 F8
Ford Heath Shrops....149 G8
Ford Hill Northumb....263 B11
Fordhouses W Mid....133 C8
Fordingbridge Hants....31 E10
Fordley T&W....243 C7
Fordon E Yorks....217 D10
Fordoun Aberds....293 F9
Ford's Green E Sus....36 B6
Fordstreet Essex....107 F8
Ford Street Som....27 D11
Fordton Devon....14 B2
Fordwater Devon....28 G4
Fordwells Oxon....82 C4
Fordwich Kent....55 B7
Fordyce Aberds....302 C5
Forebridge Staffs....151 E8
Foredale N Yorks....212 F6
Forehill S Ayrs....257 E8
Foreland Fields IoW....21 D9
Foreland Ho Argyll....274 G3
Foremark Derbys....152 D6
Forest Becks Lancs....203 C11
Forestburn Gate
Northumb....252 D3
Forest Coal Pit Mon....96 G5
Forestdale London....67 G11
Foresterseat Moray....301 D11
Forest Gate London....68 C2
Forest Green Glos....80 E4
Sur....50 E6
Forest Hall Cumb....221 E10
T&W....243 D7
Forest Head Cumb....240 F3
Forest Hill Oxon....83 D9
Wilts....63 F8
Forest Holme Lancs....195 B10
Forest-in-Teesdale
Durham....232 F4
Forest Lane Head
N Yorks....206 B2

Forest Lodge Argyll....284 C6
Perth....291 F11
Forest Mill Clack....279 C9
Forest Moor N Yorks....206 B2
Forestreet Devon....24 E5
Forest Row E Sus....52 G2
Forestside W Sus....34 E3
Forest Side IoW....20 D5
Forest Town Notts....171 C9
Forewoods Common
Wilts....61 G10
Forfar Angus....287 B8
Forgandenny Perth....286 F4
Forge Corn....4 F3
Powys....128 D5
Forge Hammer Torf....78 F3
Forge Side Torf....78 D2
Forgewood N Lanark....268 D4
Forgie Moray....302 D3
Forgie Ho Aberds....302 E6
Forglen Aberds....302 D6
Forhill Worcs....117 B11
Formby Mers....193 F10
Forncett End Norf....142 E2
Forncett St Mary Norf...142 E3
Forncett St Peter Norf...142 E3
Forneth Perth....286 C4
Fornham All Saints Suff..124 D6
Fornham St Genevieve
Suff....124 D6
Fornham St Martin Suff..125 D7
Fornighty Highld....301 D9
Forrabury Corn....11 C7
Forres Moray....301 D10
Forrestfield N Lanark....269 B7
Forrest Lodge Dumfries 246 F3
Forry's Green Essex....106 E5
Forsbrook Staffs....169 G7
Forse Highld....310 F6
Forse Ho Highld....310 F6
Forsham Heath Warks...117 C11
Forsinain Highld....310 E3
Forsinard Highld....310 E2
Forsinard Station Highld 310 E2
Forstal Kent....53 B8
Forston Dorset....17 B9
Fort Augustus Highld....290 C5
Forteviot Perth....286 F4
Fort George Highld....301 D7
Forth S Lnrk....269 E8
Forthampton Glos....99 E7
Forthay Glos....80 F2
Forth Road Bridge Edin 280 F2
Fortis Green London....67 B9
Fort Matilda Invclyd....276 F5
Forton Hants....33 G10
Lancs....202 C5
Shrops....149 F8
Som....28 G5
Staffs....150 D5
Forton Heath Shrops....149 F8
Fortrie Aberds....302 E6
Aberds....303 D7
Fortrose Highld....301 D7
Fortuneswell Dorset....17 G9
Fort William Highld....290 F3
Forty Green Bucks....84 G3
Bucks....84 G6
Forty Hill London....86 F4
Forward Green Suff....125 F11
Forwood Glos....80 E5
Fosbury Wilts....47 B10
Foscot Oxon....100 G4
Foscote Bucks....102 D4
Northants....102 B3
Fosdyke Lincs....156 B6
Fosdyke Bridge Lincs....156 C6
Foss Perth....285 B11
Foss Cross Glos....81 D9
Fossebridge Glos....81 C9
Fostall Kent....70 G5
Fosten Green Kent....53 F10
Foster's Booth
Northants....120 G3
Fosterhouses S Yorks....199 E7
Foster's Green Worcs....117 D9
Foster Street Essex....87 D7
Foston Derbys....152 C3
Leics....136 D2
Lincs....172 G5
N Yorks....216 F3
Foston on the Wolds
E Yorks....209 B8
Fotherby Lincs....190 C4
Fothergill Cumb....228 E6
Fotheringhay Northants 137 E11
Foubister Orkney....314 F5
Foul Anchor Cambs....157 F9
Foulbridge Cumb....230 B4
Foulden Borders....273 D8
Norf....140 D5
Foulford Hants....31 F11
Foulis Castle Highld....300 C5
Foul Mile E Sus....23 B10
Foulridge Lancs....204 D3
Foulsham Norf....159 E11
Foundry Corn....2 B3
Foundry Hill Norf....159 D11
Fountain Bridgend....57 E11
Fountainhall Borders....271 F7
Four Ashes Bucks....84 F5
Staffs....132 G6
Staffs....133 B8
Suff....125 C10
W Mid....118 B3
Four Crosses Powys....129 E11
Powys....133 D8
Staffs....133 B7
Wrex....166 E3
Four Elms Devon....28 F3
Kent....52 D2
Four Foot Som....44 G5
Four Forks Som....43 F8
Four Gates Gtr Man....194 F6
Four Gotes Cambs....157 F8
Four Houses Corner
W Berks....64 F6
Four Lane End S Yorks...197 G9
Four Lane Ends Blkburn..195 B7
Four Lanes Corn....2 B5
Fourlanes End Ches E....168 D4
Four Marks Hants....49 G7
Four Mile Bridge
Anglesey....178 F3
Four Mile Elm Glos....80 C4
Four Oaks E Sus....38 D5
Glos....98 F3
Kent....70 G3
W Mid....134 D2

Four Oaks Park W Mid....134 D2
Fourpenny Highld....311 K2
Four Points W Berks....64 D5
Four Pools Worcs....99 C10
Four Roads Carms....74 D6
IoM....192 F3
Fourstones Northumb....241 D9
Four Throws Kent....38 B3
Four Wantz Essex....87 C10
Four Wents Kent....53 G9
Fovant Wilts....31 B8
Foveran Aberds....303 G9
Fowey Corn....6 E2
Fowlers Plot Som....43 F10
Fowley Common Warr....183 B11
Fowlis Angus....287 D7
Fowlis Wester Perth....286 E3
Fowlmere Cambs....105 B8
Fownhope Hereford....97 E11
Foxash Estate Essex....107 E11
Foxbar Renfs....267 C9
Foxbury London....68 E2
Foxcombe Hill Oxon....83 E7
Fox Corner C Beds....103 F8
Sur....50 B2
Foxcote Glos....81 B8
Som....45 B8
Foxcotte Hants....47 D10
Foxdale IoM....192 E3
Foxdown Hants....48 C4
Foxearth Essex....106 C6
Foxendown Kent....69 F7
Foxfield Cumb....210 B4
Foxford W Mid....135 G7
Foxham Wilts....62 D3
Fox Hatch Essex....87 F9
Foxhills Hants....32 E4
Fox Hole Swansea....56 D5
Foxhole Corn....5 D9
Norf....142 D6
Foxholes N Yorks....217 E10
Foxhunt Green E Sus....23 B8
Fox Lane Hants....49 B11
Foxley Hereford....97 B8
Norf....159 E10
Staffs....168 E3
Wilts....61 B11
Fox Royd W Yorks....197 D8
Foxt Staffs....169 F8
Foxton Cambs....105 B8
Durham....234 F3
Leics....136 F3
N Yorks....225 G7
Foxup N Yorks....213 D7
Foxwist Green Ches W....167 B10
Foxwood Shrops....116 B2
Foy Hereford....97 F11
Foyers Highld....300 G4
Foynesfield Highld....301 D8
Fraddam Corn....2 C3
Fraddon Corn....5 D8
Fradley Staffs....152 F2
Fradley Junction Staffs..152 F2
Fradswell Staffs....151 D9
Fraisthorpe E Yorks....218 G3
Framfield E Sus....37 C7
Framingham Earl Norf...142 C5
Framingham Pigot Norf 142 C5
Framlingham Suff....126 E5
Frampton Dorset....17 B8
Lincs....156 B6
Frampton Cotterell
S Glos....61 C7
Frampton Court Glos....99 E10
Frampton End S Glos....61 C7
Frampton Mansell Glos..80 E6
Frampton on Severn
Glos....80 D2
Frampton West End
Lincs....174 G3
Framsden Suff....126 F3
Framwellgate Moor
Durham....233 C11
France Lynch Glos....80 E6
Frances Green Lancs....203 F7?
Frandley Ches W....183 F10
Frankby Mers....182 D2
Frankfort Norf....160 E6
Franklands Gate
Hereford....97 B10
Frankley Worcs....133 G9
Frankley Green Worcs....133 G9
Frankley Hill Worcs....117 B9
Frank's Bridge Powys....114 F2
Frankton Warks....119 C8
Frans Green Norf....160 G2
Fraserburgh Aberds....303 C9
Frating Essex....107 G11
Frating Green Essex....107 G11
Fratton Ptsmth....21 B9
Freasley Warks....134 D4
Freathy Corn....7 E8
Frecheville S Yorks....186 E6
Freckenham Suff....124 C3
Freckleton Lancs....194 B3
Fredley Sur....51 C7
Freebirch Derbys....186 G4
Freeby Leics....154 E6
Freefolk Hants....48 C3
Freehay Staffs....169 G8
Freeland Oxon....82 C6
Renfs....267 B9
Freeland Corner Norf....160 F3
Freester Shetland....313 H6
Freethorpe Norf....143 B8
Free Town Gtr Man....195 E10
Freezy Water London....86 F5
Freiston Lincs....174 G5
Freiston Shore Lincs....174 G5
Fremington Devon....40 G4
N Yorks....223 F11
Frenchay S Glos....60 D6
Frenchbeer Devon....13 D9
Frenches Green Essex....106 G3
Frenchmoor Hants....32 B3
French Street Kent....52 C2
Frenchwood Lancs....194 B4
Frenich Stirl....285 G8
Frensham Sur....49 E10
Frenze Norf....142 G2
Fresgoe Highld....310 C3
Freshbrook Swindon....62 C6
Freshfield Mers....193 F9
Freshford Bath....61 G9
Freshwater IoW....20 D2
Freshwater Bay IoW....20 D2
Freshwater East Pembs..73 F8
Fressingfield Suff....126 B5
Freston Suff....108 D3
Freswick Highld....310 C7
Fretherne Glos....80 D2
Frettenham Norf....160 F4

Freuchie Fife....286 G6
Freuchies Angus....292 G4
Freystrop Pembs....73 C7
Friarn Som....43 F7
Friar Park W Mid....133 E10
Friars Cliff Dorset....19 C5
Friar's Gate E Sus....52 G3
Friar's Hill E Sus....38 E5
Friarton Perth....286 E5
Friday Bridge Cambs....139 B9
Friday Hill London....86 G5
Friday Street E Sus....23 E10
Suff....126 F6
Suff....127 E7
Sur....50 D6
Fridaythorpe E Yorks....208 B3
Friendly W Yorks....196 C5
Friern Barnet London....86 G3
Friesland Argyll....288 D3
Friesthorpe Lincs....189 E9
Frieston Lincs....172 F6
Frieth Bucks....84 G3
Friezeland Notts....171 E7
Frilford Oxon....82 F6
Frilford Heath Oxon....82 F6
Frilsham W Berks....64 E4
Frimley Sur....49 B11
Frimley Green Sur....49 B11
Frimley Ridge Sur....49 B11
Frindsbury Medway....69 E8
Fring Norf....158 C4
Fringford Oxon....102 F2
Friningham Kent....53 B10
Frinkle Green Essex....106 C4
Frinsted Kent....53 B11
Frinton-on-Sea Essex....108 G4
Friockheim Angus....287 C9
Friog Gwyn....146 G2
Frisby Leics....136 C4
Frisby on the Wreake
Leics....154 F3
Friskney Lincs....175 D7
Friskney Eaudyke Lincs..175 D7
Friskney Tofts Lincs....175 E7
Friston E Sus....23 E9
Suff....127 E8
Fritchley Derbys....170 E5
Frith Kent....54 B2
Hants....32 E2
Frith Bank Lincs....174 F4
Fritham Hants....32 E3
Frith Common Worcs....116 D3
Frithelstock Devon....25 D7
Frithelstock Stone Devon 25 D7
Frithend Hants....49 E10
Frith-hill Bucks....84 E6
Frith Hill Sur....50 E3
Frithsden Herts....85 D8
Frithville Lincs....174 E4
Frittenden Kent....53 E10
Frittiscombe Devon....8 G6
Fritton Norf....142 E4
Norf....143 D9
Norf....161 F8
Fritwell Oxon....101 F10
Frizinghall W Yorks....205 F9
Frizington Cumb....219 B10
Frizzeler's Green Suff....124 E5
Frobost W Isles....297 J3
Frocester Glos....80 E3
Frochas Powys....148 G5
Frodesley Shrops....131 C10
Frodingham N Lincs....199 D11
Frodsham Ches W....183 F8
Frogden Borders....263 D8
Frog End Cambs....123 G10
Cambs....123 F8
Froggatt Derbys....186 F2
Froghall Staffs....169 F8
Frogham Hants....31 E11
Kent....55 C9
Froghole Kent....52 C2
Frogholt Kent....55 F7
Frogland Cross S Glos....60 C6
Frogmore Devon....8 G5
Hants....49 B11
Herts....85 D11
Frognall Lincs....156 G2
Frogpool Corn....4 G5
Frogs' Green Essex....105 D11
Frogshail Norf....160 B5
Frogwell Corn....6 B6
Frolesworth Leics....135 E9
Frome Som....45 D9
Fromebridge Glos....80 D3
Fromefield Som....45 D9
Frome St Quintin Dorset 29 G9
Fromes Hill Hereford....98 B3
Fron Denb....165 D11
Gwyn....145 B7
Gwyn....163 G7
Powys....113 D11
Powys....129 C9
Powys....130 C4
Powys....130 D2
Shrops....148 B5
Fron-Bache Denb....166 G3
Froncysyllte Wrex....166 G3
Fron-deg Wrex....166 F3
Frongoch Gwyn....147 B8
Fron Isaf Wrex....166 G3
Frost Devon....26 E3
Frostenden Suff....143 G9
Frostenden Corner Suff 143 G9
Frosterley Durham....232 D6
Frost Hill N Som....60 G3
Frostlane Hants....32 F6
Frost Row Norf....141 C11
Froxfield C Beds....103 D8
Wilts....63 F9
Froxfield Green Hants....34 B2
Froyle Hants....49 E8
Fryern Hill Hants....32 C6
Fryerning Essex....87 E11
Fryerns Essex....69 B8
Fryton N Yorks....216 E3
Fugglestone St Peter
Wilts....46 G5
Fulbeck Lincs....172 E6
Northumb....252 F5
Fulbourn Cambs....123 F10
Fulbrook Oxon....82 C3
Fulford Som....28 B2
Staffs....151 B8
York....207 D8
Fulham London....67 D9
Fulking W Sus....36 E2
Fullabrook Devon....40 E4
Fullarton Glasgow....268 C2
N Ayrs....257 B8
Fuller's End Essex....105 F10
Fuller's Moor Ches W....167 D7
Fuller Street Essex....88 B2
Kent....52 B5
Fullerton Hants....47 F11

Fulletby Lincs....190 G3
Fullshaw S Yorks....197 G8
Full Sutton E Yorks....207 B10
Fullwell Cross London....86 G6
Fullwood E Ayrs....267 E8
  Gtr Man....196 F2
Fulmer Bucks....66 B3
Fulmodeston Norf....159 C9
Fulneck W Yorks....205 G10
Fulnetby Lincs....189 F9
Fulney Lincs....156 E5
Fulready Warks....100 B5
Fulshaw Park Ches E....184 E4
Fulstone W Yorks....197 F7
Fulstow Lincs....190 B4
Fulthorpe Stockton....234 G4
Fulwell Oxon....101 G7
  T&W....243 F9
Fulwood Lancs....202 G6
  Som....28 C2
  S Yorks....186 D4
Fundenhall Norf....142 D3
Fundenhall Street Norf....142 D2
Funtington W Sus....22 B1
Funtley Hants....33 F9
Funtullich Perth....285 E11
Funzie Shetland....312 D8
Furley Devon....28 G3
Furnace Argyll....284 G4
  Carms....74 E6
  Carms....75 E8
  Ceredig....128 D3
  Highld....299 B9
Furnace End Warks....134 E4
Furnace Green W Sus....51 F9
Furnace Wood W Sus....51 F11
Furneaux Pelham Herts....105 F8
Furner's Green E Sus....36 B6
Furness Vale Derbys....185 E8
Furneux Pelham Herts....105 F8
Furnham Som....28 F4
Further Ford End Essex....105 F9
Further Quarter Kent....53 F11
Furtho Northants....102 C5
Furze Devon....25 B10
Furzebrook Dorset....18 E4
Furzedown Hants....32 B5
  London....67 E9
Furzehill Devon....41 D8
  Dorset....31 G8
Furze Hill Hants....31 E11
Furzeley Corner Hants....33 E11
Furze Platt Windsor....65 C11
Furzey Lodge Hants....32 G5
Furzley Hants....32 D3
Furzton M Keynes....102 D6
Fyfett Som....28 E2
Fyfield Essex....87 D9
  Glos....82 E2
  Hants....47 D9
  Oxon....82 F6
  Wilts....45 B11
  Wilts....63 G7
Fylingthorpe N Yorks....227 D8
Fyning W Sus....34 C4
Fyvie Aberds....303 F7

G

Gabalfa Cardiff....59 D7
Gabhsann bho Dheas
  W Isles....304 C6
Gabhsann bho Thuath
  W Isles....304 C6
Gable Head Hants....21 B10
Gablon Highld....309 K7
Gabroc Hill E Ayrs....267 E9
Gadbrook Sur....51 D8
Gaddesby Leics....154 G3
Gadebridge Herts....85 D8
Gadfa Anglesey....179 D7
Gadfield Elm Worcs....98 E5
Gadlas Shrops....149 B7
Gadlys Rhondda....77 E7
Gadshill Kent....69 E8
Gaer Newport....59 B9
  Powys....96 G3
Gaer-fawr Mon....78 F6
Gaerllwyd Mon....78 F6
Gaerwen Anglesey....179 G7
Gagingwell Oxon....101 G8
Gaick Lodge Highld....291 E9
Gailey Staffs....151 G8
Gailey Wharf Staffs....151 G8
Gainfield Oxon....82 F4
Gainford Durham....224 B3
Gain Hill Kent....53 D8
Gainsborough Lincs....188 C4
  Suff....108 C3
Gainsford End Essex....106 D4
Gairletter Argyll....276 E3
Gairloch Highld....299 B8
Gairlochy Highld....290 E3
Gairney Bank Perth....280 C2
Gairnshiel Lodge
  Aberds....292 C4
Gaisgill Cumb....222 D2
Gaitsgill Cumb....230 B3
Galadean Borders....271 G11
Galashiels Borders....261 B11
Galdlys Flint....182 G2
Gale Gtr Man....196 D2
Galhampton Som....29 B10
Gallaberry Dumfries....247 G11
Gallachoille Argyll....275 E8
Gallanach Argyll....288 C4
  Argyll....289 G10
  Highld....294 G6
Gallantry Bank Ches E....167 E8
Gallatown Fife....280 C5
Galley Common Warks....134 E6
Galleyend Essex....88 E2
Galley Hill Cambs....122 D6
  Lincs....190 F6
Galleywood Essex....88 E2
Gallin Perth....285 C9
Gallovie Highld....291 E7
Gallowfauld Angus....287 C8
Gallowhill Glasgow....267 D11
  Renfs....267 B9
Gallowhills Aberds....303 D10
Gallows Corner London....87 G8
Gallows Green Torf....78 D3
Gallows Green Essex....106 F2
  Essex....107 F8
  Staffs....169 G9
  Worcs....117 E8
Gallows Inn Derbys....171 G7
Gallowstree Common
  Oxon....65 C7
Galltair Highld....295 C10
Galltegfa Denb....165 D10

Galmpton Devon....8 G3
  Torbay....9 D7
Galon Uchaf M Tydf....77 D9
Galphay N Yorks....214 E5
Galston E Ayrs....258 B2
Galtrigill Highld....296 F1
Gam Corn....11 F7
Gamble Hill W Yorks....205 G11
Gamblesby Cumb....231 D8
Gamble's Green Essex....88 C3
Gamesley Derbys....185 C8
Gamlingay Cambs....122 G4
Gamlingay Cinques
  Cambs....122 G4
Gamlingay Great Heath
  Cambs....122 G4
Gammaton Devon....25 B7
Gammaton Moor Devon....25 B7
Gammersgill N Yorks....213 C11
Gamston Notts....154 B2
  Notts....188 F2
Ganarew Hereford....79 B8
Ganavan Argyll....289 F10
Ganders Green Glos....98 G4
Ganllwyd Gwyn....146 E4
Gannets Dorset....30 D3
Gannochy Angus....293 F7
  Perth....286 E5
Gansclet Highld....310 E7
Ganstead E Yorks....209 G9
Ganthorpe N Yorks....216 E3
Ganton N Yorks....217 D9
Gants Hill London....68 B2
Gappah Devon....14 F3
Garafad Highld....298 C4
Garamor Highld....295 F8
Garbat Highld....300 C4
Garbhallt Argyll....275 D11
Garbole Highld....301 G7
Garboldisham Norf....141 G10
Garden City Flint....166 B4
Gardeners Green
  Wokingham....65 F10
Gardenstown Aberds....303 C7
Garden Village Swansea....56 B5
  S Yorks....186 B3
  Wrex....166 E4
  W Yorks....206 G4
Garderhouse Shetland....313 J5
Gardham E Yorks....208 E5
Gardie Shetland....312 D7
Gardin Shetland....312 G6
  Shetland....312 G6
Gare Hill Som....45 E9
Garelochhead Argyll....276 C4
Garford Oxon....82 E6
Garforth W Yorks....206 G4
Gargrave N Yorks....204 C4
Gargunnock Stirl....278 C4
Garizim Conwy....179 F11
Garker Corn....5 E10
Garlandhayes Devon....27 D11
Garlands Cumb....239 G10
Garleffin S Ayrs....244 G3
Garlic Street Norf....142 G4
Garliford Devon....26 B3
Garlieston Dumfries....236 E6
Garlinge Kent....71 F10
Garlinge Green Kent....54 C6
Garlogie Aberds....293 C9
Garmelow Staffs....150 D5
Garmond Aberds....303 D8
Garmondsway Durham....234 E2
Garmony Argyll....289 E8
Garmouth Moray....302 C3
Garmston Shrops....132 B2
Garn Powys....130 G2
Garnant Carms....75 C11
Garndiffaith Torf....78 D4
Garndolbenmaen Gwyn....163 G7
Garnedd Conwy....164 E2
Garnett Bridge Cumb....221 F10
Garnetts Essex....87 B10
Garnfadryn Gwyn....144 C5
Garnkirk N Lnrk....268 B3
Garnlydan Bl Gwent....77 C11
Garnswllt Swansea....75 D10
Garn-swllt Swansea....75 D10
Garn-yr-erw Torf....78 C2
Garrabost W Isles....304 E7
Garrachra Argyll....275 E11
Garra Eallabus Argyll....274 F3
Garralburn Moray....302 D4
Garraron Argyll....275 C9
Garras Corn....2 E6
Garreg Flint....181 E10
  Gwyn....163 G10
Garrets Green W Mid....134 F2
Garrick Perth....286 F2
Garrigill Cumb....231 C10
Garriston N Yorks....224 G3
Garroch Dumfries....246 G3
Garrogie Lodge Highld....291 B7
Garros Highld....298 C4
Garrow Perth....286 C2
Garrowhill Glasgow....268 C3
Garryaloch Highld....290 C3
Garryhorn Dumfries....246 E2
Garsdale Cumb....212 B4
Garsdale Head Cumb....222 G5
Garsdon Wilts....62 B3
Garshall Green Staffs....151 C9
Garsington Oxon....83 E9
Garstang Lancs....202 D5
Garston Herts....85 F10
  Mers....182 E6
Garswood Gtr Man....183 B9
Gartachoil Stirl....277 C10
Gartbreck Argyll....254 B3
Gartcosh N Lnrk....268 B3
Garth Bridgend....57 C11
  Ceredig....111 B11
  Flint....181 E10
  Gwyn....179 E9
  Newport....59 B9
  Perth....285 B11
  Powys....95 B9
  Powys....114 C5
Garth Row Cumb....221 F10
Garthamlock Glasgow....268 B3
Garthbrengy Powys....95 E10
Gartheli Ceredig....111 F11
Garthmyl Powys....130 D3
Garthorpe Leics....154 E6
  N Lincs....199 D11
Garth Owen Powys....130 E2
Garth Trevor Wrex....166 G3
Gartlea N Lnrk....268 C5
Gartloch Glasgow....268 B3

Gartly Aberds....302 F5
Gartmore Stirl....277 B10
Gartmore Ho Stirl....277 B10
Gartnagrenach Argyll....255 B8
Gartness N Lnrk....268 C5
  Stirl....277 D10
Garton E Yorks....209 G11
Garton-on-the-Wolds
  E Yorks....208 B5
Gartsherrie N Lnrk....268 B4
Gartur Stirl....277 B11
Gartymore Highld....311 H4
Garvald E Loth....281 G11
Garvamore Highld....291 D7
Garvard Argyll....274 D4
Garvault Hotel Highld....308 F7
Garve Highld....300 C3
Garvestone Norf....141 B10
Garvock Aberds....293 F9
  Invclyd....276 G5
Garvock Hill Fife....280 D2
Garway Hereford....97 G9
Garway Hill Hereford....97 F8
Gaskan Highld....289 B9
Gasper Wilts....45 G9
Gastard Wilts....61 F11
Gasthorpe Norf....141 G9
Gaston Green Essex....87 B7
Gatacre Park Shrops....132 F5
Gatcombe IoW....20 D5
Gateacre Mers....182 D6
Gate Burton Lincs....188 E4
Gateford Notts....187 E9
Gateford Common
  Notts....187 E9
Gateforth N Yorks....198 B5
Gatehead E Ayrs....257 B9
Gate Helmsley N Yorks....207 B9
Gatehouse Northumb....251 F7
Gatehouse of Fleet
  Dumfries....237 D8
Gatelawbridge
  Dumfries....247 D10
Gateley Norf....159 E9
Gatenby N Yorks....214 B6
Gatesgarth Cumb....220 B3
Gateshead T&W....243 E7
Gatesheath Ches W....167 C7
Gateside Aberds....293 B7
  Angus....287 C8
  Dumfries....248 E4
  E Renf....267 D9
  Fife....286 G5
  N Ayrs....267 E7
  Shetland....312 F4
Gatewen Wrex....166 E4
Gatherley Devon....12 E3
Gathurst Gtr Man....194 F4
Gatlas Newport....78 G4
Gatley Gtr Man....184 D4
Gatley End Cambs....104 C5
Gatton Sur....51 C9
Gattonside Borders....262 B2
Gatwick Airport W Sus....51 E9
Gaufron Powys....113 D9
Gaulby Leics....136 C3
Gauldry Fife....287 E7
Gauntons Bank Ches E....167 F9
Gaunt's Common Dorset....31 F8
Gaunt's Earthcott S Glos....60 C6
Gaunt's End Essex....105 F10
Gautby Lincs....189 G11
Gavinton Borders....272 E5
Gawber S Yorks....197 F10
Gawcott Bucks....102 E3
Gawsworth Ches E....168 B5
Gawthorpe W Yorks....197 C9
Gawthrop Cumb....212 B3
Gawthwaite Cumb....210 C5
Gay Bowers Essex....88 E3
Gaydon Warks....119 G7
Gayfield Orkney....314 A4
Gayhurst M Keynes....103 B7
Gayle N Yorks....213 B7
Gayles N Yorks....224 D2
Gay Street W Sus....35 C9
Gayton Mers....182 E3
  Norf....158 F4
  Northants....120 G4
  Staffs....151 D9
Gayton Engine Lincs....191 D7
Gayton le Marsh Lincs....190 D2
Gayton le Wold Lincs....190 D2
Gayton Thorpe Norf....158 F4
Gaywood Norf....158 E2
Gazeley Suff....124 E4
Geanies House Highld....301 B8
Gearraidh Bhailteas
  W Isles....297 J3
Gearraidh Bhaird
  W Isles....304 F5
Gearraidh Dubh W Isles....296 F4
Gearraidh na h-Aibhne
  W Isles....304 E4
Gearraidh na Monadh
  W Isles....297 K3
Gearraidh Sheilidh
  W Isles....297 J3
Geary Highld....298 C2
Geat Wolford Warks....100 E4
Geddes House Highld....301 D8
Gedding Suff....125 F9
Geddington Northants....137 G7
Gedgrave Hall Suff....109 B8
Gedintailor Highld....295 B7
Gedling Notts....171 G10
Gedney Lincs....157 E8
Gedney Broadgate Lincs....157 E8
Gedney Drove End
  Lincs....157 D9
Gedney Dyke Lincs....157 D9
Gedney Hill Lincs....156 G6
Gee Cross Gtr Man....185 C7
Geeston Rutland....137 C7
Gegin Wrex....166 E3
Geilston Argyll....276 F6
Geinas Denb....165 B9
Geirinis W Isles....297 G3
Geise Highld....310 C5
Geisiadar W Isles....304 E3
Geldeston Norf....143 E7
Gell Conwy....164 B5
Gelli Pembs....73 B9
  Rhondda....77 G7
Gellideg M Tydf....77 D8
Gellifor Denb....165 C10
Gelligaer Caerph....77 F10
Gelligaer Neath....57 C9
Gelligroes Caerph....77 G11
Gelligron Neath....76 E2
Gellilydan Gwyn....146 B3
Gellinudd Neath....76 E2
Gellyburn Perth....286 D4
Gellywen Carms....92 G5

Gelsmoor Leics....153 F8
Gelston Dumfries....237 D9
  Lincs....172 G6
Gembling E Yorks....209 B8
Gemini Warr....183 C9
Gendros Swansea....56 B6
Genesis Green Suff....124 F4
Georgefield Dumfries....249 E7
Georgeham Devon....40 F3
George Nympton Devon....26 C2
Georgetown Bl Gwent....77 D10
Georgia Corn....1 B5
Gergask Highld....291 D8
Gerlan Gwyn....163 B10
Germansweek Devon....12 C4
Germiston Glasgow....268 B2
Gernon Bushes Essex....87 E7
Gerrans Corn....3 B9
Gerrard's Bromley
  Staffs....150 C5
Gerrards Cross Bucks....66 B4
Gerrick Redcar....226 C4
Geseilfa Powys....129 E8
Gestingthorpe Essex....106 D6
Gesto Ho Highld....294 B5
Geuffordd Powys....148 G4
Geufron Powys....129 F7
Gibbet Hill Warks....135 G10
  W Mid....118 C6
Gibb Hill Ches W....183 F10
Gibbshill Dumfries....237 B9
Gib Heath W Mid....133 F11
Gibraltar Beds....103 B10
  Bucks....84 C3
  Kent....55 F8
  Lincs....175 D8
  Oxon....83 B7
Gibshill Invclyd....276 G6
Giddeahall Wilts....61 E11
Giddy Green Dorset....18 D2
Gidea Park London....68 B4
Gidleigh Devon....13 D9
Giffard Park M Keynes....103 C7
Giffnock E Renf....267 D11
Gifford E Loth....271 B10
Giffordland N Ayrs....266 F5
Giffordtown Fife....286 F6
Gigg Gtr Man....195 F10
Giggetty Staffs....133 E7
Giggleswick N Yorks....212 G6
Gignog Pembs....91 G7
Gilberdyke E Yorks....199 B10
Gilbert's Coombe Corn....4 G3
Gilbert's End Worcs....98 C6
Gilbert's Green Warks....118 C2
Gilberstone W Mid....134 G2
Gilbert Street Hants....49 G7
Gilchriston E Loth....271 B9
Gilcrux Cumb....229 D8
Gildersome W Yorks....197 B8
Gildersome Street
  W Yorks....197 B8
Gildingwells S Yorks....187 D9
Gilesgate Durham....233 C11
Gilesgate Moor
  Durham....233 C11
Gileston V Glam....58 F4
Gilfach Caerph....77 F11
  Hereford....96 E6
Gilfach Goch Rhondda....58 B3
Gilfachrheda Ceredig....111 F8
Gilgarran Cumb....228 G6
Gill N Yorks....204 E5
Gillamoor N Yorks....216 B3
Gillan Corn....3 E7
Gillar's Green Mers....183 B7
Gillbank Cumb....221 F7
Gillbent Gtr Man....184 E5
Gillen Highld....298 D2
Gillesbie Dumfries....248 E5
Gilling East N Yorks....216 D2
Gillingham Dorset....30 B4
  Medway....69 F9
  Norf....143 E8
Gilling West N Yorks....224 D3
Gillmoss Mers....182 B6
Gillock Highld....310 D6
Gillow Heath Staffs....168 D5
Gills Highld....310 B7
Gill's Green Kent....53 B10
Gillway Staffs....134 C4
Gilmanscleuch Borders....261 E8
Gilmerton Edin....270 B5
  Perth....286 E2
Gilmonby Durham....223 C9
Gilmorton Leics....135 F11
Gilmourton S Lnrk....268 G4
Gilnow Gtr Man....195 F8
Gilroyd S Yorks....197 G10
Gilsland Northumb....240 D4
Gilsland Spa Cumb....240 D4
Gilson Warks....134 E3
Gilstead W Yorks....205 F8
Gilston Borders....271 D8
  Herts....86 C6
Gilwern Mon....78 C2
Gimingham Norf....160 B5
Giosla W Isles....304 F3
Gipping Suff....125 E11
Gipsey Bridge Lincs....174 E3
Gipsy Row Suff....107 D11
Gipsyville Hull....200 B5
Girdle Toll N Ayrs....266 G6
Girlington W Yorks....205 G8
Girlsta Shetland....313 H6
Girsby N Yorks....225 D7
Girt Som....29 C10
Girthon Dumfries....237 D8
Girton Cambs....123 E8
  Notts....172 B4
Girvan S Ayrs....244 D5
Gisburn Lancs....204 D2
Gisleham Suff....143 F10
Gislingham Suff....125 C11
Gissing Norf....142 F3
Gittisham Devon....27 G10
Givons Grove Sur....51 C7
Glack of Midthird Moray....302 E3
Gladestry Powys....114 F4
Gladsmuir E Loth....281 G10
Glais Swansea....76 E2
Glaisdale N Yorks....226 D5

Glame Highld....298 E5
Glamis Angus....287 C7
Glanaber Terrace
  Highld....309 J4
Glancat Highld....293 D7
Glan Adda Gwyn....179 G9
Glanafon Pembs....73 B7
Glanaman Carms....75 C11
Glan-Conwy Conwy....164 E4
Glandford Norf....177 E7
Glandwr Caerph....77 E11
  Pembs....92 F3
Glan-Duar Carms....93 C10
Glandy Cross Carms....92 F2
Glandyfi Ceredig....128 D3
Glan Gors Carms....179 F7
Glangrwyney Powys....78 B2
Glanhanog Powys....129 D8
Glanmule Powys....130 E3
Glanrafon Ceredig....128 G2
Glanrhyd Gwyn....144 B5
  Pembs....92 C2
Glan-rhyd Gwyn....163 D7
  Powys....76 D3
Glantlees Northumb....252 B4
Glanton Northumb....264 G3
Glanton Pike Northumb....264 G3
Glan-traeth Anglesey....178 F3
Glantwymyn / Cemmaes
  Road Powys....128 C2
Glanvilles Wootton
  Dorset....29 F11
Glanwern Ceredig....128 F2
Glanwydden Conwy....180 E4
Glan-y-don Flint....181 F11
Glan y Ffer / Ferryside
  Carms....74 C5
Glan-y-llyn Rhondda....58 C6
Glan-y-môr Carms....74 E5
Glan-y-nant Caerph....77 F10
  Powys....129 G8
Glan-yr-afon Anglesey....179 E11
  Flint....181 E10
  Gwyn....164 G6
  Gwyn....165 G8
  Shrops....148 E4
Glan-y-wern Gwyn....146 C2
Glapthorn Northants....137 E10
Glapwell Derbys....171 B7
Glas-allt Shiel Aberds....292 E4
Glasbury Powys....96 D3
Glaschoil Highld....301 F10
Glascoed Denb....181 G7
  Mon....78 E5
  Powys....148 G2
  Wrex....166 E3
Glascorrie Aberds....292 D5
  Perth....286 E2
Glascote Staffs....134 C4
Glascwm Powys....114 G3
Glasdir Flint....181 E10
Glasdrum Argyll....284 C4
Glasfryn Conwy....164 E6
Glasgoed Ceredig....92 B6
Glasgoforest Aberds....293 B10
Glasgow Glasgow....267 B11
Glashvin Highld....298 C4
Glasinfryn Gwyn....163 B9
Glaslaw Aberds....293 E10
Glasllwch Newport....59 B9
Glasnacardoch Highld....295 F8
Glasnakille Highld....295 D7
Glasphein Highld....297 D7
Glaspwll Powys....128 D4
Glassburn Highld....300 F3
Glassenbury Kent....53 F8
Glasserton Dumfries....236 F6
Glassford S Lnrk....268 F4
Glassgreen Moray....302 C2
Glass Houghton
  W Yorks....198 C2
Glasshouse Glos....98 G4
Glasshouse Hill Glos....98 G4
Glasshouses N Yorks....214 F3
Glasslie Fife....286 G6
Glasson Cumb....239 E7
  Lancs....202 B4
Glassonby Cumb....231 D7
Glasterlaw Angus....287 B9
Glaston Rutland....137 C7
Glastonbury Som....44 F4
Glatton Cambs....138 F3
Glazebrook Warr....183 C11
Glazebury Warr....183 B11
Glazeley Shrops....132 F4
Gleadless S Yorks....186 E5
Gleadless Valley
  S Yorks....186 E5
Gleadsmoss Ches E....168 B4
Gleann Tholàstaidh
  W Isles....304 D7
Gleaston Cumb....210 E5
Glebe Hants....33 D9
  Shetland....313 J6
  T&W....243 F8
Glecknabae Argyll....275 G11
Gledhow W Yorks....206 F2
Gledrid Shrops....148 B5
Gleiniant Powys....129 E9
Glemsford Suff....106 B6
Glen Dumfries....237 D10
  Dumfries....237 D7
Glenald Argyll....276 C4
Glenamachrie Argyll....289 G11
Glen Auldyn IoM....192 C5
Glenbarr Argyll....255 D7
Glenbeg Highld....289 C8
  Highld....301 G10
Glenbernisdale Highld....298 E4
Glenbervie Aberds....293 E9
  Falk....279 E7
Glenboig N Lnrk....268 B5
Glenborrodale Highld....289 C8
Glenbranter Argyll....276 B2
Glenbreck Borders....260 D3
Glenbrein Lodge Highld....290 B6
Glenbrittle House
  Highld....294 C6
Glenbuchat Castle
  Aberds....292 B5
Glenbuchat Lodge
  Aberds....292 B5
Glenbuck E Ayrs....259 D7
Glenburn Renfs....267 C9
Glenbyre Argyll....289 G7
Glencalvie Lodge
  Highld....309 L4
Glencanisp Lodge
  Highld....307 G4
Glencaple Dumfries....237 C11
Glencarron Lodge
  Highld....299 D10
Glencarse Perth....286 E5

Glencassley Castle
  Highld....309 J4
Glencat Aberds....293 D7
Glenceitlein Highld....284 C5
Glencoe Highld....284 B4
Glencraig Fife....280 B3
Glencripesdale Highld....289 D8
Glencrosh Dumfries....247 F7
Glendavan Ho Aberds....292 C6
Glendearg Borders....262 B2
Glendevon Perth....286 G3
Glendoebeg Highld....290 C6
Glendoe Lodge Highld....290 C6
Glendoick Perth....286 E6
Glendoll Lodge Angus....292 F4
Glendoune S Ayrs....244 D5
Glenduckie Fife....286 F6
Glendye Lodge Aberds....293 E8
Gleneagles Hotel Perth....286 F3
Gleneagles House Perth....286 G3
Glenearn Perth....286 F5
Glenegedale Argyll....254 B4
Glenelg Highld....295 D10
Glenernie Moray....301 E10
Glenfarg Perth....286 F5
Glenfarquhar Lodge
  Aberds....293 E9
Glenferness House
  Highld....301 E9
Glenfeshie Lodge
  Highld....291 D10
Glenfield Leics....135 B10
Glenfinnan Highld....295 G10
Glenfinnan Lodge
  Highld....295 G11
Glenfoot Perth....286 F5
Glenfyne Lodge Argyll....284 F6
Glengap Dumfries....237 D8
Glengarnock N Ayrs....266 E6
Glengolly Highld....310 C5
Glengorm Castle Argyll....288 D6
Glengoulandie Perth....285 B11
Glengrasco Highld....298 E4
Glenhead Farm Angus....292 G4
Glen Ho Borders....261 C7
Glenhoul Plym....7 C10
Glenhurich Highld....289 C10
Glenkerry Borders....261 G7
Glenkiln Dumfries....237 B10
Glenkindie Aberds....292 B6
Glenlair Dumfries....237 B9
Glenlatterach Moray....301 D11
Glenlee Dumfries....246 G4
Glenleigh Park E Sus....38 F2
Glenleraig Highld....306 F6
Glenlichorn Perth....285 F11
Glenlivet Moray....301 G11
Glenlochar Dumfries....237 C9
Glenlochsie Perth....292 F2
Glenlocksie Lodge
  Perth....292 F2
Glenloig N Ayrs....255 D10
Glenlomond Perth....286 G5
Glenluce Dumfries....236 D3
Glenlussa Ho Argyll....255 E8
Glenmallan Argyll....276 B5
Glenmark Angus....292 E6
Glenmarkie Lodge
  Angus....292 G4
Glenmarksie Highld....300 D3
Glenmassan Argyll....276 B2
Glenmavis N Lnrk....268 B5
Glenmaye IoM....192 E3
Glenmeanie Highld....300 D2
Glenmidge Dumfries....247 F10
Glenmoidart Ho Highld....289 B9
Glen Mona IoM....192 D5
Glen Mor Highld....301 B10
Glenmore Argyll....275 C10
  Highld....298 E4
Glenmore Lodge
  Highld....291 C11
Glenmoy Angus....292 G6
Glen Nevis House Highld....290 F3
Glennoe Argyll....284 D4
Glen of Newmill Moray....302 D4
Glenogil Angus....292 G6
Glenowen Pembs....73 D7
Glen Parva Leics....135 D11
Glenprosen Lodge
  Angus....292 G4
Glenprosen Village
  Angus....292 G5
Glenquaich Lodge
  Perth....286 D2
Glenquiech Angus....292 G6
Glenquithie Aberds....303 C8
Glenrath Borders....260 C6
Glenrazie Dumfries....236 C5
Glenreasdell Mains
  Argyll....255 B9
Glenree N Ayrs....255 E10
Glenridding Cumb....221 B7
Glenrossal Highld....309 J4
Glenrothes Fife....286 G6
Glensanda Highld....289 E10
Glensaugh Aberds....293 F8
Glensgaich Highld....300 C5
Glenshero Lodge Highld....290 D6
Glenshoe Lodge Perth....292 G3
Glen Sluain Argyll....275 D11
Glenstockadale
  Dumfries....236 C2
Glenstriven Argyll....275 F11
Glentaggart S Lnrk....259 D8
Glen Tanar House
  Aberds....292 D6
Glentarkie Perth....286 F5
Glenternie Borders....260 B6
Glentham Lincs....189 C7
Glentirranmuir Stirl....278 C3
Glenton Aberds....302 G6
Glentress Borders....261 B7
Glentromie Lodge
  Highld....291 D9
Glen Trool Lodge
  Dumfries....245 G10
Glentrool Village
  Dumfries....236 B5
Glentruan IoM....192 B5
Glentruim House Highld....291 D8
Glentworth Lincs....188 D6
Glenuig Highld....289 B8
Glenure Argyll....284 C4
Glenurquhart Highld....301 C7
Glen Vic Askill Highld....298 E3
Glen Village Falk....279 C7
Glen Vine IoM....192 E4
Glespin S Lnrk....259 D8
Gletness Shetland....313 H6
Glewstone Hereford....97 G11

Glinton Pboro....138 B3
Globe Town London....67 C11
Glodwick Gtr Man....196 G2
Glogue Pembs....92 E4
Glooston Leics....136 D4
Glororum Northumb....264 C5
Glossop Derbys....185 C8
Gloster Hill Northumb....253 C7
Gloucester Glos....80 B4
Gloup Shetland....312 C7
Gloweth Corn....4 G5
Glusburn N Yorks....204 E6
Glutt Lodge Highld....310 F3
Glutton Bridge Staffs....169 B8
Gluvian Corn....5 C8
Glympton Oxon....101 G8
Glyn Mon....79 F7
  Powys....129 F8
Glynarthen Ceredig....92 B6
Glynbrochan Powys....129 G8
Glyncoch Rhondda....77 G9
Glyncorrwg Neath....57 B11
Glyn-cywarch Gwyn....146 C2
Glynde E Sus....23 D7
Glyndebourne E Sus....23 C7
Glyndyfrdwy Denb....165 G10
Glynedd / Glyn neath
  Neath....76 D5
Glyn Etwg Bridgend....58 B3
Glyn-neath / Glynedd
  Neath....76 D5
Glynogwr Bridgend....58 B3
Glyntaff Rhondda....58 B5
Glyntawe Powys....76 C4
Gnosall Staffs....150 E6
Gnosall Heath Staffs....150 E6
Goadby Leics....136 D4
Goadby Marwood Leics....154 D5
Goatacre Wilts....62 D4
Goatham Green E Sus....38 C4
Goathill Dorset....29 D11
Goathland N Yorks....226 E6
Goathurst Som....43 G9
Goathurst Common
  Kent....52 C3
Goat Lees Kent....54 D4
Gobernuisgach Lodge
  Highld....308 E4
Gobernuisgeach Highld....310 F3
Gobhaig W Isles....305 H2
Gobley Hole Hants....48 D6
Gobowen Shrops....148 C6
Godalming Sur....50 E3
Goddards Bucks....84 G3
Goddard's Corner Suff....126 E5
Goddard's Green
  W Berks....64 G4
  W Sus....36 C3
Goddards' Green
  W Sus....36 C3
Godden Green Kent....52 B5
Goddington London....68 F3
Godford Cross Devon....27 G10
Godleybrook Staffs....169 G7
Godley Gtr Man....185 C7
Godley Hill Gtr Man....185 C7
Godmanchester
  Cambs....122 C4
Godmanstone Dorset....17 B9
Godmersham Kent....54 C5
Godney Som....44 E3
Godolphin Cross Corn....2 C4
Godre'r-graig Neath....76 D3
God's Blessing Green
  Dorset....31 G8
Godshill Hants....31 E11
  IoW....20 E6
Godstone Sur....51 C10
Godswinscroft Hants....19 B9
Godwell Devon....8 D2
Godwinscroft Hants....19 B9
Goetre Mon....78 D4
Goferydd Anglesey....178 E2
Goff's Oak Herts....86 E4
Gogar Edin....280 G3
Goginan Ceredig....128 G3
Goirtean a'Chladaich
  Highld....290 F2
Goirtein Argyll....275 E10
Golan Gwyn....163 G8
Golant Corn....6 E2
Golberdon Corn....12 G2
Golborne Gtr Man....183 B10
Golcar W Yorks....196 D6
Goldcliff Newport....59 C11
Golden Balls Oxon....83 F9
Golden Cross E Sus....23 C8
Golden Green Kent....52 D6
Golden Grove Carms....75 C9
Goldenhill Stoke....168 E5
Golden Hill Bristol....60 D5
  Hants....19 B11
  Pembs....73 E7
Golden Park Devon....24 C2
Golden Pot Hants....49 E8
Golden Valley Derbys....170 E6
  Glos....99 G8
  Hereford....97 D7
Golder Field Hereford....115 E11
Golders Green London....67 B9
Goldfinch Bottom
  W Berks....64 G4
Goldhanger Essex....88 D5
Gold Hill Dorset....30 E4
  Cambs....139 D9
Golding Shrops....131 C10
Goldington Beds....121 G11
Goldsborough N Yorks....206 B3
  N Yorks....226 B5
Gold's Cross Bath....60 G5
Goldsithney Corn....2 C3
Goldstone Kent....55 B10
  Shrops....150 D4
Goldthorn Park W Mid....133 D8
Goldthorpe S Yorks....198 G2
Goldworthy Devon....24 C5
Golford Kent....53 F9
Golftyn Flint....182 G3
Gollawater Corn....4 E5
Gollinglith Foot
  N Yorks....214 C3
Golly Wrex....166 D4
Golsoncott Som....42 F4
Golspie Highld....311 J2
Golval Highld....310 C2
Golynos Torf....78 E3
Gomeldon Wilts....47 F7
Gomersal W Yorks....197 B8
Gometra Ho Argyll....288 E5
Gomshall Sur....50 D6
Gonachan Cottage
  Stirl....278 D3
Gonalston Notts....171 F11
Gonamena Corn....11 G11
Gonerby Hill Foot Lincs....155 B8

Gonfirth Shetland....313 G5
Good Easter Essex....87 C10
Gooderstone Norf....140 C5
Goodleigh Devon....40 G6
Goodley Stock Kent....52 C2
Goodmanham E Yorks....208 E4
Goodmayes London....68 B3
Goodnestone Kent....55 C9
  Kent....70 G4
Goodrich Hereford....79 B9
Goodrington Torbay....9 D7
Good's Green Worcs....132 G5
Goodshaw Lancs....195 B10
Goodshaw Chapel
  Lancs....195 B10
Goodshaw Fold Lancs....195 B10
Goodstone Devon....13 G11
Goodwick / Wdig Pembs....91 D8
Goodworth Clatford
  Hants....47 E11
Goodyers End Warks....134 F6
Goodyhills Cumb....229 B8
Goole E Yorks....199 C8
Goom's Hill Worcs....117 G10
Goonabarn Corn....5 E9
Goonbell Corn....4 E4
Goon Gumpas Corn....4 F4
Goonhavern Corn....4 E5
Goonhusband Corn....2 D5
Goonlaze Corn....2 B6
Goonown Corn....4 E4
Goonpiper Corn....3 B8
Goonvrea Corn....4 E4
Gooseberry Green
  Essex....87 F11
Goose Eye W Yorks....204 E6
Gooseford Devon....13 C9
Goose Green Cumb....211 C10
  Gtr Man....194 G5
  Hants....32 F4
  Herts....86 D5
  Kent....52 C6
  Kent....53 F10
  Lancs....194 C3
  Norf....142 F2
  S Glos....61 C8
  W Sus....35 D10
Gooseham Mill Devon....24 D2
Goosehill W Yorks....197 C11
Goose Hill Hants....64 G4
Goosehill Green Worcs....117 E8
Goosemoor Staffs....150 F6
Goosemoor Green
  Staffs....151 G11
Goosenford Som....28 B2
Goosewell Devon....13 C9
Goosey Oxon....82 G5
Goosnargh Lancs....203 F7
Goostrey Ches E....184 G3
Gorbals Glasgow....267 C11
Gorcott Hill Warks....117 D11
Gord Shetland....313 L6
Gordding Conwy....179 G11
Gordon Borders....272 G2
Gordonbush Highld....311 J2
Gordonsburgh Moray....302 C4
Gordonstoun Moray....301 C11
Gordonstown
  Aberds....302 D5
  Aberds....303 F7
Gore Dorset....29 D9
  Kent....55 B10
Gorebridge Midloth....270 C6
Gore Cross Wilts....46 C4
Gore End Hants....64 G2
Gorefield Cambs....157 G8
Gorehill W Sus....35 C7
Gore Pit Essex....88 B5
Gore Street Kent....71 F9
Gorgie Edin....280 G4
Gorhambury Herts....85 D10
Goring Oxon....64 C6
Goring-by-Sea W Sus....35 G10
Goring Heath Oxon....65 D7
Gorleston-on-Sea
  Norf....143 C10
Gornalwood W Mid....133 E8
Gorrachie Aberds....303 D7
Gorran Churchtown Corn....5 G9
Gorran Haven Corn....5 G10
Gorran High Lanes Corn....5 G9
Gorrenberry Borders....249 D11
Gorrig Ceredig....93 C8
Gorsedd Flint....181 F11
Gorse Hill Gtr Man....184 B4
  Swindon....63 B7
Gorseinon Swansea....56 B5
Gorseness Orkney....314 E4
Gorsethorpe Notts....171 B9
Gorseybank Derbys....170 E3
Gorsgoch Ceredig....111 G9
Gorslas Carms....75 C9
Gorsley Glos....98 F3
Gorsley Common
  Hereford....98 F3
Gorsley Ley Staffs....133 B11
Gorstage Ches W....183 G10
Gorstan Highld....300 C3
Gorstanvorran Highld....289 B10
Gorsty Common Hereford....97 D8
Gorstyhill Ches E....168 E3
Gorsty Hill Staffs....152 D3
Gortan Argyll....274 G3
Gortantaoid Argyll....274 F4
Gortenacullish Highld....295 G8
Gorteneorn Highld....289 C8
Gortenfern Highld....289 C8
Gortinanane Argyll....255 C8
Gorton Gtr Man....184 B5
Gortonallister N Ayrs....256 D2
Gosbeck Suff....126 F3
Gosberton Lincs....156 B4
Gosberton Cheal Lincs....156 C4
Gosberton Clough Lincs....156 D3
Goseley Dale Derbys....152 D6
Gosfield Essex....106 F5
Gosford Hereford....115 D10
  Oxon....83 C7
Gosford Green W Mid....118 B6
Gosforth Cumb....219 D11
  T&W....242 D6
Gosland Green Suff....124 G3
Gosling Green Suff....107 C9
Gosmere Kent....54 B4
Gosmore Herts....104 F3
Gospel Ash Staffs....132 G6
Gospel End Village
  Staffs....133 E7
Gospel Green W Sus....50 G2
Gospel Oak London....67 B9
Gosport Hants....21 B8
  Hants....32 C5

Gossabrough Shetland 312 E7
Gossard's Green C Beds 103 C9
Gossington Glos 80 E2
Gossops Green W Sus 51 F9
Goswick Northumb 273 F11
Gotham Dorset 31 E9
 E Sus 38 F2
 Notts 153 C10
Gothelney Green Som 43 F9
Gotherington Glos 99 F9
Gothers Corn 5 D9
Gott Argyll 288 E2
 Shetland 313 J6
Gotton Som 28 B2
Goudhurst Kent 53 F8
Goukstone Moray 302 D4
Goulceby Lincs 190 F3
Goulton N Yorks 225 E9
Gourdas Aberds 303 E7
Gourdon Aberds 293 F10
Gourock Invclyd 276 F4
Govan Glasgow 267 B11
Govanhill Glasgow 267 C11
Gover Hill Kent 52 C6
Goverton Notts 172 E2
Goveton Devon 8 F5
Govilon Mon 78 C3
Gowanhill Aberds 303 C10
Gowanwell Aberds 303 E8
Gowdall E Yorks 198 C6
Gowerton / Tre-Gwyr
 Swansea 56 B5
Gowhole Derbys 185 E8
Gowkhall Fife 279 D11
Gowkthrapple N Lnrk 268 E5
Gowthorpe E Yorks 207 C11
Goxhill E Yorks 209 E9
 N Lincs 200 C6
Goxhill Haven N Lincs 200 B6
Goybre Neath 57 D9
Goytre Neath 57 D9
Gozzard's Ford Oxon 83 F7
Grabhair W Isles 305 G5
Graby Lincs 155 D11
Gracca Corn 5 D10
Gracemount Edin 270 B5
Grade Corn 2 G6
Graffham W Sus 34 D6
Grafham Cambs 122 D3
 Sur 50 E4
Grafton Hereford 97 D9
 N Yorks 215 G8
 Oxon 82 E3
 Shrops 149 F8
 Worcs 99 D9
 Worcs 115 E11
Grafton Flyford Worcs 117 F9
Grafton Regis Northants 102 B5
Grafton Underwood
 Northants 137 G8
Grafty Green Kent 53 D11
Grahamston Falk 279 E7
Graianrhyd Denb 166 D2
Graig Carms 74 E6
 Conwy 180 G4
 Denb 181 G9
 Rhondda 58 B5
 Wrex 148 B4
Graig-Fawr Swansea 75 E10
Graig-fechan Denb 165 E10
Graig Felen Swansea 75 E11
Graig Penllyn V Glam 58 D3
Graig Trewyddfa Swansea 57 B7
Grain Medway 69 D11
Grains Bar Gtr Man 196 F3
Grainsby Lincs 190 B3
Grainthorpe Lincs 190 B5
Grainthorpe Fen Lincs 190 B5
Graiselound N Lincs 188 B3
Grampound Corn 5 F8
Grampound Road Corn 5 E8
Gramsdal W Isles 296 F4
Granborough Bucks 102 F5
Granby Notts 154 B5
Grandborough Warks 119 D9
Grandpont Oxon 83 D8
Grandtully Perth 286 B3
Grange Cumb 220 B5
 Dorset 31 G8
 E Ayrs 257 B10
 Fife 287 G8
 Halton 183 E8
 Lancs 203 G7
 Medway 69 F9
 Mers 182 D2
 NE Lincs 201 F9
 N Yorks 223 G8
 Perth 286 E6
 Warr 183 C10
Grange Crossroads
 Moray 302 D4
Grange Estate Dorset 31 G10
Grange Hall Moray 301 C10
Grange Hill Durham 233 F10
 Essex 86 G6
Grangemill Derbys 170 D2
Grange Moor W Yorks 197 D8
Grangemouth Falk 279 E8
Grangemuir Fife 287 G9
Grange of Cree
 Dumfries 236 D6
Grange of Lindores Fife 286 F6
Grange-over-Sands
 Cumb 211 D8
Grangepans Falk 279 E10
Grange Park London 86 F4
 Mers 183 C7
 Northants 120 F5
 Swindon 62 C6
Grangetown Cardiff 59 E7
 Redcar 235 G7
 T&W 243 G10
Grange Villa Durham 242 G6
Grange Village Glos 79 C11
Granish Highld 291 B11
Gransmoor E Yorks 209 B8
Gransmore Green
 Essex 106 G3
Granston / Treopert
 Pembs 91 E7
Grantchester Cambs 123 F8
Grantham Lincs 155 B8
Grantley N Yorks 214 F4
Grantley Hall N Yorks 214 F4
Grantlodge Aberds 293 B9
Granton Dumfries 248 B3
 Edin 280 F4
Grantown Aberds 302 D5
Grantown-on-Spey
 Highld 301 G10
Grantsfield Hereford 115 E10
Grantshouse Borders 272 B6
Grant Thorold NE Lincs 201 F9
Graplin Dumfries 237 E8
Grappenhall Warr 183 D10
Grasby Lincs 200 G5
Grasmere Cumb 220 D6
Grasscroft Gtr Man 196 G3
Grassendale Mers 182 D5
Grassgarth Cumb 221 F8
 Cumb 230 C2
Grass Green Essex 106 D4
Grassholme Durham 232 G4
Grassington N Yorks 213 G10
Grassmoor Derbys 170 B6
Grassthorpe Notts 172 B3
Grasswell T&W 243 G8
Grateley Hants 47 E9
Gratton Devon 24 E5
Gratwich Staffs 151 C10
Gravel Ches W 167 B11
Gravel Castle Kent 55 D8
Graveley Cambs 122 E4
 Herts 104 F4
Gravelhill Shrops 149 G9
Gravel Hill Bucks 85 G8
Gravel Hole Gtr Man 196 F2
 Shrops 149 B7
Gravelly Hill W Mid 134 E2
Gravels Shrops 130 D6
Gravelsbank Shrops 130 C6
Graven Shetland 312 F6
Graveney Kent 70 G5
Gravenhunger Moss
 Shrops 168 G2
Gravesend Herts 105 F8
 Kent 68 E6
Grayingham Lincs 188 B6
Grayrigg Cumb 221 F11
Grays Thurrock 68 D6
Grayshott Hants 49 F11
Grayson Green Cumb 228 F5
Grayswood Sur 50 G2
Graythorp Hrtlpl 234 F6
Grazeley Wokingham 65 F7
Grazeley Green W Berks 65 F7
Greagdhubh Lodge
 Highld 291 D8
Greamchary Highld 310 F2
Greasbrough S Yorks 186 B6
Greasby Mers 182 D3
Greasley Notts 171 F7
Great Abington Cambs 105 B10
Great Addington
 Northants 121 B9
Great Alne Warks 118 F2
Great Altcar Lancs 193 F10
Great Amwell Herts 86 C5
Great Asby Cumb 222 C3
Great Ashfield Suff 125 D9
Great Ashley Wilts 61 G10
Great Ayton N Yorks 225 C11
Great Baddow Essex 88 E2
Great Bardfield Essex 106 E3
Great Barford Beds 122 G2
Great Barrington Glos 82 C2
Great Barrow Ches W 167 B7
Great Barton Suff 125 D7
Great Barugh N Yorks 216 D4
Great Bavington
 Northumb 251 G11
Great Bealings Suff 108 B4
Great Bedwyn Wilts 63 G9
Great Bentley Essex 108 G2
Great Berry Essex 69 B7
Great Billing Northants 120 E6
Great Bircham Norf 158 C5
Great Blakenham Suff 126 G2
Great Blencow Cumb 230 E5
Great Bolas Telford 150 E2
Great Bookham Sur 50 C6
Great Bosullow Corn 1 C4
Great Bourton Oxon 101 B9
Great Bowden Leics 136 F4
Great Bower Kent 54 C4
Great Bradley Suff 124 G3
Great Braxted Essex 88 C5
Great Bricett Suff 125 G10
Great Brickhill Bucks 103 E8
Great Bridge W Mid 133 E9
Great Bridgeford Staffs 151 D7
Great Brington
 Northants 120 D3
Great Bromley Essex 107 F11
Great Broughton Cumb 229 E7
 N Yorks 225 D10
Great Buckland Kent 69 G7
Great Budworth
 Ches W 183 F11
Great Burdon Darl 224 B6
Great Burgh Sur 51 B8
Great Burstead Essex 87 G11
Great Busby N Yorks 225 D10
Great Canfield Essex 87 B9
Great Carlton Lincs 190 D6
Great Casterton Rutland 137 B9
 Rutland 137 B10
Great Cellws Powys 113 E11
Great Chalfield Wilts 61 G11
Great Chart Kent 54 E3
Great Chatwell Staffs 150 G5
Great Chell Stoke 168 E5
Great Chesterford
 Essex 105 C10
Great Cheveney Kent 53 E8
Great Cheverell Wilts 46 C3
Great Chilton Durham 233 E11
Great Chishill Cambs 105 D8
Great Clacton Essex 89 B11
Great Claydons Essex 88 E3
Great Cliff W Yorks 197 D10
Great Clifton Cumb 228 F6
Great Coates NE Lincs 201 F8
Great Comberton Worcs 99 C9
Great Common Suff 143 F7
 W Sus 35 B8
Great Corby Cumb 239 G11
Great Cornard Suff 107 C7
Great Cowden E Yorks 209 E10
Great Coxwell Oxon 82 G3
Great Crakehall
 N Yorks 224 G4
Great Cransley
 Northants 120 B6
Great Cressingham
 Norf 141 C7
Great Crosby Mers 182 B4
Great Crosthwaite
 Cumb 229 G11
Great Cubley Derbys 152 B3
Great Dalby Leics 154 G4
Great Denham Beds 103 B10
Great Doddington
 Northants 121 E7
Great Doward Hereford 79 B9
Great Dunham Norf 159 G7
Great Dunmow Essex 106 G2
Great Durnford Wilts 46 F6
Great Easton Essex 106 F2
 Leics 136 E6
Great Eccleston Lancs 202 E4
Great Edstone N Yorks 216 C4
Great Ellingham Norf 141 D10
Great Elm Som 45 D8
Great Eppleton T&W 234 B3
Greater Doward Hereford 79 B9
Great Eversden Cambs 123 G7
Great Fencote N Yorks 224 G5
Greatfield Wilts 62 B5
Great Finborough Suff 125 F10
Greatford Lincs 155 G11
Great Fransham Norf 159 G7
Great Gaddesden Herts 85 C8
Greatgap Bucks 84 B6
Greatgate Staffs 169 G9
Great Gate Staffs 169 G9
Great Gidding Cambs 138 G2
Great Givendale
 E Yorks 208 C2
Great Glemham Suff 126 E6
Great Glen Leics 136 D3
Great Gonerby Lincs 155 B7
Great Gransden Cambs 122 F5
Great Green Cambs 104 C5
 Norf 142 F5
 Suff 125 B11
 Suff 125 F8
 Suff 126 B2
Great Habton N Yorks 216 D5
Great Hale Lincs 173 G10
Great Hallingbury Essex 87 B8
Greatham Hants 49 G9
 Hrtlpl 234 F5
 W Sus 35 D8
Great Hampden Bucks 84 E4
Great Harrowden
 Northants 121 C7
Great Harwood Lancs 203 G10
Great Haseley Oxon 83 E10
Great Hatfield E Yorks 209 E9
Great Haywood Staffs 151 E9
 Staffs 151 E10
Great Heath W Mid 134 G6
Great Heck N Yorks 198 C5
Great Henny Essex 107 D7
Great Hinton Wilts 46 B2
Great Hivings Bucks 85 E7
Great Hockham Norf 141 E9
Great Holcombe Oxon 83 F10
Great Holland Essex 89 B12
Great Hollands Brack 65 F11
Great Holm M Keynes 102 D6
Great Honeyborough
 Pembs 73 D7
Great Horkesley Essex 107 E9
Great Hormead Herts 105 F7
Great Horton W Yorks 205 G8
Great Horwood Bucks 102 E5
Great Houghton
 Northants 120 F5
 S Yorks 198 F2
Great Howarth Gtr Man 196 D2
Great Hucklow Derbys 185 F11
Great Job's Cross Kent 38 B4
Great Kelk E Yorks 209 B8
Great Kendale E Yorks 217 G10
Great Kimble Bucks 84 D4
Great Kingshill Bucks 84 F5
Great Langton N Yorks 224 F5
Great Lea Common
 Reading 65 F8
Great Leighs Essex 88 B2
Great Lever Gtr Man 195 F8
Great Limber Lincs 200 F6
Great Linford M Keynes 103 C7
Great Livermere Suff 125 C7
Great Longstone Derbys 186 G2
Great Lumley Durham 233 B11
Great Lyth Shrops 131 B9
Great Malgraves Thurrock 69 C7
Great Malvern Worcs 98 B5
Great Maplestead Essex 106 E6
Great Marton Blkpool 202 F2
Great Marton Moss
 Blkpool 202 G2
Great Massingham Norf 158 E5
Great Melton Norf 142 B2
Great Milton Oxon 83 E10
Great Missenden Bucks 84 E5
Great Mitton Lancs 203 F10
Great Mongeham Kent 55 C10
Greatmoor Bucks 102 G4
Great Moor Gtr Man 184 D6
 Staffs 132 D6
Great Moulton Norf 142 E3
Great Munden Herts 105 G7
Great Musgrave Cumb 222 C5
Greatness Kent 52 B4
Great Ness Shrops 149 F7
Great Notley Essex 106 G4
Great Oak Mon 78 D5
Great Oakley Essex 108 F3
 Northants 137 F7
Great Offley Herts 104 F2
Great Ormside Cumb 222 B4
Great Orton Cumb 239 G8
Great Ouseburn
 N Yorks 215 G8
Great Oxendon
 Northants 136 G4
Great Oxney Green
 Essex 87 D11
Great Palgrave Norf 158 G6
Great Parndon Essex 86 D6
Great Pattenden Kent 53 E8
Great Paxton Cambs 122 E4
Great Plumpton Lancs 202 G3
Great Plumstead Norf 160 G6
Great Ponton Lincs 155 C8
Great Preston W Yorks 198 B2
Great Purston
 Northants 101 D10
Great Raveley Cambs 138 G5
Great Rissington Glos 81 B11
Great Rollright Oxon 100 E6
Great Ryburgh Norf 159 D9
Great Ryle Northumb 264 G2
Great Ryton Shrops 131 C9
Great Saling Essex 106 F4
Great Salkeld Cumb 231 D7
Great Sampford Essex 106 D2
Great Sankey Warr 183 D9
Great Saredon Staffs 133 B9
Great Saxham Suff 124 E5
Great Shefford W Berks 63 E11
Great Shelford Cambs 123 G9
Great Shoddesden Hants 47 D9
Great Smeaton N Yorks 224 E6
Great Snoring Norf 159 C8
Great Somerford Wilts 62 C3
Great Stainton Darl 234 G2
Great Stambridge Essex 88 G5
Great Staughton Cambs 122 E2
Great Steeping Lincs 174 C6
Great Stoke S Glos 60 C6
Great Stonar Kent 55 B10
Greatstone-on-Sea Kent 39 C9
Great Stretton Leics 136 C3
Great Strickland Cumb 231 G7
Great Stukeley Cambs 122 C4
Great Sturton Lincs 190 F2
Great Sutton Ches W 182 F5
 Shrops 131 G10
Great Swinburne
 Northumb 241 B10
Great Tew Oxon 101 F7
Great Tey Essex 107 F7
Great Thirkleby N Yorks 215 D9
Great Thurlow Suff 124 G3
Great Torrington Devon 25 D7
Great Tosson Northumb 252 C2
Great Totham Essex 88 C5
Great Tows Lincs 190 C2
Great Tree Corn 6 D5
Great Urswick Cumb 210 E5
Great Wakering Essex 70 B2
Great Waldingfield Suff 107 C8
Great Walsingham Norf 159 B8
Great Waltham Essex 87 C11
Great Warley Essex 87 G9
Great Washbourne Glos 99 E9
Great Weeke Devon 13 D10
Great Weldon Northants 137 F8
Great Welnetham Suff 125 F7
Great Wenham Suff 107 D11
Great Whittington
 Northumb 242 C2
Great Wigborough Essex 89 C7
Great Wilbraham
 Cambs 123 F10
Great Wilne Derbys 153 C8
Great Wishford Wilts 46 F5
Great Witchingham
 Norf 160 E2
Great Witcombe Glos 80 C6
Great Witley Worcs 116 D5
Great Wolford Warks 100 E4
Greatworth Northants 101 C11
Great Wratting Suff 106 B3
Great Wymondley Herts 104 F4
Great Wyrley Staffs 133 B9
Great Wytheford
 Shrops 149 F11
Great Yarmouth Norf 143 B10
Great Yeldham Essex 106 D5
Greave Gtr Man 184 C6
 Lancs 195 C11
Grebby Lincs 174 B6
Greeba IoM 192 D4
Green Denb 165 B9
 Pembs 73 E7
 Powys 130 E5
Greenacres Gtr Man 196 F2
Greenan Argyll 275 G11
Greenbank Ches W 183 G10
 Falk 279 F7
 Shetland 312 C7
Green Bank Cumb 211 C7
Green Bottom Corn 4 F5
 Glos 79 B11
Greenburn W Loth 269 C8
Green Close N Yorks 212 F4
Green Clough W Yorks 205 G7
Green Crize Hereford 97 D10
Greencroft Durham 242 G5
Green Cross Sur 49 F11
Greendale Ches E 184 F5
Greendikes Northumb 264 D3
Greendown Som 44 C5
Green Down Devon 28 G3
Greendykes Northumb 264 D3
Greenend N Lnrk 268 C4
 Oxon 100 G6
Green End Beds 103 B10
 Beds 121 E11
 Beds 122 E2
 Beds 122 G2
 Bucks 84 F4
 Bucks 103 E8
 Cambs 122 C4
 Cambs 123 F7
 C Beds 103 D11
 Herts 85 D8
 Herts 104 E5
 Herts 104 E6
 Herts 104 G6
 Herts 105 F7
 Lancs 204 D4
 N Yorks 226 E6
 Warks 134 F5
Greenfaulds N Lnrk 278 G5
Greenfield C Beds 103 E11
 Glasgow 268 C2
 Gtr Man 196 G3
 Highld 289 D11
 Highld 290 C4
 Oxon 84 G2
Greenfield / Maes-Glas
 Flint 181 F11
Greenfoot N Lnrk 268 B4
Greenford London 66 C6
Greengairs N Lnrk 278 G5
Greengarth Hall Cumb 219 E11
Greengate Gtr Man 196 D2
 Norf 159 F10
Green Gate Devon 27 D8
Greengates W Yorks 205 F9
Greengill Cumb 229 D8
Green Hailey Bucks 84 E4
Greenhalgh Lancs 202 F4
Greenhall S Lnrk 268 D3
Greenham Dorset 28 G6
 Som 27 C9
 W Berks 64 F3
Green Hammerton
 N Yorks 206 B5
Greenhaugh Northumb 251 F7
Green Haworth Lancs 195 B9
Greenhead Borders 261 D11
 Dumfries 247 D9
 N Lnrk 268 E6
 Northumb 240 D5
 Staffs 169 F7
Green Head Cumb 230 B3
Green Heath Staffs 151 G9
Greenheys Gtr Man 195 G8
Greenhill Dumfries 238 B4
 Durham 234 B3
 Falk 278 F6
 Hereford 98 B4
 Kent 71 F7
 Leics 153 G8
 London 67 B7
 S Yorks 186 E4
 Worcs 99 B10
 Worcs 116 B6
Green Hill Kent 53 C9
 Lincs 155 B8
 Wilts 62 B5
 W Yorks 206 F4
Greenhill Bank Shrops 149 B7
Greenhillocks Derbys 170 F6
Greenhills N Ayrs 267 E7
 S Lnrk 268 E2
Greenhithe Kent 68 E5
Greenholm E Ayrs 258 B2
Greenholme Cumb 221 D11
Greenhouse Borders 262 E3
Greenhow N Yorks 214 G2
Greenhow Hill N Yorks 214 G2
Greenigoe Orkney 314 F4
Greenland Highld 310 C6
 S Yorks 186 D5
Greenland Mains Highld 310 C6
Greenlands Bucks 65 B9
 Worcs 117 D11
Green Lane Devon 13 F11
 Hereford 98 B2
 Powys 130 E3
 Warks 117 E11
 Warks 118 B6
Greenlaw Aberds 302 D6
 Borders 272 F4
Greenlaw Mains Midloth 270 C4
Greenlea Dumfries 238 B2
Greenley M Keynes 102 C6
Greenloaning Perth 286 G2
Greenlooms Ches W 167 C7
Greenman's Lane Wilts 62 C3
Greenmeadow Swindon 62 B6
 Torf 78 F3
Green Moor S Yorks 186 B3
Greenmount Gtr Man 195 E9
Greenmow Shetland 313 L6
Greenoak E Yorks 199 B10
Greenock Invclyd 276 F5
Greenock West Invclyd 276 F5
Greenodd Cumb 210 C6
Green Ore Som 44 C5
Green Parlour Bath 45 C8
Green Quarter Cumb 221 E9
Greenrigg W Loth 269 C8
Greenrow Cumb 238 G4
Greens Borders 249 F11
Green St Green London 68 G3
Greensforge Staffs 133 F7
Greensgate Norf 160 F2
Greenside Cumb 222 E4
 Derbys 186 F5
 Gtr Man 184 B6
 T&W 242 E4
 W Yorks 197 D7
Green Side W Yorks 197 E7
 W Yorks 205 G11
Greensidehill Northumb 263 F11
Greens Norton
 Northants 102 B3
Greensplat Corn 5 D9
Greenstead Essex 107 F10
Greenstead Green Essex 106 F6
Greensted Essex 87 E8
Greensted Green Essex 87 E8
Green Street Essex 87 F10
 E Sus 38 E3
 Glos 80 B5
 Glos 80 E3
 Herts 85 F11
 Herts 105 G9
 Worcs 99 B7
 Worcs 99 C7
 W Sus 35 C10
Greenstreet Green
 Suff 107 B10
Green Street Green Kent 68 E5
 London 68 G3
Green Tye Herts 86 B6
Greenway Hereford 98 E4
 Pembs 91 E11
 Som 27 B11
 V Glam 58 E5
 Worcs 116 C4
Greenwell Cumb 240 F2
Greenwells Borders 262 C3
Greenwich London 67 D11
 Suff 108 C3
 Wilts 46 G2
Greenwith Common Corn 4 G5
Greenwoods Essex 87 F11
Greeny Orkney 314 D2
Greep Highld 298 E2
Greet Glos 99 E10
 Kent 54 B2
Greete Shrops 115 C11
Greetham Lincs 190 G4
 Rutland 155 G8
Greetland W Yorks 196 C5
Greetland Wall Nook
 W Yorks 196 C5
Greetwell N Lincs 200 G2
Gregg Hall Cumb 221 G9
Gregson Lane Lancs 194 B5
Gregynog Powys 129 D11
Grèin W Isles 297 L2
Greinetobht W Isles 296 D4
Greinton Som 44 F2
Gremista Shetland 313 J6
Grenaby IoM 192 E3
Grendon Northants 121 E7
 Warks 134 C5
Grendon Bishop
 Hereford 115 F11
Grendon Common
 Warks 134 D5
Grendon Green
 Hereford 115 F11
Grendon Underwood
 Bucks 102 G3
Grenofen Devon 12 G5
Grenoside S Yorks 186 C4
Greosabhagh W Isles 305 J3
Gresford Wrex 166 E5
Gresham Norf 160 B3
Greshornish Highld 298 D3
Gressenhall Norf 159 F9
Gressingham Lancs 211 F11
Gresty Green Ches E 168 E2
Greta Bridge Durham 223 C11
Gretna Dumfries 239 D8
Gretna Green Dumfries 239 D8
Gretton Glos 99 E10
 Northants 137 E7
 Shrops 131 D10
Gretton Fields Glos 99 E10
Grewelthorpe N Yorks 214 D4
Greyfield Bath 44 B6
Greygarth N Yorks 214 E3
Grey Green N Lincs 199 F9
Greylake Som 43 G11
Greylake Fosse Som 44 F2
Greynor Carms 75 D9
Greynor-isaf Carms 75 D9
Greyrigg Dumfries 248 F3
Greys Green Oxon 65 C8
Greysouthen Cumb 229 F7
Greystead Northumb 251 F7
Greystoke Cumb 230 E4
Greystoke Gill Cumb 230 F4
Greystone Aberds 292 D6
 Aberds 302 F6
 Angus 287 C9
 Cumb 211 D10
 Dumfries 237 B11
Greystonegill N Yorks 212 F3
Greystones S Yorks 186 D4
 Warks 99 B11
Greytree Hereford 97 F11
Greywell Hants 49 C8
Griais W Isles 304 D6
Grianan W Isles 304 E6
Gribb Dorset 28 G5
Gribthorpe E Yorks 207 F11
Gridley Corner Devon 12 C3
Griff Warks 135 F7
Griffins Hill W Mid 133 G10
Griffithstown Torf 78 F3
Griffydam Leics 153 F8
Griggs Kent 53 E11
Griggs Green Hants 49 G10
Grillis Corn 2 B5
Grilstone Devon 26 C2
Grimbister Orkney 314 E3
Grimblethorpe Lincs 190 D2
Grimeford Village Lancs 194 E6
Grimes Hill Worcs 117 B11
Grimesthorpe S Yorks 186 C5
Grimethorpe S Yorks 198 F2
Griminis W Isles 296 D3
 W Isles 296 F3
Grimister Shetland 312 D6
Grimley Worcs 116 E6
Grimness Orkney 314 G4
Grimoldby Lincs 190 D5
Grimpo Shrops 149 D7
Grimsargh Lancs 203 G7
Grimsbury Oxon 101 C9
Grimsby NE Lincs 201 E9
Grimscote Northants 120 G3
Grimscott Corn 24 F3
Grimshaw Blkburn 195 C8
Grimshaw Green Lancs 194 E3
Grimsthorpe Lincs 155 E10
Grimston E Yorks 209 F11
 Leics 154 E3
 Norf 158 E4
 York 207 C8
Grimstone Dorset 17 C8
Grimstone End Suff 125 D8
Grinacombe Moor Devon 12 C4
Grindale E Yorks 218 E2
Grindigar Orkney 314 F5
Grindiscol Shetland 313 K6
Grindle Shrops 132 C5
Grindleford Derbys 186 F2
Grindleton Lancs 203 D11
Grindley Staffs 151 D10
Grindley Brook Shrops 167 G8
Grindlow Derbys 185 F11
Grindon Northumb 273 G8
 Staffs 169 E9
 Stockton 234 F3
 T&W 243 G9
Grindonmoor Gate
 Staffs 169 E9
Grindsbrook Booth
 Derbys 185 D10
Gringley on the Hill
 Notts 188 C2
Grinsdale Cumb 239 F9
Grinshill Shrops 149 E10
Grinstead Hill Suff 125 G11
Grinton N Yorks 223 F10
Griomasaigh W Isles 297 G4
Griomsidar W Isles 304 F5
Grisdale Cumb 222 G5
Grishipoll Argyll 288 D3
Grisling Common E Sus 36 C6
Gristhorpe N Yorks 217 C11
Griston Norf 141 D8
Gritley Orkney 314 F5
Grittenham Wilts 62 C4
Grittlesend Hereford 98 B4
Grittleton Wilts 61 C11
Grizebeck Cumb 210 C4
Grizedale Cumb 220 G6
Groam Highld 300 E5
Grobister Orkney 314 D6
Grobsness Shetland 313 G5
Groby Leics 135 B10
Groes Conwy 165 C8
 Neath 57 D9
Groes Efa Denb 165 B10
Groes-faen Rhondda 58 C5
Groes-fawr Denb 165 B10
Groesffordd Gwyn 144 B5
 Powys 95 F11
Groesffordd Marli Denb 181 G8
Groeslon Gwyn 163 C8
 Gwyn 163 D7
Groes-lwyd Mon 96 G6
 Powys 148 G4
Groespluan Powys 130 B4
Groes-wen Caerph 58 B6
Grogport Argyll 255 C9
Gromford Suff 127 F7
Gronant Flint 181 E9
Gronwen Shrops 148 D5
Groombridge E Sus 52 F4
Grosmont Mon 97 G8
 N Yorks 226 D6
Gross Green Warks 119 F7
Grotaig Highld 300 G4
Groton Suff 107 C9
Grotton Gtr Man 196 G3
Grougfoot Falk 279 F10
Grove Bucks 103 G8
 Dorset 17 G10
 Hereford 98 C2
 Kent 71 G8
 Notts 188 F2
 Oxon 82 G6
 Pembs 73 E7
Grove End Kent 69 G11
 Warks 100 D6
 Warks 134 D3
Grove Green Kent 53 B9
Grovehill E Yorks 208 F6
 Herts 85 D9
Grove Hill E Sus 23 C10
 Kent 71 G8
Grove Park London 67 D8
 London 68 E2
Groves Kent 55 B9
Grovesend Swansea 75 E9
Grove Town W Yorks 198 C3
Grove Vale W Mid 133 E10
Grubb Street Kent 68 F5
Grub Street Staffs 150 D5
Grudie Highld 300 C3
Gruids Highld 309 J5
Gruinard House Highld 307 K4
Gruinards Highld 309 K5
Grula Highld 294 C5
Gruline Argyll 289 E7
Gruline Ho Argyll 289 F7
Grumbeg Highld 308 F6
Grumbla Corn 1 D4
Grunasound Shetland 313 K5
Grundisburgh Suff 126 G4
Grunsagill Lancs 203 C11
Gruting Shetland 313 J4
Grutness Shetland 313 N6
Gryn Goch Gwyn 162 F6
Gualachulain Highld 284 C5
Gualin Ho Highld 308 D3
Guardbridge Fife 287 F8
Guard House W Yorks 204 E6
Guarlford Worcs 98 B6
Guay Perth 286 C4
Gubbion's Green Essex 88 B2
Gubblecote Herts 84 C6
Guesachan Highld 289 B10
Guestling Green E Sus 38 E5
Guestling Thorn E Sus 38 D5
Guestwick Norf 159 D11
Guestwick Green Norf 159 D11
Guide Blkburn 195 B8
Guide Bridge Gtr Man 184 B6
Guide Post Northumb 253 F7
Guilden Morden Cambs 104 C5
Guilden Sutton Ches W 166 B6
Guildford Sur 50 D3
Guildford Park Sur 50 D3
Guildiehaugh W Loth 269 B9
Guildtown Perth 286 D5
Guilford Pembs 73 D7
Guilsborough Northants 120 C3
Guilsfield / Cegidfa
 Powys 148 G4
Guilthwaite S Yorks 187 D7
Guilton Kent 55 B9
Guineaford Devon 40 F5
Guisachan Highld 300 G3
Guisborough Redcar 226 B2
Guiseley W Yorks 205 E9
Guist Norf 159 D9
Guith Orkney 314 C5
Guiting Power Glos 99 G11
Gulberwick Shetland 313 K6
Gullane E Loth 281 E9
Guller's End Worcs 99 D7
Gulling Green Suff 124 F6
Gullom Holme Cumb 231 F9
Gulval Corn 1 C5
Gulworthy Devon 12 G4
Gumfreston Pembs 73 E10
Gumley Leics 136 E3
Gummow's Shop Corn 5 D7
Gunby E Yorks 207 F10
 Lincs 155 E8
 Lincs 175 B7
Gundenham Som 27 C10
Gundleton Hants 48 G6
Gun Green Kent 53 G9
Gun Hill E Sus 23 C9
Gunn Devon 40 G6
Gunnersbury London 67 D7
Gunnerside N Yorks 223 F9
Gunnerton Northumb 241 C10
Gunness N Lincs 199 E10
Gunnislake Corn 12 G4
Gunnista Shetland 313 J7
Gunstone Staffs 133 C7
Guns Village W Mid 133 E9
Gunter's Bridge W Sus 35 C7
Gunthorpe Lincs 188 B4
 Norf 159 C10
 Notts 171 G11
 Pboro 138 C3
 Rutland 137 B7
Gunton Suff 143 D10
Gunville IoW 20 D5
Gunwalloe Corn 2 E5
Gunwalloe Fishing Cove
 Corn 2 E5
Gupworthy Som 42 F3
Gurnard IoW 20 B5
Gurnett Ches E 184 G6
Gurney Slade Som 44 D6
Gurnos M Tydf 77 D8
 Powys 76 D3
Gushmere Kent 54 B4
Gussage All Saints Dorset 31 E8
Gussage St Andrew
 Dorset 31 E7
Gussage St Michael
 Dorset 31 E7
Gustard Wood Herts 85 B11
Guston Kent 55 E10
Gutcher Shetland 312 D7
Guthram Gowt Lincs 156 E3
Guthrie Angus 287 B9
Guyhirn Cambs 139 C7
Guyhirn Gull Cambs 139 C7
Guy's Cliffe Warks 118 D5
Guy's Head Lincs 157 D9
Guy's Marsh Dorset 30 C4
Guyzance Northumb 252 C6
Gwaelod-y-garth Cardiff 58 C6
Gwaenysgor Flint 181 E9
Gwalchmai Anglesey 178 F5
Gwalchmai Uchaf
 Anglesey 178 F5
Gwallon Corn 2 C2
Gwastad Pembs 91 G10
Gwastadgoed Gwyn 145 G11
Gwastadnant Gwyn 163 D10
Gwaun-Cae-Gurwen
 Neath 76 C2
Gwaun-Leision Neath 76 C2
Gwavas Corn 2 D5
 Corn 2 G6
Gwbert Ceredig 92 B3
Gwedna Corn 2 C4
Gweek Corn 2 D6
Gwehelog Mon 78 E5
Gwenddwr Powys 95 C11
Gwennap Corn 2 B6
Gwenter Corn 2 F6
Gwernaffield-y-Waun
 Flint 166 C2
Gwernafon Powys 129 E8
Gwerneirin Powys 129 F10
 Powys 130 G3
Gwernesney Mon 78 E6
Gwernogle Carms 93 E10
Gwernol Denb 166 E2
Gwern y brenin Shrops 148 D6
Gwernydd Powys 129 C11
Gwernymynydd Flint 166 C2
Gwern-y-Steeple V Glam 58 D5
Gwersyllt Wrex 166 E4
Gwespyr Flint 181 E10
Gwills Corn 4 D6
Gwinear Corn 2 B3
Gwinear Downs Corn 2 C4
Gwithian Corn 2 A3
Gwredog Anglesey 178 D6
Gwrhay Caerph 77 F11
Gwyddelwern Denb 165 F9
Gwyddgrug Carms 93 D9
Gwynfryn Wrex 166 E3
Gwystre Powys 113 D11
Gwytherin Conwy 164 C5
Gyfelia Wrex 166 F4
Gyffin Conwy 180 F3
Gylen Park Argyll 289 G10
Gyre Orkney 314 F3
Gyrn Denb 165 D11
Gyrn-goch Gwyn 162 F6

H

Habberley Shrops 131 C7
 Worcs 116 B6
Habergham Lancs 204 G2
Habertoft Lincs 175 B8
Habin W Sus 34 C4
Habrough NE Lincs 200 E6
Haccombe Devon 14 G3
Haceby Lincs 155 B10
Hacheston Suff 126 F6
Hackbridge London 67 F9
Hackenthorpe S Yorks 186 E6
Hackford Norf 141 C11
Hackforth N Yorks 224 G4
Hack Green Ches E 167 F10
Hackland Orkney 314 D3
Hackleton Northants 120 F6
Hacklinge Kent 55 C10
Hackman's Gate Worcs 117 B7
Hackness N Yorks 227 G9
 Orkney 314 G3
 Som 43 D10
Hackney London 67 C10
Hackney Wick London 67 C11
Hackthorn Lincs 189 E7
 Wilts 47 D7
Hackthorpe Cumb 230 G6
Haclait W Isles 297 G4
Haconby Lincs 156 D2
Hacton London 68 B4
Haddacott Devon 25 C8
Hadden Borders 263 B7
Haddenham Bucks 84 D2
 Cambs 123 B9
Haddenham End Field
 Cambs 123 B9
Haddington E Loth 281 G10
 Lincs 172 C6
Haddiscoe Norf 143 D8
Haddoch Aberds 302 E5
Haddon Cambs 138 E2
 Ches E 169 B7
Hade Edge W Yorks 196 F6
Hademore Staffs 134 B3
Haden Cross W Mid 133 F9
Hadfield Derbys 185 B8
Hadham Cross Herts 86 B6
Hadham Ford Herts 105 G8
Hadleigh Essex 69 B10
 Suff 107 C10
Hadleigh Heath Suff 107 C9
Hadley London 86 F2
 Telford 150 G3
 Worcs 117 E7
Hadley Castle Telford 150 G3
Hadley End Staffs 152 E2
Hadley Wood London 86 F3
Hadlow Kent 52 D6
Hadlow Down E Sus 37 C8
Hadlow Stair Kent 52 D6
Hadnall Shrops 149 F10
Hadspen Som 45 G7
Hadstock Essex 105 C11
Hadston Northumb 253 D7
Hady Derbys 186 G5
Hadzor Worcs 117 E8
Haffenden Quarter Kent 53 E11
Hafod Swansea 57 C7
Hafod-Dinbych Conwy 164 E5
Hafod Grove Pembs 92 C2
Hafodiwan Ceredig 111 G7
Hafod-lom Conwy 180 G5
Hafod-y-Green Denb 181 G8
Hafodyrynys Bl Gwent 78 F2
Hag Fold Gtr Man 195 G7
Haggate Gtr Man 196 F2
 Lancs 204 F3
Haggbeck Cumb 239 C11
Haggersta Shetland 313 J5
Haggerston London 67 C10
 Northumb 273 G10
Hagginton Hill Devon 40 D5
Haggrister Shetland 312 F5
Haggs Falk 278 F5
Haghill Glasgow 268 B2
Hagley Hereford 97 C11
 Worcs 133 G8
Hagloe Glos 79 D11
Hagmore Green Suff 107 D9
Hagnaby Lincs 174 C4
 Lincs 191 F7
Hagnaby Lock Lincs 174 D4
Hague Bar Derbys 185 D7
Hagworthingham Lincs 174 B4
Haigh Gtr Man 194 F6
 S Yorks 197 E9
Haigh Moor W Yorks 197 C9
Haighton Green Lancs 203 G7
Haighton Top Lancs 203 G7
Haile Cumb 219 D10
Hailes Glos 99 E10
Hailey Herts 86 C5
 Oxon 64 B6
 Oxon 82 C5
Hailsham E Sus 23 D9
Hailstone Hill Wilts 81 G9
Hail Weston Cambs 122 E3
Haimer Highld 310 C5
Haimwood Powys 148 F6
Hainault London 87 G7
Haine Kent 71 F11
Hainford Norf 160 F4
Hains Dorset 30 D3
Hainton Lincs 189 E11
Hainworth W Yorks 205 F7
Hainworth Shaw
 W Yorks 205 F7
Hairmyres S Lnrk 268 E2
Haisthorpe E Yorks 218 G2
Hakeford Devon 40 F6
Hakin Pembs 72 D5
Halabezack Corn 2 C6
Halam Notts 171 E11
Halamanning Corn 2 C3
Halbeath Fife 280 D2
Halberton Devon 27 E8
Halcon Som 28 B2
Halcro Highld 310 C6
Haldens Herts 86 C2
Hale Cumb 211 D10
 Gtr Man 184 D3
 Halton 183 E7
 Hants 31 D11
 Kent 71 F9
 Medway 69 F9
 Som 30 B3
 Sur 49 D10
Hale Bank Halton 183 E7
Hale Barns Gtr Man 184 D3
Halecommon W Sus 34 C4
Hale Coombe N Som 44 B2
Hale End London 86 G5
Hale Green E Sus 23 C9
Hale Mills Corn 4 G5
Hale Nook Lancs 202 E3
Hales Norf 143 D7
 Staffs 150 C4
Hales Bank Hereford 116 G2
Halesfield Telford 132 C4
Halesgate Lincs 156 D6
Hales Green Derbys 169 G11
 Norf 143 D7
Halesowen W Mid 133 G9
Hales Park Worcs 116 B5
Hales Place Kent 54 B6
Hales Street Norf 142 F3
Hale Street Kent 53 D7
Halesworth Suff 127 B7
Halewood Mers 183 D7
Half Moon Village Devon 14 B3
Halford Shrops 131 G8
 Warks 100 B5
Halfpenny Cumb 211 B10
Halfpenny Furze Carms 74 C3
Halfpenny Green Staffs 132 E6
Halfway Carms 75 E8
 Carms 94 E2
 Carms 94 E6
 S Yorks 186 E6
 W Berks 64 F2
 Wilts 45 D11
Halfway Bridge W Sus 34 C6
Halfway House Shrops 148 G6

Halfway Houses
Gtr Man 195 F9
Kent 70 E2
Halfway Street Kent 55 D9
Halgabron Corn 11 D7
Halifax W Yorks 196 B5
Halkburn Borders 271 G9
Halket E Ayrs 267 E8
Halkirk Highld 310 D5
Halkyn / Helygain Flint 182 G2
Halkyn Mountain Flint 182 G2
Hallam Fields Derbys 153 B9
Halland E Sus 23 B8
Hallaton Leics 136 D5
Hallatrow Bath 44 B6
Hallbankgate Cumb 240 F3
Hall Bower W Yorks 196 E6
Hall Broom S Yorks 186 D3
Hall Cross Lancs 202 G4
Hall Dunnerdale Cumb 220 F4
Halleaths Dumfries 248 G3
Hallen S Glos 60 C5
Hallend Warks 118 D2
Hall End Beds 103 B10
C Beds 103 D11
Lincs 174 E6
S Glos 61 B8
Warks 134 C5
Hallew Corn 5 D10
Hallfield Gate Derbys 170 D5
Hall Flat Worcs 117 C9
Hallgarth Durham 234 C2
Hall Garth York 207 C9
Hallglen Falk 279 F7
Hall Green Ches E 168 D4
Essex 106 D5
Lancs 194 C3
Lancs 194 F4
W Mid 133 E10
W Mid 134 G2
W Mid 135 G7
Wrex 167 G7
W Yorks 197 D10
Hall Grove Herts 89 C8
Halliburton Borders 261 B11
Borders 272 F3
Hallin Highld 298 D2
Halling Medway 69 G8
Hallingbury Street Essex 87 B8
Hallington Lincs 190 D4
Northumb 241 B11
Hall i' th' Wood Gtr Man 195 E8
Halliwell Gtr Man 195 E8
Hall of Clestrain Orkney 314 F2
Hall of Tankerness
Orkney 314 F5
Hall of the Forest
Shrops 130 G4
Hallon Shrops 132 D5
Hallonsford Shrops 132 D5
Halloughton Notts 171 E11
Hallow Worcs 116 F6
Hallowes Derbys 186 F5
Hallow Heath Worcs 116 F6
Hallowsgate Ches W 167 B8
Hallrule Borders 262 G3
Halls E Loth 282 G3
Hallsands Devon 9 G11
Hall Santon Cumb 220 E2
Hall's Cross E Sus 23 D11
Hallsford Bridge Essex 87 E9
Halls Green Essex 86 D6
Hall's Green Herts 104 F5
Kent 52 D4
Hallspill Devon 25 C7
Hallthwaites Cumb 210 B3
Hall Waberthwaite
Cumb 220 F2
Hallwood Green Glos 98 E3
Hallworthy Corn 11 D9
Hallyards Borders 260 B6
Hallyburton House
Perth 286 D6
Hallyne Borders 270 G3
Halmer End Staffs 168 F3
Halmond's Frome
Hereford 98 B3
Halmore Glos 79 E11
Halmyre Mains Borders 270 F3
Halnaker W Sus 22 B6
Halsall Lancs 193 E11
Halse Northants 101 C11
Som 27 B10
Halsetown Corn 2 B2
Halsfordwood Devon 14 C3
Halsham E Yorks 201 B9
Halsinger Devon 40 F4
Halstead Essex 106 E6
Kent 68 G3
Leics 136 B4
Halstock Dorset 29 F8
Halsway Som 42 F6
Haltcliff Bridge Cumb 230 D3
Halterworth Hants 32 C5
Haltham Lincs 174 C2
Haltoft End Lincs 174 F5
Halton Bucks 84 C5
Halton 183 E8
Lancs 211 G10
Northumb 241 D11
Wrex 148 B6
W Yorks 206 G2
Halton Barton Corn 7 B8
Halton Brook Halton 183 E8
Halton East N Yorks 204 C6
Halton Fenside Lincs 174 C6
Halton Gill N Yorks 213 D7
Halton Green Lancs 211 F10
Halton Holegate Lincs 174 B6
Halton Lea Gate
Northumb 240 F5
Halton Moor W Yorks 206 G2
Halton Shields
Northumb 242 D2
Halton View Halton 183 D8
Halton West N Yorks 204 C2
Haltwhistle Northumb 240 E6
Halvergate Norf 143 B8
Halvosso Corn 2 C6
Halwell Devon 8 E5
Halwill Devon 12 B4
Halwill Junction Devon 24 G6
Halwin Corn 2 C5
Ham Devon 28 G2
Glos 79 F11
Glos 99 G9
Highld 310 B6
Kent 55 C10
London 67 E7
Plym 7 D9
Shetland 313 K1
Som 27 C11
Som 28 B3
Som 28 E3
Som 45 D7
Wilts 63 G10
Hamar Shetland 312 F5
Hamarhill Orkney 314 C5
Hamars Shetland 313 G6
Hambleden Bucks 65 B9
Hambledon Hants 33 E10
Sur 50 F3
Hamble-le-Rice Hants 33 F7
Hambleton Lancs 202 E3
N Yorks 205 C7
N Yorks 207 G7
Hambleton Moss Side
Lancs 202 E3
Hambridge Som 28 C5
Hambrook S Glos 60 D6
W Sus 22 B3
Ham Common Dorset 30 B4
Hameringham Lincs 174 B4
Hamerton Cambs 122 B2
Hametoun Shetland 313 K1
Ham Green Bucks 83 B11
Hants 48 G2
Hereford 98 C4
Kent 38 B5
Kent 69 F10
N Som 60 D4
Wilts 61 G11
Worcs 117 E10
Ham Hill Kent 69 G8
Hamilton S Lnrk 268 D3
Hamister Shetland 313 G7
Hamlet Dorset 29 F9
Hammer W Sus 49 G11
Hammer Bottom Hants 49 G11
Hammerfield Herts 85 D8
Hammerpot W Sus 35 F9
Hammersmith Derbys 170 E5
London 67 D8
Hammerwich Staffs 133 B11
Hammerwood E Sus 52 F2
Hammill Kent 55 B9
Hammond Street Herts 86 E4
Hammoon Dorset 30 E4
Ham Moor Sur 66 G5
Hamnavoe Shetland 312 E4
Shetland 312 E6
Shetland 312 F6
Shetland 313 K5
Hamnish Clifford
Hereford 115 F10
Hamp Som 43 F10
Hampden Park E Sus 23 E10
Hampen Glos 81 B9
Hamperden End Essex 105 E11
Hamperley Shrops 131 F8
Hampers Green W Sus 35 C7
Hampeth Northumb 252 B5
Hampnett Glos 81 B10
Hampole S Yorks 198 E4
Hampreston Dorset 19 B7
Hampsfield Cumb 211 C8
Hampson Green Lancs 202 C5
Hampstead London 67 B9
Hampstead Garden Suburb
London 67 B9
Hampstead Norreys
W Berks 64 D4
Hampsthwaite N Yorks 205 B11
Hampton Kent 71 F7
London 66 F6
Shrops 132 F4
Swindon 81 G11
Worcs 99 C10
Hampton Bank Shrops 149 C9
Hampton Beech Shrops 130 B6
Hampton Bishop
Hereford 97 D11
Hampton Fields Glos 80 F5
Hampton Gay Oxon 83 B7
Hampton Green Ches W 167 F8
Glos 80 E5
Hampton Hargate Pboro 138 E3
Hampton Heath Ches W 167 F7
Hampton Hill London 66 E6
Hampton in Arden
W Mid 134 G4
Hampton Loade Shrops 132 F5
Hampton Lovett Worcs 117 D7
Hampton Lucy Warks 118 F5
Hampton Magna Warks 118 D5
Hampton on the Hill
Warks 118 E5
Hampton Park Hereford 97 D10
Soton 32 D6
Hampton Poyle Oxon 83 B8
Hamptons Kent 52 C6
Hampton Wick London 67 F7
Hamptworth Wilts 32 D2
Hamrow Norf 159 E8
Hamsey E Sus 36 E6
Hamsey Green London 51 B10
Hamshill Glos 80 E3
Hamstall Ridware Staffs 152 F2
Hamstead IoW 20 C4
W Mid 133 E10
Hamstead Marshall
W Berks 64 F2
Hamsterley Durham 233 E8
Durham 242 F4
Hamstreet Kent 54 G4
Ham Street Som 44 G5
Hamworthy Poole 18 C5
Hanbury Staffs 152 D3
Worcs 117 E9
Hanbury Woodend
Staffs 152 D3
Hanby Lincs 155 C10
Hanchett Village Suff 106 B3
Hanchurch Staffs 168 G4
Handbridge Ches W 166 B6
Handcross W Sus 36 B3
Handforth Ches E 184 E5
Hand Green Ches W 167 C8
Handless Shrops 131 E7
Handley Ches W 167 D7
Derbys 170 C5
Handley Green Essex 87 E11
Handsacre Staffs 151 F11
Handside Herts 86 C2
Handsworth S Yorks 186 D6
W Mid 133 E10
Handsworth Wood
W Mid 133 E11
Handy Cross Bucks 84 G5
Devon 24 B6
Som 42 G6
Hanford Dorset 30 E4
Stoke 168 G5
Hangersley Hants 31 F11
Hanging Bank Kent 52 C3
Hanging Heaton
W Yorks 197 C9
Hanging Houghton
Northants 120 C5
Hanging Langford Wilts 46 F4
Hangingshaw Borders 261 C9
Dumfries 248 F4
Hangleton Brighton 36 F3
W Sus 35 G9
Hangsman Hill S Yorks 199 E7
Hanham S Glos 60 E6
Hanham Green S Glos 60 E6
Hankelow Ches E 167 F11
Hankerton Wilts 81 G7
Hankham E Sus 23 D10
Hanley Stoke 168 F5
Hanley Castle Worcs 98 C6
Hanley Child Worcs 116 E3
Hanley Swan Worcs 98 C6
Hanley William Worcs 116 D3
Hanlith N Yorks 213 G8
Hanmer Wrex 149 B9
Hannaford Devon 25 B10
Hannafore Corn 6 E5
Hannah Lincs 191 F8
Hanningfields Green
Suff 125 G7
Hannington Hants 48 B4
Northants 120 C6
Swindon 81 G11
Hannington Wick
Swindon 81 F11
Hanscombe End C Beds 104 E2
Hansel Devon 8 F6
Hansel Village S Ayrs 257 C9
Hansley Cross Staffs 169 G9
Hanslope M Keynes 102 B6
Hanthorpe Lincs 155 E11
Hanwell London 67 C7
Oxon 101 C8
Hanwood Shrops 131 B8
Hanwood Bank Shrops 149 G8
Hanworth Brack 65 F11
London 66 E6
Norf 160 B3
Happendon S Lnrk 259 C9
Happisburgh Norf 161 C7
Happisburgh Common
Norf 161 D7
Hapsford Ches W 183 G7
Som 45 D9
Hapton Lancs 203 G11
Norf 142 D3
Hararden / Penarlâg
Flint 166 B4
Harberton Devon 8 D5
Harbertonford Devon 8 D5
Harbledown Kent 54 B6
Harborne W Mid 133 G10
Harborough Magna
Warks 119 B9
Harborough Parva
Warks 119 B9
Harbottle Northumb 251 C10
Harbour Heights E Sus 36 G6
Harbourland Kent 53 B9
Harbourneford Devon 8 C4
Harbours Hill Worcs 117 D9
Harbour Village Pembs 91 D8
Harbridge Hants 31 E10
Harbridge Green Hants 31 E10
Harburn W Loth 269 C10
Harbury Warks 119 F7
Harby Leics 154 C4
Notts 188 G5
Harcombe Devon 14 E3
Devon 15 C9
Harcourt Corn 3 B8
Harcourt Hill Oxon 83 E7
Hardbreck Orkney 314 F4
Hardeicke Glos 80 C4
Harden S Yorks 197 G7
W Mid 133 C10
W Yorks 205 F7
Hardendale Cumb 221 C11
Hardenhuish Wilts 62 E2
Harden Park Ches E 184 F4
Hardgate Aberds 293 C9
Dumfries 237 C10
N Yorks 214 G5
W Dunb 277 G10
Hardham W Sus 35 D8
Hardhorn Lancs 202 F3
Hardingham Norf 141 C10
Hardings Booth Staffs 169 C9
Hardingstone Northants 120 F5
Hardings Wood Staffs 168 E4
Hardington Som 45 C8
Hardington Mandeville
Som 29 E8
Hardington Marsh Som 29 F8
Hardington Moor Som 29 E8
Hardiston Perth 279 B11
Hardisworthy Devon 24 C2
Hardley Hants 32 G6
Hardley Street Norf 143 C7
Hardmead M Keynes 103 B8
Hardrow N Yorks 223 G7
Hardstoft Derbys 170 C6
Hardstoft Common
Derbys 170 C6
Hardway Hants 33 G10
Som 45 G8
Hardwick Bucks 84 B4
Cambs 122 D3
Cambs 123 F7
Norf 142 F4
Norf 158 F2
Northants 121 D7
Oxon 82 D5
Oxon 101 C8
Oxon 101 F11
Shrops 131 E7
Stockton 234 G4
S Yorks 187 D7
W Mid 133 D11
Hardwicke Glos 80 C3
Glos 99 F8
Hereford 96 C5
Hardwick Green Worcs 98 E6
Hardwick Village Notts 187 F10
Hardy's Green Essex 107 G8
Hare Som 28 D3
Hare Appletree Lancs 202 B6
Hareby Lincs 174 B4
Harecroft W Yorks 205 F7
Hareden Lancs 203 C8
Hare Edge Derbys 186 G4
Harefield London 85 G9
Soton 33 E7
Harefield Grove London 85 G9
Haregate Staffs 169 D7
Hare Green Essex 107 G11
Hare Hatch Wokingham 65 D10
Harehill Derbys 152 B3
Harehills W Yorks 206 G2
Harehope Borders 270 G4
Northumb 264 E3
Harelaw Durham 242 G5
Hareleeshill S Lnrk 268 E5
Hareplain Kent 53 F10
Haresceugh Cumb 231 C8
Harescombe Glos 80 C4
Haresfield Glos 80 C4
Swindon 82 G2
Haresfinch Mers 183 B8
Hareshaw N Lnrk 268 C6
Hareshaw Head
Northumb 251 F9
Harestanes E Dunb 278 G3
Harestock Hants 48 G3
Hare Street Essex 86 D6
Herts 104 E6
Herts 105 F7
Harewood W Yorks 206 D2
Harewood End Hereford 97 F10
Harewood Hill W Yorks 204 F6
Harford Carms 94 C2
Devon 8 D2
Devon 40 G6
Hargate Norf 142 E2
Hargate Hill Derbys 185 C8
Hargatewall Derbys 185 F10
Hargrave Ches W 167 C7
Northants 121 C10
Suff 124 F5
Harker Cumb 239 E9
Harker Marsh Cumb 229 E7
Harkland Shetland 312 E6
Harknett's Gate Essex 86 D6
Harkstead Suff 108 E3
Harlaston Staffs 152 G4
Harlaw Ho Aberds 303 G7
Harlaxton Lincs 155 C7
Harlech Gwyn 145 C11
Harlequin Notts 154 B3
Harlescott Shrops 149 F10
Harlesden London 67 C8
Harlesthorpe Derbys 187 F7
Harleston Devon 8 F5
Norf 142 G4
Suff 125 F10
Harlestone Northants 120 E4
Harle Syke Lancs 204 F3
Harley Shrops 131 C11
S Yorks 186 B5
Harleyholm S Lnrk 259 B10
Harley Shute E Sus 38 F3
Harleywood Glos 80 F4
Harling Road Norf 141 F9
Harlington C Beds 103 E10
London 66 D5
S Yorks 198 G3
Harlosh Highld 298 E2
Harlow Essex 86 C6
Harlow Carr N Yorks 205 C11
Harlow Green T&W 243 F7
Harlow Hill Northumb 242 D3
N Yorks 205 C11
Harlthorpe E Yorks 207 F10
Harlton Cambs 123 G7
Harlyn Corn 10 F3
Harman's Corner Kent 69 G11
Harman's Cross Dorset 18 E5
Harmans Water Brack 65 F11
Harmby N Yorks 214 B2
Harmer Green Herts 86 B3
Harmer Hill Shrops 149 E9
Harmondsworth London 66 D5
Harmston Lincs 173 C7
Harnage Shrops 131 C11
Harnham Northumb 242 B3
Wilts 31 B10
Wilts 31 B11
Harnhill Glos 81 E9
Harold Hill London 87 G8
Harold Park London 87 G9
Haroldston West Pembs 72 B5
Haroldswick Shetland 312 B8
Harold Wood London 87 G8
Harome N Yorks 216 C2
Harpenden Herts 85 C10
Harpenden Common
Herts 85 C10
Harper Green Gtr Man 195 F8
Harperley Durham 242 G5
Harper's Gate Staffs 169 D7
Harper's Green Norf 159 E8
Harpford Devon 15 C7
Harpham E Yorks 217 G11
Harpley Norf 158 D5
Worcs 116 E3
Harpole Northants 120 E3
Harpsdale Highld 310 D5
Harpsden Oxon 65 C9
Harpsden Bottom Oxon 65 C9
Harpswell Lincs 188 D6
Harpton Powys 114 F4
Harpurhey Gtr Man 195 G11
Harpur Hill Derbys 185 G9
Harraby Cumb 239 G10
Harracott Devon 25 B9
Harrapool Highld 295 C8
Harras Cumb 219 B9
Harraton T&W 243 G7
Harrier Shetland 313 J1
Harrietfield Perth 286 E3
Harrietsham Kent 53 C11
Harringay London 67 B10
Harrington Cumb 228 F5
Lincs 190 G5
Northants 136 G5
Harringworth Northants 137 D8
Harris Highld 294 F5
Harriseahead Staffs 168 D5
Harriston Cumb 229 C9
Harrogate N Yorks 206 C2
Harrold Beds 121 F8
Harrop Dale Gtr Man 196 F4
Harrow Highld 310 B6
London 67 B7
Harrowbarrow Corn 7 B7
Harrowbeer Devon 7 B10
Harrowby Lincs 155 B8
Harrowden Beds 103 B11
Harrowgate Hill Darl 224 B5
Harrowgate Village
Darl 224 B5
Harrow Green Suff 125 G7
Harrow Hill Glos 79 B10
Harrow on the Hill
London 67 B7
Harrow Street Suff 107 D9
Harrow Weald London 85 G11
Harry Stoke S Glos 60 D6
Harston Cambs 123 G8
Leics 154 C6
Harswell E Yorks 208 E2
Hart Hrtlpl 234 E5
Hartbarrow Cumb 221 G8
Hartburn Northumb 252 F3
Stockton 225 B8
Hartcliffe Bristol 60 F5
Hart Common Gtr Man 194 F6
Hartest Suff 124 G6
Hartest Hill Suff 124 G6
Hartfield E Sus 52 F3
Highld 299 E7
Hartford Cambs 122 C5
Ches W 183 G10
Som 27 B7
Hartfordbeach
Ches W 183 G10
Hartfordbridge Hants 49 B9
Hartford End Essex 87 B11
Hartforth N Yorks 224 D3
Hartgrove Dorset 30 D4
Hartham Herts 86 C4
Harthill Ches W 167 D8
N Lnrk 269 C8
S Yorks 187 E7
Hart Hill Luton 104 G2
Hartington Derbys 169 C10
Hartland Devon 24 C3
Hartle Worcs 117 B8
Hartlebury Shrops 132 D4
Worcs 116 C6
Hartlebury Common
Worcs 116 C6
Hartlepool Hrtlpl 234 E6
Hartley Cumb 222 D5
Kent 53 G9
Kent 68 F6
Northumb 243 B8
Plym 7 D9
Hartley Green Kent 68 F6
Staffs 151 D9
Hartley Mauditt Hants 49 F8
Hartley Westpall Hants 49 B7
Hartley Wintney Hants 49 B9
Hartlington N Yorks 213 G10
Hartlip Kent 69 G10
Hartmoor Dorset 30 C3
Hartmount Highld 301 B7
Hartoft End N Yorks 226 G5
Harton N Yorks 216 G4
Shrops 131 F9
T&W 243 E9
Hartpury Glos 98 F5
Hartsgreen Shrops 132 G5
Hart's Green Suff 125 F7
Hartshead W Yorks 197 C7
Hartshead Green
Gtr Man 196 G3
Hartshead Moor Side
W Yorks 197 C7
Hartshead Moor Top
W Yorks 197 B7
Hartshead Pike
Gtr Man 196 G3
Hartshill Stoke 168 F5
Warks 134 E6
Hart's Hill W Mid 133 F8
Hartshill Green Warks 134 E6
Hartshorne Derbys 152 E6
Hartsop Cumb 221 C8
Hart Station Hrtlpl 234 D5
Hartswell Som 27 B9
Hartwell Northants 120 G5
Staffs 151 B8
Hartwith N Yorks 214 G4
Hartwood Lancs 194 D5
N Lnrk 268 D6
Hartwoodburn Borders 261 D11
Harvel Kent 68 G6
Harvest Hill W Mid 134 G5
Harvieston Stirl 277 D11
Harvills Hawthorn
W Mid 133 E9
Harvington Worcs 99 B11
Worcs 117 C7
Harvington Cross Worcs 99 B11
Harvington Hill Worcs 99 B10
Harwell Notts 187 C11
Oxon 64 B3
Harwich Essex 108 E5
Harwood Durham 232 E2
Gtr Man 195 E8
Harwood Dale N Yorks 227 F9
Harwood Lee Gtr Man 195 E8
Harwood on Teviot
Borders 249 B10
Harworth Notts 187 C10
Hasbury W Mid 133 G9
Hascombe Sur 50 E3
Haselbech Northants 120 B4
Haselbury Plucknett Som 29 E7
Haseley Warks 118 D4
Haseley Green Warks 118 D4
Haseley Knob Warks 118 C4
Haselor Warks 118 F2
Hasfield Glos 98 F6
Hasguard Pembs 72 D5
Haskayne Lancs 193 F11
Hasketon Suff 126 G4
Hasland Derbys 170 B5
Haslemere Sur 50 G2
Haslingbourne W Sus 35 C7
Haslingden Lancs 195 C9
Haslingfield Cambs 123 G8
Haslington Ches E 168 D2
Hasluck's Green W Mid 118 B2
Hassall Ches E 168 D3
Hassall Green Ches E 168 D3
Hassell Street Kent 54 D5
Hassendean Borders 262 E2
Hassingham Norf 143 B7
Hassocks W Sus 36 D3
Hassop Derbys 186 G2
Haster Highld 310 D7
Hasthorpe Lincs 175 B7
Hastigrow Highld 310 C6
Hasting Hill T&W 243 G9
Hastingleigh Kent 54 E5
Hastings E Sus 38 F4
Som 28 D4
Hastingwood Essex 87 D7
Hastoe Herts 84 D6
Haston Shrops 149 E10
Haswell Durham 234 C3
Haswell Moor Durham 234 C3
Haswell Plough Durham 234 C3
Haswellsykes Borders 260 B6
Hatch C Beds 104 B3
Devon 8 F4
Hants 49 C7
Wilts 30 B6
Hatch Beauchamp Som 28 C4
Hatch Bottom Hants 33 E7
Hatch End Beds 121 E11
London 85 G10
Hatchet Gate Hants 32 G5
Hatchet Green Hants 31 D11
Hatch Farm Hill W Sus 34 B6
Hatch Green Som 28 D4
Hatching Green Herts 85 C10
Hatchmere Ches W 183 G9
Hatch Warren Hants 48 D6
Hatcliffe NE Lincs 201 G8
Hateley Heath W Mid 133 E10
Hatfield Hereford 115 F11
Herts 86 D2
S Yorks 199 F7
Worcs 117 G7
Hatfield Broad Oak Essex 87 B8
Hatfield Chase S Yorks 199 E8
Hatfield Garden Village
Herts 86 D2
Hatfield Heath Essex 87 B8
Hatfield Hyde Herts 86 C2
Hatfield Peverel Essex 88 C3
Hatfield Woodhouse
S Yorks 199 F7
Hatford Oxon 82 G4
Hatherden Hants 47 C10
Hatherleigh Devon 25 G8
Hatherley Glos 99 G8
Hathern Leics 153 E9
Hatherop Glos 81 D11
Hathersage Derbys 186 E2
Hathersage Booths
Derbys 186 E2
Hathershaw Gtr Man 196 G2
Hatherton Ches E 167 F11
Staffs 151 G9
Hatley St George Cambs 122 G5
Hatston Orkney 314 E4
Hatt Corn 7 C7
Hatterseat Aberds 303 G9
Hattersley Gtr Man 185 C7
Hatt Hill Hants 32 B4
Hattingley Hants 48 F6
Hatton Aberds 303 F10
Angus 287 D9
Derbys 152 D4
Lincs 189 F11
London 66 D5
Moray 301 D11
Shrops 131 E9
Warks 118 D4
Warr 183 E9
Hattonburn Aberds 293 C9
Hatton Castle Aberds 303 E7
Hattoncrook Aberds 303 G8
Hatton Grange Shrops 132 C5
Hatton Heath Ches W 167 C7
Hatton Hill Sur 66 G2
Hattonknowe Borders 270 F4
Hatton of Fintray
Aberds 293 B10
Hatton Park Northants 121 D7
Haugh E Ayrs 257 D11
Gtr Man 196 E2
Lincs 190 F6
Haugham Lincs 190 E4
Haugh-head Borders 261 B8
Haugh Head Northumb 264 D2
Haughland Orkney 314 E5
Haughley Suff 125 E10
Haughley Green Suff 125 E10
Haughley New Street
Suff 125 E10
Haugh of Glass Moray 302 F4
Haugh of Kilnmaichlie
Moray 301 F11
Haugh of Urr Dumfries 237 C10
Haughs of Clinterty
Aberdeen 293 B10
Haughton Ches E 167 D9
Notts 187 G11
Powys 148 F6
Shrops 132 B4
Shrops 132 D3
Shrops 149 D7
Shrops 149 F11
Staffs 151 E7
Haughton Castle
Northumb 241 C10
Haughton Green
Gtr Man 184 C6
Haughton Le Skerne
Darl 224 B6
Haughurst Hill W Berks 64 G5
Haulkerton Aberds 293 F9
Haultwick Herts 104 G6
Haunn Argyll 288 E5
W Isles 297 K3
Haunton Staffs 152 G4
Hauxton Cambs 123 G8
Havannah Ches E 168 C5
Havant Hants 22 B2
Haven Hereford 97 B11
Hereford 115 G8
Haven Bank Lincs 174 E2
Haven Side E Yorks 201 B7
Havenstreet IoW 21 C7
Havercroft W Yorks 197 E11
Haverfordwest / Hwlffordd
Pembs 73 B7
Haverhill Suff 106 B3
Haverigg Cumb 210 D3
Havering-atte-Bower
London 87 G8
Haveringland Norf 160 E3
Haversham M Keynes 102 C6
Haverthwaite Cumb 210 C6
Haverton Hill Stockton 234 G5
Haviker Street Kent 53 D8
Havyatt Som 44 F4
Havyatt Green N Som 60 G3
Hawarden / Penarlâg
Flint 166 B4
Hawbridge Worcs 99 B8
Hawbush Green Essex 106 G5
Hawcoat Cumb 210 E4
Hawcross Glos 98 E5
Hawddamor Gwyn 146 F3
Hawen Ceredig 92 B6
Hawes N Yorks 213 B7
Hawes' Green Norf 142 D4
Hawes Side Blkpool 202 G2
Hawford Worcs 116 E6
Hawgreen Shrops 150 D2
Hawick Borders 262 F2
Hawkchurch Devon 28 G4
Hawkcombe Som 41 D11
Hawkedon Suff 124 G5
Hawkenbury Kent 52 F5
Kent 53 E10
Hawkeridge Wilts 45 C11
Hawkerland Devon 15 D7
Hawkesland Cross
Hereford 97 B10
Hawkesbury S Glos 61 B9
Warks 135 G7
Hawkesbury Upton
S Glos 61 B9
Hawkes End W Mid 134 G6
Hawkesley W Mid 117 B10
Hawk Green Gtr Man 185 D7
Hawkhill Northumb 264 G6
Hawk Hill Cumb 228 F6
Hawkhope Northumb 250 F6
Hawkhurst Kent 53 G9
Hawkhurst Common
E Sus 23 B8
Hawkinge Kent 55 F8
Hawkin's Hill Essex 106 E3
Hawkley Gtr Man 194 G5
Hants 34 B2
Hawkridge Som 41 G11
Hawksdale Cumb 230 B3
Hawks Green Staffs 151 G9
Hawkshaw Blkburn 195 D9
Hawkshead Cumb 221 F7
Hawkshead Hill Cumb 220 F6
Hawks Hill Bucks 66 B2
Hawk's Hill Sur 51 B7
Hawksland S Lnrk 259 B8
Hawkspur Green Essex 106 E3
Hawks Stones W Yorks 196 B2
Hawkswick N Yorks 213 E9
Hawksworth Notts 172 G3
W Yorks 205 E9
W Yorks 205 F11
Hawkwell Essex 88 G4
Northumb 242 C3
Hawley Hants 49 B11
Kent 68 E4
Hawley Bottom Devon 28 G2
Hawley Lane Hants 49 B11
Hawling Glos 99 G11
Hawn Orkney 314 D4
Hawnby N Yorks 215 B10
Haworth W Yorks 204 F6
Haws Bank Cumb 220 F6
Hawstead Suff 125 F7
Hawstead Green Suff 125 F7
Hawthorn Durham 234 B4
Hants 49 G7
Rhondda 58 B6
Wilts 61 F11
Hawthorn Corner Kent 71 F8
Hawthorn Hill Brack 65 E11
Lincs 174 D2
Hawthorns Staffs 168 F4
Hawthorpe Lincs 155 D10
Hawton Notts 172 E3
Haxby York 207 B8
Haxey N Lincs 188 B3
N Lincs 199 G9
Haxey Carr N Lincs 199 G9
Haxted Sur 52 D2
Haxton Wilts 46 D6
Hay Corn 10 G5
Haybridge Shrops 116 C2
Som 44 D4
Telford 150 G3
Hayden Glos 99 G8
Haydock Mers 183 B9
Haydon Bath 45 C7
Dorset 29 D11
Som 28 C3
Som 44 D5
Swindon 62 B6
Haydon Bridge
Northumb 241 E8
Haydon Wick Swindon 62 B6
Haye Corn 7 B7
Haye Fm Corn 6 B6
Hayes Bromley 68 F2
Hillingdon 66 C6
Staffs 169 C9
Hayes End London 66 C5
Hayes Knoll Wilts 81 G10
Hayes Town London 66 C6
Hayfield Derbys 185 D8
Fife 280 C5
Hay Field S Yorks 187 B10
Hayfield Green
S Yorks 187 B11
Haygate Telford 150 G2
Haygrass Som 28 C2
Hay Green Essex 87 E10
Herts 104 D6
Norf 157 F10
Hayhill E Ayrs 257 F11
Hayhillock Angus 287 C9
Haylands IoW 21 C7
Hayle Corn 2 B3
Hayley Green W Mid 133 G8
Hay Mills W Mid 134 G2
Haymoor End Som 28 B4
Haymoor Green
Ches E 167 E11
Hayne Devon 26 F5
Haynes C Beds 103 C11
Haynes Church End
C Beds 103 C11
Haynes West End
C Beds 103 C11
Hay-on-Wye Powys 96 C4
Hayscastle Pembs 91 F7
Hayscastle Cross Pembs 91 G8
Haysford Pembs 91 G8
Hayshead Angus 287 C10
Hayston E Dunb 278 G2
Haystoun Borders 261 B7
Hay Street Herts 105 F7
Haythorne Dorset 31 F8
Hayton Aberdeen 293 C11
Cumb 229 C8
Cumb 240 F2
E Yorks 208 D2
Notts 188 E2
Hayton's Bent Shrops 131 G10
Haytor Vale Devon 13 F11
Haytown Devon 24 E5
Haywards Heath W Sus 36 C4
Haywood S Lnrk 269 E9
S Yorks 198 E5
Haywood Oaks Notts 171 D10
Hazard's Green E Sus 23 C11
Hazelbank S Lnrk 268 F6
Hazelbeach Pembs 72 E6
Hazelbury Bryan Dorset 30 F2
Hazeleigh Essex 88 E4
Hazel End Essex 105 G9
Hazeley Hants 49 B8
Hazeley Bottom Hants 49 B9
Hazeley Heath Hants 49 B9
Hazeley Lea Hants 49 B8
Hazelgrove Notts 171 F8
Hazel Grove Gtr Man 184 D6
Hazelhurst Gtr Man 195 D9
Gtr Man 195 G9
Gtr Man 196 G3
Hazelslack Cumb 211 D9
Hazelslade Staffs 151 G10
Hazel Street Kent 53 B11
Kent 53 F7
Hazel Stub Suff 106 C3
Hazelton Glos 81 B9
Hazelton Walls Fife 287 E7
Hazelwood Derbys 170 F4
Devon 8 E4
London 68 G2
Hazlehead S Yorks 197 G7
Hazlemere Bucks 84 F5
Hazler Shrops 131 E9
Hazlerigg T&W 242 C6
Hazles Staffs 169 F8
Hazlescross Staffs 169 F8
Hazleton Glos 81 B9
Hazlewood N Yorks 205 C7
Hazon Northumb 252 C5
Heacham Norf 158 B3
Headbourne Worthy
Hants 48 G3
Headbrook Hereford 114 F6
Headcorn Kent 53 E10
Headingley W Yorks 205 F11
Headington Oxon 83 D8
Headington Hill Oxon 83 D8
Headlam Durham 224 B3
Headless Cross Cumb 211 D7
Worcs 117 D10
Headley Hants 49 F10
Hants 64 G4
Sur 51 C8
Headley Down Hants 49 F10
Headley Heath Worcs 117 B11
Headley Park Bristol 60 F5
Head of Muir Falk 278 E6
Headon Devon 24 G5
Notts 188 F2
Heads S Lnrk 268 F4
Headshaw Borders 261 E11
Heads Nook Cumb 239 F11
Headstone London 66 B6
Headwell Fife 279 D11
Heady Hill Gtr Man 195 E10
Heage Derbys 170 E5
Healaugh N Yorks 206 D5
N Yorks 223 F10
Heald Green Gtr Man 184 D4
Healds Green Gtr Man 195 F11
Heale Devon 40 D6
Som 28 B5
Som 28 D2
Som 45 E7
Healey Gtr Man 195 D11
Northumb 242 F2
N Yorks 214 C3
W Yorks 197 C8
W Yorks 197 D9
Healey Cote Northumb 252 C4
Healeyfield Durham 233 B7
Healey Hall Northumb 242 F2
Healing NE Lincs 201 E8
Heamoor Corn 1 C5
Heaning Cumb 221 F8
Heanish Argyll 288 E2
Heanor Derbys 170 F6
Heanor Gate Derbys 170 F6
Heanton Punchardon
Devon 40 F4
Heap Bridge Gtr Man 195 E10
Heapham Lincs 188 D5
Hearn Hants 49 F10
Hearnden Green Kent 53 D10
Hearthstane Borders 260 D4
Hearthstone Derbys 170 D4
Hearts Delight Kent 69 G11
Heasley Mill Devon 41 G8
Heast Highld 295 D8
Heath Cardiff 59 D7
Derbys 170 B6
Halton 183 E8
Heath and Reach
C Beds 103 F8
Heath Charnock Lancs 194 E5
Heath Common W Sus 35 E10
W Yorks 197 D11
Heathcot Aberds 293 C10
Heathcote Derbys 169 C10
Shrops 150 D3
Warks 118 E6
Heath Cross Devon 13 B10
Devon 14 C2
Heath End Bucks 84 F5
Bucks 85 D7
Derbys 153 E7
Hants 64 G2
Hants 64 G5
S Glos 61 B7
Sur 49 D10
Warks 118 E4
W Mid 133 C10
W Sus 35 D7
Heather Leics 153 G7
Heathercombe Devon 13 E10
Heatherfield Highld 298 E4
Heather Row Hants 49 C8
Heatherside Sur 50 B2
Heatherwood Park
Highld 311 K2
Heatherybanks Aberds 303 E7
Heathfield Cambs 105 B9
Devon 14 F2
E Sus 37 C9
Glos 80 F2
Hants 33 F9
Lincs 189 C10
N Yorks 214 F2
S Ayrs 257 E9
Som 27 B11
Som 43 G7
Heathfield Village Oxon 83 B8
Heath Green Hants 48 F6
Worcs 117 C11
Heathhall Dumfries 237 B11
Heath Hayes Staffs 151 G10
Heath Hill Shrops 150 G5
Heath House Som 44 D2
Heathlands Wokingham 65 F10
Heath Lanes Telford 150 E2
Heath Park London 68 B4
Heathrow Airport
London 66 D5
Heath Side Kent 68 E4
Heathstock Devon 28 G2
Heathton Shrops 132 E6
Heathtop Derbys 152 C4
Heath Town W Mid 133 D8
Heathwaite Cumb 221 F8
N Yorks 225 E9
Heatley Staffs 151 D11
Warr 184 D2
Heaton Gtr Man 195 F7
Lancs 211 G8
Staffs 169 C7
T&W 243 D7
W Yorks 205 G8
Heaton Chapel Gtr Man 184 C5
Heaton Mersey Gtr Man 184 C5
Heaton Moor Gtr Man 184 C5
Heaton Norris Gtr Man 184 C5
Heaton Royds W Yorks 205 F8
Heaton's Bridge Lancs 194 E2
Heaton Shay W Yorks 205 F8
Heaven's Door Som 29 C10
Heaverham Kent 52 B5
Heaviley Gtr Man 184 D6
Heavitree Devon 14 C4
Hebburn T&W 243 E8
Hebburn Colliery T&W 243 D8
Hebburn New Town
T&W 243 E8
Hebden N Yorks 213 G10
Hebden Bridge W Yorks 196 B3
Hebden Green Ches W 167 B10
Hebing End Herts 104 G6
Hebron Anglesey 179 E7
Carms 92 F3
Northumb 252 F5
Heck Dumfries 248 G3
Heckdyke N Lincs 188 B3
Heckfield Hants 65 G8
Heckfield Green Suff 126 B3
Heckfordbridge Essex 107 G8
Heckingham Norf 143 D7
Heckington Lincs 173 G10
Heckmondwike
W Yorks 197 C8
Heddington Wilts 62 F3
Heddington Wick Wilts 62 F3
Heddle Orkney 314 E3
Heddon Devon 25 B11
Heddon-on-the-Wall
Northumb 242 D4
Hedenham Norf 142 E6
Hedge End Dorset 30 F4
Hants 33 E7
Hedgehog Bridge Lincs 174 F3
Hedgerley Bucks 66 B3
Hedgerley Green Bucks 66 B3
Hedgerley Hill Bucks 66 B3
Hedging Som 28 B4
Hedley Hill Durham 233 C9
Hedley on the Hill
Northumb 242 F3
Hednesford Staffs 151 G9
Hedon E Yorks 201 B7
Hedsor Bucks 66 B2
Hedworth T&W 243 E8
Heelands M Keynes 102 D6
Heeley S Yorks 186 E5
Hegdon Hill Hereford 115 G11
Heggerscales Cumb 222 C6
Heggle Lane Cumb 230 D3

Heglibister Shetland 313 H5
Heighington Darl 233 G11
Lincs 173 B8
Heighley Staffs 168 F3
Height End Lancs 195 C9
Heightington Worcs 116 C5
Heights Gtr Man 196 F3
Heights of Brae Highld 300 C5
Heights of Kinlochewe
Highld 299 C10
Heilam Highld 308 C4
Heiton Borders 262 C6
Helbeck Cumb 222 B5
Hele Devon 12 C2
Devon 13 G10
Devon 27 G7
Devon 40 D4
Som 27 C11
Torbay 9 B8
Helebridge Corn 24 G2
Helensburgh Argyll 276 E5
Helford Corn 3 D7
Helford Passage Corn 3 D7
Helham Green Herts 86 B5
Helhoughton Norf 159 D7
Helions Bumpstead
Essex 106 C3
Hellaby S Yorks 187 C8
Helland Corn 11 G7
Som 28 C4
Hellandbridge Corn 11 G7
Hell Corner W Berks 63 G11
Hellesdon Norf 160 G4
Hellesveor Corn 2 A2
Hellidon Northants 119 F10
Hellifield N Yorks 204 B3
Hellifield Green
N Yorks 204 B3
Hellingly E Sus 23 C9
Hellington Norf 142 C6
Hellister Shetland 313 J5
Hellman's Cross Essex 87 B9
Helm Northumb 252 D5
N Yorks 223 G8
Helmburn Borders 261 E9
Helmdon Northants 101 C11
Helme W Yorks 196 E5
Helmingham Suff 126 F3
Helmington Row
Durham 233 D9
Helmsdale Highld 311 H4
Helmshore Lancs 195 C9
Helmside Cumb 212 B3
Helmsley N Yorks 216 C2
Helperby N Yorks 215 F8
Helperthorpe N Yorks 217 E9
Helpringham Lincs 173 G10
Helpston Pboro 138 B2
Helsby Ches W 183 F7
Helscott Corn 24 G2
Helsey Lincs 191 G8
Helston Corn 2 D5
Helstone Corn 11 E7
Helston Water Corn 4 G5
Helton Cumb 230 G6
Helwith Bridge N Yorks 212 F6
Helygain / Halkyn Flint 182 G2
Hemblington Norf 160 G6
Hemblington Corner
Norf 160 G6
Hembridge Som 44 F5
Hemel Hempstead Herts 85 D9
Hemerdon Devon 7 D11
Hemford Shrops 130 C6
Hem Heath Stoke 168 G5
Hemingbrough N Yorks 207 G9
Hemingby Lincs 190 G2
Hemingfield S Yorks 197 G11
Hemingford Abbots
Cambs 122 C5
Hemingford Grey
Cambs 122 C5
Hemingstone Suff 126 G3
Hemington Leics 153 D9
Northants 137 F11
Som 45 C8
Hemley Suff 108 C5
Hemlington Mbro 225 C10
Hemp Green Suff 127 D7
Hempholme E Yorks 209 C7
Hempnall Norf 142 E4
Hempnall Green Norf 142 E4
Hempriggs House
Highld 310 E7
Hemp's Green Essex 107 F8
Hempshill Vale Notts 171 G8
Hempstead Essex 106 D2
Medway 69 G9
Norf 160 B2
Norf 161 D8
Hempsted Glos 80 B4
Hempton Norf 159 D8
Oxon 101 E8
Hempton Wainhill
Oxon 84 E3
Hemsby Norf 161 F9
Hemsted Kent 54 E6
Hemswell Lincs 188 C6
Hemswell Cliff Lincs 188 D6
Hemsworth Dorset 31 F7
S Yorks 186 E5
W Yorks 198 E2
Hemyock Devon 27 E10
Henaford Devon 24 D2
Hen Bentref Llandegfan
Anglesey 179 G9
Henbrook Worcs 117 D8
Henbury Bristol 60 D5
Ches E 184 G5
Dorset 18 B5
Hendomen Powys 130 D4
Hendon London 67 B8
T&W 243 F10
Hendra Corn 2 B6
Corn 2 C5
Corn 2 D3
Corn 2 F6
Corn 5 C9
Corn 5 D9
Corn 11 E7
Hendrabridge Corn 6 B5
Hendraburnick Corn 11 D8
Hendra Croft Corn 4 D5
Hendre Flint 165 B11
Gwyn 110 B2
Powys 129 D9
Hendre-ddu Conwy 164 B5
Hendredenny Park
Caerph 58 B6
Hendreforgan Rhondda 58 B3
Hendrerwydd Denb 165 C10
Hendrewen Swansea 75 D10
Hendy Carms 75 E9
Hendy-Gwyn Carms 74 B2
Hendy Gwyn / Whitland
Carms 73 B11
Hên-efail Denb 165 C9
Heneglwys Anglesey 178 F6
Hen-feddau fawr Pembs 92 E4
Henfield S Glos 61 D7
W Sus 36 D2
Henford Devon 12 C3
Henfords Marsh Wilts 45 E11
Henghurst Kent 54 F3
Hengoed Caerph 77 F10
Denb 165 D9
Powys 114 G4
Shrops 148 C5
Hengrave Norf 160 F2
Suff 124 D6
Hengrove Bristol 60 F6
Hengrove Park Bristol 60 F5
Henham Essex 105 F10
Heniarth Powys 130 B2
Henlade Som 28 C3
Henleaze Bristol 60 D5
Henley Dorset 29 G11
Glos 80 B6
Shrops 115 B10
Shrops 131 F9
Som 44 G2
Suff 126 G3
Wilts 47 B10
Wilts 61 F10
W Sus 34 B5
Henley Common W Sus 34 B5
Henley Green W Mid 135 G7
Henley-in-Arden Warks 118 D3
Henley-on-Thames Oxon 65 C9
Henley's Down E Sus 38 E2
Henley Street Kent 69 F7
Henllan Ceredig 93 C7
Denb 165 B8
Henllan Amgoed Carms 92 G3
Henlle Shrops 148 C6
Henllys Torf 78 G3
Henllys Vale Torf 78 G3
Henlow C Beds 104 D3
Hennock Devon 14 E2
Henny Street Essex 107 D7
Henryd Conwy 180 G3
Henry's Moat Pembs 91 F10
Hensall N Yorks 198 C5
Henshaw Northumb 241 E7
W Yorks 205 E10
Hensingham Cumb 219 B9
Hensington Oxon 83 B7
Henstead Suff 143 F9
Hensting Hants 33 C7
Henstridge Devon 40 E5
Som 30 D2
Henstridge Ash Som 30 C2
Henstridge Bowden
Som 29 C11
Henstridge Marsh Som 30 C2
Henton Oxon 84 E3
Som 44 D3
Henwood Corn 11 G11
Oxon 83 E7
Henwood Green Kent 52 E6
Heogan Shetland 313 J6
Heol-ddu Carms 75 E7
Swansea 56 B6
Heolgerrig M Tydf 77 D8
Heol-laethog Bridgend 58 C2
Heol-las Bridgend 58 C2
Swansea 57 B7
Heol Senni Powys 95 G8
Heol-y-gaer Powys 96 D3
Heol-y-mynydd V Glam 57 G11
Hepburn Northumb 264 E3
Hepple Northumb 251 C11
Hepscott Northumb 252 G6
Hepthorne Lane Derbys 170 C6
Heptonstall W Yorks 196 B3
Hepworth Suff 125 C9
W Yorks 197 F7
Herbrandston Pembs 72 D5
Hereford Hereford 97 C10
Heribusta Highld 298 B4
Heriot Borders 271 E7
Hermiston Edin 280 G3
Hermitage Borders 250 D2
Dorset 29 F10
W Berks 64 E4
W Sus 22 B3
Hermitage Green Mers 183 C10
Hermit Hill S Yorks 197 G10
Hermit Hole W Yorks 205 F7
Hermon Anglesey 162 B5
Carms 93 E7
Carms 94 F3
Pembs 92 E4
Herne Kent 71 F7
Herne Bay Kent 71 F7
Herne Common Kent 71 F7
Herne Hill London 67 E10
Herne Pound Kent 53 C7
Herner Devon 25 B9
Hernhill Kent 70 G5
Herniss Corn 2 C6
Herodsfoot Corn 6 C4
Heron Cross Stoke 168 G5
Heronden Kent 55 C9
Herongate Essex 87 G10
Heronsford S Ayrs 244 G4
Heronsgate Herts 85 G8
Heron's Ghyll E Sus 37 B7
Herons Green Bath 44 B5
Heronston Bridgend 58 D2
Herra Shetland 312 D8
Herriard Hants 49 D7
Herringfleet Suff 143 D9
Herring's Green Beds 103 C11
Herringswell Suff 124 C4
Herringthorpe S Yorks 186 C6
Hersden Kent 71 G8
Hersham Corn 24 F3
Sur 66 G6
Herstmonceux E Sus 23 C10
Herston Dorset 18 F6
Orkney 314 G4
Hertford Herts 86 C4
Hertford Heath Herts 86 C4
Hertingfordbury Herts 86 C4
Hesketh Bank Lancs 194 C2
Hesketh Lane Lancs 203 E8
Hesketh Moss Lancs 194 C2
Hesket Newmarket
Cumb 230 D2
Heskin Green Lancs 194 D4
Hesleden Durham 234 D4
Hesleyside Northumb 251 G8
Heslington York 207 C8
Hessay York 206 C6
Hessenford Corn 6 D6
Hessett Suff 125 E8
Hessle E Yorks 200 B4
W Yorks 198 D2
Hest Bank Lancs 211 F9
Hester's Way Glos 99 G8
Hestinsetter Shetland 313 J4
Heston London 66 D6
Hestwall Orkney 314 E2
Heswall Mers 182 E3
Hethe Oxon 101 F11
Hethel Norf 142 C3
Hethelpit Cross Glos 98 F5
Hethersett Norf 142 C3
Hethersgill Cumb 239 D11
Hetherside Cumb 239 D10
Hetherson Green
Ches W 167 F8
Hethpool Northumb 263 D9
Hett Durham 233 D11
Hetton N Yorks 204 B5
Hetton Downs T&W 234 B3
Hetton-le-Hill T&W 234 B3
Hetton-le-Hole T&W 234 B3
Hetton Steads Northumb 264 B2
Heugh Northumb 242 C3
Heugh-head Aberds 292 B5
Heveningham Suff 126 C6
Hever Kent 52 E3
Heversham Cumb 211 C9
Hevingham Norf 160 E3
Hewas Water Corn 5 F9
Hewelsfield Glos 79 E9
Hewelsfield Common
Glos 79 E8
Hewer Hill Cumb 230 D3
Hew Green N Yorks 205 B10
Hewish N Som 60 G2
Som 28 F6
Hewood Dorset 28 G5
Heworth T&W 243 E7
York 207 C8
Hexham Northumb 241 E10
Hextable Kent 68 E4
Hexthorpe S Yorks 198 G5
Hexton Herts 104 E2
Hexworthy Devon 13 G9
Hey Lancs 204 E3
Heybridge Essex 87 F10
Essex 88 D5
Heybridge Basin Essex 88 D5
Heybrook Bay Devon 7 F10
Heydon Cambs 105 C8
Norf 160 D2
Heydour Lincs 155 B10
Hey Green W Yorks 196 E4
Heyheads Gtr Man 196 G3
Hey Houses Lancs 193 B10
Heylipol Argyll 288 E1
Heylor Shetland 312 E4
Heyope Powys 114 C4
Heyrod Gtr Man 185 B7
Heysham Lancs 211 G8
Heyshaw N Yorks 214 G3
Heyshott W Sus 34 D5
Heyshott Green W Sus 34 D5
Heyside Gtr Man 196 F2
Heytesbury Wilts 46 E2
Heythrop Oxon 101 F7
Heywood Gtr Man 195 E11
Wilts 45 C11
Hibaldstow N Lincs 200 G3
Hibb's Green Suff 125 G7
Hickford Hill Essex 106 C5
Hickleton S Yorks 198 F3
Hickling Norf 161 E8
Notts 154 D3
Hickling Green Norf 161 E8
Hickling Heath Norf 161 E8
Hickling Pastures Notts 154 D3
Hickmans Green Kent 54 B5
Hicks Forstal Kent 71 G7
Hicks Gate Bath 60 F6
Hick's Mill Corn 4 G5
Hickstead W Sus 36 C3
Hidcote Bartrim Glos 100 C3
Hidcote Boyce Glos 100 C3
Hifnal Shrops 132 D4
Higginshaw Gtr Man 196 F2
High Ackworth W Yorks 198 D2
Higham Derbys 170 D5
Fife 286 F6
Kent 69 E8
Lancs 204 F2
Suff 107 D10
Suff 124 E4
S Yorks 197 F10
Higham Common
S Yorks 197 F10
Higham Dykes Northumb 242 B4
Higham Ferrers
Northants 121 D9
Higham Gobion C Beds 104 E2
Higham Hill London 86 G5
Higham on the Hill
Leics 135 D7
Highampton Devon 25 G7
Highams Park London 86 G5
Higham Wood Kent 52 D5
High Angerton Northumb 252 F3
High Bankhill Cumb 231 C7
High Banton N Lnrk 278 E4
High Barn Lincs 174 C5
High Barnes T&W 243 F9
High Barnet London 86 F2
High Beach Essex 86 F6
High Bentham N Yorks 212 F3
High Bickington Devon 25 C10
High Biggins Cumb 212 D2
High Birkwith N Yorks 212 D5
High Birstwith N Yorks 205 B10
High Blantyre S Lnrk 268 D3
High Bonnybridge Falk 278 F6
High Bradfield S Yorks 186 C3
High Bradley N Yorks 204 D6
High Bray Devon 41 G7
Highbridge Cumb 230 C3
Hants 33 C7
Highld 290 E3
Som 43 D10
W Mid 133 C10
Highbrook W Sus 51 G11
High Brooms Kent 52 E5
High Brotheridge Glos 80 C5
High Bullen Devon 25 C8
Highburton W Yorks 197 E7
Highbury London 67 B10
Ptsmth 33 G11
Som 45 D7
Highbury Vale
Nottingham 171 G8
High Buston Northumb 252 B6
High Callerton
Northumb 242 C5
High Cark Cumb 211 C7
High Casterton Cumb 212 D2
High Catton E Yorks 207 C10
High Church Northumb 252 F5
Highclere Hants 64 G2
Highcliffe Derbys 186 F2
Dorset 19 C10
High Cogges Oxon 82 D5
High Common Norf 141 B9
High Coniscliffe Darl 224 B4
High Crompton Gtr Man 196 F2
High Cross Cambs 123 F8
Corn 2 D6
E Sus 37 B9
Hants 34 B2
Herts 85 F10
Herts 86 B5
Newport 59 B9
Warks 118 D3
W Sus 36 D2
High Crosshill S Lnrk 268 C2
High Cunsey Cumb 221 G7
High Dubmire T&W 234 B2
High Dyke Durham 232 F5
High Easter Essex 87 C10
High Eggborough
N Yorks 198 C5
High Eldrig Dumfries 236 C4
High Ellington N Yorks 214 C3
Higher Alham Som 45 E7
Higher Ansty Dorset 30 G3
Higher Ashton Devon 14 E3
Higher Audley Blkburn 195 B7
Higher Bal Corn 4 E4
Higher Ballam Lancs 202 G3
Higher Bartle Lancs 202 G6
Higher Bebington Mers 182 D4
Higher Berry End
C Beds 103 E9
Higher Blackley
Gtr Man 195 G10
Higher Boarshaw
Gtr Man 195 F11
Higher Bockhampton
Dorset 17 C10
Higher Bojewyan Corn 1 C3
Higher Boscaswell Corn 1 C3
Higher Brixham Torbay 9 D8
Higher Broughton
Gtr Man 195 G10
Higher Burrow Som 28 C6
Higher Burwardsley
Ches W 167 D8
High Ercall Telford 149 F11
Higher Chalmington
Dorset 29 G9
Higher Cheriton Devon 27 G10
Higher Chillington Som 28 E5
Higher Chisworth
Derbys 185 C7
Highercliff Corn 6 D4
Higher Clovelly Devon 24 C4
Higher Condurrow Corn 2 B5
Higher Crackington Corn 11 B9
Higher Cransworth Corn 5 B9
Higher Croft Blkburn 195 B7
Higher Denham Bucks 66 B4
Higher Dinting Derbys 185 C8
Higher Disley Ches E 185 E7
Higher Downs Corn 2 C3
Higher Durston Som 28 B3
Higher End Gtr Man 194 G4
Higher Folds Gtr Man 195 G7
Higherford Lancs 204 E3
Higher Gabwell Torbay 9 B8
Higher Green Gtr Man 195 G8
Higher Halstock Leigh
Dorset 29 F8
Higher Heysham Lancs 211 G8
Higher Hogshead
Lancs 195 C11
Higher Holton Som 29 B11
Higher Hurdsfield
Ches E 184 G6
Higher Kingcombe
Dorset 16 B6
Higher Kinnerton Flint 166 C4
Higher Land Corn 12 G3
Higher Marsh Som 30 C2
Higher Melcombe Dorset 30 G2
Higher Menadew Corn 5 D10
Higher Molland Devon 41 G8
Higher Muddiford Devon 40 F5
Higher Nyland Dorset 30 C2
Higher Penwortham
Lancs 194 B4
Higher Pertwood Wilts 45 F11
Higher Porthpean Corn 5 E10
Higher Poynton Ches E 184 E6
Higher Prestacott Devon 12 B3
Higher Rads End
C Beds 103 E9
Higher Ridge Shrops 149 C7
Higher Rocombe Barton
Devon 9 B8
Higher Row Dorset 31 G8
Higher Runcorn Halton 183 E8
Higher Sandford Dorset 29 C10
Higher Shotton Flint 166 B4
Higher Shurlach
Ches W 183 G11
Higher Slade Devon 40 D4
Higher Street Som 42 E6
Higher Tale Devon 27 G9
Higher Tolcarne Corn 5 B7
Higher Totnell Dorset 29 F10
Highertown Corn 4 G6
Corn 11 E8
Higher Town Corn 5 C10
Scilly 1 F4
Som 42 D3
Higher Tremarcoombe
Corn 6 B5
Higher Vexford Som 42 F6
Higher Walreddon Devon 12 G5
Higher Walton Lancs 194 B5
Warr 183 D9
Higher Wambrook Som 28 F3
Higher Warcombe Devon 40 D3
Higher Weaver Devon 27 G9
Higher Whatcombe
Dorset 30 G4
Higher Wheelton Lancs 194 C6
Higher Whitley
Ches W 183 E10
Higher Wincham
Ches W 183 F11
Higher Woodsford
Dorset 17 D11
Higher Wraxall Dorset 29 G9
Higher Wych Ches W 167 G7
High Etherley Durham 233 F9
High Ferry Lincs 174 F5
Highfield E Yorks 207 F10
Glos 79 E10
Gtr Man 194 G5
Gtr Man 195 F8
Herts 85 D9
N Ayrs 266 E6
Oxon 101 G11
Soton 32 E6
S Yorks 186 D5
T&W 242 F4
High Field Lancs 203 C10
Highfields Cambs 123 F7
Derbys 170 B6
Essex 88 B5
Glos 80 F3
Leicester 136 C2
Northumb 273 E9
Staffs 151 E8
S Yorks 198 F4
High Flatts W Yorks 197 F8
High Forge Durham 242 G6
High Friarside Durham 242 F5
High Gallowhill E Dunb 278 G2
High Garrett Essex 106 F5
Highgate E Sus 52 G2
Kent 53 G9
London 67 B9
Powys 130 D2
S Yorks 198 G3
W Mid 133 F11
High Grange Durham 233 E9
High Grantley N Yorks 214 F4
High Green Cumb 221 E8
Norf 141 B8
Norf 142 B2
Norf 159 G8
Shrops 132 G4
Suff 125 E7
S Yorks 186 B4
Worcs 99 B7
W Yorks 197 E7
High Halden Kent 53 F11
High Halstow Medway 69 D9
High Ham Som 44 G2
High Handenhold
Durham 242 G6
High Harrington Cumb 228 F6
High Harrogate N Yorks 206 B2
High Haswell Durham 234 C3
High Hatton Shrops 150 E2
High Hauxley Northumb 253 C7
High Hawsker N Yorks 227 D8
High Heath Shrops 150 D3
W Mid 133 C10
High Hesket Cumb 230 C5
High Hesleden Durham 234 D5
High Hill Cumb 229 G11
High Houses Essex 87 C11
High Hoyland S Yorks 197 E9
High Hunsley E Yorks 208 F4
High Hurstwood E Sus 37 B7
High Hutton N Yorks 216 F5
High Ireby Cumb 229 D10
High Kelling Norf 177 E10
High Kilburn N Yorks 215 D10
High Lands Durham 233 F8
Highlane Ches E 168 B5
Derbys 186 E6
High Lane Gtr Man 185 D7
Worcs 116 E3
Highlanes Corn 10 G4
Staffs 150 C5
High Lanes Corn 2 B3
High Laver Essex 87 D8
Highlaws Cumb 229 B8
Highleadon Glos 98 G5
High Legh Ches E 184 E2
Highleigh W Sus 22 D4
High Leven Stockton 225 C8
Highley Shrops 132 G4
High Littleton Bath 44 B6
High Longthwaite
Cumb 229 B11
High Lorton Cumb 229 F9
High Marishes N Yorks 216 D6
High Marnham Notts 188 G4
High Melton S Yorks 198 G4
High Mickley Northumb 242 E3
High Mindork Dumfries 236 D5
Highmoor Cumb 229 B11
Oxon 65 B8
High Moor Derbys 187 E7
Lancs 194 E4
Highmoor Cross Oxon 65 C8
Highmoor Hill Mon 60 B3
High Moorsley T&W 234 B2
Highnam Glos 80 B3
Highnam Green Glos 98 G5
High Nash Glos 79 C9
High Newton Cumb 211 C8
High Newton-by-the-Sea
Northumb 264 D6
High Nibthwaite Cumb 210 B5
Highoak Norf 141 C11
High Oaks Cumb 222 G2
High Offley Staffs 150 D5
High Ongar Essex 87 E9
High Onn Staffs 150 F6
High Onn Wharf Staffs 150 F6
High Park Cumb 221 G10
Mers 193 D11
Highridge Bristol 60 F5
High Risby N Lincs 200 E2
Highroad Well Moor
W Yorks 196 B5
High Roding Essex 87 B10
High Rougham Suff 125 E8
High Row Cumb 230 D3
Cumb 230 G3
High Salvington W Sus 35 F10
High Scales Cumb 229 B9
High Sellafield Cumb 219 E10
High Shaw N Yorks 223 G7
High Shields T&W 243 D9
High Shincliffe Durham 233 C11
High Side Cumb 229 E10
High Southwick T&W 243 F9
High Spen T&W 242 F4
High Stakesby N Yorks 227 C7
Highstead Kent 71 F8
Highsted Kent 70 G2
High Stoop Durham 233 C8
Highstreet Kent 70 G5
High Street Corn 5 E9
Kent 53 G8
Pembs 73 B11
Suff 107 B7
Suff 127 C8
Suff 127 F8
Suff 143 G7
Highstreet Green Essex 106 E5
Sur 50 F3
High Street Green Suff 125 F10
High Sunderland
Borders 261 C11
Hightae Dumfries 238 B3
Highter's Heath W Mid 117 B11
High Throston Hrtlpl 234 E5
High Tirfergus Argyll 255 F7
Hightown Ches E 168 C5
Hants 31 G11
Mers 193 G10
Soton 33 E7
Wrex 166 F4
W Yorks 197 C7
High Town Luton 103 G11
Shrops 132 E4
Staffs 151 G9
Hightown Green Suff 125 F9
Hightown Heights
W Yorks 197 C7
High Toynton Lincs 174 B3
High Trewhitt Northumb 252 B2
High Urpeth Durham 242 G6
High Valleyfield Fife 279 D10
High Walton Cumb 219 C9
High Warden Northumb 241 D10
High Water Head Cumb 220 F6
Highway Corn 4 G4
Hereford 97 B9
Som 29 C7
Wilts 62 E4
Windsor 65 C11
Highweek Devon 14 G2
High Westwood Durham 242 F4
High Whinnow Cumb 239 G8
Highwood Devon 27 F10
Dorset 18 D3
Essex 87 E10
Hants 31 F11
Worcs 116 D3
Highwood Hill London 86 G2
High Woolaston Glos 79 F9
High Worsall N Yorks 225 D7
Highworth Swindon 82 G2
Highworthy Devon 24 F6
High Wray Cumb 221 F7
High Wych Herts 87 C7
High Wycombe Bucks 84 G5
Hilborough Norf 140 C6
Hilborough Ho Norf 140 C6
Hilcot Glos 81 B7
Hilcote Derbys 171 D7
Hilcot End Glos 81 E9
Hilcott Wilts 46 B6
Hildenborough Kent 52 D5
Hilden Park Kent 52 D5
Hildersham Cambs 105 B10
Hildersley Hereford 98 G2
Hilderstone Staffs 151 C8
Hilderthorpe E Yorks 218 F3
Hilfield Dorset 29 F10
Hilgay Norf 140 D2
Hill S Glos 79 G10
Warks 119 D9
W Mid 134 D2
Hillam N Yorks 198 B4
Hillbeck Cumb 222 B5
Hillblock Pembs 73 B8
Hillborough Kent 71 F8
Hill Bottom Oxon 64 D6
Hillbourne Poole 18 C6
Hillbrae Aberds 302 E6
Aberds 303 G7
Hill Brow W Sus 34 B3
Hillbutts Dorset 31 G7
Hill Chorlton Staffs 150 B5
Hillcliffe Warr 183 D10
Hillclifflane Derbys 170 F3
Hillcommon Som 27 B11
Hill Common Norf 161 E8
Hill Corner Som 45 D10
Hill Croome Worcs 99 C7
Hillcross Derbys 152 C6
Hill Dale Lancs 194 E3
Hill Deverill Wilts 45 E11
Hilldyke Lincs 174 F4
Hill Dyke Lincs 174 F4
Hillend Fife 280 E2
N Lnrk 268 B6
N Som 43 B11
Shrops 132 E6
Swansea 56 C2
Hill End Durham 232 D6
Fife 279 B10
Glos 99 D8
London 85 G8
N Yorks 205 C7
Som 29 E8
Worcs 117 E8
Hillend Green Glos 98 F4
Hillersland Glos 79 C9
Hillerton Devon 13 B10
Hillesden Bucks 102 F3
Hillesden Hamlet Bucks 102 E3
Hillesley Glos 61 B9
Hillfarance Som 27 C11
Hillfarrance Som 27 C11
Hillfield Devon 8 E6
W Mid 118 B2
Hillfields S Glos 60 D6
W Mid 118 B6
Hillfoot Aberds 303 D9
W Yorks 205 G10
Hillfoot End C Beds 104 E2
Hill Furze Worcs 99 B9
Hill Gate Hereford 97 F9
Hillgreen W Berks 64 D3
Hill Green Essex 105 E9
Kent 69 G10
Hillgrove W Sus 34 B6
Hillhampton Hereford 97 B11
Hillhead Aberds 302 F5
Aberds 303 G8
Corn 5 C11
Devon 9 E8
E Ayrs 257 B10
S Ayrs 257 F10
Hill Head Hants 33 G8
Northumb 241 D10
Hillhead of Auchentumb
Aberds 303 D9
Hillhead of Blairy
Aberds 302 D6
Hillhead of Cocklaw
Aberds 303 E10
Hill Hoath Kent 52 E3
Hill Hook W Mid 134 C2
Hillhouse Borders 271 D10
Hill Houses Shrops 116 B2
Hilliard's Cross Staffs 152 G3
Hilliclay Highld 310 C5
Hillingdon London 66 C5
Hillingdon Heath London 66 C5
Hillington Glasgow 267 C10
Norf 158 D4
Hillis Corner IoW 20 C5
Hillmoor Devon 27 E10
Hillmorton Warks 119 C10
Hill Mountain Pembs 73 D7
Hillockhead Aberds 292 B6
Aberds 292 C5
Hillock Vale Lancs 195 B9
Hill of Beath Fife 280 C3
Hill of Drip Stirl 278 B5
Hill of Fearn Highld 301 B8
Hill of Keillor Angus 286 C6
Hill of Mountblairy
Aberds 302 D6
Hill of Overbrae Aberds 303 C8
Hill Park Hants 33 F9
Kent 52 B2
Hillpool Worcs 117 B7
Hillpound Hants 33 D9
Hill Ridware Staffs 151 F11
Hillsborough S Yorks 186 C4
Hillside Aberds 293 D11
Angus 293 G9
Devon 8 C4
Devon 27 F11
Hants 49 C9
Mers 193 E10
Orkney 314 D3
Orkney 314 G4
Shetland 313 G6
Shrops 131 F11
Wilts 81 G9
Hill Side Hants 34 B3
S Yorks 197 G8
Worcs 116 E5
W Yorks 197 D7
Hill Somersal Derbys 152 C2
Hills Town Derbys 171 B7
Hillstreet Hants 32 D4
Hill Street Kent 54 D6
Hillswick Shetland 312 F4
Hilltop Bl Gwent 77 D11
Bucks 85 E7
Derbys 170 C4
Hill Top Derbys 186 F5
Durham 232 G5
Durham 233 C10
Durham 242 G5
Gtr Man 195 G8
Hants 32 G6
Notts 171 F7
N Yorks 214 G3
N Yorks 214 G5
Staffs 133 B7
S Yorks 186 C5
S Yorks 186 D3
S Yorks 187 B7
S Yorks 197 F9
Warks 134 E5
Warks 135 E7
W Mid 133 E9
W Sus 34 C5
W Yorks 196 E5
W Yorks 197 D10
W Yorks 205 G7
W Yorks 205 G11
Hillview T&W 243 G9
Hill View Dorset 18 B5
Hillway IoW 21 D8
Hillwell Shetland 313 M5
Hill Wood W Mid 134 C2
Hill Wootton Warks 118 D6
Hillyfields Hants 32 D5
Hilmarton Wilts 62 D4
Hilperton Wilts 45 B11
Hilperton Marsh Wilts 45 B11
Hilsea Ptsmth 33 G11
Hilston E Yorks 209 G11
Hiltingbury Hants 32 C6
Hilton Aberds 303 F9
Borders 273 E7
Cambs 122 D5
Cumb 231 G10
Derbys 152 C4
Dorset 30 G3
Durham 233 G9
Highld 309 L7
Highld 311 L3
Shrops 132 D5
Staffs 133 B11
Stockton 225 C9
Hilton House Gtr Man 194 F6
Hilton Lodge Highld 300 G2
Hilton of Cadboll Highld 301 B8
Hilton Park Gtr Man 195 G10
Himbleton Worcs 117 F8
Himley Staffs 133 E7
Hincaster Cumb 211 C10
Hinchley Wood Sur 67 F7
Hinchliffe Mill W Yorks 196 F6
Hinchwick Glos 100 E2
Hinckley Leics 135 E8
Hinderclay Suff 125 B10
Hinderton Ches W 182 F4
Hinderwell N Yorks 226 B5
Hindford Shrops 148 C6
Hindhead Sur 49 F11
Hindle Fold Lancs 203 G10
Hindley Gtr Man 194 G6
Northumb 242 F2
Hindley Green Gtr Man 194 G6
Hindlip Worcs 117 F7
Hindolveston Norf 159 D10
Hindon Wilts 46 G2
Hindpool Cumb 210 F3
Hindringham Norf 159 B9
Hindsford Gtr Man 195 G7
Hingham Norf 141 C10
Hinstock Shrops 150 D3
Hintlesham Suff 107 C11
Hinton Glos 79 E11
Hants 19 B10
Hereford 96 D6
Northants 119 G10
S Glos 61 D8
Shrops 131 B8
Som 29 C9
Hinton Ampner Hants 33 B9
Hinton Blewett Bath 44 B5
Hinton Charterhouse
Bath 45 B9
Hinton Cross Worcs 99 C10
Hinton-in-the-Hedges
Northants 101 D11
Hinton Martell Dorset 31 F8
Hinton on the Green
Worcs 99 C10
Hinton Parva Dorset 31 G7
Swindon 63 C8
Hinton St George Som 28 E6
Hinton St Mary Dorset 30 D3
Hinton Waldrist Oxon 82 F5
Hints Shrops 116 C2
Staffs 134 C3
Hinwick Beds 121 E8
Hinwood Shrops 131 B7
Hinxhill Kent 54 E5
Hinxton Cambs 105 B9
Hinxworth Herts 104 C4
Hipperholme W Yorks 196 B6
Hipplecote Worcs 116 F4
Hipsburn Northumb 264 G6
Hipswell N Yorks 224 F3
Hirael Gwyn 179 G9
Hiraeth Carms 92 G3
Hirn Aberds 293 C9
Hirnant Powys 147 E11
Hirst N Lnrk 269 C7
Northumb 253 F7
Hirst Courtney N Yorks 198 C6
Hirwaen Denb 165 C10
Hirwaun Rhondda 77 D7
Hirwaun Common
Bridgend 58 C2
Hiscott Devon 25 B8
Hislop Borders 249 C9
Hisomley Wilts 45 D11
Histon Cambs 123 E8
Hitcham Suff 125 G9
Hitchill Dumfries 238 D4
Hitchin Herts 104 F3
Hitchin Hill Herts 104 F3
Hitcombe Bottom Wilts 45 E10
Hither Green London 67 E11
Hittisleigh Devon 13 C10
Hittisleigh Barton Devon 13 B10
Hive E Yorks 208 G2
Hixon Staffs 151 D10
Hoaden Kent 55 B9
Hoar Cross Staffs 152 E2
Hoarwithy Hereford 97 F10
Hoath Kent 71 G8
Hoath Corner Kent 52 E3
Hobarris Shrops 114 B6
Hobbister Orkney 314 F3
Hobble End Staffs 133 B10
Hobbles Green Suff 124 G4
Hobbs Cross Essex 87 C7
Essex 87 F7
Hobbs Wall Bath 61 G7
Hob Hill Ches W 167 E7
Hobkirk Borders 262 G3
Hobroyd Derbys 185 C8
Hobson Durham 242 F5
Hoby Leics 154 F3
Hoccombe Som 27 B10
Hockenden London 68 F3
Hockerill Herts 105 G9
Hockering Norf 159 G11
Hockering Heath Norf 159 G11
Hockerton Notts 172 D2
Hockholler Som 27 C11
Hockholler Green Som 27 C11
Hockley Ches E 184 E6
Essex 88 G4
Kent 54 B3
Staffs 134 C4
W Mid 118 B5
Hockley Heath W Mid 118 C3
Hockliffe C Beds 103 F9
Hockwold cum Wilton
Norf 140 F4
Hockworthy Devon 27 D8
Hocombe Hants 32 C6
Hoddesdon Herts 86 D5
Hoddlesden Blkburn 195 C8
Hoddomcross Dumfries 238 C5
Hoddom Mains Dumfries 238 C5
Hoden Worcs 99 B11
Hodgefield Staffs 168 E6
Hodgehill Ches E 168 B4
W Mid 134 F2
Hodgeston Pembs 73 F8
Hodley Powys 130 E3
Hodnet Shrops 150 D2
Hodnetheath Shrops 150 D2
Hodsock Notts 187 D10
Hodsoll Street Kent 68 G6
Hodson Swindon 63 C7
Hodthorpe Derbys 187 F8
Hoe Hants 33 D9
Norf 159 F9
Sur 50 D5
Hoe Benham W Berks 64 F2
Hoe Gate Hants 33 E10
Hoff Cumb 222 B3
Hoffleet Stow Lincs 156 B4
Hogaland Shetland 312 F5
Hogben's Hill Kent 54 B4
Hogganfield Glasgow 268 B2
Hoggard's Green Suff 125 F7
Hoggeston Bucks 102 G6
Hoggington Wilts 45 B10
Hoggrill's End Warks 134 E4
Hogha Gearraidh
W Isles 296 D3
Hog Hatch Sur 49 D10
Hoghton Lancs 194 B6
Hoghton Bottoms Lancs 194 B6
Hogley Green W Yorks 196 F6
Hognaston Derbys 170 E2
Hogpits Bottom Herts 85 E8
Hogsthorpe Lincs 191 G8
Hogstock Dorset 31 F7
Holbeach Lincs 157 E7
Holbeach Bank Lincs 157 D7
Holbeach Clough Lincs 156 D6
Holbeach Drove Lincs 156 G6
Holbeache Worcs 116 B5
Holbeach Hurn Lincs 157 D7
Holbeach St Johns
Lincs 156 F6
Holbeach St Marks
Lincs 157 C7
Holbeach St Matthew
Lincs 157 C8
Holbeck Notts 187 G8
W Yorks 205 G11
Holbeck Woodhouse
Notts 187 G8
Holberrow Green
Worcs 117 F10
Holbeton Devon 8 E2
Holborn London 67 C10
Holborough Kent 69 G8
Holbrook Derbys 170 G5
Suff 108 D3
S Yorks 186 E6
Holbrook Common
S Glos 61 E7
Holbrook Moor Derbys 170 F5
Holbrooks W Mid 134 G6
Holburn Northumb 264 B2
Holbury Hants 32 G6
Holcombe Devon 14 G5
Gtr Man 195 D9
Som 45 D7
Holcombe Brook
Gtr Man 195 E9
Holcombe Rogus Devon 27 D9
Holcot Northants 120 D5
Holdbrook London 86 F5
Holden Lancs 203 D11
Holdenby Northants 120 D3
Holden Fold Gtr Man 196 F2
Holdenhurst Bmouth 19 B8
Holder's Green Essex 106 F2
Holders Hill London 86 G2
Holdfast Worcs 99 D7
Holdgate Shrops 131 F11
Holdingham Lincs 173 F9
Holditch Dorset 28 G4
Holdsworth W Yorks 196 B5
Holdworth S Yorks 186 C3
Hole Devon 24 D4
W Yorks 204 F6
Hole Bottom W Yorks 196 C2
Holefield Borders 263 C8
Holehills N Lnrk 268 B5
Holehouse Derbys 185 C8
Holehouses Ches E 184 F2
Hole-in-the-Wall
Hereford 98 F2
Holemill Aberdeen 293 C10
Holemoor Devon 24 F6
Hole's Hole Devon 7 B8
Holestane Dumfries 247 D9
Holestone Derbys 170 C4
Hole Street W Sus 35 E10
Holewater Devon 41 F8
Holford Som 43 E7
Holgate York 207 C7
Holker Cumb 211 D7
Holkham Norf 176 E5
Hollacombe Devon 24 G5
Devon 26 G4
Hollacombe Hill Devon 7 E10
Holland Orkney 314 A4
Orkney 314 D6
Sur 52 C2
Holland Fen Lincs 174 F2
Holland Lees Lancs 194 F4
Holland-on-Sea Essex 89 B12
Hollands Som 29 D9
Hollandstoun Orkney 314 A7
Hollee Dumfries 239 D7
Hollesley Suff 109 C7
Hollicombe Torbay 9 C7
Hollies Common Staffs 150 E6
Hollinfare Warr 183 C11
Hollingbourne Kent 53 B10
Hollingbury Brighton 36 F4
Hollingdean Brighton 36 F4
Hollingdon Bucks 103 F7
Hollingrove E Sus 37 C11
Hollingthorpe W Yorks 197 D10
Hollington Derbys 152 B4
E Sus 38 E3
Hants 48 B2

Staffs ... 151 B11
Hollington Cross Hants ... 48 B2
Hollington Grove Derbys ... 152 B4
Hollingwood Derbys ... 186 G6
Hollingworth Gtr Man ... 185 B8
Hollin Hall Lancs ... 204 F4
Hollin Park W Yorks ... 206 F2
Hollins Cumb ... 222 G3
 Derbys ... 186 G4
 Gtr Man ... 195 F8
 Gtr Man ... 195 F11
 Gtr Man ... 168 G6
 Staffs ... 168 E4
 Staffs ... 169 F7
Hollinsclough Staffs ... 169 B9
Hollins End S Yorks ... 186 E5
Hollinsgreen Ches E ... 168 C2
Hollins Green Warr ... 183 C11
Hollins Lane Lancs ... 202 C5
 Shrops ... 149 B10
Hollinswood Telford ... 132 B4
Hollinthorpe W Yorks ... 206 G3
Hollinwood Gtr Man ... 196 G2
 Shrops ... 149 B10
Hollis Green Devon ... 27 F9
Hollis Head Devon ... 27 G7
Hollocombe Devon ... 25 E10
Hollocombe Town Devon ... 25 E10
Holloway Derbys ... 170 D4
 Wilts ... 45 G11
 Windsor ... 65 C10
Holloway Hill Sur ... 50 E3
Hollow Brook Bath ... 60 G5
Hollowell Northants ... 120 C3
Hollow Meadows S Yorks ... 186 D2
Hollowmoor Heath Ches W ... 167 B7
Hollow Oak Dorset ... 18 C2
Hollows Dumfries ... 239 B9
Hollow Street Kent ... 71 G8
Holly Bank W Mid ... 133 C11
Hollybed Common W Mid ... 134 G5
Holly Brook Som ... 16 G2
Hollybush Caerph ... 77 E11
 E Ayrs ... 257 G9
 Stoke ... 168 G5
 Torf ... 78 G3
 Worcs ... 98 D5
Holly Bush Wrex ... 166 E4
Hollybush Corner Bucks ... 66 B3
 Suff ... 125 F8
Hollybushes Kent ... 54 B2
Hollybush Hill Bucks ... 66 C3
 Essex ... 89 B10
Hollycroft Leics ... 135 E8
Holly End Norf ... 139 B9
Holly Green Bucks ... 84 F6
 Worcs ... 99 C7
Holly Hill N Yorks ... 224 E3
 Warks ... 135 F7
Hollyhurst Shrops ... 131 D9
Hollym E Yorks ... 201 B10
Hollywaste Shrops ... 116 B2
Hollywater Hants ... 49 G10
Hollywood Worcs ... 117 B11
Holmacott Devon ... 25 B8
Holman Clavel Som ... 28 D2
Holmbridge W Yorks ... 196 F6
Holmbury St Mary Sur ... 50 E6
Holmbush Corn ... 5 E10
 Dorset ... 28 G5
Holmcroft Staffs ... 151 D8
Holme Cambs ... 138 F3
 C Beds ... 104 C3
 Cumb ... 211 D10
 N Lincs ... 200 F2
 Notts ... 172 D4
 W Yorks ... 215 C7
 W Yorks ... 196 F6
 W Yorks ... 205 G9
Holmebridge Dorset ... 18 D3
Holme Chapel Lancs ... 195 B11
Holme Green C Beds ... 104 C3
 N Yorks ... 207 E7
 Wokingham ... 65 F10
Holme Hale Norf ... 141 B7
Holme Hill NE Lincs ... 201 F9
Holme Lacy Hereford ... 97 D11
Holme Lane Notts ... 154 B2
Holme Marsh Hereford ... 114 G6
Holme Mills Cumb ... 211 D10
Holme next the Sea Norf ... 176 E2
Holme-on-Spalding-Moor E Yorks ... 208 F2
Holme on the Wolds E Yorks ... 208 D5
Holme Pierrepont Notts ... 154 B2
Holmer Hereford ... 97 C10
Holmer Green Bucks ... 84 F6
Holmes Lancs ... 194 D2
Holme St Cuthbert Cumb ... 229 B8
Holmes Chapel Ches E ... 168 B3
Holmesdale Derbys ... 186 F4
Holmesfield Derbys ... 186 F4
Holme Slack Lancs ... 203 G7
Holme's Hill E Sus ... 23 C8
Holmeswood Lancs ... 194 D2
Holmethorpe Sur ... 51 C9
Holme Wood W Yorks ... 205 G9
Holmfield W Yorks ... 196 F5
Holmfirth W Yorks ... 196 F6
Holmhead Angus ... 293 F7
 Dumfries ... 246 F6
 E Ayrs ... 258 A3
Holmhill Dumfries ... 247 D9
Holmisdale Highld ... 297 G7
Holmley Common Derbys ... 186 F5
Holmpton E Yorks ... 201 C11
Holmrook Cumb ... 219 F11
Holmsgarth Shetland ... 313 J6
Holmside Durham ... 233 B10
Holmsleigh Green Devon ... 28 G2
Holmston S Ayrs ... 257 E9
Holmwrangle Cumb ... 230 B6
Holne Devon ... 8 B4
Holnest Dorset ... 29 E11
Holnicote Som ... 42 D2
Holsworthy Devon ... 24 G4
Holsworthy Beacon Devon ... 24 F5
Holt Dorset ... 31 G8
 Mers ... 183 C7
 Norf ... 159 B11
 Wilts ... 61 G11
 Worcs ... 116 E6
 Wrex ... 166 E6
Holtby York ... 207 C9
Holt End Hants ... 49 F7
 Worcs ... 117 D11
Holt Fleet Worcs ... 116 E6

Holt Green Lancs ... 193 G11
Holt Head W Yorks ... 196 E5
Holt Heath Dorset ... 31 G9
 Staffs ... 152 D2
Holt Hill Kent ... 53 B8
Holton Oxon ... 83 D10
 Som ... 29 B11
 Suff ... 127 B7
Holton cum Beckering Lincs ... 189 E10
Holton Heath Dorset ... 18 C4
Holton le Clay Lincs ... 201 G9
Holton le Moor Lincs ... 200 G4
Holton St Mary Suff ... 107 D11
Holt Park W Yorks ... 205 E11
Holt Pound Hants ... 49 E10
Holts Gtr Man ... 196 G3
Holtspur Bucks ... 84 G6
Holt Wood Dorset ... 31 F8
Holtye E Sus ... 52 F3
Holway Dorset ... 28 G5
 Dorset ... 29 C10
 Flint ... 181 F11
 Som ... 28 C2
Holwell Dorset ... 30 E2
 Herts ... 104 E3
 Leics ... 154 E4
 Oxon ... 82 D2
 Som ... 45 D8
Holwellbury C Beds ... 104 E3
Holwick Durham ... 232 F4
Holworth Dorset ... 17 E11
Holybourne Hants ... 49 E8
Holy City Devon ... 28 G3
Holy Cross T&W ... 243 D8
 Worcs ... 117 B8
Holyfield Essex ... 86 E5
Holyhead / Caergybi Anglesey ... 178 E2
Holy Island Northumb ... 273 B11
Holylee Borders ... 261 B9
Holymoorside Derbys ... 170 B4
Holyport Windsor ... 65 D11
Holystone Northumb ... 251 C11
Holytown N Lnrk ... 268 C5
Holy Vale Scilly ... 1 G4
Holywell Cambs ... 122 C6
 C Beds ... 85 B8
 Corn ... 4 D5
 Dorset ... 29 G9
 E Sus ... 23 F9
 Glos ... 80 G3
 Hereford ... 97 C7
 Herts ... 85 F9
 Northumb ... 243 C8
 Som ... 29 E8
 Warks ... 118 D3
Holywell Bridge W Yorks ... 197 D9
Holywell Green W Yorks ... 196 D5
Holywell Lake Som ... 27 C10
Holywell Row Suff ... 124 B4
Holywell / Treffynnon Flint ... 181 F11
Holywood Dumfries ... 247 G10
Homedowns Glos ... 99 E8
Homer Shrops ... 132 C2
Homer Green Mers ... 193 G10
Homersfield Suff ... 142 F5
Homerton London ... 67 B11
Hom Green Hereford ... 97 G11
Homington Wilts ... 31 B10
Honeyborough Pembs ... 72 D6
Honeybourne Worcs ... 100 C2
Honeychurch Devon ... 25 G10
Honeydon Beds ... 122 F2
Honey Hall N Som ... 60 G2
Honeyhill Wokingham ... 65 F10
Honey Hill Kent ... 70 G6
Honey Street Wilts ... 62 G6
Honey Tye Suff ... 107 D9
Honeywick C Beds ... 103 G9
Honicknowle Plym ... 7 D10
Honiley Warks ... 118 C4
Honing Norf ... 160 D6
Honingham Norf ... 160 G2
Honington Lincs ... 172 G6
 Suff ... 125 C8
 Warks ... 100 C5
Honiton Devon ... 27 G11
Honkley Wrex ... 166 D4
Honley W Yorks ... 196 E6
Honley Moor W Yorks ... 196 E6
Honnington Telford ... 150 F4
Honor Oak London ... 67 E11
Honor Oak Park London ... 67 E11
Honresfeld Gtr Man ... 196 D2
Hoo Kent ... 71 G9
Hoober S Yorks ... 186 B6
Hoobrook Worcs ... 116 C6
Hood Green S Yorks ... 197 G10
Hood Hill S Yorks ... 186 B5
Hood Manor Warr ... 183 D9
Hooe E Sus ... 23 D11
 Plym ... 7 E10
Hooe Common E Sus ... 23 C11
Hoofield Ches W ... 167 C8
Hoo Green Ches E ... 184 E2
Hoohill Blkpool ... 202 F2
Hoo Hole W Yorks ... 196 B4
Hook Cambs ... 139 C8
 Devon ... 28 F4
 E Yorks ... 199 B9
 Hants ... 33 F8
 Hants ... 49 C8
 London ... 67 G7
 Pembs ... 73 C7
 Wilts ... 62 C5
Hook-a-gate Shrops ... 131 B9
Hook Bank Worcs ... 98 C6
Hooke Dorset ... 16 B6
Hook End Essex ... 87 F9
 Oxon ... 65 C7
 W Mid ... 134 G4
Hook Green Kent ... 53 F7
 Kent ... 68 F6
Hook Heath Sur ... 50 B3
Hookgate Staffs ... 150 B4
Hook Green Kent ... 53 F7
Hook Norton Oxon ... 101 E7
Hook Park Hants ... 33 G7
Hook's Cross Herts ... 104 G5
Hook Street Glos ... 79 F11
 Wilts ... 62 C5
Hooksway W Sus ... 34 D4
Hookway Devon ... 14 B3
Hookwood Sur ... 51 E9
 Staffs ... 151 D7
Hoole Ches W ... 166 B6
Hoole Bank Ches W ... 166 B6
Hooley Sur ... 51 B9
Hooley Bridge Gtr Man ... 195 E11
Hooley Brow Gtr Man ... 195 E11
Hooley Hill Gtr Man ... 184 B6
Hoo Meavy Devon ... 7 B11
Hoop Mon ... 79 D8
Hoopers Pool Wilts ... 45 C10
Hoops Devon ... 24 C5
Hoo St Werburgh Medway ... 69 E9
Hooton Ches W ... 182 F5

Hooton Levitt S Yorks ... 187 C8
Hooton Pagnell S Yorks ... 198 F3
Hooton Roberts S Yorks ... 187 B7
Hopcroft's Holt Oxon ... 101 F9
Hope Derbys ... 185 E11
 Devon ... 9 G8
 Highld ... 308 D4
 Powys ... 130 B5
 Shrops ... 130 C6
 Staffs ... 169 D10
Hope Bagot Shrops ... 115 C11
Hope Bowdler Shrops ... 131 E9
Hopedale Staffs ... 169 D10
Hope End Green Essex ... 105 G11
Hope Green Ches E ... 184 E6
Hopeman Moray ... 301 C11
Hope Mansell Hereford ... 79 B10
Hope Park Shrops ... 130 C6
Hopesay Shrops ... 131 G7
Hopesgate Shrops ... 130 C6
Hope's Green Essex ... 69 B9
Hope's Rough Hereford ... 98 B2
Hopetown W Yorks ... 197 C11
Hope under Dinmore Hereford ... 115 G10
Hope / Yr Hôb Flint ... 166 D4
Hopgoods Green W Berks ... 64 F4
Hopkinstown Rhondda ... 77 G9
Hopley's Green Hereford ... 114 G6
Hopperton N Yorks ... 206 B4
Hop Pole Lincs ... 156 G3
Hopsford Warks ... 135 G8
Hopstone Shrops ... 132 E5
Hopton Derbys ... 170 E3
 Shrops ... 149 D11
 Shrops ... 149 E7
 Staffs ... 151 D8
 Suff ... 125 B9
Hoptonbank Shrops ... 116 B2
Hopton Cangeford Shrops ... 131 G10
Hopton Castle Shrops ... 115 B7
Hoptongate Shrops ... 131 G10
Hoptonheath Shrops ... 115 B7
Hopton Heath Staffs ... 151 D9
Hopton on Sea Norf ... 143 D10
Hopton Wafers Shrops ... 116 B2
Hopwas Staffs ... 134 B3
Hopwood Gtr Man ... 195 F11
 Worcs ... 117 B10
Hopworthy Devon ... 24 G4
Horam E Sus ... 23 B9
Horbling Lincs ... 156 B2
Horbury W Yorks ... 197 D9
Horbury Bridge W Yorks ... 197 D9
Horbury Junction W Yorks ... 197 D10
Horcott Glos ... 81 E11
Horden Durham ... 234 C4
Horderley Shrops ... 131 F8
Hordle Hants ... 19 B11
Hordley Shrops ... 149 C7
Horeb Carms ... 75 D7
 Carms ... 93 F10
 Ceredig ... 93 C7
 Flint ... 166 D3
Horfield Bristol ... 60 D6
Horgabost W Isles ... 305 J2
Horham Suff ... 126 C4
Horkesley Heath Essex ... 107 F9
Horkstow N Lincs ... 200 D3
Horkstow Wolds N Lincs ... 200 D3
Horley Oxon ... 101 C8
 Sur ... 51 E9
Horn Ash Dorset ... 28 G5
Hornblotton Som ... 44 G5
Hornblotton Green Som ... 44 G5
Hornby Lancs ... 211 F11
 N Yorks ... 224 E4
 N Yorks ... 225 D7
Horncastle Lincs ... 174 B3
Hornchurch London ... 68 B4
Horncliffe Northumb ... 273 F11
Horndean Borders ... 273 F7
 Hants ... 34 E2
Horndon Devon ... 12 F6
Horndon on the Hill Thurrock ... 69 C7
Horne Sur ... 51 E10
Horne Row Essex ... 88 E3
Horner's Green Suff ... 107 C10
Hornestreet Essex ... 107 E10
Horney Common E Sus ... 37 B7
Horn Hill Som ... 43 E8
Hornick Corn ... 5 E9
Horniehaugh Angus ... 292 G6
Horning Norf ... 160 F6
Horninghold Leics ... 136 D6
Horninglow Staffs ... 152 D4
Horningsea Cambs ... 123 E9
Horningsham Wilts ... 45 E10
Horningtoft Norf ... 159 E8
Horningtops Corn ... 6 C5
Hornsbury Som ... 28 E4
Hornsby Cumb ... 240 G2
Hornsbygate Cumb ... 230 G6
Horns Corner Kent ... 38 B2
Horns Cross Devon ... 24 C5
 E Sus ... 38 C4
Hornsea E Yorks ... 209 D10
Hornsea Bridge E Yorks ... 209 D10
Hornsea Burton E Yorks ... 209 D10
Hornsey London ... 67 B10
Hornsey Vale London ... 67 B10
Horns Green Kent ... 52 B3
Horn Street Kent ... 55 F7
 Kent ... 69 G7
Hornton Oxon ... 101 B7
Horpit Swindon ... 63 C8
Horrabridge Devon ... 7 A11
Horringer Suff ... 124 E6
Horringford IoW ... 20 D6
Horrocks Fold Gtr Man ... 195 E8
Horrocksford Lancs ... 203 E11
Horsalls Kent ... 53 C11
Horsebridge Devon ... 12 G4
 Hants ... 47 G10
 Shrops ... 131 B7
Horse Bridge Staffs ... 169 E7
Horsebrook Devon ... 8 D4
 Staffs ... 151 G7
Horsecastle N Som ... 60 F2
Horsedown Wilts ... 61 D10
Horsedowns Corn ... 2 C4
Horsehay Telford ... 132 B3
Horseheath Cambs ... 106 B2
Horseholm Dumfries ... 238 C2
Horsehouse N Yorks ... 213 C10
Horseley Heath W Mid ... 133 E9
Horsell Sur ... 50 B3
Horsell Birch Sur ... 50 B3
Horseman's Green Wrex ... 166 G6
Horseman Side Essex ... 87 F8

Horsemere Green W Sus ... 35 G7
Horsenden Bucks ... 84 E3
Horsepools Glos ... 80 C4
Horseway Cambs ... 139 F8
Horseway Head Hereford ... 114 C6
Horsey Norf ... 161 E9
Horsey Corner Norf ... 161 E9
Horsey Down Wilts ... 81 G9
Horsford Norf ... 160 F3
Horsforth W Yorks ... 205 F10
Horsforth Woodside W Yorks ... 205 F10
Horsham Worcs ... 116 F4
 W Sus ... 51 G7
Horsham St Faith Norf ... 160 F4
Horsington Lincs ... 174 C2
 Som ... 30 C2
Horsley Derbys ... 170 G5
 Glos ... 80 F4
 Northumb ... 242 D3
 Northumb ... 251 D8
Horsley Cross Essex ... 108 F2
Horsleycross Street Essex ... 108 F2
Horsleyhill Borders ... 262 F2
Horsley Hill T&W ... 243 D9
Horsleyhope Durham ... 233 B7
Horsleys Green Bucks ... 84 F3
Horsley Woodhouse Derbys ... 170 G5
Horsmonden Kent ... 53 E7
Horspath Oxon ... 83 E9
Horstead Norf ... 160 F5
Horsted Green E Sus ... 23 B7
Horsted Keynes W Sus ... 36 B5
Horton Bucks ... 84 B6
 Dorset ... 31 F8
 Kent ... 54 B6
 Lancs ... 204 C3
 Northants ... 120 G6
 S Glos ... 61 C9
 Shrops ... 149 D9
 Som ... 28 E4
 Staffs ... 168 D6
 Swansea ... 56 D3
 Telford ... 150 G3
 Wilts ... 62 G5
 Windsor ... 66 D4
Horton Common Dorset ... 31 F8
Horton Cross Som ... 28 D4
Horton-cum-Studley Oxon ... 83 C9
Horton Green Ches W ... 167 F7
Horton Heath Dorset ... 31 F9
 Hants ... 33 D7
Horton in Ribblesdale N Yorks ... 212 E6
Horton Kirby Kent ... 68 F5
Hortonlane Shrops ... 149 G8
Horton Wharf Bucks ... 84 B6
Hortonwood Telford ... 150 G3
Horwich Gtr Man ... 195 E7
Horwich End Derbys ... 185 E8
Horwood Devon ... 25 B8
Horwood Riding S Glos ... 61 B8
Hoscar Lancs ... 194 E3
Hose Leics ... 154 D4
Hoselaw Borders ... 263 C8
Hoses Cumb ... 220 G4
Hosey Hill Kent ... 52 C3
Hosh Perth ... 286 E2
Hosta W Isles ... 296 D3
Hoswick Shetland ... 313 L6
Hotham E Yorks ... 208 G3
Hothfield Kent ... 54 D3
Hotley Bottom Bucks ... 84 E5
Hoton Leics ... 153 E11
Hotwells Bristol ... 60 E5
Houbans Shetland ... 312 F5
Houbie Shetland ... 312 D8
Houdston S Ayrs ... 244 B5
Hough Argyll ... 288 E1
 Ches E ... 168 E2
 Ches E ... 184 F5
Hougham Lincs ... 172 G5
Hough Green Halton ... 183 D7
Hough-on-the-Hill Lincs ... 172 F6
Hough Side W Yorks ... 205 G10
Houghton Cambs ... 122 C5
 Cumb ... 239 F10
 Hants ... 47 G10
 Northumb ... 242 D4
 Pembs ... 73 D7
 W Sus ... 35 E8
Houghton Bank Darl ... 233 G10
Houghton Conquest C Beds ... 103 C10
Houghton Green E Sus ... 38 C6
 Warr ... 183 C10
Houghton-le-Side Darl ... 233 G10
Houghton-le-Spring T&W ... 234 B2
Houghton on the Hill Leics ... 136 C3
Houghton Regis C Beds ... 103 G10
Houghton St Giles Norf ... 159 B8
Houghwood Mers ... 194 G4
Houlland Shetland ... 312 B7
 Shetland ... 312 F7
 Shetland ... 313 H5
Houlsyke N Yorks ... 226 D4
Hound Hants ... 33 F7
Hound Green Hants ... 49 B8
Hound Hill Dorset ... 31 G7
Houndmills Hants ... 48 C6
Houndscroft Glos ... 80 E5
Houndslow Borders ... 272 F2
Houndsmoor Som ... 27 B10
Houndstone Som ... 29 D8
Houndwood Borders ... 273 C7
Hounsdown Hants ... 32 E5
Hounsley Batch N Som ... 60 G4
Hounslow London ... 66 D6
Hounslow Green Essex ... 87 B11
Hounslow West London ... 66 D5
Hourston Orkney ... 314 E2
Housabister Shetland ... 313 H6
Housay Shetland ... 312 F8
Househill Highld ... 301 D8
House of Daviot Highld ... 301 E7
House of Glenmuick Aberds ... 292 D5
Houses Hill W Yorks ... 197 D7
Housetter Shetland ... 312 E5
Housham Tye Essex ... 87 C8
Houss Shetland ... 313 K5
Houston Renfs ... 267 B8
Houstry Highld ... 310 F5
Houton Orkney ... 314 F3
Hove Brighton ... 36 G3
Hove Edge W Yorks ... 196 C6
Hoveringham Notts ... 171 F11
Hoveton Norf ... 160 F6
Hovingham N Yorks ... 216 D3

How Cumb ... 240 F2
Howbeck Bank Ches E ... 167 F11
Howbrook S Yorks ... 186 B4
How Caple Hereford ... 98 E2
Howden Borders ... 262 E5
 E Yorks ... 199 B8
 W Loth ... 269 B11
Howden Clough W Yorks ... 197 B8
Howden-le-Wear Durham ... 233 E9
Howdon T&W ... 243 D8
Howdon Pans T&W ... 243 D8
Howe Highld ... 310 C7
 Norf ... 142 C5
 N Yorks ... 214 C6
Howe Bridge Gtr Man ... 195 G7
Howegreen Essex ... 88 E4
Howe Green Essex ... 87 B8
 Warks ... 134 F6
Howell Lincs ... 173 F10
How End Beds ... 103 C10
 N Yorks ... 218 D2
Howe of Teuchar Aberds ... 303 E7
Howe Street Essex ... 87 C11
 Essex ... 106 E3
Howey Powys ... 113 F11
Howford Borders ... 261 B8
 Borders ... 261 E9
Howgate Cumb ... 228 G5
 Midloth ... 270 D4
Howgill N Yorks ... 222 F2
 Lancs ... 204 D2
Howick Mon ... 79 F8
 Northumb ... 265 F7
Howick Cross Lancs ... 194 B4
Howle Durham ... 233 F7
 Telford ... 150 E3
Howleigh Som ... 28 D2
Howlett End Essex ... 105 E11
Howley Glos ... 80 G2
 Som ... 28 F3
 Warr ... 183 D11
Hownam Borders ... 263 F7
Hownam Mains Borders ... 263 E7
Howpasley Borders ... 249 B8
Howsen Worcs ... 116 G5
Howsham N Lincs ... 200 G4
 N Yorks ... 216 G4
Howslack Dumfries ... 248 B3
Howt Green Kent ... 69 F11
Howton Hereford ... 97 F8
Howtown Cumb ... 221 B8
Howwood Renfs ... 267 C7
How Wood Herts ... 85 E10
Hoxne Suff ... 126 B3
Hoxton London ... 67 C10
Hoy Orkney ... 314 F2
Hoylake Mers ... 182 D2
Hoyland S Yorks ... 197 G11
Hoylandswaine S Yorks ... 197 G9
Hoyle W Sus ... 34 D6
Hoyle Mill S Yorks ... 197 F11
Hubbard's Hill Kent ... 52 C4
Hubberholme N Yorks ... 213 D8
Hubberston Pembs ... 72 D5
Hubbersty Head Cumb ... 221 G8
Hubberton Green W Yorks ... 196 C4
Hubbert's Bridge Lincs ... 174 G3
Huby N Yorks ... 205 D11
 N Yorks ... 215 F11
Hucclecote Glos ... 80 B5
Hucking Kent ... 53 B10
Hucknall Notts ... 171 E8
Huddersfield W Yorks ... 196 D6
Huddington Worcs ... 117 F8
Huddlesford Staffs ... 134 B3
Hud Hey Lancs ... 195 C9
Hudnall Herts ... 85 C8
Hudnalls Glos ... 79 E8
Hudswell N Yorks ... 224 E3
Huggate E Yorks ... 208 B3
Hugglepit Devon ... 24 C4
Hugglescote Leics ... 153 G8
Hughenden Valley Bucks ... 84 F5
Hughley Shrops ... 131 D11
Hugh Mill Lancs ... 195 C10
Hugh Town Scilly ... 1 G4
Hugus Corn ... 4 G5
Huish Devon ... 25 E8
 Devon ... 25 G8
 Wilts ... 62 G6
Huish Champflower Som ... 27 B9
Huish Episcopi Som ... 28 B6
Huisinis W Isles ... 305 G2
Hulcote Northants ... 102 B4
Hulcott Bucks ... 84 B5
Hulham Devon ... 14 D5
Hulland Derbys ... 170 F2
Hulland Moss Derbys ... 170 F3
Hulland Ward Derbys ... 170 F3
Hullavington Wilts ... 61 C11
Hullbridge Essex ... 88 G4
Hull End Derbys ... 185 E9
Hulme Gtr Man ... 184 B4
 Staffs ... 168 F6
Hulme End Staffs ... 169 D10
Hulme Walfield Ches E ... 168 B4
Hulseheath Ches E ... 184 E2
Hulverstone IoW ... 20 E3
Hulver Street Suff ... 143 F9
Humber Devon ... 14 G3
 Hereford ... 115 F10
Humber Bridge N Lincs ... 200 C4
Humberston NE Lincs ... 201 F10
Humberstone Leicester ... 136 B2
Humberston Fitties NE Lincs ... 201 F10
Humbie E Loth ... 271 C9
Humbledon T&W ... 243 F9
Humble Green Suff ... 107 B8
Humbleton E Yorks ... 209 G10
 Northumb ... 263 D11
Humby Lincs ... 155 D10
Hume Borders ... 272 G4
Humehall Borders ... 272 G4
Hummersknott Darl ... 224 C5
Humshaugh Northumb ... 241 C10
Huna Highld ... 310 B7
Huncoat Lancs ... 203 G11
Huncote Leics ... 135 D10
Hundalee Borders ... 262 F4
Hundall Derbys ... 186 F5
Hunderthwaite Durham ... 232 G5
Hundle Houses Lincs ... 174 E3
Hundleshope Borders ... 260 B6
Hundleton Pembs ... 73 E7
Hundon Suff ... 106 B4
Hundred Acres Hants ... 33 E9

Hundred End Lancs ... 194 C2
 E Yorks ... 208 C3
 Lancs ... 194 B3
 N Som ... 43 B11
Hundred House Powys ... 114 G2
Hungarton Leics ... 136 B3
Hungate N Yorks ... 197 B11
Hungerford Hants ... 31 E11
 Shrops ... 131 F11
 Som ... 42 E4
 W Berks ... 63 F10
 Windsor ... 65 B10
Hungerford Green W Berks ... 64 D5
Hungerford Newtown W Berks ... 63 E11
Hunger Hill Gtr Man ... 195 F8
 Lancs ... 194 E4
Hungershall Park Kent ... 52 F5
Hungerstone Hereford ... 97 D8
Hungerton Lincs ... 155 D7
Hungladder Highld ... 298 B3
Hungreyhatton Shrops ... 150 D3
Hunmanby N Yorks ... 217 D11
Hunmanby Moor N Yorks ... 218 D2
Hunningham Warks ... 119 D7
Hunningham Hill Warks ... 119 D7
Hunnington Worcs ... 133 G9
Hunny Hill IoW ... 20 D5
Hunsdon Herts ... 86 C6
Hunsdonbury Herts ... 86 C6
Hunsingore N Yorks ... 206 C4
Hunslet W Yorks ... 206 G2
Hunslet Carr W Yorks ... 206 G2
Hunsonby Cumb ... 231 D7
Hunspow Highld ... 310 B6
Hunstanton Norf ... 175 G11
Hunstanworth Durham ... 232 B5
Hunston W Sus ... 22 C5
 Suff ... 125 D9
Hunston Green Suff ... 125 D9
Hunstrete Bath ... 60 G6
Hunsworth W Yorks ... 197 B7
Hunt End Worcs ... 117 E10
Huntenhull Green Wilts ... 45 D10
Huntercombe End Oxon ... 65 B7
Hunters Forstal Kent ... 71 F7
Hunter's Quay Argyll ... 276 F3
Huntham Som ... 28 B4
Hunthill Lodge Angus ... 292 F6
Huntingdon Cambs ... 122 C4
Huntingfield Suff ... 126 C6
Huntingford Dorset ... 45 G9
 S Glos ... 80 G2
Huntington Ches W ... 166 C6
 E Loth ... 281 F9
 Hereford ... 97 C9
 Hereford ... 114 G5
 Staffs ... 151 G9
 Telford ... 132 B3
 York ... 207 B8
Hunt's Corner Norf ... 141 F11
Hunt's Cross Mers ... 182 D6
Hunts Green Warks ... 134 D3
 W Berks ... 64 E3
 Bucks ... 84 F5
Huntsham Devon ... 27 C8
Huntshaw Devon ... 25 C8
Huntshaw Water Devon ... 25 C8
Hunt's Hill Bucks ... 84 F4
Hunt's Lane Leics ... 135 C9
Huntspill Som ... 43 D10
Huntstile Som ... 43 G9
Huntworth Som ... 43 G10
Hunwick Durham ... 233 E9
Hunworth Norf ... 159 C11
Hurcott Som ... 28 E5
 Som ... 29 B8
 Worcs ... 117 B7
Hurdcott Wilts ... 47 G7
Hurdley Powys ... 130 E5
Hurdsfield Ches E ... 184 G6
Hurgill N Yorks ... 224 E3
Hurlet Glasgow ... 267 C10
Hurley Warks ... 134 D4
 Windsor ... 65 C10
Hurley Bottom Windsor ... 65 C10
Hurley Common Warks ... 134 D4
Hurlford E Ayrs ... 257 B11
Hurliness Orkney ... 314 H2
Hurlston Green Lancs ... 193 E11
Hurn Dorset ... 19 B8
Hurn's End Lincs ... 174 F6
Hursey Dorset ... 28 G5
Hursley Hants ... 32 B6
Hurst Cumb ... 230 C4
 Dorset ... 17 C11
 Gtr Man ... 196 G3
 N Yorks ... 223 E10
 Som ... 29 D7
 Wokingham ... 65 D8
Hurstbourne Priors Hants ... 48 D2
Hurstbourne Tarrant Hants ... 47 C11
Hurst Green E Sus ... 38 B2
 Essex ... 88 B2
 Lancs ... 203 F11
 Sur ... 51 F7
 W Mid ... 133 F9
Hurst Hill W Mid ... 133 E8
Hurstley Hereford ... 97 B7
Hurst Park Sur ... 66 F6
Hurstpierpoint W Sus ... 36 D3
Hurst Wickham W Sus ... 36 D3
Hurstwood Lancs ... 204 G3
Hurtmore Sur ... 50 D3
Hurworth-on-Tees Darl ... 224 D6
Hurworth Place Darl ... 224 D5
Hury Durham ... 223 B9
Husabost Highld ... 298 D2
Husbands Bosworth Leics ... 136 G2
Husborne Crawley C Beds ... 103 D9
Husthwaite N Yorks ... 215 D10
Hutcherleigh Devon ... 8 E5
Hutchesontown Glasgow ... 267 C11
Hutchwns Bridgend ... 57 F10
Huthwaite Notts ... 171 D7
 N Yorks ... 225 G8
Huttock Top Lancs ... 195 C11
Huttoft Lincs ... 191 F7
Hutton Borders ... 273 E8
 Cumb ... 230 F4

 E Yorks ... 208 C6
 Lancs ... 194 B3
 N Som ... 43 B11
Hutton Bonville N Yorks ... 224 E6
Hutton Buscel N Yorks ... 217 C9
Hutton Conyers N Yorks ... 214 E6
Hutton Cranswick E Yorks ... 208 C6
Hutton End Cumb ... 230 D4
Hutton Gate Redcar ... 225 B11
Hutton Hang N Yorks ... 214 B3
Hutton Henry Durham ... 234 D4
Hutton-le-Hole N Yorks ... 226 G4
Hutton Magna Durham ... 224 C2
Hutton Mount Essex ... 87 G10
Hutton Roof Cumb ... 211 D11
 Cumb ... 230 E3
Hutton Rudby N Yorks ... 225 D9
Huttons Ambo N Yorks ... 216 F5
Hutton Sessay N Yorks ... 215 D9
Hutton Village Redcar ... 225 B11
Hutton Wandesley N Yorks ... 206 C6
Huxham Devon ... 14 B4
Huxham Green Som ... 44 F5
Huxley Ches W ... 167 C8
Huxter Shetland ... 313 G7
 Shetland ... 313 H3
 Shetland ... 313 H5
Huxton Borders ... 273 C8
Huyton Mers ... 182 C6
Huyton Park Mers ... 182 C6
Huyton Quarry Mers ... 183 C7
Hwlffordd / Haverfordwest Pembs ... 73 B7
Hycemoor Cumb ... 210 B1
Hyde Glos ... 99 F11
 Glos ... 80 E5
 Gtr Man ... 184 B6
 Hants ... 31 E11
 Hants ... 48 G3
 Hereford ... 115 F9
Hyde Chase Essex ... 88 E4
Hyde End W Berks ... 64 G5
Hyde Heath Bucks ... 84 E6
Hyde Lea Staffs ... 151 E8
Hyde Park S Yorks ... 198 G5
Hydestile Sur ... 50 E3
Hykeham Moor Lincs ... 172 B6
Hylton Castle T&W ... 243 F9
Hylton Red House T&W ... 243 F9
Hyltons Crossways Norf ... 160 F5
Hyndburn Bridge Lancs ... 203 G10
Hyndford Bridge S Lnrk ... 269 G8
Hyndhope Borders ... 261 E9
Hynish Argyll ... 288 F1
Hyssington Powys ... 130 E6
Hystfield Glos ... 79 F11
Hythe Hants ... 32 F6
 Kent ... 55 F7
 Som ... 44 C2
 Sur ... 66 E4
Hythe End Windsor ... 66 E4
Hythie Aberds ... 303 D10
Hyton Cumb ... 210 B1

I

Iarsiadar W Isles ... 304 E3
Ibberton Dorset ... 30 F3
Ible Derbys ... 170 D2
Ibsley Hants ... 31 F11
Ibstock Leics ... 153 G8
Ibstone Bucks ... 84 G3
Ibthorpe Hants ... 47 C11
Iburndale N Yorks ... 227 D7
Ibworth Hants ... 48 C5
Icelton N Som ... 59 F11
Ichrachan Argyll ... 284 D4
Ickburgh Norf ... 140 E6
Ickenham London ... 66 B5
Ickenthwaite Cumb ... 210 B6
Ickford Bucks ... 83 D11
Ickham Kent ... 55 B8
Ickleford Herts ... 104 E3
Icklesham E Sus ... 38 D5
Ickleton Cambs ... 105 C9
Icklingham Suff ... 124 C5
Ickornshaw N Yorks ... 204 E5
Ickwell C Beds ... 104 B3
Ickwell Green C Beds ... 104 B3
Icomb Glos ... 100 G4
Icy Park Devon ... 8 F3
Idbury Oxon ... 82 B2
Iddesleigh Devon ... 25 F9
Ide Devon ... 14 C3
Ideford Devon ... 14 G3
Ide Hill Kent ... 52 C3
Iden E Sus ... 38 C5
Iden Green Kent ... 53 F8
 Kent ... 53 G9
Idle W Yorks ... 205 F9
Idle Moor W Yorks ... 205 F9
Idless Corn ... 4 F6
Idlicote Warks ... 100 C5
Idmiston Wilts ... 47 F7
Idole Carms ... 74 B6
Idridgehay Derbys ... 170 F3
Idridgehay Green Derbys ... 170 F3
Idrigill Highld ... 298 C3
Idstone Oxon ... 63 C9
Idvies Angus ... 287 C9
Iet-y-bwlch Carms ... 92 F3
Iffley Oxon ... 83 E8
Ifield W Sus ... 51 F8
Ifield Green W Sus ... 51 F9
Ifieldwood W Sus ... 51 F8
Ifold W Sus ... 50 G4
Iford Bmouth ... 19 C8
 E Sus ... 36 F6
Ifton Heath Shrops ... 148 B6
Ightfield Shrops ... 149 B11
Ightfield Heath Shrops ... 149 B11
Ightham Kent ... 52 B5
Iken Suff ... 127 F8
Ilam Staffs ... 169 E10
Ilchester Som ... 29 C8
Ilchester Mead Som ... 29 C8
Ilderton Northumb ... 264 E2
Ileden Kent ... 55 C8
Ilford London ... 68 B2
 Som ... 28 D5
Ilfracombe Devon ... 40 D4
Ilkeston Derbys ... 171 G7
Ilketshall St Andrew Suff ... 143 F7
Ilketshall St Lawrence Suff ... 143 G7
Ilketshall St Margaret Suff ... 142 F6
Ilkley W Yorks ... 205 D8
Illand Corn ... 11 F11
Illey W Mid ... 133 G9
Illidge Green Ches E ... 168 C3
Illington Norf ... 141 F8
Illingworth W Yorks ... 196 B5
Illogan Corn ... 4 G3
Illogan Highway Corn ... 4 G3

Illshaw Heath W Mid ... 118 C2
Illston on the Hill Leics ... 136 D4
Ilmer Bucks ... 84 D3
Ilmington Warks ... 100 C4
Ilminster Som ... 28 E5
Ilsington Devon ... 13 G11
Ilston Swansea ... 56 C5
Ilton N Yorks ... 214 D3
 Som ... 28 D5
Imachar N Ayrs ... 255 C9
Imber Wilts ... 46 D3
Immeralval Argyll ... 254 C4
Immervoulin Stirl ... 285 F9
Immingham NE Lincs ... 201 E7
Impington Cambs ... 123 E9
Ince Ches W ... 183 F7
Ince Blundell Mers ... 193 G10
Ince in Makerfield Gtr Man ... 194 G5
Inchbae Lodge Highld ... 300 C4
Inchbare Angus ... 293 G8
Inchberry Moray ... 302 D3
Inchbraoch Angus ... 287 B11
Inchbrook Glos ... 80 E4
Inchcape Highld ... 309 J6
Incheril Highld ... 299 C10
Inchgrundle Angus ... 292 F6
Inchina Highld ... 307 K4
Inchinnan Renfs ... 267 B9
Inchkinloch Highld ... 308 E5
Inchlaggan Highld ... 290 C3
Inchlumpie Highld ... 300 B5
Inchmore Highld ... 300 E3
 Highld ... 300 E5
Inchnacardoch Hotel Highld ... 290 B5
Inchnadamph Highld ... 307 G2
Inchock Angus ... 287 C10
Inch of Arnhall Aberds ... 293 F8
Inchree Highld ... 290 G2
Inchrory Moray ... 292 C3
Inchs Corn ... 5 C9
Inchture Perth ... 286 E6
Inchyra Perth ... 286 E5
Indian Queens Corn ... 5 D8
Inerval Argyll ... 254 C4
Ingatestone Essex ... 87 F11
Ingbirchworth S Yorks ... 197 F8
Ingerthorpe N Yorks ... 214 F5
Ingestre Staffs ... 151 E9
Ingham Lincs ... 188 E6
 Norf ... 161 D7
 Suff ... 125 C7
Ingham Corner Norf ... 161 D7
Ingleborough Norf ... 157 F9
Ingleby Derbys ... 152 D6
 Lincs ... 188 F5
Ingleby Arncliffe N Yorks ... 225 E8
Ingleby Barwick Stockton ... 225 C9
Ingleby Cross N Yorks ... 225 E9
Ingleby Greenhow N Yorks ... 225 D11
Ingleigh Green Devon ... 25 F10
Inglemire Hull ... 209 G7
Inglesbatch Bath ... 61 G8
Inglesham Swindon ... 82 F2
Ingleton Durham ... 233 G9
 N Yorks ... 212 E3
Inglewhite Lancs ... 202 E6
Ingmanthorpe N Yorks ... 206 C4
Ingoe Northumb ... 242 C2
Ingol Lancs ... 202 G6
Ingoldisthorpe Norf ... 158 C3
Ingoldmells Lincs ... 175 B9
Ingoldsby Lincs ... 155 C10
Ingon Warks ... 118 F4
Ingram Northumb ... 264 F2
Ingrams Green W Sus ... 34 C4
Ingrave Essex ... 87 G10
Ingrow W Yorks ... 205 F7
Ings Cumb ... 221 F8
Ingst S Glos ... 60 B5
Ingworth Norf ... 160 D3
Inham's End Cambs ... 138 D5
Inhurst Hants ... 64 G5
Inkberrow Worcs ... 117 F10
Inkerman Durham ... 233 D8
Inkersall Derbys ... 186 G6
Inkersall Green Derbys ... 186 G6
Inkford Worcs ... 117 C11
Inkpen W Berks ... 63 G11
Inkpen Common W Berks ... 63 G11
Inkstack Highld ... 310 B6
Inlands W Sus ... 22 B3
Inmarsh Wilts ... 62 G2
Inn Cumb ... 221 D8
Innellan Argyll ... 276 G3
Inner Hope Devon ... 9 G8
Innerleithen Borders ... 261 B8
Innerleven Fife ... 287 G7
Innermessan Dumfries ... 236 C2
Innerwick E Loth ... 282 G4
 Perth ... 285 C9
Innie Argyll ... 275 B9
Inninbeg Highld ... 289 E8
Innis Chonain Argyll ... 284 E5
Innistrynich Argyll ... 284 E5
Innox Hill Som ... 45 D9
Innsworth Glos ... 99 G7
Insch Aberds ... 302 G6
Insh Highld ... 291 C10
Inshegra Highld ... 306 D7
Inshore Highld ... 308 C3
Inskip Lancs ... 202 F5
Inskip Moss Side Lancs ... 202 F5
Instoneville S Yorks ... 198 E5
Instow Devon ... 40 G3
Insworke Corn ... 7 E8
Intack Blkburn ... 195 B8
Intake S Yorks ... 198 G5
 S Yorks ... 198 G5
Interfield Worcs ... 98 B5
Intwood Norf ... 142 C3
Inver Aberds ... 292 D4
 Highld ... 311 L2
 Perth ... 286 C4
Inverailort Highld ... 295 C9
Inveraldie Angus ... 287 D8
Inveralligin Highld ... 299 D8
Inverallochy Aberds ... 303 C10
Inveran Highld ... 309 K5
Inveraray Argyll ... 284 G4
Inverarish Highld ... 295 B7
Inverarity Angus ... 287 C8
Inverarnan Stirl ... 285 F7
Inverasdale Highld ... 307 L3
Inverawe Ho Argyll ... 284 D4
Inverbeg Argyll ... 276 B6
Inverbervie Aberds ... 293 F10
Inverboyndie Aberds ... 302 C6
Inverbroom Highld ... 307 L6

Invercarron Mains
Highld 309 K5
Invercassley Highld 309 J4
Invercauld House
Aberds 292 D3
Inverchaolain Argyll 275 F11
Invercharnan Highld 284 C5
Inverchoran Highld 300 D2
Invercreran Argyll 284 C4
Inverdruie Highld 291 B11
Inverebrie Aberds 303 F9
Invereck Argyll 276 E2
Inverernan Ho Aberds 292 B5
Invereshie House
Highld 291 C10
Inveresk E Loth 280 G6
Inverey Aberds 292 E2
Inverfarigaig Highld 300 G5
Invergarry Highld 290 C5
Invergelder Aberds 292 D4
Invergeldie Perth 285 E11
Invergordon Highld 301 C7
Invergowrie Perth 287 D7
Inverguseran Highld 295 E9
Inverhadden Perth 285 B10
Inverhaggernie Stirl 285 E7
Inverharroch Moray 302 F3
Inverherive Stirl 285 E7
Inverie Highld 295 F9
Inverinan Argyll 275 B10
Inverinate Highld 295 C11
Inverkeilor Angus 287 C10
Inverkeithing Fife 280 E2
Inverkeithny Aberds 302 E6
Inverkip Invclyd 276 G4
Inverkirkaig Highld 307 H5
Inverlael Highld 307 L6
Inverleith Edin 280 F4
Inverliever Lodge Argyll 275 C9
Inverliver Argyll 284 D4
Inverlochlarig Stirl 285 F8
Inverlochy Argyll 284 E5
Highld 290 F3
Moray 301 G11
Inverlounin Argyll 276 B4
Inverlussa Argyll 275 E7
Inver Mallie Highld 290 E3
Invermark Lodge Angus 292 E6
Invermoidart Highld 289 B8
Invermoriston Highld 290 B6
Invernaver Highld 308 C7
Inverneill Argyll 275 E9
Inverness Highld 300 E6
Invernettie Aberds 303 E11
Invernoaden Argyll 276 B2
Inveronich Argyll 284 G6
Inveroran Hotel Argyll 284 C6
Inverpolly Lodge Highld 307 H5
Inverquharity Angus 287 B8
Inverquhomery Aberds 303 E10
Inverroy Highld 290 E4
Inversanda Highld 289 D11
Invershiel Highld 295 D11
Invershin Highld 309 K5
Invershore Highld 310 F6
Inversnaid Hotel Stirl 285 G7
Invertrossachs Stirl 285 G9
Inverugie Aberds 303 E11
Inveruglas Argyll 285 G7
Inveruglass Highld 291 C10
Inverurie Aberds 303 G7
Invervar Perth 285 C10
Inverythan Aberds 303 E7
Inwardleigh Devon 13 B7
Inwood Shrops 131 D9
Inworth Essex 88 B5
Iochdar W Isles 297 G3
Iping W Sus 34 C5
Ipplepen Devon 8 B6
Ipsden Oxon 64 B6
Ipsley Worcs 117 D11
Ipstones Staffs 169 F8
Ipswich Suff 108 C3
Irby Mers 182 E3
Irby in the Marsh Lincs 175 C7
Irby upon Humber
NE Lincs 201 G7
Irchester Northants 121 D8
Ireby Cumb 229 D10
Lancs 212 D3
Ireland C Beds 104 C2
Orkney 314 F3
Shetland 313 L5
Wilts 45 C10
Ireland's Cross Shrops 168 G2
Ireland Wood W Yorks 205 F11
Ireleth Cumb 210 D4
Ireshopeburn Durham 232 D3
Ireton Wood Derbys 170 F3
Irlam Gtr Man 184 C2
Irlams o' th' Height
Gtr Man 195 G9
Irnham Lincs 155 D10
Iron Acton S Glos 61 C7
Ironbridge Telford 132 C3
Iron Bridge Cambs 139 D9
Iron Cross Warks 117 G11
Irongray Dumfries 237 B11
Iron Lo Highld 299 G10
Ironmacannie Dumfries 237 B8
Irons Bottom Sur 51 D9
Ironside Aberds 303 D8
Ironville Derbys 170 E6
Irstead Norf 161 E7
Irstead Street Norf 161 F7
Irthington Cumb 239 E11
Irthlingborough
Northants 121 C8
Irton N Yorks 217 C10
Irvine N Ayrs 257 B8
Irwell Vale Lancs 195 C9
Isabella Pit Northumb 253 G8
Isallt Bach Anglesey 178 F3
Isauld Highld 310 C3
Isbister Orkney 314 D2
Orkney 314 E3
Shetland 312 D5
Shetland 313 G7
Isel Cumb 229 E9
Isfield E Sus 36 D6
Isham Northants 121 C7
Ishriff Argyll 289 F8
Isington Hants 49 E9
Island Carr N Lincs 200 F3
Islands Common
Cambs 122 E3
Islay Ho Argyll 274 G4
Isle Abbotts Som 28 C5
Isle Brewers Som 28 C5
Isleham Cambs 124 C2
Isle of Axholme N Lincs 199 F9
Isle of Dogs London 67 D11
Isle of Man Dumfries 238 B2
Isle of Whithorn
Dumfries 236 F6
Isleornsay Highld 295 D9
Islesburgh Shetland 312 G5
Islesteps Dumfries 237 B11
Isleworth London 67 D7
Isley Walton Leics 153 D8
Islibhig W Isles 304 F1
Islington London 67 C10
Telford 150 E4
Islip Northants 121 B9
Oxon 83 C8
Isombridge Telford 150 G2
Istead Rise Kent 68 F6
Isycoed Wrex 166 E6
Itchen Soton 32 E6
Itchen Abbas Hants 48 G4
Itchen Stoke Hants 48 G5
Itchingfield W Sus 35 B10
Itchington S Glos 61 B7
Itteringham Norf 160 C2
Itteringham Common
Norf 160 D3
Itton Devon 13 B9
Mon 79 F7
Itton Common Mon 79 F7
Ivegill Cumb 230 C4
Ivelet N Yorks 223 F8
Iver Bucks 66 C4
Iver Heath Bucks 66 C4
Iverley Staffs 133 G7
Iveston Durham 242 G4
Ivinghoe Bucks 84 B6
Ivinghoe Aston Bucks 85 B7
Ivington Hereford 115 F9
Ivington Green Hereford 115 F9
Ivybridge Devon 8 D2
Ivy Chimneys Essex 86 E6
Ivychurch Kent 39 B8
Ivy Cross Dorset 30 C5
Ivy Hatch Kent 52 C5
Ivy Todd Norf 141 B7
Iwade Kent 69 F11
Iwerne Courtney or Shroton
Dorset 30 E5
Iwerne Minster Dorset 30 E5
Iwood N Som 60 G3
Ixworth Suff 125 C8
Ixworth Thorpe Suff 125 C8

J

Jackfield Telford 132 C3
Jack Green Lancs 194 B5
Jack Hayes Staffs 168 F6
Jack Hill N Yorks 205 C10
Jack in the Green Devon 14 B6
Jacksdale Notts 170 E6
Jack's Green Essex 105 G11
Glos 80 D5
Jack's Hatch Essex 86 D6
Jackson Bridge
W Yorks 197 F7
Jackstown Aberds 303 F7
Jacobstow Corn 11 B9
Jacobstowe Devon 25 G9
Jacobs Well Sur 50 C3
Jagger Green W Yorks 196 D5
Jameston Pembs 73 F9
Jamestown Dumfries 249 D8
Highld 300 D4
W Dunb 277 E7
Jamphlars Fife 280 B4
Janetstown Highld 310 C4
Janke's Green Essex 107 F8
Jarrow T&W 243 D8
Jarvis Brook E Sus 37 B8
Jasper's Green Essex 106 F4
Java Argyll 289 F9
Jawcraig Falk 278 F6
Jaw Hill W Yorks 197 C9
Jaywick Essex 89 C11
Jealott's Hill Brack 65 E11
Jeaniefield Borders 271 G10
Jedburgh Borders 262 E5
Jedurgh Borders 262 F5
Jeffreyston Pembs 73 D9
Jellyhill E Dunb 278 G2
Jemimaville Highld 301 C7
Jennetts Hill W Berks 64 E5
Jennyfield N Yorks 205 B11
Jericho Gtr Man 195 E10
Jersey Farm Herts 85 D11
Jersey Marine Neath 57 C8
Jerviswood S Lnrk 269 F7
Jesmond T&W 243 D7
Jevington E Sus 23 E9
Jewell's Cross Corn 24 G3
Jingle Street Mon 79 C7
Jockey End Herts 85 C8
Jodrell Bank Ches E 184 G3
Johnby Cumb 230 E4
John O'Gaunt Leics 136 B4
John O'Gaunts
W Yorks 197 B11
John o'Groats Highld 310 B7
John's Cross E Sus 38 C2
Johnshaven Aberds 293 G9
Johnson Fold Gtr Man 195 E7
Johnson's Hillock Lancs 194 C5
Johnson Street Norf 161 F7
Johnston Pembs 72 C6
Johnstone Renfs 267 C8
Johnstonebridge
Dumfries 248 E3
Johnstone Mains
Aberds 293 F9
Johnstown Carms 74 B6
Wrex 166 F4
Jolly's Bottom Corn 4 F5
Joppa Corn 2 B3
Edin 280 G6
S Ayrs 257 F10
Jordan Green Norf 159 E11
Jordanhill Glasgow 267 B10
Jordans Bucks 85 G7
Jordanston Pembs 91 E8
Jordanthorpe S Yorks 186 E5
Jordon S Yorks 186 C6
Joyford Glos 79 C9
Joy's Green Glos 79 B10
Jubilee Gtr Man 196 E2
Notts 170 E6
Jugbank Staffs 150 B5
Jump S Yorks 197 G11
Jumpers Common Dorset 19 C8
Jumpers Green Dorset 19 C8
Jumper's Town E Sus 52 G3
Junction N Yorks 204 D6
Juniper Northumb 241 F10
Juniper Green Edin 270 B3
Jurby East IoM 192 C4
Jurby West IoM 192 C4
Jurston Devon 13 E9
Jury's Gap E Sus 39 D7

K

Kaber Cumb 222 C5
Kaimend S Lnrk 269 F9
Kaimes Edin 270 B5
Kaimrig End Borders 269 G11
Kalemouth Borders 262 D6
Kame Fife 287 G7
Kames Argyll 275 B9
Argyll 275 F10
E Ayrs 258 D5
Kates Hill W Mid 133 E9
Kea Corn 4 G6
Keadby N Lincs 199 E10
Keal Cotes Lincs 174 C5
Kearby Town End
N Yorks 206 D2
Kearnsey Kent 55 E9
Kearsley Gtr Man 195 F9
Kearstwick Cumb 212 C2
Kearton N Yorks 223 F9
Kearvaig Highld 306 B7
Keasden N Yorks 212 F4
Kebroyd W Yorks 196 C4
Keckwick Halton 183 E9
Keddington Lincs 190 D4
Keddington Corner
Lincs 190 D5
Kedington Suff 106 B4
Kedleston Derbys 170 G4
Kedslie Borders 271 G11
Keekle Cumb 219 B10
Keelars Tye Essex 107 G11
Keelby Lincs 201 E7
Keele Staffs 168 F4
Keeley Green Beds 103 B10
Keelham W Yorks 205 G7
Keenley Northumb 241 F7
Keenthorne Som 43 F8
Keeres Green Essex 87 C9
Keeston Pembs 72 B6
Keevil Wilts 46 B2
Kegworth Leics 153 D9
Kehelland Corn 4 G2
Keig Aberds 293 B8
Keighley W Yorks 205 E7
Keil Highld 289 D11
Keilarsbrae Clack 279 C7
Keilhill Aberds 303 D7
Keillmore Argyll 275 E7
Keillor Perth 286 C6
Keillour Perth 286 E3
Keills Argyll 274 G5
Keils Argyll 274 G6
Keinton Mandeville Som 44 G4
Keir Mill Dumfries 247 E9
Keisby Lincs 155 D10
Keiss Highld 310 C7
Keistle Highld 298 D4
Keith Moray 302 D4
Keith Hall Aberds 303 G7
Keith Inch Aberds 303 E11
Keithock Angus 293 G8
Kelbrook Lancs 204 E4
Kelby Lincs 173 G8
Kelcliffe W Yorks 205 E9
Keld Cumb 221 C11
N Yorks 223 E7
Keldholme N Yorks 216 B4
Keld Houses N Yorks 214 G2
Kelfield N Lincs 199 G10
N Yorks 207 F7
Kelham Notts 172 D3
Kelhurn Argyll 276 F6
Kellacott Devon 12 D4
Kellamergh Lancs 194 B2
Kellan Argyll 289 E7
Kellas Angus 287 D8
Moray 301 D11
Kellaton Devon 9 G11
Kellaways Wilts 62 D3
Kelleth Cumb 222 D3
Kelleythorpe E Yorks 208 B5
E Yorks 208 B6
Kelling Norf 177 E9
Kellingley N Yorks 198 C4
Kellington N Yorks 198 C5
Kelloe Durham 234 D2
Kelloholm Dumfries 258 G6
Kells Cumb 219 B9
Kelly Corn 10 G6
Devon 12 E3
Kelly Bray Corn 12 G3
Kelmarsh Northants 120 B4
Kelmscott Oxon 82 F3
Kelsale Suff 127 D7
Kelsall Ches W 167 B8
Kelsall Hill Ches W 167 B8
Kelsay Argyll 254 B2
Kelshall Herts 104 D6
Kelsick Cumb 238 G5
Kelso Borders 262 C6
Kelstedge Derbys 170 C4
Kelstern Lincs 190 C3
Kelsterton Flint 182 G3
Kelston Bath 61 F8
Keltneyburn Perth 285 C11
Kelton Dumfries 237 B11
Durham 232 G4
Kelty Fife 280 C2
Keltybridge Fife 280 B2
Kelvedon Essex 88 B5
Kelvedon Hatch Essex 87 F9
Kelvin S Lnrk 268 E2
Kelvindale Glasgow 267 B11
Kelvinside Glasgow 267 B11
Kelynack Corn 1 D3
Kemacott Devon 41 D7
Kemback Fife 287 F8
Kemberton Shrops 132 C4
Kemble Glos 81 F7
Kemble Wick Glos 81 F7
Kemerton Worcs 99 D8
Kemeys Commander
Mon 78 E4
Kemincham Ches E 168 B4
Kemnay Aberds 293 B9
Kempe's Corner Kent 54 D4
Kempie Highld 308 D4
Kempley Glos 98 F3
Kempley Green Glos 98 F3
Kempsey Worcs 99 B7
Kempsford Glos 81 F11
Kemps Green Warks 118 C2
Kempshott Hants 48 C6
Kempston Beds 103 B10
Kempston Church End
Beds 103 B10
Kempston Hardwick
Beds 103 C10
Kempston West End
Beds 103 B9
Kempton Shrops 131 G7
Kemp Town Brighton 36 G4
Kemsing Kent 52 B4
Kemsley Kent 70 F2
Kemsley Street Kent 69 G10
Kenardington Kent 54 G3
Kenchester Hereford 97 C8
Kencot Oxon 82 E3
Kendal Cumb 221 G10
Kendal End Worcs 117 C10
Kendleshire S Glos 61 D7
Kendon Caerph 77 F11
Kendoon Dumfries 246 F4
Kendray S Yorks 197 F11
Kenfig Bridgend 57 E10
Kenfig Hill Bridgend 57 E10
Kengharair Argyll 288 E6
Kenilworth Warks 118 C5
Kenknock Stirl 285 D8
Kenley London 51 B10
Shrops 131 C11
Kenmore Argyll 284 G4
Highld 299 D7
Perth 285 C11
Kenmure Dumfries 237 B8
Kenn Devon 14 D4
N Som 60 F2
Kennacley W Isles 305 J3
Kennacraig Argyll 275 G9
Kennards House Corn 11 E11
Kenneggy Corn 2 D3
Kenneggy Downs Corn 2 D3
Kennerleigh Devon 26 F4
Kennet Clack 279 C8
Kennet End Suff 124 D4
Kennethmont Aberds 302 G5
Kennett Cambs 124 D3
Kennford Devon 14 D4
Kenninghall Norf 141 F10
Kenninghall Heath
Norf 141 G10
Kennington Kent 54 E4
London 67 D10
Oxon 83 E8
Kenn Moor Gate N Som 60 F2
Kennoway Fife 287 G7
Kenny Som 28 D4
Kenny Hill Suff 124 B3
Kennythorpe N Yorks 216 F5
Kenovay Argyll 288 E1
Kensaleyre Highld 298 D4
Kensal Green London 67 C8
Kensal Rise London 67 C8
Kensal Town London 67 C8
Kensary Highld 310 E6
Kensington London 67 D9
Mers 182 C5
Kensworth C Beds 85 B8
Kentallen Highld 284 B4
Kentchurch Hereford 97 F8
Kentford Suff 124 D4
Kentisbeare Devon 27 F9
Kentisbury Devon 40 E6
Kentisbury Ford Devon 40 E6
Kentish Town London 67 C9
Kentmere Cumb 221 E9
Kenton Devon 14 E5
London 67 B7
Suff 126 D3
T&W 242 D6
Kenton Bankfoot T&W 242 D6
Kenton Bar T&W 242 D6
Kenton Corner Suff 126 D4
Kenton Green Glos 80 C3
Kentra Highld 289 C8
Kentrigg Cumb 221 G10
Kents Corn 11 B9
Kents Bank Cumb 211 D7
Kent's Green Glos 98 G4
Kents Hill M Keynes 103 D7
Kent's Oak Hants 32 C4
Kent Street E Sus 38 D3
Kent 53 C7
W Sus 36 C2
Kenwick Shrops 149 C8
Kenwick Park Shrops 149 D8
Kenwyn Corn 4 F6
Kenyon Warr 183 B10
Keoldale Highld 308 C3
Keonchulish Ho Highld 307 K6
Kepdowrie Stirl 277 C11
Kepnal Wilts 63 G7
Keppanach Highld 290 G2
Keppoch Highld 295 C11
Keprigan Argyll 255 F7
Kepwick N Yorks 225 G9
Kerchesters Borders 263 B7
Kerdiston Norf 159 E11
Keresforth Hill S Yorks 197 F10
Keresley W Mid 134 G6
Keresley Newlands
Warks 134 G6
Kerfield Borders 270 G5
Kerley Downs Corn 4 G5
Kernborough Devon 8 G5
Kerne Bridge Hereford 79 B9
Kernsary Highld 299 B8
Kerridge Ches E 184 F6
Kerridge-end Ches E 184 F6
Kerris Corn 1 D4
Kerry / Ceri Powys 130 F2
Kerrycroy Argyll 266 C2
Kerry Hill Staffs 168 F6
Kerrysdale Highld 299 B8
Kerry's Gate Hereford 97 E7
Kersal Gtr Man 195 G10
Kersall Notts 172 C2
Kersbrook Cross Corn 12 F2
Kerscott Devon 25 B10
Kersey Suff 107 C10
Kersey Tye Suff 107 C9
Kersey Upland Suff 107 C9
Kershopefoot Cumb 249 G11
Kersoe Worcs 99 D9
Kerswell Devon 27 F9
Kerswell Green Worcs 99 B7
Kerthen Wood Corn 2 C3
Kesgrave Suff 108 B4
Kessingland Suff 143 F10
Kessingland Beach
Suff 143 F10
Kessington E Dunb 277 G11
Kestle Corn 5 F9
Kestle Mill Corn 5 D7
Keston London 68 G2
Keston Mark London 68 F2
Keswick Cumb 229 G11
Norf 142 C4
Norf 161 C7
Kete Pembs 72 E4
Ketford Glos 98 E4
Ketley Telford 150 G3
Ketley Bank Telford 150 G3
Ketsby Lincs 190 F5
Kettering Northants 121 B7
Ketteringham Norf 142 C3
Kettins Perth 286 D6
Kettlebaston Suff 125 G9
Kettlebridge Fife 287 G7
Kettlebrook Staffs 134 C4
Kettleburgh Suff 126 E5
Kettle Corner Kent 53 C8
Kettle Green Herts 86 B6
Kettlehill Fife 287 G7
Kettleholm Dumfries 238 B4
Kettleness N Yorks 226 B6
Kettleshulme Ches E 185 F7
Kettleshume Ches E 185 F7
Kettlesing N Yorks 205 B10
Kettlesing Bottom
N Yorks 205 B10
Kettlesing Head
N Yorks 205 B10
Kettlestone Norf 159 C9
Kettlethorpe Lincs 188 F4
W Yorks 197 D10
Kettletoft Orkney 314 C6
Kettlewell N Yorks 213 E9
Ketton Rutland 137 C9
Kevingtown London 68 F3
Kew London 67 D7
Keward Som 44 E4
Kew Bridge London 67 D7
Kewstoke N Som 59 G10
Kexbrough S Yorks 197 F9
Kexby Lincs 188 D5
York 207 C10
Keybridge Corn 11 G7
Keycol Kent 69 G11
Keyford Som 45 D9
Key Green Ches E 168 C5
N Yorks 226 E6
Keyham Leics 136 B3
Keyhaven Hants 20 C2
Keyingham E Yorks 201 B8
Keymer W Sus 36 D4
Keynsham Bath 61 F7
Keysers Estate Essex 86 D5
Key's Green Kent 53 F7
Keysoe Beds 121 E11
Keysoe Row Beds 121 E11
Keyston Cambs 121 B10
Key Street Kent 69 G11
Keyworth Notts 154 C2
Khantore Aberds 292 D4
Kibbear Som 28 C2
Kibblesworth T&W 242 F6
Kibworth Beauchamp
Leics 136 E3
Kibworth Harcourt
Leics 136 E3
Kidbrooke London 68 D2
Kidburngill Cumb 229 G7
Kiddal Lane End
W Yorks 206 F4
Kiddemore Green Staffs 133 B7
Kidderminster Worcs 116 B6
Kiddington Oxon 101 G8
Kidd's Moor Norf 142 C2
Kidlington Oxon 83 C7
Kidmore End Oxon 65 D7
Kidnal Ches W 167 F7
Kidsdale Dumfries 236 F6
Kidsgrove Staffs 168 E4
Kidstones N Yorks 213 C9
Kidwelly / Cydweli
Carms 74 D6
Kiel Crofts Argyll 289 F11
Kielder Northumb 250 E4
Kierfiold Ho Orkney 314 E2
Kiff Green W Berks 64 F5
Kilbagie Fife 279 D8
Kilbarchan Renfs 267 C8
Kilbeg Highld 295 E8
Kilberry Argyll 275 G8
Kilbirnie N Ayrs 266 E6
Kilbowie W Dunb 277 G10
Kilbraur Highld 311 H2
Kilbride Argyll 254 C4
Argyll 275 D9
Argyll 289 G10
Argyll 289 G11
Highld 295 C7
Kilbridemore Argyll 275 D11
Kilbryde Castle Stirl 285 G11
Kilburn Angus 292 G5
Derbys 170 F5
London 67 C9
N Yorks 215 D10
Kilby Leics 136 D2
Kilby Bridge Leics 136 D2
Kilchamaig Argyll 275 G9
Kilchattan Argyll 274 D4
Kilchattan Bay Argyll 266 E2
Kilchenzie Argyll 255 E7
Kilcheran Argyll 289 F10
Kilchiaran Argyll 274 G3
Kilchoan Argyll 275 B8
Highld 288 C6
Kilchoman Argyll 274 G3
Kilchrenan Argyll 284 E4
Kilconquhar Fife 287 G8
Kilcot Glos 98 F3
Kilcoy Highld 300 D5
Kilcreggan Argyll 276 E4
Kildale N Yorks 226 D2
Kildalloig Argyll 255 F8
Kildary Highld 301 B7
Kildaton Ho Argyll 254 C5
Kildavanan Argyll 275 G11
Kildermorie Lodge
Highld 300 B5
Kildonan Dumfries 236 D2
Highld 298 D3
N Ayrs 256 E2
Kildonan Lodge Highld 311 G3
Kildonnan Highld 294 G6
Kildrum N Lnrk 278 F5
Kildrummy Aberds 292 B6
Kildwick N Yorks 204 D6
Kilfinan Argyll 275 F10
Kilfinnan Highld 290 D4
Kilgetty Pembs 73 D10
Kilgour Fife 286 G6
Kilgrammie S Ayrs 245 C7
Kilgwrrwg Common Mon 79 F7
Kilhallon Corn 5 E11
Kilham E Yorks 217 G11
Northumb 263 C9
Kilkeddan Argyll 255 E8
Kilkenneth Argyll 288 E1
Kilkenny Glos 81 B8
Kilkerran Argyll 255 F8
Kilkhampton Corn 24 E3
Killamarsh Derbys 187 E7
Killaworgey Corn 5 C8
Killay Swansea 56 C6
Killbeg Argyll 289 E8
Killean Argyll 255 C7
Killearn Stirl 277 D10
Killegruer Argyll 255 D7
Killen Highld 300 D6
Killerby Darl 224 B3
Killichonan Perth 285 B9
Killiechoinich Argyll 289 G10
Killiechonate Highld 290 E4
Killiechronan Argyll 289 E7
Killiecrankie Perth 291 G11
Killiemor Argyll 288 F6
Killiemore House Argyll 288 G6
Killilan Highld 295 B11
Killimster Highld 310 D7
Killin Stirl 285 D9
Killinallan Argyll 274 F4
Killingbeck W Yorks 206 G2
Killinghall N Yorks 205 B11
Killington Cumb 212 B2
Devon 41 D7
Killingworth T&W 243 C7
Killingworth Moor T&W 243 C7
Killingworth Village
T&W 243 C7
Killin Lodge Highld 291 C7
Killivose Corn 2 B4
Killmahumaig Argyll 275 D8
Killochyett Borders 271 F9
Killocraw Argyll 255 D7
Killundine Highld 289 E7
Killylung Dumfries 247 G11
Kilmacolm Invclyd 267 B7
Kilmaha Argyll 275 C10
Kilmahog Stirl 285 G10
Kilmalieu Highld 289 D10
Kilmaluag Highld 298 B4
Kilmany Fife 287 E7
Kilmarie Highld 295 D7
Kilmarnock E Ayrs 257 B10
Kilmaron Castle Fife 287 F7
Kilmartin Argyll 275 D9
Kilmaurs E Ayrs 267 G8
Kilmelford Argyll 275 B9
Kilmeny Argyll 274 G4
Kilmersdon Som 45 C7
Kilmeston Hants 33 B9
Kilmichael Argyll 255 E7
Argyll 275 F10
Kilmichael Glassary
Argyll 275 D9
Kilmichael of Inverlussa
Argyll 275 E8
Kilmington Devon 15 B11
Wilts 45 F9
Kilmington Common
Wilts 45 F9
Kilmoluaig Argyll 288 E1
Kilmonivaig Highld 290 E3
Kilmorack Highld 300 E4
Kilmore Argyll 289 G10
Highld 295 E8
Kilmory Argyll 275 F8
Highld 289 B7
Highld 294 E5
N Ayrs 255 E10
Kilmory Lodge Argyll 275 C8
Kilmote Highld 311 H3
Kilmuir Highld 298 B3
Highld 298 E2
Highld 300 E6
Highld 301 B7
Kilmun Argyll 275 B10
Argyll 276 E3
Kilnave Argyll 274 F3
Kilncadzow S Lnrk 269 F7
Kilndown Kent 53 G8
Kiln Green Hereford 79 B10
Wokingham 65 D10
Kilnhill Cumb 229 E10
Kilnhurst S Yorks 187 B7
Kilninian Argyll 288 E5
Kilninver Argyll 289 G10
Kiln Pit Hill Northumb 242 G2
Kilnsea E Yorks 201 D12
Kilnsey N Yorks 213 F9
Kilnwick E Yorks 208 D5
Kilnwick Percy E Yorks 208 C2
Kiloran Argyll 274 D4
Kilpatrick N Ayrs 255 E10
Kilpeck Hereford 97 E8
Kilphedir Highld 311 H3
Kilpin E Yorks 199 B9
Kilpin Pike E Yorks 199 B9
Kilrenny Fife 287 G9
Kilsby Northants 119 C11
Kilspindie Perth 286 E6
Kilsyth N Lnrk 278 F4
Kiltarlity Highld 300 E5
Kilton Notts 187 F9
Redcar 226 B4
Som 43 E7
Kilton Thorpe Redcar 226 B3
Kiltyrie Perth 285 D10
Kilvaxter Highld 298 C3
Kilve Som 43 E7
Kilvington Notts 172 G3
Kilwinning N Ayrs 266 G6
Kimberley Norf 141 C11
Notts 171 G8
Kimberworth S Yorks 186 C6
Kimberworth Park
S Yorks 186 C6
Kimblesworth Durham 233 B11
Kimble Wick Bucks 84 D4
Kimbolton Cambs 121 D11
Hereford 115 E10
Kimbridge Hants 32 B4
Kimcote Leics 135 F11
Kimmeridge Dorset 18 F4
Kimmerston Northumb 263 B11
Kimpton Hants 47 D9
Herts 85 B11
Kimworthy Devon 24 E4
Kinabus Argyll 254 C3
Kinbeachie Highld 300 C6
Kinbrace Highld 310 F2
Kinbuck Stirl 285 G11
Kincaidston S Ayrs 257 F9
Kincaple Fife 287 F8
Kincardine Fife 279 D8
Highld 309 L6
Kincardine Bridge Falk 279 D8
Kincardine O'Neil
Aberds 293 D7
Kinclaven Perth 286 D5
Kincorth Aberdeen 293 C11
Kincorth Ho Moray 301 C10
Kincraig Highld 291 C10
Kincraigie Perth 286 C3
Kindallachan Perth 286 C3
Kine Moor S Yorks 197 G9
Kineton Glos 99 F11
Warks 118 G6
Kineton Green W Mid 134 G2
Kinfauns Perth 286 E5
Kingairloch Highld 289 D10
Kingarth Argyll 255 B11
Kingates IoW 20 F6
Kingbeare Corn 11 G11
Kingcoed Mon 78 D6
Kingdown N Som 60 G4
King Edward Aberds 303 D7
Kingerby Lincs 189 C9
Kingfield Sur 50 B4
Kingford Devon 24 F3
Devon 25 D10
Kingham Oxon 100 G5
Kinghay Wilts 30 B5
Kingholm Quay
Dumfries 237 B11
Kinghorn Fife 280 D5
Kingie Highld 290 C3
Kinglassie Fife 280 B4
Kingledores Borders 260 D4
Kingoodie Perth 287 E7
King's Acre Hereford 97 C9
Kingsand Corn 7 E8
Kingsash Bucks 84 D5
Kingsbarns Fife 287 F9
Kingsbridge Devon 8 G4
Som 42 F3
King's Bromley Staffs 152 F2
Kingsburgh Highld 298 D3
Kingsbury London 67 B8
Warks 134 D4
Kingsbury Episcopi Som 28 C6
Kingsbury Regis Som 29 D11
King's Caple Hereford 97 F11
Kingscauseway Highld 301 B7
Kingscavil W Loth 279 F10
Kingsclere Hants 48 B4
Kingsclere Woodlands
Hants 64 G4
King's Cliffe Northants 137 D10
Kings Clipstone Notts 171 C10
Kingscote Glos 80 F4
Kingscott Devon 25 D8
King's Coughton Warks 117 F11
Kingscourt Glos 80 E4
Kingscross N Ayrs 256 D2
Kingsditch Glos 99 G8
Kingsdon Som 29 B8
Kingsdown Kent 54 B2
Kent 55 D11
Swindon 63 B7
Wilts 61 F10
King's Dyke Cambs 138 D4
Kingseat Fife 280 C2
Kingseathill Fife 280 D2
King's End Worcs 116 G6
Kingsett Devon 12 E6
Kingsey Bucks 84 D2
Kingsfield Hereford 97 B10
Kingsfold Lancs 194 B4
W Sus 51 F7
Kingsford Aberds 293 B7
E Ayrs 267 F8
Worcs 132 G6
Kingsforth N Lincs 200 D4
King's Furlong Hants 48 C6
Kingsgate Kent 71 E11
King's Green Glos 98 E5
Worcs 116 E5
Kingshall Green Suff 125 E8
Kingshall Street Suff 125 E8
Kingsheanton Devon 40 F5
King's Heath Northants 120 E4
W Mid 133 G11
Kings Hedges Cambs 123 E9
Kingshill Glos 80 F3
Swindon 62 C6
Kings Hill Glos 81 E8
King's Hill Kent 53 C7
W Mid 133 D9
Kingsholm Glos 80 B4
Kingshouse Hotel
Highld 284 B6
Kingshurst W Mid 134 F3
Kingside Hill Cumb 238 G5
Kingskerswell Devon 9 B7
Kingskettle Fife 287 G7
Kingsknowe Edin 280 G4
Kingsland Anglesey 178 E2
Hereford 115 E8
London 67 C10
Shrops 149 G9
Kings Langley Herts 85 E9
Kingsley Ches W 183 G9
Hants 49 F9
Staffs 169 F8
Kingsley Green W Sus 49 G11
Kingsley Holt Staffs 169 F8
Kingsley Moor Staffs 169 F7
Kingsley Park Northants 120 E5
Kingslow Shrops 132 D5
King's Lynn Norf 158 E2
King's Meaburn Cumb 231 G8
Kingsmead Hants 33 E9
Kingsmere Oxon 101 G11
King's Mills Derbys 153 D8
Wrex 166 F4
Kingsmoor Essex 86 D6
Kings Moss Mers 194 G4
Kingsmuir Angus 287 C8
Fife 287 G9
Kings Muir Borders 261 B7
King's Newnham Warks 119 B9
King's Newton Derbys 153 D7
Kingsnordley Shrops 132 F5
Kingsnorth Kent 54 F4
King's Norton Leics 136 C3
W Mid 117 B11
King's Nympton Devon 25 D11
King's Pyon Hereford 115 G8
Kings Ripton Cambs 122 B5
King's Somborne Hants 47 G11
King's Stag Dorset 30 E2
King's Stanley Glos 80 E4
King's Sutton Northants 101 D9
King's Tamerton Plym 7 D9
Kingstanding W Mid 133 E11
Kingsteignton Devon 14 G3
Kingsteps Highld 301 D9
King Sterndale Derbys 185 G9
King's Thorn Hereford 97 E10
Kingsthorpe Northants 120 E5
Kingsthorpe Hollow
Northants 120 E5
Kingston Cambs 122 F6
Devon 8 F2
Devon 9 E8
Dorset 18 F5
Dorset 30 F3
E Loth 281 E10
Gtr Man 184 B6
Hants 31 G11
IoW 20 E5
Kent 55 C7
M Keynes 103 D8
Moray 302 C3
Ptsmth 33 G11
Suff 108 B5
Kingston Bagpuize Oxon 82 F6
Kingston Blount Oxon 84 F2
Kingston by Sea W Sus 36 G2
Kingston Deverill Wilts 45 F10
Kingstone Hereford 97 D8
Hereford 98 G2
Som 28 E5
Staffs 151 D11
S Yorks 197 F10
Kingstone Winslow Oxon 63 B9
Kingston Gorse W Sus 35 G9
Kingston Lisle Oxon 63 B10
Kingston Maurward
Dorset 17 C10
Kingston near Lewes
E Sus 36 F5
Kingston on Soar
Notts 153 D10
Kingston Park T&W 242 D6
Kingston Russell Dorset 17 C7
Kingston St Mary Som 28 B2
Kingston Seymour
N Som 60 F2
Kingston Stert Oxon 84 E2
Kingston upon Hull Hull 200 B5
Kingston upon Thames
London 67 F7
Kingston Vale London 67 E8
Kingstown Cumb 239 F9
King Street Essex 87 E9
King's Walden Herts 104 G3
Kingsway Bath 61 G8
Halton 183 D8
Kingswear Devon 9 E7
Kingswells Aberdeen 293 C10
Kingswinford W Mid 133 F7
Kingswood Bucks 83 B11
Essex 69 B8
Glos 80 G2
Hereford 114 G5
Herts 85 E10
Kent 53 C10
Powys 130 C4
S Glos 60 E6
Som 42 F6
Sur 51 B8
Warks 118 C3
Warr 183 C9
Kingswood Brook
Warks 118 C3
Kingswood Common
Staffs 132 C6
Worcs 116 D4
Kings Worthy Hants 48 G3
Kingthorpe Lincs 189 F10
Kington Hereford 114 F5
S Glos 79 G10
Worcs 117 F9
Kington Langley Wilts 62 D2
Kington Magna Dorset 30 C3
Kington St Michael Wilts 62 D2
Kingussie Highld 291 C9
Kingweston Som 44 G4
Kinhrive Highld 301 B7
Kininvie Ho Moray 302 E3
Kinkell Bridge Perth 286 F3
Kinknockie Aberds 303 E10
Aberds 303 G9
Kinkry Hill Cumb 240 B2
Kinlet Shrops 132 G4
Kinloch Fife 286 F6
Highld 289 D8
Highld 294 F5
Highld 295 D8
Highld 308 F3
Perth 286 C5
Perth 286 C6
Kinlochan Highld 289 C10
Kinlochard Stirl 285 G8
Kinlochbeoraid Highld 295 G10
Kinlochbervie Highld 306 D7
Kinloch Damph Highld 299 E8
Kinlocheil Highld 289 B11
Kinlochewe Highld 299 C10
Kinloch Hourn Highld 295 E11
Kinloch Laggan Highld 291 E7
Kinlochleven Highld 290 G3
Kinloch Lodge Highld 308 D5
Kinlochmoidart Highld 289 B9
Kinlochmorar Highld 295 F10
Kinlochmore Highld 290 G3
Kinloch Rannoch Perth 285 B10
Kinlochspelve Argyll 289 G8
Kinloid Highld 295 G8
Kinloss Moray 301 C10
Kinmel Bay / Bae Cinmel
Conwy 181 E7
Kinmuck Aberds 293 B10
Kinmundy Aberds 293 B10
Kinnadie Aberds 303 E9
Kinnaird Perth 286 B3
Perth 286 E6
Kinnaird Castle Angus 287 B10
Kinnauld Highld 309 J7
Kinneff Aberds 293 F10
Kinneil Falk 279 E9
Kinnelhead Dumfries 248 C2
Kinnell Angus 287 B10
Kinnerley Shrops 148 E6
Kinnersley Hereford 96 B6
Worcs 99 C7
Kinnerton Powys 114 E4
Kinnerton Green Flint 166 C4
Kinnesswood Perth 286 G5
Kinninvie Durham 233 G7
Kinnordy Angus 287 B7
Kinoulton Notts 154 C3
Kinross Perth 286 G5
Kinrossie Perth 286 D5
Kinsbourne Green Herts 85 B10
Kinsey Heath Ches E 167 G11
Kinsham Hereford 115 E7
Worcs 99 D8
Kinsley W Yorks 198 E2
Kinson Bmouth 19 B7
Kintallan Argyll 275 E8
Kintbury W Berks 63 F11
Kintessack Moray 301 C9
Kintillo Perth 286 F5
Kintocher Aberds 293 C7
Kinton Hereford 115 C8
Shrops 149 F7
Kintore Aberds 293 B9
Kintour Argyll 254 B5
Kintra Argyll 254 C4
Argyll 288 G5
Kintradwell Highld 311 J3
Kintraw Argyll 275 C9
Kinuachdrachd Argyll 275 D8
Kinveachy Highld 291 B11
Kinver Staffs 132 G6
Kinwalsey Warks 134 F5
Kip Hill Durham 242 G6
Kiplin N Yorks 224 F5
Kippax W Yorks 206 G4
Kippen Stirl 278 C3
Kippford or Scaur
Dumfries 237 D10
Kippilaw Borders 262 D2
Kippilaw Mains Borders 262 D2
Kipping's Cross Kent 52 F6
Kippington Kent 52 C4
Kirbister Orkney 314 D6
Orkney 314 E2
Orkney 314 F3
Kirbuster Orkney 314 D2
Kirby Bedon Norf 142 B5
Kirby Bellars Leics 154 F4
Kirby Cane Norf 143 E7
Kirby Corner W Mid 118 B5
Kirby Cross Essex 108 G4
Kirby Fields Leics 135 C10
Kirby Green Norf 143 E7
Kirby Grindalythe
N Yorks 217 F8
Kirby Hill N Yorks 215 F7
N Yorks 224 D2
Kirby Knowle N Yorks 215 B9
Kirby-le-Soken Essex 108 G4
Kirby Misperton
N Yorks 216 D5
Kirby Moor Cumb 240 E2
Kirby Muxloe Leics 135 C10
Kirby Row Norf 143 E7
Kirby Sigston N Yorks 225 G8
Kirby Underdale
E Yorks 208 B2
Kirby Wiske N Yorks 215 C7
Kirdford W Sus 35 B8
Kirk Highld 310 D6
Kirkabister Shetland 312 G6
Shetland 313 K6
Kirkandrews Dumfries 237 E8
Kirkandrews-on-Eden
Cumb 239 F9
Kirkapol Argyll 288 E2
Kirkbampton Cumb 239 F8
Kirkbean Dumfries 237 D11
Kirkborough Cumb 229 D7
Kirkbrae Orkney 314 B4
Kirk Bramwith S Yorks 198 E6
Kirkbride Cumb 238 F6
Kirkbridge N Yorks 224 G5

Kirkbuddo Angus 287 C9
Kirkburn Borders 261 B7
— E Yorks 208 B5
Kirkburn W Yorks 197 E7
Kirkby Lincs 189 C9
— Mers 182 B6
— N Yorks 225 D10
Kirkby Fenside Lincs 174 C4
Kirkby Fleetham N Yorks 224 G5
Kirkby Green Lincs 173 D9
Kirkby Hill N Yorks 215 F7
Kirkby in Ashfield Notts 171 D8
Kirkby-in-Furness Cumb 210 C4
Kirkby la Thorpe Lincs 173 F10
Kirkby Lonsdale Cumb 212 E2
Kirkby Malham N Yorks 213 G7
Kirkby Mallory Leics 135 C9
Kirkby Malzeard N Yorks 214 E4
Kirkby Mills N Yorks 216 B4
Kirkbymoorside N Yorks 216 B3
Kirkby on Bain Lincs 174 C2
Kirkby Overblow N Yorks 206 D2
Kirkby Stephen Cumb 222 D4
Kirkby Thore Cumb 231 F8
Kirkby Underwood Lincs 155 D11
Kirkby Wharfe N Yorks 206 E6
Kirkby Woodhouse Notts 171 E7
Kirkcaldy Fife 280 C5
Kirkcambeck Cumb 240 D2
Kirkcarswell Dumfries 237 E9
Kirkcolm Dumfries 236 C2
Kirkconnel Dumfries 258 G6
Kirkconnell Dumfries 237 C11
Kirkcowan Dumfries 236 C5
Kirkcudbright Dumfries 237 D8
Kirkdale Mers 182 C4
Kirk Deighton N Yorks 206 C3
Kirk Ella E Yorks 200 B4
Kirkfieldbank S Lnrk 269 G7
Kirkforthar Feus Fife 286 G6
Kirkgunzeon Dumfries 237 C10
Kirk Hallam Derbys 171 G7
Kirkham Lancs 202 G4
— N Yorks 216 F4
Kirkhamgate W Yorks 197 C9
Kirk Hammerton N Yorks 206 B5
Kirkhams Gtr Man 195 F10
Kirkharle Northumb 252 G4
Kirkheaton Northumb 242 B2
— W Yorks 197 D7
Kirkhill Angus 293 G8
— E Renf 267 D11
— Highld 300 E5
— Midloth 270 C4
— Moray 302 F2
— W Loth 279 G11
Kirkholt Gtr Man 195 E11
Kirkhope Borders 261 E9
Kirkhouse Borders 261 C8
— Cumb 240 F3
Kirkiboll Highld 308 D5
Kirkibost Highld 295 D7
Kirkinch Angus 287 C7
Kirkinner Dumfries 236 D6
Kirkintilloch E Dunb 278 G3
Kirk Ireton Derbys 170 E3
Kirkland Cumb 229 B11
— Cumb 231 E8
— Dumfries 247 E10
— Dumfries 258 G6
— S Ayrs 244 E6
Kirkland Guards Cumb 229 C9
Kirk Langley Derbys 152 B5
Kirkleatham Redcar 235 G7
Kirklees Gtr Man 195 E10
Kirklevington Stockton 225 D8
Kirkley Suff 143 E10
Kirklington Notts 171 D11
— N Yorks 214 C6
Kirklinton Cumb 239 D10
Kirkliston Edin 280 G2
Kirkmaiden Dumfries 236 F3
Kirk Merrington Durham 233 E11
Kirkmichael Perth 286 B4
— S Ayrs 245 B8
Kirk Michael IoM 192 C4
Kirkmichael Mains Dumfries 248 F2
Kirkmuirhill S Lnrk 268 G5
Kirknewton Northumb 263 C10
— W Loth 270 B2
Kirkney Aberds 302 F5
Kirk of Shotts N Lnrk 268 C6
Kirkoswald Cumb 231 C7
— S Ayrs 244 B6
Kirkpatrick Dumfries 247 E10
Kirkpatrick Durham Dumfries 237 B9
Kirkpatrick-Fleming Dumfries 239 C7
Kirk Sandall S Yorks 198 F6
Kirksanton Cumb 210 C2
Kirkshaw N Lnrk 268 C4
Kirk Smeaton N Yorks 198 D4
Kirkstall W Yorks 205 F11
Kirkstead Borders 261 E7
— Lincs 173 C11
Kirkstile Aberds 302 F5
Kirkstyle Highld 310 B7
Kirkthorpe W Yorks 197 C11
Kirkton Aberds 302 E6
— Aberds 303 D7
— Angus 286 C6
— Angus 287 C8
— Angus 287 D8
— Argyll 275 G4
— Borders 262 G2
— Dumfries 247 G10
— Fife 280 G4
— Fife 287 E7
— Highld 295 C10
— Highld 299 E9
— Highld 301 D7
— Highld 309 K7
— Perth 286 F3
— S Lnrk 259 E10
— Stirl 285 G9
— W Loth 269 B10
Kirktonhill Borders 271 E9
— W Dunb 277 F7
Kirkton Manor Borders 260 B6
Kirkton of Airlie Angus 287 B7
Kirkton of Auchterhouse Angus 287 D7
Kirkton of Auchterless Aberds 303 E7
Kirkton of Barevan Highld 301 E8
Kirkton of Bourtie Aberds 303 G8

Kirkton of Collace Perth 286 D5
Kirkton of Craig Angus 287 B11
Kirkton of Culsalmond Aberds 302 F6
Kirkton of Durris Aberds 293 D9
Kirkton of Glenbuchat Aberds 292 B5
Kirkton of Glenisla Angus 292 G4
Kirkton of Kingoldrum Angus 287 B7
Kirkton of Lethendy Perth 286 C5
Kirkton of Logie Buchan Aberds 303 G9
Kirkton of Maryculter Aberds 293 D10
Kirkton of Menmuir Aberds 293 G7
Kirkton of Monikie Angus 287 D9
Kirkton of Oyne Aberds 302 G6
Kirkton of Rayne Aberds 302 G6
Kirkton of Skene Aberds 293 C10
Kirkton of Tough Aberds 293 B8
Kirktown Aberds 303 D10
Kirktown of Alvah Aberds 302 C6
Kirktown of Deskford Moray 302 C5
Kirktown of Fetteresso Aberds 293 E10
Kirktown of Mortlach Moray 302 F3
Kirktown of Slains Aberds 303 G10
Kirkurd Borders 270 G2
Kirkwall Orkney 314 E4
Kirkwhelpington Northumb 251 G11
Kirmington N Lincs 200 E6
Kirmond le Mire Lincs 189 C11
Kirn Argyll 276 F3
Kirriemuir Angus 287 B7
Kirstead Green Norf 142 D5
Kirtlebridge Dumfries 238 C6
Kirtleton Dumfries 249 G2
Kirtling Cambs 124 F3
Kirtling Green Cambs 124 F3
Kirtlington Oxon 83 B7
Kirtomy Highld 308 C7
Kirton Lincs 156 B6
— Notts 171 B11
— Suff 143 E10
Kirton Campus W Loth 269 B10
Kirton End Lincs 174 G3
Kirton Holme Lincs 174 G3
Kirton in Lindsey N Lincs 188 B6
Kiskin Cumb 210 B1
Kislingbury Northants 120 F3
Kitbridge Devon 28 G4
Kitchenroyd W Yorks 197 F8
Kitebrook Warks 100 E4
Kite Green Warks 118 D3
Kite Hill IoW 21 C7
Kites Hardwick Warks 119 D9
Kit Hill Dorset 30 D4
Kitley Som 80 E5
Kit's Coty Kent 69 G8
Kitt Green Gtr Man 194 F5
Kittisford Som 27 C9
Kittle Swansea 56 D5
Kitts End Herts 86 F2
Kitt's Moss Gtr Man 184 E5
Kittwhistle Dorset 28 G5
Kittybrewster Aberdeen 293 C11
Kitwell W Mid 133 G10
Kitwood Hants 49 G7
Kiveton Park S Yorks 187 E7
Kives of Elrick Aberds 302 D6
Knaith Lincs 188 E4
Knaith Park Lincs 188 D4
Knap Corner Dorset 30 C4
Knaphill Hants 50 B3
Knapp Hants 32 C6
— Perth 286 D6
— Som 28 B4
— Wilts 31 B8
Knapp Hill Wilts 30 B5
Knapthorpe Notts 172 D2
Knaptoft Leics 136 F2
Knapton Norf 160 C6
— N Yorks 207 C7
Knapton Green Hereford 115 G8
Knapwell Cambs 122 E6
Knaresborough N Yorks 206 B3
Knarsdale Northumb 240 G5
Knatts Valley Kent 68 G5
Knauchland Moray 302 D5
Knaven Aberds 303 E8
Knave's Ash Kent 71 G7
Knaves Green Suff 126 D2
Knavesmire York 207 D7
Knayton N Yorks 215 B8
Knebworth Herts 104 G5
Knedlington E Yorks 199 B8
Kneesall Notts 172 C2
Kneesworth Cambs 104 C6
Kneeton Notts 172 F2
Knelston Swansea 56 D3
Knenhall Staffs 151 B8
Knettishall Suff 141 G9
Knightacott Devon 41 F7
Knightcote Warks 119 G7
Knightcott N Som 43 B11
Knightley Staffs 150 D6
Knightley Dale Staffs 150 E6
Knighton Devon 7 F10
— Dorset 29 E10
— Leicester 135 C11
— Poole 18 B6
— Som 43 F7
— Staffs 150 D4
— Staffs 168 G2
— Wilts 63 G9
— W Loth 269 B10
Knighton / Tref-y-Clawdd Powys 114 C5
Knighton Fields Leicester 135 C11
Knighton on Teme Worcs 116 D2
Knightor Corn 5 D10
Knightsbridge Glos 99 F7
— London 67 D9
Knight's End Cambs 139 E8

Knightsmill Corn 11 E7
Knightside W Loth 269 D9
Knightswood Glasgow 267 B10
Knightwick Worcs 116 F4
Knill Hereford 114 E5
Knipe Fold Cumb 220 F6
Knipoch Argyll 289 G10
Knipton Leics 154 C6
Knitsley Durham 233 B8
Kniveton Derbys 170 E2
Knock Argyll 289 F7
— Cumb 231 F9
— Moray 302 D5
Knockally Highld 311 G5
Knockan Highld 307 H6
Knockandhu Moray 302 G2
Knockando Moray 301 E11
Knockando Ho Moray 302 E2
Knockandoo Highld 301 G7
Knockbain Highld 300 D6
Knockbreck Highld 298 C2
Knockbrex Dumfries 237 E7
Knockcarrach Highld 290 B6
Knockdee Highld 310 C5
Knockdolian S Ayrs 244 F4
Knockdow Argyll 276 G2
Knockdown Glos 61 B10
Knockenbaird Aberds 302 G6
Knockenkelly N Ayrs 256 D2
Knockentiber E Ayrs 257 B9
Knockerdown Derbys 170 E2
Knockfarrel Highld 300 D5
Knockglass Dumfries 236 D2
Knockhall Kent 68 E5
Knockholt Kent 52 B3
Knockholt Pound Kent 52 B3
Knockie Lodge Highld 290 B6
Knockin Shrops 149 E7
Knockin Heath Shrops 149 E7
Knockinlaw E Ayrs 257 B10
Knockinnon Highld 310 F5
Knocklearn Dumfries 237 B9
Knocknaha Argyll 255 F7
Knocknain Dumfries 236 C1
Knockothie Aberds 303 F9
Knockrome Argyll 274 F6
Knocksharry IoM 192 D3
Knockstapplemore Argyll 255 F7
Knockvologan Argyll 274 A4
Knodishall Suff 127 E8
Knokan Argyll 288 G6
Knole Som 29 B7
Knollbury Mon 60 B2
Knoll Green Som 43 F8
Knolls Green Ches E 184 F4
Knoll Top N Yorks 214 F3
Knolton Wrex 149 B7
Knolton Bryn Wrex 149 B7
Knook Wilts 46 E2
Knossington Leics 136 B6
Knotbury Staffs 169 B8
Knott End-on-Sea Lancs 202 D3
Knotting Beds 121 E10
Knotting Green Beds 121 E10
Knottingley W Yorks 198 C2
Knott Lanes Gtr Man 196 G2
Knott Oak Som 28 E4
Knott Cumb 230 G4
— Lancs 203 C11
Knotty Ash Mers 182 C6
Knotty Corner Devon 24 B6
Knotty Green Bucks 115 C11
Knowbury Shrops 115 C11
Knowe Dumfries 236 B5
— Shetland 313 G5
Knowefield Cumb 239 F10
Knowehead Aberds 293 C7
— Aberds 302 D5
— Dumfries 246 E4
Knowes of Elrick Aberds 302 D6
Knoweton N Lnrk 268 D5
Knowetop N Lnrk 268 D5
Knowhead Aberds 303 D9
Knowl Bank Staffs 168 F4
Knowle Bristol 60 E6
— Devon 15 E7
— Devon 26 G3
— Devon 40 F3
— Hants 33 F9
— Shrops 115 C11
— Som 43 F10
— W Mid 63 G7
Knowle Fields Warks 117 C10
Knowle Green Essex 107 E7
— Lancs 203 F8
Knowle Grove W Mid 118 B3
Knowle Hill Sur 66 F3
Knowle Park W Yorks 205 E7
Knowle St Giles Som 28 E4
Knowles Hill Devon 14 G3
Knowl Green Essex 106 C5
Knowl Hill Windsor 65 D10
Knowlton Dorset 31 E8
— Kent 55 C9
Knowl Wall Staffs 151 B7
Knowl Wood W Yorks 196 C2
Knowsley Mers 182 B6
Knowstone Devon 26 C4
Knox Bridge Kent 53 E9
Knucklas Powys 114 C5
Knuston Northants 121 D8
Knutsford Ches E 184 F3
Knutton Staffs 168 F4
Knypersley Staffs 168 D5
Kraiknish Highld 294 C5
Krumlin W Yorks 196 D5
Kuggar Corn 2 F6
Kyleakin Highld 295 C9
Kyle of Lochalsh Highld 295 C9
Kylepark N Lnrk 268 C3
Kylerhea Highld 295 C10
Kyles Scalpay / Caolas Scalpaigh W Isles 305 J4
Kylesknoydart Highld 295 F10
Kylesmorar Highld 295 F10
Kylestrome Highld 306 F7
Kyllachy House Highld 301 G7
Kymin Hereford 97 H11
— Mon 79 C8
Kynaston Hereford 97 F10
— Shrops 149 E7
Kynnersley Telford 150 F3
Kyre Worcs 116 E2
Kyre Green Worcs 116 E2

Kyre Magna Worcs 116 E2
Kyre Park Worcs 116 E2
Kyrewood Worcs 116 D2

L

Labost W Isles 304 D4
Lacasaidh W Isles 304 E5
Lacasdal W Isles 304 E6
Laceby NE Lincs 201 F8
Laceby Acres NE Lincs 201 F8
Lacey Green Bucks 84 F4
— Ches E 184 E4
Lach Dennis Ches W 184 G2
Lache Ches W 166 C5
Lackenby Redcar 225 B11
Lackford Suff 124 C5
Lacock Wilts 62 F2
Lacock Green Wilts 62 F2
Ladbroke Warks 119 F8
Laddingford Kent 53 D7
Lade Kent 39 C9
Lade Bank Lincs 174 E5
Ladies Riggs N Yorks 214 F2
Ladmanlow Derbys 185 G8
Ladock Corn 5 E7
Ladwell Hants 32 C6
Lady Orkney 314 B6
Ladybank Fife 287 F7
Ladybrook Notts 171 C8
Ladyburn Invclyd 276 F6
Ladycross Corn 11 C4
Ladyes Hills Warks 118 C5
Lady Green Mers 193 G10
Lady Hall Cumb 210 B3
Lady Halton Shrops 115 B9
Ladykirk Borders 273 F7
Ladyoak Shrops 131 C7
Lady Park T&W 242 F6
Ladyridge Hereford 97 E11
Ladysford Aberds 303 C9
Lady's Green Suff 124 F5
Ladywell London 67 E11
— Shrops 149 C9
— W Loth 269 B10
Ladywood Telford 132 C3
— W Mid 133 F11
Lady Wood W Yorks 206 F2
Laffak Mers 183 B8
Laga Highld 289 C8
Lagafater Lodge Dumfries 236 B3
Lagalochan Argyll 275 B9
Lagavulin Argyll 254 C5
Lagg Argyll 274 F6
— N Ayrs 255 E10
Laggan Highld 254 B3
— Highld 289 B9
— Highld 290 D4
— Highld 291 D10
— S Ayrs 245 G7
Lagganlia Highld 291 C10
Laggan Lodge Argyll 289 G8
Lagganmullan Dumfries 237 D7
Lagganulva Argyll 288 E6
Lagness W Sus 22 C5
Laide Highld 307 K3
Laig Highld 294 D6
Laigh Carnduff S Lnrk 268 F3
Laigh Fenwick E Ayrs 267 G9
Laigh Glengall S Ayrs 257 F8
Laighmuir E Ayrs 267 F9
Laighstonehall S Lnrk 268 E4
Laindon Essex 69 B7
Lair Highld 299 E10
— Perth 292 G3
Laira Plym 7 D10
Lairg Highld 309 J5
Lairg Lodge Highld 309 J5
Lairgmore Highld 300 F5
Lairg Muir Highld 309 J5
Laisterdyke W Yorks 205 G9
Laithes Cumb 230 E5
Laithkirk Durham 232 G5
Laity Moor Corn 4 F3
Lake Devon 12 D6
— Devon 24 F6
— Devon 40 G5
— IoW 21 E7
— Poole 18 C5
— Wilts 46 F6
Lake End Bucks 66 D2
Lakenham Norf 142 B4
Lakenheath Suff 140 G4
Laker's Green Sur 50 F4
Lakesend Norf 139 D10
Lakeside Cumb 211 B7
— Thurrock 68 D5
Laleham Sur 66 F5
Laleston / Trelales Bridgend 57 F11
Lamanva Corn 3 D7
Lamarsh Essex 107 D7
Lamas Norf 160 E4
Lamb Corner Essex 107 E10
Lambden Borders 272 G4
Lamberden Kent 38 B4
Lamberhead Green Gtr Man 194 G4
Lamberhurst Kent 53 F7
Lamberhurst Quarter Kent 53 F7
Lamberton Borders 273 D8
Lambert's End W Mid 133 E9
Lambeth London 67 D10
Lambfair Green Suff 124 G4
Lambfoot Cumb 229 E8
Lambhill Glasgow 267 B11
Lambley Northumb 240 F5
— Notts 171 F10
Lambourn W Berks 63 D10
Lambourne Corn 4 E5
— Essex 87 G7
Lambourne End Essex 87 G7
Lambourn Woodlands W Berks 63 D10
Lambridge Bath 61 F9
Lamb's Cross Kent 53 D9
Lambs Green W Sus 51 F8
Lamb's Green Dorset 18 B5
Lambston Pembs 72 B6
Lambton T&W 243 G2
Lamellion Corn 6 C4
Lamerton Devon 12 F5
Lamesley T&W 243 F7
Laminess Orkney 314 C6
Lamington Highld 301 B7
— S Lnrk 259 C11
Lamlash N Ayrs 256 C2
Lamledra Corn 5 G10
Lamloch Dumfries 246 D2
Lammack Blkburn 195 B7
Lamonby Cumb 230 D4
Lamorick Corn 5 C10
Lamorna Corn 1 E4
Lamorran Corn 5 G7
Lampardbrook Suff 126 E5

Lampeter / Llanbedr Pont Steffan Ceredig 93 B11
Lampeter Velfrey Pembs 73 C11
Lamphey Pembs 73 E8
Lamplugh Cumb 229 G7
Lamport Northants 120 C5
Lampton London 66 D6
Lamyatt Som 45 F7
Lana Devon 12 B2
— Devon 24 F4
Lanark S Lnrk 269 G7
Lancaster Lancs 211 G9
Lanchester Durham 233 B9
Lancing W Sus 35 G11
Landbeach Cambs 123 D9
Landcross Devon 25 C7
Landerberry Aberds 293 C9
Landewednack Corn 2 G6
Landford Wilts 32 D3
Landford Manor Wilts 32 C3
Landfordwood Wilts 32 C3
Land Gate Gtr Man 194 G5
Landguard Manor IoW 21 E7
Landhill Devon 12 C3
Landican Mers 182 D3
Landimore Swansea 56 C3
Landkey Devon 40 G5
Landkey Newland Devon 40 G5
Landore Swansea 57 B7
Landport E Sus 36 E6
— Ptsmth 33 G10
Landrake Corn 7 C7
Land's End Corn 1 E3
Landscove Devon 8 C5
Land Shipping Pembs 73 C8
Landshipping Quay Pembs 73 C8
Landslow Green Gtr Man 185 B7
Landulph Corn 7 C8
Landwade Suff 124 D2
Landywood Staffs 133 B9
Lane Corn 4 C6
Laneast Corn 11 E10
Lane Bottom Lancs 204 F3
Lane End Bucks 84 G4
— Cumb 210 C6
— Cumb 220 G2
— Derbys 170 C6
— Devon 18 C3
— Dorset 18 D2
— Flint 166 C3
— Glos 79 B10
— Hants 33 B9
— Hants 33 B11
— IoW 21 D9
— Kent 68 E5
— Lancs 204 D3
— Sur 49 E10
— S Yorks 186 B6
— Wilts 45 D10
— N Yorks 204 F6
Lane Ends Ches E 168 G2
— Derbys 152 C4
— Gtr Man 185 C7
— Lancs 203 C11
— Lancs 203 G9
— N Yorks 204 E5
Lane Green Staffs 133 C7
Laneham Notts 188 F4
Lanehead Durham 232 C2
— Northumb 251 F7
Lane Head Derbys 185 F11
— Durham 224 C2
— Gtr Man 183 B11
— W Mid 133 C9
— W Yorks 197 F7
Lane Heads Lancs 202 F4
Lanehouse Dorset 17 F9
Lanercost Cumb 240 E3
Lanescot Corn 5 D11
Lanesend Pembs 73 E8
Lanes End Bucks 84 D6
Lane's End Shrops 132 G2
Lanesfield W Mid 133 D8
Laneshaw Bridge Lancs 204 E4
Lane Side Lancs 195 C9
Laney Green Staffs 133 B9
Lanfach Caerph 78 F2
Langaford Devon 12 B4
Langage Devon 7 E11
Langal Highld 289 C9
Langaller Som 28 B3
Langar Notts 154 C4
Langbank Renfs 277 G7
Langbar N Yorks 205 C7
Langbaurgh N Yorks 225 C11
Langburnshiels Borders 250 C2
Langcliffe N Yorks 212 G6
Langdale End N Yorks 227 G8
Langdon Corn 11 E4
— Corn 11 D4
Langdon Beck Durham 232 E3
Langdon Hills Essex 69 B7
Langdown Hants 32 F6
Langdyke Dumfries 238 C3
— Fife 287 G7
Langenhoe Essex 89 B8
Langford C Beds 104 C3
— Devon 14 B4
— Devon 27 G8
— Essex 88 D4
— Norf 177 E8
— Notts 172 D4
— Oxon 82 E4
— Som 28 B3
Langford Budville Som 27 C10
Langford Green N Som 44 B3
Langham Dorset 30 B3
— Essex 107 E10
— Norf 177 E8
— Rutland 154 G6
— Som 28 B2
— Suff 125 D10
Langhaugh Borders 260 C5
Langho Lancs 203 G10
Langholm Dumfries 249 G10
Langleeford Northumb 263 E10
Langley Ches E 184 G3
— Derbys 170 F6
— Essex 105 D8
— Glos 99 F10
— Gtr Man 195 F11
— Hants 32 G6
— Herts 104 G5
— Kent 53 C10
— Northumb 241 E8
— Oxon 82 B4
— Slough 66 D4
Langley Burrell Wilts 62 D2
Langley Corner Bucks 66 B4
Langley Common Derbys 152 B5
— Wokingham 65 F9
Langley Corner Derbys 152 B5
— Essex 107 G2
— Warks 118 E3
— W Mid 133 F9
Langley Heath Kent 53 C10
Langley Marsh Som 27 B9
Langley Mill Derbys 170 F6
Langley Moor Durham 233 C11
Langley Park Durham 233 C10
Langley Street Norf 143 C7
Langley Vale Sur 51 B8
Langloan N Lnrk 268 C4
Langney E Sus 23 E10
Langold Notts 187 D9
Langore Corn 11 E10
Langport Som 28 B6
Langrick Lincs 174 F3
Langrick Bridge Lincs 174 F3
Langridge Bath 61 F8
Langridge Ford Devon 25 C9
Langrigg Cumb 229 B9
Langrish Hants 34 C2
Langsett S Yorks 197 G8
Langshaw Borders 262 B2
Langshawburn Borders 248 D4
Langside Glasgow 267 C11
— Perth 285 F11
Langskaill Orkney 314 B4
Langstone Devon 13 D10
— Hants 22 C2
— Newport 78 G5
Langthorne N Yorks 224 G5
Langthorpe N Yorks 215 F7
Langthwaite N Yorks 223 E10
Langtoft E Yorks 217 F10
— Lincs 156 G2
Langton Durham 224 B3
— Lincs 174 B2
— Lincs 190 G5
— N Yorks 216 F5
Langton by Wragby Lincs 189 F11
Langton Green Kent 52 F4
— Suff 126 D4
Langton Herring Dorset 17 E8
Langton Long Blandford Dorset 30 F5
Langton Matravers Dorset 18 F6
Langtree Devon 25 D7
Langtree Week Devon 25 D7
Langwathby Cumb 231 E7
Langwell Ho Highld 311 G5
Langwell Lodge Highld 307 J6
Langwith Derbys 171 B8
Langwith Junction Derbys 171 B8
Langworth Lincs 189 F9
Lanham Green Essex 106 G5
Lanivet Corn 5 C10
Lanjeth Corn 5 E9
Lank Corn 11 F7
Lanlivery Corn 5 D11
Lanner Corn 4 G3
Lanreath Corn 6 D3
Lansallos Corn 6 E3
Lansbury Park Caerph 59 B7
Lansdown Bath 61 F8
— Glos 99 G8
Lanstephan Corn 12 D2
Lanteglos Corn 11 E7
Lanteglos Highway Corn 6 E3
Lanton Borders 262 E5
— Northumb 263 D10
Lantuel Corn 5 B9
Lantyan Corn 6 D2
Lapal W Mid 133 G9
Lapford Devon 26 F2
Lapford Cross Devon 26 F2
Laphroaig Argyll 254 C4
Lapley Staffs 151 G7
Lapworth Warks 118 C3
Larachbeg Highld 289 E8
Larbert Falk 279 E7
Larbreck Lancs 202 E4
Larches Lancs 202 G6
Larden Green Ches E 167 E9
Largie Aberds 302 F6
Largiebaan Argyll 255 F7
Largiemore Argyll 275 E10
Largoward Fife 287 G8
Largs N Ayrs 266 D4
Largue Aberds 302 E6
Largybeg N Ayrs 256 D2
Largymeanoch N Ayrs 256 D2
Largymore N Ayrs 256 D2
Larkfield Involyd 276 F4
— Kent 53 B8
Larkhall Bath 61 F9
— S Lnrk 268 E5
Larkhill Wilts 46 E6
Lark Hill Gtr Man 195 G7
Larklands Derbys 171 G7
Larks' Hill Suff 108 B3
Larling Norf 141 F9
Larport Hereford 97 D11
Larrick Corn 12 F2
Larriston Borders 250 E2
Lartington Durham 223 B10
Lary Aberds 292 C5
Lasborough Glos 80 G4
Lasham Hants 49 E7
Lashbrook Devon 24 F6
— Oxon 65 D8
Lashenden Kent 53 E10
Lask Edge Staffs 168 D6
Lassington Glos 98 G5
Lassodie Fife 280 C2
Lastingham N Yorks 226 G4
Latcham Som 44 D2
Latchbrook Corn 7 D7
Latchford Herts 105 G7
— Oxon 83 E11
Latchingdon Essex 88 E5
Latchley Corn 12 G4
Lately Common Warr 183 B11
Lathallan Mill Fife 287 G8
Lathbury M Keynes 103 B7
Latheron Highld 310 F5
Latheronwheel Highld 310 F5
Latheronwheel Ho Highld 310 F5
Lathom Lancs 194 E3
Lathones Fife 287 G8
Latimer Bucks 85 F8

— Som 27 B9
— Warks 118 E3
— W Mid 133 F9
— W Sus 34 B4
Latteridge S Glos 61 C7
Lattiford Som 29 B11
Latton Wilts 81 F9
Latton Bush Essex 87 D7
Lauchintilly Aberds 293 B9
Laudale Ho Highld 289 D9
Lauder Borders 271 F10
Lauder Barns Borders 271 F10
Laugharne / Talacharn Carms 74 C4
Laughern Hill Worcs 116 F5
Laughterton Lincs 188 F4
Laughton E Sus 23 C7
— Leics 136 F3
— Lincs 155 C11
— Lincs 188 C4
Laughton Common S Yorks 187 D8
Laughton en le Morthen S Yorks 187 D8
Launcells Corn 24 F2
Launcells Cross Corn 24 F3
Launceston Corn 12 D2
Launcherley Som 44 E4
Laund Lancs 195 C10
Launton Oxon 102 G2
Laurencekirk Aberds 293 F9
Laurieston Dumfries 237 C8
— Falk 279 F8
Lavendon M Keynes 121 G8
Lavenham Suff 107 B8
Laverackloch Moray 301 C11
Laverhay Dumfries 248 D4
Laverlay Borders 261 B7
Laverley Som 44 E5
Lavernock V Glam 59 F7
Laversdale Cumb 239 E11
Laverstock Wilts 47 G7
Laverstoke Hants 48 D3
Laverton Glos 99 D11
— N Yorks 214 E4
— Som 45 C9
Lavington Sands Wilts 46 B4
Lavister Wrex 166 D5
Law S Lnrk 269 E7
Lawers Perth 285 E11
— Perth 285 F11
Lawford Essex 107 E11
— Som 43 F7
Lawford Heath Warks 119 C9
Lawhill Perth 286 F3
Law Hill S Lnrk 268 E6
Lawhitton Corn 12 E3
Lawkland N Yorks 212 F5
Lawkland Green N Yorks 212 F5
Lawley Telford 132 B3
Lawley Bank Telford 132 B3
Lawn Swindon 63 C7
Lawnhead Staffs 150 E6
Lawns W Yorks 197 C10
Lawnswood W Yorks 205 F11
Lawnt Denb 165 B8
Lawrence Hill Newport 59 B10
Lawrenny Pembs 73 D8
Lawrenny Quay Pembs 73 D8
Lawshall Suff 125 G7
Lawshall Green Suff 125 G7
Lawton Hereford 115 F8
Lawton-gate Ches E 168 D4
Lawton Heath End Ches E 168 D3
Laxey IoM 192 D5
Laxfield Suff 126 C5
Laxfirth Shetland 313 H6
— Shetland 313 J6
Laxford Bridge Highld 306 E7
Laxo Shetland 313 G6
Laxobigging Shetland 312 F6
Laxton E Yorks 199 B9
— Northants 137 D8
— Notts 172 B2
Laycock W Yorks 204 E6
Layer Breton Essex 88 B6
Layer de la Haye Essex 89 B7
Layer Marney Essex 88 B6
Layerthorpe York 207 C8
Layham Suff 107 C10
Laymore Dorset 28 G5
Layters Green Bucks 85 G7
Laytham E Yorks 207 F10
Layton Blkpool 202 F2
Lazenby Redcar 225 B11
Lazonby Cumb 230 D6
Lea Derbys 170 D4
— Hereford 98 G3
— Lincs 188 D4
— Shrops 131 F7
— Shrops 131 C7
— Wilts 62 B2
Lea Bridge London 67 B11
Leabrooks Derbys 170 E6
Lea by Backford Ches W 182 G5
Lea End Worcs 117 B10
Leadburn Midloth 270 D4
Leadendale Staffs 151 B8
Leaden Roding Essex 87 C9
Leadgate Cumb 231 C10
— Durham 242 G4
— T&W 242 F4
Leadhills S Lnrk 259 G9
Leadingcross Green Kent 53 C11
Leadmill Derbys 186 E2
— Flint 166 C2
Leafield Oxon 82 B4
— Wilts 45 B10
Lea Forge Ches E 168 F2
Leagrave Luton 103 G10
Leagreen Hants 19 C11
Lea Green Mers 183 C8
Lea Hall W Mid 134 F2
Lea Heath Staffs 151 D10
Leake Lincs 174 F6
— N Yorks 225 G8
Leake Commonside Lincs 174 E5
Leake Fold Hill Lincs 174 E6
Lealholm N Yorks 226 D5
Lealholm Side N Yorks 226 D5
Lealt Argyll 275 D7
— Highld 298 C5
Leam Derbys 186 F2
Lea Marston Warks 134 E4
Leamington Hastings Warks 119 D8
Leamonsley Staffs 134 B2
Leamoor Common Shrops 131 F9
Leamore W Mid 133 C10
Leamside Durham 234 B2

Leanach Argyll 275 D11
Leanachan Highld 290 F4
Leanaig Highld 300 D5
Leapgate Worcs 116 C6
Leargybreck Argyll 274 F6
Lease Rigg N Yorks 226 E6
Leasey Bridge Herts 85 C11
Leasgill Cumb 211 C9
Leasingham Lincs 173 F9
Leasingthorne Durham 233 F11
Leason Swansea 56 C3
Leasowe Mers 182 C3
Leatherhead Sur 51 B7
Leatherhead Common Sur 51 B7
Leathern Bottle Glos 80 E2
Leathley N Yorks 205 D11
Leaths Dumfries 237 C9
Leaton Shrops 149 F9
— Telford 150 G2
Leaton Heath Shrops 149 F9
Lea Town Lancs 202 G5
Lea Valley Herts 85 E11
Leaveland Kent 54 C4
Leavenheath Suff 107 D9
Leavening N Yorks 216 G5
Leaves Green London 68 G2
Lea Yeat Cumb 212 B5
Leazes Durham 242 F5
Lebberston N Yorks 217 C11
Leburnick Corn 12 E3
Lechlade-on-Thames Glos 82 F2
Leck Lancs 212 D2
Leckford Hants 47 F11
Leckfurin Highld 308 D7
Leckgruinart Argyll 274 G3
Leckhampstead Bucks 102 D4
— W Berks 64 D2
Leckhampstead Thicket W Berks 64 D2
Leckhampton Glos 80 B6
Leckie Highld 299 C10
Leckmelm Highld 307 K6
Leckuary Argyll 275 D9
Leckwith V Glam 59 E7
Leconfield E Yorks 208 E6
Ledaig Argyll 289 F11
Ledburn Bucks 103 G8
Ledbury Hereford 98 D4
Ledcharrie Stirl 285 E9
Leddington Glos 98 E3
Ledgemoor Hereford 115 G8
Ledgowan Highld 299 D11
Ledicot Hereford 115 E8
Ledmore Angus 293 G7
— Highld 307 H7
Lednagullin Highld 308 C7
Ledsham Ches W 182 G5
— W Yorks 198 B2
Ledston W Yorks 198 B2
Ledstone Devon 8 F4
Ledston Luck W Yorks 206 G4
Ledwell Oxon 101 F8
Lee Argyll 288 G6
— Devon 40 D3
— Devon 40 F5
— Hants 32 D5
— Lancs 203 C8
— London 67 E11
— Northumb 241 G10
— Shrops 149 C8
Leeans Shetland 313 J5
Lee Bank W Mid 133 F11
Leebotten Shetland 313 L6
Leebotwood Shrops 131 D9
Lee Brockhurst Shrops 149 D10
Leece Cumb 210 F4
Leechpool Pembs 72 C6
Leedon Bucks 103 F8
Leeds Kent 53 C10
— W Yorks 205 G11
Leedstown Corn 2 C4
Leeford Devon 41 D9
Lee Gate Bucks 84 D5
Leegomery Telford 150 G3
Lee Ground Hants 33 F8
Lee Head Derbys 185 C8
Leeholme Durham 233 F10
Leek Staffs 169 D7
Leekbrook Staffs 169 E7
Leek Wootton Warks 118 D5
Lee Mill Devon 8 D2
Leeming N Yorks 214 B5
— W Yorks 204 G6
Leeming Bar N Yorks 224 G5
Leemings Lancs 203 D10
Lee Moor Devon 7 C11
— W Yorks 197 B10
Lee-on-the-Solent Hants 33 G8
Lee-over-Sands Essex 89 C10
Lees Derbys 152 B5
— Gtr Man 196 G3
— W Yorks 204 F6
Leeswood / Coed-Llai Flint 166 D3
Leetown Perth 286 E6
Leftwich Ches W 183 G11
Legar Powys 78 B2
Legbourne Lincs 190 E5
Legburthwaite Cumb 220 B6
Legerwood Borders 271 G11
Leggatt Hill W Sus 34 C5
Legsby Lincs 189 D11
Leicester Leicester 135 C11
Leicester Forest East Leics 135 C10
Leicester Grange Warks 135 E8
Leigh Dorset 26 E6
— Dorset 29 F10
— Dorset 30 F3
— Glos 99 F7
— Gtr Man 195 G7
— Kent 52 D5
— Shrops 130 C6
— Sur 51 D8
— Wilts 81 G9
— Worcs 116 G5
Leigh Beck Essex 69 C10
Leigh Common Som 30 B1
Leigh Delamere Wilts 61 D11
Leigh Green Kent 54 G2
Leighland Chapel Som 42 F4
Leigh-on-Sea Sthend 69 B10
Leigh Park Hants 22 B2
Leigh Sinton Worcs 116 G5
Leighswood W Mid 133 C11
Leighterton Glos 80 G4
Leighton N Yorks 214 D3
— Powys 130 B4
— Shrops 132 B2
— Som 45 E8

Leighton Bromswold
Cambs. 122 B2
Leighton Buzzard
C Beds. 103 F8
Leighton / Tre'r llai
Powys. 130 B5
Leigh upon Mendip Som. .45 D7
Leigh Woods N Som. ...60 E5
Leinthall Earls Hereford. 115 D8
Leinthall Starkes
Hereford. 115 D8
Leintwardine Hereford. 115 D8
Leire Leics. 135 E10
Leirinmore Highld. 308 C4
Leiston Suff. 127 E8
Leitfie Perth. 286 C6
Leith Edin. 280 F5
Leithenhall Dumfries. .248 D4
Leitholm Borders. 272 G5
Lelant Corn. 2 B2
Lelant Downs Corn. ...2 B2
Lelley E Yorks. 209 G10
Lem Hill Worcs. 116 C4
Lemington T&W. 242 E5
Lemmington Hall
Northumb. 264 G4
Lempitlaw Borders. ...263 C7
Lemsford Herts. 86 C2
Lenacre Cumb. 212 B3
Lenborough Bucks. ...102 E3
Lenchwick Worcs. 99 B10
Lendalfoot S Ayrs. ...244 F4
Lendrick Lodge Stirl. .285 G10
Lenham Kent. 53 C11
Lenham Forstal Kent. .54 C2
Lenham Heath Kent. ..54 C2
Lennel Borders. 273 G7
Lennoxtown E Dunb. .278 F2
Lent Bucks. 66 C2
Lenten Pool Denb. ...165 B8
Lenton Lincs. 155 C10
Nottingham. 153 B11
Lenton Abbey
Nottingham. 153 B10
Lentran Highld. 300 E5
Lent Rise Bucks. 66 C2
Lenwade Norf. 159 F11
Leny Ho Stirl. 285 G10
Lenzie E Dunb. 278 G3
Lenziemill N Lnrk. ...278 G5
Leoch Angus. 287 D7
Leochel-Cushnie
Aberds. 293 B7
Leominster Hereford. .115 F9
Leomonsley Staffs. ...134 G2
Leonard Stanley Glos. .80 E4
Leonardston Pembs. ..72 D6
Leorin Argyll. 254 C4
Lepe Hants. 20 B5
Lephin Highld. 297 G7
Lephinchapel Argyll. .275 D10
Lephinmore Argyll. ...275 D10
Leppington N Yorks. ..216 G5
Lepton W Yorks. 197 D8
Lepton Edge W Yorks. 197 D8
Lerigoilugan Argyll. ..275 C9
Lerrocks Stirl. 285 G11
Lerryn Corn. 6 D2
Lerwick Shetland. 313 J6
Lesbury Northumb. ...264 G6
Leschangie Aberds. ..293 B9
Le Skerne Haughton
Darl. 224 B6
Leslie Aberds. 302 G5
Fife. 286 G6
Lesmahagow S Lnrk. .259 B8
Lesnewth Corn. 11 C8
Lessendrum Aberds. ..302 E5
Lessingham Norf. 161 D7
Lessness Heath London. .68 D3
Lessonhall Cumb. 238 G6
Leswalt Dumfries. ...236 C2
Letchmore Heath Herts. .85 F11
Letchworth Herts. ...104 E4
Letcombe Bassett Oxon. .63 B11
Letcombe Regis Oxon. .63 B11
Letham Angus. 287 C9
Falk. 279 D7
Fife. 287 F7
Perth. 286 E4
Letham Grange Angus .287 C10
Lethem Borders. 250 B5
Lethen Ho Highld. ...301 D9
Lethenty Aberds. 303 E8
Aberds. 303 G7
Letheringham Suff. ..126 F5
Letheringsett Norf. ..159 B11
Lettaford Devon. 13 E10
Lettan Orkney. 314 B7
Letter Aberds. 293 B9
Letterewe Highld. ...299 B9
Letterfearn Highld. ..295 C10
Letterfinlay Highld. ..290 D4
Lettermay Argyll. 284 G5
Lettermorar Highld. ..295 G9
Lettermore Argyll. ...288 E6
Letters Highld. 307 L6
Letterston / Treletert
Pembs. 91 F8
Lettoch Highld. 292 B2
Highld. 301 F10
Moray. 302 F3
Perth. 291 G11
Letton Hereford. 96 B6
Hereford. 115 C7
Letton Green Norf. ..141 B9
Lett's Green Kent. ...52 B3
Letty Brongu Bridgend .57 D11
Letty Green Herts. ..86 C3
Letwell S Yorks. 187 D9
Leuchars Fife. 287 E8
Leuchars Ho Moray. .302 C2
Leumrabhagh W Isles .305 G5
Levalsa Meor Corn. ..5 F10
Levan Inclyd. 276 F4
Levaneap Shetland. ..313 G6
Levedale Staffs. 151 F7
Level of Mendalgief
Newport. 59 B10
Level's Green Essex. .105 G9
Leven E Yorks. 209 D8
Fife. 287 G8
Levencorroch N Ayrs. .256 E2
Levenhall E Loth. ...281 G7
Levens Cumb. 211 B9
Levens Green Herts. .105 G7
Levenshulme Gtr Man .184 C5
Leventhorpe W Yorks. .205 G8
Levenwick Shetland. .313 M5
Lever-Edge Gtr Man. .195 F8
Leverington Cambs. ..157 G8
Leverington Common
Cambs. 157 G8
Leverstock Green Herts .85 D9
Leverton Lincs. 174 F6
W Berks. 63 E10
Leverton Highgate Lincs .174 F6

Leverton Lucasgate
Lincs. 174 F6
Leverton Outgate Lincs .174 F6
Levington Suff. 108 D4
Levisham N Yorks. ...226 G6
Levishie Highld. 290 B6
Lew Oxon. 82 D4
Lewannick Corn. 11 E11
Lewcombe Dorset. ...29 F9
Lewdown Devon. 12 D4
Lewes E Sus. 36 E6
Leweston Pembs. 91 G8
Lewisham London. ...67 D11
Lewiston Highld. 300 G5
Lewistown Bridgend. .58 B2
Lewknor Oxon. 84 F2
Leworthy Devon. 24 G4
Devon. 27 F9
Lewson Street Kent. .70 G3
Lewth Lancs. 202 F5
Lewthorn Cross Devon .13 F11
Lexden Essex. 107 G9
Ley Aberds. 293 B7
Corn. 6 D2
Som. 41 F10
Leybourne Kent. 53 B7
Leyburn N Yorks. ...224 G2
Leycett Staffs. 168 F3
Leyfields Staffs. 134 B4
Ley Green Herts. 104 G3
Ley Hill Bucks. 85 E7
S Glos. 79 G11
Ley Hill W Mid. 134 D2
Leyland Lancs. 194 C4
Leylodge Aberds. ...293 B9
Leymoor W Yorks. ..196 D6
Leys Aberds. 303 D10
Aberds. 303 D10
Cumb. 219 B11
Perth. 286 D6
Staffs. 169 F8
Leys Castle Highld. ..300 E6
Leysdown-on-Sea Kent .70 E4
Leys Hill Hereford. ..79 B9
Leysmill Angus. 287 C10
Leys of Cossans Angus .287 B7
Leysters Hereford. ...115 E11
Leysters Pole Hereford .115 E11
Leyton London. 67 B11
Leytonstone London. .67 B12
Lezant Corn. 12 F2
Lezerea Corn. 2 C5
Leziate Norf. 158 F3
Lhanbryde Moray. ...302 C2
Liatrie Highld. 300 F2
Libanus Powys. 95 F9
Libberton S Lnrk. ...269 G9
Libbery Worcs. 117 F9
Liberton Edin. 270 B5
Liceasto W Isles. ...305 J3
Lichfield Staffs. 134 B2
Lick Perth. 286 B2
Lickey Worcs. 117 B9
Lickey End Worcs. ..117 C9
Lickfold W Sus. 34 B6
Lickhill Worcs. 116 C6
Licklehead Castle
Aberds. 302 G6
Liddaton Devon. 12 E5
Liddel Orkney. 314 H4
Liddesdale Highld. ...289 D9
Liddeston Pembs. ...72 D5
Liddington Swindon. .63 C8
Liden Swindon. 63 C7
Lidgate Suff. 124 F4
Lidget S Yorks. 199 G2
Lidget Green W Yorks .205 G8
Lidgett Notts. 171 B10
Lidgett Park W Yorks .206 F2
Lidham Hill E Sus. ..38 D4
Lidlington C Beds. ...103 D9
Lidsey W Sus. 22 C6
Lidsing Kent. 69 G9
Lidstone Oxon. 101 G7
Lieurary Highld. 310 C4
Liff Angus. 287 D7
Lifford W Mid. 117 B11
Lifton Devon. 12 D3
Liftondown Devon. ..12 D3
Lightcliffe W Yorks. .196 B6
Lighteach Shrops. ...149 C10
Lightfoot Green Lancs .202 G5
Lighthorne Warks. ..118 F6
Lighthorne Heath Warks .119 F7
Lighthouse Rough
Warks. 118 F6
Lightmoor Telford. ..132 B3
Light Oaks Staffs. ...168 E6
Lightpill Glos. 80 E4
Lightwater Sur. 66 G2
Lightwood Shrops. ..132 E2
Shrops. 150 D3
Stoke. 168 G6
S Yorks. 186 E5
Lightwood Green
Ches E. 167 G10
Wrex. 166 G5
Lilbourne Northants. .119 B11
Lilburn Tower Northumb .264 E2
Lilford Gtr Man. 195 G7
Lillesdon Som. 28 C4
Lilleshall Telford. ...150 F4
Lilley Herts. 104 F2
W Berks. 64 D2
Lilliesleaf Borders. ..262 E2
Lillingstone Dayrell
Bucks. 102 D4
Lillingstone Lovell
Bucks. 102 D4
Lillington Dorset. ...29 E10
Warks. 118 D6
Lilliput Poole. 18 C6
Lilstock Som. 43 E7
Lilybank Inclyd. 276 G6
Lilyhurst Shrops. ...150 G4
Lilyvale Kent. 54 F5
Limbrick Lancs. 194 D6
Limbury Luton. 103 G11
Limebrook Hereford. .115 D7
Limefield Gtr Man. ..195 E10
Limehouse London. ..67 C11
Limehurst Gtr Man. .196 G2
Limekilnburn S Lnrk. .268 E4
Limekiln Field Derbys .187 G7
Limekilns Fife. 279 E11
Limerigg Falk. 279 G7
Limerstone IoW. 20 E4
Lime Side Gtr Man. ..196 G2
Limestone Brae
Northumb. 231 B11
Lime Street Worcs. ..98 E6
Lime Tree Park W Mid .118 B5
Limington Som. 29 C8
Limpenhoe Norf. ...143 C7
Limpenhoe Hill Norf. .143 C8
Limpers Hill Wilts. ..45 G10
Limpley Stoke Wilts. .61 G9

Limpsfield Sur. 52 C2
Limpsfield Chart Sur. .52 C2
Limpsfield Common Sur .52 C2
Linbriggs Northumb. .251 B9
Linburn W Loth. 270 B2
Linby Notts. 171 E8
Linchmere W Sus. ...49 G11
Lincluden Dumfries. .237 B11
Lincoln Lincs. 189 G7
Lincomb Worcs. 116 D6
Lincombe Devon. ...8 D4
Devon. 40 D3
Lindale Cumb. 211 C8
Lindal in Furness Cumb .210 D5
Lindean Borders. ...261 C11
Linden Glos. 80 B4
Lindfield W Sus. 36 B4
Lindford Hants. 49 F10
Lindifferon Fife. 287 F7
Lindley N Yorks. 205 D10
W Yorks. 196 D6
Lindley Green N Yorks .205 D10
Lindores Fife. 286 F6
Lindow End Ches E. .184 F4
Lindridge Worcs. ...116 D3
Lindsell Essex. 106 F2
Lindsey Suff. 107 C9
Lindsey Tye Suff. ...107 B9
Lindwell W Yorks. ..196 C5
Linfitts Gtr Man. 196 F3
Linford Hants. 31 F11
Thurrock. 69 D7
Lingague IoM. 192 E3
Lingards Wood W Yorks .196 E5
Lingbob W Yorks. ..205 F7
Lingdale Redcar. 226 B3
Lingen Hereford. ...115 D7
Lingfield Darl. 224 C6
Sur. 51 E11
Lingfield Common Sur. .51 E11
Lingley Green Warr. .183 D9
Lingley Mere Warr. .183 D10
Lingreabhagh W Isles .296 C6
Lingwood Norf. 143 B7
Linhope Borders. ...249 C10
Northumb. 263 F11
Liniclate W Isles. ...296 C3
Linicro Highld. 298 C4
Link N Som. 44 B3
Linkend Worcs. 98 E6
Linkenholt Hants. ...47 B11
Linkhill Kent. 38 B4
Linkhorne Corn. 12 G2
Linkinhorne Corn. ..12 G2
Linklater Orkney. ...314 H4
Linklet Orkney. 314 A7
Linksness Orkney. ...314 E2
Orkney. 314 F2
Linktown Fife. 280 C5
Linley Shrops. 131 E7
Shrops. 132 D3
Linley Brook Shrops. .132 D3
Linleygreen Shrops. .132 D3
Linley Green Hereford .116 G3
Linlithgow W Loth. .279 F10
Linlithgow Bridge
W Loth. 279 F9
Linndhu Ho Argyll. ..289 D7
Linns Angus. 292 F3
Linnyshaw Gtr Man. .195 G8
Linshiels Northumb. .251 B9
Linsiadar W Isles. ..304 E4
Linsidemore Highld. .309 K5
Linslade C Beds. 103 F8
Linstead Parva Suff. .126 B6
Linstock Cumb. 239 F10
Linthorpe Mbro. 225 B9
Linthurst Worcs. ...117 C9
Linthwaite W Yorks. .196 E6
Lintlaw Borders. 272 E6
Lintmill Moray. 302 C5
Linton Borders. 263 D7
Cambs. 105 B11
Derbys. 152 F5
Hereford. 98 F3
Kent. 53 D9
N Yorks. 213 G9
W Yorks. 206 D3
Linton Heath Derbys. .152 F5
Linton Hill Hereford. .98 G3
Linton-on-Ouse
N Yorks. 215 G9
Lintridge Glos. 98 E4
Lintz Durham. 242 F5
Lintzford T&W. 242 F4
Lintzgarth Durham. .232 C4
Linwood Hants. 31 F11
Lincs. 189 D10
Renfs. 267 C8
Lionacleit W Isles. ..297 G3
Lional W Isles. 304 B7
Lions Green E Sus. ..23 B9
Liphook Hants. 49 G10
Lipley Shrops. 150 C4
Lippitts Hill Essex. ..86 F5
Liquo or Bowhousebog
N Lnrk. 269 D7
Liscard Mers. 182 C4
Liscombe Som. 41 G11
Liskeard Corn. 6 C5
Liss Hants. 34 B3
Lissett E Yorks. 209 B8
Liss Forest Hants. ...34 B3
Lissington Lincs. ...189 E10
Lisson Grove London .67 C9
Listerdale S Yorks. ..187 C7
Listock Som. 28 C4
Listoft Lincs. 191 G8
Liston Essex. 106 C6
Liston Garden Essex. .106 B6
Lisvane Cardiff. 59 C7
Liswerry Newport. ..59 B10
Litcham Norf. 159 F7
Litchard Bridgend. ..58 C2
Litchborough Northants .120 G2
Litchfield Hants. ...48 C3
Litherland Mers. ...182 B4
Litlington Cambs. ...104 C6
E Sus. 23 E8
Litmarsh Hereford. ..97 B10
Little Abington Cambs .105 B10
Little Addington
Northants. 121 C9
Little Airmyn N Yorks .199 B8
Little Almshoe Herts. .104 F3
Little Alne Warks. ..118 E2
Little Altcar Mers. ..193 F10
Little Ann Hants. ...47 D11
Little Arowry Wrex. .167 G7
Little Asby Cumb. ..222 D3
Little Ashley Wilts. .61 G10
Little Aston Staffs. ..133 C11
Little Atherfield IoW. .20 E5
Little Ayre Orkney. ..314 G3
Little Ayre Shetland. .313 G5
Little-ayre Shetland. .313 G5

Little Ayton N Yorks. .225 C11
Little Baddow Essex. .88 D3
Little Badminton S Glos .61 C10
Little Ballinluig Perth. .286 B3
Little Bampton Cumb. .238 G6
Little Bardfield Essex. .106 E3
Little Barford Beds. ..122 F3
Little Barningham Norf .160 C2
Little Barrington Glos. .82 C2
Little Barrow Ches W. .183 G7
Little Barugh N Yorks. .216 D5
Little Bavington
Northumb. 241 B11
Little Bayham E Sus. .52 F6
Little Bealings Suff. .108 B4
Little Beckford Glos. .99 E9
Little Bedwyn Wilts. .63 F10
Little Bentley Essex. .108 F2
Little Berkhamsted Herts .86 D3
Little Billing Northants .120 E6
Little Billington C Beds .103 G8
Little Birch Hereford. .97 E10
Little Bispham Blkpool .202 E2
Little Blakenham Suff. .108 B2
Little Blencow Cumb. .230 E5
Little Bloxwich W Mid .133 C10
Little Bognor W Sus. .35 C8
Little Bolehill Derbys. .170 E3
Little Bollington Ches E .184 D2
Little Bolton Gtr Man. .184 B3
Little Bookham Sur. ..50 C6
Littleborough Devon. .26 E4
Gtr Man. 196 D2
Notts. 188 E4
Little Bourton Oxon. .101 C9
Little Bowden Leics. .136 F4
Little Boys Heath Bucks .84 F6
Little Bradley Suff. ..124 G3
Little Braithwaite
Cumb. 229 G10
Little Brampton Shrops .131 G7
Little Braxted Essex. .88 C4
Little Bray Devon. ..41 F7
Little Brechin Angus. .293 G7
Littlebredy Dorset. ..17 D7
Little Brickhill
M Keynes. 103 E8
Little Bridgeford Staffs .151 D7
Little Brington Northants .120 E3
Little Bristol S Glos. .80 G2
Little Britain Warks. .118 G2
Little Bromley Essex. .107 F11
Little Bromwich W Mid .134 F2
Little Broughton Cumb. .229 E7
Little Budworth Ches W .167 B8
Little Burstead Essex. .87 G11
Little Bytham Lincs. .155 F10
Little Cambridge Essex .106 F2
Little Canfield Essex. .105 G11
Little Canford Poole. .18 B6
Little Carleton Lancs. .202 F2
Little Carlton Lincs. .190 D5
Notts. 172 D3
Little Casterton
Rutland. 137 B10
Little Catwick E Yorks .209 E8
Little Catworth Cambs .122 C2
Little Cawthorpe Lincs .190 E5
Little Chalfield Wilts. .61 G11
Little Chalfont Bucks. .85 F7
Little Chart Kent. ...54 D2
Little Chart Forstal Kent .54 D3
Little Chell Stoke. ...168 E5
Little Chesterford Essex .105 C10
Little Chesterton Oxon .101 G11
Little Cheveley Wilts. .46 C3
Little Chishill Cambs. .105 D9
Little Clacton Essex. .89 B11
Little Clanfield Oxon. .82 E3
Little Clifton Cumb. .229 F7
Little Coates NE Lincs .201 F8
Little Colp Aberds. ..303 E7
Little Comberton Worcs .99 C9
Little Comfort Corn. .12 E2
Little Common E Sus. .38 F2
Little Comp Kent. ...52 B6
Little Corby Cumb. ..239 F11
Little Cornard Suff. .107 D7
Littlecott Wilts. 46 C6
Little Cowarne Hereford .116 G2
Little Coxwell Oxon. .82 G3
Little Crakehall N Yorks .224 G4
Little Cransley Northants .120 C6
Little Crawley M Keynes .103 B8
Little Creaton Northants .120 C4
Little Creich Highld. .309 L6
Little Cressingham Norf .141 D7
Little Crosby Mers. ..193 G10
Little Cubley Derbys. .152 B3
Little Dalby Leics. ..154 G5
Little Dawley Telford. .132 B3
Littledean Glos. 79 C11
Littledean Hill Glos. .79 C11
Little Dens Aberds. .303 E10
Little Dewchurch
Hereford. 97 E10
Little Ditton Cambs. .124 F3
Little Doward Hereford .79 B8
Littledown Bmouth. .19 C8
Little Downham Cambs .139 G10
Little Drayton Shrops. .150 C3
Little Driffield E Yorks .208 B6
Little Drybrook Glos. .79 D9
Little Dunham Norf. .159 G7
Little Dunkeld Perth. .286 C4
Little Dunmow Essex. .106 G3
Little Durnford Wilts. .46 G6
Little Easton Essex. .106 F2
Little Eaton Derbys. .170 G5
Little Eccleston Lancs. .202 E4
Little Ellingham Norf. .141 D10
Little End Cambs. ...122 F3
Essex. 87 E8
Little Everdon
Northants. 119 F11
Little Eversden Cambs .123 G7
Little Faringdon Oxon. .82 E2
Little Fencote N Yorks .224 G4
Little Fenton N Yorks. .206 G6
Littleferry Highld. ...311 J3
Little Finborough Suff. .125 G10

Little Fransham Norf. .159 G8
Little Frith Kent. 54 B2
Little Gaddesden Herts .85 C7
Littlegain Shrops. ...132 D5
Little Gidding Cambs. .138 G2
Little Gight Aberds. .303 F8
Little Glemham Suff. .126 F6
Little Glenshee Perth. .286 D3
Little Gorsley Glos. ..98 F3
Little Gransden Cambs .122 G5
Little Green Cambs. .104 B5
Lancs. 203 E10
Notts. 172 G2
Som. 45 D8
Suff. 125 C11
Wrex. 167 G7
Little Grimsby Lincs. .190 C5
Little Gringley Notts. .188 E3
Little Gruinard Highld. .307 L4
Little Habton N Yorks .216 D4
Little Hadham Herts. .105 G8
Little Hale Lincs. ...173 G10
Norf. 141 B8
Little Hallam Derbys. .171 G7
Little Hallingbury Essex .87 B7
Littleham Devon. ...14 E6
Devon. 24 C6
Little Hampden Bucks. .84 E4
Littlehampton W Sus. .35 G8
Little Haresfield Glos. .80 D4
Little Harrowden
Northants. 121 C7
Little Harwood Blkburn .195 B7
Little Haseley Oxon. .83 E10
Little Hatfield E Yorks. .209 E8
Little Hautbois Norf. .160 E5
Little Haven Pembs. ..72 C5
W Sus. 51 G7
Little Hay Staffs. ...134 C2
Little Hayfield Derbys. .185 D8
Little Haywood Staffs. .151 E10
Little Heath Ches E. .167 G11
Ches W. 166 B6
Herts. 85 B8
London. 68 B3
Staffs. 151 F8
Sur. 66 G6
W Berks. 64 E6
W Mid. 134 G6
Little Heck N Yorks. .198 C5
Littlehempston Devon. .8 C6
Little Henham Essex. .105 E10
Little Henny Essex. .107 D7
Little Herbert's Glos. .81 B7
Little Hereford
Hereford. 115 D11
Little Hill Hereford. ..97 F9
Som. 28 E3
Little Holbury Hants. .32 G6
Little Honeyborough
Pembs. 73 D7
Little Hoole Moss Houses
Lancs. 194 C3
Little Horkesley Essex .107 E9
Little Hormead Herts. .105 F8
Little Horsted E Sus. .23 B7
Little Horton W Yorks .205 G9
Wilts. 62 G4
Little Horwood Bucks. .102 E5
Littlehoughton
Northumb. 264 F6
Little Houghton
Northants. 120 F6
S Yorks. 198 G2
Little Hucklow Derbys .185 F11
Little Hulton Gtr Man. .195 G8
Little Humber E Yorks .201 C8
Little Hungerford
W Berks. 64 E4
Little Ilford London. .68 B2
Little Ingestre Staffs. .151 E9
Little Inkberrow Worcs .117 F10
Little Irchester
Northants. 121 D8
Little Keyford Som. ..45 D8
Little Kimble Bucks. .84 D4
Little Kineton Warks. .118 G6
Little Kingshill Bucks. .84 F5
Little Knowles Green
Suff. 124 F5
Little Langdale Cumb. .220 E6
Little Langford Wilts. .46 F4
Little Laver Essex. ..87 D9
Little Lawford Warks. .119 B9
Little Layton Blkpool. .202 F2
Little Leigh Ches W. .183 F10
Little Leighs Essex. ..88 B2
Little Lepton W Yorks .197 E8
Little Leven E Yorks. .209 D8
Little Lever Gtr Man. .195 F9
Little Limber Lincs. .200 E6
Little Linford M Keynes .102 C6
Little Load Som. 29 C7
Little London Bucks. .83 C10
Bucks. 84 D5
Cambs. 139 D8
Essex. 106 D3
E Sus. 23 B9
Glos. 80 B2
Hants. 47 D11
Hants. 48 B6
Lincs. 156 D6
Lincs. 157 E8
Lincs. 189 D10
Norf. 140 F4
Norf. 160 C2
Norf. 160 E3
Oxon. 83 E8
Powys. 129 F10
Shrops. 146 B6
Suff. 124 G3
W Yorks. 205 F10
Little Longstone
Derbys. 185 G11
Little Lynturk Aberds. .293 B7
Little Lyth Shrops. ..131 B9
Little Madeley Staffs. .168 F3
Little Malvern Worcs. .98 C5
Little Mancot Flint. ..166 B4
Little Maplestead Essex .106 E6
Little Marcle Hereford. .98 D3
Little Marlow Bucks. .65 B11
Little Marsh Bucks. ..102 G6
Norf. 159 B8
Little Marton Blkpool. .202 G2
Little Massingham Norf .158 E5
Little Melton Norf. ..142 B3
Little Mill Kent. 53 D7
Mon. 78 E4

Little Mill Newport. ..59 B11
Little Milton Oxon. ..83 E10
Little Minster Oxon. .82 C4
Little Missenden Bucks .84 F6
Little Mongeham Kent .55 C10
Littlemoor Derbys. ..170 C5
Dorset. 17 E9
Little Moor End Lancs .195 B8
Littlemore Oxon. 83 E8
Little Moor Lancs. ...203 E10
Little Morrell Warks. .118 F6
Littlemoss Gtr Man. .184 B6
Little Mountain Flint. .166 C3
Little Musgrave Cumb. .222 C5
Little Ness Shrops. ..149 F8
Little Neston Ches W. .182 F3
Little Newcastle Pembs .91 F9
Little Newsham Durham .224 B2
Little Norlington E Sus .23 C7
Little Norton Som. ..29 D7
Little Oakley Essex. .108 F4
Northants. 137 F7
Little Odell Beds. ...121 F9
Little Offley Herts. ..104 F2
Little Onn Staffs. ...150 F6
Little Ormside Cumb. .222 B4
Little Orton Cumb. ..239 F9
Leics. 134 B6
Little Ouse Norf. ...140 F2
Little Ouseburn N Yorks .215 G8
Littleover Derby. ...152 C6
Little Overton Wrex. .166 G5
Little Oxney Green
Essex. 87 D11
Little Packington Warks .134 G4
Little Parndon Essex. .86 C6
Little Paxton Cambs. .122 E3
Little Petherick Corn. .10 G4
Little Pitlurg Moray. .302 E4
Little Plumpton Lancs. .202 G3
Little Plumstead Norf. .160 G6
Little Ponton Lincs. .155 C8
Littleport Cambs. ...139 F11
Little Posbrook Hants. .33 G8
Little Poulton Lancs. .202 F3
Little Preston Kent. ..53 B8
W Yorks. 206 G3
Little Raveley Cambs. .122 B5
Little Reedness
E Yorks. 199 C10
Little Reynoldston
Swansea. 56 D3
Little Ribston N Yorks .206 C3
Little Rissington Glos. .81 B11
Little Rogart Highld. .309 J7
Little Rollright Oxon. .100 E5
Little Ryburgh Norf. .159 D9
Little Ryle Northumb. .264 G2
Little Ryton Shrops. .131 C9
Little Salkeld Cumb. .231 D7
Little Sampford Essex. .106 E3
Little Sandhurst Brack. .65 G10
Little Saredon Staffs. .133 B8
Little Saxham Suff. ..124 E5
Little Scatwell Highld. .300 D3
Little Scotland Gtr Man .194 E6
Little Sessay N Yorks. .215 E9
Little Shelford Cambs. .123 G9
Little Shoddesden Hants .47 D9
Little Shrewley Warks. .118 D4
Little Singleton Lancs. .202 F3
Little Skillymarno
Aberds. 303 D9
Little Skipwith N Yorks .207 F9
Little Smeaton N Yorks .198 D4
N Yorks. 224 E6
Little Snoring Norf. .159 C9
Little Sodbury S Glos. .61 C9
Little Sodbury End
S Glos. 61 C8
Little Somborne Hants. .47 G11
Little Somerford Wilts. .62 C3
Little Soudley Shrops. .150 D4
Little Stainforth
N Yorks. 212 F6
Little Stainton Darl. .234 G2
Little Stanmore London .85 G11
Little Stanney Ches W. .182 G6
Little Staughton Beds. .122 E2
Littlestead Green Oxon. .65 D8
Little Steeping Lincs. .174 C6
Little Stoke S Glos. ..60 C6
Staffs. 151 B8
Littlestone-on-Sea Kent .39 C9
Little Stonham Suff. .126 E2
Little Stretton Leics. .136 C3
Shrops. 131 E9
Little Strickland Cumb. .221 B11
Little Studley N Yorks. .214 E6
Little Stukeley Cambs. .122 B4
Little Sugnall Staffs. .150 C6
Little Sutton Ches W. .182 F5
Lincs. 157 E8
Shrops. 131 G10
Little Swinburne
Northumb. 241 B10
Little Swinton
Borders. 272 F5
Little Tarrington Hereford .98 C2
Little Tew Oxon. 101 F7
Little Tey Essex. 107 G7
Little Thetford Cambs. .123 B10
Little Thirkleby N Yorks .215 D9
Little Thornage Norf. .159 B11
Little Thornton Lancs. .202 E3
Littlethorpe Leics. ..135 D11
N Yorks. 214 F6
Little Thorpe Durham. .234 C4
W Yorks. 197 C7
Little Thurlow Suff. .124 G3
Little Thurlow Green
Suff. 124 G3
Little Thurrock Thurrock .68 D6
Littleton Bath. 60 G5
Ches W. 166 B6
Dorset. 30 G5
Guildford, Sur. 50 D3
Hants. 48 G3
Perth. 286 D6
Som. 44 G3
V Glam. 58 F4
Littleton Common Sur. .66 E5
Littleton Drew Wilts. .61 C10
Littleton Pannell Wilts. .46 C4
Littleton-upon-Severn
S Glos. 79 G10
Little Torboll Highld. .309 K7
Little Torrington Devon .25 D7
Little Totham Essex. .88 C4
Little Toux Aberds. ..302 D5
Little Town Cumb. ..220 B4
Lancs. 203 F8
Warr. 183 C10
Little Tring Herts. ..84 C6
Little Urswick Cumb. .210 E5
Little Vantage W Loth. .270 C2
Little Wakering Essex. .70 B2
Little Walden Essex. .105 C10
Little Waldingfield Suff .107 B8
Little Walsingham Norf .159 B8
Little Waltham Essex. .88 C2
Little Warley Essex. .87 G10
Little Warton Warks. .134 C5
Little Washbourne Glos .99 E9
Little Weighton E Yorks .208 G5
Little Weldon Northants .137 F8
Little Welland Worcs. .98 D6
Little Welnetham Suff. .125 E7
Little Welton Lincs. .190 D4
Little Wenham Suff. .107 D11
Little Wenlock Telford. .132 B2
Little Weston Som. ..29 B10
Little Whitehouse IoW .20 C5
Little Whittingham Green
Suff. 126 B5
Littlewick Green
Windsor. 65 D10
Little Wigborough Essex .89 B7
Little Wilbraham
Cambs. 123 F10
Littlewindsor Dorset. .28 G6
Little Wisbeach Lincs. .156 C2
Little Witcombe Glos. .80 B6
Little Witley Worcs. .116 E5
Little Wittenham Oxon .83 G9
Little Wolford Warks. .100 D5
Littlewood Staffs. ...133 B9
Little Wood Corner Bucks .84 E6
Little Woodcote London .67 G9
Little Woolgarston
Dorset. 18 E5
Littleworth Beds. ...103 C11
Glos. 80 E4
Glos. 100 G4
Oxon. 82 F4
Oxon. 83 D9
Staffs. 151 E10
Staffs. 151 G10
S Yorks. 187 B10
Warks. 117 E11
Worcs. 99 B8
Worcs. 117 E7
W Sus. 35 C11
Littleworth Common
Bucks. 66 B2
Little Worthen Shrops. .130 B6
Littleworth End Warks. .134 D3
Little Wratting Suff. .106 B3
Little Wymington Beds .121 D9
Little Wymondley Herts .104 F4
Little Wyrley Staffs. .133 C10
Little Wytheford
Shrops. 149 F11
Little Yeldham Essex. .106 D5
Littley Green Essex. .87 B11
Litton Derbys. 185 F11
N Yorks. 213 E8
Som. 44 C5
Litton Cheney Dorset. .17 C7
Litton Mill Derbys. ..185 G11
Liurbost W Isles. ...304 F5
Livermead Torbay. ...9 C7
Liverpool Mers. 182 C4
Liverpool Airport Mers .182 D6
Liversedge W Yorks. .197 C8
Liverton Devon. 14 F2
Redcar. 226 B4
Liverton Mines Redcar. .226 B4
Liverton Street Kent. .53 C11
Livesey Street Kent. .53 C8
Livingshayes Devon. .27 G7
Livingston W Loth. ..269 B11
Livingston Village
W Loth. 269 B11
Lix Toll Stirl. 285 D9
Lixwm Flint. 181 G11
Lizard Corn. 2 G6
Llaingoch Anglesey. .178 E2
Llaithddu Powys. ...129 G11
Llampha V Glam. 58 D2
Llan Powys. 129 C7
Llanaber Gwyn. 146 F2
Llanaelhaearn Gwyn. .162 G5
Llanafan Ceredig. ...112 C3
Llanafan-fawr Powys. .113 F9
Llanafan-fechan
Powys. 113 F11
Llanallgo Anglesey. .179 D7
Llananno Powys. 113 C11
Llanarmon Gwyn. ...145 B8
Llanarmon Dyffryn Ceiriog
Wrex. 148 C3
Llanarmon Mynydd-mawr
Powys. 148 D2
Llanarmon-yn-Ial
Denb. 165 D11
Llanarth Ceredig. ...111 F8
Mon. 78 C5
Llanarthne Carms. ..93 G10
Llanasa Flint. 181 E10
Llanbabo Anglesey. .178 D5
Llanbad Rhondda. ...58 C3
Llanbadarn Fawr
Ceredig. 128 G2
Llanbadarn Fynydd
Powys. 114 B2
Llanbadarn-y-Garreg
Powys. 96 B2
Llanbadoc Mon. 78 E5
Llanbadrig Anglesey. .178 C5
Llanbeder Newport. ..78 G5
Llanbedr Gwyn. 145 D11
Powys. 96 D3
Powys. 96 E2
Llanbedr-Dyffryn-Clwyd
Denb. 165 D10
Llanbedrgoch Anglesey .179 E7
Llanbedrog Gwyn. ..144 C6
Llanbedr Pont Steffan /
Lampeter Ceredig. ..93 B11
Llanbedr-y-cennin
Conwy. 164 B3
Llanberis Gwyn. 163 D9
Llanbethery / Llanbydderi
V Glam. 58 F4
Llanbister Powys. ..114 C2
Llanblethian / Llanfleiddan
V Glam. 58 E3
Llanboidy Carms. ...92 G4
Llanbradach Caerph. .77 G10
Llanbrynmair Powys. .129 C7
Llancadle / Llancatal
V Glam. 58 F4
Llancaiach Caerph. ..77 F10
Llancarfan V Glam. ..58 E4

Llancatal / Llancadle
V Glam. 58 F4
Llancayo Mon. 78 E5
Llancloudy Hereford. .97 G9
Llancowrid Powys. ..130 E3
Llancynfelyn Ceredig. .128 E2
Llan-dafal Bl Gwent. .77 E11
Llandaff Cardiff. 59 D7
Llandaff North Cardiff. .59 D7
Llandanwg Gwyn. ..145 D11
Llandarcy Neath. ...57 B8
Llandawke Carms. ...74 C3
Llanddaniel Fab
Anglesey. 179 G7
Llanddarog Carms. ..75 C9
Llanddeiniol Ceredig. .111 C11
Llanddeiniolen Gwyn. .163 B8
Llandderfel Gwyn. ..147 B10
Llanddeusant Anglesey .178 D4
Carms. 94 G5
Llanddew Powys. ...95 E11
Llanddewi Swansea. .56 D3
Llanddewi-Brefi Ceredig .112 F3
Llanddewi Fach Mon. .78 F4
Llanddewi'r Cwm Powys .95 B10
Llanddewi Rhydderch
Mon. 78 C5
Llanddewi Skirrid Mon .78 B4
Llanddewi Velfrey
Pembs. 73 B10
Llanddewi Ystradenni
Powys. 114 D2
Llanddoged Conwy. .164 C4
Llanddona Anglesey. .179 F9
Llanddowror Carms. .74 C3
Llanddulas Conwy. ..180 F6
Llanddwywe Gwyn. .145 E11
Llanddyfnan Anglesey .179 F7
Llandecwyn Gwyn. ..146 B2
Llandefaelog Fach
Powys. 95 E10
Llandefaelog-tre'r-graig
Powys. 96 E2
Llandefalle Powys. ..96 E2
Llandegai Gwyn. 179 G9
Llandegfan Anglesey. .179 G9
Llandegla Denb. 165 D11
Llandegley Powys. ..114 E2
Llandegveth Mon. ...78 F4
Llandegwning Gwyn. .144 C5
Llandeilo Carms. ...94 G2
Llandeilo Graban Powys .95 C11
Llandeilo'r Fan Powys. .95 E7
Llandeloy Pembs. ...91 F7
Llandenny Mon. 78 E5
Llandenny Walls Mon. .78 E5
Llandevaud Newport. .78 G5
Llandevenny Mon. ...60 B2
Llandewi Ystradenny
Powys. 114 D2
Llandilo Pembs. 92 F2
Llandinabo Hereford. .97 F10
Llandinam Powys. ..129 F10
Llandissilio Pembs. ..92 G2
Llandogo Mon. 79 E8
Llandough V Glam. ..58 E3
V Glam. 59 E7
Llandovery / Llanymddyfri
Carms. 94 E4
Llandow / Llandw
V Glam. 58 E2
Llandre Carms. 94 C3
Ceredig. 128 F2
Llandrillo Denb. 147 B10
Llandrillo-yn-Rhôs
Conwy. 180 E4
Llandrindod Wells
Powys. 113 E11
Llandrinio Powys. ..148 F5
Llandruidion Pembs. .90 G5
Llandudno Conwy. ..180 E3
Llandudno Junction /
Cyffordd Llandudno
Conwy. 180 F3
Llandudoch / St Dogmaels
Pembs. 92 B3
Llandw / Llandow
V Glam. 58 E2
Llandwrog Gwyn. ...163 D7
Llandybie Carms. ...75 C10
Llandyfaelog Carms. .74 C6
Llandyfan Carms. ...75 B10
Llandyfriog Ceredig. .92 C6
Llandyfrydog Anglesey .178 D6
Llandygwydd Ceredig. .92 C4
Llandynan Denb. ...165 F11
Llandyrnog Denb. ..165 B10
Llandysilio Powys. ..148 F5
Llandyssil Powys. ...130 D3
Llandysul Ceredig. ..93 C8
Llanedeyrn Cardiff. ..59 C8
Llanedi Carms. 75 D9
Llanedwen Anglesey. .163 B8
Llanefydd Conwy. ..181 G7
Llanegryn Gwyn. ...128 B2
Llanegwad Carms. ..93 G10
Llaneilian Anglesey. .179 C7
Llanelian yn-Rhôs
Conwy. 180 F5
Llanelidan Denb. ...165 E10
Llanelieu Powys. ...96 E2
Llanellen Mon. 78 C4
Llanelli Carms. 56 B4
Llanelltyd Gwyn. ...146 F4
Llanelly Mon. 78 C2
Llanelly Hill Mon. ..78 C2
Llanelwedd Powys. .113 G11
Llanelwy / St Asaph
Denb. 181 G8
Llanenddwyn Gwyn. .145 E11
Llanengan Gwyn. ...144 D5
Llanerch Powys. 130 D6
Llanerchymedd
Anglesey. 178 D6
Llanerfyl Powys. ...129 B11
Llaneuddog Anglesey .179 C7
Llan eurgain / Northop
Flint. 166 B2
Llanfabon Caerph. ..77 G10
Llanfachraeth Anglesey .178 E4
Llanfachreth Gwyn. .146 E5
Llanfaelog Anglesey. .178 F4
Llanfaelrhys Gwyn. .144 D4
Llanfaenor Mon. ...78 B6
Llanfaes Anglesey. ..179 F10
Powys. 95 F10
Llanfaethlu Anglesey. .178 D4
Llanfaglan Gwyn. ...163 C7
Llanfair Gwyn. 145 D11
Llanfair Caereinion
Powys. 130 B2
Llanfair Clydogau
Ceredig. 112 F3
Llanfair-Dyffryn-Clwyd
Denb. 165 D10

Llanfair-Nant-Gwyn Pembs....92 D3
Llanfairpwll-gwyngyll Anglesey....179 G8
Llanfair Talhaiarn Conwy....180 G6
Llanfair Waterdine Shrops....114 B4
Llanfairyneubwll Anglesey....178 F3
Llanfairynghornwy Anglesey....178 C4
Llanfallteg Carms....73 B11
Llanfallteg West Carms....73 B10
Llanfaredd Powys....113 G11
Llanfarian Ceredig....111 B11
Llanfechain Powys....148 E3
Llanfechell Anglesey....178 C5
Llanferres Denb....165 C11
Llan Ffestiniog Gwyn....164 G2
Llanfflewyn Anglesey....178 D5
Llanfigael Anglesey....178 E4
Llanfihangel-ar-arth Carms....93 D9
Llanfihangel-Crucorney Mon....96 G6
Llanfihangel Glyn Myfyr Conwy....165 F7
Llanfihangel-helygen Powys....113 E10
Llanfihangel Nant Bran Powys....95 E8
Llanfihangel-nant-Melan Powys....114 F3
Llanfihangel Rhydithon Powys....114 D3
Llanfihangel Rogiet Mon....60 B2
Llanfihangel Tal-y-llyn Powys....96 F2
Llanfihangel Tor y Mynydd Mon....79 E7
Llanfihangel-uwch-Gwili Carms....93 G9
Llanfihangel-y-Creuddyn Ceredig....112 B3
Llanfihangel-yng-Ngwynfa Powys....147 F11
Llanfihangel yn Nhowyn Anglesey....178 F4
Llanfihangel-y-pennant Gwyn....128 B3
  Gwyn....163 F8
Llanfilo Powys....96 E2
Llanfleiddan / Llanblethian V Glam....58 E3
Llanfoist Mon....78 C3
Llanfor Gwyn....147 B8
Llanfrechfa Torf....78 G4
Llanfrothen Gwyn....163 G10
Llanfrynach Powys....95 F11
Llanfwrog Anglesey....178 E4
  Denb....165 D10
Llanfyllin Powys....148 F2
Llanfynydd Carms....93 F11
  Flint....166 D3
Llanfyrnach Pembs....92 C4
Llangadfan Powys....147 G10
Llangadog Carms....74 D6
  Carms....94 F4
Llangadwaladr Anglesey....162 B5
  Powys....148 C3
Llangaffo Anglesey....162 B6
Llangain Carms....74 B5
Llangammarch Wells Powys....95 B8
Llangan V Glam....58 D3
Llangarron Hereford....97 G10
Llangasty Talyllyn Powys....96 F2
Llangathen Carms....93 G11
Llangattock Powys....78 B2
Llangattock Lingoed Mon....97 G7
Llangattock nigh Usk Mon....78 D4
Llangattock-Vibon-Avel Mon....79 B7
Llangedwyn Powys....148 E3
Llangefni Anglesey....179 F7
Llangeinor Bridgend....58 B2
Llangeitho Ceredig....112 F2
Llangeler Carms....93 D7
Llangendeirne Carms....75 C7
Llangennech Carms....75 E9
Llangennith Swansea....56 C2
Llangenny Powys....78 B2
Llangernyw Conwy....164 B5
Llangeview Mon....78 E5
Llangewydd Court Bridgend....57 E11
Llangian Gwyn....144 D5
Llangiwg Neath....76 D1
Llanglydwen Carms....92 F3
Llangoed Anglesey....179 F10
Llangoedmor Ceredig....92 B3
Llangollen Denb....166 G3
Llangolman Pembs....92 F2
Llangors Powys....96 F2
Llangorwen Ceredig....128 G2
Llangovan Mon....79 D7
Llangower Gwyn....147 C8
Llangranog Ceredig....110 G6
Llangristiolus Anglesey....178 G6
Llangrove Hereford....79 B8
Llangua Mon....97 F7
Llangunllo Powys....114 C4
Llangunnor Carms....74 B6
Llangurig Powys....113 B8
Llangwm Conwy....165 G7
  Mon....78 E6
  Pembs....73 D7
Llangwnnadl Gwyn....144 C4
Llangwyfan Denb....165 B10
Llangwyfan-isaf Anglesey....162 B4
Llangwyllog Anglesey....178 F6
Llangwyryfon Ceredig....111 C11
Llangybi Ceredig....112 G2
  Gwyn....162 G6
  Mon....78 F5
Llangyfelach Swansea....57 C7
Llangyndeyrn Carms....75 C7
Llangynhafal Denb....165 C10
Llangynidr Powys....77 B11
Llangynin Carms....74 B4
Llangynog Carms....74 B4
  Powys....147 E11
Llangynwyd Bridgend....57 D11
Llanhamlach Powys....95 F11
Llanharan Rhondda....58 C4
Llanharry Rhondda....58 C4
Llanhennock Mon....78 G5
Llanhilleth Bl Gwent....78 E3
Llanhowel Pembs....90 F6
Llanidloes Powys....129 G7
Llaniestyn Gwyn....144 C5
Llanifyny Powys....129 F11
Llanigon Powys....96 D4
Llanilar Ceredig....112 C2
Llanilid Rhondda....58 C3
Llanilltud Fawr / Llantwit Major V Glam....58 F3

Llanilltud Fawr / Llantwit Major V Glam....58 F3
Llanio Ceredig....112 F2
Llanion Pembs....73 E7
Llanishen Cardiff....59 C7
  Mon....79 E7
Llanllawddog Carms....93 F9
Llanllechid Gwyn....163 B10
Llanllowell Mon....78 F5
Llanllugan Powys....129 C11
Llanllwch Carms....74 B5
Llanllwchaiarn Powys....130 E2
Llanllwni Carms....93 D9
Llanllwyd Shrops....130 G3
Llanllyfni Gwyn....163 E7
Llanmadoc Swansea....56 C2
Llanmaes Cardiff....58 F3
  V Glam....58 F3
Llanmartin Newport....59 B11
Llanmerwig Powys....130 E2
Llanmihangel V Glam....58 E3
Llan-mill Pembs....73 C10
Llanmiloe Carms....74 D3
Llanmorlais Swansea....56 C4
Llannefydd Conwy....181 G7
Llannerch-y-nor Flint....181 F11
Llannon Carms....75 D8
  V Glam....58 F3
Llan-non / Llanon Ceredig....111 D10
Llannor Gwyn....145 B7
Llanon Pembs....90 E6
Llanover Mon....78 D4
Llanpumsaint Carms....93 F8
Llanreath Pembs....73 E7
Llanreithan Pembs....91 F7
Llanrhaeadr Denb....165 C9
Llanrhaeadr-ym-Mochnant Powys....148 D2
Llanrhian Pembs....90 E6
Llanrhidian Swansea....56 C3
Llanrhos Conwy....180 E3
Llanrhyddlad Anglesey....178 C4
Llanrhystud Ceredig....111 D10
Llanrosser Hereford....96 D5
Llanrothal Hereford....79 B7
Llanrug Gwyn....163 C8
Llanrumney Cardiff....59 C8
Llanrwst Conwy....164 C4
Llansadurnen Carms....74 C3
Llansadwrn Anglesey....179 F9
  Carms....94 E3
Llansaint Carms....74 D5
Llansamlet Swansea....57 B7
Llansanffraid Glan Conwy Conwy....180 F4
Llansannan Conwy....164 B6
Llansannor V Glam....58 D3
Llansantffraed Ceredig....111 D10
  Powys....96 F2
Llansantffraed Cwmdeuddwr Powys....113 D9
Llansantffraed-in-Elwel Powys....113 G11
Llansantffraid-ym-Mechain Powys....148 E4
Llansawel Carms....94 D2
  Neath....57 C8
Llansilin Powys....148 D4
Llansoy Mon....78 E6
Llanspyddid Powys....95 F10
Llanstadwell Pembs....72 D6
Llansteffan Carms....74 C5
Llanstephan Powys....96 D3
Llantarnam Torf....78 G4
Llanteems Pembs....73 C11
Llanteg Pembs....73 D11
Llanthony Mon....96 F6
Llantilio Crossenny Mon....78 C5
Llantilio Pertholey Mon....78 C4
Llantood Pembs....92 C3
Llantrisant Anglesey....178 E5
  Mon....78 F5
  Rhondda....58 C4
Llantrithyd V Glam....58 E4
Llantwit Neath....57 B9
Llantwit Fardre Rhondda....58 B5
Llantwit Major / Llanilltud Fawr V Glam....58 F3
Llanuwchllyn Gwyn....147 C7
Llanvaches Newport....78 G6
Llanvair Discoed Mon....78 G6
Llanvapley Mon....78 C5
Llanvetherine Mon....78 B5
Llanveynoe Hereford....96 E6
Llanvihangel Crucorney Mon....96 G6
Llanvihangel Gobion Mon....78 D4
Llanvihangel-Ystern-Llewern Mon....78 C6
Llanwarne Hereford....97 F10
Llanwddyn Powys....147 F10
Llanwenarth Mon....78 C3
Llanwenog Ceredig....93 B9
Llanwern Newport....59 B10
Llanwinio Carms....92 F5
Llanwnda Gwyn....163 D7
  Pembs....91 D8
Llanwnnen Ceredig....93 B10
Llanwnog Powys....129 E10
Llanwrda Carms....94 E4
Llanwrin Powys....128 C5
Llanwrthwl Powys....113 D9
Llanwrtud / Llanwrtyd Wells Powys....95 B7
Llanwrtyd Wells / Llanwrtud Powys....95 B7
Llanwyddelan Powys....129 C11
Llanyblodwel Shrops....148 E4
Llanybri Carms....74 C4
Llanybydder Carms....93 C10
Llanycefn Pembs....91 G11
Llanychaer Pembs....91 D9
Llanycil Gwyn....147 C8
Llanycrwys Carms....94 B2
Llanymawddwy Gwyn....147 F8
Llanymddyfri / Llandovery Carms....94 E4
Llanymynech Powys....148 E5
Llanynghenedl Anglesey....178 E4
Llanynys Denb....165 C10
Llan-y-pwll Wrex....166 E5
Llanyrafon Torf....78 G4
Llanyre Powys....113 E10
Llanystumdwy Gwyn....145 B9
Llanywern Powys....96 F2
Llawhaden Pembs....73 C9
Llawnt Shrops....148 C5
Llawr-y-glyn Powys....129 E8
Llay Wrex....166 D4
Llechcynfarwy Anglesey....178 E5
Llecheiddior Gwyn....163 F7
Llechfaen Powys....95 F11
Llechryd Caerph....77 D10
  Ceredig....92 C4
Llechrydau Powys....148 C4

Llechwedd Conwy....180 F3
Lledrod Ceredig....112 C2
Llidiad Nenog Carms....93 D10
Llidiardau Gwyn....147 B7
Llidiart-y-parc Denb....165 G10
Llithfaen Gwyn....162 G5
Lloc Flint....181 F10
Llong Flint....166 C3
Llowes Powys....96 C3
Lloyney Powys....114 B4
Llugwy Powys....128 C3
Llundain-fach Ceredig....111 F11
Llwydcoed Rhondda....77 E7
Llwyn Denb....165 G5
  Shrops....130 G5
Llwyncelyn Ceredig....111 F8
Llwyndafydd Ceredig....111 F7
Llwyn-derw Powys....129 G8
Llwyn-du Mon....78 C3
Llwynduris Ceredig....92 C4
Llwyneinion Wrex....166 F3
Llwyngwril Gwyn....110 B2
Llwynhendy Carms....56 B4
Llwynmawr Wrex....148 B4
Llwyn-on Village M Tydf....77 C8
Llwyn-y-brain Carms....73 C11
Llwyn-y-go Powys....148 E6
Llwynygog Powys....129 E7
Llwyn-y-groes Ceredig....111 F11
Llwynypia Rhondda....77 G7
Llwyn-yr-hwrdd Pembs....92 E4
Llynclys Shrops....148 E5
Llysfaen Conwy....180 F5
Llyswen Powys....96 D2
Llysworney V Glam....58 E3
Llys-y-frân Pembs....91 G10
Llywel Powys....95 E7
Llwyernog Ceredig....128 G4
Load Brook S Yorks....186 D3
Loan Falk....279 F9
Loandhu Highld....301 B8
Loanend Northumb....273 E8
Loanhead Aberds....302 D6
  Midloth....270 B5
  Perth....286 D5
Loanreoch Highld....300 B6
Loans S Ayrs....257 C8
Loans of Tullich Highld....301 B8
Lobb Devon....40 F3
Lobhillcross Devon....12 D5
Lobley Hill T&W....242 E6
Lobthorpe Lincs....155 E9
Loch a Charnain W Isles....297 G4
Loch a' Ghainmhich W Isles....304 F4
Lochailort Highld....295 G9
Lochaline Highld....289 E8
Lochanhully Highld....301 G9
Lochans Dumfries....236 D2
Locharbriggs Dumfries....247 G11
Lochassynt Lodge Highld....307 G6
Lochavich Ho Argyll....275 B10
Lochawe Argyll....284 E5
Loch Baghasdail W Isles....297 K3
Lochbuie Ho Argyll....289 G8
Lochcallater Lodge Aberds....292 E3
Lochcarron Highld....295 B10
Loch Choire Lodge Highld....308 F6
Lochdhu Highld....310 E4
Lochdochart House Stirl....285 E8
Lochdon Argyll....289 F9
Lochdrum Highld....300 B2
Lochead Argyll....275 E11
  Argyll....275 F8
Lochearnhead Stirl....285 E9
Lochee Dundee....287 D7
Loch Eil Highld....290 F2
Lochend Edin....280 G5
  Highld....300 F5
  Highld....310 C6
Lochend Ho Stirl....277 B11
Locherben Dumfries....247 D11
Lochetive Ho Highld....284 C5
Loch Euphort W Isles....296 E4
Lochfoot Dumfries....237 B10
Lochgair Argyll....275 D10
Lochgarthside Highld....291 B7
Lochgelly Fife....280 C3
Lochgilphead Argyll....275 E9
Lochgoilhead Argyll....284 G6
Loch Head Dumfries....236 E5
  Dumfries....245 E11
Lochhill Moray....302 C2
Lochhussie Highld....300 D4
Lochinch Castle Dumfries....236 C3
Lochindorb Lodge Highld....301 F9
Lochinver Highld....307 G5
Lochlane Perth....286 E2
Lochletter Highld....300 G4
Lochluichart Highld....300 C3
Lochmaben Dumfries....248 G3
Lochmore Cottage Highld....310 E4
Lochmore Lodge Highld....306 F7
Loch nam Madadh W Isles....296 E5
Lochnell Ho Argyll....289 F10
Lochore Fife....280 B3
Lochportain W Isles....296 D5
Lochran Perth....280 B2
Lochranza N Ayrs....255 B10
Lochs Crofts Moray....302 C3
Loch Sgioport W Isles....297 H4
Lochside Aberds....293 G9
  Highld....301 D8
  Highld....308 D4
  Highld....310 D2
Lochslin Highld....311 L2
Lochstack Lodge Highld....306 F7
Lochton Aberds....293 D9
Lochty Angus....293 G7
  Fife....287 G8
  Perth....286 E4
Lochuisge Highld....289 D9
Lochurr Dumfries....247 F7
Lochwinnoch Renfs....267 D7
Lochwood Dumfries....248 D3
  Glasgow....268 B3
Lochyside Highld....290 F3

Lockengate Corn....5 C10
Lockerbie Dumfries....248 G4
Lockeridge Wilts....62 F6
Lockeridge Dene Wilts....62 F6
Lockerley Hants....32 B3
Lockhills Cumb....230 D6
Locking N Som....43 B11
Locking Stumps Warr....183 C10
Lockington E Yorks....208 D5
Lockleywood Shrops....150 D3
Locksbottom London....68 F2
Locksbrook Bath....61 G8
Locks Heath Hants....33 F8
Lockton N Yorks....226 G6
Lockwood W Yorks....196 D6
Loddington Leics....136 C5
  Northants....120 B6
Loddiswell Devon....8 F4
Loddon Norf....143 D7
Loddon Ingloss Norf....142 D6
Lode Cambs....123 E10
Lode Heath W Mid....134 G3
Loders Dorset....16 C6
Lodge Green N Yorks....223 F9
Lodge Green W Mid....134 G5
Lodge Hill Corn....6 C4
Lodge Lees Kent....55 D8
Lodge Moor S Yorks....186 D3
Lodge Park Worcs....117 D10
Lodsworth W Sus....34 C6
Lodsworth Common W Sus....34 C6
Lodway Bristol....60 D4
Lofthouse N Yorks....214 E2
  W Yorks....197 B10
Lofthouse Gate W Yorks....197 C10
Loftus Redcar....226 B4
Logan E Ayrs....258 E3
Loganlea W Loth....269 C9
Loggerheads Denb....165 C11
  Staffs....150 B4
Logie Angus....293 G8
  Fife....287 E8
  Moray....301 D10
Logie Coldstone Aberds....292 C6
Logie Hill Highld....301 B7
Logie Newton Aberds....302 F6
Logie Pert Angus....293 G8
Logierait Perth....286 B3
Logiealmond Lodge Perth....286 D3
Login Carms....92 G3
Logmore Green Sur....50 D6
Loidse Mhorsgail W Isles....304 F3
Lolworth Cambs....123 E7
Lomeshaye Lancs....204 F2
Lôn Gwyn....147 C7
Lonbain Highld....298 D6
Londesborough E Yorks....208 D3
London Apprentice Corn....5 E10
London Beach Kent....53 F11
London Colney Herts....85 E11
Londonderry N Yorks....214 B6
  W Mid....133 F10
London End Cambs....121 D11
London Fields W Mid....133 E8
London Minstead Hants....32 E3
Londonthorpe Lincs....155 B9
Londubh Highld....307 L3
Lonemore Highld....299 B7
  Highld....309 L7
Long Ashton N Som....60 E5
Long Bank Worcs....116 C5
Longbar N Ayrs....266 E6
Longbarn Warr....183 C10
Longbenton T&W....243 D7
Longborough Glos....100 F3
Long Bredy Dorset....17 C7
Longbridge Plym....7 D10
  Warks....118 E5
  W Mid....117 B10
Longbridge Deverill Wilts....45 E11
Longbridge Hayes Stoke....168 E5
Longbridgemuir Dumfries....238 D3
Long Buckby Northants....120 D2
Long Buckby Wharf Northants....120 D2
Longburgh Cumb....239 F8
Longburton Dorset....29 E11
Longcause Devon....8 C5
Long Clawson Leics....154 D4
Longcliffe Derbys....170 D2
Long Common Hants....33 E8
Long Compton Staffs....151 E7
  Warks....100 E5
Longcot Oxon....82 G3
Long Crendon Bucks....83 D11
Long Crichel Dorset....31 E7
Longcroft Cumb....238 F6
  Falk....278 F5
Longcross Devon....12 F4
  Sur....66 F3
Long Cross Wilts....45 G9
Longdale Cumb....222 D2
Longdales Cumb....230 C5
Long Dean Wilts....61 D11
Longden Shrops....131 B8
Longden Common Shrops....131 B8
Long Ditton Sur....67 F7
Longdon Staffs....151 G11
  Worcs....98 D6
Longdon Green Staffs....151 G11
Longdon on Tern Telford....150 F2
Longdown Devon....14 C3
Longdowns Corn....2 C6
Long Drax N Yorks....199 B7
Long Duckmanton Derbys....186 G6
Long Eaton Derbys....153 C9
Longfield Kent....68 F6
  Shetland....313 M5
  Wilts....45 B11
Longfield Hill Kent....68 F6
Longfleet Poole....18 C6
Longford Derbys....152 B5
  Glos....98 G6
  Kent....52 B4
  London....66 D6
  Shrops....150 B2
  Telford....150 F3
  W Mid....135 G7
Longfordlane Derbys....152 B5

Longforgan Perth....287 E7
Longformacus Borders....272 D3
Longframlington Northumb....252 C4
Long Gardens Essex....106 D6
Long Green Ches W....183 F11
  Suff....125 B11
  Worcs....98 E6
Longham Dorset....19 B7
  Norf....159 F8
Long Hanborough Oxon....82 C6
Longhaven Aberds....303 F11
Longhedge Wilts....45 E11
Longhill Aberds....303 D10
Longhirst Northumb....252 F6
Longhope Glos....79 B11
  Orkney....314 G3
Longhorsley Northumb....252 E5
Longhoughton Northumb....264 G6
Long Itchington Warks....119 D8
Longlands Cumb....229 D11
  London....68 E2
Longlane Derbys....152 B5
  W Berks....64 E4
Long Lane Telford....150 F2
Long Lawford Warks....119 B9
Long Lee W Yorks....205 E7
Longlevens Glos....99 G7
Longley W Yorks....196 F5
Longley Estate S Yorks....186 C5
Longley Green Worcs....116 G4
Longleys Perth....286 C6
Long Load Som....29 C7
Longmanhill Aberds....303 C7
Long Marston Herts....84 B5
  N Yorks....206 C6
  Warks....100 B3
Long Marton Cumb....231 G9
Long Meadow Cambs....123 E10
Long Meadowend Shrops....131 G8
Long Melford Suff....106 C6
Longmoor Camp Hants....49 G9
Longmorn Moray....302 D2
Longmoss Ches E....184 G5
Long Newnton Glos....80 G6
Longnewton Borders....262 D3
  Stockton....225 B7
Long Newton E Loth....271 C10
Longney Glos....80 C3
Longniddry E Loth....281 F8
Longnor Shrops....131 C9
  Staffs....169 C9
Longnor Park Shrops....131 C9
Long Oak Shrops....149 E7
Longparish Hants....48 E2
Longpark Cumb....239 E10
  E Ayrs....257 B10
Long Park Hants....48 G2
Long Preston N Yorks....204 B2
Longridge Lancs....203 F8
  Staffs....151 F8
  W Loth....269 C9
Longridge End Glos....98 G6
Longriggend N Lnrk....278 G6
Long Riston E Yorks....209 E8
Longrock Corn....1 C5
Longsdon Staffs....169 E7
Longshaw Gtr Man....194 G4
  Staffs....169 F9
Longside Aberds....303 E10
Longsight Gtr Man....184 B5
Long Sight Gtr Man....196 F2
Longslow Shrops....150 B3
Longsowerby Cumb....239 G9
Longstanton Cambs....123 D7
Longstock Hants....47 F11
Longstone Corn....11 G7
  Pembs....73 D10
  Som....28 B5
Longstowe Cambs....122 G6
Long Stratton Norf....142 E3
Longstreet Wilts....46 C6
Long Street M Keynes....102 B5
Long Sutton Hants....49 D8
  Lincs....157 E8
  Som....29 C7
Longthorpe Pboro....138 D3
Long Thurlow Suff....125 D10
Longthwaite Cumb....230 G4
Longton Lancs....194 B3
  Stoke....168 G6
Longtown Cumb....239 D9
  Hereford....96 F6
Longtownmail Orkney....314 H4
Longview Mers....182 C6
Longville in the Dale Shrops....131 D10
Long Way Bank Derbys....170 E4
Longwell Green S Glos....61 E7
Long Whatton Leics....153 E9
Longwick Bucks....84 D3
Long Wittenham Oxon....83 G8
Longwitton Northumb....252 F3
Longwood Shrops....132 B2
Longworth Oxon....82 F5
Longwood Edge W Yorks....196 D6
Longyester E Loth....271 B10
Lon-las Swansea....57 B8
Lonmay Aberds....303 D10
Lonmore Highld....298 E2
Looe Corn....6 E5
Looe Mills Corn....6 E5
Loose Kent....53 C9
Loosegate Lincs....156 D6
Loose Hill Kent....53 C9
Loosley Row Bucks....84 E4
Lopcombe Corner Wilts....47 F9
Lopen Som....28 E6
Lopen Head Som....28 E6
Loppergarth Cumb....210 D5
Loppington Shrops....149 D9
Lopwell Devon....7 C9
Lorbottle Northumb....252 C2
Lorbottle Hall Northumb....252 C2
Lordington W Sus....34 F2
Lord's Hill Soton....32 D5
Lordshill Common Sur....50 E4
Lordswood Soton....32 D5
Lords Wood Medway....69 G9
Lornty Perth....286 C5
Loscoe Derbys....170 F6
  N Yorks....198 D2
Loscombe Dorset....16 B6
Losgaintir W Isles....305 J2
Lossiemouth Moray....302 B2
Lossit Argyll....254 B2

Lossit Lodge Argyll....274 G5
Lostford Shrops....150 C2
Lostock Gralam Ches W....183 F11
Lostock Green Ches W....183 G11
Lostock Hall Lancs....194 B4
Lostock Junction Gtr Man....195 F7
Lostwithiel Corn....6 D2
Loth Orkney....314 C6
Lothbeg Highld....311 H3
Lothersdale N Yorks....204 D5
Lothianbridge Midloth....270 C6
Lothmore Highld....311 H3
Lottisham Som....44 G5
Loudwater Bucks....84 G5
Loughborough Leics....153 F10
Loughor Swansea....56 B5
Loughton Essex....86 F6
  M Keynes....102 D6
  Shrops....132 G2
Lound Lincs....155 F11
  Notts....187 D11
  Suff....143 D10
Lount Leics....153 F7
Louth Lincs....190 D4
Love Clough Lancs....195 B10
Lovedean Hants....33 E11
Love Green Bucks....66 C5
Lover Wilts....32 C2
Loversall S Yorks....187 B9
Loves Green Essex....87 E10
Lovesome Hill N Yorks....225 F7
Loveston Pembs....73 D9
Lovington Som....44 G5
Low Ackworth W Yorks....198 D3
Low Angerton Northumb....252 G3
Lowbands Glos....98 E5
Low Barlings Lincs....189 G9
Low Bentham N Yorks....212 F2
Low Bradfield S Yorks....186 C3
Low Bradley N Yorks....204 D6
Low Braithwaite Cumb....230 D4
Lowbridge House Cumb....221 D11
Low Brunton Northumb....241 C10
Low Burnham N Lincs....199 G9
Low Burton N Yorks....214 C4
Low Buston Northumb....252 B6
Lowca Cumb....228 G5
Low Catton E Yorks....207 C10
Low Clanyard Dumfries....236 F3
Low Common Norf....142 D2
Low Coniscliffe Darl....224 C5
Low Cotehill Cumb....239 G11
Low Coylton S Ayrs....257 F10
Low Crosby Cumb....239 F10
Low Dalby N Yorks....216 B6
Low Dinsdale Darl....224 C6
Lowdham Notts....171 F11
Low Dinsdale Darl....224 C6
Low Ellington N Yorks....214 C4
Lowe Shrops....149 C10
Lowe Hill Staffs....169 D7
Low Eggborough N Yorks....198 C5
Low Ellington N Yorks....214 C4
Low Etherley Durham....233 F9
Low Fell T&W....243 F7
Low Fulney Lincs....156 E5
Low Gate Northumb....241 D10
Low Green N Yorks....205 C9
  Suff....125 D7
Low Habberley Worcs....116 B6
Low Ham Som....28 B6
Low Hameringham Lincs....190 G5
Low Hauxley Northumb....253 C7
Low Hawsker N Yorks....227 D8
Low Hesket Cumb....230 C5
Low Hesleyhurst Northumb....252 D3
Low Hutton N Yorks....216 G5
Low Laithe N Yorks....214 G4
Lowlands Torf....78 E3
Low Leighton Derbys....185 D8
Low Lorton Cumb....229 F9
Low Marishes N Yorks....216 C6
Low Marnham Notts....188 G4
Low Mill N Yorks....226 F3
Low Moor Lancs....203 E10
  W Yorks....197 B7
Low Moorsley T&W....234 B2
Low Newton Cumb....211 C8
Low Newton-by-the-Sea Northumb....264 E6
Lownie Moor Angus....287 C9
Low Row Cumb....229 C7
  Cumb....240 E4
  N Yorks....223 F10
Low Salchrie Dumfries....236 B2
Low Smerby Argyll....255 E8
Lowsonford Warks....118 D4
Low Street Norf....160 G5
Lowther Cumb....230 G6
Lowthorpe E Yorks....217 G11
Lowton Devon....26 F2
  Gtr Man....183 B10
  Som....27 D11
Lowton Common Gtr Man....183 B10
Low Torry Fife....279 D10
Low Toynton Lincs....190 G4
Low Valleyfield Fife....279 D10
Low Worsall N Yorks....225 D7
Low Wood Cumb....210 C6
Low Wray Cumb....221 E7
Loxbeare Devon....27 E7
Loxhill Sur....50 F4
Loxhore Devon....40 F6
Loxley S Yorks....186 D4
  Warks....118 F5
Loxley Green Staffs....151 B10
Loxton N Som....43 C11
Loxwood W Sus....50 G4
Lower Achachenna Argyll....284 E4
Lower Aisholt Som....43 F8
Lower Allscot Shrops....132 D4
Lower Altofts W Yorks....197 C11
Lower Amble Corn....10 G5
Lower Ansty Dorset....30 G3
Lower Arncott Oxon....83 B10
Lower Ashton Devon....14 E2
Lower Assendon Oxon....65 C8
Lower Badcall Highld....306 E6
Lower Ballam Lancs....202 G3
Lower Bartle Lancs....202 G5
Lower Basildon W Berks....64 D6
Lower Bassingthorpe Lincs....155 D9
Lower Bearwood Hereford....115 F7
Lower Bebington Mers....182 E4
Lower Beeding W Sus....36 B2
Lower Benefield Northants....137 F9
Lower Bentley Worcs....117 D9
Lower Beobridge Shrops....132 E5
Lower Berry Hill Glos....79 C9
Lower Binton Warks....118 G2
Lower Birchwood Derbys....170 E6
Lower Bitchet Kent....52 C5
Lower Blandford St Mary Dorset....30 F5
Lower Blunsdon Swindon....81 G10
Lower Bobbingworth Green Essex....87 D8
Lower Bockhampton Dorset....17 C10
Lower Boddington Northants....119 G9
Lower Bodham Norf....160 B2
Lower Bodinnar Corn....1 C4
Lower Bois Bucks....85 E7
Lower Bordean Hants....33 C11
Lower Boscaswell Corn....1 C3
Lower Bourne Sur....49 E10
Lower Bradley W Mid....133 D9
Lower Brailes Warks....100 D6
Lower Breakish Highld....295 C8
Lower Bredbury Gtr Man....184 C6
Lower Broadheath Worcs....116 F6
Lower Broughton Gtr Man....184 B4
Lower Brynamman Neath....76 C2
Lower Brynn Corn....5 C7
Lower Buckenhill Hereford....98 E2
Lower Buckland Hants....20 B2
Lower Bullingham Hereford....97 D10
Lower Bullington Hants....48 D3
Lower Bunbury Ches E....167 D9
Lower Burgate Hants....31 D11
Lower Burrow Som....28 C6

Lower Burton Hereford....115 F7
Lower Bush Medway....69 F7
Lower Caldecote C Beds....104 B3
Lower Cam Glos....80 E2
Lower Canada N Som....43 B11
Lower Carden Ches W....167 E7
Lower Catesby Northants....119 F10
Lower Caversham Reading....65 E8
Lower Chapel Powys....95 D10
Lower Chedworth Glos....81 C9
Lower Cheriton Devon....27 G10
Lower Chicksgrove Wilts....46 G3
Lower Chute Wilts....47 C10
Lower Clapton London....67 B11
Lower Clent Worcs....117 B8
Lower Clicker Corn....6 C5
Lower Clopton Warks....118 F3
Lower Common Hants....48 E6
  Hants....65 G9
  Mon....78 B2
  Mon....78 B4
  Shrops....131 B9
Lower Copthurst Lancs....194 C5
Lower Cotburn Aberds....303 D7
Lower Cousley Wood E Sus....53 G7
Lower Cox Street Kent....69 G10
Lower Cragabus Argyll....254 C4
Lower Creedy Devon....26 G4
Lower Croan Corn....10 G6
Lower Crossings Derbys....185 E8
Lower Cumberworth W Yorks....197 F8
Lower Cwm-twrch Powys....76 C3
Lower Daggons Hants....31 E9
Lower Darwen Blkburn....195 B7
Lower Dean Beds....121 D10
  Devon....8 C4
Lower Dell Highld....292 B2
Lower Denby W Yorks....197 F8
Lower Denzell Corn....5 B7
Lower Deuchries Aberds....302 D6
Lower Diabaig Highld....299 C7
Lower Dicker E Sus....23 C9
Lower Dinchope Shrops....131 G9
Lower Dowdeswell Glos....81 B8
Lower Down Shrops....130 G6
Lower Drift Corn....1 D4
Lower Dunsforth N Yorks....215 G8
Lower Durston Som....28 B3
Lower Earley Wokingham....65 E9
Lower East Carleton Norf....142 C3
Lower Eastern Green W Mid....118 B5
Lower Edmonton London....86 G4
Lower Egleton Hereford....98 B2
Lower Elkstone Staffs....169 D9
Lower Ellastone Staffs....169 G10
Lower End Bucks....83 D11
  Bucks....102 A4
  C Beds....103 D8
  C Beds....103 G9
  Glos....81 E7
  Northants....120 C6
  Northants....121 E7
  Oxon....82 B4
Lower Everleigh Wilts....47 C7
Lower Eythorne Kent....55 D9
Lower Failand N Som....60 E4
Lower Faintree Shrops....132 F3
Lower Falkenham Suff....108 D5
Lower Farringdon Hants....49 F8
Lower Feltham London....66 E5
Lower Fittleworth W Sus....35 D8
Lowerford Lancs....204 F3
Lower Forge Shrops....132 F4
Lower Foxdale IoM....192 E3
Lower Frankton Shrops....149 C7
Lower Freystrop Pembs....73 C7
Lower Froyle Hants....49 E9
Lower Gabwell Devon....9 B8
Lower Gledfield Highld....309 K5
Lower Godney Som....44 E3
Lower Goldstone Kent....71 G9
Lower Gornal W Mid....133 E8
Lower Grange W Yorks....205 G8
Lower Gravenhurst C Beds....104 D2
Lower Green Essex....88 E2
  Essex....106 E4
  Gtr Man....184 B2
  Herts....104 E4
  Kent....52 E5
  Kent....52 E6
  Norf....159 B9
  Staffs....133 B8
  Suff....124 D6
  Warks....119 D10
  W Berks....64 F2
Lower Grove Common Hereford....97 F11
Lower Hacheston Suff....126 F6
Lower Halistra Highld....298 D2
Lower Halliford Sur....66 F5
Lower Halstock Leigh Dorset....29 F8
Lower Halstow Kent....69 F11
Lower Hamworthy Poole....18 C6
Lower Hardres Kent....55 C7
Lower Hartshay Derbys....170 E5
Lower Hartwell Bucks....84 C3
Lower Hatton Staffs....150 B6
Lower Hawthwaite Cumb....210 B4
Lower Haysden Kent....52 D5
Lower Hayton Shrops....131 G11
Lower Hazel S Glos....60 B6
Lower Heppington Kent....54 C6
Lower Hergest Hereford....114 F5
Lower Heyford Oxon....101 G9
Lower Heysham Lancs....211 G8
Lower Higham Kent....69 E8
Lower Highmoor Oxon....65 B8
Lower Holbrook Suff....108 E4
Lower Holditch Dorset....28 G4
Lower Holloway London....67 B10
Lower Holwell Dorset....31 E9
Lower Hook Worcs....98 C6
Lower Hookner Devon....13 E11
Lower Hopton Shrops....149 D7

Lower Hordley Shrops....149 D7
Lower Horncroft W Sus....35 D8
Lower Horsebridge E Sus....23 C9
Lowerhouse Ches E....184 F6
Lower House Halton....183 D8
  Lancs....204 G2
Lower Houses W Yorks....197 D7
Lower Howsell Worcs....98 B5
Lower Illey Worcs....133 G9
Lower Island Kent....70 F6
Lower Kersal Gtr Man....195 G10
Lower Kilburn Derbys....170 F5
Lower Kilcott Glos....61 B9
Lower Killeyan Argyll....254 C3
Lower Kingcombe Dorset....17 B7
Lower Kingswood Sur....51 C8
Lower Kinnerton Ches W....166 C4
Lower Kinsham Hereford....115 E7
Lower Knapp Som....28 B4
Lower Knightley Staffs....150 E5
Lower Knowle Bristol....60 E5
Lower Langford N Som....60 G4
Lower Largo Fife....287 G8
Lower Layham Suff....107 C10
Lower Ledwyche Shrops....115 C10
Lower Leigh Staffs....151 B10
Lower Lemington Glos....100 E4
Lower Lenie Highld....300 G5
Lower Lode Glos....99 E7
Lower Lovacott Devon....25 B8
Lower Loxhore Devon....40 F6
Lower Lydbrook Glos....79 B9
Lower Lye Hereford....115 D8
Lower Machen Newport....59 B8
Lower Maes-coed Hereford....96 E6
Lower Mains Clack....279 B9
Lower Mannington Dorset....31 F9
Lower Marston Som....45 D9
Lower Meend Glos....79 E9
Lower Menadue Corn....5 D10
Lower Merridge Som....43 G8
Lower Mickletown W Yorks....198 B2
Lower Middleton Cheney Northants....101 C10
Lower Midway Derbys....152 E6
Lower Mill Corn....3 B10
Lower Milovaig Highld....296 F1
Lower Milton Som....44 D4
Lower Moor W Mid....81 B9
  Worcs....99 B9
Lower Morton S Glos....79 G10
Lower Mountain Flint....166 D4
Lower Nazeing Essex....86 D5
Lower Netchwood Shrops....132 E2
Lower Netherton Devon....14 G3
Lower New Inn Torf....78 E4
Lower Ninnes Corn....1 C5
Lower Nobut Staffs....151 C10
Lower North Dean Bucks....84 F5
Lower Norton Warks....118 E4
Lower Nyland Dorset....30 C2
Lower Ochrwyth Caerph....59 B8
Lower Odcombe Som....29 D7
Lower Oddington Glos....100 F4
Lower Ollach Highld....295 B7
Lower Padworth W Berks....64 F6
Lower Penarth V Glam....59 F7
Lower Penn Staffs....133 D7
Lower Pennington Hants....20 C2
Lower Penwortham Lancs....194 B4
Lower Peover Ches W....184 G3
Lower Pexhill Ches E....184 G5
Lower Pilsley Derbys....170 C6
Lower Pitkerrie Highld....311 L2
Lower Place Gtr Man....196 F2
Lower Pollicott Bucks....84 C2
Lower Porthkerry V Glam....58 F5
Lower Porthpean Corn....5 E10
Lower Quinton Warks....100 B3
Lower Rabber Hereford....114 G5
Lower Race Torf....78 E3
Lower Radley Oxon....83 F8
Lower Rainham Medway....69 F10
Lower Ratley Hants....32 C4
Lower Raydon Suff....107 D10
Lower Rea Glos....80 B4
Lower Ridge Devon....28 G4
Lower Rochford Worcs....116 D2
Lower Rose Corn....4 E5
Lower Row Dorset....31 G8
Lower Sapey Worcs....116 E3
Lower Seagry Wilts....62 C3
Lower Sheering Essex....87 C7
Lower Shelton C Beds....103 C9
Lower Shiplake Oxon....65 D9
Lower Shuckburgh Warks....119 E10
Lower Sketty Swansea....56 C6
Lower Slackstead Hants....32 B5
Lower Slade Devon....40 D4
Lower Slaughter Glos....100 G3
Lower Soar Pembs....90 E3
Lower Soothill W Yorks....197 C9
Lower Soudley Glos....79 D11
Lower Southend Essex....98 C3
Lower Stanton St Quintin Wilts....62 C2
Lower Stoke Medway....69 D10
  W Mid....119 B7
Lower Stondon C Beds....104 D3
Lower Stone Glos....79 G11
Lower Stonnall Staffs....133 C11
Lower Stow Bedon Norf....141 E9
Lower Stratton Som....28 D6
  Swindon....63 B7
Lower Street E Sus....23 C11
  Norf....160 B5
  Norf....160 C5
  Suff....108 C4
  Suff....124 G5
Lower Strensham Worcs....99 C8
Lower Stretton Warr....183 E10
Lower Studley Wilts....45 B11
Lower Sundon C Beds....103 F10
Lower Swainswick Bath....61 F9
Lower Swanwick Hants....33 F7
Lower Swell Glos....100 F3
Lower Sydenham London....67 E11

Lower Thorpe
Northants....101 B10
Lower Threapwood
Wrex....166 G6
Lower Thurlton Norf....143 D8
Lower Thurnham Lancs.202 C5
Lower Thurvaston
Derbys....152 B4
Lower Todding Hereford 115 B8
Lower Tote Highld....298 C5
Lowertown Corn....5 C11
Corn....2 D5
Devon....12 E5
Lower Town Devon....27 E8
Hereford....98 C2
Pembs....91 D9
Worcs....117 F7
W Yorks....206 F2
Lower Trebullett Corn..12 F2
Lower Tregunnon Corn.11 E10
Lower Treworrick Corn..6 B4
Lower Tuffley Glos....80 C4
Lower Twitchen Devon..24 E5
Lower Twydall Medway.69 F10
Lower Tysoe Warks....100 B6
Lower Upham Hants....33 D8
Lower Upnor Medway...69 E9
Lower Vexford Som....42 F6
Lower Wainhill Oxon....84 E3
Lower Walton Warr....183 D10
Lower Wanborough
Swindon....63 C8
Lower Weacombe Som..42 E6
Lower Weald M Keynes..102 D5
Lower Wear Devon....14 D4
Lower Weare Som....44 C2
Lower Weedon
Northants....120 F2
Lower Welson Hereford 114 G5
Lower Westholme Som..44 E5
Lower Westhouse
N Yorks....212 E3
Lower Westmancote
Worcs....99 D8
Lower Weston Som....61 F8
Lower Whatcombe
Dorset....30 G4
Lower Whatley Som....45 D8
Lower Whitley Ches W.183 F10
Lower Wick Glos....80 F2
Worcs....116 G6
Lower Wield Hants....48 E6
Lower Willingdon E Sus..23 E9
Lower Winchendon or
Nether Winchendon
Bucks....84 C2
Lower Withington
Ches E....168 B4
Lower Wolverton Worcs 117 G8
Lower Woodend Aberds 293 B8
Bucks....65 B10
Lower Woodford Wilts..46 G6
Lower Woodley Corn....5 D8
Lower Woodside Herts..86 D2
Lower Woolston Som...29 B11
Lower Woon Corn....5 C10
Lower Wraxall Dorset..29 G9
Wilts....61 G10
Lower Wych Ches W....167 G7
Lower Wyche Worcs....98 C5
Lower Wyke W Yorks...197 B7
Lower Yelland Devon...40 G3
Lower Zeals Wilts....45 G9
Lowes Barn Durham...233 C11
Lowesby Leics....136 B4
Lowestoft Suff....143 E10
Loweswater Cumb....229 G8
Low Etherley Durham..233 F9
Low Fell T&W....243 F7
Lowfield S Yorks....186 D5
Lowfield Heath W Sus...51 E9
Low Fold W Yorks....205 F10
Lowford Hants....33 E7
Low Fulney Lincs....156 E5
Low Garth N Yorks....226 D4
Low Gate Northumb....241 E10
N Yorks....214 F5
Low Grantley N Yorks..214 E4
Low Green N Yorks....205 B10
Suff....125 E7
W Yorks....205 D10
Low Greenside T&W...242 E4
Low Habberley Worcs..116 B6
Low Ham Som....28 B6
Low Hauxley Northumb.253 C7
Low Hawsker N Yorks..227 D8
Low Hesket Cumb....230 B5
Low Hesleyhurst
Northumb....252 D3
Low Hill W Mid....133 C8
Low Hutton N Yorks....216 F5
Lowick Cumb....210 B5
Northants....137 G9
Northumb....264 B2
Lowick Bridge Cumb...210 B5
Lowick Green Cumb....210 B5
Low Knipe Cumb....230 G6
Low Laithe N Yorks....214 G3
Low Laithes S Yorks....197 G11
Lowlands Torf....78 F3
Low Leighton Derbys..185 D8
Low Lorton Cumb....229 F9
Low Marishes N Yorks.216 D6
Low Marnham Notts...172 B4
Low Mill N Yorks....226 F3
Low Moor Lancs....203 E10
W Yorks....197 B7
Lowmoor Row Cumb...231 F8
Low Moorsley T&W....234 B2
Low Moresby Cumb....228 G5
Lowna N Yorks....226 G3
Low Newton Cumb....211 C8
Low Newton-by-the-Sea
Northumb....264 E6
Lownie Moor Angus...287 C8
Lowood Borders....262 B2
Low Prudhoe Northumb.242 E4
Low Risby N Yorks....200 E2
Low Row Cumb....229 C9
Cumb....240 E3
N Yorks....223 F9
Low Salchrie Dumfries.236 C2
Low Smerby Argyll....255 E8
Low Snaygill N Yorks..204 D5
Lowsonford Warks....118 D3
Low Street Norf....141 B10
Thurrock....69 D7
Low Tharston Norf....142 D3
Lowther Cumb....230 G6
Lowthertown Dumfries.238 D3
Lowthorpe E Yorks....217 G11
Lowton Devon....8 E4
Hereford....115 F7

Lowton Gtr Man....183 B10
Som....27 D11
Lowton Common
Gtr Man....183 B10
Lowton Heath Gtr Man 183 B10
Lowton St Mary's
Gtr Man....183 B10
Low Torry Fife....279 D10
Low Town Som....132 E4
Low Toynton Lincs....190 G3
Low Valley S Yorks....198 G2
Low Valleyfield Fife...279 D10
Low Walton Cumb....219 C9
Low Wood Cumb....210 C6
Low Worsall N Yorks...225 C7
Low Wray Cumb....221 E7
Loxbeare Devon....26 D6
Loxford London....68 B2
Loxhill Sur....50 F4
Loxhore Devon....40 F6
Loxhore Cott Devon....40 F6
Loxley S Yorks....186 D4
Warks....118 G5
Loxley Green Staffs....151 C11
Loxter Hereford....98 C4
Loxton N Som....43 B11
Loxwood W Sus....50 G4
Loyter's Green Essex...87 C8
Loyterton Kent....70 G3
Lozells W Mid....133 F11
Lubachlaggan Highld..300 B3
Lubachoinnich Highld..309 K4
Lubberland Shrops....116 B2
Lubcroy Highld....309 J3
Lubenham Leics....136 F4
Lubinvullin Highld....308 C5
Lucas End Herts....86 F3
Lucas Green Lancs....194 C5
Sur....50 B2
Luccombe Som....42 E2
Luccombe Village IoW..21 F7
Lucker Northumb....264 C5
Luckett Corn....12 G3
Lucking Street Essex...106 E6
Luckington Wilts....61 C10
Lucklawhill Fife....287 E8
Luckwell Bridge Som...42 F2
Lucton Hereford....115 E8
Ludag W Isles....297 K3
Ludborough Lincs....190 B3
Ludbrook Devon....8 E3
Ludchurch Pembs....73 C10
Luddenden W Yorks...196 B4
Luddenden Foot
W Yorks....196 C4
Ludderburn Cumb....221 G8
Luddesdown Kent....69 F7
Luddington N Lincs....199 D10
Warks....118 G3
Luddington in the Brook
Northants....138 G2
Lude House Perth....291 G10
Ludford Lincs....190 D2
Shrops....115 C10
Ludgershall Bucks....83 B11
Wilts....47 C9
Ludgvan Corn....2 C2
Ludham Norf....161 F7
Ludlow Shrops....115 C10
Ludney Lincs....190 B5
Som....28 E5
Ludstone Shrops....132 E6
Ludwell Wilts....30 C6
Ludworth Durham....234 C3
Luffenhall Herts....104 F5
Luffincott Devon....12 C2
Lufton Som....29 D8
Lugar E Ayrs....258 E3
Lugate Borders....271 G8
Luggate Burn E Loth...282 G2
Lugg Green Hereford...115 E9
Luggiebank N Lanark...278 G5
Lugsdale Halton....183 D8
Lugton E Ayrs....267 E8
Lugwardine Hereford...97 C11
Luib Highld....295 C7
Luibeilt Highld....290 G4
Lulham Hereford....97 C8
Lullenden Sur....52 E2
Lullington Derbys....152 G5
Som....45 C9
Sur....64 F4
Lulsgate Bottom N Som.60 F4
Lulsley Worcs....116 G5
Lulworth Camp Dorset..18 E2
Lumb Lancs....195 C10
Lancs....195 D9
W Yorks....196 C4
W Yorks....197 E7
Lumb Foot W Yorks....204 F6
Lumburn Devon....12 G5
Lumbutts W Yorks....196 C3
Lumley N Yorks....206 G5
Lumley W Sus....22 B3
Lumley Thicks Durham.243 G8
Lumloch E Dunb....268 B2
Lumphanan Aberds....293 C7
Lumphinnans Fife....280 C3
Lumsdaine Borders....273 B7
Lumsden Aberds....302 G4
Lunan Angus....287 B10
Lunanhead Angus....287 B8
Luncarty Perth....286 E4
Lund E Yorks....208 D5
N Yorks....207 G9
Shetland....312 C7
Lundal W Isles....304 E3
Lundavra Highld....290 G2
Lunderton Aberds....303 E11
Lundie Angus....286 D6
Highld....290 B3
Lundin Links Fife....287 G8
Lundwood S Yorks....197 F11
Lundy Green Norf....142 E4
Lunga Argyll....275 C8
Lunna Shetland....312 G6
Lunning Shetland....312 G7
Lunnister Shetland....312 F5
Lunnon Swansea....56 D4
Lunsford Kent....53 B8
Lunsford's Cross E Sus..38 E2
Lunt Mers....193 G10
Luntley Hereford....115 F7
Lunts Heath Halton....183 D8
Lupin Staffs....152 F2
Luppitt Devon....27 F11
Lupridge Devon....8 E4
Lupset W Yorks....197 D10
Lupton Cumb....211 C11
Lurg Aberds....293 C8
Lurgashall W Sus....34 B6
Lurignich Argyll....289 D11
Lurley Devon....26 E6
Lusby Lincs....174 B4
Luscombe Devon....8 E5
Lushcott Shrops....131 D11
Luson Devon....8 F2
Luss Argyll....277 C7

Lussagiven Argyll....275 E7
Lusta Highld....298 D2
Lustleigh Devon....13 E11
Lustleigh Cleave Devon.13 E11
Luston Hereford....115 E9
Lusty Som....45 G7
Luthermuir Aberds....293 G8
Luthrie Fife....287 F7
Lutley W Mid....133 G8
Luton Devon....14 E4
Devon....27 G9
Luton....103 G11
Medway....69 F9
Lutsford Devon....24 D3
Lutterworth Leics....135 G10
Luxborough Som....42 F3
Luxley Glos....98 G3
Luxted London....68 G2
Luxton Devon....28 E2
Luxulyan Corn....5 D11
Luzley Gtr Man....196 G3
Luzley Brook Gtr Man..196 F2
Lyatts Som....29 E8
Lybster Highld....310 F6
Lydbury North Shrops..131 F7
Lydcott Devon....41 F7
Lydd Kent....39 C8
Lydden Kent....55 D9
Kent....71 F11
Lyddington Rutland....137 D7
Lydd on Sea Kent....39 C9
Lyde Orkney....314 E3
Shrops....130 C6
Lydeard St Lawrence
Som....42 G6
Lye Cross Hereford....97 C10
Lye Green Hants....49 B8
S Glos....61 D7
Lydford Devon....12 E6
Lydford Fair Place Som..44 G5
Lydford-on-Fosse Som..44 G5
Lydgate Derbys....186 F4
Gtr Man....196 G3
W Yorks....196 B2
Lydham Shrops....130 E6
Lydiard Green Wilts....62 B5
Lydiard Millicent Wilts.62 B5
Lydiard Plain Wilts....62 B5
Lydiard Tregoze Swindon 62 C6
Lydiate Mers....193 G11
Lydiate Ash Worcs....117 B9
Lydlinch Dorset....30 E2
Lydmarsh Som....28 F5
Lydney Glos....79 E10
Lydstep Pembs....73 F9
Lye W Mid....133 G8
Lye Green Bucks....85 E7
E Sus....52 G4
Warks....118 D3
Wilts....45 B10
Lye Head Worcs....116 C5
Lye Hole N Som....60 G4
Lyewood Common E Sus.52 F4
Lyford Oxon....82 G5
Lymbridge Green Kent..54 E6
Lyme Green Ches E....184 G6
Lyme Regis Dorset....16 C2
Lymiecleuch Borders...249 C9
Lyminge Kent....55 E7
Lymington Hants....20 B2
Lyminster W Sus....35 G8
Lymm Warr....183 D11
Lymore Hants....19 C11
Lympne Kent....54 F6
Lympsham Som....43 C10
Lympstone Devon....14 E5
Lynbridge Devon....41 D8
Lynch Hants....48 D4
Som....42 D2
Lynchat Highld....291 C9
Lynchgate Shrops....131 F7
Lynch Hill Hants....48 D3
Slough....66 C2
Lyndale Ho Highld....298 D3
Lyndhurst Hants....32 F4
Lyndon Rutland....137 C8
Lyndon Green W Mid...134 F2
Lyne Borders....270 G4
Sur....66 F4
Lyneal Shrops....149 C8
Lyneal Mill Shrops....149 C9
Lyneal Wood Shrops...149 C9
Lyne Down Hereford....98 E2
Lyneham Devon....10 C3
Wilts....62 D4
Lynemore Highld....301 G10
Lynemouth Northumb..253 E7
Lyne of Gorthleck
Highld....300 G5
Lyne of Skene Aberds..293 B9
Lyness Orkney....314 G3
Lyne Station Borders...260 B6
Lynford Norf....140 E6
Lyng Norf....159 F11
Som....28 B4
Lyngate Norf....160 C5
Lyngford Som....28 B2
Lynmore Highld....301 F10
Lynmouth Devon....41 D8
Lynn Staffs....133 C11
Telford....150 F5
Lynsore Bottom Kent...55 D7
Lynsted Kent....70 G2
Lynstone Corn....24 F2
Lynton Devon....41 D8
Lynwilg Highld....291 B10
Lynworth Glos....99 G9
Lyons T&W....234 B3
Lyon's Gate Dorset....29 E11
Lyon's Green Norf....159 G8
Lyonshall Hereford....114 F6
Lyons Hall Essex....88 B2
Lypiatt Glos....80 D6
Lyrabus Argyll....274 G3
Lytchett Matravers
Dorset....18 B4
Lytchett Minster Dorset.18 C5
Lyth Highld....310 C6
Lytham Lancs....193 B11
Lytham St Anne's
Lancs....193 B10
Lythbank Shrops....131 B9
Lythe N Yorks....226 C6
Lythes Orkney....314 H4
Lythmore Highld....310 C4

M
Maam Argyll....284 F5
Mabe Burnthouse Corn..3 C7
Mabie Dumfries....237 B11
Mabledon Kent....52 E5

Mablethorpe Lincs....191 D8
Macclesfield Ches E....184 G6
Macclesfield Forest
Ches E....185 G7
Macduff Aberds....303 C7
Mace Green Suff....108 C2
Machan S Lanark....268 E5
Macharioch Argyll....255 G8
Machen Caerph....59 B8
Machrie N Ayrs....255 D9
Machrie Hotel Argyll...254 C4
Machrihanish Argyll....255 E7
Machrins Argyll....274 D4
Machynlleth Powys....128 C4
Machynys Carms....56 B4
Mackerel's Common
W Sus....35 B8
Mackerye End Herts....85 B11
Mackham Devon....27 F11
Mackney Oxon....64 B5
Mackside Borders....262 G4
Mackworth Derbys....152 B6
Macmerry E Loth....281 G8
Madderty Perth....286 E3
Maddington Wilts....46 E5
Maddiston Falk....279 F8
Maddox Moor Pembs...73 C7
Madehurst W Sus....35 E7
Madeley Staffs....168 G3
Telford....132 C3
Madeley Heath Staffs...168 F3
Worcs....117 B9
Madeley Park Staffs....168 G3
Madeleywood Telford...132 C3
Maders Corn....12 G2
Madford Devon....27 E10
Madingley Cambs....123 E7
Madjeston Dorset....30 B4
Madley Hereford....97 D8
Madresfield Worcs....98 B6
Madron Corn....1 C5
Maenaddwyn Anglesey.179 E7
Maenclochog Pembs....91 F11
Maendy V Glam....58 D4
Maenporth Corn....3 D7
Maentwrog Gwyn....163 G11
Maen-y-groes Ceredig..111 F7
Maer Corn....24 F2
Staffs....150 B5
Maerdy Carms....94 G2
Conwy....165 G8
Rhondda....77 F7
Maes-bangor Ceredig..128 G3
Maesbrook Shrops....148 E5
Maesbury Shrops....148 D6
Maesbury Marsh Shrops.148 D6
Maesgeirchen Gwyn....179 G9
Maes-glas Newport....59 B9
Maes Glas / Greenfield
Flint....181 F11
Maesgwyn-Isaf Powys..148 G3
Maeshafn Denb....166 C2
Maesllyn Ceredig....93 C7
Maes llyn Ceredig....93 C7
Maesmynis Powys....95 B10
Maes Pennant Flint....181 F11
Maesteg Bridgend....57 C10
Maes-Treylow Powys...114 D5
Maesybont Carms....75 B9
Maesycrugiau Carms....93 C9
Maesycwmmer Caerph..77 G11
Maesymeillion Ceredig..93 B8
Maespndy Powys....129 D9
Maesyrhandir Powys....129 E11
Magdalen Laver Essex..87 D8
Maggieknockater Moray 302 E3
Maggots End Essex....105 F9
Magham Down E Sus...23 C10
Maghull Mers....193 G11
Magor Mon....60 B2
Magpie Green Suff....125 B11
Maida Vale London....67 C9
Maidenbower W Sus....51 F9
Maiden Bradley Wilts...45 E10
Maidenhall Suff....108 C3
Maidenhead Windsor...65 C11
Maiden Head N Som....60 F5
Maidenhead Court
Windsor....66 C2
Maiden Law Durham...233 B9
Maiden Newton Dorset..17 B7
Maidenpark Falk....279 E9
Maidens S Ayrs....244 B6
Maidensgrave Suff....108 B5
Maiden's Green Brack...65 F11
Maidensgrove Oxon....65 B8
Maiden's Hall Northumb.252 D6
Maidenwell Corn....11 G8
Lincs....190 F4
Maiden Wells Pembs....73 F7
Maidford Northants....120 G2
Maids Moreton Bucks...102 D4
Maidstone Kent....53 B9
Maidwell Northants....120 B4
Mail Shetland....313 L6
Mailand Shetland....312 C8
Mailingsland Borders...270 G4
Main Powys....148 F3
Mainholm S Ayrs....257 E9
Mains Cumb....210 C5
Mainsforth Durham....234 E2
Mains of Airies
Dumfries....236 C1
Mains of Allardice
Aberds....293 F10
Mains of Annochie
Aberds....303 E9
Mains of Ardestie
Angus....287 D9
Mains of Arnage Aberds 303 F9
Mains of Auchoynanie
Moray....302 E4
Mains of Baldoon
Dumfries....236 D6
Mains of Ballhall Angus.287 B9
Mains of Ballindarg
Angus....287 B8
Mains of Balnakettle
Aberds....293 F8
Mains of Birness Aberds 303 F9
Mains of Blackhall
Aberds....303 G7
Mains of Burgie Moray.301 D10
Mains of Cairnbrogie
Aberds....303 G8
Mains of Cairnty Moray.302 D3
Mains of Clunas Highld.301 E8
Mains of Crichie Aberds.303 E9
Mains of Daltulich
Highld....301 E7
Mains of Delavaird
Aberds....293 F9
Mains of Drum Aberds..293 D10

Mains of Edingight
Moray....302 D5
Mains of Fedderate
Aberds....303 E8
Mains of Flichity Highld.300 G6
Mains of Hatton Aberds 303 D9
Mains of Inkhorn Aberds 303 F9
Mains of Innerpeffray
Perth....286 F3
Mains of Kirktonhill
Aberds....293 G8
Mains of Laithers
Aberds....303 E7
Mains of Mayen Moray.302 E5
Mains of Melgund
Angus....287 B9
Mains of Taymouth
Perth....285 C11
Mains of Thornton
Aberds....293 F8
Mains of Towie Aberds.303 E7
Mains of Ulster Aberds.310 E7
Mains of Watten Highld.310 D6
Mainsriddle Dumfries...237 D11
Mainstone Shrops....130 F5
Maisemore Glos....98 G6
Maitland Park London...67 C9
Major's Green W Mid...118 B2
Makeney Derbys....170 F5
Makerstoun Borders....262 C4
Malacleit W Isles....296 D3
Malborough Devon....9 G9
Malcoff Derbys....185 E8
Malden Rushett London.67 G7
Maldon Essex....88 D4
Malehurst Shrops....131 B7
Malham N Yorks....213 G8
Maligar Highld....298 C4
Malinbridge S Yorks....186 D4
Malinslee Telford....132 B3
Malkin's Bank Ches E...168 D3
Mallaig Highld....295 F8
Mallaig Bheag Highld..295 F8
Malleny Mills Edin....270 B3
Malling Stirl....285 G9
Malltraeth Anglesey....162 B6
Mallwyd Gwyn....147 G2
Malmesbury Wilts....62 B2
Malmsmead Devon....41 D9
Malpas Ches W....167 F7
Corn....4 G6
Newport....78 G4
Malswick Glos....98 F4
Maltby Lincs....190 E4
Stockton....225 C9
S Yorks....187 D8
Maltby le Marsh Lincs..191 E7
Malting End Suff....124 G4
Malting Green Essex...107 G9
Maltings Angus....293 G9
Maltman's Hill Kent....54 E2
Malton N Yorks....216 E5
Malvern Common Worcs.98 C5
Malvern Link Worcs....98 B5
Malvern Wells Worcs...98 C5
Mambeg Argyll....276 D4
Mamble Worcs....116 C3
Mamhilad Mon....78 E4
Manaccan Corn....3 E7
Manadon Plym....7 D9
Manafon Powys....130 C2
Manais W Isles....296 C7
Manar Ho Aberds....303 G7
Manaton Devon....13 E11
Manby Lincs....190 D5
Mancetter Warks....134 D6
Manchester Gtr Man...184 B4
Manchester Airport
Gtr Man....184 D4
Mancot Flint....166 B4
Mancot Royal Flint....166 B4
Mandally Highld....290 C4
Manea Cambs....139 F9
Maney W Mid....134 D2
Manfield N Yorks....224 C4
Mangaster Shetland....312 F5
Mangotsfield S Glos....61 D7
Mangrove Green Herts..104 G2
Mangurstadh W Isles...304 E2
Manhay Corn....2 C5
Manian-fawr Pembs....92 B3
Manian-glas Caerph....77 G11
Manley Ches W....183 G8
Manley Common
Ches W....183 G8
Manmoel Caerph....77 E11
Man-moel Caerph....77 E11
Mannal Argyll....288 E1
Mannamead Plym....7 D9
Mannerston W Loth....279 F10
Manningford Abbots
Wilts....46 B6
Manningford Bohune
Wilts....46 B6
Manningford Bruce Wilts.46 B6
Manningham W Yorks..205 G9
Manning's Heath W Sus.35 C11
Mannings Heath W Sus.35 C11
Mannington Dorset....31 F9
Manningtree Essex....107 E11
Mannofield Aberdeen...293 C11
Manor London....68 C2
Manorbier Pembs....73 F9
Manorbier Newton
Pembs....73 F8
Manordeilo Carms....94 F3
Manor Estate S Yorks...186 D5
Manor Hill Corner Lincs.157 F8
Manor House W Mid....134 D4
Manor Park Bucks....84 C4
Ches W....167 B11
E Sus....37 C7
London....68 B2
Slough....66 C3
S Yorks....186 D5
W Yorks....205 G9
Manorowen Pembs....91 D8
Manor Parsley Corn....4 F4
Manor Royal W Sus....51 F9
Man's Cross Essex....106 D5
Mansegate Dumfries...247 G9
Manselfield Swansea...56 D5
Mansell Gamage
Hereford....97 C7
Mansell Lacy Hereford..97 C8
Mansergh Cumb....212 C2
Mansewood Glasgow...267 C11
Mansfield E Ayrs....258 G4
Notts....171 C8
Mansfield Woodhouse
Notts....171 C8
Mansriggs Cumb....210 C5
Manston Dorset....30 D4
Kent....71 F10

W Yorks....206 F3
Manswood Dorset....31 F7
Manthorpe Lincs....155 B8
Lincs....155 F11
Mantles Green Bucks....85 F7
Manton N Lincs....200 G3
Notts....187 F9
Rutland....137 C7
Wilts....63 F7
Manton Warren N Lincs.200 F2
Manuden Essex....105 F9
Manwood Green Essex..87 C8
Manywells Height
W Yorks....205 F7
Maperton Som....29 B11
Maplebeck Notts....172 C2
Maple Cross Herts....85 G8
Mapledurham Oxon....65 D7
Mapledurwell Hants....49 C7
Maple End Essex....105 D11
Maplehurst W Sus....35 C11
Maplescombe Kent....68 G5
Mapleton Derbys....169 F11
Mapperley Derbys....170 G6
Nottingham....171 G9
Mapperley Park
Nottingham....171 G9
Mapperton Dorset....16 B6
Dorset....18 B6
Mappleborough Green
Warks....117 D11
Mappleton E Yorks....209 E10
Mapplewell S Yorks....197 F10
Mappowder Dorset....30 F2
Maraig W Isles....305 H3
Marazanvose Corn....4 E6
Marazion Corn....2 C2
Marbhig W Isles....305 G6
Marbrack Dumfries....246 E3
Marbury Ches E....167 F8
March Cambs....139 D8
S Lanark....259 G11
Marcham Oxon....83 F7
Marchamley Shrops....149 D11
Marchamley Wood
Shrops....149 C11
Marchington Staffs....152 C2
Marchington Woodlands
Staffs....152 D2
Marchroes Gwyn....144 D6
Marchwiel Wrex....166 F5
Marchwood Hants....32 E5
Marcross V Glam....58 F2
Marden Hereford....97 B10
T&W....243 C9
Wilts....46 B5
Marden Ash Essex....87 E9
Marden Beech Kent....53 E8
Marden's Hill E Sus....52 G3
Marden Thorn Kent....53 E9
Mardleybury Herts....86 B3
Mardu Shrops....130 G5
Mardy Mon....78 B4
Marefield Leics....136 B4
Mareham le Fen Lincs..174 C3
Mareham on the Hill
Lincs....174 B3
Marehay Derbys....170 F5
Marehill W Sus....35 D9
Maresfield E Sus....37 C7
Maresfield Park E Sus...37 C7
Marfleet Hull....200 B6
Marford Wrex....166 D5
Margam Neath....57 D9
Margaret Marsh Dorset..30 D4
Margaret Roding Essex..87 C9
Margaretting Essex....87 E11
Margaretting Tye Essex.87 E11
Margate Kent....71 E11
Margery Sur....51 D9
Margnaheglish N Ayrs..256 C2
Margreig Dumfries....237 B10
Margrove Park Redcar..226 B3
Marham Norf....158 G4
Marhamchurch Corn....24 G2
Marholm Pboro....138 C2
Marian Flint....181 F9
Marian Cwm Denb....181 F9
Mariandyrys Anglesey..179 E10
Marianglas Anglesey...179 E8
Marian-glas Anglesey...179 E8
Mariansleigh Devon....26 C2
Marian y de / South Beach
Gwyn....145 C7
Marian y mor / West End
Gwyn....145 C7
Marine Town Kent....70 E2
Marionburgh Aberds....293 C9
Marishader Highld....298 C4
Marjoriebanks Dumfries 248 G3
Mark Dumfries....236 D3
S Ayrs....236 B2
Som....43 D11
Markbeech Kent....52 E2
Markby Lincs....191 F7
Mark Causeway Som....43 D11
Mark Cross E Sus....23 B9
E Sus....52 G5
Markeaton Derbys....152 B6
Market Bosworth Leics 135 C8
Market Deeping Lincs..138 B2
Market Drayton Shrops.150 C3
Market Harborough
Leics....136 F4
Markethill Perth....286 D6
Market Lavington Wilts..46 C4
Market Overton Rutland 155 F7
Market Rasen Lincs....189 D10
Market Stainton Lincs..190 D2
Market Warsop Notts...171 B9
Market Weighton
E Yorks....208 D2
Market Weston Suff....125 B9
Markfield Leics....153 G9
Mark Hall North Essex..87 C7
Mark Hall South Essex..87 C7
Markham Caerph....77 E11
Markham Moor Notts...188 F2
Markinch Fife....286 G6
Markington N Yorks....214 F5
Markland Hill Gtr Man..195 F7
Markle E Loth....281 F11
Marksbury Bath....61 G7
Mark's Corner IoW....20 C5
Marks Gate London....68 B3
Marks Tey Essex....107 G8
Markyate Herts....85 B9
Marland Gtr Man....195 E11
Marlas Hereford....97 G8
Marl Bank Worcs....98 C5
Marlborough Wilts....63 F8
Marlbrook Hereford....115 G10
Worcs....117 C9
Marlcliff Warks....117 G11
Marldon Devon....9 C7
Marle Green E Sus....23 C9
Marle Hill Glos....99 G9
Marlesford Suff....126 F6

Marley Kent....55 C7
Kent....55 C10
Marley Green Ches E....167 F8
Marley Heights W Sus..49 G11
Marley Hill T&W....242 F6
Marley Pots T&W....243 F9
Marlingford Norf....142 G2
Mar Lodge Aberds....292 D2
Marlow Bucks....65 B10
Hereford....115 B8
Marlow Bottom Bucks...65 B11
Marlow Common Bucks.65 B10
Marlpit Hill Kent....52 E2
Marlpits E Sus....38 E2
Marlpool Derbys....170 F6
Marnhull Dorset....30 D3
Marnock N Lanark....268 B4
Marple Gtr Man....185 D7
Marple Bridge Gtr Man.185 D7
Marpleridge Gtr Man...185 D7
Marr S Yorks....198 F4
Marr Green Wilts....63 G8
Marrel Highld....311 H4
Marrick N Yorks....223 F11
Marrister Shetland....313 G7
Marros Carms....74 D2
Marsden T&W....243 E9
W Yorks....196 E4
Marsden Height Lancs..204 F3
Marsett N Yorks....213 B8
Marsh Bucks....84 D4
Devon....28 E3
W Yorks....204 F6
Marshall Meadows
Northumb....273 D9
Marshall's Cross Mers..183 C8
Marshall's Elm Som....44 G3
Marshall's Heath Herts..85 B11
Marshalsea Dorset....28 G5
Marshalswick Herts....85 D11
Marsham Norf....160 E3
Marshaw Lancs....203 C7
Marsh Baldon Oxon....83 F9
Marsh Benham W Berks.64 F2
Marshborough Kent....55 B10
Marshbrook Shrops....131 F8
Marshchapel Lincs....190 B5
Marsh Common S Glos..60 C5
Marsh Gate W Berks....63 F10
Marsh Gibbon Bucks...102 G2
Marsh Green Ches W...183 F8
Devon....14 C6
Gtr Man....194 F5
Kent....52 E2
Staffs....168 D5
Telford....150 G2
Marsh Houses Lancs....202 C5
Marshland St James
Norf....139 B10
Marsh Lane Derbys....186 F6
Glos....79 D9
Marsh Mills Som....43 F7
Marshmoor Herts....86 D2
Marshside Kent....71 F8
Mers....193 D11
Marsh Side Norf....176 E3
Marsh Street Som....42 E4
Marshwood Dorset....16 B3
Marske N Yorks....224 E2
Marske-by-the-Sea
Redcar....235 G8
Marston Ches W....183 F11
Hereford....115 F7
Lincs....172 G5
Oxon....83 D8
Staffs....150 E6
Staffs....151 D8
Warks....134 E4
Wilts....46 B3
Marston Bigot Som....45 E8
Marston Doles Warks...119 F9
Marston Gate Som....45 D9
Marston Green W Mid..134 F3
Marston Hill Glos....81 F10
Marston Jabbett Warks.135 F7
Marston Magna Som....29 C9
Marston Meysey Wilts..81 F10
Marston Montgomery
Derbys....152 B3
Marston Moretaine
C Beds....103 C9
Marston on Dove
Derbys....152 D4
Marston St Lawrence
Northants....101 C10
Marston Stannett
Hereford....115 F11
Marston Trussell
Northants....136 F3
Marstow Hereford....79 B9
Marsworth Bucks....84 C6
Marten Wilts....47 B9
Marthall Ches E....184 F4
Martham Norf....161 F9
Marthwaite Cumb....222 G2
Martin Hants....31 D9
Kent....55 D10
Lincs....173 D10
Lincs....174 B2
Martin Drove End Hants.31 C9
Martindale Cumb....221 B8
Martin Dales Lincs....173 C10
Martinhoe Devon....41 D7
Martinhoe Cross Devon.41 D7
Martin Hussingtree
Worcs....117 E7
Martin Mill Kent....55 D10
Martinscroft Warr....183 D11
Martin's Moss Ches E...168 C4
Martinstown or
Winterbourne St Martin
Dorset....17 D8
Martlesham Suff....108 B4
Martlesham Heath Suff.108 B4
Martletwy Pembs....73 C8
Martley Worcs....116 F5
Martock Som....29 D7
Marton Ches E....168 B5
Ches W....167 B10
Cumb....210 D4
E Yorks....209 F9
Lincs....188 E4
Mbro....225 B10
N Yorks....216 F2
Shrops....130 C5
Shrops....131 B7
Warks....119 D8
Marton Green Ches W...167 B10

Marton Grove Mbro....225 B10
Marton-in-the-Forest
N Yorks....215 F11
Marton-le-Moor
N Yorks....215 E7
Marton Moor Warks....119 D8
Marton Moss Side
Blackpool....202 G2
Martyr's Green Sur....50 B5
Martyr Worthy Hants....48 G4
Marwick Orkney....314 D2
Marwood Devon....40 F4
Marybank Highld....300 D4
Highld....301 B7
Maryburgh Highld....300 D5
Maryfield Aberds....293 C7
Corn....7 D8
Maryhill Glasgow....267 B11
Marykirk Aberds....293 G8
Maryland Mon....79 D8
Marylebone Gtr Man...194 F5
London....67 C9
Marypark Moray....301 F11
Maryport Cumb....228 E6
Dumfries....236 F3
Mary Tavy Devon....12 F6
Maryton Angus....287 B10
Angus....287 B8
Marywell Aberds....293 D8
Aberds....293 D11
Angus....287 C10
Masbrough S Yorks....186 C6
Mascle Bridge Pembs...73 D7
Masham N Yorks....214 C4
Mashbury Essex....87 C11
Masongill N Yorks....212 D3
Masonhill S Ayrs....257 E9
Mastin Moor Derbys....187 F7
Mastrick Aberdeen....293 C10
Matchborough Worcs...117 D11
Matching Essex....87 C8
Matching Green Essex..87 C8
Matching Tye Essex....87 C8
Matfen Northumb....242 C2
Matfield Kent....53 E7
Mathern Mon....79 G8
Mathon Hereford....98 B4
Mathry Pembs....91 E7
Matlaske Norf....160 C3
Matley Gtr Man....185 B7
Matlock Derbys....170 C3
Matlock Bank Derbys...170 C3
Matlock Bath Derbys...170 D3
Matlock Bridge Derbys.170 C3
Matlock Cliff Derbys....170 C4
Matlock Dale Derbys....170 D3
Matshead Lancs....202 E6
Matson Glos....80 B5
Matterdale End Cumb...230 G3
Mattersey Notts....187 D11
Mattersey Thorpe
Notts....187 D11
Matthewsgreen
Wokingham....65 F10
Mattingley Hants....49 B8
Mattishall Norf....159 G11
Mattishall Burgh Norf..159 G11
Mauchline E Ayrs....257 D11
Maud Aberds....303 E9
Maudlin Corn....5 C11
W Sus....22 B5
Maudlin Cross Dorset...28 F5
Maugersbury Glos....100 F4
Maughold IoM....192 C5
Mauld Highld....300 F4
Maulden C Beds....103 D11
Maulds Meaburn Cumb 222 B2
Maunby N Yorks....215 B7
Maund Bryan Hereford.115 G11
Maundown Som....27 B9
Mauricewood Midloth..270 C5
Mautby Norf....161 G9
Mavesyn Ridware
Staffs....151 F11
Mavis Enderby Lincs....174 B5
Maviston Highld....301 D9
Mawbray Cumb....229 B7
Mawdesley Lancs....194 E3
Mawdlam Bridgend....57 E10
Mawgan Corn....2 D6
Mawgan Porth Corn....5 B7
Maw Green Ches E....168 D2
Mawla Corn....4 F4
Mawnan Corn....3 D7
Mawnan Smith Corn....3 D7
Mawsley Northants....120 B6
Mawson Green S Yorks.198 D6
Mawthorpe Lincs....191 F7
Maxey Pboro....138 B2
Maxstoke Warks....134 F4
Maxted Street Kent....54 E6
Maxton Borders....262 C4
Kent....55 E10
Maxwellheugh Borders 262 C6
Maxwelltown Dumfries.237 B11
Maxworthy Corn....11 C11
Mayals Swansea....56 C6
May Bank Staffs....168 F5
Maybole S Ayrs....257 G9
Maybury Sur....50 B4
Maybush Soton....32 E5
Mayer's Green W Mid...133 E10
Mayes Green Sur....50 F6
Mayeston Pembs....73 E8
Mayfair London....67 C9
Mayfield E Sus....37 B9
Midloth....271 C7
Northumb....243 D7
Staffs....169 F11
W Loth....269 B8
Mayford Sur....50 B3
Mayhill Swansea....56 C6
May Hill Mon....79 C9
May Hill Village Glos....98 G4
Mayland Essex....88 E6
Maylandsea Essex....88 E6
Maynard's Green E Sus..23 C9
Mayne Ho Moray....302 C2
Mayon Corn....1 D3
Maypole Bromley....68 G3
Dartford....68 E4
Kent....71 G7
Mon....79 C7
Scilly....1 G4
Maypole Green Essex...107 G9
Norf....143 E8
Suff....125 B11
Suff....126 C5
Mays Green Oxon....65 C8
Sur....50 B5
Mayshill S Glos....61 C7
Maythorn S Yorks....197 F7
Maythorne Notts....171 D11
Maywick Shetland....313 L5
Mead Devon....24 D3
Devon....24 G2
Mead End Hants....19 B11
Hants....33 C11
Meadgate Bath....45 B7

Meadle Bucks 84 D4
Meadowbank Ches W 167 B11
Edin 280 G5
Meadowfield Durham 233 D10
Meadowfoot N Ayrs 266 F4
Meadow Green Hereford 116 F4
Meadow Hall S Yorks 186 C5
Meadow Head S Yorks 186 E4
Meadowley Shrops 132 E3
Meadowmill E Loth 281 G8
Meadows Nottingham 153 B11
Meadowtown Shrops 130 C6
Meads E Sus 23 F10
Meadside Oxon 83 G9
Mead Vale Sur 51 D9
Meadwell Devon 12 E4
Meaford Staffs 151 B7
Meagill N Yorks 205 B9
Mealabost W Isles 304 E6
Mealabost Bhuirgh W Isles 304 C6
Mealasta W Isles 304 F1
Meal Bank Cumb 221 F10
Meal Hill W Yorks 197 F7
Mealrigg Cumb 229 B8
Mealsgate Cumb 229 C10
Meanwood W Yorks 205 F11
Mearbeck N Yorks 212 G6
Meare Som 44 E3
Meare Green Som 28 B4
Som 28 C3
Mearns Bath 45 B7
E Renf 267 D10
Mears Ashby Northants 120 D6
Measborough Dike S Yorks 197 F11
Measham Leics 152 G6
Meath Green Sur 51 E9
Meathop Cumb 211 C8
Meaux E Yorks 209 F7
Meaver Corn 2 F5
Meavy Devon 7 B10
Medbourne Leics 136 E5
M Keynes 102 D6
Medburn Northumb 242 C4
Meddon Devon 24 D3
Meden Vale Notts 171 B9
Medhurst Row Kent 52 D3
Medlam Lincs 174 D4
Medlar Lancs 202 F4
Medlicott Shrops 131 E8
Medlyn Corn 2 C6
Medmenham Bucks 65 C10
Medomsley Durham 242 G4
Medstead Hants 49 F7
Meerbrook Staffs 169 C7
Meer Common Hereford 115 G7
Meer End W Mid 118 C4
Meerhay Dorset 29 G7
Meers Bridge Lincs 191 D7
Meersbrook S Yorks 186 E5
Meesden Herts 105 E8
Meeson Telford 150 E3
Meeson Heath Telford 150 E3
Meeth Devon 25 F8
Meethe Devon 25 C11
Meeting Green Suff 124 F4
Meeting House Hill Norf 160 D6
Meggernie Castle Perth 285 C9
Meggethead Borders 260 E5
Meidrim Carms 92 G5
Meifod Denb 165 D8
Powys 148 G3
Meigle N Ayrs 266 B3
Perth 286 C6
Meikle Earnock S Lnrk 268 E4
Meikle Ferry Highld 309 L7
Meikle Forter Angus 292 G3
Meikle Gluich Highld 309 L6
Meikle Obney Perth 286 D4
Meikleour Perth 286 D5
Meikle Pinkerton E Loth 282 F4
Meikle Strath Aberds 293 F8
Meikle Tarty Aberds 303 G9
Meikle Wartle Aberds 303 F7
Meinciau Carms 75 C7
Meir Stoke 168 G6
Meir Heath Staffs 168 G6
Melbourn Cambs 105 C7
Melbourne Derbys 153 D7
E Yorks 207 E11
S Lnrk 269 G11
Melbury Abbas Dorset 30 C5
Melbury Bubb Dorset 29 F9
Melbury Osmond Dorset 29 F9
Melbury Sampford Dorset 29 F9
Melby Shetland 313 H3
Melchbourne Beds 121 D10
Melcombe Som 43 G9
Melcombe Bingham Dorset 30 G3
Melcombe Regis Dorset 17 E9
Meldon Devon 13 C7
Northumb 252 G4
Meldreth Cambs 105 B7
Meldrum Ho Aberds 303 G8
Melfort Argyll 275 B9
Melgarve Highld 290 D6
Meliden / Gallt Melyd Denb 181 E9
Melinbyrhedyn Powys 128 D6
Melin Caiach Caerph 77 F10
Melincourt Neath 76 E4
Melincryddan Neath 57 B8
Melinsey Corn 3 B10
Melin-y-coed Conwy 164 C4
Melin-y-ddôl Powys 129 B11
Melin-y-grug Powys 129 B11
Melin-y-Wig Denb 165 F8
Melkington Northumb 273 G7
Melkinthorpe Cumb 231 F7
Melkridge Northumb 240 E6
Melksham Wilts 62 G2
Melksham Forest Wilts 62 G2
Mellangaun Highld 307 L3
Mellangoose Corn 2 D5
Melldalloch Argyll 275 F10
Mell Green W Berks 64 D3
Mellguards Cumb 230 B4
Melling Lancs 211 E11
Mers 193 G11
Mellingey Corn 10 G4
Melling Mount Mers 194 G2
Mellis Suff 126 C2
Mellis Green Suff 125 C11
Mellon Charles Highld 307 K3
Mellon Udrigle Highld 307 K3
Mellor Gtr Man 185 D7
Lancs 203 G9
Mellor Brook Lancs 203 G8
Mells Som 45 D8
Suff 127 B8
Mells Green Som 45 D8
Melmerby Cumb 231 D8
N Yorks 213 B11
N Yorks 214 D6
Melon Green Suff 124 F6
Melplash Dorset 16 B5
Melrose Borders 262 C2
Melsetter Orkney 314 H2
Melsonby N Yorks 224 D3
Meltham W Yorks 196 E6
Meltham Mills W Yorks 196 E6
Melton E Yorks 200 B3
Suff 126 G5
Meltonby E Yorks 207 C11
Melton Constable Norf 159 C10
Melton Mowbray Leics 154 F5
Melton Ross N Lincs 200 E5
Melvaig Highld 307 L2
Melverley Shrops 148 F6
Melverley Green Shrops 148 F6
Melvich Highld 310 C2
Membland Devon 7 F11
Membury Devon 28 G3
Memsie Aberds 303 C9
Memus Angus 287 B8
Mena Corn 5 C10
Menabilly Corn 5 E11
Menadarva Corn 4 G2
Menagissey Corn 4 F4
Menai Bridge / Porthaethwy Anglesey 179 G9
Mendham Suff 142 G5
Mendlesham Suff 126 D2
Mendlesham Green Suff 125 E11
Menethorpe N Yorks 216 F5
Mengham Hants 21 B10
Menheniot Corn 6 C5
Menherion Corn 2 B6
Menithwood Worcs 116 D4
Menna Corn 5 E8
Mennock Dumfries 247 B8
Menston W Yorks 205 E9
Menstrie Clack 278 B6
Mentmore Bucks 84 B6
Menzion Borders 260 E3
Meoble Highld 295 G9
Meole Brace Shrops 149 G9
Meols Mers 182 C2
Meon Hants 33 G8
Meonstoke Hants 33 D10
Meopham Kent 68 F6
Meopham Green Kent 68 F6
Meopham Station Kent 68 F6
Mepal Cambs 139 G8
Meppershall C Beds 104 D2
Merbach Hereford 96 B6
Mercaton Derbys 170 G3
Merchant Fields W Yorks 197 B7
Merchiston Edin 280 G4
Mere Ches E 184 E2
Wilts 45 G10
Mere Brow Lancs 194 D2
Mereclough Lancs 204 G3
Mere Green W Mid 134 D2
Worcs 117 E9
Merehead Wrex 149 B9
Mere Heath Ches W 183 G11
Meresborough Medway 69 G10
Mereside Blkpool 202 G2
Meretown Staffs 150 E5
Mereworth Kent 53 C7
Mergie Aberds 293 E9
Meriden Herts 85 F10
W Mid 134 G4
Merkadale Highld 294 B5
Merkland Dumfries 237 B9
N Ayrs 256 B2
S Ayrs 244 E6
Merkland Lodge Highld 309 G4
Merle Common Sur 52 D2
Merley Poole 18 B6
Merlin's Bridge Pembs 72 C6
Merlin's Cross Pembs 73 F7
Merridale W Mid 133 D7
Merridge Som 43 G8
Merrie Gardens IoW 21 E7
Merrifield Devon 8 F6
Devon 24 G3
Merrington Shrops 149 E9
Merrion Pembs 72 F6
Merriott Dorset 16 B6
Som 28 E6
Merriottsford Som 28 E6
Merritown Dorset 19 B8
Merrivale Devon 12 F6
Hereford 98 G2
Merrow Sur 50 C4
Merrybent Darl 224 C4
Merry Field Hill Dorset 31 G8
Merry Hill Herts 85 G10
W Mid 133 D7
Merryhill Green Wokingham 65 E9
Merrylee E Renf 267 D11
Merry Lees Leics 135 B9
Merrymeet Corn 6 B5
Merry Meeting Corn 11 G7
Merry Oak Soton 32 E6
Mersham Kent 54 F5
Merstham Sur 51 C9
Merston W Sus 22 C5
Merstone IoW 20 E6
Merther Corn 5 G7
Merther Lane Corn 5 G7
Merthyr Carms 93 G7
Merthyr Cynog Powys 95 D9
Merthyr-Dyfan V Glam 58 F6
Merthyr Mawr Bridgend 57 F11
Merthyr Tydfil M Tydf 77 D8
Merthyr Vale M Tydf 77 F9
Merton Devon 25 E8
London 67 E9
Norf 141 D8
Oxon 83 B9
Merton Park London 67 F9
Mervinslaw Borders 262 G5
Meshaw Devon 26 D3
Messing Essex 88 B5
Messingham N Lincs 199 G11
Mesty Croft W Mid 133 E9
Mesur-y-dorth Pembs 87 E11
Metal Bridge Durham 233 E11
Metfield Suff 142 G5
Metherell Corn 7 B8
Metheringham Lincs 173 C9
Methersgate Suff 108 B5
Methil Fife 281 B7
Methilhill Fife 281 B7
Methlem Gwyn 144 C3
Methley W Yorks 197 B11
Methley Junction W Yorks 197 B11
Methley Lanes W Yorks 197 B11
Methlick Aberds 303 F8
Methven Perth 286 E4
Methwold Norf 140 E4
Methwold Hythe Norf 140 E4
Mettingham Suff 143 F7
Metton Norf 160 B3
Mevagissey Corn 5 G10
Mewith Head N Yorks 212 F4
Mexborough S Yorks 187 B7
Mey Highld 310 B6
Meyrick Park Bmouth 19 C7
Meysey Hampton Glos 81 F10
Miabhag W Isles 305 H2
W Isles 305 J3
Miabhig W Isles 304 E2
Mial Highld 299 B7
Michaelchurch Hereford 97 F10
Michaelchurch Escley Hereford 96 E6
Michaelchurch on Arrow Powys 114 G4
Michaelston-le-Pit V Glam 59 E7
Michaelston-y-Fedw Newport 59 C8
Michaelstow Corn 11 F7
Michealston-super-Ely Cardiff 58 D6
Michelcombe Devon 8 B3
Micheldever Hants 48 F4
Michelmersh Hants 32 B4
Mickfield Suff 126 E2
Micklebring S Yorks 187 C8
Mickleby N Yorks 226 C6
Micklefield Bucks 84 G5
W Yorks 206 G4
Micklefield Green Herts 85 F8
Mickleham Sur 51 C7
Micklehurst Gtr Man 196 G3
Mickleover Derby 152 C6
Micklethwaite Cumb 239 G7
W Yorks 205 E8
Mickleton Durham 232 G5
Glos 100 C3
Mickletown W Yorks 197 B11
Mickle Trafford Ches W 166 B6
Mickley Derbys 186 F4
N Yorks 214 D5
Shrops 150 C2
Mickley Green Suff 124 F6
Mickley Square Northumb 242 E3
Midanbury Hants 33 E7
Mid Ardlaw Aberds 303 C9
Mid Auchinleck Invclyd 276 G6
Midbea Orkney 314 B4
Mid Beltie Aberds 293 C8
Mid Calder W Loth 269 B11
Mid Cloch Forbie Aberds 303 D7
Mid Clyth Highld 310 F6
Middle Assendon Oxon 65 B8
Middle Aston Oxon 101 F9
Middle Balnald Perth 286 B4
Middle Barton Oxon 101 F8
Middle Bickenhill W Mid 134 G4
Middlebie Dumfries 238 B6
Middle Bockhampton Dorset 19 B9
Middle Bourne Sur 49 E10
Middle Bridge N Som 60 D3
Middle Burnham Som 43 D10
Middle Cairncake Aberds 303 E8
Middlecave N Yorks 216 E5
Middle Chinnock Som 29 E7
Middle Claydon Bucks 102 F4
Middle Cliff Staffs 169 E8
Middlecliffe S Yorks 198 F2
Middlecott Devon 13 D10
Devon 24 F6
Devon 26 F3
Middle Crackington Corn 11 B9
Middlecroft Derbys 186 G6
Middle Drums Angus 287 B9
Middle Duntisbourne Glos 81 D7
Middlefield Falk 279 E7
Middleforth Green Lancs 194 B4
Middle Green Bucks 66 C4
Som 27 D10
Suff 124 D4
Middleham N Yorks 214 B2
Middle Handley Derbys 186 F6
Middle Harling Norf 141 F9
Middle Herrington T&W 243 G9
Middlehill Corn 6 B5
Wilts 61 F10
Middle Hill Pembs 73 C7
Staffs 133 B9
Middlehope Shrops 131 F9
Middle Kames Argyll 275 E10
Middle Littleton Worcs 99 B11
Middle Luxton Devon 28 E2
Middle Madeley Staffs 168 F3
Middle Maes-coed Hereford 96 E6
Middlemarsh Dorset 29 F11
Middle Marwood Devon 40 F4
Middle Mayfield Staffs 169 G10
Middle Mill Pembs 87 F11
Middlemoor Devon 12 G5
Middlemuir Aberds 303 D9
Aberds 303 E8
Aberds 303 G9
Middleport Stoke 168 F5
Middle Quarter Kent 53 F11
Middle Rainton T&W 234 B2
Middle Rasen Lincs 189 D9
Middle Rigg Perth 286 G4
Middle Rocombe Devon 9 B8
Middlesbrough Mbro 234 G5
Middlesceugh Cumb 230 C4
Middleshaw Cumb 211 B11
Middle Side Durham 232 F4
Middlesmoor N Yorks 213 E11
Middle Stoford Som 27 C11
Middle Stoke Devon 13 G9
Medway 69 D10
W Mid 119 B7
Middlestone Durham 233 E11
Middlestone Moor Durham 233 E10
Middle Stoughton Som 44 D2
Middlestown W Yorks 197 D9
Middle Strath W Loth 279 G8
Middle Street Glos 80 E3
Middle Taphouse Corn 6 C3
Middlethird Borders 272 G3
Middlethorpe York 207 D7
Middleton Aberds 293 B10
Argyll 288 E1
Cumb 212 B2
Derbys 169 C11
Derbys 170 D3
Essex 107 D7
Gtr Man 195 F11
Hants 48 E2
Hereford 115 D10
Hrtlpl 234 E6
IoW 20 D2
Lancs 202 B4
Midloth 271 D7
Norf 158 F3
Northants 136 F6
Northumb 252 F3
Northumb 264 B4
N Yorks 204 E5
N Yorks 205 D8
N Yorks 216 B5
Perth 286 C5
Perth 286 F2
Perth 286 G5
Shrops 115 B10
Shrops 130 D5
Shrops 148 D6
Suff 127 D8
Swansea 56 D2
Warks 134 D3
W Yorks 197 B10
Middleton Baggot Shrops 132 E2
Middleton Cheney Northants 101 C9
Middleton Green Staffs 151 B9
Middleton Hall Northumb 263 D11
Middleton-in-Teesdale Durham 232 F4
Middleton Junction Gtr Man 195 G11
Middleton Moor Suff 127 D8
Middleton of Rora Aberds 303 E10
Middleton One Row Darl 225 C7
Middleton-on-Leven N Yorks 225 D9
Middleton-on-Sea W Sus 35 G7
Middleton on the Hill Hereford 115 E10
Middleton-on-the-Wolds E Yorks 208 D4
Middleton Place Cumb 219 G11
Middleton Priors Shrops 132 E2
Middleton Quernhow N Yorks 214 D6
Middleton St George Darl 224 C6
Middleton Scriven Shrops 132 F3
Middleton Stoney Oxon 101 G10
Middleton Tyas N Yorks 224 D4
Middletown Cumb 219 D9
N Som 60 E3
Powys 148 G6
Warks 117 E11
Middle Town Scilly 1 F4
Middle Tysoe Warks 100 C6
Middle Wallop Hants 47 F9
Middle Weald M Keynes 102 D5
Middlewich Ches E 167 B11
Middlewick Wilts 61 E11
Middle Wick Glos 80 F2
Middle Winterslow Wilts 47 G8
Middlewood Ches E 184 E6
Corn 11 F11
S Yorks 186 C4
Middle Woodford Wilts 46 F6
Middlewood Green Suff 125 E11
Middleyard Glos 80 E4
Middlezoy Som 43 G11
Middridge Durham 233 F11
Midelney Som 28 C6
Midfield Highld 308 C5
Midford Bath 61 G9
Midgard Borders 262 F3
Mid Garrary Dumfries 237 B7
Midge Hall Lancs 194 C4
Midgehole W Yorks 196 B3
Midgeholme Cumb 240 F4
Midgham W Berks 64 F5
Midgham Green W Berks 64 F5
Midgley W Yorks 196 B4
W Yorks 197 E9
Mid Holmwood Sur 51 D7
Midhopestones S Yorks 186 B2
Midhurst W Sus 34 C5
Mid Lambrook Som 28 D6
Midland Orkney 314 F3
Mid Lavant W Sus 22 B5
Midlem Borders 262 D2
Mid Letter Argyll 284 G4
Midlock S Lnrk 259 E11
Mid Main Highld 300 F4
Midmar Aberds 293 C8
Midmuir Argyll 289 G11
Mid Murthat Dumfries 248 D3
Midpark Argyll 255 B11
Midplaugh Aberds 302 E5
Midsomer Norton Bath 45 C7
Midton Invclyd 276 F4
Midtown Highld 307 L3
Highld 308 C5
Midtown of Buchromb Moray 302 E3
Midtown of Glass Aberds 302 E4
Mid Urchany Highld 301 E8
Midville Lincs 174 D5
Mid Walls Shetland 313 H4
Midway Ches E 184 E6
Som 45 D7
Mid Yell Shetland 312 D7
Miekle Toux Aberds 302 D5
Migdale Highld 309 K6
Migvie Aberds 292 C6
Milarrochy Stirl 277 C8
Milber Devon 14 G3
Milborne Port Som 29 D11
Milborne St Andrew Dorset 18 B2
Milborne Wick Som 29 C11
Milbourne Northumb 242 B4
Wilts 62 B2
Milburn Aberds 302 E5
Aberds 302 F6
Cumb 231 F9
Milbury Heath S Glos 79 G11
Milby N Yorks 215 F8
Milch Hill Essex 106 G4
Milcombe Corn 6 D4
Oxon 101 E8
Milden Suff 107 B9
Mildenhall Suff 124 C4
Wilts 63 F8
Milebrook Powys 114 C6
Milebush Kent 53 D9
Mile Cross Norf 160 G4
Mile Elm Wilts 62 F3
Mile End Cambs 140 G2
Devon 14 G2
Essex 107 F9
Glos 79 C9
London 67 C11
Suff 124 G6
Mileham Norf 159 F8
Mile Oak Brighton 36 F2
Kent 53 E7
Shrops 148 D6
Staffs 134 C3
Miles Green Staffs 168 F4
Sur 50 B3
Miles Hill W Yorks 205 F11
Milesmark Fife 279 D11
Miles Platting Gtr Man 184 B5
Miles's Green W Berks 64 F4
Mile Town Kent 70 E2
Milfield Northumb 263 C10
Milford Derbys 170 F5
Devon 24 C2
Powys 129 E11
Shrops 149 E8
Staffs 151 E9
Sur 50 E2
Wilts 31 B11
Milford Haven Pembs 72 D6
Milford on Sea Hants 19 C11
Milkhouse Water Wilts 63 G7
Milkieston Borders 270 F4
Milkwall Glos 79 D9
Milkwell Wilts 30 C6
Milland W Sus 34 B4
Millarston Renfs 267 C9
Millbank Aberds 303 E11
Highld 310 C5
Kent 71 F8
Mill Bank W Yorks 196 C4
Millbeck Cumb 229 F11
Millbounds Orkney 314 C5
Millbreck Aberds 303 E10
Millbridge Sur 49 E10
Millbrook C Beds 103 D10
Corn 7 E8
Devon 41 G9
Gtr Man 185 B7
Soton 32 E5
Mill Brow Gtr Man 185 D7
Millburn S Ayrs 257 D10
Millcombe Devon 8 F6
Mill Common Norf 142 C6
Suff 143 G8
Mill Corner E Sus 38 C4
Milldale Staffs 169 E10
Mill Dam N Yorks 212 F3
Millden Lodge Angus 293 F7
Milldens Angus 287 B9
Millend Glos 80 D3
Glos 80 F3
Mill End Bucks 65 C9
Cambs 124 F3
Glos 81 C10
Herts 85 G8
Herts 104 E6
Mill End Green Essex 106 F2
Millendreath Corn 6 E5
Millerhill Midloth 270 B6
Miller's Dale Derbys 185 G10
Miller's Green Derbys 170 E3
Essex 87 D9
Millersneuk E Dunb 278 G3
Millerston Glasgow 268 B2
Mill Farm Aberds 303 C8
Millfield Pboro 138 C3
T&W 243 F9
Millgate Lancs 195 D11
Norf 160 D3
Millgillhead Cumb 229 G7
Mill Green Cambs 106 B2
Essex 87 E10
Hants 64 G4
Herts 86 D2
Norf 142 G2
Shrops 150 D3
Suff 107 C9
Suff 125 F9
Suff 126 E2
W Mid 133 C11
Millhalf Hereford 96 B5
Millhall Kent 53 B8
Mill Hall Dumfries 237 E8
Millhayes Devon 27 E10
Devon 28 G2
Millhead Lancs 211 E9
Millheugh S Lnrk 268 E5
Millhill Devon 12 G5
Mill Hill Blkburn 195 B7
Essex 88 G4
E Sus 23 D10
Glos 79 D10
Gtr Man 195 F8
Kent 55 C11
Lincs 175 B8
London 86 G2
Suff 125 G7
Mill Hills Suff 108 B5
Mill Hirst N Yorks 214 G3
Millholme Cumb 221 G11
Millhouse Argyll 275 F10
Cumb 230 D3
Millhousebridge Dumfries 248 F4
Millhouse Green S Yorks 197 G8
Millhouses S Yorks 186 E4
S Yorks 198 G2
Millikenpark Renfs 267 C8
Millin Cross Pembs 73 C7
Millington E Yorks 208 C2
Millington Green Derbys 170 F3
Mill Lane Hants 49 C9
Mill Meads London 67 C11
Millmeece Staffs 150 C6
Millmoor Devon 27 E10
Millness Cumb 211 C10
Mill of Brydock Aberds 302 D6
Mill of Chon Stirl 285 G8
Mill of Haldane W Dunb 277 E8
Mill of Kingoodie Aberds 303 G8
Mill of Lynebain Aberds 302 F4
Mill of Muiresk Aberds 302 E6
Mill of Rango Orkney 314 E2
Mill of Sterin Aberds 292 D5
Mill of Uras Aberds 293 E10
Millom Cumb 210 C3
Millook Corn 11 B9
Millow C Beds 104 C4
Mill Park Argyll 255 G8
Mill Place N Lincs 200 F3
Millpool Corn 2 C3
Corn 11 G8
Millport N Ayrs 266 E3
Millquarter Dumfries 246 G4
Mill Shaw W Yorks 205 G11
Mill Side Cumb 211 C8
Mill Street Kent 53 B7
Norf 159 F11
Suff 107 D9
Millthorpe Derbys 186 F4
Lincs 156 C2
Mill Throop Bmouth 19 B8
Millthrop Cumb 222 G3
Milltimber Aberdeen 293 C10
Milltown Aberds 292 C4
Corn 6 B2
Corn 6 D2
Derbys 170 C5
Devon 40 F5
Highld 301 E9
Milltown of Aberdalgie Perth 286 E4
Milltown of Auchindoun Moray 302 E3
Milltown of Craigston Aberds 303 D7
Milltown of Edinvillie Moray 302 E2
Milltown of Kildrummy Aberds 292 B6
Milltown of Rothiemay Moray 302 E5
Milltown of Towie Aberds 292 B6
Millwall London 67 D11
Milnathort Perth 286 G5
Milner's Heath Ches W 167 C7
Milngavie E Dunb 277 G11
Milnquarter Falk 278 F6
Milnrow Gtr Man 196 E2
Milnsbridge W Yorks 196 D6
Milnshaw Lancs 195 B9
Milnthorpe Cumb 211 C9
W Yorks 197 D10
Milnwood N Lnrk 268 D4
Milo Carms 75 B9
Milson Shrops 116 C2
Milstead Kent 54 B2
Milston Wilts 47 D7
Milthorpe Northants 101 B11
Milton Angus 287 C7
Angus 292 E6
Cambs 123 E9
Cumb 211 C10
Cumb 240 E3
Derbys 152 D6
Dumfries 236 D4
Dumfries 237 B10
Dumfries 247 G8
Fife 287 E8
Glasgow 267 B11
Highld 299 E7
Highld 300 D3
Highld 300 E5
Highld 300 F4
Highld 301 B7
Highld 301 E7
Highld 310 D7
Kent 69 E7
Moray 292 B3
Moray 302 C5
Notts 188 G2
N Som 59 G10
Oxon 83 G7
Oxon 101 E8
Pembs 73 E8
Perth 286 F3
Powys 114 G4
Ptsmth 21 B9
Som 29 C7
Stirl 285 G9
Stoke 168 E6
S Yorks 197 G11
W Dunb 277 G8
Wilts 45 G11
Milton Abbas Dorset 30 G4
Milton Bridge Midloth 270 C4
Milton Bryan C Beds 103 E9
Milton Clevedon Som 45 F7
Milton Coldwells Aberds 303 F9
Milton Combe Devon 7 B9
Milton Common Oxon 83 E11
Milton Coombe Devon 7 B9
Milton Damerel Devon 24 E5
Miltonduff Moray 301 C11
Milton End Glos 80 C2
Glos 81 E10
Milton Ernest Beds 121 F10
Milton Green Ches W 167 D7
Devon 12 F4
Milton Heights Oxon 83 G7
Miltonhill Moray 301 C10
Milton Hill Devon 14 F4
Oxon 83 G7
Miltonise Dumfries 236 B3
Milton Keynes M Keynes 103 D7
Milton Keynes Village M Keynes 103 D7
Milton Lilbourne Wilts 63 G7
Milton Malsor Northants 120 F4
Milton Morenish Perth 285 D10
Milton of Auchinhove Aberds 293 C7
Milton of Balgonie Fife 287 G7
Milton of Buchanan Stirl 277 C8
Milton of Campfield Aberds 293 C8
Milton of Campsie E Dunb 278 F3
Milton of Corsindae Aberds 293 C8
Milton of Cullerlie Aberds 293 C9
Milton of Cultoquhey Perth 286 E2
Milton of Cushnie Aberds 293 B7
Milton of Dalcapon Perth 286 B3
Milton of Drimmie Perth 286 B5
Milton of Edradour Perth 286 B3
Milton of Gollanfield Highld 301 D7
Milton of Lesmore Aberds 302 G4
Milton of Logie Aberds 292 C6
Milton of Machany Perth 286 F3
Milton of Mathers Aberds 293 G9
Milton of Murtle Aberdeen 293 C10
Milton of Noth Aberds 302 G5
Milton of Tullich Aberds 292 D5
Milton on Stour Dorset 30 B3
Milton Regis Kent 70 F2
Milton Street E Sus 23 E8
Milton under Wychwood Oxon 82 B3
Milverton Som 27 B10
Warks 118 D6
Milwich Staffs 151 C9
Milwr Flint 181 G11
Mimbridge Sur 66 G3
Minard Argyll 275 D10
Minard Castle Argyll 275 D10
Minchington Dorset 31 E7
Minchinhampton Glos 80 E5
Mindrum Northumb 263 C8
Minehead Som 42 D3
Minera Wrex 166 E3
Mineshope Corn 11 B9
Minety Wilts 81 G8
Minffordd Gwyn 145 B11
Gwyn 146 G4
Gwyn 179 G9
Mingarrypark Highld 289 C8
Mingoose Corn 4 F4
Miningsby Lincs 174 C4
Minions Corn 11 G11
Minishant S Ayrs 257 G8
Minllyn Gwyn 147 G7
Minnes Aberds 303 G9
Minngearraidh W Isles 297 J3
Minnigaff Dumfries 236 C6
Minnonie Aberds 303 C7
Minnow End Essex 88 C2
Minnygap Dumfries 248 D2
Minshull Vernon Ches E 167 C11
Minskip N Yorks 215 G7
Minstead Hants 32 E3
Minsted W Sus 34 C5
Minster Kent 70 E3
Kent 71 G10
Minsterley Shrops 131 C7
Minster Lovell Oxon 82 C4
Minsterworth Glos 80 B3
Minterne Magna Dorset 29 G11
Minterne Parva Dorset 29 G11
Minting Lincs 189 G11
Mintlaw Aberds 303 E10
Minto Borders 262 E3
Minto Kames Borders 262 E3
Minton Shrops 131 E8
Mintsfeet Cumb 221 G10
Minwear Pembs 73 C8
Minworth W Mid 134 E3
Mirbister Orkney 314 E2
Mirehouse Cumb 219 B9
Mireland Highld 310 C7
Mirfield W Yorks 197 D8
Miserden Glos 80 D6
Misery Corner Norf 142 F5
Miskin Rhondda 58 C4
Rhondda 77 F8
Misselfore Wilts 31 C8
Misson Notts 187 C11
Misterton Leics 135 G11
Notts 188 C3
Som 29 F7
Misterton Soss Notts 188 B3
Mistley Essex 108 E2
Mistley Heath Essex 108 E2
Mitcham London 67 F9
Mitcheldean Glos 79 B11
Mitchell Corn 5 E7
Mitchell Hill Borders 260 C3
Mitchellslacks Dumfries 247 D11
Mitchelston Borders 271 F9
Mitchel Troy Mon 79 C7
Mitcheltroy Common Mon 79 D7
Mite Houses Cumb 219 F11
Mitford Northumb 252 F5
Mithian Corn 4 E4
Mithian Downs Corn 4 F4
Mitton Staffs 151 F7
Worcs 99 E8
Mixbury Oxon 102 E2
Mixenden W Yorks 196 B5
Mixtow Corn 6 E2
Moat Cumb 239 C10
Moats Tye Suff 125 F10
Mobberley Ches E 184 F3
Staffs 169 G8
Moblake Ches E 167 G11
Mobwell Bucks 84 E5
Moccas Hereford 97 C7
Mochdre Conwy 180 F4
Powys 129 F11
Mochrum Dumfries 236 E5
Mockbeggar Hants 31 F11
Kent 54 E6
Medway 69 E8
Mockerkin Cumb 229 G7
Moclett Orkney 314 B4
Modbury Devon 8 E3
Moddershall Staffs 151 B8
Model Village Derbys 187 G8
Warks 119 E8
Modest Corner Kent 52 E5
Moelfre Anglesey 179 D8
Conwy 181 G7
Powys 148 D3
Moel Tryfan Gwyn 163 D8
Moel-y-crio Flint 165 B11
Moffat Dumfries 248 B3
Moffat Mills N Lnrk 268 C5
Mogador Sur 51 C8
Moggerhanger C Beds 104 B2
Mogworthy Devon 26 D5
Moira Leics 152 F6
Moity Powys 96 C3
Molash Kent 54 C4
Mol-chlach Highld 294 D6
Mold Flint 166 C2
Moldgreen W Yorks 197 D7
Molehill Green Essex 105 G11
Essex 106 G4
Molescroft E Yorks 208 E6
Molesden Northumb 252 G4
Molesworth Cambs 121 B11
Molinnis Corn 5 D10
Moll Highld 295 B7
Molland Devon 26 B4
Mollington Ches W 182 G5
Oxon 101 B8
Mollinsburn N Lnrk 278 G4
Monachty Ceredig 111 E10
Monachylemore Stirl 285 F8
Monar Lodge Highld 300 E2
Monaughty Powys 114 D4
Monboddo House Aberds 293 F9
Mondaytown Shrops 130 B6
Mondynes Aberds 293 F9
Monemore Stirl 285 D9
Monevechadan Argyll 284 G5
Monewden Suff 126 F4
Moneyacres E Ayrs 267 E8
Moneydie Perth 286 E4
Moneyhill Herts 85 G8
Money Hill Leics 153 F7
Moneyrow Green Windsor 65 D11
Moneystone Staffs 169 F9
Mongleath Corn 3 C7
Moniaive Dumfries 247 E7
Monifieth Angus 287 D8
Monikie Angus 287 D8
Monimail Fife 286 F6
Monington Pembs 92 C2
Monk Bretton S Yorks 197 F11
Monk End N Yorks 224 D5
Monken Hadley London 86 F3
Monkerton Devon 14 C5
Monk Fryston N Yorks 198 B4
Monk Hesleden Durham 234 D5
Monkhide Hereford 98 C2
Monkhill Cumb 239 F8
W Yorks 198 C3
Monkhopton Shrops 132 E2
Monkland Hereford 115 F9
Monkleigh Devon 25 C7
Monknash V Glam 58 E2
Monkokehampton Devon 25 F9
Monkscross Corn 12 G3
Monkseaton T&W 243 C8
Monks Eleigh Suff 107 B9
Monk's Gate W Sus 36 B2
Monks Heath Ches E 184 G4
Monk Sherborne Hants 48 B6
Monkshill Aberds 303 E7
Monks Hill Kent 53 E11
Monksilver Som 42 F5
Monks Kirby Warks 135 G9
Monk Soham Suff 126 D4
Monks Orchard London 67 F11
Monk's Park Wilts 61 F11
Monkspath W Mid 118 B2
Monks Risborough Bucks 84 E4
Monksthorpe Lincs 174 B6
Monkston Park M Keynes 103 D7
Monk Street Essex 106 F2
Monkswood Midloth 270 C6
Mon 78 E4
W Yorks 206 F2
Monkton Devon 27 G11
Kent 71 G9
Pembs 73 E7
S Ayrs 257 D9
T&W 243 E8
V Glam 58 E2
Monkton Combe Bath 61 G9
Monkton Deverill Wilts 45 F11
Monkton Farleigh Wilts 61 F10
Monktonhall E Loth 280 G6
Monkton Heathfield Som 28 B3
Monkton Up Wimborne Dorset 31 E8
Monkwearmouth T&W 243 F9
Monkwood Hants 49 G7
Monkwood Green Worcs 116 E6
Monmarsh Hereford 97 B10
Monmore Green W Mid 133 D8
Monmouth Cap Mon 97 F7
Monmouth / Trefynwy Mon 79 C8
Monnington on Wye Hereford 97 C7
Monreith Dumfries 236 E5
Monreith Mains Dumfries 236 E5
Montacute Som 29 D7
Montcliffe Gtr Man 195 E7
Montcoffer Ho Aberds 302 C6
Montford Argyll 266 C2
Shrops 149 G8
Montford Bridge Shrops 149 F8
Montgarrie Aberds 293 B7
Montgomery Powys 130 D4
Montgomery Lines Hants 49 C11
Monton Gtr Man 184 B3
Montpelier Bristol 60 E5
Montrave Fife 287 G7
Montrose Angus 287 B11
Montsale Essex 89 F8
Monwode Lea Warks 134 E5
Monxton Hants 47 E10
Monyash Derbys 169 B11
Monymusk Aberds 293 B8
Monzie Perth 286 E2
Monzie Castle Perth 286 E2
Moodiesburn N Lnrk 278 G3
Moolham Som 28 E5
Moon's Green Kent 38 B5
Moon's Moat Worcs 117 D11
Moonzie Fife 287 F7
Moor Som 28 D6
Mooradale Shetland 312 F6
Moor Allerton W Yorks 205 F11
Mooray Wilts 46 G3
Moorby Lincs 174 C3
Moorclose Cumb 228 F5
Gtr Man 195 F11
Moor Common Bucks 84 G4
Moorcot Hereford 115 F7
Moor Crichel Dorset 31 F7
Moor Cross Devon 8 D2
Moordown Bmouth 19 C7
Moore Halton 183 E9
Moor Edge W Yorks 205 F7
Moorend Cumb 239 G8
Derbys 170 F2
Dumfries 239 C7
Glos 80 C5
Glos 80 E2
Gtr Man 185 D7
S Glos 61 D7
Moor End Bucks 84 G4
Cambs 105 B7
C Beds 103 G9
Durham 234 C2
E Yorks 208 F2
Glos 99 G9
Lancs 202 E3
N Yorks 207 F7
N Yorks 215 G7
S Yorks 197 G9
Worcs 117 E8
W Yorks 196 B5
W Yorks 206 D4
York 207 B9
Moorend Cross Hereford 98 B4
Moor End Field N Yorks 215 F8
Moorends S Yorks 199 D7
Moorfield Derbys 185 C8
Moorgate Norf 160 C3
S Yorks 186 C6
Moorgreen Hants 33 D7
Notts 171 F7
Moor Green Herts 104 F6
Staffs 169 G7
Wilts 61 F11
W Mid 133 G11
Moorhaigh Notts 171 C8
Moorhall Derbys 186 G4
Moor Hall W Mid 134 D2
Moorhampton Hereford 97 B7
Moorhaven Village Devon 8 D3
Moorhayne Devon 28 F2
Moorhead W Yorks 205 F8
Moor Head W Yorks 197 B8
W Yorks 197 E8
Moorhey Gtr Man 196 G2
Moorhole S Yorks 186 E6
Moorhouse Cumb 239 F8
Cumb 239 G7
Notts 172 B3
S Yorks 198 E3
Moorhouse Bank Sur 52 C2
Moorhouses Lincs 174 D3
Moorland or Northmoor Green Som 43 G10
Moorledge Bath 60 G5
Moorlinch Som 43 F11
Moor Monkton N Yorks 206 B6
Moor Monkton Moor N Yorks 206 B6
Moor of Balvack Aberds 293 B8
Moor of Granary Moray 301 D10
Moor of Ravenstone Dumfries 236 E5
Moor Park Cumb 229 D7
Hereford 97 C9

Moor Park *continued*

Herts.	85	G9
Sur.	49	D11
Moor Row Cumb.	219	C10
Cumb.	229	B10
Moorsholm Redcar.	226	C3
Moorside Ches W.	182	F3
Dorset.	30	D3
Durham.	233	B7
Gtr Man.	195	G9
Gtr Man.	196	F3
W Yorks.	197	B8
W Yorks.	205	H10
Moor Side Lancs.	202	F5
Lancs.	202	G4
Lincs.	174	D2
Lincs.	190	D6
W Yorks.	197	B7
W Yorks.	204	F6
Moorstock Kent.	54	F6
Moor Street Kent.	69	F10
Moorswater Corn.	6	C4
Moorthorpe W Yorks.	198	E3
Moor Top W Yorks.	197	C7
Moortown Devon.	12	B2
Devon.	12	G6
Devon.	25	C8
Hants.	31	G11
IoW.	20	E4
Lincs.	189	B9
Telford.	150	F2
W Yorks.	206	F2
Morangie Highld.	309	L7
Morar Highld.	295	F8

Moravian Settlement

Derbys.	153	B8
Morawelon Anglesey.	178	E3
Morayhill Highld.	301	E7
Morborne Cambs.	138	E2
Morchard Bishop Devon.	26	F3
Morchard Road Devon.	26	G3
Morcombelake Dorset.	16	C4
Morcott Rutland.	137	C8
Morda Shrops.	148	D5
Morden Dorset.	18	B4
London.	67	F9
Morden Green Cambs.	104	C5
Morden Park London.	67	E8
Mordiford Hereford.	97	D11

Mordington Holdings

Borders.	273	D8
Mordon Durham.	234	F2
More Shrops.	130	E6
Morebath Devon.	27	C7
Morebattle Borders.	263	E7
Morecambe Lancs.	211	G8
More Crichel Dorset.	31	F7
Moredon Swindon.	62	B6
Moredun Edin.	280	B5
Morefield Highld.	307	K6
Morehall Kent.	55	F8
Morelaggan Argyll.	284	G6
Moreleigh Devon.	8	E5
Morenish Perth.	285	D9
Moresby Cumb.	228	G5
Moresby Parks Cumb.	219	B9
Morestead Hants.	33	B8
Moreton Dorset.	18	D2
Essex.	87	D8
Hereford.	115	D10
Mers.	182	C3
Oxon.	82	E6
Oxon.	83	E11
Staffs.	150	F5
Staffs.	152	D2

Moreton Corbet

Shrops.	149	E11

Moretonhampstead

Devon.	13	D11
Moreton-in-Marsh Glos.	100	E4

Moreton Jeffries

Hereford.	98	B2
Moreton Morrell Warks.	118	F6

Moreton on Lugg

Hereford.	97	B10
Moreton Paddox Warks.	118	G6

Moreton Pinkney

Northants.	101	B11
Moreton Say Shrops.	150	C2
Moreton Valence Glos.	80	D3
Moretonwood Shrops.	150	C2
Morfa Carms.	56	B4
Carms.	75	C9
Ceredig.	110	G6
Gwyn.	144	C3
Morfa Bach Carms.	74	C5
Morfa Bychan Gwyn.	145	B10
Morfa Dinlle Gwyn.	162	D6
Morfa Glas Neath.	76	D5
Morfa Nefyn Gwyn.	162	G3
Morfydd Denb.	165	E10
Morganstown Cardiff.	58	C6
Morgan's Vale Wilts.	31	C11
Moriah Ceredig.	112	B2
Mork Glos.	79	D9
Morland Cumb.	231	G7
Morley Ches E.	184	E4
Derbys.	170	G5
Durham.	233	F8
W Yorks.	197	B9
Morley Green Ches E.	184	E4
Morleymoor Derbys.	170	G5
Morley Park Derbys.	170	F5

Morley St Botolph

Norf.	141	D11
Morley Smithy Derbys.	170	G5
Mornick Corn.	12	G2
Morningside Edin.	280	G3
N Lnrk.	268	D6
Morningthorpe Norf.	142	E4
Morpeth Northumb.	252	F6
Morphie Aberds.	293	G9
Morrey Staffs.	152	F2
Morridge Side Staffs.	169	E8
Morrilow Heath Staffs.	151	B9
Morris Green Essex.	106	E4

Morriston / Treforys

Swansea.	57	B7
Morristown V Glam.	59	E7
Morston Norf.	177	E8
Mortehoe Devon.	40	D3
Morthen S Yorks.	187	D7
Mortimer W Berks.	65	G7

Mortimer's Cross

Hereford.	115	E8

Mortimer West End

Hants.	64	G6
Mortlake London.	67	D8
Mortomley S Yorks.	186	B4
Morton Cumb.	230	D4
Cumb.	239	G9
Derbys.	170	C6
IoW.	21	D8
Lincs.	155	E11
Lincs.	172	C5
Lincs.	188	C4
Norf.	160	F2
Notts.	172	E2
S Glos.	79	G10
Shrops.	148	E5

Morton Bagot Warks.	118	E2
Morton Common Shrops.	148	E5
Morton Mains Dumfries.	247	D9
Morton Mill Shrops.	149	E11

Morton-on-Swale

N Yorks.	224	G6
Morton Spirit Warks.	117	G10

Morton Tinmouth

Durham.	233	G9

Morton Underhill

Worcs.	117	F10
Morvah Corn.	1	B4
Morval Corn.	6	D5
Morven Lodge Aberds.	292	C5
Morvich Highld.	295	C11
Highld.	309	J7
Morville Shrops.	132	E3
Morville Heath Shrops.	132	E3
Morwellham Quay Devon.	7	B8
Morwenstow Corn.	24	E2
Mosborough S Yorks.	186	E6
Moscow E Ayrs.	267	G9
Mose Shrops.	132	E5
Mosedale Cumb.	230	E3
Moseley W Mid.	133	D8
W Mid.	116	F6
Worcs.	117	E10

Moses Gate Gtr Man. | 195 | F8 |

Mosley Common

Gtr Man.	195	G8
Moss Argyll.	288	E1
Highld.	289	C8
S Yorks.	198	E5
Wrex.	166	E4
Mossat Aberds.	292	B6
Mossbank Shetland.	312	F6
Moss Bank Halton.	183	D8
Mers.	183	B8
Mossbay Cumb.	228	F5
Mossblown S Ayrs.	257	E10
Mossbrow Gtr Man.	184	D2
Mossburnford Borders.	262	F5
Mossdale Dumfries.	237	B8
Mossedge Cumb.	239	D11
Moss Edge Lancs.	202	D4
Lancs.	202	E4
Moss End Brack.	65	E11
Ches E.	183	F11
Mosser Mains Cumb.	229	F8
Mossfield Highld.	300	B6
Mossgate Staffs.	151	B8
Mossgiel E Ayrs.	257	D11
Mosshouses Borders.	262	B2
Moss Houses Ches E.	184	G5
Mossley Ches E.	287	B8
Moss Lane Ches E.	184	G6
Mossley Ches E.	168	C5
Gtr Man.	196	G3
Mossley Brow Gtr Man.	196	G3
Mossley Hill Mers.	182	D5
Moss Nook Gtr Man.	184	D4
Mers.	183	C8

Moss of Barmuckity

Moray.	302	C2
Moss of Meft Moray.	302	C2
Mosspark Glasgow.	267	C10
Moss Pit Staffs.	151	E8
Moss Side Cumb.	238	G5
Lancs.	184	B4
Moss-side Highld.	301	D8
Moss Side Lancs.	193	G11
Lancs.	194	C4
Lancs.	202	G3
Mers.	182	B6
Moss-side Moray.	302	D5
Mosstodloch Moray.	302	D3
Mosston Angus.	287	C9
Mossy Lea Lancs.	194	E4
Mosterton Dorset.	29	F7
Moston Ches E.	168	C2
Ches W.	182	G6
Gtr Man.	195	G11
Shrops.	149	D11
Moston Green Ches E.	168	C2
Mostyn Flint.	181	E11
Mostyn Quay Flint.	181	E11
Motcombe Dorset.	30	B5
Mothecombe Devon.	8	F2
Motherby Cumb.	230	F4
Motherwell N Lnrk.	268	D5
Motspur Park London.	68	E2
Mottingham London.	68	E2
Mottisfont Hants.	32	B4
Mottistone IoW.	20	E4

Mottram in Longdendale

Gtr Man.	185	B7
Mottram Rise Gtr Man.	185	B7

Mottram St Andrew

Ches E.	184	F5
Mott's Green Essex.	87	B8
Mott's Mill E Sus.	52	F4
Mouldsworth Ches W.	183	G8
Moulin Perth.	286	B3
Moulsecoomb Brighton.	36	F4
Moulsford Oxon.	64	C5
Moulsham Essex.	88	D2
Moulsoe M Keynes.	103	C8
Moultavie Highld.	300	B6
Moulton Ches W.	167	B11
Lincs.	156	E6
Northants.	120	D5
N Yorks.	224	E4
Suff.	124	E3
V Glam.	58	E5
Moulton Chapel Lincs.	156	F5
Moulton Eaugate Lincs.	156	F6
Moulton Park Northants.	120	E5
Moulton St Mary Norf.	143	B7
Moulton Seas End Lincs.	156	D6
Moulzie Angus.	292	F4
Mounie Castle Aberds.	303	G7
Mount Corn.	4	D5
Corn.	6	B2
Highld.	301	E9
W Yorks.	196	D5
Mountain Anglesey.	178	G2
W Yorks.	205	G7
Mountain Air Bl Gwent.	77	D11

Mountain Ash / Aberpennar

Rhondda.	77	F8
Mountain Bower Wilts.	61	D10
Mountain Cross Borders.	270	F2
Mountain Street Kent.	54	C5
Mountain Water Pembs.	91	G8
Mount Ambrose Corn.	4	G4
Mount Ballan Mon.	60	B3
Mount Batten Plym.	7	E9
Mountbenger Borders.	261	D8

Mountbengerburn

Borders.	261	D8
Mountblow W Dunb.	277	G9
Mount Bovers Essex.	88	G4
Mount Bures Essex.	107	E8
Mount Canisp Highld.	301	B7
Mount Charles Corn.	5	B10
Corn.	5	E10
Mount Cowdown Wilts.	47	C9
Mount End Essex.	87	E7
Mount Ephraim E Sus.	23	B7

Mounters Dorset.	30	D3
Mountfield E Sus.	38	C2
Mountgerald Highld.	300	C5
Mount Gould Plym.	7	D9
Mount Hawke Corn.	4	F4
Mount Hermon Corn.	2	F6
Sur.	50	B4
Mount Hill S Glos.	61	E7
Mountjoy Corn.	5	C7
Mount Lane Devon.	12	B3
Mountnessing Essex.	87	F10
Mounton Mon.	79	G8
Mount Pleasant Bucks.	102	E3
Ches E.	168	D4
Corn.	5	C10
Derbys.	152	D6
Derbys.	152	F5
Derbys.	170	F4
Devon.	27	G11
Durham.	233	E11
E Sus.	23	E7
E Sus.	36	D6
Flint.	182	G2
Hants.	19	B11
Kent.	71	F10
London.	85	G8
M Tydf.	77	F9
Neath.	57	B9
Norf.	141	E9
Pembs.	73	D8
Shrops.	149	G9
Stockton.	234	G4
Stoke.	168	G5
Suff.	106	B4
T&W.	243	E7
Warks.	135	F7
Worcs.	99	D10
Worcs.	117	E10
Mount Sion Wrex.	166	E3
Mount Skippett Oxon.	82	B5
Mountsolie Aberds.	303	D9
Mountsorrel Leics.	153	F11
Mount Sorrel Wilts.	31	C8
Mount Tabor W Yorks.	196	B5
Mount Vernon Glasgow.	268	C3
Mount Wise Corn.	7	E9
Mousehill Sur.	50	E2
Mousehole Corn.	1	D5
Mousen Northumb.	264	C4
Mousley End Warks.	118	D4
Mouswald Dumfries.	238	C3
Mouth Mill Devon.	24	B3
Mowbreck Lancs.	202	G4
Mow Cop Ches E.	168	D5
Mowden Darl.	224	B5
Essex.	88	C3
Mowhaugh Borders.	263	E8

Mowmacre Hill

Leicester.	135	B11
Mowshurst Kent.	52	D3
Mowsley Leics.	136	F2
Moxby N Yorks.	215	F11
Moxley W Mid.	133	D9
Moy Argyll.	255	E8
Highld.	290	E6
Highld.	301	F7
Moy Hall Highld.	301	F7
Moy Ho Moray.	301	C10
Moyles Court Hants.	31	F11

Moylgrove / Trewyddel

Pembs.	92	C2
Moy Lodge Highld.	290	E6
Muasdale Argyll.	255	C7
Muchalls Aberds.	293	D11
Much Birch Hereford.	97	E10
Much Cowarde Hereford.	98	B1
Much Cowarne Hereford.	98	B2

Much Dewchurch

Hereford.	97	E9
Muchelney Som.	28	C6
Muchelney Ham Som.	28	C6
Much Hadham Herts.	86	B5
Much Hoole Lancs.	194	C3

Much Hoole Moss Houses

Lancs.	194	C3

Much Hoole Town

Lancs.	194	C3
Muchlarnick Corn.	6	D4
Much Marcle Hereford.	98	E3
Muchrachd Highld.	300	F2
Much Wenlock Shrops.	132	C2
Muckairn Argyll.	289	F11
Muckernich Aberds.	300	D5
Mucking Thurrock.	69	C7
Muckle Breck Shetland.	312	G7
Muckleford Dorset.	17	C8
Mucklestone Staffs.	150	B4
Muckleton Norf.	158	B6
Shrops.	149	E11
Muckletown Aberds.	302	G5
Muckley Shrops.	132	D2
Muckley Corner Staffs.	133	B11
Muckley Cross Shrops.	132	D2
Muckton Lincs.	190	E5
Muckton Bottom Lincs.	190	E5
Mudale Highld.	308	F5
Mudd Ches E.	185	C7
Muddiford Devon.	40	F5
Muddlebridge Devon.	40	G4
Muddles Green E Sus.	23	C8
Mudeford Dorset.	19	C9
Mudford Som.	29	D9
Mudford Sock Som.	29	D9
Mudgley Som.	44	D2
Mugdock Stirl.	277	F11
Mugeary Highld.	294	B6
Muggington Derbys.	170	G3

Muggintonlane End

Derbys.	170	G3
Muggleswick Durham.	232	B6
Mugswell Sur.	51	C9
Muie Highld.	309	J6
Muir Aberds.	292	E2
Muirden Aberds.	303	D7
Muirdrum Angus.	287	D9
Muiredge Fife.	281	B7
Muirend Glasgow.	267	C11
Muirhead Angus.	287	D7
Fife.	286	G6
Fife.	287	F8
N Lnrk.	268	B3
S Ayrs.	257	C8
Muirhouse Edin.	280	F4
N Lnrk.	268	D5
Muirhouselaw Borders.	262	D4
Muirhouses Falk.	279	E10
Muirkirk E Ayrs.	258	E5
Muirmill Stirl.	278	E4
Muir of Alford Aberds.	293	B7
Muir of Fairburn Highld.	300	D4
Muir of Fowlis Aberds.	293	B7
Muir of Kinellar		
Aberds.	293	B10
Muir of Miltonduff		
Moray.	301	D11
Muir of Ord Highld.	300	D5
Muir of Pert Angus.	287	D8
Muirshearlich Highld.	290	E3
Muirskie Aberds.	293	D10

Muirtack Aberds.	303	F9
Aberds.	303	D7
Highld.	301	C7
Perth.	286	C5
Perth.	286	F3
Muirton Mains Highld.	300	D4

Muirton of Ardblair

Perth.	286	C5

Muirton of Ballochy

Angus.	293	G8
Muiryfold Aberds.	303	D7
Muker N Yorks.	223	F8
Mulbarton Norf.	142	C3
Mulben Moray.	302	D3
Mulberry Corn.	5	B10
Mulfra Corn.	1	C5
Mulindry Argyll.	254	B4
Mulla Shetland.	313	G6
Mulladoch House		
Highld.	300	F2
Mullenspond Hants.	47	D9
Mullion Corn.	2	B2
Mullion Cove Corn.	2	F5
Mumbles Hill Swansea.	56	D6
Mumby Lincs.	191	G8
Mumps Gtr Man.	196	F2
Mundale Moray.	301	D10
Munderfield Row		
Hereford.	116	G2
Munderfield Stocks		
Hereford.	116	G2
Mundesley Norf.	160	B6
Mundford Norf.	140	E6
Mundham Norf.	142	D6
Mundon Essex.	88	E5
Mundurno Aberdeen.	293	B11
Mundy Bois Kent.	54	D2
Munerigie Highld.	290	C4
Muness Shetland.	312	C8
Mungasdale Highld.	307	K4
Mungrisdale Cumb.	230	E3
Munlochy Highld.	300	D6
Munsary Cottage Highld.	310	E6
Munsley Hereford.	98	C3
Munslow Shrops.	131	F10
Munstone Hereford.	97	C10
Murch V Glam.	59	E7
Murchington Devon.	13	D9
Murcot Worcs.	99	C11
Murcott Oxon.	83	B9
Wilts.	81	G7
Murdieston Stirl.	278	B3
Murdishaw Halton.	183	E9
Murieston W Loth.	269	C11
Murkle Highld.	310	C5
Murlaggan Highld.	290	D2
Highld.	290	E5
Murra Orkney.	314	F2
Murrayfield Edin.	280	G4
Murrayshall Perth.	286	E5
Murraythwaite Dumfries.	238	C4
Murrell Green Hants.	49	B8
Murrell's End Glos.	98	E4
Glos.	98	G5
Murrion Shetland.	312	F4
Murrow Cambs.	139	B7
Mursley Bucks.	102	F6
Murston Kent.	70	G2
Murthill Angus.	287	B8
Murthly Perth.	286	D4
Murton Cumb.	231	G10
Durham.	234	B3
Northumb.	273	F9
Swansea.	56	D5
T&W.	243	G8
York.	207	C8

Murton Grange

N Yorks.	215	B10
Murtwell Devon.	8	D5
Musbury Devon.	15	C11
Muscliff Bmouth.	19	B7
Muscoates N Yorks.	216	C3
Muscott Northants.	120	E2
Musdale Argyll.	289	G11

Mushroom Green

W Mid.	133	F8
Musselburgh E Loth.	280	G6
Musselwick Pembs.	72	D4
Mustard Hyrn Norf.	161	F8
Muston Leics.	154	B6
N Yorks.	217	D11
Mustow Green Worcs.	117	C7
Muswell Hill London.	86	G3
Mutehill Dumfries.	237	E8
Mutford Suff.	143	F9
Muthill Perth.	286	F2
Mutley Plym.	7	D9
Mutterton Devon.	27	G8
Mutton Hall E Sus.	37	C8
Muxton Telford.	150	G4
Mwdwl-eithin Flint.	181	F11
Mwynbwll Flint.	165	B11
Mybster Highld.	310	D5
Myddfai Carms.	94	F5
Myddle Shrops.	149	E9
Myddlewood Shrops.	149	E9
Myddyn-fych Carms.	75	C10
Mydroilyn Ceredig.	111	F9
Myerscough Lancs.	202	F5

Myerscough Smithy

Lancs.	203	G8
Mylor Bridge Corn.	3	B8
Mylor Churchtown Corn.	3	B8
Mynachdy Cardiff.	59	D7
Rhondda.	77	F8
Mynachog-ddu Pembs.	92	C2
Mynydd Cardiff.	59	C7
Mynd Llandegau		
Gwyn.	163	B10
Myndtown Shrops.	131	F7
Mynydd Bach Ceredig.	112	B4
Mynydd-bach Mon.	79	G7
Swansea.	57	B7
Mynydd-bach-y-glo		
Swansea.	56	B6
Mynydd Bodafon		
Anglesey.	179	D7
Mynydd Fflint / Flint		
Mountain Flint.	182	G2
Mynydd Gilan Gwyn.	144	E5
Mynydd-isa Flint.	166	C3
Mynyddislwyn Caerph.	77	G11
Mynydd-llan Flint.	181	G11
Mynydd Marian Conwy.	180	F5
Mynydd Mechell		
Anglesey.	178	D5
Mynyddygarreg Carms.	74	D6
Mynytho Gwyn.	144	C6
Myrebird Aberds.	293	D9
Myreside Perth.	286	E6
Myrtle Hill Carms.	94	E5
Mytchett Sur.	49	B11
Mytchett Place Sur.	49	C11
Mytholm W Yorks.	196	B3
Mytholmes W Yorks.	204	F6
Mytholmroyd W Yorks.	196	B4
Mythop Lancs.	202	G3
Mytice Aberds.	302	F4
Myton N Yorks.	118	E6
Myton Hall N Yorks.	215	F8

Myton-on-Swale

N Yorks.	215	F8
Mytton Shrops.	149	F8

N

Naast Highld.	307	L3
Nab Hill W Yorks.	197	D7
Nab's Head Lancs.	194	B6
Nab Wood W Yorks.	205	F8
Naburn York.	207	D7
Naccolt Kent.	54	E4
Nackington Kent.	55	C7
Nacton Suff.	108	C4
Nadderwater Devon.	14	C3
Nafferton E Yorks.	209	B7
Na Gearrannan W Isles.	304	D3
Nag's Head Glos.	80	F5
Naid-y-march Flint.	181	F11
Nailbridge Glos.	79	B10
Nailsbourne Som.	28	B2
Nailsea N Som.	60	D3
Nailstone Leics.	135	B8
Nailsworth Glos.	80	F5
Nailwell Bath.	61	G8
Nairn Highld.	301	D8
Nalderswood Sur.	51	E8
Nance Corn.	4	G3
Nanceddan Corn.	2	C2
Nancegollan Corn.	2	C5
Nancemellin Corn.	4	G2
Nancenoy Corn.	2	D6
Nancledra Corn.	1	C5
Nangreaves Lancs.	195	D10
Nanhoron Gwyn.	144	C5
Nanhyfer / Nevern		
Pembs.	91	D11
Nannau Gwyn.	146	E4
Nannerch Flint.	165	B11
Nanpantan Leics.	153	F10
Nanpean Corn.	5	D9
Nanquidno Corn.	1	D3
Nanstallon Corn.	5	B10
Nant Carms.	74	B6
Denb.	165	D11
Nant Alyn Flint.	165	B11
Nant-ddu Powys.	77	B8
Nanternis Ceredig.	111	F7
Nantgaredig Carms.	93	G9
Nantgarw Rhondda.	58	B6
Nant-glas Powys.	113	E9
Nantglyn Denb.	165	C8
Nantgwyn Powys.	113	B9
Nantithet Corn.	2	E5
Nantlle Gwyn.	163	E8
Nantmawr Shrops.	148	E5
Nantmel Powys.	113	D10
Nantmor Gwyn.	163	F10
Nant Peris / Old Llanberis		
Gwyn.	163	D10
Nantserth Powys.	113	C9
Nant Uchaf Denb.	165	D8
Nantwich Ches E.	167	E11
Nant-y-Bai Carms.	94	C5
Nant-y-Bwch Bl Gwent.	77	D10
Nant-y-cafn Neath.	76	D4
Nantycaws Carms.	75	B7
Nant-y Caws Shrops.	148	D5
Nant-y-ceisiad Caerph.	59	B8
Nant-y-derry Mon.	78	D4
Nant-y-felin Conwy.	179	G11
Nant-y-ffin Carms.	93	E11
Nantyffyllon Bridgend.	57	C11
Nantyglo Bl Gwent.	77	D11
Nant-y-gollen Shrops.	148	D5
Nant-y-moel Bridgend.	76	G6
Nant-y-pandy Conwy.	179	G11
Nant-y-Rhiw Conwy.	164	D4

Nantyronen Station

Ceredig.	112	B3
Napchester Kent.	55	D10
Naphill Bucks.	84	F4
Napleton Worcs.	99	B7
Napley Staffs.	150	B4
Napley Heath Staffs.	150	B4
Nappa N Yorks.	204	C3
Nappa Scar N Yorks.	223	G9
Napton on the Hill		
Warks.	119	E10
Narberth / Arberth		
Pembs.	73	C10
Narberth Bridge Pembs.	73	C10
Narborough Leics.	135	D10
Norf.	158	G4
Narkurs Corn.	6	D6
Narracott Devon.	25	D7

Narrowgate Corner

Norf.	161	F8
Nasareth Gwyn.	163	E7
Naseby Northants.	120	B3
Nash Bucks.	102	E5
Hereford.	114	E6
Kent.	55	B9
London.	68	G2
Newport.	59	C10
Shrops.	116	C2
Som.	29	B8
Nashend Glos.	80	D5
Nash End Worcs.	132	G5
Nashes Green Hants.	49	D7
Nash Lee Bucks.	84	D4
Nash Mills Herts.	85	D9
Nash Street Sus.	23	C8
Kent.	68	F6
Nassington Northants.	137	D11
Nastend Glos.	80	D3
Nast Hyde Herts.	86	D2
Nasty Herts.	105	G7
Natcott Devon.	24	C3
Nateby Cumb.	222	D5
Lancs.	202	E5
Nately Scures Hants.	49	C8
Natland Cumb.	211	B10
Natton Glos.	99	E8
Naughton Suff.	107	B10
Naunton Glos.	100	G2
Naunton Beauchamp		
Worcs.	117	G9
Navant Hill W Sus.	34	B6
Navenby Lincs.	173	D7
Navestock Heath Essex.	87	F8
Navestock Side Essex.	87	F9
Navidale Highld.	311	H4
Navity Highld.	301	C7
Nawton N Yorks.	216	C3
Nayland Suff.	107	E9
Nazeing Essex.	86	D6
Nazeing Gate Essex.	86	D6
Nazeing Long Green		
Essex.	86	E6
Nazeing Mead Essex.	86	D5
Neacroft Hants.	19	B9
N Som.	60	G4
Neal's Green Warks.	134	G5
Neames Forstal Kent.	54	B5
Neap Shetland.	313	H7

Near Hardcastle

N Yorks.	214	F2
Near Sawrey Cumb.	221	F7
Nearton End Bucks.	102	F6
Neasden London.	67	B8
Neasham Darl.	224	C6
Neat Enstone Oxon.	101	G7
Neath / Castell-nedd		
Neath.	57	B8
Neatishead Norf.	160	E6
Neaton Norf.	141	C8
Nebo Anglesey.	179	C7
Ceredig.	111	D10
Conwy.	164	D5
Gwyn.	163	E7
Necton Norf.	141	B7
Nedd Highld.	306	F6
Nedderton Northumb.	252	G6
Nedge Hill Telford.	132	B4
Nedging Suff.	107	B9
Nedging Tye Suff.	107	B10
Needham Norf.	142	G4
Needham Green Essex.	87	B9
Needham Market Suff.	125	G11
Needham Street Suff.	124	D4
Needingworth Cambs.	122	C6
Needwood Staffs.	152	E3
Neen Savage Shrops.	116	B3
Neen Sollars Shrops.	116	C3
Neenton Shrops.	132	F2
Nefod Shrops.	148	B6
Nefyn Gwyn.	162	G4
Neighbourne Som.	44	D6
Neight Hill Worcs.	117	F8
Neilston E Renf.	267	D9
Neinthirion Powys.	129	B9
Neithrop Oxon.	101	C8

Nelly Andrews Green

Powys.	130	B5
Nelson Caerph.	77	F10
Lancs.	204	F3
Nelson Village Northumb.	243	B7
Nemphlar S Lnrk.	269	G7

Nempnett Thrubwell

N Som.	60	G4
Nene Terrace Lincs.	138	B5
Nenthall Cumb.	231	B11
Nenthead Cumb.	231	C11
Nenthorn Borders.	262	B5
Neopardy Devon.	13	B11
Nepcote W Sus.	35	F10
Nepgill Cumb.	229	F7
Nep Town W Sus.	36	D2
Nerabus Argyll.	254	B3
Nercwys Flint.	166	C2
Nerston S Lnrk.	268	D2
Nesbit Northumb.	263	C11
Ness Ches W.	182	F4
Orkney.	314	C4
Nesscliffe Shrops.	149	F7
Nessholt Ches W.	182	F4
Nesstoun Orkney.	314	A7
Neston Ches W.	182	F3
Wilts.	61	F11
Netchells Green		
W Mid.	133	F11
Netham Bristol.	60	E6
Nethanfoot S Lnrk.	268	F6
Nether Alderley Ches E.	184	F4
Netheravon Wilts.	46	D6
Nether Blainslie		
Borders.	271	G10
Nether Booth Derbys.	185	D10
Netherbrae Aberds.	303	D7
Netherbrough Orkney.	314	E3
Nether Broughton Leics.	154	D3
Netherburn S Lnrk.	268	F6
Nether Burrow Lancs.	212	D2
Nether Burrows Derbys.	152	B5
Netherbury Dorset.	16	B6
Netherby Cumb.	239	C9
N Yorks.	206	D3
Nether Cassock		
Dumfries.	248	C6
Nether Cerne Dorset.	17	B9
Nether Chanderhill		
Derbys.	186	G4
Netherclay Som.	28	C3
Nether Compton Dorset.	29	D9
Nethercote Oxon.	101	C9
Warks.	119	E10
Nethercott Devon.	40	F3
Devon.	25	G9
Som.	42	G6
Nether Crimond Aberds.	303	G8
Netherdale Shetland.	313	H3
Nether Dalgliesh		
Borders.	249	B7
Nether Dallachy Moray.	302	C3
Nether Edge S Yorks.	186	E4
Netherend Glos.	79	E9
Nether End Derbys.	186	G3
Leics.	154	G4
S Yorks.	197	F8
Nether Exe Devon.	26	G6
Netherfield E Sus.	38	D2
M Keynes.	103	D7
Notts.	171	G10
Nethergate Norf.	159	D11
Nether Glasslaw Aberds.	303	D8
Nether Hall Leicester.	136	B2
Netherhampton Wilts.	31	B10
Nether Handley Derbys.	186	F6
Nether Handwick Angus.	287	C7
Nether Haugh S Yorks.	186	B6
Nether Headon Notts.	188	F2
Nether Heage Derbys.	170	E5
Nether Heyford		
Northants.	120	F3
Nether Hindhope		
Borders.	263	G7
Nether Horsburgh		
Borders.	261	B8
Nether Howecleuch S		
Lnrk.	260	G2
Nether Kellet Lancs.	211	F10
Nether Kidston Borders.	270	G4
Nether Kinmundy		
Aberds.	303	E10
Nether Kirton E Renf.	267	D9
Nether Langwith Notts.	187	G8
Netherlaw Dumfries.	237	E9
Netherlay Dorset.	28	F6
Nether Leask Aberds.	303	F10
Netherlee E Renf.	267	D11
Nether Lenshie Aberds.	302	E6
Netherley Aberds.	293	D10
Mers.	182	D6
W Yorks.	196	E4
Nether Loads Derbys.	170	B4
Nethermill Dumfries.	248	F2
Nethermills Moray.	302	D5

Nether Monynut

Borders.	272	C4
Nether Moor Derbys.	170	B5
Nethermuir Aberds.	303	E9
Netherne on-the-Hill		
Sur.	51	B9
Netheroyd Hill W Yorks.	196	D6
Nether Padley Derbys.	186	F3
Nether Park Aberds.	303	D10
Netherplace E Renf.	267	D10
Nether Poppleton York.	207	B7
Netherraw Borders.	262	E3
Nether Row Cumb.	230	D2
Nether Savock Aberds.	303	E10
Netherseal Derbys.	152	G5
Nether Shiels Borders.	271	F8
Nether Skyborry Shrops.	114	C5
Nether Stowe Staffs.	152	G2
Netherstoke Dorset.	29	E8
Nether Stowey Som.	43	F7
Nether Street Essex.	87	C9
Herts.	86	B6
Netherthird E Ayrs.	258	F3
Netherthong W Yorks.	196	F6
Netherthorpe Derbys.	186	G6
S Yorks.	187	E8
Netherton Angus.	287	B9
Ches W.	183	F8
Corn.	11	G11
Cumb.	228	D6
Devon.	14	G3
Glos.	81	G11
Hants.	47	B11
Hereford.	97	F10
Mers.	193	G11
N Lnrk.	268	C5
Northumb.	251	B11
Oxon.	82	F6
Perth.	286	B5
Shrops.	132	G4
W Mid.	133	F8
Worcs.	99	C9
W Yorks.	196	E6
W Yorks.	197	D9
Netherton of Lonmay		
Aberds.	303	C10
Netherton of Lonmay		
Highld.	310	H7
Staffs.	152	F2
Nether Urquhart Fife.	286	G5
Nether Wallop Hants.	47	G10
Nether Warden		
Northumb.	241	D10
Nether Wasdale Cumb.	220	E2
Nether Welton Cumb.	230	D3
Nether Westcote Glos.	100	G4
Nether Whitacre Warks.	134	E4
Nether Winchendon or		
Lower Winchendon		
Bucks.	84	C2
Netherwitton Northumb.	252	E4
Netherwood E Ayrs.	258	D5
Nether Worton Oxon.	101	E8
Nether Yeadon		
W Yorks.	205	F9
Nethy Bridge Highld.	301	G10
Netley Hants.	33	F7
Netley Hill Soton.	33	E7
Netley Marsh Hants.	32	E4
Nettacott Devon.	14	B4
Netteswell Essex.	87	C7
Nettlebed Oxon.	65	B8
Nettlebridge Som.	44	D6
Nettlecombe Dorset.	16	B6
IoW.	20	F6
Nettleden Herts.	85	C8
Nettleham Lincs.	189	F8
Nettlestead Kent.	53	C7
Suff.	107	B11
Nettlestead Green Kent.	53	C7
Nettlestone IoW.	21	C8
Nettlesworth Durham.	233	B11
Nettleton Glos.	80	G6
Lincs.	200	G6
Wilts.	61	D10
Nettleton Green Wilts.	61	D10
Nettleton Hill W Yorks.	196	D5
Nettleton Shrub Wilts.	61	D10
Nettleton Top Lincs.	189	B10
Netton Devon.	7	F11
Wilts.	46	F6
Neuadd Carms.	94	G3
Nevendon Essex.	88	G2
Nevern / Nanhyfer		
Pembs.	91	D11
Nevilles Cross Durham.	233	C11
New Abbey Dumfries.	237	C11
New Aberdour Aberds.	303	C8
New Addington London.	67	G11
Newall W Yorks.	205	D10
Newall Green Gtr Man.	184	D4
New Alresford Hants.	48	G5
New Alyth Perth.	286	C6
Newark Orkney.	314	B7
Pboro.	138	C4
Newark-on-Trent Notts.	172	E3
New Arley Warks.	134	F5
New Arram E Yorks.	208	E6
Newarthill N Lnrk.	268	D5
New Ash Green Kent.	68	F6
Newball Lincs.	189	F9
New Barn Kent.	68	F6
New Barnet London.	86	F3
New Barnetby N Lincs.	200	E5
Newbarns Cumb.	210	E4
New Barton Northants.	121	E7
New Basford Nottingham.	171	G9
Newbattle Midloth.	270	B6
New Beaupre V Glam.	58	E4

New Beckenham

London.	67	E11
New Bewick Northumb.	264	E3
Newbie Dumfries.	238	D5
Newbiggin Cumb.	210	F5
Cumb.	211	D11
Cumb.	219	G11
Cumb.	231	B7
Cumb.	231	F8
Durham.	232	F4
Durham.	233	B8
N Yorks.	213	B9
N Yorks.	223	G8

Newbiggin-by-the-Sea

Northumb.	253	G8
Newbigging Aberds.	303	G7
Angus.	287	D8
Borders.	262	F6
Edin.	270	C6
S Lnrk.	269	F10

Newbiggin Hall Estate

T&W.	242	D6

Newbiggin-on-Lune

Cumb.	222	D4
New Bilton Warks.	119	B9
Newbold Derbys.	186	G5
Gtr Man.	196	E2
Leics.	136	B5
Leics.	153	F7
Newbold Heath Leics.	135	B8
Newbold on Avon		
Warks.	119	B9
Newbold on Stour		
Warks.	100	A4
Newbold Pacey Warks.	118	F5
Newbolds W Mid.	133	C8
Newbold Verdon Leics.	135	C8
New Bolingbroke Lincs.	174	D4
New Bolsover Derbys.	187	G7
Newborough Pboro.	138	B4
Staffs.	152	E2
New Boston Mers.	183	B9
New Botley Oxon.	83	D7
Newbottle Northants.	101	D10
T&W.	243	G8
New Boultham Lincs.	189	G7
Newbourne Suff.	108	C5
New Bradwell M Keynes.	102	C6
New Brancepeth		
Durham.	233	C10
Newbridge Bath.	61	F8
Caerph.	78	F2
Ceredig.	111	F10
Corn.	1	C4
Corn.	4	G5
Corn.	7	B7
Dumfries.	237	B11
Edin.	280	G2
IoW.	20	D4
N Yorks.	216	B6
Oxon.	82	E6
Pembs.	91	B8
Shrops.	148	B6
W Mid.	133	D7
Wrex.	166	G3
Newbridge Green Worcs.	98	D6
Newbridge-on-Usk Mon.	78	G5
Newbridge-on-Wye		
Powys.	113	F10
New Brighton Flint.	166	B3
Flint.	182	G2
Hants.	34	C3
Wrex.	166	E3
W Sus.	22	B3
W Yorks.	197	B9
W Yorks.	205	F8
New Brimington Derbys.	186	G6
New Brinsley Notts.	171	E7
New Brotton Redcar.	235	G4
Newbrough Northumb.	241	D9
New Broughton Wrex.	166	E4
New Buckenham Norf.	141	E11
New Buildings Devon.	26	G3
Dorset.	18	B5
Newburgh Aberds.	303	D9
Aberds.	303	G9
Borders.	261	F8
Fife.	286	F6
Lancs.	194	E3
Newburn T&W.	242	D5
Newbury Kent.	54	E2
W Berks.	64	F3
Wilts.	45	D11
New Bury Gtr Man.	195	F8
Newbury Park London.	68	B2
Newby Cumb.	231	G7
Lancs.	204	D2
N Yorks.	205	D11
N Yorks.	212	E4
N Yorks.	215	F7
N Yorks.	225	C11
N Yorks.	227	G10
Newby Bridge Cumb.	211	B7
Newby Cote N Yorks.	212	E4
Newby East Cumb.	239	F11
Newby Head Cumb.	231	G7
New Byth Aberds.	303	D8
Newby West Cumb.	239	G9
Newby Wiske N Yorks.	215	B7
Newcastle Bridgend.	58	C2
Mon.	78	B6
Shrops.	130	G4
Newcastle Emlyn / Castell		
Newydd Emlyn Carms.	92	C6
Newcastleton or Copshaw		
Holm Borders.	249	E11
Newcastle-under-Lyme		
Staffs.	168	F4
Newcastle upon Tyne		
T&W.	242	E6
New Catton Norf.	160	G4
Newchapel Powys.	129	G9
Staffs.	168	E5
Sur.	51	E11
Newchapel / Capel Newydd		
Pembs.	92	D4
New Charlton London.	68	D2
New Cheltenham S Glos.	61	E7
New Cheriton Hants.	33	B9
Newchurch Bl Gwent.	77	C11
Carms.	93	G7
Hereford.	115	G7
IoW.	21	D7
Kent.	54	G5
Lancs.	195	C11
Mon.	79	F7
Powys.	114	G4
Staffs.	152	E2
Newchurch in Pendle		
Lancs.	204	F3
New Clipstone Notts.	171	C9
New Costessey Norf.	160	G3
Newcott Devon.	28	F2
New Coundon Durham.	233	E10
New Cowper Cumb.	229	B8
Newcraighall Edin.	280	G6
New Crofton W Yorks.	197	D11
New Cross Ceredig.	112	B2
London.	67	D11
Oxon.	65	D9
Som.	28	D6
New Cross Gate London.	67	D11
New Cumnock E Ayrs.	258	G4
New Deer Aberds.	303	E8
New Delaval Northumb.	243	B7
New Delph Gtr Man.	196	F3
New Denham Bucks.	66	C4
Newdigate Sur.	51	E7
New Downs Corn.	1	C3
Corn.	4	E4
New Duston Northants.	120	E4
New Earswick York.	207	B8
New Eastwood Notts.	171	F7
New Edlington S Yorks.	187	B8
New Elgin Moray.	302	C2
New Ellerby E Yorks.	209	F9
New Eltham London.	68	E2
New End Lincs.	190	G2

Warks 118 E2
Worcs 117 F11
Newenden Kent 38 B4
New England Essex 106 C4
Lincs 175 D8
Pboro 138 C3
Som 28 E4
Newent Glos 98 F4
Newerne Glos 79 E10
New Farnley W Yorks 205 G10
New Ferry Mers 182 D4
Newfield Durham 233 E10
Durham 242 G6
Highld 301 B7
Stoke 168 E6
New Fletton Pboro 138 D3
Newford Scilly 1 G4
Newfound Hants 48 C5
New Fryston W Yorks 198 B3
Newgale Pembs 90 G6
New Galloway Dumfries 237 B8
Newgarth Orkney 314 E2
Newgate Lancs 194 F4
Norf 177 E9
Newgate Corner Norf 161 G8
Newgate Street Herts 86 D4
New Gilston Fife 287 G8
New Greens Herts 85 D10
New Grimsby Scilly 1 F3
New Ground Herts 85 C7
Newgrounds Hants 31 E11
Newhailes Edin 280 G6
New Hainford Norf 160 F4
Newhall Ches E 167 F10
Derbys 152 E5
Newhall Green Warks 134 F5
New Hall Hey Lancs 195 C10
Newhall House Highld 300 C6
Newhall Point Highld 301 C7
Newham Lincs 174 E3
Northumb 264 D5
New Hartley Northumb 243 B8
Newhaven Derbys 169 C11
Devon 24 C5
Edin 280 F5
E Sus 36 G6
New Haw Sur 66 G5
Newhay N Yorks 207 G9
New Headington Oxon 83 D9
New Heaton Northumb 273 G7
New Hedges Pembs 73 E10
New Herrington T&W 243 G8
Newhey Gtr Man 196 E2
Newhill Fife 286 F6
Perth 286 G5
S Yorks 186 B6
Newhills Aberdeen 293 C10
New Hinksey Oxon 83 E8
New Ho Durham 232 D3
New Holkham Norf 159 B7
New Holland N Lincs 200 C5
W Yorks 205 F7
Newholm N Yorks 227 C7
New Horwich Derbys 185 E8
New Houghton Derbys 171 B7
Norf 158 D5
Newhouse Borders 262 E2
N Lnrk 268 C5
Shetland 313 G6
New House Kent 68 E6
Newhouses Borders 271 G10
New Houses Gtr Man 194 G5
N Yorks 212 E6
New Humberstone
Leicester 136 B2
New Hunwick Durham 233 E9
New Hutton Cumb 221 G11
New Hythe Kent 53 B8
Newick E Sus 36 C6
Newingreen Kent 54 F6
Newington Edin 280 G5
Kent 55 F7
Kent 69 G11
Kent 71 F11
London 67 D10
Notts 187 C11
Oxon 83 F10
Shrops 131 G8
Newington Bagpath Glos 80 G4
New Inn Carms 93 D9
Devon 24 F6
Mon 79 E7
Pembs 91 E11
Torf 78 F4
New Invention Shrops 114 B5
W Mid 133 C9
New Kelso Highld 299 E9
New Kingston Notts 153 D10
New Kyo Durham 242 G5
New Ladykirk Borders 273 F7
New Lanark S Lnrk 269 G7
Newland Cumb 210 D6
E Yorks 199 B10
Glos 79 D9
Hull 209 G7
N Yorks 199 C7
Oxon 82 C5
Worcs 98 B5
Newland Bottom Cumb 210 C5
Newland Common
Worcs 117 E8
Newland Green Kent 54 D2
Newlandrig Midloth 271 C7
Newlands Borders 250 E2
Borders 262 E2
Cumb 229 G10
Cumb 230 D2
Derbys 170 F6
Dumfries 247 F11
Glasgow 267 C11
Highld 301 E7
Moray 302 D3
Northumb 242 F3
Notts 171 C9
Staffs 151 E11
Newlands Corner Sur 50 D4
Newlandsmuir S Lnrk 268 E2
Newlands of Geise
Highld 310 C4
Newlands of Tynet
Moray 302 C3
Newlands Park Anglesey 178 E3
New Lane Lancs 194 E2
New Lane End Warr 183 B10
New Langholm Dumfries 249 G9
New Leake Lincs 174 D6
New Leeds Aberds 303 D9
Newliston Edin 280 G2
Fife 280 C5
New Lodge S Yorks 197 F10
New Longton Lancs 194 B4
Newlot Orkney 314 E5
New Luce Dumfries 236 C3
Newlyn Corn 1 D5
Newmachar Aberds 293 B10
Newmains N Lnrk 268 D6
New Malden London 67 F8
Newman's End Essex 87 C8
Newman's Green Suff 107 C7
Newman's Place Hereford 96 B5
Newmarket Glos 80 F4
Suff 124 E2
W Isles 304 E6
New Marske Redcar 235 G8
New Marston Oxon 83 D8
New Marton Shrops 148 C6
New Micklefield
W Yorks 206 G4
Newmill Borders 261 G11
Corn 1 C5
Moray 302 D4
New Mill Aberds 293 E9
Borders 262 G2
Corn 1 C5
Corn 4 F6
Cumb 219 E11
Herts 84 C6
Wilts 63 G7
W Yorks 197 F7
Newmillerdam
W Yorks 197 D10
Newmill of Inshewan
Angus 292 G6
Newmills Corn 11 D11
Fife 279 D10
Highld 300 C6
New Mills Borders 271 F10
Ches E 184 E3
Corn 5 E7
Derbys 185 D7
Glos 79 E10
Hereford 98 D4
New Mills / Felin Newydd
Powys 129 C11
Newmills of Boyne
Aberds 302 D5
Newmiln Perth 286 D5
Newmilns E Ayrs 258 B2
New Milton Hants 19 B10
New Mistley Essex 108 E2
New Moat Pembs 91 F11
Newmore Highld 300 B6
Highld 300 D5
New Moston Gtr Man 195 G11
Newnes Shrops 149 C7
Newney Green Essex 87 D11
Newnham Cambs 123 F8
Glos 79 C11
Hants 49 C8
Herts 104 D4
Kent 54 B3
Northants 119 F11
Warks 118 E3
Newnham Bridge Worcs 116 D2
New Ollerton Notts 171 B11
New Oscott W Mid 133 E11
New Pale Ches W 183 G8
Newpark Fife 287 F8
New Park N Yorks 205 B11
New Parks Leicester 135 B11
New Passage S Glos 60 B4
New Pitsligo Aberds 303 D8
New Polzeath Corn 10 F4
Newpool Staffs 168 D5
Newport Corn 12 D2
Devon 40 G5
Dorset 18 C3
Essex 105 E10
E Yorks 208 G3
Glos 79 F11
Highld 311 G5
IoW 20 D6
Newport 59 B10
Norf 161 F10
Som 28 C4
Telford 150 F4
Newport-on-Tay Fife 287 E8
Newport Pagnell
M Keynes 103 C7
Newport / Trefdraeth
Pembs 91 D11
Newpound Common
W Sus 35 B9
Newquay Corn 4 C6
New Quay / Ceinewydd
Ceredig 111 F7
New Rackheath Norf 160 G5
New Radnor Powys 114 E4
New Rent Cumb 230 D5
New Ridley Northumb 242 F3
New Road Side N Yorks 204 E5
W Yorks 197 B7
New Romney Kent 39 C9
New Rossington
S Yorks 187 B10
New Row Ceredig 112 C4
Lancs 203 F8
N Yorks 226 B3
Newsam Green
W Yorks 206 G3
New Sarum Wilts 46 G6
New Sawley Derbys 153 C9
Newsbank Ches E 168 B4
New Scarbro W Yorks 205 G10
Newseat Aberds 303 E10
Aberds 303 F7
Newsells Herts 105 D7
Newsham Lancs 202 F6
Northumb 243 B8
N Yorks 215 C7
N Yorks 224 C2
New Sharlston
W Yorks 197 C11
Newsholme E Yorks 199 B8
Lancs 204 C2
W Yorks 204 F6
New Silksworth T&W 243 G9
New Skelton Redcar 226 B3
New Smithy Derbys 185 E9
Newsome W Yorks 196 E6
New Southgate London 86 G3
New Springs Gtr Man 194 F6
New Sprowston Norf 160 G4
New Stanton Derbys 153 B9
Newstead Borders 262 C3
Northumb 264 D5
Notts 171 E8
Staffs 168 G5
W Yorks 197 E11
New Stevenston N Lnrk 268 D5
New Street Kent 68 G6
Staffs 169 E9
Newstreet Lane Shrops 150 B2
New Swanage Dorset 18 E6
New Swannington Leics 153 F8
Newtake Devon 14 G3
New Thirsk N Yorks 215 C8
Newthorpe Notts 171 F7
N Yorks 206 G5
Newthorpe Common
Notts 171 F7
New Thundersley Essex 69 B9
Newtoft Lincs 189 D8
Newton Argyll 275 D11
Borders 262 E2
Borders 262 F2
Bridgend 57 F10
Cambs 105 B8
Cambs 157 G8
Cardiff 59 D8
C Beds 104 C4
Ches W 166 B6
Ches W 167 D8
Ches W 183 F8
Corn 5 C11
Cumb 210 E4
Derbys 170 D6
Dorset 30 E3
Dumfries 239 C7
Dumfries 248 E4
Gtr Man 185 B7
Hereford 96 C5
Hereford 96 E6
Hereford 115 D7
Hereford 115 G10
Highld 301 C7
Highld 301 E7
Highld 306 F7
Highld 310 F7
Lancs 202 F2
Lancs 202 G4
Lancs 203 C9
Lancs 211 E11
Lincs 155 B10
Mers 182 D2
Moray 301 C11
Norf 158 F6
Northants 137 G7
Northumb 242 E2
Notts 171 G11
Perth 286 D2
S Glos 79 G10
Shetland 312 E5
Shetland 313 K5
Shrops 132 D4
Shrops 149 C8
S Lnrk 259 C10
S Lnrk 268 C3
Som 42 F6
Staffs 151 D10
Suff 107 C8
Swansea 56 D6
S Yorks 198 G5
Warks 119 B10
Wilts 32 C2
W Loth 279 F11
W Mid 133 E10
Newton Abbot Devon 14 G3
Newtonairds Dumfries 247 G9
Newton Arlosh Cumb 238 F5
Newton Aycliffe
Durham 233 G11
Newton Bewley Hrtlpl 234 F5
Newton Blossomville
M Keynes 121 G8
Newton Bromswold
Northants 121 D9
Newton Burgoland
Leics 135 B7
Newton by Toft Lincs 189 D9
Newton Cross Pembs 91 F7
Newton Ferrers Devon 7 F10
Newton Flotman Norf 142 D4
Newtongrange Midloth 270 C6
Newton Green Mon 79 G8
Newton Hall Durham 233 B11
Northumb 242 D2
Newton Harcourt Leics 136 D2
Newton Heath
Gtr Man 195 G11
Newtonhill Aberds 293 D11
Highld 300 E5
Newton Hill W Yorks 197 C10
Newton Ho Aberds 302 G6
Newton Hurst Staffs 151 D11
Newtonia Ches E 167 B11
Newton Ketton Darl 234 G2
Newton Kyme N Yorks 206 E5
Newton-le-Willows
Mers 183 B9
N Yorks 214 B4
Newton Longville Bucks 102 E6
Newton Mearns
E Renf 267 D10
Newtonmill Angus 293 G8
Newtonmore Highld 291 D9
Newton Morrell
N Yorks 224 D4
Oxon 102 F2
Newton Mulgrave
N Yorks 226 B5
Newton of Ardtoe
Highld 289 B8
Newton of Balcanquhal
Perth 286 F5
Newton of Balcormo
Fife 287 G9
Newton of Falkland
Fife 286 G6
Newton of Mountblairy
Aberds 302 D6
Newton of Pitcairns
Perth 286 F4
Newton on Ayr S Ayrs 257 E8
Newton on Ouse
N Yorks 206 B6
Newton-on-Rawcliffe
N Yorks 226 G6
Newton on the Hill
Shrops 149 E9
Newton on the Moor
Northumb 252 B5
Newton on Trent Lincs 188 G4
Newton Park Argyll 266 B2
Mers 183 C9
Newton Peveril Dorset 18 B4
Newton Poppleford
Devon 15 D7
Newton Purcell Oxon 102 E2
Newton Regis Warks 134 B5
Newton Reigny Cumb 230 E5
Newton Rigg Cumb 230 E5
Newton St Boswells
Borders 262 C3
Newton St Cyres Devon 14 B3
Newton St Faith Norf 160 F4
Newton St Loe Bath 61 G8
Newton St Petrock Devon 24 E6
Newton Solney Derbys 152 D5
Newton Stacey Hants 48 E2
Newton Stewart
Dumfries 236 C6
Newton Tony Wilts 47 E8
Newton Tracey Devon 25 B8
Newton under Roseberry
Redcar 225 C11
Newton Underwood
Northumb 252 F4
Newton upon Derwent
E Yorks 207 D10
Newton Valence Hants 49 G8
Newton with Scales
Lancs 202 G4
New Town Gtr Man 184 B6
New Totley S Yorks 186 F4
Newtown Argyll 284 G4
Bl Gwent 77 C11
Bucks 85 E7
Caerph 78 G2
Cambs 121 D11
Shetland 313 G7
Ches E 184 E6
Ches W 183 F8
Corn 2 D3
Corn 11 F11
Cumb 229 B7
Cumb 239 F9
Cumb 240 E2
Derbys 185 E7
Devon 26 B3
Dorset 29 G7
Falk 279 E9
Glos 79 E11
Glos 80 D3
Glos 99 E8
Gtr Man 194 F5
Gtr Man 195 G9
Hants 21 B8
Hants 32 C4
Hants 32 E3
Hants 33 D8
Hants 33 E10
Hants 33 F7
Hants 49 F8
Hants 49 G10
Hants 64 G3
Hereford 97 E10
Hereford 98 C2
Highld 290 C5
IoM 192 E4
IoW 20 C4
Mers 183 F7
Norf 143 B10
Northumb 252 C2
Northumb 263 C11
Northumb 264 D2
Oxon 65 G9
Poole 18 C6
Powys 130 E2
Rhondda 77 F9
Shrops 132 C2
Shrops 149 C9
Shrops 149 E8
Som 28 E3
Som 43 F9
Staffs 133 C9
Staffs 168 C6
Staffs 169 C9
Wilts 30 B6
Wilts 63 G10
W Mid 133 F11
Worcs 116 F5
Worcs 117 E7
New Town Bath 45 B9
Bath 60 G5
Dartford 68 E4
Dorset 30 C3
Dorset 30 D6
Dorset 31 D7
Dorset 31 F7
Edin 280 G4
Edin 280 G5
E Loth 281 G8
E Sus 37 C7
Glos 99 E10
Lancs 203 F8
Luton 103 G11
Maidstone 53 B7
Medway 69 G8
Oxon 100 F5
Reading 65 E8
Shetland 312 E6
Som 29 D9
Som 29 D11
Som 44 D3
Soton 33 E7
Swindon 63 C7
T&W 234 B2
T&W 243 E8
W Berks 64 D6
Wilts 46 C6
Wilts 47 G8
W Mid 133 B11
W Mid 133 E9
W Sus 35 B11
W Yorks 198 C3
Newtown-in-St Martin
Corn 2 E6
Newtown Linford Leics 135 B10
Newtown St Boswells
Borders 262 C3
Newtown Unthank Leics 135 C9
New Tredegar Caerph 77 E10
New Trows S Lnrk 259 B8
Newtyle Angus 286 C6
New Ulva Argyll 275 E8
New Village E Yorks 209 G7
S Yorks 198 F5
New Walsoken Cambs 139 B9
New Waltham NE Lincs 201 G9
New Well Powys 113 B11
New Wells Powys 130 D3
New Whittington Derbys 186 F5
New Wimpole Cambs 104 B6
New Winton E Loth 281 G8
New Woodhouses
Shrops 167 G9
New Works Telford 132 B3
New Wortley W Yorks 205 G11
New Yatt Oxon 82 C5
Newyears Green London 66 B5
New York Lincs 174 D2
N Yorks 214 G3
New Zealand Wilts 62 D4
Nextend Hereford 114 F6
Neyland Pembs 73 D7
Niarbyl IoM 192 E3
Nib Heath Shrops 149 F8
Nibley Glos 79 D11
S Glos 61 C7
Nibley Green Glos 80 F2
Nibon Shetland 312 F5
Nicholashayne Devon 27 D10
Nicholaston Swansea 56 D4
Nidd N Yorks 214 G6
Niddrie Edin 280 G5
Nigg Aberdeen 293 C11
Highld 301 B8
Nigg Ferry Highld 301 C7
Nightcott Som 26 B5
Nilig Denb 165 D8
Nimble Nook Gtr Man 196 G2
Nimlet S Glos 61 E8
Nimmer Som 28 E4
Nine Ashes Essex 87 E9
Ninebanks Northumb 241 G7
Nine Elms London 67 D9
Swindon 62 B6
Nine Maidens Downs Corn 2 B5
Nine Mile Burn Midloth 270 D3
Nineveh Worcs 116 C3
Worcs 116 E2
Ninewells Glos 79 C9
Nine Wells Pembs 90 G5
Ninfield E Sus 38 E2
Ningwood IoW 20 D3
Ningwood Common IoW 20 D3
Ninnes Bridge Corn 2 B2
Nisbet Borders 262 D5
Nisthouse Orkney 314 E3
Shetland 313 G7
Nithbank Dumfries 247 D9
Niton IoW 20 F6
Nitshill Glasgow 267 C10
Noah's Arks Kent 52 B5
Noah's Green Worcs 117 E10
Noak Bridge Essex 87 G11
Noak Hill Essex 87 G11
London 87 G8
Nob End Gtr Man 195 F9
Nobland Green Herts 86 B5
Noblethorpe S Yorks 197 F9
Nobold Shrops 149 G9
Nobottle Northants 120 E3
Nob's Crook Hants 33 C7
Nocton Lincs 173 C9
Noctorum Mers 182 D3
Nodmore W Berks 64 D2
Noel Park London 86 G4
Nogdam End Norf 143 C7
Nog Tow Lancs 202 G6
Noke Oxon 83 C8
Noke Street Medway 69 E8
Nolton Pembs 72 B5
Nolton Haven Pembs 72 B5
No Man's Heath Ches W 167 F8
Warks 134 B5
Nomansland Devon 26 E4
Herts 85 C11
Wilts 32 D3
No Man's Land Corn 6 D5
Hants 33 B8
Noneley Shrops 149 D9
Noness Shetland 313 L6
Nonikiln Highld 300 B6
Nonington Kent 55 C9
Nook Cumb 211 C10
Noon Nick W Yorks 205 F8
Noonsbrough Shetland 313 H4
Noonsun Ches E 184 F4
Noonvares Corn 2 C3
Noranside Angus 292 G6
Norbiton London 67 F7
Norbreck Blkpool 202 E2
Norbridge Hereford 98 C4
Norbury Ches E 167 F9
Derbys 169 G10
London 67 F10
Shrops 131 E7
Staffs 150 E5
Norbury Common
Ches E 167 F9
Norbury Junction Staffs 150 E5
Norbury Moor Gtr Man 184 D6
Norby N Yorks 215 C8
Shetland 313 H3
Norchard Worcs 116 D6
Norcote Glos 81 E8
Norcott Brook Ches W 183 E10
Norcross Blkpool 202 E2
Nordelph Norf 139 C11
Nordelph Corner Norf 141 C10
Norden Dorset 18 E4
Gtr Man 195 E11
Norden Heath Dorset 18 E4
Nordley Shrops 132 D3
Norham Northumb 273 F8
Norham West Mains
Northumb 273 F8
Nork Sur 51 B8
Norland Town W Yorks 196 C5
Norleaze Wilts 45 C11
Norley Ches W 183 G9
Devon 25 G8
Norley Common Sur 50 E4
Norleywood Hants 20 B3
Norlington E Sus 36 E6
Normacot Stoke 168 G6
Normanby N Lincs 199 D11
N Yorks 216 C4
Redcar 225 B10
Normanby-by-Spital
Lincs 189 D7
Normanby by Stow
Lincs 188 E5
Normanby le Wold
Lincs 189 B10
Norman Cross Cambs 138 E3
Normandy Sur 50 C2
Norman Hill Glos 80 F3
Norman's Bay E Sus 23 D11
Norman's Green Devon 27 G9
Normanston Suff 143 E10
Normanton Derby 152 C6
Leics 172 G4
Lincs 172 F6
Notts 172 E2
Rutland 137 B8
Wilts 46 E6
W Yorks 197 C11
Normanton le Heath
Leics 153 G7
Normanton on Soar
Notts 153 E10
Normanton-on-the-Wolds
Notts 154 C2
Normanton on Trent
Notts 172 B3
Normanton Spring
S Yorks 186 E6
Normanton Turville
Leics 135 D9
Normoss Lancs 202 F2
Norney Sur 50 E2
Norr W Yorks 205 F7
Norrington Common
Wilts 61 G11
Norris Green Corn 7 B8
Mers 182 C5
Norris Hill Leics 152 F6
Norristhorpe W Yorks 197 C8
Norseman Orkney 314 E3
Northacre Norf 141 D9
North Acton London 67 C8
Northall Bucks 103 G9
Northallerton N Yorks 225 G7
Northall Green Norf 159 G9
Northam Devon 24 B6
Soton 32 E6
Northampton Northants 120 E5
North Anston S Yorks 187 E8
North Ascot Brack 66 F2
North Aston Oxon 101 F9
Northaw Herts 86 E3
Northay Devon 28 G5
Som 28 E3
North Ayre Shetland 312 F6
North Baddesley Hants 32 D5
North Ballachulish
Highld 290 G2
North Barrow Som 29 B10
North Barsham Norf 159 C8
North Batsom Som 41 G10
Northbeck Lincs 173 G9
North Beer Corn 12 C2
North Benfleet Essex 69 B9
North Bersted W Sus 22 C6
North Berwick E Loth 281 D11
North Bitchburn Durham 233 E9
North Blyth Northumb 253 G8
North Boarhunt Hants 33 E10
North Bockhampton
Dorset 19 B9
Northborough Pboro 138 B3
Northbourne Bmouth 19 B7
Kent 55 C10
North Bovey Devon 13 E10
North Bradley Wilts 45 C11
North Brentor Devon 12 E5
North Brewham Som 45 F8
Northbridge Street
E Sus 38 C2
Northbrook Dorset 17 C11
Hants 33 D9
Hants 48 F5
Oxon 101 G9
Wilts 46 C4
North Brook End Cambs 104 C5
North Broomage Falk 279 E7
North Buckland Devon 40 E3
North Burlingham Norf 161 G7
North Cadbury Som 29 B10
North Cairn Dumfries 236 B1
North Camp Hants 49 C11
North Carlton Lincs 188 F6
Notts 187 E9
North Carrine Argyll 255 G7
North Cave E Yorks 208 G3
North Cerney Glos 81 D8
North Chailey E Sus 36 C5
Northchapel W Sus 35 B7
North Charford Wilts 31 D11
North Charlton
Northumb 264 E5
North Cheam London 67 F8
North Cheriton Som 29 B11
Northchurch Herts 85 D7
North Cliff E Yorks 209 D10
North Cliffe E Yorks 208 F3
North Clifton Notts 188 G4
North Close Durham 233 E11
North Cockerington
Lincs 190 C5
North Coker Som 29 E8
North Collafirth
Shetland 312 E5
North Common S Glos 61 E7
Suff 125 B9
North Connel Argyll 289 F11
North Cornelly Bridgend 57 E10
North Corner Corn 3 F7
S Glos 61 C7
North Corriegills
N Ayrs 256 C2
North Corry Highld 289 D10
Northcote Devon 27 G11
North Cotes Lincs 201 G11
Northcott Corn 24 F2
Devon 12 C2
Devon 27 E9
Devon 27 F10
North Country Corn 4 G3
Northcourt Oxon 83 F8
North Court Som 41 F11
North Cove Suff 143 F9
North Cowton N Yorks 224 E5
North Craigo Angus 293 G8
North Crawley
M Keynes 103 C8
North Cray London 68 E3
North Creake Norf 159 B7
North Curry Som 28 B4
North Dalton E Yorks 208 C4
North Darley Corn 11 G11
North Dawn Orkney 314 F4
North Deighton N Yorks 206 C3
North Denes Norf 161 G10
Northdown Kent 71 E11
North Dronley Angus 287 D7
North Drumachter Lodge
Highld 291 F8
North Duffield N Yorks 207 F9
Northdyke Orkney 314 D2
North Dykes Cumb 230 D6
North Eastling Kent 54 B3
Northedge Derbys 170 B5
North Elham Kent 55 E7
North Elkington Lincs 190 C3
North Elmham Norf 159 E9
North Elmsall W Yorks 198 E3
North Elmshall W Yorks 198 E3
North Elphinestone
E Loth 281 G7
Northend Bath 61 F9
Bucks 84 G2
Essex 89 E7
Essex 105 D10
Warks 119 G7
North End Bath 60 G6
Beds 121 F10
Bexley 68 D4
Bucks 102 F4
Bucks 102 F6
Camden 67 B9
Cumb 239 F8
Devon 27 D10
Dorset 30 B4
Durham 233 C11
Essex 87 B11
Essex 106 D5
E Yorks 209 C9
E Yorks 209 E9
E Yorks 209 G11
Hants 31 D10
Hants 33 B9
Hants 64 G2
Leics 153 F11
Lincs 174 G2
Lincs 189 B8
Lincs 190 C5
Lincs 190 D6
Lincs 191 D7
Lincs 201 G10
N Lincs 200 C6
Norf 141 E10
Northumb 252 C4
N Som 60 F2
Ptsmth 33 G11
Som 28 B3
Wilts 81 G8
W Sus 35 F10
W Sus 35 G7
W Sus 51 F11
Northenden Gtr Man 184 C4
Northern Moor Gtr Man 184 C4
North Erradale Highld 307 L2
North Evington
Leicester 136 C2
North Ewster N Lincs 199 G10
North Fambridge Essex 88 F5
North Fearns Highld 295 B7
North Featherstone
W Yorks 198 C2
North Feltham London 66 E6
North Feorline N Ayrs 255 E10
North Ferriby E Yorks 200 B3
Northfield Aberdeen 293 C11
Borders 262 D3
Borders 273 B8
Edin 280 G5
E Yorks 200 B4
Highld 301 B7
M Keynes 103 C7
Northants 137 E7
Som 43 F9
W Mid 117 B10
Northfields Hants 33 B7
Lincs 137 B10
North Finchley London 86 G3
Northfleet Kent 68 E6
Northfleet Green Kent 68 E6
North Flobbets Aberds 303 F7
North Frodingham
E Yorks 209 C8
Northgate Lincs 156 D3
Som 27 B9
W Sus 51 F9
North Gluss Shetland 312 F5
North Gorley Hants 31 E11
North Green Norf 141 B10
Norf 142 F4
Suff 126 B6
Suff 126 E6
Suff 127 D7
North Greetwell Lincs 189 G8
North Grimston N Yorks 216 F6
North Halley Orkney 314 F5
North Halling Medway 69 F8
North Harrow London 66 B6
North Hayling Hants 22 C2
North Hazelrigg
Northumb 264 C3
North Heasley Devon 41 G8
North Heath W Berks 64 E3
W Sus 35 C9
North Hill Corn 11 F11
North Hillingdon London 66 C5
North Hinksey Oxon 83 D7
North Hinksey Village
Oxon 83 D7
North Ho Shetland 313 J5
North Holmwood Sur 51 D7
North Houghton Hants 47 G10
Northhouse Borders 249 B10
North Howden E Yorks 207 G11
North Huish Devon 8 D4
North Hyde London 66 D6
North Hykeham Lincs 172 B6
North Hylton T&W 243 F8
Northiam E Sus 38 B4
Northill C Beds 104 B2
Northington Glos 80 D2
Hants 48 F5
North Kelsey Lincs 200 G4
North Kelsey Moor
Lincs 200 G5
North Kensington London 67 C8
North Kessock Highld 300 E6
North Killingholme
N Lincs 200 D6
North Kilvington
N Yorks 215 B8
North Kilworth Leics 136 G2
North Kingston Hants 31 G11
North Kirkton Aberds 303 D11
North Kiscadale N Ayrs 256 D2
North Kyme Lincs 173 E11
North Laggan Highld 290 D4
North Lancing W Sus 35 F11
North Landing E Yorks 218 E4
Northlands Lincs 174 E4
Northlea Durham 243 G10
Northleach Glos 81 C10
North Lee Bucks 84 D4
North Lees N Yorks 214 E6
Northleigh Devon 15 B9
Devon 40 G6
North Leigh Kent 54 D6
Oxon 82 C5
North Leverton with
Habblesthorpe Notts 188 E3
Northlew Devon 12 B6
North Littleton Worcs 99 B11
North Looe Sur 67 G8
North Lopham Norf 141 G10
North Luffenham
Rutland 137 C8
North Marden W Sus 34 D4
North Marston Bucks 102 G5
North Middleton
Midloth 271 D7
Northumb 264 E2
North Millbrex Aberds 303 E8
North Molton Devon 26 B2
Northmoor Devon 24 D4
Oxon 82 E6
Northmoor Corner Som 43 G10
Northmoor Green or
Moorland Som 43 G10
North Moreton Oxon 64 B5
North Mosstown
Aberds 303 D10
North Motherwell N
Lnrk 268 D4
North Moulsecoomb
Brighton 36 F4
Northmuir Angus 287 B7
North Mundham W Sus 22 C5
North Muskham Notts 172 D3
North Newbald E Yorks 208 F4
North Newington Oxon 101 D8
North Newnton Wilts 46 B6
North Newton Som 43 G9
Northney Hants 22 C2
North Nibley Glos 80 F2
North Oakley Hants 48 C4
North Ockendon London 68 C5
Northolt London 66 C6
Northop Hall Flint 166 B3
Northop / Llan-eurgain
Flint 166 B2
North Ormesby Mbro 234 G6
North Ormsby Lincs 190 C3
Northorpe Lincs 155 F11
Lincs 156 B4
Lincs 188 B5
W Yorks 197 C8
North Otterington
N Yorks 215 B7
Northover Som 29 C8
Som 44 F3
North Owersby Lincs 189 C9
Northowram W Yorks 196 B6
Northpark Argyll 275 G11
North Perrott Som 29 F7
North Petherton Som 43 G9
North Petherwin Corn 11 D11
North Pickenham Norf 141 B7
North Piddle Worcs 117 G9
North Poorton Dorset 16 B6
Northport Dorset 18 D4
North Port Argyll 284 E4
North Poulner Hants 31 F11
Northpunds Shetland 313 L6
North Queensferry Fife 280 E2
North Radworthy Devon 41 G9
North Rauceby Lincs 173 F8
North Reddish Gtr Man 184 C5
Northrepps Norf 160 B4
North Reston Lincs 190 E5
North Rigton N Yorks 205 D11
North Ripley Hants 19 B9
North Rode Ches E 168 B5
North Roe Shetland 312 E5
North Row Cumb 229 E10
North Runcton Norf 158 F2
North Sandwick
Shetland 312 D7
North Scale Cumb 210 F3
North Scarle Lincs 172 B5
North Seaton Northumb 253 F7
North Seaton Colliery
Northumb 253 F7
North Sheen London 67 D7
North Shian Argyll 289 E11
North Shields T&W 243 D9
North Shoebury S'thend 70 B2
North Shore Blkpool 202 F2
Northside Aberds 303 D8
Orkney 314 D2
North Side Cumb 228 F6
Pboro 138 D5
North Skelmanae
Aberds 303 D9
North Skelton Redcar 226 B3
North Somercotes Lincs 190 B6
North Stainley N Yorks 214 D5
North Stainmore Cumb 222 B6
North Stifford Thurrock 68 C6
North Stoke Bath 61 F8
Oxon 64 B6
W Sus 35 E8
North Stoneham Hants 32 D6
North Street Hants 31 D11
Hants 48 G6
Kent 54 B4
Medway 69 E10
W Berks 64 E6
North Sunderland
Northumb 264 C6
North Synton Borders 261 E11
North Tamerton Corn 12 B2
North Tawton Devon 25 G11
North Thoresby Lincs 190 B3
North Tidworth Wilts 47 D8
North Togston Northumb 252 C6
Northton Aberds 293 C9
Northtown Orkney 314 G4
Shetland 313 M5
North Town Devon 25 F8
Hants 49 C11
Som 29 B10
Som 44 E5
Windsor 65 C11
North Tuddenham
Norf 159 G10
Northumberland Heath
London 68 D4
Northville Torf 78 F3
North Walbottle T&W 242 D5
North Walney Cumb 210 F3
North Walsham Norf 160 C5
North Waltham Hants 48 D5
North Warnborough
Hants 49 C8
North Water Bridge
Angus 293 G8
North Waterhayne Devon 28 F3
North Watford Herts 85 F10
North Watten Highld 310 D6
Northway Devon 24 C5
Glos 99 E8
Som 27 B10
Swansea 56 D5
North Weald Bassett
Essex 87 E7
North Weirs Hants 32 G3
North Wembley London 67 B7
North Weston N Som 60 D3
Oxon 83 D11
North Wheatley Notts 188 D3
North Whilborough Devon 9 B7
North Whiteley Moray 302 E4
Northwich Ches W 183 G11
Northwick S Glos 60 B5
Som 43 D11
Worcs 116 F6
North Wick Bath 60 F5
North Widcombe Bath 44 B5
North Willingham
Lincs 189 D11
North Wingfield Derbys 170 B6
North Witham Lincs 155 E8
Northwold Norf 140 D5
Northwood Derbys 170 C3
IoW 20 C5
Kent 71 F11
London 85 G9
Mers 182 B6
Shrops 149 C9
Staffs 168 G5
Stoke 168 F5
Northwood Green Glos 80 B2
Northwood Hills London 85 G9
North Woolwich London 68 D2
North Wootton Dorset 29 E11
Norf 158 E2
Som 44 E5
North Wraxall Wilts 61 D10
North Wroughton
Swindon 63 C7
Norton Devon 9 E7
Devon 24 B3
E Sus 23 E7
Glos 99 G7
Halton 183 E9
Herts 104 E4
IoW 20 D2
Mon 78 B6
Northants 120 E2
Notts 187 G9
N Som 59 G10
Powys 114 D6
Shrops 131 B11
Shrops 131 G9
Shrops 132 C4
Stockton 234 G4
Suff 125 D9
Swansea 56 D3
Swansea 56 D6
S Yorks 186 E5
S Yorks 198 D4
Wilts 61 C11
W Mid 133 G7
Worcs 99 B10
Worcs 117 G7
W Sus 22 B6
W Sus 22 D5
Norton Ash Kent 70 G3
Norton Bavant Wilts 46 E2
Norton Bridge Staffs 151 C7
Norton Canes Staffs 133 B10
Norton Canon Hereford 97 B7
Norton Corner Norf 159 D11
Norton Disney Lincs 172 D5
Norton East Staffs 133 B10
Norton Ferris Wilts 45 F9
Norton Fitzwarren
Som 27 B11
Norton Green Herts 104 G4
IoW 20 D2
Staffs 168 E6
W Mid 118 C3
Norton Hawkfield Bath 60 G5
Norton Heath Essex 87 E10

Norton in Hales Shrops 150 B4
Norton-in-the-Moors
Stoke 168 E5
Norton-Juxta-Twycross
Leics 134 B6
Norton-le-Clay N Yorks 215 E8
Norton Lindsey Warks 118 E4
Norton Little Green
Suff 125 D9
Norton Malreward Bath 60 F6
Norton Mandeville Essex 87 E9
Norton-on-Derwent
N Yorks 216 E5
Norton St Philip Som 45 B9
Norton Subcourse Norf 143 D8
Norton sub Hamdon Som 29 D7
Norton's Wood N Som 60 E2
Norton Woodseats
S Yorks 186 E5
Norwell Notts 172 C3
Norwell Woodhouse
Notts 172 C2
Norwich Norf 142 B4
Norwick Shetland 312 B8
Norwood Derbys 187 E7
Dorset 29 F8
Norwood End Essex 87 D9
Norwood Green London 66 D6
W Yorks 196 B6
Norwood Hill Sur 51 E8
Norwood New Town
London 67 E10
Norwoodside Cambs 139 D8
Noseley Leics 136 D4
Noss Highld 310 D7
Shetland 313 M5
Noss Mayo Devon 7 F11
Nosterfield N Yorks 214 C5
Nosterfield End Cambs 106 C2
Nostie Highld 295 C10
Notgrove Glos 100 G2
Nottage Bridgend 57 F10
Notter Corn 7 C7
Nottingham Nottingham 153 B11
Notting Hill London 67 C8
Nottington Dorset 17 E9
Notton Wilts 62 F2
W Yorks 197 E10
Nounsley Essex 88 C3
Noutard's Green Worcs 116 D5
Novar House Highld 300 C6
Nova Scotia Ches W 167 B10
Novers Park Bristol 60 F5
Noverton Glos 99 G9
Nowton Suff 125 E7
Nox Shrops 149 G8
Noyadd Trefawr Ceredig 92 B5
Noyadd Wilym Ceredig 92 C4
Nuffield Oxon 65 B7
Nun Appleton N Yorks 207 F7
Nunburnholme E Yorks 208 D2
Nuncargate Notts 171 E8
Nunclose Cumb 230 B5
Nuneaton Warks 135 E7
Nuneham Courtenay
Oxon 83 F9
Nuney Green Oxon 65 D7
Nunhead London 67 D11
Nun Hills Lancs 195 C11
Nun Monkton N Yorks 206 B6
Nunney Som 45 D8
Nunney Catch Som 45 E8
Nunnington N Yorks 216 D3
Nunnykirk Northumb 252 E3
Nunsthorpe NE Lincs 201 F9
Nunthorpe Mbro 225 C10
York 207 C8
Nunton Wilts 31 B11
Nunwick N Yorks 214 E6
Nupdown S Glos 79 F10
Nupend Glos 80 D3
Glos 80 F4
Nup End Bucks 84 B5
Herts 86 B2
Nuper's Hatch Essex 87 G8
Nuppend Glos 79 E10
Nuptown Brack 65 E11
Nursling Hants 32 D5
Nursted Hants 34 C3
Nursteed Wilts 62 G4
Nurston V Glam 58 F5
Nurton Staffs 132 D6
Nurton Hill Staffs 132 D6
Nutbourne W Sus 22 B3
W Sus 35 D9
Nutbourne Common
W Sus 35 D9
Nutburn Hants 32 C5
Nutcombe Sur 49 G11
Nutfield Sur 51 C10
Nut Grove Mers 183 C7
Nuthall Notts 171 G8
Nuthampstead Herts 105 E8
Nuthurst Warks 118 C3
W Sus 35 B11
Nutley E Sus 36 B6
Hants 48 E6
Nuttall Gtr Man 195 D9
Nutwell S Yorks 198 G6
Nybster Highld 310 C7
Nye N Som 60 G2
Nyetimber W Sus 22 D5
Nyewood W Sus 34 C4
Nyland Som 44 C3
Nymet Rowland Devon 26 F2
Nymet Tracey Devon 26 G2
Nympsfield Glos 80 E4
Nynehead Som 27 C10
Nythe Som 44 G2
Swindon 63 B7
Nyton W Sus 22 B6

O

Oadby Leics 136 C2
Oad Street Kent 69 G11
Oakall Green Worcs 116 E6
Oakamoor Staffs 169 G9
Oakbank W Loth 269 B11
Oak Bank Gtr Man 195 F10
Oak Cross Devon 12 B6
Oakdale Caerph 77 F11
N Yorks 205 B11
Poole 18 C6
Oake Som 27 B11
Oake Green Som 27 B11
Oaken Staffs 133 C7
Oakenclough Lancs 202 D6
Oakengates Telford 150 G4
Oakenholt Flint 182 G3
Oakenshaw Durham 233 D10
Lancs 203 G10
W Yorks 197 B7
Oakerthorpe Derbys 170 E5
Oakes W Yorks 196 D6
Oakfield Herts 104 F3
IoW 21 C7
Torf 78 G4
Oakford Ceredig 111 F9
Devon 26 C6
Oakfordbridge Devon 26 C6
Oakgrove Ches E 168 B6
M Keynes 103 D7
Oakham Rutland 137 B7
W Mid 133 F9
Oakhanger Ches E 168 E3
Hants 49 F9
Oakhill Som 44 D6
W Sus 51 G7
Oak Hill Stoke 168 G5
Suff 109 B7
Oakhurst Kent 52 C4
Oakington Cambs 123 E8
Oaklands Carms 74 B6
Herts 86 B2
Powys 113 G10
Oakleigh Park London 86 G3
Oakle Street Glos 80 B3
Oakley Beds 121 G10
Bucks 83 C10
Fife 279 D10
Glos 99 G9
Hants 48 C5
Oxon 84 E3
Poole 18 B6
Staffs 150 B4
Suff 126 B3
Oakley Court Oxon 64 B6
Oakley Green Windsor 66 D2
Oakley Park Powys 129 F9
Suff 126 B3
Oakley Wood Oxon 64 B6
Oakmere Ches W 167 B9
Oakridge Glos 80 E6
Hants 48 C6
Oakridge Lynch Glos 80 E6
Oaks Shrops 131 C8
Oaksey Wilts 81 G7
Oaks Green Derbys 152 C3
Oakshaw Ford Cumb 240 B2
Oakshott Hants 34 B2
Oaks in Charnwood
Leics 153 F9
Oakthorpe Leics 152 G6
Oak Tree Darl 225 C7
Oakwell W Yorks 197 B8
Oakwood Derby 153 B7
London 86 F3
Northumb 241 D10
Warr 183 C11
W Yorks 206 F2
Oakwoodhill Sur 50 F6
Oakworth W Yorks 204 F6
Oape Highld 309 J4
Oare Kent 70 G4
Som 41 D10
W Berks 64 E4
Wilts 63 G7
Oareford Som 41 D10
Oasby Lincs 155 B10
Oath Som 28 B5
Oathill Dorset 28 F6
Oathlaw Angus 287 B8
Oatlands Glasgow 267 C11
N Yorks 205 C11
Oatlands Park Sur 66 G5
Oban Argyll 289 G10
Highld 295 G10
W Isles 305 H3
Obley Shrops 114 B6
Oborne Dorset 29 D11
Obthorpe Lincs 155 F11
Obthorpe Lodge Lincs 156 F2
Occlestone Green
Ches W 167 C11
Occold Suff 126 C3
Ocean Village Soton 32 E6
Ochiltree E Ayrs 258 E2
Ochr-y-foel Denb 181 F9
Ochtermuthill Perth 286 F2
Ochtertyre Perth 286 E2
Ochtow Highld 309 J4
Ockbrook Derbys 153 B8
Ocker Hill W Mid 133 E9
Ockeridge Worcs 116 E5
Ockford Ridge Sur 50 E3
Ockham Sur 50 B5
Ockle Highld 289 B7
Ockley Sur 50 F6
Ocle Pychard Hereford 97 B11
Octon E Yorks 217 F10
Octon Cross Roads
E Yorks 217 F10
Odam Barton Devon 26 D2
Odcombe Som 29 D8
Odd Down Bath 61 G8
Oddendale Cumb 221 C11
Odder Lincs 188 G6
Oddingley Worcs 117 F8
Oddington Glos 100 F4
Oxon 83 C9
Odell Beds 121 F9
Odham Devon 25 G7
Odie Orkney 314 D6
Odiham Hants 49 C8
Odsal W Yorks 197 B7
Odsey Cambs 104 D5
Odstock Wilts 31 B10
Odstone Leics 135 B7
Offchurch Warks 119 D7
Offenham Worcs 99 B11
Offenham Cross Worcs 99 B11
Offerton Gtr Man 184 D6
T&W 243 F8
Offerton Green Gtr Man 184 D6
Offham E Sus 36 E5
Kent 53 B7
W Sus 35 F8
Offleyhay Staffs 150 D5
Offleymarsh Staffs 150 D5
Offleyrock Staffs 150 D5
Offord Cluny Cambs 122 D4
Offord D'Arcy Cambs 122 D4
Offton Suff 107 B11
Offwell Devon 15 B9
Ogbourne Maizey Wilts 63 E7
Ogbourne St Andrew
Wilts 63 E7
Ogbourne St George
Wilts 63 E8
Ogden W Yorks 205 G7
Ogdens Hants 31 E11
Ogil Angus 292 G6
Ogle Northumb 242 B4
Ogmore V Glam 57 F11
Ogmore-by-Sea / Aberogwr
V Glam 57 F11
Ogmore Vale Bridgend 76 G6
Okeford Fitzpaine
Dorset 30 E4
Okehampton Devon 13 B7
Okehampton Camp
Devon 13 C7
Oker Derbys 170 C3
Okewood Hill Sur 50 F6
Okle Green Glos 98 F5
Okraquoy Shetland 313 K6
Okus Swindon 62 C6
Olchard Devon 14 F3
Old Northants 120 C5
Old Aberdeen
Aberdeen 293 C11
Old Alresford Hants 48 G5
Oldany Highld 306 F6
Old Arley Warks 134 E5
Old Balornock Glasgow 268 B2
Old Basford Nottingham 171 G8
Old Basing Hants 49 C7
Oldbelses Borders 262 E3
Oldberrow Warks 118 D2
Old Bewick Northumb 264 E3
Old Bexley London 68 E3
Old Blair Perth 291 G10
Old Bolingbroke Lincs 174 B4
Oldborough Devon 26 F3
Old Boston Mers 183 B9
Old Bramhope
W Yorks 205 E10
Old Brampton Derbys 186 G4
Old Bridge of Tilt
Perth 291 G10
Old Bridge of Urr
Dumfries 237 C9
Oldbrook M Keynes 103 D7
Old Buckenham Norf 141 E11
Old Burdon T&W 243 G9
Old Burghclere Hants 48 B3
Oldbury Kent 52 B5
Shrops 132 E4
Warks 134 E6
W Mid 133 F9
Oldbury Naite S Glos 79 G10
Oldbury-on-Severn
S Glos 79 G10
Oldbury on the Hill Glos 61 B10
Old Byland N Yorks 215 B11
Old Cambus Borders 272 B6
Old Cardinham Castle
Corn 6 B2
Old Carlisle Cumb 229 B11
Old Cassop Durham 234 D2
Oldcastle Mon 96 G6
Oldcastle Heath Ches W 167 F7
Old Castleton Borders 250 E2
Old Catton Norf 160 G4
Old Chalford Oxon 100 F6
Old Church Stoke
Powys 130 E5
Old Clee NE Lincs 201 F9
Old Cleeve Som 42 E4
Old Colwyn Conwy 180 F5
Old Coppice Shrops 131 B9
Old Corry Highld 295 C8
Oldcotes Notts 187 D9
Old Coulsdon London 51 B10
Old Country Hereford 98 C4
Old Craig Aberds 303 G9
Angus 292 G4
Oldcroft Glos 79 D10
Old Crombie Aberds 302 D5
Old Cryals Kent 53 E7
Old Cullen Moray 302 C5
Old Dailly S Ayrs 244 D6
Old Dalby Leics 154 E3
Old Dam Derbys 185 F10
Old Deer Aberds 303 E9
Old Denaby S Yorks 187 B7
Old Ditch Som 44 D4
Old Dolphin W Yorks 205 G8
Old Down S Glos 60 B6
Old Duffus Moray 301 C11
Old Edlington S Yorks 187 B8
Old Eldon Durham 233 F10
Old Ellerby E Yorks 209 F9
Oldend Glos 80 D3
Old Fallings W Mid 133 C8
Oldfallow Staffs 151 G9
Old Farm Park
M Keynes 103 D8
Old Felixstowe Suff 108 D6
Oldfield Cumb 229 F7
Shrops 132 F3
Worcs 116 E6
W Yorks 196 E6
W Yorks 204 F6
Old Field Shrops 115 B9
Oldfield Brow Gtr Man 184 D3
Oldfield Park Bath 61 G8
Old Fletton Pboro 138 D3
Old Fold T&W 243 E7
Oldford Som 45 C9
Old Ford London 67 C11
Old Forge Hereford 79 B9
Oldfurnace Staffs 169 G8
Old Furnace Torf 78 E3
Old Gate Lincs 157 E8
Old Glossop Derbys 185 C8
Old Goginan Ceredig 128 G3
Old Goole E Yorks 199 C8
Old Gore Hereford 98 F2
Old Graitney Dumfries 239 D8
Old Grimsby Scilly 1 F3
Oldhall Renfs 267 C10
Old Hall Powys 129 G8
Oldhall Green Suff 125 F7
Old Hall Green Herts 105 G7
Oldhall Ho Highld 310 D6
Old Hall Street Norf 160 C6
Oldham Gtr Man 196 F2
Oldham Edge Gtr Man 196 F2
Oldhamstocks E Loth 282 G4
Old Harlow Essex 87 C7
Old Hatfield Herts 86 D2
Old Heath Essex 107 G10
Old Heathfield E Sus 37 C9
Old Hill W Mid 133 F9
Old Hills Worcs 98 B6
Old Hunstanton Norf 175 G11
Oldhurst Cambs 122 B6
Old Hurst Cambs 122 B5
Old Hutton Cumb 211 B11
Oldington Shrops 132 D4
Old Johnstone Dumfries 248 D6
Old Kea Corn 4 G6
Old Kilpatrick W Dunb 277 G9
Old Kinnernie Aberds 293 C9
Old Knebworth Herts 104 G4
Oldland S Glos 61 E7
Oldland Common S Glos 61 E7
Old Langho Lancs 203 F10
Old Laxey IoM 192 D5
Old Leake Lincs 174 E6
Old Leckie Stirl 278 C3
Old Lindley W Yorks 196 D5
Old Linslade C Beds 103 F8
Old Llanberis / Nant Peris
Gwyn 163 D10
Old Malden London 67 F8
Old Malton N Yorks 216 E5
Old Marton Shrops 148 C6
Old Mead Essex 105 F10
Oldmeldrum Aberds 303 G8
Old Micklefield
W Yorks 206 G4
Old Mill Corn 12 G3
Old Milton Hants 19 C10
Old Milverton Warks 118 D5
Oldmixon N Som 43 B10
Old Monkland N Lnrk 268 C4
Old Nenthorn Borders 262 B5
Old Netley Hants 33 F7
Old Neuadd Powys 129 F11
Old Newton Suff 125 E11
Old Oak Common London 67 C8
Old Park Corn 6 B4
Telford 132 B3
Old Passage S Glos 60 B5
Old Perton Staffs 133 D7
Old Philpstoun W Loth 279 F11
Old Polmont Falk 279 F8
Old Portsmouth Ptsmth 21 B8
Old Quarrington
Durham 234 D2
Old Radnor Powys 114 F5
Old Rattray Aberds 303 D10
Old Rayne Aberds 302 G6
Old Romney Kent 39 B8
Old Shirley Soton 32 E5
Oldshore Beg Highld 306 D6
Old Shoreham W Sus 36 F2
Oldshoremore Highld 306 D7
Old Snydale W Yorks 198 C2
Old Sodbury S Glos 61 C9
Old Somerby Lincs 155 C9
Oldstead N Yorks 215 C10
Old Stillington Stockton 234 G3
Old Storridge Common
Worcs 116 G4
Old Stratford Northants 102 C5
Old Struan Perth 291 G10
Old Swan Mers 182 C5
Old Swarland Northumb 252 C5
Old Swinford W Mid 133 G8
Old Tame Gtr Man 196 F3
Old Tebay Cumb 222 D2
Old Thirsk N Yorks 215 C8
Old Tinnis Borders 261 D9
Old Toll S Ayrs 257 E9
Oldtown Aberds 293 C7
Aberds 302 G5
Highld 309 L5
Old Town Cumb 211 C11
Cumb 230 C5
Edin 280 G5
E Sus 23 F9
E Sus 38 F2
E Sus 38 F4
E Yorks 218 F3
Herts 104 F4
Scilly 1 G4
Swindon 63 C7
W Yorks 196 B3
Oldtown of Ord Aberds 302 D6
Old Trafford Gtr Man 184 B4
Old Tree Kent 71 G8
Old Tupton Derbys 170 B5
Oldwalls Swansea 56 C3
Old Warden C Beds 104 C2
Old Warren Flint 166 C4
Oldway Swansea 56 D5
Torbay 9 C7
Old Way Som 28 D5
Oldways End Devon 26 B5
Old Weston Cambs 121 B11
Old Wharf Hereford 98 D4
Oldwhat Aberds 303 D8
Old Whittington Derbys 186 G5
Oldwich Lane W Mid 118 C4
Old Wick Highld 310 D7
Old Wimpole Cambs 122 G6
Old Windsor Windsor 66 E3
Old Wingate Durham 234 D3
Old Wives Lees Kent 54 C5
Old Woking Sur 50 B4
Old Wolverton
M Keynes 102 C6
Oldwood Worcs 115 D11
Old Woodhall Lincs 174 B2
Old Woodhouses
Shrops 167 G9
Old Woodstock Oxon 82 B6
Olgrinmore Highld 310 D4
Olive Green Staffs 152 F2
Oliver's Battery Hants 33 B7
Ollaberry Shetland 312 E5
Ollag W Isles 297 G3
Ollerbrook Booth
Derbys 185 D10
Ollerton Ches E 184 F3
Notts 171 B11
Shrops 150 D2
Ollerton Fold Lancs 194 C6
Ollerton Lane Shrops 150 D3
Olmarch Ceredig 112 F2
Olmstead Green Essex 106 C2
Olney M Keynes 121 G7
Olrig Ho Highld 310 C5
Olton W Mid 134 G2
Olveston S Glos 60 B6
Olwen Ceredig 93 B11
Ombersley Worcs 116 E6
Ompton Notts 171 B11
Omunsgarth Shetland 313 J5
Onchan IoM 192 E4
Onecote Staffs 169 D9
Onehouse Suff 125 F10
Onen Mon 78 C6
Onesacre S Yorks 186 C3
Ongar Hill Norf 157 E11
Ongar Street Hereford 115 D7
Onibury Shrops 115 B9
Onich Highld 290 G2
Onllwyn Neath 76 C4
Onneley Staffs 168 G3
Onslow Village Sur 50 D3
Onthank E Ayrs 267 G8
Onziebust Orkney 314 D4
Openshaw Gtr Man 184 B5
Openwoodgate Derbys 170 F5
Opinan Highld 299 B7
Highld 307 K3
Orange Lane Borders 272 G5
Orange Row Norf 157 E10
Orasaigh W Isles 305 G5
Orbiston N Lnrk 268 D4
Orbliston Moray 302 D3
Orbost Highld 298 E2
Orby Lincs 175 B7
Orchard Hill Devon 24 B6
Orchard Leigh Bucks 85 E7
Orchard Portman Som 28 C2
Orcheston Wilts 46 D5
Orcop Hereford 97 F9
Orcop Hill Hereford 97 F9
Ord Highld 295 D8
Ordale Shetland 312 C8
Ordhead Aberds 293 B8
Ordie Aberds 292 C6
Ordiequish Moray 302 D3
Ordiqhill Aberds 302 D5
Ordley Northumb 241 F10
Ordsall Gtr Man 184 B4
Notts 187 E11
Ore E Sus 38 E4
Oreston Plym 7 E10
Oreton Shrops 132 G3
Orford Suff 109 B8
Warr 183 C10
Organford Dorset 18 C4
Orgreave Staffs 152 F3
S Yorks 186 D6
Oridge Street Glos 98 F5
Orlandon Pembs 72 D4
Orlestone Kent 54 G3
Orleton Hereford 115 D9
Worcs 116 D3
Orleton Common
Hereford 115 D9
Orlingbury Northants 121 C7
Ormacleit W Isles 297 H3
Ormathwaite Cumb 229 F11
Ormesby Redcar 225 B10
Ormesby St Margaret
Norf 161 G9
Ormesby St Michael
Norf 161 G9
Ormiclate Castle
W Isles 297 H3
Ormidale Lodge Argyll 275 F11
Ormiscaig Highld 307 K3
Ormiston Borders 262 G2
E Loth 271 B8
Ormsaigbeg Highld 288 C6
Ormsaigmore Highld 288 C6
Ormsary Argyll 275 F8
Ormsgill Cumb 210 E3
Ormskirk Lancs 194 F2
Ornsby Hill Durham 233 B9
Orpington London 68 F3
Orrell Gtr Man 194 F4
Mers 182 B4
Orrell Post Gtr Man 194 G4
Orrisdale IoM 192 C4
Orrock Fife 280 D4
Orroland Dumfries 237 E9
Orsett Thurrock 68 C6
Orsett Heath Thurrock 68 D6
Orslow Staffs 150 F6
Orston Notts 172 G3
Orthwaite Cumb 229 E11
Ortner Lancs 202 C6
Orton Cumb 222 D2
Northants 120 B6
Staffs 133 D7
Orton Brimbles Pboro 138 D3
Orton Goldhay Pboro 138 D3
Orton Longueville
Pboro 138 D3
Orton Malborne Pboro 138 D3
Orton-on-the-Hill Leics 134 C6
Orton Rigg Cumb 239 G8
Orton Southgate Pboro 138 E2
Orton Waterville Pboro 138 D3
Orton Wistow Pboro 138 D2
Orwell Cambs 123 G7
Osbaldeston Lancs 203 G8
Osbaldeston Green
Lancs 203 G8
Osbaldwick York 207 C8
Osbaston Leics 135 C8
Shrops 148 E6
Telford 149 F11
Osbaston Hollow Leics 135 B8
Osbournby Lincs 155 B11
Oscroft Ches W 167 B8
Ose Highld 298 E3
Osea Island Essex 88 D6
Osehill Green Dorset 29 F11
Osgathorpe Leics 153 F8
Osgodby Lincs 189 C9
N Yorks 207 G8
N Yorks 217 C11
Osgodby Common
N Yorks 207 F8
Osidge London 86 G3
Oskaig Highld 295 B7
Oskamull Argyll 288 E6
Osleston Derbys 152 B4
Osmaston Derby 153 C7
Derbys 170 G2
Osmington Dorset 17 E10
Osmington Mills Dorset 17 E10
Osmondthorpe W Yorks 206 G2
Osmotherley N Yorks 225 F9
Osney Oxon 83 D8
Ospisdale Highld 309 L7
Ospringe Kent 70 G4
Ossaborough Devon 40 E3
Ossemsley Hants 19 B10
Osset Spa W Yorks 197 D9
Ossett W Yorks 197 C9
Ossett Street Side
W Yorks 197 C9
Ossington Notts 172 C3
Ostend Essex 88 F6
Norf 161 C7
Osterley London 66 D6
Oswaldkirk N Yorks 216 D2
Oswaldtwistle Lancs 195 B8
Oswestry Shrops 148 D5
Otby Lincs 189 C10
Oteley Shrops 149 C8
Otford Kent 52 B4
Otham Kent 53 C9
Otham Hole Kent 53 C10
Otherton Staffs 151 G8
Othery Som 43 G11
Otley Suff 126 F4
W Yorks 205 D10
Otterbourne Hants 33 C7
Otterburn Northumb 251 E9
N Yorks 204 B3
Otterburn Camp
Northumb 251 D9
Otterden Place Kent 54 C2
Otter Ferry Argyll 275 E10
Otterford Som 28 E2
Otterham Corn 11 C9
Otterhampton Som 43 E8
Otterham Quay Kent 69 F10
Otterham Station Corn 11 D9
Otter Ho Argyll 275 F10
Ottershaw Sur 66 G4
Otterspool Mers 182 D5
Otterswick Shetland 312 E7
Otterton Devon 15 D7
Otterwood Hants 32 G6
Ottery St Mary Devon 15 B8
Ottinge Kent 55 E7
Ottringham E Yorks 201 C9
Oughterby Cumb 239 F7
Oughtershaw N Yorks 213 C7
Oughterside Cumb 229 C8
Oughtibridge S Yorks 186 C4
Oughtrington Warr 183 D11
Oulston N Yorks 215 E10
Oulton Cumb 238 G6
Norf 160 D2
Staffs 150 E5
Staffs 151 B8
Suff 143 D10
W Yorks 197 B11
Oulton Broad Suff 143 E10
Oultoncross Staffs 151 C8
Oulton Grange Staffs 151 B8
Oulton Heath Staffs 151 B8
Oulton Street Norf 160 D3
Oundle Northants 137 F10
Ounsdale Staffs 133 E7
Ousby Cumb 231 E8
Ousdale Highld 311 G4
Ousden Suff 124 F4
Ousefleet E Yorks 199 C10
Ousel Hole W Yorks 205 E8
Ouston Durham 243 G7
Northumb 241 G7
Northumb 242 C3
Outcast Cumb 210 D6
Out Elmstead Kent 55 C8
Outer Hope Devon 8 G3
Outertown Orkney 314 E2
Outgate Cumb 221 F7
Outhgill Cumb 222 E5
Outhill Warks 118 D2
Outhills Aberds 303 D10
Outlands Staffs 150 C5
Outlane W Yorks 196 D5
Outlane Moor W Yorks 196 D5
Outlet Village Ches W 182 G6
Outmarsh Wilts 61 G11
Out Newton E Yorks 201 C11
Out Rawcliffe Lancs 202 E4
Outwell Norf 139 C10
Outwick Hants 31 D10
Outwood Gtr Man 195 F9
Som 28 B4
Sur 51 D10
W Yorks 197 C10
Outwoods Leics 153 F8
Staffs 150 F5
Staffs 152 E4
Warks 134 G4
Ouzlewell Green
W Yorks 197 B10
Ovenden W Yorks 196 B5
Ovenscloss Borders 261 C11
Over Cambs 123 C7
Ches W 167 B10
Glos 80 B4
S Glos 60 C5
Overa Farm Stud Norf 141 F9
Overbister Orkney 314 B6
Over Burrow Lancs 212 D2
Over Burrows Derbys 152 B5
Overbury Worcs 99 D9
Overcombe Dorset 17 E9
Over Compton Dorset 29 D9
Overend W Mid 133 G9
Over End Cambs 137 E11
Derbys 186 G3
Overgreen Derbys 186 G4
Over Green W Mid 134 E3
Over Haddon Derbys 170 B2
Over Hulton Gtr Man 195 F7
Over Kellet Lancs 211 E10
Over Kiddington Oxon 101 G8
Over Knutsford Ches E 184 F3
Over Langshaw
Borders 271 G10
Overleigh Som 44 F3
Overley Staffs 152 F3
Overley Green Warks 117 F11
Over Monnow Mon 79 C8
Overmoor Staffs 169 F7
Over Norton Oxon 100 F6
Over Peover Ches E 184 G3
Overpool Ches W 182 F5
Overs Shrops 131 D7
Overscaig Hotel Highld 309 G4
Overseal Derbys 152 F5
Over Silton N Yorks 225 G9
Overslade Warks 119 C9
Oversland Kent 54 B5
Oversley Green Warks 117 F11
Overstone Northants 120 D6
Over Stowey Som 43 F7
Overstrand Norf 160 A4
Over Stratton Som 28 D6
Over Tabley Ches E 184 E2
Overthorpe Northants 101 C9
W Yorks 197 D8
Overton Aberdeen 293 B10
Aberds 293 B9
Ches W 183 F8
Dumfries 237 C11
Glos 80 C2
Hants 48 D4
Invclyd 276 G5
Lancs 202 B4
N Yorks 207 B7
Shrops 115 C10
Staffs 151 B10
Swansea 56 D3
W Yorks 197 D9
Overton Bridge Wrex 166 G5
Overton / Owrtyn Wrex 166 G5
Overtown Lancs 212 D2
N Lnrk 268 E6
Swindon 63 D7
W Yorks 197 D11
Over Town Lancs 195 B11
Over Wallop Hants 47 F9
Over Whitacre Warks 134 E5
Over Worton Oxon 101 F8
Oving Bucks 102 G5
W Sus 22 C6
Ovingdean Brighton 36 G5
Ovingham Northumb 242 E3
Ovington Durham 224 C2
Essex 106 C5
Hants 48 G5
Norf 141 C8
Northumb 242 E3
Owen's Bank Staffs 152 D4
Ower Hants 32 D4
Owermoigne Dorset 17 D11
Owlbury Shrops 130 E6
Owlcotes Derbys 170 B6
Owl End Cambs 122 B4
Owler Bar Derbys 186 F3
Owlerton S Yorks 186 D4
Owlet W Yorks 205 F9
Owlpen Glos 80 F4
Owl's Green Suff 126 D5
Owlsmoor Brack 65 G11
Owlswick Bucks 84 D3
Owlthorpe S Yorks 186 E6
Owmby Lincs 200 G5
Owmby-by-Spital Lincs 189 D8
Ownham W Berks 64 E2
Owrtyn / Overton Wrex 166 G5
Owslebury Hants 33 C8
Owston Leics 136 B5
S Yorks 198 E5
Owston Ferry N Lincs 199 G10
Owstwick E Yorks 209 G11
Owthorne E Yorks 201 B10
Owthorpe Notts 154 C3
Owton Manor Hrtlpl 234 F5
Oxborough Norf 140 C4
Oxclose S Yorks 186 E6
T&W 243 F7
Oxcombe Lincs 190 F4
Oxcroft Derbys 187 G7
Oxcroft Estate Derbys 187 G7
Oxen End Essex 106 F3
Oxenhall Glos 98 F4
Oxenholme Cumb 211 B10
Oxenhope W Yorks 204 F6
Oxen Park Cumb 210 B6
Oxenpill Som 44 E2
Oxenton Glos 99 E9
Oxenwood Wilts 47 B10
Oxford Oxon 83 D8
Stoke 168 E5
Oxgang E Dunb 278 G3
Oxgangs Edin 270 B4
Oxhey Herts 85 F10
Oxhill Durham 242 G5
Warks 100 B6
Oxlease Herts 86 D2
Oxley W Mid 133 C8
Oxley Green Essex 88 C6
Oxley's Green E Sus 37 C11
Oxlode Cambs 139 F9
Oxnam Borders 262 F5
Oxnead Norf 160 E4
Oxshott Sur 66 G6
Oxspring S Yorks 197 G9
Oxted Sur 51 C11
Oxton Borders 271 E9
Mers 182 D3
Notts 171 E10
N Yorks 206 E6
Oxton Rakes Derbys 186 G4
Oxwich Swansea 56 D3
Oxwich Green Swansea 56 D3
Oxwick Norf 159 D8
Oykel Bridge Highld 309 J3
Oyne Aberds 302 G6
Oystermouth Swansea 56 D6
Ozleworth Glos 80 G3

P

Pabail Iarach W Isles 304 E7
Pabail Uarach W Isles 304 E7
Pabo Conwy 180 F4
Pace Gate N Yorks 205 C8
Pachesham Park Sur 51 B7
Packers Hill Dorset 30 E2
Packington Leics 153 G7
Packmoor Staffs 168 E5
Packmores Warks 118 D5
Packwood W Mid 118 C3
Packwood Gullet
W Mid 118 C3
Padanaram Angus 287 B8
Padbury Bucks 102 E4
Paddington London 67 C9
Warr 183 D10
Paddlesworth Kent 55 F7
Kent 69 G7
Paddock Kent 54 C3
W Yorks 196 D6
Paddockhaugh Moray 302 D2
Paddockhill Ches E 184 F4
Paddockhole Dumfries 248 G6
Paddock Wood Kent 53 E7
Paddolgreen Shrops 149 C10
Padfield Derbys 185 B8
Padgate Warr 183 D10
Padham's Green Essex 87 F10
Padiham Lancs 203 G11
Padney Cambs 123 C10
Padog Conwy 164 E4
Padside N Yorks 205 B9
Padside Green N Yorks 205 B9
Padson Devon 13 B7
Padstow Corn 10 F4
Padworth W Berks 64 F6
Padworth Common
Hants 64 G6
Paganhill Glos 80 D4
Page Bank Durham 233 D10
Page Moss Mers 182 C6
Page's Green Suff 126 D2
Pagham W Sus 22 D5
Paglesham Churchend
Essex 88 G6
Paglesham Eastend
Essex 88 G6
Paibeil W Isles 296 E3
Paible W Isles 305 J2
Paignton Torbay 9 C7
Pailton Warks 135 G9
Painleyhill Staffs 151 C10
Painscastle Powys 96 B3
Painshawfield Northumb 242 E3
Pains Hill Sur 52 C2
Painsthorpe E Yorks 208 B2
Painswick Glos 80 D5
Painter's Forstal Kent 54 B3
Painters Green Wrex 167 G8
Painter's Green Herts 86 B3
Painthorpe W Yorks 197 D10
Paintmoor Som 28 F4
Pairc Shiaboist W Isles 304 D4
Paisley Renfs 267 C9
Pakefield Suff 143 E10
Pakenham Suff 125 D8
Pale Gwyn 147 B9
Pale Green Essex 106 C3
Palehouse Common
E Sus 23 B7
Palestine Hants 47 E9
Paley Street Windsor 65 D11
Palfrey W Mid 133 D10
Palgowan Dumfries 245 G9
Palgrave Suff 126 B2
Pallaflat Cumb 219 C9
Pallington Dorset 17 C11
Pallion T&W 243 F9
Pallister Mbro 225 B10
Palmarsh Kent 54 G6
Palmer Moor Derbys 152 C2
Palmersbridge Corn 11 F9
Palmers Cross Staffs 133 C7
Sur 50 E4
Palmer's Flat Glos 79 D9
Palmers Green London 86 G4
Palmer's Green Kent 53 E7
Palmerstown V Glam 58 F6
Palmersville T&W 243 C7
Palmstead Kent 55 D7
Palnackie Dumfries 237 D10
Palnure Dumfries 236 C6
Palterton Derbys 171 B7
Pamber End Hants 48 B6
Pamber Green Hants 48 B6
Pamber Heath Hants 64 G6
Pamington Glos 99 E8
Pamphill Dorset 31 G7
Pampisford Cambs 105 B9
Pan IoW 20 D6
Orkney 314 G3
Panborough Som 44 D3
Panbride Angus 287 D9
Pancakehill Glos 81 C9
Pancrasweek Devon 24 F3
Pancross V Glam 58 F4
Pandy Gwyn 128 C2
Gwyn 146 F4
Gwyn 147 D7
Mon 96 G6
Powys 129 C8
Wrex 148 B3
Wrex 166 G6
Pandy'r Capel Denb 165 E9
Pandy Tudur Conwy 164 C5
Panfield Essex 106 F4
Pangbourne W Berks 64 D6
Panhall Fife 280 C6
Panks Bridge Hereford 98 B2
Pannal N Yorks 206 C2
Pannal Ash N Yorks 205 C11
Pannel's Ash Essex 106 C5
Panpunton Powys 114 C5
Panshanger Herts 86 C3
Pant Denb 166 E2
Flint 181 G10
Gwyn 144 C4
M Tydf 77 D9
Powys 129 C11
Shrops 148 E5
Wrex 166 D5
Wrex 166 F3
Pantasaph Flint 181 F11
Pantdu Neath 57 C9
Panteg Ceredig 111 E9
Torf 78 F4
Pantersbridge Corn 6 B3
Pant-glas Gwyn 163 F7
Pant-glâs Powys 128 D5
Pant-glas Shrops 148 C5
Pantgwyn Carms 93 F11
Ceredig 92 B4
Pant-lasau Swansea 57 B7
Pantmawr Cardiff 58 C6
Pant Mawr Powys 129 G7
Panton Lincs 189 F11
Pant-pastynog Denb 165 C8
Pantperthog Gwyn 128 C4
Pantside Caerph 78 F2
Pant-teg Carms 93 F9
Pant-y-Caws Carms 92 F3
Pant-y-crûg Ceredig 112 B3
Pant-y-dwr Powys 113 B9
Powys 113 C9
Pant-y-ffridd Powys 130 C3
Pantyffynnon Carms 75 C10
Pantygasseg Torf 78 F3
Pantymwyn Flint 165 C11
Pant-y-pyllau Bridgend 58 C2
Pant-yr-awel Bridgend 58 B2
Pant-y-Wacco Flint 181 F10
Panxworth Norf 161 G7
Papcastle Cumb 229 E8
Papermill Bank Shrops 149 D11
Papigoe Highld 310 D7
Papil Shetland 313 K5
Papley Northants 138 F2
Orkney 314 G4
Papple E Loth 281 G11
Papplewick Notts 171 E8
Papworth Everard
Cambs 122 E5
Papworth St Agnes
Cambs 122 E5
Papworth Village Settlement
Cambs 122 E5
Par Corn 5 E11
Paradise Glos 80 C5
Paradise Green Hereford 97 B10
Paramoor Corn 5 F9
Paramour Street Kent 71 G9
Parbold Lancs 194 E3
Parbrook Som 44 F5
W Sus 35 B9
Parc Gwyn 147 C7
Parc Erissey Corn 4 G3
Parc-hendy Swansea 56 B4
Parchey Som 43 F10
Parciau Anglesey 179 E7
Parcllyn Ceredig 110 G4
Parc Mawr Caerph 77 G10
Parc-Seymour Newport 78 G6
Parc-y-rhôs Carms 93 B11
Pardown Hants 48 D5
Pardshaw Cumb 229 G7
Pardshaw Hall Cumb 229 F8
Parham Suff 126 E6
Park Corn 10 G6
Devon 14 B2
Dumfries 247 E10
Som 44 G5
Swindon 63 C7
Park Barn Sur 50 C3
Park Bottom Corn 4 G3
Park Bridge Gtr Man 196 G2
Park Broom Cumb 239 F10
Park Close Lancs 204 E3
Park Corner Bath 45 B9
E Sus 23 C8
E Sus 52 F4
Oxon 65 B7
Windsor 65 C11
Parkend Glos 79 D10
Glos 80 C3
Park End Beds 121 G9
Cambs 123 E11
Mbro 225 B10
Northumb 241 B9
Som 43 G7
Staffs 168 E3
Worcs 116 C5
Parkengear Corn 5 F8
Parker's Corner W Berks 64 E6
Parker's Green Herts 104 F6
Kent 52 D6
Parkeston Essex 108 E4
Parkfield Corn 6 B6
S Glos 61 D7
W Mid 133 D8
Parkfoot Falk 278 F6
Parkgate Ches E 184 G3
Ches W 182 F3
Cumb 229 B10
Dumfries 248 F2
Essex 87 B11
Kent 53 G11
Sur 51 E8
S Yorks 186 B6
Park Gate Dorset 30 F2
Hants 33 F8
Kent 55 D7
Suff 124 F4
Worcs 117 C8
W Yorks 197 E8
Park Green Essex 105 F9
Parkhall W Dunb 277 G9
Park Hall Shrops 148 C6
Parkham Devon 24 C5
Parkham Ash Devon 24 C5
Parkhead Cumb 230 C2
Glasgow 268 C2
S Yorks 186 E4
Park Head Cumb 231 C7
Derbys 170 E5
W Yorks 197 F7
Parkhill Aberds 303 E10
Invclyd 277 G7
Park Hill Glos 79 F9
Kent 54 G3
Mers 194 G3
Notts 171 E11
N Yorks 214 F6
S Yorks 186 D5
Parkhill Ho Aberds 293 B10
Parkhouse Mon 79 E7
Parkhouse Green
Derbys 170 C6
Parkhurst IoW 20 C5
Parklands W Yorks 206 F3

Park Lane Staffs 133 B7
Wrex 149 B8
Park Langley London 67 F11
Park Mains Renfs 277 G9
Parkmill Swansea 56 D4
Park Mill W Yorks 197 E9
Parkneuk Aberds 293 F9
Fife 279 D11
Park Royal London 67 C7
Parkside C Beds 103 G10
Cumb 219 B10
Durham 234 B4
N Lnrk 268 D6
Staffs 151 D8
Wrex 166 D5
Parkstone Poole 18 C6
Park Street Herts 85 E10
W Sus 50 G6
Park Town Luton 103 G11
Oxon 83 D8
Park Village Northumb 240 E5
W Mid 133 C8
Park Villas W Yorks 206 F2
Parkway Hereford 98 D4
Som 29 C9
Park Wood Kent 53 C9
Medway 69 G10
Parkwood Springs
S Yorks 186 D4
Parley Cross Dorset 19 B7
Parley Green Dorset 19 B7
Parliament Heath Suff 107 C9
Parlington W Yorks 206 F4
Parmoor Bucks 65 B9
Parnacott Devon 24 F4
Parney Heath Essex 107 E10
Parr Mers 183 C8
Parracombe Devon 41 E7
Parr Brow Gtr Man 195 G8
Parrog Pembs 91 D10
Parsley Hay Derbys 169 C10
Parslow's Hillock Bucks 84 E4
Parsonage Green Essex 88 D2
Parsonby Cumb 229 D8
Parson Cross S Yorks 186 C5
Parson Drove Cambs 139 B7
Parsons Green London 67 D9
Parson's Heath Essex 107 F10
Partick Glasgow 267 B11
Partington Gtr Man 184 C2
Partney Lincs 174 B6
Parton Cumb 228 G5
Cumb 239 G7
Dumfries 237 B8
Glos 99 G7
Hereford 96 B6
Partridge Green W Sus 35 D11
Partrishow Powys 96 G5
Parwich Derbys 169 E11
Pasford Staffs 132 D6
Passenham Northants 102 D5
Passfield Hants 49 G10
Passingford Bridge Essex 87 F8
Passmores Essex 86 D6
Paston Norf 160 C6
Pboro 138 C3
Paston Green Norf 160 C6
Pasturefields Staffs 151 D9
Patchacott Devon 12 B5
Patcham Brighton 36 F4
Patchetts Green Herts 85 F10
Patching W Sus 35 F9
Patchole Devon 40 E6
Patchway S Glos 60 C6
Pategill Cumb 230 F6
Pateley Bridge N Yorks 214 F3
Paternoster Heath Essex 88 C6
Pathe Som 43 G11
Pather N Lnrk 268 D5
Pathfinder Village Devon 14 C2
Pathhead Aberds 293 G9
E Ayrs 258 G4
Fife 280 C5
Midloth 271 C7
Path Head T&W 242 E5
Pathlow Warks 118 F3
Path of Condie Perth 286 F4
Patient End Herts 105 F8
Patmore Heath Herts 105 F8
Patney Wilts 46 B5
Patrick IoM 192 D3
Patrick Brompton
N Yorks 224 G4
Patricroft Gtr Man 184 B3
Patrington E Yorks 201 C10
Patrington Haven
E Yorks 201 C10
Patrixbourne Kent 55 B7
Patsford Devon 40 F4
Patterdale Cumb 221 B7
Pattiesmuir Fife 279 E11
Pattingham Staffs 132 D6
Pattishall Northants 120 G3
Pattiswick Essex 106 G6
Patton Shrops 131 E11
Patton Bridge Cumb 221 F11
Paul Corn 1 D5
Paulerspury Northants 102 B4
Paull E Yorks 201 B7
Paul's Green Corn 2 C4
Paulsgrove Ptsmth 33 F10
Paulton Bath 45 B7
Paulville W Loth 269 B9
Pave Lane Telford 150 F5
Pavenham Beds 121 F9
Pawlett Som 43 E10
Pawlett Hill Som 43 E9
Pawston Northumb 263 C9
Paxford Glos 100 D3
Paxton Borders 273 E8
Payden Street Kent 54 C2
Payhembury Devon 27 G9
Paynes Green Sur 50 F6
Paynter's Cross Corn 7 C7
Paynter's Lane End Corn 4 G3
Paythorne Lancs 204 C2
Payton Som 27 C10
Peacehaven E Sus 36 G6
Peacehaven Heights
E Sus 36 G6
Peacemarsh Dorset 30 B4
Peak Dale Derbys 185 F9
Peak Forest Derbys 185 F10
Peak Hill Lincs 156 F5
Peakirk Pboro 138 B3
Pean Hill Kent 70 G6
Pear Ash Som 45 G9
Pearsie Angus 287 B7
Pearson's Green Kent 53 E7
Peartree Herts 86 C2
Pear Tree Derby 153 C7
Peartree Green Essex 87 F9
Hereford 97 E11
Soton 32 E6
Sur 50 F3
Peas Acre W Yorks 205 E8
Peasedown St John Bath 45 B8
Peasehill Derbys 170 F6
Peaseland Green Norf 159 F11

Peasemore W Berks 64 D3
Peasenhall Suff 127 D7
Pease Pottage W Sus 51 G9
Peaslake Sur 50 E5
Peasley Cross Mers 183 C8
Peasmarsh E Sus 38 C5
Som 28 E4
Sur 50 D3
Peaston E Loth 271 B8
Peastonbank E Loth 271 B8
Peathill Aberds 303 C9
Peat Inn Fife 287 G8
Peatling Magna Leics 135 E11
Peatling Parva Leics 135 F11
Peaton Shrops 131 G10
Peatonstrand Shrops 131 G10
Peats Corner Suff 126 E3
Pebmarsh Essex 107 E7
Pebsham E Sus 38 F3
Pebworth Worcs 100 B2
Pecket Well W Yorks 196 B3
Peckforton Ches E 167 D8
Peckham London 67 D10
Peckham Bush Kent 53 D7
Peckingell Wilts 62 E2
Pecking Mill Som 44 F6
Peckleton Leics 135 C9
Pedair-ffordd Powys 148 E2
Pedham Norf 160 G6
Pedlars End Essex 87 D8
Pedlar's Rest Shrops 131 G8
Pedlinge Kent 54 F6
Pedmore W Mid 133 G8
Pednormead End Bucks 85 F7
Pedwell Som 44 F2
Peebles Borders 270 G5
Peel Borders 261 B10
IoM 192 D3
Lancs 202 G3
Peel Common Hants 33 G9
Peel Green Gtr Man 184 B4
Peel Hall Gtr Man 184 D4
Peel Hill Lancs 202 G3
Peel Park S Lnrk 268 E2
Peene Kent 55 F7
Peening Quarter Kent 38 B5
Peggs Green Leics 153 F8
Pegsdon C Beds 104 E2
Pegswood Northumb 252 F6
Pegwell Kent 71 G11
Peinaha Highld 298 D4
Peinchorran Highld 295 B7
Peingown Highld 298 B4
Peinlich Highld 298 D4
Pelaw T&W 243 E7
Pelcomb Pembs 72 B6
Pelcomb Bridge Pembs 72 B6
Pelcomb Cross Pembs 72 B6
Peldon Essex 89 B7
Pelhamfield IoW 21 C7
Pell Green E Sus 52 G6
Pellon W Yorks 196 B5
Pelsall W Mid 133 C10
Pelsall Wood W Mid 133 C10
Pelton Durham 243 G7
Pelton Fell Durham 243 G7
Pelutho Corn 229 B8
Pelynt Corn 6 D4
Pemberton Carms 75 E8
Gtr Man 194 G5
Pembles Cross Kent 53 D11
Pembre / Pembrey
Carms 74 E6
Pembrey / Pembre
Carms 74 E6
Pembridge Hereford 115 F7
Pembroke Pembs 73 E7
Pembroke Dock / Doc
Penfro Pembs 73 E7
Pembroke Ferry Pembs 73 E7
Pembury Kent 52 E6
Pempwell Corn 12 F3
Penallt Mon 79 C8
Pen-allt Hereford 97 F11
Penally / Penalun
Pembs 73 F10
Penalt Hereford 97 F11
Penalun / Penally
Pembs 73 F10
Penare Corn 5 G9
Penarlâg / Hawarden
Flint 166 B4
Penarron Powys 130 F2
Penarth V Glam 59 E7
Penarth Moors Cardiff 59 E7
Plym 7 D9
Penbeagle Corn 2 B2
Penbedw Flint 165 B11
Pen-bedw Pembs 92 D4
Penbeth Corn 1 E4
Penbidwal Mon 96 G6
Penboyr Carms 93 D7
Penbryn Ceredig 110 G5
Pencader Carms 93 D8
Pencaenewydd Gwyn 162 G6
Pencaerau Neath 57 C8
Pencaitland E Loth 271 B8
Pencarnisiog Anglesey 178 G4
Pencarreg Carms 93 B10
Pencarrow Corn 11 E8
Pencelli Powys 95 F11
Pen-clawdd Swansea 56 C3
Pencoed Bridgend 58 C3
Pencombe Hereford 115 G11
Pen-common Powys 76 D6
Pencoyd Hereford 97 F10
Pencoys Corn 2 B5
Pencraig Anglesey 179 F7
Hereford 97 G11
Powys 147 D10
Pencroesoped Mon 78 D4
Pendas Fields W Yorks 206 F3
Pendeen Corn 1 C3
Penderyn Rhondda 77 D7
Pendine / Pentywyn
Carms 74 D2
Pendlebury Gtr Man 195 G9
Pendleton Gtr Man 184 B4
Lancs 203 F11
Pendock Worcs 98 E5
Pendomer Som 29 E8
Pendoylan V Glam 58 D5
Pendre Bridgend 58 C2
Penegoes Powys 128 C4
Penelewey Corn 4 G6
Penenden Heath Kent 53 B9
Penffordd Pembs 91 G11

Penffordd Lâs / Staylittle
Powys 129 D2
Pengam Caerph 77 F11
Penge London 67 E11
Pengegon Corn 2 B5
Pengelly Corn 11 E7
Pengenffordd Powys 96 E3
Pengersick Corn 2 D3
Pengold Corn 11 C8
Pengorffwysfa Anglesey 179 C7
Pengover Green Corn 6 B5
Pen-groes-oped Mon 78 D4
Penguithal Hereford 97 G10
Pengwern Denb 181 F8
Penhale Corn 5 D8
Corn 5 G8
Penhale Jakes Corn 2 D4
Penhallick Corn 3 F7
Corn 4 G3
Penhallow Corn 4 E5
Penhalurick Corn 2 B6
Penhalvean Corn 2 B6
Penhelig Gwyn 128 D2
Penhill Devon 40 G4
Swindon 63 B7
Penhow Newport 78 G6
Penhurst E Sus 23 B11
Peniarth Gwyn 128 B2
Penicuik Midloth 270 C4
Peniel Carms 93 G8
Denb 165 C8
Penifiler Highld 298 E4
Peninver Argyll 255 E8
Penisa'r Waun Gwyn 163 C9
Penistone S Yorks 197 G8
Penjerrick Corn 3 C7
Penketh Warr 183 D9
Penkhull Stoke 168 G5
Penkill S Ayrs 244 D6
Penknap Wilts 45 D11
Penkridge Staffs 151 G8
Pen-lan Swansea 56 B6
Pen-Lan-mabws Pembs 91 F7
Penleigh Wilts 45 C11
Penley Wrex 149 B8
Penllech Gwyn 144 C4
Penllergaer Swansea 56 B6
Penllwyn Caerph 77 F11
Ceredig 128 G3
Pen-llyn V Glam 58 D3
Pen-llyn Anglesey 178 E4
Pen-lon Anglesey 162 B6
Penmachno Conwy 164 E3
Penmaen Caerph 77 F11
Swansea 56 D4
Penmaenan Conwy 180 F2
Penmaenmawr Conwy 180 F2
Penmaenpool Gwyn 146 F3
Penmaen Rhôs Conwy 180 F5
Penmark V Glam 58 F5
Penmarth Corn 2 B6
Penmayne Corn 10 F4
Pen Mill Som 29 D9
Penmon Anglesey 179 E10
Penmore Mill Argyll 288 D6
Penmorfa Ceredig 110 G6
Gwyn 163 G8
Penmynydd Anglesey 179 G8
Penn Bucks 84 G6
W Mid 133 D7
Pennal Gwyn 128 C4
Pennan Aberds 303 C8
Pennance Corn 4 G4
Pennant Ceredig 111 E10
Conwy 164 D5
Denb 147 C10
Denb 165 G8
Powys 129 D7
Pennant Melangell
Powys 147 D10
Pennar Pembs 73 E7
Pennard Swansea 56 D5
Pennar Park Pembs 72 E6
Penn Bottom Bucks 84 G6
Pennerley Shrops 131 D7
Pennington Cumb 210 D5
Gtr Man 183 B11
Hants 20 C2
Pennington Green
Gtr Man 194 F6
Penn Street Bucks 84 F6
Pennsylvania Devon 14 C4
S Glos 61 B8
Penny Bridge Cumb 210 C6
Pennycross Argyll 289 G7
Plym 7 D9
Pennygate Norf 160 E6
Pennygown Argyll 289 E7
Penny Green Derbys 187 F8
Penny Hill Lincs 157 D7
W Yorks 196 D5
Pennylands Lancs 194 F3
Pennymoor Devon 26 E5
Pennypot Kent 54 G6
Penny's Green Norf 142 D3
Pennytinney Corn 10 G5
Pennywell T&W 243 F9
Pen-onn V Glam 58 F5
Penparc Ceredig 92 B4
Pembs 91 E7
Penparcau Ceredig 111 B11
Penpedairheol Caerph 77 F10
Mon 78 E4
Penpergym Mon 78 C4
Penperlleni Mon 78 D4
Penpethy Corn 11 D7
Penpillick Corn 5 D11
Penpol Corn 3 B8
Corn 6 E2
Penponds Corn 2 B4
Penpont Corn 11 G7
Dumfries 247 D8
Powys 95 F9
Penprysg Bridgend 58 C3
Penquit Devon 8 E2
Penrallt Gwyn 145 B7
Powys 129 F9
Penrherber Carms 92 D5
Penrhiw Caerph 78 G2
Pen-Rhiw-fawr Neath 76 C2
Penrhiwceiber Rhondda 77 F8
Penrhiwgarreg Bl Gwent 78 E2
Penrhiw-llan Ceredig 93 C7
Penrhiw-pal Ceredig 92 B6
Penrhiwtyn Neath 57 B8
Penrhos Anglesey 178 E3
Gwyn 144 C6
Hereford 114 F6
Mon 78 C6
Powys 76 C3
Wrex 166 E3
Penrhosfeilw Anglesey 178 E2
Penrhos-garnedd Gwyn 179 G9
Penrhyd Lastra Anglesey 178 C6
Penrhyn Bay / Bae-Penrhyn
Conwy 180 E5
Penrhyn Castle Pembs 92 B2

Penrhyn-coch Ceredig 128 G2
Penrhyndeudraeth
Gwyn 146 B2
Penrhynside Conwy 180 E4
Penrhyn side Conwy 180 E4
Penrhys Rhondda 77 F8
Penrice Swansea 56 D4
Penrith Cumb 230 E6
Penrose Corn 10 G3
Corn 11 F7
Penrose Hill Corn 2 D4
Penryn Corn 3 C7
Pensarn Carms 74 B6
Conwy 181 F7
Pen-sarn Gwyn 145 C11
Gwyn 162 G6
Pensax Worcs 116 D4
Pensby Mers 182 E3
Penselwood Som 45 G9
Pensford Bath 60 G6
Pensham Worcs 99 C8
Penshaw T&W 243 G8
Penshurst Kent 52 E4
Pensilva Corn 6 B5
Pensnett W Mid 133 F8
Penston E Loth 281 G8
Penstone Devon 26 G3
Pentewan Corn 5 F10
Pentir Gwyn 163 B9
Pentire Corn 4 C5
Pentiry Corn 4 G4
Pentirvin Shrops 130 C6
Pentlepoir Pembs 73 D10
Pentlow Essex 106 B6
Pentlow Street Essex 106 B6
Pentney Norf 158 G4
Penton Corner Hants 47 D10
Penton Grafton Hants 47 D10
Penton Mewsey Hants 47 D10
Pentonville London 67 C10
Pentowin Carms 74 B3
Pentraeth Anglesey 179 F8
Pentrapeed Caerph 77 E11
Pentre Carms 75 B7
Denb 165 D10
Flint 181 E11
Flint 166 B4
Flint 166 C2
Powys 129 F11
Powys 130 B4
Powys 130 C5
Powys 147 D11
Powys 148 G3
Rhondda 77 F7
Shrops 148 B6
Shrops 149 F7
Wrex 148 B2
Wrex 166 G3
Pentrebach Carms 94 E6
M Tydf 77 D8
Rhondda 58 B5
Swansea 75 D10
Pentre-bâch Ceredig 93 B11
Pentre-bach Powys 95 E8
Pentrebane Cardiff 58 D6
Pentrebeirdd Powys 148 G3
Pentre-bont Conwy 164 E2
Pentre Broughton Wrex 166 E4
Pentre Bychan Wrex 166 F4
Pentrecagal Carms 92 C6
Pentre-cefn Shrops 148 D5
Pentre-celyn Denb 165 D11
Powys 129 B7
Pentre-chwyth Swansea 57 B7
Pentre Cilgwyn Wrex 148 B4
Pentre-clawdd Shrops 148 C5
Pentre-cwrt Carms 93 D7
Pentre Dolau-Honddu
Powys 95 C9
Pentredwr Denb 165 F11
Pentre-dwr Swansea 57 B7
Pentrefelin Anglesey 179 C7
Carms 93 G11
Ceredig 94 B2
Conwy 180 G4
Denb 166 G2
Gwyn 145 B10
Pentre-Ffwrndan Flint 182 G3
Pentrefoelas Conwy 164 E5
Pentref-y-groes Caerph 77 F11
Pentregalar Pembs 92 E3
Pentre-Gwenlais Carms 75 B11
Pentre Gwynfryn Gwyn 145 D11
Pentre Halkyn Flint 182 G2
Pentreheyling Shrops 130 E4
Pentre Hodre Shrops 114 B6
Pentre Isaf Conwy 164 B5
Pentre Llanrhaeadr
Denb 165 C9
Pentre Llifior Powys 130 D2
Pentrellwyn Ceredig 93 C8
Pentre-llwyn-llwyd
Powys 113 G9
Pentre-llyn cymmer
Conwy 165 D7
Pentre Maelor Wrex 166 F5
Pentre Meyrick V Glam 58 D3
Pentre-newydd Shrops 148 B5
Pentre-Piod Torf 78 E3
Pentre-Poeth Carms 75 E8
Newport 59 B9
Pentre'r beirdd Powys 148 G3
Pentre'r Felin Conwy 164 B4
Pentre'r-felin Denb 165 B10
Powys 95 E8
Pentre-rhew Ceredig 112 G3
Corn 55 B9
W Mid 133 E11
Pentre-tafarn-y-fedw
Conwy 164 C4
Pentre-ty-gwyn Carms 94 D6
Pentreuchaf Gwyn 145 B7
Pentre-uchaf Conwy 180 F5
Pentrich Derbys 170 E5
Pentridge Dorset 31 D8
Pentrisil Pembs 91 E11
Pentwyn Caerph 77 E10
Cardiff 59 C8
Som 43 F9
Torf 78 E3
Wilts 62 B3
Pentwyn Berthlwyd
Caerph 77 F10
Pentwyn-mawr Caerph 77 F11
Pentyrch Cardiff 58 C6
Penuchadre V Glam 57 G11
Pen-Uchar Plwyf Flint 181 G11
Penuwch Ceredig 111 E11
Penwartha Corn 4 E5
Penwartha Coombe Corn 4 E5
Penweathers Corn 4 G6
Penwithick Corn 5 D10
Penwood Hants 64 G2

Penwortham Lane
Lancs 194 B4
Penwyllt Powys 76 B5
Pen-y-Ball Top Flint 181 F11
Penybanc Carms 75 C10
Carms 93 G10
Pen-y-banc Carms 93 G8
Penybont Carms 94 G2
Powys 114 E2
Pen-y-Bont Bl Gwent 78 D2
Carms 92 F6
Gwyn 128 C4
Gwyn 146 D2
Powys 148 E5
Pen-y-bont-fawr Powys 147 E10
Pen-y-bryn Gwyn 145 B9
Gwyn 146 F3
Pembs 92 C3
Powys 130 C3
Swansea 56 B3
Wrex 166 F3
Pen-y-cae Bridgend 58 C2
Neath 57 D9
Powys 76 C4
Pen-y-cae-mawr Mon 78 F6
Penycaerau Gwyn 144 D3
Pen-y-cefn Flint 181 F10
Pen-y-clawdd Mon 79 D7
Pen-y-coed Shrops 148 E5
Pen-y-coedcae Rhondda 58 B5
Penycwm Pembs 90 G6
Pen-y-Darren M Tydf 77 D9
Pen-y-fai Bridgend 57 E11
Carms 75 E7
Pen-y-fan Mon 79 B8
Penyffordd Pembs 91 F7
Pen-y-felin Flint 165 B11
Penyffordd Flint 166 C4
Pen-y-ffordd Denb 181 E11
Flint 181 E10
Pen y Foel Shrops 148 E5
Pen-y-garn Carms 93 E11
Ceredig 128 F2
Penygarnedd Powys 148 E2
Pen-y-garnedd
Anglesey 179 F8
Penygelli Powys 130 E2
Pen-y-gop Conwy 164 G6
Penygraig Rhondda 77 G7
Pen-y-graig Gwyn 144 C3
Penygraigwen Anglesey 178 D6
Penygroes Carms 75 C9
Gwyn 163 E7
Pen-y-groeslon Gwyn 144 C4
Pen-y-Gwryd Hotel
Gwyn 163 D11
Pen-y-lan Cardiff 59 D7
Newport 59 B9
V Glam 58 D3
Pen-y-maes Flint 181 F11
Pen-y-Mynydd Carms 75 E7
Penymynydd Flint 166 C4
Pen-y-Park Hereford 96 C5
Pen-yr-englyn Rhondda 76 F6
Pen-yr-heol Bridgend 58 C2
Mon 78 C6
Pen-yr-Heolgerrig
M Tydf 77 D8
Pen-y-rhiw Rhondda 58 B5
Penysarn Anglesey 179 C7
Pen-y-stryt Denb 165 E11
Penywaun Rhondda 77 E7
Pen-y-wern Shrops 114 B6
Penzance Corn 1 C5
Peopleton Worcs 117 G8
Peover Heath Ches E 184 G3
Peper Harow Sur 50 E2
Peppercombe Devon 24 C5
Pepper Hill Som 43 F7
W Yorks 196 B6
Pepperstock C Beds 85 B9
Perceton N Ayrs 267 G7
Percie Aberds 293 D7
Percyhorner Aberds 303 C9
Percy Main T&W 243 D8
Perham Down Wilts 47 D9
Periton Som 42 D3
Perivale London 67 C7
Perkhill Aberds 293 C7
Perkinsville Durham 243 G7
Perlethorpe Notts 187 G11
Perranarworthal Corn 3 B7
Perrancoombe Corn 4 E5
Perran Downs Corn 2 C3
Perranporth Corn 4 E5
Perranuthnoe Corn 2 D2
Perranwell Corn 3 B7
Corn 4 E5
Perranwell Station Corn 3 B7
Perranzabuloe Corn 4 E5
Perrott's Brook Glos 81 D8
Perry Devon 26 F5
Kent 55 B9
W Mid 133 E11
Perry Barr W Mid 133 E11
Perry Beeches W Mid 133 E11
Perry Common W Mid 133 E11
Perry Crofts Staffs 134 C4
Perryfields Worcs 117 C8
Perryfoot Derbys 185 E10
Perry Green Essex 106 G4
Herts 86 B6
Som 43 F9
Wilts 62 B3
Perrymead Bath 61 G9
Perry Street Kent 68 E6
Som 28 E4
S Yorks 197 G10
Pershall Staffs 150 C6
Pershore Worcs 99 B8
Pert Angus 293 G8
Pertenhall Beds 121 D11
Perth Perth 286 E5
Perthcelyn Rhondda 77 F9
Perthy Shrops 149 C7
Perton Hereford 97 C11
Staffs 133 D7
Pertwood Wilts 45 E11
Pested Kent 54 C4
Peter's Green Herts 85 B10

Peterburn Highld 307 L2
Peterchurch Hereford 96 D6
Peterculter Aberden 293 C10
Peterhead Aberds 303 E11
Peterlee Durham 234 C4
Petersburn N Lnrk 268 C5
Petersfield Hants 34 C2
Peter's Finger Devon 12 D3
Peter's Green Herts 85 B10
Petersham London 67 E7
Northants 137 G10
Rutland 137 C8
Som 44 E5
Peterstone Wentlooge
Newport 59 C9
Peterston-super-Ely
V Glam 58 D5
Peterstow Hereford 97 G11
Peter Tavy Devon 12 F6
Peterton Orkney 314 F3
Peterville Corn 4 E4
Petham Kent 54 C6
Petherwin Gate Corn 11 D11
Petrockstow Devon 25 F8
Petsoe End M Keynes 103 B7
Pett E Sus 38 E5
Pettaugh Suff 126 F3
Pett Bottom Kent 54 E6
Corn 55 C7
Petteridge Kent 53 E7
Pettinain S Lnrk 269 G9
Pettings Kent 68 G6
Pettistree Suff 126 G5
Pett Level E Sus 38 E5
Petton Devon 27 C8
Shrops 149 D8
Petts Wood London 68 F2
Petty Aberds 303 F7
Pettycur Fife 280 D5
Petty France S Glos 61 B9
Pettymuick Aberds 303 G9
Pettywell Norf 159 E11
Petworth W Sus 35 C7
Pevensey E Sus 23 E10
Pevensey Bay E Sus 23 E11
Peverell Plym 7 D9
Pewsey Wilts 63 G7
Pewsey Wharf Wilts 63 G7
Pewterspear Warr 183 E10
Phantassie E Loth 281 F11
Pharisee Green Essex 106 G2
Pheasants Bucks 65 B9
Pheasant's Hill Bucks 65 B9
Pheasey W Mid 133 D11
Phocle Green Hereford 98 F2
Phoenix Green Hants 49 B9
Phoenix Row Durham 233 F9
Phorp Moray 301 D10
Pibsbury Som 28 B6
Pibwrlwyd Carms 74 B6
Pica Cumb 228 G5
Piccadilly S Yorks 187 B7
Warks 134 D4
Piccadilly Corner Norf 142 F5
Piccotts End Herts 85 D9
Pickburn S Yorks 198 F4
Picken End Worcs 98 C6
Pickering N Yorks 216 C5
Pickering Nook Durham 242 F5
Picket Hill Hants 31 F11
Picket Piece Hants 47 D11
Picket Post Hants 31 F11
Pickford W Mid 134 G5
Pickford Green W Mid 134 G5
Pickhill N Yorks 214 C6
Picklenash Glos 98 F4
Picklescott Shrops 131 D8
Pickles Hill W Yorks 204 F6
Pickletillem Fife 287 E8
Pickley Green Gtr Man 195 G7
Pickmere Ches E 183 F11
Pickney Som 27 B11
Pickstock Telford 150 E4
Pickup Bank Blkburn 195 C8
Pickwell Devon 40 E3
Leics 154 G5
Pickwick Wilts 61 E11
Pickworth Lincs 155 C10
Rutland 155 G9
Picton Ches W 182 G6
Flint 181 E10
N Yorks 225 D8
Pict's Hill Som 28 B6
Piddinghoe E Sus 36 G6
Piddington Bucks 84 G4
Northants 120 G6
Oxon 83 B10
Piddlehinton Dorset 17 B10
Piddletrenthide Dorset 17 B10
Pidley Cambs 122 B6
Pidney Dorset 30 F2
Piece Corn 2 B4
Piercebridge Darl 224 B4
Piercing Hill Essex 86 F6
Pierowall Orkney 314 A4
Piff's Elm Glos 99 F8
Pigdon Northumb 252 F5
Pig Oak Dorset 31 G8
Pigstye Green S Yorks 87 D10
Pikehall Derbys 169 D11
Pike Hill Lancs 204 G3
Pike Law W Yorks 196 D4
Pikeshill Hants 32 F3
Pilford Dorset 31 G8
Pilgrims Hatch Essex 87 F9
Pilham Lincs 188 C4
Pill N Som 60 D4
Pillaton Corn 7 C7
Staffs 151 G8
Pillerton Hersey Warks 100 B5
Pillerton Priors Warks 100 B5
Pilleth Powys 114 D4
Pilley Hants 20 B2
S Yorks 197 G10
Pilley Bailey Hants 20 B2
Pilgwenlly Newport 59 B10
Pilling Lancs 202 D4
Pilling Lane Lancs 202 D3
Pillmouth Devon 25 C7
Pillowell Glos 79 D10
Pillows Green Glos 98 F5
Pill Moor Hereford 97 C10
Pillwell Dorset 30 D3
Pilmuir Borders 261 G11
Pilning S Glos 60 C5
Pilrig Edin 280 F5
Pilsbury Derbys 169 C10
Pilsdon Dorset 16 B4

Pilsdon Dorset 16 B4
Pilsgate Pboro 137 B11
Pilsley Derbys 170 G6
Derbys 186 G2
Pilson Green Norf 161 G7
Piltdown E Sus 36 C6
Pilton Devon 40 G5
Edin 280 F4
Northants 137 G10
Rutland 137 C8
Som 44 E5
Pilton Green Swansea 56 D2
Piltown 44 F5
Pimhole Gtr Man 195 E10
Pimlico Herts 85 D9
Lancs 203 E10
London 67 D9
Northants 102 C2
Pimperne Dorset 30 F6
Dorset 30 E6
Pin Green Herts 104 F4
Pinchbeck Lincs 156 D4
Pinchbeck Bars Lincs 156 D3
Pinchbeck West Lincs 156 E4
Pincheon Green
S Yorks 199 D7
Pinckney Green Wilts 61 G10
Pincock Lancs 194 D5
Pineham Kent 55 D10
M Keynes 103 C7
Pinehurst Swindon 63 B7
Pinfarthings Glos 80 E5
Pinfold Lancs 193 E11
Pinfold Hill S Yorks 197 G9
Pinfoldpond C Beds 103 E8
Pinford End Suff 124 F6
Pinged Carms 74 E6
Pingewood W Berks 65 F7
Pin Green Herts 104 F4
Pinhoe Devon 14 C5
Pinkett's Booth W Mid 134 G5
Pink Green Worcs 117 D9
Pinkie Braes E Loth 281 G7
Pinkney Wilts 61 B11
Pinkneys Green Windsor 65 C11
Pinksmoor Som 27 D10
Pinley W Mid 119 B7
Pinley Green Warks 118 D4
Pin Mill Suff 108 D4
Pinminnoch Dumfries 236 D2
S Ayrs 244 E5
Pinmore S Ayrs 244 E6
Pinmore Mains S Ayrs 244 E6
Pinnacles Essex 86 D6
Pinner London 66 B6
Pinner Green London 85 G10
Pinnerwood Park
London 85 G10
Pinsley Green Ches E 167 F9
Pinstones Shrops 131 F9
Pinvin Worcs 99 B9
Pinwall Leics 134 C6
Pinwherry S Ayrs 244 E5
Pipe and Lyde Hereford 97 C10
Pipe Aston Hereford 115 C9
Pipe Gate Shrops 168 G2
Pipehill Staffs 133 B11
Pipehouse Bath 45 B9
Piperhall Argyll 266 D2
Piperhill Highld 301 D8
Pipe Ridware Staffs 151 F11
Piper's End Worcs 98 E6
Piper's Ash Ches W 166 B6
Piper's Hill Worcs 117 D9
Piper's Pool Corn 11 E11
Pipewell Northants 136 F6
Pippacott Devon 40 F4
Pippin Street Lancs 194 C5
Pipsden Kent 53 G9
Pipton Powys 96 D3
Pirbright Sur 50 B2
Pirbright Camp Sur 50 B2
Pirnmill N Ayrs 255 C9
Pirton Herts 104 E2
Worcs 99 B7
Pisgah Ceredig 112 B3
Stirl 285 G11
Pishill Oxon 65 B8
Pishill Bank Oxon 84 G2
Pismire Hill S Yorks 186 C5
Pistyll Gwyn 162 G4
Pit Hon 78 D5
Pitagowan Perth 291 G10
Pitblae Aberds 303 C9
Pitcairngreen Perth 286 E4
Pitcalnie Highld 301 B8
Pitcaple Aberds 303 G7
Pitch Green Bucks 84 E3
Pitchcombe Glos 80 D5
Pitchcott Bucks 102 G5
Pitcher's Green Suff 125 F8
Pitchford Shrops 131 C10
Pitch Place Sur 49 F11
Sur 50 C3
Pitcombe Som 45 G7
Pitcot Som 45 B7
Pitcur Perth 286 D6
Pitfancy Aberds 302 E5
Pitfichie Aberds 293 B8
Pitforthie Aberds 293 F10
Pitgair Aberds 303 D7
Pitgrudy Highld 309 K7
Pithmaduthy Highld 301 B7
Pitkennedy Angus 287 B9
Pitkevy Fife 286 G6
Pitkierie Fife 287 G9
Pitlessie Fife 287 G7
Pitlochry Perth 286 B3
Pitmachie Aberds 302 G6
Pitmain Highld 291 C9
Pitmedden Aberds 303 G8
Pitminster Som 28 D2
Pitmuies Angus 287 C9
Pitmunie Aberds 293 B8
Pitney Som 29 B7
Pitroddie Perth 286 E6
Pitscottie Fife 287 F8
Pitsea Essex 69 B8
Pitses Gtr Man 196 G2
Pitsford Northants 120 D5
Pitsford Hill Som 42 G6
Pitsmoor S Yorks 186 D5
Pitstone Bucks 84 B6
Pitstone Green Bucks 84 B6
Pitt Hants 33 B7
Pittachar Perth 286 E2
Pitt Court Glos 80 F2
Pittendreich Moray 301 C11
Pittentrail Highld 309 J7
Pittenweem Fife 287 G9
Pitteuchar Fife 280 B5
Pittington Durham 234 C2
Pittodrie Aberds 302 G6

Pitton Swansea 56 D2
Wilts 47 G8
Pitts Hill Stoke 168 E5
Pittswood Kent 52 E6
Pittulie Aberds 303 C9
Pittville Glos 99 G9
Pityme Corn 10 F5
Pity Me Durham 233 B11
Pityoulish Highld 291 B11
Pixey Green Suff 126 B4
Pixham Sur 51 C7
Worcs 98 B6
Pixley Hereford 98 D3
Shrops 150 D3
Pizien Well Kent 53 C7
Place Newton N Yorks 217 E7
Plaidy Aberds 303 D7
Corn 6 E5
Plain-an-Gwarry Corn 4 G5
Plain Dealings Pembs 73 B9
Plains N Lnrk 268 B5
Plainsfield Som 43 F7
Plain Spot Notts 171 E7
Plaish Shrops 131 D10
Plaistow Bromley 68 E2
Newham 68 C2
W Sus 50 G4
Plaistow Green Essex 106 F6
Plaitford Wilts 32 D3
Plaitford Green Hants 32 D3
Plank Lane Gtr Man 194 G6
Plas Shrops 238 D3
Plantation Bridge Cumb 221 F9
Plantationfoot Dumfries 248 E4
Plardiwick Staffs 150 E6
Plasau Shrops 149 E7
Plas Berwyn Denb 165 G11
Plas-canol Gwyn 145 E11
Plas Coch Wrex 166 E4
Plas Dinam Powys 129 F10
Plas Gogerddan Ceredig 128 G2
Plashett Carms 74 D3
Plasiolyn Powys 129 C11
Plas Llwyngwern Powys 128 C5
Plas Meredydd Powys 130 D3
Plas Nantyr Wrex 148 B3
Plasnewydd Powys 129 D9
Plaster's Green Bath 60 G4
Plastow Green Hants 64 G4
Plas-yn-Cefn Denb 181 G8
Platt Kent 52 B6
Platt Bridge Gtr Man 194 G6
Platt Lane Shrops 149 B10
Platts Common
S Yorks 197 G11
Platt's Heath Kent 53 C11
Plawsworth Durham 233 B11
Plaxtol Kent 52 C6
Playden E Sus 38 C6
Playford Suff 108 B4
Play Hatch Oxon 65 D8
Playing Place Corn 4 G6
Playley Green Glos 98 E5
Plealey Shrops 131 B8
Pleamore Cross Som 27 D10
Plean Stirl 278 D6
Pleasant Valley Pembs 73 D10
Pleasington Blkburn 194 B6
Pleasley Derbys 171 C8
Pleasleyhill Notts 171 C8
Pleck Dorset 30 D3
Dorset 30 E2
W Mid 133 D9
Pleckgate Blkburn 203 G9
Pleck or Little Ansty
Dorset 30 G3
Pledgdon Green Essex 105 F11
Pledwick W Yorks 197 D10
Plemstall Ches W 183 G7
Plenmeller Northumb 240 E6
Pleshey Essex 87 C11
Plockton Highld 295 B10
Plocrapol W Isles 305 J3
Plot Gate Som 44 G4
Plot Street Som 44 F5
Ploughhill Hereford 97 C7
Plough Hill Warks 134 E6
Plowden Shrops 131 F7
Ploxgreen Shrops 131 C7
Pluckley Kent 54 E2
Pluckley Thorne Kent 54 E2
Plucks Gutter Kent 71 G9
Plumbland Cumb 229 D8
Plumbley S Yorks 186 E6
Plumford Kent 54 B4
Plumley Ches E 184 F2
Plump Hill Glos 79 B11
Plumpton Cumb 230 D5
E Sus 36 E5
Northants 101 B11
Plumpton End
Northants 102 B4
Plumpton Foot Cumb 230 D5
Plumpton Green E Sus 36 D5
Plumpton Head Cumb 230 E6
Plumstead London 68 D3
Norf 160 C2
Plumstead Common
London 68 D3
Plumstead Green Norf 160 C2
Plumtree Notts 154 C2
Plumtree Green Kent 53 D10
Plumtree Park Notts 154 C2
Plungar Leics 154 C5
Plush Dorset 30 G2
Plushabridge Corn 12 G2
Plusha Corn 11 E11
Plusterwine Glos 79 F9
Plwmp Ceredig 111 G7
Plymouth Plym 7 E9
Plympton Plym 7 D10
Plymstock Devon 7 E10
Plymtree Devon 27 G9
Pobgreen Gtr Man 196 F4
Pochin Houses Caerph 77 E11
Pocket Nook Gtr Man 183 B10
Pockley N Yorks 216 C3
Pocklington E Yorks 208 D2
Pockthorpe Norf 141 D8
Norf 158 D6
Norf 159 F11
Pode Hole Lincs 156 E4
Podimore Som 29 C8
Podington Beds 121 E8
Podmore Norf 159 G9
Staffs 150 B5
Podsmead Glos 80 B4
Poffley End Oxon 82 C5
Pogmoor S Yorks 197 F10
Point Corn 3 B8
Point Clear Essex 89 C9
Pointon Lincs 156 C2
Pokesdown Bmouth 19 C8
Pol a Charra W Isles 297 K3
Polbae Dumfries 236 B4

Polbain Highld 307 H4
Polbathic Corn 7 D7
Polbeth W Loth 269 C10
Polbrock Corn 7 C7
Polchar Highld 291 C10
Polebrook Northants . . 137 F11
Pole Elm Worcs 98 B6
Polegate E Sus 23 D9
Pole Moor W Yorks 196 D5
Poles Highld 309 K7
Polesden Lacey Sur 50 C6
Poleshill Som 27 C9
Pole's Hole Wilts 45 C10
Polesworth Warks 134 C5
Polgear Corn 2 B5
Polgigga Corn 1 E3
Polglass Highld 307 J5
Polgooth Corn 5 E9
Poling W Sus 35 G8
Poling Corner W Sus 35 F8
Polkerris Corn 5 E11
Polla Highld 308 D3
Polladras Corn 2 C4
Pollard Street Norf . . . 160 C6
Pollhill Kent 53 C11
Poll Hill Mers 182 E3
Pollie Highld 309 H7
Pollington E Yorks 198 D6
Polloch Highld 289 C9
Pollok Glasgow 267 C10
Pollokshields Glasgow 267 C11
Polmaily Highld 300 F4
Polmarth Corn 2 B6
Polmassick Corn 5 F9
Polmear Corn 5 E11
Polmont Falk 279 F8
Polmorla Corn 10 G5
Polnessan E Ayrs 257 G10
Polnish Highld 295 G9
Polopit Northants 121 B10
Polpenwith Corn 2 D6
Polpeor Corn 2 E1
Polperro Corn 6 E4
Polruan Corn 6 E2
Polsham Som 44 E4
Polsloe Devon 14 C4
Polstead Suff 107 C9
Polstead Heath Suff . . 107 C9
Poltalloch Argyll 275 D9
Poltesco Corn 2 F6
Poltimore Devon 14 B5
Polton Midloth 270 C4
Polwarth Borders 272 E4
Polwheveral Corn 2 D6
Polyphant Corn 11 E11
Polzeath Corn 10 F4
Pomeroy Derbys 169 B10
Pomphlett Plym 7 E10
Ponciau Wrex 166 F3
Pond Close Som 27 B10
Ponde Powys 96 D2
Pondersbridge Cambs . 138 E5
Ponders End London 86 F5
Pond Park Bucks 85 E7
Pond Street Essex 105 D9
Pondtail Hants 49 C10
Pondwell IoW 21 C8
Poniou Corn 1 B4
Ponjeravah Corn 2 D6
Ponsanooth Corn 3 B7
Ponsford Devon 27 F8
Ponsonby Cumb 219 D11
Ponsongath Corn 3 F7
Ponsworthy Devon 13 G10
Pont Corn 6 E2
Pont Aber Carms 94 G4
Pont Aber-Geirw Gwyn 146 D5
Pontamman Carms 75 C10
Pontantwn Carms 74 C6
Pontardawe Neath 76 E2
Pontarddulais Swansea .75 E9
Pontarfynach / Devils
  Bridge Ceredig 112 B4
Pont ar Hydfer Powys . .95 F7
Pont-ar-llechau Carms . 94 G4
Pontarsais Carms 93 F8
Pontblyddyn Flint 166 C3
Pontbren Araeth Carms .94 F3
Pontbren Llwyd Rhondda .76 D6
Pontcanna Cardiff 59 D7
Pont Cyfyng Conwy . . . 163 D7
Pont Cysyllte Wrex 166 G3
Pontdolgoch Powys . . . 129 E10
Pont Dolydd Prysor
  Gwyn 146 B4
Pontefract W Yorks . . . 198 D3
Ponteland Northumb . . 242 C5
Ponterwyd Ceredig . . . 128 G4
Pontesbury Shrops 131 B8
Pontesbury Hill Shrops 131 B8
Pontesford Shrops 131 B8
Pontfadog Wrex 148 B4
Pontfaen Pembs 91 E10
Pont-faen Powys 95 E9
  Shrops 148 B5
Pont Fronwydd Gwyn . 146 D6
Pont-garreg Pembs 92 C2
Pontgarreg Ceredig . . . 110 G6
Ponthen Shrops 148 F6
Pont-Henri Carms 75 D7
Ponthirwaun Ceredig . . .92 B5
Pont Hwfa Anglesey . . 178 D2
Pontiago Pembs 91 B8
Pont iets / Pontyates
  Carms 75 D7
Pontithel Powys 96 D3
Pontllanfraith Caerph . .77 F11
Pontlliw Swansea 75 E11
Pont-Llogel Powys 147 F10
Pontllyfni Gwyn 162 E6
Pontlottyn Caerph 77 E10
Pontneddfechan Powys .76 D6
Pontnewydd Torf 78 F3
Pont-newydd Carms 74 E3
  Flint 165 B11
Pontnewynydd Torf 78 E3
Pont Pen-y-benglog
  Gwyn 163 D6
Pont Rhydgaled Powys 128 G6
Pont Rhyd-goch
  Conwy 163 C11
Pont-Rhyd-sarn Gwyn . 147 D7
Pont-rhyd-y-berry
  Powys 95 D9
Pont Rhyd-y-cyff
  Bridgend 57 D11
Pontrhydyfen Neath . . . 57 C9
Pont-rhyd-y-groes
  Ceredig 112 C4
Pontrhydyrun Torf 78 F3
Pont-Rhythallt Gwyn . . 163 C8
Pontrilas Hereford 97 F7

Pontrobert Powys 148 G2
Pont-rug Gwyn 163 C8
Pont Senni / Sennybridge
  Powys 95 F8
Ponts Green E Sus 23 B11
Pontshill Hereford 98 G2
Pont-siân Ceredig 93 B8
Pont Siôn Norton
  Rhondda 77 G9
Pontsticill M Tydf 77 C9
Pont-Walby Neath 76 D5
Pontwgan Conwy 180 G3
Pontyates / Pont-iets
  Carms 75 D7
Pontyberem Carms 75 C8
Pont-y-blew Shrops . . . 148 B6
Pontyclun Rhondda 58 C4
Pontycymer Bridgend . . 76 D6
Pontyglasier Pembs 92 D2
Pont-y-gwaith Rhondda .77 G8
Pont-y-pant Conwy . . . 164 E3
Pont y Pennant Gwyn . 147 E8
Pontypool Torf 78 E3
Pontypridd Rhondda . . . 58 B5
Pont yr Afon-Gam
  Gwyn 164 G2
Pont-yr-hafod Pembs . . 91 F8
Pont-y-rhyl Bridgend . . 58 B2
Pont-Ystrad Denb 165 C9
Pont-y-wal Powys 96 D2
Pontywaun Caerph 78 G2
Pooksgreen Hants 32 E5
Pool Corn 4 G3
  W Yorks 205 D10
Poole Dorset 18 C6
  Som 27 C10
Poole Keynes Glos 81 F8
Poolend Staffs 169 D7
Poolewe Highld 307 L3
Pooley Bridge Cumb . . 230 G5
Pooley Street Norf 141 G11
Poolfold Staffs 168 D5
Poolhead Hereford 115 G11
Pool Hey Lancs 193 D11
Poolhill Glos 98 F4
Poolmill Hereford 97 G11
Pool o' Muckhart Clack 286 G4
Pool Quay Powys 148 G5
Poolsbrook Derbys 186 G6
Poolside Moray 302 E4
Pooltown Som 42 F3
Pootings Kent 52 D3
Pope's Hill Glos 79 C11
Popeswood Brack 65 F10
Popham Devon 9 B7
  Hants 48 E5
Poplar London 67 C11
Poplar Grove Lincs . . . 190 B6
Poplars Glos 104 G5
Popley Hants 48 C6
Porchester Nottingham 171 G9
Porchfield IoW 20 C4
Porin Highld 300 D3
Poringland Norf 142 C5
Porkellis Corn 2 C5
Porlock Som 41 D11
Porlockford Som 41 D11
Porlock Weir Som 41 D11
Portachoillan Argyll . . 275 B8
Port Allen Perth 286 E6
Port Ann Argyll 275 E10
Port Appin Argyll 289 E11
Port Arthur Shetland . . 313 K5
Portavadie Argyll 275 G10
Port Askaig Argyll 274 G5
Port Bannatyne Argyll 275 G11
Port Brae Corn 280 C5
Port Bridge Devon 9 D7
Portbury N Som 60 D4
Port Carlisle Cumb 239 E8
Port Charlotte Argyll . . 254 B3
Portchester Hants 33 F10
Portclair Highld 290 B6
Port Dinorwic / Y Felinheli
  Gwyn 163 B8
Port Driseach Argyll . . 275 F10
Port Dundas Glasgow . 267 B11
Porteath Corn 10 F5
Port Edgar Edin 280 F2
Port Ellen Argyll 254 C4
Port Elphinstone Aberds 293 B9
Portencalzie Dumfries . 236 B2
Portencross N Ayrs . . . 266 F3
Porterfield Renfs 267 B9
Port Erin IoM 192 F2
Port Erroll Aberds 303 F10
Porter's End Herts 85 B11
Portesham Dorset 17 D8
Portessie Moray 302 C4
Port e Vullen IoM 192 C5
Port-Eynon Swansea . . . 56 D3
Portfield Argyll 289 G9
  Som 28 B6
  W Sus 22 B5
Portfield Gate Pembs . . 72 B6
Portgate Devon 12 D4
Port Gaverne Corn 10 F6
Port Glasgow Inyclyd . . 276 G6
Portgordon Moray 302 C3
Portgower Highld 311 H4
Porth Corn 4 C4
  Rhondda 77 G8
Porthallow Corn 3 E7
  Corn 6 E4
Porthcawl Bridgend . . . 57 F10
Porth Colmon Gwyn . . 144 C3
Porthcothan Corn 10 G3
Porthcurno Corn 1 E3
Porth Dinllaen Gwyn . 144 C4
Portheiddy Pembs 90 E6
Porthgain Pembs 90 E6
Porthgwarra Corn 1 E3
Porthhallow Corn 3 E7
Porthill Shrops 149 G9
  Staffs 168 F5
Port Hill Oxon 65 B7
Porth Kea Corn 4 G5
Porthkerry V Glam 58 F5
Porthleven Corn 2 D5
Porthllechog / Bull Bay
  Anglesey 178 C6
Porthloo Scilly 1 G4
Porthmadog Gwyn . . . 145 B11
Porthmeor Corn 1 B4
Porth Navas Corn 3 D7
Porthoustock Corn 3 E8
Porthpean Corn 5 E10
Porthtowan Corn 4 F3
Porth Tywyn / Burry Port
  Carms 74 E6

Devon 26 F5
Poulner Hants 31 F11
Poulshot Wilts 46 B3
Poulton Ches W 166 G5
  Glos 81 E10
  Mers 182 E4
Poulton-le-Fylde Lancs 202 F2
Pound Bank Worcs 98 B5
  Worcs 116 C4
Poundbury Dorset 17 C9
Poundffald Swansea . . . 56 C5
Poundfield E Sus 52 G4
Poundgate E Sus 37 B7
Poundgreen Wokingham .65 F7
Pound Green E Sus 37 C8
  Hants 48 B5
  IoW 20 D2
  Suff 124 G4
  Worcs 116 B5
Pound Hill W Sus 244 F5
Poundland S Ayrs 244 F5
Poundon Bucks 102 F2
Poundsbridge Kent 52 E4
Poundsgate Devon 13 G10
Poundstock Corn 11 B10
Pound Street Hants 64 G3
Pountley Corn 17 B7
Povey Cross Sur 51 E9
Powburn Northumb . . 264 F3
Powderham Devon 14 E5
Powder Mills Kent 52 D5
Powers Hall End Essex 88 B4
Powerstock Dorset 16 B6
Powfoot Dumfries 238 D4
Pow Green Hereford . . . 98 C4
Powhill Cumb 238 F6
Powick Worcs 116 G6
Powler's Piece Devon . . 24 D5
Powmill Perth 279 B10
Pownall Park Ches E . . 184 E4
Pountley Copse Hants . .49 E8
Poxwell Dorset 17 E10
Poyle Slough 66 D4
Poynings W Sus 36 E3
Poynton Ches E 184 E6
  Telford 149 F11
Poynton Green Telford 149 F11
Poyntzfield Highld 301 C7
Poyston Pembs 73 B7
Poyston Cross Pembs . . 73 B7
Poystreet Green Suff . . 125 F9
Praa Sands Corn 2 D3
Pratling Street Kent . . . 53 B8
Pratt's Bottom London . 68 G3
Praze Corn 2 B4
Praze-an-Beeble Corn . .2 B4
Predannack Wollas Corn . .2 F5
Prees Shrops 149 C11
Preesall Lancs 202 D3
Preesall Park Lancs . . . 202 D3
Prees Green Shrops . . . 149 C11
Preesgweene Shrops . . 148 B5
Prees Heath Shrops . . . 149 B11
Preeshenlle Shrops . . . 148 C6
Prees Higher Heath
  Shrops 149 B11
Prees Lower Heath
  Shrops 149 C11
Prees Wood Shrops . . . 149 C11
Prenbrigog Flint 166 C3
Prendergast Borders . . 273 D8
  Pembs 90 G6
Prendwick Northumb . 264 G2
Pren-gwyn Ceredig 93 C8
Prenteg Gwyn 163 D9
Prenton Mers 182 D4
Prescot Mers 183 C7
Prescott Devon 27 E9
  Glos 99 F9
  Shrops 132 G3
  Shrops 149 E8
Presdales Herts 86 C5
Preshome Moray 302 C4
Press Derbys 170 B5
Pressen Northumb 263 B8
Prestatyn Denb 181 E9
Prestbury Ches E 184 F6
  Glos 99 G9
Presteigne Powys 114 E6
Presthope Shrops 131 D11
Prestleigh Som 44 E6
Prestolee Gtr Man 195 F9
Preston Borders 272 D5
  Brighton 36 F4
  Devon 14 G3
  Dorset 17 E10
  E Loth 281 F11
  E Loth 281 G7
  E Yorks 209 G9
  Glos 81 E8
  Glos 98 E5
  Herts 104 G3
  Kent 71 G8
  Lancs 194 B4
  London 67 B7
  Northumb 264 D5
  Rutland 137 C7
  Shrops 149 G10
  Torbay 9 C7
  T&W 243 D8
  Wilts 62 D4
  Wilts 63 F9
Preston Bagot Warks . . 118 D3
Preston Bissett Bucks . 102 F3
Preston Bowyer Som . . 27 B10
Preston Brockhurst
  Shrops 149 E10
Preston Brook Halton . 183 E9
Preston Candover Hants .48 E6
Preston Capes
  Northants 119 G11
Preston Crowmarsh
  Oxon 83 G10
Preston Deanery
  Northants 120 F5
Prestonfield Edin 280 G5
Preston Fields Warks . . 118 D3
Preston Grange T&W . . 243 D8
Preston Green Warks . . 118 D3
Preston Gubbals Shrops 149 F9
Preston-le-Skerne
  Durham 234 G2
Preston Marsh Hereford 97 B11
Prestonmill Dumfries . . 237 D11
Preston Montford
  Shrops 149 G8
Preston on Stour Warks 118 G4
Preston-on-Tees
  Stockton 225 B8
Preston on the Hill
  Halton 183 E9
Preston on Wye Hereford .97 B11
Prestonpans E Loth . . . 281 G7
Preston Pastures Worcs 100 B3

Preston Plucknett Som . 29 D8
Preston St Mary Suff . . 125 G8
Preston-under-Scar
  N Yorks 223 G11
Preston upon the Weald
  Moors Telford 150 F3
Preston Wynne Hereford 97 B11
Prestwich Gtr Man 195 G10
Prestwick Northumb . . 242 C5
  S Ayrs 257 D9
Prestwold Leics 153 E11
Prestwood Bucks 84 E5
  Staffs 133 F7
  Staffs 169 G10
Prey Heath Sur 50 B3
Price Town Bridgend . . 76 G6
Prickwillow Cambs . . . 139 G11
Priddy Som 44 C4
Pride Park Derbys 153 B7
Priestacott Devon 24 F6
Priestcliffe Derbys 185 G10
Priestcliffe Ditch
  Derbys 185 G10
Priest Down Bath 60 G6
Priestfield W Mid 133 D8
  Worcs 98 C6
Priesthaugh Borders . . 249 C11
Priest Hill Lancs 203 G8
Priesthill Glasgow 267 C10
Priestland E Ayrs 258 B3
Priest Weston Shrops . . 130 D5
Priestwood Brack 65 F11
  Kent 69 G7
Priestwood Green Kent . 69 G7
Primethorpe Leics 135 E10
Primrose T&W 243 E8
Primrose Corner Norf . 160 G6
Primrose Green Norf . . 159 F11
Primrose Hill Bath 61 F8
  Derbys 170 F6
  Lancs 193 F11
  London 67 C9
  W Mid 133 F8
Primrose Valley
  N Yorks 218 D2
Primsland Worcs 117 E8
Prince Hill Ches E 168 G2
Prince Royd W Yorks . . 196 D6
Princes End W Mid . . . 133 E9
Prince's Marsh Hants . . 34 B3
Princes Gate Pembs . . . 73 B9
Princethorpe Warks . . . 119 C8
Princetown Caerph 77 C10
  Devon 13 G7
Prinsted W Sus 22 B3
Printstile Kent 52 E5
Prion Denb 165 C9
Prior Muir Fife 287 F9
Prior Park Northumb . . 273 E9
Prior Rigg Cumb 239 D11
Priors Frome Hereford . 97 D11
Priors Halton Shrops . . 115 B9
Priors Hardwick Warks 119 F9
Priorslee Telford 150 G4
Priors Marston Warks . 119 F9
Prior's Norton Glos 99 G7
Priorswood Som 28 B2
Priory Pembs 72 D6
Priory Green Suff 107 C8
Priory Heath Suff 108 C3
Priory Wood Hereford . 96 B5
Prisk V Glam 58 D4
Pristacott Devon 25 B8
Priston Bath 61 G7
Pristow Green Norf . . . 142 F2
Prittlewell Sthend 69 B11
Privett Hants 21 B7
  Hants 33 B11
  Kent 69 E11
Prixford Devon 40 F4
Probus Corn 5 F7
Proncy Highld 309 K7
Prospect Cumb 229 C8
Prospect Village Staffs 151 G10
Prospidnick Corn 2 C4
Provanmill Glasgow . . 268 B2
Prowse Devon 26 F4
Prudhoe Northumb . . . 242 E3
Prussia Cove Corn 2 D3
Ptarmigan Lodge Stirl 285 C8
Pubil Perth 285 C8
Publow Bath 60 G6
Puckeridge Herts 105 G7
Puckington Som 28 D5
Pucklechurch S Glos . . . 61 D7
Pucknall Hants 32 C5
Puckrup Glos 99 D7
Puckshole Glos 80 D4
Puddaven Devon 8 C5
Puddinglake Ches W . . 184 G2
Puddinglane Hants 48 B5
Puddington Ches W . . 182 G4
  Devon 26 E4
Puddle Corn 5 D11
Puddledock Hextable . . 68 E4
  Norf 141 E11
  Westerham 52 C3
Pudleston Hereford . . . 115 F11
Pudleigh Som 28 E4
Pudsey W Yorks 196 B5
Pulborough W Sus 35 D8
Pulcree Dumfries 237 D7
Pule Hill W Yorks 196 B5
Puleston Telford 150 E4
Pulford Ches W 166 D5
Pulham Dorset 30 F2
Pulham Market Norf . . 142 F3
Pulham St Mary Norf . 142 F4
Pullens Green S Glos . . . 79 G10
Pulley Shrops 131 B9
Pullington Kent 53 G10
Pulloxhill C Beds 103 E11
Pulverbatch Shrops . . . 131 C8
Pumpherston W Loth . 269 B11
Pumsaint Carms 94 C3
Puncheston / Cas-Mael
  Pembs 91 F10
Puncknowle Dorset 16 D6
Punnett's Town E Sus . . 37 C11
Purbrook Hants 33 F11
Purewell Dorset 19 C9
Purfleet Thurrock 68 D5
Puriton Som 43 E10
Purleigh Essex 88 E4
Purley London 67 G10
Purley on Thames
  W Berks 65 D7
Purlogue Shrops 114 B5
Purlpit Wilts 61 G11
Purls Bridge Cambs . . . 139 F9

Purn N Som 43 B10
Purse Caundle Dorset . . 29 D11
Purslow Shrops 130 G6
Purston Jaglin W Yorks 198 D2
Purtington Som 28 E5
Purton Glos 79 E11
  W Berks 64 D3
  Wilts 62 B5
Purton Common Wilts . .62 B5
Purton Stoke Wilts 81 G9
Purwell Herts 104 F4
Pury End Northants . . . 102 B4
Pusey Oxon 82 F5
Putley Hereford 98 D2
Putley Common Hereford .98 D2
Putley Green Hereford . 98 D3
Putloe Glos 80 D3
Putney London 67 D8
Putney Heath London . . 67 E8
Putney Vale London . . . 67 E8
Putsborough Devon . . . 40 E3
Putson Hereford 97 D10
Puttenham Herts 84 C5
  Sur 50 D2
Puttock End Essex 106 C6
Puttock's End Essex 87 B9
Putton Dorset 17 E9
Puxey Dorset 30 E3
Puxley Northants 102 C5
Puxton N Som 60 G2
Puttenham Herts 84 C5
Pwll Carms 75 E7
  Powys 130 C3
Pwll-clai Flint 181 G11
Pwllcrochan Pembs 72 E6
Pwll-glas Denb 165 D10
Pwllgloyw Powys 95 E10
Pwllheli Gwyn 145 B7
Pwll-Mawr Cardiff 59 D8
Pwll-melyn Flint 181 G11
Pwllmeyric Mon 79 G8
Pwll-trap Carms 74 B3
Pwll-y-glaw Neath 57 C9
Pwllypant Caerph 59 B7
Pye Bridge Derbys 170 E6
Pye Corner Devon 14 B4
  Kent 53 D11
  Newport 59 B9
  S Glos 60 D6
Pye Green Staffs 151 G9
Pye Hill Notts 170 E6
Pyewipe NE Lincs 201 E9
Pyle IoW 20 F5
  Swansea 56 D5
Pylehill Hants 33 D7
Pyle / Y Pîl Bridgend . . 57 E10
Pylle Som 44 F6
Pymore or Pymoor
  Cambs 139 F9
Pype Hayes W Mid 134 E2
Pyrford Sur 50 B4
Pyrford Green Sur 50 B4
Pyrford Village Sur 50 B4
Pyrland Som 28 B2
Pyrton Oxon 83 F11
Pytchley Northants . . . 121 C7
Pyworthy Devon 24 G4

Q

Quabbs Shrops 130 G4
Quabrook E Sus 52 G2
Quadring Lincs 156 C4
Quadring Eaudike Lincs 156 C4
Quags Corner W Sus . . . 34 C5
Quainton Bucks 84 B2
Quaker's Yard M Tydf . . 77 F9
Quaking Houses
  Durham 242 G5
Quality Corner Cumb . . 219 B9
Quarhouse Glos 80 E5
Quarley Hants 47 E9
Quarmby W Yorks 196 D6
Quarndon Derbys 170 G4
Quarndon Common
  Derbys 170 G4
Quarrelton Renfs 267 C8
Quarrendon Bucks 84 B4
Quarr Hill IoW 21 C7
Quarriers Village
  Inyclyd 267 B7
Quarrington Lincs 173 G9
Quarrington Hill
  Durham 234 D2
Quarrybank Ches W . . 167 B8
Quarry Bank W Mid . . . 133 F8
Quarryford E Loth 271 B11
Quarryhead Aberds . . . 303 C9
Quarry Heath Staffs . . . 151 E8
Quarryhill Highld 309 L7
Quarry Hill Staffs 134 C4
Quarrywood Moray . . . 301 C11
Quarter S Lnrk 268 E4
Quartley Devon 27 B7
Quatford Shrops 132 E4
Quatt Shrops 132 F5
Quebec Durham 233 C9
  W Sus 34 D5
Quedgeley Glos 80 C4
Queen Adelaide Cambs 139 G11
Queenborough Kent . . . 70 E2
Queen Camel Som 29 C9
Queen Charlton Bath . . 60 F6
Queen Dart Devon 26 D5
Queenhill Worcs 99 D7
Queen Oak Dorset 45 G9
Queen's Bower IoW 21 E7
Queensbury London . . . 67 B7
  W Yorks 205 G8
Queen's Corner W Sus . 34 B5
Queensferry Edin 280 F2
  Flint 166 B4
Queen's Head Shrops . 148 D6
Queenslie Glasgow . . . 268 B3
Queen's Park Beds 103 B10
  Blkburn 195 B7
  Ches W 166 B6
  Essex 87 F11
  Northants 120 E4
Queenstown Blkpool . . 202 F2
Queen Street Kent 53 E7
  Wilts 62 B4
Queensville Staffs 151 E8
Queenzieburn N Lnrk . 278 F3
Quemerford Wilts 62 F4
Quendale Shetland . . . 313 M5
Quendon Essex 105 E10
Queniborough Leics . . 154 G2
Quenington Glos 81 E10
Quernmore Lancs 202 B6
Quethiock Corn 6 C6
Quholm Orkney 314 E2
Quick Gtr Man 196 G3
Quick Edge Gtr Man . . 196 G3

Quicks Green W Berks . . 64 D5
Quidenham Norf 141 F10
Quidhampton Hants . . . 48 C4
  Wilts 46 G6
Quina Brook Shrops . . 149 C10
Quinbury End Northants 120 G2
Quindry Orkney 314 G4
Quinton Northants 120 G5
  W Mid 133 G9
Quintrell Downs Corn . .5 C7
Quixhill Staffs 169 G10
Quoditch Devon 12 B4
Quoig Perth 286 E2
Quoisley Ches E 167 F8
Quoit Corn 5 C8
Quorndon or Quorn
  Leics 153 F11
Quothquan S Lnrk 259 B11
Quoyloo Orkney 314 D2
Quoynee Highld 310 D6
Quoyness Orkney 314 F2
Quoys Shetland 312 B8
  Shetland 313 G6

R

Raasay Ho Highld 295 B7
Rabbit's Cross Kent 53 D9
Rableyheath Herts 86 B2
Raby Cumb 238 G5
  Mers 182 F4
Racecourse Suff 108 C3
Racedown Hants 47 E9
Rachan Mill Borders . . 260 C4
Rachub Gwyn 163 B10
Rackenford Devon 26 D5
Rackham W Sus 35 E9
Rackheath Norf 160 G5
Rackley Som 43 C11
Racks Dumfries 238 C2
Rackwick Orkney 314 B4
  Orkney 314 G2
Radbourne Derbys 152 B5
Radcliffe Gtr Man 195 F9
  Northumb 253 C7
Radcliffe on Trent Notts 154 B2
Radclive Bucks 102 E3
Radcot Oxon 82 F3
Raddery Highld 301 D7
Radernie Fife 287 G8
Radfall Kent 70 G6
Radford Bath 45 B7
  Nottingham 171 G9
  Oxon 101 G8
  W Mid 118 B6
  Worcs 117 F10
Radfordbridge Oxon . . 101 G8
Radford Semele Warks 118 E6
Radipole Dorset 17 E9
Radlet Som 43 F8
Radlett Herts 85 F11
Radley Oxon 83 F8
Radley Green Essex 87 D10
Radley Park Oxon 83 F8
Radlith Shrops 131 B8
Radmanthwaite Notts . 171 C8
Radmoor Shrops 150 D2
Radmore Green Ches E 167 D9
Radmore Wood Staffs 151 D11
Radnage Bucks 84 F3
Radnor Corn 4 G4
Radnor Park W Dunb . 277 G9
Radstock Bath 45 C7
Radstone Northants . . 101 C11
Radway Warks 119 G7
Radway Green Ches E . 168 E2
Radwell Herts 104 D4
  Beds 121 F10
Radwinter Essex 106 D2
Radwinter End Essex . . 106 D2
Radyr Cardiff 58 C6
Raehills Dumfries 248 E3
Raera Argyll 289 G10
Rafborough Hants 49 B11
Rafford Moray 301 D10
Raga Shetland 312 D6
Ragdale Leics 154 F3
Ragdon Shrops 131 E9
Raggalds W Yorks 205 G7
Ragged Appleshaw
  Hants 47 D10
Raginnis Corn 1 D5
Raglan Mon 78 D6
Ragmere Norf 141 E11
Ragnall Notts 188 G4
Rahane Argyll 276 D4
Rahoy Highld 289 D8
Raigbeg Highld 301 G8
Rails S Yorks 186 D3
Rainbow Hill Worcs . . . 117 F7
Rainford Mers 194 G3
Rainford Junction Mers 194 G3
Rainham London 68 C4
  Medway 69 F10
Rainhill Mers 183 C7
Rainhill Stoops Mers . . 183 C8
Rainow Ches E 185 F7
Rainowlow Ches E 185 F7
Rain Shore Gtr Man . . . 195 D11
Rainsough Gtr Man . . . 195 G10
Rainton Dumfries 237 D8
  N Yorks 215 D7
Rainton Bridge T&W . . 234 B2
Rainton Gate Durham . 234 B2
Rainworth Notts 171 D9
Raisbeck Cumb 222 D3
Raise Cumb 231 B10
Rait Perth 286 E6
Raithby Lincs 190 E4
Raithby by Spilsby Lincs 174 B5
Rake W Sus 34 B4
Rake End Staffs 151 F11
Rakeheath Lancs 195 C10
Rakes Dale Staffs 169 G9
Rakeway Staffs 169 G8
Rakewood Gtr Man . . . 196 E2
Raleigh Devon 40 G5
Ralia Lodge Highld . . . 291 D9
Rallt Swansea 56 C4
Ram Carms 93 B11
Ram Alley Wilts 63 G8
Ramasaig Highld 297 G2
Rame Corn 2 C6
  Corn 7 F8
Ram Hill S Glos 61 D7
Ram Lane Kent 54 D3
Rameldry Mill Bank
  Fife 287 G7
Rampisham Dorset 29 G9
Rampside Cumb 210 F4
Rampton Cambs 123 D8
  Notts 188 F3

Ramsbottom Gtr Man . 195 D9
Ramsburn Moray 302 D5
Ramsbury Wilts 63 E9
Ramscraigs Highld . . . 311 G5
Ramsdean Hants 34 C2
Ramsdell Hants 48 B5
Ramsden London 68 F3
  Oxon 82 B5
  Worcs 99 B8
Ramsden Bellhouse
  Essex 88 G2
Ramsden Heath Essex . 88 F2
Ramsden Wood
  W Yorks 196 C2
Ramsey Cambs 138 F5
  Essex 108 E4
  IoM 192 C5
Ramsey Forty Foot
  Cambs 138 F5
Ramsey Heights Cambs 138 F5
Ramsey Island Essex . . 89 D7
Ramsey Mereside
  Cambs 138 F5
Ramsey St Mary's
  Cambs 138 F5
Ramsgate Kent 71 G11
Ramsgill N Yorks 214 E2
Ramshaw Durham 232 B5
  Durham 233 F8
Ramshorn Staffs 169 F9
Ramsley Devon 13 C8
Ramsnest Common Sur 50 G2
Ranais W Isles 304 F6
Ranby Lincs 190 F2
  Notts 187 E11
Rand Lincs 189 F10
Randwick Glos 80 D4
Ranfurly Renfs 267 C7
Rangag Highld 310 E5
Rangemore Staffs 152 E3
Rangeworthy S Glos . . . 61 B7
Rankinston E Ayrs 257 G11
Rank's Green Essex 88 B3
Ranmoor S Yorks 186 D4
Ranmore Common Sur . 50 C6
Rannerdale Cumb 220 B3
Rannoch Lodge Perth . 285 B9
Rannoch Station Perth 285 B8
Ranochan Highld 295 G10
Ranskill Notts 187 D11
Ranton Staffs 151 E7
Ranton Green Staffs . . 150 E6
Ranworth Norf 161 G7
Rapkyns W Sus 50 G6
Raploch Stirl 278 C5
Rapness Orkney 314 B5
Rapps Som 28 D4
Rascal Moor E Yorks . . 208 F2
Rascarrel Dumfries . . . 237 E9
Rashielee Renfs 277 G9
Rashiereive Aberds . . . 303 G9
Raskelf N Yorks 215 E9
Rassau Bl Gwent 77 C11
Rastrick W Yorks 196 C6
Ratagan Highld 295 D11
Ratby Leics 135 B10
Ratcliffe Corn 67 C11
Ratcliffe Culey Leics . . 134 D5
Ratcliffe on Soar Leics 153 D9
Ratcliffe on the Wreake
  Leics 154 G2
Ratford Wilts 62 E3
Ratfyn Wilts 47 E7
Rathen Aberds 303 C10
Rathillet Fife 287 E7
Rathmell N Yorks 204 B2
Ratho Edin 280 G2
Ratho Station Edin . . . 280 G2
Rathven Moray 302 C4
Ratlake Hants 32 C6
Ratley Warks 101 B7
Ratlinghope Shrops . . . 131 D8
Ratsloe Devon 14 B5
Rattar Highld 310 B6
Ratten Row Cumb 230 B3
  Cumb 230 C2
  Lancs 202 E4
  Norf 157 G10
Rattery Devon 8 C4
Rattlesden Suff 125 F9
Rattray Perth 286 C5
Raughton Cumb 230 B3
Raughton Head Cumb . 230 B3
Raunds Northants 121 C9
Ravelston Edin 280 G4
Ravenfield S Yorks 187 B7
Ravenglass Cumb 219 G11
Ravenhead Mers 183 C8
Ravenhills Green Worcs 116 G4
Raveningham Norf 143 D7
Ravenscar N Yorks 227 G9
Ravenscliffe Stoke 168 E4
  W Yorks 205 F9
Ravenscraig Inyclyd . . 276 F5
Ravensdale IoM 192 C4
Ravensden Beds 121 G11
Ravenseat N Yorks 223 F7
Ravenshall Staffs 168 F3
Ravenshead Notts 171 E9
Raven's Green Essex . . 108 G2
Ravensmoor Ches E . . . 167 E10
Ravensthorpe Northants 120 C3
  Pboro 138 C3
  W Yorks 197 C8
Ravenstone Leics 153 G8
  M Keynes 120 G6
Ravenstonedale Cumb 222 E4
Ravenstown Cumb 211 D7
Ravensworth N Yorks . 224 D2
Raw N Yorks 227 D8
Rawcliffe E Yorks 199 C7
  York 207 C7
Rawcliffe Bridge
  E Yorks 199 C7
Rawdon W Yorks 205 F10
Rawdon Carrs W Yorks 205 F10
Rawfolds W Yorks 197 C7
Rawgreen Northumb . . 241 F10
Raw Green S Yorks 197 F9
Rawmarsh S Yorks 186 B6
Rawnsley Staffs 151 G10
Rawreth Essex 88 G3
Rawreth Shot Essex . . . 88 G3
Rawridge Devon 28 F2
Rawson Green Derbys . 170 F5
Rawtenstall Lancs 195 C10
Rawthorpe W Yorks . . . 197 D7
Rawyards N Lnrk 268 B5
Raxton Aberds 303 F8
Raydon Suff 107 D11
Raygill N Yorks 204 D4
Raylees Northumb 251 E10

Rayleigh Essex 88 G4
Rayne Essex 106 G4
Rayners Lane London 66 B6
Raynes Park London 67 F8
Reabrook Shrops 131 C7
Reach Cambs 123 D11
Read Lancs 203 G11
Reader's Corner Essex 88 E2
Reading Reading 65 E8
Readings Glos 79 B10
Reading Street Kent 54 G2
  Kent 71 F11
Readymoney Corn 6 E2
Ready Token Glos 81 E10
Reagill Cumb 222 B2
Rearquhar Highld 309 K7
Rearsby Leics 154 G3
Reasby Lincs 189 F9
Rease Heath Ches E 167 E10
Reaster Highld 310 C6
Reaulay Highld 299 D7
Reawick Shetland 313 J5
Reawla Corn 2 B4
Reay Highld 310 C3
Rechullin Highld 299 D8
Reculver Kent 71 F8
Red Ball Devon 27 D7
Redberth Pembs 73 E9
Redbourn Herts 85 C10
Redbournbury Herts 85 C10
Redbourne N Lincs 189 B7
  N Lincs 200 G3
  London 68 B2
  Soton 32 E5
Red Bridge Lancs 211 D9
Redbrook Mon 79 C8
  Wrex 167 G8
Red Bull Ches E 168 D4
  Staffs 150 B4
Redburn Highld 300 C5
  Highld 301 G9
  Northumb 241 E7
Redcar Redcar 235 G8
Redcastle Angus 287 B10
  Highld 300 E5
Redcliff Bay N Som 60 D2
Redcroft Dumfries 237 B9
Redcross Worcs 117 C7
Red Dial Cumb 229 B11
Reddicap Heath W Mid 134 D2
Redding Falk 279 F8
Reddingmuirhead Falk 279 F8
Reddish Gtr Man 184 C5
  Warr 183 D11
Redditch Worcs 117 D10
Redenhall Norf 142 G5
Redenham Hants 47 D10
Redesdale Camp
  Northumb 251 D8
Redesmouth Northumb 251 G9
Redford Aberds 293 F9
  Angus 287 C9
  Dorset 29 F11
  Durham 233 E7
  W Sus 34 B5
Redfordgreen Borders 261 F9
Redgorton Perth 286 E4
Redgrave Suff 125 B10
Redheugh Angus 292 G6
Redhill Aberds 293 C9
  Aberds 302 F6
  Herts 104 E6
  Notts 171 F9
  N Som 60 G4
  Shrops 131 B9
  Shrops 150 G4
  Staffs 150 D6
  Sur 51 C9
  Telford 150 G4
Red Hill Bmouth 19 B7
  Hants 34 E2
  Hereford 97 D10
  Kent 53 C7
  Leics 135 D10
  Pembs 73 E9
  Warks 118 F2
  Worcs 117 G7
  W Yorks 198 B2
Redhills Cumb 230 F6
  Devon 14 C4
Redhouse Argyll 275 G9
Red House Common
  E Sus 36 C5
Redhouses Argyll 274 G4
Redisham Suff 143 G8
Red Lake Telford 150 G3
Redland Bristol 60 D5
  Orkney 314 D3
Redland End Bucks 84 E4
Redlands Dorset 17 E8
  Som 44 G3
  Swindon 81 G11
Redlane Som 28 E2
Redlingfield Suff 126 C3
Red Lodge Suff 124 C3
Red Lumb Gtr Man 195 D10
Redlynch Som 45 G8
  Wilts 32 C2
Redmain Cumb 229 E8
Redmarley D'Abitot Glos 98 E5
Redmarshall Stockton 234 G3
Redmile Leics 154 B5
Redmire N Yorks 223 G10
Redmonsford Devon 24 D4
Redmoor Corn 5 C11
Redmoss Aberds 303 F8
Rednal Shrops 149 D7
  W Mid 117 B10
Redpath Borders 262 B3
Red Pits Norf 159 D11
Redpoint Highld 299 C7
Red Post Corn 24 F3
  Corn 5 E9
Red Rail Hereford 97 F10
Red Rice Hants 47 E10
Red Rock Gtr Man 194 F5
Red Roses Carms 74 C2
Red Row Northumb 253 D7
Redruth Corn 4 G3
Red Scar Lancs 203 G7
Redscarhead Borders 270 G4
Redstocks Wilts 62 G2
Red Street Staffs 168 E4
Redtye Corn 5 D10
Redvales Gtr Man 195 F10
Red Wharf Bay Anglesey 179 E8
  S Glos 60 B4
Redwick Newport 60 C2
  S Glos 60 B4
Redwith Shrops 148 E6
Redworth Darl 233 G10
Reed Herts 105 D7
Reed End Herts 104 D6
Reedham Lincs 174 D2
  Norf 143 C8
Reedley Lancs 204 F2
Reedness E Yorks 199 C9
Reed Point Lincs 174 E2
Reeds Beck Lincs 174 B2
Reedsford Northumb 263 C9
Reeds Holme Lancs 195 C10

Reedy Devon 14 D2
Reen Manor Corn 4 E5
Reepham Lincs 189 G8
  Norf 159 E11
Rees Green W Mid 118 B5
Reeves Green W Mid 118 B5
Refail Powys 130 C3
Regaby IoM 192 C5
Regil Bath 60 G4
Regoul Highld 301 D8
Reiff Highld 307 H4
Reigate Sur 51 C8
Reigate Heath Sur 51 C8
Reighton N Yorks 218 D2
Reighton Gap N Yorks 218 D2
Reinigeadal W Isles 305 H4
Reisque Aberds 293 B10
Reiss Highld 310 D7
Rejerrah Corn 4 D5
Releath Corn 2 C3
Relubbus Corn 2 C3
Relugas Moray 301 E9
Remenham Wokingham 65 C9
Remenham Hill
  Wokingham 65 C9
Remony Perth 285 C11
Rempstone Notts 153 E11
Remusaig Highld 309 J7
Rendcomb Glos 81 D8
Rendham Suff 126 E6
Rendlesham Suff 126 G6
Renfrew Renfs 267 B10
Renhold Beds 121 G11
Renishaw Derbys 186 F6
Renmure Angus 287 B10
Rennington Northumb 264 F6
Renton W Dunb 277 F7
Renwick Cumb 231 C7
Repps Norf 161 F8
Repton Derbys 152 D6
Reraig Highld 295 C10
Reraig Cot Highld 295 B10
Rerwick Shetland 313 M5
Rescassa Corn 3 B9
Rescobie Angus 287 B9
Rescorla Corn 5 D10
Resipole Highld 289 C9
Reskadinnick Corn 4 G2
Resolis / Resolfen
  Neath 76 E4
Resolis Highld 300 C6
Resolven / Resolfen
  Neath 76 E4
Restalrig Edin 280 G5
Reston Borders 273 C7
  Cumb 221 F9
Restronguet Passage Corn 3 B8
Restrop Wilts 62 B5
Resugga Green Corn 5 D10
Reswallie Angus 287 B9
Retew Corn 5 D8
Retford Notts 188 E2
Retire Corn 5 C10
Rettendon Essex 88 F3
Rettendon Place Essex 88 F3
Revesby Lincs 174 C3
Revesby Bridge Lincs 174 C4
Revidge Blkburn 195 B7
Rew Devon 13 G11
  Devon 29 F11
Rewe Devon 14 B4
Rew Street IoW 20 C5
Rexon Devon 12 D4
Rexon Cross Devon 12 D4
Reybridge Wilts 62 F2
Reydon Suff 127 B9
Reydon Smear Suff 127 B9
Reymerston Norf 141 B10
Reynalton Pembs 73 D9
Reynoldston Swansea 56 C3
Rezare Corn 12 F3
Rhadyr Mon 78 E5
Rhaeadr Gwy / Rhayader
  Powys 113 D9
Rhandir Conwy 180 G4
Rhandirmwyn Carms 94 C5
Rhayader / Rhaeadr Gwy
  Powys 113 D9
Rhedyn Gwyn 144 C5
Rhegreanoch Highld 307 H5
Rhemore Highld 289 D7
Rhencullen IoM 192 C4
Rhenetra Highld 298 D4
Rhes-y-cae Flint 181 G11
Rhewl Denb 165 C10
  Denb 165 F11
  Shrops 148 C6
  Wrex 149 B7
Rhewl-fawr Flint 181 E10
Rhewl-Mostyn Flint 181 E11
Rhian Highld 309 H5
Rhicarn Highld 307 G5
Rhiconich Highld 306 D7
Rhicullen Highld 300 B6
Rhidorroch Ho Highld 307 K6
Rhiews Shrops 150 B3
Rhifail Highld 308 E7
Rhigolter Highld 308 D3
Rhigos Rhondda 76 D6
Rhilochan Highld 309 J7
Rhippinllwyd Ceredig 92 C5
  Ceredig 110 G6
Rhiroy Highld 307 L6
Rhitongue Highld 308 D6
Rhivichie Highld 306 D7
Rhiw Gwyn 144 D4
Rhiwabon / Ruabon
  Wrex 166 G4
Rhiwbebyll Denb 165 B10
Rhiwbina Cardiff 59 C7
Rhiwbryfdir Gwyn 163 F11
Rhiwceiliog Bridgend 58 C3
Rhiwderin Newport 59 B9
Rhiwen Gwyn 163 C9
Rhiwfawr Neath 76 C2
Rhiwinder Rhondda 58 B4
Rhiwlas Gwyn 147 B8
  Gwyn 163 B9
  Powys 148 C3
Rhode Som 43 G9
Rhode Common Kent 54 B5
Rhodes Gtr Man 195 F11
Rhodesia Notts 187 F9
Rhodes Minnis Kent 55 E7
Rhodiad Pembs 90 F5
Rhonadale Argyll 255 D8
Rhondda Rhondda 77 F7
Rhonehouse or Kelton Hill
  Dumfries 237 D9
Rhoose V Glam 58 F5
Rhos Carms 93 D7
Rhôs Denb 165 C10
  Neath 76 E2
Rhos Powys 148 B5
Rhosaman Carms 76 C2
Rhosbeirio Anglesey 178 C5
Rhoscefnhir Anglesey 179 F8
Rhoscolyn Anglesey 178 F3

Rhôs Common Powys 148 F5
Rhoscrowther Pembs 72 E6
Rhosddu Wrex 166 E4
Rhos-ddû Gwyn 144 B5
Rhosdylluan Gwyn 147 D7
Rhosesmor Flint 166 B2
Rhosfach Pembs 92 F2
Rhos-fawr Gwyn 145 B7
Rhosgadfan Gwyn 163 D8
Rhosgoch Anglesey 178 D6
  Powys 96 B3
Rhos-goch Powys 163 G7
Rhosgyll Powys 163 G7
Rhos Haminiog Ceredig 111 E10
Rhos-hill Pembs 92 C3
Rhoshirwaun Gwyn 144 D3
Rhos Isaf Gwyn 163 D7
Rhoslan Gwyn 163 G7
Rhoslefain Gwyn 110 B2
Rhosllanerchrugog
  Wrex 166 F3
Rhôs Lligwy Anglesey 179 D7
Rhosmaen Carms 94 G2
Rhosmeirch Anglesey 178 G4
Rhosneigr Anglesey 178 G4
Rhosnesni Wrex 166 E4
Rhos-on-Sea Conwy 180 E4
Rhosrobin Wrex 166 E4
Rhossili Swansea 56 D2
Rhosson Pembs 90 F4
Rhostrehwfa Anglesey 178 G6
Rhostryfan Gwyn 163 D7
Rhostyllen Wrex 166 F4
Rhoswiel Shrops 148 B5
Rhosybol Anglesey 178 D6
Rhos-y-brithdir Powys 148 E2
Rhoscyaerau Pembs 91 D8
Rhosygadair Newydd
  Ceredig 92 B4
Rhosygadfa Shrops 148 C6
Rhos-y-garth Ceredig 112 C2
Rhos-y-gwaliau Gwyn 147 C8
Rhos-y-llan Gwyn 144 B4
Rhos-y-Madoc Wrex 166 G4
Rhosymedre Wrex 166 G3
Rhos-y-meirch Powys 114 D5
Rhosyn-coch Carms 92 G5
Rhu Argyll 275 D11
  Argyll 276 E5
Rhualt Denb 181 F9
Rhubodach Argyll 275 F11
Rhuddall Heath Ches W 167 C9
Rhuddlan Ceredig 93 C9
  Denb 181 F8
Rhue Highld 307 K5
Rhulen Powys 96 B2
Rhunahaorine Argyll 255 C8
Rhyd Ceredig 111 D11
  Gwyn 163 G10
Rhydaman / Ammanford
  Carms 75 C10
Rhydargaeau Carms 93 F8
Rhydcymerau Carms 93 D11
Rhydd Worcs 98 B6
Rhyd-Ddu Gwyn 163 E9
Rhydding Neath 57 B8
Rhydfudr Ceredig 111 D11
Rhydgaled Conwy 165 C8
Rhydgaled / Chancery
  Ceredig 111 B11
Rhydlewis Ceredig 92 B6
Rhydlios Gwyn 144 C3
Rhydlydan Conwy 164 E5
  Powys 129 E11
Rhydmoelddu Powys 113 B11
Rhydness Powys 96 C2
Rhydowen Ceredig 93 B8
Rhyd-Rosser Ceredig 111 D11
Rhydspence Hereford 96 B4
Rhydtalog Flint 166 D2
Rhyd-uchaf Gwyn 147 B8
Rhydwen Gwyn 146 F4
Rhydwyn Anglesey 178 C4
Rhyd-y-Brown Pembs 91 G11
Rhyd-y-clafdy Gwyn 144 B6
Rhydycroesau Powys 148 C4
Rhyd-y-cwm Shrops 130 G3
Rhydyfelin Ceredig 111 B11
  Rhondda 58 B5
Rhyd-y-foel Conwy 180 F6
Rhyd-y-fro Neath 76 D2
Rhydygwystl Gwyn 145 B8
Rhyd-y-gwin Swansea 75 E11
Rhyd-y-meirch Mon 78 D4
Rhyd-y-meudwy Denb 165 D10
Rhydymwyn Flint 166 B2
Rhyd-y-pandy Swansea 75 E11
Rhyd-yr-onen Gwyn 128 C2
Rhyd-y-sarn Gwyn 163 G11
Rhydywrach Carms 73 B11
Rhyl Denb 181 E8
Rhymney Caerph 77 D10
Rhyn Wrex 148 B6
Rhynd Fife 287 E8
  Perth 286 E5
Rhynie Aberds 302 G4
  Highld 301 B8
Ribbesford Worcs 116 C5
Ribblehead N Yorks 212 D5
Ribbleton Lancs 203 G7
Ribby Lancs 202 G4
Ribchester Lancs 203 F8
Riber Derbys 170 D4
Ribigill Highld 308 D5
Riby Lincs 201 F7
Riby Cross Roads Lincs 201 F7
Riccall N Yorks 207 F8
Riccarton E Ayrs 257 B10
Richards Castle
  Hereford 115 D9
Richborough Port Kent 71 G10
Richings Park Bucks 66 D4
Richmond London 67 E7
  N Yorks 224 E3
  S Yorks 186 D6
Richmond's Green
  Essex 106 F2
Rich's Holford Som 42 G6
Rickard's Down Devon 24 B6
Rickarton Aberds 293 E10
Rickerby Cumb 239 F10
Rickerscote Staffs 151 E8
Rickford N Som 44 B3
Rickham Devon 7 F7
Rickinghall Suff 125 C10
Rickleton T&W 243 G7
Rickling Essex 105 E9
Rickling Green Essex 105 F10
Rickmansworth Herts 85 G9
Rickney E Sus 23 D10
Riddell Borders 262 E2
Riddings Derbys 170 E6

Riddlecombe Devon 25 E10
Riddlesden W Yorks 205 E7
Riddrie Glasgow 268 B2
Ridgacre W Mid 133 G10
Ridge Bath 44 B5
  Dorset 18 D4
  Hants 32 D4
  Herts 86 E2
  Lancs 211 G9
  Som 28 F3
  Wilts 46 G3
Ridgebourne Powys 113 E10
Ridge Common Hants 34 C2
Ridge Green Sur 51 D10
Ridge Hill Gtr Man 185 B7
Ridgehill N Som 60 G4
Ridge Lane Warks 134 E5
Ridgemarsh Herts 85 G8
Ridgeway Bristol 60 D6
  Derbys 170 E5
  Derbys 186 E6
  Kent 54 E5
  Newport 59 B9
  Pembs 73 D10
  Som 45 D8
  Staffs 168 F5
Ridgeway Cross Hereford 98 B4
Ridgeway Moor Derbys 186 E6
Ridgewell Essex 106 C4
Ridgewood E Sus 23 B7
Ridgmont C Beds 103 D9
Ridgway Shrops 131 F7
  Sur 50 B4
Riding Gate Som 30 B2
Riding Mill Northumb 242 E2
Ridley Kent 68 G6
  Northumb 241 E7
Ridley Stokoe Northumb 250 F6
Ridleywood Wrex 166 E6
Ridlington Norf 160 C6
  Rutland 136 C6
Ridlington Street Norf 160 C6
Ridsdale Northumb 251 G10
Riechip Perth 286 C4
Riemore Perth 286 C4
Rienachait Highld 306 F5
Rievaulx N Yorks 215 B11
Riff Orkney 314 E4
Riffin Aberds 303 E7
Rifle Green Torf 78 D3
Rift House Hrtlpl 234 E5
Rigg Dumfries 239 D7
Riggend N Lnrk 278 G5
Rigsby Lincs 190 F6
Rigside S Lnrk 259 B9
Riley Green Lancs 194 B6
Rileyhill Staffs 152 F2
Rilla Mill Corn 11 G11
Rillaton Corn 11 G11
Rillington N Yorks 217 E7
Rimac Lincs 191 C7
Rimington Lancs 204 D2
Rimpton Som 29 C10
Rimswell E Yorks 201 B10
Rimswell Valley
  E Yorks 201 B10
Rinaston Pembs 91 F9
Rindleford Shrops 132 D4
Ringasta Shetland 313 M5
Ringford Dumfries 237 D8
Ringing Hill Leics 153 F9
Ringinglow S Yorks 186 E3
Ringland Newport 59 B11
  Norf 160 G2
Ringles Cross E Sus 37 C7
Ringlestone Kent 53 B9
  Kent 53 B11
Ringley Gtr Man 195 F9
Ringmer E Sus 36 E6
Ringmore Devon 8 F3
Ring o' Bells Lancs 194 E3
Ringorm Moray 302 E2
Ring's End Cambs 139 C7
Ringsfield Suff 143 F9
Ringsfield Corner Suff 143 F9
Ringshall Herts 85 C7
  Suff 125 G10
Ringshall Stocks Suff 125 G10
Ringstead Norf 176 E2
  Northants 121 B9
Ringtail Green Essex 87 B11
Ringwood Hants 31 F11
Ringwould Kent 55 D11
Rinmore Aberds 292 B6
Rinnigill Orkney 314 G3
Rinsey Corn 2 D4
Rinsey Croft Corn 2 D4
Riof W Isles 304 E3
Ripe E Sus 23 D8
Ripley Derbys 170 E5
  Hants 19 B9
  N Yorks 214 G5
  Sur 50 B5
Riplingham E Yorks 208 G5
Ripon N Yorks 214 E6
Ripper's Cross Kent 54 E4
Rippingale Lincs 155 D11
Ripple Kent 55 D11
  Worcs 99 D7
Ripponden W Yorks 196 D4
Rireavach Highld 307 K5
Risabus Argyll 254 C4
Risbury Hereford 115 G10
Risby E Yorks 208 G5
  Lincs 189 C10
  Suff 124 D5
Rise E Yorks 209 E8
Rise Carr Darl 224 B5
Riseden E Sus 52 G6
  Kent 53 F8
Risegate Lincs 156 D4
Riseholme Lincs 189 F7
Risehow Cumb 228 E6
Riseley Beds 121 E10
  Wokingham 65 G8
Rise Park London 87 G8
  Nottingham 171 F9
Rishangles Suff 126 D3
Rishton Lancs 203 G10
Rishworth W Yorks 196 D4
Rising Bridge Lancs 195 B9
Risley Derbys 153 B9
  Warr 183 C11
Risplith N Yorks 214 F4
Rispond Highld 308 C4
Rivar Wilts 63 G10
Rivenhall Essex 88 B4
Rivenhall End Essex 88 B4
River Kent 55 E10
  W Sus 34 C6
River Bank Cambs 123 D10
Riverhead Kent 52 B4
Rivers' Corner Dorset 30 E2
Riverside Cardiff 59 D7
  Plym 7 D8
  Herts 104 E6
Riverside Docklands
  Lancs 194 B4
Riverton Devon 40 G6
Riverview Park Kent 69 E7
Rivington Lancs 194 E6
Rixon Dorset 30 E3
Rixton Warr 183 C11
Roach Bridge Lancs 194 B5
Roaches Gtr Man 196 G3
Roachill Devon 26 C4
Roade Northants 120 G5
Road Green Norf 142 E5
Roadhead Cumb 240 C2
Roadmeetings S Lnrk 269 F7
Roadside Highld 310 C5
Roadside of Catterline
  Aberds 293 F10
Roadside of Kinneff
  Aberds 293 F10
Roadwater Som 42 F4
Road Weedon Northants 120 F2
Roag Highld 298 E2
Roa Island Cumb 210 G4
Roast Green Essex 105 E9
Roath Cardiff 59 D7
Roath Park Cardiff 59 D7
Roberton Borders 261 G10
  S Lnrk 259 D10
Robertsbridge E Sus 38 C2
Robertstown Moray 302 E2
  Rhondda 77 E8
Roberttown W Yorks 197 C7
Robeston Back Pembs 72 D5
Robeston Cross Pembs 72 D5
Robeston Wathen Pembs 73 C9
Robeston West Pembs 72 D5
Robhurst Kent 54 G2
Robin Hill Staffs 168 D6
Robin Hood Derbys 186 G3
  Lancs 194 E4
  W Yorks 197 B10
Robinhood End Essex 106 D4
Robin Hood's Bay
  N Yorks 227 D9
Robins W Sus 34 B4
Robinson's End Warks 134 E6
Roborough Devon 7 C10
  Devon 25 D9
Roby Mers 182 C6
Roby Mill Lancs 194 F4
Rocester Staffs 152 B2
Roch Pembs 91 G7
Rochdale Gtr Man 195 E11
Roche Corn 5 C9
Roche Grange Staffs 169 C7
Rochester Medway 69 F8
  Northumb 251 D8
Rochford Essex 88 G5
  Worcs 116 D2
Roch Gate Pembs 91 G7
Rock Caerph 77 F11
  Corn 10 G4
  Devon 28 G3
  Neath 57 D9
  Northumb 264 G6
  Som 28 C4
  W Sus 35 E10
  Worcs 116 C4
Rockbeare Devon 14 C6
Rockbourne Hants 31 D10
Rockcliffe Cumb 239 E9
  Dumfries 237 D10
Rockcliffe Cross Cumb 239 E8
Rock End Staffs 168 E5
Rock Ferry Mers 182 D4
Rockfield Highld 311 L3
  Mon 79 C7
Rockford Devon 41 D9
  Hants 31 F11
Rockgreen Shrops 115 B10
Rockhampton S Glos 79 G11
Rockhead Corn 11 E7
Rockhill Shrops 114 B5
Rockingham Northants 137 E7
Rockland All Saints
  Norf 141 D9
Rockland St Mary Norf 142 C6
Rockland St Peter Norf 141 D9
Rockley Notts 188 G2
  Wilts 63 E7
Rockness Glos 80 F4
Rockrobin E Sus 52 G6
Rocks Park E Sus 37 C7
Rockstowes Glos 80 F3
Rockville Argyll 276 C4
Rockwell End Bucks 65 B9
Rockwell Green Som 27 C10
Rocky Hill Scilly 1 G4
Rodbaston Staffs 151 G8
Rodborough Glos 80 E4
Rodbourne Swindon 62 B6
  Wilts 62 B4
Rodbourne Bottom Wilts 62 C2
Rodbourne Cheney
  Swindon 62 B6
Rodd Hereford 114 E6
Roddam Northumb 264 E2
Rodden Dorset 17 E8
Rodd Hurst Hereford 114 E6
Roddymoor Durham 233 D9
Rode Som 45 C10
Rodeheath Ches E 168 B5
Rode Heath Ches E 168 D3
Roden Telford 149 F11
Rodford S Glos 61 C7
Rodgrove Som 30 C2
Rodhuish Som 42 F4
Rodington Telford 149 F11
Rodington Heath
  Telford 149 G11
Rodley Glos 80 C2
  W Yorks 205 F10
Rodmarton Glos 80 F6
Rodmell E Sus 36 F6
Rodmer Clough
  W Yorks 196 B3
Rodmersham Kent 70 G2
Rodmersham Green Kent 70 G2
Rodney Stoke Som 44 C3
Rodsley Derbys 170 G2
Rodway Som 43 F9
  Telford 150 F2
Rodwell Dorset 17 F8
Roe Cross Gtr Man 185 B7
Roe End Herts 85 B8
Roedean Brighton 36 G4
Roe Green Herts 86 E3
  Herts 104 E6
Roehampton London 67 E8

Roe Lee Blkburn 203 G9
Roesound Shetland 312 G5
Roestock Herts 86 D2
Roffey W Sus 51 G7
Rogart Highld 309 J7
Rogart Station Highld 309 J7
Rogate W Sus 34 C4
Roger Ground Cumb 221 F7
Rogerstone Newport 59 B9
Rogerton S Lnrk 268 D2
Roghadal W Isles 296 C6
Rogiet Mon 60 B3
Rogue's Alley Cambs 139 B7
Roke Oxon 83 G10
Rokemarsh Oxon 83 G10
Roker T&W 243 F10
Rollesby Norf 161 F8
Rolleston Leics 136 C4
  Notts 172 E2
Rolleston Camp Wilts 46 E5
Rolleston-on-Dove
  Staffs 152 D4
Rolls Mill Dorset 30 E3
Rolston E Yorks 209 D10
Rolstone N Som 59 G11
Rolvenden Kent 53 G11
Rolvenden Layne Kent 53 G11
Romaldkirk Durham 232 G5
Romanby N Yorks 225 G7
Romannobridge Borders 270 F3
Romansleigh Devon 26 C2
Rome Angus 293 G7
Romesdal Highld 298 D4
Romford Dorset 31 F9
  Kent 52 E6
  London 68 B4
Romiley Gtr Man 184 C6
Romney Street Kent 68 G4
Rompa Shetland 313 L6
Romsey Hants 32 C5
Romsey Town Cambs 123 F9
Romsley Shrops 132 G5
  Worcs 117 B9
Romsley Hill Worcs 117 B9
Ronague IoM 192 E3
Ronachan Ho Argyll 255 B8
Rood End W Mid 133 F10
Rookby Cumb 222 C6
Rook End Essex 105 E11
Rookhope Durham 232 C4
Rookley IoW 20 E6
Rookley Green IoW 20 E6
Rooks Bridge Som 43 C11
Rooksey Green Suff 125 G8
Rooks Hill Kent 52 C5
Rooksmoor Glos 80 E4
Rook's Nest Som 42 G5
Rook Street Wilts 45 G10
Rookwith N Yorks 214 B4
Rookwood W Sus 21 B11
Roos E Yorks 209 G11
Roose Cumb 210 F4
Roosebeck Cumb 210 F4
Roosecote Cumb 210 F4
Roost End Essex 106 C4
Rootham's Green Beds 122 F2
Rootpark S Lnrk 269 E9
Ropley Hants 48 G6
Ropley Dean Hants 48 G6
Ropley Soke Hants 49 G7
Ropsley Lincs 155 C9
Rora Aberds 303 D10
Rorandle Aberds 293 B8
Rorrington Shrops 130 C5
Rosarie Moray 302 E3
Roscroggan Corn 4 G3
Rose Corn 4 D4
Rose-an-Grouse Corn 2 B3
Roseacre Kent 53 B9
  Lancs 202 F4
Rose Ash Devon 26 C3
Rosebank E Dunb 278 G3
  S Lnrk 268 F6
Rosebery Midloth 270 D5
Rosebrae Moray 301 C11
Rosebrough Northumb 264 D4
Rosebush Pembs 91 F11
Rosecare Corn 11 B9
Rosedale Herts 86 E4
Rosedale Abbey
  N Yorks 226 F4
Roseden Northumb 264 E2
Rosedinnick Corn 5 C8
Rosedown Devon 24 C3
Rosefield Highld 301 D8
Rose Green Essex 107 F8
  Suff 107 D9
  Suff 107 C9
  W Sus 22 D6
Rose Grove Lancs 204 G3
Rosehall Highld 309 J4
  N Lnrk 268 C4
Rosehaugh Mains
  Highld 300 D6
Rosehearty Aberds 303 C9
Rosehill Blkburn 195 C8
  Corn 1 C5
  Corn 5 C10
  Gtr Man 184 D3
  Herts 104 E6
  Pembs 73 B7
  Shrops 150 B2
  Shrops 150 C3
  T&W 243 D8
Rose Hill Bucks 66 C2
  Derbys 153 B7
  E Sus 37 C7
  Lancs 204 G2
  Oxon 83 E8
  Suff 108 C3
  Sur 51 D7
Roseisle Moray 301 C11
Roseland Corn 6 C5
Roselands E Sus 23 E10
Rosemarket Pembs 73 D7
Rosemarkie Highld 301 D7
Rosemary Lane Devon 27 E11
Rosemelling Corn 5 D10
Rosemergy Corn 1 B4
Rosemount Perth 286 C5
Rosenannon Corn 5 C8
Rosenithon Corn 3 E8
Roser's Cross E Sus 37 C9
Rose Valley Pembs 73 E8
Rosevean Corn 5 D10
Rosevear Corn 2 E5
Roseville W Mid 133 E8
Rosewarne Corn 2 B4
  Corn 4 G3
Rosewell Midloth 270 C5
Roseworth Stockton 234 G4

Roseworthy Corn 2 B4
  Corn 4 F5
Roseworthy Barton Corn 2 B4
Rosgill Cumb 221 B10
Rosherville Kent 68 E6
Roshven Highld 289 B9
Roskear Croft Corn 4 G3
Roskill House Highld 300 D6
Roskorwell Corn 3 E7
Rosley Cumb 230 B2
Roslin Midloth 270 C5
Rosliston Derbys 152 F4
Rosneath Argyll 276 E5
Ross Borders 273 C9
  Dumfries 237 E8
  Northumb 264 B4
  Perth 285 E11
Rossett Wrex 166 D5
Rossett Green N Yorks 206 C2
Ross Green Worcs 116 E5
Rossie Ochill Perth 286 F4
Rossie Priory Perth 286 D6
Rossington S Yorks 187 B10
Rosskeen Highld 300 C6
Rossland Renfs 277 G8
Rossmore Poole 19 C7
Ross-on-Wye Hereford 98 G2
Roster Highld 310 F6
Rostherne Ches E 184 E2
Rostholme S Yorks 198 F5
Rosthwaite Cumb 220 C5
  Cumb 220 G4
Roston Derbys 169 G10
Rosudgeon Corn 2 D3
Rosyth Fife 280 E2
Rotchfords Essex 107 E8
Rotcombe Bath 44 B6
Rothbury Northumb 252 C3
Rotherbridge W Sus 35 C7
Rotherby Leics 154 F3
Rotherfield E Sus 37 B9
Rotherfield Greys Oxon 65 C8
Rotherfield Peppard
  Oxon 65 C8
Rotherham S Yorks 186 C6
Rotherhithe London 67 D11
Rotherwick Hants 49 B8
Rothersthorpe Northants 120 F4
Rotherwas Hereford 97 D10
Rothes Moray 302 E2
Rothesay Argyll 275 G11
Rothiebrisbane Aberds 303 F7
Rothiemay Crossroads
  Moray 302 E5
Rothiemurchus Lodge
  Highld 291 C11
Rothienorman Aberds 303 F7
Rothiesholm Orkney 314 D6
Rothley Leics 153 G11
  Northumb 252 E2
Rothley Plain Leics 153 G11
Rothley Shield East
  Northumb 252 E2
Rothmaise Aberds 302 F6
Rothwell Lincs 189 B11
  Northants 136 G6
  W Yorks 197 B10
Rothwell Haigh
  W Yorks 197 B10
Rotsea E Yorks 209 C7
Rottal Angus 292 G5
Rotten End Essex 106 F4
  Suff 127 D7
Rotten Green Hants 49 B9
Rotten Row W Berks 64 E5
  W Mid 118 B3
Rottingdean Brighton 36 G5
Rottington Cumb 219 C9
Roud IoW 20 E6
Rougham Norf 158 E5
  Suff 125 E8
Rougham Green Suff 125 E8
Rough Bank Gtr Man 196 E2
Roughbirchworth
  S Yorks 197 G9
Roughburn Highld 290 E5
Rough Close Staffs 151 B8
Rough Common Kent 54 B6
Roughcote Staffs 168 G6
Rough Haugh Highld 308 E7
Rough Hay Staffs 152 E4
Roughlee Lancs 204 E2
Roughley W Mid 134 D2
Roughmoor Som 28 B2
  Swindon 62 B6
Roughrigg N Lnrk 278 G6
Roughsike Cumb 240 B2
Roughton Lincs 174 C2
  Norf 160 B4
  Shrops 132 E5
Roughton Moor Lincs 174 C2
Roundbush Essex 88 E5
Round Bush Herts 85 F10
Roundbush Green Essex 87 C9
Round Green Luton 103 G11
Roundham Som 28 F6
Roundhay W Yorks 206 F2
Round Maple Suff 107 C9
Round Oak Shrops 131 G7
  W Mid 133 F8
Round's Green W Mid 133 F9
Roundshaw London 67 G10
Roundstreet Common
  W Sus 35 B9
Roundswell Devon 40 G4
Roundthorn Gtr Man 184 D4
Roundthwaite Cumb 222 E2
Roundway Wilts 62 G4
Roundyhill Angus 287 B7
Rousdon Devon 15 C11
Rousham Oxon 101 G9
Rous Lench Worcs 117 G10
Routenburn N Ayrs 266 C3
Routh E Yorks 209 E7
Rout's Green Bucks 84 F3
Row Corn 11 F7
  Cumb 211 B8
Rowanburn Dumfries 239 B10
Rowanfield Glos 99 G8
Rowardennan Stir 277 B7
Rowarth Derbys 185 D8
Row Ash Hants 33 E8
Rowberrow Som 44 B3
Row Brow Cumb 229 D7
Rowde Wilts 62 G3
Rowden Devon 13 B8
  N Yorks 205 B11
Rowe Head Cumb 210 D5
Rowen Conwy 180 G3
Rowfoot Northumb 240 E5
Rowford Som 28 B2

Row Green Essex 106 G4
Row Heath Essex 89 B10
Rowhedge Essex 107 G10
Rowhill Sur 66 G4
Rowhook W Sus 50 G6
Rowington Warks 118 D4
Rowington Green
  Warks 118 D4
Rowland Derbys 186 G2
Rowlands Castle Hants 34 E2
Rowlands Gill T&W 242 F5
Rowland's Green
  Hereford 98 D3
Rowledge Sur 49 E10
Rowlestone Hereford 97 F7
Rowley E Yorks 208 G5
  Shrops 130 B6
Rowley Green London 86 F2
Rowley Hill W Yorks 197 E7
Rowley Park Staffs 151 E8
Rowley Regis W Mid 133 F9
Rowley's Green W Mid 134 G6
Rowling Kent 55 C9
Rowly Sur 50 E4
Rownall Staffs 169 F7
Rowner Hants 33 G9
Rowney Green Worcs 117 C10
Rownhams Hants 32 D5
Row-of-trees Ches E 184 F4
Rowrah Cumb 219 B11
Rowsham Bucks 84 B4
Rowsley Derbys 170 B3
Rowstock Oxon 64 B3
Rowston Lincs 173 D9
Rowthorne Derbys 171 C7
Rowton Ches W 166 C6
  Shrops 149 G7
  Shrops 150 F2
  Telford 150 F2
Row Town Sur 66 G4
Roxburgh Borders 262 C5
Roxburgh Mains
  Borders 262 C5
Roxby N Lincs 200 D2
  N Yorks 226 B5
Roxeth London 66 B6
Roxton Beds 122 G3
Roxwell Essex 87 D11
Royal British Legion Village
  Kent 53 B8
Royal Leamington Spa
  Warks 118 D6
Royal Oak Darl 233 G10
  Lancs 194 G2
  N Yorks 218 D2
Royal's Green Ches E 167 G10
Royal Tunbridge Wells /
  Tunbridge Wells 52 F5
Royal Wootton Bassett
  Wilts 62 C5
Roybridge Highld 290 E4
Royd S Yorks 197 G8
Roydhouse W Yorks 197 E8
Royd Moor S Yorks 197 G8
  W Yorks 198 E2
Roydon Essex 86 D6
  Norf 141 G11
  Norf 158 E4
Roydon Hamlet Essex 86 D6
Royds Green W Yorks 197 B11
Royston Glasgow 268 B2
  Herts 105 C7
  S Yorks 197 E10
Royston Water Som 28 E2
Royton Gtr Man 196 F2
Ruabon / Rhiwabon
  Wrex 166 G4
Ruaig Argyll 288 E2
Ruan High Lanes Corn 3 B10
Ruan Lanihorne Corn 5 G7
Ruan Major Corn 2 F6
Ruan Minor Corn 2 F6
Ruarach Highld 295 C11
Ruardean Glos 79 B10
Ruardean Hill Glos 79 B10
Ruardean Woodside
  Glos 79 B10
Rubery Worcs 117 B9
Rubha Ghaisinis
  W Isles 297 G4
Rubha Stoer Highld 306 F5
Ruchazie Glasgow 268 B2
Ruchill Glasgow 267 B11
Ruckcroft Cumb 230 C6
Ruckhall Hereford 97 D9
Ruckinge Kent 54 G4
Ruckland Lincs 190 F4
Rucklers Lane Herts 85 E9
Ruckley Shrops 131 C10
Rudbaxton Pembs 91 G9
Rudby N Yorks 225 D9
Ruddington Notts 153 C11
Ruddle Glos 79 C11
Rudford Glos 98 G5
Rudge Shrops 132 D6
  Som 45 C10
Rudge Heath Shrops 132 D5
Rudgeway S Glos 60 B6
Rudgwick W Sus 50 G5
Rudhall Hereford 98 F2
Rudheath Ches W 183 G11
  Ches W 184 G2
Rudhja Garbh Argyll 289 E11
Rudley Green Essex 88 E4
Rudloe Wilts 61 E10
Rudry Caerph 59 B7
Rudston E Yorks 217 F11
Rudyard Staffs 169 D7
Ruewood Shrops 149 D9
Rufford Lancs 194 D3
Rufforth York 206 C6
Ruffs Notts 171 F8
Rugby Warks 119 B10
Rugeley Staffs 151 F10
Ruggin Som 27 D11
Ruglen S Ayrs 245 C7
Rugley Northumb 264 G5
Ruilick Highld 300 E5
Ruishton Som 28 C3
Ruisigearraidh W Isles 296 C5
Ruislip London 66 B5
Ruislip Common London 66 B5
Ruislip Manor London 66 B6
Ruiton W Mid 133 E8
Ruloe Ches W 183 G9
Rumach Highld 295 G8
Rumbling Bridge
  Perth 279 B10
Rumbow Cottages
  Worcs 117 B8
Rumburgh Suff 142 G6
Rumbush W Mid 118 B2
Rumer Hill Staffs 133 B9
Rumford Corn 10 G3
  Falk 279 F8
Rumney Cardiff 59 D8
Rumsam Devon 40 G5

Runwell Som 27 C11
Runcorn Halton 183 E8
Runcton W Sus 22 C5
Runcton Holme Norf 140 B2
Rundlestone Devon 13 G7
Runfold Sur 49 D11
Runhall Norf 141 B11
Runham Norf 143 B10
Norf 161 G9
Runham Vauxhall Norf 143 B10
Running Hill Head
Gtr Man 196 F4
Runnington Som 27 C10
Running Waters Durham 234 C2
Runsell Green Essex 88 D3
Runshaw Moor Lancs 194 D4
Runswick Bay N Yorks 226 B6
Runwell Essex 88 G2
Ruscombe Glos 80 D4
Wokingham 65 D9
Ruscote Oxon 101 C8
Rushall Hereford 98 E2
Norf 142 G3
Wilts 46 B6
W Mid 133 C10
Rushbrooke Suff 125 E7
Rushbury Shrops 131 E10
Rushcombe Bottom
Poole 18 B5
Rushden Herts 104 E6
Northants 121 D9
Rushenden Kent 70 E2
Rusher's Cross E Sus 37 B10
Rushey Mead Leicester 136 B2
Rushford Devon 12 F4
Norf 141 G8
Rushgreen Warr 183 D11
Rush Green Essex 89 B11
Herts 86 C5
Herts 104 G4
London 68 B4
Norf 141 B11
Rush-head Aberds 303 E8
Rush Hill Bath 61 G8
Rushington Hants 32 E5
Rushlake Green E Sus 23 B10
Rushland Cross Cumb 210 B6
Rushley Green Essex 106 D5
Rushmere C Beds 103 F8
Suff 143 F9
Rushmere St Andrew
Suff 108 B4
Rushmere Street Suff 108 B4
Rushmoor Sur 49 E11
Telford 150 G2
Rushmore Hants 33 E11
Rushmore Hill London 68 G3
Rushock Hereford 114 F6
Worcs 117 C7
Rusholme Gtr Man 184 B5
Rushton Ches W 167 C9
Dorset 18 D3
Northants 136 G6
N Yorks 217 C9
Shrops 132 B2
Rushton Spencer Staffs 168 C6
Rushwick Worcs 116 G6
Rushyford Durham 233 F11
Rushy Green E Sus 23 C7
Ruskie Stirl 285 G10
Ruskington Lincs 173 E9
Rusland Cumb 210 B6
Rusling End Herts 104 G4
Rusper W Sus 51 F8
Ruspidge Glos 79 C11
Russel Highld 299 E8
Russell Hill London 67 G10
Russell's Green E Sus 38 E2
Russell's Hall W Mid 133 F8
Russell's Water Oxon 65 B8
Russel's Green Suff 126 C5
Russ Hill Sur 51 E8
Rusthall Kent 52 F5
Rustington W Sus 35 G9
Ruston N Yorks 217 C9
Ruston Parva E Yorks 217 G11
Ruswarp N Yorks 227 D7
Ruthall Shrops 131 F11
Rutherford Borders 262 C4
Rutherglen S Lnrk 268 C2
Ruthernbridge Corn 5 B10
Ruthin Denb 165 D10
V Glam 58 D3
Ruthrieston Aberdeen 293 C11
Ruthven Aberds 302 E5
Angus 286 C6
Highld 291 D9
Highld 301 F8
Ruthven House Angus 287 C7
Ruthvoes Corn 5 C8
Ruthwaite Cumb 229 D10
Ruthwell Dumfries 238 D3
Ruxley London 68 E3
Ruxton Hereford 97 F11
Ruxton Green Hereford 79 B8
Ruyton-XI-Towns
Shrops 149 E7
Ryal Northumb 242 C2
Ryal Fold Blkburn 195 C7
Ryall Dorset 16 C4
Worcs 99 C7
Ryarsh Kent 53 B7
Rychraggan Highld 300 F4
Rydal Cumb 221 D7
Ryde IoW 21 C7
Rydens Sur 66 F6
Rydeshill Sur 50 C3
Rydon Devon 14 G3
Rye E Sus 38 C6
Ryebank Shrops 149 C10
Rye Common Hants 49 C9
Ryecroft S Yorks 186 B6
W Yorks 205 F7
Ryecroft Gate Staffs 168 C6
Ryeford Glos 80 E4
Rye Foreign E Sus 38 C5
Rye Harbour E Sus 38 D6
Ryehill E Yorks 201 B8
Ryeish Green Wokingham 65 F8
Ryelands Hereford 115 F9
Rye Park Herts 86 C5
Rye Street Worcs 98 D5
Ryeworth Glos 99 G9
Ryhall Rutland 155 G10
Ryhill W Yorks 197 E11
Ryhope T&W 243 G10
Rylah Derbys 171 B7
Rylands Notts 153 B10
Rylstone N Yorks 204 B5
Ryme Intrinseca Dorset 29 E9
Ryther N Yorks 207 F7
Ryton Glos 98 E4
N Yorks 216 D5
Shrops 132 C5
T&W 242 E5
Warks 135 F7
Ryton-on-Dunsmore
Warks 119 C7
Ryton Woodside T&W 242 E4

S

Sabden Lancs 203 F11
Sabine's Green Essex 87 F8
Sackers Green Suff 107 D8
Sacombe Herts 86 B4
Sacombe Green Herts 86 B4
Sacriston Durham 233 B10
Sadberge Darl 224 B6
Saddell Argyll 255 D8
Saddell Ho Argyll 255 D8
Saddington Leics 136 E3
Saddle Bow Norf 158 F2
Saddlescombe W Sus 36 E3
Saddle Street Dorset 28 G5
Sadgill Cumb 221 D9
Saffron's Cross
Hereford 115 G10
Saffron Walden Essex 105 D10
Sageston Pembs 73 E9
Saham Hills Norf 141 C8
Saham Toney Norf 141 C8
Saighdinis W Isles 296 E4
Saighton Ches W 166 C6
Sain Dunwyd / St Donats
V Glam 58 F2
St Abbs Borders 273 B8
St Abb's Haven Borders 273 B8
St Agnes Corn 4 E4
Scilly 1 H3
St Albans Herts 85 D10
St Allen Corn 4 E6
St Andrews Fife 287 F9
St Andrew's Major
V Glam 58 E6
St Andrew's Wood Devon 27 F9
St Annes Lancs 193 B10
St Anne's Park Bristol 60 E6
St Ann's Dumfries 248 E3
Nottingham 171 G9
St Ann's Chapel Corn 12 G4
Devon 8 F3
St Anthony Corn 3 C9
St Anthony-in-Meneage
Corn 3 D7
St Anthony's T&W 243 E7
St Anthony's Hill E Sus 23 E10
St Arvans Mon 79 F8
St Asaph / Llanelwy
Denb 181 G8
St Athan / Sain Tathon
V Glam 58 F4
Sain Tathon / St Athan
V Glam 58 F4
St Augustine's Kent 54 C6
St Austell Corn 5 E10
St Austins Hants 20 B2
St Bees Cumb 219 C9
St Blazey Corn 5 E11
St Blazey Gate Corn 5 E11
St Boswells Borders 262 C3
St Breock Corn 10 G5
St Breward Corn 11 F7
St Briavels Glos 79 E9
St Briavels Common Glos 79 E8
St Bride's Pembs 72 C4
St Brides Major / Saint-y-Brid V Glam 57 G11
St Bride's Netherwent
Mon 60 B2
St Brides-super-Ely
V Glam 58 D5
St Brides Wentlooge
Newport 59 C9
Saintbridge Glos 80 B5
St Budeaux Plym 7 D8
Saintbury Glos 100 D2
St Buryan Corn 1 D4
St Catherine Bath 61 E9
St Catherine's Argyll 284 G5
St Catherine's Hill Dorset 19 B8
St Chloe Glos 80 E4
St Clears / Sanclêr
Carms 74 B3
St Cleer Corn 6 B5
St Clement Corn 4 G6
St Clether Corn 11 E10
St Colmac Argyll 275 G11
St Columb Major Corn 5 C8
St Columb Minor Corn 4 C6
St Columb Road Corn 5 D8
St Combs Aberds 303 C10
St Cross Hants 33 B7
St Cross South Elmham
Suff 142 G5
St Cyrus Aberds 293 G9
St David's Perth 286 E3
St David's / Tyddewi
Pembs 90 F5
St Day Corn 4 G4
St Decumans Som 42 E5
St Dennis Corn 5 D9
St Denys Soton 32 E6
St Devereux Hereford 97 E8
St Dials Torf 78 G3
St Dogmaels / Llandudoch
Pembs 92 B3
St Dominick Corn 7 B8
St Donat's / Sain Dunwyd
V Glam 58 F2
St Edith's Wilts 62 G3
St Endellion Corn 10 F5
St Enoder Corn 5 D7
St Erme Corn 4 E6
St Erney Corn 7 D7
St Erth Corn 2 B3
St Erth Praze Corn 2 B3
St Ervan Corn 10 G3
St Eval Corn 5 B7
St Ewe Corn 5 F9
St Fagans Cardiff 58 D6
St Fergus Aberds 303 D10
St Fillans Perth 285 E10
St Florence Pembs 73 E9
St Gennys Corn 11 B8
St George Bristol 60 E6
Conwy 181 F7
St George in the East
London 67 C10
St Georges N Som 59 G11
St George's Gtr Man 184 B4
Telford 150 G4
V Glam 58 D5
St George's Hill Sur 66 G5
St George's Well Devon 27 F8
St Germans Corn 7 D7
St Giles Lincs 189 G7
London 67 C10
St Giles in the Wood
Devon 25 D8
St Giles on the Heath
Devon 12 C3
St Giles's Hill Hants 33 B7
St Gluvias Corn 3 C7
St Godwalds Worcs 117 D9
St Harmon Powys 113 C9
St Helena Warks 134 C5
St Helen Auckland
Durham 233 F9
St Helens Cumb 228 E6
IoW 21 D8
Mers 183 B8
St Helen's E Sus 38 E4
S Yorks 197 F11
St Helen's Wood E Sus 38 E4
St Helier London 67 F9
St Hilary Corn 2 C3
V Glam 58 E4
Saint Hill Devon 27 F9
W Sus 51 F11
St Ibbs Herts 104 F3
St Illtyd Bl Gwent 78 E2
St Ippollytts Herts 104 F3
St Ishmael's Pembs 72 D4
St Issey Corn 10 G4
St Ive Corn 6 B6
St Ive Cross Corn 6 B6
St Ives Cambs 122 C6
Corn 2 A2
Dorset 31 G10
St James Dorset 30 C5
London 67 C9
Norf 160 E5
St James's End
Northants 120 E4
St James South Elmham
Suff 142 G6
St Jidgey Corn 5 B8
St John Corn 7 E8
St Johns London 67 D11
Warks 118 C5
St John's E Sus 52 G4
IoM 192 D3
Sevenoaks 52 B4
Southborough 52 E5
Sur 50 B3
Worcs 116 G6
W Yorks 206 F4
St John's Chapel Devon 25 B8
Durham 232 D3
St John's Fen End
Norf 157 G10
St John's Highway
Norf 157 G10
St John's Park IoW 21 C8
St John's Town of Dalry
Dumfries 246 G4
St John's Wells Aberds 303 F7
St John's Wood London 67 C9
St Judes IoM 192 C4
St Julians Herts 85 D10
Newport 59 B10
St Just Corn 1 C3
St Justinian Pembs 90 F4
St Just in Roseland Corn 3 B9
St Katharines Wilts 63 G9
St Katherine's Aberds 303 F7
St Keverne Corn 3 E7
St Kew Corn 10 F6
St Kew Highway Corn 10 F6
St Keyne Corn 6 C4
St Lawrence Corn 5 B10
Essex 89 E7
IoW 20 F6
Kent 71 F11
St Leonards Dorset 31 G10
E Sus 38 F3
S Lnrk 268 E2
St Leonard's Bucks 84 D6
St Leonard's Street Kent 53 B7
St Levan Corn 1 E3
St Luke's Derby 152 B6
London 67 C10
St Lythans V Glam 58 E6
St Mabyn Corn 10 G6
St Madoes Perth 286 E5
St Margarets Herts 86 C5
London 67 E7
St Margaret's Hereford 97 E7
St Margaret's at Cliffe
Kent 55 E11
St Margaret's Hope
Orkney 314 G4
St Margaret South Elmham
Suff 142 G6
St Mark's Glos 99 G8
IoM 192 E3
St Martin Corn 2 E6
Corn 6 E5
St Martins Perth 286 D5
St Martin's Shrops 148 B6
St Martin's Moor Shrops 148 B6
St Mary Bourne Hants 48 C2
St Marychurch Torbay 9 B8
St Mary Church V Glam 58 E4
St Mary Cray London 68 F3
St Mary Hill V Glam 58 D3
St Mary Hoo Medway 69 D10
St Mary in the Marsh
Kent 39 B9
St Mary's Orkney 314 F4
St Mary's Bay Kent 39 B9
St Maughans Mon 79 B7
St Maughans Green Mon 79 B7
St Mawes Corn 3 C8
St Mawgan Corn 5 B7
St Mellion Corn 7 B7
St Mellons Cardiff 59 C8
St Merryn Corn 10 G3
St Mewan Corn 5 E9
St Michael Caerhays Corn 5 G9
St Michael Church Som 43 G10
St Michael Penkevil Corn 5 G7
St Michaels Kent 53 F11
Torbay 9 C7
Worcs 115 D11
St Michael's Hamlet
Mers 182 D5
St Michael's on Wyre
Lancs 202 E5
St Michael South Elmham
Suff 142 G6
St Minver Corn 10 F5
St Monans Fife 287 G9
St Neot Corn 6 B3
St Neots Cambs 122 E3
St Newlyn East Corn 4 D6
St Nicholas Herts 104 F5
Pembs 91 D7
V Glam 58 E5
St Nicholas at Wade Kent 71 F9
St Nicholas South Elmham
Suff 142 G6
St Nicolas Park Warks 135 E7
St Ninians Stirl 278 C5
St Olaves Norf 143 D9
St Osyth Essex 89 B10
St Osyth Heath Essex 89 B10
St Owens Cross
Hereford 97 G10
St Pancras London 67 C10
St Paul's Glos 80 B4
St Paul's Cray London 68 F3
St Paul's Walden Herts 104 G3
St Peters Kent 71 F11
St Peter's Glos 99 G8
T&W 243 E7
St Peter South Elmham
Suff 142 G6
St Peter The Great
Worcs 117 G7
St Petrox Pembs 73 F7
St Pinnock Corn 6 C4
St Quivox S Ayrs 257 E9
St Ruan Corn 2 F6
Saint's Hill Kent 52 E4
St Stephen Corn 5 E8
St Stephens Corn 7 D8
Herts 85 D10
St Stephen's Corn 12 D2
St Teath Corn 11 E7
St Thomas Devon 14 C4
Swansea 57 C7
St Tudy Corn 11 F7
St Twynnells Pembs 73 F7
St Veep Corn 6 E2
St Vigeans Angus 287 C10
St Vincent's Hamlet
Essex 87 G9
St Wenn Corn 5 C9
St Weonards Hereford 97 G9
St Winnow Corn 6 D2
Saint y Brid / St Brides Major V Glam 57 G11
St y-Nyll V Glam 58 D5
Saith ffynnon Flint 181 F11
Salcombe Devon 9 G9
Salcombe Regis Devon 15 D9
Salcott-cum-Virley
Essex 88 C6
Salden Bucks 102 F6
Sale Gtr Man 184 C3
Saleby Lincs 191 F7
Sale Green Worcs 117 F8
Salehurst E Sus 38 C2
Salem Carms 94 F2
Ceredig 128 G3
Corn 4 G4
Salen Argyll 289 E7
Highld 289 C8
Salendine Nook
W Yorks 196 D6
Salenside Borders 261 E11
Salesbury Lancs 203 G9
Saleway Worcs 117 F8
Salford C Beds 103 D8
Gtr Man 184 B4
Oxon 100 F5
Salford Ford C Beds 103 D8
Salford Priors Warks 117 G11
Salfords Sur 51 D9
Salhouse Norf 160 G6
Saligo Argyll 274 G3
Salisbury Wilts 31 B10
Salkeld Dykes Cumb 230 D6
Sallachan Highld 289 C11
Sallachy Highld 295 B11
Highld 309 J5
Salle Norf 160 E2
Salmans Kent 52 E4
Salmonby Lincs 190 G4
Salmond's Muir Angus 287 D9
Salmonhutch Devon 14 B2
Salperton Glos 99 G11
Salperton Park Glos 81 B9
Salph End Beds 121 G11
Salsburgh N Lnrk 268 C6
Salt Staffs 151 D9
Salta Cumb 229 B7
Saltaire W Yorks 205 F8
Saltash Corn 7 D8
Saltburn Highld 301 C7
Saltburn-by-the-Sea
Redcar 235 G9
Saltby Leics 155 D7
Salt Coates Cumb 238 G5
Saltcoats Cumb 219 F11
E Loth 281 E9
N Ayrs 266 G4
Saltcotes Lancs 193 B11
Saltdean Brighton 36 G5
Salt End E Yorks 201 B7
Salter Lancs 212 G2
Salterbeck Cumb 228 F5
Salterforth Lancs 204 D3
Salters Heath Hants 48 B6
Saltershill Shrops 150 D2
Salters Lode Norf 139 C11
Salter Street W Mid 118 C2
Salterswall Ches W 167 B10
Salterton Wilts 46 F6
Saltfleet Lincs 191 C7
Saltfleetby All Saints
Lincs 191 C7
Saltfleetby St Clement
Lincs 191 C7
Saltfleetby St Peter
Lincs 190 D6
Saltford Bath 61 F7
Salt Hill Slough 66 C3
Salthouse Cumb 210 F4
Norf 177 E9
Saltley W Mid 133 F11
Saltmarsh Newport 59 C11
Saltmarshe E Yorks 199 C9
Saltness Orkney 314 G2
Shetland 313 J4
Saltney Flint 166 B5
Salton N Yorks 216 D4
Saltrens Devon 25 C7
Saltwell T&W 243 E7
Saltwick Northumb 242 B5
Saltwood Kent 55 F7
Salum Argyll 288 E2
Salvington W Sus 35 F10
Salwarpe Worcs 117 E7
Salwayash Dorset 16 B5
Sambourne Warks 117 E11
Wilts 45 E11
Sambrook Telford 150 E4
Samhla W Isles 296 E3
Samlesbury Lancs 203 G7
Samlesbury Bottoms
Lancs 194 B6
Sampford Arundel Som 27 D10
Sampford Brett Som 42 E5
Sampford Chapple
Devon 25 G10
Sampford Courtenay
Devon 25 G10
Sampford Moor Som 27 D10
Sampford Peverell Devon 27 E8
Sampford Spiney Devon 12 G6
Sampool Bridge Cumb 211 B9
Samuel's Corner Essex 70 B3
Samuelston E Loth 281 G9
Sanachan Highld 299 E8
Sanaigmore Argyll 274 F3
Sanclêr / St Clears
Carms 74 B3
Sancreed Corn 1 D4
Sancton E Yorks 208 F4
Sand Highld 307 K4
Shetland 313 J5
Som 44 D2
Sandaig Highld 295 E9
Sandal W Yorks 197 D10
Sandale Cumb 229 C10
Sandal Magna
W Yorks 197 D10
Sandavore Highld 294 G6
Sandbach Ches E 168 C3
Sandbach Heath Ches E 168 C3
Sandbank Argyll 276 E3
Sandbanks Kent 70 G4
Poole 18 D6
Sandborough Staffs 152 F2
Sandbraes Lincs 200 G6
Sandend Aberds 302 C5
Sanderstead London 67 G10
Sandfields Glos 99 G8
Neath 57 C8
Staffs 134 B2
Sandford Cumb 222 B4
Devon 26 G4
Dorset 18 D4
Hants 31 G11
IoW 20 E6
N Som 44 B2
Shrops 148 E6
Shrops 149 C11
S Lnrk 268 G4
Worcs 99 B7
W Yorks 205 F11
Sandford Batch N Som 44 B2
Sandfordhill Aberds 303 E11
Sandford Hill Stoke 168 G6
Sandford on Thames
Oxon 83 E8
Sandford Orcas Dorset 29 C10
Sandford St Martin
Oxon 101 F8
Sandgate Kent 55 G7
Sand Gate Cumb 211 D7
Sandgreen Dumfries 237 D7
Sandhaven Aberds 303 C9
Argyll 276 E3
Sandhead Dumfries 236 E2
Sandhill Bucks 102 F4
Cambs 139 F11
S Yorks 198 F2
Sandhills Dorset 29 E11
Dorset 29 G9
Mers 182 C4
Oxon 83 D9
Sur 50 F2
W Yorks 206 F3
Sandhoe Northumb 241 D11
Sandhole Argyll 275 D11
Sand Hole E Yorks 208 F2
Sandholme E Yorks 208 G2
Lincs 156 B6
Sandhurst Brack 65 G10
Glos 98 G6
Kent 38 B3
Sandhurst Cross Kent 38 B3
Sandhutton N Yorks 215 C7
Sand Hutton N Yorks 207 B9
Sandiacre Derbys 153 B9
Sandilands Lincs 191 E8
S Lnrk 259 B9
Sandiway Ches W 183 G10
Sandleheath Hants 31 E10
Sandling Kent 53 B9
Sandlow Green Ches E 168 B3
Sandness Shetland 313 H3
Sandon Essex 88 E2
Herts 104 E6
Staffs 151 C8
Sandonbank Staffs 151 D8
Sandown IoW 21 E7
Sandown Park Kent 52 E6
Sandpit Dorset 28 G6
Sandpits Glos 98 F6
Sandplace Corn 6 D5
Sandridge Herts 85 C11
Wilts 62 F2
Sandringham Norf 158 D3
Sands Bucks 84 G4
Sandsend N Yorks 227 C7
Sands End London 67 D9
Sandside Cumb 210 D6
Cumb 211 C9
Orkney 314 F2
Sand Side Cumb 210 C4
Lancs 202 C4
Sandside Ho Highld 310 C3
Sandsound Shetland 313 J5
Sandtoft N Lincs 199 F8
Sandvoe Shetland 312 D5
Sandway Kent 53 C11
Sandwell W Mid 133 F10
Sandwich Kent 55 B10
Sandwich Bay Estate
Kent 55 B11
Sandwick Cumb 221 B8
Orkney 314 H4
Shetland 313 L6
Sandwith Cumb 219 C9
Sandwith Newtown
Cumb 219 C9
Sandy Carms 75 E7
C Beds 104 B3
Sandybank Orkney 314 C5
Sandy Bank Lincs 174 E3
Sandy Carrs Durham 234 C3
Sandycroft Flint 166 B4
Sandy Cross E Sus 37 C9
Sur 49 D11
Sandy Down Hants 20 B2
Sandyford Dumfries 248 E6
Stoke 168 E5
Sandygate Devon 14 G3
IoM 192 C4
S Yorks 186 D4
Sandy Gate Devon 14 C5
Sandy Haven Pembs 72 D5
Sandyhills Dumfries 237 D10
Sandylake Corn 6 C2
Sandylands Lancs 211 G8
Som 27 C10
Sandylane Swansea 56 D5
Sandy Lane Wilts 62 F3
Wrex 166 G5
W Yorks 205 F8
Sandypark Devon 13 D10
Sandysike Cumb 239 D9
Sandy Way IoW 20 E5
Sangobeg Highld 308 C4
Sangomore Highld 308 C4
Sanham Green W Berks 63 F10
Sankey Bridges Warr 183 D9
Sankyns Green Worcs 116 E5
Sanna Highld 288 C6
Sanndabhaig W Isles 297 G4
W Isles 304 E6
Sannox N Ayrs 255 C11
Sanquhar Dumfries 247 B7
Sansaw Heath Shrops 149 E10
Santon Cumb 220 E2
N Lincs 200 E2
Santon Bridge Cumb 220 E2
Santon Downham Suff 140 F6
Sapcote Leics 135 E9
Sapey Bridge Worcs 116 F4
Sapey Common
Hereford 116 E4
Sapiston Suff 125 B8
Sapley Cambs 122 C4
Sapperton Derbys 152 C3
Glos 80 E6
Lincs 155 C10
Saracen's Head Lincs 156 D6
Sarclet Highld 310 E7
Sardis Carms 75 D9
Pembs 73 D10
Sarisbury Hants 33 F8
Sarn Bridgend 58 C2
Flint 181 F10
Powys 130 E4
Sarnau Carms 74 B4
Ceredig 110 G6
Gwyn 147 B9
Powys 95 E10
Powys 148 F4
Sarn Bach Gwyn 144 D6
Sarnesfield Hereford 115 G7
Sarn Meyllteyrn Gwyn 144 C4
Saron Carms 75 C10
Carms 93 D7
Denb 165 C8
Gwyn 163 B8
Gwyn 163 D7
Sarratt Herts 85 F8
Sarratt Bottom Herts 85 F8
Sarre Kent 71 G9
Sarsden Oxon 100 G5
Sarsden Halt Oxon 100 G5
Sarsgrum Highld 308 C3
Sasaig Highld 295 E8
Sascott Shrops 149 G8
Satley Durham 233 C8
Satmar Kent 55 F9
Satran Highld 294 B6
Satron N Yorks 223 F8
Satterleigh Devon 25 C11
Satterthwaite Cumb 220 G6
Satwell Oxon 65 C8
Sauchen Aberds 293 B8
Saucher Perth 286 D5
Sauchie Clack 279 C7
Sauchieburn Aberds 293 G8
Saughall Ches W 182 G5
Saughall Massie Mers 182 D3
Saughton Edin 280 G4
Saughtree Borders 250 D3
Saul Glos 80 D2
Saundby Notts 188 D3
Saundersfoot Pembs 73 E10
Saunderton Bucks 84 E3
Saunderton Lee Bucks 84 F4
Saunton Devon 40 F3
Sausthorpe Lincs 174 B5
Saval Highld 309 J5
Savary Highld 289 E8
Saveock Corn 4 F5
Saverley Green Staffs 151 B9
Savile Park W Yorks 196 C5
Savile Town W Yorks 197 C8
Sawbridge Warks 119 D10
Sawbridgeworth Herts 87 B7
Sawdon N Yorks 217 B8
Sawley Derbys 153 C9
Lancs 203 D11
N Yorks 214 F4
Sawood W Yorks 204 G6
Sawston Cambs 105 B9
Sawtry Cambs 138 G3
Sawyers Hill Wilts 81 G8
Sawyer's Hill Som 27 C11
Saxby Leics 154 F6
Lincs 189 D8
W Sus 35 G7
Saxby All Saints N Lincs 200 D3
Saxelbye Leics 154 E4
Saxham Street Suff 125 E11
Saxilby Lincs 188 F5
Saxlingham Norf 159 B10
Saxlingham Green Norf 142 D4
Saxlingham Nethergate
Norf 142 D4
Saxlingham Thorpe
Norf 142 D4
Saxmundham Suff 127 E7
Saxondale Notts 154 B3
Saxon Street Cambs 124 F3
Saxtead Suff 126 D5
Saxtead Green Suff 126 E5
Saxtead Little Green
Suff 126 D5
Saxthorpe Norf 160 C2
Saxton N Yorks 206 F5
Sayers Common W Sus 36 D3
Scackleton N Yorks 216 E2
Scadabhagh W Isles 305 J3
Scaftworth Notts 187 C11
Scagglethorpe N Yorks 216 E6
Scaitcliffe Lancs 195 B9
Scaladal W Isles 305 G3
Scalan Moray 292 B4
Scalasaig Argyll 274 D4
Scalby E Yorks 199 B10
N Yorks 227 G10
Scald End Beds 121 F10
Scaldwell Northants 120 C5
Scaleby Cumb 239 E11
Scalebyhill Cumb 239 E10
Scale Hall Lancs 211 G9
Scale Houses Cumb 231 B7
Scales Cumb 210 E5
Cumb 230 F2
Cumb 231 C7
Lancs 202 G5
Scalford Leics 154 E5
Scaling Redcar 226 C4
Scaliscro W Isles 304 F3
Scallasaig Highld 295 D10
Scallastle Argyll 289 F8
Scalloway Shetland 313 K6
Scalpay W Isles 305 J4
Scalpay Ho Highld 295 C8
Scalpsie Argyll 255 B11
Scamadale Highld 295 F9
Scamblesby Lincs 190 F3
Scamland E Yorks 207 E11
Scammadale Argyll 289 G10
Scamodale Highld 289 B10
Scampston N Yorks 217 D7
Scampton Lincs 189 F7
Scaniport Highld 300 F6
Scapa Orkney 314 F4
Scapegoat Hill W Yorks 196 D5
Scar Orkney 314 B6
Scarborough N Yorks 217 B10
Scarcewater Corn 5 E8
Scarcliffe Derbys 171 B7
Scarcroft W Yorks 206 E3
Scarcroft Hill W Yorks 206 E3
Scardroy Highld 300 D2
Scarff Shetland 312 E4
Scarfskerry Highld 310 B6
Scargill Durham 223 C11
Scar Head Cumb 220 G5
Scarinish Argyll 288 E2
Scarisbrick Lancs 193 E11
Scarness Cumb 229 E10
Scarning Norf 159 G9
Scarrington Notts 172 G2
Scarth Hill Lancs 194 F2
Scarthingwell N Yorks 206 F5
Scartho NE Lincs 201 F9
Scarvister Shetland 313 J5
Scarwell Orkney 314 D2
Scatness Shetland 313 M5
Scatraig Highld 301 F7
Scatwell Ho Highld 300 D3
Scawby N Lincs 200 F3
Scawsby S Yorks 198 G5
Scawthorpe S Yorks 198 F5
Scawton N Yorks 215 C10
Scayne's Hill W Sus 36 C5
Scethrog Powys 96 F2
Scholar Green Ches E 168 D4
Scholemoor W Yorks 205 G8
Scholes Gtr Man 194 F5
S Yorks 186 B5
W Yorks 197 B7
W Yorks 197 F7
W Yorks 204 F6
W Yorks 206 F3
Scholey Hill W Yorks 197 B11
School Aycliffe
Durham 233 G11
Schoolgreen Wokingham 65 F8
School Green Ches W 167 C10
Essex 106 E4
IoW 20 D2
W Yorks 205 G8
Schoolhill Aberds 293 D11
School House Dorset 28 G5
Sciberscross Highld 309 H7
Scilly Bank Cumb 219 B9
Scissett W Yorks 197 E8
Scleddau Pembs 91 E8
Scofton Notts 187 E10
Scole Norf 126 B2
Scole Common Norf 142 G2
Scolpaig W Isles 296 D3
Scone Perth 286 E5
Sconser Highld 295 B7
Scoonie Fife 287 G7
Scoor Argyll 274 B5
Scopwick Lincs 173 D9
Scoraig Highld 307 K5
Scorborough E Yorks 208 D6
Scorrier Corn 4 G4
Scorriton Devon 8 B4
Scorton Lancs 202 D6
N Yorks 224 E5
Sco Ruston Norf 160 E5
Scotbheinn W Isles 296 F4
Scotby Cumb 239 G10
Scotch Corner N Yorks 224 E4
Scotches Derbys 170 F4
Scotforth Lancs 202 B5
Scotgate W Yorks 196 E6
Scot Hay Staffs 168 F4
Scothern Lincs 189 F8
Scotland Leics 136 D3
Leics 153 E7
Lincs 155 C10
W Berks 64 F5
Scotland End Oxon 100 E6
Scotland Gate Northumb 253 G7
Scotlands W Mid 133 C8
Scotland Street Suff 107 D9
Scotlandwell Perth 286 G5
Scot Lane End Gtr Man 194 F6
Scotsburn Highld 301 B7
Scotscalder Station
Highld 310 D4
Scotscraig Fife 287 E8
Scots' Gap Northumb 252 F2
Scotston Aberds 293 F9
Perth 286 C3
Scotstoun Glasgow 267 B10
Scotstown Highld 289 C10
Scotswood T&W 242 E5
Windsor 66 F2
Scottas Highld 295 E9
Scotter Lincs 199 G11
Scotterthorpe Lincs 199 G11
Scottlethorpe Lincs 155 E11
Scotton Lincs 188 B5
N Yorks 206 B2
N Yorks 224 F3
Scottow Norf 160 E5
Scott Willoughby Lincs 155 B11
Scoughall E Loth 282 E2
Scoulag Argyll 266 D2
Scoulton Norf 141 C9
Scounslow Green
Staffs 151 D11
Scourie Highld 306 E6
Scourie More Highld 306 E6
Scousburgh Shetland 313 M5
Scout Dike S Yorks 197 G8
Scout Green Cumb 221 D11
Scouthead Gtr Man 196 F3
Scowles Glos 79 C9
Scrabster Highld 310 B4
Scraesburgh Borders 262 F5
Scrafield Lincs 174 B4
Scragged Oak Kent 69 G10
Scrainwood Northumb 251 B11
Scrane End Lincs 174 G5
Scrapsgate Kent 70 E2
Scraptoft Leics 136 B2
Scrapton Som 28 E3
Scratby Norf 161 F10
Scrayingham N Yorks 216 G4
Scredda Corn 5 E10
Scredington Lincs 173 G9
Screedy Som 27 B9
Scremby Lincs 174 B6
Scremerston Northumb 273 F10
Screveton Notts 172 G2
Scrivelsby Lincs 174 B3
Scriven N Yorks 206 B2
Scronkey Lancs 202 D4
Scrooby Notts 187 C11
Scropton Derbys 152 C3
Scrub Hill Lincs 174 D2
Scruton N Yorks 224 G5
Scrwgan Powys 148 E3
Scuddaborg Highld 298 C3
Scuggate Cumb 239 C10
Sculcoates Hull 209 G7
Sculthorpe Norf 159 C7
Scunthorpe N Lincs 199 E11
Scurlage Swansea 56 D3
Sea Som 28 E4
Seaborough Dorset 28 F6
Seabridge Staffs 168 G4
Seabrook Kent 55 G7
Seaburn T&W 243 F10
Seacombe Mers 182 C4
Seacox Heath Kent 53 G8
Seacroft Lincs 175 C9
W Yorks 206 F3
Seadyke Lincs 156 B6
Seafar N Lnrk 278 G5
Seafield Highld 311 L3
Midloth 270 C5
S Ayrs 257 E8
W Loth 269 B10
Seaford E Sus 23 F7
Seaforth Mers 182 B4
Seagrave Leics 154 F2
Seagry Heath Wilts 62 C3
Seaham Durham 234 B4
Seahouses Northumb 264 C6
Seal Kent 52 B4
Sealand Flint 166 B5
Seale Sur 49 D11
Seamer N Yorks 217 C10
N Yorks 225 C9
Seamill N Ayrs 266 F4
Sea Mill Cumb 210 F5
Sea Mills Bristol 60 D5
Corn 10 G4
Sea Palling Norf 161 D8
Searby Lincs 200 F5
Seasalter Kent 70 F5
Seascale Cumb 219 E10
Seathorne Lincs 175 B9
Seathwaite Cumb 220 C4
Cumb 220 F4
Seatle Cumb 211 C7
Seatoller Cumb 220 C4
Seaton Corn 6 E6
Cumb 228 E6
Devon 15 C10
Durham 243 G9
E Yorks 209 D9
Kent 55 B8
Northumb 243 B8
Rutland 137 D8
Seaton Burn T&W 242 C6
Seaton Carew Hrtlpl 234 F6
Seaton Delaval
Northumb 243 B8
Seaton Ross E Yorks 207 E11
Seaton Sluice Northumb 243 B8
Seatown Aberds 302 C5
Aberds 303 D11
Dorset 16 C4
Seaureaugh Moor Corn 2 B6
Seave Green N Yorks 225 E11
Seaview IoW 21 C8
Seaville Cumb 238 G5
Seavington St Mary Som 28 E6
Seavington St Michael
Som 28 D6
Seawick Essex 89 C10
Sebastopol Torf 78 F3
Sebay Orkney 314 F5
Sebergham Cumb 230 C3
Sebiston Velzian Orkney 314 D2
Seckington Warks 134 B5
Second Coast Highld 307 K4
Second Drove Cambs 139 F10
Sedbergh Cumb 222 G3
Sedbury Glos 79 G8
Sedbusk N Yorks 223 G7
Seddington C Beds 104 B3
Sedgeberrow Worcs 99 D10
Sedgebrook Lincs 155 B7
Sedgefield Durham 234 F3
Sedgeford Norf 158 B4
Sedgehill Wilts 30 B5
Sedgemere W Mid 118 B4
Sedgley W Mid 133 E8
Sedgley Park Gtr Man 195 G10
Sedgwick Cumb 211 B10
Sedlescombe E Sus 38 D3
Sedlescombe Street
E Sus 38 D3
Sedrup Bucks 84 C3
Seed Kent 54 B2
Seed Lee Lancs 194 C5
Seedley Gtr Man 184 B4
Seend Wilts 62 G2
Seend Cleeve Wilts 62 G2
Seend Head Wilts 62 G2
Seer Green Bucks 85 G7
Seething Norf 142 D6
Seething Wells London 67 F7
Sefton Mers 193 G11
Segensworth Hants 33 F8
Seggat Aberds 303 E7
Seghill Northumb 243 C7
Seifton Shrops 131 G9
Seighford Staffs 151 D7
Seilebost W Isles 305 J2
Seion Gwyn 163 B8
Seisdon Staffs 132 E6
Seisiadar W Isles 304 E7
Selattyn Shrops 148 C5
Selborne Hants 49 G8
Selby N Yorks 207 G8
Selgrove Kent 54 B4
Selham W Sus 34 C6
Selhurst London 67 F10
Selkirk Borders 261 D11
Sellack Hereford 97 F11
Sellack Boat Hereford 97 F11
Sellafirth Shetland 312 D7
Sellan Corn 1 C4
Sellibister Orkney 314 B7
Sellick's Green Som 28 D2
Sellindge Kent 54 F6
Selling Kent 54 B4
Sells Green Wilts 62 G3
Selly Hill N Yorks 227 D7
Selly Oak W Mid 133 G10
Selly Park W Mid 133 G11
Selmeston E Sus 23 D8
Selsdon London 67 G10
Selsey W Sus 22 E5
Selsfield Common
W Sus 51 G10
Selside Cumb 221 F10
N Yorks 212 D5
Selsley Glos 80 E4
Selsmore Hants 21 B10
Selson Kent 55 B10
Selsted Kent 55 E8
Selston Notts 171 E7
Selston Common Notts 171 E7
Selston Green Notts 171 E7
Selwick Orkney 314 F2
Selworthy Som 42 D2
Semblister Shetland 313 H5
Semer Suff 107 B9
Semington Wilts 61 G11
Semley Wilts 30 B5
Sempringham Lincs 156 C2
Send Sur 50 B4
Send Grove Sur 50 C4
Send Marsh Sur 50 B4
Senghenydd Caerph 77 G10
Sennen Corn 1 D3
Sennen Cove Corn 1 D3
Sennybridge / Pont Senni
Powys 95 F8
Serlby Notts 187 D10
Serrington Wilts 46 F5
Sessay N Yorks 215 D9
Setchey Norf 158 G2
Setley Hants 32 G4
Seton E Loth 281 G8
Seton Mains E Loth 281 F8
Setter Shetland 312 E6
Shetland 313 H5
Shetland 313 J7
Shetland 313 L6
Settiscarth Orkney 314 E3
Settle N Yorks 212 G6
Settrington N Yorks 216 E6
Seven Ash Som 43 G7

Sevenhampton Glos....99 G10
Swindon....82 G2
Seven Kings London....68 B3
Sevenoaks Kent....52 C4
Sevenoaks Common
Kent....52 C4
Sevenoaks Weald Kent....52 C4
Seven Sisters / Blaendulais
Neath....76 D4
Seven Springs Glos....81 B7
Seven Star Green Essex....107 F8
Severn Beach S Glos....60 B4
Severnhampton Swindon....82 G2
Severn Stoke Worcs....99 C7
Sevick End Beds....121 G11
Sevington Kent....54 E4
Sewards End Essex....105 D11
Sewardstone Essex....86 F5
Sewardstonebury Essex....86 F5
Sewell C Beds....103 G9
Sewerby E Yorks....218 F3
Seworgan Corn....2 C6
Sewstern Leics....155 E7
Sexhow N Yorks....225 D9
Sezincote Glos....100 E3
Sgarasta Mhor W Isles....305 J2
Sgiogarstaigh W Isles....304 B7
Sgiwen / Skewen Neath....57 B8
Shabbington Bucks....83 D11
Shab Hill Glos....80 B6
Shackerley Shrops....132 B6
Shackerstone Leics....135 B7
Shacklecross Derbys....153 C8
Shackleford Sur....50 D2
Shackleton W Yorks....196 B3
Shacklewell London....67 C10
Shacklford Sur....50 D2
Shade W Yorks....196 C2
Shadforth Durham....234 C2
Shadingfield Suff....143 G8
Shadoxhurst Kent....54 E4
Shadsworth Blkburn....195 B8
Shadwell Glos....80 F3
London....67 C11
Norf....141 G8
W Yorks....206 F2
Shaffalong Staffs....169 E7
Shaftenhoe End Herts....105 D8
Shaftesbury Dorset....30 C5
Shafton S Yorks....197 E11
Shafton Two Gates
S Yorks....197 E11
Shaggs Dorset....18 E3
Shakeford Shrops....150 D3
Shakerley Gtr Man....195 G7
Shakesfield Glos....98 E3
Shalbourne Wilts....63 G10
Shalden Hants....49 E7
Shalden Green Hants....49 E7
Shaldon Devon....14 G4
Shalfleet IoW....20 D4
Shalford Essex....106 F4
Som....45 G8
Sur....50 D4
Shalford Green Essex....106 F4
Shallock Moray....302 D3
Shallowford Devon....25 B11
Devon....41 E8
Staffs....151 D8
Shalmsford Street Kent....54 C5
Shalstone Bucks....102 D2
Shamley Green Sur....50 E4
Shandon Argyll....276 D5
Shandwick Highld....301 B8
Shangton Leics....136 D4
Shankhouse Northumb....243 B7
Shanklin IoW....21 E7
Shannochie N Ayrs....255 E10
Shannochill Stirl....277 B10
Shanquhar Aberds....302 F5
Shanwell Fife....287 E8
Shanzie Perth....286 B6
Shap Cumb....221 B11
Shapridge Glos....79 B11
Shapwick Dorset....30 G6
Som....44 F2
Sharcott Wilts....46 B6
Shard End W Mid....134 F3
Shardlow Derbys....153 C8
Shareshill Staffs....133 B8
Sharlston W Yorks....197 D11
Sharlston Common
W Yorks....197 D11
Sharmans Cross W Mid....118 B2
Sharnal Street Medway....69 E9
Sharnbrook Beds....121 F9
Sharneyford Lancs....195 C11
Sharnford Leics....135 E9
Sharnhill Green Dorset....18 B2
Sharoe Green Lancs....202 G6
Sharow N Yorks....214 E6
Sharpenhoe C Beds....103 E11
Sharperton Northumb....251 C11
Sharples Gtr Man....195 E8
Sharpley Heath Staffs....151 B9
Sharpness Glos....79 E11
Sharpsbridge E Sus....36 C6
Sharp's Corner E Sus....23 B9
Sharpstone Bath....45 B9
Sharp Street Norf....161 E7
Sharpthorne W Sus....51 G11
Sharptor Corn....11 G11
Sharpway Gate Worcs....117 D9
Sharrington Norf....159 B10
Sharston Gtr Man....184 D4
Shatterford Worcs....132 G5
Shatterling Kent....55 B9
Shatton Derbys....185 E11
Shaugh Prior Devon....7 C10
Shavington Ches E....168 E2
Shaw Gtr Man....196 F2
Swindon....62 B6
W Berks....64 F3
Wilts....61 F11
W Yorks....204 F6
Shawbank Shrops....131 G9
Shawbirch Telford....150 G2
Shawbury Shrops....149 E11
Shawclough Gtr Man....195 E11
Shaw Common....98 F3
Shawdon Hall Northumb....264 G3
Shawell Leics....135 G10
Shawfield Gtr Man....195 E11
Staffs....169 C9
Shawfield Head
N Yorks....205 C11
Shawford Hants....33 C7
Som....45 C9
Shawforth Lancs....195 C11
Shaw Green Herts....104 E5
Lancs....194 D4
N Lnrk....268 C4
Shaw Heath Ches E....184 F3
Gtr Man....184 D5
Shawhead Dumfries....238 B1

Shaw Mills N Yorks....214 G5
Shawsburn S Lnrk....268 E5
Shaw Side Gtr Man....196 F2
Shawton S Lnrk....268 F3
Shawtonhill S Lnrk....268 F3
Shay Gate W Yorks....205 F8
Sheandow Moray....302 F2
Shear Cross Wilts....45 E11
Sheardley Lane....217 D9
Shearington Dumfries....238 D2
Shearsby Leics....136 E2
Shearston Som....43 G9
Shebbear Devon....24 F6
Shebdon Staffs....150 D5
Shebster Highld....310 C4
Sheddens E Renf....267 D11
Shedfield Hants....33 E9
Sheen Staffs....169 C10
Sheepbridge Derbys....186 G5
Sheepdrove W Berks....63 D10
Sheep Hill Durham....242 F5
Sheeplane C Beds....103 E8
Sheepridge Bucks....65 B11
W Yorks....197 D7
Sheepscar W Yorks....206 G2
Sheepscombe Glos....80 C5
Sheepstor Devon....7 B11
Sheepwash Devon....25 F7
Northumb....253 F7
Sheepway N Som....60 D3
Sheepy Magna Leics....134 C6
Sheepy Parva Leics....134 C6
Sheering Essex....87 C8
Sheerness Kent....70 E2
Sheerwater Sur....66 G4
Sheet Hants....34 C3
Shrops....115 C8
Sheets Heath Sur....50 B2
Sheffield Corn....1 D5
S Yorks....186 D5
Sheffield Bottom
W Berks....65 F7
Sheffield Green E Sus....36 C6
Sheffield Park
E Sus....186 D5
Sheffield Woodlands
W Berks....63 E11
Sheigra Highld....306 C6
Sheinton Shrops....132 C2
Shelderton Shrops....115 B8
Sheldon Derbys....169 B11
Devon....27 F10
W Mid....134 G3
Sheldwich Kent....54 B4
Sheldwich Lees Kent....54 B4
Shelf Bridgend....58 C2
W Yorks....196 B6
Shelfanger Norf....142 G2
Shelfield Warks....118 E2
W Mid....133 C10
Shelfield Green Warks....118 E2
Shelfleys Northants....120 F4
Shelford Notts....171 G11
Warks....135 F8
Shell Worcs....117 F9
Shelland Suff....125 E9
Shellbrook Leics....152 F6
Shelley Essex....87 E9
Suff....107 D10
W Yorks....197 E8
Shelley Woodhouse
W Yorks....197 E8
Shell Green Halton....183 D8
Shellingford Oxon....82 G4
Shellow Bowells Essex....87 D10
Shellwood Cross Sur....51 D8
Shelsley Beauchamp
Worcs....116 E4
Shelsley Walsh Worcs....116 E4
Shelthorpe Leics....153 F10
Shelton Beds....121 D10
Norf....142 E4
Notts....172 G3
Shrops....149 G9
Stoke....168 F5
Shelton Green Norf....142 E4
Shelton Lock Derby....153 C7
Shelton under Harley
Staffs....150 B6
Shelve Shrops....130 D6
Shelvin Devon....27 G11
Shelvingford Kent....71 F8
Shelwick Hereford....97 C10
Shelwick Green
Hereford....97 C10
Shenfield Essex....87 G10
Shennington Oxon....101 C7
Shenley Herts....85 E11
Shenley Brook End
M Keynes....102 D6
Shenleybury Herts....85 E11
Shenley Church End
M Keynes....102 D6
Shenley Fields W Mid....133 G10
Shenley Lodge
M Keynes....102 D6
Shenley Wood
M Keynes....102 D6
Shenmore Hereford....97 D7
Shennanton Dumfries....236 C5
Shennanton Ho
Dumfries....236 C5
Shenstone Staffs....134 C2
Worcs....117 C7
Shenstone Woodend
Staffs....134 C2
Shenton Leics....135 C7
Shenval Highld....300 G4
Moray....302 G2
Shepeau Stow Lincs....156 G6
Shephall Herts....104 G5
Shepherd Hill W Yorks....196 C6
Shepherd's Bush London....67 C8
Shepherd's Gate Norf....157 F11
Shepherd's Green Oxon....65 C8
Shepherd's Hill Sur....50 G2
Shepherd's Patch Glos....80 E2
Shepherd's Port Norf....158 C3
Shepherdswell or
Sibertswold Kent....55 D9
Shepley W Yorks....197 F7
Shepperdine S Glos....79 F10
Shepperton Sur....66 F5
Shepperton Green Sur....66 F5
Shepreth Cambs....105 B7
Shepshed Leics....153 F9
Shepton Beauchamp
Som....28 D6
Shepton Mallet Som....45 E7
Shepton Montague Som....45 G7
Shepway Kent....53 C9
Sheraton Durham....234 D4
Sherborne Dorset....29 D10
Glos....81 B11
Sherborne St John Hants....48 B6
Sherbourne Warks....118 E5
Sherbourne Street Suff....107 C9
Sherburn Durham....234 C2

N Yorks....217 D9
Sherburn Grange
Durham....234 C2
Sherburn Hill Durham....234 C2
Sherburn in Elmet
N Yorks....206 G5
Shere Sur....50 D5
Shereford Norf....159 D7
Sherfield English Hants....32 C3
Sherfield on Loddon
Hants....49 B7
Sherfin Lancs....195 B9
Sherford Devon....8 G5
Dorset....18 C4
Som....28 C2
Sheriffhales Shrops....150 G5
Sheriff Hill T&W....243 E7
Sheriff Hutton N Yorks....216 F3
Sheriff's Lench Worcs....99 B10
Sheringham Norf....177 E11
Sheringwood Norf....177 E11
Shermanbury W Sus....36 D2
Shernal Green Worcs....117 E8
Shernborne Norf....158 C4
Sherrard's Green Worcs....98 B5
Sherrardspark Herts....86 C2
Sherriffhales Shrops....150 G5
Sherrington Suff....46 F3
Wilts....46 E2
Sherston Wilts....61 B11
Sherwood Nottingham....171 G9
Sherwood Green Devon....25 C9
Sherwood Park Kent....52 E6
Shettleston Glasgow....268 C2
Shevington Gtr Man....194 F4
Shevington Moor
Gtr Man....194 E4
Shevington Vale
Gtr Man....194 F4
Sheviock Corn....7 D7
Shewalton N Ayrs....257 B8
Shibden Head W Yorks....196 B5
Shide IoW....20 D5
Shiel Bridge Highld....295 D11
Shieldaig Highld....299 D8
Highld....299 D8
Shieldhall Glasgow....267 B10
Shieldhill Dumfries....248 F2
Falk....279 F7
S Lnrk....269 G10
Shield Row Durham....242 G6
Shielfoot Highld....289 C8
Shielhill Angus....287 B8
Inclyd....276 G4
Shifford Oxon....82 E5
Shifnal Shrops....132 B4
Shilbottle Northumb....252 B5
Shilbottle Grange
Northumb....252 B6
Shildon Durham....233 F10
Shillford E Renf....267 D8
Shillingford Devon....27 C7
Oxon....83 G9
Shillingford Abbot Devon....14 D4
Shillingford St George
Devon....14 D4
Shillingstone Dorset....30 E4
Shillington C Beds....104 E2
Shillmoor Northumb....251 B9
Shilton Oxon....82 D3
Warks....135 G8
Shilvington Northumb....252 G5
Shimpling Norf....142 G3
Suff....125 G7
Shimpling Street Suff....125 G7
Shincliffe Durham....233 C11
Shiney Row T&W....243 G8
Shinfield Wokingham....65 F8
Shingay Cambs....104 B6
Shingham Norf....140 C5
Shingle Street Suff....109 C7
Shinner's Bridge Devon....8 C5
Shinness Highld....309 H5
Shipbourne Kent....52 C5
Shipdham Norf....141 B9
Shipdham Airfield Norf....141 B9
Shipham Som....44 B2
Shiphay Torbay....9 B7
Shiplake Oxon....65 D9
Shiplake Bottom Oxon....65 C8
Shiplake Row Oxon....65 D9
Shiplate N Som....43 B11
Shiplaw Borders....270 F4
Shipley Derbys....170 G6
Northumb....264 F4
Shrops....132 D6
W Sus....35 C10
W Yorks....205 F8
Shipley Bridge Sur....51 E10
Shipley Common
Derbys....171 G7
Shipley Shiels Northumb....251 E7
Shipmeadow Suff....143 F7
Shipping Pembs....73 D10
Shippon Oxon....83 F7
Shipston-on-Stour
Warks....100 C5
Shipton Bucks....102 F5
Glos....81 B8
N Yorks....207 B7
Shrops....131 E11
Shipton Bellinger Hants....47 D8
Shipton Gorge Dorset....16 C5
Shipton Green W Sus....22 C4
Shipton Lee Bucks....102 G4
Shipton Moyne Glos....61 B11
Shipton Oliffe Glos....81 B8
Shipton on Cherwell
Oxon....83 B7
Shipton Solers Glos....81 B8
Shiptonthorpe E Yorks....208 E3
Shipton-under-Wychwood
Oxon....82 B3
Shirburn Oxon....83 F11
Shirdley Hill Lancs....193 E11
Shirebrook Derbys....171 B8
Shirecliffe S Yorks....186 C4
Shiregreen S Yorks....186 C5
Shirehampton Bristol....60 D4
Shiremoor T&W....243 C8
Shirenewton Mon....79 G7
Shireoak W Mid....133 C11
Shireoaks Derbys....185 E9
Notts....187 E9
Shires Mill Fife....279 D10
Shirkoak Kent....54 F2
Shirland Derbys....170 D6
Shirlett Shrops....132 D3
Shirley Derbys....170 G2
Hants....19 B9
London....67 F11
Soton....32 E6
W Mid....118 B2
Shirley Heath W Mid....118 B2
Shirl Heath Hereford....115 F8
Shirrell Heath Hants....33 E9
Shirwell Devon....40 F5
Shirwell Cross Devon....40 F5

Shiskine N Ayrs....255 E10
Shobdon Hereford....115 E8
Shobley Hants....31 F11
Shobnall Staffs....152 E4
Shobrooke Devon....26 G5
Shoby Leics....154 F3
Shocklach Ches W....166 F6
Shocklach Green
Ches W....166 F6
Shoeburyness Sthend....70 C6
Sholden Kent....55 C11
Sholing Soton....32 E6
Sholing Common Soton....33 E7
Sholver Gtr Man....196 F3
Shootash Hants....32 C4
Shooters Hill London....68 D2
Shootersway Herts....85 D7
Shoot Hill Shrops....149 G8
Shop Corn....10 G3
Corn....24 E5
Shop Corner Suff....108 E4
Shopford Cumb....240 C3
Shopnoller Som....43 G7
Shopp Hill W Sus....34 B6
Shopwyke W Sus....22 B5
Shore Gtr Man....196 B2
Shore Bottom Devon....28 G2
Shoregill Cumb....222 E5
Shoreham Kent....68 G4
Shoreham Beach W Sus....36 G2
Shoreham-by-Sea
W Sus....36 G2
Shore Mill Highld....301 C7
Shoresdean Northumb....273 F11
Shores Green Oxon....82 D5
Shoreside Shetland....313 J4
Shoreswood Northumb....273 F8
Shoreton Highld....300 C6
Shorley Hants....33 B8
Shorncliffe Camp Kent....55 F7
Shorncote Glos....81 F8
Shorne Kent....69 E7
Shorne Ridgeway Kent....69 E7
Shorne West Kent....69 E7
Shortacombe Devon....12 D6
Shortacross Corn....6 D5
Short Cross W Mid....133 G9
Shortfield Common N Sur....49 E10
Shortgate E Sus....23 B7
Short Green Norf....141 F11
Shortheath Hants....49 F9
Sur....49 E10
W Mid....133 E9
Short Heath Derbys....152 G6
W Mid....133 D9
Shorthampton Oxon....100 G6
Shortheath Hants....49 F9
Sur....49 E10
Shorthill Shrops....131 B8
Shortlands London....67 F11
Shortlanesend Corn....4 F6
Shortlees E Ayrs....257 B10
Shortmoor Dorset....28 G2
Dorset....28 G2
Shorton Torbay....9 C7
Shortroods Renfs....267 B9
Shortstanding Glos....79 C9
Shortstown Beds....103 B11
Short Street Wilts....45 D10
Shortwood Glos....80 F4
S Glos....61 D7
Shorwell IoW....20 E5
Shoscombe Bath....45 B8
Shoscombe Vale Bath....45 B8
Shotatton Shrops....149 E7
Shotesham Norf....142 D5
Shotgate Essex....88 G3
Shotley Suff....108 D4
Shotleyfield Durham....242 G3
Shotley Bridge Durham....242 G3
Shotley Gate Suff....108 E4
Shottenden Kent....54 C4
Shottermill Sur....49 G11
Shottery Warks....118 G3
Shotteswell Warks....101 C8
Shottisham Suff....108 C6
Shottle Derbys....170 F4
Shottlegate Derbys....170 F4
Shotton Durham....234 B4
Durham....234 F3
Flint....166 B4
Northumb....242 B6
Northumb....263 C8
Shotton Colliery
Durham....234 C3
Shotts N Lnrk....269 C7
Shotwick Ches W....182 G4
Shouldham Norf....140 B3
Shouldham Thorpe Norf....140 B3
Shoulton Worcs....116 F6
Shover's Green E Sus....53 G7
Shraleybrook Staffs....168 F3
Shrawardine Shrops....149 F8
Shrawley Worcs....116 E6
Shrewley Warks....118 D4
Shrewley Common
Warks....118 D4
Shrewsbury Shrops....149 G9
Shrewton Wilts....46 E5
Shripney W Sus....22 C6
Shrivenham Oxon....63 B8
Shropham Norf....141 E9
Shroton or Iwerne Courtney
Dorset....30 E5
Shrub End Essex....107 G9
Shrubs Hill Sur....66 F3
Shrutherhill S Lnrk....268 F5
Shucknall Hereford....97 C11
Shudy Camps Cambs....106 C2
Shulishadermor Highld....298 E4
Shulista Highld....298 B4
Shuna Ho Argyll....275 C8
Shurdington Glos....80 B6
Shurlock Row Windsor....65 E10
Shurnock Worcs....117 E10
Shurrey Highld....310 D4
Shurrery Lodge Highld....310 D4
Shurton Som....43 E8
Shustoke Warks....134 E4
Shute Devon....15 B11
Devon....26 G5
Shute End Wilts....31 B11
Shutford Oxon....101 C7
Shut Heath Staffs....151 E7
Shuthonger Glos....99 D7
Shutlanger Northants....120 G4
Shutta Corn....6 E5
Shutt Green Staffs....133 B7
Shutton Hill Hereford....61 E8
Shutton Som....29 E10
Shuttlesfield Kent....55 E7
Shuttleworth Gtr Man....195 D10
Shutt Green Staffs....133 B7
Siabost N Ayrs....255 E10

Siabost bho Dheas
W Isles....304 D4
Siabost bho Thuath
W Isles....304 D4
Siadar W Isles....304 C5
Siadar Iarach W Isles....304 C5
Siadar Uarach W Isles....304 C5
Sibbaldbie Dumfries....248 F4
Sibbertoft Northants....136 G3
Sibdon Carwood Shrops....131 G8
Sibford Ferris Oxon....101 D7
Sibford Gower Oxon....101 D7
Sible Hedingham Essex....106 E5
Sibley's Green Essex....106 F2
Sibsey Lincs....174 E5
Sibsey Fen Side Lincs....174 E5
Sibson Cambs....137 D11
Leics....135 C7
Sibster Highld....310 D7
Sibthorpe Notts....172 F3
Sibton Suff....127 D7
Sibton Green Suff....127 C7
Sicklesmere Suff....125 E7
Sicklinghall N Yorks....206 D3
Sid Devon....15 D8
Sidbrook Som....28 B3
Sidbury Devon....15 C8
Shrops....132 F3
Sidcot N Som....44 B2
Sidcup London....68 E3
Siddal W Yorks....196 C6
Siddick Cumb....228 E6
Siddington Ches E....184 G4
Glos....81 F8
Siddington Heath
Ches E....184 G4
Sidemoor Worcs....117 C9
Sidestrand Norf....160 B5
Sideway Stoke....168 G5
Sidford Devon....15 C8
Sidlesham W Sus....22 D5
Sidlesham Common
W Sus....22 D5
Sidley E Sus....38 F2
Sidlow Sur....51 D9
Sidmouth Devon....15 D8
Sidway Staffs....150 B5
Sigford Devon....13 G11
Sigglesthorne E Yorks....209 D9
Sighthill Edin....280 G3
Sigingstone / Tresigin
V Glam....58 E3
Signet Oxon....82 C2
Sigwells Som....29 C10
Silchester Hants....64 G6
Sildinis W Isles....305 G4
Sileby Leics....153 F11
Silecroft Cumb....210 C2
Silfield Norf....142 D2
Silford Devon....24 B6
Silian Ceredig....111 G11
Silkstead Hants....32 C6
Silkstone S Yorks....197 F9
Silkstone Common
S Yorks....197 G9
Silk Willoughby Lincs....173 G9
Silloth Cumb....238 G4
Sills Northumb....251 C8
Sillyearn Moray....302 D5
Siloh Carms....94 D4
Silpho N Yorks....227 G9
Silsden W Yorks....204 D6
Silsoe C Beds....103 D11
Silton Dorset....30 B3
Silverburn Midloth....270 C4
Silverdale Lancs....211 E9
Staffs....168 F4
Silverdale Green Lancs....211 E9
Silver End Essex....88 B4
W Mid....133 F8
Silvergate Norf....160 D3
Silverhill E Sus....38 E3
Silverhillocks Aberds....303 C8
Silver Hill E Sus....38 C3
Silverhill Park E Sus....38 E3
Silver Knap Som....29 C11
Silverknowes Edin....280 F4
Silverley's Green Suff....126 B5
Silvermuir S Lnrk....269 F8
Silverstone Northants....102 C3
Silver Street Glos....80 E3
Kent....69 G11
Som....44 G4
Worcs....117 B11
Silverton Devon....27 G7
W Dunb....277 F8
Silvertonhill S Lnrk....268 E4
Silvertown London....68 D2
Silverwell Corn....4 F4
Silvington Shrops....116 B2
Silwick Shetland....313 J4
Sim Hill S Yorks....197 G9
Simister Gtr Man....195 F10
Simmondley Derbys....185 C8
Simm's Cross Halton....183 D8
Simm's Lane End Mers....194 G4
Simonburn Northumb....241 C9
Simonsbath Som....41 F9
Simonsburrow Devon....27 D10
Simonside T&W....243 E8
Simonstone Lancs....203 G11
N Yorks....223 G7
Simprim Borders....272 F6
Simpson M Keynes....103 D7
Simpson Cross Pembs....72 B5
Simpson Green S Yorks....205 F9
Sinclair's Hill Borders....272 E6
Sinclairston E Ayrs....257 F11
Sinclairtown Fife....280 C5
Sinderby N Yorks....214 C6
Sinderhope Northumb....241 G8
Sinderland Green
Gtr Man....184 D2
Sindlesham Wokingham....65 F9
Sinfin Derby....152 C6
Sinfin Moor Derby....153 C7
Singdean Borders....250 C3
Singleborough Bucks....102 E5
Single Hill Bath....45 B8
Singleton Lancs....202 F3
W Sus....34 E5
Singlewell Kent....69 E7
Singret Wrex....166 D5
Sinkhurst Green Kent....53 E11
Sinnahard Aberds....292 B6
Sinnington N Yorks....216 B4
Sinton Worcs....116 E6
Sinton Green Worcs....116 E6
Sipson London....66 D5
Sir Hill Staffs....61 F8
Sirhowy BI Gwent....77 C11
Sisland Norf....142 D6
Sissinghurst Kent....53 F9
Sisterpath Borders....272 F5
Siston S Glos....61 D7

Sithney Corn....2 D4
Sithney Common Corn....2 D4
Sithney Green Corn....2 D4
Sittingbourne Kent....70 G2
Six Ashes Staffs....132 F5
Six Bells BI Gwent....78 E2
Six Hills Leics....154 E2
Sixhills Lincs....189 D11
Six Mile Bottom Cambs....123 F11
Sixpenny Handley Dorset....31 D7
Sixty Acres....173 F9
Sizewell Suff....127 E9
Skaigh Devon....13 C8
Skail Highld....308 E7
Skaill Orkney....314 C4
Orkney....314 E2
Orkney....314 F5
Skares E Loth....282 F4
Skateraw E Loth....282 F4
Skaw Shetland....312 B8
Shetland....312 G7
Skeabost Highld....298 E4
Skeabrae Orkney....314 D2
Skelberry Shetland....313 G6
Shetland....313 M5
Skelbo Highld....309 K7
Skelbo Street Highld....309 K7
Skelbrooke S Yorks....198 E4
Skeldon E Ayrs....257 G9
Skeldyke Lincs....156 B6
Skelfhill Borders....249 C11
Skellingthorpe Lincs....188 G6
Skellister Shetland....313 H6
Skellorn Green Ches E....184 E6
Skellow S Yorks....198 E4
Skelmanthorpe W Yorks....197 E8
Skelmersdale Lancs....194 F3
Skelmonae Aberds....303 F8
Skelmorlie N Ayrs....266 B3
Skelmuir Aberds....303 E9
Skelpick Highld....308 D7
Skelton Cumb....230 D4
E Yorks....199 B9
N Yorks....223 B11
Redcar....226 B3
York....207 B7
Skelton-on-Ure
N Yorks....215 F7
Skelwick Orkney....314 B4
Skelwith Bridge Cumb....220 E6
Skendleby Lincs....174 B6
Skendleby Psalter Lincs....190 G6
Skene Ho Aberds....293 C9
Skenfrith Mon....97 G9
Skerne E Yorks....208 B6
Skerne Park Darl....224 C5
Skeroblingarry Argyll....255 E8
Skerray Highld....308 C6
Skerricha Highld....306 D7
Skerryford Pembs....72 C6
Skerton Lancs....211 G9
Sketchley Leics....135 E8
Sketty Swansea....56 C6
Skewen / Sgiwen Neath....57 B8
Skewes Corn....5 B9
Skewsby N Yorks....216 E2
Skeyton Norf....160 D4
Skeyton Corner Norf....160 D5
Skiag Bridge Highld....307 G7
Skibo Castle Highld....309 L7
Skidbrooke Lincs....190 C6
Skidbrooke North End
Lincs....190 B6
Skidby E Yorks....208 G6
Skilgate Som....27 B7
Skilington Lincs....155 D7
Skinburness Cumb....238 F4
Skinflats Falk....279 E8
Skinidin Highld....298 E2
Skinnergate Darl....160 D6
Skinner's Bottom Corn....4 F4
Skinners Green W Berks....64 F2
Skinnet Highld....308 C5
Skinningrove Redcar....226 B4
Skipness Argyll....255 B9
Skippool Lancs....202 E3
Skiprigg Cumb....230 B3
Skipsea E Yorks....209 C9
Skipsea Brough E Yorks....209 C9
Skipton N Yorks....204 C5
Skipton-on-Swale
N Yorks....215 D7
Skipwith N Yorks....207 F9
Skirbeck Lincs....174 G4
Skirbeck Quarter Lincs....174 G4
Skirethorns N Yorks....213 G9
Skirlaugh E Yorks....209 F8
Skirling Borders....260 B3
Skirmett Bucks....65 B9
Skirpenbeck E Yorks....207 B10
Skirwith Cumb....231 E8
N Yorks....212 E4
Skirza Highld....310 C7
Skitby Cumb....239 D10
Skitham Lancs....202 E4
Skittle Green Bucks....84 E3
Skulamus Highld....295 C8
Skullomie Highld....308 C6
Skyborry Green Shrops....114 C5
Skye Green Essex....107 G7
Skye of Curr Highld....301 G9
Skyfog Pembs....90 F6
Skyreholme N Yorks....213 G11
Slack Derbys....170 C4
W Yorks....196 B3
Slackcote Gtr Man....196 F3
Slackhall Derbys....185 E9
Slackhead Moray....302 C4
Slack Head Cumb....211 D9
Slackholme End Lincs....191 G8
Slacks of Cairnbanno
Aberds....303 E8
Slad Glos....80 D5
Slade Glos....80 F5
Devon....40 D4
Kent....55 G11
Pembs....72 B6
Slade End Oxon....83 G9
Slade Green London....68 D4
Slade Heath Staffs....133 B8
Slade Hooton S Yorks....187 D8
Sladesbridge Corn....10 G6
Slades Green Worcs....99 D7
Slaggyford Northumb....240 G5
Slaidburn Lancs....203 C10
Slaithwaite W Yorks....196 D5
Slaley Derbys....170 D3
Northumb....241 F11
Slamannan Falk....279 G7
Slangford Orkney....72 B6
Slapewath Redcar....226 B3
Slapton Bucks....103 G8
Devon....8 G6
Northants....102 B3
Snails Hill Som....29 E7

Slateford Edin....280 G4
Slate Haugh Moray....302 C4
Slatepit Dale Derbys....170 B4
Slattocks Gtr Man....195 F11
Slaugham W Sus....36 B3
Slaughterbridge Corn....11 D8
Slaughterford Wilts....61 E10
Slaughter Hill Ches E....168 D2
Slawston Leics....136 E5
Sleaford Hants....49 F10
Lincs....173 F9
S Yorks....198 G2
Sleagill Cumb....221 B11
Sleap Shrops....149 D9
Sleapford Telford....150 F2
Sleapshyde Herts....86 D2
Sleastary Highld....309 K6
Slebech Pembs....73 B8
Sledge Green Worcs....98 E6
Sledmere E Yorks....217 G8
Sleetbeck Cumb....240 B2
Sleet Moor Derbys....170 E6
Sleight Dorset....18 B5
Sleights N Yorks....227 D7
Slepe Dorset....18 C4
Sliabh na h-Airde
W Isles....296 F3
Slickly Highld....310 C6
Sliddery N Ayrs....255 E10
Slideslow Worcs....117 C9
Slindon Staffs....150 C6
W Sus....35 F7
Slinfold W Sus....50 G6
Sling Gwent....79 D9
Gwyn....163 B10
Slingsby N Yorks....216 E3
Slioch Aberds....302 F5
Slip End C Beds....85 B9
Herts....104 D5
Slipper's Ford W Yorks....204 E6
Slipton Northants....121 B9
Slitting Mill Staffs....151 F10
Slochd Highld....301 G8
Slockavullin Argyll....275 D9
Slogan Argyll....302 E3
Sloley Norf....160 E5
Sloncombe Devon....13 D10
Sloothby Lincs....191 G7
Slough Slough....66 D3
Slough Green W Sus....36 B3
Som....28 C3
Slough Hill Suff....125 G7
Sluggan Highld....301 G8
Sluggans Highld....298 E4
Slumbay Highld....295 B10
Sly Corner Kent....54 G3
Slyfield Sur....50 C3
Slyne Lancs....211 F9
Smailholm Borders....262 B4
Smallbridge Gtr Man....196 D2
Smallbrook Glos....14 B3
Glos....79 E9
Smallburgh Norf....160 E6
Smallburn E Ayrs....258 D5
Aberds....303 E10
Smalldale Derbys....185 F9
Derbys....185 F9
Small Dole W Sus....36 E2
Small End Lincs....174 D6
Smalley Derbys....170 G6
Smalley Common
Derbys....170 G6
Smalley Green Derbys....170 G6
Smallfield Sur....51 E10
Smallford Herts....85 D11
Small Heath W Mid....134 F2
Smallholm Dumfries....238 B4
Small Hythe Kent....53 F11
Smallmarsh Devon....25 C10
Smallrice Staffs....151 C9
Smallridge Devon....28 G4
Smallshaw Gtr Man....196 G2
Smallthorne Stoke....168 E5
Small Way Som....44 G6
Smallwood Ches E....168 C4
Worcs....117 D10
Smallwood Green Suff....125 F8
Smallwood Hey Lancs....202 D3
Smallworth Norf....141 G10
Smannell Hants....47 D11
Smardale Cumb....222 D4
Smarden Kent....53 E11
Smarden Bell Kent....53 E11
Smart's Hill Kent....52 E4
Smaull Argyll....274 G3
Smeatharpe Devon....28 E2
Smeaton Fife....280 C5
Smeeth Kent....54 F5
Smeeth E....54 F5
Smeeton Westerby
Leics....136 E3
Smelthouses N Yorks....214 G3
Smercleit W Isles....297 K3
Smerral Highld....310 F5
Smestow Staffs....133 E7
Smethcott Shrops....131 D9
Smethwick W Mid....133 F10
Smethwick Green
Ches E....168 C4
Smirisary Highld....289 B8
Smisby Derbys....152 F6
Smite Hill Worcs....117 F7
Smith End Green Worcs....116 G5
Smithfield Cumb....239 D10
Smith Green Lancs....202 C5
Smithies S Yorks....197 F11
Smithincott Devon....27 E9
Smithley S Yorks....197 G11
Smith's End Herts....105 D8
Smith's Green Essex....106 G2
Essex....105 C11
Smith's Green Ches E....168 E3
Smithstown Aberds....302 G5
Smithstown Highld....299 B7
Smithton Highld....301 E7
Smithwood Green Suff....125 G8
Smithy Bridge Gtr Man....196 D2
Smithy Gate Flint....181 F11
Smithy Green Ches E....184 G2
Gtr Man....184 D5
Smithy Houses Derbys....170 F5
Smithy Lane Ends Lancs....194 E2
Smock Alley W Sus....35 D9
Smockington Leics....135 F9
Smoky Row Bucks....84 D4
Smug Oak Herts....85 E10
Smyrton S Ayrs....244 G4
Smythe's Green Essex....88 B6
Snagshall E Sus....38 C3
Snaigow House Perth....286 C4
Snailbeach Shrops....131 C7
Snailbeach N Ayrs....255 E10

Snailswell Herts....104 E3
Snailwell Cambs....124 D2
Snainton N Yorks....217 C8
Snaith E Yorks....198 C6
Snape N Yorks....214 C5
Suff....127 F7
Snape Green Lancs....193 E11
Snape Hill Derbys....186 F5
S Yorks....198 G2
Snapper Devon....40 G5
Snarestone Leics....134 B6
Snarford Lincs....189 E9
Snargate Kent....39 C7
Snarraness Shetland....313 H4
Snatchwood Torf....78 E3
Snave Kent....39 B8
Sneachill Worcs....117 G8
Snead Powys....130 E6
Snead Common Worcs....116 D4
Sneads Green Worcs....117 D7
Sneath Common Norf....142 F3
Sneaton N Yorks....227 D7
Sneatonthorpe N Yorks....227 D8
Snedshill Telford....132 B4
Sneinton Nottingham....153 B11
Snelland Lincs....189 E9
Snelston Derbys....169 G11
Snettertom Norf....141 E9
Snettisham Norf....158 C3
Sneyd Green Stoke....168 F5
Sneyd Park Bristol....60 D5
Snibston Leics....153 G8
Snig's End Glos....98 F5
Snipeshill Kent....70 G2
Snitterby Lincs....189 C7
Sniseabhal W Isles....297 H3
Snitter Northumb....252 C2
Snitterby Lincs....189 C7
Snitterfield Warks....118 F4
Snittergate Norf....142 E4
Snitton Shrops....115 B11
Snittongate Shrops....115 B11
Snodhill Hereford....96 C6
Snodland Kent....69 G7
Snods Edge Northumb....242 G3
Snowden Hill S Yorks....197 G9
Snowdown Kent....55 C8
Snow End Herts....105 E8
Snow Hill Ches E....167 E10
W Yorks....197 C10
Snow Lea W Yorks....196 C5
Snowshill Glos....99 E11
Snow Street Norf....141 G11
Snydale W Yorks....198 D2
Soake Hants....33 E11
Soar Anglesey....178 G5
Carms....94 F2
Devon....9 G9
Gwyn....146 B2
Powys....95 E9
Soar-y-Mynydd
Ceredig....112 G5
Soberton Hants....33 D10
Soberton Heath Hants....33 E10
Sockbridge Cumb....230 F6
Sockburn Darl....224 D6
Sodom Denb....181 F7
Shetland....313 G7
Sodylt Bank Shrops....148 B6
Soham Cambs....123 C11
Soham Cotes Cambs....123 B11
Soho London....67 C9
Som....45 D7
W Mid....133 F10
Solas W Isles....296 D4
Soldon Cross Devon....24 E4
Soldridge Hants....49 G7
Sole Street Kent....54 D5
Kent....69 G7
Solihull W Mid....118 B2
Solihull Lodge W Mid....117 B11
Sollers Dilwyn Hereford....115 F8
Sollers Hope Hereford....98 E2
Sollom Lancs....194 D3
Solva / Solfach Pembs....90 G5
Somerby Leics....154 G5
Lincs....200 F5
Somercotes Derbys....170 E6
Somerdale Bath....61 F7
Somerford Ches E....168 B4
Dorset....19 C9
Somerford Keynes Glos....81 G8
Somerley W Sus....22 D4
Somerleyton Suff....143 D9
Somersal Herbert
Derbys....152 B2
Somersby Lincs....190 G4
Somersham Cambs....123 B7
Suff....107 B11
Somers Town London....67 C9
Ptsmth....21 B8
Somerton Newport....59 B10
Oxon....101 F9
Som....29 B7
Suff....124 G6
Somerton Hill Som....29 B7
Somerwood Shrops....149 G11
Sompting W Sus....35 G10
Sompting Abbots
W Sus....35 F11
Sonning Wokingham....65 D9
Sonning Common Oxon....65 C8
Sonning Eye Oxon....65 D9
Sontley Wrex....166 F4
Sookholme Notts....171 B9
Sopley Hants....19 B9
Sopwell Herts....85 D11
Sopworth Wilts....61 B10
Sorbie Dumfries....236 E6
Sordale Highld....310 C5
Sorisdale Argyll....288 C4
Sorley Devon....8 E4
Sorn E Ayrs....258 D3
Sornhill E Ayrs....258 C2
Sortat Highld....310 C6
Sotby Lincs....190 F2
Sots Hole Lincs....173 C10
Sotterley Suff....143 G9
Soudley Shrops....131 E11
Shrops....150 D4
Soughley S Yorks....197 G7
Soughton / Sychdyn
Flint....166 B2
Soulbury Bucks....103 F7
Soulby Cumb....222 B4
Cumb....230 E6
Souldern Oxon....101 E10
Souldrop Beds....121 E9
Sound Ches E....167 F10
Shetland....313 H5
Shetland....313 J6
Sound Heath Ches E....167 F10
Soundwell S Glos....60 D6

Sourhope Borders 263 E8
Sourin Orkney 314 C4
Sourlie N Ayrs 266 G6
Sour Nook Cumb. 230 C3
Sourton Devon. 12 C6
Soutergate Cumb. 210 C4
South Acre Norf 158 G6
South Acton London. 67 D7
South Alkham Kent 55 E8
Southall London 66 C6
South Allington Devon. 9 G10
South Alloa Falk. 279 C7
Southam Cumb. 219 C9
  Glos. 99 F9
  Warks 119 E8
South Ambersham W Sus 34 C6
Southampton Soton 32 E6
South Anston S Yorks 187 E8
South Ascot Windsor 66 F2
South Ashford Kent 54 E4
South Auchmachar Aberds 303 E9
Southay Som 28 D4
South Baddesley Hants 20 B3
South Ballachulish Highld 284 M4
South Balloch S Ayrs 245 D8
South Bank Redcar 234 G6
  York 207 C7
South Barrow Som. 29 B10
South Beach Northum. 243 B8
South Beach / Marian-y-de Gwyn. 145 C2
South Beddington London 67 G9
South Benfleet Essex 69 B9
South Bents T&W. 243 E10
South Bersted W Sus. 22 C6
South Blainslie Borders 271 G10
South Bockhampton Dorset. 19 B9
Southborough Bromley 68 F2
  Kent. 52 E6
  Kingston-upon-Thames 67 F7
Southbourne Bmouth 19 C8
  W Sus. 22 B3
South Bramwith S Yorks 198 E6
South Brent Devon. 8 D3
South Brewham Som 45 F8
South Bromley London 67 C11
Southbrook Wilts. 45 G8
South Broomage Falk. 279 E7
Southbroomhill Northumb 252 D6
Southburgh Norf. 141 C9
South Burlingham Norf. 143 B7
Southburn E Yorks 208 C5
South Cadbury Som 29 B10
South Cairn Dumfries 236 C1
South Carlton Lincs. 189 F7
  Notts 187 E9
South Carne Corn. 11 E10
South Cave E Yorks 208 G4
South Cerney Glos. 81 F8
South Chailey E Sus. 36 D5
South Chard Som 28 F4
South Charlton Northumb 264 C5
South Cheriton Som 29 C11
Southchurch Sthend 70 B2
South Church Durham. 233 F10
South Cliffe E Yorks 208 F3
South Clifton Notts 188 G4
South Clunes Highld 300 E5
South Cockerington Lincs 190 D5
South Common Devon 28 G4
Southcoombe Oxon. 100 F6
South Cornelly Bridgend 57 E10
South Corriegills N Ayrs 256 C2
South Correlaw Dumfries 248 G5
Southcote Reading. 65 E7
Southcott Corn. 11 B9
  Devon 24 D6
  Wilts 47 B7
Southcourt Bucks 84 C4
South Cove Suff 143 G9
South Creagan Argyll 289 E11
South Creake Norf 159 B7
Southcrest Worcs 117 D10
South Crosland W Yorks 196 E6
South Croxton Leics 154 G3
South Croydon London 67 G10
South Cuil Highld 298 C3
South Dalton E Yorks 208 D5
South Darenth Kent 68 E5
Southdean Borders 250 B4
Southdene Mers. 182 B6
South Denes Norf 143 C10
Southdown Bath 61 G8
  Corn. 7 E8
South Down Hants 33 C7
  Som 28 E2
South Duffield N Yorks 207 G9
South Dunn Highld 310 D5
South Earlswood Sur 51 D9
Southease E Sus. 36 G6
South Elkington Lincs 190 D3
South Elmsall W Yorks 198 E3
South Elphinstone E Loth 281 G7
Southend Argyll 255 G7
  Bucks. 65 B9
  Glos. 80 F2
  London 67 E11
  Oxon 83 E9
  W Berks 64 D2
  Wilts 63 E7
South End Beds. 103 B10
  Bucks. 103 F7
  Cumb 210 G4
  E Yorks 209 E9
  Hants 31 D10
South-end Herts 86 B6
South End N Lincs 200 C6
  Norf 141 E9
Southend-on-Sea Sthend 69 B11
Southerhouse Shetland 313 K6
Southerly Devon 12 D6
Southernby Cumb 230 D3
Southern Cross Brighton 36 F3
Southernden Kent 53 D11
Southerndown V Glam 57 G11
Southerness Dumfries 237 D11
Southern Green Herts 104 E6
South Erradale Highld. 299 B7
Southery Norf 140 E2
Southey Green Essex 106 E5
South Fambridge Essex 88 F4

South Farnborough Hants 49 C11
South Fawley W Berks 63 C11
South Ferriby N Lincs 200 C3
Southfield Northumb 243 B7
South Field E Yorks 200 B4
  Windsor 66 D3
Southfields London 67 E9
  Thurrock 69 C7
Southfleet Kent 68 E6
South Flobbets Aberds. 303 F7
Southford IoW 20 E6
South Garth Shetland 312 D7
South Garvan Highld 289 B11
Southgate Ceredig. 111 A11
  London 86 G3
  Norf. 159 C7
  Norf. 160 E2
  Swansea 56 D5
  W Sus. 51 F9
South Glendale W Isles 297 K3
South Gluss Shetland 312 F5
South Godstone Sur 51 D11
South Gorley Hants 31 E11
South Gosforth T&W 242 D6
South Green Essex 87 G11
  Essex 89 B8
  Kent. 69 G11
  Norf 157 F10
  Norf 159 G11
  Suff 126 B3
South Gyle Edin. 280 G3
South-haa Shetland 312 E5
South Hackney London 67 C11
South Ham Hants 48 C6
South Hampstead London 67 C9
South Hanningfield Essex 88 F2
South Harefield London. 66 B5
South Harrow London 66 B6
South Harting W Sus. 34 D3
South Hayling Hants 21 B10
South Hazelrigg Northumb 264 C3
South Heath Bucks. 84 E6
  Essex 89 B10
South Heighton E Sus. 23 E7
South-heog Shetland 312 E6
South Hetton Durham. 234 B3
South Hiendley W Yorks 197 E11
South Hill Corn. 12 G2
  N Som 43 B10
  Pembs 72 C4
South Hinksey Oxon 83 E8
South Hole Devon. 24 C2
South Holme N Yorks 216 D3
South Holmwood Sur 51 D7
South Hornchurch London 68 C4
South Huish Devon. 8 G3
South Hykeham Lincs. 172 C6
South Hylton T&W. 243 F9
Southill C Beds 104 C3
  Dorset. 17 E9
Southington Hants 48 D4
South Kelsey Lincs. 189 C9
South Kensington London 67 D9
South Kessock Highld. 300 E6
South Killingholme N Lincs 201 D7
South Kilvington N Yorks 215 C8
South Kilworth Leics 136 G2
South Kirkby W Yorks 198 E3
South Kirkton Aberds. 293 C9
South Kiscadale N Ayrs 256 D2
South Knighton Devon. 14 G2
  Leicester 136 C2
South Kyme Lincs. 173 F11
South Lambeth London. 67 D10
South Lancing W Sus. 35 G11
Southlands Dorset. 17 F9
South Lane E Yorks 197 F9
South Leigh Devon. 82 D5
South Leverton Notts 188 E3
South Littleton Worcs. 99 B11
South Lopham Norf. 141 G10
South Luffenham Rutland 137 C8
South Malling E Sus. 36 E6
Southmarsh Som 45 G8
South Marston Swindon 63 B7
Southmead Bristol. 60 D5
South Merstham Sur 51 C9
South Middleton Northumb 263 E11
South Milford N Yorks 206 G5
South Millbrex Aberds. 303 E8
South Milton Devon. 8 G4
South Mimms Herts 86 E2
Southminster Essex 89 F7
South Molton Devon. 26 C4
Southmoor Oxon. 82 F5
South Moor Durham. 242 G5
South Moreton Oxon. 64 B5
South Mundham W Sus. 22 C5
South Muskham Notts 172 D3
South Newbald E Yorks. 208 F4
South Newbarns Cumb. 210 F4
South Newington Oxon. 101 E8
South Newsham Northumb 243 B8
South Newton Wilts. 46 G5
South Normanton Derbys 170 D6
South Norwood London 67 G10
South Nutfield Sur 51 D10
South Ockendon Thurrock 68 C5
Southoe Cambs. 122 E3
Southolt Suff. 126 D3
South Ormsby Lincs 190 F5
Southorpe Pboro 137 C11
South Ossett W Yorks 197 D9
South Otterington N Yorks 215 B7
Southover Dorset. 17 C8
  E Sus. 23 C8
  E Sus. 37 B11
South Owersby Lincs 189 C9
Southowram W Yorks 196 B6
South Oxhey Herts. 85 G10
South Park Sur 51 D8
South Pelaw Durham. 243 G7
South Perrott Dorset. 28 F6
South Petherton Som. 28 D6
South Petherwin Corn. 11 E11
South Pickenham Norf 141 C7
South Pill Corn. 7 D8
South Pool Devon. 8 G5
South Poorton Dorset. 16 B6
Southport Mers. 193 D10
South Port Argyll 284 E4
Southpunds Shetland 313 L6
South Quilquox Aberds. 303 F8
South Radworthy Devon. 41 G9
South Raceby Lincs 173 H8
South Raynham Norf 159 E7
South Reddish Gtr Man. 184 C5

South Reston Lincs 190 E6
Southrey Lincs. 173 B10
Southrop Glos. 81 E11
  Oxon 101 E7
South Ruislip London 66 B6
South Runcton Norf 140 B2
South Scarle Notts 172 C4
Southsea Ptsmth 21 B8
  Wrex 166 E4
South Shian Argyll 289 E11
South Shields T&W 243 D9
South Shore Blkpool 202 G2
South Side Durham 233 F8
  Orkney 314 G5
South Somercotes Lincs 190 C6
South Stainley N Yorks 214 G6
South Stainmore Cumb. 222 C6
South Stanley Durham. 242 G5
South Stifford Thurrock 68 D6
Southstoke Bath. 61 G8
South Stoke Oxon 64 C6
  W Sus. 35 F8
South Stour E Sus. 54 F4
South Street E Sus. 36 D6
  Kent. 54 B5
  Kent. 69 G10
  Kent. 70 F6
  London 52 B2
South Tawton Devon. 13 C9
South Tehidy Corn. 4 G3
South Thoresby Lincs 190 F6
South Tidworth Wilts. 47 D8
South Tottenham London 67 B10
Southtown Norf. 143 B10
  Orkney 314 G4
  Som 44 B5
South Town Devon. 14 E5
  Hants 49 F7
South Twerton Bath 61 G8
South Ulverston Cumb. 210 D6
South View Hants 48 C6
Southville Devon 8 G4
  Torf 78 F3
South Voxter Shetland 313 G5
South Walsham Norf 161 G7
Southwark London 67 D10
South Warnborough Hants 49 D8
Southwater W Sus. 35 C11
Southwater Street W Sus. 35 B11
Southway Plym. 7 C9
  Som 44 E4
South Weald Essex 87 G9
South Weirs Hants 32 G3
Southwell Dorset. 17 G9
  Notts 172 E2
South Weston Oxon 84 C2
South Wheatley Corn. 11 C10
  Notts 188 D3
South Whiteness Shetland 313 J5
Southwick Hants 33 D10
  Northants 137 E10
  Som 43 D9
  T&W 243 F9
  Wilts 45 B10
  W Sus. 36 F2
South Widcombe Bath 44 B5
South Wigston Leics. 135 D11
South Willesborough Kent 54 E4
South Willingham Lincs 189 E11
South Wimbledon London 67 E9
South Wingate Durham 234 E4
South Wingfield Derbys. 170 D5
South Witham Lincs 155 F8
South Wonston Hants 48 F3
Southwood Derbys 152 F6
  Hants 49 B10
  Norf 143 A8
  Som 44 G5
  Worcs 116 E4
South Woodford London 86 G6
South Woodham Ferrers Essex 88 F4
South Wootton Norf 158 E2
South Wraxall Wilts 61 G10
South Yardley W Mid 134 G2
South Yarrows Highld 310 E6
Sow Devon. 25 G8
South Zeal Devon 13 C9
Soval Lodge W Isles 304 F5
Sowber Gate N Yorks 215 B7
Sowerby N Yorks 215 C8
  W Yorks 196 C4
Sowerby Bridge W Yorks 196 C5
Sowerby Row Cumb 230 D3
Sower Carr Lancs 202 E3
Sowley Green Suff 124 G4
Sowood W Yorks 196 D5
Sowood Green W Yorks 196 D5
Sowton Devon 14 C5
Sowton Barton Devon 14 D2
Soyal Highld 309 K5
Soyland Town W Yorks 196 C4
Spacey Houses N Yorks 206 C2
Spa Common Norf 160 C5
Spalding Lincs 156 E4
Spaldington E Yorks 207 G11
Spaldwick Cambs 122 C2
Spalford Notts 172 B4
Spanby Lincs 155 B11
Spango Invclyd 276 G4
Spanish Green Hants 49 B7
Sparham Norf 159 F11
Sparhamhill Norf 159 F11
Spark Bridge Cumb 210 C6
Sparkbrook W Mid 133 G11
Sparket Cumb 230 G6
Sparkford Som 29 C10
Sparkhill W Mid 133 G11
Sparkwell Devon 7 D11
Sparl Shetland 312 G5
Sparnon Corn 1 E3
Sparnon Gate Corn 4 G3
Sparrow Green Norf 159 G9
Sparrow Hill Som 44 C2
Sparrowpit Derbys 185 E9
Sparrow's Green E Sus. 52 G6
Sparsholt Hants 48 G3
  Oxon 63 B10
Spartylea Northumb 232 B3
Spath Staffs 151 B11
Spaunton N Yorks 216 G4
Spaxton Som 43 F8
Spean Bridge Highld 290 E4
Spear Hill W Sus 35 D10
Spearywell Hants 32 B4
Speckington Som 29 C9
Speddoch Dumfries 247 F9
Speed Gate Kent 68 F5
Speedwell Bristol 60 E6
Speen Bucks 84 F4
  W Berks 64 F3
Speeton N Yorks 218 E2
Speke Mers. 182 G6
Speldhurst Kent. 52 E5
Spellbrook Herts. 87 B7
Spelsbury Oxon. 101 G7
Spelter Bridgend 57 C11
Spen W Yorks 197 B7
Spencers Wood Wokingham 65 F8
Spennells Worcs. 116 C6
Spennithorne N Yorks 214 B2
Spennymoor Durham 233 E11
Spernall Warks 117 E11
Spetchley Worcs. 117 G7
Spetisbury Dorset. 30 G6
Spexhall Suff 143 G7
Speybank Highld 291 C10
Spey Bay Moray 302 C3
Speybridge Highld 301 G10
Speyview Moray 302 E2
Spillardsford Aberds. 303 D10
Spilsby Lincs 174 B6
Spindlestone Northumb 264 C5
Spinkhill Derbys 187 F7
Spinney Hill Northants 120 E5
Spinney Hills Leicester 136 C2
Spinningdale Highld 309 L6
Spion Kop Notts 171 B9
Spirthill Wilts 62 D3
Spital Mers. 182 E4
  Windsor 66 D3
Spitalbrook Herts. 86 D5
Spitalfields London 67 C10
Spital Hill S Yorks 187 C10
  Lincs 189 D7
Spital in the Street Lincs 189 D7
Spital Tongues T&W 242 D6
Spithurst E Sus. 36 D6
Spittal Dumfries 236 D5
  E Loth. 281 F9
  Highld 310 D5
  Northumb 273 E10
  Pembs 91 G9
  Stirl 277 D10
Spittalfield Perth. 286 C5
Spittal Houses S Yorks 186 B5
Spittal of Glenmuick Aberds. 292 E5
Spittal of Glenshee Perth. 292 F3
Spittlegate Lincs. 155 C8
Spixworth Norf. 160 F4
Splatt Corn. 10 F4
  Corn. 11 D10
  Devon 25 F10
  Som 43 F8
Splayne's Green E Sus. 36 C6
Splott Cardiff 59 D7
Spofforth N Yorks 206 C3
Spondon Derby 153 B8
Spon End W Mid. 118 B6
Spon Green Flint. 166 C3
Spooner Row Norf. 141 D11
Spoonleygate Shrops 132 D6
Sporle Norf. 158 G6
Spotland Bridge Gtr Man. 195 E11
Spott E Loth. 282 F3
Spratton Northants 120 C4
Spreakley Sur 49 E10
Spreyton Devon. 13 B9
Spriddlestone Devon 7 E10
Spridlington Lincs 189 E8
Sprig's Alley Oxon 84 F3
Springbank Glos. 99 G8
Spring Bank Cumb 229 G10
Springboig Glasgow 268 C3
Springbourne Bmouth 19 C8
Springburn Glasgow 268 B2
Spring Cottage Leics 152 F6
Spring End N Yorks 223 G9
Springfield Argyll 275 F11
  Caerph. 77 F11
  Dumfries 239 D8
  Essex 88 D2
  Fife 287 F7
  Gtr Man 194 F5
  Highld 300 E6
  M Keynes 103 D7
  Moray 301 D10
  W Mid. 133 D8
  W Mid. 133 F11
  W Mid. 133 G11
Springfields Stoke. 168 G5
Spring Gardens Som. 45 D9
Spring Green Lancs. 204 E4
Spring Grove London 67 D7
Springhead Gtr Man. 196 G3
Springhill Renf. 267 D10
  IoW 20 B6
  N Lnrk 269 D7
  Staffs 133 B11
  Staffs. 133 C9
Spring Hill Gtr Man. 196 F2
  Lancs 195 B8
  W Mid. 133 D7
Springholm Dumfries 237 C10
Springkell Dumfries 239 B7
Spring Park London 67 G11
Springside N Ayrs 257 B9
Springthorpe Lincs 188 D5
Spring Vale S Yorks 197 G9
Spring Valley IoM 192 E4
Springwell Essex 105 C10
  T&W. 243 F7
  T&W. 243 F7
Springwells Dumfries 248 E3
Sproatley E Yorks 209 G9
Sproston Green W Mid. 168 B2
Sprotbrough S Yorks 198 G4
Sproughton Suff. 108 C2
Sprouston Borders 263 B7
Sprowston Norf 160 G4
Sproxton Leics 155 E7
  N Yorks 216 C2
Spurlands End Bucks. 84 F5
Spurstow Ches E 167 D9
Spurtree Shrops 116 D2
Spynie Moray 302 C2
Spyway Dorset. 17 D8
Square and Compass Pembs. 90 E6
Squires Gate Blkpool 202 G2
Squirrel's Heath London 68 B4
Sraid Ruadh Argyll 288 E1
Srannda W Isles 296 C6
Sronphadruig Lodge Perth. 291 F9
Stableford Shrops 132 D5
  Staffs. 150 B6
Stacey Bank S Yorks 186 C3
Stackhouse N Yorks 212 F6
Stackpole Pembs 73 F7
Stackpole Quay Pembs. 73 F7
Stacksford Norf 141 E11
Stacksteads Lancs. 195 C10

Stackyard Green Suff 107 B9
Staddiscombe Plym 7 E10
Staddlethorpe E Yorks 199 B10
Staddon Devon 24 C3
  Devon 24 G5
Staden Derbys 185 G9
Stadhampton Oxon 83 F10
Stadhlaigearraidh W Isles 297 H3
Stadmorslow Staffs 168 D5
Staffield Cumb 230 C6
Staffin Highld 298 C4
Stafford Staffs 151 E8
Stafford Park Telford 132 B4
Stafford's Corner Essex 89 B7
Stagbatch Hereford 115 F9
Stagden Cross Essex 87 C10
Stagehall Borders 271 G9
Stagsden Beds 103 B9
Stagsden West End Beds 103 B9
Stag's Head Devon 25 B11
Stainburn Cumb 229 F7
  N Yorks 205 D10
Stainby Lincs 155 E8
Staincliffe W Yorks 197 C8
Staincross S Yorks 197 E10
Staindrop Durham 233 G8
Staines-upon-Thames Sur 66 E4
Stainfield Lincs 155 D11
  Lincs 189 B10
Stainforth N Yorks 212 F6
  S Yorks 198 E6
Staining Lancs 202 F3
Stainland W Yorks 196 D5
Stainsacre N Yorks 227 D8
Stainsby Derbys 170 B6
  Lincs 190 G4
Stainton Cumb 211 B10
  Cumb 230 F5
  Cumb 239 F9
  Durham 223 B11
  Mbro 225 C9
  N Yorks 224 F2
  S Yorks 187 C9
Stainton by Langworth Lincs 189 F9
Stainton le Vale Lincs 189 C11
Stainton with Adgarley Cumb 210 E5
Stair Cumb 229 G10
  E Ayrs 257 E10
Stairfoot S Yorks 197 F11
Stairhaven Dumfries 236 D4
Staithes N Yorks 226 B5
Stakeford Northumb 253 F7
Stake Hill Gtr Man 195 F11
Stakenbridge Worcs 117 B7
Stake Pool Lancs 202 D4
Stalbridge Dorset 30 D2
Stalbridge Weston Dorset 30 D2
Stalham Norf 161 D7
Stalham Green Norf 161 E7
Stalisfield Green Kent 54 C3
Stallen Dorset 29 D10
Stalling Busk N Yorks 213 B8
Stallingborough NE Lincs 201 E7
Stallington Staffs 151 B8
Stalmine Lancs 202 D3
Stalmine Moss Side Lancs 202 D3
Stalybridge Gtr Man 185 B7
Stambermill W Mid 133 G8
Stamborough Som 42 F4
Stambourne Essex 106 D4
Stambourne Green Essex 106 D4
Stamford Lincs 137 B10
  Northumb 264 E6
Stamford Bridge Ches W 167 B7
  E Yorks 207 B10
Stamfordham Northumb 242 C3
Stamford Hill London 67 B10
Stamperland E Renf 267 D11
Stamshaw Ptsmth 33 G10
Stanah Cumb 220 B6
  Lancs 202 E3
Stanborough Herts 86 C2
Stanbridge C Beds 103 G9
  Dorset 31 G8
Stanbridgeford C Beds 103 G9
Stanbrook Essex 106 F2
  Worcs 98 B6
Stanbury W Yorks 204 F6
Stand Gtr Man 195 F9
  N Lnrk 268 B5
Standburn Falk 279 G8
Standeford Staffs 133 B8
Standen Lancs 203 E10
Standen Hall Lancs 203 E10
Standen Street Kent 53 G10
Standerwick Som 45 D10
Standford Hants 49 G10
Standford Bridge Telford 150 E4
Standingstone Cumb 229 B11
  Cumb 229 G7
Standish Glos 80 D4
  Gtr Man 194 E5
Standish Lower Ground Gtr Man 194 F5
Standlake Oxon 82 E5
Standon Hants 32 B6
  Herts 105 G7
  Staffs 150 B6
Standon Green End Herts 86 C5
Stane N Lnrk 269 D7
Stanecastle N Ayrs 257 B8
Stanfield Norf 159 E8
  Suff 124 F5
Stanford C Beds 104 C3
  Kent 54 F6
  Norf 141 E7
  Shrops 148 F6
Stanford Bishop Hereford 116 G3
Stanford Bridge Worcs 116 D4
Stanford Dingley W Berks 64 E4
Stanford End Wokingham 65 G8
Stanford Hills Notts 153 D10
Stanford in the Vale Oxon 82 G5
Stanford-le-Hope Thurrock 69 C7
Stanford on Avon Northants 119 B10
Stanford on Soar Notts 153 E10
Stanford on Teme Worcs 116 D4
Stanford Rivers Essex 87 E8
Stanfree Derbys 187 F7
Stanground Pboro 138 D3
Stanhill Lancs 195 B8

Stanhoe Norf 158 B6
Stanhope Borders 260 D4
  Durham 232 D5
  Kent 54 E3
Stanion Northants 137 F8
Stank Cumb 210 E4
Stanklyn Worcs 117 C7
Stanks W Yorks 206 F3
Stanley Durham 242 G5
  Lancs 194 F3
  Notts 171 C7
  Perth 286 D5
  Shrops 132 G3
  Shrops 132 G5
  Staffs 168 E6
  Wilts 62 E3
  W Yorks 197 C10
Stanley Common Derbys 170 G6
Stanley Crook Durham 233 D9
Stanley Downton Glos 80 E4
Stanley Ferry W Yorks 197 C11
Stanley Gate Lancs 194 G2
Stanley Green Ches E 184 E5
  Poole 18 C6
  Shrops 149 B10
Stanley Hill Hereford 98 C3
Stanley Moor Staffs 168 E6
Stanley Pontlarge Glos 99 E9
Stanleytown Rhondda 77 G8
Stanlow Ches W 182 F6
  Staffs 132 D5
Stanmer Brighton 36 F4
Stanmore Hants 33 B7
  London 85 G11
  W Berks 64 D3
Stannergate Dundee 287 D8
Stannersburn Northumb 250 F6
Stanners Hill Sur 66 G3
Stanningfield Suff 125 F7
Stanningley W Yorks 205 G10
Stannington Northumb 242 B6
  S Yorks 186 D4
Stanpit Dorset 19 C9
Stansbatch Hereford 114 E6
Stansfield Suff 124 G5
Stanshope Staffs 169 E10
Stanstead Suff 106 B6
Stanstead Abbotts Herts 86 C5
Stansted Kent 68 G6
Stansted Airport Essex 105 G11
Stansted Mountfitchet Essex 105 G10
Stanthorne Ches W 167 B11
Stanton Glos 99 E11
  Mon 96 G6
  Northumb 252 F4
  Staffs 169 F10
  Suff 125 C9
Stanton by Bridge Derbys 153 D7
Stanton-by-Dale Derbys 153 B9
Stanton Chare Suff 125 C9
Stanton Drew Bath 60 G5
Stanton Fitzwarren Swindon 81 G11
Stanton Gate Notts 153 B9
Stanton Harcourt Oxon 82 D6
Stanton Hill Notts 171 C7
Stanton in Peak Derbys 170 C2
Stanton Lacy Shrops 115 B9
Stanton Lees Derbys 170 C3
Stanton Long Shrops 131 E11
Stanton-on-the-Wolds Notts 154 C2
Stanton Prior Bath 61 G7
Stanton St Bernard Wilts 62 G5
Stanton St John Oxon 83 D9
Stanton St Quintin Wilts 62 D2
Stanton Street Suff 125 D9
Stanton under Bardon Leics 153 G9
Stanton upon Hine Heath Shrops 149 E11
Stanton Wick Bath 60 G5
Stanwardine in the Fields Shrops 149 E8
Stanwardine in the Wood Shrops 149 D8
Stanway Essex 107 G8
  Glos 99 E11
Stanway Green Essex 107 G8
  Suff 126 C4
Stanwell Sur 66 E5
Stanwell Moor Sur 66 E5
Stanwick Northants 121 C9
Stanwick-St-John N Yorks 224 C3
Stanwix Cumb 239 F10
Stanycliffe Gtr Man 195 F11
Stanydale Shetland 313 H4
Staoinebrig W Isles 297 H3
Stape N Yorks 226 G5
Stapehill Dorset 31 G9
Stapeley Ches E 167 F11
Stapenhill Staffs 152 E5
Staple Kent 55 B9
  Som 42 F6
Staplecross E Sus 38 C3
Staple Cross Devon 27 C8
Staplefield W Sus 36 B3
Staple Fitzpaine Som 28 D3
Stapleford Cambs 123 G9
  Herts 86 B4
  Leics 154 F6
  Lincs 172 D5
  Notts 153 B9
  Wilts 46 G5
Stapleford Abbotts Essex 87 G8
Stapleford Tawney Essex 87 F8
Staplegrove Som 28 B2
Staplehay Som 28 C2
Staple Hill S Glos 61 D7
Staplehurst Kent 53 E9
Staple Lawns Som 28 D3
Staplers IoW 20 D6
Staplestreet Kent 70 G5
Stapleton Bristol 60 D6
  Cumb 240 C2
  Hereford 114 D6
  Leics 135 D8
  N Yorks 224 C5
  Shrops 131 C9
  Som 28 C6
  Som 29 C7
Stapley Som 27 E11
Staploe Beds 122 E2
Staplow Hereford 98 C3
Star Fife 287 G7
  Pembs 92 D4
  Som 43 B11

Starbotton N Yorks 213 E9
Starcross Devon 14 E5
Stareton Warks 118 C6
Stargate T&W 242 E5
Star Hill Mon 79 E7
Starkholmes Derbys 170 D4
Starling Gtr Man 195 E9
Starling's Green Essex 105 E9
Starr's Green E Sus 38 D3
Starston Norf 142 G4
Start Devon 8 G6
Startforth Durham 223 B10
Start Hill Essex 105 G10
Startley Wilts 62 C2
Startop's End Bucks 84 C6
Starveall Bristol 61 B9
Starvecrow Kent 52 D5
Statenborough Kent 55 B10
Statford St Andrew Suff 127 E7
Statham Warr 183 D11
Stathe Som 28 B5
Stathern Leics 154 C5
Station Hill Cumb 229 B11
Station Town Durham 234 D4
Statland Common Norf 141 D10
Staughton Green Cambs 122 D2
Staughton Highway Cambs 122 E2
Staunton Glos 79 C8
  Glos 98 F5
Staunton in the Vale Notts 172 G4
Staunton on Arrow Hereford 115 E7
Staunton on Wye Hereford 97 B7
Staupes N Yorks 205 B10
Staveley Cumb 211 B7
  Cumb 221 F9
  Derbys 186 G6
  N Yorks 215 G7
Staveley-in-Cartmel Cumb 211 B7
Staverton Devon 8 C5
  Glos 99 G7
  Northants 119 E10
  Wilts 61 G11
Staverton Bridge Glos 99 G7
Stawell Som 43 F11
Stawley Som 27 C9
Staxigoe Highld 310 D7
Staxton N Yorks 217 D10
Staylittle / Penffordd-Lâs Powys 129 E7
Staynall Lancs 202 E3
Staythorpe Notts 172 E3
Stead W Yorks 205 D8
Steam Mills Glos 79 B10
Stean N Yorks 213 E11
Steanbow Som 44 F5
Stearsby N Yorks 216 E2
Steart Som 29 B9
  Som 43 D9
  W Yorks 205 F8
Stebbing Essex 106 G2
Stebbing Green Essex 106 G3
Stechford W Mid 134 F2
Stedham W Sus 34 C5
Stede Quarter Kent 53 F11
Steel Northumb 241 D10
  Northumb 251 G9
Steel Bank S Yorks 186 D4
Steel Cross E Sus 52 G4
Steelend Fife 279 C10
Steele Road Borders 250 E2
Steeleroad-end Borders 250 E2
Steel Green Cumb 210 D3
Steen's Bridge Hereford 115 F11
Steep Hants 34 B2
Steephill IoW 21 F7
Steep Lane W Yorks 196 C4
Steeple Dorset 18 E4
  Essex 88 E6
Steeple Ashton Wilts 46 B2
Steeple Aston Oxon 101 F9
Steeple Barton Oxon 101 G8
Steeple Bumpstead Essex 106 C3
Steeple Claydon Bucks 102 F3
Steeple Gidding Cambs 138 G2
Steeple Langford Wilts 46 F5
Steeple Morden Cambs 104 C5
Steep Marsh Hants 34 B3
Steeraway Telford 132 B3
Steeton W Yorks 204 E6
Stein Highld 298 D2
Steinmanhill Aberds 303 E7
Stella T&W 242 E5
Stelling Minnis Kent 54 D6
Stelvio Newport 59 B9
Stembridge Som 28 C6
Stemster Highld 310 C5
Stemster Ho Highld 310 C5
Stenalees Corn 5 D10
Stenaquoy Orkney 314 C5
Stencoose Corn 4 F4
Stenhill Devon 27 E9
Stenhouse Dumfries 247 E8
  Edin 280 G4
Stenhousemuir Falk 279 E7
Stenigot Lincs 190 D3
Stennack Corn 2 B5
Stenness Shetland 312 F4
Stenscholl Highld 298 C4
Stenso Orkney 314 D3
Stenson Derbys 152 D6
Stenton E Loth 282 G2
  Fife 280 B5
Stentwood Devon 27 F10
Stenwith Lincs 154 B6
Stepaside Corn 5 F9
  Pembs 73 D10
  Powys 129 F11
Stepping Hill Gtr Man 184 D6
Steppingley C Beds 103 D10
Stepps N Lnrk 268 B3
Sterndale Moor Derbys 169 B10
Sternfield Suff 127 E7
Sterridge Devon 40 D5
Stert Wilts 46 B4
Sterte Dorset 18 C6
Stetchworth Cambs 124 F2
Stevenage Herts 104 G4
Steven's Crouch E Sus 38 D2
Stevenston N Ayrs 266 G5
Stevenstone Devon 25 D8
Steventon Hants 48 D4
  Oxon 83 G7
Steventon End Essex 105 C11
Stevington Beds 121 F9
Stewards Essex 87 D7
Steward's Green Essex 87 E7
Stewartby Beds 103 C10
Stewarton Argyll 255 F7
  E Ayrs 267 F8

Stewkley Bucks 103 E8
Stewkley Dean Bucks 102 E8
Stewley Som 28 D4
Stewton Lincs 190 E5
Steyne Cross IoW 21 D8
Steyning W Sus 35 E11
Steynton Pembs 72 D6
Stibb Corn 24 D2
Stibbard Norf 159 D9
Stibb Cross Devon 24 E6
Stibb Green Wilts 63 G8
Stibbington Cambs 137 D11
Stichill Borders 262 B6
Sticker Corn 5 E9
Stickford Lincs 174 D5
Stick Hill Kent 52 E2
Sticklepath Devon 13 C8
  Devon 40 G5
  Som 28 C4
  Som 42 F4
Sticklinch Som 44 F5
Stickling Green Essex 105 E9
Stickney Lincs 174 D4
Stiffkey Norf 177 E7
Stifford's Bridge Hereford 98 B4
Stiff Street Kent 69 G11
Stileway Som 44 E3
Stillingfleet N Yorks 207 E7
Stillington N Yorks 215 F11
  Stockton 234 G3
Stilton Cambs 138 F3
Stinchcombe Glos 80 F2
Stinsford Dorset 17 C10
Stiperstones Shrops 131 C7
Stirchley Telford 132 B4
  W Mid 133 G11
Stirling Aberds 303 E11
  Stirl 278 C5
Stirtloe Cambs 122 D3
Stirton N Yorks 204 C5
Stisted Essex 106 G5
Stitchcombe Wilts 63 F8
Stitchin's Hill Worcs 116 G5
Stithians Corn 2 B6
Stittenham Highld 300 B6
Stivichall W Mid 118 B6
Stixwould Lincs 173 B11
Stoak Ches W 182 G6
Stobhill Northumb 252 G6
Stobhillgate Northumb 252 F6
Stobo Borders 260 B6
Stoborough Dorset 18 D4
Stoborough Green Dorset 18 D4
Stobs Castle Borders 250 B2
Stobshiel E Loth 271 C8
Stobswood Northumb 252 E6
Stock Essex 87 F11
  Lancs 204 D3
  N Som 60 G3
Stockbridge Hants 47 G11
  S Yorks 198 F5
  W Sus 22 C5
  W Yorks 205 E8
Stockbridge Village Mers 182 C6
Stockbury Kent 69 G10
Stockcross W Berks 64 F2
Stockdalewath Cumb 230 C4
Stockend Glos 80 D4
Stocker's Head Kent 54 C3
Stockerston Leics 136 D6
Stockfield W Mid 134 G2
Stock Green Worcs 117 F9
Stockheath Hants 22 B2
Stock Hill Suff 125 C10
Stockholes Turbary N Lincs 199 F10
Stockiemuir Stirl 277 E10
Stocking Hereford 98 E2
Stockingford Warks 134 E6
Stocking Green Essex 105 E9
Stocking Pelham Herts 105 F9
Stockland Bristol Som 43 E8
Stockland Green Kent 52 E5
  W Mid 133 E11
Stockleigh English Devon 26 F6
Stockleigh Pomeroy Devon 26 G5
Stockley Wilts 62 E4
Stocklinch Som 28 D5
Stockport Gtr Man 184 C5
Stocksbridge S Yorks 186 B3
Stocksfield Northumb 242 E2
Stock's Green Kent 52 D5
Stockstreet Essex 106 G6
Stockton Hereford 115 E10
  Norf 143 E7
  Shrops 130 C6
  Shrops 132 D5
  Telford 150 F4
  Warks 119 E8
  Wilts 46 F3
Stockton Brook Staffs 168 E6
Stockton Heath Warr 183 D10
Stockton-on-Tees Stockton 225 B8
Stockton on Teme Worcs 116 D4
Stockton on the Forest York 207 B8
Stockwell Devon 27 G7
  Glos 80 C6
  London 67 D10
Stockwell End W Mid 133 C7
Stockwell Heath Staffs 151 E11
Stockwitch Cross Som 29 C9
Stockwood Bristol 60 F6
  Dorset 29 F9
Stock Wood Worcs 117 F10
Stockwood Vale Bath 60 F6
Stodday Lancs 211 G9
Stodmarsh Kent 71 G8
Stody Norf 159 C11
Stoer Highld 307 G5
Stoford Som 29 E9
  Wilts 46 G5
Stoford Water Devon 27 F9
Stogumber Som 42 F5
Stogursey Som 43 E8
Stoke Devon 24 C2
  Hants 22 C2
  Hants 48 C3
  Medway 69 D10
  Plym 7 D9
  Suff 108 C3
Stoke Abbott Dorset 29 G7
Stoke Aldermoor W Mid 119 B8
Stoke Ash Suff 126 C2
Stoke Bardolph Notts 171 G11
Stoke Bishop Bristol 60 D5
Stoke Bliss Worcs 116 E3
Stoke Bruerne Northants 102 B4
Stoke by Clare Suff 106 C4
Stoke-by-Nayland Suff 107 B10

Stoke Canon Devon....14 B4
Stoke Charity Hants....48 F3
Stoke Climsland Corn....12 G3
Stoke Common Hants....33 C7
Stoke Cross Hereford....116 G2
Stoke D'Abernon Sur....50 B6
Stoke Doyle Northants....137 F10
Stoke Dry Rutland....137 D7
Stoke Edith Hereford....98 C2
Stoke End Warks....134 D3
Stoke Farthing Wilts....31 B9
Stoke Ferry Norf....140 D4
Stoke Fleming Devon....9 F7
Stokeford Dorset....18 D3
Stoke Gabriel Devon....9 E6
Stoke Gifford S Glos....60 D6
Stoke Goldington M Keynes....102 B4
Stokegorse Shrops....131 G11
Stoke Green Bucks....66 C3
Stokeham Notts....188 F3
Stoke Hammond Bucks....103 F7
Stoke Heath Shrops....150 D3
W Mid....135 G7
Worcs....117 D8
Stoke Hill Devon....14 C4
Hereford....98 C2
Stoke Holy Cross Norf....142 C4
Stokeinteignhead Devon....14 G4
Stoke Lacy Hereford....98 B2
Stoke Lane Hereford....116 G2
Stoke Lyne Oxon....101 F11
Stoke Mandeville Bucks....84 F3
Stokenchurch Bucks....84 F3
Stoke Newington London....67 B10
Stokenham Devon....8 G6
Stoke on Tern Shrops....150 D2
Stoke-on-Trent Stoke....168 F5
Stoke Orchard Glos....99 F8
Stoke Park Bucks....108 C3
Stoke Poges Bucks....66 C3
Stoke Pound Worcs....117 D9
Stoke Prior Hereford....115 F10
Worcs....117 D8
Stoke Rivers Devon....40 F6
Stoke Rochford Lincs....155 D8
Stoke Row Oxon....65 C7
Stoke St Gregory Som....28 B4
Stoke St Mary Som....28 C3
Stoke St Michael Som....45 D7
Stoke St Milborough Shrops....131 G11
Stokesay Shrops....131 G8
Stokesby Norf....161 G8
Stokesley N Yorks....225 D10
Stoke sub Hamdon Som....29 D7
Stoke Talmage Oxon....83 F11
Stoke Trister Som....30 B2
Stoke Wake Dorset....30 F3
Stoke Water Dorset....29 G7
Stoke Wharf Worcs....117 D9
Stokoe Northumb....250 F6
Stolford Som....43 D8
Stondon Massey Essex....87 E9
Stone Bucks....84 C3
Glos....79 F11
Kent....38 B6
Kent....68 E5
Som....44 B5
Staffs....151 C8
S Yorks....187 D9
Worcs....117 B7
W Mid....134 G4
Stonea Cambs....139 E9
Stoneacton Shrops....131 E10
Stone Allerton Som....44 C2
Ston Easton Som....44 C6
Stonebow Worcs....99 B8
Stonebridge Essex....70 B2
London....67 C8
Norf....141 E8
N Som....43 B11
Sur....51 D7
W Mid....134 G4
Stone Bridge Corner Pboro....138 C5
Stonebridge Green Kent....54 D2
Stonebroom Derbys....170 D6
Stonebyres Holdings S Lnrk....268 G6
Stone Chair W Yorks....196 B6
Stoneclough Gtr Man....195 F9
Stonecombe Devon....40 E6
Stone Cross E Sus....23 E10
E Sus....37 B8
E Sus....52 G6
Kent....52 F4
Kent....54 F4
Kent....55 B10
W Mid....133 E10
Stonecrouch Kent....53 G7
Stonedge Borders....250 B3
Stone-edge Batch N Som....60 E3
Stoneferry Hull....209 G8
Stonefield Argyll....289 F11
S Lnrk....268 D3
Staffs....151 C7
Stonefield Castle Hotel Argyll....275 F9
Stonegate E Sus....37 B11
N Yorks....226 D5
Stonegrave N Yorks....216 D3
Stonegravels Derbys....186 G5
Stonehall Kent....55 D9
Worcs....99 B7
Stonehaugh Northumb....241 B7
Stonehaven Aberds....293 E10
Stone Head N Yorks....204 E4
Stone Heath Staffs....151 B9
Stonehill Sur....66 F4
Stone Hill Kent....54 D2
Kent....54 F5
S Glos....60 E6
S Yorks....199 F7
Stonehills Hants....33 G7
Stonehouse Aberds....303 F8
Glos....80 D4
Northumb....240 F5
Plym....7 E9
S Lnrk....268 F5
Stone House Cumb....212 B5
Stonehouses Staffs....169 G7
Stone in Oxney Kent....38 B6
Stoneleigh London....67 G8
Warks....118 C6
Stoneley Green Ches E....167 E10
Stonely Cambs....122 D2
Stonepits Worcs....117 F10
Stonequarry W Sus....52 F2
Stone Raise Cumb....230 B4
Stoner Hill Hants....34 B2
Stonesby Leics....154 E6
Stonesfield Oxon....82 B5
Stones Green Essex....108 F3
Stone Street Kent....52 C5
Suff....107 D9
Suff....143 G7

Stoneton Warks....119 G9
Stonewells Moray....302 C2
Stonewood Kent....68 E5
Stoneyard Green Hereford....98 C4
Stoneybank E Loth....280 G6
Stoneybreck Shetland....313 N2
Stoneyburn W Loth....269 C9
Stoneycombe Devon....9 B7
Stoneycroft Mers....182 C5
Stoney Cross Hants....32 E3
Stoneyfield Gtr Man....195 E11
Moray....301 D11
Stoneyford Derbys....170 F6
Devon....27 F8
Stoneygate Aberds....303 F10
Leicester....136 C2
Stoney Hill Worcs....117 C9
Stoneyhills Essex....88 F6
Stoneykirk Dumfries....236 D2
Stoneylane Shrops....115 B11
Stoney Middleton Derbys....186 F2
Stoney Royd W Yorks....196 C5
Stoney Stanton Leics....135 E9
Stoney Stoke Som....45 F7
Stoney Stratton Som....45 F7
Stoney Stretton Shrops....131 B7
Stonewood Aberdeen....293 B10
Stonganess Shetland....312 C7
Stonham Aspal Suff....126 F3
Stonnall Staffs....133 C11
Stonor Oxon....65 B8
Stonton Wyville Leics....136 D4
Stony Batter Hants....32 B3
Stony Cross Devon....25 B8
Hereford....98 B4
Hereford....115 D10
Stony Dale Notts....172 G2
Stonyfield Highld....300 B6
Stonyford Hants....32 D4
Stony Gate T&W....243 G9
Stony Green Bucks....84 F5
Stony Heap Durham....242 G4
Stony Heath Hants....48 B5
Stony Houghton Derbys....171 B7
Stony Knaps Dorset....28 G5
Stonyland Devon....25 B8
Stony Littleton Bath....45 B8
Stonymarsh Hants....32 C4
Stony Stratford M Keynes....102 C5
Stoodleigh Devon....26 D6
Stop-and-Call Pembs....91 D8
Stopes S Yorks....186 D3
Stopgate Devon....28 F2
Stopham W Sus....35 D8
Stopper Lane Lancs....204 D2
Stopsley Luton....104 G2
Stoptide Corn....10 F4
Stores Corner Suff....109 B7
Storeton Mers....182 E4
Storiths N Yorks....205 C7
Stormontfield Perth....286 E5
Stormore Wilts....45 D10
Stornoway W Isles....304 E6
Storridge Hereford....98 B4
Storrington W Sus....35 E9
Storrs Cumb....221 G7
S Yorks....186 D3
Storth Cumb....211 C9
Stotfield Moray....302 B2
Stotfold C Beds....104 D4
Stottesdon Shrops....132 G3
Stoughton Leics....136 C2
Sur....50 C3
W Sus....34 E4
Stoughton Cross Som....44 D2
Stoul Highld....295 F9
Stoulton Worcs....99 B8
Stourbridge W Mid....133 G8
Stourpaine Dorset....30 F5
Stourport on Severn Worcs....116 C6
Stour Provost Dorset....30 C3
Stour Row Dorset....30 C4
Stourton Staffs....133 F7
Warks....100 D5
Wilts....45 G9
N Yorks....226 E4
Stourton Caundle Dorset....30 D2
Stourton Hill Warks....100 D6
Stout Som....44 G2
Stove Orkney....314 C6
Shetland....313 L6
Stoven Suff....143 G8
Stow Borders....271 G9
Lincs....155 B11
Lincs....188 E5
Stow Bardolph Norf....140 B2
Stow Bedon Norf....141 D9
Stowbridge Norf....140 B2
Stow cum Quy Cambs....123 E10
Stowe Glos....79 D9
Hereford....96 B5
Lincs....156 G2
Shrops....114 C6
Staffs....152 G2
Stowe-by-Chartley Staffs....151 D10
Stowe Green Glos....79 D9
Stowell Glos....81 C9
Som....29 C11
Stowey Bath....44 B5
Stowford Devon....12 B4
Devon....12 D4
Devon....24 E3
Devon....25 B10
Devon....41 E7
Stowgate Lincs....156 G3
Stowlangtoft Suff....125 D9
Stow Longa Cambs....122 C2
Stow Maries Essex....88 F4
Stowmarket Suff....125 F11
Stow-on-the-Wold Glos....100 F3
Stow Park Newport....59 B10
Stowting Kent....54 E6
Stowting Common Kent....54 E6
Stowting Court Kent....54 E6
Stowupland Suff....125 F11
Straad Argyll....275 G11
Strachan Aberds....293 D8
Stradbroke Suff....126 C4
Stradishall Suff....124 G4
Stradsett Norf....140 C3
Stragglethorpe Lincs....172 E6
Straid S Ayrs....244 E4
Straight Soley Wilts....63 E10
Straith Dumfries....247 F8
Straiton Edin....270 B5
S Ayrs....245 C9
Straloch Aberds....303 G8
Perth....292 G2
Stramshall Staffs....151 B11
Strand Glos....80 C2

London....67 C10
Strands Cumb....210 C3
Strang IoM....192 E4
Strangeways Gtr Man....184 B4
Strangford Hereford....97 F11
Stranghow Redcar....226 B3
Strangways Wilts....46 E4
Stranog Aberds....293 D10
Stranraer Dumfries....236 C2
Strata Florida Ceredig....112 C4
Stratfield Mortimer W Berks....65 G7
Stratfield Saye Hants....65 G7
Stratfield Turgis Hants....49 B7
Stratford C Beds....104 B3
Glos....99 D7
London....67 C11
Stratford Marsh London....67 C11
Stratford New Town London....67 C11
Stratford St Andrew Suff....127 E7
Stratford St Mary Suff....107 E10
Stratford Sub Castle Wilts....46 F6
Stratford Tony Wilts....31 B9
Stratford-upon-Avon Warks....118 F3
Strath Highld....299 B7
Highld....310 D6
Strathallan Castle Perth....286 F3
Strathan Highld....295 F11
Highld....307 G5
Highld....308 C5
Strathan Skerray Highld....308 C6
Strathaven S Lnrk....268 G4
Strathavon Lo Moray....301 G11
Strathblane Stirl....277 F11
Strathcanaird Highld....307 J6
Strathcarron Highld....299 E9
Strathcoil Argyll....289 F8
Strathcoul Highld....310 D5
Strathdon Aberds....292 B5
Strathellie Aberds....303 C10
Strathgarve Lodge Highld....300 C4
Strathkinness Fife....287 F8
Strathmashie House Highld....291 D7
Strathmiglo Fife....286 F6
Strathmore Lodge Highld....310 E5
Strathpeffer Highld....300 D4
Strathrannoch Highld....300 B3
Strathtay Perth....286 B3
Strathvaich Lodge Highld....300 B3
Strathwhillan N Ayrs....256 B2
Strathy Highld....300 B6
Highld....310 C2
Strathyre Stirl....285 F9
Stratton Corn....24 F2
Dorset....17 C9
Glos....81 E8
Stratton Audley Oxon....102 F2
Stratton Chase Bucks....85 G7
Stratton-on-the-Fosse Som....45 C7
Stratton St Margaret Swindon....63 B7
Stratton St Michael Norf....142 E4
Stratton Strawless Norf....160 E4
Stravithie Fife....287 F9
Strawberry Bank Cumb....211 B8
Strawberry Hill E Sus....52 F5
London....67 E7
W Yorks....198 C2
Street E Sus....36 E6
Som....34 E4
Suff....143 G8
N Yorks....226 C4
Street Ash Som....28 E3
Street Ashton Warks....135 G9
Street Dinas Shrops....148 B6
Street End Hants....33 D9
Kent....54 C6
W Sus....34 E4
Street Gate T&W....242 F6
Streethay Staffs....152 G2
Streethouse W Yorks....197 C11
Street Houses N Yorks....206 D6
Streetlam N Yorks....224 F6
Streetly W Mid....133 D11
Street Lydan Wrex....149 B8
Streetly End Cambs....106 B2
Street of Kincardine Highld....291 B11
Street on the Fosse Som....44 F6
Strefford Shrops....131 G9
Strelley Notts....171 G8
Strensall York....216 G2
Strensham Worcs....99 C8
Stretch Down Devon....26 E4
Stretcholt Som....43 E9
Strete Devon....8 F6
Stretford Gtr Man....184 C4
Hereford....97 B9
Stretford Court Hereford....115 F8
Strethall Essex....105 D9
Stretham Cambs....123 C10
Strettington W Sus....22 B5
Stretton Ches W....166 E6
Derbys....170 C5
Rutland....155 F8
Staffs....151 G7
Staffs....152 D5
Warr....183 E10
Stretton en le Field Leics....152 G6
Stretton Grandison Hereford....98 C2
Stretton-on-Dunsmore Warks....119 C8
Stretton-on-Fosse Warks....100 D4
Stretton Sugwas Hereford....97 C9
Stretton under Fosse Warks....135 G8
Stretton Westwood Shrops....131 D11
Strichen Aberds....303 D9
Strines Gtr Man....185 D7
Stringston Som....43 E7
Strixton Northants....121 E8
Stroat Glos....79 F9
Strode Devon....60 G4
Strom Shetland....313 J5
Stromeferry Highld....295 B10
Stromemore Highld....295 B10
Stromness Orkney....314 F2

Stronaba Highld....290 E4
Stronachlachar Stirl....285 F8
Stronachullin Lodge Argyll....275 F9
Stronchreggan Highld....290 F2
Stronchrubie Highld....307 H7
Strone Argyll....255 F7
Argyll....274 G6
Highld....290 E3
Highld....290 F5
Highld....291 D9
Inyclyd....276 G5
Stronenaba Highld....290 E4
Stroneskar Argyll....275 C9
Stronmachair Stirl....285 G8
Stronmilchan Argyll....284 E5
Stronord Dumfries....236 C6
Stronsaul Argyll....276 F2
Strontian Highld....289 C10
Stronvar Stirl....285 E9
Strood Kent....53 G11
Medway....69 F8
Strood Green Sur....51 B8
Sur....35 C8
Sur....50 G6
W Sus....35 D7
Strothers Dale Northumb....241 F11
Stroud Glos....80 D4
Hants....34 C2
Stroude Sur....66 F4
Strouden Bmouth....19 C8
Stroud Green Essex....88 G5
Glos....80 D4
London....67 B10
Stroul Argyll....276 E4
Stroupster Highld....310 C7
Stroxton Lincs....155 C8
Stroxworthy Devon....24 D4
Struan Highld....294 B5
Perth....291 G10
Strubby Lincs....191 E7
Strugg's Heath Wilts....56 B5
Strumpshaw Norf....142 B6
Strutherhill S Lnrk....268 F5
Struthers Fife....287 G7
Struy Highld....300 F3
Stryd Anglesey....178 E2
Stryd y Facsen Anglesey....178 E4
Stryt-issa Wrex....166 F3
Stuartfield Aberds....303 E9
Stubb Norf....161 E8
Stubbermere W Sus....22 B3
Stubber's Green W Mid....133 C10
Stubbings Windsor....65 C10
Stubbing's Green Suff....125 C11
Stubbington Hants....33 G8
Stubbins Lancs....195 D9
Lancs....202 E6
Stubble Green Cumb....219 F11
Stubbs Cross Kent....54 F3
Stubbs Green Norf....143 D7
Stubb's Green Norf....142 D5
Stubhampton Dorset....30 E6
Stubshaw Cross Gtr Man....194 G5
Stubton Lincs....172 F5
Stubwood Staffs....151 B11
Stuckgowan Argyll....285 G7
Stuckton Hants....31 E11
Studdal Kent....55 D10
Studd Hill Kent....71 F7
Studfold N Yorks....212 E6
Stud Green Ches E....168 C2
Windsor....65 D11
Studham C Beds....85 B8
Studland Dorset....18 E6
Studley Warks....117 E11
Wilts....62 E3
Studley Green Bucks....84 F3
Wilts....45 B10
Studley Roger N Yorks....214 E5
Studley Royal N Yorks....214 E5
Stump Cross Essex....105 C10
Stumps Cross Glos....99 E11
Stuntney Cambs....123 B11
Stunts Green E Sus....23 C10
Sturbridge Staffs....150 C6
Sturford Wilts....45 E10
Sturgate Lincs....188 D5
Sturmer Essex....106 C3
Sturminster Common Dorset....30 E3
Sturminster Marshall Dorset....31 G7
Sturminster Newton Dorset....30 E3
Sturry Kent....71 G7
Sturston Derbys....170 F2
Sturton N Lincs....200 G3
Sturton by Stow Lincs....188 E5
Sturton le Steeple Notts....188 E3
Stuston Suff....126 B2
Stutton N Yorks....206 E5
Suff....108 E3
Styal Ches E....184 E4
Styants Bottom Kent....52 B5
Stydd Lancs....203 F9
Styrrup Notts....187 C10
Suainebost W Isles....304 B6
Suardail W Isles....304 E6
Succoth Aberds....302 F4
Argyll....284 G6
Suckley Worcs....116 G4
Suckley Green Worcs....116 G4
Suckley Knowl Worcs....116 G4
Suckquoy Orkney....314 H4
Sucksted Green Essex....105 F11
Sudborough Northants....137 G9
Sudbourne Suff....127 G8
Sudbrook Lincs....173 G7
Mon....60 B4
Sudbrooke Lincs....189 F8
Sudbury Derbys....152 C3
London....67 C7
Suff....107 C7
W Sus....35 D7
Sudden Gtr Man....195 E11
Suddie Highld....300 D6
Sudgrove Glos....80 D6
Suffield Norf....160 C4
N Yorks....227 G9
Sugnall Staffs....150 C5
Sugwas Pool Hereford....97 C9
Suisnish Highld....295 C7
Suladale Highld....298 D3
Sulaisiadar W Isles....304 E7
Sulby IoM....192 C4
Sulgrave Northants....101 B11
Sulham W Berks....64 D6
Sulhamstead W Berks....64 F6
Sulhamstead Abbots W Berks....64 F6
Sulhamstead Bannister Upper End W Berks....64 F6

Sulhamstead W Berks....64 F6
Sulland Orkney....314 B6
Sullington W Sus....35 E9
Sullington Warren W Sus....35 E9
Sullom Shetland....312 F5
Sullom Voe Oil Terminal Shetland....312 F5
Sully V Glam....59 F7
Sumburgh Shetland....313 N6
Summerbridge N Yorks....214 G4
Summer Bridge N Yorks....214 G4
Summercourt Corn....5 D7
Summerfield Kent....55 B9
Norf....158 B5
Worcs....116 C6
Summerfield Park W Mid....133 F10
Summergangs Hull....209 G8
Summer Heath Bucks....84 G2
Summerhill Newport....59 B10
Pembs....73 D11
Staffs....133 B11
Telford....150 F4
W Mid....116 B6
Wrex....166 E4
Summer Hill E Sus....23 D9
W Mid....133 E9
Summerhouse Darl....224 B4
Summerlands Cumb....211 B10
Som....29 D8
Summerleaze Mon....60 B2
Summerley Derbys....186 F5
Summerscales N Yorks....205 C8
Summerseat Gtr Man....195 E9
Summerston Glasgow....277 G11
Summerstown Som....102 G3
Summertown Oxon....83 D8
Summit Gtr Man....195 E10
Gtr Man....196 D2
Gtr Man....196 D2
Sunbrick Cumb....210 E5
Sunbury Common Sur....66 F5
Sunbury-on-Thames Sur....66 F5
Sundayshill S Glos....79 G11
Sundaywell Dumfries....247 G8
Sunderland Argyll....274 G3
Cumb....229 D9
Lancs....202 B4
T&W....243 F9
Sunderland Bridge Durham....233 D11
Sundhope Borders....261 D8
Sundon Park Luton....103 F11
Sundridge Kent....52 B3
London....68 E2
Sun Green Gtr Man....185 B7
Sunhill Glos....81 E10
Sunipol Argyll....288 D5
Sunken Marsh Essex....69 C10
Sunk Island E Yorks....201 D9
Sunningdale Windsor....66 F3
Sunninghill Windsor....66 F3
Sunningwell Oxon....83 E7
Sunniside Durham....233 D8
T&W....242 F6
Sunny Bank Gtr Man....195 F10
Sunny Bower Lancs....203 G10
Sunnybrow Durham....233 E9
Sunnyfields S Yorks....198 F4
Sunny Hill Derby....152 C6
Sunnyhurst Blkburn....195 C7
Sunnylaw Stirl....278 B5
Sunnymead Oxon....83 D8
Sunnymede Essex....87 G11
Sunnyside S Yorks....187 C7
W Sus....51 F11
Sunset Hereford....114 F6
Sunton Wilts....47 C8
Surbiton London....67 F7
Surby IoM....192 E3
Surfleet Lincs....156 D5
Surfleet Seas End Lincs....156 D5
Surlingham Norf....142 B6
Surrex Essex....107 G7
Suspension Bridge Norf....139 E10
Sustead Norf....160 B3
Susworth Lincs....199 G10
Sutcombe Devon....24 E4
Sutcombemill Devon....24 E4
Sutherland Grove Argyll....289 E11
Suton Norf....141 D11
Sutors of Cromarty Highld....301 C8
Sutterby Lincs....190 G5
Sutterton Lincs....156 B5
Sutterton Dowdyke Lincs....156 C5
Sutton Bucks....66 D4
Cambs....123 B8
C Beds....104 B4
Devon....8 G4
Devon....23 F7
London....67 G9
Kent....55 D10
Mers....183 C8
N Som....44 B4
Norf....161 E7
Notts....154 B5
Notts....187 G11
N Yorks....198 B3
Pboro....137 D11
Pembs....72 B6
Shrops....132 F4
Shrops....149 D7
Shrops....149 G10
Shrops....150 C3
Som....29 B11
Staffs....150 E5
Suff....108 B4
Sur....50 D5
S Yorks....198 E5
W Sus....35 D7
Sutton Abinger Sur....50 D6
Sutton at Hone Kent....68 E5
Sutton Bassett Northants....136 E5
Sutton Benger Wilts....62 D2
Sutton Bingham Som....29 E8
Sutton Bonington Notts....153 D10
Sutton Bridge Lincs....157 E9
Sutton Cheney Leics....135 C8
Sutton Coldfield W Mid....134 D2
Sutton Corner Lincs....157 D8
Sutton Courtenay Oxon....83 G8
Sutton Crosses Lincs....157 D8
Sutton Cum Lound Notts....187 E11
Sutton End W Sus....35 D7
Sutton Forest Side Notts....171 D8
Sutton Gault Cambs....123 B8

Sutton Green Ches W....182 G5
Sur....50 C4
Wrex....166 F6
Sutton Hall Shrops....132 C4
Sutton Heath Mers....183 C8
Sutton Hill Telford....132 C4
Sutton Holms Dorset....31 F9
Sutton Howgrave N Yorks....214 D6
Sutton in Ashfield Notts....171 D7
Sutton-in-Craven N Yorks....204 E6
Sutton Ings Hull....209 G8
Sutton in the Elms Leics....135 E10
Sutton Lakes Hereford....97 C11
Sutton Lane Ends Ches E....184 G6
Sutton Leach Mers....183 C8
Sutton Maddock Shrops....132 C4
Sutton Mallet Som....43 F11
Sutton Mandeville Wilts....31 B7
Sutton Manor Mers....183 C8
Sutton Marsh Hereford....97 C10
Sutton Mill N Yorks....204 E6
Sutton Montis Som....29 C10
Sutton on Hull Hull....209 G8
Sutton on Sea Lincs....191 E8
Sutton-on-the-Forest N Yorks....215 G11
Sutton on the Hill Derbys....152 C4
Sutton on Trent Notts....172 B3
Sutton Poyntz Dorset....17 E10
Sutton Row Wilts....31 B7
Sutton St Edmund Lincs....157 G7
Sutton St James Lincs....157 F7
Sutton St Michael Hereford....97 B10
Sutton St Nicholas Hereford....97 B10
Sutton Scarsdale Derbys....170 B6
Sutton Scotney Hants....48 F3
Sutton Street Suff....108 C6
Sutton under Brailes Warks....100 D6
Sutton under Whitestonecliffe N Yorks....215 C9
Sutton upon Derwent E Yorks....207 D10
Sutton Valence Kent....53 D10
Sutton Veny Wilts....45 E11
Sutton Waldron Dorset....30 D5
Sutton Weaver Ches W....183 F8
Sutton Wick Bath....44 B5
Oxon....83 G7
Swaby Lincs....190 F5
Swadlincote Derbys....152 F6
Swaffham Norf....140 B5
Swaffham Bulbeck Cambs....123 E11
Swaffham Prior Cambs....123 E11
Swafield Norf....160 C5
Swaile's Green E Sus....38 C3
Swainby N Yorks....225 E9
Swain House W Yorks....205 F9
Swainshill Hereford....97 C9
Swainsthorpe Norf....142 C4
Swainswick Bath....61 F9
Swalcliffe Oxon....101 D7
Swalecliffe Kent....70 F6
Swallow Lincs....201 G7
Swallow Beck Lincs....173 B7
Swallowcliffe Wilts....31 B7
Swallowfield Wokingham....65 F8
Swallowfields Devon....8 C5
Swallowhurst Cumb....220 G2
Swallownest S Yorks....187 E7
Swallows Cross Essex....87 F10
Swampton Hants....48 C2
Swanage Dorset....18 F6
Swanbach Ches E....167 G11
Swanbister Orkney....314 F3
Swanborough Swindon....81 G11
Swan Bottom Bucks....84 D6
Swanbourne Bucks....102 F6
Swanbridge V Glam....59 F7
Swan Green Ches W....184 G2
Suff....126 C5
Swanland E Yorks....200 B4
Swanley Kent....68 F4
Swanley Bar Herts....86 E3
Swanley Village Kent....68 F4
Swanmore Hants....33 D9
IoW....21 C7
Swannay Orkney....314 D2
Swannington Leics....153 F8
Norf....160 F2
Swanpool Lincs....189 G7
Swanscombe Kent....68 E6
Swansea / Abertawe Swansea....56 C6
Swanside Mers....182 C6
Swanston Edin....270 B4
Swan Street Essex....107 F7
Swanton Abbott Norf....160 D5
Swanton Hill Norf....160 D5
Swanton Morley Norf....159 F10
Swanton Novers Norf....159 C10
Swanton Street Kent....53 B11
Swan Village W Mid....133 E9
Swanwick Derbys....170 E6
Hants....33 F8
Swanwick Green Ches E....167 F9
Swarby Lincs....173 G9
Swarcliffe W Yorks....206 F3
Swardeston Norf....142 C4
Swarister Shetland....312 E7
Swarkestone Derbys....153 D7
Swarland Northumb....252 C5
Swarraton Hants....48 F5
Swartha W Yorks....205 D7
Swarthmoor Cumb....210 D5
Swartland Orkney....314 D2
Swathwick Derbys....170 B5
Swaton Lincs....156 B3
Swavesey Cambs....123 D7
Sway Hants....19 B11
Swayfield Lincs....155 E9
Swaythling Soton....32 D6
Sweet Green Worcs....116 D2
Sweetham Devon....14 B3
Sweethaws E Sus....37 B8
Sweethay Som....28 C2
Sweetholme Cumb....221 B11
Sweethouse Corn....5 C11
Sweets Corn....11 B9
Sweetshouse Corn....5 C11
Swefling Suff....126 E6
Swell Som....28 C5
Swelling Hill Hants....49 G7
Swepstone Leics....153 F7
Swerford Oxon....101 E7
Swettenham Ches E....168 B4
Swetton N Yorks....214 E3
Swffryd Caerph....78 F2

Swiftsden E Sus....38 G2
Sur....50 C4
Wrex....166 F6
Swift's Green Kent....53 E11
Swilland Suff....126 G3
Swillbrook Lancs....202 G5
Swillington W Yorks....206 G3
Swillington Common W Yorks....206 G3
Swimbridge Devon....40 G6
Swimbridge Newland Devon....40 G6
Swinbrook Oxon....82 C3
Swincliffe N Yorks....205 B10
W Yorks....197 B8
Swincombe Devon....41 E7
Swinden N Yorks....204 C3
Swinderby Lincs....172 C5
Swindon Glos....99 G8
Staffs....133 F7
Swine E Yorks....209 F8
Swinefleet E Yorks....199 C7
Swineford S Glos....61 F7
Swineshead Beds....121 D11
Lincs....174 G2
Swineshead Bridge Lincs....174 G2
Swinethorpe Lincs....172 B5
Swiney Highld....310 F6
Swinford Leics....119 B11
Oxon....82 D6
Swingate Notts....171 G8
Swingbrow Cambs....139 F7
Swingfield Minnis Kent....55 E8
Swingfield Street Kent....55 E8
Swingleton Green Suff....107 B9
Swinhoe Northumb....264 D6
Swinhope Lincs....190 B2
Swining Shetland....312 G6
Swinister Shetland....312 E5
Shetland....313 L6
Swinithwaite N Yorks....213 B10
Swinmore Common Hereford....98 C3
Swinnie Borders....262 F4
Swinnow Moor W Yorks....205 G10
Swinscoe Staffs....169 F10
Swinside Townfoot Borders....262 F6
Swinstead Lincs....155 E10
Swinton Borders....272 F6
Glasgow....268 C3
Gtr Man....195 G9
N Yorks....214 D4
N Yorks....216 E5
S Yorks....186 B6
Swinton Bridge S Yorks....187 B7
Swinton Hill Borders....272 F6
Swintonmill Borders....272 F6
Swinton Park Gtr Man....195 G9
Swiss Valley Carms....75 E8
Swithland Leics....153 G10
Swordale Highld....300 C5
Swordland Highld....295 F9
Swordly Highld....308 C7
Sworton Heath Ches E....183 E11
Swyddffynnon Ceredig....112 D3
Swynnerton Staffs....151 B7
Swyre Dorset....16 C6
Sycamore Devon....28 F3
Sychdyn / Soughton Flint....166 B2
Sychtyn Powys....129 B9
Sydallt Wrex....166 D4
Syde Glos....81 C7
Sydenham London....67 E11
Oxon....84 E2
Som....43 F10
Sydenham Damerel Devon....12 F4
Syderstone Norf....158 C6
Sydling St Nicholas Dorset....17 B8
Sydmonton Hants....48 B3
Sydney Ches E....168 D2
Syerston Notts....172 F2
Syke Gtr Man....195 D11
Sykehouse S Yorks....198 D6
Sykes Lancs....203 C8
Syleham Suff....126 B4
Sylen Carms....75 D8
Symbister Shetland....313 G7
Symington Borders....271 F8
S Ayrs....257 B8
S Lnrk....259 B11
Symondsbury Dorset....16 C4
Symonds Green Herts....104 F4
Symonds Yat Hereford....79 B9
Synderford Dorset....28 G5
Synod Inn / Post Mawr Ceredig....111 G8
Synton Borders....261 E11
Synton Mains Borders....261 E11
Syreford Glos....99 G9
Syresham Northants....102 C2
Syston Leics....154 G2
Lincs....172 G6
Sytchampton Worcs....116 D6
Sytch Ho Green Shrops....132 E5
Sytch Lane Telford....150 E2
Sywell Northants....120 D6

T

Taagan Highld....299 C10
Tabley Hill Ches E....184 F2
Tabor Gwyn....146 F5
Tàbost W Isles....304 B7
Tàbost W Isles....305 G6
Tachbrook Mallory Warks....118 E6
Tacker Street Som....42 F4
Tackley Oxon....101 G9
Tacleit W Isles....304 E3
Tacolneston Norf....142 D2
Tadcaster N Yorks....206 E5
Tadden Dorset....31 G7
Taddington Derbys....185 G10
Glos....99 E11
Taddiport Devon....25 D7
Tadhill Som....45 D7
Tadley Hants....64 G4
Oxon....64 B4
Tadlow C Beds....104 B5
Tadmarton Oxon....101 D7
Tadnoll Dorset....17 D11
Tadwick Bath....61 E8
Tadworth Sur....51 B8
Tafarn-y-bach Bl Gwent....77 C10
Tafarnaubach Bl Gwent....77 C10
Tafarn-y-bwlch Pembs....91 E11
Tafarn-y-gelyn Denb....165 C11
Taff Merthyr Garden Village M Tydf....77 F10

Taff's Well Rhondda....58 C6
Tafolwern Powys....129 C7
Taharacon Neath....57 D9
Tai-bach Powys....148 D3
Taigh a Ghearraidh W Isles....296 D3
Taigh Bhalaigh W Isles....296 D3
Tai-mawr Conwy....165 G7
Tai-morfa Gwyn....144 D5
Tain Highld....309 L7
Highld....310 C6
Tai-nant Wrex....166 F3
Tainlon Gwyn....162 E6
Tairbeart W Isles....305 H3
Tai'r-Bull Powys....95 F9
Tairgwaith Neath....76 C2
Tai'r-heol Caerph....77 G10
Tai'r-ysgol Swansea....57 B7
Tai-Ucha Denb....165 D8
Takeley Essex....105 G11
Takeley Street Essex....105 G10
Talacharn / Laugharne Carms....74 C4
Talachddu Powys....95 E11
Talacre Flint....181 E10
Talardd Gwyn....147 D7
Talaton Devon....15 B7
Talbenny Pembs....72 C4
Talbot Green Rhondda....58 C4
Talbot Heath Poole....19 C7
Talbot's End S Glos....80 G2
Talbot Village Poole....19 C7
Talbot Woods Bmouth....19 C7
Tale Devon....27 G9
Talerddig Powys....129 C8
Talgarreg Ceredig....111 G8
Talgarth Powys....96 E2
Talgarth's Well Swansea....56 D2
Talisker Highld....294 B5
Talke Staffs....168 E4
Talke Pits Staffs....168 E4
Talkin Cumb....240 F3
Talladale Highld....299 B9
Talla Linnfoots Borders....260 E4
Tallaminnoch S Ayrs....245 D10
Talland Corn....6 E4
Tallarn Green Wrex....166 G6
Tallentire Cumb....229 D8
Talley Carms....94 E2
Tallington Lincs....137 B11
Talmine Highld....308 C5
Talog Carms....92 F6
Talsarn Ceredig....111 F10
Carms....94 F5
Tal-sarn Ceredig....111 F10
Talsarnau Gwyn....146 B2
Talskiddy Corn....5 B8
Talwrn Anglesey....179 F7
Wrex....166 F3
Tal-y-bont Ceredig....128 F3
Conwy....164 B3
Gwyn....145 E11
Gwyn....179 G10
Talybont-on-Usk Powys....96 G2
Tal-y-cafn Conwy....180 G3
Tal-y-coed Mon....78 B6
Talygarn Rhondda....58 C4
Talyllyn Powys....96 F2
Tal-y-llyn Gwyn....128 B4
Tal-y-wern Powys....128 C6
Tamanabhagh W Isles....304 F2
Tame Bridge N Yorks....225 D10
Tamer Lane End Gtr Man....194 G6
Tamerton Foliot Plym....7 C9
Tame Water Gtr Man....196 F3
Tamfourhill Falk....279 E7
Tamworth Staffs....134 C4
Tamworth Green Lincs....174 G5
Tancred N Yorks....206 B5
Tandem W Yorks....197 D7
Tanden Kent....54 F2
Tandlehill Renfs....267 C8
Tandridge Sur....51 C11
Tanerdy Carms....93 G8
Tanfield Durham....242 F5
Tanfield Lea Durham....242 G5
Tang N Yorks....205 B10
Tangasdal W Isles....297 M2
Tang Hall York....207 C8
Tangiers Pembs....73 B7
Tangley Hants....47 C10
Tanglwst Carms....92 E6
Tangmere W Sus....22 B6
Tangwick Shetland....312 F4
Tangy Argyll....255 E7
Tan Hills Durham....233 B11
Tan Hinon Powys....129 F7
Tanhouse Lancs....194 F3
Tanis Wilts....62 G3
Tankersley S Yorks....197 G10
Tankerton Kent....70 F6
Tanlan Flint....181 E10
Tan-lan Conwy....164 C3
Gwyn....163 F10
Tanlan Banks Flint....181 E10
Tannach Highld....310 E7
Tannachie Aberds....293 E9
Tannadice Angus....287 B8
Tanner's Green Worcs....117 C11
Tannington Suff....126 D4
Tannington Place Suff....126 D4
Tannochside N Lnrk....268 C4
Tan Office Suff....126 E2
Tan Office Green Suff....124 F5
Tansley Derbys....170 D4
Tansley Hill W Mid....133 F9
Tansley Knoll Derbys....170 C4
Tansor Northants....137 E11
Tanterton Lancs....202 G6
Tantobie Durham....242 G5
Tanton N Yorks....225 C10
Tanwood Worcs....117 C8
Tanworth-in-Arden Warks....118 C2
Tan-y-bwlch Gwyn....163 G11
Tanyfron Wrex....166 E3
Tan-y-fron Conwy....165 D7
Tan-y-graig Anglesey....179 F8
Gwyn....144 B6
Tangysiau Gwyn....163 F11
Tanygrisiau Gwyn....163 F11
Tanygroes Ceredig....92 B5
Tan-y-pistyll Powys....147 D11
Tan-yr-allt Denb....181 E9
Gwyn....163 E7
Tanyrhydiau Ceredig....112 D4
Taobh a Chaolais W Isles....297 K3
Taobh a Deas Loch Aineort W Isles....297 J3
Taobh a Thuath Loch Aineort W Isles....297 J3

Taobh a Tuath Loch
Baghasdail W Isles 297 J3
Taobh Siar W Isles 305 H3
Taobh Tuath W Isles 296 C5
Taplow Bucks 66 C2
Tapnage Hants 33 E9
Tapton Derbys 186 G5
Tapton Hill S Yorks 186 G5
Tarbat Ho Highld 301 B7
Tarbert Argyll 255 B7
  Argyll 275 E7
  Argyll 275 G8
Tarbet Argyll 285 C11
  Highld 295 F9
  Highld 306 E6
Tarbock Green Mers 183 D7
Tarbolton S Ayrs 257 D10
Tarbrax S Lnrk 269 D10
Tardebigge Worcs 117 D10
Tardy Gate Lancs 194 B4
Tarfside Angus 292 F6
Tarland Aberds 292 C6
Tarleton Lancs 194 C3
Tarleton Moss Lancs 194 C3
Tarlogie Highld 309 L7
Tarlscough Lancs 194 E2
Tarlton Glos 81 F7
Tarn W Yorks 205 F9
Tarnbrook Lancs 203 B7
Tarnock Som 43 C11
Tarns Cumb 229 B8
Tarnside Cumb 221 G8
Tarporley Ches W 167 C9
Tarpots Essex 69 B9
Tarr Som 42 G6
Tarraby Cumb 239 F10
Tarrant Crawford Dorset 30 E6
Tarrant Gunville Dorset 30 E6
Tarrant Hinton Dorset 30 E6
Tarrant Keyneston
  Dorset 30 G6
Tarrant Launceston
  Dorset 30 F6
Tarrant Monkton Dorset 30 F6
Tarrant Rawston Dorset 30 F6
Tarrant Rushton Dorset 30 F6
Tarrel Highld 311 L2
Tarring Neville E Sus 36 G6
Tarrington Hereford 98 C2
Tarrington Common
  Hereford 98 D2
Tarryblake Ho Moray 302 E5
Tarsappie Perth 286 E5
Tarskavaig Highld 295 E7
Tarts Hill Shrops 149 B8
Tarves Aberds 303 F8
Tarvie Highld 300 D4
  Perth 292 G2
Tarvin Ches W 167 B7
Tarvin Sands Ches W 167 B7
Tasburgh Norf 142 D4
Tasley Shrops 132 E3
Taston Oxon 101 G7
Tat Bank W Mid 133 F9
Tatenhill Staffs 152 E4
Tatenhill Common
  Staffs 152 E3
Tathall End M Keynes 102 B6
Tatham Lancs 212 F2
Tathwell Lincs 190 E4
Tatling End Bucks 66 B4
Tatsfield Sur 52 B2
Tattenhall Ches W 167 D7
Tattenhoe M Keynes 102 E6
Tatterford Norf 159 D7
Tattersett Norf 158 C6
Tattershall Lincs 174 D2
Tattershall Bridge
  Lincs 173 D11
Tattershall Thorpe
  Lincs 174 D2
Tattingstone Suff 108 D2
Tattingstone White Horse
  Suff 108 D2
Tattle Bank Warks 118 E3
Tatton Dale Ches E 184 E2
Tatworth Som 28 F4
Taunton Gtr Man 196 G2
  Som 28 C2
Taverham Norf 160 G3
Taverners Green Essex 87 B9
Tavernspite Pembs 73 C11
Tavistock Devon 12 G5
Taw Green Devon 13 B9
Tawstock Devon 25 C8
Taxal Derbys 185 F8
Tay Bridge Dundee 287 E8
Tayinloan Argyll 255 C7
Taymouth Castle Perth 285 C11
Taynish Argyll 275 D8
Taynton Glos 98 G4
  Oxon 82 C2
Taynuilt Argyll 284 D4
Tayport Fife 287 E8
Tayvallich Argyll 275 D8
Tea Green Herts 104 G2
Tealby Lincs 189 C11
Tealing Angus 287 D8
Teams T&W 242 E6
Team Valley T&W 242 E6
Teamford Staffs 169 G8
Teangue Highld 295 E8
Teanna Mhachair
  W Isles 296 E3
Teasley Mead E Sus 52 F4
Tebay Cumb 222 E2
Tebworth C Beds 103 F9
Tedburn St Mary Devon 14 C2
Teddington Glos 99 E9
  London 67 E7
Teddington Hands
  Worcs 99 E9
Tedsmore Shrops 149 D7
Tedstone Delamere
  Hereford 116 F3
Tedstone Wafer
  Hereford 116 F3
Teesville Redcar 225 B10
Teeton Northants 120 C3
Teffont Evias Wilts 46 G3
Teffont Magna Wilts 46 G3
Tegryn Pembs 92 E4
Teigh Rutland 155 F7
Teigncombe Devon 13 D9
Teigngrace Devon 14 G2
Teignmouth Devon 14 G4
Teign Village Devon 14 C2
Telham E Sus 38 E3
Tellisford Som 45 B10
Telscombe E Sus 36 G6
Telscombe Cliffs E Sus 36 G5
Templand Dumfries 248 F3
Temple Corn 11 G8
  Glasgow 267 B10
  Midloth 270 D6
  Wilts 45 C10
  Windsor 65 C10
Temple Balsall W Mid 118 B4

Temple Bar Carms 75 B9
  Ceredig 111 G10
  W Sus 22 B5
Templeborough
  S Yorks 186 C6
Temple Cloud Bath 44 B6
Templecombe Som 30 C2
Temple Cowley Oxon 83 E8
Temple End Essex 106 C6
  Suff 124 G3
Temple Ewell Kent 55 E9
Temple Fields Essex 87 C7
Temple Grafton Warks 118 G2
Temple Guiting Glos 99 F11
Templehall Fife 280 C5
Temple Herdewyke
  Warks 119 G7
Temple Hill Kent 68 D5
Temple Hirst N Yorks 198 C6
Templeman's Ash Dorset 28 G6
Temple Normanton
  Derbys 170 B6
Temple Sowerby Cumb 231 F8
Templeton Devon 26 E5
  Pembs 73 C10
  W Berks 63 F11
Templeton Bridge Devon 26 E5
Templetown Durham 242 G4
Tempsford C Beds 122 G3
Ten Acres W Mid 133 G11
Tenandry Perth 291 G11
Tenbury Wells Worcs 115 D11
Tenby / Dinbych-y-Pysgod
  Pembs 73 D10
Tencreek Corn 6 E4
Tendring Essex 108 G2
Tendring Green Essex 108 F2
Tendring Heath Essex 108 F2
Ten Mile Bank Norf 140 D2
Tenston Orkney 314 E2
Tenterden Kent 53 G11
Terfyn Conwy 180 F6
  Gwyn 163 C9
Terhill Som 43 G7
Terling Essex 88 B3
Ternhill Shrops 150 C2
Terpersie Castle Aberds 302 G5
Terras Corn 5 E8
Terregles Banks
  Dumfries 237 B11
Terrible Down E Sus 23 B7
Terrick Bucks 84 D4
Terriers Bucks 84 G5
Terrington N Yorks 216 E3
Terrington St Clement
  Norf 157 E10
Terrington St John
  Norf 157 G10
Terryhorn Aberds 302 F4
Terry's Green Warks 118 C2
Terwick Common W Sus 34 C4
Teston Kent 53 C8
Testwood Hants 32 E5
Tetbury Glos 80 G5
Tetbury Upton Glos 80 F5
Tetchill Shrops 149 C7
Tetchwick Bucks 83 B11
Tetcott Devon 12 B2
Tetford Lincs 190 G4
Tetley N Lincs 199 E9
Tetney Lincs 201 G10
Tetney Lock Lincs 201 G10
Tetsworth Oxon 83 E11
Tettenhall W Mid 133 D7
Tettenhall Wood W Mid 133 D7
Tetworth Cambs 122 G4
Teuchan Aberds 303 F10
Teversal Notts 171 C7
Teversham Cambs 123 F9
Teviothead Borders 249 B10
Tewel Aberds 293 E10
Tewin Herts 86 C3
Tewin Wood Herts 86 B3
Tewkesbury Glos 99 E7
Teynham Kent 70 G3
Teynham Street Kent 70 G3
Thackley W Yorks 205 F9
Thackley End W Yorks 205 F9
Thackthwaite Cumb 229 G8
Thainston Aberds 293 F8
Thakeham W Sus 35 D10
Thame Oxon 84 D2
Thames Ditton Sur 67 F7
Thames Haven Thurrock 69 C8
Thames Head Glos 81 F7
Thamesmead London 68 C3
Thanington Kent 54 B6
Thankerton S Lnrk 259 B11
Tharston Norf 142 E3
Thatcham W Berks 64 F4
Thatto Heath Mers 183 C8
Thaxted Essex 106 E2
The Aird Highld 298 D4
Thealby N Lincs 199 D11
Theale Som 44 D3
  W Berks 64 E6
The Alders Staffs 134 C3
The Arms Norf 141 D7
The Bage Hereford 96 C5
The Balloch Perth 286 F2
The Bank Ches E 168 D4
  Shrops 132 D2
The Banks Gtr Man 185 D7
  Wilts 62 D4
The Barony Ches E 167 E11
  Orkney 314 D2
The Barton Wilts 62 D5
The Batch S Glos 61 E7
The Beeches Glos 81 D8
The Bell Gtr Man 194 F4
The Bents Staffs 151 C10
Theberton Suff 127 D8
The Blythe Staffs 151 D10
The Bog Shrops 131 D7
The Borough Dorset 30 E2
  London 67 D10
The Bourne Sur 49 E10
  Worcs 117 F9
The Bows Bris 285 G11
The Braes Highld 295 B7
The Brampton Staffs 168 F4
The Brand Leics 153 G10
The Bratch Staffs 133 E7
The Breck Orkney 314 F3
The Brents Kent 70 G4
The Bridge Dorset 30 G3
The Broad Hereford 115 E9
The Brook Suff 125 B11
The Bryn Mon 78 D4
The Burf Worcs 116 D6
The Butts Glos 49 F8
  Som 45 D9
The Camp Glos 80 D6
  Herts 85 D11
The Cape Warks 118 D5
The Chart Sur 52 C3
The Chequer Wrex 167 G7

The City Bucks 84 F3
The Cleaver Hereford 97 F10
The Close W Isles 305 J1
The Colony Oxon 100 D6
The Common Bath 60 G6
  Bucks 102 E5
  Dorset 30 E3
  Shrops 150 B1
  Suff 108 B2
  Wilts 47 G8
  Wilts 61 G11
  Wilts 62 C4
  W Sus 51 G7
The Corner Kent 53 E8
  Shrops 131 F8
The Cot Mon 79 F8
The Craigs Highld 309 K4
The Crofts E Yorks 218 E4
The Cronk IoM 192 C4
The Cross Hands Leics 134 C6
The Cwm Mon 79 G7
Theddingworth Leics 136 F3
Theddlethorpe All Saints
  Lincs 191 D7
Theddlethorpe St Helen
  Lincs 191 D7
The Dell Suff 143 D9
The Delves W Mid 133 D10
The Den N Ayrs 266 E6
The Dene Durham 242 G4
  Hants 47 C11
The Down Kent 53 F7
The Downs Sur 50 F3
The Dunks Wrex 166 E4
The Eals Northumb 251 F7
The Eaves Glos 79 D10
The Fall N Yorks 197 B10
The Fence Glos 79 D8
The Flat Glos 80 B3
The Flatt Cumb 240 B3
The Flourish Derbys 153 B8
The Folly Herts 85 C11
  S Glos 61 B8
The Fording Hereford 98 F3
The Forge Hereford 114 F6
The Forstal Kent 54 F4
The Forties Derbys 152 F6
The Four Alls Shrops 150 C3
The Fox Wilts 62 B6
The Foxholes Shrops 132 G2
The Frenches Hants 32 C4
The Frythe Herts 86 C2
The Garths Shetland 312 B8
The Gibb Wilts 61 D10
The Glack Borders 260 B6
The Gore Shrops 131 G11
The Grange Norf 160 G2
  N Yorks 225 F11
The Green Cambs 122 D5
  C Beds 85 B8
  Cumb 210 C3
  Cumb 211 D7
  Essex 88 B3
  Hants 32 B3
  M Keynes 103 C7
  Norf 141 C11
  Norf 159 B11
  Northants 102 C5
  Oxon 101 F9
  Shrops 130 G6
  S Yorks 197 G8
  Warks 118 C4
  Wilts 45 G11
The Grove Dumfries 237 B11
  Durham 242 G3
  Herts 85 D9
  Shrops 131 B7
  Shrops 131 G8
  Worcs 99 C7
The Gutter Shrops 170 F5
  W Sus 117 B9
The Hacket S Glos 61 B7
The Hague Derbys 185 C8
The Hall Shetland 312 D8
The Hallands N Lincs 200 C5
The Ham Wilts 45 C11
The Handfords Staffs 151 E7
The Harbour Kent 53 D10
Thainstone Aberds 293 B8
The Haven W Sus 50 G5
The Headland Hrtlpl 234 E6
The Heath Norf 159 D8
  Norf 160 E3
  Norf 160 E4
  Staffs 151 C11
  Suff 108 D2
The Hem Shrops 132 B4
The Hendre Mon 79 C7
The Herberts V Glam 58 E3
The Hermitage Cambs 123 C7
The High Essex 86 C6
The Highlands E Sus 38 F2
The Hill Cumb 210 C3
The Hobbins Shrops 132 E4
The Hollands Staffs 168 D6
The Hollies Notts 172 E4
The Holmes Derbys 153 B7
The Holt Wokingham 65 D10
The Hook Worcs 98 C6
The Hope Shrops 115 B10
The Howe Cumb 211 B9
  IoM 192 F2
The Humbers Telford 150 G3
The Hundred Hereford 115 E10
The Hyde London 67 B8
  Worcs 98 B6
The Hythe Essex 107 G10
The Inch Edin 280 G5
The Knab Swansea 56 D6
The Knap V Glam 58 F5
The Knapp Hereford 116 G3
Thicket Mead Bath 45 B7
Thick Hollins W Yorks 196 E6
Thickthorn Hall Norf 142 B3
Thickwood Wilts 61 E10
Thimbleby Lincs 190 G2
  N Yorks 225 F7
Thimble End W Mid 134 E2
Thinford Durham 233 E11
Thingley Wilts 61 E11
Thingwall Mers 182 E3
Thirdpart N Ayrs 266 F3
Thirlby N Yorks 215 C9
Thirlestane Borders 271 F11
Thirn N Yorks 214 B4
Thirsk N Yorks 215 C8
Thirtleby E Yorks 209 G9
Thistleton Lancs 202 F4
  Rutland 155 F8
Thistley Green Essex 88 B2
Thixendale N Yorks 216 G6
Thockrington Northumb 241 B11
Tholomas Drove Cambs 139 B7
Tholthorpe N Yorks 215 F9
Thomas Chapel Pembs 73 D10
Thomas Close Cumb 230 C4
Thomastown Aberds 302 F5
  Rhondda 58 B4
Thompson Norf 141 D8

Suff 125 B11
Suff 126 B2
Suff 62 C5
Wilts 62 C4
Themelthorpe Norf 159 E11
The Middles Durham 242 G6
The Mint Hants 33 C7
The Moor Flint 166 B4
  Kent 38 B3
Theobald's Green Wilts 62 F4
The Mumbles / Y Mwmbwls
  Swansea 56 D6
The Murray S Lnrk 268 E2
The Mythe Glos 99 E7
The Nant Wrex 166 E3
The Narth Mon 79 D8
The Neuk Aberds 293 D9
Thenford Northants 101 C10
The Node Herts 86 B3
The Nook Shrops 149 C11
  Shrops 150 B13
The North Mon 79 D8
The North Moor Norf 141 B9
The Oval Bath 61 G8
The Park Glos 99 G8
The Parks S Yorks 198 F6
The Pitts Wilts 31 B9
The Platt E Sus 23 B10
The Pludds Glos 79 B10
The Point Devon 14 E5
The Pole of Itlaw
  Aberds 302 D6
The Port of Felixstowe
  Suff 108 E5
The Potteries Stoke 168 F5
The Pound Glos 98 G4
The Quarry Glos 80 F2
  Shrops 149 G9
The Quarter Kent 53 E11
  Kent 53 G11
The Rampings Worcs 99 E7
The Rectory Lincs 156 G2
The Reddings Glos 99 G8
Therfield Herts 104 D6
The Rhos Pembs 73 C8
The Rhydd Hereford 97 E9
The Riddle Hereford 115 E9
The Ridge Wilts 61 F11
The Ridges Wokingham 65 G10
The Ridgeway Herts 86 E3
The Riding Northumb 241 D10
The Riggs Borders 261 C8
The Rink Borders 261 C11
The Rise Windsor 66 F2
The Rock Telford 132 B3
The Rocks Kent 53 B8
  S Glos 61 C8
The Roe Denb 181 G8
The Rookery Herts 85 G10
  Staffs 168 D5
The Row Lancs 211 D9
The Rowe Staffs 150 B6
The Ryde Herts 86 D2
The Sands Sur 49 D11
The Scarr Glos 98 F4
The Shoe Wilts 61 E10
The Shruggs Staffs 151 C8
The Slack Durham 233 F8
The Slade W Berks 64 F4
The Smeeth Norf 157 G10
  Gtr Man 195 F11
Thornham Magna Suff 126 C2
Thornham Parva Suff 126 C2
The Spa Wilts 62 G2
The Spring Warks 118 C5
The Square Torf 78 F3
  Wilts 62 G2
The Stocks Kent 38 B6
  Wilts 62 G2
The Straits Hants 49 F9
  W Mid 133 E8
The Strand Wilts 46 B2
The Swillett Herts 85 F8
The Sydnall Shrops 150 C3
Thetford Lincs 156 F2
  Norf 141 G7
The Thrift Cambs 104 D6
Thornhill Edge W Yorks 197 D8
Thornhill Lees W Yorks 197 D8
Thornhill Park Hants 33 E7
  N Yorks 197 C7
The Town Scilly 1 F3
The Towans Corn 2 B3
The Twittocks Glos 99 D7
The Tynings Glos 80 B6
The Vale W Mid 133 G11
  Durham 233 D8
  Durham 234 D3
Thornley Durham 233 D8
Thornliebank E Renf 267 D10
Thornly Park Renfs 267 C9
Thornroan Aberds 303 F8
Thorns N Yorks 223 E7
  Suff 124 F4
Thornsett Derbys 185 D8
The Village Newport 78 G4
  Windsor 66 E3
  W Mid 133 F7
The Walshes Worcs 116 C6
The Warren Kent 54 E3
  Wilts 63 F8
The Waterwheel Shrops 131 C7
The Weaven Hereford 97 E10
The Wells Sur 67 G7
The Wern Wrex 166 E3
The Willows NE Lincs 201 F8
The Wood Shrops 148 E6
  Shrops 149 C8
  Leics 135 B9
  Leics 202 E2
  Leics 174 B2
The Woodlands Leics 136 D3
  Suff 107 C11
  Suff 108 D3
The Woods W Mid 133 G10
The Wrangle Bath 44 B4
The Wrythe London 67 F9
The Wyke Shrops 132 B4
The Wymm Hereford 97 B10
Theydon Bois Essex 86 F6
Theydon Garnon Essex 87 F7
Theydon Mount Essex 87 F7
The Yeld Shrops 131 G11

Thomshill Moray 302 D2
Thong Kent 69 E7
Thongsbridge W Yorks 196 F6
Thoralby N Yorks 213 B10
Thoresby Notts 187 G9
Thoresthorpe Lincs 191 F7
Thoresway Lincs 189 B11
Thorganby Lincs 190 B2
  N Yorks 207 E9
Thorgill N Yorks 226 F4
Thorington Suff 127 C8
Thorington Street Suff 107 D10
Thorlby N Yorks 204 C5
Thorley Herts 87 B7
  IoW 20 D3
Thorley Houses Herts 105 G9
Thorley Street Herts 87 B7
  IoW 20 D3
Thormanby N Yorks 215 E9
Thornaby on Tees
  Stockton 225 B9
Thornage Norf 159 B11
Thornborough Bucks 102 E4
  N Yorks 214 D5
Thornbury Devon 24 F6
  Hereford 116 F2
  S Glos 79 G10
  W Yorks 205 G9
Thornby Cumb 239 G7
  Northants 120 B3
Thorncliff W Yorks 197 E8
Thorncliffe Staffs 169 D8
Thorncombe Dorset 28 G5
  Dorset 30 G5
Thorncombe Street Sur 50 E4
Thorncote Green
  C Beds 104 B3
Thorncross IoW 20 E4
Thorndon Suff 126 D2
Thorndon Cross Devon 24 G2
Thorne Corn 24 E2
  S Yorks 199 E7
Thorne Coffin Som 29 D8
Thornehillhead Devon 24 E6
Thorne Moor Devon 12 D3
Thorner W Yorks 206 E3
Thornes Staffs 133 C11
  W Yorks 197 D10
Thorne St Margaret Som 27 C9
Thorney Bucks 66 D4
  Notts 188 G5
  Pboro 138 C5
  Som 28 C6
Thorney Close Stockton 243 G9
Thorney Crofts E Yorks 201 C8
Thorney Green Suff 125 E11
Thorney Hill Hants 19 B9
Thorney Island W Sus 22 C3
Thorney Toll Pboro 138 C5
Thorneywood Notts 171 G9
Thornfalcon Som 28 C3
Thornford Dorset 29 E10
Thorngrafton Northumb 241 D7
Thorngrove Som 43 G11
Thorngumbald E Yorks 201 B8
Thornham Norf 176 E2
Thornham Fold
  Gtr Man 195 F11
Thornham Magna Suff 126 C2
Thornham Parva Suff 126 C2
Thornhaugh Pboro 137 C11
Thornhill Cardiff 59 C7
  Cumb 219 D10
  Derbys 185 E11
  Dumfries 247 D9
  Soton 33 E7
  Stir 278 B3
  Torf 78 F3
  W Yorks 197 D9
Thornhill Edge W Yorks 197 D8
Thornhill Lees W Yorks 197 D8
Thornhill Park Hants 33 E7
  N Yorks 197 C7
Thornholme E Yorks 218 G2
Thornicombe Dorset 30 G5
Thornielee Borders 261 B10
Thornley Durham 233 D8
  Durham 234 D3
Thornliebank E Renf 267 D10
Thornly Park Renfs 267 C9
Thornroan Aberds 303 F8
Thorns N Yorks 223 E7
  Suff 124 F4
Thornsett Derbys 185 D8
Thorns Green Ches E 184 E3
Thornthwaite Cumb 229 F10
  N Yorks 205 B9
Thornton Angus 287 C7
  Bucks 102 D5
  E Yorks 207 D11
  Fife 280 B5
  Lancs 202 E2
  Leics 135 B9
  Mbro 225 C9
  Mers 193 G10
  Northumb 273 F8
  Pembs 72 D6
  W Yorks 205 G8
Thornton Curtis N Lincs 200 D5
Thornton Heath London 67 F10
Thornton Hough Mers 182 E4
Thornton in Craven
  N Yorks 204 D4
Thornton in Lonsdale
  N Yorks 212 E3
Thornton-le-Beans
  N Yorks 225 G7
Thornton-le-Clay
  N Yorks 216 F3
Thornton-le-Dale
  N Yorks 216 C6
Thornton le Moor Lincs 189 B10
Thornton-le-Moor
  N Yorks 215 B7
Thornton-le-Moors
  Ches W 182 G6
Thornton-le-Street
  N Yorks 215 B8
Thorntonloch E Loth 282 F6
Thornton Park Northumb 273 F8
Thornton Rust N Yorks 213 B9
Thornton Steward
  N Yorks 214 B3
Thornton Watlass
  N Yorks 214 B4
Thornydykes Borders 272 F2
Thornyhill Aberds 293 F8
Thornythwaite Cumb 230 G4
Thoroton Notts 172 G2
Thorp Gtr Man 196 F2
Thorp Arch W Yorks 206 D4
Thorpe Cumb 230 G2
  Derbys 169 E11
  E Yorks 208 D5
  Lincs 191 E7
  Norf 143 D8
  Notts 172 D3
  N Yorks 213 G10
  Sur 66 F4
Thorpe Abbotts Norf 126 B3
Thorpe Acre Leics 153 E10
Thorpe Arnold Leics 154 E5
Thorpe Audlin W Yorks 198 D2
Thorpe Bassett N Yorks 217 E7
Thorpe Bay Sthend 70 B2
Thorpe by Water
  Rutland 137 E7
Thorpe Common Suff 108 D3
  S Yorks 186 B5
Thorpe Constantine
  Staffs 134 B5
Thorpe Culvert Lincs 175 C7
Thorpe Edge W Yorks 205 F9
Thorpe End Norf 160 G5
Thorpe Fendykes Lincs 175 C7
Thorpe Green Essex 108 G3
  Lancs 194 C5
  Suff 125 G8
Thorpe Hamlet Norf 142 B4
Thorpe Hesley S Yorks 186 B5
Thorpe in Balne
  S Yorks 198 E5
Thorpe in the Fallows
  Lincs 188 E6
Thorpe Langton Leics 136 E4
Thorpe Larches Durham 234 F3
Thorpe Latimer Lincs 156 B2
Thorpe Lea Sur 66 E4
Thorpe-le-Soken Essex 108 G3
Thorpe le Street
  E Yorks 208 E2
Thorpe le Vale Lincs 190 C2
Thorpe Malsor
  Northants 120 B6
Thorpe Mandeville
  Northants 101 B10
Thorpe Market Norf 160 B4
Thorpe Marriot Norf 160 F3
Thorpe Morieux Suff 125 G8
Thorpeness Suff 127 F9
Thorpe on the Hill
  Lincs 172 C6
  W Yorks 197 B10
Thorpe Row Norf 141 B9
Thorpe St Andrew Norf 142 B5
Thorpe St Peter Lincs 175 C7
Thorpe Salvin S Yorks 187 E8
Thorpe Satchville Leics 154 G4
Thorpe Street Suff 125 B10
Thorpe Thewles
  Stockton 234 G4
Thorpe Tilney Lincs 173 D10
Thorpe Underwood
  Northants 136 G5
  N Yorks 206 B5
Thorpe Waterville
  Northants 137 G10
Thorpe Willoughby
  N Yorks 207 G7
Thorp Wood N Yorks 207 G7
Thorrington Essex 89 B9
Thorverton Devon 26 G6
Thoulstone Wilts 45 D10
Thrandeston Suff 126 B2
Thrapston Northants 121 B9
Thrashbush N Lnrk 268 B5
Threapland Cumb 229 D9
  N Yorks 213 G9
Threapwood Ches W 166 F6
  Staffs 169 G8
Three Ashes Hants 64 G6
  Hereford 97 G10
  Shrops 115 B7
  Som 45 D7
Three Bridges Argyll 284 F4
  Lincs 190 D6
  W Sus 51 F9
Three Burrows Corn 4 G4
Three Chimneys Kent 53 F10
Three Cocked Hat Norf 143 D8
Three Cocks / Aberllynfi
  Powys 96 D3
Three Crosses Swansea 56 C5
Three Cups Corner
  E Sus 37 C10
Three Fingers Wrex 167 G7
Three Gates Dorset 29 F10
Threehammer Common
  Norf 160 F6
Three Hammers Corn 11 D10
Three Holes Norf 139 C10
Three Holes Cross Corn 10 G6
Threekingham Lincs 155 B11
Three Leg Cross E Sus 53 G7
Three Legged Cross
  Dorset 31 F9
Threelows Staffs 169 F8
Three Maypoles W Mid 118 B2
Threemile Cross
  Wokingham 65 F8
Three Mile Cross
  Wokingham 65 F8
Threemilestone Corn 4 G5
Threemiletown W Loth 279 F11
Three Oaks E Sus 38 E4
Threepwood Borders 271 G10
Three Sisters Denb 165 C9
Threewaters Corn 5 B8
Threlkeld Cumb 230 F2
Threshers Bush Essex 87 D7
Threshfield N Yorks 213 G9
Thrigby Norf 161 G9
Thringarth Durham 232 G4
Thringstone Leics 153 F8
Thrintoft N Yorks 224 G6
Thriplow Cambs 105 B8
Throapham S Yorks 187 D8
Throckenholt Lincs 139 B7
Throcking Herts 104 E6
Throckley T&W 242 D5
Throckmorton Worcs 99 B9
Throop Dorset 18 C2
Throphill Northumb 252 F5
Thropton Northumb 252 C2
Throsk Stir 279 C8
Througham Glos 80 D6
Throughgate Dumfries 247 G9
Throwleigh Devon 13 C9
Throwley Kent 54 C3
Throwley Forstal Kent 54 C3
Throxenby N Yorks 217 B10
Thrumpton Notts 153 C10
  Notts 188 E2
Thrumster Highld 310 E7
Thrunton Northumb 264 G3
Thrupe Som 44 D6
Thrupp Glos 80 E5
  Oxon 82 B7
  Oxon 83 B7
Thruscross N Yorks 205 B9
Thrushelton Devon 12 D4
Thrussington Leics 154 F2
Thruxton Hants 47 D9
  Hereford 97 E8

Thrybergh S Yorks 187 B7
Thulston Derbys 153 C8
Thunder Bridge
  W Yorks 197 E7
Thundergay N Ayrs 255 C9
Thunder Hill Norf 161 F8
Thundersley Essex 69 B9
Thundridge Herts 86 B5
Thurcaston Leics 153 G11
Thurcroft S Yorks 187 D7
Thurdon Corn 24 E3
Thurgarton Norf 160 C3
  Notts 171 F11
Thurgoland S Yorks 197 G9
Thurlaston Leics 135 D10
  Warks 119 C9
Thurlbear Som 28 C3
Thurlby Lincs 156 F2
  Lincs 172 C6
  Lincs 191 F7
Thurleigh Beds 121 F11
Thurlestone Devon 8 G3
Thurloxton Som 43 G9
Thurlstone S Yorks 197 G8
Thurlton Norf 143 D8
Thurlton Links Norf 143 D8
Thurlwood Ches E 168 D4
Thurmaston Leics 136 B2
Thurnby Leics 136 C2
Thurne Norf 161 F8
Thurnham Kent 53 B10
Thurning Norf 159 D11
  Northants 137 G11
Thurnscoe S Yorks 198 F3
Thurnscoe East S Yorks 198 F3
Thursby Cumb 239 G8
Thursden Lancs 204 G3
Thursford Norf 159 C9
Thursford Green Norf 159 C9
Thursley Sur 50 F2
Thurso Highld 310 C5
Thurso East Highld 310 C5
Thurstaston Mers 182 E2
Thurston Suff 125 D8
Thurston Clough
  Gtr Man 196 F3
Thurston End Suff 124 F5
Thurstonfield Cumb 239 F8
Thurstonland W Yorks 197 E7
Thurton Norf 142 C6
Thurvaston Derbys 152 B3
  Derbys 152 B4
Thuxton Norf 141 B10
Thwaite N Yorks 223 F7
  Suff 126 D2
Thwaite Flat Cumb 210 E4
Thwaite Head Cumb 220 G6
Thwaites W Yorks 205 E7
Thwaite St Mary Norf 142 E6
Thwaites Brow W Yorks 205 E7
Thwing E Yorks 217 E11
Tibberton Glos 98 G5
  Telford 150 E2
  Worcs 117 F8
Tibbermore Perth 286 E4
Tibenham Norf 142 F2
Tibshelf Derbys 170 C6
Tibshelf Wharf Notts 171 C7
Tibthorpe E Yorks 208 B5
Ticehurst E Sus 53 G7
Tichborne Hants 48 G5
Tickencote Rutland 137 B9
Tickenham N Som 60 E3
Ticket Wood Devon 8 G4
Tickford End M Keynes 103 C7
Tickhill S Yorks 187 C9
Ticklerton Shrops 131 E9
Tickmorend Glos 80 F4
Ticknall Derbys 153 E7
Tickton E Yorks 209 E7
Tidbury Green W Mid 117 B11
Tidcombe Wilts 47 B9
Tiddington Oxon 83 E11
  Warks 118 F4
Tidebrook E Sus 37 B10
Tideford Corn 6 D6
Tideford Cross Corn 6 D6
Tidenham Glos 79 F9
Tidenham Chase Glos 79 F9
Tideswell Derbys 185 F11
Tidmarsh W Berks 64 E6
Tidmington Warks 100 D5
Tidnor Hereford 97 D11
Tidpit Hants 31 D9
Tidworth Wilts 47 D8
Tiers Cross Pembs 72 C6
Tiffield Northants 120 G3
Tifty Aberds 303 E7
Tigerton Angus 293 G7
Tigh-na-Blair Perth 285 F11
Tighnabruaich Argyll 275 F10
Tighnacachla Argyll 274 G3
Tighnafiline Highld 307 L3
Tigley Devon 8 C5
Tilbrook Cambs 121 D11
Tilbury Thurrock 68 D6
Tilbury Green Essex 106 C4
Tilbury juxta Clare
  Essex 106 C5
Tile Cross W Mid 134 F3
Tile Hill W Mid 118 B5
Tilehouse Green W Mid 118 B3
Tilehurst Reading 65 E7
Tilekiln Green Essex 105 G10
Tiley Dorset 29 E11
Tilford Sur 49 E11
Tilford Common Sur 49 E11
Tilford Reeds Sur 49 E11
Tilgate W Sus 51 G9
Tilgate Forest Row
  W Sus 51 G9
Tilkey Essex 106 G6
Tillan Corn 6 C6
Tillathrowie Aberds 302 F4
Tillers' Green Glos 98 E3
Tilley Shrops 149 D10
Tilley Green Shrops 149 D10
Tillicoultry Clack 279 B8
Tillietudlem S Lnrk 268 F6
Tillingham Essex 89 E7
Tillington Hereford 97 B9
  Staffs 151 E8
  W Sus 35 C7
Tillington Common
  Hereford 97 B9
Tillislow Devon 12 C3
Tilly Down Hants 47 D10
Tillyarblet Angus 293 G7
Tillybirloch Aberds 293 C8
Tillycorthie Aberds 303 G8
Tillydrone Aberdeen 293 B11
Tillyfar Aberds 303 E9
Tillyfour Aberds 293 B8
Tillyfourie Aberds 293 B8
Tillygarmond Aberds 293 D8
Tillygreig Aberds 303 G8
Tillykerrie Aberds 303 G8

Tilly Lo Aberds 293 C7
Tillynaught Aberds 302 C5
Tilmanstone Kent 55 C10
Tilney All Saints Norf 157 F11
Tilney cum Islington
  Norf 157 G11
Tilney Fen End Norf 157 G11
Tilney High End Norf 157 F11
Tilney St Lawrence
  Norf 157 G10
Tilsdown Glos 80 F2
Tilshead Wilts 46 D4
Tilsmore E Sus 37 C9
Tilsop Shrops 116 C2
Tilstock Shrops 149 B10
Tilston Ches W 167 E7
Tilstone Bank Ches W 167 C9
  Ches W 167 C9
Tilston Fearnall
  Ches W 167 C9
Tilsworth C Beds 103 G9
Tilton on the Hill Leics 136 B4
Tilts S Yorks 198 F5
Tiltups End Glos 80 F4
Tilty Essex 105 F11
Timberden Bottom Kent 68 G4
Timberhonger Worcs 117 C8
Timberland Lincs 173 D10
Timbersbrook Ches E 168 C5
Timberscombe Som 42 E3
Timble N Yorks 205 C9
Timbold Hill Kent 54 B2
Timbrelham Corn 12 E3
Timperley Gtr Man 184 D3
Timsbury Bath 45 B7
  Hants 32 C4
Timsgearraidh W Isles 304 E2
Timworth Suff 125 D7
Timworth Green Suff 125 D7
Tincleton Dorset 17 C11
Tindale Cumb 240 F4
Tindale Crescent
  Durham 233 F9
Tindon End Essex 106 E2
Tingewick Bucks 102 E3
Tingley W Yorks 197 B9
Tingon Shetland 312 E4
Tingrith C Beds 103 E10
Tingwall Orkney 314 D3
Tinhay Devon 12 E3
Tinkers End Bucks 102 E5
Tinshill W Yorks 205 F11
Tinsley S Yorks 186 C6
Tinsley Green W Sus 51 F9
Tintagel Corn 11 D7
Tintern Parva Mon 79 E8
Tintinhull Som 29 D8
Tintwistle Derbys 185 B8
Tinwald Dumfries 248 G3
Tinwell Rutland 137 B10
Tipner Ptsmth 33 G10
Tippacott Devon 41 D9
Tipperty Aberds 302 C6
  Aberds 303 G9
Tipple Cross Devon 12 D3
Tipps End Norf 139 D10
Tip's Cross Essex 87 E9
Tiptoe Hants 19 B11
Tipton W Mid 133 E8
Tipton Green W Mid 133 E9
Tipton St John Devon 15 C7
Tiptree Essex 88 B5
Tiptree Heath Essex 88 B5
Tirabad Powys 95 C7
Tiraghoil Argyll 288 G5
Tircanol Swansea 57 B7
Tirdeunaw Swansea 57 B7
Tirinie Perth 291 G10
Tirley Glos 98 F6
Tirley Knowle Glos 98 F6
Tiroran Argyll 288 G6
Tirphil Caerph 77 E10
Tirril Cumb 230 F6
Tirryside Highld 309 H5
Tir-y-berth Caerph 77 F11
Tir-y-dail Carms 75 C10
Tisbury Wilts 30 B6
Tisman's Common
  W Sus 50 G5
Tissington Derbys 169 E11
Titchberry Devon 24 B2
Titchfield Hants 33 F8
Titchfield Common Hants 33 F8
Titchfield Park Hants 33 F8
Titchmarsh Northants 121 B10
Titchwell Norf 176 E3
Titcomb W Berks 63 F11
Tithby Notts 154 B3
Tithebarn Staffs 169 G8
Tithe Barn Hillock Mers 183 B9
Titley Hereford 114 E6
Titlington Northumb 264 F4
Titmore Green Herts 104 F4
Titsey Sur 52 C2
Titson Corn 24 G2
Tittenhurst Windsor 66 F3
Tittensor Staffs 151 B7
Titterhill Shrops 131 G10
Tittle Row Windsor 65 C11
Tittleshall Norf 159 E7
Titton Worcs 116 D6
Titty Hill W Sus 34 B5
Tiverton Ches W 167 C9
  Devon 27 D7
Tivetshall St Margaret
  Norf 142 F3
Tivetshall St Mary Norf 142 F3
Tividale W Mid 133 E9
Tivington Som 42 E3
Tivington Knowle Som 42 E2
Tivoli Cumb 228 G5
Tivy Dale S Yorks 197 F9
Tixall Staffs 151 E9
Tixover Rutland 137 C9
Toab Orkney 314 F5
  Shetland 313 M5
Toadmoor Derbys 170 E4
Toad Row Suff 143 F10
Tobermory Argyll 289 D7
Toberonochy Argyll 275 C8
Tobha Beag W Isles 296 D5
Tobha Mor W Isles 297 H3
Tobhtanardi W Isles 304 E3
Tobson W Isles 304 E3
Toby's Hill Lincs 191 C7
Tocher Aberds 302 F6
Tockenham Wilts 62 D4
Tockenham Wick Wilts 62 C4
Tockholes Blackburn 195 C7
Tockington S Glos 60 B6
Tockwith N Yorks 206 C5
Todber Dorset 30 C4
  Lancs 204 C2
Toddington C Beds 103 F10
  Glos 99 E10
Todenham Glos 100 D4
Todhill Angus 287 C8
Todhills Cumb 239 E9

Durham 233 E10
Todlachie Aberds 293 B8
Todmorden W Yorks 196 C2
Todpool Corn 4 G4
Todrig Borders 261 D11
Todwick S Yorks 187 E7
Toft Cambs 123 F7
Lincs 155 F11
Shetland 312 F6
Warks 119 C9
Toft Hill Durham 233 F9
Lincs 174 C2
Toft Monks Norf 143 E8
Toft next Newton Lincs 189 D8
Toftrees Norf 159 D7
Tofts 310 C7
Toftshaw W Yorks 197 B7
Toftwood Norf 159 G9
Togston Northumb 252 C6
Tokavaig Highld 295 D8
Tokers Green Oxon 65 D8
Tokyngton London 67 C7
Tolastadh a Chaolais W Isles 304 E3
Tolastadh bho Thuath W Isles 304 D7
Tolborough Corn 11 F9
Corn 2 B5
Tolcarne Corn 2 B5
Tolcarne Wartha Corn 2 B5
Toldish Corn 5 D8
Tolgus Mount Corn 4 G3
Tolhurst E Sus 53 G7
Tolladine Worcs 116 F7
Tolland Som 42 G6
Tollard Farnham Dorset 30 D6
Tollard Royal Wilts 30 D6
Toll Bar Mers 183 C7
Rutland 137 B10
S Yorks 198 F5
Tollbar End W Mid 119 B7
Toll End W Mid 133 E9
Tollerford Dorset 17 B7
Toller Fratrum Dorset 17 B7
Toller Porcorum Dorset 17 B7
Tollerton Notts 154 C2
N Yorks 215 G10
Toller Whelme Dorset 29 G8
Tollesbury Essex 89 C7
Tollesby Mbro 225 B10
Tolleshunt D'Arcy Essex 88 C6
Tolleshunt Knights Essex 88 C6
Tolleshunt Major Essex 88 C6
Tollie Highld 300 D5
Toll of Birness Aberds 303 F10
Tolm W Isles 304 E6
Tolmers Herts 86 E4
Tolpuddle Dorset 17 C11
Tolskithy Corn 4 G3
Tolvaddon Downs Corn 4 G3
Tolvah Highld 291 D10
Tolworth London 67 F7
Tomaknock Perth 286 E2
Tom an Fhuadain W Isles 305 G5
Tomatin Highld 301 G8
Tombreck Highld 300 F6
Tombui Perth 286 B2
Tomchrasky Highld 290 B4
Tomdoun Highld 290 C3
Tomich Highld 300 D4
Highld 300 G3
Tomich House Highld 300 E5
Tomintoul Aberds 292 D3
Moray 292 B3
Tomlow Warks 119 E9
Tomnaven Moray 302 F4
Tomnavoulin Moray 302 G2
Tomperrow Corn 4 G5
Tompkin Staffs 168 E6
Tompset's Bank E Sus 52 G2
Tomsleibhe Argyll 289 F8
Tomthorn Derbys 185 F9
Ton Mon 78 F5
Ton Breigam V Glam 58 D3
Tonbridge Kent 52 D5
Tonderghie Dumfries 236 F6
Tondu Bridgend 57 E11
Tone Som 27 C10
Tonedale Som 27 C10
Tone Green Som 27 C11
Tong Kent 53 D10
Shrops 132 B5
W Yorks 205 G10
Tonge Leics 153 E8
Tonge Corner Kent 70 F2
Tonge Fold Gtr Man 195 F8
Tonge Moor Gtr Man 195 E8
Tong Forge Shrops 132 B5
Tong Green Kent 54 C3
Tongham Sur 49 D11
Tongland Dumfries 237 D8
Tong Norton Shrops 132 B5
Tong Park W Yorks 205 F9
Tong Street W Yorks 205 G9
Tongue Highld 308 D5
Tongue End Lincs 156 F3
Tongwell M Keynes 103 C7
Tongwynlais Cardiff 58 C6
Tonmawr Neath 57 B10
Tonna / Tonnau Neath 57 B9
Tonnau / Tonna Neath 57 B9
Ton-Pentre Rhondda 77 F7
Ton-teg Rhondda 58 B5
Tontine Lancs 194 G4
Tonwell Herts 86 B4
Tonypandy Rhondda 77 G7
Ton-y-pistyll Caerph 77 F11
Tonyrefail Rhondda 58 B4
Toot Baldon Oxon 83 E9
Toothill Hants 32 D5
Swindon 62 C6
W Yorks 196 C6
Toot Hill Essex 87 E8
Staffs 169 G9
Tooting Graveney London 67 E9
Topcliffe N Yorks 215 D8
W Yorks 197 B9
Topcroft Norf 142 E5
Topcroft Street Norf 142 E5
Top End Beds 121 E10
Top Green Notts 172 F3
Topham S Yorks 198 D6
Topleigh W Sus 34 D6
Top Lock Gtr Man 194 F6
Top of Hebers Gtr Man 195 F11
Top o' th' Lane Lancs 194 C5
Top o' th' Meadows Gtr Man 196 F3
Toppesfield Essex 106 D4
Toppings Gtr Man 195 E8
Topsham Devon 14 D5
Top Valley Nottingham 171 F9
Torbeg N Ayrs 255 E10
Torboll Farm Highld 309 K7
Torbreck Highld 309 J7
Torbrex Stirl 278 C5
Torbryan Devon 8 B6
Torbush N Lnrk 268 D5

Torcross Devon 8 G6
Torcroy Highld 291 D9
Tore Highld 300 D6
Torefrey Corn 6 E2
Torgyle Highld 290 B5
Torinturk Argyll 275 G9
Torkington Gtr Man 184 D6
Torksey Lincs 188 F4
Torlum W Isles 296 F3
Torlundy Highld 290 F3
Tormarton S Glos 61 D9
Tormisdale Argyll 254 B2
Tormitchell S Ayrs 244 E6
Tormore Highld 295 E8
N Ayrs 255 D9
Tornagrain Highld 301 E7
Tornahaish Aberds 292 C4
Tornapress Highld 299 E8
Tornaveen Aberds 293 C8
Torness Highld 300 G5
Toronto Durham 233 E9
Torpenhow Cumb 229 D10
Torphichen W Loth 279 G9
Torphin Edin 270 B4
Torphins Aberds 293 C8
Torpoint Corn 7 E8
Torquay Torbay 9 C8
Torquhan Borders 271 F8
Torr Devon 7 E11
Devon 8 C2
Torra Argyll 254 B4
Torran Argyll 275 C9
Highld 298 E5
Highld 301 B7
Torrance E Dunb 278 G2
Torrans Argyll 288 G6
Torranyard N Ayrs 267 G7
Torre Som 42 E4
Torbay 9 C8
Torridon Highld 299 D9
Torridon Ho Highld 299 D8
Torries Aberds 293 B8
Torrin Highld 295 C7
Torrisdale Highld 308 C6
Torrisdale Castle Argyll 255 D8
Torrisdale-Square Argyll 255 D8
Torrish Highld 311 H3
Torrisholme Lancs 211 G9
Torroble Highld 309 J5
Torroy Highld 309 K5
Torrpark Corn 11 D10
Torry Aberdeen 293 C11
Aberds 302 F4
Torryburn Fife 279 D10
Torsonce Borders 271 G8
Torsonce Mains Borders 271 G9
Torterston Aberds 303 E10
Torthorwald Dumfries 238 B2
Tortington W Sus 35 F8
Torton Worcs 116 C6
Tortworth S Glos 80 G2
Torvaig Highld 298 E4
Torver Cumb 220 G5
Torwood Falk 278 E6
Torwoodlee Mains Borders 261 B11
Torworth Notts 187 D11
Tosberry Devon 24 C3
Toscaig Highld 295 B9
Toseland Cambs 122 E4
Tosside N Yorks 203 B11
Tostock Suff 125 E9
Totaig Highld 295 C10
Highld 298 D2
Totardor Highld 294 B5
Tote Highld 298 E4
Tote Highld 310 C2
Tote Hill Hants 34 C4
W Sus 34 C5
Totford Hants 48 F5
Totham Hill Essex 88 C5
Totham Plains Essex 88 C5
Tothill Lincs 190 E6
Tot Hill Hants 64 G3
Totland IoW 20 D2
Totley S Yorks 186 F4
Totley Brook S Yorks 186 F4
Totley Rise S Yorks 186 F4
Totmonslow Staffs 151 B9
Totnell Dorset 29 F10
Totnes Devon 8 C6
Toton Notts 153 C10
Totronald Argyll 288 D3
Totscore Highld 298 C3
Tottenham London 86 G4
Tottenhall Norf 158 G2
Tottenham Hale London 67 B10
Tottenhill Norf 158 G2
Tottenhill Row Norf 158 G2
Totteridge Bucks 84 G5
London 86 G2
Totternhoe C Beds 103 G9
Tottington Gtr Man 195 E9
Norf 141 D7
Tottleworth Lancs 203 G10
Totton Hants 32 E5
Touchen End Windsor 65 D11
Toulston N Yorks 206 E5
Toulton Som 43 G7
Toulvaddie Highld 311 L2
Tournaig Highld 307 L3
Tovaig W Isles 303 D9
Tovil Kent 53 C9
Towan Corn 10 G3
Towan Cross Corn 4 F4
Toward Argyll 266 B2
Towcester Northants 102 B3
Towednack Corn 2 C3
Towerage Bucks 84 G4
Tower End Norf 158 F3
Tower Hamlets Kent 55 E10
Towerhead N Som 44 B2
Tower Hill Ches E 184 F6
Devon 12 C3
Essex 85 E8
Herts 85 E8
Mers 194 G2
Sur 51 D7
W Mid 133 E11
W Sus 35 B11
Towersey Oxon 84 D2
Tow House Northumb 241 E7
Towie Aberds 292 B6
Aberds 302 C6
Aberds 303 C8
Towiemore Moray 302 E3
Tow Law Durham 233 D8
Town Barton Devon 14 C2
Townend Derbys 185 E9
Staffs 169 F11
W Dunb 277 F8
Town End Bucks 84 F3
Cambs 139 D8
Cumb 211 B7
Cumb 211 C8
Cumb 212 C2

Cumb 220 D6
Cumb 221 D8
Cumb 221 D7
Cumb 231 F8
Derbys 185 F11
E Yorks 207 C10
Mers 183 D7
W Yorks 196 D5
Townfield Durham 232 B5
Town Fields Ches W 167 B10
Towngate Cumb 230 B6
Cumb 229 D7
Cumb 230 D6
Cumb 231 E8
Dumfries 237 E8
N Lnrk 268 B4
Northumb 251 E9
S Ayrs 244 C6
Corn 1 E3
Town Green Gtr Man 183 B9
Lancs 194 F2
Norf 161 G7
Town Head Cumb 220 B6
Cumb 221 B8
Cumb 222 C2
Cumb 222 C3
Cumb 231 B7
Cumb 231 F11
Derbys 185 G11
N Yorks 204 F2
N Yorks 212 F5
Staffs 169 F8
W Yorks 204 D6
Townhead of Greenlaw Dumfries 237 C9
Townhill Fife 280 D2
Swansea 56 C6
Townhill Park Hants 33 E7
Town Kelloe Durham 234 D3
Townlake Devon 12 G4
Townland Green Kent 54 G2
Town Lane Gtr Man 183 B11
Town Littleworth E Sus 36 E6
Town of Lowton Mers 183 B10
Town Park Telford 132 B3
Town Row E Sus 52 G5
Townsend Bath 44 B5
Bucks 84 D2
Devon 25 B10
Herts 85 D10
Oxon 63 B11
Pembs 72 D4
Som 44 C4
Stoke 168 F6
Wilts 46 B3
Wilts 46 B4
Towns End Hants 48 B5
Som 30 D2
Town's End Bucks 102 G2
Dorset 18 B3
Dorset 18 E5
Dorset 29 F9
Som 45 D7
Townsend Fold Lancs 195 C10
Townshend Corn 2 C3
Town Street Glos 98 F6
Townwell S Glos 79 G11
Town Yetholm Borders 263 D8
Towthorpe E Yorks 217 G8
York 207 B8
Towton N Yorks 206 F5
Towyn Conwy 181 F7
Toxteth Mers 182 D5
Toynton All Saints Lincs 174 C5
Toynton Fen Side Lincs 174 C5
Toynton St Peter Lincs 174 C6
Toy's Hill Kent 52 C3
Trabboch E Ayrs 257 E10
Traboe Corn 2 E6
Trabrown Borders 271 F10
Tracebridge Som 27 C9
Tradespark Highld 301 D8
Orkney 314 F4
Trafford Park Gtr Man 184 B3
Traigh Ho Highld 295 F8
Trallong Powys 95 F9
Trallwn Rhondda 77 G9
Tram Inn Hereford 97 E9
Tramagenna Corn 11 E7
Tranch Torf 78 E3
Tranent E Loth 281 G8
Tranmere Mers 182 D4
Trantlebeg Highld 310 D2
Trantlemore Highld 310 D2
Tranwell Northumb 252 G5
Trapp Carms 75 B11
Traprain E Loth 281 F11
Trap's Green Warks 118 D2
Trapshill W Berks 63 G11
Traquair Borders 261 C8
Trash Green W Berks 65 F7
Travellers' Rest Carms 74 B5
Trawden Lancs 204 F4
Trawscoed Powys 95 E11
Trawsfynydd Gwyn 146 B4
Trawsnant Ceredig 111 D11
Treadam Mon 78 C6
Treaddow Hereford 97 G10
Treal Corn 2 F6
Trealaw Rhondda 77 G8
Treales Lancs 202 G4
Trearddur Anglesey 178 F3
Treaslane Highld 298 D3
Treath Corn 3 D7
Treator Corn 10 F4
Tre-Aubrey V Glam 58 E4
Trebanog Rhondda 77 G8
Trebanos Neath 76 E2
Trebarber Corn 4 C6
Trebartha Corn 11 F11
Trebarwith Corn 11 D7
Trebarwith Strand Corn 11 D6
Trebeath Corn 11 E11
Tre-Beferad V Glam 58 F3
Trebell Green Corn 5 C11
Treberfydd Powys 96 F2
Trebetherick Corn 10 F4
Trebilcock Corn 5 C9
Tre-boeth Swansea 57 B7
Treborough Som 42 F4
Trebudannon Corn 5 C7
Trebullett Corn 12 F2
Treburgett Corn 11 F7
Treburley Corn 12 F2
Treburrick Corn 10 G3
Trebyan Corn 5 C11
Trecastle Powys 95 F7
Trecenydd Caerph 58 B6
Trecott Devon 25 G10
Trecwn Pembs 91 E9
Trecynon Rhondda 77 E7
Tredannick Corn 10 G6
Tredaule Corn 11 E10

Tredavoe Corn 1 D5
Treddiog Pembs 91 F7
Tredegar Bl Gwent 77 D10
Trederwen Powys 148 F5
Tre-derwen Powys 148 F4
Tredethy Corn 5 B9
Tredington Glos 99 F8
Warks 100 C5
Tredinnick Corn 1 C4
Corn 5 D10
Corn 6 B3
Corn 10 G4
Corn 11 G9
Tredogan V Glam 58 F5
Tredomen Caerph 77 G10
Powys 96 E2
Tredown Devon 24 D2
Tredizzick Corn 10 F5
Tredunnock Mon 78 G5
Tredustan Powys 96 E2
Tredworth Glos 80 B4
Treen Corn 1 E4
Corn 1 E3
Treesmill Corn 5 D11
Treeton S Yorks 186 D6
Trefasser Pembs 91 D7
Trefdraeth Anglesey 178 G6
Trefdraeth / Newport Pembs 91 D11
Trefecca Powys 96 E2
Trefechan Ceredig 111 A11
M Tydf 77 D8
Trefeglwys Powys 129 E9
Trefeitha Powys 96 E2
Trefenter Ceredig 112 D2
Treffgarne Pembs 91 G9
Treffynnon Pembs 90 F6
Treffynnon / Holywell Flint 181 F11
Trefgarn Owen Pembs 91 F7
Trefil Bl Gwent 77 C10
Trefilan Ceredig 111 F11
Trefin / Trevine Pembs 90 E6
Treflach Shrops 148 D5
Trefnanney Powys 148 F4
Trefnant Denb 181 G9
Trefonen Shrops 148 D5
Trefor Anglesey 178 E5
Gwyn 162 F5
Treforda Corn 11 E7
Treforest Rhondda 58 B5
Treforgan Ceredig 92 B4
Tre-Forgan Neath 76 D3
Trefrew Conwy 164 C3
Trefrize Corn 12 F2
Tref y Clawdd / Knighton Powys 114 C5
Trefynwy / Monmouth Mon 79 C8
Tregada Corn 12 E2
Tregadgwith Corn 1 D4
Tregadillett Corn 12 E2
Tre-gagle Mon 79 D8
Tregaian Anglesey 178 F6
Tregajorran Corn 4 G4
Tregamere Corn 5 C8
Tregare Mon 78 C6
Tregarland Corn 6 D5
Tregarne Corn 3 E7
Tregaron Ceredig 112 F3
Tregarrick Mill Corn 6 D4
Tregarth Gwyn 163 B10
Tregaswith Corn 5 C7
Tregatillian Corn 5 C8
Tregatta Corn 11 D7
Tregavarah Corn 1 D4
Tregear Corn 5 C7
Tregeare Corn 11 E10
Tregeiriog Wrex 148 C3
Tregele Anglesey 178 C5
Tregellist Corn 10 F6
Tregeseal Corn 1 C3
Tregew Corn 3 C8
Tre-Gibbon Rhondda 77 E7
Tregidden Corn 3 E7
Tregiskey Corn 5 F10
Treglemais Pembs 90 G6
Tregole Corn 11 B9
Tregolls Corn 4 E4
Tregolwyn / Colwinston V Glam 58 D2
Tregona Corn 5 B7
Tregonce Corn 10 G4
Tregonetha Corn 5 C9
Tregonning Corn 5 D7
Tregony Corn 5 G8
Tregoodwell Corn 11 E8
Tregorden Corn 10 G6
Tregorrick Corn 5 E10
Tregoss Corn 5 C9
Tregowris Corn 3 E7
Tregoyd Powys 96 D4
Tregoyd Mill Powys 96 D3
Tregreenwell Corn 11 E7
Tregrehan Mills Corn 5 E10
Tregroes Ceredig 93 C8
Tregullon Corn 5 C11
Tregunna Corn 10 G5
Tregurrian Corn 5 B7
Tregurtha Downs Corn 2 C2
Tre Gwyr / Gowerton Swansea 56 B5
Tregyddulan Pembs 91 D7
Tregynon Powys 129 D11
Tre-gynwr Carms 74 B6
Trehafod Rhondda 77 G8
Trehafren Powys 129 E11
Trehan Corn 7 D8
Treharris M Tydf 77 F9
Trehemborne Corn 10 G3
Treherbert Rhondda 76 F6
Tre-hill V Glam 58 E5
Trehunist Corn 6 C6
Trekeivesteps Corn 11 G10
Trekenner Corn 12 F2
Trekenning Corn 5 C8
Treknow Corn 11 D7

Trelill Corn 10 F6
Trelion Corn 5 E8
Treliske Corn 4 F6
Trelissick Corn 3 B8
Trellech Mon 79 E7
Trelleck Grange Mon 79 E7
Trelogan Flint 181 E10
Treloquithack Corn 2 D5
Trelowia Corn 6 D5
Trelowth Corn 5 E9
Trelystan Powys 130 C5
Tremadog Gwyn 163 G9
Tremail Corn 11 D9
Tremain Ceredig 92 B4
Tremaine Corn 11 D10
Tremains Bridgend 58 D2
Tremar Corn 6 C5
Trematon Corn 7 D7
Trematon Castle Corn 7 D8
Tremayne Corn 2 C4
Trembraze Corn 6 C5
Tremedda Corn 2 B3
Tremeirchion Denb 181 G9
Tremethick Cross Corn 1 C4
Tremore Corn 5 C10
Tremorebridge Corn 5 C10
Tremorfa Cardiff 59 D8
Tre-Mostyn Flint 181 F10
Trenance Corn 4 C6
Corn 5 C9
Corn 10 G4
Corn 10 G4
Trenarren Corn 5 F10
Trenay Corn 6 B3
Trench Telford 150 G3
Trench Green Oxon 65 D7
Trench Wood Kent 52 D5
Trencreek Corn 4 C6
Corn 2 B2
Trendeal Corn 5 E7
Trenear Corn 2 D5
Trenerth Corn 2 C3
Trenewan Corn 6 E3
Trengune Corn 11 C9
Treninnick Corn 4 C6
Trenoon Corn 2 F6
Trenoweth Corn 3 C7
Trent Dorset 29 D9
Trentham Stoke 168 G5
Trentishoe Devon 40 D6
Trentlocks Derbys 153 C9
Trenwheal Corn 2 C4
Treoes V Glam 58 D2
Treopert / Granston Pembs 91 E7
Treorchy / Treorci Rhondda 77 F7
Treorci / Treorchy Rhondda 77 F7
Trequite Corn 10 F6
Tre'r-ddôl Ceredig 128 E3
Trerhyngyll V Glam 58 D4
Trerise Corn 2 F6
Trer Ilai / Leighton Powys 130 B4
Trerulefoot Corn 6 D6
Tresaith Ceredig 110 G5
Tresamble Corn 3 B7
Tresarrett Corn 11 F7
Tresawsen Corn 4 E5
Tresawle Corn 5 F7
Trescoll Corn 5 C10
Trescott Staffs 132 D6
Trescowe Corn 2 C3
Tresean Corn 4 D5
Tresevern Croft Corn 2 B6
Tresham Glos 80 G3
Tresigin / Sigingstone V Glam 58 E3
Tresillian Corn 5 F7
Tresimwn / Bonvilston V Glam 58 E5
Tresinney Corn 11 E8
Tresinwen Pembs 91 C7
Treskerby Corn 4 G4
Treskillard Corn 2 B5
Treskilling Corn 5 D10
Treskinnick Cross Corn 11 B10
Treslothan Corn 2 B5
Tresmeer Corn 11 E10
Tresowes Green Corn 2 D3
Tresoweshill Corn 2 D4
Tresparrett Corn 11 C8
Tresparrett Posts Corn 11 C8
Tressady Highld 309 J7
Tressait Perth 291 G10
Tresta Shetland 312 D8
Shetland 313 H5
Treswell Notts 188 F3
Treswithian Corn 4 G2
Treswithian Downs Corn 4 G2
Tre-Taliesin Ceredig 128 E3
Trethellan Water Corn 2 B6
Trethevy Corn 11 D7
Trethewell Corn 3 B9
Trethewey Corn 1 E3
Trethillick Corn 10 F4
Trethomas Caerph 59 B7
Trethosa Corn 5 E8
Trethowel Corn 5 E10
Trethurgy Corn 5 E10
Tretio Pembs 90 F5
Tretire Hereford 97 G10
Tretower Powys 96 G3
Treuddyn Flint 166 D3
Trevadlock Corn 11 F11
Trevail Corn 4 D5
Trevalga Corn 11 D7
Trevalyn Wrex 166 D5
Trevance Corn 10 G5
Trevanger Corn 10 F5
Trevanson Corn 10 G5
Trevarrack Corn 1 C5
Trevarren Corn 5 C8
Trevarrian Corn 5 B7
Trevarrick Corn 5 G9
Trevaughan Carms 73 B11
Carms 93 G7
Tre-vaughan Carms 93 G8
Treveal Corn 1 A5
Treveighan Corn 11 F7
Trevellas Corn 4 E4
Trevelmond Corn 6 C4
Trevelver Corn 10 G5
Treveor Corn 5 G9
Treverbyn Corn 5 D10
Corn 6 B3
Treverva Corn 3 C7
Trevescan Corn 1 E3
Trevethin Torf 78 E3
Trevia Corn 11 E7
Trevigro Corn 6 B6
Trevilder Corn 10 G6
Trevilla Corn 3 B8
Trevilson Corn 4 D6
Trevine Corn 3 B7
Trevine / Trefin Pembs 90 E6
Treviscoe Corn 5 D8
Treviskey Corn 2 B6
Trevithal Corn 1 D5
Trevoll Corn 4 D6
Trevone Corn 10 F3
Trevor Wrex 166 G3
Trevor Uchaf Denb 166 G2
Trevowah Corn 4 D5
Trevowhan Corn 1 B4
Trew Corn 2 D4
Trewalder Corn 11 E7
Trewarmett Corn 11 D7
Trewartha Corn 2 B2
Corn 3 B10
Trewassa Corn 11 D9
Treween Corn 11 E10
Trewellard Corn 1 C3
Trewen Corn 11 E11
Mon 79 C7
Trewennack Corn 2 D5
Trewennan Corn 11 E7
Trewern Powys 148 G5
Trewethern Corn 10 F6
Trewethen Corn 10 F6
Trewey Corn 1 B5
Trewidland Corn 6 D5
Trewindle Corn 6 C2
Trewint Corn 11 B9
Corn 11 E10
Trewithian Corn 3 B9
Trewithick Corn 2 D5
Trewoofe Corn 1 D4
Trewoon Corn 2 F5
Corn 5 E9
Treworga Corn 5 G7
Treworgan Common Mon 78 D6
Treworlas Corn 3 B9
Treworld Corn 11 C8
Treworrick Corn 6 B4
Treworthal Corn 3 B9
Trewyddel / Moylgrove Pembs 92 C2
Trewyn Devon 24 G4
Tre-wyn Mon 96 G6
Treyarnon Corn 10 G3
Treyford W Sus 34 D4
Trezaise Corn 5 D9
Trezelah Corn 1 C5
Triangle Glos 79 E8
Staffs 133 B11
W Yorks 196 C4

Trevena Corn 2 D4
Trevenen Corn 2 D5
Trevenen Bal Corn 2 D5
Trevenning Corn 11 F7
Treveor Corn 6 B4
Trickett's Cross Dorset 31 G9
Triffleton Pembs 91 G9
Trillacott Corn 11 D11
Trimdon Durham 234 D3
Trimdon Colliery Durham 234 D3
Trimdon Grange Durham 234 D3
Trimingham Norf 160 B5
Trimley Lower Street Suff 108 D5
Trimley St Martin Suff 108 D5
Trimley St Mary Suff 108 D5
Trimpley Worcs 116 B5
Trimsaran Carms 75 E7
Trims Green Herts 87 B7
Trimstone Devon 40 E3
Trinafour Perth 291 G9
Trinant Caerph 78 E2
Tring Herts 84 C6
Tringford Herts 84 C6
Tring Wharf Herts 84 C6
Trinity Angus 293 G8
Devon 27 E7
Edin 280 F4
Trinity Fields Staffs 151 B8
Trisant Ceredig 112 B4
Triscombe Som 43 F7
Som 42 G6
Trislaig Highld 290 F2
Trispen Corn 4 E6
Tritlington Northumb 252 E6
Troan Corn 5 D8
Trochry Perth 286 C3
Trodigal Argyll 255 E7
Troedrhiwdalar Powys 113 G9
Troedrhiwfenyd Ceredig 93 C8
Troedrhiwfuwch Caerph 77 E10
Troedyraur Ceredig 92 B6
Troedyrhiw M Tydf 77 E9
Trofarth Conwy 180 G5
Trolliloes E Sus 23 C10
Trondavoe Shetland 312 F5
Troon Corn 2 C4
S Ayrs 257 C8
Trooper's Inn Pembs 73 C7
Trosaraidh W Isles 297 K3
Trossachs Hotel Stirl 285 G9
Troston Suff 125 C7
Trostre Carms 56 B4
Trostrey Common Mon 78 E5
Troswell Corn 11 C11
Trottiscliffe Kent 68 G6
Trotton W Sus 34 C4
Trough Gate Lancs 195 C11
Troutbeck Cumb 221 E8
Cumb 230 G4
Troutbeck Bridge Cumb 221 F8
Troway Derbys 186 F5
Trowbridge Cardiff 59 C8
Wilts 45 B11
Trowell Notts 153 B9
Trowle Common Wilts 45 B10
Trowley Bottom Herts 85 C9
Trows Borders 262 C5
Trowse Newton Norf 142 B4
Troydale W Yorks 205 G10
Troy Town Kent 52 D2
Kent 54 C5
Medway 69 F8

Truas Corn 11 D7
Trub Gtr Man 195 F11
Trudoxhill Som 45 E8
Trueman's Heath Worcs 117 B11
True Street Devon 8 C6
Trull Som 28 C2
Trumaisgearraidh W Isles 296 E4
Trumfleet S Yorks 198 E6
Trumpan Highld 298 C2
Trumpet Hereford 98 D3
Trumpington Cambs 123 F8
Trumpsgreen Sur 66 F3
Trunch Norf 160 C5
Trunnah Lancs 202 E2
Truro Corn 4 F6
Truscott Corn 12 D2
Trusham Devon 14 D3
Trusley Derbys 152 B5
Trussall Corn 2 D5
Trussell Corn 11 D10
Trusthorpe Lincs 191 E8
Truthan Corn 4 E6
Truthwall Corn 2 C2
Trwstllewelyn Powys 130 D3
Tryfil Anglesey 178 E6
Trysull Staffs 133 E7
Trythall Corn 1 C5
Tubbs Mill Corn 5 G9
Tubney Oxon 82 F6
Tubslake Kent 53 G9
Tuckenhay Devon 8 D6
Tuckermarsh Devon 7 B8
Tuckerton Som 28 B3
Tuckhill Shrops 132 F5
Tuckingmill Corn 4 G3
Wilts 30 B6
Tucking Mill Bath 61 G9
Tuckton Bmouth 19 C8
Tuddenham Suff 108 B3
Suff 124 C4
Tuddenham St Martin Suff 108 B3
Tudeley Kent 52 D6
Tudeley Hale Kent 52 D6
Tudhay Devon 28 G3
Tudhoe Durham 233 D11
Tudhoe Grange Durham 233 D11
Tudor Hill W Mid 134 D2
Tudorville Hereford 97 G11
Tudweiliog Gwyn 144 B4
Tuebrook Mers 182 C5
Tuesley Sur 50 E3
Tuesnoad Kent 54 E2
Tuffley Glos 80 C4
Tufnell Park London 67 B9
Tufton Hants 48 D3
Pembs 91 F10
Tugby Leics 136 C5
Tugford Shrops 131 F11
Tughall Northumb 264 D6
Tulchan Lodge Angus 292 F3
Tullecombe W Sus 34 B4
Tullibardine Perth 286 F3
Tullibody Clack 279 B7
Tullich Argyll 284 F4
Highld 299 E9
Highld 300 G6
Tullich Muir Highld 301 B7
Tulliemet Perth 286 B3
Tulloch Aberds 293 F9
Aberds 303 F8
Highld 290 E5
Perth 286 E4
Tulloch Castle Highld 300 C5
Tullochgorm Argyll 275 D10
Tulloch-gribban Highld 301 G9
Tullochvenus Aberds 293 C7
Tulloes Angus 287 C9
Tullybannocher Perth 285 E11
Tullybelton Perth 286 D4
Tullycross Stirl 277 D9
Tullyfergus Perth 286 C6
Tullymurdoch Perth 286 B5
Tullynessle Aberds 293 B7
Tulse Hill London 67 E10
Tumble / Y Tymbl Carms 75 C8
Tumbler's Green Essex 106 F6
Tumby Lincs 174 D2
Tumby Woodside Lincs 174 D3
Tumpy Green Glos 80 E2
Tumpy Lakes Hereford 97 B10
Tunbridge Wells / Royal Tunbridge Wells Kent 52 F5
Tunga W Isles 304 E6
Tungate Norf 160 D5
Tunley Bath 45 B7
Glos 80 E6
Tunnel Hill Worcs 98 C6
Tunnel Pits N Lincs 199 G8
Tunshill Gtr Man 196 E2
Tunstall E Yorks 209 G12
Kent 69 G11
Lancs 212 E2
Norf 143 B8
N Yorks 224 F4
Staffs 150 D5
Stoke 168 E5
Suff 127 G7
T&W 243 F9
Tunstead Derbys 185 G10
Gtr Man 196 G4
Norf 160 E5
Tunworth Hants 49 D7
Tupsley Hereford 97 C10
Tupton Derbys 170 B5
Turbary Common Poole 19 C7
Turfdown Corn 5 B11
Turf Hill Gtr Man 196 E2
Turfholm S Lnrk 259 B8
Turfmoor Devon 28 G3
Shrops 149 F7
Turgis Green Hants 49 B7
Turin Angus 287 B9
Turkdean Glos 81 B10
Turkey Island Hants 33 D9
W Sus 34 D3
Turkey Tump Hereford 97 F10
Tur Langton Leics 136 E4
Turleigh Wilts 61 G10
Turleygreen Shrops 132 F5
Turlin Moor Poole 18 C5
Turmer Hants 31 F10
Turnalt Argyll 275 C9
Turnastone Hereford 97 D7
Turnberry S Ayrs 244 B6
Turnchapel Plym 7 E9
Turnditch Derbys 170 F3
Turner Green Lancs 203 G8
Turner's Green E Sus 23 B10
E Sus 52 G6
Warks 118 D3
W Berks 64 F4
Turners Hill W Sus 51 F10

Turners Puddle Dorset 18 C2
Turnerwood S Yorks 187 E8
Turnford Herts 86 E5
Turnhouse Edin 280 G3
Turnhurst Stoke 168 E5
Turnstead Milton Derbys 185 E8
Turnworth Dorset 30 F4
Turrerich Perth 286 D2
Turriff Aberds 303 D7
Tursdale Durham 234 D2
Turton Bottoms Blkburn 195 D8
Turves Cambs 138 D6
Turves Green W Mid 117 B10
Turvey Beds 121 G8
Turville Bucks 84 G3
Turville Heath Bucks 84 G2
Turweston Bucks 102 D2
Tushielaw Borders 261 F8
Tutbury Staffs 152 D4
Tutnall Worcs 117 C9
Tutnalls Glos 79 G8
Tutshill Glos 79 G8
Tutt Hill Kent 54 E3
Tuttington Norf 160 D4
Tutts Clump W Berks 64 E5
Tutwell Corn 12 F3
Tuxford Notts 188 G2
Twatt Orkney 314 D2
Shetland 313 H5
Twechar E Dunb 278 F4
Tweedale Telford 132 C4
Tweeddaleburn Borders 270 C5
Tweedmouth Northumb 273 E9
Tweedsmuir Borders 260 E3
Twelve Heads Corn 4 G5
Twelve Oaks E Sus 37 C11
Twelvewoods Corn 6 B4
Twemlow Green Ches E 168 B3
Twenties Kent 71 F10
Twenty Lincs 156 E3
Twerton Bath 61 G8
Twickenham London 67 E7
Twigworth Glos 98 G6
Twineham W Sus 36 D3
Twineham Green W Sus 36 D3
Twinhoe Bath 45 B8
Twinstead Essex 107 D7
Twinstead Green Essex 106 D6
Twiss Green Warr 183 B11
Twiston Lancs 204 E2
Twitchen Devon 41 G8
Shrops 115 B7
Twitchen Mill Devon 41 G9
Twitham Kent 55 B9
Twitton Kent 52 B4
Two Bridges Devon 13 G8
Glos 79 D11
Two Burrows Corn 4 F4
Two Dales Derbys 170 C3
Two Gates Staffs 134 C4
Two Mile Ash M Keynes 102 D6
W Sus 35 B10
Two Mile Oak Cross Devon 8 B6
Two Mills Ches W 182 G5
Two Pots Devon 40 E4
Two Waters Herts 85 D9
Twr Anglesey 178 E2
Twycross Leics 134 C6
Twydall Medway 69 F9
Twyford Bucks 102 F2
Derbys 152 D6
Dorset 30 D5
Hants 33 C7
Leics 154 G4
Lincs 155 E8
Norf 159 E10
Wokingham 65 D9
Twyford Common Hereford 97 D10
Twyn-Allws Mon 78 C3
Twynholm Dumfries 237 D8
Twyning Glos 99 D7
Twyning Green Glos 99 D8
Twynllanan Carms 94 G5
Twynmynydd Carms 75 C11
Twyn Shôn-Ifan Caerph 77 G11
Twynyrodyn M Tydf 77 D9
Twyn-yr-odyn V Glam 58 E6
Twyn-y-Sheriff Mon 78 D6
Twywell Northants 121 B9
Tyberton Hereford 97 D7
Tyburn W Mid 134 E2
Tyby Norf 159 D11
Ty-coch Swansea 56 C6
Tycroes Carms 75 C10
Tycrwyn Powys 148 F2
Tyddewi / St Davids Pembs 90 F5
Tydd Gote Lincs 157 F7
Tydd St Giles Cambs 157 F8
Tydd St Mary Lincs 157 F8
Tye Hants 22 C2
Tye Common Essex 87 G11
Tyegate Green Norf 161 G7
Tye Green Essex 87 C10
Essex 87 C11
Essex 105 D11
Essex 105 G10
Essex 106 G5
Tyersal W Yorks 205 G9
Ty-fry Mon 78 F6
Tyganol V Glam 58 E4
Ty-hen Carms 92 G6
Gwyn 144 C3
Ty-isaf Carms 75 C7
Tyla Mon 78 C2
Tylagwyn Bridgend 58 B2
Tyldesley Gtr Man 195 G7
Tyle Carms 94 F3
Tyle-garw Rhondda 58 C4
Tyler Hill Kent 70 G6
Tylers Causeway Herts 86 D3
Tylers Green Essex 86 G6
Tyler's Green Essex 87 D8
Sur 51 C11
Tyler's Hill Bucks 85 E7
Tylorstown Rhondda 77 F8
Tylwch Powys 129 G9
Ty-mawr Anglesey 179 D7
Carms 93 C10
Ty Mawr Carms 93 C10
Ty-mawr Conwy 181 F7
Ty Mawr Cwm Conwy 164 F6
Tynant Conwy 165 G11
Ty-nant Conwy 165 G11
Gwyn 147 D8

Tyncelyn Ceredig 112 E2
Tyndrum Stirl 285 D7
Tyne Dock T&W 243 D9
Tyneham Dorset 18 E3
Tynehead Midloth 271 D7
Tynemouth T&W 243 D9
Tyne Tunnel T&W 243 D8
Tynewydd Ceredig 92 B4
Neath 76 D4
Rhondda 76 F6
Ty-Newydd Ceredig 111 D10
Tyning Bath 45 B7
Tyninghame E Loth 282 F2
Tyn-lon Gwyn 163 D7
Tynron Dumfries 247 E8
Tyntesfield N Som 60 E4
Tyntetown Rhondda 77 F9
Ty'n-y-bryn Rhondda 58 B4
Tyn-y-celyn Wrex 148 B3
Tyn-y-coed Shrops 148 D4
Ty'n-y-coedcae Caerph 59 B7
Tyn-y-cwm Swansea 75 E10
Tynyfedw Conwy 165 B7
Ty'n-y-fedwen Powys 148 C2
Ty'n-y-ffordd Denb 181 G8
Tyn-y-ffridd Powys 148 C2
Ty'n-y-garn Bridgend 57 E11
Tynygongl Anglesey 179 E8
Tynygraig Ceredig 112 D3
Tyn-y-graig Powys 113 G10
Ty'n-y-groes Conwy 180 G3
Ty'n-y-maes Gwyn 163 C10
Tyn-y-pwll Anglesey 178 D6
Ty'n-yr-eithin Ceredig 112 E3
Tynyrwtra Powys 129 F7
Tyrells End C Beds 103 E9
Tyrell's Wood Sur 51 B7
Ty^r-felin-isaf Conwy 164 C5
Ty Rhiw Rhondda 58 C6
Tyrie Aberds 303 C9
Tyringham M Keynes 103 B7
Tyseley W Mid 134 G2
Ty-Sign Caerph 78 G2
Tythecott Devon 24 D6
Tythegston Bridgend 57 F11
Tytherington Ches E 184 F6
S Glos 61 B7
Som 45 D9
Wilts 46 E2
Tytherleigh Devon 28 G4
Tytherton Lucas Wilts 62 E2
Tyttenhanger Herts 85 D11
Ty-uchaf Powys 147 E10
Tywardreath Corn 5 E11
Tywardreath Highway
Corn 5 D11
Tywyn Conwy 180 F3
Gwyn 110 C2

U

Uachdar W Isles 296 F3
Uags Highld 295 B9
Ubberley Stoke 168 F6
Ubbeston Green Suff 126 C6
Ubley Bath 44 B4
Uckerby N Yorks 224 E4
Uckfield E Sus 37 C7
Uckinghall Worcs 99 D7
Uckington Glos 99 G8
Shrops 131 B11
Uddingston S Lnrk 268 C3
Uddington S Lnrk 259 C9
Udimore E Sus 38 D5
Udley N Som 60 G3
Udny Green Aberds 303 G8
Udny Station Aberds 303 G9
Udston S Lnrk 268 D3
Udstonhead S Lnrk 268 F4
Uffcott Wilts 62 D6
Uffculme Devon 27 E9
Uffington Lincs 137 B11
Oxon 63 B10
Shrops 149 G10
Ufford Pboro 137 C11
Suff 126 G5
Ufton Warks 119 E7
Ufton Green W Berks 64 F6
Ufton Nervet W Berks 64 F6
Ugadale Argyll 255 E8
Ugborough Devon 8 D3
Ugford Wilts 46 G5
Uggeshall Suff 143 G8
Ugglebarnby N Yorks 227 D7
Ughill S Yorks 186 C3
Ugley Essex 105 F10
Ugley Green Essex 105 F10
Ugthorpe N Yorks 226 C5
Uidh W Isles 297 M2
Uig Argyll 276 E2
Argyll 288 D3
Highld 296 F7
Highld 298 C3
Uigen W Isles 304 E2
Uigshader Highld 298 E4
Uisken Argyll 274 B4
Ulaw Aberds 303 G9
Ulbster Highld 310 E7
Ulcat Row Cumb 230 G4
Ulceby Lincs 190 G6
N Lincs 200 E6
Ulceby Skitter N Lincs 200 E6
Ulcombe Kent 53 D10
Uldale Cumb 229 D10
Uley Glos 80 F3
Ulgham Northumb 252 E6
Ullapool Highld 307 K6
Ullcombe Devon 28 F2
Ullenhall Warks 118 D2
Ullenwood Glos 80 B6
Ulleskelf N Yorks 206 E6
Ullesthorpe Leics 135 F10
Ulley S Yorks 187 D7
Ullingswick Hereford 97 B11
Ullington Worcs 100 B2
Ullinish Highld 294 B5
Ullock Cumb 229 G7
Cumb 229 G10
Ulnes Walton Lancs 194 D4
Ulpha Cumb 220 G3
Ulrome E Yorks 209 B9
Ulshaw N Yorks 214 B2
Ulsta Shetland 312 E6
Ulva House Argyll 288 F6
Ulverley Green W Mid 134 G2
Ulverston Cumb 210 D5
Ulwell Dorset 18 E6
Umberleigh Devon 25 C10
Unapool Highld 306 F7
Unasary W Isles 297 J3
Under Bank W Yorks 196 F6
Underbarrow Cumb 221 G9
Undercliffe W Yorks 205 G9
Underdale Shrops 149 G10
Underdown Devon 14 D3
Underhill London 86 F3
Wilts 45 G11
Underhoull Shetland 312 C7
Underling Green Kent 53 D9
Underriver Kent 52 C5
Underriver Ho Kent 52 C5
Under the Wood Kent 71 F8
Under Tofts S Yorks 186 D4
Underton Shrops 132 E3
Underwood Newport 59 B11
Notts 171 E7
Pembs 73 C7
Plym 7 D10
Undley Suff 140 G3
Undy Mon 60 B2
Ungisiadar W Isles 304 F3
Unifirth Shetland 313 H4
Union Cottage Aberds 293 D10
Union Mills IoM 192 E4
Union Street E Sus 53 G8
United Downs Corn 4 G4
Unstone Derbys 186 F5
Unstone Green Derbys 186 F5
Unsworth Gtr Man 195 F10
Unthank Cumb 230 B3
Cumb 230 D5
Cumb 231 C8
Derbys 186 F4
Unthank End Cumb 230 D5
Upavon Wilts 46 C6
Up Cerne Dorset 29 G11
Upchurch Kent 69 F10
Upcott Devon 24 D2
Devon 25 F9
Devon 25 F11
Devon 40 F3
Hereford 114 G6
Som 27 C11
Upend Cambs 124 F3
Up End M Keynes 103 B8
Up Exe Devon 26 G6
Upgate Norf 160 F2
Upgate Street Norf 141 E11
Norf 142 E5
Up Green Hants 65 G9
Uphall Dorset 29 G9
W Loth 279 G11
Uphall Station W Loth 279 G11
Upham Devon 26 F5
Hants 33 C8
Uphampton Hereford 115 E7
Worcs 116 E6
Up Hatherley Glos 99 G8
Uphempston Devon 8 C6
Uphill N Som 43 B10
Uphill Manor N Som 43 B10
Up Holland Lancs 194 F4
Uplands Glos 80 D5
Swansea 56 C6
Uplawmoor E Renf 267 D8
Upleadon Glos 98 F5
Upleadon Court Glos 98 F5
Upleatham Redcar 226 B2
Uplees Kent 70 G3
Uploders Dorset 16 C6
Uplowman Devon 27 D8
Uplyme Devon 16 C2
Up Marden W Sus 34 E3
Upminster London 68 B5
Up Mudford Som 29 D9
Up Nately Hants 49 C7
Upnor Medway 69 E9
Upottery Devon 28 F2
Uppacott Devon 25 B9
Uppat Highld 311 J2
Uppend Essex 105 F9
Upper Affcot Shrops 131 F8
Upper Ardchronie
Highld 309 L6
Upper Ardgrain Aberds 303 F9
Upper Ardroscadale
Argyll 275 G11
Upper Arley Worcs 132 G5
Upper Armley W Yorks 205 G11
Upper Arncott Oxon 83 B10
Upper Astley Shrops 149 F10
Upper Aston Shrops 132 E6
Upper Astrop
Northants 101 D10
Upper Badcall Highld 306 E6
Upper Bangor Gwyn 179 G9
Upper Basildon W Berks 64 D5
Upper Batley W Yorks 197 B8
Upper Battlefield
Shrops 149 F10
Upper Beeding W Sus 35 E11
Upper Benefield
Northants 137 F9
Upper Bentley Worcs 117 D9
Upper Bighouse Highld 310 D2
Upper Birchwood
Derbys 170 E6
Upper Blainslie
Borders 271 G10
Upper Boat Rhondda 58 B6
Upper Boddam Aberds 302 F6
Upper Boddington
Northants 119 G9
Upper Bogrow Highld 309 L7
Upper Bogside Moray 302 D2
Upper Bonchurch IoW 21 F7
Upper Booth Derbys 185 D10
Upper Borth Ceredig 128 F2
Upper Boyndlie Aberds 303 C9
Upper Brailes Warks 100 D6
Upper Brandon Parva
Norf 141 B10
Upper Breakish Highld 295 C8
Upper Breinton
Hereford 97 C9
Upper Broadheath
Worcs 116 F6
Upper Brockholes
W Yorks 196 B5
Upper Broughton Notts 154 D3
Upper Broxwood
Hereford 115 G7
Upper Bruntingthorpe
Leics 136 F2
Upper Brynamman
Carms 76 C2
Upper Buckenhill
Hereford 97 E11
Upper Bucklebury
W Berks 64 F4
Upper Bullington Hants 48 E3
Upper Burgate Hants 31 D11
Upper Burnhaugh
Aberds 293 D10
Upper Bush Medway 69 F7
Upperby Cumb 239 G10
Upper Caldecote
C Beds 104 B3
Upper Cam Glos 80 F3
Upper Canada N Som 43 B11
Upper Canterton Hants 32 E3
Upper Catesby
Northants 119 F10
Upper Catshill Worcs 117 C9
Upper Chapel Powys 95 C10
Upper Cheddon Som 28 B2
Upper Chicksgrove
Wilts 31 B7
Upper Church Village
Rhondda 58 B5
Upper Chute Wilts 47 C9
Upper Clapton London 67 B10
Upper Clatford Hants 47 E11
Upper Coberley Glos 81 B7
Upper College Shrops 149 C11
Upper Colwall Hereford 98 C5
Upper Common Hants 48 D6
Upper Cotburn Aberds 303 D7
Upper Cotton Staffs 169 F9
Upper Coullie Aberds 293 B9
Upper Cound Shrops 131 C11
Upper Coxley Som 44 E4
Upper Cudworth
S Yorks 197 F11
Upper Culphin Aberds 302 D6
Upper Cumberworth
W Yorks 197 F8
Upper Cwmbran Torf 78 F3
Upper Cwm-twrch Powys 76 C3
Upperdale Derbys 185 G11
Upper Dallachy Moray 302 C3
Upper Deal Kent 55 C11
Upper Dean Beds 121 D10
Devon 8 C4
Upper Denby W Yorks 197 D8
W Yorks 197 F8
Upper Denton Cumb 240 D4
Upper Derraid Highld 301 F10
Upper Diabaig Highld 299 C8
Upper Dicker E Sus 23 D9
Upper Dinchope Shrops 131 G9
Upper Dormington
Hereford 97 D11
Upper Dounreay Highld 310 C4
Upper Dovercourt Essex 108 E4
Upper Dowdeswell Glos 81 B8
Upper Druimfin Argyll 289 D7
Upper Dunsforth
N Yorks 215 G8
Upper Dunsley Herts 84 C6
Upper Eashing Sur 50 E3
Upper Eastern Green
W Mid 134 G5
Upper Eathie Highld 301 C7
Upper Edmonton London 86 G4
Upper Egleton Hereford 98 C2
Upper Elkstone Staffs 169 D9
Upper Ellastone Staffs 169 G10
Upper Elmers End
London 67 F11
Upper End Derbys 185 F9
Glos 81 C10
Glos 81 D8
Leics 154 G4
Upper Enham Hants 47 D11
Upper Farmcote Shrops 132 E5
Upper Farringdon Hants 49 F8
Upper Feorlig Highld 298 E2
Upper Fivehead Som 28 C4
Upper Forge Shrops 132 F4
Upper Framilode Glos 80 C3
Upper Froyle Hants 49 E9
Upper Gambolds Worcs 117 D9
Upper Gills Highld 310 B7
Upper Glenfintaig
Highld 290 E4
Upper Godney Som 44 E3
Upper Goldstone Kent 71 G9
Upper Gornal W Mid 133 E8
Upper Gravenhurst
C Beds 104 D2
Upper Green Essex 105 E8
Mon 78 B5
Suff 124 E4
W Berks 63 G11
W Mid 135 G7
W Yorks 197 B9
Upper Grove Common
Hereford 97 F11
Upper Guist Norf 159 D10
Upper Hackney Derbys 170 C3
Upper Hale Sur 49 D10
Upper Halistra Highld 298 D2
Upper Halliford Sur 66 F5
Upper Halling Medway 69 G7
Upper Ham Worcs 99 D7
Upper Hambleton
Rutland 137 B8
Upper Hamnish
Hereford 115 F10
Upper Harbledown Kent 54 B6
Upper Hardres Court
Kent 55 C7
Upper Hardwick
Hereford 115 F8
Upper Hartfield E Sus 52 G3
Upper Hartshay Derbys 170 E5
Upper Haselor Worcs 99 C10
Upper Hatton Staffs 150 B6
Upper Haugh S Yorks 186 B6
Upper Hawkhillock
Aberds 303 F10
Upper Hayesden Kent 52 E5
Upper Hayton Shrops 131 G10
Upper Heath Shrops 131 F11
Upper Heaton W Yorks 197 D7
Upper Hellesdon Norf 160 G4
Upper Helmsley
N Yorks 207 B9
Upper Hengoed Shrops 148 C5
Upper Hergest Hereford 114 G5
Upper Heyford
Northants 120 F3
Oxon 101 F9
Upper Hill Glos 79 F11
Hereford 115 G9
Upper Hindhope
Borders 251 B7
Upper Holloway London 67 B9
Upper Holton Suff 127 B8
Upper Hopton W Yorks 197 D7
Upper Horsebridge
E Sus 23 C9
Upper Howsell Worcs 98 B5
Upper Hoyland
S Yorks 197 G11
Upper Hulme Staffs 169 C8
Upper Hyde IoW 21 E7
Upper Ifold Sur 50 G4
Upper Inglesham Swindon 82 F2
Upper Inverbrough
Highld 301 F8
Upper Kergord Shetland 313 H6
Upper Kidston Borders 270 G4
Upper Kilcott Glos 61 B9
Upper Killay Swansea 56 C5
Upper Killeyan Argyll 254 C3
Upper Kinsham
Hereford 115 D7
Upper Knockando
Moray 301 E11
Upper Lambourn
W Berks 63 C10
Upper Landywood
Staffs 133 B9
Upper Langford N Som 44 B3
Upper Langwith Derbys 171 B8
Upper Layham Suff 107 C10
Upper Leigh Staffs 151 B10
Upper Lenie Highld 300 G5
Upper Littleton N Som 60 G5
Upper Loads Derbys 170 B4
Upper Lochton Aberds 293 D8
Upper Lode Worcs 99 E7
Upper Longdon Staffs 151 G11
Upper Longwood
Shrops 132 B2
Upper Ludstone Shrops 132 D6
Upper Lybster Highld 310 F6
Upper Lydbrook Glos 79 B10
Upper Lyde Hereford 97 C9
Upper Lye Hereford 115 D7
Upper Maes-coed
Hereford 96 D6
Upper Marsh W Yorks 204 F6
Upper Midhope S Yorks 186 B2
Upper Midway Derbys 152 E5
Uppermill Gtr Man 196 F3
Upper Milovaig Highld 297 G7
Upper Milton Oxon 82 B3
Som 44 D4
Upper Minety Wilts 81 G8
Upper Mitton Worcs 116 C6
Upper Moor Worcs 99 B9
Upper Moor Side
W Yorks 205 G10
Upper Morton S Glos 79 G11
Upper Nash Pembs 73 E8
Upper Netchwood
Shrops 132 E2
Upper Newbold Derbys 186 G5
Upper Nobut Staffs 151 B10
Upper North Dean Bucks 84 F4
Upper Norwood London 67 F10
W Sus 34 D6
Upper Obney Perth 286 D4
Upper Ochrwyth Caerph 59 B8
Upper Oddington Glos 100 F4
Upper Ollach Highld 295 B7
Upper Padley Derbys 186 F2
Upper Pickwick Wilts 61 E11
Upper Pollicott Bucks 84 C2
Upper Poppleton York 207 C7
Upper Port Highld 301 G10
Upper Postern Kent 52 D6
Upper Quinton Warks 100 B3
Upper Race Torf 78 F3
Upper Ratley Hants 32 C4
Upper Ridinghill
Aberds 303 D10
Upper Rissington Glos 82 B2
Upper Rochford Worcs 116 D2
Upper Rodmersham
Kent 70 G2
Upper Sandaig Highld 295 D9
Upper Sanday Orkney 314 F5
Upper Sapey Hereford 116 E3
Upper Saxondale Notts 154 B3
Upper Seagry Wilts 62 C2
Upper Shelton C Beds 103 C9
Upper Sheringham
Norf 177 E10
Upper Shirley London 67 G11
Soton 32 E6
Upper Siddington Glos 81 F8
Upper Skelmorlie
N Ayrs 266 B4
Upper Slackstead Hants 32 B5
Upper Slaughter Glos 100 G3
Upper Solva Pembs 90 G5
Upper Soudley Glos 79 C11
Uppersound Shetland 313 J6
Upper Stanton Drew
Bath 60 G6
Upper Staploe Beds 122 F2
Upper Stoke Norf 142 C5
W Mid 135 G7
Upper Stondon C Beds 104 D2
Upper Stowe Northants 120 F2
Upper Stratton Swindon 63 B7
Upper Street Hants 31 D11
Norf 142 G3
Norf 160 B5
Norf 160 E6
Norf 160 F6
Norf 161 F7
Suff 108 E2
Suff 124 G5
Suff 126 G2
Upper Strensham Worcs 99 D8
Upper Studley Wilts 45 B10
Upper Sundon C Beds 103 F10
Upper Swainswick Bath 61 F9
Upper Swanmore Hants 33 D9
Upper Swell Glos 100 F3
Upper Sydenham
London 67 E10
Upper Tankersley
S Yorks 186 B4
Upper Tean Staffs 151 B10
Upperthong W Yorks 196 F6
Upperthorpe Derbys 187 E7
N Lincs 199 G9
Upper Threapwood
Ches W 166 F6
Upper Thurnham Lancs 202 C5
Upper Tillyrie Perth 286 G5
Upperton E Sus 23 E10
Oxon 83 G11
W Sus 35 C7
Upper Tooting London 67 E9
Upper Tote Highld 298 D5
Uppertown Derbys 170 C4
Highld 300 F4
Highld 310 B7
Northumb 241 C9
Orkney 314 G4
Upper Town Derbys 170 D3
Derbys 170 E2
Durham 233 D7
Hereford 97 B11
N Som 60 F4
Suff 125 D8
Wilts 62 D3
W Yorks 204 G6
Upper Treverward
Shrops 114 B5
Upper Tysoe Warks 100 C6
Upper Up Glos 81 F8
Upper Upham Wilts 63 D8
Upper Upnor Medway 69 E9
Upper Vobster Som 45 D8
Upper Walthamstow
London 67 B11
Upper Wardington Oxon 101 B9
Upper Wardley W Sus 34 B4
Upper Weald M Keynes 102 D5
Upper Weedon
Northants 120 F2
Upper Welland Worcs 98 C5
Upper Wellingham E Sus 36 E6
Upper Welson Hereford 114 G5
Upper Westholme Som 44 E5
Upper Weston Bath 61 F8
Upper Weybread Suff 126 B4
Upper Whiston S Yorks 187 D7
Upper Wick Glos 80 F2
Worcs 116 G6
Upper Wield Hants 48 F6
Upper Wigginton
Shrops 148 B6
Upper Winchendon
Bucks 84 C2
Upper Witton W Mid 133 E11
Upper Wolvercote Oxon 83 D7
Upper Wolverton Worcs 117 G8
Upperwood Derbys 170 D3
Upper Woodend Aberds 293 B8
Upper Woodford Wilts 46 F6
Upper Woolhampton
W Berks 64 F5
Upper Wootton Hants 48 C5
Upper Wraxall Wilts 61 E10
Upper Wyche Hereford 98 C5
Uppincott Devon 26 G5
Uppingham Rutland 137 D7
Uppington Dorset 31 F8
Shrops 132 B2
Upsall N Yorks 215 B9
Upsher Green Suff 107 C8
Upshire Essex 86 E6
Up Somborne Hants 47 G11
Upstreet Kent 71 G8
Up Sydling Dorset 29 G10
Upthorpe Glos 80 E3
Suff 125 C9
Upton Bucks 84 C3
Cambs 122 B3
Ches W 166 B6
Corn 11 G11
Corn 24 G2
Cumb 230 D2
Devon 8 G4
Devon 27 G9
Dorset 17 E10
Dorset 18 C5
E Yorks 209 C8
Hants 32 D5
Hants 47 B11
IoW 21 C7
Kent 71 F11
Leics 135 D7
Lincs 188 D5
London 68 C2
Mers 182 D3
Mers 183 D7
Norf 161 G7
Northants 120 E4
Notts 172 E2
Notts 188 F2
Oxon 64 B4
Oxon 82 C2
Pboro 138 C2
Slough 66 D3
Som 27 B7
Som 29 B7
Warks 118 F2
Wilts 45 G11
W Yorks 198 E3
Upton Bishop Hereford 98 F2
Upton Cheyney S Glos 61 F7
Upton Cressett Shrops 132 E3
Upton Crews Hereford 98 F2
Upton Cross Corn 11 G11
Upton End C Beds 104 E2
Upton Field Notts 172 E2
Upton Green Norf 161 G7
Upton Grey Hants 49 D7
Upton Heath Ches W 166 B6
Upton Hellions Devon 26 G4
Upton Lea Bucks 66 C3
Upton Lovell Wilts 46 E2
Upton Magna Shrops 149 G11
Upton Noble Som 45 F8
Upton Park London 68 C2
Upton Pyne Devon 14 B4
Upton Rocks Halton 183 D8
Upton St Leonards Glos 80 C5
Upton Scudamore Wilts 45 D11
Upton Snodsbury Worcs 117 G8
Upton upon Severn
Worcs 99 C7
Upton Warren Worcs 117 D8
Upwaltham W Sus 34 E6
Upware Cambs 123 C10
Upwell Norf 139 C9
Upwey Dorset 17 E9
Upwick Green Herts 105 G9
Upwood Cambs 138 G5
Uradale Shetland 313 K6
Urafirth Shetland 312 F5
Uragaig Argyll 274 D4
Urchfont Wilts 46 B4
Urdimarsh Hereford 97 B10
Ure Shetland 312 F4
Ure Bank N Yorks 214 E6
Urgashay Som 29 C9
Urgha W Isles 305 J3
Urgha Beag W Isles 305 H3
Urishay Common
Hereford 96 D6
Urlar Perth 286 C2
Urlay Nook Stockton 225 C7
Urmston Gtr Man 184 C3
Urpeth Durham 242 G6
Urquhart Highld 300 D5
Moray 302 C2
Urra N Yorks 225 E11
Urray Highld 300 D5
Ushaw Moor Durham 233 C10
Usk Mon 78 E5
Usselby Lincs 189 C9
Usworth T&W 243 F8
Utkinton Ches W 167 B8
Utley W Yorks 204 E6
Uton Devon 14 B2
Utterby Lincs 190 C4
Uttoxeter Staffs 151 C11
Uwchmynydd Gwyn 144 D3
Uxbridge London 66 C5
Uxbridge Moor London 66 C5
Uyea Shetland 312 D5
Uyeasound Shetland 312 C7
Uzmaston Pembs 73 C7

V

Vachelich Pembs 90 F5
Vadlure Shetland 313 J4
Vagg Som 29 D8
Vaila Hall Shetland 313 J4
Vaivoe Shetland 312 G7
Vale W Yorks 196 B2
Vale Down Devon 12 D6
Vale of Health London 67 B9
Valeswood Shrops 149 E7
Valleyfield Dumfries 237 D8
Valley Park Hants 32 C6
Valley Truckle Corn 11 E7
Valley / Y Fali Anglesey 178 F3
Valsgarth Shetland 312 B8
Valtos Highld 298 C5
Van Caerph 59 B7
Powys 129 F9
Vange Essex 69 B8
Vanlop Shetland 313 M5
Varchoel Powys 148 G4
Varfell Corn 2 C2
Varteg Torf 78 D3
Vassa Shetland 313 H6
Vastern Wilts 62 C5
Vatsetter Shetland 312 E7
Shetland 313 L5
Vatten Highld 298 E2
Vaul Argyll 288 E2
Vauxhall London 67 D10
Mers 182 C4
W Mid 133 F11
Vaynol Hall Gwyn 163 B8
Vaynor M Tydf 77 C8
Veensgarth Shetland 313 J6
Velator Devon 40 F3
Veldo Hereford 97 C11
Velindre Powys 96 D3
Vellanoweth Corn 2 C2
Vellow Som 42 F5
Velly Devon 24 C3
Veness Orkney 314 D5
Venn Devon 8 F4
Venngreen Devon 24 E5
Venn Green Devon 24 E5
Vennington Shrops 130 B6
Venn Ottery Devon 15 C7
Venn's Green Hereford 97 B10
Venny Tedburn Devon 14 B2
Venterdon Corn 12 G3
Vention Devon 40 E3
Ventnor IoW 21 F7
Venton Devon 7 D11
Ventongimps Corn 4 E5
Ventonleague Corn 2 B3
Venus Hill Herts 85 E8
Veraby Devon 26 B3
Vermentry Shetland 313 H5
Vernham Bank Hants 47 B10
Vernham Dean Hants 47 B10
Vernham Row Hants 47 B10
Vernham Street Hants 47 B11
Vernolds Common
Shrops 131 G9
Verwood Dorset 31 F9
Veryan Corn 3 B10
Veryan Green Corn 5 G8
Vicarage Devon 15 D10
Vicarscross Ches W 166 B6
Vickerstown Cumb 210 F3
Victoria Corn 5 C9
S Yorks 197 F7
Victoria Dock Village
Hull 200 B6
Victoria Park Bucks 84 C4
Victory Gardens Renfs 267 B10
Vidlin Shetland 312 G6
Viewpark N Lnrk 268 C4
Vigo W Mid 133 C10
Vigo Village Kent 68 G6
Vinegar Hill Mon 60 B2
Vinehall Street E Sus 38 C3
Vines Cross E Sus 23 B9
Viney Hill Glos 79 D11
Vinney Green S Glos 61 D7
Virginia Water Sur 66 F3
Virginstow Devon 12 C3
Viscar Corn 2 C6
Vobster Som 45 D8
Voe Shetland 312 E5
Shetland 313 G6
Vogue Corn 4 G4
Vole Som 43 D11
Vowchurch Hereford 97 D7
Vowchurch Common
Hereford 97 D7
Voxmoor Som 27 D10
Voxter Shetland 312 F5
Voy Orkney 314 E2
Vron Gate Shrops 130 B6
Vulcan Village Mers 183 C9

W

Waberthwaite Cumb 220 G2
Wackerfield Durham 233 G9
Wacton Hereford 116 F2
Norf 142 E3
Wacton Common Norf 142 F3
Wadbister Shetland 313 J6
Wadborough Worcs 99 B8
Wadbrook Devon 28 G4
Waddesdon Bucks 84 B2
Waddeton Devon 9 D7
Waddicar Mers 182 B5
Waddicombe Devon 26 B5
Waddingham Lincs 189 B7
Waddington Lancs 203 E10
Lincs 173 C7
Waddingworth Lincs 189 G11
Waddon Devon 14 F3
London 67 G10
Wadebridge Corn 10 G5
Wadeford Som 28 E4
Wade Hall Lancs 194 C4
Wadenhoe Northants 137 G10
Wades Green Ches E 167 C11
Wadesmill Herts 86 B5
Wadhurst E Sus 52 G6
Wadshelf Derbys 186 G4
Wadsley S Yorks 186 C4
Wadsley Bridge S Yorks 186 C4
Wadswick Wilts 61 F10
Wadwick Hants 48 C2
Wadworth S Yorks 187 B9
Waen Denb 165 B10
Denb 165 C7
Flint 181 G11
Powys 129 E9
Waen Aberwheeler
Denb 165 B9
Waen-fâch Powys 148 F4
Waen Goleugoed Denb 181 G9
Waen-pentir Gwyn 163 B9
Waen-wen Gwyn 163 B9
Wag Highld 311 G4
Wagbeach Shrops 131 C7
Wagg Som 28 B6
Waggersley Staffs 151 B7
Waggs Plot Devon 28 G4
Wainfelin Torf 78 E3
Wainfleet All Saints
Lincs 175 D7
Wainfleet Bank Lincs 175 D7
Wainfleet St Mary Lincs 175 D8
Wainfleet Tofts Lincs 175 D7
Wainford Norf 142 E6
Waingroves Derbys 170 F6
Wainhouse Corner Corn 11 B9
Wain Lee Staffs 168 D5
Wainscott Medway 69 E8
Wainstalls W Yorks 196 B4
Waitby Cumb 222 D5
Waithe Lincs 201 G9
Wakefield W Yorks 197 C10
Wake Green W Mid 133 G11
Wake Hill N Yorks 214 E3
Wake Lady Green
N Yorks 226 F3
Wakeley Herts 104 F6
Wakerley Northants 137 D9
Wakes Colne Essex 107 F7
Wakes Colne Green
Essex 107 E7
Walberswick Suff 127 C9
Walberton W Sus 35 F7
Walbottle T&W 242 D5
Walby Cumb 239 E10
Walcombe Som 44 D5
Walcot Bath 61 F9
Lincs 155 B11
N Lincs 199 C11
Oxon 82 B4
Shrops 130 F6
Swindon 63 C7
Telford 149 G11
Worcs 99 B8
Walcote Leics 135 G11
Warks 118 F2
Walcot Green Norf 142 G2
Walcott Lincs 173 D10
Norf 161 C7
Walden N Yorks 213 C10
Walden Head N Yorks 213 C9
Walden Stubbs N Yorks 198 D5
Waldersey Cambs 139 C8
Waldershaigh S Yorks 186 B3
Walderslade Medway 69 G9
Walderton W Sus 34 E3
Walditch Dorset 16 C5
Waldley Derbys 152 B2
Waldridge Durham 243 G7
Waldringfield Suff 108 C5
Waldringfield Heath
Suff 108 B5
Waldron E Sus 23 B8
Waldron Down E Sus 37 C8
Wales Som 29 C9
S Yorks 187 E7
Wales Bar S Yorks 187 E7
Walesby Lincs 189 C10
Notts 187 G11
Walesby Grange Lincs 189 C10
Wales End Suff 106 B5
Waleswood S Yorks 187 E7
Walford Hereford 97 G11
Hereford 115 C7
Shrops 149 E8
Som 28 B3
Staffs 150 C6
Walford Heath Shrops 149 F8
Walgherton Ches E 167 F11
Walgrave Northants 120 C6
Walham Glos 98 G6
Walham Green London 67 D9
Walhampton Hants 20 B2
Walkden Gtr Man 195 G8
Walker T&W 243 E7
Walker Barn Ches E 185 G7
Walkerburn Borders 261 B9
Walker Fold Lancs 203 E9
Walkeringham Notts 188 C3
Walkerith Lincs 188 C3
Walkern Herts 104 F5
Walker's Green Hereford 97 B10
Walker's Heath W Mid 117 B11
Walkerville N Yorks 224 F4
Walkford Dorset 19 C10
Walkhampton Devon 7 B10
Walkington E Yorks 208 F5
Walkley S Yorks 186 D4
Walkmill Shrops 131 E7
Walk Mill Lancs 204 G3
Walkmills Shrops 131 D9
Wall Corn 2 B4
Northumb 241 D10
Staffs 134 B2
Wallacestone Falk 279 F8
Wallaceton Dumfries 247 F8
Wallacetown S Ayrs 245 C7
S Ayrs 257 E8
Shetland 313 H5
Wallands Park E Sus 36 E6
Wallasey Mers 182 C4
Wallbank Lancs 195 D11
Wall Bank Shrops 131 E10
Wallbrook W Mid 133 E8
Wallcrouch E Sus 53 G7
Wallend London 68 C2
Wall End Cumb 210 C4
Kent 71 G8
Waller's Green Hereford 98 D3
Walley's Green Ches E 167 C11
Wall Heath W Mid 133 F7
Wall Hill Gtr Man 196 F3
Wallingford Oxon 64 B6
Wallington Hants 33 F9
Herts 104 E5
London 67 G9
Wallington Heath
W Mid 133 C9
Wallingwells Notts 187 E9
Wallis Pembs 91 F10
Wallisdown Poole 19 C7
Walliswood Sur 50 F6
Wall Mead Bath 45 B7
Wall Nook Durham 233 B10
Wallow Green Glos 80 F4
Wallridge Northumb 242 B3
Walls Shetland 313 J4
Wallsend T&W 243 D7
Wallston V Glam 58 E6
Wallsuches Gtr Man 195 E7
Wallsworth Glos 98 G6
Wall under Heywood
Shrops 131 E10
Wallyford E Loth 281 G7
Walmer Kent 55 C11
Walmer Bridge Lancs 194 C3
Walmersley Gtr Man 195 E10
Walmgate Stray York 207 C8
Walmley W Mid 134 E2
Walmsgate Lincs 190 F5
Walnut Grove Perth 286 E5
Walnut Tree M Keynes 103 D7
Walnuttree Green Herts 105 G9
Walpole Som 43 E10
Suff 127 C7
Walpole Cross Keys
Norf 157 F10
Walpole Highway Norf 157 G10
Walpole Marsh Norf 157 F9
Walpole St Andrew
Norf 157 F10
Walpole St Peter Norf 157 F9
Walrow Som 43 D10
Walsal End W Mid 118 B4
Walsall W Mid 133 D10
Walsall Wood W Mid 133 C10
Walsden W Yorks 196 C2
Walsgrave on Sowe
W Mid 135 G7
Walsham le Willows
Suff 125 C9
Walshaw Gtr Man 195 E9
Walshford N Yorks 206 C4
Walsoken Cambs 157 G9
Walson Mon 97 G8
Walston S Lnrk 269 F11
Walsworth Herts 104 E4
Walters Ash Bucks 84 F4
Walter's Green Kent 52 E4
Walterston V Glam 58 E5
Walterstone Hereford 96 F6
Waltham Kent 54 D6
NE Lincs 201 G9
Waltham Abbey Essex 86 E5
Waltham Chase Hants 33 D9
Waltham Cross Herts 86 E5
Waltham on the Wolds
Leics 154 D6
Waltham St Lawrence
Windsor 65 D10
Waltham's Cross Essex 106 E3
Walthamstow London 67 B11
Walton Bucks 84 C4
Cumb 240 E2
Derbys 170 B5
Leics 135 F11
Mers 182 C5
M Keynes 103 D7
Pboro 138 C3
Powys 114 F5
Shrops 115 B9
Som 44 F3
Staffs 151 C7
Staffs 151 D7
Suff 108 D5
Telford 149 F11
Warks 118 G5
W Yorks 197 D11
W Yorks 206 D4
Walton Cardiff Glos 99 E8
Walton Court Bucks 84 C4
Walton East Pembs 91 G10
Walton Elm Dorset 30 D3
Walton Grounds
Northants 101 E10
Walton Heath Hants 33 F10
Walton Highway Norf 157 G9
Walton in Gordano
N Som 60 E2
Walton-le-Dale Lancs 194 B5
Walton Manor Oxon 83 D8
Walton-on-Thames Sur 66 F6
Walton on the Hill
Staffs 151 E9
Sur 51 B8
Walton-on-the-Naze
Essex 108 G5
Walton on the Wolds
Leics 153 F11
Walton-on-Trent
Derbys 152 F4
Walton Pool Worcs 117 B8
Walton St Mary N Som 60 E2
Walton Summit Lancs 194 B5
Walton Warren Norf 158 F4
Walton West Pembs 72 C5
Walwen Flint 181 F10
Flint 181 G11
Flint 182 F2
Walwick Northumb 241 C10
Walworth Darl 224 B4
London 67 D10
Walworth Gate Darl 233 G10
Walwyn's Castle Pembs 72 C5
Wambrook Som 28 F3
Wampool Cumb 238 G6
Wanborough Sur 50 D2
Swindon 63 C8
Wandel Dyke S Lnrk 259 D11
Wandle Park London 67 F10
Wandon End Herts 104 G2
Wandsworth London 67 E9
Wangford Suff 127 B9
Wanlip Leics 154 G2
Wanlockhead Dumfries 259 G9
Wannock E Sus 23 E9
Wansford E Yorks 209 B7
Pboro 137 D11
Wanshurst Green Kent 53 D9
Wanson Corn 24 G1
Wanstead London 68 B2
Wanstrow Som 45 E8
Wanswell Glos 79 E11
Wantage Oxon 63 B11
Wants Green Worcs 116 F5
Wapley S Glos 61 D8
Wappenbury Warks 119 D7
Wappenham Northants 102 B2
Wapping London 67 C10
Warbleton E Sus 23 B10
Warblington Hants 22 B2
Warborough Oxon 83 G9
Warboys Cambs 138 G6
Warbreck Blkpool 202 F2
Warbstow Corn 11 C10
Warbstow Cross Corn 11 C10
Warburton Gtr Man 184 D2
Warburton Green
Gtr Man 184 E3
Warcop Cumb 222 B4
Warden Kent 70 E4
Northumb 241 D10
Powys 114 E6
Ward End W Mid 134 F2
Warden Hill Glos 99 G8
Warden Point IoW 20 D2
Warden Street C Beds 104 C2
Ward Green Suff 125 E10
S Yorks 197 G10
Ward Green Cross
Lancs 203 F8
Wardhedges C Beds 103 D11
Wardhill Orkney 314 D6
Wardington Oxon 101 B9
Wardlaw Borders 261 F7
Wardle Ches E 167 D10
Gtr Man 196 D2
Wardle Bank Ches E 167 D10
Wardley Gtr Man 195 G9
Rutland 136 C6
T&W 243 E7
W Sus 34 B4
Wardlow Derbys 185 G11
Wardour Wilts 30 B6
Wardpark N Lnrk 278 F5
Wardrobes Bucks 84 E4
Wardsend Ches E 184 E6
Wardy Hill Cambs 139 G9
Ware Herts 86 C5
Kent 71 G9
Wareham Dorset 18 D4
Warehorne Kent 54 G3
Warenford Northumb 264 D4
Waren Mill Northumb 264 C4
Warenton Northumb 264 C4
Wareside Herts 86 B5
Waresley Cambs 122 G4
Worcs 116 C6
Ware Street Kent 53 B9
Warfield Brack 65 E11
Warfleet Devon 9 E7
Wargate Lincs 156 C4
Wargrave Mers 183 C9
Wokingham 65 D9
Warham Hereford 97 D9
Norf 176 E6
Warhill Gtr Man 185 B7
Waring's Green W Mid 118 C2
Wark Northumb 241 B9
Northumb 263 B8
Wark Common
Northumb 263 B8
Warkleigh Devon 25 C10
Warkton Northants 121 B7

Warkworth Northants 101 C9
Northumb 252 B6
Warlaby N Yorks 224 G6
Warland W Yorks 196 C2
Warleggan Corn 6 B3
Warleigh Bath 61 G9
Warley Essex 87 G9
Warley Town W Yorks 196 B5
Warley Woods W Mid 133 F10
Warlingham Sur 51 B11
Warmbrook Derbys 170 E3
Warmfield W Yorks 197 C11
Warmingham Ches E 168 C2
Warminghurst W Sus 35 D10
Warmington Northants 137 E11
Warks 101 B8
Warminster Wilts 45 D11
Warminster Common
Wilts 45 E11
Warmlake Kent 53 C10
Warmley S Glos 61 E7
Warmley Hill S Glos 61 E7
Warmley Tower S Glos 61 E7
Warmonds Hill
Northants 121 D9
Warmsworth S Yorks 198 G4
Warmwell Dorset 17 D11
Warnborough Green
Hants 49 C8
Warndon Worcs 117 F7
Warners End Herts 85 D8
Warnford Hants 33 C10
Warnham W Sus 51 G7
Warningcamp W Sus 35 F8
Warninglid W Sus 36 B2
Warpsgrove Oxon 83 F10
Warren Ches E 184 G5
Dorset 18 C3
Pembs 72 F6
S Yorks 186 B5
Warrenby Redcar 235 F7
Warren Corner Hants 34 B2
Hants 49 D10
Warren Heath Suff 108 C4
Warren Row Windsor 65 C10
Warren's Green Herts 104 F5
Warren Street Kent 54 C2
Warrington M Keynes 121 G7
Warr 183 D10
Warsash Hants 33 F7
Warslow Staffs 169 D9
Warsop Vale Notts 171 B8
Warstock W Mid 117 B11
Warstone Staffs 133 B9
Warter E Yorks 208 C3
Warthermarske N Yorks 214 D4
Warthill N Yorks 207 B9
Wartle Aberds 293 C7
Wartling E Sus 23 D11
Wartnaby Leics 154 E4
Warton Lancs 194 B2
Lancs 211 E9
Northumb 252 C2
Warks 134 C5
Warton Bank Lancs 194 B2
Warwick Warks 118 E5
Warwick Bridge Cumb 239 F11
Warwick on Eden
Cumb 239 F11
Warwicksland Cumb 239 B10
Warwick Wold Sur 51 C10
Wasbister Orkney 314 C3
Wasdale Head Cumb 220 D3
Wash Derbys 185 E9
Washall Green Herts 105 E8
Washaway Corn 5 B10
Washbourne Devon 8 E5
Washbrook Som 44 C2
Suff 108 C2
Washbrook Street Suff 108 C2
Wash Common W Berks 64 G3
Wash Dyke Norf 157 F10
Washerwall Staffs 168 F6
Washfield Devon 26 D6
Washfold N Yorks 223 E11
Washford Som 42 E5
Worcs 117 D11
Washford Pyne Devon 26 E4
Washingborough Lincs 189 G8
Washingley Cambs 138 F2
Washington T&W 243 F8
W Sus 35 E10
Washington Village
T&W 243 F8
Washmere Green Suff 107 B8
Washpit W Yorks 196 F6
Wash Water W Berks 64 G3
Washwood Heath
W Mid 134 F2
Wasing W Berks 64 G5
Waskerley Durham 233 B7
Wasperton Warks 118 F5
Wasp Green Sur 51 D10
Wasps Nest Lincs 173 C9
Wass N Yorks 215 D11
Waste Green Warks 118 D4
Wastor Devon 8 F2
Watchet Som 42 E5
Watchfield Oxon 63 B8
Som 43 D10
Watchgate Cumb 221 F10
Watchhill Cumb 229 C9
Watch House Green
Essex 106 G3
Watchill Dumfries 238 D6
Dumfries 248 G3
Watcombe Torbay 9 B8
Watendlath Cumb 220 B5
Water Devon 13 E11
Lancs 195 B10
Waterbeach Cambs 123 D9
W Sus 22 B5
Waterbeck Dumfries 238 B6
Waterdale Herts 85 E10
Waterden Norf 159 B7
Waterditch Hants 19 B9
Water Eaton M Keynes 103 E7
Oxon 83 C8
Waterend Bucks 84 F3
Cumb 229 G8
Glos 80 C3
Herts 86 C2
Water End Beds 104 B2
C Beds 103 D11
C Beds 104 B5
Essex 105 C11
E Yorks 207 F11
Hants 49 C7
Herts 85 C8
Herts 86 E2
Waterfall Staffs 169 E9
Waterfoot Argyll 255 D9
Cumb 230 G5
E Renf 267 D11
Lancs 195 C10
Waterford Hants 20 B2
Herts 86 C4
Water Fryston W Yorks 198 B3
Water Garth Nook Cumb 210 F3
Watergate Corn 6 E4
Corn 11 E8
Watergore Som 28 D6
Waterhales Essex 87 F8
Waterham Kent 70 G5
Waterhay Wilts 81 G9
Waterhead Angus 292 F6
Cumb 221 E7
Devon 8 F3
Dumfries 248 E5
Waterhead on Minnoch
S Ayrs 245 E9
Waterheads Borders 270 E4
Waterheath Norf 143 E8
Waterhouses Durham 233 C9
Staffs 169 E9
Water Houses N Yorks 213 F7
Wateringbury Kent 53 C7
Waterlane Glos 80 E6
Waterlip Som 45 E7
Waterloo Blkburn 195 B7
Corn 11 G8
Derbys 170 C6
Gtr Man 196 G2
Highld 295 C8
Mers 182 B4
N Lnrk 268 E6
Norf 126 B2
Norf 143 E8
Norf 160 F4
Pembs 73 E7
Perth 286 D4
Poole 18 C6
Shrops 149 C9
Waterloo Park Mers 182 B4
Waterloo Port Gwyn 163 C7
Waterlooville Hants 33 F11
Waterman Quarter Kent 53 E10
Watermead Glos 80 B5
Watermeetings S Lnrk 259 G11
Watermill E Sus 38 E2
Watermillock Cumb 230 G4
Watermoor Glos 81 E8
Water Newton Cambs 138 D2
Water Orton Warks 134 E3
Waterperry Oxon 83 D10
Waterrow Som 27 B9
Watersfield W Sus 35 D8
Watersheddings
Gtr Man 196 F2
Waterside Aberds 292 B5
Aberds 303 G10
Blkburn 195 C8
Bucks 85 E7
Cumb 229 B10
Derbys 185 E8
E Ayrs 245 B10
E Ayrs 267 G9
E Dunb 278 G3
E Renf 267 D10
Sur 51 D11
S Yorks 199 E7
Telford 150 F2
Waterslack Lancs 211 D9
Water's Nook Gtr Man 195 F7
Waterstein Highld 297 G7
Waterstock Oxon 83 D10
Waterston Pembs 72 D6
Water Stratford Bucks 102 E3
Waters Upton Telford 150 F2
Waterthorpe S Yorks 186 E6
Waterton Aberds 303 F9
Bridgend 58 D2
Water Yeat Cumb 210 B5
Watford Herts 85 F10
Northants 120 D2
Watford Gap Staffs 134 C2
Watford Heath Herts 85 G10
Watford Park Caerph 58 B6
Wath Cumb 222 D3
N Yorks 214 D6
N Yorks 214 F2
N Yorks 216 D3
Wath Brow Cumb 219 C10
Watherston Borders 271 F8
Wath upon Dearne
S Yorks 198 G2
Watledge Glos 80 E4
Watley's End S Glos 61 C7
Watlington Norf 158 G2
Oxon 83 G11
Watnall Notts 171 F8
Watsness Shetland 313 H3
Watten Highld 310 D6
Wattisfield Suff 125 C10
Wattisham Suff 125 G10
Wattisham Stone Suff 125 G10
Wattlefield Norf 142 D2
Wattlesborough Heath
Shrops 149 G7
Watton E Yorks 208 C6
Norf 141 C8
Watton at Stone Herts 86 B4
Watton Green Norf 141 C8
Watton's Green Essex 87 F8
Wattston N Lnrk 268 B5
Wattstown Rhondda 77 G8
Wattsville Caerph 78 G2
Wauchan Highld 295 G11
Waulkmill Lodge Orkney 314 F3
Waun Gwyn 163 C9
Powys 148 F4
Waunarlwydd Swansea 56 B6
Waun Beddau Pembs 90 F5
Waunclunda Carms 94 E3
Waunfawr Gwyn 163 D8
Waun Fawr Ceredig 128 G2
Waungilwen Carms 92 D6
Waungron Swansea 75 E9
Waunlwyd Bl Gwent 77 D11
Waun-Lwyd Bl Gwent 77 D11
Waun-y-clyn Carms 75 E7
Waun y Gilfach Bridgend 57 D10
Wavendon M Keynes 103 D8
Wavendon Gate
M Keynes 103 D8
Waverbridge Cumb 229 B10
Waverton Ches W 167 C7
Cumb 229 B10
Wavertree Mers 182 D5
Wawcott W Berks 63 F11
Wawne E Yorks 209 F7
Waxham Norf 161 D8
Waxholme E Yorks 201 B10
Way Kent 71 F10
Waye Devon 13 G11
Wayend Street Hereford 98 D4
Wayfield Medway 69 F9
Wayford Som 28 F6
Waymills Shrops 167 G9
Wayne Green Mon 78 B6
Way's Green Ches W 167 B10
Waytown Devon 24 C5
Devon 40 G5
Way Village Devon 26 E5
Way Wick N Som 59 G11
Wdig / Goodwick Pembs 91 D8
Weachyburn Aberds 302 D6
Weacombe Som 42 E6
Weald Oxon 82 E4
Wealdstone London 67 B7
Wearde Corn 7 D8
Weardley W Yorks 205 E11
Weare Som 44 C2
Weare Giffard Devon 25 C7
Wearhead Durham 232 D3
Wearne Som 28 B6
Weasdale Cumb 222 E3
Weasenham All Saints
Norf 158 E6
Weasenham St Peter
Norf 159 E7
Weaste Gtr Man 184 B4
Weatherhill Sur 51 E10
Weatheroak Hill Worcs 117 C11
Weaverham Ches W 183 G10
Weavering Street Kent 53 B9
Weaverslake Staffs 152 F2
Weaverthorpe N Yorks 217 E9
Webbington Som 43 B11
Webheath Worcs 117 D10
Webscott Shrops 149 E9
Wecock Hants 33 E11
Wedderlairs Aberds 303 F8
Wedderlie Borders 272 E2
Weddington Kent 55 B9
Warks 135 E7
Wedhampton Wilts 46 B5
Wedmore Som 44 D2
Wednesbury W Mid 133 D9
Wednesbury Oak
W Mid 133 E9
Wednesfield W Mid 133 C8
Weecar Notts 172 B4
Weedon Bucks 84 B4
Weedon Bec Northants 120 F2
Weedon Lois Northants 102 B2
Weeford Staffs 134 C2
Week Devon 8 C5
Devon 12 E5
Devon 25 B9
Devon 26 D2
Weeke Devon 26 F3
Hants 48 G3
Week Green Corn 11 B10
Weekley Northants 137 G7
Weekmoor Som 27 B10
Weeks IoW 21 C7
Week St Mary Corn 11 B10
Weel E Yorks 209 F7
Weeley Essex 108 G2
Weeley Heath Essex 108 G3
Weelsby NE Lincs 201 F9
Weem Perth 286 C2
Weeping Cross Staffs 151 E8
Weethley Warks 117 F11
Weethley Bank Warks 117 G11
Weethley Gate Warks 117 G11
Weeting Norf 140 F5
Weeton E Yorks 201 C11
Lancs 202 G3
N Yorks 205 D11
Weetwood W Yorks 205 F11
Weetwood Common
Ches W 167 B8
Weetwood Hall
Northumb 264 D2
Weir Essex 69 B10
Lancs 195 B11
Weirbrook Shrops 148 E6
Weir Quay Devon 7 C8
Welborne Norf 159 G11
Welborne Common
Norf 141 B11
Welbourn Lincs 173 E7
Welburn N Yorks 216 C3
N Yorks 216 F4
Welbury N Yorks 225 E7
Welby Lincs 155 B9
Welches Dam Cambs 139 F9
Welcombe Devon 24 D2
Weld Bank Lancs 194 D5
Weldon Northants 137 F8
Northumb 252 D4
Welford Northants 136 G2
W Berks 64 E2
Welford-on-Avon
Warks 118 G3
Welham Leics 136 E5
Notts 188 E2
Som 45 G7
Welhambridge
E Yorks 207 G11
Welham Green Herts 86 D2
Well Hants 49 D9
Lincs 190 G6
N Yorks 214 C5
Welland Worcs 98 C5
Welland Stone Worcs 98 D6
Wellbank Angus 287 D8
Well Bottom Dorset 30 D6
Wellbrook E Sus 37 B9
Welldale Dumfries 238 D5
Well End Bucks 65 B11
Herts 86 F2
Weller's Town Kent 52 E4
Wellesbourne Warks 118 F5
Well Green Gtr Man 184 D3
Wellheads Aberds 302 F4
Well Heads W Yorks 205 G7
Well Hill Kent 68 G3
Wellhouse W Berks 64 E4
W Yorks 196 E5
Welling London 68 D3
Wellingborough
Northants 121 D7
Wellingham Norf 159 E7
Wellingore Lincs 173 D7
Wellington Cumb 219 E11
Hereford 97 B9
Som 27 C10
Telford 150 G3
Wellington Heath
Hereford 98 C4
Wellington Hill W Yorks 206 F2
Wellisford Som 27 C9
Wellow Bath 45 B8
IoW 20 D3
NE Lincs 201 F9
Notts 171 B11
Wellow Wood Hants 32 C3
Well Place Oxon 65 B7
Wellpond Green Herts 105 G8
Wellroyd W Yorks 205 F10
Wells Som 44 D5
Wellsborough Leics 135 C7
Wells Green Ches E 167 E11
Wells-Next-The-Sea
Norf 176 E6
Wellsprings Som 28 B2
Well Street Kent 53 B7
Wellstye Green Essex 87 B10
Wellswood Torbay 9 C8
Welltown Corn 6 B2
Well Town Devon 26 F6
Wellwood Fife 279 D11
Welney Norf 139 E10
Welsford Devon 24 C3
Welshampton Shrops 149 B8
Welsh Bicknor Hereford 79 B9
Welsh End Shrops 149 B10
Welsh Frankton Shrops 149 C7
Welsh Harp London 67 B8
Welsh Hook Pembs 91 F8
Welsh Newton Hereford 79 B7
Welsh Newton Common
Hereford 79 B8
Welshpool Powys 130 B4
Welsh St Donats V Glam 58 D4
Welshwood Park Essex 107 F10
Welstor Devon 13 G10
Welton Bath 45 C7
Cumb 230 C3
E Ayrs 258 D2
E Yorks 200 B3
Lincs 189 F8
Northants 119 D11
Welton Hill Lincs 189 E8
Welton le Marsh Lincs 175 B7
Welton le Wold Lincs 190 D3
Welwick E Yorks 201 C10
Welwyn Herts 86 B2
Welwyn Garden City
Herts 86 C2
Wem Shrops 149 D10
Wembdon Som 43 F9
Wembley London 67 B7
Wembley Park London 67 B7
Wembury Devon 7 F10
Wembworthy Devon 25 F11
Wemyss Bay Invclyd 266 B3
Wenallt Ceredig 112 C3
Gwyn 146 F4
Gwyn 165 G7
Wendens Ambo Essex 105 D10
Wendlebury Oxon 83 B9
Wendling Norf 159 G8
Wendover Bucks 84 D5
Wendover Dean Bucks 84 E5
Wendron Corn 2 C5
Wendy Cambs 104 B6
Wenfordbridge Corn 11 F7
Wenhaston Suff 127 B8
Wenhaston Black Heath
Suff 127 C8
Wennington Cambs 122 B4
Lancs 212 E2
London 68 C4
Wensley Derbys 170 C3
N Yorks 213 B11
Wentbridge W Yorks 198 D3
Wentnor Shrops 131 E7
Wentworth Cambs 123 B9
S Yorks 186 B5
Wenvoe V Glam 58 E6
Weobley Hereford 115 G8
Weobley Marsh
Hereford 115 G8
Weoley Castle W Mid 133 G10
Wepham W Sus 35 F8
Wepre Flint 166 B3
Wereham Norf 140 C3
Wereham Row Norf 140 C3
Wereton Staffs 168 E3
Wergs W Mid 133 C7
Wern Gwyn 145 B10
Powys 77 B10
Powys 147 G9
Powys 148 E5
Powys 148 G5
Shrops 148 C5
Swansea 56 C4
Wern ddu Shrops 148 D4
Werneth Gtr Man 196 G2
Werneth Low Gtr Man 185 C7
Wernffrwd Swansea 56 C4
Wern-Gifford Mon 96 G6
Wernlas Shrops 148 E6
Wern-olau Swansea 56 B5
Wernrheolydd Mon 78 C5
Wern Tarw Bridgend 58 C3
Wern-y-cwrt Mon 78 D5
Wern-y-gaer Flint 166 B2
Wernyrheolydd Mon 78 C5
Werrington Corn 12 D2
Pboro 138 C3
Staffs 168 F6
Wervin Ches W 182 G6
Wescoe Hill N Yorks 205 D11
Wesham Lancs 202 G4
Wessington Derbys 170 D5
West Aberthaw V Glam 58 F4
Westacott Devon 40 G5
West Acre Norf 158 F5
West Acton London 67 C7
West Adderbury Oxon 101 D9
West Allerdean
Northumb 273 F9
West Allotment T&W 243 C8
West Alvington Devon 8 G4
West Amesbury Wilts 46 E6
West Anstey Devon 26 B5
West Appleton N Yorks 224 G4
West Ardhu Argyll 288 D6
West Ardsley W Yorks 197 B9
West Ardwell Dumfries 236 E2
West Arthurlie E Renf 267 D9
West Ashby Lincs 190 G3
West Ashford Devon 40 F4
West Ashling W Sus 22 B4
West Ashton Wilts 45 B11
West Auckland Durham 233 F9
West Ayton N Yorks 217 C9
West Bagborough Som 43 G7
West Bank Bl Gwent 78 D2
Halton 183 E8
West Barkwith Lincs 189 E11
West Barnby N Yorks 226 C6
West Barnes London 67 F8
West Barns E Loth 282 F3
West Barsham Norf 159 C8
West Bay Dorset 16 C5
West Beckham Norf 160 B2
West Bedfont Sur 66 E5
West Benhar N Lnrk 269 C7
Westbere Kent 71 G7
West Bergholt Essex 107 F9
West Bexington Dorset 16 D6
West Bilney Norf 158 F4
West Blackdene Durham 232 D3
West Blackdown Devon 12 E5
West Blatchington
Brighton 36 F3
West Bold Borders 261 B9
West Boldon T&W 243 E9
Westborough Lincs 172 G5
Westbourne Bmouth 19 C7
Suff 108 B2
W Sus 22 B3
Westbourne Green
London 67 C9
West Bourton Dorset 30 B3
West Bowling W Yorks 205 G9
West Bradford Lancs 203 E10
West Bradley Som 44 F5
West Bretton W Yorks 197 E9
West Bridgford Notts 153 B11
West Brompton London 67 D9
West Bromwich
W Mid 133 E10
Westbrook Hereford 96 C5
Kent 71 E10
Sur 50 E3
Warr 183 C9
W Berks 64 E2
Wilts 62 F3
Westbrook Green Norf 142 G2
Westbrook Hay Herts 85 D8
West Broughton Derbys 152 C2
West Buckland Devon 41 G7
Som 27 C11
West Burnside Aberds 293 F8
West Burrafirth
Shetland 313 H4
West Burton N Yorks 213 B10
W Sus 35 E7
Westbury Bucks 102 D2
Shrops 131 B7
Wilts 45 C11
Westbury Leigh Wilts 45 C11
Westbury-on-Severn
Glos 80 C2
Westbury on Trym Bristol 60 D5
Westbury Park Bristol 60 D5
Westbury-sub-Mendip
Som 44 D4
West Butsfield Durham 233 C8
West Butterwick
N Lincs 199 F10
Westby Lancs 202 G3
Lincs 155 D9
West Byfleet Sur 66 G4
West Caister Norf 161 G10
West Calder W Loth 269 C10
West Camel Som 29 C9
West Carlton W Yorks 205 E10
West Carr Hull 209 G7
N Lincs 199 F8
West Chadsmoor Staffs 151 G9
West Challow Oxon 63 B11
West Charleton Devon 8 G5
West Chelborough Dorset 29 F8
West Chevington
Northumb 252 D6
West Chiltington W Sus 35 D9
West Chiltington Common
W Sus 35 D9
West Chinnock Som 29 E7
West Chirton T&W 243 D8
West Chisenbury Wilts 46 C6
West Clandon Sur 50 C4
West Cliff Bmouth 19 C7
N Yorks 227 C7
West Cliffe Kent 55 E10
Westcliff-on-Sea
Sthend 69 B11
West Clyne Highld 311 J2
Highld 311 J2
West Clyth Highld 310 F6
Highld 310 F6
West Coker Som 29 E8
Westcombe Som 29 B7
Som 45 F7
West Common Hants 32 G6
West Compton Dorset 17 C7
Som 44 E5
West Cornforth Durham 234 E2
Westcot Oxon 63 B10
Westcote Glos 100 G4
Westcotes Leicester 135 C11
Westcott Bucks 84 B2
Devon 27 G8
Shrops 131 C8
Sur 50 D6
Westcott Barton Oxon 101 F8
Westcourt Wilts 63 G8
West Cowick E Yorks 199 C7
West Cranmore Som 45 E7
Westcroft M Keynes 102 E6
W Mid 133 C8
West Cross Kent 53 G10
Swansea 56 D6
West Crudwell Wilts 80 G6
West Cullery Aberds 293 C9
West Curry Corn 11 C11
West Curthwaite Cumb 230 B2
West Darlochan Argyll 255 E7
Westdean E Sus 23 F8
West Dean Wilts 32 B3
W Sus 34 E5
West Deeping Lincs 138 B2
West Denant Pembs 72 C6
Westdene Brighton 36 F3
West Denton T&W 242 D5
West Derby Mers 182 C5
West Dereham Norf 140 C3
West Didsbury Gtr Man 184 C4
West Down Devon 40 E4
Hants 47 F11
Westdown Camp Wilts 46 D4
Westdowns Corn 11 E7
West Downs Corn 5 C10
West Drayton London 66 D5
Notts 188 G2
West Dulwich London 67 E10
West Ealing London 67 C7
West Edge Derbys 170 C4
West Ella E Yorks 200 B4
Westend Oxon 100 G6
S Glos 79 G10
West End Beds 121 E11
Beds 121 G9
Brack 65 E11
Bracknell 66 G2
Caerph 78 F2
Cumb 239 F8
Dorset 30 G6
E Yorks 201 B9
E Yorks 208 G4
E Yorks 209 B9
E Yorks 209 G9
E Yorks 217 G11
Glos 80 F5
Hants 33 E7
Hants 33 F9
Hants 48 F6
Herts 86 D3
Kent 54 B2
Kent 71 F7
Lancs 195 B8
Lancs 211 G8
Leics 153 F8
Lincs 174 F5
Lincs 190 B5
Mon 78 F6
Norf 141 B8
Norf 161 G10
N Som 60 F3
N Yorks 205 B8
N Yorks 206 E6
N Yorks 207 F7
Oxon 64 B5
Oxon 82 E6
S Glos 61 B8
S Lnrk 269 F9
Som 44 C5
Som 45 G7
Suff 143 G9
Surrey Heath 49 E10
S Yorks 199 F7
Wilts 30 C6
Wilts 31 C7
Wilts 62 D3
Windsor 65 D10
Worcs 99 D11
W Sus 36 D2
W Yorks 197 B7
W Yorks 205 F10
West End Esher, Sur 66 G6
West End Green Hants 65 G7
West End / Marian-y-mor
Gwyn 145 C7
Westend Town
Northumb 241 D7
West-end Town V Glam 58 F3
Westenhanger Kent 54 F6
Wester Aberchalder
Highld 300 G5
Wester Arboll Highld 311 L2
Wester Auchinloch N
Lnrk 278 G3
Wester Auchnagallin
Highld 301 F10
Wester Balgedie Perth 286 G5
Wester Brae Highld 300 C6
Wester Broomhouse
E Loth 282 F3
Wester Craiglands
Highld 301 D7
Wester Culbeuchly
Aberds 302 C6
Westerdale Highld 310 D5
N Yorks 226 D3
Wester Dalvoult Highld 291 B11
Wester Dechmont
W Loth 269 B10
Wester Deloraine
Borders 261 E8
Wester Denoon Angus 287 C7
Wester Ellister Argyll 254 B2
Wester Essendy Perth 286 C5
Wester Essenside
Borders 261 E10
Wester Feddal Perth 286 G2
Westerfield Shetland 313 H5
Suff 108 B3
Wester Fintray Aberds 293 B10
Westerfolds Moray 301 C11
Wester Galgantray
Highld 301 E8
Westergate W Sus 22 C6
Wester Gospetry Fife 286 G5
Wester Gruinards
Highld 309 K5
Wester Hailes Edin 270 B4
Westerham Kent 52 C2
Westerhope T&W 242 D5
Wester Housebyres
Borders 262 B2
Wester Kershope
Borders 261 D9
Wester Lealty Highld 300 B6
Westerleigh S Glos 61 D8
Westerleigh Hill S Glos 61 D8
Wester Lix Stirl 285 E9
Wester Milton Highld 301 D9
Wester Mosshead
Aberds 302 F5
Western Bank Cumb 229 B10
Western Downs Staffs 151 E8
Wester Newburn Fife 287 G8
Western Heights Kent 55 E10
Western Hill Durham 233 C11
Western Park Leicester 135 C11
Wester Ord Aberds 293 C10
Wester Parkgate
Dumfries 248 F2
Wester Quarff Shetland 313 K6
Wester Skeld Shetland 313 J4
Wester Strath Highld 300 D6
Westerton Aberds 293 B9
Aberds 302 E5
Angus 287 B10
Durham 233 E10
Moray 302 D3
W Sus 22 B5
Westertown Aberds 303 F7
Wester Watten Highld 310 D6
Westerwick Shetland 313 J4
West Ewell Sur 67 G8
West Farleigh Kent 53 C8
West Farndon
Northants 119 G10
West Felton Shrops 148 D6
West Fenton E Loth 281 E9
West Ferry Dundee 287 D8
Westfield Bath 45 C7
Cumb 228 F5
E Sus 38 D4
Hants 21 B10
Hereford 98 B4
Highld 310 C4
N Lnrk 278 G4
Norf 141 B9
Redcar 235 G7
Sur 50 B4
S Yorks 186 E6
W Loth 279 G8
W Yorks 197 C8
W Yorks 205 E9
West Field N Lincs 200 D6
York 207 C7
Westfields Dorset 30 F2
Hereford 97 C9
West Fields W Berks 64 F3
Westfields of Rattray
Perth 286 C5
Westfield Sole Kent 69 G9
West Firle E Sus 23 D7
West Fleetham
Northumb 264 D5
West Flodden
Northumb 263 C10
Westford Som 27 C10
West Garforth W Yorks 206 G3
Westgate Durham 232 D4
N Lincs 199 F9
Norf 176 E4
Norf 177 E7
Westgate Hill W Yorks 197 B8
Westgate on Sea Kent 71 E10
Westgate Street Norf 160 E3
West Ginge Oxon 64 B2
West Gorton Gtr Man 184 B5
West Grafton Wilts 63 G8
West Green Hants 49 B8
London 67 B10
S Yorks 197 F11
W Sus 51 F9
West Greenskares
Aberds 303 C7
West Grimstead Wilts 32 B2
West Grinstead W Sus 35 C11
West Haddlesey
N Yorks 198 B5
West Haddon Northants 120 C2
West Hagbourne Oxon 64 B4
West Hagley Worcs 133 G8
Westhall Aberds 302 G6
Suff 143 G8
West Hall Cumb 240 D3
West Hallam Derbys 170 G6
Westhall Hill Oxon 82 C3
West Halton N Lincs 200 C2
Westham Dorset 17 F9
E Sus 23 E10
Som 44 D2
West Ham Hants 48 C6
London 68 C2
Westhampnett W Sus 22 B5
West Hampstead London 67 B9
West Handley Derbys 186 F5
West Hanney Oxon 82 G6
West Hanningfield Essex 88 F2
West Hardwick
W Yorks 198 D2
West Harling Norf 141 G9
West Harlsey N Yorks 225 F8
West Harnham Wilts 31 B10
West Harptree Bath 44 B5
West Harrow London 66 B6
West Harting W Sus 34 C3
West Harton T&W 243 E9
West Hatch Som 28 C3
Wilts 30 B6
Westhay Som 44 E2
Westhead Lancs 194 F2
West Head Norf 139 B11
West Heath Ches E 168 C4
Hants 48 B5
Hants 49 B11
London 68 D3
W Mid 117 B10
West Helmsdale Highld 311 H4
West Hendon London 67 B8
West Hendred Oxon 64 B2
West Herrington T&W 243 G8
West Heslerton N Yorks 217 D8
West Hewish N Som 59 G11
Westhide Hereford 97 C11
Westhill Aberds 293 C10
E Yorks 209 F10
Highld 301 E7
West Hill Devon 15 C7
E Sus 38 E4
E Yorks 218 F3
London 67 E8
N Som 60 D3
Som 30 B2
Staffs 151 G9
Wilts 61 F11
W Sus 51 G10
West Hoathly W Sus 51 G11
West Holme Dorset 18 D3
West Holywell T&W 243 C8
Westhope Hereford 115 G9
Shrops 131 F9
West Horndon Essex 68 B6
Westhorp Northants 119 G10
Westhorpe Lincs 156 C4
Notts 171 E11
Suff 125 D10
West Horrington Som 44 D5
West Horsley Sur 50 C5
West Horton Northumb 264 C2
West Hougham Kent 55 E9
Westhoughton Gtr Man 195 F7
West Houlland Shetland 313 H4
Westhouse N Yorks 212 E3
Westhouses Derbys 170 D6
West Houses Lincs 174 E4
West Howe Bmouth 19 B7
West Howetown Som 42 G2
Westhumble Sur 51 C7
West Huntington York 207 B8
West Huntspill Som 43 E10
West Hurn Dorset 19 B8
West Hyde Herts 85 G8
West Hynish Argyll 288 F1
West Hythe Kent 54 G6
West Ilkerton Devon 41 D8
West Ilsley W Berks 64 C3
Westing Shetland 312 C7
Westington Glos 100 D2
West Itchenor W Sus 22 C3
West Jesmond T&W 243 D7
West Keal Lincs 174 C5
West Kennett Wilts 62 F6
West Kensington London 67 D8
West Kilbride N Ayrs 266 F4
West Kilburn London 67 C8
West Kingsdown Kent 68 G5
West Kingston W Sus 35 G9
West Kington Wilts 61 D10
West Kington Wick
Wilts 61 D10
West Kinharrachie
Aberds 303 F9
West Kirby Mers 182 D2
West Kirkby Mers 182 D2
West Knapton N Yorks 217 D7
West Knighton Dorset 17 D10
West Knoyle Wilts 45 G11
West Kyloe Northumb 273 G11
West Kyo Durham 242 G5
Westlake Devon 8 E2
West Lambrook Som 28 D6
Westland Argyll 275 G11
Westland Green Herts 105 G8
Westlands Staffs 168 G4
Worcs 117 E7
West Langdon Kent 55 D10
West Langwell Highld 309 J6
West Lavington Wilts 46 C4
W Sus 34 C5
West Layton N Yorks 224 D2
Westlea Northumb 252 G6
Swindon 62 C6
West Lea Durham 234 B4
West Leake Notts 153 D10
West Learmouth
Northumb 263 B9
Westleigh Devon 25 B7
Devon 27 D9
Gtr Man 194 G6
West Leigh Devon 25 F11
Hants 22 B2
Som 42 G6
Westleton Suff 127 D8
West Lexham Norf 158 F6
Westley Shrops 131 B7
Suff 124 E6
Westley Heights Essex 69 B7
Westley Waterless
Cambs 124 F2
West Lilling N Yorks 216 F2
Westlington Bucks 84 C3
Westlinton Cumb 239 E9
West Linton Borders 270 E2
West Liss Hants 34 B3
West Littleton S Glos 61 D9
West Lockinge Oxon 64 B2
West Looe Corn 6 E5
West Luccombe Som 41 D11
West Lulworth Dorset 18 E2
West Lutton N Yorks 217 F8
West Lydford Som 44 G5
West Lydiatt Hereford 97 C11
West Lyn Devon 41 D8
West Lyng Som 28 B4
West Lynn Norf 158 E2
West Mains Borders 271 F11
S Lnrk 268 E2
West Malling Kent 53 B7
West Malvern Worcs 98 B5
Westmancote Worcs 99 D8
West Marden W Sus 34 E3
West Marina E Sus 38 F3
West Markham Notts 188 G2
Westmarsh Kent 71 G9
West Marsh NE Lincs 201 E9
West Marton N Yorks 204 C3
West Mathers Aberds 293 G9
West Melbury Dorset 30 C5
West Melton S Yorks 198 G2
West Meon Hants 33 C10
West Meon Woodlands
Hants 33 B10
West Merkland Highld 308 F3
West Mersea Essex 89 C8
Westmeston E Sus 36 E4
Westmill Herts 104 E3
Herts 105 F7
West Milton Dorset 16 B6
Westminster London 67 D10
West Minster Kent 70 E2
West Molesey Sur 66 F6
West Monkseaton T&W 243 C8
West Monkton Som 28 B3
West Moor T&W 243 C7
Westmoor End Cumb 229 D8
West Moors Dorset 31 G9
West Morden Dorset 18 B4
West Morriston Borders 272 G2
West Morton W Yorks 205 E7
West Mudford Som 29 C9
Westmuir Angus 287 B7
West Muir Angus 293 G7
West Myreriggs Perth 286 C6
Westness Orkney 314 D3
West Ness N Yorks 216 D3
West Newham Northumb 242 B3
Westnewton Cumb 229 C8
Northumb 263 C10
West Newton E Yorks 209 F9
Norf 158 D3
Som 28 B3
West Norwood London 67 E10
Westoe T&W 243 D9
West Ogwell Devon 14 G2
Weston Bath 61 F8
Ches E 168 E2
Ches E 184 G5
Devon 15 D9
Devon 27 G10
Dorset 17 G9
Dorset 29 F8
Halton 183 E8
Hants 34 C2
Hereford 115 F7
Herts 104 E5
Lincs 156 D5
Northants 101 B11
Notts 172 B3
N Yorks 205 D9
Pembs 73 C8
Shrops 114 C6
Shrops 131 E11
Shrops 148 D5
Shrops 149 D11
S Lnrk 269 F10
Soton 32 E6
Staffs 151 D9
Suff 143 F8
W Berks 63 E11
Weston Bampfylde Som 29 C10
Weston Beggard
Hereford 97 C11
Westonbirt Glos 61 B11
Weston by Welland
Northants 136 E5
Weston Colley Hants 48 F4
Weston Colville Cambs 124 G2
Westoncommon Shrops 149 D8
Weston Common Soton 33 E7
Weston Corbett Hants 49 D7
Weston Coyney Stoke 168 G6
Weston Ditch Suff 124 B3
Weston Favell Northants 120 E5
Weston Green Cambs 124 G2
Norf 160 G2
Sur 67 F7
Weston Heath Shrops 150 G5
Weston Hills Lincs 156 E5
Weston in Arden Warks 135 F7
Westoning C Beds 103 E10
Weston-in-Gordano
N Som 60 E2
Weston Jones Staffs 150 E5
Weston Longville Norf 160 F2
Weston Lullingfields
Shrops 149 E8
Weston Manor IoW 20 D2
Weston Mill Plym 7 D9
Weston-on-Avon
Warks 118 G3
Weston-on-the-Green
Oxon 83 B8
Weston-on-Trent
Derbys 153 D8
Weston Park Bath 61 F8
Weston Patrick Hants 49 D7
Weston Point Halton 183 E7
Weston Rhyn Shrops 148 B5
Weston-sub-Edge Glos 100 C2
Weston-super-Mare
N Som 59 G10
Weston Town Som 45 E8
Weston Turville Bucks 84 C5
Weston under Lizard
Staffs 150 G6
Weston under Penyard
Hereford 98 G2
Weston under Wetherley
Warks 119 D7
Weston Underwood
Derbys 170 G3
M Keynes 121 G7
Westonwharf Shrops 149 D8
Westonzoyland Som 43 G11
West Orchard Dorset 30 D4
West Overton Wilts 62 F6
Westow N Yorks 216 F5
Westowe Som 42 G6
Westown Devon 27 E10
Perth 286 E6
West Panson Devon 12 C2
West Park Hrtlpl 234 E5
Hull 200 B5
Mers 183 B7
T&W 243 D9
W Yorks 205 F11
West Parley Dorset 19 B7
West Pasture Durham 232 G4
West Peckham Kent 52 C6
West Pelton Durham 242 G6
West Pennard Som 44 F4
West Pentire Corn 4 C5
West Perry Cambs 122 D2
West Pontnewydd Torf 78 F3
West Poringland Norf 142 C5
West Porlock Som 41 D11
Westport Argyll 255 E7
Som 28 D5

West Portholland Corn 5 G9
West Porton Renfs 277 G8
West Pulham Dorset 30 F2
West Putford Devon 24 D5
West Quantoxhead Som 42 E6
Westquarter Falk 279 F8
Westra V Glam 58 E6
West Rainton Durham 234 B2
West Rasen Lincs 189 D9
West Ravendale
NE Lincs 190 B2
West Raynham Norf 159 D7
West Retford Notts 187 E11
Westridge Green
W Berks 64 D5
Westrigg W Loth 269 B8
Westrip Glos 80 D4
Westrop Wilts 61 E11
Westrop Green W Berks 64 E4
West Rounton N Yorks 225 E8
West Row Suff 124 B3
West Royd W Yorks 205 F9
West Rudham Norf 158 D6
West Ruislip London 66 B5
Westrum N Lincs 200 F4
West Runton Norf 177 E11
Westruther Borders 272 F2
Westry Cambs 139 D7
West Saltoun E Loth 271 B9
West Sandford Devon 26 G4
West Sandwick Shetland 312 E6
West Scholes W Yorks 205 G7
West Scrafton N Yorks 213 C11
West Shepton Som 44 E6
West Side Bl Gwent 77 D11
Orkney 314 C5
West Skelston Dumfries 247 F8
West Sleekburn
Northumb 253 G7
West Somerton Norf 161 F9
West Southbourne
Bmouth 19 C8
West Stafford Dorset 17 D10
West Stockwith Notts 188 C3
West Stoke Devon 13 G9
Som 29 D7
W Sus 22 B4
West Stonesdale
N Yorks 223 E7
West Stoughton Som 44 D2
West Stour Dorset 30 C3
West Stourmouth Kent 71 G9
West Stow Suff 124 C6
West Stowell Wilts 62 G6
West Strathan Highld 308 C5
West Stratton Hants 48 E4
West Street Kent 54 C2
Kent 55 C10
Medway 69 D8
Suff 125 C9
West Tanfield N Yorks 214 D5
West Taphouse Corn 6 C3
West Tarbert Argyll 275 G9
West Tarring W Sus 35 G10
West Third Borders 262 B4
West Thirston
Northumb 252 D5
West Thorney W Sus 22 C3
Westthorpe Derbys 187 F7
West Thurrock Thurrock 68 D5
West Tilbury Thurrock 69 D7
West Tisted Hants 33 B11
West Tofts Norf 140 E6
Perth 286 D5
West Tolgus Corn 4 G3
West Torrington Lincs 189 E10
West Town Bath 60 G4
Devon 14 B3
Devon 24 C4
Hants 21 B10
Hereford 115 E8
N Som 60 F3
Som 44 F4
W Sus 36 D3
West Tytherley Hants 32 B3
West Tytherton Wilts 62 E2
Westvale Mers 182 B6
West Vale W Yorks 196 C5
West View Hrtlpl 234 D5
West Village V Glam 58 E3
Westville Devon 8 G4
Notts 171 F8
West Walton Norf 157 G9
West Walton Highway
Norf 157 G9
Westward Cumb 229 C11
Westward Ho! Devon 24 B6
West Watergate Corn 6 E4
West Watford Herts 85 F10
West Weekmoor Devon 12 C4
Westwell Kent 54 D3
Oxon 82 D2
Westwell Leacon Kent 54 D3
West Wellow Hants 32 D3
Westwells Wilts 61 F11
West Wemyss Fife 280 C6
Westwick Cambs 123 D8
Durham 223 B11
Norf 160 D5
West Wick N Som 59 G11
West Wickham Cambs 106 B2
London 67 F11
Westwick Row Herts 85 D9
West Williamston
Pembs 73 D8
West Willoughby Lincs 173 G7
West Winch Norf 158 F2
West Winterslow Wilts 47 G8
West Wittering W Sus 21 B11
West Witton N Yorks 213 B11
Westwood Devon 14 B6
Devon 14 E5
Kent 55 D7
Kent 71 F11
Notts 171 E7
Pboro 138 D3
S Lnrk 268 E2
Wilts 45 B10
Wilts 46 G6
West Woodburn
Northumb 251 F9
West Woodhay W Berks 63 G11
Westwood Heath
W Mid 118 B5
West Woodlands Som 45 E9
Westwood Park Essex 107 E9
Gtr Man 184 B3
Westwoodside N Lincs 188 B3
West Worldham Hants 49 F8
West Worlington Devon 26 E3
West Worthing W Sus 35 G10
West Wratting Cambs 124 G2
West Wycombe Bucks 84 G4
West Wylam Northumb 242 E4
Westy Warr 183 D10
West Yatton Wilts 61 E11
West Yell Shetland 312 E6
West Yeo Som 43 G10
West Yoke Kent 68 F5
West Youlstone Corn 24 D3
Wetham Green Kent 69 F10
Wetheral Cumb 239 G11
Wetheral Plain Cumb 239 F11
Wetherby W Yorks 206 D4
Wetherden Suff 125 E10
Wetherden Upper Town
Suff 125 D10
Wetheringsett Suff 126 D2
Wethersfield Essex 106 E4
Wethersta Shetland 312 G5
Wetherup Street Suff 126 E2
Wetley Rocks Staffs 169 F7
Wetmore Staffs 152 E5
Wettenhall Ches E 167 C10
Wettenhall Green
Ches E 167 C10
Wettles Shrops 131 F8
Wetton Staffs 169 D10
Wetwang E Yorks 208 B4
Wetwood Staffs 150 C5
Wexcombe Wilts 47 B9
Wexham Street Bucks 66 C3
Weybourne Norf 177 E10
Sur 49 D11
Weybread Suff 142 G4
Weybridge Sur 66 G5
Weycroft Devon 16 B2
Weydale Highld 310 C5
Weyhill Hants 47 D10
Weymouth Dorset 17 F9
Weythel Powys 114 F4
Whaddon Bucks 102 E6
Cambs 104 B6
Glos 80 C4
Glos 99 G9
Wilts 31 B11
Wilts 61 G11
Whaddon Gap Cambs 104 B6
Whale Cumb 230 G6
Whaley Derbys 187 G8
Whaley Bridge Derbys 185 E8
Whaley Thorns Derbys 187 G8
Whaligoe Highld 310 E7
Whalley Lancs 203 F10
Whalley Banks Lancs 203 F10
Whalley Range Gtr Man 184 C4
Whalleys Lancs 194 F3
Whalton Northumb 252 G4
Wham N Yorks 212 G5
Whaplode Lincs 156 E6
Whaplode Drove Lincs 156 G6
Whaplode St Catherine
Lincs 156 E6
Wharf Warks 119 G8
Wharfe N Yorks 212 F5
Wharles Lancs 202 F4
Wharley End C Beds 103 C8
Wharmley Northumb 241 D9
Wharncliffe Side
S Yorks 186 C3
Wharram le Street
N Yorks 217 F7
Wharram Percy
N Yorks 217 G7
Wharton Ches W 167 B11
Hereford 115 F10
Lincs 188 C4
Wharton Green
Ches W 167 B11
Whashton N Yorks 224 D3
Whasset Cumb 211 C10
Whatcombe Dorset 30 G4
Whatcote Warks 100 C6
Whatcroft Ches W 167 B11
Whateley Staffs 134 D4
Whatfield Suff 107 B10
Whatley Som 28 F5
Som 45 D8
Whatlington E Sus 38 D3
Whatmore Shrops 116 C2
Whatsole Street Kent 54 E6
Whatstandwell Derbys 170 E4
Whatton Notts 154 B4
Whauphill Dumfries 236 E6
Whaw N Yorks 223 E9
Wheal Alfred Corn 2 B3
Wheal Baddon Corn 4 G5
Wheal Busy Corn 4 G4
Wheal Frances Corn 4 E5
Wheal Kitty Corn 4 E4
Wheal Rose Corn 4 G4
Wheatacre Norf 143 E9
Wheatcroft Derbys 170 D5
Wheatenhurst Glos 80 D3
Wheathall Shrops 131 C9
Wheathampstead Herts 85 C11
Wheathill Shrops 132 G2
Som 44 G5
Wheat Hold Hants 64 G5
Wheatley Devon 14 C4
Hants 49 E9
Oxon 83 D9
S Yorks 198 G5
W Yorks 196 B5
Wheatley Hill Durham 234 D3
Wheatley Hills S Yorks 198 G6
Wheatley Lane Lancs 204 F2
Wheatley Park S Yorks 198 F5
Wheaton Aston Staffs 151 G7
Wheddon Cross Som 42 F2
Wheedlemont Aberds 302 G4
Wheelbarrow Town Kent 55 D7
Wheeler End Bucks 84 G4
Wheelerstreet Sur 50 E2
Wheelock Ches E 168 D3
Wheelock Heath
Ches E 168 D2
Wheelton Lancs 194 C5
Lancs 194 C6
Lancs 194 D5
Lancs 194 D6
Wheen Angus 292 F5
Wheldale W Yorks 198 B3
Wheldrake York 207 D9
Whelford Glos 81 F11
Whelley Gtr Man 194 F5
Whelpley Hill Herts 85 E7
Whelpo Cumb 230 D2
Whelp Street Suff 107 B8
Whelston Flint 182 F2
Whempstead Herts 104 G6
Whenby N Yorks 216 F2
Whepstead Suff 124 F6
Wherry Town Corn 1 D5
Wherstead Suff 108 C3
Wherwell Hants 47 E11
Wheston Derbys 185 F10
Whetley Cross Dorset 29 G7
Whetsted Kent 53 D7
Whetstone Leics 135 D11
London 86 G3
Whettleton Shrops 131 G8
Whicham Cumb 210 C2
Whichford Warks 100 E6
Whickham T&W 242 E6
Whickham Fell T&W 242 F6
Whiddon Devon 40 F5
Whiddon Down Devon 13 C9
Whifflet N Lnrk 268 C4
Whigstreet Angus 287 C8
Whilton Northants 120 E2
Whilton Locks Northants 120 E2
Whimble Devon 24 G5
Whim Farm Borders 270 E4
Whimple Devon 14 B6
Whimpwell Green Norf 161 D7
Whinburgh Norf 141 B10
Whinfield Darl 224 B6
Whinhall N Lnrk 268 B5
Whin Lane End Lancs 202 E3
Whinmoor W Yorks 206 F3
Whinney Hill Stockton 225 B7
S Yorks 187 C7
Whinnieliggate
Dumfries 237 D9
Whinnyfold Aberds 303 F10
Whinny Heights Blkburn 195 B7
Whins of Milton Stirl 278 C5
Whins Wood W Yorks 205 F7
Whipcott Devon 27 D9
Whippendell Botton
Herts 85 E9
Whippingham IoW 20 C6
Whipsiderry Corn 4 C6
Whipsnade C Beds 85 B8
Whipton Devon 14 C5
Whirley Grove Ches E 184 F5
Whirlow S Yorks 186 E4
Whisby Lincs 172 B6
Whissendine Rutland 154 G6
Whissonsett Norf 159 E8
Whisterfield Ches E 184 G4
Whistlefield Argyll 276 C2
Argyll 276 C4
Whistley Green
Wokingham 65 E9
Whistlow Oxon 101 F9
Whiston Mers 183 C7
Northants 120 E6
Staffs 151 G7
Staffs 169 F8
S Yorks 186 D6
Whiston Cross Mers 183 C7
Shrops 132 C5
Whitacre Heath Warks 134 E4
Whitbarrow Village
Cumb 230 F4
Whitbeck Cumb 210 C2
Whitbourne Hereford 116 F4
Whitbourne Moor Wilts 45 D10
Whitburn T&W 243 E10
W Loth 269 C8
Whitburn Colliery
T&W 243 E10
Whitby Ches W 182 F5
N Yorks 227 C7
Whitbyheath Ches W 182 F5
Whitchurch Bath 60 F6
Bucks 102 G5
Cardiff 59 C7
Devon 12 G5
Hants 48 D3
Hereford 79 B9
Pembs 90 F5
Shrops 167 G8
Som 30 C2
Whitchurch Canonicorum
Dorset 16 B3
Whitchurch Hill Oxon 64 D6
Whitchurch-on-Thames
Oxon 64 D6
Whitcombe Dorset 17 D10
Som 29 C10
Whitcot Shrops 131 E7
Whitcott Keysett Shrops 130 G5
Whiteacen Moray 302 E2
Whiteacre Kent 54 D6
Whiteacre Heath Warks 134 E4
Whiteash Green Essex 106 E5
White Ball Som 27 D9
Whitebirk Blkburn 195 B8
Whitebog Highld 301 C7
Whitebridge Highld 290 B6
Whitebrook Mon 79 D8
Whiteburn Borders 271 F11
Whitebushes Sur 51 D9
Whitecairn Dumfries 236 D4
Whitecairns Aberds 293 B11
Whitecastle S Lnrk 269 G10
Whitechapel Lancs 203 E7
London 67 C10
Whitechurch Maund
Hereford 97 B11
Whitecleat Orkney 314 F5
Whitecliff Glos 79 C9
Whiteclosegate Cumb 239 F10
White Colne Essex 107 F7
White Coppice Lancs 194 D6
Whitecote W Yorks 205 F10
Whitecraig E Loth 281 G7
Whitecraigs E Renf 267 D11
Whitecroft Glos 79 D10
Whitecrook W Dunb 267 B10
Whitecross Corn 2 C2
Corn 6 E2
Corn 10 G5
Falk 279 F9
Som 28 C6
Staffs 151 E7
White Cross Bath 44 B5
Bath 44 B6
Corn 2 E5
Corn 5 D7
Hereford 97 C9
Som 43 D10
Wilts 45 G9
White Cross Hill Cambs 123 B9
White End Worcs 98 E5
Whiteface Highld 309 L7
Whitefarland N Ayrs 255 C9
Whitefaulds S Ayrs 245 B7
Whitefield Aberds 303 G7
Dorset 18 C4
Gtr Man 195 F10
Perth 286 D5
Som 27 B9
Whitefield Lane End
Mers 183 D7
Whiteflat E Ayrs 258 D2
Whiteford Aberds 303 G7
Whitegate Ches W 167 B10
White Gate Gtr Man 195 G11
Som 28 F4
White Grit Shrops 130 D6
Whitehall Blkburn 195 C7
Bristol 60 E6
Devon 27 E10
Devon 40 F4
Hants 49 C8
Herts 104 E6
W Sus 35 C10
White Hall Herts 104 G5
Whitehall Village
Orkney 314 D6
Whitehaven Cumb 219 B9
Shrops 148 E5
Whitehawk Brighton 36 G4
Whiteheath Gate W Mid 133 F9
Whitehill E Sus 37 B8
Hants 49 G9
Kent 54 B4
Midloth 271 B7
Moray 302 D5
S Lnrk 268 D4
Staffs 168 E3
White Hill Bath 45 B8
Wilts 45 G10
W Yorks 204 E6
Whitehills Aberds 302 C6
S Lnrk 268 E2
T&W 243 E7
White Hills Northants 120 E4
Whiteholme Blkpool 202 E2
Whitehough Derbys 185 E8
Whitehouse Aberds 293 B8
Argyll 275 G9
White House Suff 108 B2
Whitehouse Common
W Mid 134 D2
Whitehouse Green
W Berks 65 F7
White Houses Notts 188 F2
Whiteinch Glasgow 267 B10
Whitekirk E Loth 281 E10
Whiteknights Reading 65 E8
Whiteknowes Aberds 293 C7
Whitelackington Som 28 D5
White Lackington
Dorset 17 B10
White Ladies Aston
Worcs 117 G8
Whitelaw S Lnrk 268 G2
Whiteleaf Bucks 84 E4
Whiteleas T&W 243 E9
Whiteleaved Oak Glos 98 D5
Whitelee Borders 262 C3
Northumb 250 B6
White Lee W Yorks 197 B8
Whitelees S Ayrs 257 C9
White-le-Head Durham 242 G5
Whiteley Bank IoW 21 E7
Whiteley Green Ches E 184 F6
Whiteley Village Sur 66 G5
White Lund Lancs 211 G8
Whitelye Mon 79 E8
Whitemans Green W Sus 36 B4
White Mill Carms 93 G9
Whitemire Moray 301 D9
Whitemoor Corn 5 D9
Nottingham 171 G8
Warks 118 C5
White Moor Derbys 170 F5
Whitemore Staffs 168 C5
Whitenap Hants 32 C5
White Ness Shetland 313 J5
White Notley Essex 88 B3
White Oak Kent 68 F4
Whiteoak Green Oxon 82 C4
White Ox Mead Bath 45 B8
Whiteparish Wilts 32 C2
White Pit Lincs 190 F5
Whitepits Wilts 45 F10
White Post Kent 52 E4
Notts 171 D10
Whiterashes Aberds 303 G8
Whiterigg Borders 262 C3
Whiterock Bridgend 58 D2
White Rocks Hereford 97 G8
White Roding or White
Roothing Essex 87 C9
Whiterow Highld 310 E7
White's Green W Sus 34 B6
Whiteshill Glos 80 D4
S Glos 60 D6
Whiteside Northumb 240 D6
W Loth 269 B9
Whitesmith E Sus 23 C8
Whitespots Dumfries 247 F10
White Stake Lancs 194 B4
Whitestaunton Som 28 E3
Whitestone Aberds 293 D8
Devon 14 C3
Devon 40 D3
Warks 135 F7
White Stone Hereford 97 C11
Whitestones Aberds 303 D8
Whitestreet Green Suff 107 D9
Whitewall Common Mon 60 B2
Whitewall Corner
N Yorks 216 E5
White Waltham Windsor 65 D10
Whiteway Bath 61 G8
Dorset 18 E3
Glos 80 C6
Glos 80 F4
Whitewell Aberds 303 C9
Corn 11 E7
Highld 291 C11
Lancs 203 D9
Wrex 167 G7
Whitewell Bottom
Lancs 195 C10
Whiteworks Devon 13 G8
Whitfield Kent 55 D10
Northants 102 D2
Northumb 241 F7
S Glos 79 G11
Whitfield Court Sur 50 B3
Whitfield Hall Northumb 241 F7
Whitford Devon 15 B11
Whitford / Chwitffordd
Flint 181 F10
Whitgift E Yorks 199 C10
Whitgreave Staffs 151 D7
Whithaugh Borders 249 F11
Whithebeir Orkney 314 C5
Whithorn Dumfries 236 E6
Whiting Bay N Ayrs 256 D2
Whitington Norf 140 D4
Whitkirk W Yorks 206 G3
Whitland / Hendy-Gwyn
Carms 73 B11
Whitlaw Borders 271 F9
Whitleigh Plym 7 C9
Whitletts S Ayrs 257 E9
Whitley Gtr Man 194 F5
N Yorks 198 C5
Reading 65 E8
S Yorks 186 C4
Wilts 61 F11
W Mid 119 B7
Whitley Bay T&W 243 C9
Whitley Bridge N Yorks 198 C5
Whitley Chapel
Northumb 241 F10
Whitley Head W Yorks 204 E6
Whitley Heath Staffs 150 D6
Whitley Lower W Yorks 197 D8
Whitley Reed Ches W 183 E10
Whitley Row Kent 52 C3
Whitley Sands T&W 243 C9
Whitley Thorpe N Yorks 198 C5
Whitley Wood Reading 65 F8
Whitlock's End W Mid 118 B2
Whitminster Glos 80 D3
Whitmoor Devon 27 E9
Whitmore Dorset 31 F9
Staffs 168 G4
Whitmore Park W Mid 134 G6
Whitnage Devon 27 D8
Whitnash Warks 118 E6
Whitnell Som 43 F8
Whitney Bottom Som 28 E4
Whitney-on-Wye
Hereford 96 B5
Whitrigg Cumb 229 D10
Cumb 238 F6
Whitriggs Borders 262 F3
Whitsbury Hants 31 D10
Whitslaid Borders 271 G11
Whitsome Borders 273 E7
Whitsomehill Borders 273 F7
Whitson Newport 59 C11
Whitstable Kent 70 F6
Whitstone Corn 11 B11
Whittingham Northumb 264 G3
Whittingslow Shrops 131 F8
Whittington Glos 99 G10
Lancs 212 D2
Norf 140 D4
Shrops 148 C6
Staffs 133 G7
Staffs 134 B3
Staffs 150 C5
Warks 134 D5
Worcs 117 G7
Whittington Moor
Derbys 186 G5
Whittlebury Northants 102 C3
Whittleford Warks 134 E6
Whittle-le-Woods
Lancs 194 C5
Whittlesey Cambs 138 D5
Whittlesford Cambs 105 B9
Whittlestone Head
Blkburn 195 D8
Whitton Borders 263 E7
Hereford 115 C8
London 66 E6
N Lincs 200 C2
Northumb 252 C3
Powys 114 D5
Shrops 115 C11
Stockton 234 G3
Suff 108 B2
Whittonditch Wilts 63 E9
Whittonstall Northumb 242 F3
Whittytree Shrops 115 B8
Whitway Hants 48 B3
Whitwell Derbys 187 F8
Herts 104 G3
IoW 20 F6
N Yorks 224 F5
Rutland 137 B8
Whitwell-on-the-Hill
N Yorks 216 F4
Whitwell Street Norf 160 E2
Whitwick Leics 153 F8
Whitwood W Yorks 198 C2
Whitworth Lancs 195 D11
Whixall Shrops 149 C10
Whixley N Yorks 206 B4
Whoberley W Mid 118 B6
Wholeflats Falk 279 E8
Whome Orkney 314 G3
Whorlton Durham 224 C2
N Yorks 225 E9
Whydown E Sus 38 F2
Whygate Northumb 241 B7
Whyke W Sus 22 C5
Whyle Hereford 115 E11
Whyteleafe Sur 51 B10
Wibdon Glos 79 F9
Wibsey W Yorks 205 G8
Wibtoft Leics 135 F9
Wichenford Worcs 116 E5
Wichling Kent 54 B2
Wick Bmouth 19 C8
Devon 27 G11
Highld 310 D7
S Glos 61 E8
Shetland 313 K6
Som 28 B6
Som 43 C10
Som 43 E8
V Glam 58 E2
Wilts 31 C11
Worcs 99 B9
W Sus 35 G8
Wicken Cambs 123 C11
Northants 102 D4
Wicken Bonhunt Essex 105 E9
Wickenby Lincs 189 E9
Wicken Green Village
Norf 158 C6
Wick Episcopi Worcs 116 G6
Wickersley S Yorks 187 C7
Wicker Street Green
Suff 107 C9
Wickford Essex 88 G3
Wickham Hants 33 E9
W Berks 63 E11
Wickham Bishops Essex 88 C4
Wickhambreaux Kent 55 B8
Wickhambrook Suff 124 G4
Wickhamford Worcs 99 C11
Wickham Green Suff 125 D11
W Berks 63 E11
Wickham Heath W Berks 64 F2
Wickham Market Suff 126 F6
Wickhampton Norf 143 B8
Wickham St Paul Essex 106 D6
Wickham's Cross Som 44 G4
Wickham Skeith Suff 125 D11
Wickham Street Suff 124 G5
Suff 125 D11
Wick Hill Brack 65 E11
Kent 53 E10
Wokingham 65 G9
Wickhurst Kent 52 D4
Wicklane Bath 45 B7
Wicklewood Norf 141 C11
Wickmere Norf 160 C3
Wickridge Street Glos 98 F6
Wick Rocks S Glos 61 E8
Wick St Lawrence
N Som 59 F11
Wickstreet E Sus 23 D8
Wick Street Glos 80 D5
Wickwar S Glos 61 B8
Widbrook Wilts 45 B10
Widcombe Bath 61 G9
Widdington Essex 105 E10
Widdrington Northumb 253 D7
Widdrington Station
Northumb 252 E6
Widecombe in the Moor
Devon 13 F10
Widegates Corn 6 D5
Widemarsh Hereford 97 C10
Widemouth Bay Corn 24 G2
Wideopen T&W 242 C6
Widewall Orkney 314 G4
Widewell Plym 7 C9
Widford Essex 87 D11
Herts 86 B6
Widgham Green Cambs 124 F3
Widham Wilts 62 B5
Widley Hants 33 F11
Widmer End Bucks 84 F5
Widmerpool Notts 154 D2
Widmoor Bucks 66 B2
Widmore London 68 F2
Widnes Halton 183 D8
Wierton Kent 53 D9
Wig Powys 130 F2
Wigan Gtr Man 194 F5
Wiganthorpe N Yorks 216 E3
Wigbeth Dorset 31 F8
Wigborough Som 28 D6
Wig Fach Bridgend 57 F10
Wiggaton Devon 15 C8
Wiggenhall St Germans
Norf 157 G11
Wiggenhall St Mary
Magdalen Norf 157 G11
Wiggenhall St Mary the
Virgin Norf 157 G11
Wiggenhall St Peter
Norf 158 G2
Wiggens Green Essex 106 C3
Wiggington Staffs 134 B4
Wigginstall Staffs 169 C9
Wigginton Herts 84 C6
Oxon 101 E7
Shrops 148 B6
Staffs 134 B4
York 207 B7
Wigginton Bottom Herts 84 D6
Wigginton Heath Oxon 101 D7
Wigglesworth N Yorks 204 B2
Wiggonby Cumb 239 G7
Wiggonholt W Sus 35 D9
Wighill N Yorks 206 D5
Wighton Norf 159 B8
Wightwick Manor Staffs 133 D7
Wigley Derbys 186 G4
Hants 32 D4
Wigmarsh Shrops 149 D7
Wigmore Hereford 115 D8
Medway 69 G10
Wigsley Notts 188 G5
Wigsthorpe Northants 137 G10
Wigston Leics 136 D2
Wigston Magna Leics 136 D2
Wigston Parva Leics 135 F9
Wigthorpe Notts 187 E9
Wigtoft Lincs 156 B5
Wigton Cumb 229 B11
Wigtown Dumfries 236 D6
Wigtwizzle S Yorks 186 B2
Wike W Yorks 206 E2
Wike Well End S Yorks 199 E7
Wilbarston Northants 136 F6
Wilberfoss E Yorks 207 C10
Wilberlee W Yorks 196 E5
Wilburton Cambs 123 C9
Wilby Norf 141 F10
Northants 121 D7
Suff 126 C4
Wilcot Wilts 62 G6
Wilcott Shrops 149 F7
Wilcott Marsh Shrops 149 F7
Wilcove Corn 7 D8
Wilcrick Newport 60 B2
Wilday Green Derbys 186 G4
Wildboarclough Ches E 169 B7
Wilden Beds 121 F11
Worcs 116 C6
Wildern Hants 33 E7
Wildernesse Kent 52 B4
Wilderspool Warr 183 D10
Wilderswood Gtr Man 194 E6
Wilde Street Suff 124 B4
Wildhern Hants 47 C11
Wildhill Herts 86 D3
Wildmanbridge S Lnrk 268 E6
Wild Mill Bridgend 58 C2
Wildmoor Hants 49 B7
Oxon 83 F7
Worcs 117 B9
Wildridings Brack 65 F11
Wildsworth Lincs 188 B4
Wildwood Staffs 151 E8
Wilford Nottingham 153 B11
Wilgate Green Kent 54 B3
Wilkesley Ches E 167 G10
Wilkhaven Highld 311 L3
Wilkieston W Loth 270 B2
Wilkinthroop Som 29 C11
Wilkin Throop Som 29 C11
Wilksby Lincs 174 C3
Willacy Lane End Lancs 202 F5
Willand Devon 27 E8
Som 27 E11
Willand Moor Devon 27 E8
Willard's Hill E Sus 38 C2
Willaston Ches E 167 E11
Ches W 182 F4
Shrops 149 B11
Willen M Keynes 103 C7
Willenhall W Mid 119 B7
W Mid 133 D9
Willerby E Yorks 208 G6
N Yorks 217 D10
Willersey Glos 100 D2
Willersley Hereford 96 B6
Willesborough Kent 54 E4
Willesborough Lees
Kent 54 E4
Willesden London 67 C8
Willesden Green London 67 C8
Willesley Leics 152 G6
Wilts 61 B11
Willett Som 42 G6
Willey Shrops 132 D3
Warks 135 G9
Willey Green Sur 50 C2
Williamhope Borders 261 C10
Williamscott Oxon 101 B9
William's Green Suff 107 C9
Williamslee Borders 270 G6
Williamstown Rhondda 77 G8
Williamthorpe Derbys 170 B6
William Herts 104 E4
Willicote Pastures
Worcs 100 B3
Willingale Essex 87 D9
Willingcott Devon 40 E3
Willingdon E Sus 23 E9
Willingham Cambs 123 C8
Suff 143 G8
Willingham by Stow
Lincs 188 E5
Willingham Green
Cambs 124 G2
Willington Beds 104 B2
Derbys 152 D5
Durham 233 D9
Kent 53 C9
T&W 243 D8
Warks 100 D5
Willington Corner
Ches W 167 B8
Willington Quay T&W 243 D8
Willisham Suff 125 G11
Willisham Tye Suff 125 G11
Willitoft E Yorks 207 F10
Williton Som 42 E5
Willoughbridge Staffs 168 G3
Willoughby Lincs 191 G7
Warks 119 D10
Willoughby Hills Lincs 174 F4
Willoughby-on-the-Wolds
Notts 154 D2
Willoughby Waterleys
Leics 135 E11
Willoughton Lincs 188 C6
Willowbank Bucks 66 B5
Willow Green Ches W 183 F10
Worcs 116 F5
Willow Holme Cumb 239 F9
Willows Gtr Man 195 F8
Willows Green Essex 88 B2
Willowtown Bl Gwent 77 C11
Will Row Lincs 191 D7
Willsbridge S Glos 61 E7
Willslock Staffs 151 C11
Willstone Shrops 131 D9
Willsworthy Devon 12 E6
Wilmcote Warks 118 F3
Wilmington Bath 61 G7
Devon 15 B10
E Sus 23 E8
Kent 68 E4
Wilmington Green E Sus 23 D8
Wilminstone Devon 12 F5
Wilmslow Ches E 184 E4
Wilmslow Park Ches E 184 E5
Wilnecote Staffs 134 C4
Wilney Green Norf 141 G11
Wilpshire Lancs 203 G9
Wilsden W Yorks 205 F7
Wilsden Hill W Yorks 205 F7
Wilsford Lincs 173 G8
Wilts 46 B6
Wilts 46 F6
Wilsham Devon 41 D9
Wilshaw W Yorks 196 F6
Wilsic S Yorks 187 B9
Wilsill N Yorks 214 G3
Wilsley Green Kent 53 F9
Wilsley Pound Kent 53 F9
Wilson Hants 49 F8
Wilson Hereford 97 G11
Leics 153 E8
Wilsontown S Lnrk 269 D9
Wilstead Beds 103 C11
Wilsthorpe Derbys 153 C9
Lincs 155 G11
Wilstone Herts 84 C6
Wilstone Green Herts 84 C6
Wilthorpe S Yorks 197 F10
Wilton Borders 261 G11
Cumb 219 C10
Hereford 97 G11
N Yorks 217 C7
Redcar 225 B11
Som 28 C2
Wilts 46 G5
Wilts 63 G9
Wilton Park Bucks 85 G7
Wiltown Devon 27 D11
Som 28 C5
Wimbish Essex 105 D11
Wimbish Green Essex 106 D2
Wimblebury Staffs 151 G10
Wimbledon London 67 E8
Wimble Hill Hants 49 D10
Wimblington Cambs 139 E8
Wimboldsley Ches W 167 C11
Wimbolds Trafford
Ches W 182 G6
Wimborne Minster
Dorset 18 B6
Wimborne St Giles
Dorset 31 E8
Wimbotsham Norf 140 B2
Wimpole Cambs 104 B6
Wimpson Soton 32 E5
Wimpstone Warks 100 B4
Wincanton Som 30 B2
Winceby Lincs 174 B4
Wincham Ches W 183 F11
Winchburgh W Loth 279 G11
Winchcombe Glos 99 F10
Winchelsea E Sus 38 D6
Winchelsea Beach E Sus 38 D6
Winchester Hants 33 B7
Winchestown Bl Gwent 77 C11
Winchet Hill Kent 53 E8
Winchfield Hants 49 C9
Winchfield Hurst Hants 49 C9
Winchmore Hill Bucks 84 G6
London 86 G4
Wincle Ches E 169 B7
Wincobank S Yorks 186 C5
Winder Cumb 219 B10
Windermere Cumb 221 F8
Winderton Warks 100 C6
Windhill Highld 300 E5
S Yorks 198 G3
W Yorks 205 F9
Wind Hill Cumb 210 E5
Pembs 73 F9
Windhouse Shetland 312 D6
Winding Wood W Berks 63 E11
Windle Hill Ches W 182 F4
Windlehurst Gtr Man 185 D7
Windlesham Sur 66 G2
Windley Derbys 170 F4
Windmill Corn 10 G3
Flint 181 G11
Flint 182 G2
Windmill Hill Bristol 60 E5
E Sus 23 C10
Halton 183 E9
Kent 69 F10
Som 28 D4
Worcs 99 B8
W Yorks 197 D11
Windrush Glos 81 C11
Windsor N Lincs 199 E9
Windsor 66 D3
Windsoredge Glos 80 E4
Windsor Green Suff 125 G7
Windwhistle Som 28 F5
Windy Arbor Mers 183 D7
Windy Arbour Warks 118 C5
Windydoors Borders 261 B10
Windygates Fife 287 G7
Windyharbour Ches E 184 G4
Windy Hill Wrex 166 E4
Windyknowe W Loth 269 B9
Windy Nook T&W 243 E7
Windywalls Borders 263 C7
Windy-Yett E Ayrs 267 E9
Wineham W Sus 36 C2
Winestead E Yorks 201 C9
Winewall Lancs 204 E4
Winfarthing Norf 142 F2
Winford IoW 21 E7
N Som 60 F4
Winforton Hereford 96 B5
Winfrith Newburgh
Dorset 18 E2
Wing Bucks 103 G7
Rutland 137 C7
Wingate Durham 234 D4
Wingates Gtr Man 195 F7
Northumb 252 D4
Wingerworth Derbys 170 B5
Wingfield C Beds 103 F10
Suff 126 B4
S Yorks 186 B6
Wilts 45 B10
Wingfield Green Suff 126 B4
Wingfield Park Derbys 170 E5
Wingham Kent 55 B8
Wingham Green Kent 55 B8
Wingham Well Kent 55 B8
Wingmore Kent 55 D7
Wingrave Bucks 84 B5
Winkburn Notts 172 D2
Winkfield Brack 66 E2
Winkfield Place Brack 66 E2
Winkfield Row Brack 65 E11
Winkhill Staffs 169 E9
Winkhurst Green Kent 52 D3
Winklebury Hants 48 C6
Winkleigh Devon 25 F10
Winksley N Yorks 214 E5
Winkton Dorset 19 B9
Winlaton T&W 242 E5
Winlaton Mill T&W 242 E5
Winless Highld 310 D7
Winllan Powys 148 E4
Winmarleigh Lancs 202 D5
Winmarleigh Moss
Lancs 202 D4
Winnal Hereford 97 E9
Winnal Common Hereford 97 E9
Winnall Hants 33 B7
Worcs 116 D6
Winnard's Perch Corn 5 B8
Winnersh Wokingham 65 E9
Winnington Ches W 183 G10
Staffs 150 B4
Winnington Green
Shrops 148 G6
Winnothdale Staffs 169 G8
Winscales Cumb 228 F6
Winscombe N Som 44 B2
Winsdon Hill Luton 103 G11
Winsford Ches W 167 B10
Som 42 G2
Winsham Devon 40 F3
Som 28 F5
Winshill Staffs 152 E5
Winsh-wen Swansea 57 B7
Winsick Derbys 170 B6
Winskill Cumb 231 D7
Winslade Devon 24 D5
Hants 49 D7
Winsley N Yorks 214 G4
Wilts 61 G10
Winslow Bucks 102 F5
Winslow Mill Hereford 98 D2
Winson Glos 81 D9
Winson Green W Mid 133 F10
Winsor Hants 32 E4
Winstanley Gtr Man 194 G5
Winstanleys Gtr Man 194 F5
Winster Cumb 221 G8
Derbys 170 C2
Winston Durham 224 B2
Suff 126 E3
Winstone Glos 81 D7
Winston Green Suff 126 E3
Winswell Devon 25 E7
Winterborne Bassett
Wilts 62 E6
Winterborne Came
Dorset 17 D10
Winterborne Clenston
Dorset 30 G4
Winterborne Herringston
Dorset 17 D9
Winterborne Houghton
Dorset 30 G4
Winterborne Kingston
Dorset 18 B3
Winterborne Monkton
Wilts 62 E6
Winterborne Muston
Dorset 18 B3
Winterborne Stickland
Dorset 30 G4
Winterborne Tomson
Dorset 18 B3
Winterborne Whitechurch
Dorset 30 G4
Winterborne Zelston
Dorset 18 B3
Winterbourne Kent 54 B5
S Glos 60 C6
W Berks 64 E3
Winterbourne Abbas
Dorset 17 C8
Winterbourne Bassett
Wilts 62 E6
Winterbourne Dauntsey
Wilts 47 G7
Winterbourne Down
S Glos 61 D7
Winterbourne Earls Wilts 47 G7
Winterbourne Gunner
Wilts 47 F7
Winterbourne Monkton
Dorset 17 D9
Winterbourne Steepleton
Dorset 17 D8
Winterbourne Stoke
Wilts 46 E5
Winterbrook Oxon 64 B6
Winterburn N Yorks 204 B4
Winterfield Bath 45 B7
Winter Gardens Essex 69 C9
Winterhay Green Som 28 D5
Winterhead N Som 44 B2
Winteringham N Lincs 200 C2
Winterley Ches E 168 D2
Wintersett W Yorks 197 D11
Wintershill Hants 33 D8
Winterton N Lincs 200 D2
Winterton-on-Sea Norf 161 F9
Winter Well Som 28 C3
Winthorpe Lincs 175 B9
Notts 172 D4
Winton Bmouth 19 C7
Cumb 222 C5
E Sus 23 E8
Gtr Man 184 B3
N Yorks 225 F8
Wintringham N Yorks 217 E7
Winwick Cambs 138 G2
Northants 120 C2
Warr 183 C10
Winwick Quay Warr 183 C10
Winyard's Gap Dorset 29 F7
Winyates Worcs 117 D11
Winyates Green Worcs 117 D11
Wirksworth Derbys 170 E3
Wirksworth Moor
Derbys 170 E4
Wirswall Ches E 167 G8
Wisbech Cambs 139 B9
Wisbech St Mary Cambs 139 B8
Wisborough Green
W Sus 35 B8
Wiseton Notts 188 D2
Wishanger Glos 80 D6
Wishaw N Lnrk 268 D5
Warks 134 E3
Wisley Sur 50 B5

Wispington Lincs . . . 190 G2
Wissenden Kent . . . 54 E2
Wissett Suff . . . 127 B7
Wistanstow Shrops . . . 131 F8
Wistanswick Shrops . . . 150 D3
Wistaston ChesE . . . 167 E11
Wistaston Green
ChesE . . . 167 E11
Wiston Pembs . . . 73 B8
S Lnrk . . . 259 C11
W Sus . . . 35 E10
Wiston Mains S Lnrk . . . 259 C11
Wistow Cambs . . . 138 G5
Leics . . . 136 D2
N Yorks . . . 207 F7
Wiswell Lancs . . . 203 F10
Witcham Cambs . . . 139 G9
Witchampton Dorset . . . 31 F7
Witchford Cambs . . . 123 B10
Witcombe Som . . . 29 C7
Withacott Devon . . . 24 D6
Witham Essex . . . 88 C4
Witham Friary Som . . . 45 E18
Witham on the Hill
Lincs . . . 155 F11
Witham St Hughs Lincs . . . 172 C5
Withcall Lincs . . . 190 E3
Withdean Brighton . . . 36 F4
Witherenden Hill ESus . . . 37 B10
Withergate Norf . . . 160 D5
Witheridge Devon . . . 26 E4
Witheridge Hill Oxon . . . 65 C7
Witherley Leics . . . 134 D6
Withermarsh Green
Suff . . . 107 D10
Withern Lincs . . . 190 E6
Withernsea E Yorks . . . 201 B10
Withernwick E Yorks . . . 209 E9
Withersdale Street Suff 142 G5
Withersdane Kent . . . 54 D5
Withersfield Suff . . . 106 B3
Witherslack Cumb . . . 211 C8
Witherwack T&W . . . 243 F9
Withial Som . . . 44 F5
Withiel Corn . . . 5 B9
Withiel Florey Som . . . 42 G3
Withielgoose Corn . . . 5 B10
Withielgoose Mills Corn . . 5 B10
Withington Glos . . . 81 B8
Gtr Man . . . 184 C5
Hereford . . . 97 C11
Shrops . . . 149 G11
Staffs . . . 151 B10
Withington Green
ChesE . . . 184 G4
Withington Marsh
Hereford . . . 97 C11
Withleigh Devon . . . 26 E6
Withnell Lancs . . . 194 C6
Withnell Fold Lancs . . . 194 C6
Withybed Green Worcs 117 C10
Withybrook Som . . . 45 D7
Warks . . . 135 G8
Withybush Pembs . . . 73 B7
Withycombe Som . . . 41 F11
Som . . . 42 E4
Withycombe Raleigh
Devon . . . 14 E6
Withyditch Bath . . . 45 B8
Withyham ESus . . . 52 F3
Withy Mills Bath . . . 45 B7
Withypool Village
W Mid . . . 133 F8
Withypool Som . . . 41 F10
Withystakes Staffs . . . 169 F7
Withywood Bristol . . . 60 F5
Witley Sur . . . 50 F2
Witnells End Worcs . . . 132 G5
Witnesham Suff . . . 126 G3
Witney Oxon . . . 82 C5
Wittersford Hants . . . 137 C11
Wittering Pboro . . . 137 C11
Wittersham Kent . . . 38 B5
Witton Angus . . . 293 F7
Norf . . . 142 B6
W Mid . . . 133 E11
Worcs . . . 117 F7
Witton Bridge Norf . . . 160 C6
Witton Gilbert Durham 233 B10
Witton Hill Worcs . . . 116 E5
Witton-le-Wear
Durham . . . 233 E8
Witton Park Durham 233 E9
Wiveliscombe Som . . . 27 B9
Wivelrod Hants . . . 49 F7
Wivelsfield ESus . . . 36 C4
Wivelsfield Green ESus . 36 C5
Wivenhoe Essex . . . 107 G10
Wivenhoe Cross Essex 107 G10
Wiveton Norf . . . 177 E8
Wix Essex . . . 108 F3
Wixams Beds . . . 103 C10
Wixford Warks . . . 117 G11
Wixhill Shrops . . . 149 D11
Wixoe Suff . . . 106 C4
Woburn C Beds . . . 103 E8
Woburn Sands
M Keynes . . . 103 D8
Wofferwood Common
Hereford . . . 116 G3
Wokefield Park W Berks 65 F7
Woking Sur . . . 50 B4
Wokingham Wokingham 65 F10
Wolborough Devon . . . 14 G3
Woldhurst W Sus . . . 22 C5
Woldingham Sur . . . 51 B11
Woldingham Garden
Village Sur . . . 51 B11
Wold Newton E Yorks . 217 E10
NE Lincs . . . 190 B2
Wolfclyde S Lnrk . . . 260 B2
Wolferd Green Norf . . 142 D5
Wolferlow Hereford . . . 116 E3
Wolferton Norf . . . 158 D3
Wolfhampcote Warks . 119 D10
Wolfhill Perth . . . 286 D5
Wolf's Castle Pembs . . 91 F9
Wolfsdale Pembs . . . 91 G8
Wolfsdale Hill Pembs . . 91 G8
Woll Borders . . . 261 G11
Wollaston Northants . . 121 E8
Shrops . . . 148 G6
W Mid . . . 133 G7
Wollaton Nottingham . 153 B10
Wollerton Shrops . . . 150 C2
Wollerton Wood Shrops 150 C2
Wollescote W Mid . . . 133 G8
Wollrig Borders . . . 261 G11
Wolsingham Durham . . 233 D7
Wolstanton Staffs . . . 168 F5

Wolstenholme
Gtr Man . . . 195 D11
Wolston Warks . . . 119 B8
Wolsty Cumb . . . 238 G4
Wolterton Norf . . . 160 C3
Wolvercote Oxon . . . 83 D7
Wolverham ChesW . . 182 F6
Wolverhampton W Mid . 133 D8
Wolverley Shrops . . . 149 C9
Worcs . . . 116 B6
Wolverstone Devon . . . 8 D4
Wolverton Hants . . . 48 B5
Kent . . . 55 E9
M Keynes . . . 102 C6
Shrops . . . 131 F9
Warks . . . 118 E4
Wilts . . . 45 G9
Wolverton Common
Hants . . . 48 B5
Wolvesnewton Mon . . . 79 F7
Wolvey Warks . . . 135 F8
Wolvey Heath Warks . . 135 F8
Wolviston Stockton . . . 234 F5
Womaston Powys . . . 114 E5
Wombleton N Yorks . . . 216 C3
Wombourne Staffs . . . 133 D7
Wombridge Telford . . . 150 G3
Wombwell S Yorks . . . 197 G11
Womenswold Kent . . . 55 C8
Womersley N Yorks . . . 198 D4
Wonastow Mon . . . 79 C7
Wonderstone N Som . . 43 B10
Wonersh Sur . . . 50 D4
Wonford Devon . . . 14 C4
Wonson Devon . . . 13 D9
Wonston Dorset . . . 30 F2
Hants . . . 48 F3
Wooburn Bucks . . . 66 B2
Wooburn Green Bucks . 66 B2
Wood Pembs . . . 91 G7
Som . . . 28 D4
Woodacott Devon . . . 24 E5
Woodacott Cross Devon . 24 E5
Woodale N Yorks . . . 213 D10
Woodbank Argyll . . . 255 F7
ChesW . . . 182 G5
Shrops . . . 131 F11
Som . . . 28 B5
Woodbastwick Norf . . . 160 F6
Woodbeck Notts . . . 188 F3
Wood Bevington
Warks . . . 117 G11
Woodborough Notts . . 171 F10
Wilts . . . 46 B6
Woodbridge Dorset . . . 30 D5
Dorset . . . 30 E2
Glos . . . 81 C8
Suff . . . 108 B5
Woodbridge Hill Sur . . 50 C3
Woodbridge Walk Suff . 109 B7
Wood Burcote Northants 102 C3
Woodburn Common
Bucks . . . 66 B2
Woodburn Moor Bucks . 84 G6
Woodbury Devon . . . 14 D6
Woodbury Salterton
Devon . . . 14 D6
Woodchester Glos . . . 80 E4
Woodchurch Kent . . . 54 G2
Mers . . . 182 D3
Woodcock Wilts . . . 45 E11
Woodcock Heath
Staffs . . . 151 D11
Woodcock Hill Herts . . 85 G9
W Mid . . . 133 G10
Woodcombe Som . . . 42 D3
Woodcot Hants . . . 33 G9
Woodcote London . . . 67 G10
Oxon . . . 64 C6
Sur . . . 51 B8
Telford . . . 150 F5
Woodcote Green London 67 G10
Worcs . . . 117 C8
Woodcott Hants . . . 48 C2
Woodcroft Glos . . . 79 F8
Woodcutts Dorset . . . 31 D7
Wood Dalling Norf . . . 159 D11
Woodeaton Oxon . . . 83 C8
Wood Eaton Staffs . . . 150 F6
Wooden Pembs . . . 73 D10
Woodend ChesE . . . 185 D7
Cumb . . . 219 C10
Cumb . . . 220 F3
Cumb . . . 229 F10
Essex . . . 87 C9
Fife . . . 280 B4
Northants . . . 102 B2
Notts . . . 171 C7
Staffs . . . 152 D3
W Loth . . . 279 F11
W Sus . . . 22 B4
Wood End Beds . . . 103 B10
Beds . . . 121 D11
Beds . . . 103 C9
C Beds . . . 103 C9
Gtr Man . . . 184 B4
Herts . . . 104 F6
Warks . . . 118 C2
Warks . . . 134 D4
Warks . . . 134 F5
Windsor . . . 66 E2
W Mid . . . 133 C8
W Mid . . . 135 G2
Wood Enderby Lincs . . 174 C3
Woodend Green Essex . 105 F11
Northants . . . 102 B2
Wood End Green London 66 C5
Woodfalls Wilts . . . 31 C11
Woodfield Glos . . . 80 F2
Oxon . . . 101 G11
S Ayrs . . . 257 E8
Wood Field Sur . . . 51 B7
Woodford Corn . . . 24 E2
Devon . . . 8 E5
Glos . . . 79 F11
Gtr Man . . . 184 E5
London . . . 86 G6
Northants . . . 121 B9
Plym . . . 7 D10
Som . . . 42 F5
Woodford Bridge London 86 G6
Woodford Green London 86 G6
Woodford Halse
Northants . . . 119 G10

Woodford Wells London . 86 G6
Woodgate Devon . . . 27 D10
Norf . . . 159 F10
W Mid . . . 133 G9
Worcs . . . 117 D9
W Sus . . . 22 C6
Wood Gate Staffs . . . 152 D3
Woodgate Hill Gtr Man . 195 E10
Woodgates End Essex . 105 F11
Woodgates Green
W Mid . . . 116 C2
Woodgate Valley
W Mid . . . 133 G10
Woodgreen Hants . . . 31 D11
Oxon . . . 82 C5
Wood Green Essex . . . 86 E6
London . . . 86 G4
Norf . . . 142 E4
W Mid . . . 133 D9
Worcs . . . 116 D6
Woodhall Herts . . . 86 C2
Invclyd . . . 276 G6
N Yorks . . . 207 G9
N Yorks . . . 223 G9
Wood Hall Essex . . . 88 C3
Woodhall Hills
W Yorks . . . 205 F10
Woodhall Spa Lincs . . 173 C11
Woodham Bucks . . . 84 B2
Durham . . . 233 F11
Sur . . . 66 G4
Woodham Ferrers Essex . 88 F3
Woodham Mortimer
Essex . . . 88 E4
Woodham Walter Essex . 88 D4
Woodhatch Sur . . . 51 D9
Wood Hayes W Mid . . . 133 C8
Woodhaven Fife . . . 287 E8
Woodhead Aberds . . . 303 F7
Woodheads Borders . . 271 F10
Woodhey Gtr Man . . . 195 D9
Woodhey Green ChesE . 167 E9
Woodhill Essex . . . 88 E3
N Som . . . 60 D3
Shrops . . . 132 G4
Som . . . 28 B5
Woodhorn Northumb . . 253 F7
Woodhouse Cumb . . . 211 C10
Cumb . . . 219 B9
Hants . . . 47 D11
Leics . . . 153 F10
N Lincs . . . 199 F9
Perth . . . 286 D6
Shrops . . . 130 G6
Telford . . . 132 C3
W Mid . . . 133 F8
W Yorks . . . 196 B6
Woodhouse Down SGlos . 60 B6
Woodhouse Eaves
Leics . . . 153 G10
Woodhouse Green
Staffs . . . 168 C6
Woodhouselee Midloth . 270 C4
Woodhouselees
Dumfries . . . 239 C9
Woodhouse Mill
S Yorks . . . 186 D6
Woodhouse Park
Gtr Man . . . 184 D4
Woodhouses ChesW . . 183 F8
Cumb . . . 239 G8
Gtr Man . . . 184 C3
Gtr Man . . . 196 G2
Leics . . . 153 F10
Staffs . . . 152 F3
Woodhurst Cambs . . . 122 B6
Woodingdean Brighton . 36 F5
Woodington Hants . . . 32 C4
Woodkirk W Yorks . . . 197 C9
Woodlake Dorset . . . 18 C3
Woodland Cumb . . . 210 B4
Devon . . . 8 B5
Devon . . . 8 D2
Durham . . . 233 F7
Kent . . . 54 E6
Woodland Head Devon . 13 B11
Woodlands Aberdeen . 293 B10
Aberds . . . 293 D9
Dorset . . . 31 F9
Dumfries . . . 238 B3
Gtr Man . . . 185 B7
Hants . . . 32 E4
Highld . . . 300 C5
Kent . . . 68 G5
N Yorks . . . 206 C2
Som . . . 43 F7
S Yorks . . . 198 F4
Wokingham . . . 65 C9
W Yorks . . . 196 B5
Woodlands Common
Dorset . . . 31 F9
Woodlands Park
Windsor . . . 65 D11
Woodlands St Mary
W Berks . . . 63 E10
Woodlane Shrops . . . 150 D3
Staffs . . . 152 E2
Wood Lane Shrops . . . 149 C8
Staffs . . . 168 E4
Wood Lanes ChesE . . . 184 E6
Woodleigh Devon . . . 8 F4
Woodlesford W Yorks . 197 B11
Woodley Gtr Man . . . 184 C6
Hants . . . 32 C5
Wokingham . . . 65 E9
Woodley Green
Wokingham . . . 65 E9
Woodleys Oxon . . . 82 B6
Woodlinkin Derbys . . . 170 F6
Woodloes Park Warks . 118 D5
Woodmancote Glos . . . 80 F3
Glos . . . 81 D8
Glos . . . 99 C8
W Sus . . . 22 B3
W Sus . . . 36 E2
Woodmancott Hants . . 48 E5
Woodmansey E Yorks . 209 F7
Woodmansgreen W Sus . 34 B5
Woodmans Green E Sus . 38 D3
Woodmansterne Sur . . 51 B9
Woodmill Staffs . . . 152 E2
Woodminton Wilts . . . 31 C8
Woodnesborough Kent . 55 B10
Woodnewton Northants 137 E10
Woodnook Lincs . . . 155 C8

Woodnook Lancs . . . 195 B9
Lincs . . . 155 C8
Wood Norton Norf . . . 159 D10
Worcs . . . 99 B10
Woodplumpton Lancs . 202 G6
Woodram Som . . . 28 D2
Woodridsing Norf . . . 141 C9
Woodrow Bucks . . . 84 F6
Cumb . . . 229 B10
Dorset . . . 30 E3
Dorset . . . 30 F2
Worcs . . . 117 B7
Woodrow Bucks . . . 84 F6
Wood Row W Yorks . . 197 B11
Woods Hereford . . . 96 B5
Woods Bank W Mid . . 133 D9
Wood's Corner ESus . . 23 B11
Woodsden Kent . . . 53 G9
Woodseats Derbys . . . 185 C7
Wood Seats S Yorks . . 186 B4
Woodseaves Shrops . . 150 C3
Staffs . . . 150 D5
Woodsend Pembs . . . 72 C5
Wilts . . . 63 D8
Woods End Gtr Man . . 184 B2
Woodsetton W Mid . . 133 D8
Woodsetts S Yorks . . . 187 E9
Woodsfield Worcs . . . 98 B6
Woodsfold Lancs . . . 202 F5
Wood's Green ESus . . 52 G6
Woodside Aberdeen . . 293 C11
Aberds . . . 303 E10
Beds . . . 121 G11
Brack . . . 66 E2
C Beds . . . 85 B9
ChesE . . . 167 C10
Derbys . . . 183 G8
Derbys . . . 170 G5
Derbys . . . 187 G7
Dumfries . . . 238 B2
Durham . . . 233 F9
Fife . . . 287 G8
Hants . . . 20 C2
Herts . . . 85 E10
Herts . . . 86 D3
Herts . . . 86 D3
IoW . . . 20 C6
London . . . 67 F10
N Lincs . . . 199 G8
Perth . . . 286 D6
Shrops . . . 132 C3
Telford . . . 132 C3
W Mid . . . 133 D8
W Yorks . . . 196 B6
W Yorks . . . 205 E7
W Yorks . . . 205 F11
Woodside Green Essex . 87 B8
Kent . . . 54 C2
Woodside of Arbeadie
Aberds . . . 293 D9
Woodside Park London . 86 G3
Woods Moor Gtr Man . 184 D6
Woodspeen W Berks . . 64 F2
Woodspring Priory
N Som . . . 59 F10
Wood Stanway Glos . . 99 E11
Woodstock Kent . . . 70 G2
Oxon . . . 82 B6
Pembs . . . 91 F10
Woodston Pboro . . . 138 D3
Wood Street Norf . . . 161 E7
Sur . . . 50 C3
Wood Street Village Sur . 50 C3
Woodthorpe Derbys . . 187 G7
Leics . . . 153 F10
Lincs . . . 190 E6
Notts . . . 171 G9
York . . . 207 D7
Woodton Norf . . . 142 E5
Woodtown Devon . . . 24 C6
Devon . . . 25 B7
Woodvale Mers . . . 193 E10
Woodville Derbys . . . 152 F6
Dorset . . . 30 C4
Woodville Feus Angus . 287 C10
Woodwall Green Staffs . 150 C5
Woodway Oxon . . . 64 C4
Woodway Park W Mid . 135 G2
Woodwell Northants . . 121 B9
Woodwick Orkney . . . 314 D3
Woodworth Green
ChesE . . . 167 D9
Woodyates Dorset . . . 31 D8
Woody Bay Devon . . . 41 D7
Wooferton Shrops . . . 115 D10
Wookey Som . . . 44 D4
Wookey Hole Som . . . 44 D4
Wool Dorset . . . 18 D2
Woolacombe Devon . . 40 E3
Woolage Green Kent . . 55 D10
Woolage Village Kent . . 55 C8
Woolaston Glos . . . 79 E10
Woolaston Common Glos . 79 E9
Woolaston Slade Glos . 79 E9
Woolaston Woodside
Glos . . . 79 E9
Woolavington Som . . . 43 E10
Woolbeding W Sus . . 34 C5
Wooldale W Yorks . . . 197 F7
Wooler Northumb . . . 263 D11
Woolfall Heath Mers . . 182 C6
Woolfardisworthy Devon . 26 F4
Woolfardisworthy or
Woolsery Devon . . . 24 C4
Woolfold Gtr Man . . . 195 E9
Woolfords Cottages S
Lnrk . . . 269 D10
Woolford's Water Dorset 29 F11
Woolgarston Dorset . . 18 E5
Woolgreaves W Yorks . 197 D10
Woolhampton W Berks . 64 F5
Woolhope Hereford . . . 98 D2
Woolland Dorset . . . 30 F3
Woolland Bath . . . 60 G6
Woollaston Staffs . . . 151 F7
Woollaton Devon . . . 25 E7
Woollensbrook Herts . . 86 C5
Woolley Bath . . . 61 F8
Cambs . . . 122 C3
Corn . . . 24 D3
Derbys . . . 170 C5
Wilts . . . 61 G10
W Yorks . . . 197 E10
Woolley Bridge Gtr Man 185 B8
Woolley Green Wilts . . 61 G11
Windsor . . . 65 C11
Woolmere Green Worcs 117 E9

Woolmer Green Herts . . 86 B3
Woolmer Hill Sur . . . 49 G11
Woolmersdon Som . . . 43 G9
Woolminstone Som . . . 28 F6
Woolpack Corner Kent . . 53 F11
Woolpit Suff . . . 125 E9
Woolpit Green Suff . . . 125 E9
Wood Road Gtr Man . . 195 E9
Woolpit Heath Suff . . . 125 E9
Woolridge Glos . . . 98 G6
Woolscott Warks . . . 119 D9
Woolsery or
Woolfardisworthy
Devon . . . 24 C4
Devon . . . 26 G3
Woolsgrove Devon . . . 26 G3
Woolsington T&W . . . 242 D5
Woolstanwood ChesE . 167 D11
Woolstaston Shrops . . 131 D9
Woolsthorpe Lincs . . . 155 E8
Woolsthorpe by Belvoir
Lincs . . . 154 C6
Woolsthorpe-by-
Colsterworth Lincs . . 155 E8
Woolston Corn . . . 6 B5
Devon . . . 8 G4
Shrops . . . 131 B8
Shrops . . . 148 E6
Som . . . 29 B10
Som . . . 42 F5
Soton . . . 32 E6
Warr . . . 183 D10
Woolston Green Devon . 8 B5
Woolton Mers . . . 182 D6
Woolton Hill Hants . . . 64 G2
Woolverstone Suff . . . 108 D3
Woolverton Som . . . 45 C9
Woolwell Devon . . . 7 C10
Woolwich London . . . 68 D2
Woolwich Ferry London . 68 D2
Woon Corn . . . 5 D10
Woonton Hereford . . . 115 E10
Hereford . . . 115 G7
Wooperton Northumb . 264 E2
Woopaw Borders . . . 272 C6
Woore Shrops . . . 168 G2
Wooton Shrops . . . 115 C11
Wootten Green Suff . . 126 C4
Wootton Beds . . . 103 B10
Hants . . . 19 B11
Hereford . . . 97 D11
Hereford . . . 114 C6
IoW . . . 20 C6
Kent . . . 55 D8
N Lincs . . . 200 D5
Northants . . . 120 F5
Oxon . . . 82 B6
Oxon . . . 83 C7
Shrops . . . 115 B9
Shrops . . . 148 D6
Staffs . . . 150 D6
Staffs . . . 169 F10
Wootton Bourne End
Beds . . . 103 B9
Wootton Bridge IoW . . 20 C6
Wootton Broadmead
Beds . . . 103 C10
Wootton Common IoW . 20 C6
Wootton Courtenay Som . 42 E3
Wootton Fitzpaine Dorset . 16 B3
Wootton Green Beds . . 103 C9
W Mid . . . 118 B4
Wootton Rivers Wilts . . 63 G7
Wootton St Lawrence
Hants . . . 48 C5
Wootton Wawen Warks . 118 E3
Worbarrow Dorset . . . 18 E3
Worcester Worcs . . . 117 F7
Worcester Park London . 67 F8
Wordsley W Mid . . . 133 F7
Wordwell Suff . . . 124 C6
Worfield Shrops . . . 132 D5
Worgret Dorset . . . 18 D4
Work Orkney . . . 314 E4
Workhouse Common
Norf . . . 161 E7
Workhouse End Beds . . 122 G2
Workhouse Green Suff . 107 D8
Workhouse Hill Essex . 107 F9
Workington Cumb . . . 228 F5
Worksop Notts . . . 187 F9
Worlaby Lincs . . . 190 F4
N Lincs . . . 200 E4
Worlds End Hants . . . 33 E10
W Mid . . . 134 G2
World's End Bucks . . . 84 D5
London . . . 86 F4
Suff . . . 125 F9
W Sus . . . 36 D4
Worle N Som . . . 59 G11
Worleston ChesE . . . 167 D11
Worley Glos . . . 80 F4
Worlingham Suff . . . 143 F8
Worlingdown Corn . . . 12 D2
Worlington Devon . . . 40 G3
Suff . . . 124 C3
Worlingworth Suff . . . 126 D4
Wormadale Shetland . . 313 J5
Wormald Green
N Yorks . . . 214 G6
Wormbridge Hereford . 97 E8
Wormbridge Common
Hereford . . . 97 E8
Wormegay Norf . . . 158 G3
Wormelow Tump
Hereford . . . 97 E9
Wormhill Derbys . . . 185 G10
Wormingford Essex . . 107 E8
Worminghall Bucks . . 83 D10
Wormington Glos . . . 99 D10
Worminster Som . . . 44 E5
Wormiston Ho Fife . . . 287 G10
Wormit Fife . . . 287 E7
Wormleighton Warks . . 119 G7
Wormley Herts . . . 86 D5
Sur . . . 50 F2
Wormleybury Herts . . 86 D5
Wormley West End Herts 86 D4
Worms Ash Worcs . . . 117 C8
Wormshill Kent . . . 53 B11
Worms Hill Kent . . . 53 F8
Wormsley Hereford . . . 97 B8
Worplesdon Sur . . . 50 C3
Worrall S Yorks . . . 186 C4

Worrall Hill Glos . . . 79 C10
Worsbrough S Yorks . . 197 G11
Worsbrough Bridge
S Yorks . . . 197 G11
Worsbrough Common
S Yorks . . . 197 G11
Worsbrough Dale
S Yorks . . . 197 G11
Worsham Oxon . . . 82 C3
Worsley Gtr Man . . . 195 G8
Worsley Hall Gtr Man . 194 F5
Worsley Mesnes
Gtr Man . . . 194 G5
Worstead Norf . . . 160 D6
Worsthorne Lancs . . . 204 G3
Worston Devon . . . 7 E11
Lancs . . . 203 E11
Worswell Devon . . . 7 F10
Worten Kent . . . 54 E3
Worth Kent . . . 55 B10
Som . . . 44 D4
Som . . . 51 F9
Worth Abbey W Sus . . 51 G10
Wortham Suff . . . 125 B11
Worthen Shrops . . . 130 C6
Worthenbury Wrex . . . 166 F6
Worthing Norf . . . 159 F9
W Sus . . . 35 G10
Worthington Leics . . . 153 E8
Worth Matravers Dorset . 18 F5
Worthy Som . . . 41 D11
Worthybrook Mon . . . 79 C7
Worthy Hants . . . 80 G3
Wortley Glos . . . 80 G3
S Yorks . . . 186 B4
W Yorks . . . 205 G11
Worton N Yorks . . . 223 G9
Oxon . . . 83 C7
Wilts . . . 46 B3
Wortwell Norf . . . 142 G5
Wotherton Shrops . . . 130 C5
Wothorpe Pboro . . . 137 B10
Wotter Devon . . . 7 C11
Wotton Glos . . . 80 B4
Sur . . . 50 D6
Wotton-under-Edge
Glos . . . 80 G3
Wotton Underwood
Bucks . . . 83 B11
Woughton on the Green
M Keynes . . . 103 D7
Woughton Park
M Keynes . . . 103 D7
Wouldham Kent . . . 69 G8
Woundale Shrops . . . 132 E5
Wrabness Essex . . . 108 E3
Wraes Aberds . . . 302 F5
Wrafton Devon . . . 40 F3
Wragby Lincs . . . 189 F10
Worcs . . . 198 D2
Wragholme Lincs . . . 190 B5
Wramplingham Norf . . 142 B2
Wrangaton Devon . . . 8 D2
Wrangbrook W Yorks . 198 E3
Wrangham Aberds . . . 302 F6
Wrangle Lincs . . . 174 E6
Wrangle Bank Lincs . . 174 E6
Wrangle Low Ground
Lincs . . . 174 E6
Wrangway Som . . . 27 D10
Wrantage Som . . . 28 C4
Wrawby N Lincs . . . 200 F4
Wraxall Dorset . . . 29 G9
N Som . . . 60 E3
Som . . . 44 F6
Wray Lancs . . . 212 F2
Wray Common Sur . . . 51 C9
Wraysbury Windsor . . 66 E4
Wrayton Lancs . . . 212 E2
Wrea Green Lancs . . . 202 G3
Wreaks End Cumb . . . 210 B4
Wreath Som . . . 28 F2
Wreay Cumb . . . 230 B4
Cumb . . . 230 G4
Wrecclesham Sur . . . 49 D10
Wrekenton T&W . . . 243 F7
Wrelton N Yorks . . . 216 B5
Wrenbury ChesE . . . 167 F9
Wrenbury cum Frith
ChesE . . . 167 F9
Wrench Green N Yorks . 217 B9
Wreningham Norf . . . 142 D3
Wrentham Suff . . . 143 G9
Wrenthorpe W Yorks . . 197 C10
Wrentnall Shrops . . . 131 C8
Wressle E Yorks . . . 207 G10
N Lincs . . . 200 E4
Wrestlingworth C Beds . 104 B5
Wretham Norf . . . 141 F8
Wretton Norf . . . 140 D3
Wrexham Wrex . . . 166 E4
Wreyland Devon . . . 13 E11
Wribbenhall Worcs . . 116 B5
Wrickton Shrops . . . 132 F2
Wrightington Bar Lancs . 194 E4
Wrights Green Warr . . 183 E10
Wright's Green Essex . 87 B8
Wrinehill Staffs . . . 168 F3
Wrington N Som . . . 60 G4
Wriothsgdown Corn . . 12 D2
Wrington N Som . . . 60 G3
Wrinkleberry Devon . . 24 C4
Writhlington Bath . . . 45 C8
Writtle Essex . . . 87 D11
Wrockwardine Telford . 150 G2
Wrockwardine Wood
Telford . . . 150 G4
Wroot N Lincs . . . 199 G8
Wrose W Yorks . . . 205 F9
Wrotham Kent . . . 52 B6
Wrotham Heath Kent . . 52 B6
Wroughton Swindon . . 62 C6
Wroxall IoW . . . 21 F7
Warks . . . 118 C4
Wroxeter Shrops . . . 131 B11
Wroxhall Warks . . . 118 C4
Wroxham Norf . . . 160 F6
Wroxton Oxon . . . 101 C8
Wstrws Ceredig . . . 93 B7
Wyatt's Green Essex . . 87 F9
Wyaston Derbys . . . 169 G11
Wybers Wood NE Lincs . 201 F8
Wyberton Lincs . . . 174 G4
Wyboston Beds . . . 122 F3
Wybunbury ChesE . . . 168 F2
Wychbold Worcs . . . 117 D8
Wych Cross ESus . . . 52 G2
Wychnor Staffs . . . 152 F3
Wychnor Bridges Staffs . 152 F3
Wyck Hants . . . 49 F7
Wyck Rissington Glos . 100 G3

Wycliffe Durham . . . 224 C2
Wycoller Lancs . . . 204 F4
Wycomb Leics . . . 154 E5
Wycombe Marsh Bucks . 84 G5
Wyddial Herts . . . 105 E7
Wye Kent . . . 54 D5
Wyebanks Kent . . . 54 C2
Wyegate Green Glos . . 79 D9
Wyesham Mon . . . 79 C8
Wyfordby Leics . . . 154 F5
Wyke Dorset . . . 30 B3
Shrops . . . 132 C2
Sur . . . 50 C2
W Yorks . . . 197 B7
Wyke Champflower
Som . . . 44 F6
Wykeham Lincs . . . 156 D5
N Yorks . . . 216 C6
N Yorks . . . 217 C9
Wyken Shrops . . . 132 E5
W Mid . . . 135 G2
Wyke Regis Dorset . . . 17 F9
Wykey Shrops . . . 149 E7
Wykin Leics . . . 135 D8
Wylam Northumb . . . 242 E4
Wylde Hereford . . . 115 C9
Wylde Green W Mid . . 134 E2
Wyllie Caerph . . . 77 G11
Wylye Wilts . . . 46 F4
Wymans Brook Glos . . 99 G8
Wymbush M Keynes . . 102 D6
Wymering Ptsmth . . . 33 F10
Wymeswold Leics . . . 154 E2
Wymington Beds . . . 121 E9
Wymondham Leics . . . 155 F7
Norf . . . 142 C2
Wymondley Bury Herts . 104 F4
Wymott Lancs . . . 194 C4
Wyndham Bridgend . . 76 G6
Wyndham Park V Glam . 58 D5
Wynds Point Hereford . 98 C5
Wynford Eagle Dorset . 17 B7
Wyng Orkney . . . 314 G3
Wynn's Green Hereford . 98 B2
Wynyard Village
Stockton . . . 234 F4
Wyre Piddle Worcs . . . 99 B9
Wysall Notts . . . 154 D2
Wyson Hereford . . . 115 D10
Wythall Worcs . . . 117 B11
Wytham Oxon . . . 83 D7
Wythburn Cumb . . . 220 C6
Wythenshawe Gtr Man . 184 D4
Wythop Mill Cumb . . . 229 F9
Wyton Cambs . . . 122 C5
E Yorks . . . 209 G9
Wyverstone Suff . . . 125 D10
Wyverstone Green
Suff . . . 125 D10
Wyverstone Street
Suff . . . 125 D10
Wyville Lincs . . . 155 D7
Wyvis Lodge Highld . . 300 B4

Y

Yaddlethorpe N Lincs . 199 F11
Yafford IoW . . . 20 E4
Yafforth N Yorks . . . 224 G6
Yair Borders . . . 261 C11
Yalberton Torbay . . . 9 D7
Yalding Kent . . . 53 C7
Yanley N Som . . . 60 F5
Yanworth Glos . . . 81 C9
Yapham E Yorks . . . 207 C11
Yapton W Sus . . . 35 G7
Yarberry N Som . . . 43 B11
Yarborough NE Lincs . 201 F9
Yarbridge IoW . . . 21 D8
Yarburgh Lincs . . . 190 C5
Yarcombe Devon . . . 28 F2
Yard Som . . . 42 F5
Yarde Som . . . 42 F5
Yardhurst Kent . . . 54 E3
Yardley W Mid . . . 134 F2
Yardley Gobion
Northants . . . 102 C5
Yardley Hastings
Northants . . . 121 F7
Yardley Wood W Mid . 118 B2
Yardro Powys . . . 114 F4
Yarford Som . . . 28 B2
Yarhampton Worcs . . 116 D5
Yarhampton Cross
Worcs . . . 116 D5
Yarkhill Hereford . . . 98 C2
Yarlet Staffs . . . 151 D8
Yarley Som . . . 44 D4
Yarlington Som . . . 29 B11
Yarlside Cumb . . . 210 F4
Yarm Stockton . . . 225 C8
Yarmouth IoW . . . 20 D3
Yarnacott Devon . . . 40 G6
Yarnbrook Wilts . . . 45 C11
Yarnfield Staffs . . . 151 C7
Yarningale Common
Warks . . . 118 D3
Yarnscombe Devon . . 25 C9
Yarnton Oxon . . . 83 C7
Yarpole Hereford . . . 115 E9
Yarrow Borders . . . 261 D9
Northumb . . . 251 E8
Som . . . 43 D11
Yarrow Feus Borders . . 261 D9
Yarrowford Borders . . 261 D10
Yarsop Hereford . . . 97 B8
Yarwell Northants . . . 137 D11
Yate S Glos . . . 61 C8
Yateley Hants . . . 65 G10
Yate Rocks S Glos . . . 61 C8
Yatesbury Wilts . . . 62 E5
Yattendon W Berks . . 64 E5
Yatton Hereford . . . 115 D8
N Som . . . 60 G3
Yatton Keynell Wilts . . 61 D11
Yaverland IoW . . . 21 D8
Yawthorpe Lincs . . . 188 C5
Yaxham Norf . . . 159 G10
Yaxley Cambs . . . 138 E2
Suff . . . 126 C2

Yealand Redmayne
Lancs . . . 211 D10
Yealand Storrs Lancs . 211 D9
Yealmbridge Devon . . . 7 E11
Yealmpton Devon . . . 7 E11
Yearby Redcar . . . 235 G8
Yearngill Cumb . . . 229 C8
Yearsley N Yorks . . . 215 E11
Yeaton Shrops . . . 149 F8
Yeaveley Derbys . . . 169 G11
Yeavering Northumb . . 263 D11
Yedingham N Yorks . . 217 D7
Yelden Beds . . . 121 D10
Yeldersley Hollies
Derbys . . . 170 G2
Yeldon Beds . . . 121 D10
Yelford Oxon . . . 82 E5
Yelland Devon . . . 40 G3
Yelling Cambs . . . 122 E5
Yelsted Kent . . . 69 G10
Yelvertoft Northants . . 119 B11
Yelverton Devon . . . 7 B10
Norf . . . 142 C5
Yenston Som . . . 30 C2
Yeoford Devon . . . 13 B11
Yeolmbridge Corn . . . 12 D2
Yeo Mill Devon . . . 26 B4
Yeo Vale Devon . . . 24 C6
Yeovil Som . . . 29 D9
Yeovil Marsh Som . . . 29 D8
Yeovilton Som . . . 29 C8
Yerbeston Pembs . . . 73 D9
Yesnaby Orkney . . . 314 E2
Yetlington Northumb . . 252 B2
Yetminster Dorset . . . 29 E9
Yett N Lnrk . . . 268 D5
Yettington Devon . . . 15 D7
Yetts o' Muckhart Clack . 286 G4
Yew Green Warks . . . 118 D4
Yewhedges Kent . . . 54 B3
Yew Tree Gtr Man . . . 185 B7
W Mid . . . 133 D10
Yewtree Cross Kent . . 55 E7
Y Fali / Valley Anglesey . 178 F3
Y Felinheli / Port Dinorwic
Gwyn . . . 163 B8
Y Ferwig Ceredig . . . 92 B3
Y Ffôr Gwyn . . . 145 B7
Y-Ffrith Denb . . . 181 E8
Y Gors Ceredig . . . 112 B2
Y Gribyn Powys . . . 129 C8
Yieldshields S Lnrk . . 269 E7
Yiewsley London . . . 66 C5
Yinstay Orkney . . . 314 E5
Y Mwmbwls / The Mumbles
Swansea . . . 56 D6
Ynus-tawelog Swansea . 75 D10
Ynys Gwyn . . . 145 B11
Ynysboeth Rhondda . . 77 F9
Ynysddu Caerph . . . 77 G11
Ynysforgan Swansea . . 57 B7
Ynysgyfflog Gwyn . . . 146 G2
Ynyshir Rhondda . . . 77 G8
Ynys-isaf Powys . . . 76 C3
Ynyslas Ceredig . . . 128 E2
Ynysmaerdy Neath . . 57 B8
Rhondda . . . 58 A4
Ynysmeudwy Neath . . 76 D2
Neath . . . 76 D2
Ynys Tachwedd Ceredig . 128 E2
Ynystawe Swansea . . 75 E11
Ynyswen Powys . . . 76 C3
Rhondda . . . 77 F7
Ynysybwl Rhondda . . 77 G9
Ynysygwas Neath . . . 57 C9
Yockenthwaite N Yorks . 213 D8
Yockleton Shrops . . . 149 G7
Yodercott Devon . . . 27 E9
Yokefleet E Yorks . . . 199 C10
Yoker W Dunb . . . 267 B10
Yonder Bognie Aberds . 302 E5
Yonder Bognie Devon . 7 D11
Yopps Green Kent . . . 52 C6
York Lancs . . . 203 G10
York . . . 207 C7
Yorkletts Kent . . . 70 G5
Yorkley Glos . . . 79 D10
Yorkley Slade Glos . . 79 D10
York Town Sur . . . 65 G11
Yorton Shrops . . . 149 E10
Yorton Heath Shrops . . 149 E10
Yottenfews Cumb . . . 219 D10
Youlgrave Derbys . . . 170 C2
Youlstone Devon . . . 24 D3
Youlthorpe E Yorks . . 207 B11
Youlton N Yorks . . . 215 G9
Youngsbury Herts . . . 86 B5
Young's End Essex . . . 88 B2
Young Wood Lincs . . . 189 G10
Yoxall Staffs . . . 152 F2
Yoxford Suff . . . 127 D7
Y Pîl / Pyle Bridgend . . 57 E10
Yr Hôb / Hope Flint . . 166 D4
Ysbyty Cynfyn Ceredig . 112 B5
Ysbyty Ifan Conwy . . 164 F4
Ysbyty Ystwyth Ceredig . 112 C4
Ysceifiog Flint . . . 181 G11
Ysgeibion Denb . . . 165 D9
Yspitty Carms . . . 56 B5
Ystalyfera Neath . . . 76 D3
Ystrad Rhondda . . . 77 F7
Ystrad Aeron Ceredig . 111 F10
Ystradfellte Powys . . 76 C5
Ystradffin Carms . . . 94 B6
Ystradgynlais Powys . 76 C3
Ystradmeurig Ceredig . 112 D4
Ystrad-mynach Caerph . 77 G10
Ystradowen Carms . . 76 C2
V Glam . . . 58 D4
Ystrad Uchaf Powys . . 129 C11
Ystumtuen Ceredig . . 112 B4
Ythanbank Aberds . . . 303 F9
Ythanwells Aberds . . 302 F6
Ythsie Aberds . . . 303 F8
Y Tymbl / Tumble Carms . 75 D10
Y Waun / Chirk Wrex . . 148 B5

Z

Zeal Monachorum Devon 26 G2
Zeals Wilts . . . 45 G9
Zelah Corn . . . 4 E5
Zennor Corn . . . 1 B5
Zoar Corn . . . 3 F7
Zouch Notts . . . 153 E10

County and unitary authority boundaries

Ordnance Survey National Grid

The blue lines which divide the Navigator map pages into squares for indexing match the Ordnance Survey National Grid and correspond to the small squares on the boundary map below. Each side of a grid square measures 10km on the ground.

The National Grid 100-km square letters and kilometre values are indicated for the grid intersection at the outer corners of each page. For example, the intersection SE6090 at the upper right corner of page 215 is 60km East and 90km North of the south-west corner of National Grid square SE.

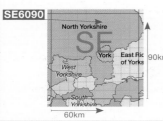

Using GPS with Navigator mapping

Since Navigator Britain is based on Ordnance Survey mapping, and rectified to the National Grid, it can be used with in-car or handheld GPS for locating identifiable waypoints such as road junctions, bridges, railways and farms, or assessing your position in relation to any of the features shown on the map.

On your receiver, choose British Grid as the location format and for map datum select Ordnance Survey (this may be described as Ord Srvy GB or similar, or more specifically as OSGB36). Your receiver will automatically convert the latitude/longitude co-ordinates transmitted by GPS into compatible National Grid data.

Positional accuracy of any particular feature is limited to 50–100m, due to the limitations of the original survey and the scale of Navigator mapping.

For further information see www.gps.gov.uk

Greater London

1 City and County of the City of London	16 Lewisham
2 Hackney	17 Merton
3 Tower Hamlets	18 Richmond upon Thames
4 Southwark	19 Hounslow
5 Lambeth	20 Ealing
6 Wandsworth	21 Brent
7 Hammersmith and Fulham	22 Barnet
8 Royal Borough of Kensington and Chelsea	23 Enfield
	24 Redbridge
9 City of Westminster	25 Barking and Dagenham
10 Camden	26 Havering
11 Islington	27 Bexley
12 Haringey	28 Bromley
13 Waltham Forest	29 Croydon
14 Newham	30 Sutton
15 Greenwich	31 Kingston upon Thames
	32 Hillingdon
	33 Harrow

1 Central Scotland

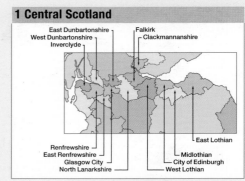

2 Northern England

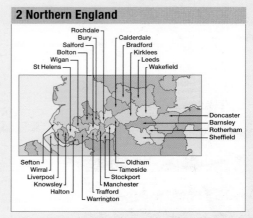

3 West Midlands

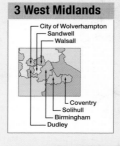

4 South Wales and Bristol area

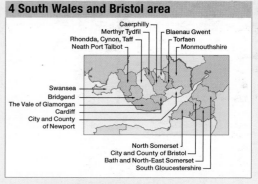

5 Thames Valley

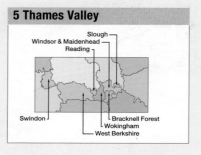

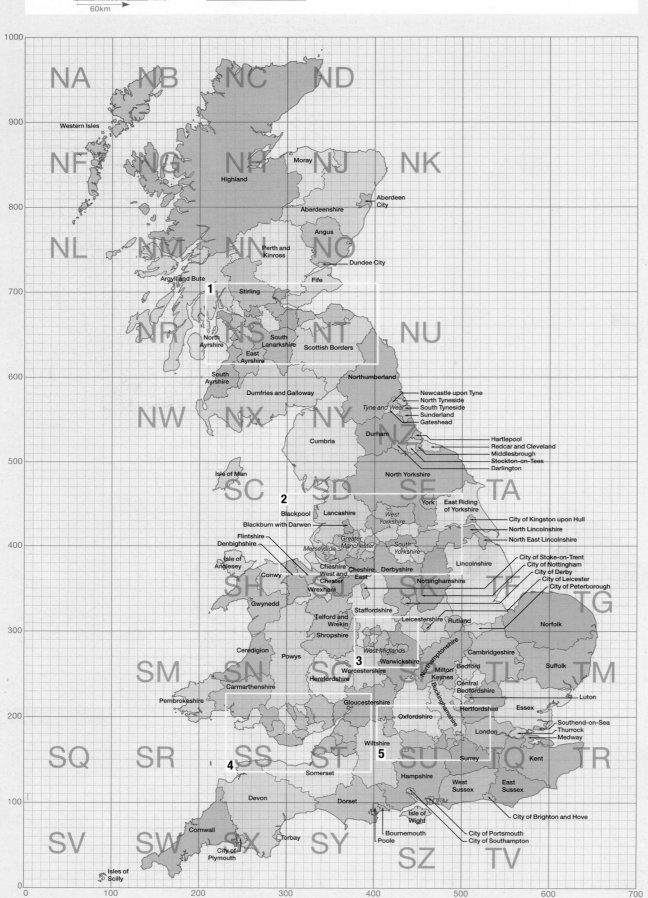